the
AMERICANA ANNUAL

1987

GROLIER

AN ENCYCLOPEDIA OF THE EVENTS OF 1986
YEARBOOK OF THE ENCYCLOPEDIA AMERICANA

This annual has been prepared as a yearbook for general encyclopedias. It is also published as *Encyclopedia Year Book.*

© GROLIER INCORPORATED 1987

Copyright in Canada © by Grolier Limited

Library of Congress Catalog Card Number: 23-10041

ISBN: 0-7172-0218-6

ISSN: 0196-0180

Printed and manufactured in the United States of America

Grolier Enterprises, Inc. offers a varied selection of both adult and children's book racks. For details on ordering, please write:

Grolier Enterprises, Inc.
Sherman Turnpike
Danbury, CT 06816
Attn: Premium Department

Contents

Feature Articles of the Year

The Alphabetical Section

Entries on the continents, major nations of the world, U.S. states, Canadian provinces, and chief cities will be found under their own alphabetical headings.

Sygma

The Year in Review

On Feb. 26, 1986, the new president of the Philippines, Corazon Aquino, could declare to her people: "The long agony is over. A new life starts for our country tomorrow." In a ground swell of "People Power," the long-ruling Ferdinand Marcos had been swept from office and replaced by a soft-spoken widow who dressed in yellow and symbolized the democratic process.

Among the major events of 1986, the peaceful revolution in the Philippines would prove to be one of the few bright spots. Many of the year's biggest headlines went to tragedy and turmoil, dashed hope and broken trust.

Nothing in a long time was as devastating to the American psyche as the sudden explosion of the space shuttle *Challenger* and the loss of its seven crew members on January 28.

In April, Moscow confirmed that a serious accident had taken place at the Chernobyl nuclear power plant in the Ukraine, releasing a cloud of radiation into the atmosphere.

Also in April, after months of escalating international terrorism and growing evidence of Libyan state sponsorship, the United States launched a bombing raid on that country. Terrorist attacks seemed to slacken, but only briefly. In Lebanon, meanwhile, two Americans and five Frenchmen were freed from captivity, but at least 16 Westerners were still being held hostage at year's end.

In superpower relations, an October "mini-summit" between U.S. President Ronald Reagan and Soviet General Secretary Mikhail Gorbachev in Reykjavik, Iceland (*photo*), nearly produced a major arms-control agreement but fell apart over the U.S. Strategic Defense Initiative ("Star Wars").

The disappointment of Reykjavik was followed by a domestic setback for President Reagan: in November elections the Democrats gained control of the Senate, 55–45. Then came political disaster: news that the administration had made secret arms sales to Iran, with the proceeds going to "contra" rebels in Nicaragua. Reagan's popularity plummeted.

In the Soviet Union, the high-profile Gorbachev orchestrated a campaign of *glasnost* (publicity, openness); Anatoly Shcharansky and other dissidents were allowed to leave; and Andrei Sakharov was released from internal exile. But the extent of substantive change remained to be seen.

In other world developments, international pressure continued to mount on the stubbornly repressive white regime in South Africa; OPEC scrambled for an antidote to tumbling oil prices. Haiti's despotic President-for-Life Jean-Claude Duvalier was forced to flee; Sweden's popular Prime Minister Olof Palme was assassinated. Concentration camp survivor and author Elie Wiesel won the Nobel Peace Prize; former UN Secretary-General Kurt Waldheim was accused of Nazi war crimes but was elected president of Austria.

On the U.S. scene, the high point was a Fourth of July extravaganza to mark the centennial of the restored Statue of Liberty. There was landmark tax reform and immigration legislation. William Rehnquist replaced Warren Burger as chief justice of the Supreme Court; another conservative, Antonin Scalia, was named to the bench. Interest rates were down, but the trade deficit reached a record high.

It was a boom year on Wall Street, but there was scandal involving insider trading. In sports, successes by veterans Jack Nicklaus and Bill Shoemaker were overshadowed by the cocaine death of young basketball star Len Bias. Skywatchers said good-bye to Halley's Comet—another disappointment.

By way of respite, and irony, the year ended with an act of heroic achievement. Aboard a plane called *Voyager,* Dick Rutan and Jeana Yeager completed the first nonstop flight around the world on a single load of fuel.

THE EDITORS

January

1 U.S. President Ronald Reagan and Soviet General Secretary Mikhail Gorbachev deliver five-minute messages of peace that are televised in each other's country.

Spain and Portugal officially join the European Community.

Aruba secedes from the Netherlands Antilles and becomes a self-ruling member of the Kingdom of the Netherlands.

3 President Reagan and Mexico's President Miguel de la Madrid Hurtado discuss trade and debt issues in talks at Mexicali, Mexico.

6 Gen. Samuel K. Doe is sworn in as civilian president of Liberia.

Paul N. Carlin is removed as U.S. postmaster general and replaced by Albert V. Casey.

7 Accusing Libya of supporting terrorist attacks on the Rome and Vienna 1985 airports in December 1985, President Reagan severs economic ties and orders all Americans still in Libya to leave at once.

13 Fighting breaks out between rival Christian militias in east Beirut, Lebanon, jeopardizing the Syrian-mediated, multilateral peace agreement signed in December 1985.

14 Marco Vinicio Cerezo Arévalo is inaugurated as Guatemala's first civilian president in 16 years.

15 Ecuador's President León Febres Cordero concludes a three-day visit to the United States.

16 The fourth round of U.S.-Soviet arms talks opens in Geneva. The Soviets present a proposal, announced by General Secretary Gorbachev one day earlier, to ban nuclear weapons worldwide by the year 2000.

Shock and mourning: In Washington, DC, flags are flown at half-staff for the seven astronauts killed in the space shuttle "Challenger" explosion.

18 The U.S. space shuttle *Columbia* completes a six-day scientific mission that had been postponed seven times.

20 Prime Minister Leabua Jonathan of Lesotho is ousted in a coup.

France and Great Britain agree on the construction of twin rail tunnels connecting the two countries under the English Channel.

Martin Luther King Day is observed as a U.S. federal holiday for the first time.

22 Three Sikhs are convicted of the October 1984 assassination of India's Prime Minister Indira Gandhi and are sentenced to hang.

23 With world oil prices declining rapidly, some crudes fall below $20 per barrel.

24 Britain's Minister of Trade and Industry Leon Brittan resigns in a dispute over the rescue of the Westland helicopter manufacturer. Minister of Defence Michael Heseltine resigned January 9.

The U.S. space probe Voyager 2 passes within 51,000 mi (82 000 km) of the planet Uranus.

25 After a 12-day civil war between rival Marxist factions, South Yemen's President Ali Nasir Muhammad al-Hasani is ousted. Former Prime Minister Haydar Abu Bakr al-Attas becomes interim president.

26 The Chicago Bears rout New England, 46–10, in Super Bowl XX.

27 José Azcona Hoyo is sworn in as president of Honduras.

28 The U.S. space shuttle *Challenger* explodes shortly after takeoff from Cape Canaveral, FL. All seven crew members are killed.

Angolan rebel leader Jonas Savimbi arrives in the United States for a ten-day visit and receives a warm official welcome.

29 Yoweri Museveni of Uganda declares himself president after his rebel group overthrew the ruling military council.

President Reagan names Richard E. Lyng as secretary of agriculture. John R. Block announced his resignation January 7.

Ugandan rebel leader Yoweri Museveni declared himself president after a violent three-day coup in late January. He promised to return the country to parliamentary democracy.

© W. Campbell/Sygma

9

February

1 Pope John Paul II begins a ten-day tour of India.

2 Oscar Arias Sanchez of the ruling National Liberation Party is elected president of Costa Rica.

4 After a one-week delay because of the space shuttle disaster, President Reagan delivers his fifth State of the Union message. On February 3, Reagan appointed a special commission, headed by former Secretary of State William P. Rogers, to investigate the accident.

Israeli fighter planes intercept a civilian Libyan jetliner between Tripoli and Damascas and force it to land. After an unsuccessful search for terrorists, the plane is allowed to go on.

5 President Reagan sends the U.S. Congress a $994 billion federal budget proposal for fiscal 1987.

7 One week after calling a state of siege to quell antigovernment protests, Haiti's President-for-Life Jean-Claude Duvalier is forced to flee the country. A military-civilian council takes power.

Former U.S. Central Intelligence Agency analyst Larry Wu-Tai Chin is convicted of spying for China.

8 A woman in Peekskill, NY, dies after taking a Tylenol pain-relief capsule laced with cyanide poison.

10 Libyan-backed rebels attack government forces in central Chad, setting off the worst fighting in that country since 1984.

A trial of some 474 Mafia suspects, the largest in history, opens in Palermo, Italy.

The city of Port-au-Prince, Haiti, broke out in joyful celebration when President-for-Life Jean Claude Duvalier fled the country February 7. After months of growing unrest, "Baby Doc" flew to France aboard a U.S. Air Force jet.

11 The Soviet Union frees Jewish dissident Anatoly Shcharansky in a nine-prisoner exchange between East and West in Berlin. Shcharansky travels to Israel, where he receives a hero's welcome.

In one of the major thrusts of its ongoing war with Iraq, Iran captures the oil port of Fao, near Kuwait.

16 Former Prime Minister Mário Soares, a Socialist, is elected Portugal's first civilian president in 60 years.

17 Israel launches a large-scale military operation in southern Lebanon following the capture of two of its soliders there.

In the first meeting of its kind, representatives of 41 French-speaking nations open a three-day summit in Versailles, France.

19 Jordan's King Hussein announces that he is abandoning his joint effort with the PLO to revive the Arab-Israeli peace process.

The U.S. Senate ratifies a UN treaty outlawing genocide.

20 Petroleum prices continue to fall on international markets, with benchmark crudes dropping below $15 per barrel.

24 President Reagan proposes that the United States and Soviet Union eliminate all medium-range nuclear missiles over three years.

26 Philippines' President Ferdinand Marcos flees the country, ending 20 years in power. The departure comes ten days after the National Assembly declared him the winner of disputed February 7 presidential elections and opposition candidate Corazon Aquino announced a campaign of nonviolent "active resistance."

28 Sweden's Prime Minister Olof Palme is shot and killed on a Stockholm street.

© Joel Fishman/Black Star

Soviet Jewish dissident Anatoly Shcharansky gets a tumultuous welcome in Israel after his release February 11. Shcharansky, 38, had spent nearly nine years in prison and forced labor.

March

4 Evidence surfaces that former UN Secretary-General Kurt Waldheim, currently running for president of Austria, had been a member of Nazi organizations and had served under a war criminal during World War II.

6 The 27th Congress of the Soviet Communist Party ends in Moscow. The nine-day congress was highlighted by changes in party leadership and ratification of economic and political programs.

A commission in Philadelphia concludes that Mayor W. Wilson Goode had been "grossly negligent" in failing to prevent a fatal police confrontation with the radical group MOVE in May 1985.

President Reagan names James C. Fletcher as administrator of the National Aeronautics and Space Administration (NASA), a post he held from 1971 to 1977.

7 South Africa's President Pieter W. Botha lifts the state of emergency declared in riot-stricken black areas in July 1985.

12 In a national referendum, Spanish voters call for continued membership in the North Atlantic Treaty Organization (NATO).

13 Former U.S. Congressman Barber B. Conable, Jr., is nominated by President Reagan to head the World Bank.

14 The European Space Agency probe *Giotto* passes within 335 mi (539 km) of the core of Halley's Comet. In recent days, two Soviet and one Japanese spacecraft also made their closest approaches.

18 Canada's Prime Minister Brian Mulroney arrives in Washington for two days of talks with President Reagan.

20 Jacques Chirac, the mayor of Paris and a leader of France's right wing, is sworn in as prime minister and names a new, conservative government. The Socialist Party of President François Mitterrand had been defeated by the right in March 15 National Assembly elections, creating the unusual power-sharing arrangement.

23 In South Korea's largest antigovernment rally since President Chun Doo Hwan assumed power in 1980, tens of thousands of demonstrators cheer dissident leader Kim Young Sam in Pusan.

Acid rain, free trade, and defense were among the bilateral issues discussed by President Reagan and Canada's Prime Minister Brian Mulroney during two days of Washington talks.

AP/Wide World

Antigovernment protests in South Korea grew increasingly violent throughout the spring. Opponents of President Chun Doo Hwan called for sweeping constitutional reforms.

24 Libya fires antiaircraft missiles at U.S. war planes over the Gulf of Sidra. With a Navy task force positioned in and near the gulf, the United States retaliates with air attacks against Libyan ships and a missile installation on the mainland.

The Organization of the Petroleum Exporting Countries (OPEC) ends a nine-day meeting in Geneva without taking action to counteract the continuing decline in world oil prices.

25 Newly elected President Corazon Aquino of the Philippines abolishes the National Assembly, abrogates the 1973 constitution, and temporarily assumes legislative power.

27 At their joint semiannual meeting, held in Washington, DC, the International Monetary Fund and World Bank approve a new $3.1 billion loan pool to aid the world's poorest nations.

29 Three Bulgarians and three Turks charged in the 1981 assassination attempt against Pope John Paul II, are acquitted by an Italian court for "lack of evidence."

31 The Louisville Cardinals defeat the Duke Blue Devils, 72–69, to win the NCAA Division I men's college basketball championship.

April

2 A bomb explodes aboard a TWA jetliner en route from Rome to Athens, killing four American passengers.

6 Six currencies of the European Monetary System are realigned.

7 U.S. Vice-President George Bush concludes a three-day visit to Saudi Arabia, where he expressed concern over the low price of oil on the international market.

After three days of discussions in Panama, a meeting of Contadora Group nations breaks up without agreement on how to revive Central American peace negotiations.

10 In Italy, at least 20 persons are reported dead in recent weeks after drinking wine contaminated with methanol. U.S. consumers are warned not to drink Italian wine until it has been tested.

The U.S. House of Representatives vote to ease gun control restrictions; the Senate passed a similar measure in 1985.

11 In Miami, FL, two FBI agents are killed and five wounded in a street shootout with suspected armed robbers.

12 China's National People's Congress approves the nation's seventh five-year economic plan, for 1986–1990.

13 Japan's Prime Minister Yasuhiro Nakasone arrives in Washington for two days of talks with President Reagan.

Pope John Paul II visits Rome's main synagogue, in what is believed to be the first papal visit to a Jewish house of worship.

14 U.S. fighter planes bomb "terrorist centers" in a night attack on Tripoli and Benghazi, Libya. President Reagan says the attacks are in retaliation for Libya's proven role in the April 5 bombing of a West Berlin discotheque in which a U.S. serviceman was killed.

16 Soviet General Secretary Gorbachev arrives in East Berlin for the 11th Congress of the Socialist Unity (Communist) Party of East Germany. It is Gorbachev's first visit to the country since taking power.

China rejects a proposed summit to discuss normalized relations with the Soviet Union.

18 South Africa's President Pieter W. Botha announces the repeal of "pass laws" that restricted the movement of blacks and required them to carry special passbooks.

A U.S. Titan 34-D rocket and its military payload explode seconds after liftoff from Vandenberg Air Force Base in California.

21 Foreign ministers of the Economic Community agree on a package of measures aimed at limiting Libya's ability to sponsor terrorist attacks.

28 The Soviet Union confirms that a serious accident has taken place at the Chernobyl nuclear power plant north of Kiev, releasing a cloud of radiation into the atmosphere.

AP/Wide World

Russian-born pianist Vladimir Horowitz, 81, returned to the Soviet Union after an absence of 61 years, giving April recitals in Moscow and Leningrad. The two concerts were part of a cultural exchange agreement between the United States and Soviet Union.

May

1 On a 13-day trip to the Far East, President Reagan meets in Bali, Indonesia, with foreign ministers of the Association of Southeast Asian Nations (ASEAN) and with Indonesia's President Suharto.

In Tucson, AZ, a federal jury convicts eight Christian activists of smuggling Central American aliens into the United States.

2 Expo 86, a world's fair, opens in Vancouver, BC, Canada.

3 Ferdinand wins the 112th running of the Kentucky Derby.

4 Afghanistan's leader Babrak Karmal steps down and is replaced by Najibullah, former head of the Afghan secret police.

5 At the 12th annual economic summit of major industrial democracies, held May 4–6 in Tokyo, the seven national leaders issue a joint statement pledging to combat international terrorism.

Syria's President Hafez al-Assad arrives in Jordan for a two-day visit, his first in nine years, with King Hussein.

6 Sudan's ruling military council hands over power to a civilian coalition government. Multiparty elections were held April 1–12.

Israel becomes the third U.S. ally, following Great Britain and West Germany, to announce its participation in the Strategic Defense Initiative.

10 Louisiana's Gov. Edwin W. Edwards (D) and four codefendants are acquitted by a New Orleans jury on fraud and racketeering charges.

15 Two members of a climbing group lost in a blizzard on Oregon's Mt. Hood are found alive after a two-day search. Nine died in the storm.

16 Three members of Argentina's former military junta are found guilty of negligence in losing the 1982 Falklands War.

17 China and Taiwan open their first direct talks since the Communists took power on the mainland in 1949. The talks concern the return of a Taiwanese plane hijacked to China by its pilot May 3.

19 South Africa attacks guerrilla strongholds of the African National Congress (ANC) in Botswana, Zambia, and Zimbabwe.

20 The Soviet Union names Yuri V. Dubinin, its chief UN delegate, to succeed Anatoly Dobrynin as ambassador to the United States.

21 In the Netherlands, the coalition of Prime Minister Ruud Lubbers retains its parliamentary majority in national elections.

In Bangladesh, the progovernment Jatiya Party is declared the winner of May 7 parliamentary elections.

At the Teamsters union convention in Las Vegas, NV, President Jackie Presser is elected to a five-year term. Five days earlier, Presser was indicted on federal racketeering charges.

May 4, Tokyo: The leaders of Canada, France, Great Britain, Italy, Japan, West Germany, and the United States open their 12th annual economic summit conference. It was widely regarded as the most successful to date.

© Robert Wallis/JB Pictures

© Charlie Archambault/Picture Group

24 Britain's Margaret Thatcher begins a three-day visit to Israel, the first ever by a British prime minister.

The Montreal Canadiens win hockey's Stanley Cup championship, defeating the Calgary Flames in Game 5 of the play-off finals.

25 Virgilio Barco Vargas wins presidential elections in Colombia.

The presidents of five Central American countries conclude a two-day summit in Esquipulas, Guatemala, to discuss regional peace; differences persist.

In "Hands Across America," organized to focus attention on the problems of poverty and homelessness, more than five million persons form a human chain across the United States.

26 In the Dominican Republic, former President Joaquin Balaguer is declared the winner of May 16 presidential elections.

27 President Reagan tentatively affirms U.S. compliance with the 1979 Strategic Arms Limitation Treaty (SALT II) but warns that continued Soviet violations would force a change in policy.

The United Nations General Assembly opens a six-day special session on the economic crisis in Africa.

29 An independent counsel is appointed to investigate conflict-of-interest and influence-peddling charges against lobbyist Michael Deaver, formerly a top aide to President Reagan.

From Battery Park in New York City to the dock of the "Queen Mary" in Long Beach, CA, the Hands Across America chain was 4,150 mi (6 680 km) long. Officially, 5,441,960 people took part in the event, which raised up to $100 million for the poor and homeless.

June

3 Leftist rebels in El Salvador accept a government offer to re-open peace talks, stalled since 1984.

William R. Graham is named chief science adviser to President Reagan.

4 Former U.S. Navy Intelligence analyst Jonathan Jay Pollard pleads guilty to spying for Israel.

5 The U.S. Senate sustains President Reagan's veto of a resolution barring an advanced missile sale to Saudi Arabia.

Ronald W. Pelton, a former employee of the U.S. National Security Agency, is found guilty of spying for the Soviet Union.

President Reagan announces big changes in the U.S. Supreme Court: Warren Burger (far right) steps down as chief justice, Associate Justice William Rehnquist (second from right) is appointed to succeed him, and Judge Antonin Scalia (far left) is appointed to the body.

8 Former UN Secretary-General Kurt Waldheim is elected president of Austria despite charges of Nazi activity during World War II.

The Boston Celtics win their 16th National Basketball Association championship, defeating the Houston Rockets in the play-off finals.

9 After a four-month investigation, the president's commission on the space shuttle disaster submits its report. The rocket manufacturer and the space administration are severely criticized.

11 Leaders of the Warsaw Pact countries conclude a two-day summit in Budapest, Hungary.

12 The white minority government of South Africa, anticipating black violence related to the upcoming tenth anniversary of the Soweto uprising, declares a nationwide state of emergency.

17 Warren E. Burger announces his retirement as chief justice of the U.S. Supreme Court. President Reagan names Associate Justice William H. Rehnquist as his successor and appoints federal appeals court Judge Antonin Scalia to the vacant seat.

19 Richard W. Miller, a former agent of the U.S. Federal Bureau of Investigation, is found guilty of spying for the Soviet Union.

20 President Reagan has two small polyps removed from his colon.

22 Spain's Prime Minister Felipe González wins reelection, as his Socialist Workers' Party retains a solid parliamentary majority.

24 The U.S. Senate overwhelmingly approves a sweeping tax-reform bill. The House had passed its own tax bill in December 1985; a joint conference now would consider differences between the two bills.

Cocaine overdose is identified as the cause of death, June 19, of college basketball star Len Bias.

25 In a reversal of a March vote, the U.S. House of Representatives approves $100 million in aid to Nicaraguan "contra" rebels.

26 Irish voters overwhelmingly reject a measure to end the nation's ban on divorce.

27 The International Court of Justice rules that the United States had broken international law and violated Nicaragua's national sovereignty by aiding antigovernment rebels.

Italy's Prime Minister Bettino Craxi announces the resignation of his goverment.

Citing differences over nuclear policy, U.S. Secretary of State George Shultz informs New Zealand Prime Minister David Lange that the United States would no longer be bound to defend New Zealand under the ANZUS treaty.

29 Argentina defeats West Germany, 3-2, to win soccer's World Cup.

30 The U.S. Supreme Court rules, 5-4, that the constitution does not protect private homosexual acts between consenting adults.

Two days after being chosen by the Boston Celtics in the NBA's annual college draft, former University of Maryland basketball standout Len Bias, 22, died of a cocaine overdose.

July

1 Pope John Paul II arrives in Colombia for a six-day visit.

3 On the first day of "Liberty Weekend" in New York City, President Reagan relights the torch of the Statue of Liberty. The four-day celebration marks the statue's restoration and 100th anniversary.

The 10th congress of Poland's United Workers' (Communist) Party concludes in Warsaw with the reelection of Gen. Wojciech Jaruzelski as first secretary and with sweeping changes in the policy-making Politburo.

4 Athletes from 70 nations gather in Moscow for the opening of the first Goodwill Games, a 16-day Olympic-type competition.

6 West Germany's Boris Becker successfully defends his Wimbledon men's singles tennis title. Martina Navratilova won her fifth straight women's singles crown on July 5.

Japan's ruling Liberal Democratic Party (LDP), headed by Prime Minister Yasuhiro Nakasone, wins a landslide victory in parliamentary elections.

7 Loyalists of former Philippines President Ferdinand Marcos abandon a short-lived rebellion. The Marcos supporters, including several hundred troops, occupied a Manila hotel the previous day.

France and New Zealand announce the settlement of differences over the July 1985 sinking of the Greenpeace vessel *Rainbow Warrior* by French agents in Auckland harbor.

The U.S. Supreme Court rules that a key provision of the Gramm-Rudman budget-balancing law, the mechanism for automatic spending cuts, is unconstitutional.

10 Eleven men charged in the October 1985 hijacking of the cruise ship *Achille Lauro* are convicted by an Italian court.

14 In Vietnam, Truong Chinh is chosen to succeed Le Duan, who died on July 10, as secretary of the nation's Communist Party.

15 U.S. officials announce that Army troops and equipment have been sent to Bolivia to help in the war on drug trafficking.

20 As part of a Soviet effort to improve relations with Western Europe, the Kremlin welcomes West German Foreign Minister Hans-Dietrich Genscher to Moscow. Earlier in the month, France's President François Mitterrand visited the USSR, and Soviet Foreign Minister Eduard Shevardnadze traveled to London.

21 Israel's Prime Minister Shimon Peres arrives in Morocco for two days of talks with King Hassan II.

22 In a major policy speech on South Africa, President Reagan calls for the Pretoria government to negotiate an end to apartheid, but he rejects any new U.S. economic sanctions.

23 At London's Westminster Abbey, Great Britain's Prince Andrew marries Sarah Ferguson.

24 As a protest against Great Britain's policies toward South Africa, more than 30 nations and colonies boycott the Commonwealth Games in Edinburgh, Scotland.

26 After being held hostage for nearly 19 months, the Rev. Lawrence Jenco is freed by Lebanese Shiite Muslim extremists.

28 Soviet General Secretary Gorbachev announces that the USSR will withdraw six military units, or up to 7,500 troops, from Afghanistan by year's end.

29 A U.S. federal jury in New York City finds that the National Football League had violated antitrust law, but it awards the United States Football League only $1 (trebled) in damages.

31 U.S. and Japanese representatives sign a five-year accord resolving a bitter trade dispute over computer chips.

The Rev. Lawrence Jenco of Joliet, IL, enters the U.S. Air Force hospital in Wiesbaden, West Germany, after his release by Lebanese Shiite Muslims on July 26. The 51-year-old priest had been held hostage in Lebanon for nearly 19 months. He was found to be in good health.

AP/Wide World

August

1 Ending a month-long government crisis, Socialist Bettino Craxi is sworn in as prime minister of Italy.

President Reagan backs a plan for the United States to subsidize exports of 4 million metric tons of wheat to the USSR.

3 Thailand's Prem Tinsulanonda agrees to stay on as prime minister, heading a coalition formed after July 27 elections.

4 Breaking a long deadlock, the Organization of the Petroleum Exporting Countries (OPEC) agrees on cuts in oil production.

5 At a summit of seven Commonwealth heads of state, Britain's Prime Minister Margaret Thatcher agrees to two limited economic sanctions against South Africa but resists tougher action.

Preston R. Tisch is named U.S. postmaster general, replacing Albert V. Casey.

6 William J. Schroeder, the longest surviving artificial heart recipient, dies 620 days after the device was implanted.

7 The Soviet news agency Tass reports that fugitive U.S. CIA agent Edward Lee Howard has been granted asylum in the USSR.

© Sahm Doherty/''Time'' Magazine

The British government came under mounting pressure, both from demonstrators at home and from other Commonwealth nations, to declare economic sanctions against South Africa. Prime Minister Thatcher steadfastly opposed strong action, arguing that sanctions would hurt South African blacks and fail to destroy apartheid.

12 Mexico's President Miguel de la Madrid Hurtado begins a three-day visit to the United States.

13 The U.S. Senate votes to approve President Reagan's request for $100 million in aid to Nicaraguan contra rebels; the House passed an identical measure in June.

In separate ceremonies, leaders of East and West Germany mark the 25th anniversary of the start of the construction on the Berlin Wall.

18 Soviet General-Secretary Mikhail Gorbachev announces that Moscow's yearlong moratorium on nuclear testing, which expired August 6, will continue to Jan. 1, 1987.

Israeli and Soviet officials meet in Helsinki, Finland, to discuss possible resumption of consular diplomatic ties. It is the first formal contract between the two nations in some 19 years.

20 In one of the worst mass-murder attacks in U.S. history, part-time mail carrier Patrick Sherrill opens fire in the Edmonds, OK, post office, killing 14 workers; he also kills himself.

21 More than 1,700 persons are killed in the African country of Cameroon, as poisonous gas erupts from volcanic Lake Nios and drifts over nearby villages.

25 A special conference called by the International Atomic Energy Agency convenes in Vienna, Austria, to study the causes and effects of the Chernobyl nuclear power plant accident in the Soviet Ukraine. A formal report issued by the Soviet Union on August 21 cited human error as the cause.

28 The government of Bolivia declares a state of siege to quell growing labor unrest.

Jerry A. Whitworth is sentenced to 365 years in prison for his role in a spy ring that sold U.S. naval secrets to the USSR.

30 Nicholas Daniloff, a correspondent for *U.S. New & World Report* magazine, is arrested in Moscow under suspicion of spying. The move is seen as a retaliation for the arrest in New York one week earlier of alleged Soviet spy Gennadi Zakharov.

AP/Wide World

The 47-year-old former U.S. Navy radioman Jerry Whitworth, who was convicted in July of selling code and communications secrets to the Soviet Union, was sentenced by a California federal judge to 365 years in prison.

September

1 A Soviet freighter and cruise ship collide on the Black Sea. Some 835 people are rescued, but 398 are dead or missing.

5 Four Arab terrorists storm a Pan Am jet in Karachi, Pakistan. After a 16-hour standoff, the gunmen open fire and kill 21 passengers. The hijackers are captured in a raid by Pakistani troops.

6 Two Arab terrorists open fire inside a Jewish synagogue in Istanbul, Turkey, killing 21 worshipers and themselves.

7 Chile's President Augusto Pinochet survives an assassination attempt on a road outside Santiago. Hours later, he declares a state of siege.

The eighth summit of the Nonaligned Movement concludes in Harare, Zimbabwe. Discussions of South African apartheid and U.S. foreign policy dominated the conference.

Ivan Lendl and Martina Navratilova win the men's and women's singles titles, respectively, at the U.S. Open tennis tournament at Flushing Meadow, NY.

8 Pakistani opposition leader Benazir Bhutto, the daughter of former President Zulfikar Ali Bhutto who had been arrested in a sweeping government crackdown August 14, is released from custody. Bhutto returned from exile in April.

9 Brazil's President José Sarney becomes that country's first civilian president in more than 30 years to visit the United States.

10 Thomas Wyman resigns as chairman and president of CBS Inc. Laurence Tisch, the company's largest stockholder, takes over as chief executive. Company founder William Paley is named acting chairman.

11 Egypt's President Hosni Mubarak and Israel's Prime Minister Shimon Peres begin a two-day conference in Alexandria, Egypt. It is the first summit between the two nations in five years.

The Dow Jones industrial stock average drops a record 86.61 points, falling to 1792.89. Less than a week earlier, the index hit an all-time high of 1919.71.

12 A yearlong strike by meatpackers against the Hormel Company ends as workers vote to approve a new contract.

14 In a televised address, President Reagan and First Lady Nancy Reagan appeal for a "national crusade" against drug abuse.

15 Texas Air Corp. agrees to purchase ailing People Express Inc.

16 Foreign ministers of the 12 European Community nations agree to a package of economic sanctions against South Africa.

The 41st session of the UN General Assembly opens in New York.

17 A terrorist bomb blast in Paris, France, the fifth to rip the city in ten days, leaves five persons dead.

18 During a nine-day visit to the United States, Philippines' President Corazon Aquino addresses a joint session of Congress.

22 After 32 months of negotiations in Stockholm, Sweden, the 35-nation Conference on Confidence- and Security-Building Measures and Disarmament in Europe (CDE) adopts a final document to reduce the risk of war.

26 William H. Rehnquist is sworn in as U.S. chief justice; Antonin Scalia is sworn in as associate justice of the Supreme Court. Both nominations were approved by the Senate September 17.

30 Under a diplomatic arrangement between Washington and Moscow two days earlier, accused Soviet spy Gennadi Zakharov is released from U.S. custody. American journalist Nicholas Daniloff, arrested in Moscow on August 30, was set free September 29.

AP/Wide World

In an address to a joint session of the U.S. Congress on September 18, Philippines President Corazon Aquino (bottom) focused on her handling of the Communist insurgency. House Speaker Tip O'Neill (left) called it "the finest speech I've heard in my 34 years in Congress."

October

2 According to a White House memo uncovered by the press, the Reagan administration had planned and launched a media "disinformation" campaign to convince Libyan leader Muammar el-Qaddafi that he would be ousted in a coup or that the United States would launch another retaliatory bombing raid.

India's Prime Minister Rajiv Gandhi is unharmed in an assassination attempt by a lone gunman in Delhi.

3 The World Bank and International Monetary Fund conclude their annual joint meeting in Washington, DC. The World Bank will increase its aid to poor Third World countries by 14%.

5 Nicaraguan forces shoot down a U.S. cargo plane carrying arms to "contra" rebels in southern Nicaragua. Two U.S. crew members are killed, and a third, Eugene Hasenfus, a 45-year-old native of Marinette, WI, is captured.

6 A Soviet nuclear-powered submarine sinks in the Atlantic Ocean after an on-board explosion that killed three crew members.

7 Soviet dissidents Yuri Orlov and Irina Valitova are welcomed at the White House. Their release October 5 was part of the deal between Washington and Moscow for the exchange of accused Soviet spy Gennadi Zakharov and U.S. journalist Nicholas Daniloff.

9 The U.S. Senate convicts District Court Judge Harry E. Claiborne on three articles of impeachment. He had been convicted of tax evasion in 1984 but refused to resign from the bench.

Soviet world chess champion Gary Kasparov retains his title with a final draw in a 24-game rematch with Anatoly Karpov.

10 An earthquake in San Salvador, the capital of El Salvador, leaves an estimated 1,500 people dead and 300,000 homeless.

12 President Reagan and Soviet General Secretary Mikhail Gorbachev conclude two days of talks at Reykjavik, Iceland. A major arms control agreement fell through over differences regarding the future of the U.S. Strategic Defense Initiative, or "Star Wars" program.

Great Britain's Queen Elizabeth II arrives in China in the first state visit to that country by a British monarch.

14 Author, educator, and human-rights activist Elie Wiesel is named the winner of the Nobel Prize for Peace.

15 President Hussain Mohammad Ershad of Bangladesh easily wins reelection, as opposition parties boycott the balloting.

16 An Israeli warplane is shot down during an air strike on Palestinian guerrilla bases in southern Lebanon. The raid came one day after a terrorist grenade attack in Jerusalem.

17 President Reagan signs into law a five-year, $9 billion Superfund toxic waste cleanup bill.

19 President Samora Machel of Mozambique is killed in a plane crash en route from Zambia.

20 In a power rotation agreement reached in 1984, Yitzhak Shamir is sworn in as prime minister of Israel. He replaces Shimon Peres, who takes over his post as foreign minister.

21 International Business Machines (IBM) Corporation announces that it is suspending business in South Africa. General Motors Corporation announced its pullout the day before.

22 In an escalating series of diplomatic expulsions, the Soviet Union orders five U.S. diplomats to leave the country. One day earlier Washington expelled 55 Soviets, in retaliation for Moscow's ouster of five Americans on October 19.

President Reagan signs into law a sweeping reform of the U.S. tax code.

© J.L. Atlan/Sygma

In an October 22 ceremony on the White House lawn, administration officials and key members of the Senate and House gathered to watch President Reagan sign the Tax Reform Act of 1986. He called it "less a reform . . . than a revolution."

24 A jury in Great Britain convicts Palestinian Nezar Hindawi of packing a bomb in the bag of his Irish girlfriend, who was boarding a flight from London to Tel Aviv, Israel, in April. Citing links between Hindawi and the Syrian government, Great Britain severs diplomatic relations with Damascus.

27 A major deregulation of the London Stock Exchange, being called the "Big Bang," goes into effect.

The New York Mets win baseball's World Series with an 8–5 victory over the Boston Red Sox in Game 7.

28 A quiet ceremony on Liberty Island in New York Harbor marks the official 100th birthday of the Statue of Liberty.

29 Saudi Arabia's King Fahd dismisses the nation's longtime oil minister, Sheik Ahmed Zaki Yamani.

31 The United States and Japan announce a broad economic cooperation agreement.

Prince Souphanouvong of Laos steps down as president. Phoumi Vongvichit is named temporary president.

November

1 A fire at a chemical warehouse near Basel, Switzerland, causes a chemical spill that seriously pollutes the Rhine River.

2 American hostage David Jacobsen, the director of American University Hospital in Beirut, who had been held in Lebanon for 18 months, is freed by Shiite Muslim extremists.

4 In U.S. midterm elections, the Democrats win a 55–45 majority in the Senate and increase their majority in the House to 258–177. The Republicans gain eight governorships.

In Vienna, Austria, the 35-nation Conference on Security and Cooperation opens its third major review of the 1975 Helsinki Accords. U.S. Secretary of State George Shultz and Soviet Foreign Minister Eduard Shevardnadze confer on arms control but make no progress.

5   Three U.S. Navy ships dock in Qingdao, China, in the first U.S. naval port call to that country since the Communist takeover in 1949.

6   President Reagan signs what he calls "the most comprehensive reform of our immigration laws since 1952." He vetoes a bill to provide $18 billion for sewer projects and the cleaning up of U.S. waterways.

John A. Walker, Jr., the convicted leader of a spy ring that sold important military secrets to the Soviet Union, is sentenced to life in prison.

General Motors Corporation announces that it will close 11 plants, employing some 29,000 people, by 1990.

13 President Reagan confirms reports that the United States has sent shipments of arms and military spare parts to Iran.

14 Ivan Boesky, a major Wall Street stock investor, agrees to pay a $100 million penalty for insider trading.

15 The ruling party of Brazil's President José Sarney wins a landslide victory in congressional and state elections.

17 Georges Blesse, the president of France's state-owned automobile maker Renault, is killed by leftist extremists.

18 Earlier reports of the assassination of North Korea's President Kim Il Sung are proven false, as he makes a public appearance.

The Chinese Navy welcomed visitors from the United States on November 5 in Qingdao. The docking of the USS "Reeves," "Rentz," and "Oldendorf" marked the first U.S. naval port call to the People's Republic.

19 The International Monetary Fund approves a $1.68 billion standby loan to Mexico.

20 U.S. Senate Democrats name Robert C. Byrd (WV) as the body's new majority leader.

The World Health Organization announces a major international campaign against Acquired Immune Deficiency Syndrome (AIDS).

23 Amid reports of a planned coup attempt by military officers loyal to Defense Minister Juan Ponce Enrile, President Corazon Aquino of the Philippines asks for the resignation of her entire cabinet and immediately replaces Enrile.

25 U.S. Attorney General Edwin Meese III reports that up to $30 million in proceeds from secret U.S. weapons sales to Iran had been diverted to Nicaraguan "contra" rebels. President Reagan says that he "was not fully informed" of the activities and therefore has accepted the resignation of National Security Adviser John M. Poindexter and fired a key aide, Lt. Col. Oliver L. North.

Soviet General-Secretary Mikhail Gorbachev arrives in India for a three-day visit, the first by a leader of the USSR since 1980.

Austria's Chancellor Franz Vranitzky and his government resign. In national elections two days earlier, his Socialist Party retained a plurality in the National Council but lost ten seats.

Bronx (NY) Democratic leader Stanley Friedman and three co-defendants are convicted of racketeering and conspiracy charges related to a corruption scandal in the New York City Parking Violations Bureau.

27 The Philippine government and Communist rebels sign a 60-day cease-fire.

The West German government imposes diplomatic sanctions against Syria one day after two Palestinians with links to Damascus were convicted of the March 29 bombing of a club in West Berlin.

28 By deploying a B-52 bomber capable of carrying cruise missiles, the United States officially violates the 1979 Strategic Arms Limitation Treaty (SALT II).

30 Sikh extremists in the Indian state of Punjab commandeer a public bus and kill 22 Hindu passengers.

Lt. Col. Oliver North invoked his 5th Amendment rights and refused to testify before House and Senate committees investigating the Iran-contra affair. The key question was whether he acted alone or with the approval of higher administration officials.

December

1 Pope John Paul II concludes a five-nation, 31,000-mi (50 000-km) tour of Asia and the Pacific, the longest trip of his papacy.

4 Chief White House spokesman Larry Speakes announces that he is resigning, effective Feb. 1, 1987.

6 Honduran planes and ground forces attack Nicaraguan troops along the border between the two countries after the Sandinistas had entered Honduras in a mission against "contra" rebels based there. U.S. helicopters are deployed to airlift Honduran troops.

In Taiwan the opposition Democratic Progressive Party wins a surprising 23 of 44 contested seats in legislative elections.

8 After more than two weeks of often violent student protests, French Prime Minister Jacques Chirac announces that he will withdraw his disputed legislative bill on university reform.

U.S. Rep. Jim Wright (TX) is elected by Democratic colleagues as speaker of the House, succeeding the retiring Rep. Thomas P. (Tip) O'Neill (MA).

10 The government of South Africa imposes strict new regulations on news reporting of black unrest.

15 Two days of ethnic rioting in Karachi, Pakistan, leave at least 150 persons dead.

16 Agriculture ministers of the European Community (EC) reach a major agreement on farm policy, aimed specifically at reducing dairy and beef surpluses.

17 Eugene Hasenfus, the American flyer shot down over Nicaragua while carrying arms supplies to "contra" rebels in October and later sentenced to 30 years in prison, is set free. Five days earlier, another American, self-styled counterterrorist Sam Nesley Hall, was arrested in Nicaragua and charged with spying.

18 Moscow announces that it will end its moratorium on underground nuclear testing upon the first U.S. test in 1987.

The Soviet news agency Tass reports an outbreak of anti-Russian rioting in Alma-Ata, the capital of Kazakhstan province, USSR.

Nguyen Van Linh is named head of the Communist Party of Vietnam. He replaces Truong Chinh, who resigned two days earlier.

19 Soviet dissident Andrei Sakharov and his wife, human-rights campaigner Yelena Bonner, are released from internal exile in Gorky and allowed to return to Moscow. Another prominent dissident, Anatoly Marchenko, died in a Soviet prison December 8.

20 Meeting in Geneva, members of the Organization of the Petroleum Exporting Countries (OPEC) agree to cut oil production and raise prices to $18 per barrel.

Some 50,000 students march in the streets of Shanghai, China, calling for broader democratic rights.

23 Richard G. Rutan and Jeana Yeager, flying the experimental plane *Voyager,* complete the first nonstop flight around the world on a single load of fuel. The nine-day trip began and ended at Edwards Air Force Base in California.

24 Shiite Muslim extremists in Lebanon free French hostage Aureal Cornéa, who had been held for more than nine months.

25 A hijacked Iraqi jetliner crashes on a desert airstrip in Saudi Arabia, killing 62 persons.

26 One day after a new military offensive by Iran, Iraqi troops recapture four small islands in the strategic Shatt al Arab frontier waterway. Both sides suffer heavy casualties.

31 Nearly 100 people are killed in a New Year's Eve fire at the Dupont Plaza Hotel in San Juan, Puerto Rico. Arson is suspected.

AP/Wide World

Soviet dissident Andrei Sakharov meets with reporters upon returning to Moscow after seven years of exile in Gorky. The 65-year-old physicist, who apparently was released without condition, condemned the USSR's continued presence in Afghanistan and called for freedom for all jailed dissidents.

© Andy Hernandez/Sygma

THE PHILIPPINES
A NATION IN CHANGE

By Leonard Casper and Gretchen Casper

The Philippine presidential election campaign began during December 1985. Corazon Aquino (above left), the wife of the assassinated opposition leader Benigno Aquino, and her running mate, Salvador Laurel (right), traveled throughout the nation to convey their message.

On the evening of Feb. 25, 1986, Corazon C. Aquino, the principal figure in the peaceful revolution that ousted Philippines President Ferdinand Marcos after 20 years in power—and the newly inaugurated successor to the presidency—made a brief statement on national television: "A new life starts for our country tomorrow," she declared, "a life filled with hope and I believe a life that will be blessed with peace and progress."

For the Southeast Asian nation of 58 million people, the transfer of power culminated several years of increasingly active anti-Marcos sentiment, especially since the mysterious August 1983 assassination of Mrs. Aquino's husband, opposition leader and former Sen. Benigno S. Aquino, Jr. As the developments of 1986 quite clearly demonstrated, however, the installation of "Cory" Aquino and her 17-member cabinet also marked the beginning of a difficult and precarious period of transition.

The Elections. The historic events of 1986 in the Philippines began with a presidential election campaign early in the year. Constitutionally, Marcos was not required to hold an election until 1987. However, under pressure from foreign interest in a stable government and from local reformers, the 68-year-old Marcos agreed to test his popular mandate at an earlier date. His ability to rule was being questioned on several grounds: the state of his health; his closeness with Chief of Staff Gen. Fabian C. Ver, who although acquitted in December 1985 of involvement in the assassination of Benigno Aquino, was still connected in the minds of some with the murder; continuing economic decline despite general growth in the rest of Pacific Asia; and the steady escalation of armed Communist insurgency, blamed in part on Marcos' regime. In November 1985 he suddenly announced that a "snap election" would be held on Feb. 7, 1986. A coalition of opposition parties persuaded Corazon Aquino, the senator's widow, to run against Marcos, with Salvador Laurel of the United Democratic Opposition (UNIDO) as the vice-presidential candidate.

Although the period for campaigning was brief, the Filipino people did not need extraordinary measures to be aroused. Under Marcos there had been martial law from 1972 to 1981 and rule by decree since then. There also was widespread official corruption, a steady flight of capital (especially since the Aquino assassination), a 20% rate of unemployment, and poverty for more than two thirds of the population. Aquino supporters were asking only for an honest tally of their votes. Jaime Cardinal Sin, the Roman Catholic archbishop of Manila, who previously had maintained a position of "critical collaboration" with Marcos, now urged the people to vote their consciences. The possibility of an anti-Marcos election result had become evident when, in the National Assembly elections of 1984, the opposition took 56 of the 183 available seats.

This time, mindful of Aquino's popularity, Marcos' New Society Movement (KBL)—despite the presence of official foreign observers and worldwide media—was reported to have resorted to the kinds of strategies that had kept him in power for 20 years. Election day saw widespread terrorism at the polls, bribes, fraud, "flying voters," stolen ballot boxes, and disenfranchisement of hundreds of thousands of Aquino backers. Nevertheless the nonpartisan National Citizens' Movement for Free Elections (NAMFREL), which guarded the ballots and ran its own tallies, declared on February 8 that Aquino was winning the vote count, 55%–45%. The next day the government's Committee on Elections (COMELEC) put President Marcos in the lead. Giving credence to the charges of manipulation, 30 COMELEC computer operators deserted their machines rather than be accomplices to apparent vote fraud.

On February 9, Marcos hinted that, should Aquino appear to win the election, he would bar the Assembly from proclaiming her president. Two days later word came from the province of Antique that the popular Evelio Javier, Aquino's local campaign manager, had been murdered by gunmen in a public square.

Information Highlights

Official Name: Republic of the Philippines.

Location: Southeast Asia.

Area: 116,000 sq mi (300 440 km²).

Population: (mid-1986 est.): 58,100,000.

Chief Cities (1980 census): Manila, the capital, 1,630,485; Quezon City, 1,165,865; Davao, 610,375; Cebu, 490,281.

Government: *Head of state and government,* Corazon C. Aquino, president (took office Feb. 25, 1986).

Monetary Unit: Peso (20.4 pesos equal U.S. $1, Dec. 5, 1986).

Gross National Product (1985 prelim. U.S.$): $33,590,000,000.

Economic Index (1985): *Consumer Prices* (1980 = 100), all items, 253.9; food, 249.7.

Foreign Trade (1985): *Imports,* $5,261,000,000; *exports,* $4,544,000,000.

About the Authors: Dr. Leonard Casper is a professor of English at Boston College in Chestnut Hill, MA, and his daughter Gretchen teaches political science at Grinnell College in Grinnell, IA. Both are keen observers of current developments in the Philippines and have traveled throughout the country. Dr. Leonard Casper was twice the recipient of Fulbright grants to lecture in the Philippines, and he has written or edited several important works on the nation's literature.

The sitation continued to deteriorate. On February 14 the Roman Catholic Bishops Conference called the election fraud unparalleled. U.S. President Ronald Reagan's special emissary, Philip Habib, arrived the next day to assess the possibility of reconciliation, but Corazon Aquino had already proclaimed that "The people and I have won, and we know it. Nothing can take our victory from us."

On February 16 the National Assembly declared Marcos the winner with 53.8% of the vote. The same day NAMFREL had Aquino ahead in its unofficial count and claimed that at least 3.3 million of her supporters had been prevented from voting. Declaring herself president, Aquino announced a nonviolent resistance campaign to bring down the Marcos regime. She called for a one-day general strike, should he be inaugurated, and a boycott of banks and businesses controlled by his government. Marcos stood firm, threatening demonstrators and boycotters with charges of sedition and rebellion.

The Changeover. On February 22, while Aquino was in Cebu rallying her supporters, Defense Minister Juan Ponce Enrile and Deputy Chief of the Armed Forces Lt. Gen. Fidel Ramos defected from the Marcos ranks and, surrounded by several hundred troops, took over Camp Aguinaldo, the defense ministry headquarters in Quezon City. Both Ramos and Enrile had reason to feel slighted by the administration they had served. Ramos, one of several Filipino military officers to be graduated from West Point, felt that he, not General Ver, should be chief of staff. General Ver had been appointed chief of staff in 1981 and recently had become de facto commander of the Philippine Constabulary. While Ver was being tried, Ramos was made acting chief of staff, but in name only. Ver,

At campaign rallies such as the one in Caloocan (below), Ferdinand Marcos regularly predicted that he would defeat Mrs. Aquino overwhelmingly.

© Andy Hernandez/Sygma

through an alliance with the politically powerful Imelda Marcos, the president's wife, also had relegated Enrile to so insignificant a role that the defense minister had offered to resign. What further motivated the two defectors was their closeness to a growing reform movement within the military and to several coup attempts under consideration. The reformists, who had anonymously endorsed Mrs. Aquino, were predominantly junior officers who sought an end to corruption and political cronyism in the military. Abuses by the armed forces, desperate economic conditions, and land ownership by a relative few were widely believed to have spurred the growth of the Communist insurgency, called the New People's Army (NPA), over the years. Insurgent forces increased from an estimated 500 in 1965 to 16,000 regulars in 1985, gaining control of about 20% of the nation's 40,000 villages.

At first Enrile and Ramos had the active backing of less than 300 troops. Then Cardinal Sin appealed to the Filipino people on Radio Veritas to bring food and supplies to the garrisons at Camp Aguinaldo and nearby Camp Crame. Half a million citizens responded to the plea and formed human barriers around the camps. When Marcos' tanks and marines arrived on February 23, they could not bring themselves to massacre the assemblies of nuns and priests, unarmed businessmen, and students offering flowers. Ver urged an assault, however bloody; but Marcos delayed.

The following day armed helicopters joined Enrile at Camp Crame, and Ramos reported that he had gained the support of most field commanders. Marcos requested that Malacañang, the presidential palace, not be stormed and that he be allowed to remain as a figurehead president until 1987, after which he would no longer seek elective office. He was promised only a

The National Assembly, which counted the ballots, proclaimed President Marcos the election winner early on February 16.

After declaring herself president, announcing a nonviolent "active resistance" campaign to bring down the Marcos government, and winning some key support, Cory Aquino was sworn in by Supreme Court Justice Claudio Teehankee at the Club Filipino on February 25. Her mother-in-law held the bible.

© Greg Smith/Picture Group

safe departure. Nations around the world, including the United States, withdrew their support and called on him to resign.

On the morning of February 25, Corazon Aquino was sworn in as president. A few hours later at Malacañang Palace, Marcos quietly held his own inauguration ceremony, after which his entourage was taken by helicopter to Clark Field, where they boarded a U.S. Air Force transport plane for Guam. President Aquino declared a "new life" for the Philippines.

Aftermath and the New Government. By February 26 the Marcos entourage—including some 90 relatives and supporters—had arrived in Hawaii. Among their baggage were the equivalent of $1.5 million in new peso bills and jewelry worth $5–$10 million, most of which was confiscated by U.S. Customs as undeclared. In addition they carried documents eventually made available to the Philippine government as evidence of bank deposits and properties around the world. Before year's end several million dollars had been recovered by the Aquino government's new Presidential Commission on

Good Government; Marcos' children, along with General Ver, were being investigated by U.S. courts for possible embezzlement of economic and military aid; and, in an unusual move, Swiss banks disclosed secret Marcos holdings. Facing confiscations and years of litigation, the Marcoses requested refuge in other countries, but only several small West African nations made offers.

While many Filipino people rejoiced at Marcos' removal, the joy was quickly tempered by the realization that removing the effects of two decades of increasingly authoritarian rule and the alleged plundering of their national treasury might require years of concerted effort and good will. The question arose whether the change in power would be an "unfinished revolution" like that against Spain in 1896 (which was followed by U.S. annexation rather than independence). In a culture so long governed by privilege and patronage, would there be a return to rule by an all-powerful elite or would the republic-in-name become a sociopolitical fact?

Aquino's inauguration on the patrician grounds of the exclusive Club Filipino in Manila was worrisome even to some of her closest supporters. She sought to offset the impression of elitism by opening Malacañang Palace to the public, while setting up office in the guest house and living elsewhere entirely. On March 2 habeas corpus was restored, and by March 5 hundreds of political prisoners, including Communist leaders José Maria Sison and Bernabe Buscayno, were released; amnesty was offered to other rebels in return for pledges of nonviolence.

After lengthy cabinet discussions on how to legitimize her administration in the absence of a definitive vote tally, President Aquino on March 25 proclaimed a provisional "freedom constitution" based on popular mandate. Under the document the National Assembly was abolished, and President Aquino would be the sole legislator until a new charter was written and submitted to a referendum, and legislative elections were held. She limited her power by reinstating the bill of rights and allowing full judicial review. Within 60 days, Aquino prom-

AP/Wide World

President Marcos fled the Philippines shortly after being inaugurated privately for another term in Malacañang Palace on February 25. He and his wife Imelda (above) flew to Guam and then settled in Hawaii.

Mrs. Aquino's first task as president was to name a government. A key figure in her 17-member cabinet was Defense Minister Juan Ponce Enrile (far left). In subsequent months, a rift developed between Aquino and Enrile, and before year's end he was dismissed.

© Sandro Tucci/"Time" Magazine

ised, she would appoint a Constitutional Commission to draw up a new charter. Another 60 days after the charter was completed, it would be referred to a plebiscite, after which a general election would be held.

The commission convened on June 2, its 48 delegates having been selected by Aquino from among 1,000 nominees. Among them were lawyers, religious and social activists, student and peasant leaders, and such former KBL stalwarts as Blas Ople, now reorganizing the Nationalist Party. To preside over the commission the delegates chose retired Supreme Court Justice Cecilia Muñoz-Palma, a counselor to Aquino but also a critic of her broad powers.

To provide as wide a spectrum of advice as possible, Aquino named a 17-member cabinet whose members often disagreed with one another. Salvador Laurel, who was elected vice-president, also became the foreign minister, and Enrile was named defense minister. (Ramos earlier had been designated chief of staff, a noncabinet post.) Having no formal party of her own and depending more on popular appeal than on organized support, Aquino had difficulty controlling the political aspirations of her own appointees. Minister of Local Government Aquilino Pimentel, for example, replaced local KBL officials with members of his own Filipino Democratic (PDP)/LABAN Party, who sometimes were less popular or competent than the original officials. In some instances he tried to wrest positions from UNIDO members, to the particular dismay of Laurel, who found his own political base shrinking after he had already sacrificed his presidential aspirations in order to let Aquino run.

Instability. Disunity within the new government grew as Enrile challenged the president more directly in public rallies. His principal complaint was that Aquino was too soft on Communism. First, she refused to set a deadline for NPA acceptance of a cease-fire, while the Philippine military (now called the New Armed Forces) was reduced to a defensive posture and continued to suffer casualties. Secondly, Enrile complained, she was offering amnesty to NPA members accused of brutal slayings while threatening to prosecute military officers charged with similar crimes.

Heartened by this confusion and urged on by Marcos from Hawaii, Arturo Tolentino, the KBL's vice-presidential candidate, seized the Manila Hotel with the help of several hundred troops on July 6. Tolentino took the oath of office as acting president and offered cabinet positions to Enrile and Ramos. When they declined, most of the soldiers surrendered. Tolentino himself was pardoned after swearing allegiance to the "freedom constitution" and renouncing future use of violence.

Burdened by attacks from opportunists within and outside the new government, Aquino's pace seemed to slacken. On August 22, Cardinal Sin warned that the gains of the revolution were "little by little" being lost. The Communist Party, whose leadership had made the mistake of boycotting the presidential election, regained a degree of prominence on Au-

One of the prime movers in the change of government was Lt. Gen. Fidel Ramos, the deputy chief of the armed forces under President Marcos. His defection, along with that of Defense Minister Enrile, to the Aquino camp was the turning point. Later in the year he was reported to block a move against the Aquino government by troops loyal to Enrile.

AP/Wide World

The funeral procession in Manila for Rolando Olalia, a leftist trade-union leader found slain November 13, was an outpouring of support for the Aquino government.

gust 30, when Sison and Buscayno announced the formation of the People's Party in time for the 1987 elections. Nevertheless, Aquino managed to set up peace talks with Muslim separatist leader Nur Misuari of the Moro National Liberation Front (MNLF), who had been in Middle Eastern exile for ten years. And on September 13, she signed a truce with Conrado Balweg of the Cordillera People's Liberation Army, an NPA splinter group.

In addition to ensuring a workable democratic government and defusing the Communist insurgency, restoring a battered economy was the major challenge facing President Aquino. In 1985 the nation's economic growth rate was a negative 3.5%, almost half of the nation's 21 million workers were underemployed, and the foreign debt totaled $26.2 billion. That such an ailing economy belonged to one of Southeast Asia's potentially richest countries suggested profound corruption among a profiteering few. To be successful President Aquino would need to achieve peace with the insurgents, establish a responsible and diverse group of cabinet advisers, and carry out her pledge of ending monopolies on sugar, coconut, and timber.

Some help came during President Aquino's nine-day visit to the United States in September. Among her achievements there was a widely applauded address to Congress, which later voted the Philippines $200 million in additional aid. She also received a promise of up to $600 million in new loans from the World Bank, as well as pledges of support from Filipinos across America. In late October the International Monetary Fund formally approved $519.4 million in loans.

©Manuel Cene/Black Star

© Andy Hernandez/Sygma

The insurgent New People's Army (NPA) numbered more than 16,000 regulars in 1986 and controlled 20% or more of the nation's villages. The communist NPA refused to take part in the February elections, but on November 27, after an ultimatum from President Aquino, agreed to sign a 60-day cease-fire, to begin December 10.

Shortly after Aquino's return home, Rodolfo Salas, the chairman of the Communist Party, was captured in Manila. At first the National Democratic Front (NDF), the political arm of the communist insurgents, broke off cease-fire negotiations, but it soon resumed them. Aquino already had convinced the U.S. Congress that every attempt at peaceful reconciliation had to be made before "taking up the sword" against the insurgents, but convincing Enrile was less easy.

On October 15, Aquino signed the draft charter presented by the Constitutional Commission. The document was more than a month late, but it had been passed almost unanimously by the commission delegates. Among its recommendations were a House of Representatives with 250 members and a Senate with 24, to be elected in May 1987; strong measures of social justice; economic guidelines; the dismantling of Marcos' Civilian Home Defense Forces, which had been accused of widespread abuse; and six-year presidential terms, with Aquino and Laurel permitted to remain in office until 1992.

It was this final provision which most alienated Defense Minister Enrile. He had considered running for president at the next election, but the proposed constitution, if ratified in the February 1987 plebiscite, would postpone his chances until 1992. Belatedly he challenged the legitimacy of the commission on the grounds that it had been appointed rather than elected. Salvador Laurel also urged that presidential as well as legislative elections be held in May. In addition to having sacrificed his own ambitions to the Aquino candidacy, he had seen his role as vice-president and foreign minister gradually diminished and his UNIDO coalition robbed of appointments. He was anxious to bring to the polls whatever power he could preserve.

The rift between Aquino and Enrile widened during October and early November, as the defense minister grew increasingly and more openly critical of the government's handling of the insurgency. Communist and government leaders met November 5 to discuss a 100-day cease-fire proposed by the NPA, but the two sides adjourned without an agreement. Amid rumors of an imminent coup attempt and against the urgings of her advisers, President Aquino departed November 10 on a four-day visit to Japan, where she negotiated another $649 million in aid. On the day of her return Rolando Olalia, a leftist political leader and the head of the nation's largest labor union, was found slain in Manila. Members of his party and union blamed the military and demanded Enrile's resignation.

The tensions came to a head on the night of November 22, when Chief of Staff Ramos blocked a reported move against the government by forces loyal to Enrile. The next day President Aquino dismissed the defense minister and named retired Lt. Gen. Rafael Ileto, Enrile's deputy, as his replacement. Saying "we need a fresh start," President Aquino also asked for the pro-forma resignations of her other cabinet members. She later dismissed three of them, including Pimentel, and promised other changes in due course. Pimental later was named a presidential adviser for national affairs.

Simultaneously with Enrile's firing, President Aquino also issued a stern warning to the insurgents. They would have seven days to agree to a cease-fire or all further negotiations would be terminated. The ultimatum apparently worked. Three days later the two sides agreed to a 60-day cease-fire, the first formal cessation of hostilities in 17 years of the guerrilla war. The cease-fire would take effect on December 10, with wider negotiations to begin 30 days later.

The signing of the accords took place on November 27, the birthday of Mrs. Aquino's late husband, at the Club Filipino, where she was sworn in as president in February. Mrs. Aquino did not actually attend the ceremony, but she issued a statement in which she expressed hope for a lasting settlement built on "the spirit of a genuine desire for peace." The February 2 plebiscite, as a vote of confidence, may finally permit the newly strengthened chief executive to get on with the "unfinished revolution."

As the year came to a close, the Philippines looked ahead to a February 1987 plebiscite on a new constitution. The proposed charter called for a 250-member House of Representatives, 24-member Senate, and six-year presidential term.

AP/Wide World

The Loss of
"CHALLENGER"
and AMERICA'S
FUTURE IN SPACE

By U.S. Rep. Bill Nelson (D-FL)

The sudden explosion of the U.S. space shuttle *Challenger* and the death of its seven crew members on Jan. 28, 1986, shattered the nation's innocent view of space travel and provided a grim lesson in its inherent dangers. The shockwaves will reverberate for years.

After 24 successful missions, most Americans had become convinced that the space shuttle system was eminently safe and reliable. The launching of *Challenger* from Cape Canaveral, FL, was expected to be another major highlight in the 25-year history of manned U.S. space flight. A private citizen —a person who could have been anyone's neighbor—for the first time was a crew member. Millions of students looked forward to lessons from space by Christa McAuliffe, a high-school teacher from Concord, NH. Flight commander Richard Scobee and pilot Michael Smith, along with payload specialist Gregory Jarvis and mission specialists Judith Resnick, Ellison Onizuka, and Ronald McNair (*see* pages 40–41), were to perform complex tasks which had become routine—launch a satellite and conduct dozens of experiments in zero gravity.

The crew and the thousands of people who worked to make the launch possible knew that every flight is dangerous. At 11:39 on that cold January morning, the entire nation—and the world—came to understand that space flight is risky business. Americans watched in stunned disbelief as footage of the accident, photographed with agonizing clarity, was shown repeatedly on television. Never before had the National Aeronautics and Space Administration (NASA) suffered a worse accident or setback. Never before had Americans related as closely to an astronaut as they did to Christa.

Yet, after their shock and sadness subsided, children showed a redoubled interest in space flight. National leaders spoke of a strong resolve to learn from the accident and resume the shuttle program. Americans realized that a return to safe space flight and to America's leadership position in space would be a most fitting tribute to the *Challenger* crew.

At 11:38 A.M. on Jan. 28, 1986, the space shuttle "Challenger" was launched from Cape Canaveral, FL, with a crew of seven on board (photo, page 36).

About the Author: Bill Nelson (D-FL) has been a member of the U.S. House of Representatives since January 1979. As chairman of the House Subcommittee on Space Science and Applications, he was involved in the investigation of the "Challenger" disaster. The congressman was a member of the crew of the "Columbia" space shuttle mission, Jan. 12–18, 1986 (*left*). A former lawyer, he served for six years in Florida's legislature. Cape Canaveral is in his congressional district.

AP/Wide World

Only seconds after the shuttle was launched, an orange ball of fire appeared at the base of the "Challenger's" fuel tank. Then more fire flickered ·around the tank, and the shuttle was engulfed in a cloud of fire and smoke. The seven astronauts were believed to have died instantly.

The Disaster—Causes and Consequences. Less than a week after the *Challenger* explosion, President Ronald Reagan appointed a 12-member independent commission, headed by former Secretary of State William P. Rogers, to investigate the possible causes. In a painstaking four-month probe, the panel reassembled the chain of events leading up to the accident. In its final report, presented June 9, the commission detailed a complex series of mistakes, oversights, and misjudgments. It blamed the loss of *Challenger* on flaws in the shuttle system itself and stated that the accident was avoidable. The disclosure of these problems stripped the patina from NASA's reputation as a model of efficiency and safety.

The Rogers Commission identified two main reasons for the loss of *Challenger*. First, engineers at Morton Thiokol Inc., the manufacturer of the shuttle rockets, and at NASA's Marshall Space Flight Center in Huntsville, AL, had incorrectly designed the seals ("O-rings") used to join sections of the two solid-rocket boosters on either side of the shuttle. The function of the seals was to keep hot gases from escaping through gaps in the joints between the sections. Neither NASA nor Morton Thiokol acted quickly enough to fix persistent problems with the seals that developed during several previous flights—largely because engineers had greatly underestimated the seriousness of these problems.

Secondly, the shuttle was launched in 36°F (2°C) weather, about 15°F (8°C) colder than any previous launch. While later tests showed that the seals could fail even in warmer weather, the cold did exacerbate inherent problems with their design. Warnings from some engineers to delay lift-off until warmer weather were never-passed on to officials responsible for the final launch decision. The rubber seals between the two lower sections of the right solid-rocket booster were stiffened by the cold and could not seat properly. At ignition, white-hot gases from the burning fuel shot between sections of the rocket, damaging the seals. Then the O-rings were temporarily seated.

About 58 seconds after lift-off, however, after strong winds buffeted the spacecraft, the seals apparently reopened. Tongues of flame jetted between the joint of two booster sections and burned a hole in the large external fuel tank, which was filled with the liquid hydrogen and liquid oxygen used to fuel *Challenger*'s three main engines. The external tank ruptured. Seventy-four seconds after lift-off, *Challenger* became enveloped in the explosive burn of the escaping fuel. The spacecraft broke apart under extreme aerodynamic pressure, its pieces falling 60,000 ft (18 300 m) to the Atlantic Ocean.

The Rogers Commission also found that NASA, striving to make the shuttle live up to self-imposed launch demands, had stopped putting safety first. In a similar finding, the Science and Technology Committee of the U.S. House of Representatives concluded that NASA's drive to meet a schedule of 24 shuttle flights per year created pressures that directly contributed to unsafe launch operations. Congress and the Reagan administration had determined that the shuttle system should be the principal U.S. space launch vehicle as well as an internationally competitive system for putting commercial payloads into orbit. Pressures within NASA to evolve from a research and development agency into a quasi-competitive business—performing the fastest manned launch rates in history—influenced it to put performance before safety.

President and Mrs. Reagan joined family members, some 90 congressmen, and other dignitaries at a special memorial service for the lost astronauts at the Johnson Space Center in Houston, January 31. In his eulogy, the president said: "To reach out for new goals, and even greater achievements, that is the way we shall commemorate our seven 'Challenger' heroes."

© Arthur Grace/Sygma

NASA

The "CHALLENGER" Crew

A Portrait of the Seven—(Front row, from left): *Michael J. Smith, pilot; Francis R. (Dick) Scobee, flight commander; and Ronald E. McNair, mission specialist. (Back row, from left): Ellison O. Onizuka, mission specialist; S. Christa McAuliffe, payload specialist; Gregory B. Jarvis, payload specialist; and Judith A. Resnick, mission specialist.*

MICHAEL J. SMITH

Navy Cmdr. Michael John Smith, the pilot of *Challenger,* had logged more than 4,300 hours in the air and waited five years before his first mission as an astronaut. Born on April 30, 1945, he grew up on his parents' chicken farm in Beaufort, NC. He learned to fly as a teenager and, after graduating from Beaufort High School, attended the U.S. Naval Academy.

A decorated veteran of Vietnam, where he served in an attack squadron aboard an aircraft carrier, Smith went on to become a jet training instructor and an instructor of Navy test pilots. In 1980 he was selected by NASA for astronaut training, attaining the rank of full commander two years later. He is survived by a wife, Jane Anne Jarrell Smith, and three children.

FRANCIS R. SCOBEE

Flight commander Francis Richard (Dick) Scobee was born on May 19, 1939, in Cle Elum, WA. The son of a railroad engineer, he enlisted in the Air Force right out of high school. Trained as a mechanic, engineer, and pilot, he earned his B.A. from the University of Arizona in 1965 and won his wings the following year. As a combat pilot (in Vietnam)

and test pilot, he logged more than 6,500 hours of flight in 45 different types of aircraft.

Scobee retired from the Air Force in 1979 and became the first enlisted man to be named an astronaut. In April 1984 he was the pilot on a one-week *Challenger* mission. The father of two—and a new grandfather—Scobee lived near Houston with his wife, June Kent Scobee.

RONALD E. McNAIR

A laser physicist, Ronald Erwin McNair became the second black American to fly in space aboard *Challenger* in February 1984. On his 1986 mission he was to have launched a small science platform to study Halley's Comet.

McNair was born on Oct. 21, 1950, in Lake City, SC. He attended North Carolina A&T University on a scholarship and earned his Ph.D. in physics from the Massachusetts Institute of Technology in 1976. After working as a staff physicist for the Hughes Research Laboratories in California, he was selected as an astronaut in 1978.

McNair was married to the former Cheryl Moore and was the father of two. He played saxophone in a swing band and taught karate at his church.

ELLISON S. ONIZUKA

Trained as an aeronautical engineer and test pilot, Air Force Lt. Col. Ellison Shoji Onizuka was the first Hawaiian, the first Japanese-American, and the first Buddhist astronaut. He flew on the secret Defense Department mission of the space shuttle *Discovery* in January 1985 and was one of the three mission specialists aboard *Challenger*.

Born on June 24, 1946, in Kealakekua, HI, Onizuka studied engineering at the University of Colorado and later attended the Air Force Test Pilot School at Edwards Air Force Base, CA, where he stayed on as an instructor. He was selected for astronaut training in 1978. Onizuka was married to the former Lorna Yoshida and had two daughters. They lived in Houston.

S. CHRISTA McAULIFFE

A high-school social-studies teacher from Concord, NH, Sharon Christa McAuliffe was selected from more than 11,000 applicants to be the first private citizen in space. Aboard *Challenger* she was to have taught science lessons on television to schoolchildren across the country.

Born in Boston, MA, on Sept. 2, 1948, McAuliffe was raised in nearby Framingham, where she attended a Catholic prep school. After graduating from Framingham State College in 1970, she was married to Steven McAuliffe and the couple moved to Maryland. She taught junior high school there until 1978 and earned a master's degree in teaching administration from Bowie State College. McAuliffe was the mother of two—a son, Scott, and a daughter, Caroline.

GREGORY B. JARVIS

Bumped from two previous shuttle missions, Gregory Bruce Jarvis was making his first spaceflight. As a payload specialist aboard *Challenger,* he was to have conducted experiments on fluid dynamics in an orbiting spacecraft. An engineer, he was employed by the Hughes Aircraft Company.

Jarvis was born on Aug. 24, 1944, in Detroit, MI, and was raised in the town of Mohawk, NY. He attended the State University of New York at Buffalo and earned an M.A. in electrical engineering from Northeastern University in 1969. Until 1973 he worked on advanced communications satellites for the Air Force. Discharged as a captain, he went to work for Hughes.

Jarvis lived with his wife, the former Marcia Jarboe, in Hermosa Beach, CA.

JUDITH A. RESNICK

An electrical engineer before joining the space program in 1978, Judith Arlene Resnick was described by a NASA colleague as "an astronaut's astronaut." She became the second American woman in space aboard the shuttle *Discovery* in August 1984.

Born on April 5, 1949, in Akron, OH, Resnick attended Firestone High School there and graduated from Carnegie Tech with a degree in engineering in 1970. While working for the Radio Corporation of America, she earned a master's degree from the University of Pennsylvania and her doctorate in electrical engineering from the University of Maryland in 1977.

"J.R.," as her friends called her, was also an accomplished classical pianist and was divorced.

AP/Wide World

The design changes deemed necessary to make the shuttle safe forced a two-year halt in manned launches, with the next shuttle mission set for early 1988. The delay has severely hampered U.S. access to space, creating a tremendous backlog of defense payloads and scientific experiments. Some of the national security needs can be met with the use of unmanned rockets, but the delay has been a major setback in the pursuit of scientific objectives.

The Space Program—Priorities and Resources. Based on the findings of the Rogers Commission and the House Science and Technology Committee, it appears that NASA was trying to do too many things with too few resources. The agency's major tasks included flying the shuttle—and marketing itself as a launcher of commercial satellites; developing a space station; exploring nearby planets; building and operating space platforms, such as the Hubble Space Telescope; and performing increasingly complicated scientific research. As its budget became tighter, NASA had greater difficulty carrying out all of its varied tasks.

On August 15, President Reagan instructed NASA to build a new shuttle to replace *Challenger* but told the agency to drop out of "the business of launching private satellites." He did allow NASA to honor prior commitments to launch some 20 commercial satellites, but he wants the space agency to return to its original task of research and development. The new policy has left some companies without a domestic vehicle for launching their multimillion-dollar satellites that serve the needs of today's high-technology world. Thus, a race is on to create a private launch system, using NASA launchpads, before too many American businesses are forced to use foreign carriers.

A major task for the United States will be to restore its previously unquestioned dominance in space flight and technology. A potential loss of space leadership would undermine U.S. prestige and add to its national trade deficit. Competition from Western Europe's Arianespace company, despite several of its own launch failures, already is pulling commercial launch business away from the United States. The Soviet Union and China have announced their desire to carry commercial payloads aboard their own unmanned rockets, and Japan wants to offer its launch services to the open market.

To maintain U.S. leadership in space, companies must move quickly into the private rocket-launching business and handle the great excess of commercial payloads from the shuttle program. This will be an expensive and risky venture for private industry. As America began to rely on the shuttle for its space transportation needs, production lines for most unmanned rockets were being shut down. Now companies need some assurance that the tremendous risk and start-up costs will pay off in the long run. The Air Force is developing a new rocket capable of carrying the heavy payloads that the shuttle would have launched; current plans call for the Air Force to purchase 23 of the first rockets off the assembly line. In addition the Air Force is developing a medium-lift-capability rocket that could have many commercial applications. It remains to be seen whether this financial boost will be enough to launch unsubsidized American companies into the commercial payload-delivery business at a competitive price.

Among the mistakes highlighted by the *Challenger* accident was the reliance of the U.S. space program on only one type of space vehicle. Since the decision to build the shuttle

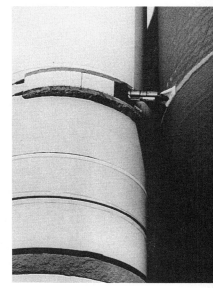

The above photo, released by NASA on March 21, shows how the solid-booster rocket (left) was attached to the bottom of "Challenger's" fuel tank. Flames first emerged from the attach-point. To collect as much evidence as possible about the causes of the accident, an extensive effort was made to retrieve the shuttle's debris. The vehicle's right-front section (below) was among the items pulled from the Atlantic.

Photos AP/Wide World

was made in the early 1970s, the government had planned to phase out the use of such unmanned rockets as the Atlas-Centaur and the Delta. The decision was made in an attempt to maximize the use of the shuttle. But in order to meet the nation's space needs through the year 2000, America must have several types of unmanned rockets, plus the reusable space shuttle, in its stable of launch vehicles. Access to space is vital to America's national security and technological prowess. Having several types of rockets decreases the chance that the failure of one type will take away that access.

The reliance on the shuttle program was based largely on the fact that some of its costs could be recouped by charging money to launch commercial satellites, do research in near-zero gravity, and perform other tasks in earth orbit. Before the *Challenger* accident, NASA had planned on earning $320 million in launch fees during 1986, carrying commercial and Defense Department payloads. Without this income, future U.S. space exploration will rely almost totally on government support. This financial burden comes at a time of fiscal restraint, as lawmakers struggle to reduce the national debt.

The NASA budget for 1987 is $10.5 billion, up 43% from 1986. About $2.1 billion of the increase will be used to build the replacement for *Challenger,* expected to be completed in about 1991. The hard fight for money to replace *Challenger* was won partly because America needs a fleet of four shuttles to build a space station by 1992 and, at the same time, to meet the nation's defense and scientific needs in space.

Toward a Vibrant Future. Despite the U.S. budget difficulties, sufficient money must be found to keep the space program strong and vibrant. Space technology and its valuable practical spin-offs must be aggressively pursued, or the United States will languish behind the well-funded efforts of other countries. America must reemphasize basic scientific research to make sure that it has the information on which to develop the technological wonders needed in the next phase of space exploration. Research to be performed in the space station could lead to new wonder drugs, space-based manufacturing, improved metals, and other valuable innovations.

AP/Wide World

Americans were shocked and stunned by the tragic disaster. The loss of New Hampshire schoolteacher Christa McAuliffe, selected as NASA's first citizen-in-space, particularly affected students.

America's goals in space through the year 2000 are manifold. They include construction of a space station to serve as an international research laboratory and development of new space transportation technologies. By the 1990s, engineers will be able to determine the feasibility of a national "aerospace plane"—a spaceship capable of taking off from a conventional runway, accelerating to low earth orbit, and landing at an airport.

NASA now also must begin planning projects which will follow the space station. Now is the time to determine the future directions of the civilian space program.

One option is a manned mission to Mars. The President's National Commission on Space, which issued an excellent report in 1986, identified manned exploration of Mars as an important goal which should be pursued by the U.S. space program. A wide range of detailed engineering studies on manned and unmanned Mars missions is now under way in the United States and the Soviet Union. Five unmanned spacecraft—four Soviet and one American—are scheduled to be launched to Mars from 1988 to 1992. These follow the U.S. Viking 1 and 2 probes, which reached the red planet in 1976 and sent back photographs and scientific information.

The cost of a manned venture to Mars would be substantial. A joint mission with the Soviet Union, the European Space Agency, Japan, and other space-faring nations would put the world's best minds on a valuable common goal. It could go a long way toward improving relations between countries, with a potentially profound influence on the geopolitics of the planet Earth.

The shuttle accident raised new questions about the future of the space program. In May, NASA unveiled a new draft of its $8 billion manned space station that it plans to assemble in orbit during the 1990s in conjunction with several other nations.

THE LIABILITY
INSURANCE CRISIS

By Mary H. Cooper

About the Author. Mary H. Cooper is a staff writer for *Editorial Research Reports,* a news service published by Congressional Quarterly in Washington, DC. Ms. Cooper's interesting and detailed article on the "Liability Insurance Squeeze" appeared in the Dec. 5, 1985, issue of the publication.

As the subway train pulled into the station, a man jumped off the platform into its path. Because the engineer failed to stop the train in time, the man was injured seriously. Although he clearly had intended to commit suicide, the man brought suit against the transit authority and came away not only with his life, but with $650,000 from an out-of-court settlement to boot. While remarkable in its circumstances, this case is not unusual either for the size of the award for damages or for the seemingly innocent persons held ultimately liable for wrongful or neglectful acts—in this case the taxpayers of New York.

It also has been cited as but one of a deluge of liability suits brought before the U.S. courts in the last few years. Once regarded as an occupational hazard to physicians alone, other professionals, businesses, and government entities are increasingly finding themselves targets of liability suits. Not only are plaintiffs winning these cases, but they are being awarded unprecedented amounts of money by sympathetic juries. As a result, insurance companies that offer liability coverage have canceled policies outright or hiked their premiums to the point where many can no longer afford coverage.

Physicians have long held liability insurance to protect themselves from medical malpractice suits. Today, however, many physicians—especially obstetricians and orthopedic surgeons, who are most commonly sued for malpractice—are no longer able to afford the premiums, and some have abandoned their practices altogether. Other health professionals, such as nurse-midwives, who rarely have been taken to court, suddenly are unable to obtain insurance at any price. Rising liability insurance rates are contributing to the continuing increase in health-care costs, while certain areas of the United States are experiencing shortages of qualified professionals.

Small towns and counties have been especially hard hit by the liability insurance crunch. New York City, with its large tax base, can afford to be self-insured and pay awards to complainants, such as the would-be suicide victim, from its operating budget. But small municipalities must depend on commercial insurers for coverage. As premiums continued to rise in 1986, many localities were forced to drain public swimming pools and close playgrounds, beaches, and other facilities that present the risk of physical injury.

The loss of many private services also can be traced to the liability insurance squeeze. Alarmed by a spate of child-molestation cases in 1984, insurers have shied away from day-care centers or have raised their rates beyond the reach of small operations, which represent the vast majority of day-care centers. Many can no longer afford to remain open at a time when more and more mothers of small children are going to work and must depend on day care to keep their jobs. Other small enterprises also have been faced with the choice of going out of business or "going bare," continuing to operate uninsured.

The growing number of U.S. day-care centers, especially the smaller ones, face a major problem—the unavailability or high cost of liability insurance. Child-abuse cases are the fear of the insurance companies.

Bars and restaurants serving alcoholic beverages have found their "liquor liability" premiums drastically increased or lost coverage altogether in 38 states where such establishments are held liable for the actions of intoxicated patrons even after they leave the premises.

Big business is being squeezed by the insurance crunch in a different way. Among U.S. manufacturers, only the tobacco industry—whose products are recognized widely to cause cancer—seems immune to defeat in product liability lawsuits. Their immunity was bolstered in April 1986 when a federal appeals court ruled that the warning labels that have appeared on cigarette packs since 1965 protect the companies from charges that they fail to provide adequate warning of the potential dangers of smoking. In contrast, A.H. Robins Co., maker of the Dalkon Shield, filed for bankruptcy after it was found liable for injuries caused by the intrauterine device (IUD) and faced some $1 billion in claims awarded the thousands of women affected. The court decision led G.D. Searle & Co. to announce in early 1986 that it would stop selling the Copper-7, the most widely used IUD in the United States, and continue to produce it for export only. Successful product-liability suits are thus a double-edged sword for consumers: while the first case proved beneficial to consumers by compensating for injuries caused by a flawed product and removing it from circulation, it also set a court precedent that reduced the availability of similar products, harmful or otherwise.

Bars and restaurants in some 38 states now are liable for the actions of their customers. "Liquor liability" insurance premiums have risen accordingly. To dramatize the situation, some 400 watering places in New Hampshire sponsored an Unhappy Hour, charging exorbitant prices for their various beverages.

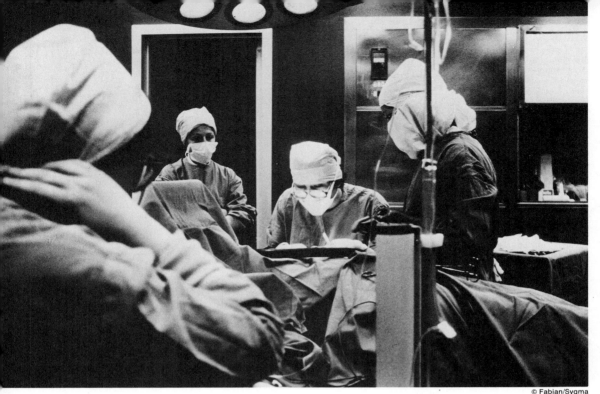

Assessing Blame. What is behind the liability insurance squeeze? Each player involved has a different answer. The insurance industry blames lawyers, who often pocket one third or more of jury awards in liability cases, and the legal system which allows them to do it. Lawyers, together with consumer advocates, blame the insurance industry which, they say, has conjured up a "crisis" as a cover to justify outlandish hikes in premiums.

Everyone agrees that the insurance industry has been going through the low point of one of its periodic "boom-and-bust" cycles, which typically range over 6 to 10 years. As their profits rise, insurers tend to lower premium rates in an effort to win new clients. Eventually, claims against their policies begin to outpace the profits earned from premiums, and the insurers hike rates once again to recoup their losses. It is at this point that the industry has found itself since the early 1980s.

But this cycle, which began in the mid-1970s, is different in several respects from its predecessors. In setting their rates, insurance companies must estimate the likelihood that premiums will exceed claims by a sufficient margin to assure a profit. The U.S. economic environment of the late 1970s, with its high inflation and unpredictable interest rates, made it especially hard for insurers to set their rates and make investment decisions. Eager to reap high interest earnings on investments made out of policyholders' premiums, the insurers competed for customers by slashing their rates for all lines of insurance, including liability. As a result, the nation's 3,468 property and casualty insurers—the companies that underwrite liability insurance—wrote more than $144 billion in total net premiums in 1985, up from $50 billion in 1975.

Lawsuits against doctors, especially such specialists as neurosurgeons, obstetricians, and orthopedists, have caused some premiums for malpractice insurance to exceed $50,000 annually.

Rising insurance premiums have forced many ski operators to increase the price of their lift tickets by $2 or $3. Most residents of Roosevelt Island, NY, travel to their Manhattan jobs on a tramway (below). Early in 1986, the tram's liability insurance premiums soared, forcing the system to stop operating until the state assumed responsibility for the tram's insurance. In the interim, the 5,200 islanders had to spend an extra two hours for their daily commute. Unable to afford the high cost of insurance, many communities, including Chicago's Northwest Side (bottom), have had no choice but to dismantle their public playgrounds.

© Rick Browne/Picture Group

© Joe Azzara/The Image Bank

© Kevin Horan/Picture Group

In the early 1980s, however, interest rates began to fall and, with them, returns on the insurance industry's investments. At the same time, claims mounted in the wake of a growing number of court decisions in favor of victims of asbestos and environmental pollution as well as medical malpractice. Since 1983, the industry has sustained record losses; by 1985, underwriting losses exceeded investment income by $5.4 billion.

Consumer advocates and lawyers shed no tears for the insurers. The industry showed signs of improvement in 1986 and posted a $500 million profit in the first quarter. But it did not immediately pass this improvement on to consumers and business clients in the form of lower premiums and wider insurance availability. Some industry critics say the insurance industry has only its own greed to blame for its financial problems. In their view, the "boom-and-bust" cycle could easily be avoided altogether if insurers maintained steady rates instead of engaging in cutthroat competition for the premium dollar.

Ask the holders of liability insurance who is to blame for the squeeze, and many will point to the U.S. legal system. Especially to blame, they say, is the tradition of tort law, under which a person may bring a civil suit alleging that someone else's wrongful action caused injury to himself or damage to his property. Corporate executives and physicians in particular blame this system for encouraging lawsuits and forcing the insurers to hike rates to cover the rising number of claims or cease offering coverage for businesses or professionals that have been found liable in court cases. Even when the fault of an injury may be open to question, they say, the size of awards granted in recent liability cases may make the recourse to trial too attractive for many people to resist. The upshot, say critics, is that tort law, as practiced in the United States, has transformed Americans into a "litigious society," ready to sue anyone on the chance of reaping a windfall.

Another flaw in the system, critics say, is the diversity of product liability statutes among the states. Since both federal courts and, more commonly, state courts handle liability cases, decisions regarding similar cases often vary widely. Robert H. Malott, chairman of the board and chief executive officer of the Chicago-based FMC Corp., recalled a case in Illinois in which a construction worker drove an FMC-manufactured crane into high-voltage lines. FMC was held liable for damages because the crane lacked sufficient safety warnings. Malott said, however, that courts in other states had dismissed similar cases on the grounds that high-voltage wires constitute an obvious danger for which no warnings are necessary.

Some state courts have made it easier for plaintiffs to win product liability suits by adopting "comparative fault" standards, which allow individuals to sue manufacturers for damages incurred while using a product, even when the users themselves contributed by their own actions to their injuries. Critics also point to the courts' expanding interpretation of "strict liability" for injury or damages incurred during the use

Courtesy of the
Insurance Information Institute

The nonprofit Insurance Information Institute believes that lawsuits have gotten out of hand and has taken to advertising to make the point.

of defective products. While manufacturers could initially be held liable only for physical flaws in their products, strict liability has been broadened to include the lack of safety warnings, as shown in the crane incident. Because of their vast financial resources, critics charge, manufacturers and their insurers are attractive targets for consumers and lawyers eager to "go for the deep pocket."

Many critics of the legal system hold lawyers largely responsible for the problem. Lawyers are paid on a contingency basis in liability cases, which means they receive a percentage of whatever award may be granted. This system, critics say, naturally encourages lawyers to seek the highest amounts possible. But lawyers reject this criticism, emphasizing that they get no fee at all for their services if they lose a case, and must pay the court expenses to boot. They also deny that Americans are more litigious and say the big awards are justified, since they are granted only to people who have been victimized severely by malpractice or defective products.

Reform Efforts Such finger-pointing among the various players in the liability insurance game grew more vehement as the year progressed. In 1986, state legislatures and the U.S. Congress reacted to the liability insurance crunch with a flurry of proposals to reform tort law, change insurance standards, or both. In April, the state of Washington passed a tort reform

Faced with a rising tide of popular protest against big damage awards and skyrocketing liability insurance premiums, many states passed or considered reform legislation during 1986.

measure that caps the amount plaintiffs may be awarded for noneconomic damages and banned any payment to plaintiffs who were injured because they were intoxicated or while they were committing a crime. In addition, the legislature limited the "deep-pockets doctrine," which can force a manufacturer or other wealthy defendant to pay damages even if they were less responsible than other parties for damage or injuries. In June, California voters followed suit by overwhelmingly approving Proposition 51, which also limits the deep-pockets doctrine. California's "joint-and-several" liability provision limits each defendant's liability for pain and suffering and for punitive damages to the proportion of harm the defendant actually caused, as determined by the court.

Lawyers' contingency fees were the focus of a tort-reform measure signed into law in Connecticut in June. Under the new law, lawyers may receive no more than one third of awards of up to $300,000. It is hoped that such limits on one aspect or another of tort law will encourage insurers to lower their rates and broaden their coverage, since their losses to claims should be reduced greatly. Experience in other states, however, gives little encouragement. In July, only months after the Maryland legislature imposed a $350,000 cap on "pain and suffering" awards, the state's insurance commissioner approved a 50% increase in medical malpractice premiums.

Florida is taking no chances. In June its legislature passed the most sweeping measure to date to deal with the insurance squeeze. In addition to tort reforms, including a $450,000 cap on awards for noneconomic damages, the law required insurance companies to cut their rates for liability coverage by 40% by the end of 1986.

While the states pursued their reform efforts in 1986, some observers said that the insurance crisis required federal action. The Reagan administration agreed and lent its support to a measure introduced by Sen. Bob Kasten (R-WI) and approved by the Senate Commerce Committee in June. Both the Senate and the House were lobbied heavily by consumer groups, who opposed liability restrictions contained in the bill and favored coupling tort reform with insurance rate cuts as Florida had done; by lawyers, who opposed the measure's contingency fee caps; and by the insurance industry, which was eager to prevent the Florida action from spreading across the United States. In September the bill, which would have established the first nationwide standards for liability, was pulled before it could be voted on by the full Senate when Sen. Ernest F. Hollings (D-SC) threatened a filibuster. Hollings, a former trial lawyer who blamed the insurance industry for the liability crisis, opposed the bill's provisions that would have limited court awards in product liability cases and thus curtail lawyer contingency fees.

With a Democratic majority once again in control of the Senate following the November elections, Senator Hollings was to assume the chairmanship of the Commerce Committee, effectively dooming any measure brought up before the 100th Congress that includes national tort reform.

© Cynthia Johnson/"Time" Magazine

As part of their "Operation Product Liability Reform," representatives of the National Association of Manufacturers converged on Capitol Hill in March to promote their cause.

THE BUSINESS OF ADVICE

by Isadore Barmash

When Thales, the earliest of the Greek philosophers, was asked what was difficult, he replied, "To know one's self." And what was easy? "To advise another."

In a trend peaking in the mid-1980s, Americans have become a people of advice-seekers. As technological, social, and just plain living pressures mounted, Americans were seeking help from professional experts and pop-experts on all manner of questions. Whether it was buying a new or secondhand auto or a new or second home, finding the right prep school or college, redecorating one's home, or clarifying a delicate sex problem, they found advisers readily at hand, as easily as in the yellow pages of their telephone books or on radio and television.

It was as if Americans had no time to do even a quick study to solve a problem. Financial, real estate, social, home decor, and fashion columns sprouted in the nation's newspapers, while advisers in those and other fields were television or radio personalities. These included Louis Rukeyser, Adam Smith (George J. W. Goodman), and Bruce Williams on Wall Street and financial matters; "Dr. Ruth" Westheimer on sexual matters; sundry real-estate experts on radio; and Bernard Meltzer, the earthy broadcaster who, after beginning a long career as a financial adviser, found himself faced with questions on family squabbles, where and how economically to move, and how to enjoy one's retirement. A new industry, the advice business, literally blossomed and matured in the space of a few years, spanning the 1970s and 1980s, with 1986 revenues estimated at $15 billion.

The Advice Industry. One of the most dynamic segments of this new industry is financial consulting, which specializes in personal finance, including how to beat the income-tax burden and plan for retirement. More than 100,000 specialists, many of whom achieved professional credibility by certification from the Institute of Financial Planning, either dispense financial advice for a fee or both advise and recommend specific investments for a fee and commission. Another big segment is personal counseling, in which some 135,000 sociologists, psychologists, and psychiatrists offer advice on marital, parental, or sibling difficulties and emotional problems. A third is management consulting, which boomed, with not only retired senior executives but even recent MBA graduates coming directly into the field. Political and governmental consultants also are putting out their shingles in ever-increasing numbers. These experts surface not only during election periods to help aspiring or worried politicians but also rise to serve harassed bureaucrats eager to receive assistance from former government officials or those with suitable academic qualifications.

Within this advice industry, "how to" publishing has flourished. A torrent of such books—estimated at almost 10% of the 45,000 volumes of all kinds published annually in the 1980s —reflect the full spectrum of help needs Americans want from consultants and airborne gurus. The subjects are diverse indeed: how to buy a home or become a millionaire, real-estate

About the Author. Isadore Barmash has been a business writer, specializing in the retailing field, for *The New York Times* for more than 20 years. Previously he was editor in chief of Fairchild Publications and a feature writer for the New York *Herald Tribune.* Mr. Barmash is the author of several books, including *The Self-Made Man* (1969), *Welcome to Our Conglomerate: You're Fired* (1971), *The Chief Executives* (1978), and *Always Live Better Than Your Clients* (1983).

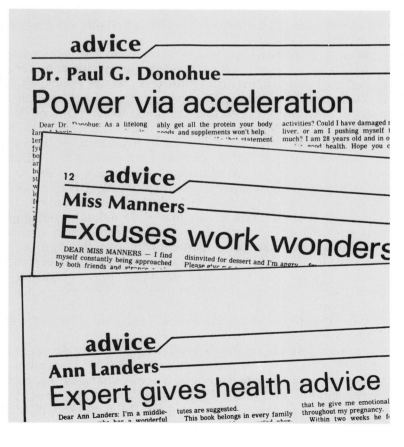

Advice is a multibillion-dollar business for the U.S. print media. Opposite page: The How-to-Do-It Bookshop in Philadelphia offers some 10,000 "how-to" books on 300 topics. An estimated 4,200 "how-to" books are published annually in the United States. Left: Syndicated newspaper advice columns cover everything from medicine and health to etiquette and the solving of personal dilemmas.

investing; general investing; how to enjoy better romantic relations as a single or married person. Cook books proliferate. Best-sellers in the first week of September 1986, according to *Publishers Weekly,* included *The Rotation Diet* by Martin Katahn; *Fit for Life* by Harvey and Marilyn Diamond; *Callanetics: 10 Years Younger in 10 Hours* by Callan Pinckney; *Medical Makeover: The Revolutionary, No-Willpower Program for Lifetime Health* by Dr. Robert M. Giller and Kathy Matthews; and *When All You've Ever Wanted Isn't Enough* by Harold S. Kushner.

In Philadelphia in 1986, the "How-to-Do-It Book Shop" stocked 10,000 different books on 300 topics and was selling about 26,000 copies yearly. And *How-To: 1,400 Best Books on Doing Almost Everything* helped to steer readers to the most appropriate volumes.

The Reasons Americans Seek Advice. Were Americans being lazy or just confused by seeking help on so many fronts? According to Dr. Leo Bogart, a marketing expert and general manager of the Newspaper Advertising Bureau, "increasingly, we [Americans] find ourselves in a world where we must manage information more than material things. We have computers, videotext, and other means of electronic aids but we all crave personal help. We are all exposed to such vastly greater information than ever before, but we find that having all that information is onerous for most of us, and that breeds the need for more or simpler information. And that, too, moves us toward the experts who help us find our way among the impersonal aids."

Many Americans seeking assistance from financial counselors, social advisers, and psychiatrists are young achievers —singles or young marrieds of both sexes whose professional or academic attainments appear to be greater than their ability to cope with the rigors of their personal lives. "One of the problems young, successful professionals have is that they can only deal with what is rational and structured for them," says Dr. George J. Breitbart, a New York psychiatrist. "But when they run out of guidelines and parameters where they have demonstrated expertise, they flounder. Why is that? Because they are only taught skills that they can master rather than survival skills. As a result, they have difficulty fulfilling their personal destiny, in terms of their sexual, social, and moral lives." An increasing number of "young, hot-shot" executives are asking for help, he said, complaining of depression, discomfiture, and some "with the most exquisitely defined terrors" because of their lack of living experience. The therapy is usually traditional—"helping them identify what their problems are, sometimes even drawing in their families to provide information"—he said.

Perhaps less important, but still vital to many people, is the need to ease money pressures and plan their financial futures. One area of growing confusion was changing income-tax regulations, first in the 1981 federal tax act and most recently in the new tax-reform provisions. William Freund, Jr., senior vice-president and a certified financial planner at Pres-

German-born sex therapist Dr. Ruth Westheimer, 58, gives frank advice in cable television and radio call-in shows. "Dr. Ruth" has also produced a video cassette, published several books, written regular newspaper and magazine columns, and marketed a board game.

Longtime media psychologist Dr. Joyce (Diane) Brothers has had several of her own TV and radio counseling shows since the late 1950s. She also continues to write a widely syndicated newspaper column. Dr. Brothers earned her Ph.D. from Columbia University in 1953.

TV Tips: *Dr. Anita Migday, left, hosts a 26-part "how-to" series on public television, "Cats & Dogs," that explores the relationship between pets and their owners. Dick Raymond, below, has cultivated a wide audience for his TV series, "The Joy of Gardening." With his wife Jan, he also has written some 16 books and handbooks on vegetables and gardening.*

The inimitable Julia (McWilliams) Child began doing her "French Chef" TV show on Boston's WGBH in 1962 and has had a weekly cooking segment on ABC-TV's "Good Morning, America." The 74-year-old California native has written six books.

© D. P. Hershkowitz/Bruce Coleman, Inc.

© Michael Hayman/Stock Boston

© Charles Gupton/Stock Boston

© Lawrence Barns/Black Star

Help! *The complexity of life in the Eighties has spawned professional advice givers in every aspect of work and leisure. Job recruiters, top, not only help with placement but may also give training in résumé writing, interviewing, and other aspects of the job search. With the proliferation of investment options in the 1980s, financial counselors, above, provide a valuable service. The deregulation of air travel and myriad tour packages have made travel clubs and agents, above, left, indispensable. And even the fitness craze has benefited from the guidance of experts—the 1–2 count of exercise instructors.*

cott, Ball & Turben, a brokerage firm in Cleveland, observed that while Americans were earning and spending more, there was surprisingly little planning involved. "People don't seem to have the time or inclination for it," he said, "and much less so for estate planning." But many are realizing this failure and seeking help, he said.

The Consultant Craze. The demand for help has created new career opportunities for those with the requisite counseling skills. This has caused such individuals to foresake their vocations and become seers with their own corners in the nation's newspapers and magazines. Readers can have wisdom along with coffee, news, and the weather. Ann Landers dominates a growing list of social counselors who have had their own columns that are syndicated widely. Bernard Gladstone has had a long career in *The New York Times* as the wise man of home repair. Other columns have had long duration in such fields as dog care, coins and stamps, sports history, food, audio, and antiques. And response surveys by the media have found that these columns have a high, continuing readership.

Career opportunities have opened for consultants. Early retirements with attractive conditions, including federally protected pensions, have led many executives and professionals to give up their regular careers and turn to consulting. It is a lively and remunerative alternative to "being put on the beach." And the trend gives the practitioners a new life, in a sense, where they combine part-time effort with part-time leisure. Besides corporate executives, those turning to this endeavor include former government officials, tenured academics, and former military officers.

The richness and pertinence of the adviser fare on radio have built loyal audiences. On a typical Saturday in New York in 1986, when consumers presumably were more inclined to turn on their radios, that medium carried ten programs featuring advisers of varied types. Most presentations were of the call-in variety. Listeners working the dial would hear Bill Flanagan, financial advice; Doug Bryan, home repair; Dr. Lawrence Balter, child psychology; Bernard Meltzer, finance, real estate, and other matters; John Scheuer, financial advice; Mike McClintock, home improvement; "Health Saturday"; Dr. Carlton Fredericks, nutrition; "Garden Hotline"; and Dr. Joy Browne, personal advice. On Sundays, some of those shows, including John Scheuer's and Bernard Meltzer's, were marathon four-hour events from 10 A.M. to 2 P.M.

On television, the rise of cable stations and networks has brought a new supply of airtime that is filled, in large part, by service programs. These, too, reflect the same need for experts that regular television and radio broadcasting had rushed to fill. Financial advisers, real-estate consultants, and social counselors are appearing on cable television with increasing frequency. In 1986, Dr. Ruth Westheimer not only delivered her often startling revelations on a two-hour NBC Radio show, *Sexually Speaking,* but also offered a nightly cable-TV rendering.

King Features

"Hints from Heloise" is a widely syndicated newspaper column that gives tips on running a household. Heloise, who uses no last name, is the daughter of the late Heloise Bowles, who began the column in 1959. Today it runs in some 500 newspapers in 20 countries.

© Faverly/Gamma-Liaison

Ann Landers (Esther P. Lederer) was born on July 4, 1918, in Sioux City, IA. She began writing her syndicated personal advice column in 1955, and today it appears in approximately 1,100 newspapers. Her twin sister is Abigail "Dear Abby" Van Buren (Pauline Friedman Phillips).

Financial adviser Bruce Williams is the top-rated radio talk-show host in the United States. His call-in program has approximately 3 million listeners in 250 cities. Williams also writes a syndicated column, "Smart Money." "I tell the listener what I would do," he says. "But that's not necessarily what anyone else should do." His own advisers include his bartender and his barber.

The 70-year-old former actress and government adviser Betty Furness gives tips to consumers on NBC News in New York City. She has served as special assistant to the president of the United States for consumer affairs (1967–69), chairman of the N.Y. State Consumer Protection Board (1970–71), and commissioner of the N.Y. Department of Consumer Affairs (1973).

In a newspaper column distributed by United Features Syndicate since 1978, "Miss Manners" —aka Judith Martin, 48, of Washington, DC—solves all those sticky problems of whom to invite and where they should sit. She is also a critic-at-large for Vanity Fair and writes for several other magazines. Miss Manners responds to letters with the greeting "Gentle Reader."

The Overview. In sum, "get me an expert!" seems to have become an American phenomenon, ranging through all segments of society. But is it a promising or disturbing trend? Does it augur for a better-informed, more decisive nation or for a hesitant, indecisive one?

The answers, among experts evaluating experts, vary. Vance Packard, the author of popular books on social mores, told *U.S. News & World Report* that "50% of it [the advice business] isn't needed." Consultants defend their function, but most complain that their customers too often follow their recommendations only in a token manner and also tend to relegate their counsel to the "future file." But, in general, it has been agreed that the most reliable advice, by its very nature, is in the "harder" or more technical matters, such as finance, vocational counseling, real estate, electronic data processing, than in the "softer" matters, such as social or emotional counseling. And the consensus is that whether the advice-seeking trend is worthwhile depends on the seeker's internal needs, drives, and self-confidence. There is, in other words, no substitute for common sense.

Will the help-seeking trend continue? "I see no diminution of it as time goes by," flatly says Dr. Leo Bogart. In a country renowned for its independence, it appears, the pace of life with its rapidly unfolding dimensions and pressures now is becoming just too much for Americans to go it alone.

Lady Liberty At 100

by Bernard A. Weisberger

It was a birthday celebration and Fourth of July gala the likes of which have rarely, if ever, been seen—speeches by the presidents of two countries, a processional salute by 22 majestic tall ships from 18 countries, and a fireworks show witnessed by up to two million people on piers, bridges, and buildings lining New York harbor—and on some 40,000 private boats and 32 naval vessels in the bay itself —as well as a television audience numbering in the tens or hundreds of millions. In addition, the four-day extravaganza included celebrity entertainment, expensive parties for the elite, and the conversion of lower Manhattan into a virtual street fair for millions of proud Americans. The party cost some $30 million, and to prepare for it the birthday girl—the 100-year-old Statue of Liberty—underwent a two-year, $70 million face-lift.

THE NEW COLOSSUS
By Emma Lazarus

Not like the brazen giant of Greek fame,
  With conquering limbs astride from land to land;
  Here at our sea-washed, sunset gates shall stand
A mighty woman with a torch, whose flame
Is the imprisoned lightning, and her name
  Mother of Exiles. From her beacon-hand
  Glows world-wide welcome; her mild eyes command
The air-bridged harbor that twin cities frame.
"Keep ancient lands, your storied pomp!" cries she
  With silent lips. "Give me your tired, your poor,
Your huddled masses yearning to breathe free,
  The wretched refuse of your teeming shore.
Send these, the homeless, tempest-tost to me,
  I lift my lamp beside the golden door!"

Photo, AP/Wide World

Ellis Island, the chief U.S. immigration station (1892–1943), was the site of a mass naturalization ceremony on Liberty Weekend 1986. Chrysler's Lee Iacocca, below, headed the fundraising campaign for the restoration of the statue and Ellis Island. In February he was fired as chairman of the Centennial Commission in a dispute over development plans for Ellis Island.

Photos, AP/Wide World

Origins. From the beginning she had been remarkable. At 151 ft (46 m) from toe to torch and weighing 225 tons (204 metric tons), she was the biggest statue ever made. At once she demonstrated a power to win the attention and affection of the American people and to embody their changing ideas about themselves and their freedoms.

The statue was built in a Paris factory between 1875 and 1885, the brainchild of Frédéric-Auguste Bartholdi, a sculptor with a taste for the colossal and a brilliant instinct for what made a public monument memorable. Bartholdi got the idea in 1865 from an America-loving French republican, Edouard de Laboulaye, who proposed a gift from the French people to the American people in celebration of the centennial of U.S. independence in 1876. Bartholdi conceived a gigantic female figure with a torch, to be called "Liberty Enlightening the World," and personally chose the location on Bedloe's Island in New York, the gateway to the New World. The statue that emerged from his workshop (missing the 1876 deadline by nine years) consisted of 300 pieces of thin copper hammered into wooden molds taken from a gigantic plaster model, then riveted together around an iron skeleton designed by Gustave Eiffel (who would build the famous tower carrying his name in 1889).

"Liberty" was first erected in Paris and opened to the French public, who had raised 600,000 francs for her by subscription and lottery, on July 4, 1885. The next spring she was dismantled, crated, and transported in a French warship to her new home, arriving in June. The pedestal, designed by the New York society architect Richard Morris Hunt, was completed at the last moment. The base structure was supposed to have been built with American contributions, but fund-raising had lagged, and it took a vigorous campaign in Joseph Pulitzer's *New York World* to gather the balance of the necessary $250,000.

Meanings and Images. The festivities of 1986 were old stuff to the statue. At her inaugural on Oct. 28, 1886, there also had been fireworks, a monster parade down Broadway, and dedication speeches by a host of dignitaries, including President Grover Cleveland. The oratory that day emphasized the themes of peace, progress, and Franco-American friendship. Very soon, however, the statue acquired a fresh meaning. In 1892, only a few hundred yards away, Ellis Island was opened as a U.S. immigration reception station. Over the next 40 years, the statue became the first sight of the Promised Land for some 18 million immigrants who arrived in New York. She now was the "Mother of Exiles," lifting her lamp beside the Golden Door just as Emma Lazarus' 1883 poem, *The New Colossus,* had prophesied (though in fact the verses were not placed on a tablet inside the pedestal until 1903).

By World War I, the statue's image had been widely used in advertisements and had shown uncanny promotional power. The U.S. government, learning by the examples, used the statue in posters to promote its "Liberty Loan" bond drives. In 1924 the statue and the island were declared a national monument, later extended to include Ellis Island.

As she neared her 50th anniversary in 1936, the statue's familiar figure had come to stand not only for freedom and asylum, but—like the bald eagle or Uncle Sam—for the

About the Author: Bernard A. Weisberger is a historian and free-lance writer whose numerous books include *The Statue of Liberty: The First Hundred Years* (1985). Dr. Weisberger taught American history for 30 years at the University of Chicago, University of Rochester, Vassar College, and other institutions. He also has written for radio and television.

© Hiroyuki Matsumoto/Black Star

The 315-ft (96-m), free-standing aluminum scaffolding that surrounded the statue during work on her exterior was entered in the Guiness Book of World Records *as the tallest ever. Restoring Lady Liberty was an engineering and artistic challenge for hundreds of American and French workers. A team of French artisans shipped in 2 tons of handmade tools for highly skilled metalwork unknown in the United States.*

The U.S. Coast Guard bark "Eagle"(top, right) led Operation Sail '86, an 18-mi (30-km) parade of ships up the Hudson River. The 256-ft (78-m) tall ship was built in Hitler's Germany in 1936 and later acquired as a war reparation. President Reagan, joined by the First Lady, took an active part in the weekend celebrations. In reviewing Op Sail, the president spoke of tall ships: "Perhaps, indeed, these vessels embody our conception of liberty itself: to have before one no impediments, only open spaces; to chart one's own course and take the adventure of life as it comes; to be free as the wind— as free as the tall ships."

United States itself. That identification was strengthened by World War II and the Cold War, and "Lady Liberty" came to be regarded as a national treasure. Bedloe's Island, renamed Liberty Island in 1956, was tidied up by the National Park Service for the growing throngs of tourists.

Restoration and Celebration. Through the decades, even as the statue took on new and stronger symbolic meaning, the physical structure itself suffered from long periods of neglect. With the approach of her 100th birthday, it seemed both natural and necessary to honor the statue with a major restoration as well as a spectacular centennial celebration. Thus, in 1982, the Statue of Liberty-Ellis Island Foundation was created to raise some $230 million for the renovation of both the Statue of Liberty and Ellis Island. The foundation was headed by Lee Iacocca, a son of Italian immigrants and the well-known chairman of the Chrysler Corporation.

Among the major jobs to be performed on the statue was the complete replacement of the leaking, badly corroded torch, which in 1916 had been pierced to accommodate dozens of panes of colored glass through which lights within might shine. The flame on the replacement torch, as Bartholdi originally intended, is gold-plated and reflects light rather than transmits it. In addition, some discolorations on the face caused by modern atmospheric pollution were cleaned up, and the crown spikes and windows were cleaned and replaced. Other changes were not externally visible. The statue's iron ribs were replaced with rustproof, stainless steel ones. Rivets rusted out by salt air were replaced. The right shoulder of Eiffel's skeleton was strengthened and the right arm slightly relocated. The interior was completely cleaned and repainted, and the stairs and lighting were refurbished. The renovation took 30 months and had 500 workmen swarming over the elaborate aluminum scaffolding that obscured the statue and kept it closed to visitors from mid-1984.

By July 3, 1986, the work was complete, and the centennial spectacle, orchestrated by Hollywood producer David L.

Wolper, could begin. On that chilly Thursday evening, U.S. President Ronald Reagan, France's President François Mitterrand, and thousands of paying guests (at $5,000 a head) sat on Governor's Island, just off the Brooklyn shore, in New York Harbor. The 2½ hours of speeches, ceremonies, and entertainment included a musical pageant on the history of immigration, hosted by an array of stars; the swearing in of some 16,000 new U.S. citizens, via television-satellite hookup with five cities, by U.S. Chief Justice Warren Burger; and the presentation of a newly created Medal of Liberty by President Reagan to 12 distinguished naturalized Americans. But the highlight of the evening was the unveiling of the statue and the lighting of her torch. At 10:55 P.M., President Reagan aimed a laser beam across the water and the statue blazed into light. Naval ships fired their guns in salute, smaller boats flashed their lights, church bells pealed, and bands played.

AP/Wide World

The fireworks display on July 4, heralded as the largest and most spectacular in U.S. history, attracted some 2 million spectators in and around New York Harbor. That afternoon on Governor's Island, as the harbor was being cleared of ships, a band entertained listeners with some Independence Day songs.

© J.L. Atlan/Sygma

Liberty Weekend continued on Friday afternoon with Operation Sail '86, an 18-mi (30-km) procession up the Hudson River of more than 250 vessels from 30 nations. Meanwhile, the streets of New York swarmed with hundreds of thousands of visitors and with vendors selling hot dogs, pizza, ice cream, ethnic foods, Liberty masks, balloons, T-shirts, miniature Statues of Liberty, as well as pens, lighters, ashtrays, and objects of any description on which the statue's image could be imprinted. That evening President Reagan boarded the U.S. aircraft carrier *John F. Kennedy* to share in a barbecue with 500 high-school students and the ship's crew, and to watch a televised concert of the Boston Pops Orchestra from Jersey City, featuring numbers by George M. Cohan, George Gershwin, and John Philip Sousa. At 9:45 the skies erupted in a spectacular fireworks display that was perhaps the largest in U.S. history. During the 28-minute show, more than 40,000 pyrotechnic shells were launched from 30 barges around the shoreline.

On Saturday a group of scholars convened for a two-day conference in New York on the future of liberty; the statue was officially reopened to the public by Mrs. Reagan and TV newsman Walter Cronkite; and in the evening, the New York Philharmonic gave a free concert on the Great Meadow of New York's Central Park.

On Sunday evening the official celebration moved to the Meadowlands Sports Complex in East Rutherford, NJ. At 6:30 there was a televised Sports Salute from the Brendan Byrne Arena by gymnasts, figure skaters, and other athletes. And at 8 P.M. came the Grand Finale, a three-hour televised extravaganza from Giants Stadium, with entertainment by country music stars, square dancers, tap dancers, and, among other events, a 500-person marching band and a 850-member drill team.

Looking Back, Looking Ahead. None of the exhausted revelers were likely soon to forget Liberty Weekend. The four-day extravaganza was not without controversy, however, as some citizens felt that the red-white-and-blue "show biz" razzle-dazzle had overshadowed the deeper meanings of liberty. The spectaculars, they charged, had buried serious reflection under commercial hype. Others defended the expression of pride and patriotism, arguing that American freedom even includes the right to tasteless extravagance if it tickles the public fancy. The last words on the issue might have been those of President Reagan in his remarks before igniting the fireworks: "The things that unite us—America's past of which we are so proud, our hopes and aspirations for the future of the world and this much loved country—these things far outweigh what little divides us."

Even more poignant were the president's words on relighting the torch. "We are the keepers of the flame of liberty," he said. "We hold it high tonight for the world to see."

Commencing a second hundred years, looking better than ever in a world of risks and changing values, the Statue of Liberty held up her flame with an ever-confident stance.

MEDAL OF LIBERTY

In honor of the centennial of the Statue of Liberty, President Ronald Reagan awarded the newly created Medal of Liberty to 12 distinguished, foreign-born Americans. Those honored were:

Irving Berlin, Russian-born composer

Franklin R. Chang-Diaz, Costa Rican-born astronaut

Kenneth Clark, born in Panama Canal Zone, educator and psychologist

Hanna Holburn Gray, German-born educator and university president

Bob Hope, English-born entertainer

Henry A. Kissinger, German-born political scientist and diplomat

I. M. Pei, Chinese-born architect

Itzhak Perlman, Israeli-born violinist

James B. Reston, Scottish-born journalist

Albert B. Sabin, Russian-born virologist

An Wang, Chinese-born geneticist, immunologist, educator

Elie Wiesel, Romanian-born author, educator, humanitarian

PHOBIAS

By Robert L. DuPont, M.D.

Snakes, heights, physical confinement, riding in elevators, and flying in airplanes are some of the most common causes. Crowds, darkness, thunder and lightning, fear itself—virtually anything—can trigger the reaction. A phobia is the irrational fear of an object, activity, or situation that does not cause anxiety for most people, and it can be the most crippling of all mental disorders.

For decades phobias were regarded as mysterious and incurable disorders that afflicted relatively few people. Phobias are perhaps no more prevalent now than they were decades ago, and researchers still disagree on where they come from—genetic predisposition, environment and upbringing, shock, stress, or some combination. Yet it has become increasingly clear that phobias are one of the most common of all mental disorders in the United States. More than 13 million Americans are affected by them, making phobias the number two mental-health problem after alcoholism. They often lead to avoidance behavior and anticipatory anxiety, which may cause severe distress and handicap in the lives of sufferers. New forms of treatment, however, offer great hope that phobic people and their families can live full, normal lives.

Ophidiophobia, the fear of snakes, is one of the most common forms of animal phobia.

About the Author: Dr. Robert L. DuPont is clinical professor of psychiatry at Georgetown University Medical School in Washington, DC. Since 1978 he also has served as president of the Center for Behavioral Medicine in Rockville, MD. Dr. DuPont is recognized widely for his work—both research and treatment—in such areas as drug abuse, criminology, and phobias. Founding president of the Phobia Society of America, he is the author of *Phobias and Panic: A Physician's Guide to Modern Treatment* (1986).

Types and Tendencies. Phobias can be divided into five major groups. The most common is the *simple phobia,* the fear of one or two specific situations or experiences. Fear of heights and fear of elevators are common examples. *Social phobia* is phobic panic caused by embarrassment. This type of fear might be limited to public speaking, for example, or it could involve any potentially embarrassing social situation—from eating in public to signing one's name in front of someone. *Animal phobias* are usually associated with a fear of snakes or spiders, but they might also involve dogs, cats, or birds. Another common form is *blood-injury phobia,* in which the person has a panic reaction to the sight of blood, the thought of injury, or routine medical or dental procedures.

Agoraphobia, the most complex form of phobia, is the fear of being away from a safe person or place. In open, public places, the agoraphobic suffers "adult separation anxiety." Severe cases of agoraphobia have caused some sufferers to be housebound for many years. Those who venture out often behave like kindergartners on the first day of school, clinging to their spouse or other support figure. Agoraphobia may also be characterized by spontaneous, generalized panic attacks that are not focused on any specific object or activity. It is the most crippling type of phobia since it involves the most ordinary experiences—shopping, traveling, or being alone.

At their root, all phobias are a form of claustrophobia, the fear of being trapped in a terrifying experience without being able to escape. The anticipation of being trapped often leads to avoidance of the fear-inducing experience. A phobia is a

The irrational fear of public speaking is one of the various "social phobias"—panic reactions caused by embarrassment.

G. French/H. Armstrong Roberts

debilitating case of the "what ifs." "What if the doctor's office is on the fifth floor and I have to take the elevator?" "What if the elevator gets stuck?" "What if I pass out or go crazy?" The vicious circle of panic, fear-inducing "what ifs," and avoidance behavior characterizes the phobic syndrome.

All phobias except the social phobias are much more common in females than in males. Although phobias can occur at any age, most start between the ages of 15 and 30. The exception is animal phobias, which characteristically begin during early childhood. Therapists have observed that people who become afflicted with phobias tend to be highly imaginative, perfectionistic, eager to please, and sensitive to criticism and the feelings of others. Many phobics have been found to have relatives who also suffer from phobias and depression.

A phobia is not associated with psychotic mental disorder, in which the patient loses contact with reality and may require hospitalization. People with phobias are usually good family members, employees, and friends. Some therapists call phobias the disease of "quality people." When not confronted by the phobic situation—or not thinking about confronting it —people with phobias are mentally quite normal. During the phobic experience, sufferers may appear normal except that they usually seek to escape. More characteristically, they try not to get into the situation in the first place.

Many phobic people are embarrassed by the disorder and feel forced to cover up for their avoidance. They might say, for example, "I don't like that restaurant," when what they feel is "I don't want to go there because I might panic and would be too embarrassed to tell anyone, so I would feel trapped." They are humiliated by the phobia but cannot explain it to other people because it is irrational; it makes no sense even to themselves.

The fear of crowds is known as ochlophobia. Overcrowded conditions, not only in cities but anywhere, also can lead to a most complex type of phobia, agoraphobia—the fear of being away from a safe place or person. Either disorder can cause many sufferers to remain housebound.

FREEWAY CONDITION 28
DON'T BE FUELISH
BE CARPOOLISH

Ave
o Fwy
½
1¼
2½

Avoidance behavior is central to the phobic process. Repetition of the panic reaction leads the sufferer to avoid the triggering situation—including such otherwise normal activities as driving a car—at all costs.

Symptoms and Reactions. Inside, phobic people in phobic situations are confronted by a storm of uncontrollable panic reactions—shortness of breath, racing heart, chest pain, choking or smothering sensations, dizziness, hot and cold flashes, sweating, and shaking. They might feel faint, have strange sensations in the hands and feet, and be overcome by a fear of dying, going crazy, or doing something bizarre and uncontrolled. This last aspect of the phobic reaction is perhaps the most upsetting. The person knows that the reaction is unreasonable but cannot help feeling that way when faced with the phobic situation.

Despite the overwhelming panic, the outcome of the phobic situation is rarely so dreadful as death, insanity, or loss of control. Phobic sufferers who panic when driving a car rarely, if ever, lose command of the vehicle. Typically, people with phobias will say they "almost" experienced such awful consequences. When pressed, they often admit that it never actually happened. As one phobic person acknowledged, "I have had a terrible life, but most of it never happened."

Still, the thoughts and feelings during a phobic experience are themselves dreadful. Phobic people commonly call the panic the "worst feeling" they have ever had, and they will do almost anything to avoid it. People who do not suffer from phobias often equate their own feelings of fear and anxiety with phobic panic, but this is a serious error. Phobic panic is far worse than ordinary feelings of distress. Indeed it is the terrible feelings themselves, rather than any "weakness" in handling ordinary fear and anxiety, that separate phobic people from non-phobic people. Phobia sufferers do not avoid phobic situations because they have "crazy" ideas about them but because the feelings they experience are so unbearable. The terrible feelings lead to abnormal—but understandable—thoughts, which in turn make the feelings even more terrible.

After the process is repeated enough times, the phobic person learns that the feelings of panic can be partially controlled by avoiding the situation that triggers them. This discovery leads to the avoidance of otherwise normal activities, such as driving a car, flying in an airplane, or going out in public. Along with avoidance behavior, another crippling consequence of the phobic process is anticipatory anxiety—an intense preoccupation with the source of the phobia even when it is not present. This is also called phobophobia, or fear of the fear. For example, elevator phobics not only suffer when actually riding an elevator. They also experience panic when thinking about the possibility of having to ride an elevator. Thus, even time away from the phobic situation is invaded by dread.

Finally, it is important to point out that phobias are not only handicapping to the phobic person but also to his or her family. Routine family life is disturbed by the avoidance behavior of the phobic member. For example, a child may become confused about his mother's love if she cannot drive him to special activities or visit his school as other mothers do. The child may be humiliated and embarrassed and feel "different" from his peers, just as children of alcoholics try to hide their family situations from friends. Similarly, a person with an elevator phobia can disturb the activities of the whole family by insisting on avoidance at all times.

Treatment. Until recent years, there were only a handful of institutions and psychologists in the United States that specialized in the research and treatment of phobias. Today there are more than 50 such clinics and hundreds of specialists in the field. Phobias, in fact, are one of the most treatable of psychiatric disorders. The current cure rate is as high as 70–80%.

"You're already worrying about the flight back, aren't you?"

© Rothco

Aviophobia, the fear of flying, is believed to cost the airline industry up to $1.5 billion a year. Several airlines therefore have sponsored programs to calm reluctant flyers.

USAir

Two new methods of treatment afford particular hope for phobic patients. One is called *exposure therapy*. In this treatment, the patient benefits from the support of other people (a therapist and other patients) who understand the nature of phobias and learns specific techniques for handling phobic panic in real-life situations. Usually lasting two to six months, exposure therapy is a group process in which phobic people help each other develop the courage to confront their panic-causing experiences. Then, accompanied by the therapist or other support person, the patient confronts a real-life phobic situation and practices using the fear-reducing techniques. Two helpful techniques are counting backward by threes from 100 and reciting the words to a song or poem when the panic hits. Another fear-reducing technique is simply to "wait and let time pass," learning that the panic will fade.

The other new form of treatment is the use of *antipanic medication,* especially antidepressant drugs. Such medicines are typically taken once a day, usually at bedtime, for 6 to 12 months. They block the panic so that the person enters the phobic situation with relatively little discomfort, thinking "This isn't as bad as I expected." After months of entering phobic situations without panic, the patient's nervous system seems to heal, and the antipanic medication often can be discontinued without recurrence of the panic. If it does recur, the medicine can be taken for another trial period.

Exposure therapy is most effective for patients whose phobic panic leads to the avoidance of routine, everyday ex-

© Paul Fusco/Magnum

Gephyrophobia is the fear of crossing a bridge or body of water. The late American author John Cheever is believed to have experienced such fear.

© Craig Blouin/Taurus

Acrophobia, the fear of heights, is just one of the many phobias that can interfere with the routine tasks of everyday life.

periences. Antipanic medicines are most effective for those who suffer "spontaneous panic"; that is, when panic arises even outside the phobic situation. This often occurs in cases of agoraphobia. In addition, some phobic people can be helped by medicines that reduce anxiety. And two specific types of phobia—fear of public speaking and flying in airplanes—can be helped by medicines that slow the heart rate.

Many other forms of phobia treatment, including psychotherapy aimed at identifying and overcoming difficult life experiences and relationships, have been tried with some success.

One obstacle in treating phobias is that many sufferers simply are not aware that the disorder has a name, a growing body of formal research, and proven methods of treatment. A recent study by the National Institute of Mental Health found that only 23% of phobic people are receiving any form of therapy for their disorder.

All in all, the future is bright for sufferers of phobias. Phobias and other anxiety disorders have become the most actively researched area in mental health, yielding important new understandings. For example, the observation that anxiety and phobic panic can be induced by chemicals in susceptible individuals gives strong support for a biological basis of such disorders. That discovery, in turn, offers hope that new medicines will be developed to treat phobias and perhaps some day prevent them. The good news for people with phobias is that their suffering is neither incomprehensible nor incurable, and that they can live full, normal lives.

FEAR OF....

A Glossary of Major Phobias

Acrophobia: high places.
Aerophobia: air, drafts, gases.
Agoraphobia: open spaces, being away from a safe place or person.
Ailurophobia: cats.
Amaxophobia: vehicles, driving.
Anthropophobia: people.
Aquaphobia: water, bathing, swimming.
Astraphobia (or tonitophobia): thunder and lightning.
Autophobia (or monophobia): being alone.
Aviophobia: flying.
Claustrophobia: confinement.
Cynophobia: dogs.
Entomophobia: insects.
Gephyrophobia: crossing a bridge or body of water.
Hematophobia: blood.
Neophobia: change, the new or unfamiliar.
Nyctophobia: darkness or night.
Ochlophobia: crowds.
Ophidiophobia: snakes.
Ornithophobia: birds.
Panophobia: anything and everything.
Phobophobia: fear.
Thanatophobia (or necrophobia): death or dying.
Xenophobia: strangers.
Zoophobia: animals in general.

THE DINER IS BACK

By Richard J.S. Gutman

About the Author: Richard J.S. Gutman is the coauthor of *American Diner* (1979), a tribute to the institution. He has a degree in architecture from Cornell University and is the owner of Slide Factor, a slide show production house in Massachusetts. He has lectured on diners to the National Trust for Historic Preservation, the Smithsonian Institution, and other groups.

For more than 100 years, the roadside diner has been a familiar fixture on the American landscape. Always mimicking the popular culture and current tastes in design and style, diners indeed have been *overly* familiar—overlooked and sometimes forgotten. A decade ago, diners seemed to be a dying breed. Now, in the mid-1980s, a diner renaissance is under way. Diners have begun to emerge from their nearly invisible familiarity to become a more visible and appreciated presence on the American scene. New ones are still being built; old ones are being restored. They are appearing in nationwide advertisements. Most of all, though some customers never left, the American consumer has rediscovered the diner. Suddenly, diners are chic.

Photo courtesy of The Diner on Sycamore

And just what is a diner? First, it must have a counter with a row of round stools, and there should be at least a few booths. Strictly speaking, the diner should be prefabricated. Most importantly, a diner must have a certain feel, a comfortable hominess. A diner is a place were camaraderie and good home-cooked food (the latter at reasonable prices) can always be found.

The predecessor of the modern diner was the horsedrawn lunch wagon, which first appeared in 1872. Born of the night worker's need for quick food in the wee hours, these mobile eateries filled a unique niche in the food-service business. Instantly popular, the Victorian dog wagon also became a gathering place for late-night revelers.

In the 20th century, the wagons grew in size to accommodate more customers and were moved onto permanent locations. The 1920s saw a boom in diners, as motorists hit the highways in record numbers. Drivers needed sustenance, and diners provided the perfect stopping place—the right fare in the right atmosphere. From early on, diners attracted customers with an image of cleanliness, a place where food was prepared right before one's eyes. And in the 1920s, the use of materials in diner design grew in synch with this image. Interiors were typified by the glistening machine-age look: white ceramic tile, white porcelain enamel stools, and a white marble counter.

Over the next several decades, the look of the diner evolved steadily. The futuristic 1930s witnessed the birth of stream-lined diners—sleek exteriors of gleaming stainless steel and porcelain enamel, shiny interiors with equally predominant stainless steel. Though the classic diner of this era was continually modified and enlarged, it remained generally in vogue until the 1950s.

Diners go where the people are, and vice versa: Cincinnati's Diner on Sycamore (opposite page), a Fifties classic, was rescued, revitalized, and moved to a new location, where it is thriving. Reflecting the more recent pop culture, Ediner (below) opened in 1982 at a shopping mall in Edina, MN. Cooking from scratch in a diner atmosphere has been a recipe for success in the Midwest.

Photos © Bert Levy

Until Papa Cantella's Diner (above and left) came along in Commerce, CA, none of the new diners looked back beyond the Art Deco era. Factory-built and handcrafted, Papa Cantella's re-creates a diner of the first hey-day, the 1920s. By contrast, the newly renovated Fog City Diner (below) in San Francisco's financial district, is a glitzy, nostalgic, post-modern diner for the 1980s. The interior (opposite page) shines with chrome, Formica, and high-polished wood. But if the look at Fog City is familiar, the menu is not. The dinner fare includes jalapeño corn muffins, black bean and sirloin chili, and calf's liver with tomatoes, leeks, and ginger. Fog City takes res-ervations, but it's booked up for a month.

Then came a double whammy: a severe Americana-style, followed by the Mediterranean look. Though these new diner-restaurants were built by the same old diner manufacturers, they created a look from which the classic diner seemed unlikely to recover. This was the era of the ungainly, out-of-scale Mansard roof and the change in exterior treatment from stainless steel to brick and stone. Though radically different in style from the previous generation, these new diner-restaurants were still enormously popular. Especially in the suburbs —where the color scheme is most often burgundy, beige, gray, and mauve, with smoked-glass windows—the emphasis is on the *restaurant,* not the diner.

But then, in the early 1980s, something happened. With the success of theme restaurants, restaurant operators across the United States seemed almost simultaneously to rediscover the diner. Looking back 40, 50, or 60 years, they found the seed of the original idea. Entrepreneurs nostalgic for the diners of their youth bypassed the manufacturers and started building large (and more profitable) versions of the diners of their dreams. In New York City, Cincinnati, and elsewhere, classic art-deco diners were restored and reopened to a new clientele.

And so the new diner chic was born. People began creating ''neo-diners'' and ''new diner concepts.'' Of course, one cannot be too strict with definitions when talking about the resurgence of diners. These new places are *like* diners—they have the look, the feel, and the menu of classic diners. But most often they are designed by architects and built on-site. They are today's interpretation of the diners of yesteryear.

While diners were traditionally concentrated on the East Coast and spread thinly across the rest of the country, the new diners have popped up everywhere. In fact, one reason for the new success of diners may be the fact that they are appearing where diners never were . . . or have not been for a long time.

Where does it lead from here? When it comes to diners, one should not speak of the future. Diners reflect the present —the popular culture and current tastes in design and style, and for now, at least, the diner is back.

Courtesy of Joseph Morozin,
The Dining Car

And then there's the Dining Car in Philadelphia. Of all the old-style diners that have opened in the new Diner Renaissance, the Dining Car is the first and only one to be built by a real diner manufacturer. It is traditional in every way—stainless steel throughout and basic home cooking.

Courtesy of Bill Higgins, Fog City Diner

People, Places, and Things

Terry Arthur/The White House

© T. Graham/Sygma

© Carol M. Highsmith

On the hill from which General Sherman watched Atlanta burn in 1864, the Carter Presidential Center (opposite page) opened on October 1, the former president's 62nd birthday. Built with $25 million in private donations, the Carter library and museum also will be used as a forum for advanced study of public policy. Mr. and Mrs. Reagan joined the former president and first lady for the dedication, which Mr. Reagan called "a celebration of the South—the new South that Jimmy Carter helped to build." Just two blocks from where the Carters and Reagans have lived, on Pennsylvania Avenue in Washington, DC, another monument was reopened in September. The Willard Hotel (right), an elegant 1901 Beaux-Arts building and legendary gathering place, was opened after a $73 million restoration. The term "lobbyist" is said to have originated from the political wangling that went on in its halls. And in the Netherlands, the presidents of France and West Germany joined Queen Beatrix and other Dutch dignitaries for the October 4 opening of a major new dike (above) in the Eastern Scheldt River. The $2.4 billion sea barrier is the costliest and most technologically advanced that the Dutch have constructed in their nine-century battle to hold back the North Sea tides.

The U.S. Congress finally stopped to smell the roses. More than 70 bills had been introduced over the years to promote a variety of flowers as the "national floral emblem," but in September 1986 the House passed a bill giving the designation to the rose. The Senate had passed the rose resolution the previous year, and President Reagan signed it into law on Oct. 7, 1986. At age 79, U.S. Navy Rear Adm. Grace Hopper (left) was the nation's oldest active military officer until her retirement in August. A former mathematics professor, "Amazing Grace" developed the widely used computer programming language COBOL. And Dodge Morgan (opposite page, bottom), a 54-year-old electronics entrepreneur from Maine, completed a nonstop solo circumnavigation of the globe in a record time of 150 days, 1 hour, and 6 minutes. He made the Bermuda-to-Bermuda voyage in a 60-ft. (18.3-m) sloop, "The American Promise."

The U.S. social event of the year was the July 19 wedding of Caroline Bouvier Kennedy, 28, the daughter of the late President John Kennedy, and Edwin A. Schlossberg, 41, in Cape Cod, MA (top left). Running as a Republican, the 55-year-old actor Clint Eastwood (above left) defeated the incumbent in April 8 elections for mayor of Carmel-by-the-Sea, CA. And off the coast of Montauk, Long Island, NY, charter boat captain Donnie Braddick caught a 17-ft. (5.2-m), 3,450-lb (1 565-kg) great white shark with just a rod and reel; it was the largest such fish ever caught in that manner.

AMERICAN PROMISE

As the centerpiece of its 100th annual Winter Carnival in February, the city of St. Paul, MN, constructed a 12-story neo-Gothic ice palace with computer-controlled lights (above). Measuring 128'9" (39 m) at the apex, it was the largest man-made ice structure ever built. It was made of 10,000 blocks of ice, each weighing up to 750 lbs (340 kg).

© J. P. Laffont/Sygma

AP/Wide World

Another American institution that turned 100 was the tuxedo (opposite page, bottom right). The style was born in 1886, when tobacco scion Griswold Lorillard showed up at his Tuxedo, NY, country club wearing a bib, tucker, and cut-off tailcoat. By 1986 annual sales exceeded $100 million, with rentals many times higher. A dress (opposite page, bottom left) *designed for Jeannette MacDonald in the 1937 film "Maytime" was part of the "Hollywood: Legend and Reality" exhibition, which began a two-year U.S. tour in 1986. The show was organized by the Smithsonian Institution Traveling Exhibition Service (SITES). Harvard University, the oldest U.S. institution of higher education, marked its 350th anniversary in September with a four-day celebration that included academic convocations, concerts, a display of fireworks, and speeches by a variety of alumni dignitaries. Britain's Prince Charles delivered the main address (above). And in Germany, August 13 marked the 25th anniversary of the construction of the Berlin Wall, separating East and West Berlin. East Germany celebrated the occasion with a military parade. On the West German side (left) Berliners laid wreaths in memory of those killed attempting to cross the wall.*

On Oct. 14, 1986, Elie Wiesel, the 58-year-old, Romanian-born author, educator, and survivor of Nazi death camps, was named the winner of the Nobel Peace Prize. "Elie Wiesel has emerged as one of the most important spiritual leaders and guides in an age when violence, repression, and racism continue to characterize the world," said Egil Aarvik, chairman of the Norwegian Nobel Committee. "Wiesel is a messenger to mankind. His message is one of peace, atonement, and human dignity. His belief that the forces fighting evil in the world can be victorious is a hard-won belief. His message is based on his own personal experience of total humiliation and of the utter contempt for humanity shown in Hitler's death camps. The message is in the form of a testimony, repeated and deepened through the works of a great author."

The Alphabetical Section

Oslo, Norway, Dec. 10, 1986

We must always take sides. Neutrality helps the oppressor, never the victim. Silence encourages the tormentor, never the tormented. Sometimes we must interfere. When human lives are endangered, when human dignity is in jeopardy, national borders and sensitivities become irrelevant. Wherever men or women are persecuted because of their race, religion, or political views, that place must—at that moment—become the center of the universe. . . .

There is so much injustice and suffering crying out for our attention: victims of hunger, or racism and political persecution, writers and poets, prisoners in so many lands governed by the left and by the right. Human rights are being violated on every continent. More people are oppressed than free. . . .

What all these victims need above all is to know that they are not alone; that we are not forgetting them, that when their voices are stifled we shall lend them ours, that while their freedom depends on ours, the quality of our freedom depends on theirs. . . .

We know that every moment is a moment of grace, every hour an offering; not to share them would mean to betray them. Our lives no longer belong to us alone; they belong to all those who need us desperately.

—Elie Wiesel, excerpts of acceptance speech for the 1986 Nobel Peace Prize

ACCIDENTS AND DISASTERS

AVIATION

Jan. 18—A jetliner crashes on its approach to South Elena airport in northern Guatemala, killing all 93 persons on board.

Jan. 28—The American space shuttle *Challenger* explodes soon after launching, killing all seven crew members aboard. (*See* page 36.)

Jan. 29—Twenty-one persons die when an airliner attempting to make an emergency landing crashes near Los Mochis, Mexico.

March 27—A French fighter jet crashes into a school in Bangui, Central African Republic, killing 22.

March 30—A twin turboprop airplane crashes soon after takeoff from Pemba, Mozambique, killing 49 persons.

March 31—A Mexican airliner crashes in a mountainous region of Central Mexico; 166 persons are dead.

June 18—A sightseeing plane and a helicopter collide over Arizona's Grand Canyon, killing all 25 persons on board the two aircraft.

Aug. 31—An Aeromexico commercial jetliner approaching the Los Angeles International airport and a small private plane collide and crash into homes in Cerritos, CA; 82 persons are dead.

Oct. 19—In South Africa a plane carrying the Mozambique leader Samora Machel crashes while en route from Zambia to Mozambique; 33 others also are killed.

Nov. 3 (reported)—An Iranian military transport plane crashes into a mountain in eastern Iran, killing all 103 persons aboard.

Nov. 6—A British civilian helicopter crashes in the North Sea off the Shetland Islands; 45 people are feared dead.

Dec. 12—A Soviet jetliner crashes in fog on approaching an East Berlin airport, killing 69 persons.

Dec. 25—An Iraqi airliner is hijacked and later crashes during an emergency landing at Arar, Saudi Arabia; 62 persons are killed.

FIRES AND EXPLOSIONS

Jan. 23—Fire in New Delhi's Siddarth Continental Hotel kills 37 persons.

Feb. 11—Fire destroys an annex of the Daitokan Hotel in Atagawa, Japan, killing 24 persons.

Feb. 17—An office building catches fire in Rio de Janeiro, killing 24 persons.

March 3—Fire at the Chilean embassy in Caracas, Venezuela, kills 15 persons.

July 16—Near Moura, Queensland, Australia, an explosion of methane gas in a coal mine is thought to have killed 12 trapped miners.

Aug. 21—A toxic gas of carbon dioxide, hydrogen, and sulfide escapes from Lake Nios, a lake at the bottom of a supposedly dormant volcano, in northwest Cameroon, killing some 1,700 people.

Sept. 5—Fire in a hotel in Kristiansand, Norway, kills 14 and injures more than 50.

Sept. 16—Fire in the Kinross gold mine, 60 mi (97 km) east of Johannesburg, South Africa, kills 177.

Nov. 1—In Devnya, Bulgaria, an explosion and fire at a chemical plant kills 17 persons.

Dec. 31—Fire, ruled as caused by arson, at the Dupont Plaza Hotel in San Juan, Puerto Rico, kills 96.

LAND AND SEA TRANSPORTATION

Jan. 17—A bus goes off a mountain road and plunges 900 ft (274 m) down a slope, killing 41 persons.

Feb. 8—A Canadian passenger train collides with a freight train near Hinton, Alberta, Canada, killing 23.

Feb. 16—A Soviet luxury liner, the *Mikhail Lermontov,* carrying more than 700 people, slams into the rocks off New Zealand's South Island, killing one seaman.

Feb. 17—Two passenger trains collide near the town of Limache, Chile; 58 persons are believed dead.

April 20—A ferry sinks on the Dhaleswari River in Bangladesh, near Dhaka, killing at least 300 people.

May 14—A schooner, *The Pride of Baltimore,* which was to have taken part in the July 4th festivities in New York, sinks north of Puerto Rico; four persons are missing.

May 19—A bus catches fire 67 mi (108 km) north of Bangkok, Thailand, killing 13 persons.

May 25—A double-decker ferry capsizes on the Meghna River, south of Dhaka, Bangladesh; 190 deaths are confirmed and as many as 500 are feared dead.

May 30—Near Walker, CA, a tour bus carrying mainly retirement-home residents plunges down an embankment into the Walker River, killing 18 persons.

June 17—A bus carrying schoolchildren returning from a camping vacation rolls down a steep gorge 90 mi (147 km) south of Lima, Peru; 20 are killed.

July 26—A collision between a passenger train and truck at a railroad crossing near Lockington, Humberside, England, kills nine persons.

Sept. 1—A Soviet passenger ship collides with a freighter and sinks into the Black Sea; 398 persons are feared dead.

Sept. 7—Two passenger ships collide off the coast of Port Harcourt, Nigeria; about 100 people are dead and five others are missing.

Nov. 11—A jammed coastal ferry sinks in rough seas near Montrouis, Haiti; as many as 200 are missing.

Dec. 23 (reported)—A boat from the Dominican Republic is swamped in waters near the coast of Rincón, Puerto Rico, killing at least eight.

Dec. 26—A British cargo ship sinks off the east coast of Iceland, killing all 12 members of the crew.

STORMS, FLOODS, AND EARTHQUAKES

Jan. 7—Landslides caused by heavy rain kill at least 21 persons in Sri Lanka's central highlands, particularly the Nuwara Eliya district.

Feb. 13–20—A massive storm system batters the Western United States causing snow, floods, mudslides, high winds, and avalanches from central California into neighboring states and Canada's British Columbia; some 17 persons are dead.

April 5—In the Cuzco area of Peru an earthquake kills at least 16 persons.

April 19—Two tornadoes hit Sweetwater, TX, killing one person and injuring about 100.

May 5—An earthquake in southeastern Turkey kills 15.

May 12–15—A snowstorm on Mt. Hood in Oregon kills nine mountain climbers; two others survive.

May 22 (reported)—Typhoon *Namu* hits the Solomon Islands, killing at least 71 persons.

July 9—A typhoon hits Luzon Island in the Philippines, killing at least 73 persons.

Aug. 22—A typhoon hits central Taiwan, killing at least 22 people; nine others are missing.

Aug. 25–26—Heavy rain from Hurricane *Charley* causes flooding of rivers and coastal towns in Ireland and Britain; 11 are feared dead.

Sept. 12 (reported)—A typhoon hits northern Vietnam in early September, killing nearly 400.

Sept. 13—In Kalamata, Greece, an earthquake kills 20 persons; 300 others are injured.

Oct. 6—Flooding following heavy rains in Manila and surrounding provinces of the Philippines kills at least 14 people; 11 others are missing.

Oct. 10—Two strong earthquakes hit the San Salvador area of El Salvador, killing 1,500; 300,000 others are homeless.

Nov. 10 (reported)—In the U.S. Northern Plains, a winter snowstorm kills at least five people.

Nov. 15—Two earthquakes shake Chungho, a Taipei suburb in Taiwan; 15 are killed and 44 are hurt.

Nov. 17 (reported)—A sudden snowstorm in the mountains above Srinagar in northern India kills at least 60.

MISCELLANEOUS

March 15—In Singapore, a six-story hotel collapses, killing 33 persons.

April 14—At least 48 people are crushed to death in a stampede during a religious pilgrimage at a Hindu festival at Hardwar, Uttar Pradesh, India.

April 20—A reservoir in northeastern Sri Lanka bursts, killing as many as 100 people.

April 28 (reported)—A nuclear power plant accident at the Chernobyl Station in the USSR causes death and radiation contamination; the site is 60 mi (97 km) north of Kiev. (*See* page 218.)

July 26—A landslide kills five in Senise, Italy.

Nov. 9—At least 32 pilgrims are trampled to death in a stampede at a Holy Hindu shrine at Ajodha in Uttar Pradesh state in India.

ADVERTISING

The year 1986 was one of enormous change and consolidation in the advertising industry.

Mergers and Acquisitions. Within a period of two weeks during the spring, the title of the world's largest ad-agency group changed hands twice, as two mergers of unprecedented size and scope were consummated. First in late April, BBDO International, the world's 6th largest ad agency, joined with Doyle Dane Bernbach Group, the 12th largest, and Needham Harper Worldwide, the 16th largest, to form Omnicom Group. With approximately $5 billion in combined worldwide billings, Omnicom became the largest agency group, surpassing The Interpublic Group. Less than three weeks later, however, the London-based agency of Saatchi & Saatchi PLC, which had already declared its goal of becoming number one, did exactly that with the purchase of Ted Bates Worldwide, which had ranked third. Saatchi & Saatchi, which had brought two other major agencies under its holding company umbrella within the two previous months (17th-ranked Dancer Fitzgerald Sample in March and 23d-ranked Backer & Spielvogel in April) now surpassed Omnicom with some $7.5 billion in worldwide billings. The purchase price of Bates was by far the highest ever paid for an ad agency—$450 million in cash.

There were other sizable mergers and acquisitions during the year, most notably Foote, Cone & Belding Communications' acquisition of Leber Katz Partners; Ally & Gargano's merger with MCA Advertising; and London-based WCRS Group's first entry into the United States with the purchase of HBM/Creamer and Della Femina, Travisano & Partners.

But it was the Omnicom and Saatchi & Saatchi deals that had the most far-reaching consequences. By bringing together so many agencies that had been handling the accounts of competitive advertisers, the mergers triggered a major outbreak of account movement. Among the major companies who moved their accounts in response to that merger activity were: Proctor & Gamble, the nation's largest advertiser, which moved about $150 million in billings; number three R.J. Reynolds/Nabisco, which moved about $200 million; Colgate-Palmolive ($100 million); American Honda Motors ($100 million); and Warner-Lambert ($68 million). Major account switches that were not merger-inspired included Kraft ($100 million), Xerox ($40 million), and TWA Airlines ($55 million). All in all, more than $1 billion—or almost 2% of total U.S. national advertising billings—changed agencies in 1986.

Ad Volume. Total 1986 U.S. ad spending was expected to break the $100 billion mark for the first time, rising 7.6% from the 1985 level to $101.9 billion. National advertising was projected to rise 7%, reaching $57.1 billion; local advertising was forecast to climb 8.2%, reaching $44.8 billion.

The projected spending figure for 1986 represented a considerable slowdown in growth rate from 1985, caused by a much lower rate of inflation and flat or trimmed ad budgets stemming from the sluggish U.S. economy. As a result of these factors, two of the major broadcast television networks, ABC and CBS, lowered their year-to-year, prime-time, commercial-rate increases for the first time ever.

Government and Legal. Amid considerable discussion—and even congressional hearings—on the banning of all tobacco advertising on television, the only concrete change was a ban on TV ads for smokeless tobacco (chewing tobacco and snuff) that went into effect August 28. Meanwhile, there was also new pressure on alcoholic-beverage advertising.

More serious challenges to the advertising industry came with less fanfare from the courts. In a case involving casino-gambling advertising in Puerto Rico, the U.S. Supreme Court ruled that governments could curb truthful advertising of an undesirable product or activity, even if it is legal. And in an unprecedented ruling, the U.S. Court of Appeals upheld an award of $40 million in damages to the U-Haul truck-rental company for a false comparative ad campaign by competitor Jartran; the ruling was believed to open the door to more comparative ad suits.

But advertisers also won new ground. Following a U.S. federal court ruling, Oklahoma media were required to accept alcoholic-beverage ads for the first time in 26 years. And W.R. Grace & Company, after a much-publicized struggle with the three major TV networks, won agreement from two of them to allow airing of a controversial anti-federal-deficit commercial.

Firsts. Television advertising took a big step into the global arena when the Gillette Company made the first single-source global TV buy, using Rupert Murdoch-owned TV stations on three continents. Of less scope but more fun, Burgerville USA, a small hamburger chain based in Vancouver, WA, claimed to air the first 3-D TV commercials.

The year also saw some unlikely associations between products and ad claims. Several companies jumped on the calcium bandwagon, introducing special supplement products. Tums, the antacid, continued to promote its calcium content, and Tab, the soft drink, joined in as "the one with calcium." Plaque removal was another rallying point for new products and ad campaigns, with such entries as Check-Up plaque-fighting chewing gum and Peridex plaque-removing oral rinse. Even Trident chewing gum began advertising research showing that chewing sugarless gum "actually neutralizes plaque acids."

STEWART ALTER, *"Advertising Age"*

© F. Hibon/Sygma

The tank regiment "Prague" was part of the Soviet Union's loudly proclaimed but token pullout from Afghanistan.

AFGHANISTAN

In its seventh year, the war between Soviet troops in Afghanistan and the rebel *mujahidin* ("holy warriors") began to tilt slightly in favor of the Soviets during 1986. The Geneva negotiations between Afghanistan and Pakistan ended in deadlock, and U.S. aid to the Afghan resistance increased. In May, Babrak Karmal resigned as general secretary of the ruling Communist Party and was replaced by Sayid Mohammad Najibullah.

Military Developments. In its first coherent and effective counterinsurgency strategy of the war, the Soviets began to utilize the *Spetsnaz,* elite commandos trained to operate in small teams at night behind enemy lines. In July, Soviet leader Mikhail Gorbachev announced that six regiments (up to 7,000 troops) would be withdrawn from the war, but the move was purely cosmetic, as Soviet troop levels had already reached 150,000.

Armaments on both sides increased in quality and quantity. In April the *mujahidin* were promised Stinger antiaircraft by the United States, but opposition in the United States and Pakistan caused delays. The Soviet strategy was to secure key urban areas and communications lines, devastate rural areas that supported the resistance, exploit tribal and factional divisions, cut supply routes from Pakistan, and undermine Pakistan's support for the resistance. The Soviets launched several major offensives in the spring. Spearheaded by Spetsnaz commandos, they swept up the Kunar Valley and destroyed the major resistance supply base at Jawar. Spetsnaz teams assassinated

several experienced guerrilla commanders, and Soviet "scorched earth" tactics eroded rural civilian support for the *mujahidin*. The loss of local supplies forced the resistance to allocate precious transport space to food instead of arms. And the resistance was further plagued by a leaky weapons pipeline through Pakistan, where up to 60% of foreign aid is diverted and sold on the black market. But the *mujahidin* struck back, reopening supply lines, recapturing and rebuilding the Jawar base, and attacking Kabul itself, where they blew up a major ammunition depot.

Soviet military problems also persisted. Desertions from the Afghan army continued: an Afghan unit of 600 men defected in Kandahar, and four Afghan generals were arrested for cooperating with the resistance. Ethnic conflict in Soviet units culminated in a mutiny by Soviet Tajiks at the Dasht-e-Abadan base in northern Afghanistan; 80 were killed.

Politics. In Afghan politics the program of Sovietization was accelerated. Some 40,000 Afghan students, including small children, were being trained in the USSR to form future Communist government cadres. Tribal leaders were subverted to oppose the resistance, and the Pushtunistan separatist cause was revived to foment dissension in the tribal areas of Pakistan. The *Khad,* the secret police modeled on the Soviet KGB, was expanded to infiltrate the resistance, increase terrorist attacks inside Pakistan, and assassinate resistance leaders.

A former head of *Khad,* and more recently the party secretary in charge of security, Najibullah replaced Babrak Karmal as general secretary of the People's Democratic (Communist)

Party on May 4. (Karmal also gave up the ceremonial post of president in November.) Declining health was cited as the reason for Karmal's resignation, but the change was seen as a Soviet effort to broaden the base of the government. Najibullah, the scion of a leading Ahmadzai Pushtun tribal family, was more acceptable to the Afghan tribes than the detribalized Karmal. Najibullah promptly offered the resistance a general amnesty and a coalition government.

War-weariness and fear of reprisals eroded political support for the resistance among the rural population. Pakistan's support also wavered in the face of increased cross-border attacks, unrest and terrorism in the Northwest Frontier Province, and resentment against the growing economic and refugee burdens.

Economy. The destruction of the economy continued. In January, President Karmal announced that damage to the nation's infrastructure amounted to $35 billion, equivalent to two thirds of all the money spent on development in the previous 20 years. Near-famine conditions were reported throughout the country. Soviet-Afghan trade rose to more than 80% of Afghanistan's total exports. Soviet aid, including wheat and other commodities from the United States, rose to $850 million, a level unprecedented in Soviet relations with any Third World country. Internal migration from the devastated countryside to the cities caused severe housing shortages and high inflation.

Diplomacy and Foreign Affairs. With the war dragging on and the new Kremlin leadership paying closer attention to international "public relations," the Soviets undertook a campaign to persuade the world that they were sincerely seeking a peaceful political settlement of the Afghan conflict. At the same time, the Soviet media covered the war in increasingly realistic terms. In March, General Secretary Gorbachev called Afghanistan a "bleeding wound," and in August he promised the withdrawal of six regiments by year's end. The theme of a political peace offensive was echoed by Najibullah's call for reconciliation with the resistance.

International reaction to the Soviet diplomatic campaign was, on the whole, negative. The United States revoked Afghanistan's most-favored-nation trading status and, during talks in Moscow in September, insisted that Soviet withdrawal from Afghanistan is a prerequisite to improved U.S.-Soviet relations. President Ronald Reagan restated the position at the United Nations later that month and intended to raise it again at the Iceland summit with Gorbachev in October, but the startling Soviet disarmament proposal there apparently diverted the talks from regional issues.

In June, President Reagan declined to extend diplomatic recognition to a visiting resistance delegation, calling the request "premature." During the year, however, Reagan did sign National Security Directive 166, which ordered a full-scale effort to expel the Soviets from Afghanistan. The U.S. Congress appropriated $450 million in military aid for the resistance and $48 million in humanitarian aid.

Other international actions repudiated the Soviet propaganda campaign. In February and October, the Organization of the Islamic Conference demanded Soviet troop withdrawal. The same call was made by the Nonaligned Movement at its April and September meetings. The West German parliament, with the approval of leftist members, condemned Soviet activities in Afghanistan. And at the United Nations, the Ermacora Human Rights report censuring the Soviet Union for atrocities in Afghanistan was presented to the General Assembly. In November the annual General Assembly resolution calling for Soviet troop withdrawal from Afghanistan was passed by a vote of 122 to 20, with 12 abstentions.

In January the United States offered to guarantee any balanced agreement reached at UN-sponsored talks, held in Geneva, between Pakistan and the Afghan Communists. The seventh and eighth rounds of those talks, in May and July, exposed the hollowness of the Soviet propaganda campaign. In a crude effort to obtain recognition by Pakistan of their legitimacy, the Afghans demanded direct talks with the Islamabad government in exchange for a withdrawal schedule. Pakistan refused, and the Afghans produced a four-year timetable for withdrawal. The Afghan side further demanded that all Pakistani aid to the resistance cease as soon as the Soviet withdrawal begins. To pressure the Islamabad government, the Soviet Union issued a formal threat, saying that it considered Pakistan's nuclear program a danger to its southern border. At the same time, cross-border raids and terrorist attacks in Pakistan increased markedly. Pakistan stood firm against these pressures and demanded a complete Soviet withdrawal within four months. The negotiations were then suspended.

LEON B. POULLADA
University of Nebraska, Omaha

AFGHANISTAN · Information Highlights

Official Name: Democratic Republic of Afghanistan.
Location: Central Asia.
Area: 249,999 sq mi (647 497 km²).
Population: (mid-1986 est.): 15,400,000.
Chief Cities (March 1982): Kabul, the capital, 1,036,407; Kandahar, 191,345; Herat, 150,497.
Government: Sayid Mohammad Najibullah, general secretary; People's Democratic Party (appointed May 1986); Soltan Ali Keshtmand, prime minister (named June 1981); Haji Mohammad Chamkani, acting president (appointed Nov. 1986).
Monetary Unit: Afghani (50.6 afghanis equal U.S.$1, June 1986).
Gross National Product (1985): $3,000,000,000.
Foreign Trade (1985 U.S.$): *Imports*, $902,000,000; *exports*, $778,000,000.

© T. Orban/Sygma

In northwest Cameroon, poisonous gas erupted from volcanic Lake Nios in August, killing some 1,700 nearby villagers.

AFRICA

The continuing political and economic uncertainties in much of Africa during 1986 underscored the fact that the continent's disadvantaged countries have had little time to develop effective and responsive political and economic institutions. Confronted by crises of poverty, extreme ethnic and religious divisiveness, illiteracy, a hostile environment, international economic pressures, and internal mismanagement and corruption, Africa's politicians, soldier-politicians, and public administrators have experimented with everything from doctrinaire Marxism to foreign-dominated corporate capitalism. While authoritarian political systems continue to far outnumber democratic states, and economic decline has made the average African poorer in 1986 than in 1960, Africa's leaders and the international community apparently are beginning to deal more realistically with the limited choices imposed on them by political, economic, and environmental circumstances.

Famine, Poverty, Debt. For most of Africa in 1986, the drought was over and sufficient rains produced better harvests. Except in war zones, the famine also was over or being brought under control. According to a 1986 report by the World Bank, the continent's overall income per capita was expected to show its first increase since 1980.

Ironically, these short-term agricultural and economic successes could result in a dangerous complacency, especially in the context of Africa's long-term recovery. For example, while the continent's total debt was smaller than that of Latin America, it was growing at a faster rate and approached $100 billion. The fact re-

mained that most of sub-Saharan Africa was poorer in 1986 than in 1960. In order to service its current debts and be able to import the same amount as in 1980, Africa as a whole is going to need $15 billion per year, according to the World Bank. In 1986 there were promises from donors of $13 billion, leaving a $2 billion shortfall.

UN Plan and IMF Loan Pool. In March the International Monetary Fund (IMF) approved a $3.1 billion loan pool for the world's poorest nations; 80% of the sum was targeted for the poorest nations in sub-Saharan Africa.

The United Nations General Assembly held a special session from May 27 to June 1 to examine the economic crisis in Africa. It was the first such meeting to consider a regional economic problem in the organization's 41-year history. The meeting was called at the request of the Organization of African Unity (OAU), and the discussions were based on a five-year plan, "Africa's Priority Program for Economic Recovery," passed by the OAU in 1985. The $128 billion plan called on Western industrialized states to provide $45.4 billion in new assistance over the next five years, and for debt forgiveness of approximately the same amount. Under the OAU program, more than 70% ($82.5 billion) of the total resources were to be provided by Africans themselves.

Instability in the Horn. In Sudan, one year after the military overthrow of President Jaafar al-Nemery, political and economic stability continued to be ravaged by a seemingly endless series of ethnic, racial, sectarian, regional, and nationalistic problems. The Transitional Military Council that took control in 1985 voluntarily relinquished power, and multiparty elections for the National Assembly were held in

April. However, the ongoing conflict between the dominant Arab Muslim north and the black African Christian and animist south prevented large numbers of southerners from registering to vote and taking part in the balloting. For the new prime minister, Sadiq al-Mahdi, the ongoing civil war was at the center of far-reaching and overwhelming difficulties. The intensity of the conflict, exacerbated by a devastating drought, was keeping several million southerners from receiving desperately needed food aid. Despite repeated pleas from the International Red Cross and the UN for a food truce, suspicions that military equipment might be disguised as shipments of food prevented the south from receiving vital supplies. Unfortunately, both the government and the rebel forces resorted to the use of hunger as a political weapon, at times blocking the airlift of food and other goods to famine victims. And the economic situation was no better than the political-military one. Sudan's record of debt-servicing was so bad that in February the IMF declared it ineligible to borrow additional monies to pay overdue interest on its old loans or even to purchase additional food and other necessities. Africa's largest country had thus become the continent's most bankrupt as well. (*See* SUDAN.)

Elsewhere in the Horn, continued external aid and an end to the drought brought relief to the famine in most of Ethiopia, although it was alleged that the regime of Lt. Col. Mengistu Haile Mariam was playing politics with food by diverting it to the military and away from areas of rebel strength. While the military stalemate between the Ethiopian government and the Tigre, Oromo, and Eritrean secessionist movements continued, peace talks were held with Somalia and negotiations were held with Sudan to end support for political opponents in exile in each others' countries.

Military Politics in West Africa. If the situation in Sudan was symptomatic of Africa's despair, Nigeria, for all its problems, remained one of the continent's best hopes. Notwithstanding six successful military coups since independence in 1960, a foreign debt estimated between $15 and $22 billion, and a slumping economy, Nigeria remained committed to civilian rule, democracy, and a free press. Economic austerity was forcing long-needed reforms in Nigeria's overvalued currency and top-heavy civil service and bureaucracy. Maj. Gen. Ibrahim Babangida's first year in power saw a vigorous national debate on IMF conditionality, a surcharge on incomes, the reopening of international borders after 20 months, a release of political detainees, and a restoration of press freedoms. On the other hand, Babangida during the year had to deal with an alleged coup plot, a serious confrontation with non-Muslim southerners over apparent plans to join the Organization of Islamic Conferences, and a precipitous decline in oil production and revenues. (*See* NIGERIA.)

Liberia's Gen. Samuel K. Doe, who first seized power in a violent coup in 1980, was sworn in as the elected president in January 1986, but under less than auspicious circumstances. In the preceding months there had been allegations that the October 1985 election which brought him to power had been fraudulent, as well as severe criticism of his handling of an unsuccessful coup attempt that November. Economic problems also continued to plague the country. In January the IMF declared Liberia ineligible for future loans because it had fallen so badly behind on repayment of its existing loans. In March, four opposition parties formed a coalition and demanded new elections. At first conciliatory, Doe imprisoned coalition leaders in August and released them only after international pressure —particularly from the U.S. Congress, which resolved to monitor human-rights violations as a precondition for U.S. aid.

In Ghana, agricultural production in 1986 increased, the balance of payments deficit was eased by increased exports, and the inflation rate dropped. Despite the nation's improving economic situation, however, Flt. Lt. Jerry Rawling's Provisional National Defense Council (PNDC) came under sharp criticism for "arbitrary and excessive use of state power" after the arrest and detention of trade union and revolutionary defense committee leaders. Political stability was threatened by several alleged coup plots uncovered by the PNDC during the course of the year, resulting in more than a dozen executions.

Southern Africa in Crisis. Southern Africa remains one of the continent's most unstable regions and yet the one with perhaps the greatest promise. It continues to be an arena for great power politics and faces the very real possibility of a major racial conflagration. Mozambique, Angola, and Zimbabwe, have to contend not only with the problems of relatively recent independence but also with neighboring South Africa, the continent's last white minority-ruled nation and the region's major destabilizing force.

By 1986, after two years of escalating violence, South Africa's internal choices seemed to have narrowed to reform or increased repression. Despite the repeal of a number of apartheid laws, events in 1986 demonstrated that whites are still firmly in control and unlikely to surrender their privileges very easily. By year's end more than 12,000 black labor, political, and religious leaders and dissidents had been detained and as many as 2,000 killed. The government's hope to restore law and order through widespread and increased repression had failed, and international criticism had increased. South African security force raids on African National Congress

(ANC) offices in Botswana, Zambia, and Zimbabwe in June was a signal to the Commonwealth Eminent Persons Group (EPG), representing British Commonwealth concerns in South Africa, and to the rest of the world that neither international criticism nor escalating black violence at home would be allowed to determine government policy. (*See* SOUTH AFRICA.)

Between August and October, members of the European Community, a host of British Commonwealth nations, the United States, and Japan all announced new sanctions against South Africa. At an August summit meeting in London, six of the seven Commonwealth heads of state in attendance—with the exception of Britain's Prime Minister Margaret Thatcher—agreed to impose a series of stiffer sanctions. One month later, Japan and the European Community announced bans on imports of coal, iron, and steel from South Africa, as well as further bank loans and landing rights for South African Airways planes. After months of debate and over a presidential veto, the U.S. Congress passed a South African sanctions bill in October which banned new public and private loans and investments and restricted a wide range of imports and exports.

Diplomatic and intelligence sources reported that the fortunes of the ten-year-old insurgent Mozambique National Resistance Movement (MNR) improved dramatically in 1986. It was widely assumed that the MNR continues to be armed by South African security forces despite prohibitions against such collaboration in the 1984 Nkomati Accords. Adding to the confusion and uncertainty in Mozambique was the sudden death of President Samora Machel in an airplane crash in October. Killed along with Machel, Mozambique's first and only president since independence in 1975, were several members of his cabinet. En route from Lusaka, Zambia, to Maputo, the capital of Mozambique, the plane went down inside the South African border, leading to widespread allegations of sabotage by the Pretoria regime. South African officials blamed bad weather and pilot error. Machel's sudden death raised serious questions about whether Mozambique would remain exclusively aligned with the Soviet Union or might begin to tilt further toward the West. It also raised questions concerning Mozambique's future relations with South Africa, whether the MNR would be contained, and the effect of proposed sanctions against South Africa on Mozambique and the region. On November 3 a special session of the Central Committee of the Mozambique Liberation Front elected 47-year-old Joaquim A. Chissano, the country's foreign minister, as the new president. For the foreseeable future, Chissano was expected to continue Machel's economic and political policies.

In Lesotho, Prime Minister Leabua Jonathan was ousted in a bloodless military coup, led by Gen. Justin Lekhanya, on January 20. Jonathan had ruled the nation since 1965. The motivation for the coup apparently was dissatisfaction with Jonathan's refusal to meet South Africa's demand for lifting its blockade of the border—expulsion of the African National Congress (ANC), which had been using Lesotho as a transit route and training base. Soon after the coup King Moshoeshoe II swore in a 14-member council of ministers, headed by General Lekhanya, that would govern in the king's name. On January 25 the South African government lifted the special security measures that it had imposed on the border, and on the same day the first group of 60 ANC members were airlifted out of Lesotho. Thus, with Mozambique, Lesotho, and Swaziland having agreed to expel ANC forces, and with Botswana having consented to use its "best en-

© François von Sury/Sygma

Prince Makhosetive Dlamini of Swaziland was installed as King Mswati III on April 25. The 18-year-old, British-educated king succeeded his father, King Sobhuza II, who died in 1982. Mswati is one of Sobhuza's nearly 70 sons.

Record high prices for ivory have led to a deepening crisis for Africa's wildlife—poaching. While the continent's elephant population is still nearly 1 million, some areas have suffered 60–90% declines. The black rhinoceros, meanwhile, has become extinct in most regions. Rangers and special police have been cracking down on illegal hunters, but herds continue to be decimated.

deavors'' to contain the group, South Africa had nearly established a protective ring around its borders.

Zimbabwe. In June, Zimbabwe's Prime Minister Robert Mugabe announced that South African forces had attacked an office building in downtown Harare used by the ANC; there were no casualties. In August the Zimbabwe government announced that it would impose sanctions against South Africa, and the Pretoria government responded by delaying traffic at the border.

In early September, Harare was the site of the eighth summit conference of the 101-member Nonaligned Movement. Prime Minister Robert Mugabe took over the three-year chairmanship of the group. He called on all members to provide economic aid to the southern African nations who would be hurt by sanctions. (*See* ZIMBABWE.)

Disaster in Cameroon. On August 21 a poisonous cloud of carbon dioxide and hydrogen sulfide gas escaped from Lake Nios, which fills the crater of an extinct volcano in northwest Cameroon, asphyxiating some 1,700 residents of nearby villages. The cloud apparently changed composition as it drifted and diffused, causing sickness, skin burns, and unconsciousness in areas farther from the lake. It was the second known disaster of this kind in Cameroon in recent years. Geologists located nearly three dozen such volcanic lakes in northwest Cameroon and recommended closer monitoring to avoid such disasters in the future. (*See also* GEOLOGY.)

AIDS. By 1986, according to conservative estimates by the World Health Organization, as many as 50,000 people in central Africa had died from Acquired Immune Deficiency Syndrome (AIDS) since the first confirmed cases less than a decade earlier. The countries most affected include Zambia, Zaire, Burundi,

Rwanda, Uganda, and Tanzania—the very ones that had tried to deny the existence or seriousness of the problem in the past. Given the suspected relationship between increased vulnerability to the disease and lower general health and poor nutrition, along with the fact that in Africa the virus apparently is being spread predominantly through heterosexual contact, some specialists fear the possibility of rampant transmission of the disease in the near future.

Sport Aid. Another ''world event'' to raise money for Africa was organized by Irish rock musician Bob Geldof with UNICEF (United Nations International Children's Emergency Fund). Sport Aid, which was expected to raise up to $150 million in pledges and sponsorships, was a week-long series of sporting events which culminated in the so-called Race Against Time on May 25, a series of amateur runs in 78 countries. An estimated 20 million people took part. Unlike Geldof's Band Aid and Live Aid concerts of 1984 and 1985, whose proceeds went largely to emergency famine relief, the money raised from Sport Aid was to be allocated primarily for long-term development projects in such areas as human services (water and sanitation systems), health education, and agricultural production.

Nobelist. Wole Soyinka, a 52-year-old Nigerian playwright, poet, and novelist, became the first African writer to be awarded the prestigious Nobel Prize for Literature. His writing has reflected his staunch criticism of the failures of black politicians, of military rule, and of white oppression in South Africa. His plays evoke what the Nobel Committee described as ''the drama of existence'' in a ''wide cultural perspective and with poetic overtones.''

PATRICK O'MEARA
N. BRIAN WINCHESTER
African Studies Program, Indiana University

© Alan S. Weiner/Gamma-Liaison

On top of a severe drought that began three months earlier, a string of record-temperature days in July dried out soil and withered crops from Pennsylvania to Louisiana. Officials expected the losses to exceed $1 billion.

AGRICULTURE

A rising tide of productivity was evidenced in 1986 by large world stocks in virtually all major food categories, including grains, oilseeds, and livestock products. World grain production as well as world oilseed production reached all-time highs for the year 1985–86. Beef production declined slightly, but pork and poultry continued upward.

At the same time, world trade in agricultural products declined sharply. As the European Community (EC) developed and protected its own bountiful agriculture, Europe was evaporating as a major market for traditional raw agricultural commodities. Such populous nations as China and India had been expected to provide new food markets, but they were meeting needs largely from their own expanding agricultures. Some other developing nations may have desired to import more food but generally lacked sufficient exchange or credit with which to purchase it.

As one result of larger production with reduced foreign markets, a severe agricultural crisis persisted in the United States, Australia, Canada, and other "exporter" countries. As prices of grains fell to 30-year lows, innovative farmers who had modernized and expanded their operations during good times found it difficult to service debts, let alone to make a profit. With some farmers unable to pay their debts, banks and other farm-credit institutions suffered enormous losses, and a large number went bankrupt. Many implement dealers and other farm businesses disappeared. Agribusiness corporations and farmer cooperatives sold off assets, merged with other firms, and in other ways adjusted in order to survive.

U.S. Policy. The plight of the farmer gained the sympathy of the American public, as opinion polls clearly revealed. In response to demands from desperate farm-state leaders, a set of generous federal programs was signed into law in December 1985 and implemented in 1986. These programs were aimed at cutting production while expanding markets and supporting farmers' incomes as this was being accomplished. Under the major new "conservation reserve" program, farmers were given ten-year rental contracts to retire marginal croplands. Under a new dairy program, producers were offered a "buyout" option, by which some could retire their entire dairy herds. For basic crops including wheat, feed grains, rice, and cotton, producers would obtain much of their net income from government payments based on the difference between low market prices and a higher "target" price level. And indeed market prices were allowed to fall during 1986, on the assumption that low prices would reduce production and increase exports. Exports were directly subsidized by the granting of exporters "bonus" commodities from government stocks. These expensive programs were intended to spur farm recovery while moving the country toward a market-oriented agriculture.

But the programs cost much more than anticipated. First-year costs, which were expected to run about $19 billion, exceeded $30 billion. Despite production controls, U.S. farmers produced huge grain crops while foreign sales declined rather than increased. With much of the 1985 U.S. grain crop still in bins, additional temporary storage space had to be created for the 1986 crop—in vacant factories, in abandoned farm buildings, even under huge vinyl canopies. Meanwhile the value of farmland and other agricultural assets continued to decline, and it seemed likely that the federal government would have to commit additional billions to cover the further losses of the farm credit system.

Viewing farm policy as a political issue, congressional incumbents had hoped that the farm program's huge subsidies would help in their 1986 reelection campaigns. The Reagan administration hoped to retain a Republican majority in the Senate by winning key races in several farm states. But the farm programs boomeranged, with opponents claiming that they were "busted" and that they had not sufficiently helped farmers. (*See* page 550.)

Despite a few bright spots—cheap grain, for example, did permit profit from livestock—U.S. agriculture faced some hard options. As a major alternative to farmers' reliance on huge federal subsidies, some were advocating firm mandatory controls on production as a means of raising domestic prices. A majority of wheat farmers voted for mandatory controls in a trial referendum conducted by the U.S. Department of Agriculture.

Another option was advocated by "alternative agriculturalists," based on the concept of reducing costly inputs—such as fertilizers, pesticides, and machinery—while preserving the work role of family farmers. "Alternative agriculture" would mean a partial return to the pattern of the general farm, with its greater variety of animals and alternating crops, but it might also look to biotechnology for new "natural" processes to provide nutrients and pest controls.

Alternative agriculturalists took aim at the unwanted side effects of agricultural chemicals. Health hazards for producers and consumers, as well as the pollution of groundwaters, were reemerging crises in U.S. agriculture. Although environmentalists and chemical companies reached a compromise on a new pesticide bill which would enable prompt and more accurate responses to pesticide hazards, the measure died as Congress adjourned in October.

Agricultural research institutions and agribusinesses repositioned themselves for major breakthroughs in biotechnology, but it was far from certain that the new knowledge would soon alleviate the economic and environmental crises in U.S. agriculture. For example, an apparent breakthrough in biotechnology was the hormone somatropin, which would be administered to dairy cows and increase their production by as much as 30%. But dairy producer groups, already burdened by surpluses, sought to prevent its certification for use.

Agricultural trade policy represented another area of possible alternative approaches. As the world's major agricultural exporter, the United States had long functioned as a price leader, stabilizing some world prices at levels corresponding to supported U.S. domestic prices. But the Reagan administration had chosen another course—aggressive price competition as a means of increasing U.S. sales. Other nations responded by protecting their domestic markets and/or subsidizing their exports, and the United States slipped into a trade war with such old friends as Canada, Australia, and the European Community.

U.S. Exports. The value of U.S. agricultural exports declined by 19% in 1985–86. Losses were suffered in agricultural sales to Europe, Japan, China, other East Asian countries, the Soviet Union, Eastern Europe, and other major U.S. markets. Only a few increases were recorded, achieved mainly through "concessional" sales to North Africa, Turkey, Pakistan, Israel, and the Philippines. Concessional sales include those made under long-term, low-interest credit, as well as sales made with foreign aid loans and grants received from the U.S. Agency for International Development.

U.S. soybean exports did experience a seasonal rise, although total projected oilseed exports were down slightly from 1984–85 and down 40% from 1982–83. Similarly, the projected U.S. share of the world wheat market was 30%, down from 53% in 1972. The U.S. share for feed grains had dropped from 62% in 1981–82 to 44% for 1985–86. Feed grains, wheat, and oilseeds continued to be the major U.S. exports, making up 50% of the nation's total commodity shipments overseas. Other commodities for which the U.S. market share was down included poultry, pork, and cotton. The U.S. market share rose for beef.

The trade disappointments for 1986 may have provided a deeper awareness of the weakening U.S. position in world agriculture. It became clear that the United States and other exporters could no longer count on a large world market. U.S. policymakers also began to wonder whether they had relied too heavily on a "Third World" sales strategy. U.S. Department of Agriculture experts were pointing out potential markets in industrial countries for some high quality foods available only to U.S. consumers.

Other Exporters. The diversified economies of the United States and Europe were in a better position to absorb losses in export income and added costs of surpluses than were those of countries specializing in a single food export, such as Canada and Australia. Canadian farmers, having experienced relatively poor harvests in 1984 and 1985, suffered low market prices in 1986. Even with the government making payments to farmers, farm bankruptcies in Canada were numerous.

Wheat growers in Canada and Australia lobbied the U.S. government for relief from low prices and the competition of subsidized exports. Meanwhile the Canadian government entered a long-term agreement for grain sales to the Soviet Union, partially displacing U.S. sales under an earlier trade treaty.

European Community. Spain and Portugal joined the European Community in January 1986, bringing with them largely complementary agricultures. The two new members would provide the other EC nations additional fruits and vegetables while offering new markets for grains, meat, milk, potatoes, and sugar. Spain and Portugal previously imported these commodities from the United States and other exporters. They joined with Italy and Greece to become an influential Mediterranean bloc within the European Community.

EC agriculture was projected to achieve high production levels in 1986. Grain surpluses remained large despite a reduced 1985 crop, and grain producers were expected to receive lower incomes because of such EC budget-cutting measures as the channeling of some surplus wheat into feed for animals. The EC again exported much of its large surplus, under heavy subsidy.

Rising farm program costs, which had already consumed much of the EC budget, necessitated additional levies on member governments. However, despite a major internal study ("The Green Report") that recommended a more market-oriented policy, the EC persisted with high supports, even on beef and other surplus commodities. The Community also subsidized the processing of foods for export, prompting retaliation from the United States and other competitors. Facing the prospect of an expanding trade war, the EC Council agreed to place a discussion of these export practices on the agenda of a forthcoming international trade conference—the 1987 meeting under the General Agreement on Tariffs and Trade (GATT).

USSR and Eastern Europe. Inadequate management of agriculture was an acknowledged shortcoming in the USSR and in other Eastern European countries, and there was growing pessimism about the effectiveness of various reform efforts. In Poland, farm-machinery production had been increased in response to a shortage, but then, due to a severe shortage of machinery parts, 25% of the grain combines were inoperative during the 1985 harvest. Fertilizer use was down in Eastern Europe because of supply shortages. And Eastern European countries lacked sufficient means to purchase U.S. insecticides and other desirable inputs.

Soviet agriculture, prodded by General Secretary Mikhail Gorbachev, offered stronger production incentives to collective farmers. Through reorganization, he also sought to make input industries more responsive to agricultural needs. A new environmental consciousness was evidenced in the rejection of some agricultural practices which had caused severe soil erosion.

Soviet grain imports declined in 1985–86 because of a good 1985 harvest and because the country's declining oil exports made food imports less affordable. The projected 1986 harvest was smaller than the 1985 harvest because of less favorable weather. The Chernobyl nuclear power plant disaster was not expected to have a significant effect on the 1986 volume of production in the Soviet Union or other affected countries, although there was some apprehension among Europeans as to the healthfulness of the fruits, vegetables, and dairy products produced in those regions through which the radiation had passed.

The Soviet Union was expected to continue purchasing large amounts of grain, although it largely ignored its obligations under a five-year agreement with the United States requiring a minimum level of grain purchases.

Latin America. Most Latin American governments encouraged both sectors of their "dualistic" agricultures: they wanted their export sectors to earn more exchange with which to service their foreign debts, and they wanted their domestic sectors to meet the challenge of feeding growing populations. However, the production increases that did occur were generally inadequate to both needs.

Higher coffee prices fortunately made up for reduced export volumes from Brazil and Mexico. Mexico, while it increased soybean and wheat production for domestic use, continued to suffer an agricultural trade deficit. Venezuela, seeking to compensate for its lost oil revenues, increased its investment in agriculture. The government of Chile pressed for greater self-sufficiency in food production. Argentina reduced its export taxes to encourage agricultural exports, but the acreage planted to wheat—Argentina's principal export crop—nevertheless declined, apparently in response to lower world prices.

Central American and Caribbean countries, while relying on such traditional exports as coffee, sugar, and bananas, were also developing "nontraditional" exports, including other fruits and vegetables.

Africa. Sub-Saharan Africa continued to recover—albeit very slowly—from the severe drought of 1984. Record crops of food grains were registered in Chad, Somalia, Sudan, Burkina Faso, and Kenya. Other products for domestic consumption, including root, tuber, and livestock, also increased. Some African governments were developing incentives for more consistent agricultural growth. Kenya, as a leading example, pursued both food self-sufficiency and export growth, using "green revolution" technology to rejuvenate its small-scale

Prison inmates in Georgia unload a shipment of hay. Farmers in the Midwest aided their counterparts in the drought-stricken South by sending truckloads of hay to feed dying livestock.

© Laura Sikes/Sygma

agriculture. Nevertheless, with hunger still widespread and the need for agricultural development still desperate, Africa remained the major focus of international assistance.

African export earnings, in the aggregate, were expected to drop in 1986, in part from the effects of restrictive trade policies of non-African nations. African agriculture also suffered from the effects of civil strife in Angola and from the floundering South African economy.

In North Africa and the Middle East, total agricultural production increased, although per-capita production continued to drop. And there was considerable variation among countries: an excellent grain harvest was projected for Morocco, Turkey, and Jordan, while serious drought reduced production in Israel and Tunisia. The agricultures of Iran and Iraq recovered somewhat from the debilitating effects of war, but both countries still suffered domestic food shortages, and the war had soured their relations with some potential trading partners.

The agricultural policies of the European Community, as well as trends in world production and consumption, caused the nations of the Middle East to reexamine their selections of agricultural export products. Especially in view of low world prices, several cotton-producing countries sought alternative crops. Israel reduced citrus production, partly in response to the lack of sufficient markets.

Asia. Despite rapid population growth, Asian nations continued their remarkable progress toward food abundance. China was the chief exemplar of this movement, having increased its per-capita grain production by 50% since the mid-1970s. It was at that time that the Beijing regime began disbanding the commune system and phasing in a limited free-market. In the years since, China has gone from a major importer to a significant exporter of both grain and soybeans. In 1986 the nation's grain output was given a further boost by the government's offer of higher prices and subsidized fertilizers. Indeed China was emerging as a major agricultural supplier to other East Asian nations. The year 1986 was expected to bring a larger agricultural surplus, which economic planners looked to as a major source of future exchange earnings. At the same time, efforts were being made to convert additional croplands to the production of fruits and vegetables. Livestock output, which had grown rapidly in 1985, increased only moderately in 1986.

Agriculture in both Japan and Korea benefited from heavy government expenditures, although per-capita output in Japan did show a decline. Both China and the United States began gearing up as major competitors for potential export markets in Japan and Korea.

DONALD F. HADWIGER
Iowa State University

ALABAMA

George Wallace's decision to retire set off a wild struggle over who would lead Alabama in the post-Wallace era.

Democratic Primary Contests. Lt. Gov. Bill Baxley led the field of five aspirants by a margin of more than 70,000 votes in the June 3 Democratic gubernatorial primary. Attorney General Charles Graddick placed second. Guy Hunt, formerly a county official and Reagan campaign manager, easily won the much smaller Republican primary. In a Democratic runoff election held on June 24, Graddick defeated Baxley by close to 9,000 votes.

Four days after the runoff a challenge was filed with the Democratic Party against Graddick on the ground that his winning margin was supplied by illegal Republican crossover votes. On July 11 a suit was filed in federal court by black voters contending that Graddick's encouragement of crossover voting violated the Voting Rights Act of 1965. A three-judge federal court agreed that there had indeed been serious violations of the 1965 law and ordered the state Democratic Party either to certify Baxley or hold another runoff. A subcommittee of the state Democratic executive committee then awarded the Democratic gubernatorial nomination to Baxley.

On August 22, Graddick launched a write-in campaign for governor, while continuing his appeals. He got some temporary help from the federal judiciary on September 17 when a Birmingham judge ordered the nomination taken from Baxley and another runoff held. This order was immediately stayed, however, by a higher appeals court which, on October 1, backed the Democratic subcommittee's selection of Baxley. The final judicial rebuff to Graddick came on October 14 when the U.S. Supreme Court refused to reverse the decision. As election day drew closer and polls showed his support among voters to be fading, Graddick dropped his candidacy.

The General Election. On November 4, Hunt easily defeated Baxley, with a winning margin of more than 160,000 votes. He would be the state's first Republican governor in 112 years. Incumbent Republican Sen. Jeremiah Denton, a member of the "Reagan class of 1980," was unsuccessful in his reelection bid, despite four presidential visits within a 14-month period prior to the election. Denton was the only Republican senator Alabama has had in the 20th century. He lost narrowly to U.S. Rep. Richard Shelby, a conservative Democrat.

In other races contested in 1986 the most notable were probably the elections of Jim Folsom, Jr., son of former Gov. James E. Folsom, as lieutenant governor and George Wallace, Jr., as state treasurer. Blacks made additional gains, including two seats on the formerly all-white state board of education.

Money Problems. The Alabama legislature met in regular and special sessions in 1986. The main work of the regular session was passing the $583.1 million general fund and $2.032 billion education budgets. Due to revenue shortfalls, however, Governor Wallace ordered proration (across-the-board reductions) in both the current and future educational and general fund budgets by margins of 3 to 15%. In a legislative session called for September 8 to deal with the emergency revenue shortages, the state assembly rejected most of the governor's new tax proposals and opted, instead, for a plan offered by Lieutenant Governor Baxley that temporarily transferred $40 million in state insurance and gubernatorial discretionary reserve funds to mental and public health, Medicaid, and human resources.

The Judiciary. On June 5, Jefferson B. Sessions III of Mobile was rejected by the Senate Judiciary Committee for the position of federal district judge. He had been accused of being racially prejudiced. In October in Mobile, a case was heard in federal court asserting that secular humanism was, in effect, being taught as a religion in Alabama schools because of insufficient emphasis on religious values in textbooks. No decision had been made by the end of 1986.

Space Disaster. NASA's Marshall Space Flight Center in Huntsville had recommended the January 28 cold-weather launch of the space shuttle *Challenger,* which ended in disaster. Managers and rocket engineers at the center were criticized severely by the commission appointed to investigate the tragedy.

Drought. The state suffered from severe drought in 1986. Long-term shortages in rainfall led to projections of $750 million in farm losses in midsummer. To meet desperate needs of feed for livestock, Midwestern farmers sent free hay to Alabama farmers in late summer.

WILLIAM H. STEWART
The University of Alabama

ALABAMA • Information Highlights

Area: 51,705 sq mi (133 915 km²).
Population (1985 est.): 4,021,000.
Chief Cities (July 1, 1984 est.): Montgomery, the capital, 184,963; Birmingham, 279,813; Mobile, 204,923; Huntsville, 149,527.
Government (1986): *Chief officers*—governor, George C. Wallace (D); lt. gov. Bill Baxley (D). *Legislature*—Senate, 35 members; House of Representatives, 105 members.
State Finances (fiscal year 1985): *Revenue,* $6,601,000,000; *expenditure,* $6,082,000,000.
Personal Income (1985): $42,913,000,000; per capita, $10,673.
Labor Force (June 1986): *Civilian labor force,* 1,895,700; *unemployed,* 190,500 (10.0% of total force).
Education: *Enrollment* (fall 1984)—public elementary schools, 514,355; public secondary, 198,231; colleges and universities, 179,343. *Public school expenditures* (1983–84), $1,469,000,000 ($2,102 per pupil).

ALABAMA / SPECIAL REPORT

The Wallace Era Ends

Alabama Gov. George C. Wallace calls for a balanced state budget at the opening of the regular session of the state legislature in January. Three months later, he announced his retirement from public life.

AP/Wide World

On April 2, 1986, George C. Wallace announced that he would not seek a fifth term as governor of Alabama. Wallace said he had "climbed [his] last political mountain" and it was necessary "to pass the rope and the pick to another climber." With the conclusion of Wallace's fourth gubernatorial term in January 1987, an era in Alabaman, as well as Southern, history would end.

George Wallace's long career in government spanned the years from segregation and the height of the battle for civil rights to a new period of biracial politics in the South. When Wallace ran for governor in 1962, he won on a tough segregationist platform. At his first inauguration, Wallace orated: "And I say— segregation now, segregation tomorrow, segregation forever." On June 11, 1963, Wallace "stood in the schoolhouse door" to prevent the entry of two black students to the University of Alabama. President John F. Kennedy used military force to see that federal judicial desegregation orders were carried out.

When the Alabama Constitution prevented Wallace from seeking a second consecutive term in 1966, the governor got his wife Lurleen elected as his "stand-in." She died in May 1968. Wallace was elected to second and third gubernatorial terms in 1970 and 1974. During his third administration he acknowledged that "segregation in public facilities is now out of the realm of discussion, and I certainly have no intention and no desire to turn back the clock." He ran for governor again in 1982 and won. The election was most notable for the large percentage of the black vote—30-40 in the pri-

mary and 80 in the general election—that Wallace received. During his last term, Governor Wallace named blacks to cabinet-level positions and supported the appointment of blacks as chairs of legislative committees.

In the later part of his career, Wallace said that he had "never been for bigotry or discrimination. I never considered myself a racist." He claimed that he resisted integration to raise a constitutional question—that the federal government was encroaching too much on the rights of the states.

Presidential Quests. George Wallace's place in national political history rests primarily on his runs for the presidency during which he appealed to working-class Americans in the North as well as in the South. He first entered national politics in 1964 when he ran in Democratic presidential primaries in three non-Southern states. In 1968, Wallace was the presidential candidate of the newly formed American Independent Party. In the November election he received almost 10 million popular votes and 46 electoral votes. His name was on the ballot in every state. Wallace believed he would have had a place on the 1972 Democratic ticket had he not been shot by Arthur H. Bremer while campaigning in Laurel, MD, on May 15, 1972. Wallace underwent surgery twice during his initial 54-day hospital stay. He was hospitalized repeatedly in subsequent years due to complications arising from the near-assassination. In announcing his retirement from public life, Wallace explained that his health was too precarious to continue.

WILLIAM H. STEWART

ALASKA

The major issue in Alaska in 1986 was the precipitous decline in state revenues due to the drop in world oil prices. The shock waves resulting from this decline spilled over into the political, educational, and social arenas, in addition to affecting the economic well-being of the state.

Politics. In the August 26 primary, incumbent Democratic Gov. William Sheffield was defeated by Fairbanks attorney Steve Cowper, who had lost the 1982 primary to Sheffield by a slim margin. Sheffield's defeat was attributed to the stigma of the 1985 state Senate hearing on whether he should be impeached and his apparent inability to deal effectively with the loss of oil revenues. The Republican primary was won by state Sen. Arliss Sturgulewski, who defeated former Gov. Walter J. Hickel and five other candidates to become the first woman to receive a gubernatorial nomination in Alaska. On primary day voters also approved a referendum calling for a freeze on nuclear weapons.

In November, in what was nominally a four-way race for the governor's seat, Cowper went on to beome Alaska's seventh governor. The Alaska Independence Party and Libertarian Party candidates placed a distant third and fourth. Cowper, who assumed office in December, faces a divided state legislature. Democrats hold a clear majority in the House for the first time in a number of years, while a Republican-led coalition controls the Senate. In other contests Congressman Don Young (R) and U.S. Sen. Frank H. Murkowski (R) easily won reelection.

Economy. Although traditional industries such as tourism, fishing, and lumbering continued to perform well and Alaskans received their annual dividends from the Permanent Fund (an investment trust financed by a percentage of oil revenues), the state loses an estimated $150 million in taxes and royalties for every $1 drop in the price of a barrel of crude oil. Total state revenues for fiscal 1987 (beginning July 1) were estimated at $2.08 billion, down from a previous estimate of $2.6 billion. Due to severe cutbacks in government spending at all levels, some of the money allocated in the $3.9 billion budget for fiscal 1986 was not spent, and the budget approved for fiscal 1987 was $2.9 billion. Further cutbacks were expected in 1987.

The state has been the major employer in Alaska for some time, and in 1986 state agencies were forced to trim personnel as well as services. These reductions had a major impact on employment levels in service industries as well as government agencies. Unemployment, always high in Alaska during the winter, promised to be even more troublesome in the winter of 1986–87, with predictions that statewide unemployment would average 10–11%. After several years in which the population of the state increased steadily, most regions, particularly Anchorage, were experiencing a net outflow of population. The housing industry was severely depressed, with record foreclosures by the Alaska Housing Finance Corporation, which used oil revenues to subsidize thousands of low-interest home mortgages. To complete the glum economic picture, both business and personal bankruptcies were reaching record levels.

Education. Because education in Alaska is largely state funded, declining state revenues led to severe cutbacks for local school districts. Some districts attempted to break teacher contracts by reducing teacher salaries or the number of teachers within the district. The University of Alaska also experienced severe budget cuts, leading to efforts to restructure the statewide system to increase efficiency without seriously reducing the delivery of educational services.

Other. Controversy continued over the use of federal lands in Alaska and proposed revisions to the Alaska Native Claims Settlement Act of 1971.

A rapid advance by Hubbard Glacier blocked the outlet of Russell Fjord, threatening the fishing industry in the Situk River valley and sea mammals trapped in the fjord. Scientists flocked to study the rare geophysical event, which received nationwide publicity. In October the ice dam created by the surging glacier finally burst.

The North Slope and south-central regions were declared federal disaster areas after storms and floods caused uninsured losses totaling approximately $15 million.

Also in 1986, the city of Anchorage was unsuccessful in its bid to host the 1992 Olympic Winter Games.

CARL E. SHEPRO
University of Alaska

ALASKA • Information Highlights

Area: 591,004 sq mi (1 530 700 km²).

Population (1985 est.): 521,000.

Chief Cities (1980 census): Juneau, the capital, 19,528; Anchorage (July 1, 1984 est.), 226,663; Fairbanks, 22,645; Sitka, 7,803.

Government (1986): *Chief Officers*—governor, Steve Cowper (D); lt. gov., Stephen McAlpine (D). *Legislature*—Senate, 20 members; House of Representatives, 40 members.

State Finances (fiscal year 1985): *Revenue,* $5,918,000,000; *expenditure,* $4,950,000,000.

Personal Income (1985): $9,476,000,000; per capita, $18,187.

Labor Force (June 1986): *Civilian labor force,* 269,300; *unemployed* 29,200 (10.8% of total force).

Education: *Enrollment* (fall 1984)—public elementary schools, 75,206; public secondary, 29,393; colleges and universities, 27,479. *Public school expenditures* (1983–84), $579,000,000 ($7,026 per pupil).

ALBANIA

In 1986, Albania showed signs of moving away from the harsh, isolated regime imposed upon it by Enver Hoxha, the Stalinist dictator who ruled it from 1946 until his death in April 1985.

Domestic Affairs. On Jan. 13, 1986, in celebration of the 40th anniversary of the proclamation of Albania as a People's Republic, the presidium of the People's Assembly declared a broad political amnesty. Those prisoners not eligible for it had their remaining sentences reduced by one fourth. At the same meeting, the state's economic plan for 1985 was described as "fulfilled and over-fulfilled" and the year's wheat and cotton crops as the largest in Albania's history. The plan adopted for 1986, based on a budget of 9.3 billion leks (about $1.3 billion), predicted that national income would increase by 10.6%, industrial production by 7.3%, agricultural production by 17%, consumer-goods production by 9.5%, labor productivity by 3.9%, and exports by 31%. The draft of Albania's Eighth Five-Year Plan (1986–1990) gave priority to the development of energy and mineral resources an new metallurgical and engineering technology.

In related political changes, Niko Gjyzari was named chairman of the State Planning Commission and replaced as minister of finance by Andrea Nako. Nexhmije Hoxha, the late dictator's widow, was elected chairwoman of the Democratic Front, a body charged with organizing election campaigns and nominating all political candidates.

Foreign Affairs. Albania took steps to improve its political relations and increase its economic contacts with the rest of the world. But it remained the only European country not to attend the international conference on European security held in Stockholm in September.

In August 1985, Greece and Albania formally ended the technical state of war that had existed between them since October 1940. The agreement effectively annulled Greece's claim to northern Epirus, an area of southern Albania inhabited by about 400,000 ethnic Greeks. In November 1985 the two countries made plans for scientific and technical cooperation and set up a joint commission on hydroelectric power. An earlier attempt to compromise obstacles to the establishment of diplomatic relations between Albania and Great Britain was unsuccessful. Direct talks foundered on Albania's demand for the return of a large amount of gold held since World War II by Britain, France, and the United States, and Britain's counterclaims for monetary compensation that had been accepted by the International Court of Justice. However, confidential talks between Albania and West Germany in Vienna in May 1986 were said to have resolved the 40-year dispute over Albanian demands for war reparations and paved the way for the normalization of diplomatic relations.

Improving relations with Italy were strained in December 1985, when an Albanian family, seeking permission to emigrate, took refuge in the Italian embassy in Tiranë. Mutual official and press polemics continued between Yugoslavia and Albania over the status of the ethnic Albanian population in the Yugoslav Autonomous Province of Kosovo. Yugoslavia remained Albania's principal trading partner, with a new five-year trade agreement for 1986–90 envisioning a 20% increase over 1981–85. In August 1986, Yugoslavia completed a stretch of railway from Titograd to Shkodër, providing Albania with its first link with the European railway network.

JOSEPH F. ZACEK
State University of New York at Albany

ALBANIA · Information Highlights

Official Name: People's Socialist Republic of Albania.
Location: Southern Europe, Balkan peninsula.
Area: 11,100 sq mi (28 748 km²).
Population (mid-1986 est.): 3,000,000.
Chief City (mid-1983): Tiranë, the capital, 206,100.
Government: *Head of state,* Ramiz Alia, chairman of the Presidium (took office November 1982) and first secretary of the Albanian Workers' Party (April 1985). *Head of government,* Adil Carçani, chairman, Council of Ministers—premier (took office January 1982). *Legislature* (unicameral)—People's Assembly, 250 members.
Monetary Unit: Lek (7 leks equals U.S.$1, June 1986).
Gross National Product (1985 est. U.S.$): $2,600,000,000–$2,800,000,000.

ALBERTA

The continuing recession in oil and agriculture preoccupied Albertans in 1986.

Government and Politics. In May, under the new leader and premier, Don Getty, the Progressive Conservative (PC) Party was successful for the fifth consecutive time since 1971 in a provincial election. But from near-monopoly control of the legislature, with 75 of the then 79 seats, the PC emerged with only 61 of the now 83 seats. The New Democrats increased their number from 2 to 16, and the Liberals won 4 seats after 18 years of no representation in the legislature. Most successful opposition candidates were from Edmonton, where six cabinet ministers were defeated, and northern Alberta. Voter turnout was about 50%, compared with 66% in 1982.

In a by-election later in the year the PC ruling federal party retained its Pembina seat, but saw its previous majority of about 35,000 shrink to approximately 200.

All Alberta municipalities held elections on October 20. No fewer than 19 smaller cities and towns returned their mayors by acclamation,

Covering 5.2 million sq ft (483,000 m²), the West Edmonton Mall in Alberta, Canada, is by far the world's largest indoor shopping complex. In addition to 836 stores and 110 restaurants, the mall includes 47 amusement park rides, 20 movie theaters, and other entertainment attractions.

and most other incumbents were reelected. Edmonton's Mayor Laurence Decore won a second term with a two-to-one majority over his closest opponent; Calgary's Ralph Klein earned a third term with 90% of the vote. Voter turnout of 34% and 37%, respectively, in these cities seemed to indicate satisfaction with the status quo.

In Fort McMurray, a plebiscite asked electors whether therapeutic abortions should become available in the city's hospitals. The result was affirmative but not binding.

Business and Labor. One of the last provinces to feel the effects of the recession of the early 1980s, Alberta has been equally slow in recovering. Unemployment has remained high because of the stagnation of the oil and gas industries caused by low world prices. Low returns from farm produce have affected agriculturally oriented industry.

The spectacular success of West Edmonton Mall, the gigantic shopping and amusement center, is attracting visitors even from outside the province but providing serious competition to downtown businesses. A fatal accident on the roller coaster closed the ride for some months.

After several years during which workers accepted minimal or no changes in their contracts, in 1986 they were faced with demands for rollbacks. The result was a rash of work stoppages in both public and private sectors, with no gains for labor. Especially bitter was the strike at Gainers Inc., an Edmonton meatpacking plant, kept open by strikebreakers. Some violence on the picket line led to extensive police intervention. With some success, the strikers attempted a nationwide boycott of the plant's production.

Agriculture. Conditions for grain production proved near ideal for the whole province, but the year was not problem-free. Wet weather in September delayed harvesting, causing some deterioration in grain quality, but a warm, dry October saved the record crop.

Disappointingly low prices resulted from subsidized grain production in Europe and the United States. A five-week grain handlers' work stoppage at the Thunder Bay (Ontario) terminals threatened delivery on overseas commitments and cancellation of contracts, developments that were narrowly averted. Apprehension that the Soviet market would be lost to subsidized production elsewhere proved unwarranted.

For the first time in many years, no sugar beets were planted or sugar produced in southern Alberta.

JOHN W. CHALMERS
Concordia College, Edmonton

ALBERTA · Information Highlights

Area: 255,286 sq mi (661 190 km²)
Population (Jan. 1986 est.): 2,373,400.
Chief Cities (1981 census): Edmonton, the capital, 532,246; Calgary, 592,743; Lethbridge, 54,072.
Government (1986): *Chief Officers*—lt. gov., Helen Hunley; premier, Don Getty (Progressive Conservative). *Legislature*—Legislative Assembly, 79 members.
Provincial Finances (1986–87 fiscal year budget): *Revenues,* $8,550,000,000; *expenditures,* $10,650,000,000.
Personal Income (average weekly earnings, May 1986): $444.36.
Labor Force (July 1986, seasonally adjusted): *Employed* workers, 15 years of age and over, 1,278,000: *Unemployed,* 132,000 (10.3%).
Education (1986–87): *Enrollment*—elementary and secondary schools, 472,290 pupils; postsecondary—universities, 42,800, community colleges, 25,880.
(All monetary figures are in Canadian dollars.)

ALGERIA

Hard hit by the steep decline of oil and natural gas prices over the first half of 1986, the Algerian government addressed most of its attention to economic policy. Passage of the new National Charter was the major political development of the year.

The Economy. A revised finance bill, higher prices, new banking and currency policies, stimulation of exports, and a campaign to discourage lavish expenditure all reflected the economic squeeze. Admonishing his compatriots for their "taste for overconsumption," President Chadli Benjedid authorized a cut in government subsidies for consumer imports and a limitation on the amount of money that Algerians may carry abroad. The Ministry of Finance instituted an option for citizens to open high-interest bank accounts denominated in foreign currency in an effort to attract the earnings of émigré workers in Europe.

The official High Islamic Council called upon Algerians to forego extravagant expenses including the traditional slaughter of a lamb on Muslim holidays, encouraging instead donations for social projects. Although agricultural production grew, shortages of key commodities caused lines in urban supermarkets.

SONATRACH, the state energy company, coped with changing market conditions by renegotiating its liquefied natural gas (LNG) contract with Distrigaz of Belgium from 5 to 3 billion cubic meters (177 to 105 billion cubic feet) per year, and adjusted its prices downward about 40% from January to July. It signed a new LNG agreement worth $100 million annually with Petrobrás of Brazil. Algeria hosted a summit meeting with Nigeria, Gabon, and Libya at which the four African members of the Organization of the Petroleum Exporting Countries (OPEC) formed the African Hydrocarbon Association.

Politics. By national referendum, the voters approved the text of a new National Charter on January 16. Thus culminated a year of grassroots and high-level meetings of the National Liberation Front (FLN), Algeria's only party, to reexamine the official doctrine of the country. The revised 1986 document has much in common with the original Charter adopted in 1976 during the presidency of Houari Boumedienne. It still insists that Algeria is committed to the development of a socialist society, but it now stresses that "Algerian socialism is not inspired by a foreign doctrine." The new text accords greater attention to Islam but also to pre-Islamic Algerian history, stressing themes of national self-reliance and social justice in the nation's historical tradition. Charter 1986 serves as well to legitimize some key Benjedid policies, notably a larger role for private enterprise and decentralization of the management of the public sector.

The government took steps to neutralize various expressions of opposition. In February, Benjedid shifted the conservative Minister of Justice Boualem Baki to the Ministry of Religious Affairs in an effort to squelch support for Muslim fundamentalist dissidents who carried out armed attacks against police stations late in 1985. He ordered the human-rights activist Abdennour Ali Yahia, found guilty in December 1985 of founding an illegal association, freed in June. The government in turn established a Human Rights League.

Foreign Affairs. Algeria welcomed the talks between the Polisario Front, whose claim to self-determination for Western Sahara it has supported, and Morocco that took place at the United Nations in April. The Algerians urged both parties to "assume their responsibilities in the interest of their two fraternal peoples," a formula designed to encourage a compromise.

At the same time Algeria exploited opportunities to coax Libya out of its 1984 treaty of union with Morocco (the Treaty of Oujda). Relations with Tripoli warmed considerably after Benjedid met with Libyan leader Muammar el-Qaddafi at In-Amenas (in the Sahara) in January. During the heightened U.S.-Libyan hostilities in March and April, Algeria expressed strong solidarity with its neighbor. The collapse of the Treaty of Oujda following Moroccan King Hassan's meeting in July with Prime Minister Shimon Peres of Israel served Algerian regional goals.

Benjedid made several trips abroad in 1986, including one for medical treatment to Belgium and another to the USSR to seal an agreement to build an armaments factory in Algeria. U.S. Assistant Secretary of Defense Richard Armitage held talks regarding U.S. arms sales during a visit to Algiers in September. The new French Prime Minister Jacques Chirac also visited Algeria as both governments sought to improve relations after a chill in 1985.

ROBERT A. MORTIMER,
Haverford College

ANTHROPOLOGY

Scientific ideas about the human family tree and the sequence of its evolutionary branching several million years ago were uprooted by a 2.5-million-year-old fossil skull recovered in East Africa. The discovery represents the oldest known hominid, or humanlike creature, not directly related to modern humans. The skull was found in 1985 in Kenya by Alan Walker of Johns Hopkins University, who analyzed it with several colleagues, including Richard Leakey of the National Museums of Kenya.

Although interpretations still differ regarding human evolution over the past 4 million years, the new find challenges the view that two lines of early hominids known as australopithecines, one of which led to modern humans, branched out from a single species that has been dubbed *Australopithecus afarensis.* The latter species includes the famous skeleton "Lucy," which was discovered in Ethiopia in 1974 by a team led by Donald Johanson, now of the Institute of Human Origins in Berkeley, CA. Previously, many anthropologists believed that *A. afarensis* progressed, in one direction, through three increasingly larger species—*africanus, robustus,* and *boisei*—which then became extinct. In the other direction, it was thought *afarensis* led to the genus *Homo,* which includes modern *Homo sapiens.*

But according to Walker, the skull he found is either an early member of *A. boisei* or part of a new species clearly related to *A. boisei.* Thus, *A. africanus,* which has been found only in southern Africa and is estimated to have arisen between 2.5 million and 3 million years ago, was a contemporary of *A. boisei.* Walker contends that *A. boisei* was a separate line of hominids evolving in parallel with the *africanus-robustus* line. Some of the new skull's features, such as its small brain case, are so primitive that it may even have existed at the same time as some *afarensis* specimens that have been uncovered, notes Walker. Yet the specimen also has the relatively advanced protruding snout and flared cheekbones of later *boisei* skulls that date to 1.2 million years ago. This surprising mix of characteristics, combined with the sparse fossil record in East Africa prior to 2 million years ago, further clouds theories about who is related to whom among early hominid species.

Early Humans. There is also uncertainty about how early human ancestors obtained food and where they consumed it. After conducting the first analysis of bone weathering among animal remains at six African hominid sites in Olduvai Gorge, Tanzania, Richard Potts of the Smithsonian Institution concluded that human ancestors transported the bones over a period of 5 to 10 years to the locations. Potts holds that stone tools were kept at the

Photo by Alan Walker © National Geographic Society

A 2.5 million-year-old skull of Australopithecus boisei *raised basic new questions about hominid evolution.*

sites, dated at between 1.70 million and 1.85 million years old, where foods were taken to be cut up or otherwise processed. The sites may have been used as temporary feeding stations, says Potts, but it is not clear how often they were used for meat-eating or what proportion of bones were the result of hunting as opposed to scavenging. Other anthropologists, the most prominent being Lewis Binford of the University of New Mexico, have suggested that the Olduvai remains represent animal death sites rather than bone collections transported by hominids. Binford asserted that hominids scrounged from carcasses abandoned by carnivores and consumed more bone marrow than meat.

Scientists also discovered some of the oldest known hominid tools, dated at 2 million to 2.5 million years old, in a rain forest in western Africa. This is the first indication that hominids inhabited Africa's Western Rift Valley, which stretches from Zaire to the Atlantic Ocean. The nearly 300 quartz tools uncovered at the site included simple cobbles, flakes, and cores. One of the researchers, John W. K. Harris of the University of Wisconsin, said it is too early to tell whether the tools were used to kill animals or butcher carcasses.

Chimpanzees. Some African chimpanzees seem to seek out the leaves of a shrub known as Aspilia not for food, but for medicine. Richard Wrangham of the University of Michigan observed more than 100 instances of Aspilia swallowing by chimpanzees in two national parks in Africa. They swallowed the leaves one at a time, occasionally with a grimace, but without chewing. Wrangham said several African tribes also swallow Aspilia leaves to ease stomachaches, and sometimes rub them on surface wounds or cuts. Scientists found that a chemical on Aspilia leaves kills common disease-causing bacteria and fungi. If the chimps are intentionally medicating themselves, said Wrangham, it indicates that there was a slowly growing use of herbal medicines by human ancestors over a period of millions of years.

BRUCE BOWER
Behavioral Sciences Editor, "Science News"

ARCHAEOLOGY

Major archaeological discoveries in 1986 gave new insights into life and society from the Ice Age to the 20th century, from Europe to China, Egypt, and Central America.

Eastern Hemisphere

Cannibals. An international team of scientists uncovered the strongest evidence to date of cannibalism during the Stone Age. The bones of six humans found in a cave in southeastern France showed signs of having been butchered by inhabitants of the cave 6,000 years ago. Animal remains at the site were processed and discarded in the same way as the human bones. Microscopic examination of cut marks on the human remains also indicated that meat was removed from the bones.

Reports of prehistoric and modern cannibalism have stirred heated debates among scientists in the past decade. There is general agreement that cannibalism took place at the French cave, but it is not yet known whether it was a one-time occurrence or part of the routine and systematic eating of human flesh.

Roman City. Working at the 16-century-old Roman city of Kourion on the island of Cyprus, archaeologists discovered the skeletons of a man, woman, and child clinging together in the ruins of a house destroyed by an earthquake. Previous digs indicated that the quake, which also created tidal waves, struck the outpost on July 21, A.D. 365. It now appears that the catastrophe was comparable to that caused by the Vesuvius volcanic eruption at Pompeii in A.D. 79, according to project director David Soren of the University of Arizona. Fifteen rooms have been unearthed in the house, including several bedrooms and a complete kitchen. Kourion should provide a detailed picture of life during the late Roman Empire.

Chinese Tomb. The huge tomb of what is thought to have been a slave-owning duke who lived more than 2,500 years ago was uncovered by Chinese archaeologists. The ten-year excavation, near the Yellow River about 600 mi (950 km) southwest of Beijing, revealed a palace-size structure holding a wealth of information about the slave society that existed in western China at the time of Confucius.

The dig has produced 180 coffins containing human remains, thought by the investigators to be those of court retainers slain or buried alive to serve the duke in the afterlife. Historical chronicles indicate that the tomb was looted several times between the 7th and 13th centuries, but tools, jewelry, and dyes for several types of metal also were found.

Bronze Age Shields. In 1985 a Swedish farmer plowing his field found two ancient shields and notified local authorities. In 1986 archaeologists returned to the site and unearthed 15 more shields. They believe the bronze shields were lowered into a lake—now farmland—in a sacrificial offering to the gods during the Nordic Bronze Age between 1,500 B.C. and 500 B.C.

Celtic Society. Excavation of a 46-acre (19-ha) hill fort in southern England, where a Celtic tribe settled 2,500 years ago, yielded evidence of a sophisticated society with clear class distinctions and complex technology. The Celtic Durotriges tribe held the fort for about 500 years and dominated the region until the Roman conquest in A.D. 43. The tribe built roads and at least 600 houses inside the fort, known as Maiden Castle. There was apparently one ruler—sometimes a king, other times a queen—who presided over an aristocracy and a peasant farming community.

Egyptian Pyramid. Egyptian authorities allowed three holes to be drilled through a wall inside the largest of the Giza's Great Pyramids in hopes of reaching one of several rooms hidden for more than 4,500 years. After boring through 6.5 ft (2 m) of hard rock, however, investigators found only pockets of sand. Three more attempts with the drill were planned inside the 450-ft-(137-m-)tall Cheops Pyramid.

French archaeologists, who initiated the quest, believe the burial chamber of the Pharaoh Cheops is hidden somewhere behind what has been identified as the Queen's Chamber. The mummy of Cheops has not been found, and some scientists have speculated that the room now referred to as the King's Chamber is a decoy designed by an ancient Egyptian architect to protect his king. Previous gravitational tests indicated that there are cavities in the vicinity in which the holes were drilled.

Western Hemisphere

Titanic. Investigators returned to the site of the sunken luxury liner *Titanic,* located in 1985 in the Atlantic Ocean off the coast of Newfoundland, and peered into the vessel's inner chambers with the help of sophisticated video equipment. A three-man submersible vehicle, called *Alvin,* cruised to the 12,500-ft (3 800-m) depth of the famous wreck and released a re-

Jade carvings and a clay pot were among the artifacts recovered from a Maya tomb in southern Belize. At least four Maya kings were believed to be buried in the tomb.

AP/Wide World

mote-controlled video camera that served as a "swimming eyeball" inside the *Titanic*.

The scientists were surprised to find no evidence of a gash in the ship's hull, thought to have been caused by the ship's collision with an iceberg and long theorized as the fatal breach. Instead, said expedition leader Robert D. Ballard of Woods Hole (MA) Oceanographic Institution, it appeared that huge steel plates in the hull had buckled, popped their rivets, and separated from adjoining plates, allowing water to seep in and sink the ship. The *Titanic* broke in two, possibly on its way to the ocean floor, and both halves are imbedded in sediment. This makes a salvage operation virtually impossible, said Ballard.

Early Settlers. Evidence of the earliest known human life in the Americas, approximately 32,000 years ago, turned up in a rock shelter in Brazil. French scientists obtained radio-carbon dates from charcoal in layers of sediment that also contained stone tools. In addition, another researcher uncovered preliminary evidence of human occupation at a Chilean site dated to about 33,000 years ago.

Before the discovery in Brazil, most archaeologists held that humans first reached the Americas from Asia between 11,500 and 20,000 years ago. There is still disagreement over whether the first immigrants crossed a land bridge from Siberia to Alaska or voyaged across the Pacific Ocean to South America and then spread northward.

Ice Age Site. A cave located within 1 mi (1.6 km) of Biscayne Bay, near Miami, FL, provided a rare glimpse of a time approximately 10,000 years ago when humans and many now-extinct animals coexisted in North America. Remains at the cave, which was exposed by a sinkhole, could provide clues as to whether the extinction of numerous animal species was caused by human population growth and intensified hunting near the end of the last Ice Age, which extended from 20,000 to 8,000 years ago.

Human bones were found along with the bones of at least 50 species of animals, including mammoths, bison, jaguars, bats, and wolves. Dade County (FL) archaeologist Robert Carr said that humans and many of the now-extinct creatures probably lived in southern Florida before the melting of Ice Age glaciers, which raised the sea level and created the Everglades and Biscayne Bay.

Ancient Mayas. Two ongoing excavations helped explode the assumption that Maya from southern highlands migrated to northern lowlands in Mexico, Honduras, Guatemala, and Belize around A.D. 100, stimulating cultural advances that led to the Classic Period, or "Golden Era." Investigations at the lowland site of El Mirador in Guatemala showed it to have been more advanced than highland centers from around 400 B.C. to A.D. 250. El Mirador contains pyramids much larger than those built hundreds of years later during the Classic Period, which lasted from A.D. 200 to A.D. 900. The Honduran site of Copan also was found to have had a period of complex culture before a decline and a rebirth around 400 B.C.

Prehistoric Panama. The west coast and interior of central Panama have been continuously occupied by humans since 6,600 B.C., about 1,600 years earlier than previously documented, according to an archaeological team that has located 300 sites formerly inhabited by humans. A major change for the regional population occurred around 5,000 B.C., they reported, with the introduction of maize farming and the first evidence of extensive fishing. Residents of the area probably moved from farm sites to coastal fishing outposts for part of each year. This way of life apparently lasted until about 1,000 B.C. Curiously, ceramic pottery—usually an indicator of new technology and a more settled lifestyle—dates to 3,000 B.C. in the area.

BRUCE BOWER
"Science News"

ARCHITECTURE

While many architects and most of the U.S. public applauded the new pluralism epitomized by Post-Modernism—the well-established use of historic styles in new and often exaggerated ways—at least one critic was not so sure. Brendan Gill, a long-time writer for *The New Yorker* and an active spokesman on architectural matters, summed up his dissent at the annual meeting of the American Institute of Architects (AIA): "Are not the allurements of Post-Modernism being seen as parody in the name of paying homage to a touchingly sincere past?"

That Post-Modernism was well established was confirmed by the completion in 1986 of a number of structures, most notably in Washington, DC, by the once preeminent designers of office buildings in the International Style, associated with the stark boxy buildings of the 1950s and 1960s. The new historic borrowings included everything from neoclassicism, the city's style of choice in the 1920s and 1930s, to the rusticated, heavy masonry arches and corbels and the squat towers of late 19th-century Richardsonian-Romanesque. Other major Post-Modern buildings announced during the year included two major commercial towers in Philadelphia by the architectural firm of Kohn Pederson Fox; Washington DC's largest private project ever, a mixed-use development designed by Arthur Cotton Moore Associates; and an office project in Boston designed by the firm that, in 1983, put the Post-Modern style in the public eye with New York City's AT&T building, John Burgee Architects, with Philip Johnson. While all the new office space seemed to counter the economic analysts who had maintained for years that office space in most cities was already overbuilt, the tallest office building in the world, Television City by architects Helmut Jahn, again in Post-Modern style, was proposed in New York. A pointed spire 150-stories tall would be the centerpiece of seven 76-story apartment towers and a production studio facing the Hudson River. And the Post-Modern style even cropped up beside highways near suburban shopping-malls, as in a speculative office building in Framingham, MA, by Robert A. M. Stern.

That the public seemed to like the new design freedom was evidenced by several proposals that won competitions for new civic projects. Architects Barton Myers Associates won the right to design the new Phoenix (AZ) Municipal Government Center over a strong field of competitors, including the famed Mexican architect Ricardo Legorreta and the Japanese architect Arata Isozaki, both of whom proposed stark modern schemes. Barton Myers' scheme, by contrast, was a hybrid of textures and architectural motifs. A similar result was the winner of the Oceanside, CA, civic center design competition: a series of small-scale buildings by Charles Moore/Urban Innovations Group that appear to have been designed in the 1920s. And, that most professionals liked the new freedom was attested to by the annual AIA awards (*see* page 109).

And where was all the interest in historic styles leading? In some cases, it led to literal reproductions of older buildings. A golf clubhouse in the Chicago suburbs was designed by architects Booth/Hansen to reproduce an earlier Colonial Revival-style building on the site.

Inge and Arvid von der Ropp

Walde Huth-Schmolz

Gottfied Boehm, a 66-year-old German architect who was trained as an engineer, was awarded the 1986 Pritzker Architecture Prize. His many works include a grouping of structures, left, combining a church, library, and youth center in Cologne-Melaten, West Germany.

A whole development of Victorian cottages by architects Orr & Taylor sprouted on the beach at Seaside, FL. And a group of architects working in France, Taller de Arquitectura, managed through the mastery of precast-concrete techniques to reproduce every refinement and detail the classic pediments, cornices, and columns of 18th-century Paris at a heroic scale for new apartment houses nearby.

One of the most difficult designs executed in 1986 was the Hood Museum of Art at Dartmouth College (NH) by Centerbrook, Architects. In the new spirit of contextualism, or blending in, the design successfully linked the Romanesque and aggressively modern buildings that flanked it with yet a third style that might be called 19th-century industrial. Perhaps the most playful design was that of the Horton Plaza in San Diego by The Jerde Partnership, Architects. This downtown shopping center invoked a variety of styles to produce a permanent carnival atmosphere. Perhaps the most innovative design was for public housing inside three former filtration plants in The Netherlands by Wytze Patijn.

With a decline in U.S. subsidy programs, housing for the poor had been an area of little building and architectural activity for some years. Indeed, one economist writing in architectural journals in 1986 suggested that the key to architects' survival in the residential market was to stick to the most expensive houses, since those alone would weather the up-and-down economic cycles. In 1986, however, a pressing new housing issue did leap to the forefront of the profession's attention—the growing number of the nation's homeless. In response, the housing committee of the American Institute of Architects (AIA) began a campaign that would not only refine a new type of architectural design—that for transient shelters —but would pressure the federal and local governments to fund them. Other activities in the general public interest included the AIA's R/UDAT program in which architects volunteer to work in ailing downtown business districts, organizing local self-help programs to bring about revitalization through improvements the architects helped design.

With the rise in international terrorist activity, security at U.S. embassies and other official buildings became an issue of architectural design. Early in the year, the House Foreign Affairs Committee recommended some $4 billion for the design and construction of 126 overseas replacement posts for the U.S. State Department and 210 offices for the Central Intelligence Agency. Recommended design features included location on larger sites, circuitous access drives, fewer windows, stronger structures to withstand blasts, and internal offices for high-level personnel. The design chal-

Bradfield Associates Inc. was honored by the American Institute of Architects for a housing complex in Charleston, SC.
© Paul G. Beswick/Bradfield Associates, Inc.

The 1,000-student Loyola Law School in Los Angeles, CA, was called a "fresh, original, and joyful" project by the AIA. Frank O. Gehry and Associates designed the award-winning structures, including separate buildings for classrooms, courtrooms, and a chapel.

© Michael Moran/Frank O. Gehry and Associates

AMERICAN INSTITUTE OF ARCHITECTS
1986 Honor Award Winners

Commercial/Institutional Projects

D. Samuel and Jean H. Gottesman Exhibition Hall, New York Public Library, New York City; Davis, Brody and Associates and Giorgio Cavaglieri Architects; ". . . has brought renewed dignity and grandeur to this exquisitely crafted 75-year-old public space"

Loyola Law School, Los Angeles; Frank O. Gehry and Associates with Brooks/Collier Inc.; "an engagingly provocative project built with a limited budget and unlimited imagination"

Kaskel Library, Hackley School, Tarrytown, NY; Keith Kroeger Associates; "This conversion . . . is so harmoniously achieved that it looks as though the building has always been just as it is now"

Battell Chapel, Yale University, New Haven, CT; Herbert S. Newman Associates; "The chapel's . . . colors and . . . detail are an inspiration"

IBM Corporate Office Building, Purchase, NY; I.M. Pei and Partners; "a finely crafted, dignified expression of Modern architecture"

Clinic Building, Cleveland Clinic Foundation, Cleveland; Cesar Pelli and Associates and van Dijk, Johnson and Partners; "[meets] both human and technical needs through the genius of its design"

Herring Hall, Rice University, Houston; Cesar Pelli and Associates; "[honors] the strong visual tradition of the existing campus plan and buildings"

Residential Projects

Private residence, Dallas; Edward Larrabee Barnes Associates and Armand P. Avakian Associates; "a thoroughly romantic architectural vision, functioning effectively within the Modernist vocabulary"

Scattered-Site Infill Public Housing, Charleston, SC; Bradfield Associates Inc.; "an example of what low-cost housing should be . . . shelter not just for the body, but for the human spirit"

Parker residence, Bainbridge Island, WA; James Cutler Architects; "a model of architectural restraint and ingenuity"

Wenglowski House, Deer Isle, ME; Peter Forbes and Associates; "[employs] many modern materials . . . yet successfully retains the imagery of its rugged location"

Steel and Glass House, Chicago; Krueck and Olsen Architects; "spartan yet luxurious, austere yet filled with dramatic spaces and rich textures"

Bergren residence, Venice, CA; Mayne and Rotondi Architects; "offers a sense of liberating openness"

500 Park Tower, New York City; James Stewart Polshek and Partners and Schuman, Lichtenstein, Claman and Efron; "one of the most refreshing and intelligent buildings to be built in New York City in recent years"

lenge was to produce buildings that are both safe and consistent with the inviting image that government and corporate facilities traditionally have sought.

For the architectural profession as a whole, the year 1986 signaled change. The highest American design award, the AIA's gold medal, went to a Canadian, Arthur Erickson. Faced with the same skyrocketing liability insurance premiums that had beset other professions (*see* page 46), the AIA passed a mandatory code of ethics of professional conduct to demonstrate architect's ability to police their own behavior. And, with high competition in the field pushing profits below even the traditional marginal levels, there was talk of limiting the number of future architects being trained.

CHARLES K. HOYT, *"Architectural Record"*

Argentina's President Raúl Alfonsin (second from right) meets with aides in October to discuss Britain's imposition of a 200-mile fishing conservation zone around the Falkland (Malvinas) Islands. Argentina was excluded from the zone.

ARGENTINA

Military trials, a faltering austerity plan, and another crisis in the Falkland (Malvinas) Islands shared the nation's attention in 1986.

Politics and Government. President Raúl Alfonsín has adopted "modernization" as a principal theme. In April and May he called for constitutional and administrative reforms. He favored changing the presidential system, with its six-year term that allowed no immediate reelection, to a parliamentary one in which many presidential powers would be transferred to a prime minister. Congress would have greater responsibilities in governing. The amendment would allow a president to be reelected.

Among other reforms proposed were: restructuring the armed forces, overhauling finances, moving the federal capital to the underpopulated and overlooked south, giving provincial status to the territory of Tierra del Fuego, and curbing the right to strike. The president threatened to decree a halt to strikes if his bill on limiting work stoppages was not approved. These administration proposals failed to draw widespread public support, and congress adjourned on October 30 without approving them. A special session of congress convened on November 15 to debate the president's recommendations.

One of the most bitterly fought political battles of 1986 ended on November 27, when the supreme court declared unconstitutional a 98-year-old law barring divorce. A bill legalizing divorce had been blocked in the Senate in October, after clearing the lower legislative house by a 176-36 margin in August. Divorce was heavily favored, according to opinion polls.

Military on Trial. To the chagrin of the armed forces and the political right, public opinion rejected even the slightest hint of amnesty for military personnel implicated in human-rights violations during the "dirty war" against left-wing 'subversion" in the 1970s. In December 1985 five top commanders had received prison terms.

Because of "unjustified delays," the armed forces' highest judicial body was forced, in June, to turn over to a federal appeals court some 300 human-rights cases that had not yet been resolved by military authorities. The most notorious of the accused, former Gen. Carlos Suárez Mason, remained a fugitive, but his principal subordinates—retired Gen. Ramón Camps and his successor as police chief Ovidio Paolo Richieri, along with four police officials from Buenos Aires province—went on trial in September on 250 charges of human-rights violations, mass murder, and torture. On December 2, Camps was sentenced to 25 years in prison (specifically for torturing the newspaperman Jacobo Timerman), and Richieri received 14 years.

Sentences were announced on May 16 by the supreme council of the armed forces in the cases of Gen. Leopoldo Galtieri, Adm. Jorge Anaya, Brig. Gen. Basilio Lami Dozo, and 13 other officers involved in the Falklands (Malvinas) conflict in 1982 that took nearly 1,000 lives. Galtieri, who was serving as president of the republic and commander in chief during the war, got a 12-year sentence on charges of negligence and lack of skill. Anaya was given 14 years in prison, and Lami Dozo received eight years. They were held responsible for Argentina's loss of the war. The 13 other officers were acquitted.

Economy. The Austral plan, the Alfonsín government program to halt inflation, faltered in 1986. The year had started well in economic terms. The first six months saw a 3% growth rate. A sharp increase in tax revenue suggested a possible reduction in the public deficit. Inflation hovered near the targeted 2–3% monthly rate. Then an attempt to reach a 1986 growth rate of 4% caused the economy to overheat. By August inflation had reached the 8.8% level, before edging downward. Annualized, that rate became 119%, well above the 1986 target of only 28%. Consequently, rigid price and wage controls were reinstituted. A new team, pledged to keep a tighter rein on the money supply, took over at the central bank in September. Cutbacks in government spending were promised. Devaluations of the austral had to be accelerated. A deficit equal to 5% of the gross domestic product (GDP) was forecast, and no growth was expected.

A complex economic pact with 11 protocols was signed in Buenos Aires on July 29 by President Alfonsín and his Brazilian counterpart, José Sarney. The accord was hailed as a new effort toward Latin American regional integration. It embraced trade, investment, binational enterprises, and transfers of technology. Initially Argentina expected to boost sales of wheat to Brazil and to purchase more coal and iron ore. A customs union was established that would increase exchanges of capital goods by 30% yearly.

Debt. Payment of the $10 billion that was due in 1986 on a $50 billion foreign debt was postponed from September until March 1987, to allow for its rescheduling. Negotiations were initiated with the International Monetary Fund (IMF) in April for a new standby arrangement of $1.6 billion. Thanks to a waiver granted in June by the IMF, Argentina was able to obtain a final payment of $237 million on a 1984 standby accord and a $600 million installment of a $4.2 billion private loan, obtained in 1985. The IMF had been concerned over Argentina's inability to limit the 1985 budget deficit to 3.6% of GDP.

The World Bank authorized $350 million in March for agricultural development. In September, Argentina sought up to $3 billion from private banks to cover the 1986 budget deficit.

Labor Unrest. While labor attempted to win salary increases that would outdistance inflation, the government tried to keep wages below the inflation rate and to outlaw strikes for the duration of collective bargaining agreements. The first general strike called in 1986 by the General Confederation of Labor (CGT) took place on January 24 and was termed by some the most effective since Alfonsín became president. Others were held in March and June. The one scheduled for July was canceled after the Alfonsín government had negotiated sectoral wage adjustments with metalworkers, state employees, and construction workers, without the participation of CGT boss Saúl Ubaldini. In doing this the government surpassed its own wage guidelines.

As inflation approached 9% for August, and topped 7% in September, the CGT began to revive a "struggle plan" of 12- and 24-hour strikes to force meaningful wage increases. Ubaldini claimed that deterioration in the labor sector's real wages had averaged 27% during the previous 15 months. Unemployment rose to 9% in some sectors. Nationwide general strikes were resumed on October 9. By official estimates, 60% of the work force was idle in Buenos Aires. Some 100,000 Peronists took to the streets in a noisy demonstration; they blasted the government for giving away "the efforts of the people" to the IMF.

Falklands (Malvinas) Controversy. The issue of sovereignty over the British-ruled Falklands (Malvinas) Islands and adjacent waters erupted in October with more intensity than at any time since 1982 when Argentina seized and lost the archipelago in a 74-day undeclared war that ended in a truce. Argentina had initialed bilateral fishing agreements with the Soviet Union and Bulgaria on July 28, allowing them to fish waters that were subsequently incorporated by Britain into a 200-mile fishing conservation zone around the Falklands. Argentina was excluded from the zone, and other nations could fish there only with British permission.

Support for Argentina poured in from other Latin American nations. The Organization of American States (OAS), meeting in Guatemala, called on November 11 for a settlement by negotiation. Alfonsín traveled to Washington on November 17 to gain support from President Ronald Reagan. Coinciding with the White House call, Argentina offered to end hostilities formally with London and initiate new negotiations on the sovereignty issue. While Britain had sought such a declaration on a cessation of hostilities from Argentina, it refused to negotiate the sovereignty issue. Therefore, on November 18, the British government found the Argentine offer unacceptable.

LARRY L. PIPPIN, *University of the Pacific*

ARGENTINA · Information Highlights

Official Name: Argentine Republic.
Location: Southern South America.
Area: 1,068,297 sq mi (2 766 889 km²).
Population (mid-1986 est.): 31,200,000.
Chief Cities (1980 census): Buenos Aires, the capital, 2,922,829; Cordoba, 983,960; Rosario, 957,301.
Government: *Head of state and government,* Raul Alfonsin, president (took office Dec. 10, 1983). *Legislature*—Senate and Chamber of Deputies.
Monetary Unit: Austral (.9174 austral equals U.S.$1, Oct. 20, 1986).
Gross Domestic Product (1984 U.S.$): $74,400,-000,000.
Economic Indexes (1985): *Consumer Prices* (1980 = 100), all items, 134,835.7; food, 130,231.5. *Industrial Production* (1980 = 100), 84.
Foreign Trade (1985 U.S.$): *Imports,* $3,814,000,000; *exports,* $8,396,000,000.

Republican Barry Goldwater, 77, retired after five terms as U.S. senator from Arizona (1953–65, 1969–87). A testimonial dinner was held in Washington on September 9.

AP/Wide World

ARIZONA

Gubernatorial, senate, and congressional races, along with environmental concerns and illegal immigration, were major issues in Arizona during 1986.

Elections. Experts were correct when they predicted that Phoenix car dealer Evan Mecham could not draw more than 40% of the vote, but it was all he needed to become the state's new Republican governor. Mecham was aided by the lowest voter turnout (52%) since 1942 and the candidacy of Bill Schulz, an independent whose late campaign split the moderate-liberal vote for Democratic nominee Carolyn Warner, giving Mecham the edge he needed. After the election, Mecham added to the consternation of Democrats when he vowed to rescind the state's Martin Luther King, Jr., holiday while promising a "U turn" in the policies of outgoing Gov. Bruce Babbitt. He will work with returning Republican majorities in both houses of the state legislature.

It was also a tough election for Democrats in other state races, as former Republican Congressman John McCain handily defeated Richard Kimball (D) for the U.S. Senate seat vacated by retiring Barry Goldwater; and Republicans Jim Kolbe, Bob Stump, Jon Kyl, and John J. Rhodes III won four of the state's five congressional seats. The only bright spot for Democrats was the reelection of Congressman Morris Udall to his fourteenth term.

Arizonans also voted on six propositions, approving two (increasing limits on school district spending and setting limits on campaign contributions), and defeating four. The defeated propositions included one that would have deregulated telephone rate schedules; another that would have given local governments more flexibility on spending limits; and a third

that would have increased the salaries of legislators from $15,000 to $20,000. The most controversial proposition by far, one that would have permitted the legislature to set limits on liability awards, was narrowly defeated.

Environmental Measures. Governor Babbitt signed into law a landmark bill to protect the state's ground water. The law creates a new department of environmental quality to restrict pollution, holds polluters liable for the cost of cleaning up pollution regardless of when it occurred, and establishes a "superfund" to pay for cleanups when the polluter cannot be identified.

In July the U.S. Environmental Protection Agency (EPA) and the Phelps Dodge Corporation announced an agreement designed to reduce air pollution in the area around the company's copper smelting plant in Douglas and set a January 1987 date for closing the plant. In the meantime, Phelps Dodge prom-

---

ARIZONA • Information Highlights

Area: 114,000 sq mi (295 260 km²).
Population (1985 est.): 3,187,000.
Chief Cities (July 1, 1984 est.): Phoenix, the capital, 853,266; Tucson, 365,422; Mesa, 193,931; Tempe, 118,336; Glendale, 113,888.
Government (1986): *Chief Officers*—governor, Bruce E. Babbitt (D); secretary of state, Rose Mofford (D). *Legislature*—Senate, 30 members; House of Representatives, 60 members.
State Finances (fiscal year 1985): *Revenue,* $5,330,000,000; *expenditure,* $4,599,000,000.
Personal Income (1985): $40,775,000,000; per capita, $12,795.
Labor Force (June 1986): *Civilian labor force,* 1,590,600; *unemployed,* 112,700 (7.1% of total force).
Education: *Enrollment* (fall 1984)—public elementary schools, 373,235; public secondary, 156,827; colleges and universities, 216,854. *Public school expenditures* (1983–84), $1,246,000,000 ($2,738 per pupil).

---

ised to abide by sulfur dioxide emissions limits established by the EPA and to pay a $400,000 fine for past violations. The company posted a $3 million letter of credit, which would be forfeited if the plant were not closed on time.

Sanctuary Trial. In May, 8 defendants, members of the Sanctuary Movement—an interdenominational group of Protestants and Catholics—were convicted of aiding Salvadoran and Guatemalan refugees entering the country illegally. Three other defendants were aquitted. Those found guilty were placed on probation and were appealing the convictions.

Economy. Despite the state's rapid population growth, state revenues were down. A shortfall of between $60 million and $150 million was projected for the state income and sales taxes for 1986. Incomes and consumer spending have not kept pace with the growth rate, some experts claim, because of the state's low wage structure.

JAMES W. CLARKE, *University of Arizona*

ARKANSAS

In 1986, Arkansas celebrated its 150th year of statehood, a sesquicentennial marked by beginnings and endings as well as by the continuing of old problems.

Public-school districts began implementing costly legislative-mandated programs designed to raise the quality of education. The family-owned, reform oriented *Arkansas Gazette,* a 167-year old Little Rock newspaper with a statewide circulation, was sold to the Gannett Co., publisher of *USA Today.* Past hardships persisted. Factories continued to close. Oil and crop prices remained low. Farm values dropped. Personal income declined. Bank and savings and loan institutions sustained large losses. Concern over environmental pollution intensified, as chemically contaminated feed required the quarantining of 122 dairy farms.

The Elections. The saturation of the media with negative campaign tactics and gimmicks produced no election upsets. Incumbents defeated challengers in the primary and general elections, usually by lopsided votes. Democrats won all state executive and federal elections except one and maintained their majorities in the General Assembly—91 of the 100 representatives and 31 of the 35 senators. Bill Clinton became the state's second fourth-term governor and the first since 1874 to win a four-year term. He defeated former Gov. Frank White with 64% of the vote. U.S. Sen. Dale Bumpers was reelected to a third term by a 62% vote. In the third congressional district, incumbent Republican John Paul Hammerschmidt was returned by an 80% vote to the U.S. House of Representatives for his 11th consecutive term. The three other incumbent Congressmen, all Democrats—Bill Alexander, Jr., Tommy F. Robinson, and Beryl F. Anthony, Jr.—won their races by big margins.

Voters approved two constitutional amendments—expanding the civil jurisdiction of municipal courts from $300 to $3,000 and reversing a state Supreme Court decision requiring popular approval of local government revenue bonds. An amendment to prohibit funding of abortions was defeated narrowly.

Administration. Gov. Bill Clinton continued to dominate state governmental affairs, despite revenue shortfalls and management problems. In a special session the legislature approved 16 of the 17 items listed in the governor's program, including an increase in workers' compensation benefits. Even with record general revenues of $1.586 billion, a 2% increase over the previous fiscal year, the governor had to order four cutbacks in state spending because collections fell below estimates. The Federal Health Care Financing Administration threatened to terminate Medicaid funding for the Booneville Human Development Center and the Medicare certification of the state hospital. Overcrowded state prisons again were the center of investigations.

The Judiciary. The U.S. Supreme Court upheld a state law banning opponents of the death penalty from juries hearing capital offense cases. Blacks challenged as racially discriminating the at-large election system of the Humnoke School District, Lonoke County, and as racially gerrymandered the justice of peace districts in Mississippi and Lee counties and the city council wards in Marianna.

James Dean Walker, with two previous convictions for the shooting death of a North Little Rock policeman in 1963, reversed by appellate courts, avoided a third trial and gained his freedom by pleading no contest to a manslaughter charge. He was sentenced to time already served.

WILLIAM C. NOLAN
Southern Arkansas University

ARKANSAS · Information Highlights

Area: 53,187 sq mi (137 754 km²).
Population (1985 est.): 2,359,000.
Chief Cities (1980 census): Little Rock, the capital (July 1, 1982 est.), 167,974; Fort Smith, 71,626; North Little Rock, 64,288; Pine Bluff, 56,636.
Government (1986): *Chief Officers*—governor, Bill Clinton (D); lt. gov. Winston Bryant (D). *General Assembly*—Senate, 35 members; House of Representatives, 100 members.
State Finances (fiscal year 1985): *Revenue,* $3,342,000,000; *expenditure,* $3,018,000,000.
Personal Income (1985): $24,707,000,000; per capita, $10,476.
Labor Force (June 1986): *Civilian labor force,* 1,068,900; *unemployed,* 95,000 (8.9% of total force).
Education: *Enrollment* (fall 1984)—public elementary schools, 304,518; public secondary, 128,150; colleges and universities, 77,958. *Public school expenditures* (1983–84), $893,000,000 ($2,198 per pupil).

ARMS CONTROL

Nineteen eighty-six was a roller coaster year for arms control and disarmament, with lowered expectations followed by high hopes, which in turn were dashed. During the early part of the year, U.S. President Ronald Reagan said that he was considering the deployment of strategic nuclear weapons in numbers beyond the limits established in the SALT II (Strategic Arms Limitation Talks II) treaty. (Such deployment materialized in November.) At the suggestion of Soviet General Secretary Mikhail Gorbachev, the leaders of the two nuclear superpowers met October 11-12 in Reykjavik, Iceland, where they came close to negotiating the most sweeping arms agreements in the four-decade-long Cold War period. The unprecedented set of potential agreements finally failed to be adopted because of disagreement over President Reagan's Strategic Defense Initiative (SDI, or "Star Wars"). A last effort to resurrect the lost opportunities of the Iceland meeting collapsed on November 6 in Vienna, Austria, where U.S. Secretary of State George Shultz and Soviet Foreign Minister Eduard Shevardnadze failed to negotiate anything. As was the case in Iceland, the Vienna impasse resulted from the inability of Washington and Moscow to reach agreement on SDI.

Problems with SALT II. In 1979, U.S. President Jimmy Carter and the late Soviet leader Leonid Brezhnev signed the SALT II treaty, which placed numerical limits on the strategic nuclear forces of both nations. Although the U.S. Senate never ratified the treaty, the Reagan administration abided by its terms. In May 1986, however, the White House announced that U.S. policy might change. President Reagan ordered the destruction of two nuclear-powered submarines (each of which carried 16 Poseidon ballistic missiles) so that the addition of a new Trident submarine to the fleet would not exceed the treaty limits. But the president also declared that the SALT II treaty was "fundamentally flawed" and stated that he would not be bound by its terms if the Soviets continued to cheat on the limits it established and if Moscow were not willing to negotiate a new arms agreement.

At the time of the president's statement, Secretary Shultz called SALT II "obsolete" and expressed hope that it would be replaced by an agreement to make deep cuts in the number of strategic nuclear weapons possessed by the two sides. In June presidential spokesman Larry Speakes announced that "the SALT treaty no longer exists," and President Reagan said that it was his intention to replace it with a "better deal."

On November 28 the United States exceeded the limits of the Salt II agreement when a B-52 bomber, newly modified to carry cruise missiles, entered active service. The idea of abandoning SALT II had created sharp disagreement among U.S. allies for months. Particularly critical were the foreign ministers of Great Britain, West Germany, and Canada. In the United States, President Reagan's statements prompted leading arms-control advocates to warn that abandonment of the treaty likely would intensify the arms race and cause the Soviets to build up their stockpile of nuclear weapons to much higher levels.

The Iceland Summit. When President Reagan and General Secretary Gorbachev, accompanied by their senior advisers, met in Reykjavik, their initial purpose was to discuss the agenda for a more detailed summit meeting, including new arms control and disarmament proposals. But when Gorbachev surprised the Americans with a detailed set of impressive arms offers—at one point described by Secretary Shultz as "breathtaking"—the U.S. delegation had high hopes for an agreement on dramatic mutual reductions in nuclear forces. After two days of intense bargaining, however, the meeting ended in bitter disappointment and recriminations.

While the exact terms of the potential arms deal were not fully set forth by either side, a general picture of what was discussed could be pieced together from the statements of those who were at Reykjavik. According to the Americans, the major terms included: near elimination of intermediate-range ballistic missiles (IRBMs) from the Eurasian continent, to only 100 for the Soviets; deep cuts in the total number of strategic nuclear missiles, possibly followed by the complete elimination of such weapons within ten years; and substantial reduction in the number of underground nuclear weapons tests, with adequate verification, possibly culminating in the complete cessation of such tests within the decade.

Both the U.S. and the Soviet negotiators later said that the basic stumbling block to an agreement was failure to agree to what kind of limitations would be placed on the U.S. Strategic Defense Initiative. According to President Reagan, the talks failed because General Secretary Gorbachev, "insisted that we sign an agreement that could deny to me and future presidents for ten years the right to develop, test, and deploy a defense against nuclear missiles for the people of the free world. This we could not and will not do."

Both the Americans and Soviets also were quick to blame each other for the failure of the Iceland talks. Secretary of State Shultz was quoted as saying, "We are deeply disappointed at this outcome." General Secretary Gorbachev was quoted as saying, "This has been a failure, and a failure when we were very close to an historic agreement." (*See also* MILITARY AFFAIRS.)

ROBERT M. LAWRENCE
Colorado State University

A Diego Rivera centennial show was held at the Detroit Institute, owner of the fresco "Detroit Industry," above.

ART

During 1986, existing art museums in both the United States and Europe continued to expand, while new museums also were opened. At the same time an increasing number of large international loan exhibitions attracted visitors, and important acquisitions were announced.

Museum News. In Paris, following the opening of the Picasso Museum in 1985, the National Museum of Modern Art moved into permanent quarters at the Pompidou Center, and the Musée d'Orsay was scheduled to be inaugurated in December. For 39 years the popular Museum of the Jeu de Paume, a former greenhouse adjacent to the Tuileries Gardens, housed the world's largest collection of French Impressionist paintings. Having long outgrown this space, the collection was moved across the Seine to a new museum created out of the vast spaces of a converted railroad station, the Gare d'Orsay. In its new quarters the collection will be combined with other 19th- and 20th-century paintings and sculpture, and other examples of the art of the time. A preview of the exhibition policy of the new museum was afforded by a loan exhibition, "From Courbet to Cezanne: A New 19th Century," at the Brooklyn (NY)

Museum in the spring. The exhibit showed Impressionist paintings in conjunction with contemporary academic art and other forms of artistic expression.

In Venice, the 18th century Palazzo Grassi was restored with the financial aid of the Italian automobile manufacturer Fiat to become a center of the arts under the direction of Pontus Hulten, well known as the successful director of the Pompidou Center, the Modern Museum of Stockholm, and the Museum of Contemporary Art in Los Angeles. Palazzo Grassi will not have a permanent collection but will house exhibitions. The museum's inaugural exhibition, "Futurismo e Futurismi," opened in May 1986 and illustrated the interaction of art and other cultural manifestations. Featured was a reconstruction of the study of Filippo Tommaso Marinetti (1876–1944), writer and founder of the futuristic movement, who began as a poet writing in French under the influence of the Symbolists and went on to formulate the Futurist Manifesto in 1909. The most important exponents of futurism, however, were the painters Gino Severini, Giacomo Balla, Carlo Carrà, and the painter-sculptor Umberto Boccioni. They were fascinated by the modern world as embodied in the speed, strength, and precision of machinery. At the 1986 exhibit, loans from four continents presented not only the accomplishments of futurism in Italy but also the work influenced by the movement in other countries. The presence of several World War I airplanes suspended in the courtyard lent a dramatic accent to the exhibit.

A new building was inaugurated for the Kunstsammlung Nordrhein-Westfalen, founded in 1962 in Düsseldorf, West Germany. Enjoying a large annual budget, this museum has succeeded in amassing a fine collection of major 20th-century works.

Plans for an ambitious expansion of the Brooklyn Museum were announced. Though overshadowed by the many institutions in Manhattan, the Brooklyn Museum ranks seventh among American museums in terms of holdings and owns a fine collection, particularly in Egyptian art, American art from pre-Columbian to contemporary, and the decorative arts. Designed by McKim, Mead and White in 1893, the building was originally planned to be much larger, but construction ceased in 1927. It is to be renovated, and a new addition, doubling its size, will provide more adequate exhibition areas, space for storage and conservation, a 1,000-seat auditorium, a library, and educational facilities. A link, planned in the original design, will connect the museum with the nearby Botanic Garden.

The naming of an American, Edmund Pillsbury, director of the Kimbell Art Museum in Fort Worth, TX, as director of the National Gallery, and of another American, Robert Venturi, as the architect of its planned extension, highlighted museum news in London. The museum's new wing is to be built to house early Renaissance paintings and temporary exhibitions. It is to include an entrance vestibule, sales space, and a restaurant, and will complement the existing structure.

Acquisitions. Deaccessioning, a practice whereby museums eliminate duplications or works of lesser quality, often randomly acquired through gifts, has become acceptable. Many American museums have sold works without protests and thereby gained funds to buy desired additions. However, one of the most remarkable new acquisitions came from one museum's own storerooms. At the Museum of Fine Arts in Boston a collection of more than 500 original printmaking woodblocks by the Japanese artist Hokusai (1760–1849) came to light. Donated in 1889, the woodblocks had been thought to have been destroyed. Most such blocks are discarded after use and are thus extremely rare.

A sixth-century B.C. statue of a naked youth or a kouros acquired by the J. Paul Getty Museum in Malibu in 1985 finally went on view after extensive restoration. The statue's exact origin is a mystery, and its authenticity has been challenged by some. However, scientific tests of the stone and its aging seem to prove its antiquity, and it is considered one of the

Collection of the Hermitage Museum, Leningrad, from the National Gallery of Art, Washington, DC

Renoir's "Portrait of the Actress Jeanne Samary" toured the United States in a cultural exchange with the Soviet Union.

most important acquisitions by a museum in recent years.

The Smithsonian Institution in Washington, DC, was able to buy intact a fabulous collection of art of the Persian Empire, amassed early in the 20th century by the Parisian jeweler Henri Vever. Last exhibited in Paris in 1931, the collection was thought to have been lost until found by chance in storage in New York where it had been shipped for safety in 1945. Its importance lies in the fact that it includes unmutilated illustrated volumes, rather than separate pages. There are also many miniatures, calligraphies, bookbindings, and textiles from the area that now includes Iran and parts of Iraq, Pakistan, and India. In order to maintain the collection intact the owner agreed to sell it for $7 million instead of the original price of $11 million. It is to be housed in galleries to be built for the Smithsonian with funds provided by Arthur M. Sackler, who also raised the money to purchase the collection.

Another important collection—more than 1,000 works by Thomas Eakins (1844–1916) which were in his studio when he died and subsequently owned by one of his students, Charles Bregler—was purchased by the Pennsylvania Academy of the Fine Arts. Eakins was director of the academy (1882–86). The collection includes paintings, drawings, photographs, manuscripts, and slides.

The Philadelphia Museum of Art was bequeathed the art collection of the late Henry P. McIlhenny, for many years curator of the decorative arts and trustee of the museum. The collection consists of paintings, including masterpieces by Ingres, Delacroix, Degas, and Chardin; lesser works by Victorian artists which he collected before they began to be appreciated; and drawings, sculpture, and furniture.

Exhibitions. The New York Metropolitan Museum of Art's most heralded show of the year was "Liechtenstein: The Princely Collection." The exhibit, which opened in late October 1985, presented paintings, sculptures, firearms, and porcelains from one of the last great European private collections never before seen in North America. Most of the works were commissioned or bought in the 17th and 18th centuries by the hereditary rulers of the principality of Liechtenstein. The high point was a cycle of eight canvases by Rubens, depicting the exploits of the Roman consul Decius Mus, painted in 1617–18 as cartoons for tapestries. Visitors also were impressed greatly by the Golden Carriage built in France in 1738 and beautifully decorated with painted panels, bronze ornaments, silk, satin, and leather.

Collection of the Metropolitan Museum of Art, New York, from the National Gallery of Art, Washington, DC

Monet's "Path Among the Poppies, Ile Saint-Martin," above, was part of a special exhibit, titled "The New Painting: Impressionism 1874–1886," that reconstructed the eight original impressionist shows held in Paris during that period. Andrew Wyeth's "Crown of Flowers," below, was one of his previously unknown paintings and drawings, done over a 15-year period, that came to light in 1986. All 240 works featured Helga, a neighbor of the Wyeths.

From mid-April through mid-June 1986 the Metropolitan Museum showed the "Gothic and Renaissance Art in Nuremberg: 1300–1550." During that period, Nuremberg attained a peak of power and wealth and a leading position in the arts with Albrecht Dürer as its foremost exponent. Jointly organized with the Germanisches National Museum which showed it after its stay in New York, the exhibit consisted of 278 objects in all media, including books and prints. Also at the Metropolitan the French artist François Boucher (1703–70) received his first retrospective in a show organized by the Detroit Institute of Arts and Réunion des Musées Nationaux de France. Eighty paintings, six tapestries, drawings, and porcelains after his designs ranged in subject from portraits and mythological and allegorical scenes to landscapes, interiors, and even religious subjects.

At the National Gallery in Washington and the Fine Arts Museums of San Francisco an unusual exhibition, organized by Charles Moffett of the latter institution, reconstructed the original eight impressionist shows held in Paris between 1874 and 1886. At the time Impressionist paintings were not accepted by the official salons. Almost all the paintings originally shown were present, including those by such famous artists as Degas, Monet, Renoir, and Cézanne.

The Museum of Modern Art in New York showed "Vienna 1900: Art, Architecture and Design," from July through October. A more comprehensive show, "Art and Reality: Vienna 1870–1930" was held in Vienna in 1985, but the importance of that city and its culture is increasingly recognized, and the New York show was amply justified. More concise and stressing art of the highest quality, it presented paintings and drawings by Gustav Klimt, Oskar Kokoschka, and Egon Schiele, as well as examples of the imaginative creativity of the artists and craftsmen who designed objects for everyday use. An unusual feature was the reconstruction of the facade of the Die Zeit telegraph office built by Otto Wagner in 1902; while in the garden the museum recreated a Viennese cafe in the style of Josef Hoffmann.

As part of the U.S.-USSR cultural exchange program, 41 paintings from the Hermitage Museum in Leningrad and the Pushkin Museum in Moscow, including masterpieces by Cézanne, Gauguin, Matisse, Monet, and Picasso, were on loan at the National Gallery, the Los Angeles County Museum, and the Metropolitan from May through October. In return the United States sent 40 of its own modern paintings to the two Russian museums, and works from the collection of American industrialist Armand Hammer, who oversaw the exchange, were viewed in the USSR.

To mark the 150th anniversary of the birth of Winslow Homer, the National Gallery exhibited 99 of his watercolors representing 30 years of his life, on loan from 60 public and private collections. The show subsequently traveled to the Amon Carter Museum in Fort Worth and the Yale University Art Gallery. The Mexican artist Diego Rivera was honored on the occasion of the centenary of his birth by a retrospective organized by the Detroit Institute of Arts, owner of *Detroit Industry,* his most important fresco outside Mexico. More than 100 paintings and 140 drawings and watercolors comprised the show which opened in Detroit and was to continue to Philadelphia, Mexico City, Madrid, and West Berlin.

Auction News. In the auction and sales rooms it was noted that American collectors are turning to Old Masters. In contrast to European collectors who always have maintained an interest in the Old Masters, Americans have preferred Dutch and Flemish 17th-century paintings to Italian Renaissance art and secular to religious subjects. Despite this trend, record prices still continued to be set for Impressionist paintings. At Christie's in London, *Rue Mosnier with Street Pavers* (1878) by Edouard Manet was auctioned for more than $11 million, the most ever for an Impressionist work. Earlier at Sotheby's, *Opera Ball* by Toulouse-Lautrec sold for some $2.86 million.

An 18th-century Philadelphia Chippendale tea table sold for $1,045,000 at Christie's. It was the highest price ever paid for a piece of American furniture. The rarity of American furniture of this style accounted for the high price. Also astonishing was the success of a sale of 100,000 pieces of blue and white Chinese porcelain salvaged from a ship wrecked in the South China Sea two centuries ago. One dealer bought $860,000 worth, and a dinner service for 144 persons was sold for $332,707. The prices were all the more surprising because most pieces were ordinary ware made for the middle-class European market of the time.

Meanwhile, Goya's *Marquesa de Santa Cruz* was returned to Spain following an agreement between the Spanish government and the owner of the portrait, Lord Wimbourne. The Spanish government claimed that the portrait left Spain illegally in 1983. Lord Wimbourne, who had bought the work in good faith, sought to sell it for a record price of $12 million. Under the agreement, the British nobleman received $6 million for the painting which now would hang in Madrid's Prado Museum.

Wyeth. The popular American painter Andrew Wyeth became the center of a minor sensation when a series of 240 drawings, paintings, and watercolors he had done between 1970 and 1985 were purchased by a Pennsylvania collector for a sum said to be in the multimillions of dollars. All of the works featured the same subject, a blond woman named Helga, and all had been kept hidden by the artist.

ISA RAGUSA, *Princeton University*

Photos courtesy of NTV Tokyo-Musei Vaticani/Scala/Art Resource

ART RESTORATION

With air pollution and natural deterioration threatening some of the world's great works of art, cleaning and restoration efforts are under way at numerous museums and other art sites. Among the treasures being restored are: the Ice Age wall paintings in the Lascaux Cave at Dordogne, France; Byzantine murals at the Kariye Camir Chapel in Istanbul; Leonardo da Vinci's *Last Supper* at Santa Maria delle Grazie in Milan; and Masaccio's *St. Peter Cycle* at the Brancacci Chapel in Florence.

But the most ambitious and widely publicized restoration project is Michelangelo's early 16th-century frescoes in the Vatican's Sistine Chapel. The $3 million cleanup began in 1980 and is scheduled for completion in 1992. As demonstrated in the photos above—"before" and "after" views of the *Eleazar and Mathan* lunette—the removal of centuries of soot and grime have revealed colors of surprising brightness. In addition to altering aesthetic appreciation of Michelangelo's masterpiece, the restoration is also providing new insights into his painting technique.

ASIA

Change was in the air across Asia in 1986, most dramatically in the Philippines. Various nations sought to enhance their political influence on the continent, although strife in Afghanistan, Cambodia, and Sri Lanka continued despite such diplomatic activity.

Changing of the Guard. The death in July of longtime Vietnamese Communist Party leader Le Duan signaled the beginning of the end of an era. His successor, veteran fellow Marxist Truong Chinh, hardly represented a new generation of leadership, but Le Duan's passing moved nearer the day when younger Vietnamese would assume power. Similarly the decision to lift martial law on Taiwan after 37 years foreshadowed the time when 76-year-old Chiang Ching-kuo (son of the late Chiang Kai-shek, whose 100th birthday was celebrated in 1986) would no longer rule the "other China."

An era did end in the Philippines in February when longtime president Ferdinand Marcos fled the country, and his rival, Corazon Aquino, was elevated to the nation's highest office on a wave of peaceful popular protests (*see* feature article, page 26). In South Korea opponents of military strongman Chun Doo Hwan also demonstrated, but Chun's regime was not as weak as its Filipino counterpart, and the country's economy was much stronger. Benazir Bhutto's attempt to spark a popular revolt in Pakistan was accompanied by the worst political violence in years, but President Mohammad Zia ul-Haq remained in power.

Familiar Faces. On a continent where most political leadership is exceptionally durable, other major figures cemented their hold on power. Japanese Prime Minister Yasuhiro Nakasone's ruling Liberal Democratic Party won July elections by the largest margin in its 30-year history, while Mahathir Mohammad's ruling National Front coalition scored a landslide victory in Malaysia in August. In Bangladesh, H. M. Ershad won a presidential election boycotted by the opposition; in November, Ershad ended four years of martial law. Elsewhere, Indonesian President Suharto was nominated for a fifth term, and Thailand's Prem Tinsulanonda became the longest-serving premier in his country's history following midyear elections.

Diplomacy. Several major powers pursued new diplomatic initiatives in Asia. The USSR took the lead, wooing Japan, the non-Communist governments of Southeast Asia, China, and North Korea. In May, Eduard Shevardnadze became the first Soviet foreign minister to visit Japan in ten years. Subsequently, Soviet leader Mikhail Gorbachev made a major speech in Vladivostok calling for an expanded Pacific role for Moscow.

U.S. President Ronald Reagan visited Indonesia en route to a seven-nation economic summit in Tokyo in May, while Secretary of State George Shultz made two trips to visit key Southeast Asian leaders. Caspar Weinberger traveled to China, Pakistan, and India—the first visit ever of a U.S. secretary of defense to the latter land. After 55 years the United States also negotiated on possible recognition of Mongolia.

China signed a consular pact with pro-Soviet Mongolia after Moscow announced troop removals from that country. A Chinese vice premier visited the non-Communist nations of Southeast Asia. Beijing also moved to renew ties with Communist Eastern Europe.

Indian Prime Minister Rajiv Gandhi made a four-nation tour of Southeast Asia seeking to end the war in Cambodia. In November he hosted the second annual summit of the South Asian Association for Regional Cooperation.

Wars and Civil Strife. Conflict in Sri Lanka worsened; the seven-year-old war in Afghanistan was stalemated; and the struggle in Cambodia dragged on without major encounters.

More than 4,000 people have died in Sri Lanka's three-year-old civil war pitting the majority Sinhalese against Tamil Indian separatists. Indian Prime Minister Gandhi sought to encourage peace talks in Sri Lanka, but little progress was made because of recurring violence and the unwillingness of more militant Tamils to participate.

Afghanistan's armed conflict, in which 150,000 Soviet troops participated, already has resulted in the flight abroad of one third of the nation's people. Losing confidence in Afghan Communist leader Babrak Karmal, the Soviets installed a new party secretary, former secret police chief Sayid Mohammad Najibullah.

Some 150,000 Vietnamese troops remained in Cambodia, where an internally divided coalition of indigenous Communists and non-Communists continued to battle Vietnamese troops and the Vietnamese-backed government in Phnom Penh. China, aiding the rebels, refused to negotiate various issues with Moscow until the Soviets persuaded Vietnam to withdraw.

Other major violence included the persisting Communist insurgency in the Philippines. In India terrorism by Sikhs continued.

Economic Developments. Japan's economic influence remained preeminent, but Southeast Asians complained that Japan was shifting its investments to Europe and the United States. China continued to reduce the government's role in industry and commerce and cut back on its budget accordingly. Asia's four "miracle" economies—South Korea, Taiwan, Hong Kong, and Singapore—all experienced slowdowns after a prolonged period of sustained growth. Economic problems afflicted all the countries of Southeast Asia, albeit less so than in many other parts of the Third World.

RICHARD BUTWELL
California State University, Dominguez Hills

The 64 m (210 ft.) radio telescope at Parkes, Australia, was the major earth station for communications with the European space probe "Giotto," which passed near Halley's Comet in mid-March.

AP/Wide World

ASTRONOMY

For the United States, the so-called year in space exploration ended on Jan. 28, 1986, just as it was getting started. The destruction of the space shuttle *Challenger* not only cost the lives of seven astronauts, but it also put the American space program on hold at least until 1988 (*see* feature article, page 36). Directly affecting astronomers were the scrubbing of the Ulysses space probe to the sun and the Galileo mission to Jupiter. Also postponed were the launch of the $1 billion Hubble Space Telescope, the Magellan space probe to Venus, and the Astro-1 ultraviolet observatory, which was to have studied Halley's Comet.

Uranus. Ironically, the *Challenger* accident occurred just four days after the Voyager 2 spacecraft made its closest approach to the planet Uranus. Before this encounter, during which Voyager 2 came within 51,000 mi (82 000 km) of Uranus' cloud tops, virtually nothing had been known about the planet.

To Voyager's cameras, Uranus appeared as a virtually featureless blue ball. However, several identifiable markings indicated that Uranus' atmosphere rotates in a period of 16.9 hours at latitude 27° and 16.0 hours at 40°. Such a differential rotation indicates that the atmosphere has currents similar to those of Jupiter and Saturn, Uranus' gas-giant neighbors. The atmosphere itself was found to consist mainly of hydrogen, though helium accounts for 15% by mass.

Voyager 2 also confirmed that Uranus has a magnetic field, about 50 times stronger than the earth's, whose axis is tipped 60° to the planet's axis of rotation. Studies of variations in the measured strength of the magnetic field allowed astronomers to estimate the rotation of the planet's rocky core, which is some 10,000 mi (16 000 km) in diameter, at 17.2 hours.

Voyager also discovered ten new moons orbiting Uranus, increasing the planet's retinue of known natural satellites to 15. And photographs of the largest, previously known orbiting ice-worlds revealed some exciting and often confounding details. On Oberon, for example, Uranus' most distant moon, a mountain at least 12 mi (19 km) high was found.

The images from Voyager also revealed complex patterns of ridges and grooves on each of Uranus' four inner moons. In particular, roughly concentric features on Miranda suggested that this satellite had been shattered several times by colossal impacts and then reassembled from the fragments. The other inner moons may have shared similar fates at least once in their history.

Stars. In 1986 it appeared that astronomers for the first time witnessed the birth of a star. According to long-held theory, stars are formed as a consequence of collapsing dense clouds of dust and molecular gas. After enough of this cold material is drawn together and compacted by gravity, thermonuclear reactions begin and the star ignites. Yet the very nature of this process means that the protostar is born deep within a dark cloud and is concealed from view. It is not surprising, therefore, that the new discovery was made at radio wavelengths, which can penetrate into such opaque regions.

A team of scientists from Arizona and Missouri studied an object called IRAS 16293-2422, which lies in the constellation of Ophiuchus, about 520 light-years (3 million billion mi; 4.8 million billion km) away. The scientists found evidence that a cold cloud of gas more than 600,000 times larger than the sun has been collapsing for about 30,000 years. If material

Halley's Comet

Halley's Comet has come and gone. During its 30th recorded passage by the sun—an event that occurs only once every 76 years—the legendary visitor was seen by many millions of people throughout the world. Thousands of viewers from the Northern Hemisphere traveled to such places as Australia and South America to see the comet in the clearest and darkest skies possible. Not since the first manned landing on the moon in 1969 had such worldwide attention been focused on one celestial object.

Millions of other would-be comet-watchers never did glimpse Halley, though they tried with binoculars and telescopes made and marketed especially for the event. Astronomers

continues to accumulate at the present rate, our galaxy should gain another star like the sun in another 100,000 years.

Astronomers also were surprised by a pair of very old stars discovered inside a rich stellar cluster on the outskirts of our galaxy. Unlike the sun, which moves alone in space, most stars occur in binary or multiple systems. These groups typically revolve around each other in periods ranging from hours to thousands of years. An enormous number of such binary systems are known, but one discovered in 1986 set a record. Known as 4U 1820-30, its components revolve around each other in only 11 minutes. For this to happen, the stars have to be tiny, since the diameter of their orbit can not be larger than one third of the moon's distance from the earth. Scientists theorized that one of the stars is an earth-size white dwarf and that the other is a neutron star perhaps 10 mi (16 km) across. The exciting prospect is that such massive objects, rapidly revolving around each other, should produce gravity waves.

Gravity waves do not result from radiation, such as that which makes up the electromagnetic spectrum. Rather, they are caused by accelerated bodies (as 4U 1820-30), which create warps in space-time, the very fabric of the universe. The detection of gravitational waves from the pair of stars would thus provide another confirmation of Albert Einstein's general theory of relativity.

Pulsars. The lighthouses of our galaxy, pulsars sweep their beams across the earth with uncanny regularity. PSR 1855+09, located in the constellation of Aquila, was one of the special astronomical discoveries of 1986: it is only one of seven pulsars known to be members of binary-star systems and one of only three from which pulses are detected every 0.001 second or less. The two neutron stars that make up this object revolve around each other in a nearly circular orbit, resulting in an extremely accurate and stable natural clock. Comparison of pulse arrival-times from this object with those from a similar pulsar, PSR 1937+21, will provide astronomers with another sensitive detector of gravity waves.

Quasars. Looking like stars but having the brightness of galaxies, quasars have allowed astronomers their farthest view across the universe. Since the first one was discovered in

had predicted that Halley would not be a spectacular sight, especially from urban areas where its dim glow would be overwhelmed by artificial lighting. It was our bad luck, due to an inopportune earth-comet alignment, that Halley would put on its worst performance in 2,000 years.

Nevertheless, the comet behaved just about as expected, reaching its greatest brightness and sporting its longest tail in April. Throughout the world, probably every telescope at every observatory pointed to Halley at this time. Yet the most excitement and media attention occurred a month earlier, when three space probes plunged through the comet's head. Two of these, called Vega 1 and 2, were from the Soviet Union. The other was a European craft named Giotto, which dashed within 375 mi (600 km) of the comet's nucleus. Two Japanese spacecraft passed Halley at larger distances, 125,000 mi (200 000 km) for Suisei and 2 million mi (3.2 million km) for Sakigake.

What fundamental discoveries emerged from this enormous international effort? Few, if any, though the voluminous data will be studied for years. Rather, the earth- and space-based observations confirmed and refined established ideas about the physical makeup of comets and about the way these bodies are affected by radiation from the sun.

In particular, a prediction made in 1950 by Fred L. Whipple that comet nuclei are "dirty snowballs" composed of ices and dust was completely vindicated. Indeed, the "Holy Grail" sought by the Vega and Giotto probes were images of Halley's nucleus. Because of their small size, no cometary nucleus had ever been seen before. The best images were obtained by Giotto, which revealed an irregularly shaped ellipsoidal nucleus about 9 x 5 x 5 mi (14.5 x 8 x 8 km) in size whose surface is pockmarked by crater-like features. Giotto also observed several jets of dust emanating from the nucleus, which appeared to be largely covered by a very dark crust only about one inch (2.5 cm) thick.

Astronomers have estimated that each time Halley passes the sun its nucleus loses some 275 million tons (250 million metric tons) of material, or roughly .25% of the comet's total bulk. They also determined that, during the spacecrafts' encounters, the sunward side of Halley's nucleus had a temperature not much different than that of Death Valley on a midsummer's day—about 120°F (49°C). Thus, to shield the interior ice from the sun's heat, the comet's crust must be an excellent insulator.

Now that observations of Halley have confirmed our basic understandings of how comets work, the next step is to sample the actual stuff of a comet. The core is believed to contain the most primitive material in the solar system, providing important clues as to how the solar system, and even life, began. Obtaining the core material would require landing on a comet, a mission already under study by several nations.

LEIF J. ROBINSON

1960, scientists have detected a total of about 3,500. A quasar recognized in 1986 may prove quite special, however, for it could confirm how these objects are born. The quasar was detected by the now-defunct but enormously successful IRAS satellite, which recorded infrared radiation in space. Known as 13349+2438 and located in the constellation of Coma Berenices, the newly discovered quasar emits most strongly at a wavelength of 0.025 millimeter, which corresponds to a temperature of −279°F (−173°C).

A team of astronomers at the California Institute of Technology surmised that the quasar might have been born during the collision of two galaxies, which produced an immense cloud of dust. Such a cloud could both emit the observed infrared radiation and feed a putative black hole—which many theorists imagine to be at the heart of quasars. Because of its infrared emission, 13349+2438 also seems related to a class of galaxies called Seyferts. Thus, the newly discovered object may be the "missing link" between quasars and galaxies.

Cosmology. Over the past several decades, astronomers have become increasingly aware that galaxies do not usually exist alone in space. Rather, they cluster—even the clusters cluster—and between such agglomerations there seem to be huge empty voids. In 1986 astronomers at the Center for Astrophysics in Cambridge, MA, announced the results of an accurate survey of the three-dimensional distribution of galaxies in space. From their sample of 1,100 galaxies, they concluded that these systems of stars are arranged as though on the surface of bubbles. The bubbles, whose interiors are the voids, are typically 80 million light-years across.

A reinterpretation of the bubble universe theory came quickly. Astronomers at Princeton and Chicago universities concluded from the same data that the large-scale structure of the universe might be sponge-like. By this theory, there is actually only one void and one cluster of galaxies. Such an arrangement would come about by the intertwining of galaxy-filled regions of the universe with empty ones. Topologically, the configuration would be like that of the body of a sponge.

LEIF J. ROBINSON
"Sky & Telescope"

AUSTRALIA

During its fourth year in office, the Labor government of Prime Minister Robert J. Hawke faced growing pressure to solve Australia's serious economic problems. Polls indicated that Labor's level of public support had fallen markedly, to about 41%, while the opposition Liberal-Country coalition moved up to about 48%. Minor parties also gained strength.

For the first time in decades a conservative movement (widely labeled the New Right) took shape, and public opinion was clearly influenced by newly formed business groups concerned about broad economic trends and the dangers of Australia's decline in international competitiveness. Many people believed that the economy was desperately in need of restructuring if the nation was to regain forward momentum and avoid what Treasurer Paul Keating warned might become permanent regression.

The overall national scene was notable for a strong stock market and for greater public attention to the pursuit of wealth. The number of Australian millionaires reportedly passed 25,000, although general living standards declined due to an 8% inflation rate, and business leaders expressed concern over corporate tax hikes.

Economic Setting. The slump in world oil prices early in the year highlighted Australia's economic vulnerability. Trade prospects were shown once again to hinge critically on the underlying world demand for Australian exports, 80% of which remained commodity-based. Coal, a range of minerals, sugar, wheat, and most other exports declined; the two exceptions to the downward trend were wool and gold. Both gold and diamond mining had a big year. Gold output reached a level not touched since 1915, and diamond output rose sharply with initial production from Western Australia's rich Argyle deposit.

The budget, released in August, received unprecedented media attention and was seen as marking the end of the "lucky country" syndrome. It focused on improving the balance of payments, decreasing the foreign debt, and dealing with inflation, but many serious commentators found it inadequate. The lowered budgetary deficit (down from A \$5.7 billion to \$3.5 billion) was achieved, in the words of opposition leader John Howard, through "tax not axe." Outlays were set at \$74.7 billion and receipts at \$71.2 billion. Revenue-raising measures included a higher sales tax on some luxury items, an increased excise duty on gasoline, a rise in the universal medical-care levy, higher business taxes, and a delay in some tax cuts. The budget forecast a 2.25%, 12-month real increase in the gross domestic product (GDP) (widely branded as overly optimistic), an 8% rise in the consumer price index, a 6% average increase in earnings, and an unemployment rate above 8%. Meanwhile an official survey offered a somber outlook for business investment, with outlays unlikely to match inflation.

The budget's release intensified public discussion of such issues as productivity and the burden imposed on industry by the trade union movement's outlook and work practices, matters widely seen as central to Australia's problems. A review team from the Organization for Economic Cooperation and Development (OECD) noted "what seems to be a widespread Australian view of technology as in some sense external to national life," rather than applicable to a broad range of economic activities.

Political Scene. Members of the left-wing faction of Hawke's party opposed him for

Australia's Prime Minister Robert Hawke (left) traveled to London in early August for a summit of seven Commonwealth heads of state. Along with India's Prime Minister Rajiv Gandhi (right) and four other leaders, Hawke agreed to impose harsh economic sanctions against South Africa. Britain's Prime Minister Margaret Thatcher did not go along with the plan.

abandoning Labor policy on various issues, including his lifting of a ban on uranium exports to France. (The ban was adopted to protest French nuclear testing in the Pacific.) Efforts to censure Hawks failed due to his effective insistence on "cabinet solidarity." The media generally left the impression that Hawke deserved more praise than blame for his handling of economic problems. By contrast Liberal Party leader John Howard was perceived as still failing to create a cohesive opposition, with sound alternative policies on the fundamental issues.

In the Senate, where Australian Democrats held the balance of voting power, some legislation was turned back or amended, including a controversial Bill of Rights that the government later abandoned. Labor still led four of the six state-level administrations.

Crime and corruption appeared to be a fading issue despite continuing court cases. High Court Justice and Labor social reformer Lionel Murphy was acquitted early in 1986 of old charges of perverting the course of justice. A midyear parliamentary inquiry into Murphy's suitability to retain his judgeship was terminated when it became known that he was suffering from terminal cancer; he died in October. In New South Wales, where a corruption investigation involving Labor leaders and court officers dragged on, the long-serving Neville Wran stepped down as premier, and by-elections showed sharply diminished support for Labor.

Foreign Affairs and Defense. The keystone of Australian foreign and defense policy remained the U.S. alliance. On a visit to Washington, DC, in April, Hawke pledged continued support for key U.S. initiatives but urged that Australia be allowed continued access to U.S. markets and receive fair treatment in competitive markets. He also pointed out that "the close friendship" between the two countries did not require that they take identical views on every international issue. Australia maintained defense ties with New Zealand outside the ANZUS pact, from which New Zealand was formally suspended in 1986 for its refusal to permit visits by nuclear ships. A government decision not to take part directly in the U.S. Strategic Defense Initiative (SDI) research was criticized by the opposition.

In May, Foreign Minister Bill Hayden visited nine nations and ministates in the South Pacific, where Australia spends some $100 million annually in direct development programs and indirect aid, and is the principal aid donor. The visit coincided with a major parliamentary inquiry into Australia's South Pacific relationships that led to a new regional emphasis in foreign policy.

In midyear a far-reaching report on defense strategy prepared by defense analyst Paul Dibb was made public. The report proposed greater self-reliance in Australia's defense, a stance backed by the government. Dibb felt geography worked to Australia's advantage, with isolation providing security. Critics questioned Dibb's view that Australia would have at least a ten-year warning of a serious military threat and considered his emphasis on building up northern defenses and responding to low-level threats to be too simplistic.

Other. International tourism had a very good year, bolstered in part by publicity surrounding the America's Cup yachting race in Perth. Work continued on the Australian National Trail, scheduled for completion for the 1988 bicentennial. The "longest tourist trail in the world" makes use of historic routes from northern Queensland to Melbourne to open up wilderness areas previously inaccessible to the public.

A private civil-aviation corporation took over air traffic control, pilot briefings, and other flight support services from the Department of Aviation. The government awarded the commercial television license for central Australia—a remote inland area where 27% of the population is Aboriginal—to Imparja Television, a group sponsored by the Central Australian Aboriginal Media Association.

Immigration for 1985 exceeded 75,000, with Asians comprising up to 45% of the arrivals. The 1986 target was raised to 90,000 and emphasized attracting new settlers from European countries.

Archaeologists found evidence of "literally hundreds of stone structures," some ceremonial and others presumed to be dwellings, on uninhabited Highcliffy Island in the Buccaneer Archipelago, off the northwest coast. Work began on dating materials from the site.

Pope John Paul II visited Australia in November.

R. M. YOUNGER
Australian Author

AUSTRALIA · Information Highlights

Official Name: Commonwealth of Australia.
Location: Southwestern Pacific Ocean.
Area: 2,967,895 sq mi (7 686 848 km²).
Population (mid-1986 est.): 15,800,000.
Chief Cities (1984 est.): Canberra, the capital, 264,300; Sydney, 3,355,300; Melbourne, 2,888, 400; Brisbane, 1,145,400.
Government: *Head of state,* Elizabeth II, queen; represented by Sir Ninian Martin Stephen, governor-general (took office July 1982). *Head of government,* Robert Hawke, prime minister (took office March 11, 1983). *Legislature*—Parliament: Senate and House of Representatives.
Monetary Unit: Australian dollar (1.5681 A$ equal U.S.$1, Oct. 20, 1986).
Gross Domestic Product (1984 U.S.$): $173,-600,000,000.
Economic Indexes (1985): *Consumer Prices* (1980 = 100), all items, 148.8; food, 145.1. *Industrial Production* (Nov. 1985, 1980 = 100), 108.
Foreign Trade (1985 U.S.$): *Imports,* $23,450,-000,000; *exports,* $22,883,000,000.

AUSTRIA

The dominant events of 1986 in Austria were the presidential and parliamentary elections.

Government. President Rudolf Kirchschläger, after two six-year terms, was ineligible to run again. To replace him in the largely ceremonial post, the Socialist Party nominated Minister for Health and the Environment Kurt Steyrer. Kurt Waldheim, former foreign minister (1968–70) and secretary-general of the United Nations (1972–81), announced on Nov. 4, 1985, that he would run as an independent with the backing of the conservative opposition People's Party (*see* BIOGRAPHY). Two other candidates entered the field: antinuclear activist Freda Meissner-Blau and Otto Scrinzi, a right-wing pan-German nationalist and former Nazi SS member.

The campaign proceeded sluggishly until March, when the World Jewish Congress publicly charged that Waldheim had belonged to Nazi organizations during World War II and, as an officer in the German army, had participated in anti-Jewish measures and committed war crimes. The charges, which aroused nationalist feelings against foreign intervention and a certain degree of latent anti-Semitism in Austria, generally worked in Waldheim's favor. On May 4, he received 49.6% of the 4,800,000 votes cast. Steyrer received 43.7%, Meissner-Blau 5.5%, and Scrinzi 1.2%. In a June 8 runoff, Waldheim received 53.6% of the vote to Steyrer's 46.1%.

Chancellor Fred Sinowatz and Foreign Minister Leopold Gratz resigned in protest, and Finance Minister Franz Vranitzky succeeded Sinowatz as head of a reorganized Socialist-Freedom Party coalition government sworn in on June 16. Waldheim took his oath of office on July 8.

On September 15, two days after the Freedom Party elected far-right nationalist Jörg Haider as its new chairman, Vranitzky dissolved the government, declaring that the Freedom Party was no longer an acceptable coalition partner. Parliamentary elections were held on November 23. The Socialists received 43.33% of the vote to 41.29% for the People's Party. The Freedom Party, with 9.72%, more than doubled the share it had received in 1983. The United Green Party capitalized on concerns raised by the Soviet nuclear accident at Chernobyl and November chemical spills into the Rhine to capture 4.63% of the vote and enter parliament for the first time. After the election Vranitzky said he would try to form a coalition government with the People's Party.

Economy. The 1986 budget anticipated a gross deficit of 106,542 million schillings (about $6.7 million), up from 94,230 million schillings (about $6 million) for 1985. The increase was the result of a wage hike for civil servants and increased expenditures for social security, pensions, education, and environmental protection. The growth of the gross domestic product (GDP), originally estimated at 2.5% for 1986, was revised upward to 3% in the summer.

Worker concerns about job security increased after Voest-Alpine, Austria's largest industrial concern, announced a $778 million loss for 1985. A new board was appointed to streamline the concern, which was granted a large government subsidy. Legislation enacted early in 1986 gave the government more direct control over all 198 nationalized companies.

Foreign Affairs. An Arab terrorist attack on the Israeli airline desk at the Vienna airport on Dec. 27, 1985, led Austria to institute additional security measures in January. The Austrian embassy in Tripoli received minor damage when U.S. planes bombed Libya on April 14 in retaliation for Libyan involvement in international terrorism.

From 1965 to 1985, some 261,000 Soviet Jews had emigrated to Israel via Austria. Waldheim's election strained relations between the two countries, however, and led Israel to recall its ambassador from Vienna.

In July, Austrians seeking to demonstrate against the building of a nuclear reprocessing plant at Wackersdorf, in the West German state of Bavaria, were turned back at the border. This led to a brief dispute between the Bavarian government and Austria. (Austria's only nuclear power plant, at Zwentendorf, had never opened and was ordered dismantled.)

The Conference on Security and Cooperation in Europe assembled in Vienna on November 4. Only 8 of the 34 foreign ministers attending this third follow-up meeting to review progress on the 1975 Helsinki declaration held protocol meetings with Waldheim.

Donald S. Lauder succeeded Helen van Damm-Fuertler as U.S. ambassador to Austria.

ERNST C. HELMREICH, *Professor of History Emeritus, Bowdoin College*

AUSTRIA • Information Highlights

Official Name: Republic of Austria.
Location: Central Europe.
Area: 32,369 sq mi (83 835 km²).
Population (mid-1986 est.): 7,600,000.
Chief Cities (1981 census): Vienna, the capital, 1,531,346; Graz, 243,166; Linz, 199,910; Salzburg, 139,426; Innsbruck, 117,287.
Government: *Head of state,* Kurt Waldheim, president (took office July 1986). *Head of government,* Franz Vranitzky, chancellor (took office June 16, 1986). *Legislature*—Federal Assembly: Federal Council and National Council.
Monetary Unit: Schilling (13.87 schillings equal U.S. $1, Oct. 20, 1986).
Gross National Product (1984 U.S.$): $64,210,000,000.
Economic Indexes (1985): *Consumer Prices* (1980 = 100), all items, 126.9; food, 122.4. *Industrial Production* (1980 = 100), 109.
Foreign Trade (1985 U.S.$): *Imports,* $20,937,000,000; *exports,* $17,226,000,000.

© Paula Kobylarz

Driven by low-interest finance incentives, U.S. auto sales reached nearly 15.9 million units in the 1986-model year. Domestic manufacturers offered the low rates to stave off competition from imports and foreign "transplants."

AUTOMOBILES

The sales upturn in new cars and trucks continued to roll in high gear during the 1986-model year, rising to a new peak of nearly 15.9 million units from the previous record of 15.6 million set the year before. Fueling the retail sales volume for nearly all of 1986, especially for domestic cars, was a succession of low-interest finance programs. The rates offered in these campaigns, far below the lending rates at financial institutions, ranged from 7.9% at the outset of the 1986-model season to "zero interest" promoted by American Motors at the end of the model year.

The need for U.S.-headquartered automakers to "incentivize" dealership sales reflected stiffening competition from foreign-based competitors and their rising number of U.S. plants assembling "transplant" cars and trucks. Domestic car sales by the auto manufacturers headquartered in Detroit managed to keep pace in the 1986-model run with 1985-model-year volume of approximately 8.2 million cars, but the importers and their U.S.-built cars accounted for nearly all the sales growth and raised their share of the total U.S. market to slightly more than 30%.

Although most domestic auto executives were forecasting a 1987-model-year decline to between 15.0 millon and 15.4 million cars and trucks, importers were expected to keep their penetration of the U.S. market on the rise as more North American plants open. The 1987-model year appeared likely to elevate the import-plus-transplant share to one car out of three, and analysts were predicting that this could reach nearly 50% by 1990.

As far as Detroit-based producers were concerned, however, the steady advance of truck and van demand offset the transfer of more domestic volume to overseas-based competitors. Nearly 4.9 million trucks and vans were sold in the United States during the 1986-

model year, up from the former record of 4.6 million in 1985. The new wave of small vans and pickup trucks, plus four-wheel-drive utility vehicles, was indisputably making inroads in the traditional passenger-car market.

Hardest hit by the stiffened competition was industry leader General Motors, whose share of the total U.S. new-car market slipped nearly three percentage points in 1986, to 41%. It was GM that initiated the sales-spurring loan incentive programs in August 1985, and it was GM again that led the wave of 1986-model build-out programs a year later. Every one of GM's five car divisions sustained sales decreases in the 1986-model year, although the Chevrolet division outsold archrival Ford by 350,000 cars and trucks. Nevertheless, Ford earned higher net profits than GM in the second quarter of the year—a rare occurrence attributed to the popularity of Ford's newly introduced "aerodynamic" midsize Ford Taurus and Mercury Sable.

Ford took 18% of 1986 sales, with Chrysler accounting for about 11%. The fastest growing of the smaller domestic producers was Honda, nearing a 2% share as its assembly plant at Marysville, OH, added Civic subcompact cars to its Accord compacts and also began installing U.S.-built engines for the first time. Chrysler arranged with American Motors, whose Renault Alliance declined sharply in sales, for AMC's plant at Kenosha, WI, to assemble Chrysler's large luxury sedans in a historic production linkup between two domestic producers. The GM-Toyota plant at Fremont, CA, began building a sporty Toyota model as well as Chevrolet Nova cars. The Volkswagen facility at New Stanton, PA, also expanded its product lines, to include Jetta models along with Golfs.

The 1987 Models. Stung by American's unabated acceptance of foreign-car shapes and features, the domestic automakers set about filling the gaps in their product offerings. An upscale two-seater coupe called the Allante and priced at about $50,000 was introduced by GM's Cadillac division to compete with comparable cars from Mercedes-Benz and Porsche. Buick was to follow in 1987 with its own upmarket two-seater, the Reatta.

The popular Taurus-Sable look, departing from the boxiness of most early 1980s cars, was evident in the new Chevrolet Corsica and Beretta compacts and the Pontiac Bonneville midsize sedan. A redesigned version of Ford's top-selling pickup truck was released, as Ford found itself selling more trucks than cars for the first time.

Chrysler tested the imports with a $5,495 edition of its Omni-Horizon subcompact. Chrysler planned a two-seater luxury coupe of its own for late 1987, after expanding its lineup of "sporty" sedans and coupes with the Plymouth Sundance, Dodge Shadow, and revised Chrysler LeBaron models.

Also going upscale was Honda, now the fourth largest domestic entry, with the imported Acura Legend and Integra cars. AMC began a three-stage launch program with the imported Alpine coupe and Medallion sedan from Renault, climaxed by the Premier intermediate car to be built by its new Bramalea (Ontario) plant in 1987.

The Imports. U.S. sales of "pure" imported cars alone rose to 2,099,576 units in the first eight months of 1986, from 1,839,661 in the same period of 1985. The gain of 14.1% occurred despite continuation of export quotas by the Japanese government for the fifth year.

Picking up more than 111,000 units of the import increase were new entrants from South Korea and Yugoslavia—Hyundai and Yugo, respectively. Hyundai's Excel subcompact, priced from $4,995, racked up more than 100,000 sales through September even though it was sold in only 31 states. Hyundai already had become Canada's leading import seller in only two years on the market. Yugo's price for its minicompact was even lower, $3,990, but quality problems held down sales.

WORLD MOTOR VEHICLE DATA, 1985

Country	Passenger Car Production	Truck and Bus Production	Motor Vehicle Registrations
Argentina	113,788	23,887	5,073,000
Australia	383,763	27,569	8,832,800
Austria	7,118	6,605	3,080,214
Belgium	229,705	36,977	3,647,760
Brazil	758,840	207,785	11,584,119
Canada	1,077,935	855,446	14,672,500
Czechoslovakia	186,950	51,150	3,052,424
France	2,631,366	384,740	23,921,000
East Germany	198,000	46,000	3,429,994
West Germany	4,166,686	279,234	27,070,934
Hungary	–	14,834	1,511,329
India	102,456	128,655	3,047,950
Italy	1,389,156	183,751	22,833,000
Japan	7,646,816	4,624,279	44,523,586
South Korea	264,458	113,704	948,319
Mexico	246,960	151,232	6,918,683
The Netherlands	108,083	20,644	5,153,876
Poland	265,000	47,000	4,237,777
Spain	1,230,071	187,533	10,397,692
Sweden	400,748	60,324	3,304,567
United Kingdom	1,047,973	262,283	18,908,719
United States	8,184,821	3,465,500	168,607,000*
USSR	1,400,000	800,000	19,250,000
Yugoslavia	217,755	40,531	3,529,105
Total	32,258,448	12,020,663	473,278,361**

* U.S. total includes 130,053,000 cars and 38,554,000 trucks and buses. U.S. total does not include Puerto Rico, which has 1,200,000 vehicles. ** World total includes 364,814,214 cars and 108,464,147 trucks and buses. Other countries with more than one million vehicle registrations include China, 1,800,000; Colombia, 1,091,751; Denmark, 1,692,710; Finland, 1,656,828; Greece, 1,769,637; Indonesia, 2,000,000; Iran, 2,103,948; Malaysia, 1,100,000; New Zealand, 1,706,744; Nigeria, 1,246,920; Norway, 1,643,761; Portugal, 1,482,000; Saudia Arabia, 3,560,698; South Africa, 4,115,689; Switzerland, 2,755,681; Thailand, 1,125,000; Turkey, 1,440,131, and Venezuela, 2,916,000. Source: Motor Vehicle Manufacturers Association of the United States, Inc.

On tap for 1987 were additional new models in the high-end and low-end segments of the import market. The upscale newcomers were the Volvo 780, the restyled Jaguar XJ6, and Ford Scorpio. Subaru's Justy minicar and Volkswagen's Fox subcompact, built in Brazil, were coming in the $5,000–$6,000 range.

In addition, the drive to lower production costs prompted Ford to import the Tracer subcompact and Festiva minicompact from Mexico and South Korea, respectively, while GM's Pontiac division was set to bring in its LeMans subcompact from South Korea.

MAYNARD M. GORDON
Editor, "Motor News Analysis"

Photo courtesy of Honda Motor Co., Inc.

Honda, the fourth largest entry in the U.S. market, took aim at upscale buyers with its new Acura-line imports, including the Integra, right.

BANGLADESH

Bangladesh in 1986 showed steady economic growth and halting progress toward civilian rule.

Politics. The major political events of the year were the May 7 parliamentary elections and a presidential election on October 18. Both were important steps in President H.M. Ershad's plan to civilianize, institutionalize, and legitimatize his martial-law regime. Ershad and his Jatiya Party (JP) were the clear winners in both contests, as expected.

The May elections were marred by widespread violence and cheating. Repolling was necessary in 36 constituencies where stealing of ballot boxes and other abuses occurred. Despite its earlier threat to boycott the elections, the 15-party alliance led by Sheikh Hasina Wajed's Awami League (AL) ultimately participated. The other major political grouping, the seven-party alliance led by the Bangladesh National Party (BNP) of Begum Khaleda Zia, abstained. The JP won a slight majority (153) of the 300 directly elected parliamentary seats and was able to augment its position by electing 30 additional members to seats reserved for women and minorities, by winning subsequent by-elections, and by other means. Its resultant strength of 210 in the 330-member parliament was just short of the two-thirds majority needed to pass constitutional amendments. The AL secured 76 seats, the Muslim fundamentalist Jamaat-i-Islami 10, and the Communist Party of Bangladesh 6. Mizanur Rahman Chowdhury was named prime minister.

In order to contest the fall presidential election as a civilian, Ershad resigned from the army and from his position as chief of army staff on August 31. As president, however, he remained chief martial law administrator and commander in chief of the armed forces. He then officially joined the JP, was elected its chairman on September 2, and became its nominee for president. Although some minority parties fielded candidates, both the AL and the BNP boycotted the elections because of Ershad's failure to lift martial law first. Voter turnout was low. Ershad said he would not lift martial law until parliament agreed to ratify a measure legalizing all the actions taken by the martial law regime. In November martial law was ended, and the Constitution was revived. That same month in a major cabinet shuffle, Ershad appointed A.K.M. Nurul Islam, a former Supreme Court judge, as vice-president. He also dismissed the home minister and five other ministers and inducted six ministers.

The Economy. The Bangladesh economy continued to show steady growth during 1986, with a 5% increase in the gross domestic product. Expansion in food grain production outpaced population growth, permitting a decrease in food imports. Industrial production, after a slump in the early 1980s, has rebounded strongly. During 1980–85, nontraditional exports grew at about 20% per year. Domestic energy sources have expanded steadily, and lower world oil prices helped to keep inflation to less than 10% during 1986. Remittances from overseas Bangladeshi workers were expected to increase from $400 million to $550 million during 1986 but to fall in fiscal 1987 because of cutbacks in the Middle East. All these factors helped to boost foreign exchange reserves by about $100 million, to about $450 million.

On the negative side unemployment in 1986 rose to 32%, and landlessness increased to more than 50%. During the last five years literacy has declined by 1% to 26%. To respond to these needs, the government adopted a five-point short-term program calling for higher economic growth; increased investment in labor-intensive projects; self-employment projects; the expansion of social services, including education and health care; and the targeting of resources to specific groups through "food for work" programs.

Ethnic Conflict and External Relations. Bangladesh suffered further ethnic conflict in the Chittagong Hill Tracts, where the predominantly Buddhist tribal population has long been resisting the intrusion of Bengali-speaking Muslims into their traditional homelands. On April 30, following guerrilla attacks on Muslim settlers and Muslim reprisals against the tribal people, some 10,000 refugees fled into the Indian states of Tripura and Mizoram. Despite tensions over these problems, relations with neighboring India improved during 1986.

In November, as part of a 14-day tour of Asia and the Pacific, Pope John Paul II visited the Roman Catholic community in Bangladesh. During his one-day visit, he advocated joint efforts among diverse religious groups in order to better the future condition of humanity.

WILLIAM L. RICHTER
Kansas State University

BANGLADESH • Information Highlights

Official Name: People's Republic of Bangladesh.
Location: South Asia.
Area: 55,598 sq mi (143 998 km^2).
Population (mid-1986 est.): 104,100,000.
Chief Cities (1981 census): Dhaka, the capital, 3,430,312; Chittagong, 1,391,877; Khulna, 646,359; Rajshahi, 253,740.
Government: *Head of state,* Hussain Mohammad Ershad, chief executive (assumed power March 24, 1982) and president (Dec. 1983). *Head of government,* Mizanur Rahman Chowdhury, prime minister (took office July 1986). *Legislature*—Parliament.
Monetary Unit: Taka (30.3 taka equal U.S.$1, June 1986).
Gross National Product (fiscal 1983 U.S.$): $11,600,000,000.
Economic Indexes: *Consumer Prices* (1985, 1980 = 100), all items, 163.3; food, 169.0.
Foreign Trade (1985, U.S.$): *Imports,* $2,170,000,000; *exports,* $927,000,000.

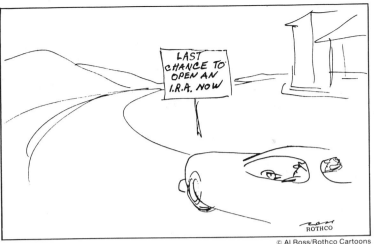

The cartoon at left illustrates the banking community's all-out effort of recent years to encourage customers to open Individual Retirement Accounts (IRAs). Under the 1986 tax law, however, the full deduction for IRAs will be limited to those workers not covered by company pension plans and to married persons with incomes up to $40,000 and single persons with incomes of less than $25,000.

BANKING AND FINANCE

The major developments in U.S. banking and finance during 1986 were the lowering of interest rates, the failure of up to 150 banks, and the continued restructuring of financial services.

Interest Rates. For the typical American, the decline in interest rates was the year's most important trend. Rates fell primarily as a consequence of the slowdown in inflation, caused by declines in energy prices, the new competition created by widespread deregulation, and the fact that foreigners were using much of the money they earned from the $180 billion U.S. balance of payments deficit to help finance the $220 billion U.S. budget deficit for fiscal year 1986.

In real terms of what money could buy, however, interest rates actually remained high. In the early 1980s, when inflation reached 18½%, the top borrowers were paying banks a prime rate of up to 21½%, yielding a "real" interest cost of only 3%. In 1986, with the prime rate at about 7½% and the inflation rate between 2% and 3%, the actual cost of borrowing, after removing the inflationary erosion of the borrowed funds' value, exceeded 5%. In real terms, savers were no longer subsidizing borrowers by accepting interest rates that did little more than offset the impact of inflation. The higher real cost of borrowing helped explain why so many more borrowers were having trouble repaying their debts and were defaulting on mortgages and business loans more than in previous years. Borrowers in certain geographical areas were no longer being bailed out by steady increases in the value of their property, as was the case in the early 1980s.

Be this as it may, many individuals who saved in 1986 still felt that they were being hurt. They generally did not see the immediate impact of lower inflation, but they did see declining rates paid on their certificates of deposit

(CDs), Individual Retirement Accounts (IRAs), and conventional savings accounts, with some banks even lowering their passbook rates below the 5½% level that had been the floor for years. Thus, savers were looking for higher-yield investment alternatives. When CD rates had been high, few depositors thought of moving funds elsewhere, but the recent decline in interest rates—while still less than the decline in inflation—had the public shopping for new savings instruments. Investment companies, in turn, began heavy marketing efforts to attract the public's funds into securities backed by the Federal National Mortgage Association (FNMA) and the Government National Mortgage Association (GNMA), as well as such other managed investments as municipal bond trusts.

The general decline in interest rates also focused considerable attention on the credit card business. For while the rates paid to savers and charged to other types of borrowers fell substantially, credit card interest rates declined only marginally. Banks justified this by saying that the cost of handling credit cards remained high and that the rate charged to customers was in part a payment for the credit card service. Nevertheless, the U.S. Congress began taking a close look at credit card rates, with talk of legislation to limit what banks can charge on outstanding credit card debts. Bankers were less worried about this than they might have been in the past, however, since the tax reforms taking effect in 1987 would encourage the public to borrow through lines of credit based on equity in their homes rather than through the use of credit cards. Under the new tax measure, interest on home equity loans remains tax deductible, while interest on credit card debts does not. (*See also* special report, page 508.)

Bank Failures. While much of the United States remained confident in its banking organizations, people in areas of economic distress

—notably agricultural and petroleum-producing regions—were worried about the health of their banks. The year 1986 was expected to see 150 or more U.S. banks go under, in most cases because poor economic conditions forced borrowers to default on loans. Failure in other cases was the result of poor management, and in a few instances due to outright fraud. In virtually every case, the federal insuring agencies —the Federal Deposit Insurance Corporation (FDIC) and the Federal Savings and Loan Insurance Corporation (FSLIC), arranged mergers with healthy institutions to protect depositors from loss of funds. Nevertheless, there was considerable fear that these insurers might run out of money. And while officials of the FDIC and FSLIC emphasized that they are government agencies and would be able to tap Federal Reserve funds to remain solvent, there was still an undertone of fear. On any rumor of trouble, many depositors were quick to move funds from one institution to another.

Another issue that hurt the image of U.S. banking in 1986 was the heavy publicity given to the practice of delaying the time between a customer's deposit and the crediting of the funds to his or her account. Because some banks have made customers wait a considerable time before the deposits are deemed collected and usable, many states passed or considered laws to limit the delay.

Structural Changes. The year 1986 also saw the continuation of major shifts in the structure of U.S. banking. Of these shifts, the most notable was the continuation of the trend toward "regional banking," under which a bank holding company acquires banks in various states within its designated region. Previous years had already seen a movement away from "unit banking," in which a bank is confined to a single building, to a system based on branch banking and holding company networks spread throughout a state. Since 1985, however, a U.S. Supreme Court ruling and new legislative action in several states have allowed banks to go interstate—usually within a geographic region. The new rules have given rise to "superregional banks," which buy up smaller banks in as many states as the laws allow.

The troubles of banking institutions in major agricultural and oil-producing areas have furthered the structural shift. In order to find saviors for troubled banks in their states, some legislatures have been forced to pass laws allowing out-of-state organizations to buy up local institutions.

With the trend expected to continue in the years to come, it seemed likely that regional banking would eventually be supplanted by nationwide banking. However, this would not mean that only a handful of giant institutions would survive, since small community banks seem to flourish alongside giant institutions. Already a large number of new banks are being chartered by local groups that feel there is a niche for smaller institutions that provide personal service in a world of impersonal banking giants. In many instances, moreover, the smaller banks are more profitable than their larger counterparts because of tighter cost control, simpler organization, and less expenditure on complex services.

Services. Despite the heavy promotion of banking in the home, bill paying by telephone, and other new services, the typical bank customer apparently still prefers traditional service by human beings instead of machines. Remote banking has continued to expand and many customers have become accustomed to automatic teller machines (ATMs), but still only about one third of U.S. bank customers make use of the machines.

To the extent allowed by law, U.S. banks in 1986 also expanded their operations in the discount brokerage and insurance businesses. And slowly but surely, the barriers that prevent banks from doing investment banking business —i.e., serving as middlemen in the placement of new securities with the public—are being broken down.

All in all, however, the breakdown of restraints on bank diversification is a two-way street. For just as banks are becoming free to compete in other financial service markets, so investment companies and others are steadily encroaching on banking's traditional territory. Through the use of so-called "nonbank banks" —organizations that eliminate one banking service and thus are not subject to banking law— such companies as Sears Roebuck and American Express are able to offer the public more and more banking services. And while some bankers have lobbied for closing the nonbank-bank loophole, Congress has taken no such action for two main reasons. Many lawmakers feel that the public benefits from the competition and the wider choice of financial service providers. And just as many lawmakers feel that banks are stronger if they can diversify, since they are no longer dependent on a single industry or service for their prosperity. Thus, it seemed unlikely that there would be any reversal of the trend in the foreseeable future.

Canada. The same trend toward diversification has been witnessed in Canada in recent years. The "four pillars" of banking and finance—banks, insurance companies, trust companies, and brokerage operations—all are expanding into services formerly reserved for the other sectors. At the same time, with structural changes similar to the ones taking place in the United States, Canadian banks have been trying to broaden their scope. All in all, "deregulation" is becoming the central theme in the Canadian financial picture, though perhaps not so rapidly as in the United States.

PAUL S. NADLER
Rutgers University

BELGIUM

Encouraged by success at the polls the preceding October, Belgium's Christian Democrat-Liberal coalition moved in 1986 to establish control over regional and communal councils throughout the country. This was achieved with little difficulty in Flanders, but in Wallonia the Socialists and Greens ("Ecolos") held enough seats to stymie the coalition. Only by successfully challenging the credentials of one member did the coalition gain a single-vote majority in the latter regional council.

Economy. The nation's domestic debt in 1985 amounted to 12% of the gross national product (GNP), while the external debt equaled 101% of the GNP. The popular Prime Minister Wilfried Martens chose Flemish Liberal leader and monetarist Guy Verhofstadt as his new budget minister, and together they proposed major austerity measures. Martens' goal for 1987 was to cut domestic deficits to 8% of GNP by reducing the size of the government and the extensive social welfare program. Hard bargaining within the cabinet produced an agreement to cut public spending over 18 months by 195 billion francs ($4.25 billion), or about 10% of the federal budget. The heaviest reductions would be made in education, social security, and subsidies to nationalized industries.

In a country where the government employs about one third of the work force, union leaders charged that the budget cuts would mean high unemployment and loss of needed services. In May and June, major strikes were called for the nation's schools, transportation system, and postal service. But the government held firm in its austerity plans, aided by the reluctance of the Confederation of Christian Trade Unions fully to support strikes against the program of a Christian Democratic prime minister.

The positive economic effect of public spending cuts also was threatened by large interest payments on the $130 billion public debt. In midsummer the government reached an agreement with Belgian banks whereby direct interest charges on $30 billion of long-term debt would be limited to 8%. The government would thereby gain an estimated savings of $2.3 billion in interest payments over five years; sources indicated that the banks were promised no new taxes until at least 1990.

Wholesale prices fell in the first half of the year, but this had scant effect on consumer prices. Exports and imports declined by July, and although industrial production showed some growth in the first half, construction starts were down. By late summer, unemployment had risen to 12.6%, with more than 532,400 persons seeking jobs.

Efforts to expand Belgium's role in the international shipping industry continued. Major dredging was undertaken to make Antwerp, already the principal container-handling port in Western Europe, accessible to carriers with 50-ft (15-m) draft. The Berendrecht lock, the largest in the world, neared completion. And at Zeebrugge, newly inaugurated harbor facilities, the result of a major engineering and construction effort, brought increased traffic as well.

Government Crisis. The austerity program and government stability itself were threatened in mid-October, when the Belgian Council of State disallowed the election of José Happart as mayor of the commune of Voerens (Fourons) because he refused to speak Flemish at official functions or to prove his bilingualism, as required by law. Happart had been elected in 1982 on a program calling for the commune to be reassigned across the linguistic border, from the province of Limburg to that of Liège, where the official language is French. Flemish Christian Democrats made Happart's dismissal a matter of principle, while Walloons of the same party refused such action. With the cabinet split, Martens offered his resignation on October 14, but King Baudouin refused to accept it. Interior Minister Charles-Ferdinand Nothomb, a French-speaking Christian Democrat who had failed in efforts to work out a compromise, then resigned. The cabinet remained intact with Joseph Michel as Nothomb's replacement, but the local problem of Voerens remained unresolved.

Other. Belgians cheered the success of their national soccer team, which reached the semifinals of the World Cup tournament in Mexico (*see* SPORTS—Soccer). Progress was made in discovering the hideouts of the terrorist Communist Combatant organization. Under pressure from the Flemish wings of the ministerial coalition, the Chambers voted to ban deployment of chemical weapons in Belgium, despite a resolution by the North Atlantic Treaty Organization (NATO) endorsing U.S. production.

J. E. HELMREICH, *Allegheny College*

BELGIUM • Information Highlights

Official Name: Kingdom of Belgium.
Location: Northwestern Europe.
Area: 11,792 sq mi (30 540 km²).
Population (mid-1986 est.): 9,900,000.
Chief Cities (Dec. 31, 1983): Brussels, the capital, 982,434; Antwerp (including suburbs), 488,425; Ghent, 235,401; Charleroi, 213,041; Liège, 203,065; Bruges, 118,146.
Government: *Head of state,* Baudouin I, king (acceded (1951). *Head of government,* Wilfried Martens, prime minister (formed new government Oct. 1985). *Legislature*—Parliament: Senate and Chamber of Representatives.
Monetary Unit: Franc (42.47 francs equal U.S.$1, Oct. 27, 1986).
Gross National Product (1984 U.S.$): $76,300,-000,000.
Economic Indexes (1985): *Consumer Prices* (1980 = 100), all items, 140.5; food, 140.6. *Industrial Production* (1980 = 100), 103.
Foreign Trade (1985 with Luxembourg, U.S.$): *Imports,* $56,130,000,000; *exports,* $53,659,000,000.

BIOCHEMISTRY

Research on the biochemistry of cancer was once again in the forefront in 1985–86. A development that promises to become a classic was the discovery that certain RNA molecules can act as biosynthetic enzymes.

Cancer. In the past several years, scientists have determined that the 30 or so cancer-causing genes (oncogenes) are in fact cellular genes that upon modification transform a normal cell into a cancerous state. Evidence exists that most oncogenes control the formation of either growth hormones or their receptors. One oncogene whose function had remained unknown was erb-A, which cooperates with the oncogene erb-B in causing leukemia, at least in chickens. This mystery was solved with the discovery that erb-A oncogene shares similarities with the gene that controls the formation of the receptor for certain steroid hormones in chickens, humans, rats, and mice. The receptor is thought to bind the steroid, and the complex then interacts with the DNA resulting in the expression of a battery of genes. It is possible that erb-A makes a defective receptor.

It also was recognized that cancer may not only be caused by oncogenes but also due to the loss of suppressor genes that constrain the growth of normal cells. Indeed, both observations may be important in cancer development. Studies demonstrated that cells that have lost part of a chromosome with the suppressor gene become cancerous when exposed to an oncogene. But the effect of such an exogenously added oncogene is nullified when the cells also are transfected with the suppressor gene. Studies were underway to determine how suppressor genes work.

In another major development with medical implications beyond cancer, a team of biochemists led by Bert Vallee at Harvard purified a protein—angiogenin—that triggers the growth of new blood vessels. That such a substance exists was suggested by the studies of Moses Judah Folkman, also of Harvard, who demonstrated in the early 1970s that solid tumors must have new blood vessels for continued growth and proposed that this is due to the release of a chemical of the tumor cells. Although Vallee's group used the culture medium in which human colon cancer cells had been grown as the starting point to purify angiogenin, it has been detected in the human liver as well. The researchers demonstrated that fertilized chicken eggs and the corneas of rabbits —which normally have no blood vessels—developed capillaries when injected with a minute amount of the pure protein.

Angiogenin is composed of a single chain of 123 amino acids and, surprisingly, bears striking resemblance to another protein ribonuclease—an enzyme that degrades RNA. However, angiogenin does not degrade RNA, and ribonuclease does not promote blood vessel growth. Using recombinant DNA technology, the researchers succeeded in cloning the gene for angiogenin, which would make it possible to produce the protein in relatively large amounts. The discovery of angiogenin has several medical implications. For example, antibodies to angiogenin might be used to block its action thereby controlling solid tumor growth; or, conversely, angiogenin could be used to increase blood supply to organs when necessary —as in the case of heart attack or stroke, or to speed up the healing of wounds.

Ribozymes. It has been an article of faith among biochemists that all enzymes are proteins, where enzymes are catalysts that accelerate metabolic reactions. However, this basic concept has been shaken within the past couple of years by the discovery that certain RNA molecules also can act as enzymes (ribozymes). Ribosomal RNA (rRNA), like other types of cellular RNA, is composed of nucleotides and is derived from a precursor RNA by the removal of a group of intervening nucleotides (called an intron) followed by splicing of the two ends. In the protozoan *Tetrahymena*, the intron is 413-nucleotides long and is precisely removed from the precursor, and then the two ends are spliced to generate the functional rRNA. In 1984, Thomas Cech and his associates at the University of Colorado made the astonishing discovery that this process occurs in the absence of a protein catalyst—in effect, RNA is capable of self-splicing by virtue of the fact that the intron snips itself out of the precursor and splices the two ends to form the mature rRNA. The extruded intron subsequently nibbles off 19 nucleotides from one of its ends to generate a shortened version.

In a series of classic research papers, published in 1986, Cech and his associates demonstrated that the shortened intron has the capacity to replicate itself in the absence of protein enzymes, and thus acts as a true biosynthetic enzyme, as well as its own template. The new discovery brings with it speculation as to the chemical events in the prebiotic world and makes the idea that life originated from RNA quite possible.

AIDS Virus. And scientists purified an enzyme from AIDS virus that is crucial to its ability to infect human cells. The key enzyme is reverse transcriptase (also found in RNA-containing cancer viruses) which permits the AIDS virus to transcribe the message contained in its genetic material (RNA) into that of DNA—a step that is essential for the virus to reproduce itself in the susceptible cells. Availability of the pure enzyme permitted scientists to test drugs that might block its action. The drug azidothymidine (AZT) was found to do just that.

See also MEDICINE AND HEALTH.

PREM P. BATRA
Wright State University

BIOGRAPHY

A selection of profiles of persons prominent in the news during 1986 appears on pages 134–46. The affiliation of the contributor is listed on pages 591-94; biographies that do not include a contributor's name were prepared by the staff. Included are sketches of:

AQUINO, Corazon Cojuangco

On Feb. 25, 1986, Corazon Cojuangco Aquino became the first woman president of the Philippines; and Ferdinand Marcos, also inaugurated for another term, fled into exile in Hawaii. Despite gross intimidation and fraud during the February 7 election and Marcos' being proclaimed winner by his National Assembly, a virtually bloodless ''people's revolution'' determined ''Cory'' Aquino's right to rule. It was the immovable and peaceful determination of the Philippine people that made Aquino's victory inevitable.

She was a reluctant presidential candidate, but once she agreed to run, she spent 16-hour days on the campaign trail and gained confidence as the campaign wore on. President Aquino selected a cabinet to oversee reforms and the recovery of national wealth allegedly plundered by her predecessors and appointed a constitutional commission to restore complete democracy.

In addition to the need for a workable, democratic government and the elimination of the nepotistic excesses of the Marcos years, a battered economy and a Communist insurgency movement were major problems facing the new president. In August, President Aquino traveled to Indonesia and Singapore. It was her first foreign trip as president. The following month, she visited the United States, where she addressed the United Nations and the U.S. Congress and met with President Reagan. Economic aid and the Communist guerrilla situation were prime topics of the presidential talks. In November, Mrs. Aquino went to Japan and was promised additional aid by the Japanese leadership. Upon her returning to the Philippines, she dismissed several members of her cabinet, including Defense Minister Juan Ponce Enrile, and the government and the insurgents signed a 60-day cease-fire. (*See* page 26.)

Background. Corazon Cojuangco was born Jan. 25, 1933, in Tarlac Province on Luzon island to a sugar-plantation family. Her grandfather had been a senator, and her father was a congressman. After attending convent schools in Manila, Philadelphia, PA, and New York, she was graduated from the College of Mount Saint Vincent in Riverdale, NY, in 1953 with a degree in French and mathematics. Back in the Philippines she met again the charismatic Benigno Aquino, who came from the same province. After their wedding on Oct. 11, 1954, she dropped out of law school and helped him campaign for mayor, governor, and senator. He expected to be chosen president in 1973, since the constitution limited President Marcos to two terms; but in 1972, Marcos declared martial law and imprisoned Aquino. In 1973, Marcos substituted a constitution giving himself indefinite rule.

Mrs. Aquino's visits with her husband during his 7½ years imprisonment transformed her. She visited Benigno several times weekly, on holidays bringing their four daughters and one son, and became his link with his followers. He coached her for press conferences that she held regularly. In 1979 when he ran unsuccessfully for the Interim Assembly from prison, she campaigned in his behalf. The opposition leader was released from prison and allowed to go to Texas for a triple heart bypass in 1980. Later the Aquinos lived quietly outside Boston. Benigno's assassination in Manila in 1983 only convinced her to continue his work for justice through nonviolence. Mrs. Aquino worked hard for the opposition during the 1984 National Assembly elections.

The 5'2" (1.57 m) president is known for her stamina, humor, and independent will. She is a devout Roman Catholic. Although as chief executive her free time will be limited, she enjoys bonsai growing and gourmet cooking. Throughout the presidential campaign and during her first days in office, Cory Aquino always dressed in yellow. She did so to commemorate her late husband.

GRETCHEN CASPER

BOGGS, Wade Anthony

In 1986, Boston Red Sox third baseman Wade Boggs won the American League (AL) batting title for the third time in his five-year career. His average of .357 raised his career standard to an amazing .352, by far the highest among active major league players. His 207 hits represented the fourth consecutive season in which he reached the 200 plateau.

The 6'2" (1.88-m), 185-lb (84-kg) Nebraska native, who hits left-handed and throws right-handed, also helped the Red Sox win the 1986 AL Eastern Division crown with a record of 95-66, as well as the AL pennant with a 4-games-to-3 defeat of the California Angels in the League Championship Series (LCS). With outstanding play at third base, an aspect of his game at which he has improved considerably over the years, and with strong (if perhaps slightly under par) hitting, he also helped bring his team to a seventh-game confrontation with the New York Mets in the World Series (*see* SPORTS —Baseball).

Background. The son of a U.S. Marine and Air Force veteran, Wade Anthony Boggs was born on June 15, 1958, in Omaha, NE. At H. B. Plant High School in Tampa, FL, he batted .522—the highest in the state—in his junior year and .485 in his senior year. As a seventh-round pick in the 1976 draft, he was offered a mere $7,500 to sign a minor league contract—an offer he quickly accepted.

After five years in the minors (batting over .300 in four of them), Boggs finally got his chance with the Red Sox in 1982. As a part-time player he batted .349 that season, and in 1983 he won his first batting crown with a .361 average (210 hits). The following year he posted figures of .325 and 203 hits, climbing to a league-high .368 and 240 hits—the most in the major leagues in 55 years—in 1985. Despite his personal and team achieve-

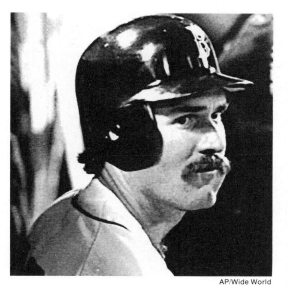

AP/Wide World

Wade Boggs

ments, 1986 was also a year of deep loss and disappointment for Boggs. After the sudden death of his mother in the spring, he dedicated the remainder of the season to her memory. The season ended with 6–5 and 8–5 losses to the New York Mets in the World Series after the Red Sox had led 3 games to 2.

Meticulous and disciplined in everything from his diet to his hitting—qualities he attributes to his father—Boggs follows the same rituals to prepare for every game. When the Red Sox play at home at night, the routine begins at 2 P.M., when the third baseman sits down with his wife Debbie and daughter Meagann for their daily chicken dinner. The Boggs' are coauthors of a chicken cookbook, *Fowl Tips* (1984). A son, Brett, was born to the couple late in 1986.

Breslin, Jimmy

Feisty, street-smart, and tough-talking, the New York newspaperman and novelist Jimmy Breslin has long been acknowledged as an authentic voice of the urban working class. His newspaper columns and books, filled with Runyonesque local color and characters like Fat Thomas and Marvin the Torch, are earmarked by their pitch-perfect vernacular, fresh points of view, and compassion for the underdog. In 1986, Breslin's journalistic and literary skills won new acclaim. He received a Pulitzer Prize and George Polk Award for his columns in the New York *Daily News* on police use of "stun guns" to torture suspects, the plight of AIDS victims, and the controversy over subway gunman Bernhard Goetz (whose action he opposed). Meanwhile, his latest novel, *Table Money*, the story of a husband and wife in Breslin's native Queens, NY, earned praises for its boisterous but sensitive dramatization of social stresses. As the year wore on, the 56-year-old maverick journalist helped break open a widespread scandal in New York City government (*see* NEW YORK CITY). In addition, ABC-TV introduced a new late-night series, *Jimmy Breslin's People,* for the fall season. (The show did not last, however.) Ever brash, often called rude, the bushy-browed Breslin already began declaring himself the winner of the 1987 Pulitzer.

Background. Jimmy Breslin was born in Jamaica, Queens, on Oct. 17, 1929. His mother was a high-school English teacher and later a social worker. Breslin attended a parochial elementary school and a public high school in Queens. He enrolled in Long Island University

in 1947, but already he was working at a newspaper. Starting out as a sportswriter, he bounced from paper to paper during the 1950s, ending up at the New York *Journal-American*. His first book, *Sunny Jim: The Life of America's Most Beloved Horseman, James Fitzsimmons* (1962), got little attention. But his second title, *Can't Anybody Here Play This Game?* (1963); about the first year of the New York Mets baseball team, was well received. Subsequent works included *The Gang That Couldn't Shoot Straight* (1969), a movie version of which appeared in 1971; *World Without End, Amen* (1973); *How The Good Guys Finally Won* (1975); and *Forsaking All Others* (1982).

Breslin became a regular columnist for the New York *Herald Tribune* in May 1963 and, after a merger two years later, for the *World Journal Tribune*. That paper folded in 1967, and Breslin began writing for *New York* magazine, which he helped launch as an independent weekly. He also wrote briefly for the New York *Post* and did some television commentary. In a brief and unsuccessful venture into politics, Breslin entered the 1969 New York Democratic primary election as a candidate for city council president, on a ticket with Norman Mailer for mayor. In July 1971 he resigned from *New York* in a dispute over the magazine's upper-class orientation. The following year he became a regular news commentator for WNBC-TV in New York, and in 1976 he took his act to the *Daily News.*

Breslin's first wife, with whom he had six children, died in 1981. He has since remarried and moved from Queens to Central Park West in Manhattan.

CHIRAC, Jacques René

On March 15, 1986, the voters of France ended five years of Socialist rule, giving a narrow parliamentary majority to a conservative alliance. Socialist President François Mitterrand, faced with choosing a prime minister from the opposition, announced his choice three days later: Jacques Chirac, 53, the hard-driving mayor of Paris, the head of France's largest conservative party—the neo-Gaullist Rally for the Republic (RPR)—and the premier for two years (1974–76) under President Valery Giscard d'Estaing. Following intense negotiations with Elysée Palace, Chirac formally accepted the premiership and announced his cabinet on March 20. "The French must understand," he said in his first declaration as prime minister, "that the moment has come to put an end to divisions and to rally for the renewal of our country."

It was a moment of unparalleled triumph for the politically ambitious, ideologically flexible Parisian native. Not only was it a vindication of his conservative platform of law-and-order and deregulation, but it put him in a unique executive power-sharing arrangement—called "cohabitation"—with the Socialist president. A first sign of Chirac's flexibility under cohabitation was his immediate acceptance of Mitterrand's veto of his choice for foreign minister, Jean Lecanuet, on the grounds that Lecanuet was too "Atlanticist." Yet in his typically forceful personal style, Chirac remained committed to reducing the role of the state in the French economy. By late autumn he had launched an economic reform program that included denationalization of three large business concerns, the easing of price and exchange controls, cutbacks in government spending, and a reduction in income taxes. In foreign affairs he favors strong ties with the United States; he traveled widely during 1986 to bolster his image as an international leader. He also struggled to cope with domestic and diplomatic problems caused by a wave of terrorist attacks in Paris.

Background. The only child of a wealthy financier, Jacques René Chirac was born on Nov. 29, 1932. After graduating from Lycée Louis-le-Grand in Paris, he made his way to the United States, where he took summer courses at Harvard University and worked as a counterboy and dishwasher at a Howard Johnson Restaurant. Upon returning to France, he attended college at the

Institut d'Etudes Politiques de Paris, served in the French Foreign Legion during Algeria's war of independence, and was graduated from the elite Ecole Nationale d'Administration in 1959.

As a protégé of former President Georges Pompidou, Chirac rose quickly through the civil-service ranks. Representing the Correze region in south-central France, where he maintains a chauteau today, Chirac was first elected to the National Assembly in 1967; he was re-elected a total of five times. He has served as minister of agriculture (1972–74), minister of the interior (1974), and prime minister—a position he resigned in protest in 1976. Chirac became head of the RPR in 1976 and was elected mayor of Paris the following year. He was re-elected in 1983 and has retained the mayoralty while prime minister.

Chirac is married to the former Bernadette Chodron de Courcel; they have two daughters.

See also FRANCE.

AXEL KRAUSE

CONABLE, Barber Benjamin, Jr.

In his first press conference after taking over as president of the World Bank on July 1, 1986, Barber B. Conable, Jr., expressed his concern about "the extent to which we seem to polarize the developed and the developing world, instead of recognizing our interdependence and our living on the world together." It was a typically conciliatory remark from a man who spent 20 years in the U.S. House of Representatives, winning a reputation as one of the wisest, most thoughtful, and most knowledgeable legislators on Capitol Hill. From 1977 until his retirement from the House in 1984, the representative of the Rochester, NY, area was the ranking Republican on the Ways and Means Committee. It was a job requiring constant mediation and compromise among strong opposing viewpoints—skills that could serve him well in his new job.

With relatively little background in banking or finance, Conable takes over a major international institution that lends more than $14 billion a year to develop the economies of 100 Third World nations. The World Bank is owned by a total of 150 governments and has a bureaucracy of more than 6,000 people. The United States, its largest contributor, has 20% of the vote on the bank's board and names the bank's president. World Bank officials hoped that Conable's knowledge of Capitol Hill might help obtain more funding for its low-cost loan affiliate, the International Development Association (IDA), as well as the bank's own capital.

Background. Barber Benjamin Conable, Jr., was born on Nov. 2, 1922, in Warsaw, NY, where he also grew up. He was graduated from Cornell University in 1942 and then enlisted in the U.S. Marine Corps. His four-year tour took him ashore on the first day of the invasion of Iwo Jima, as well as to Japan, where he served with the occupation forces. He returned to Cornell in 1946, received his law degree two years later, and then joined a law firm in Buffalo. With the outbreak of the Korean War in 1950, he went back to active military duty.

Conable made his first bid for public office in 1962, winning a seat in the New York State Senate. After two years in Albany, he was elected to the first of his ten terms as U.S. congressman from New York's 30th district. He is given considerable credit for winning passage of the revenue-sharing law of 1972 and was a strong voice in tax and trade matters.

Upon retiring from Congress in 1984, Conable said, "I would like to quit while I can still be active. I would like to be useful after leaving." President Ronald Reagan appealed to that desire in asking him to leave his 19th-century farmhouse in Alexander, NY, and his political-science professorship at the University of Rochester in order to take on the World Bank presidency.

Conable was married to Charlotte Williams of Buffalo in 1952. They have four children.

DAVID R. FRANCIS

DANILOFF, Nicholas S.

As Moscow correspondent for *U.S. News & World Report* magazine, 52-year-old Nicholas Daniloff was known for his knowledgeable, detailed, and often critical coverage of the Soviet government, as well as for his many Soviet friends and contacts. On Aug. 30, 1986, with his five-year tour of duty about to end, Daniloff met a Soviet friend, identified as "Misha," in the Lenin Hills, a wooded section of Moscow. Daniloff gave Misha two novels, and Misha handed him a sealed envelope. Misha left the scene and Daniloff was quickly surrounded by KGB agents. The correspondent was taken to Lefortovo Prison in northeast Moscow and charged with espionage. The envelope, it turned out, contained "top secret" maps of Soviet military installations.

Daniloff's detention, which came a week after the arrest in New York City of alleged Soviet spy Gennadi Zakharov, began a month-long diplomatic face-off between the White House and the Kremlin. Soviet officials insisted Daniloff was a spy; U.S. officials insisted he had been set up by the KGB. After 13 days behind bars, Daniloff was released from Lefortovo into the custody of the U.S. embassy—but still not allowed to leave the country. Finally, in a controversial diplomatic arrangement, Daniloff was set free September 29. The following day the United States released Zakharov, the Soviet Union freed longtime dissident Yuri Orlov, and the two sides announced a summit between President Ronald Reagan and General Secretary Mikhail Gorbachev in Reykjavik, Iceland, October 11–12.

Background. On the morning before his release, Nicholas Daniloff visited the Moscow grave of his great-great grandfather, a Russian who took part in the 1825 Decembrist uprising against the czar. (Daniloff is writing a book about his ancestor.) Daniloff's grandfather was a czarist general; his father was a Russian émigré; and his mother was an American. The stories he heard as a child left Daniloff with an abiding fascination and love for the Russian language (which he speaks fluently), literature, and people.

He was born in Paris on Dec. 30, 1934, and was raised in a French-speaking home. During his childhood he moved from Paris to Argentina to New Hampshire and back to Paris. He enrolled at Harvard University in 1952 and was graduated four years later. After completing two years of graduate work at Oxford University in England—where he met his future wife, Ruth—he began

Nicholas B. Daniloff

AP/Wide World

his career as a foreign correspondent. The Daniloffs were married the following year, 1959, while he was on assignment in Geneva. They have two children, Miranda, 23, and Caleb, 16.

Daniloff spent three years in Moscow with United Press International in the early 1960s, returning in 1980 as correspondent for *U.S. News.* According to his wife, he has had a "love-hate" relationship with the Soviet Union. His columns were notably critical of official policy, yet he maintained a deep appreciation of Russian culture and history. A particular fascination was the Soviet space program, about which he wrote a book, *The Kremlin and the Cosmos,* in 1972.

In Moscow, the Daniloffs lived in an apartment on Leninsky Prospekt, a main avenue leading from the central part of the city. Unlike most other buildings that house foreigners, Daniloff's was not guarded round-the-clock by Soviet police. However, his family and friends assumed that the apartment was bugged, as much to monitor his many Soviet acquaintances as Daniloff himself. As underscored by his arrest, the practice of Western-style journalism poses an inherent threat and runs an implicit risk in the Soviet Union—and indeed any Communist or other restrictive regime. (In July, *New York Times* Beijing [Peking] correspondent John F. Burns was detained for nearly a week on suspicion of espionage and expelled from the country.)

Upon his return to the United States, Nicholas Daniloff expressed the hope of some day laying more flowers on the grave of his great-great grandfather. For the time being, he signed up to cover the summit in Reykjavik for *U.S. News.*

DEAVER, Michael Keith

During his tenure as an adviser to President Ronald Reagan, Michael K. Deaver was renowned for his ability to get favorable publicity for his boss and longtime friend. But not long after he left the White House in 1985 to become a Washington lobbyist, Deaver plunged into a major controversy over conflict-of-interest allegations creating a flood of unfavorable publicity and raising the threat of criminal prosecution. The Deaver case commanded special attention because of his long and close association with President and Mrs. Reagan.

At the start of the Reagan presidency in 1981, Deaver was named deputy White House chief of staff in which post he wielded great influence over presidential public relations. His strategy of limiting and controlling access to the president was credited with helping boost Reagan's popularity. Despite his success in this job, Deaver was dissatisfied with his $70,200 salary, and talked publicly about wanting to take private employment.

Deaver resigned in May 1985, and within a year his lobbying and public-affairs firm had contracts from foreign governments worth nearly $2.5 million. In March 1986, *Time* magazine ran his picture on its cover to illustrate a story on "peddling influence" in Washington. His activities soon came under the scrutiny of the General Accounting Office and of congressional probers looking into whether he had violated the federal law that prohibits former officials from lobbying their former colleagues for a year and forbids them from ever lobbying on issues in which they have been a major participant.

The charge against Deaver that initially attracted the most attention was that he had signed on as a lobbyist for the Canadian government on acid rain and other issues, though he had been involved in administration discussions about dealing with Canada on the acid-rain problem before he resigned his post. Similar questions were raised about Deaver's activities on behalf of Rockwell International Corp. to boost purchases of the B-1 bomber and for a U.S. brokerage firm working with Japanese investors seeking Puerto Rican tax credits.

Deaver sought to dismiss the allegations against him as being politically motivated and "mean spirited." Nevertheless, the Justice Department requested a special federal court to name an independent counsel to

AP/Wide World

James C. Fletcher

investigate the charges. In May, Whitney North Seymour, Jr., a former U.S. attorney in Manhattan, was selected for the post. In August the case took on an even more serious dimension when the House Energy and Commerce Subcommittee on Oversight and Investigations recommended that Seymour consider perjury charges against Deaver growing out of his testimony before that committee. (*See also* UNITED STATES.)

Background. Michael Keith Deaver was born on April 11, 1938, in Bakersfield, CA. His father was an oil-company distributor. Deaver was graduated from San Jose State University in 1960, served six months on active duty in the Air Force, and worked as a management trainee for IBM before entering politics as a field organizer for the Republican Party in California.

Deaver joined Reagan's gubernatorial staff in 1967 and stayed for the eight years Reagan spent in the governor's mansion, winning the affection and trust of both Reagan and his wife, Nancy. In 1975, Deaver started a public-relations firm but took leaves of absence to work for Reagan's 1976 and 1980 presidential campaigns.

ROBERT SHOGAN

FLETCHER, James Chipman

On March 6, 1986, five weeks after the fatal explosion of the U.S. space shuttle *Challenger,* President Ronald Reagan nominated James C. Fletcher as the new head of the National Aeronautics and Space Administration (NASA). The position had been vacant since early December 1985, when then Administrator James M. Beggs took a leave of absence following indictment on fraud charges (relating to previous employment). Following Beggs' resignation on February 25, and with the agency facing the worst crisis in its history, Fletcher was seen as the man for the job because of his previous experience —and track record—as head of NASA from 1971 to 1977. Though he had expressed reluctance to return to the post, Fletcher accepted the appointment, won confirmation in the Senate, and took office on May 12.

Confident that "the problems can be fixed," he set about the tasks of getting the shuttle program back off the ground and restoring NASA's tarnished image. Following the release of the Rogers Commission report on the shuttle disaster, Fletcher said that American officials should not be "assigning blame" but "assigning people to fix what went wrong and make sure it doesn't happen again." He urged construction of two more shuttles, but pledged that the orbiter would not fly again until it was proven to be a "safe and effective vehicle." (*See* feature article, page 36.)

Background. James Chipman Fletcher was born June 5, 1919, in Millburn, NJ. His father was a physicist at the Bell Telephone Laboratory in New York City, of which James later became head of physics research (1970–71). Fletcher attended public high school in Queens, NY, graduating in 1937. A Mormon, he enrolled in Brigham Young University, but later transferred to Columbia University. He earned his B.A. in 1940 and was awarded a Ph.D. in physics from the California Institute of Technology in 1948. During World War II, Fletcher served as a research physicist for the Navy and later as a teaching fellow at Princeton University.

From 1948 to 1954 he served as director of the theory and analysis laboratory in the electronics division of Hughes Aircraft Company—the beginning of his career in high-technology avionics. In 1954, Dr. Fletcher was appointed associate director of the Ramo-Woolridge Corporation, soon becoming director of electronics in the guided-missile division. Four years later, he and an associate formed the Space Electronics Corporation, a manufacturer of sophisticated components. After a merger in 1961 he was elected president—and later chairman of the board—of the new Space General Corporation. In July 1964, however, he resigned those positions to become the eighth president of the University of Utah.

Having served on several government advisory groups and commissions, Fletcher was appointed the head of NASA by President Richard Nixon in March 1971. Among his key decisions was to use solid-fuel rockets—the suspected cause of the *Challenger* explosion.

After leaving NASA in 1977 he was a professor at the University of Pittsburgh and a consulting engineer. Fletcher is married to the former Fay Lee and has four children. He has won numerous awards and honorary degrees, and at the time of his reappointment to NASA he was serving on the boards of six corporations.

GALE, Robert Peter

When Dr. Robert Gale heard about the explosion at the Soviet Union's Chernobyl nuclear power plant on April 26, 1986, he realized "that they [the Soviets] would need our help. But how could I get a message to the Russians?"

Gale, a specialist in bone marrow transplants, knew that the firefighters and other people who were near the plant at the time of the explosion would have been exposed to massive doses of radiation. The radiation would destroy their bone marrow, which produces blood and disease-fighting cells. These people's only hope was to receive transplants of marrow tissue from healthy donors—a time-consuming and often risky operation.

Gale contacted Armand Hammer, chairman of Occidental Petroleum Corporation, who has long had close ties to the Soviet government. Hammer wrote to Soviet leaders describing Gale's offer of help. On May 1, Gale received a call from Oleg Sokolov, the then-acting Soviet ambassador to the United States. "How soon can you come?" asked Sokolov.

Within hours, Gale was on a plane for Moscow. Upon arrival, he went immediately to the hospital where the most severely affected victims were being treated. A few days later he was joined by several other Western doctors, plus high-tech equipment and medicine shipped in from all over the world.

An unlikely but effective alliance formed: Soviet and Western doctors, speaking different languages, using different procedures and standards, working almost around the clock to save people's lives. The doctors performed a total of 19 transplants. "It's unprecedented to have this many transplants going on simultaneously,"

noted Gale, who is regarded as a hero by the Soviet people. "There's no place in the world that could handle something like this alone. If you consider the limited nature of the accident and the tremendous medical resources that were required to respond to it, then it should put to rest any notion that we could respond effectively to a nuclear accident of a greater magnitude."

Background. Robert Peter Gale was born on Oct. 11, 1945, in New York City. He attended Hobart College in Geneva, NY, graduating with high honors in 1966. He earned an MD degree from the State University of New York at Buffalo in 1970 and a doctorate in microbiology and immunology from the University of California at Los Angeles (UCLA) in 1978.

Gale has been associated with the UCLA Department of Medicine since 1970. Currently, he is an associate professor of medicine in the division of hematology and oncology. Gale also is chairman of the advisory committee of the International Bone Marrow Transplant Registry, a consortium of 130 transplant centers in the United States and 31 other nations.

Gale and his wife, Tamar, have three children. They live in Bel Air, in the hills above the UCLA campus.

JENNY TESAR

GIAMATTI, A. Bartlett

A respected scholar of medieval and Renaissance literature, the president of Yale University for the previous eight years, and a man who once described himself as "a private type—I like to go to the library," A. Bartlett Giamatti seemed an unlikely choice to become the new president of major league baseball's National League. In June 1986, however, team owners chose Giamatti for the post, to replace Chub Feeney in December.

The choice of the 48-year-old Giamatti was not as implausible as it may have seemed. As Yale president, Giamatti had earned a reputation as a strong administrative and financial manager, reversing the organizational and fiscal instability that had begun to plague the venerated institution. Bringing a personal warmth and panache to the office, he had emerged as a national spokesman on such topics as educational excellence, the value of a traditional humanities curriculum, student funding, and the role of athletics in a college environment. Most of all, perhaps, he was a passionate and

A. Bartlett Giamatti

AP/Wide World

lifelong fan of baseball—the Boston Red Sox in particular. He had written about Tom Seaver just as he had written about the poet John Milton. In 1977, amid rumors of his impending appointment to the Yale presidency, Giamatti had quipped, "The only thing I want to be president of is the American League."

Background. Angelo Bartlett Giamatti was born on April 4, 1938, in Boston, MA. His father, a Yale graduate, was a professor of Italian at Mount Holyoke College. Young Giamatti developed a keen interest in sports—especially baseball—but he participated little and excelled not at all. His real aptitude was in languages and literature. As a child he learned Italian from his father and discussed Dante at the dinner table. He attended South Hadley (MA) High School and then spent a year at the International School of Rome in Italy, where his father was on sabbatical. After completing his secondary education at Phillips Academy in Andover, MA, he entered Yale. Majoring in English, he was graduated *magna cum laude* in 1960 and entered Yale Graduate School as a Woodrow Wilson Fellow. He received his Ph.D. in comparative literature in 1964. His dissertation, "The Earthly Paradise and the Renaissance Epic," was published in 1966 to scholarly acclaim. Later works included studies of Edmund Spenser, Milton, and other medieval and Renaissance poets.

After teaching Italian and comparative literature at Princeton University for two years, Giamatti returned to Yale in 1966 as assistant professor of English. Two years later he became associate professor, and in 1971 he was named professor of English and comparative literature. A popular teacher and respected scholar, Giamatti also took on various administrative functions both at Yale and at various literary and cultural organizations. When he assumed the Yale presidency in 1978, be became the youngest person in more than 200 years and the first person of ethnic ancestry to hold the office.

He was married in April 1960 to Toni Smith, who also became an English teacher. The Giamattis have three children.

GOLDBERG, Whoopi

A chameleon-like actress and comedienne, Whoopi Goldberg won wide recognition in 1986 for her performances in two major motion pictures and a television comedy special. She made her film debut in Steven Spielberg's *The Color Purple* (1985), earning an Academy Award nomination for best actress for her portrayal of Celie, a woman who is abused by her husband but gradually grows to self-realization and independence. In March, along with comedians Robin Williams and Billy Crystal, she cohosted a three-hour all-star comedy special, called *Comic Relief,* on the Home Box Office (HBO) cable television station; the event was designed to raise money for the nation's homeless. And in October, Goldberg appeared in a new movie, *Jumpin' Jack Flash,* starring in the comic role of a young woman who sets out to rescue a British spy trapped in an Eastern bloc country. Also in the works during 1986 was another film, called *Burglar.*

Background. Whoopi Goldberg, (whose real name reportedly is Caryn Johnson, although she seeks to keep it a secret) was born about 1949 in New York City, where she grew up in a housing project. She was fascinated by films from an early age, and she began to act in local theater groups at the age of eight. In the 1960s she dropped out of high school and joined the "hippie" scene in New York's East Village. She also became involved in civil-rights demonstrations, while finding work in the choruses of several Broadway shows. A brief marriage in the early 1970s produced a daughter, Alexandrea Martin.

In 1974, Goldberg moved with her daughter to California, where she lived on welfare and did odd jobs (including one as a beautician in a mortuary). Meanwhile, first in San Diego and later in Berkeley, she became involved in the theater. She was a founding member of

AP/Wide World

Whoopi Goldberg

the San Diego Repertory Theater and later teamed with actor Don Victor to do improvised stage skits. Her partner's failure to show up for a booking led to her first solo performance. While working with a San Francisco theater group, the Blake Street Hawkeyes, she expanded the solo act into a one-hour presentation called *The Spook Show,* which she took to New York in 1983. Director Mike Nichols saw the show there and in 1984 decided to produce a Broadway version, retitled *Whoopi Goldberg,* which received rave reviews.

Among the characters Goldberg has developed for the stage are Fontaine, a black junkie with a Ph.D. in literature; a little black girl who longs for blond hair so she can appear on the TV show *Love Boat*; a white "surfer chick" who botches an abortion; and a crippled woman who dreams of a normal life. She also has performed as the late black performer Moms Mabley.

Goldberg was married in September 1986 to the cinematographer David Claessen.

ELAINE PASCOE

HASSAN II, King

Seeking a major breakthrough in the Middle East peace process and risking his diplomatic standing in the Arab world, Morocco's King Hassan II held a surprise summit with Israel's Prime Minister Shimon Peres at the king's summer palace in Ifrane, July 22-23. It was the first such high-level contact between an Arab and Israeli leader since the series of meetings initiated by the late Egyptian President Anwar el-Sadat's visit to Jerusalem in 1977. After the two days of secret talks Peres called the summit a success, but Hassan said the Israeli leader had rejected basic Arab conditions for a Middle East peace. In the aftermath the meeting was denounced by several other Arab leaders, and Syria broke diplomatic relations with Morocco. Then on July 27, Hassan announced his resignation as chairman of the Arab League conference.

The 57-year-old monarch, who marked the 25th anniversary of his rule in February 1986, has long been considered a pro-Western moderate, friend of the United States, and something of a maverick in the Arab world regarding Israel. In 1977 he arranged for the secret meetings between Egypt and Israel that led to Sadat's visit. And in May 1984 he invited 11 members of the Israeli parliament to a meeting in Morocco honoring the country's Jewish population. He has been a frequent visitor to Washington.

Background. His Imperial Highness Moulay Hassan ben Mohammed al-Alaoui was born in Rabat, Morocco, on July 9, 1929, when the country was still a French protectorate. He was tutored at a special school in the royal palace and earned a law degree at the University of Bordeaux in France. Invested as crown prince in 1957, Hassan became commander-in-chief of the Royal Moroccan Army and served as minister of defense and vice-premier from 1960 to 1961. On Feb. 26, 1961, on the death of his father, King Mohammed V, following minor surgery, Hassan succeeded to the throne and took over the office of prime minister.

Hassan's quarter-century reign has seen a series of major political developments and crises, both domestic and foreign. One of his first acts was to promulgate a democratic constitution, which was ratified by referendum in December 1962 and led to the election of a bicameral parliament the following year. However, after antigovernment riots in Casablanca in 1965, Hassan reassumed executive and legislative power for two years. A second constitution was accepted in a referendum in 1970. Two abortive military coups shook the palace in the summers of 1971 and 1972. And a third Hassan constitution was accepted in a 1972 referendum, though new parliamentary elections (unicameral) were not held until 1977. In 1984, Hassan announced a treaty of federation with Libya, the main supplier of arms for the Polisario guerrillas seeking independence in the Western Sahara.

King Hassan is also the spiritual head of Islam in Morocco. He is married to the former Lalla Latifa, with whom he has three daughters and two sons.

KEILLOR, Garrison Edward

The "On the Air" sign flashes, and Garrison Keillor pulls the microphone close to his mouth. "Well," he begins, "it's been a quiet week in Lake Wobegon. . . . "

For the theater audience and for radio listeners across America, the introduction is a familiar one. *A Prairie Home Companion,* a two-hour anthology of humor and folk music, was first broadcast on Minnesota Public Radio in 1974. Since 1980, the show has been heard on more than 200 public radio stations throughout the country. Millions of dedicated listeners tune in on Saturday afternoons to hear the latest goings-on in Lake Wobegon, Keillor's fictional small town in Minnesota ("the little town that time forgot and the decades

Garrison Keillor

cannot improve"). His monologues about the Tollefsons, the Hockstepers, and the other folks of Lake Wobegon form the centerpiece of *A Prairie Home Companion* and have made it one of the most popular live radio shows in America.

In April 1986, Keillor for the first time welcomed a television audience to *A Prairie Home Companion.* The production celebrated the reopening of *Home Companion's* own home, the World Theater in downtown St. Paul, MN, after extensive renovation. As always, the live performance was broadcast by American Public Radio in the late afternoon, but it was also taped for airing on public television that night.

In addition, Keillor's fictional town was being introduced to the reading public in his 1985 book, *Lake Wobegon Days.* Providing a detailed history and description of community life, the title immediately hit the bestseller lists and stayed at or near the top for months.

Background. Garrison Edward Keillor was born on Aug. 7, 1942, in the small town of Anoka, MN, north of Minneapolis. His father was a carpenter and railroad mail clerk, and his mother raised six children according to the strict moral tenets of their church, the Plymouth Brethren. As a high-school student, Garrison enjoyed writing, especially poetry, and assumed he would some day work for a newspaper.

In 1965, while attending the University of Minnesota, Keillor took a job at the school's radio station. He received his B.A. in 1968, and two years later began doing a three-hour show every morning on Minnesota Public Radio. A longtime admirer of James Thurber, S.J. Perelman, E.B. White, and other writers associated with *The New Yorker,* Keillor began submitting humor pieces to that magazine. The first one was accepted in 1969, and he has been a frequent contributor ever since. A collection of his articles, *Happy to Be Here,* was published in 1982.

Keillor lives in a large Victorian house—painted black—on a hill overlooking St. Paul. He was married for the second time in December 1985 to Ulla Skaerved, a high-school classmate.

L'AMOUR, Louis

Already one of the world's three best-selling novelists (along with Harold Robbins and Irving Wallace), Louis L'Amour had another book, *Last of the Breed,* on the hardcover best-seller lists in 1986—and no less than five on the paperback lists. Some 175 million copies of L'Amour's 95 novels, including such Western classics as *Hondo* and *The Burning Hills,* are still in print around the world.

Louis L'Amour describes himself as a storyteller in the old folk tradition. His tales are characterized by their fast-paced plotting, meticulous research, and plain-speaking characters. One element notable for its absence is violence, despite the six-shooters carried by his heroes. But "I don't like being pigeonholed," L'Amour says, and not all of his books are Westerns. *Last of the Breed* is set in modern-day Siberia, its hero an Air Force pilot taken prisoner after a forced landing.

Background. Louis Dearborn LaMoore was born in Jamestown, ND, probably in 1908. As a child, he listened to tales about his great-grandfather, who was scalped by the Sioux, and his grandfather, who fought in the Civil War. When Louis was 15, he left school to drift around the West, supporting himself at various kinds of manual labor and meeting people with tales of frontier life.

While serving in the tank corps in World War II, he entertained his fellow soldiers with Western yarns. One of his listeners suggested that he write his stories down, and in the late 1940s, L'Amour began selling them to the pulps under the name Tex Burns. In 1951, "Tex Burns" published his first novel, *Hopalong Cassidy and the Riders of High Rock.* His first novel as Louis L'Amour was the ever-popular *Hondo,* in 1953. Over the next five years, L'Amour wrote 15 books for several publishers.

Louis L'Amour

© Ken Howard

Under contract to Bantam Books since 1955, he has kept up a three-book-a-year pace ever since, producing such best-sellers as *Guns of the Timberland*, *Shalako*, and *The Silver Canyon*. In his books, L'Amour celebrates the breed of "hard-shelled men" who opened the West—young, tough loners with a romantic streak and a hunger for learning and civilization. Since the 1970s, many of his books have traced the roots of three families—the Sacketts, Talons, and Chantrys—from their European roots to their lives in the West.

A burly, youthful looking man, Louis L'Amour habitually dresses in Western garb, including a string tie and Stetson hat. His many awards and citations include the Congressional Medal of Honor (1983) and Presidential Medal of Freedom (1984). L'Amour and his wife Katherine have been married since 1956; they have a son and a daughter.

LINDA TRIEGEL

LaROUCHE, Lyndon H., Jr.

On March 18, 1986, Lyndon H. LaRouche, Jr., burst into the news with the unexpected victories of two of his supporters, Janice Hart and Mark Fairchild, in the Illinois Democratic primary (*see* ILLINOIS). They were just 2 of 780 LaRouche sympathizers seeking Democratic nominations for national, state, and local office in 1986.

Scornful of ideological labels, LaRouche espouses an eclectic mix of ideas from Karl Marx, Charles Fourier, G.W.F. Hegel, Plato, and even the U.S. Founding Fathers. The core of his philosophy is the unmasking of a conspiratorial international elite consisting of among others, Zionists, the Federal Reserve Board, Jesuits, Henry Kissinger, and the British Royal family. During the 1986 campaigns, however, LaRouche candidates stressed his predictions of imminent economic collapse, attacks on drug traffickers, demands for quarantine of AIDS victims, and support for the Reagan administration's Strategic Defense Initiative.

LaRouche's organizational complex is run by a small core of fanatic loyalists, numbering only a few hundred. They raise money by telephone and public solicitations (especially at airports), publish such magazines as *The Executive Intelligence Review* and *International Journal of Fusion Energy*, and recruit candidates for public office. LaRouche's National Democratic Policy Committee receives money from thousands of voters who may not identify with him, but share his political cynicism and fondness for conspiracy theories. Money also comes from affiliated businesses, a few wealthy sympathizers, and, if federal prosecutors are correct, fraudulent loans.

Notoriety was not necessarily an asset for LaRouche in 1986. After the victories in Illinois, his candidates fared poorly, as opinion surveys revealed little public support and much opposition, and hosts of mainstream political leaders attacked his movement. Although his followers petitioned successfully to get anti-AIDS Proposition 64 on the California ballot, exploitation of this issue failed elsewhere. As 1986 ended, LaRouche suffered costly legal setbacks in litigation with federal agencies and private organizations.

Background. Lyndon H. LaRouche, Jr., was born on Sept. 8, 1922, in Rochester, NH. The son of devout Quaker parents, he had an unhappy childhood, attended Northeastern University in Boston, and was a conscientious objector in World War II. After duty in the Far East as a medical corpsman, he joined the Trotskyite Socialist Workers Party in 1948, becoming a Marxist theoretician but supporting himself as a management consultant. In the 1960s he led a radical faction aligned with Students for a Democratic Society, emerging briefly as leader of the 1968 Columbia University protests.

During the 1970's, LaRouche gradually moved to the right, creating the National Caucus of Labor Committees, the U.S. Labor Party, and the National Democratic Policy Committee as successive vehicles for his campaigns to infiltrate labor unions, fight other extremist groups, and achieve public office. LaRouche ran for president in 1976, 1980, and 1984; his best showing was 78,807 votes in 1984. Still, participation in the 1980 and 1984 Democratic primaries permitted him to qualify for and receive federal matching funds and paved the way for his subsequent drive to capture the party.

JAMES L. GUTH AND JOHN C. GREEN

LYNG, Richard Edmund

A longtime associate of President Ronald Reagan and former deputy agriculture secretary, Richard E. Lyng was named in January 1986 to replace John R. Block as U.S. secretary of agriculture. The 22d person to hold that office, he is the first from California, the nation's leading agricultural state. At age 67, he also became the oldest person to assume the post.

Lyng's selection won strong support, even among administration critics. Indeed, legislators from major farm states and both parties, including Senate majority leader Robert Dole (R-KS), had worked for his nomination. Lyng was confirmed by the Senate, 95-2 without debate, on March 6. Ideologically a "free market" advocate, he had earned a reputation for his pragmatism on specific issues and successful dealings with Congress. A loyal associate of the president, Lyng was also expected to have direct access to the White House, giving agriculture a stronger representation within the administration. The new influence of agricultural interests was demonstrated in the summer of 1986, with the approval of subsidized farm exports to the Soviet Union over the strong objection of Secretary of State George Shultz.

Background. Born on June 29, 1918, in San Francisco, Richard E. Lyng grew up in California's agriculturally rich San Joaquin Valley. His family owned a seed production and bean processing company in Modesto. Lyng attended the University of Notre Dame, graduating cum laude in 1940. After serving with the U.S. Army in the South Pacific during World War II, he returned to Modesto to manage the family business.

Lyng began his career in government in 1967 as deputy director of the California State Department of Agriculture, under then Governor Reagan. He moved to Washington in 1969 as assistant secretary of marketing and consumer services in the Department of Agriculture during the Richard Nixon administration. He resigned that post in 1973 to become president of the American Meat Institute, as well as a board member of several agribusinesses.

After Ronald Reagan won the presidential election in 1980, Lyng headed his agricultural transition team and was prominently mentioned as a candidate for secretary. Under political pressure, however, the president chose Block—a "working farmer" from the Midwest—and Lyng accepted the number two spot in the department. During his three years in that post, he managed the department's day-to-day operations and budget development. In 1984, following heart bypass surgery, he left the administration for a quieter life as an agricultural consultant and lobbyist. His return to government in 1986 came during the worst agricultural recession in decades.

Lyng and his wife, Bethyl, have two daughters and several grandchildren.

See also AGRICULTURE.

DON F. HADWIGER

MATTINGLY, Donald Arthur

In a poll during the 1986 season, major league baseball players were asked to name the best all-around performer currently in the game. Their choice was the 25-year-old first baseman of the New York Yankees, Don Mattingly. In only his third full season in the majors, Mattingly had proven that he could hit consistently for both power and average and that he could field his position with the best of them. In 1985 he earned the American League Most Valuable Player (MVP) award with hitting statistics that raised the specters of such former Yankee greats as Babe Ruth, Lou Gehrig, and Joe DiMaggio—a .324 average, 211 hits, 145 runs batted in (RBIs), and 35 home runs; he also won a Gold Glove as the league's best-fielding first baseman.

As he had in each of his previous seasons in the big leagues, Mattingly managed to improve on those heady statistics in 1986. His RBIs dropped to 113 and his homers fell off to 31 (both still among the highest in the league), but his batting average shot up to .352. In a race that went down to the season's last game, he was edged out for the league batting title by Boston's Wade Boggs (*see* BIOGRAPHY) by five points. The Yankee slugger also set an all-time team record of 238 hits in one season (breaking the mark of 231 by Earl Combs in 1927) and established another single-season Yankee standard with 53 doubles (one more than Gehrig in 1927); both totals were also the highest in the major leagues in 1986. The 6'0" (1.83-m), 175-lb (79-kg) lefty also added another Gold Glove to his trophy case and just missed winning a second consecutive MVP award. In the race for the coveted honor, he finished second to Boston Red Sox pitcher Roger Clemens. (*See also* SPORTS—Baseball.)

Background. The youngest of four brothers, all of whom excelled in sports, Donald Arthur Mattingly was born on April 21, 1961, in Evansville, IN. He attended Reitz Memorial High School in his home town and starred on the baseball, basketball, and football teams. Turning down several college scholarship offers, he decided to go into professional baseball at age 18. Only a 19th-round selection in the June 1979 draft, the fiercely competitive Mattingly compiled an overall batting average of .332 in three-and-a-half years in the minor leagues. In 1983 he played a total of 91 games for the Yankees, and by the following year he was the team's starting first baseman. His .343 average that year led the American League. Through 1986 his major league career average stood at .332, with 93 home runs and 401 RBIs.

Despite his remarkable stats, Mattingly's aim is to be a consistent player as well as "person, both on and off the field." He would rather "be able to string together a lot of good years than to be remembered for just a couple of 'monster' seasons."

Mattingly is married to the former Kim Sexton, the daughter of his high-school football coach. They have a home in the New York area but spend baseball's off-season at their other home in Evansville. They have a son, Taylor.

PAGE, Geraldine

It took eight nominations, but in 1986 Geraldine Page finally won her Oscar as best actress. As the suspense mounted during the Academy Awards ceremony on March 24, Page was clearly a sentimental favorite. She had given top caliber performances that yielded the previous seven nominations. This one was for her deeply moving portrayal of the stubborn, elderly Carrie Watts, determined to return home once more before she dies, in Horton Foote's *The Trip to Bountiful*. The tour de force synthesized her special qualities as an actress and brought to bear a lifetime of experience. The moment to honor her had surely come.

Page has long enjoyed the esteem of her peers as well as her public. She is known for her thorough craftsmanship, and in a career that has spanned some 40 years, she has moved with assurance between stage, screen, and television. She also teaches acting, and is actress-in-residence at New York's Mirror Repertory Company. Her husband is actor Rip Torn, and she is the mother of twin sons and a daughter.

Background. Page was born Nov. 22, 1924, in Kirksville, MO, to Leon and Pearl (Maize) Page. Her dramatic studies began at the Goodman School of Drama in Chicago, and she subsequently studied in New York with Herbert Berghof. After extensive work in summer stock, her big break came in 1952 with an off-Broadway production of *Summer and Smoke* by Tennessee Williams. She was hailed immediately by critics as an actress of outstanding promise. Another triumph followed in the Tennessee Williams play *Sweet Bird of Youth*. She appeared in the film versions of both. Page soon earned a reputation for definitive portrayals of Southern belles, but time and again she demonstrated her range.

Her memorable motion-picture achievements include performances in *Hondo*, *Interiors*, and *The Pope of Greenwich Village*. On stage she has excelled in such roles as the mother superior in *Agnes of God* and as the doting mother of a violent son in Sam Shepard's *Lie of the Mind*. Her television work has been honored with Emmys for performances in *A Christmas Memory* and *The Thanksgiving Visitor*.

Page is known for bringing an individual style to her "method" acting. Her voice has a distinct tone, and she rarely delivers a line not graced with unusual reflection or rhythm. She is known to fidget, and aware that idiosyncrasies stand out more on screen than on stage, she urges directors to look at daily results to be certain her mannerisms are not too pronounced. As she has grown older, Page has honed her ability to portray aging women with sensitivity and insight.

WILLIAM WOLF

Geraldine Page

AP/Wide World

William H. Rehnquist

REHNQUIST, William Hubbs

In June 1986, faced with naming a successor to retiring U.S. Chief Justice Warren E. Burger, President Ronald Reagan opted for a man who had been the voice of conservatism on the Supreme Court for 15 years, Associate Justice William H. Rehnquist. The nomination touched off a surprising confirmation battle in the Senate Judiciary Committee—far stormier than Rehnquist's confirmation hearings in 1971, when he was nominated to the high court by President Richard Nixon. In the committee hearings and floor debate of 1986, Rehnquist was criticized for his record on civil rights and individual liberties, as well as his judicial ethics. Defenders spoke of his keen intellect, demonstrated talent as a jurist, and leadership ability. The opposition fell far short of derailing the nomination, as the Senate voted 65-33 in Rehnquist's favor. However, the 33 negative votes were the most ever cast against a justice confirmed to the Supreme Court. Rehnquist was sworn in as the 16th U.S. chief justice on Sept. 26, 1986.

Background. William Hubbs Rehnquist was born on Oct. 1, 1924, in Milwaukee, WI, and was reared in the suburb of Shorewood. He attended Kenyon College for one year before joining the U.S. Army Air Corps in 1943. With the end of World War II, he entered Stanford University and graduated in 1948. He took a master's degree in political science at Harvard University in 1950, and earned his law degree from Stanford in 1952.

After working for 18 months as a law clerk to U.S. Supreme Court Justice Robert Jackson, Rehnquist entered private practice in Phoenix, AZ. There he became active in the emerging conservative wing of the Republican Party, headed by Sen. Barry Goldwater. He also became a friend and political ally of Richard G. Kleindienst. As a deputy attorney general in the Nixon administration, Kleindienst brought Rehnquist to Washington in 1969 to head the Office of Legal Counsel in the Department of Justice. Two years later, President Nixon nominated him to the Supreme Court, filling the seat of retiring Associate Justice John Marshall Harlan. Rehnquist was sworn in on Jan. 7, 1972. At age 47, he became the court's youngest member.

In his early years on the court, then still dominated by liberals from the Earl Warren era, Rehnquist often cast lone dissenting votes. Over the years, he has consistently favored the government in conflicts between the government and individuals; in conflicts between state and federal authority, he has consistently found in favor of the states. He also has repeatedly urged limiting federal judicial power. Rehnquist has displayed his conservative zeal in numerous important decisions. In 1981 he wrote the court's majority opinion that women may be excluded from military draft registration (*Rostker v.*

Goldberg). He was the author of the 1984 decision expanding police powers by allowing criminal suspects to be questioned before they are given so-called "Miranda" warnings if police act out of concern for public safety (*New York v. Quarles*). And in 1983 he was the only dissenter in the court's ruling that racially discriminatory private schools may be denied tax exemptions (*Bob Jones University v. U.S.*).

Justice Rehnquist's health became a matter of concern in late 1981 and early 1982, when he suffered a withdrawal reaction from a drug he had been taking for a chronic back problem. Doctors say he has recovered completely from the withdrawal problem.

Rehnquist was married in 1953 to Natalie Cornell, an employee of the Central Intelligence Agency when they met. They have one son and two daughters.

JIM RUBIN

RIVERS, Joan

Joan Rivers, long familiar to late-night television viewers as the substitute host for Johnny Carson on NBC's *Tonight Show,* struck out on her own in 1986 with *The Late Show Starring Joan Rivers,* a talk show that competed directly with Carson's. Rivers' new program began appearing five nights a week on independent stations in the fall, as the centerpiece of a new network, Fox Broadcasting Company, launched by the Australian-born press magnate Rupert Murdoch.

Rivers, whose brash and irreverent humor has made her one of the top stand-up comics in the United States, had received her first big show-business break as a guest on the Carson show in 1965 and had appeared on it regularly before signing on as substitute host in 1983. As reasons for making the switch, she cited NBC's unwillingness to give her a long-term contract or to consider her as a possible full-time host should Carson leave the show. Fox Broadcasting gave her a three-year, $10 million contract for the new show, which is performed live rather than taped.

Background. Joan Rivers was born Joan Molinsky in Brooklyn, NY, about 1935. One of two daughters of a well-to-do physician, she graduated from Adelphi Academy and Barnard College of Columbia University, where she studied English and anthropology and acted in school plays. After graduation in 1954, she worked as a

Joan Rivers

fashion coordinator for a chain of clothing stores but found herself unhappy in the work. Despite her parents' disapproval, she left the job to pursue a career in show business.

In the late 1950s and early 1960s, she worked a series of small "discovery" clubs and seedy bars, often without much success. In 1964 she landed a long-term engagement at the Duplex in Greenwich Village and began to reshape her act for broader appeal. Her rapid-fire, nonstop monologues, often describing her (fictional) experiences as a fat and unhappy child, seemed to strike a chord with audiences; meanwhile, she wrote material for such comedians as Bob Newhart and Phyllis Diller. It was in the guise of a comedy writer that she first appeared on *The Tonight Show* in 1965.

That show led to others, on television and in such nightclubs as New York's Downstairs at the Upstairs (where she became a regular) and San Francisco's The Hungry i. In 1968-69 she hosted her own mid-morning television talk show, *That Show,* for NBC affiliates. By the 1970s she was appearing at top Las Vegas clubs, turning her acid and irrepressible wit on every subject from Queen Elizabeth to her own weight. (Her 110 lbs— 50 kg—she says, is slightly less than she weighed at birth.)

Rivers is married to Edgar Rosenburg, a television producer who was responsible for her first series. They have a daughter and live in Los Angeles.

ELAINE PASCOE

SCALIA, Antonin

Praising him for "the depth of his understanding of our constitutional jurisprudence," President Ronald Reagan in June 1986 nominated Judge Antonin Scalia to become the newest member of the U.S. Supreme Court. As a judge on the U.S. Court of Appeals for the District of Columbia, in his speeches, and in scholarly articles, Scalia expressed views that closely paralleled positions taken by the Reagan administration on key judicial issues. He has been critical of special preferences for women and minorities, judicial activism, student busing, abortion rights, and the Freedom of Information Act.

Despite his unflinching conservatism, Senate liberals challenged Scalia in only the mildest terms during confirmation hearings in the summer of 1986. Amid effusive praise for his intellect, wit, and writing skills, Scalia won unanimous Senate approval, 98-0. He was sworn in as associate justice on September 26, filling the vacancy

Antonin Scalia

AP/Wide World

created by the retirement of Chief Justice Warren E. Burger and the elevation of Associate Justice William H. Rehnquist to that position. Scalia became the first person of Italian descent to serve on the court and, at age 50, the youngest of the nine current members.

Background. Antonin Scalia was born in Trenton, NJ, on March 11, 1936. His father, an immigrant from Sicily, was a professor of Romance languages at Brooklyn (NY) College. His mother, the daughter of Italian immigrants, was an elementary school teacher. An only child, Scalia spent his early years in Trenton, before the family moved to Queens, NY. He attended St. Francis Xavier High School in Manhattan and graduated first in his class at Georgetown University in 1957. After receiving his LL.B. from Harvard Law School in 1960, Scalia spent six years in private law practice with a leading firm in Cleveland, OH. He left in 1967 for a teaching post at the University of Virginia Law School.

Scalia entered public service in 1971 as general counsel of the White House Office of Telecommunications Policy during the Richard Nixon administration. From 1972 to 1974 he served as Chairman of the Administrative Conference of the United States, an advisory group to the government on legal matters, and then moved to the Department of Justice, where he headed the Office of Legal Counsel to the end of the Gerald Ford administration in 1977.

Returning to academia at the University of Chicago Law School, Scalia became a favorite of the Reagan administration for his conservative views. From 1979 he served as editor of *Regulation,* a magazine published by the conservative, Washington-based think tank the American Enterprise Institute. In 1982 he was appointed to the U.S. Circuit Court of Appeals for the District of Columbia, widely regarded as the second most important court in the nation.

Scalia was married in 1960 to Maureen McCarthy; they have nine children.

JIM RUBIN

SHCHARANSKY, Anatoly Borisovich

On the morning of Feb. 11, 1986, the Soviet Jewish dissident and longtime political prisoner Anatoly Shcharansky walked across Glienecke Bridge in Berlin. As he stepped over a four-inch-wide line at the center of the span, Shcharansky crossed the barrier between East and West—and between imprisonment and freedom.

Since being arrested on charges of espionage and treason in March 1977, the Ukrainian-born activist had endured nearly nine years of cold, hunger, and solitude in Soviet prison and labor camp. His emigré wife, Avital, had traveled the world campaigning for his freedom. The United States and other Western governments took up the cause and exerted pressure for his release. Finally, in early 1986, the East and West agreed to a prisoner-exchange deal involving alleged spies from several countries. Clutching a tattered copy of the *Book of Psalms,* Shcharansky walked to freedom.

Met by West German and U.S. officials, Shcharansky was taken to Munich for a tearful reunion with Avital and a flight to Israel, where they planned to settle. Arriving in Tel Aviv, the 38-year-old human-rights activist and symbol of Soviet Jewry was greeted by Prime Minister Shimon Peres and a joyous crowd of well-wishers. Three months later, on a visit to the United States, Shcharansky was hailed by President Ronald Reagan and by members of Congress. In August the USSR allowed Shcharansky's 77-year-old mother, his brother Leonid, and his brother's family to leave Moscow and go to Tel Aviv for a family reunion. On November 6 a baby girl was born to Anatoly and Avital Shcharansky.

Background. Anatoly Borisovich Shcharansky was born in the Ukraine on Jan. 20, 1948. His father was a journalist for a Communist Party newspaper. The family later moved to the town of Istra, near Moscow. Displaying a talent for mathematics, young Shcharansky graduated from secondary school into the Moscow Physical-Technical Institute. He received his training in mathe-

Anatoly B. Shcharansky

Photos, AP/Wide World

Eduard Shevardnadze

matics and computer science and, after graduation in 1972, went to work at the Oil and Gas Research Institute. Authorities later contended that the job exposed him to state secrets, making an exit visa out of the question.

Shcharansky became an active member of the dissident movement in the early 1970s, calling for open Jewish emigration, free speech, and other citizen rights. During the summer of 1974 he was married to Natalya Stiglits, the sister of a fellow activist, and the next day she left for Israel (where she changed her name to Avital). Both of them expected Anatoly to follow shortly. When an exit visa was denied, Shcharansky stepped up his dissident activities. He became a leading member of the Moscow Helsinki Watch Group, a team of citizens formed to monitor Soviet compliance with the 1975 Helsinki human rights agreement, and he spoke frequently with Western correspondents. On March 4, 1977, the government newspaper *Izvestia* published an open letter accusing him of espionage, and 11 days later he was arrested. Said Shcharansky about his nine years of forced labor: "I was much more free there in the camp than in Moscow. In the cell I could say whatever I thought."

SHEVARDNADZE, Eduard Amvrosiyevich

In the strained, often tense diplomatic maneuvering between Washington and Moscow during 1986, the most active and visible exponent of the Soviet position was Foreign Minister Eduard Shevardnadze, who had risen to the position only the year before. Underscoring his strong personal and philosophical ties with General Secretary Mikhail Gorbachev, Shevardnadze was the front man in a Kremlin effort to reinforce perceptions of a new style and dynamism in Soviet foreign policy. His meetings with U.S. President Ronald Reagan and Secretary of State George Shultz in the fall of 1985 helped pave the way for a Reagan-Gorbachev summit that November. A series of meetings with Shultz in September 1986 led to the resolution of the Nicholas Daniloff affair (*see* BIOGRAPHY) and settled the terms of a Reagan-Gorbachev "mini-summit" the following month in Reykjavik, Iceland, at which Shevardnadze himself played a central role. Other highlights in the diplomatic year of Foreign Minister Shevardnadze included visits to Japan (January), China (April), and Great Britain (July) for the purpose of strengthening ties. The concerted effort to improve relations with Western Europe also included

talks in Moscow with France's President François Mitterrand, West Germany's Foreign Minister Hans-Dietrich Genscher, and other officials.

Background. The son of a teacher, Eduard Amvrosiyevich Shevardnadze was born on Jan. 15, 1928, in the village of Mamati in the Soviet republic of Georgia. He was graduated from the Party School of the Central Committee of the Communist Party of Georgia and later earned a correspondence degree in history from the Kutaisi Pedagogical Institute. In 1946 he became an instructor in the district committee of Komsomol, the Communist youth league, and two years later joined the Communist Party.

Shevardnadze became a member of the Supreme Soviet of Georgia, its nominal legislature, in 1959 and rose rapidly through the ranks of the party and civilian police. By 1965 he became head of Georgia's ministry of public order (later, ministry of internal affairs), a post he occupied until 1972. As the republic's chief law enforcement officer, he impressed Moscow with a major crackdown on crime and corruption. In 1972 he was named first secretary of the Georgian Communist Party, and in 1976 he became a member of the Central Committee of the national Communist Party. Two years later he was elevated to the Central Committee's Politburo, the top policy-making body in the Soviet Union, as a candidate (or nonvoting) member. Then in July 1985, in a series of leadership changes that consolidated the power of newly ascended General Secretary Gorbachev, Shevardnadze became a full member of the Politburo and was the surprise choice to take over from veteran diplomat Andrei Gromyko as foreign minister. Shevardnadze made a strong impression in his international debut at the July meetings in Finland to mark the tenth anniversary of the Helsinki accords. (*See also* USSR.)

WALDHEIM, Kurt

When Kurt Waldheim was inaugurated as the president of Austria on July 8, 1986, it should have been the crowning achievement of his career as a diplomat and statesman. Then 67, Waldheim had served as Austria's foreign minister, ambassador to Canada, and representative to the United Nations, as well as secretary-general of the UN for ten years, but over all that time he made no secret of his view that the ultimate honor would be the largely ceremonial presidency of Austria.

But early in March 1986, in the midst of his campaign, there was an international uproar over charges that

Kurt Waldheim

Waldheim had belonged to two Nazi organizations as a youth, that as a German army officer in the Balkans during World War II he gave the orders that led to the massacres of Yugoslav partisans, that he knew of the deportation of Jews to death camps—and that he had lied about it all. The original charges, published in the Vienna newsmagazine *Profil*, proved to be just the tip of the iceberg. In the months that followed, the New York-based World Jewish Congress unveiled additional incriminating documents, piece by piece. Much of the evidence emerged from archives in Washington, DC, West Germany, and the UN itself. The UN file showed that in 1948 the allied War Crimes Commission had included Waldheim on a list of persons against whom there was sufficient evidence to justify prosecution.

Waldheim, who earlier had said that his active military service ended in 1942, when he was wounded on the Soviet front, now conceded that he had served as an officer in German Army Group E in the Balkans, under Gen. Alexander Loehr, who was later executed for war crimes. Waldheim insisted, however, that he had never knowingly belonged to any Nazi group and neither witnessed nor committed any war crimes.

The Austrian public was apparently satisfied with his explanation, giving him 53.9% of the vote in presidential run-off elections in June 1986. He was sworn in for a six-year term on July 8. (*See also* AUSTRIA.)

Background. Of Czechoslovak descent, Kurt Waldheim was born on Dec. 21, 1918, near Vienna, Austria. He was drafted into the German army in 1939, received his doctor of law degree from the University of Vienna in 1944, and entered the Austrian foreign service in 1945. Among his positions were delegate to negotiations on the Austrian State Treaty (1945-47), first secretary at the Austrian Embassy in Paris (1948-51), head of personnel in the ministry of foreign affairs (1951-55), permanent Austrian observer to the UN (1955-56), minister plenipotentiary to Canada (1956-58), ambassador to Canada (1958-60), director general for political affairs in the ministry of foreign affairs (1960-64), and permanent representative of Austria to the UN (1964-68). Waldheim became Austria's foreign minister in 1968, serving until 1970. The following year he lost his first bid for the Austrian presidency but won the first of his two five-year terms as UN secretary-general. His bid for a third term failed in 1981.

MICHAEL BERLIN

WALKER, Herschel Junior

When the University of Georgia running back Herschel Walker signed a multiyear contract with the New Jersey Generals of the United States Football League (USFL) in February 1983, he became the centerpiece and marquee attraction of the fledgling professional league. When the USFL suspended operations in August 1986, Walker became the most coveted of its star players to sign with a National Football League (NFL) team. After winning release from his guaranteed personal-service contract with General's owner Donald Trump, Walker penned a five-year, $5 million deal with the Dallas Cowboys (who had drafted him in 1985).

Few doubted that the 24-year-old Walker would succeed in this new phase of his career. At 6' 1½" (1.87 m), 220 lbs (100kg), he combines the strength of a weightlifter (which he is not) with the speed of a world-class sprinter (which he was). As a collegian he rushed for a total of 5,259 yards (third on the all-time list, most in a three-year career), set ten NCAA records, was voted All-America three times, and won the Heisman Trophy in his junior year (1982). In his three seasons with the Generals, Walker led the USFL in rushing yardage twice—1,812 yards in 1983 and 2,411 yards in 1985. The latter figure set a new professional record and established Walker as the league's all-time leading rusher with a total of 5,562 yards. He was the league's most valuable player in 1985.

Background. The fifth of seven children, Herschel Junior Walker was born in Augusta, GA, on March 3, 1962. The family lived in a tenant-farm shanty until he was eight, when they moved to a small wood frame house. Walker was short and chubby as a boy and, unlike his brothers and sisters, had little interest in sports. He began playing football in the fifth grade, however, and soon was dreaming of following in his brothers' footsteps as a star of the high-school varsity. Building himself with sit-ups, push-ups, and sprint running—the essence of his training even today—he developed into a powerful tailback at Johnson County High School in Wrightsville. By his senior year, he was the most highly touted high-school running back in the country. In track, Walker was all-state in the shot put, 100-yard dash, and 200-yard dash. He also played varsity basketball.

Walker began his freshman season on the University of Georgia football team as a third-stringer, but by the end of the first game, in which he scored two touchdowns, he was the regular starting tailback. He set a new NCAA freshman rushing record that year (1,616 yards) and led his team to its first championship. In 1980 he was third in the voting for the Heisman Trophy, in 1981 he finished second, and in 1982 he won the award. Walker also competed in track and was among the nation's fastest in the 100-yard dash and the 100 meters.

Herschel Walker   Photos. AP/Wide World

Bolivian troops guard a cocaine processing plant that had been raided in a joint exercise with U.S. Army forces. The American troops arrived in Bolivia in mid-July and assisted in the operation until mid-November.

BOLIVIA

The disastrous state of the economy and attempts to curb the cocaine trade, which was corrupting all levels of Bolivian society, occupied the elected government of President Victor Paz Estenssoro in 1986.

The Economy. Government-imposed austerity measures caused widespread hardship but did reduce inflation to 92% for the year ending July 31, 1986, compared with 16,259% for the year ending July 31, 1985. The collapse of world tin prices and a crackdown on the cocaine trade, however, were expected to reduce Bolivia's exports to $400 million in 1986.

A drastic reorganization of the tax structure passed by Congress in May introduced for the first time a value added tax and a wealth tax. The bill was designed to raise taxes from 1% to 12% of the gross domestic product (GDP).

In July government workers received a wage increase of 33%, their first in ten months. Earlier in the year, a majority of Bolivia's teachers had been dismissed temporarily in a salary dispute with the government.

The Labor Movement. The government announced in August that it would liquidate the money-losing government tin-mining firm, COMIBOL. A majority of the mines would be offered to the workers to run as cooperatives, and the rest would be closed. This and other drastic cutbacks led to a number of protests by tin miners during the year.

A general miners' strike at the end of August provoked the government to declare a state of siege on August 28. A nationwide curfew was imposed, political and union activities were banned, and a reported 162 persons were arrested. Some of those detained were released when the strike ended on August 30.

The pro-Soviet Communist Party had won control of the Miners Federation in May, defeating a coalition of other political factions.

Juan Lechin, who had headed the organization for 40 years, then announced that he would resign from that post and as head of the Central Obrera Boliviana (COB), the main labor group.

The labor movement generally opposed the government's economic policies. COB organized a referendum on July 25 and announced that 95% of the 300,000 people who had voted favored nonpayment of the foreign debt and opposed the new tax bill.

Politics and the Cocaine Trade. The anticipated supreme court trial of former president and suspected cocaine smuggler Luis García Meza, who was charged by Congress in February with sedition, armed revolt, and assassination, was halted in May when the court was unable to gather a quorum. Nine justices, fearing reprisals, had removed themselves from the case.

The Paz Estenssoro government tried to do something about the nation's cocaine growing and smuggling problem. In June the U.S. government decided to withhold $7.2 million in economic aid, charging that Bolivia had failed to take serious steps to curb the growing and processing of coca and its derivatives, destined for the U.S. market. In mid-July, six U.S. Army helicopters and more than 150 U.S. soldiers landed in Bolivia and cooperated with Bolivian police and soldiers in attacking and destroying coca processing plants. Few arrests were made but a steep drop in coca prices resulted. Following the withdrawal of the U.S. troops in mid-November, however, cocaine traffic was reported to be returning, and the price for the coca leaf was rising again. The Paz Estenssoro government then announced that it would ask the Bolivian Congress to outlaw the growing of coca plants and eventually to introduce an eradication program. A reorganization of the nation's narcotics police force and increased penalties for those who aid drug traffickers also were promised.

BOLIVIA · Information Highlights

Official Name: Republic of Bolivia.
Location: West-central South America.
Area: 424,163 sq mi (1 098 581 km²).
Population (mid-1986 est.): 6,400,000.
Chief Cities (1982 est.): Sucre, the legal capital, 79,941; La Paz, the actual capital, 881,404; Santa Cruz de la Sierra, 376,912; Cochabamba, 281,962.
Government: *Head of state and government,* Victor Paz Estenssoro, president (took office Aug. 6, 1985). *Legislature*—Congress: Senate and Chamber of Deputies.
Monetary Unit: Peso (1,500,000 pesos equal U.S.$1, September 1985).
Gross National Product (1985 est. U.S.$): $4,000,000,000.
Economic Index (June 1986): *Consumer Prices* (La Paz, 1980 = 100), all items, 6,921,735; food, 7,603,573.
Foreign Trade (1984 U.S.$): *Imports,* $631,000,000; *exports,* $773,000,000.

Debt. In June, Minister of Finance Juan Cariaga headed a delegation to Paris to negotiate with the governments of the Paris Club. The meeting resulted in Bolivia being given 15 years, with a ten-year grace period, to repay $400 million of the $600 million it owed to member governments. In August talks with 128 private foreign banks, aimed at rescheduling payment of $1 billion, began in Washington, DC. These efforts to settle the country's foreign debt after no payments had been made in almost two years made it possible for Bolivia to begin to receive modest new loans from a variety of sources. In June, Bolivia reached an agreement with the International Monetary Fund, contingent on the continuation of the government's economic program. It provided a $57 million standby loan, $57 million in compensatory financing, and $400 million in loans from governments and lending agencies.

ROBERT J. ALEXANDER, *Rutgers University*

BRAZIL

President José Sarney implemented a bold economic reform program that prevented the Brazilian economy from spinning out of control and ensured and impressive victory for his coalition in the first nationwide elections since the military relinquished control in 1985.

Politics and Government. Improved economic conditions lofted the popularity of Sarney, who in March 1985 became the country's first civilian chief executive in two decades. Elevated from vice-president-elect to president in April 1985 (upon the death of President-elect Tancredo Neves), Sarney during 1986 attempted to ingratiate himself with members of Neves' liberal Brazilian Democratic Movement (PMDB), who disdainfully viewed the nation's new leader as a political opportunist.

Some 30 parties participated in nationwide elections on November 15. More than 60 million Brazilians went to the polls to select governors in all 23 states, as well as 487 members of the Chamber of Deputies, 72 senators, and 947 members of provincial assemblies. The proliferation of candidates, combined with an economic upswing spurred by curbs on inflation during the preceding months, redounded to the benefit of the increasingly popular Sarney, who supported nominees of the PMDB and his own Liberal front, the right-of-center junior partner in the governing coalition.

The PMDB emerged from the election as the country's largest political force. All told, the party captured governorships in 22 of the 23 states, 51% of the seats in the lower house, and 61% of the seats in the Senate.

Especially heartening to the PMDB was the victory of its candidate, Wellington Moreira Franco, in the gubernatorial race in Rio de Janeiro. His opponent, Darcy Ribeiro, was the hand-picked choice of the flamboyant outgoing governor, Leonel Brizola, and his populist Democratic Labor Party. This setback aside, Brizola remained an important figure in Brazilian politics. In the event of deteriorating economic conditions, Brizola was well positioned to take advantage of popular frustration.

Of particular interest to Sarney and other presidential aspirants was the outcome of the legislative contests, since the members of the bicameral Congress would also form a Constituent Assembly empowered to draft a Fundamental Law to replace the one promulgated after the 1964 military coup. Central to a new constitution would be provisions for electing the chief executive and setting his term of office. The PMDB's strong presence in the assembly augured well for direct elections to replace the military-fashioned electoral college system. It remained to be seen, however, whether Sarney, who claimed he would not seek reelection, would be permitted to complete Neves' six-year term or whether a new election would be held in the late 1980s. The Constituent Assembly also was to decide on the balance of power between government branches, the role of the armed forces, the latitude allowed to foreign investors, and the economic mission of the state.

Economy. Keenly aware that economic conditions would greatly affect the legitimacy of Brazil's nascent democracy, Sarney ordered sweeping changes in late February. Precipitating this action was a surging rate of inflation, which surpassed 250% in 1985 and threatened to exceed 300% in 1986. Consequently, the president and his finance minister, Dilson Funaro, launched "a war of life and death" against higher prices. The main weapons in this conflict were a freeze on wages and prices (including rents and mortgage payments for one year) and the introduction of a new currency, the cruzado. The program, widely referred to as the Plano Tropical, also included: an increase in the minimum wage from $44 to $58 a month; unemployment benefits for individuals out of work for more than a month; and elimination of daily adjustments of Brazil's currency against the U.S. dollar, with future devaluations to be made periodically at the central bank's discretion.

The Plano Tropical had an immediate and dramatic impact. Inflation slowed to 1% per month and purchasing power increased by 30%, sparking a national shopping spree. But in late November, emboldened by its electoral triumph, the Sarney government acted to dampen what now appeared to be an overheated economy. Its decision to begin lifting the nine-month-old price freeze set off loud and bitter protests. Giving credence to Sarney's earlier warnings on the fragility of the new democratic institutions, protestors and police clashed in the first violent antigovernment protests since the end of military rule. The election tribunal received numerous calls from people wanting to change their vote.

Foreign Affairs. Encouraged by the early success of his domestic economic policy, Sarney flew to Buenos Aires in late July to enter the General Agreement on Integration and Development with Argentina's President Raúl Alfonsín. Sarney and Alfonsín championed the economic accords (which Uruguay's President Julio Maria Sanguinetti later signed) as an important step in promoting economic integration and laying the foundation for a Latin American common market.

Effective Jan. 1, 1987, the 12 protocols of the pact establish a bilateral customs union for capital goods and ensure cooperation between the two countries in biotechnology, energy, agriculture, and other areas. The initial emphasis was on capital goods, with bilateral trade anticipated to rise from $300 million to $750 million on the strength of marked expansion through the removal of trade barriers. Under the agreement, overall Argentine-Brazilian commerce was expected to double, to $3 billion, by the end of the decade. The accord also provided for the exchange of information and assistance in the event of a nuclear accident in either country.

Leaders in both nations compared the arrangement to the coal and steel pact signed by West Germany and France in the 1950s, which evolved into the European Community. Still, many businessmen, especially in Argentina, remained skeptical about the plan. Their concerns focused on the fact that Brazil, with a population four times as large as its neighbor's, boasted a dynamic economy that grew 8% in 1985, compared with negative 0.4% in Argentina, where markets were depressed and industries remained burdened by outdated equipment.

Even as trade barriers were dismantled with Argentina, Brazil continued to practice protectionism toward products from the United States and other industrialized countries. As a result commercial issues dominated talks between U.S. President Ronald Reagan and President Sarney when the latter visited Washington in September. In welcoming Brazil's first civilian chief executive to the United States in more than 30 years, Reagan lauded Brazil as an emerging "world power" that served as a model to other Latin American states. Yet, he added, Brazil's new role carried with it "global considerations and international responsibilities," including the opening of domestic markets to foreign goods and services in return for continued access to markets abroad. Uppermost in Reagan's mind was a bitter dispute sparked by Brazil's 1984 "informatics law," which barred imports of U.S.-manufactured minicomputers and microcomputers despite Brazil's $5 billion trade surplus with the United States. In the political realm officials in Washington were displeased with Brazil's renewal of diplomatic relations with Cuba and its opposition to U.S. policy in Nicaragua.

While in the United States, President Sarney stressed that only by expanding exports could his nation make payments on a $105 billion external debt, the largest in the Third World. Moreover, he pointed out, such key Brazilian products as textiles, clothing, and footwear remained subject to restrictive U.S. import practices. In a similar vein he argued that debtor nations should not import more from their creditors unless these affluent countries reduced interest rates on the debts and agreed to longer repayment periods. Such easing of debt terms would contribute to the "recovery and normalization of the world economy," he asserted.

On a different theme Sarney urged that the South Atlantic between South America and Africa be preserved as a nuclear-free zone.

GEORGE W. GRAYSON
College of William and Mary

BRAZIL · Information Highlights

Official Name: Federative Republic of Brazil.
Location: Eastern South America.
Area: 3,286,525 sq mi (8 512 100 km²).
Population (mid-1986 est.): 143,300,000.
Chief Cities (1980 census): Brasília, the capital, 1,176,908; São Paulo, 7,032,547; Rio de Janeiro, 5,090,700; Salvador, 1,491,642.
Government: *Head of state and government,* José Sarney Costa, president (took office April 21, 1985). *Legislature*—National Congress: Senate and Chamber of Deputies.
Monetary Unit: Cruzado (13.77 cruzados equal U.S. $1, Oct. 27, 1986).
Gross National Product (1984 est. U.S.$): $321,400,000,000.
Economic Indexes (1985): *Consumer Prices* (São Paulo, 1980 = 100), all items, 7178.8; food, 8387.1. *Industrial Production* (August 1985, 1980 = 100), 96.
Foreign Trade (1985 U.S.$): *Imports,* $13,167,-000,000; *exports,* $25,639,000,000.

BRITISH COLUMBIA

As had been anticipated, 1986 was an election year for British Columbia. The events that preceded the October 22 general election, however, were entirely unpredictable.

Politics and Government. Early in 1986, Premier William R. Bennett undertook a reorganization of his cabinet that saw the retirement of three veteran ministers and the establishment of a new ministry for postsecondary education. On May 22 came the surprise announcement that Bennett would step down from office. At the subsequent July 28-30 Social Credit leadership convention, William Vander Zalm, a former cabinet minister, defeated 11 other candidates for the party leadership. He won on the fourth ballot with 801 votes to the 454 cast for Attorney General Brian Smith. The new premier formed a cabinet on August 14, but within six weeks was looking for his own mandate from the electorate.

In the general election, Social Credit retained just under 50% of the popular vote and increased its representation in the enlarged 69-seat legislative assembly from 35 to 47 members. Support for the New Democratic opposition fell by 2.4 points to 42.5%.

The margins of victory were close in many ridings, and two seats changed hands following the final count of ballots cast by voters who registered on election day. The Progressive Conservatives were unable to retain the seat they had gained from the defection of a New Democrat, and no third party candidates were elected. Liberal Party support, however, rose from 2.7% to 6.7% of the popular vote.

On November 6, a new 18-member cabinet was formed. Many functions were reassigned among the ministries, and four existing members were dropped from the ''new look'' government.

BRITISH COLUMBIA • Information Highlights

Area: 365,946 sq mi (947 800 km²).
Population (Jan. 1986 est.): 2,897,900.
Chief Cities (1981 census): Victoria, the capital, 64,379; Vancouver, 414,281: Prince George, 67,559; Kamloops, 64,048; Kelowna, 59,196.
Government (1986): *Chief Officers*—lt. gov., Robert G. Rogers; premier, William Vander Zalm (Social Credit Party). *Legislature*—Legislative Assembly, 69 members.
Provincial Finances (1986–87 fiscal year budget): *Revenues,* $8,768,000,000; *expenditures,* $9,643,-000,000.
Personal Income (average weekly earnings, May 1986): $447.76.
Labor Force (July 1986, seasonally adjusted: *Employed* workers, 15 years of age and over, 1,462,000; *Unemployed,* 178,000 (12.2%).
Education (1986–87): *Enrollment*—elementary and secondary schools, 524,120 pupils; postsecondary—universities, 35,450; community colleges, 22,900.
(All monetary figures are in Canadian dollars.)

The Economy. In the provincial government's budget for fiscal year 1986-87, announced March 20, expenditures were estimated at C$9,643,000,000, and with revenues of $8,768,000,000, the annual deficit was projected to fall to $875 million from $937 million in 1985-86. Expenditure plans included $230 million from special funds for improvements in education and health care.

Tax changes to promote economic recovery included a two-stage reduction in corporate income tax rates to 14% by 1988. Insurance-premium taxes on provincial companies were to be eliminated, and property taxes on private forest lands reduced. Small business venture capital tax credits were to be extended to export-oriented service corporations.

While Expo 86, Vancouver's world's fair (*see* page 161), provided a significant boost to the tourist industry, other sectors of the economy also continued to show signs of recovery. Retail sales, urban-housing starts, manufacturing shipments, and lumber production were up in the first half of 1986. While the rate of unemployment remained high at more than 12%, it was down by nearly 2 percentage points from 1985 levels. Higher sales and prices for pulp and paper products increased earnings in the forest industry, but in July, there began a prolonged labor dispute with members of the International Woodworkers of America, shutting down logging operations and two thirds of coastal lumber-mill production.

Increased shipments to the United States were primarily responsible for a 5.6% growth in British Columbia's exports in 1985. The prospect of protectionist measures against provincial products in U.S. markets therefore continued to cause concern. In May a 35% tariff was imposed by the United States on Canadian exports of red cedar shakes and shingles. In October a preliminary ruling by the U.S. Commerce Department reversed a 1983 decision by recommending a 15% countervailing duty on softwood lumber imports to the United States from Canada.

NORMAN J. RUFF
University of Victoria

BULGARIA

A series of natural disasters, particularly a prolonged drought in the summer of 1985 and bitter cold and blizzards in early 1986, caused serious economic problems for Bulgaria. There were energy and electric-power shortages and across-the-board price increases for everything from gasoline to telephone calls. The 1985 state economic plan was not fulfilled, with severe shortfalls in major sectors and agricultural production falling 9% below 1984 figures. The government solicited a $475 million loan from the West and planned to buy Western grain.

Domestic Affairs. These problems, together with criticisms reportedly made by the Soviet Communist leader, Mikhail Gorbachev, when he visited Bulgaria in October 1985, provoked a flurry of major structural and personnel changes in the government. In March 1986, Premier Georgi (Grisha) Filipov was replaced by Georgi Atanasov. Within the Council of Ministers, three new bodies were formed: an Economic Council, a Social Council, and a Council for Intellectual Development. A new Ministry of Trade was established. The Ministry of Energy and Raw Material Reserves was divided into a Ministry of Supplies, a Ministry of Metallurgy, and a Ministry of Energy. The State Committee for Science and Technological Progress was replaced by the new State Committee on Research and Technology and given a new chairman, Stoyan Markov. Ivan Iliev was named chairman of the remodeled State Planning Commission. Other new high-level appointments included Ilcho Dimitrov as minister of national education, Georgi Georgiev as chairman of the Committee for State and People's Control, and Alexi Ivanov as minister of agriculture and forestry.

The most important event in domestic politics was the 13th Congress of the Bulgarian Communist Party (BCP), held in Sofia, April 2–5, 1986. The draft theses on the future of the party and state to the year 2000, published in February, and the addresses of Party chief Todor Zhivkov and others at the Congress stressed several major points. Bulgaria was said to have reached a crucial stage in its social-political development and would have to utilize the scientific-technological revolution to bring about a mature socialist society. Both the party and the government were exhorted to adopt a "dynamic style of work." Economic planning and management were to be modernized, with the emphasis on high professionalism for all cadres, local decision-making and initiative, competition, and wage differentials based on performance. The Eighth Five Year

Plan (1981-5) was declared a success, and the Ninth (1986-90), emphasizing technical reequipment and automation, was launched. There was to be "maximum unification" between Bulgarian economic plans and those of the Soviet Union and the Council for Mutual Economic Assistance. Zhivkov was reelected general secretary of the BCP, a post he has held since 1954.

Foreign Affairs. In March three Bulgarians accused of conspiring to assassinate Pope John Paul II in 1981 were acquitted by a court in Rome, on the grounds of insufficient evidence. Bulgaria received worldwide censure, and its relations with Turkey deteriorated over its attempt to forcibly assimilate its large ethnic Turkish minority. Bulgaria continued to insist that no coercion was being used to get ethnic Turks to adopt Slavic names. The Parliamentary Assembly of the Council of Europe and Amnesty International both denounced Bulgaria's actions.

JOSEPH FREDERICK ZACEK
State University of New York at Albany

BURMA

A drop in demand for its exports posed more of a problem for Burma in 1986 than the illness of its president or efforts at collaboration by various insurgent groups.

Politics. Formal governmental decision-making changed little on the surface in soldier-leader Ne Win's 24th year in power. At the age of 75, the veteran nationalist retained his position as chairman of the country's only political party, the Burma Socialist Program Party. He still made or reviewed all major and many minor public-policy and personnel decisions despite the fact that his chosen heir apparent, Gen. San Yu, had succeeded him as president in 1981 and been reelected to a four-year term in 1985.

Ne Win's health had been a factor in his decision to step aside as president. In 1986, however, his physical condition seemingly improved, while that of the 68-year-old San Yu appeared to falter. San Yu underwent hospitalization and treatment for an aortic aneurysm in the United States, and his recovery was visibly less than complete. In light of the health and age of both party chairman and president, speculation as to the country's ultimate leader was renewed. There was no doubt, however, that the army would continue to be the dominant element in Burmese politics.

Insurgencies. Burma's Communist and ethnic minority insurgents continued their scattered military operations against the government, but none of the rebels posed a serious threat to the regime's survival. Partly for this reason, the Communists took the lead in seeking to combine their antigovernment activity

---

BULGARIA • Information Highlights

Official Name: People's Republic of Bulgaria.
Location: Southeastern Europe.
Area: 42,823 sq mi (110 912 km²).
Population (mid-1986 est.): 9,000,000.
Chief Cities (Dec. 31, 1983): Sofia, the capital, 1,093,752; Plovdiv, 373,235; Varna, 295,218.
Government: *Head of state,* Todor Zhivkov, chairman of the State Council and general secretary of the Communist Party (took office July 1971). *Head of government,* Georgi Atanasov, chairman of the Council of Ministers (took office March 1986).
Monetary Unit: Lev (1.000 leva equal U.S.$1, June 1986).
Gross National Product (1984, 1984 U.S.$): $56,400,000,000.
Economic Index: *Industrial Production* (1985, 1980 = 100), 124.
Foreign Trade (1985 U.S.$): *Imports,* $13,647,-000,000; *exports,* $13,341,000,000.

BURMA · Information Highlights

Official Name: Socialist Republic of the Union of Burma.
Location: Southeast Asia.
Area: 261,217 sq mi (676 552 km²).
Population (mid-1986 est.): 37,700,000.
Chief City (1983 census): Rangoon, the capital, 2,458,712.
Government: *Head of state,* U San Yu, president (took office Nov. 1981). *Head of government,* U Maung Maung Kha, prime minister (took office March 1977). *Legislature* (unicameral)—National Assembly.
Monetary Unit: Kyat (7.337 kyats equal U.S.$1, June 1986).
Economic Index (Rangoon, 1985): *Consumer Prices* (1980 = 100), all items, 123.5; food, 120.8.
Foreign Trade (1985 U.S.$): *Imports,* $283,000,000; *exports,* $315,000,000.

with that of the Karen, Kachin, Shan, and other minority groups. But no joint military assaults were attempted by the Communists and those minorities willing to cooperate with them. Stepped-up army operations, in fact, resulted in the surrender of some 200 insurgents between May and August.

Economy. A decline in export earnings, dwindling foreign-exchange reserves, and a worsening debt-service ratio contrasted with optimistic official reports on gains under the Fourth Five-Year Plan, which ended March 31.

An average annual gross domestic product (GDP) increase of 5.5% was announced by the government, which also proclaimed a goal of 4.5% annual GDP growth for the Fifth Five-Year Plan, which began April 1. The reported rate of economic expansion during the 1981–86 plan was widely questioned, however, while such change as did occur was concentrated in the earlier years.

A more accurate reflection of the state of the Burmese economy was the tripling of external debt between 1979 and 1986. This debt was estimated to be as high as $3 billion. Exports declined 50% during the 1981–86 period, while foreign exchange reserves dwindled to $50 million. Although rice production increased, rice exports fell behind those of teak and hardwood in value. Because of the drop in export earnings, foreign-debt service consumed almost 60% of all export revenues.

The government's problems were worsened by an April fire in Rangoon that left 18,000 persons homeless and caused $8 million in damage.

Foreign Affairs. Burma continued to pursue a truly neutral policy in international relations. One third of its external debt was owed to Japan, while the Soviet Union purchased the largest share of Burma's grain. The United States granted a $30 million loan for construction of a rice mill and storage facility.

RICHARD BUTWELL
California State University

BUSINESS AND CORPORATE AFFAIRS

The major U.S. business stories of 1986 revolved around mergers, divestitures, and takeovers; stock market activities and illegal insider trading; and significant changes in top-level management of major corporations.

There were no major changes in the overall economic picture during the year. How one felt about the economy depended primarily on where one lived. The most hard-hit areas of the country were those dependent on petroleum, steel, and textiles. Also hard hit were agricultural areas dependent on grain crops and beef cattle. In general, however, the economic indicators were moderate to strong. The gross national product grew at a rate of nearly 3%, down slightly from 1985. Inflation during 1986 was very modest, with the Consumer Price Index—held down by the sharp drop in oil and gasoline prices—rising at an annual rate of only about 2%, and the Producer Price Index holding steady. The prime lending rate declined from 9.5% to about 7.5% during the course of the year. The unemployment rate remained approximately 7%, with total employment reaching 112 million and the number of Americans without jobs at 8.25 million. The foreign trade deficit dropped slightly as the year progressed but continued to be a serious problem. (*See also* UNITED STATES—The Economy.)

The stock market made big news in 1986. On September 4 the Dow Jones Industrial Average reached an all-time high of 1,919.71, but this was quickly followed by a record drop of 86.61 points on September 11; the 4.61% decline was the largest one-day drop since 1962. Subsequent increases brought the Dow back up to a 1986 (and another all-time) high of 1,955.57 on December 2. (*See also* STOCKS AND BONDS.)

Overall corporate profits during 1986 ran slightly ahead of 1985, but, as always, several major companies faced difficulties. LTV Corporation, the parent company of the nation's second-largest steelmaker, in July became the nation's largest industrial concern ever to file for bankruptcy. Also during the year, Union Carbide sold off some $800 million of its business; General Motors announced plans to close 11 of its plants, employing some 29,000 workers, by 1990; United Technologies announced that it would be laying off 11,000 employees; and American Telephone & Telegraph Company (AT&T) planned to eliminate 27,400 jobs. During 1986, General Motors was one of a number of U.S. companies, also including International Business Machines (IBM) and Coca-Cola, that announced discontinuation of operations in South Africa because of the political and economic uncertainties.

Mergers, Takeovers, Divestitures. The continuing trend of corporate mergers, takeovers, and divestitures had many business analysts wondering about its overall effects on the economy. Such transactions, along with insider stock trading and other financial activities, led some people to believe that business markets were being manipulated by modern-day "robber barons."

In no area did mergers and takeovers play a more significant role than the airline industry, in which federal deregulation had brought scores of new companies into the market, rampant price discounting, some huge losses, and several bankruptcies. From about mid-1985 to the end of 1986, 12 mergers were consummated or planned among U.S. airlines. Texas Air became the nation's largest carrier by acquiring Continental, Eastern, Empire, and People Express. The takeover of People Express was widely believed to have saved it from bankruptcy. People's had previously taken over Frontier, which did file for bankruptcy. In other 1986 airline deals, Northwest Orient purchased Republic, Delta took over Western, TWA bought Ozark, and USAir acquired Pacific-Southwest. Further consolidating the transportation industry, railroad companies were attempting to evolve into "megacarriers." Burlington-Northern bought six trucking companies. Norfolk Southern acquired North American Van Lines, and Union Pacific bought Overnite Transportation. (*See also* TRANSPORTATION.)

In the retailing field the major takeover was May Department Stores' purchase of Associated Dry Goods Corporation, making it the fifth largest retailer in the country. Other major mergers during the year included General Electric's takeover of Radio Corporation of America (RCA), Burroughs' acquisition of Sperry, and Campeau Corporation's (a Canadian real-estate company) purchase of Allied Stores Corporation.

Among the attempted takeovers during the year were Carl Icahn's $8 billion offer for USX (formerly U.S. Steel), Revlon's bid for Gillette, the financier James Goldsmith's effort to gain control of Goodyear Tire & Rubber Company, and First Interstate Bancorp's three separate attempts to acquire BankAmerica. Among the other deals that were consummated in 1986 were the acquisition of Celanese Corporation, a major producer of synthetic fibers, by a U.S. subsidiary of the West German chemicals company Hoechst AG; the merger of Communications Satellite Corporation (Comsat) and Contel Corporation; and Unilever's purchase of Chesebrough-Pond.

A major stimulus for much of the merger and takeover activity was the Reagan administration's "new federalism" campaign to shift power from Washington to the states. The permissiveness of the federal government in the antitrust field fueled the takeover trend. During 1986, however, a federal court did refuse to allow Coca-Cola to take over Dr. Pepper, and the U.S. Supreme Court agreed to consider the validity of an Indiana law restricting hostile takeovers of corporations established in that state. The court's ruling was eagerly awaited by the business community.

In addition to mergers and acquisitions, important divestitures took place in a variety of industries. Kroger restructured its operations by selling off its drugstore business. Dayton-Hudson Corporation sold off B. Dalton, the nation's second largest bookstore chain (later acquired by Barnes & Noble). And Transamerica sold Budget Rent-A-Car.

Insider Trading. In November the U.S. Securities and Exchange Commission (SEC) took action which, indirectly, was expected to be an important step in slowing the trend toward mergers, takeovers, and leveraged buyouts. The SEC fined Ivan F. Boesky, one of the nation's most active arbitrageurs, $100 million for the illegal use of inside information—knowledge unavailable to the public concerning proposed corporate takeovers. Boesky agreed to pay the fine and was barred for life from U.S. securities trading. The shock waves from the SEC action were still reverberating as the year ended.

Corporate Name Changes. The year 1986 saw several well-known companies change their names. U.S. Steel became USX, reflecting its de-emphasis of steel. The new computer company bringing together Burroughs and Sperry was dubbed Unisys. International Harvester became Navistar. And Standard Oil Company (Ohio)—commonly known as Sohio—dropped both names and reverted to Standard Oil Company.

Executive Changes. Among the year's new chief executive officers (CEOs) at major U.S. companies were F. Ross Johnson at RJR Nabisco, Lawrence G. Rawl at Exxon, and D. Johnson Corr at TWA (where Icahn became chairman). A.W. Clausen, the retired CEO of BankAmerica, quit his post as head of the World Bank and returned to the troubled holding company. At United Technologies, Harry J. Gray retired as chairman and was succeeded by Robert F. Daniell, already the president and CEO. At CBS Inc., Thomas H. Wyman resigned as chairman and president; company founder William S. Paley was named acting chairman, and chief stockholder Laurence A. Tisch became acting CEO. And in a highly publicized move in early December, the controversial Texas billionaire H. Ross Perot was ousted from the board of directors of General Motors, of which he was the largest stockholder; the company bought back his shares for a reported $700 million.

See also INDUSTRIAL PRODUCTION; LABOR; UNITED STATES—Privatization.

STEWART M. LEE
Geneva College

CALIFORNIA

An unusual election distinguished California in 1986. Otherwise it was an unremarkable year.

Election. Despite several emotional issues, voter turnout in the general election was near a record low. In a rare development, 3 of the 7 members of the state Supreme Court, including Chief Justice Rose E. Bird, were overwhelmingly denied further tenure in office. The principal issue involved their persistent overturning of death sentences on appeal.

Republican Gov. George Deukmejian won reelection by a 61% landslide in his rematch with Mayor Tom Bradley of Los Angeles. But Democrats won the other five elective administrative offices in California, a state where political party labels often mean little. U.S. Sen. Alan Cranston, 72, won reelection by 116,000 votes, receiving less than 50% of the total, but defeating Rep. Ed Zschau and three minor candidates. The congressional delegation remained at 27 Democrats and 18 Republicans; every incumbent who ran was reelected.

Democrats kept control of the legislature but lost two Senate and three Assembly seats. Voters also acted on several policy proposals. Approved were four ballot issues to authorize $1.8 billion in state bonds, another limiting pensions for former state officials, and three that modified the restrictions placed on the property tax by Proposition 13 of 1979. In addition two controversial propositions won easy passage: one (by 73%) to make English the official state language and another (by 63%) to place strict controls on the dumping of toxic chemicals where they might contaminate drinking water. Two other controversial measures were defeated: one (receiving only 34% support) to set salary limits for state and local officials and employees; the other (with 71% opposed) to apply quarantine laws to AIDS victims.

Budget, Tax Reform, and Banking. The governor was able to meet his goal of no general tax increases in his first term. The new budget was only 2.2% higher than the previous year, and the emphasis was on additional funds for education and toxic-waste disposal.

In September the governor signed a bill changing the state's method of taxing the income of multinational corporations. The companies would be allowed to pay a special fee to avoid the state's unitary tax system. Under the unitary method a corporation operating both in the state and overseas is taxed by California on a proportion of its worldwide income. The system had been strongly criticized by Japanese and British multinational companies.

Perhaps the most historic legislation enacted during the year ended a decade of lobbying by New York institutions to break into the vast California banking business. Local banks and consumer groups uneasily accepted com-

AP/Wide World

Controversial Chief Justice Rose Bird was denied a new 12-year term by California voters. She faced a $5 million ad campaign that attacked her record on the death penalty.

promise legislation that will open the state to all non-California banks by 1991. Meanwhile, San Francisco-based BankAmerica Corporation, the nation's second-largest bank holding company, was in difficulties and was considering takeover offers.

Prisons. Voters approved the sale of additional bonds to assist in the building of new prisons. The program, already well behind schedule, was further delayed by a conflict between the governor and legislative Democrats over the location of a prison in Los Angeles county. Legislation mandating the location of a prison there was passed in 1985; the county currently has no state prison, even though 38% of California's prison commitments are made from there. A stalemate continued.

Weather and Earthquakes. A series of storms lasting for a week in mid-February did serious crop damage in northern California and was blamed for nine deaths. A levee broke on the Yuba River north of Sacramento, causing considerable flooding. A number of moderate earthquakes struck in the Palm Springs, San Diego, and San Francisco areas during the year, causing much media attention. But all occurred on minor faults and resulted in no significant damage. The dangerous San Andreas fault remained quiet.

Immigration. By 1986 persons of Asian descent constituted 8% of the state's population and were the fastest-growing segment of it. Persons of Filipino background had replaced

CALIFORNIA · Information Highlights

Area: 158,706 sq mi (411 049 km²).
Population (1985 est.): 26,365,000.
Chief Cities (July 1, 1984 est.): Sacramento, the capital, 304,131; Los Angeles, 3,096,721; San Diego, 960,452; San Francisco, 712,753; San Jose, 686,178; Long Beach, 378,752; Oakland, 351,898.
Government (1986): *Chief Officers*—governor, George Deukmejian (R); lt. gov., Leo McCarthy (D). *Legislature*—Senate, 40 members; Assembly, 80 members.
State Finances (fiscal year 1985): *Revenue,* $57,894,000,000; *expenditure,* $51,840,000,000.
Personal Income (1985): $423,566,000,000; per capita, $16,065.
Labor Force (June 1986): *Civilian labor force,* 13,373,400; *unemployed,* 866,500 (6.5% of total force).
Education: *Enrollment* (fall 1984)—public elementary schools, 2,845,962; public secondary, 1,305,148; colleges and universities, 1,650,439. *Public school expenditures* (1983–84), $11,850,-000,000 ($2,912 per pupil).

Chinese as the largest ethnic subgroup, but there was also a strong and continuing immigration of Koreans, Thais, Cambodians, and Vietnamese.

CHARLES R. ADRIAN
University of California, Riverside

CAMBODIA

The struggle for control of Cambodia continued during 1986. Despite intense diplomatic activities involving many governments, there was little progress toward a settlement.

Political and Military Developments. The Communist government of Heng Samrin, installed in Phnom Penh in 1979, continued for the most part to carry out the orders of its Vietnamese advisers. In December, just before the Vietnamese Communist Party Congress, there was a major shuffle of cabinet posts in Phnom Penh. Prime Minister Hun Sen relinquished two of his jobs—foreign minister and chairman of the party's foreign affairs commission. The minister of defense and the minister of planning also were replaced. Some 140,000 Vietnamese troops controlled the country, despite harassment from about 50,000 rebels. The three rebel groups include the Communist Khmer Rouge guerrilla army, numbering about 30,000, and two non-Communist factions led by Prince Norodom Sihanouk and Son Sann. The resistance remained badly divided despite their formation of a nominal political and military coalition in 1982. There were reports of fighting between Communist and non-Communist rebels in some areas. Although the Heng Samrin regime has a small army of its own, desertions and poor morale continue to degrade its capabilities.

The Vietnamese continued to use Cambodian conscripts to construct barriers along the Thai border. This slowed the flow of refugees into Thailand, but did not halt rebel attacks.

Economy. Cambodia's already severe economic problems were exacerbated by disruptive guerrilla attacks. It was announced that Soviet economic aid—$138.6 million in 1985—would be doubled over the next five years. Trade with Vietnam increased, and the settlement of Vietnamese civilians in Cambodia continued.

Foreign Affairs. In March 1986, Prince Sihanouk unveiled a major peace proposal. He suggested a phased withdrawal of military forces followed by talks between the resistance coalition and the Heng Samrin regime to set up a four-party interim government in Cambodia. The next step would be free elections for a "liberal democratic" government under United Nations supervision. Presumably the elections would be followed by a complete Vietnamese withdrawal from Cambodia. The proposal differed from previous resistance peace plans in calling for an initial Vietnamese withdrawal only to the east bank of the Mekong River and in offering a governmental role for the Heng Samrin regime.

According to press reports, Vietnam rejected the coalition proposal as "rigged" by China with the "sole aim to restore the Pol Pot clique [Khmer Rouge] to power" in Cambodia. Vietnam indicated that Prince Sihanouk and Son Sann were welcome to join a government of national reconciliation but said that the resistance coalition's political and military structure would have to be dismantled in any final settlement. Interestingly, Heng Samrin's deputy foreign minister told a reporter in March that dismantling the Khmer Rouge's political structure was not a precondition for talks.

In July, Soviet leader Mikhail Gorbachev gave a speech in Vladivostok encouraging reconciliation among all Communist parties in Asia. Although Gorbachev flatly rejected the March 1986 peace proposal, he urged China and Vietnam to improve their relations. Apparently he believed that China and Vietnam could work out a solution to the Cambodian problem that would leave Vietnam virtually in control. This would open the way to improved Soviet relations with members of the Association of Southeast Asian Nations (ASEAN), who supported the resistance coalition.

PETER A. POOLE
Author, "Eight Presidents and Indochina"

CAMBODIA · Information Highlights

Official Name: People's Republic of Kampuchea.
Location: Southeast Asia.
Area: 69,898 sq mi (181 035 km²).
Population (mid-1986 est.): 6,400,000.
Chief City (1983 est.): Phnom Penh, the capital, 600,000.
Government: *Head of state,* Heng Samrin (took office 1979). *Head of government,* Hun-Sen, prime minister (took office Jan. 1985).
Monetary Unit: Riel (4 riels equal U.S.$1, 1984).

Canada's Minister of International Trade Pat Carney confers with an aide at a meeting with provincial government representatives. Canada-U.S. trade and the general "free trade" issue remained at the center of national policy debate.

Canapress Photo

CANADA

For many Canadians 1986 was a year of cheerful beginnings and frustrated finishes. The Mulroney government's Free Trade initiative began with near consensus and ended the year in recriminations and rising protectionism. Vancouver's Expo 86 (*see* page 162) defied skeptics with its imagination and verve but closed amid gloomy prognoses for the regional economy. Prairie farmers grew the best wheat crop in years, only to see grades plummet under autumn rains, collapsing prices, and exports blocked by strikes and lockouts at the shipping ports. While the Conservative government suffered a midterm slump, the opposition Liberals contemplated their own leadership and wondered whether they could ever win with former Prime Minister John Turner at the party helm.

Free Trade. Backed by the business community, nearly all the provincial premiers, and massive documentation from the Liberal-appointed MacDonald Royal Commission, Canada's Progressive Conservative (PC) government claimed a mandate to negotiate "enhanced trade" arrangements with the United States. With 25% of Canada's production exported to the United States (compared with the 2% of U.S. production that goes north), the government employed Simon Reisman, its toughest trade negotiator, to sit down with the Americans for preliminary talks. Reisman and his U.S. counterpart, Peter Murphy, spent much of 1986 exploring issues and debating whether "cultural industries," the 1965

Auto Pact, Canada's welfare program, or the low exchange rate of the Canadian dollar would be debated at any formal negotiations. During a visit to Washington in March, Prime Minister Brian Mulroney sought to reproduce the good will of the 1985 "Shamrock Summit" with unquestioning renewal of the North American Air Defence Agreement and a promise of C$800 million in Canadian support for a future U.S. space station.

A rising tide of protectionism in the United States and approaching midterm elections there made the times unpropitious for trade liberalization. The U.S. Senate narrowly agreed to "fast track" debate on any Canada-U.S. trade deal, but the vote was followed by the imposition of a tariff that virtually wiped out Canada's $250 million cedar shingle industry and ended most of its steel pipe exports to the United States. Ottawa retaliated with a tariff on imported books. In October, U.S. West Coast timber interests persuaded the Commerce Department to reverse earlier rulings and clamp a 15% tariff on Canadian softwood imports. In British Columbia and northern Ontario, thousands of workers had to be laid off, while Canadian officials, at British Columbia's insistence, sought a compromise rather than retaliation or legal challenge.

Trade squabbles split Canadian opinion on the larger free-trade issue. Free-trade enthusiasts argued that U.S. protectionism made a deal urgent; economic nationalists insisted that negotiation was hopeless. After dipping to a bare majority in midsummer, those supporting the free-trade initiative gained strength in autumn polls.

Politics. The free-trade issue was little help to a prime minister who had staked his reputation on well-publicized support for U.S. President Ronald Reagan. With U.S. elections at hand, the White House could do little to help Canada, and Mulroney's instant endorsement of Reagan policies—from the anti-drug crusade to the refusal to negotiate on "Star Wars" at the Reykjavik summit—provoked much domestic editorial criticism.

More of the government's worries grew out of its problems in Quebec, a province where Conservatives had been a minor force until their 1984 election landslide. Minister of State (Transport) Suzanne Blais-Grenier quit the cabinet early in the year to protest government neglect of Montreal's army of unemployed. A Quebec Tory member of parliament (MP) abandoned his party. The prime minister's attempt to load his own northern Quebec riding with favors climaxed with construction of a maximum-security prison at Port-Cartier, but such extravagances drew criticism from the federal auditor-general. In an even bigger gesture to the boasted "French Power" in his cabinet, the prime minister switched a $1 billion aircraft maintenance contract from the lowest bidder, a Winnipeg firm, to the Montreal-based Canadair, privatized only months before. Manitobans, who had often voted Tory because of alleged Liberal favoritism for the French-speaking province, voiced outrage. Mulroney's reference to the Winnipeg firm, Bristol Aerospace, as "foreign" gave ammunition to his critics, and the political nature of the choice worried the business community. The opposition parties, eager to keep out of regional rivalries, largely kept silent.

Quebec was not the government's only problem. A 21-day fast by Sen. Jacques Hebert failed to save Katimavik, a $20 million "domestic peace corps" for young Canadians, but media attention helped make the government look insensitive. Others complained that Hebert's tactics were as immoral as blackmail. While the prime minister was making a spring visit to the Far East, his deputy, Erik Nielsen, tried ineptly to fend off opposition charges that Minister of Regional Industrial Expansion Sinclair Stevens had negotiated business loans through his wife with firms getting extensive grants from Stevens' own department. From South Korea, where Stevens himself had friends and business links, Mulroney had to demand his minister's resignation and a judicial inquiry. The result was a summer-long investigation of Stevens' corporate connections, the easy terms given firms that would do the government's bidding, and the corresponding ease with which a minister's wife could negotiate a loan. Opinion polls at that time showed the Conservatives slumping far behind the Liberals and barely ahead of the New Democrats, Canada's socialist party.

Then Tory fortunes began to recover. In a July cabinet shuffle, Nielsen was dumped in favor of Donald Mazankowski, an able and affable Albertan. Patricia Carney, effective as energy minister, was moved to foreign trade. Perrin Beatty, a young Ontarian who had survived two minor but politically dangerous assignments—responsibility for the post office and for prisons—was promoted to minister of defense. Quebec ministers were given economic portfolios and higher profiles as a way of reviving their government's dismal standing in Quebec opinion polls. Dalton Camp, a progressive Tory and a veteran image-maker, was summoned to Ottawa, appointed a senior deputy minister, and ordered to rebuild the government's popularity. The most striking change came in September with the replacement of John Bosley as speaker of the House of Commons. Discredited after two years of rowdy debate between the huge Tory majority and the small but relentless opposition groups, Bosley was persuaded to take the unprecedented step of resigning at midterm. Using a new procedure, members of the Canadian lower house picked his successor, John Fraser, a former cabinet minister forced to resign a year earlier over a scandal in the fisheries ministry. The selection of Fraser broke the tradition of bilingual speakers, alternately from French and English Canada.

What most helped the Conservatives was the apparent plight of the former prime minister and Liberal leader, John Turner. Throughout 1986, Turner's popular support lagged far behind that of Mulroney and the overall favorite, Ed Broadbent of the New Democrats. Opinion polls showed Turner even trailing his chief intraparty rival, Jean Chrètien. A series of books by leading Liberals of the Pierre Elliott Trudeau era, including one-time organizer Keith Davey and former Agriculture Minister Eugene Whalen, gave ammunition to Turner critics. Desperate for unity and unpersuaded that a new leader would be an improvement, Liberals met at the end of November and reelected Turner as party leader with an overwhelming 76.3% of the vote. Turner told the convention that his next task was to prepare for the general election in 1988. Yet all three major parties appeared to be pleased by his continued leadership, none more so than Broadbent's New Democrats, who celebrated their 25th year of existence with their highest opinion-poll standing ever, 29%.

Government. Prime Minister Mulroney insisted that his government was doing the "big things" well and that midterm slumps were routine. While resource-producing regions in the north, east, and west were hard hit by falling world commodity prices and threats of U.S. protectionism, central Canada had a good year, inflation stayed close to 4%, and unemployment slipped below 10% nationwide, with some

THE CANADIAN MINISTRY

M. Brian Mulroney, prime minister
George H. Hees, minister of veterans affairs
Joseph Clark, secretary of state for external affairs
Flora I. MacDonald, minister of communications
John C. Crosbie, minister of transport
Roch La Salle, minister of state
Donald F. Mazankowski, deputy prime minister, president of the Queen's Privy Council for Canada, and government house leader
Elmer M. MacKay, minister of national revenue
Jake Epp, minister of national health and welfare
John Wise, minister of agriculture
Ramon J. Hnatyshyn, minister of justice and attorney general of Canada
David E. Crombie, secretary of state and minister responsible for multiculturalism
Robert R. de Cotret, president of the Treasury Board
Henry P. Beatty, minister of national defence
Michael H. Wilson, minister of finance
Harvie Andre, minister of consumer and corporate affairs
Otto J. Jelinek, minister of state (fitness and amateur sport)
Thomas E. Siddon, minister of fisheries and oceans
Charles J. Mayer, minister of state (Canadian Wheat Board)
William H. McKnight, minister of Indian affairs and northern development
Thomas M. McMillan, minister of environment
Patricia Carney, minister for international trade
André Bissonnette, minister of state (transport)
Benoît Bouchard, minister of employment and immigration
Michel Côté, minister of regional industrial expansion and minister responsible for Canada Post Corporation
James F. Kelleher, solicitor general of Canada
Marcel Masse, minister of energy, mines and resources
Barbara J. McDougall, minister of state (privatization) and minister responsible for the status of women
Gerald S. Merrithew, minister of state (forestry and mines)
Monique Vézina, minister of supply and services
Stewart McInnes, minister of public works and minister responsible for Canada Mortgage and Housing Corporation
Frank Oberle, minister of state for science and technology
Lowell Murray, leader of the government in the Senate and minister of state (federal-provincial relations)
Paul W. Dick, associate minister of national defence
Pierre Cadieux, minister of labour
Jean Charest, minister of state (youth)
Thomas Hockin, minister of state (finance)
Monique Landry, minister for external relations
Bernard Valcourt, minister of state (small businesses and tourism)
Gerry Weiner, minister of state (immigration)

cities actually reporting labor shortages. Conservative policies of "downsizing" government and "privatizing" Canada's crown corporations continued. Toronto's De-Havilland and Montreal's Canadair companies both were sold off at prices denounced by critics as giveaways.

Finance Minister Michael Wilson was almost as unhappy as Washington that the Canadian dollar was trading at close to 70 cents per U.S. dollar. In his spring budget, Wilson sought bankers' approval by pledging to trim $5 billion from the previous year's $34.3 billion deficit, largely through cost cutting and higher taxes on middle-income earners. Mulroney pledged that the government's struggle with the deficit would be "implacable, unyielding, and successful," but other priorities soon intervened. Money for the hard-pressed Atlantic provinces, the announcement of $1 billion for prairie farmers (timed to help a Tory government cling to power in Saskatchewan), and cancellation of a tax on oil and gas revenues preempted Wilson's deficit cutting. In the autumn the government began paving the way to a 1988 election with promises of U.S.-style tax reform, with cuts in personal income tax and a new "business transfer tax" modeled on the European Common Market's value-added tax.

While the government promised help to a growing list of interest groups—from working women to war veterans—cutbacks got more headlines. A task force under Montreal businessman Claude Forget proposed sharp cuts in Ottawa's $10 billion Unemployment Insurance program. To finance its high-profile part in the U.S. space program, the Canadian government slashed science projects in universities and its own National Research Council.

Law. Even without free trade in goods, American ideas and issues found a Canadian echo. Proposed Criminal Code amendments promised to make it easier to get pornography convictions, although controversy over the broad definition delayed final action. The 1985 legislation against street prostitution and juvenile offenders left many critics unappeased; police and civil-liberties leaders both had objections. Prime Minister Mulroney's brief attempt to follow President Reagan's crusade against drugs with talk of a Canadian "epidemic" foundered when experts asked for his evidence. The prime minister had more success in frustrating a majority within his own party who urged a return to the death penalty. A promised "free vote" was once again maneuvered into the future.

A more poignant test of Canadian law was posed by self-defined "political refugees" seeking asylum. Among the claimants were Sikh nationalists, alleged to be using Canada as a base for terrorism against India; thousands of fugitives from civil war in Central America; and 153 Tamils set adrift by a West German ship off Newfoundland. Canadians argued over a procedure that seemed too strict for genuine victims of tyranny and too lax for people who merely wanted to jump the immigration line.

A major goal for Mulroney was to bring his native Quebec into the 1982 constitutional accord. Robert Bourassa, the newly elected Liberal premier of the province, also wanted a settlement, but his terms included the same special recognition of Quebec as protector of the French language and culture that former Prime Minister Trudeau had angrily denounced as "ghettoization." Although John Turner promptly accepted Bourassa's terms, all three

CANADA · Information Highlights

Official Name: Canada.
Location: Northern North America.
Area: 3,849,656 sq mi (9 970 610 km²).
Population (mid-1986 est.): 25,600,000.
Chief Cities (1981 census): Ottawa, the capital, 295,163; Montreal, 980,354; Toronto, 599,217.
Government: *Head of state,* Elizabeth II, queen; represented by Jeanne Sauvé, governor-general (took office May 14, 1984). *Head of government,* M. Brian Mulroney, prime minister (took office Sept. 17, 1984). *Legislature*—Parliament: Senate and House of Commons.
Monetary Unit: Canadian dollar (1.3864 dollars equal U.S.$1, Oct. 7, 1986).
Gross Domestic Product (1985 C$, constant 1971 prices): $130,259,000,000.
Economic Index: *Consumer Prices* (May 1986, 1981 = 100), all items, 131.7; food, 125.8.
Foreign Trade (1985 C$): *Imports,* $104,914,200,000; *exports,* $119,241,300,000.

national parties feared that the issue might split their ranks and draw Trudeau from retirement. The Liberals finally reached a delicate solution, reviving Trudeau's old Victoria Charter with its offer of regional veto of future constitutional amendments. As with other issues Mulroney moved gingerly, keeping his distance and appointing Sen. Lowell Murray, a former Conservative organizer, to negotiate the issue on his behalf.

Foreign Affairs. Apart from trade relations with the United States, Canada's main external preoccupations in 1986 were the promotion of sanctions against South Africa's apartheid regime; improvement of relations with the Pacific Rim countries, symbolized by Mulroney's lengthy visit to Japan, China, and South Korea; and an obvious attempt to become a more influential member of NATO (North Atlantic Treaty Organization) without major increases in defense spending or other commitments. Since Canada's economic relations with South Africa were always limited, extensive sanctions cost little and gave Mulroney added

stature at a midsummer gathering of Commonwealth leaders in London.

Sending troops and aircraft to Norway in September cost more than the South Africa sanctions but reassured NATO leaders that Canada remembered its northern Flank commitment. The change of defense ministers—the third in two years—helped explain delays in developing a new defense policy. Politics explained delays and soaring costs in building new patrol frigates at Saint John and in acquiring other modern equipment. Also delaying a new defense policy was the general dovishness of the External Affairs department under Joe Clark, a former prime minister and Mulroney rival. Under Clark, Canada kept its distance from Washington's efforts to undermine Nicaragua's Sandinista government, contributed to humanitarian aid in Third World countries, and earned its right to criticize United Nations bureaucracy by paying its full dues.

Labor. Canadian unions lined up solidly against the government's free-trade initiative, not least because they feared that part of the "level playing field" demanded by U.S. negotiators would be the antiunion environment that had already reduced U.S. unions to half the proportional strength of Canada's organized workers. One symptom was an Ontario court case in which a teacher used the new Charter to prevent the union from using his dues for any political cause. Another omen was a year-long strike at an Edmonton packing plant owned by Peter Pocklington, a Tory leadership candidate in 1983. In July police battled strikers when strike-breakers were bused in to take their jobs.

Shirley Carr, once a stenographer in Niagara Falls, became the first woman president of the two-million member Canadian Labour Congress. She presided over a movement embroiled in strikes—from Newfoundland's civil servants to British Columbia's loggers. The aftermath of recession brought no end to em-

Canapress Photo

In May, Prime Minister Brian Mulroney (left) met with South Korea's President Chun Doo Hwan during a three-nation tour (also including Japan and China) to promote trade relations.

ployer demands for concessions, while unions fought to recover lost ground. Canada faced the worst year in the decade for strikes and lockouts.

People and Diversions. Most Canadians in 1986 enjoyed a mild winter and, at least in central Canada, had the wettest summer since the 1940s. Vancouver, normally a rainy city, rejoiced in an unusually warm, dry summer for its Expo 86. Large, happy crowds recreated at least some of the euphoria that had enveloped Montreal's Expo 67. The creator of that fair, Montreal's Mayor Jean Drapeau, finally retired after 29 years in office.

In another Montreal milestone, the Canadiens won the National Hockey League (NHL) Stanley Cup; the exuberant celebrations turned into a minor riot. Canada's soccer team, having painfully qualified for the World Cup competition in Mexico City, was eliminated in the first round. Canadian athletes did much better at the Commonwealth Games in Edinburgh, Scotland, but their gold medals were robbed of some of their glitter after a boycott by almost half the member nations.

The publicly owned Canadian Broadcasting Corporation celebrated its 50th anniversary amid criticism, budget cuts, and a report commissioned by the Conservative government that proved unexpectedly supportive of the system. Canadians, claimed commission members, had a right to choose what they see and hear, but that choice must include Canadian-made programs. Another report, by former business executive Edmund Bovey, called for a doubling of cultural spending by the year 2000, with most of the new money to be drawn from business with the incentive of generous tax concessions.

A more popular culture was served by the latest in a series of sensational murder trials. The central figure was Helmut Buxbaum, a German-born self-made millionaire and born-again Christian convicted of ordering the killing of his wife, an impediment to his secret life of drugs and prostitutes. The trial absorbed endless media coverage and generated at least two books.

The Canadian people were more happily distracted by Rick Hansen, whose "Man in Motion" campaign for muscular dystrophy had already raised money in 40 countries before he set out by wheelchair to cross Canada. Though the effort and the cause recalled earlier fundraising runs by Steve Fonyo and the late Terry Fox, Canadians seemed ready for a new hero.

By year's end Hansen was nearing the midpoint of his trans-Canada journey, John Turner was still Liberal leader, and Buxbaum and his accomplices had gone to jail. Much else, from tax reform to free trade, remained unfinished business.

DESMOND MORTON
Erindale College, University of Toronto

The Economy

A rise in real gross domestic product (GDP) during the second quarter of 1986—3.0% annual growth compared with 2.1% in the first quarter—masked emerging signs of weakness in the Canadian economy.

During 1986 average wage gains remained about 3.5%. However with the consumer price index running above the 4% mark, Canadians suffered a drop in their real income. Disposable income also was down due to Ottawa's decision to raise the personal-income tax. Consequently, consumer spending, which had remained buoyant during the previous three years, was now showing signs of fatigue. Retail sales declined, and firms accumulated inventories. That combination of circumstances stifled the growth of the manufacturing sector by reducing new orders and factory shipments in August by a hefty 5.1% and 3.2%, respectively.

Housing and Unemployment. The level of residential construction dwindled. Housing starts, which peaked in September at a seasonally adjusted annual rate of 241,000, declined to 221,000 in October. In fact sluggish growth in personal disposable income and the high unemployment rate were limiting the expansion of the housing sector.

Although the adjusted unemployment rate for August was down to 9.7% from July's 9.9%, Canadians were left with fewer jobs than what they had at the start of the year. In fact all but two of the nine major industry sectors had lower job levels in August than in January. Primary industries had the biggest employment shrinkage, 13.5%. The drop was caused by a plunge in oil prices and weakness in mining. Other sectors showing sharp decline in employment included construction, agriculture, public administration, and manufacturing.

Inflation and Profits. On the inflation front, despite the drop in energy prices, the consumer price index rose to 4.4% in October from 4.1% in September. Federal sales tax increases were working their way through the system resulting in higher consumer prices. At the same time Canadian corporate profits continued to be plagued by the drop in world oil prices.

Trade. Finally, Canada's trade balance began showing a monthly drop in April. A massive increase in imports in July pushed the trade balance, already weakened by deteriorating net foreign demand, into a deficit of $267 million for the first time in ten years. From a peak in January, the volume of merchandise exports fell by a cumulative 13.4% through June. Pending the final outcome of the Canada-U.S. trade negotiations, the future of the Canadian economy and its foreign trade remains in the doldrums.

R. P. SETH
Professor of Economics
Mount Saint Vincent University, Halifax

Expo 86

In 1978, British Columbia legislators wondered how the province might, eight years later, celebrate the centenary of its biggest city, Vancouver. The legislators decided to spend some $80 million on a modest exposition, to be called Transpo 86, with a theme of transportation. By opening day, May 2, 1986, however, the modest exposition had become a five-and-a-half month world's fair with a $1.5 billion budget, officially named "The 1986 World Exposition on Transportation and Communication," or Expo 86.

Expo 86 was a so-called "special category" world's fair, based on a specific theme and with the host country constructing the buildings and renting them to participants (as opposed to a "universal" world's fair, with no particular theme and participants erecting their own buildings). Under the theme "World in Motion, World in Touch," a total of 54 countries, 7 Canadian provinces, 3 U.S. states, and dozens of corporate exhibitors participated in Expo 86. The fair was sponsored by Canada and hosted by the provincial government of British Columbia. Vancouver businessman Jim Pattison, an organizing genius, served as president and chairman of the board. Irish-born Patrick Reid, commissioner-general of Canada's exhibits at seven previous world's fairs and a former president of the International Bureau of Expositions, served as commissioner-general.

Behind the glittering east gate of Expo 86 rises the fair's designated symbol and landmark, Expo Centre (above, left), a 17-story geodesic dome. Visitors are whisked over the grounds in a 3.35-mi (5.4-km) monorail system called Skytrain (below). The $700 million rapid-transit facility is one of the fair's permanent benefits to Vancouver.

The Expo site covers 173 acres (70 ha), with False Creek, a narrow inlet of the Pacific Ocean on its south side and downtown Vancouver to the north. Across town and jutting into Vancouver harbor is the largest Expo structure, Canada Place, the site of the Canada Pavilion and a new hotel. Its most distinctive feature is the five huge teflon sails that give it the appearance of a ship. It was designed by Toronto's Eberhard Zeidler. Modular pavilions across the fairgrounds were designed by two Vancouver architects, Bruno Freschi and Bogue Babicki.

Britain's Prince Charles and Diana, princess of Wales, officially opened the fair with a ribbon-cutting ceremony on May 2. Bolstered by Canada's largest advertising campaign ever, costing $100 million, Expo 86 surpassed the initial attendance forecast—13,750,000—on August 20. By the end of the fair on October 13, a total of 22,111,578 visitors had passed through its gates. About 60% were from Canada, 30% from the United States, and 10% from other countries.

The success of Expo 86 was attributed to its careful planning, its location in one of the world's loveliest cities, and its fun, light-hearted atmosphere. Jugglers, clowns, musicians, and acrobats provided street entertainment, and there was a huge fireworks and laser show every night.

DAVID SAVAGE

© P. Martin-Morice/Sygma

Across town from the main fairgrounds on False Creek, Canada built its own pavilion at a special site on Burrard Inlet (above). Designed in the shape of a sailing ship, Canada Place was the largest and most eye-catching pavilion at Expo 86. After the close of the fair, Canada Place was to become a convention and trade center.

© Kenne Allen

The La Scala opera company presented Verdi's "I Lombardi" in Vancouver, B.C., highlighting Canada's musical year.

© Paul Little

The Arts

The country's biggest employer of artists, the federally supported Canadian Broadcasting Corporation (CBC), gave the federal government's Task Force on Broadcasting Policy a lengthy report entitled *Let's Do It*. The report asked that almost all the American television shows it was using be replaced by Canadian shows, and that the existing CBC network be expanded, with special channels for news, sports, and regional programs. It also asked for a new and powerful TV station to beam Canadian TV programs to the United States. But Canada's federal government, faced with a lagging economy, had severe financial restrictions. Thus CBC president Pierre Juneau had to cut 350 from his staff and also reduce network programs because government funding had fallen short of CBC's expenses. But for 1986–87 the government did increase by C$22 million its grant to CBC.

Visual Arts. It was a banner season for the Vancouver Art Gallery, which in the five and one half months of Expo 86 displayed in visiting shows more international art works than any other Canadian gallery ever had in a similar period. The Norwegian government sent to the gallery the biggest ever Canadian showing of works by Edvard Munch, comprising 140 items from the Munch Museet in Oslo. The French government sent "Luxe Calme et Volupé: Aspects of French Art, 1966–1986." The Netherlands contributed "The Dutch World of Painting," which illustrated three centuries of Dutch life and included a Frans Hals and a Rembrandt. And the Italian government sent "Giacomo Balla." Balla, who died in 1958, was one of the founders of the futurist movement in Italy. "Vatican Splendor: Masterpieces of Baroque Art," 52 works of the 17th century, which opened at the National Gallery of Canada in Ottawa, moved to the Vancouver gallery as part of the Expo exhibits and then moved on to other Canadian cities. The Vancouver contribution was "Making History: Recent Art of Pacific Canada," with works by 44 British Columbia artists.

The Art Gallery of Ontario mounted a retrospective exhibition of works by the well known Canadian painter Harold Town. The Montreal Museum of Fine Arts presented "Miró in Montreal," sculptures, paintings, and prints by Spain's Joan Miró, who died in 1983. The same museum also showed "Morrice: A Painter With a View," a retrospective of more than 100 works by the late Canadian painter James Wilson Morrice. The University of British Columbia's Museum of Anthropology showed "Jack Shadbolt and the Coastal Indian Image," 50 of Shadbolt's canvases together with masks and other items by native Indians.

The British Columbia Supreme Court dismissed artist Paul Wong's action against the Vancouver Art Gallery for breach of an oral contract. Two years earlier, former Gallery director Luke Rombout had canceled Wong's exhibit entitled "Confused: Sexual Views" three days before it was due to open. The show consisted of nine hours of videotapes of people discussing their sexual experiences. The judge said the contract had included an understanding that what Wong provided for exhibition had to be acceptable to the gallery.

Performing Arts. At Stratford, Ont., artistic director John Neville, in his first season and the theater's 34th, presented in the Stratford Festival Theater three Shakespeare plays and a

163

musical based on Shakespeare's *The Comedy of Errors*. *The Winter's Tale*, directed by David William, featured actors Colm Feore and Stephen Russell. *Pericles*, directed by Richard Ouzounian, starred Nicholas Pennell and Goldie Semple. Outstanding was *Cymbeline*, set in 20th century wartime dress and directed by Robin Phillips. Much praised were the performances of Eric Donkin as the king, Susan Wright as the queen, Nicholas Pennell as Pisanio, and Colm Feore as Iachimo. *The Boys from Syracuse*, a Rodgers and Hart musical, featured Benedict Campbell and Keith Thomas.

At Niagara-on-the-Lake, Ont., the Shaw Festival celebrated its 25th year of presenting plays by George Bernard Shaw and his contemporaries. A capital fund-raising campaign was started, and two Canadian plays were commissioned, from Judith Thompson and Tom Walmsley. The festival opened with Shaw's *Arms and the Man*, directed by Leon Major and featuring Andrew Gillies and Donna Goodhand. Also shown were Shaw's *Back to Methuselah;* Agatha Christie's thriller, *Black Coffee;* English playwright Ben Travers' comedy, *Banana Ridge;* a repeat of the previous year's panoramic Noel Coward play, *Cavalcade;* and the 1930 musical comedy, *Girl Crazy*. It was Christopher Newton's seventh year as artistic director of the Shaw Festival.

Two memorable occasions, both in Vancouver, highlighted the opera scene. The first was the appearance of the La Scala opera company of Milan in four performances of Verdi's *I Lombardi* and two of his *Requiem*. Of the 39,000 seats available for the six performances, 38,900 were taken, making it the biggest ticket sale ever for an opera company's appearance in North America. At great cost and effort, the La Scala company's stagehands transformed the Pacific Coliseum, where hockey games are played, into a lush and convincing, temporary opera house. The second highlight of the opera scene was the Vancouver Opera Company's presentation of the controversial production of Bizet's *Carmen* by Romanian director Lucian Pintilie. Director Pintilie and conductor Kees Bakels disagreed in rehearsal, and Pintilie left a week before the opening because he failed to get the rehearsal time increased. The opening night audience disagreed over the performance, which some booed but most applauded. Jean Stilwell was Carmen and Tom Fox was Escamillo, with Jacques Trussel as Don José. This *Carmen* was sung in English rather than the usual French. It was the same version that raised controversy when it was first given in Wales three years earlier.

In its first appearance in North America for 22 years, the Soviet Union's Kirov Ballet gave Expo 86 its magnificent, classic *Swan Lake* and the modern *The Knight in the Tiger's Skin*. In Toronto, the National Ballet Company of Canada gave the highly praised world premiere of *Alice*, choreographed by Glen Tetley and composed by David Del Tredici. Based on Lewis Carroll's *Alice in Wonderland* and *Through the Looking Glass*, it had Karen Kain as the older Alice and Sabina Allemann and Kimberly Glasco sharing the part of the young Alice.

Film. The Canadian film, *John and the Missus*, filmed in Newfoundland, was the creation of its director and star, Gordon Pinsent. Produced by Peter O'Brian, it is about the effect of a copper mine's failure on a miner's family. Another Canadian film, *Toby McTeague*, about dogsled racing, was directed by Jean-Claude Lord, with Yannick Bisson as Toby and Winston Rekert as the father. The World Film Festival in Montreal, directed by Serge Losique, drew its biggest crowd ever. Leon Schein, founding director of the Vancouver International Film Festival, switched places with Hanna Fisher, who was running Toronto's film festival. The CBC's TV miniseries, *Anne of Green Gables*, based on Lucy Maud Montgomery's story, won the Emmy for best children's program.

DAVID SAVAGE
Free-lance Writer, Vancouver, B.C.

Monique Mojica starred in "Jessica," a play about the troubled life and spiritual growth of a Métis woman from Alberta. The Linda Griffiths' work was presented at Toronto's Theatre Passe Muraille.

In the Dominican Republic, 78-year-old Joaquin Balaguer (left) took over the presidency from Jorge Blanco (right) on August 16. Balaguer, who had served five terms previously but lost elections in 1978 and 1982, was returned to office in May voting.

AP/Wide World

CARIBBEAN

Significant political changes occurred in the Caribbean during 1986, reflecting, in part, rising impatience with depressed economic conditions and resentment of the policies of the United States toward the region. The most striking development took place in February in Haiti, when President-for-Life Jean-Claude Duvalier abruptly fled the country, ending 29 years of dictatorial rule by Duvalier and his father, François (*see* special report). Elections in Barbados and the Dominican Republic returned two veteran politicians to leadership after long periods out of office. In Jamaica, the opposition People's National Party (PNP) resoundingly defeated the governing Jamaica Labor Party (JLP), 57% to 43%, in island-wide local elections in July. Also in July an apparent plot to overthrow the government of Suriname was broken up when U.S. Federal Bureau of Investigation (FBI) agents in New Orleans arrested 14 persons described as mercenaries hired by a Surinamese rebel group. In Trinidad, a four-party opposition coalition, the National Alliance for Reconstruction, won a landslide victory in elections in December.

In the U.S. Virgin Islands, Alexander Farrelly, a Democrat, was elected governor in November. He faced a $50 million budget deficit.

Dominican Republic. Joaquin Balaguer, 78, assumed the Dominican presidency for a fifth term on August 16. He narrowly defeated former Vice-President Jacobo Majluta, the candidate of the governing Dominican Revolutionary Party (PRD), in elections held May 16.

Balaguer, long associated with former dictator Rafael Leonidas Trujillo, was appointed by Trujillo as figurehead president in 1960. When Trujillo was assassinated in 1961, Balaguer continued in office, but he was forced into exile in 1962. After the 1965 civil war, Balaguer returned to the Dominican Republic and defeated former President Juan Bosch for the presidency in 1966. He was reelected in 1970 and 1974, but lost in 1978 and 1982.

The 1986 election was held against a backdrop of severe economic problems and rising social tension. The country's mainstay industry, sugar, had been badly hurt by reductions in the U.S. sugar import quota. Sugar revenues in 1986 were estimated at $80–$90 million, compared with $575 million in 1975. The State Sugar Council announced plans to close six or seven of its 12 sugar mills in 1987.

Barbados. After being out of office for ten years, Prime Minister Errol Barrow and his Democratic Labor Party won an overwhelming victory in elections held on May 28, taking 24 of the 27 contested parliamentary seats. Barrow, 66, a fervent nationalist, had clashed frequently with the United States when he headed the Barbados government from 1961 to 1976.

In his 1986 campaign, Barrow charged the Barbados Labor Party government with being "subservient" to the United States and

Haiti

© Sygma

Haiti's President-for-Life Jean-Claude Duvalier was forced to flee February 7. "Baby Doc," who assumed the presidency from his father in 1971, took refuge in France.

Haiti is moving fitfully and uncertainly toward a return to democracy after 29 years of brutal suppression under the Duvalier family, François ("Papa Doc") and his son, Jean-Claude ("Baby Doc"). On Feb. 7, 1986, amid worsening antigovernment protests and one week after he declared a state of siege, President-for-Life Jean-Claude Duvalier was forced to flee the country. On leaving for France aboard a U.S. Air Force jet, he turned over power to an interim military-civilian government, the National Governing Council (CNG), headed by Lt. Gen. Henri Namphy.

On October 19, 41 members of a constituent assembly were elected to draft a new constitution and to prepare for national elections; another 20 assembly members were to be appointed by the CNG. Under the plans for transition to a democratically elected government, Haitians would vote for municipal officials in July 1987 and for a president four months later. The new chief executive was scheduled to be installed on Feb. 7, 1988.

By late 1986, however, it was questionable whether the electoral schedule could be followed. After decades of corrupt authoritarian rule, Haiti lacked even a rudimentary political structure. The absence of viable parties, trade unions, electoral processes, and government institutions made 1987 elections seem premature. As one example of the reigning confusion, a newspaper in Port-au-Prince, the capital, reported in July that there were 400 self-designated candidates for the presidency

pledged he would take a more independent stance. He also declared his opposition to a U.S.-backed proposal for a Regional Security System that would link the police and military systems of seven English-speaking eastern Caribbean states for the purpose of combating terrorism and civil insurrections.

Like Balaguer in the Dominican Republic, Barrow faced serious economic challenges. Barbados' unemployment rate in 1986 was 15.6%, and the sugar industry was in distress. Barrow's agriculture minister, Warwick Franklin, announced in September that land under cane cultivation would be reduced from 32,000 to 25,000 acres (12 900 to 10 100 ha) and alternate crops would be introduced. To cut government spending, Barrow lowered the salaries of his cabinet ministers by 5% and recalled government-owned cars that had been at the ministers' disposal. In a symbolic act, Barrow refused to live in a $1.5 million mansion that had been occupied by his two predecessors.

Jamaica. The Jamaican government's handling of the economy was the central issue in July municipal elections. Jamaica was suffering from high unemployment—more than 25%—a sharply rising cost of living, and depressed prices for bauxite, its main export. In an attempt to defuse criticism, Prime Minister Edward Seaga announced in May that Jamaica would disregard the austerity guidelines of the International Monetary Fund (IMF) and would reflate the economy, reduce consumer commodity prices, and cut interest rates.

Opposition leader Michael Manley claimed that the results of the July voting constituted a rejection of Seaga's policies, and called for early parliamentary elections. Seaga refused Manley's demand for elections and in September turned down an IMF request for a 10% devaluation of Jamaica's currency. Then, in a surprise announcement in mid-October, Seaga said he would retire in August 1987, a move that was retracted in early November. Seaga

but no well-organized political organizations to back them.

Most threatening to a smooth transition, however, was the violent chaos—bordering on anarchy—into which the country lapsed during the months after Duvalier's departure. Strikes, protest marches, lynchings, house burnings, robberies, and fierce fighting among neighbors occurred on an almost daily basis. The provisional government seemed powerless to cope with the disorder.

The continuing unrest was, at bottom, a reaction to the squalor and misery in which the bulk of the Haitian masses still were living. Under the Duvaliers, Haiti was the poorest country in the Western Hemisphere. Papa Doc and Baby Doc had systematically drained public and private sector funds since the elder Duvalier seized power in 1957. By one estimate, at least 15% of Haiti's annual income went into Duvalier family accounts, and Baby Doc fled the country with a nest egg estimated at $1 billion, leaving scarcely $500,000 in the public treasury. More than half the work force was unemployed. Per capita income averaged a little more than $300 a year. The national literacy rate of 36.9% was the lowest in the hemisphere. Tropical diseases abounded. Nearly two children out of ten did not live beyond five years. A 1985 survey by UNICEF found 75% of all school-age children to be suffering from some form of malnutrition.

With the downfall of Duvalier, there had been widespread—and unfounded—hope that conditions would improve. But the CNG proved hesitant and indecisive, and in the early post-Duvalier era, the country was, if possible, more destitute and desperate than ever. The economy seemed to be in a free fall. Strikes and disorder introduced an air of uncertainty in the few sectors that remained viable. The country's important light-assembly industry faced disrupted work schedules and interrupted deliveries of raw materials and finished products. At least three factories closed, and at the others production was down by an estimated 20%. Of the 50,000 light-assembly workers, 12,000 lost their jobs. Nationwide, real wages were 20% below the levels of previous years, and inflation doubled.

Haitian agriculture, long ignored by the Duvalier regime, was in a state of virtual collapse. Untimely droughts compounded the problem, but years of wasteful practices had severely damaged the land. Most of the country was denuded of trees, as destitute families had chopped down entire forests to make charcoal. Erosion was so severe that agronomists said most of Haiti would be a desert in another two decades unless massive reforestation was undertaken.

Foreign assistance trickled into Haiti after the downfall of Duvalier, but the little help that arrived was poorly utilized. The Haitian government asked the United States for emergency aid of $50 million but was told it could expect no more than $10 million. Because of serious theft problems, the U.S. Agency for International Development was distributing only half of the 700,000 meals it normally feeds daily to schoolchildren and new mothers. A proposal by the Organization of American States for the creation of an inter-American Fund for Emergency Assistance to Haiti was still pending implementation at the end of the year.

RICHARD C. SCHROEDER

---

said that economic recovery and a new IMF agreement require that he remain in office.

Economy. The depressed economic conditions of recent years persisted throughout the region in 1986. The tourist industry was a notable exception. Tourism revenues for the Caribbean as a whole reached $5 billion in 1985, an 8% gain over 1984, and tourist arrivals increased by 2% in the first half of 1986.

Results of the U.S.-sponsored Caribbean Basin Initiative (CBI), which gives duty-free entry into the United States for a wide range of Caribbean exports over a 12-year period, have been disappointing to many Caribbean governments. U.S. CBI imports from the Caribbean fell from $621.3 million in 1984 to $547.5 million in 1985.

In an effort to bolster CBI, the Commonwealth of Puerto Rico launched a "twin plant" program to encourage Puerto Rico-based companies to establish subsidiary operations on other Caribbean islands. The subsidiaries perform labor-intensive preliminary work on products which are then shipped to Puerto Rico for finishing. Twin plant products enter the United States duty free. In 1986 twin plants were in operation in the Dominican Republic and Grenada, and, according to Puerto Rican officials, were in various stages of development in at least nine other Caribbean and Central American countries. Puerto Rico's Government Development Bank provides financial assistance to companies setting up twin plants.

In a second initiative to stimulate Caribbean economies, the Reagan administration in February offered improved access to the U.S. market for Caribbean garments produced from U.S.-made fabrics. In July, Canada also began offering duty-free status to imports from Caribbean countries. And in August, Mexico and Venezuela renewed a program under which they supply petroleum on concessional terms to Caribbean and Central American countries.

RICHARD C. SCHROEDER, *"Visión" Magazine*

© Claude Urraca/Sygma

Five Central American presidents—Nicaragua's Ortega, El Salvador's Duarte, Guatemala's Cerezo, Honduras' Azcona, and Costa Rica's Arias—held talks in May on a regional peace treaty, but no agreement was forthcoming.

CENTRAL AMERICA

Peace seemed no closer in Central America in 1986 than it had in 1985, as civil war continued in Nicaragua and El Salvador. Five Central American presidents met in May at Esquipulas, Guatemala, but produced no peace. Nor did the so-called Contadora process (named for the island in Panama where the discussions were first held). The four Contadora countries—Colombia, Mexico, Panama, and Venezuela—had been trying for nearly four years to produce a peace treaty acceptable to both the United States and Nicaragua.

Inflation remained critical, unemployment was very high, and nothing of consequence was done to reduce the vast external debts of all the Central American republics. The United States allocated more than $1.3 billion in aid for Central America as a whole in 1986. Using much personal influence to overcome congressional opposition, U.S. President Ronald Reagan won approval for $100 million for the Nicaraguan "contras," who continued to fight the Sandinista government throughout the year.

In June the International Court of Justice ruled that American aid to the contras violated international law; it asked that the aid be stopped and reparations paid to Nicaragua. Alleging lack of jurisdiction by the court, the Reagan administration ignored the proceedings. Increasingly, however, the part played by the U.S. Central Intelligence Agency (CIA) and private citizens came up for discussion in Washington.

Of much concern to Central Americans was the September report of a U.S. joint congressional committee that said the U.S. trade deficit was due at least in part to lack of exports to underdeveloped Latin American countries. The conclusion seemed at odds with the needs of Central American countries, whose exports have fallen badly in recent years. There was some concern that a tariff war might develop and harm all the nations in the hemisphere.

The U.S. government was encouraged by the inauguration of several new leaders in Central American states in 1986, as a result of free elections held during the previous two years. Closely supervised and even financed in part by the United States, the elections gave Central Americans an unusual opportunity to make honest choices. Undetermined was the extent of long-range benefits, as even honest elections do not necessarily make a democracy. To strengthen grass-roots democracy, the United States financed and guided seminars and classes for judges, legislators, law enforcement personnel, and others, and sponsored a variety of technical assistance programs.

Educational exchanges between the United States and Central American countries were expanded. The education of thousands of Central American teachers and U.S. scholarships for up to 10,000 students were among the most extensive programs. Some 3,400 scholarships were granted in 1986, bringing the total allocated so far to 7,000. Most of the recipients were youngsters of nonelite background, many from rural areas, who could not otherwise afford a U.S. education, but showed potential for leadership. Since few of them spoke English, language training was provided. The students came from every Central American republic and attended a dozen or so U.S. colleges.

Belize. Prime Minister Manuel Esquivel had predicted a slight budget surplus for 1985–86, but that did not materialize. For 1986–87, his estimate was more conservative. Esquivel promised not to impose new taxes but faced the necessity of allocating nearly one fourth of the nation's budget to servicing the foreign debt. To provide a promised 10% raise for government employees, he proposed an increase in borrowing from the United States and from the private sector in Belize. He also recommended the sale of a few million dollars in government bonds to foreigners in exchange for citizenship. The chief target of this unusual sale seemed to be British citizens who lived in Hong Kong and wanted to get out before that colony's leases revert to the Chinese in 1997.

The economy showed no great change. Inflation softened a bit, and employment rose slightly. Sugar earnings declined, partly to conform with a government policy to reduce the country's longstanding dependence on sugar exports and replace it with higher-value export crops such as vegetables for the U.S. winter market. Banana and citrus production expanded.

The United States granted about $9 million in aid to Belize in 1986, and the Reagan administration sought a moderate increase for 1987. In response to charges that the young nation was a major source of marijuana, Belize accepted help from the United States to destroy vast acreages of the plant. The United States also helped with a road-building program that was expected to benefit the cattle industry.

The Reagan administration had nominated James Malone to be ambassador to Belize, but in April the appointment was rejected by the Senate Foreign Relations Committee, which questioned an apparent conflict of interest between Malone's previous work as an assistant secretary of state and as a lawyer representing several foreign firms. The Belize government announced that he would be unacceptable in any event because of his position on South Africa.

After five years Britain and Guatemala mended consular relations that had been split over the latter's refusal to recognize Belize. (Full ties have been broken since 1963.) The improved relations were made possible when Guatemala gave up most of its claims to territory in Belize, except for a small district on the Gulf of Honduras.

Direct air travel between Belize City and Houston, Los Angeles, and Washington, DC, was inaugurated in June. One of the first passengers was Esquivel, who received an honorary doctorate from his alma mater, Loyola University in New Orleans, and assurances from Michigan State University's Hotel and Restaurant Institute that it would provide technical help for Belize's infant tourist industry. Tourism was expected to be enhanced by re-

cent Mayan discoveries, which included a network of caves. The discoveries also provided a better understanding of the ruined Mayan town called Caracol. (*See* ARCHAEOLOGY.)

Costa Rica. On February 2, Oscar Arias Sánchez of the National Liberation Party defeated five other candidates for the presidency in a close but orderly election. His nearest opponent, Rafael Angel Calderón Fournier of the Social Christian Unity Party, had offered a similar platform but had more strongly opposed the Sandinistas in Nicaragua. At 45, Arias, a lawyer with a doctorate in economics and a member of a wealthy coffee-planting family, was the youngest person elected president in the nation's history. His principal handicap in the election was a charge of past corruption leveled against his party. Nevertheless, he collected 52% of the popular vote. He was inaugurated in May, the country's 49th president.

Costa Rica faced a diplomatic quandary as well as economic problems. A poll concluded that less than 40% of Costa Ricans were in favor of U.S. support of Nicaraguan contras. Yet many Nicaraguans have exiled themselves in Costa Rica, and the nation feels pressure from the United States to help in the contras' cause and to reestablish an army. Arias said

In Costa Rica, Oscar Arias Sánchez of the National Liberation Party campaigned successfully for the presidency. His margin of victory was larger than expected.

© Charles Bonnay/JB Pictures

© Shepard Sherbell/Picture Group

A giant earthquake October 10 was felt throughout El Salvador, but the effects were most devastating in San Salvador, the capital. Up to 1,500 people lost their lives.

of great austerity, the country had renegotiated much of the debt in 1985. But in early 1986, international lending agencies became dissatisfied with Costa Rican efforts at austerity and cut off loans for the immediate future. The International Monetary Fund (IMF) in particular insisted on great reductions in government subsidies and the layoff of about 5,000 government employees. (President Arias had meanwhile announced plans to subsidize training for municipal jobs.)

Arias' budget for 1986 was the largest in the nation's history, 13% higher than the 1985 budget. Some new revenue was expected to come from better coffee prices and increased water, telephone, and electric rates, while cheaper oil was expected to reduce expenses. About one fourth of the budget was earmarked for education and another fourth for servicing the debt. The president announced that his two major priorities would be jobs and housing, reflecting a 20% growth in unemployment in 1985 and estimates that one fourth of the people had inadequate housing. Despite its financial straits the government reportedly refused $1 billion in May to grant asylum to exiled Philippine President Ferdinand Marcos.

El Salvador. Disaster never seems to leave the side of the Salvadoran people. In 1986 the worst terror, for a change, was not manmade. On October 10, an earthquake, measured in different places at 5.2 to 7 on the Richter scale, struck the tiny republic. The center seemed to be about 10 mi (16 km) northwest of San Salvador, the capital, but the shock was felt everywhere in the nation. First reports revealed that an eight-story children's hospital in San Salvador had collapsed, killing 50 of the young patients. The Grand Hotel was also destroyed, and a shantytown of fugitives from the civil war was covered with mud up to 25-ft (7.6-m) deep. Authorities buried more than 1,000 people and estimated that 1,500 may have lost their lives. Rescuers continued to dig desperately through the debris as huge quantities of relief supplies poured into the nation.

The disaster only exacerbated the country's massive economic problems. Inflation and unemployment alike remained in the neighborhood of 30%. The government of President José Napoleón Duarte fought back with austerity measures. Expenditures for education, health, and jobs, for example, were lowered some 25% to 35%. Military costs continued to burden the nation, however, accounting for about one third of the budget.

When Duarte announced his austerity program in January, tens of thousands of his formerly close allies—laborers and *campesinos*—staged the largest protest march in years. The demonstrators complained in particular about increases in bus fares and gasoline prices, as well as wage increases that did not match the inflation rate. The march proved peaceful.

that he would not oppose the U.S. contra aid as long as contra bases were not located within Costa Rican boundaries. Border incidents between Costa Rica and Nicaragua have occurred frequently, and in 1985 the two countries withdrew ambassadors over one incident. In March 1986 the diplomats resumed their posts. To help prevent future problems, the two nations created a joint border commission to patrol the Rio San Juan.

The country's strategic location bordering Nicaragua has prompted the United States to grant much assistance. In 1986 U.S. economic aid was set at $155 million. Costa Rica is second only to El Salvador in aid to Latin American republics, and second only to Israel in the amount of aid per capita worldwide. From 1984 through 1986, approximately one third of the Costa Rican annual budget came from international assistance.

Costa Rica's foreign debt approached $4.5 billion, the result of financing a burgeoning welfare state during a time of easy credit. At a cost

All was not negative. Manufacturing and construction of low- and moderate-cost homes showed gains for the year. Food costs continued to rise, but coffee prices, which had dropped in 1985, looked better in 1986 because of declines in Brazilian production. And while trade within the Central American Common Market suffered, especially between El Salvador and Guatemala, nontraditional Salvadoran exports outside Central America have grown at an average of 20% in the past few years. In 1986 minimum wages were raised about 60% for rural workers and about 18% for industrial workers.

But fundamentally the nation kept afloat because of massive aid from the United States, amounting in 1986 to nearly $500 million. Only Israel received more from the Reagan administration. About one third of the funds were destined for military purposes.

The aid strengthened the army, and the rebels seemed to have been forced into using smaller, more manageable groups that attacked economic targets rather than military strongholds. But the civil war dragged on. Duarte spent much of 1986 attempting to engage in peace discussions with the guerrillas, who agreed to talk but then backed out, objecting to the presence of government soldiers at the talk site. For many weeks at a time, however, it seemed as though an unofficial truce were in effect.

Wanton killing by so-called right-wing death squads appeared to have ceased, and the president was praised when his national police broke up a kidnapping ring that possessed modern arms and secret jails. Agrarian reform entered its sixth year and continued to move slowly. The government claimed that about one fourth of the peasants and one fifth of the farmland had been affected, and that some 65,000 peasants had obtained land as a result of the program.

Guatemala. In January 1986 the Guatemalans witnessed the inauguration of President Marco Vinicio Cerezo Arévalo, the first freely elected civilian leader in a generation.

In his inaugural address, President Cerezo spoke of immediate changes, promising 40,000 new jobs and better social services from the government. To attract cooperation from all sectors of society, he announced a new process he called *concertación*, a system of consultation among labor, industry, agriculture, and the government.

The president's Christian Democratic Party also had captured control of the legislature. The new president began to carry out his promises to rectify the abuses of the military by abolishing the Department of Technical Investigation, a branch of the secret police. He was less thorough in his investigation of the disappearance of thousands of Guatemalans, suspending his own commission shortly after it began its work. Disappearances declined sharply in 1986, however.

Problems arose with the announcement of the new budget, some 36% larger than the previous year's. Partly to cope with a 37% rise in the cost of living during the first three months of 1986, Cerezo asked for a $300 million loan from the United States. He did not get it, but he did receive some smaller amounts from European countries and $47 million from the Agency for International Development (AID). To conform to requirements of international lending agencies, the government planned to phase out price controls and many hidden subsidies. Little action was taken to reduce the 45% unemployment rate or to halt the decline

© Bigwood/Gamma-Liaison

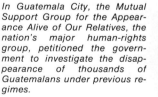

In Guatemala City, the Mutual Support Group for the Appearance Alive of Our Relatives, the nation's major human-rights group, petitioned the government to investigate the disappearance of thousands of Guatemalans under previous regimes.

José Azcona Hoyo was inaugurated on January 27 as the president of Honduras, one of the poorest nations in the Western Hemisphere. Azcona warned that there were "no magic formulas to push development and conquer poverty."

AP/Wide world

in the value of the quetzal, worth about 35 U.S. cents. The foreign debt has continued to rise for several years, and by late 1986 it approached $3 billion. But in many ways Guatemala seemed better able to service its debt than the other Central American states.

The value of traditional exports—cotton, sugar, meat—has been on the decline in recent years, but the value of nontraditional crops, such as fruits and vegetables, jumped 29% in 1986 alone. Probably because of shifting control policies, shortages arose occasionally throughout the year in staples—flour, meat, beans, and corn. The government blamed hoarding and contraband trade.

Between 1977 and 1985, Guatemala received no military assistance from the United States, largely because of charges of human-rights violations. President Reagan reinstated Guatemala's eligibility in 1986, but Cerezo declared that the nation did not need such help. However, in May, he requested $10 million for an antiterrorist program. The U.S. State Department was expected to ask for another $10 million in 1987. Guatemala also received about $100 million in economic aid from the United States in 1986.

Invited by a private university, Nicaragua's Cardinal Miguel Obando Y Bravo visited Guatemala briefly in May. The cardinal, known as a critic of the Sandinista regime, was received somewhat coolly by Guatemalan church and government officials, who appeared to be trying to remain neutral on the contra issue and avoid showing support for the cardinal's position.

Rebel activity in Guatemala declined sharply. Only a few small groups along the northern border still actively opposed the government. In May, however, the worst violence in several years broke out. Twenty-four per-

sons were killed in street rioting, and seven others disappeared. The government called the incident a matter of delinquency; opponents said it threatened the entire democratic process. Whether it was set off by Cerezo's firing of a number of policemen, by poverty, or by political extremists was uncertain. Increased liberty after years of military suppression, coupled with the bad economy, probably contributed to the disorders. More peaceful "tin pan" demonstrations in four different cities during April may have reflected some of those same feelings. Through all of this, the army remained quiet. It appeared to have accepted the president's civilian appointments as state governors and to agree with his neutrality toward Nicaragua.

Honduras. On January 27 the people of Honduras enjoyed the first peaceful transfer of the presidency between two civilians in 53 years. Although he had not won a majority of the vote, José Azcona Hoyo of the Liberal Party was declared legally elected by a national electoral tribunal, and the opposition accepted the decision. Azcona, a 59-year-old civil engineer, became the nation's 75th president in 165 years, a period with more than 300 armed rebellions that provided little tenure to chief executives. In his inaugural address, Azcona pledged continuing support for the Contadora peace process, as well as close friendship with the United States.

The new government was in many ways a coalition. The Liberal Party held a minority of seats in the legislature; so, in exchange for the privilege of nominating the legislative leaders, Azcona agreed to let the rival National Party have a majority on the Supreme Court and half of all other judicial appointments. The army, for its part, seemed to control some of the sensitive ministerial posts. Although good feelings prevailed, it was thought that the division of responsibilities might aggravate Honduras' continuing problems of high unemployment, illiteracy, and external debt and that land reform might stagnate because of the power of the National Party, which opposes the reform, in the legislature and the courts.

The country also faced problems in its relationship with the United States and the Nicaraguan contras, many of whom have been based within Honduras. That the new president faced a balancing act in foreign relations was evidenced by his letter to Nicaragua's President Daniel Ortega expressing a hope to "broaden" their "friendship," while at the same time he continued to accept friendship and influence from the United States. Agreements permit the regular presence of 1,200 U.S. troops in Honduras and up to 5,000 more during frequent maneuvers.

Honduran relations with the United States appeared unchanged in 1986. However, some Hondurans, concerned about the publicity and danger of harboring the contras, voiced fears that U.S. ties might drag the country into the Nicaraguan civil war. In March a number of Sandinista troops entered Honduras to attack contras based near the border. Between 240 and 400 people were reported killed in the fighting between the two groups, but casualty figures were not confirmed. The Honduran government ordered the contras to let the Sandinistas go home without pursuit in order to minimize the conflict; it also received from the United States $20 million in emergency military aid and help in airlifting troops to the border.

In May, Azcona took a delegation to Washington seeking $100 million in emergency aid for 15,000 Hondurans driven from the border area. Thousands of Hondurans have been moved from one 60 sq mi (155 km²) area to allow the contras to camp, and 34 villages have been abandoned. Crimes in the area have been charged to contras, and Honduran coffee-growers have claimed crop losses worth millions of dollars. Furthermore, some contras appeared to be homesteading, building houses and bringing their families from Nicaragua. These were serious irritants.

The United States has supplied the Honduran economy with more than $750 million in aid since 1981. Despite this, the country has made little progress on a number of economic fronts. Its external debt grew from $1 billion to $2 billion in the five years through 1986. Unemployment was near 40%. Honduras suffered from the highest infant mortality rate in Latin America, and more than one third of its people remained illiterate.

The new government proposed supports or tax breaks for lumber, cattle, and coffee producers. Coffee and banana exports looked healthy for the year, and declining oil prices were expected to help the economy. The Agency for International Development (AID) has helped increase production of a number of nontraditional exports, including melons, citrus, pineapples, wood products, and clothing. Honduras sought softer terms for its foreign debt in 1986; the IMF wanted imports cut back.

Nicaragua. Early in the year reports from Nicaragua indicated that the contras were losing ground and, without military aid from the United States since 1984, had been pushed onto the defensive. Their cause was damaged by the association many of their leaders had had with

Nicaraguan "contra" rebels receive training near the Honduran border. With U.S. help, steps were taken in 1986 to unify rebel groups and improve their military training.

former Nicaraguan President Anastasio Somoza and by charges of brutality and willingness to hire criminals to do their work. Nor did the contras seem to have a positive program for their nation. President Reagan used all his persuasive powers to get congressional approval for $100 million in assistance.

In March, while debate on the aid was still going on, Nicaraguan troops invaded Honduras in retaliation for hit-and-run contra raids on northern Nicaraguan villages, tobacco warehouses, and an electric plant. The contras moved farther into Honduras, making it more difficult for the Sandinistas to find them.

For some months the Reagan administration expressed concern about the lack of unity among the several contra groups. By June steps had been taken to overcome this problem. Three major contra leaders met in Miami and agreed to create a united front. Adolfo Calero, Arturo Cruz, and Alfonso Robelo planned to take two-month turns as head of the new group. The latter two men, who were more acceptable to moderates in the United States, could make appointments of civil and military leaders; Calero retained a veto over these appointments as well as over the budget, but he could be overridden.

A fourth player in the game was Edén Pastora, who waged an isolated rebellion from the Costa Rican border. Charging that the other groups were influenced by elements from the old Somoza regime, he refused to unite with them. As a result he lost money and men, and then announced his retirement and sought exile in Costa Rica. Meanwhile, the other three leaders agreed to certain reforms in their spending procedures and their human-rights policies.

In October a private American plane carrying supplies to the contras was shot down over Nicaraguan soil. Three crew members were killed, but a fourth, an American named Eugene Hasenfus, survived and was captured by Sandinista troops. He was tried in a Nicaraguan court for terrorism and other crimes and was sentenced to 30 years in prison. The U.S. government denied any responsibility for the plane, saying that only private citizens were involved. The Sandinistas, however, said that the U.S. Central Intelligence Agency had masterminded the operation.

In November the Reagan administration admitted to having made secret arms sales to Iran and transferring up to $30 million of the proceeds to the Nicaraguan contras.

On December 12, Sandinista troops captured another American, Sam Nesley Hall, a self-styled counterterrorist and the brother of U.S. Rep. Tony Hall (D-OH), in a restricted area and charged him with espionage. The Managua government announced that he would be tried in a "people's tribunal" like the one that convicted Hasenfus. Then in a surprise move on December 17, President Daniel Ortega pardoned and released Hasenfus as a "gesture of peace" to the United States.

The Sandinista government meanwhile continued the restrictions on free speech and assembly that it had imposed in October 1985, and it extended them. The only nongovernment radio station, Radio Católica, was closed in January, and the only opposition newspaper, *La Prensa,* was shut down in July. The quarrel between church and state became more bitter, too. A bishop and a priest were expelled from the country for their outspoken opposition to the government, and the government received what was called a "stinging attack" from Pope John Paul II for the expulsions. The Sandinistas said the church was supporting the contras, while the church wanted the return of the exiled clerics, the reopening of its radio station,

Eugene Hasenfus (seated, right), *an American shot down over Nicaragua while flying arms to "contra" rebels, was convicted November 15 by a People's Anti-Somocista Tribunal and sentenced to 30 years in prison. In mid-December, however, Hasenfus was released.*

and an end to the military draft. President Ortega and Cardinal Miguel Obando y Bravo met in September for the first time in 18 months to confer on these matters, but they did not appear to solve any of them.

The Interamerican Development Bank reported that many aspects of the economy had worsened. Inflation reached three digits (it had been 35% in 1984), shortages and low world prices cut into export income deeply, the foreign debt climbed toward the $5 billion mark, and some factories closed briefly because of shortages of materials. The government was able to negotiate postponements of its loan payments from European banks. To deal with food and other shortages, special worker groups were created to prevent hoarding and price-gouging, and a new ration act was adopted to regulate the sale of rice, cooking oil, sugar, salt, soap, and other staples. The Soviet Union donated 25,000 tons of rice, and Bulgaria provided wheat. At least some of the economic problems could be attributed to the civil war.

Panama. Panamanians continued to find life no easier under civilian leadership than it had been under direct military government. The 1984 election of Nicolás Ardito Barletta ended 16 years of military rule, but in September 1985 he was forced out of office by a combination of military, business, and labor groups who charged him with failure to solve Panama's economic problems. Vice-President Eric Arturo Delvalle assumed the presidency and the problems.

Panama's external debt of nearly $4 billion was perhaps the heaviest per capita in all Latin America. A major creditor, the World Bank, pressed the nation to enforce a number of austerity measures as a prerequisite for renegotiating the debt. Delvalle's plans included higher taxes on raw materials, reductions in overtime pay, privatization of some industries, and elimination or reduction of some subsidies in agriculture and industry. Workers reacted with a general strike that lasted for ten days in March and affected half the work force. Some violence accompanied the strike. Later the government lowered tariffs, eased import quotas, and curtailed price fixing. These steps improved Panama's credit rating but lowered Delvalle's popularity.

Debt payment consumed one third of the value of the nation's exports, and the economy's growth for 1985 and 1986 was tiny. Among exports, only bananas did well, a consequence of a good world price. A reduction in the government's share of the sugar and rice trade had little impact.

The face of Panama appeared to be changing, however. With more than 100 banks in Panama City alone, the country was becoming a major commercial and banking center. Very strict secrecy rules made the city one of Latin America's busiest banking communities, with assets of $37 billion. Yet at the same time landless peasants were moving into unpopulated areas, leaving behind land that had been played out or destroyed by slash-and-burn agriculture. Nearly two thirds of the forests were gone, making dangerous floods commonplace.

In 1986 the nation was also preparing for the task of taking complete control of the Panama Canal in the year 2000. The governing commission was made up of five Americans and four Panamanians, with an American administrator and a Panamanian deputy administrator. These positions were to be reversed in 1990. About 80% of the employees were Panamanians, and hundreds of people were in training or apprenticeships for future jobs. Among the newer problems faced during the year were hazardous cargoes passing through the Canal Zone and ships so large that they literally scraped their paint on the locks as they passed through. Questions for the future included the disposition of lands controlled by the U.S. military.

In all, some 12,000 Panamanians were working for the United States, putting perhaps $500 million into the economy yearly. U.S. aid for 1986 exceeded $31 million. There were points of friction between the two countries, however. Foreign Minister Jorge Abadía Arias refused permission for the United States to train contras from Nicaragua in the Canal Zone. For their part, many officials in Washington expressed their displeasure with the nation's strongman, Gen. Manuel Antonio Noriega, commander of Panama's Defense Force. They charged him with heavy involvement in illicit drug trading, money laundering, and the arms trade.

THOMAS L. KARNES
Arizona State University

CHEMISTRY

Developments in chemistry in 1986 included the discovery of a unique carbon compound believed to be shaped like a soccer ball, surprising findings in the chemistry of fluorine, and the synthesis of new compounds containing triple bonds.

Buckminsterfullerene. Few molecules recently have captured the imaginations of chemists as did an unusual cluster of 60 carbon atoms discovered by scientists at Rice University in Houston, TX. Richard E. Smalley and his coworkers originally were attempting to understand how long-chain carbon molecules might form in space near stars. To this end they subjected carbon in the form of graphite to the intense light of a laser beam, vaporizing the carbon and forcing it into a high-density flow of helium gas. In analyzing the resulting products, the scientists were surprised to find that under certain experimental conditions a stable, 60-carbon species strongly predominates. This was puzzling because a structure composed solely of 60 carbon atoms normally would be expected to contain unsatisfied valences, i.e., carbon atoms with incomplete bonding, and would be quite unstable. The scientists eventually concluded that the product must have the shape of a truncated icosahedron, a form illustrated by the seams on a soccer ball. In honor of the late Buckminster Fuller's studies of structural symmetry, they dubbed the new species "buckminsterfullerene."

The new 60-carbon species, first announced in late 1985, is believed to take the shape of a polygon with 60 vertices and 32 faces. Of the 32 faces, 20 are hexagons and 12 pentagons. Every carbon atom in such a structure is equivalent, having two single bonds and a double bond with its neighbors. Due to a property known as aromaticity, such a structure is expected to have high stability. The spherical shape of the compound provides a central cavity large enough to accommodate an additional atom. Subsequent experiments by the Rice scientists showed that single atoms of lanthanum and other elements form strong complexes with the 60-carbon clusters, suggesting that the added atoms may be inside the cavities. Although not all scientists are yet convinced of the molecule's shape, the discovery has provoked a number of new investigations.

Fluorine Chemistry. Elemental fluorine is a highly reactive, pale yellow gas. It is normally produced electrochemically at high temperatures by running an electrical current through molten fluoride salts. Fluorine is the most electro-negative, or electron-attracting, element in the periodic table, and conventional wisdom has held that the element could not be chemically liberated from its compounds. In 1986, however, chemist Karl Christe of Rockwell International in Canoga Park, CA, showed the conventional wisdom to be incorrect. Christe reacted a potassium-manganese salt of fluorine with the acid antimony pentafluoride under relatively mild conditions for one hour, and fluorine gas was produced in almost 40% yield. Although Christe's technique is unlikely to replace the customary electrochemical process for commercial purposes, it has caused inorganic chemists to reexamine their notions of fluorine chemistry. The discovery came, ironically, in the year of the 100th anniversary of the discovery of the electrochemical process for fluorine synthesis.

A team of scientists led by William B. Farnham at DuPont's Experimental Station in Wilmington, DE, reported the preparation of new fluoride salts with unusual characteristics. Salts consist of a portion bearing a positive electrical charge (the cation) and a portion with a negative charge (the anion). The DuPont scientists reported the first synthesis of a stable salt in which the anion consisted of a completely fluorinated carbon species. The nature of the cation appears to be crucial for the stability of the salt; the scientists used a cation called tris (dimethylamino) sulfonium cation, or TAS. In the course of their work, they also isolated a novel TAS salt in which a fluorine atom acts as a bridge between two halogenated (mostly fluorinated) benzene rings. A nearly linear iodine-fluorine-iodine bond was observed between the benzene rings.

Other. The synthesis of chemicals with new and interesting properties continued unabated in 1986. Workers in West Germany reported the first synthesis of a stable compound containing a carbon-arsenic triple bond. The compound was a crystalline solid with a melting point of 114°C (237°F). Another West German worker reported the synthesis of hydroxyacetylene, a highly unstable triple-bond species, in the gas phase. And a University of California, Berkeley, chemist reported that he had managed to attach six acetylene groups to benzene, yielding the compound hexaethynylbenzene. Another synthesis of note was the first total synthesis of the antibiotic tetracycline by Harry Wasserman of Yale University and his coworkers. This antibiotic is produced commercially by fermentation, but for years synthetic chemists had been unable to carry out the final step in laboratory synthesis.

The production of advanced materials, especially polymers and composites, also was a subject of intense interest in 1986. Among the hottest topics at several meetings was the quest for polymers with improved electrical properties, especially polymers that act as electrical conductors and semiconductors. Such polymers normally contain added substances which gave them their unique properties but also make them susceptible to damage from air and moisture.

PAUL G. SEYBOLD, *Wright State University*

World chess champion Gary Kasparov (right) of the Soviet Union successfully defended his title in a rematch with countryman and former champion Anatoly Karpov (left).

CHESS

In a rematch with countryman Anatoly Karpov, Soviet world chess champion Gary Kasparov retained his crown on Oct. 6, 1986, with a clinching tie in the 23d game of their 24-game title series in London and Leningrad.

For the 23-year-old Kasparov and 35-year-old Karpov, it was their third championship match—encompassing 96 games—in two years. Their first showdown began in September 1984, when Karpov, the reigning champion for ten years, took on the young challenger from the Caspian seaport of Baku. After 48 games, 40 of which ended in draws, the International Chess Federation halted the match. Then in November 1985, under a new 24-game format, Kasparov became the youngest world champion in the history of the game with a 13–11 defeat of Karpov (each game victory counting one point, each draw counting ½ point).

The 1986 rematch, based on the same 24-game format, began in July in London and moved to Leningrad after 12 games. Kasparov gained a fast advantage, moving three wins ahead after 16 games. Karpov, however, came back to gain a 9½–9½ tie. The big turning point came in Game 22, won by Kasparov. The draw in Game 23 clinched his victory, and the final game was played out to a draw—for a score of 12½–11½.

CHICAGO

After three years in office, Mayor Harold Washington gained his first working majority in the Chicago City Council in 1986. Four additional pro-Washington aldermen were selected in special elections in several wards, shifting council control away from an anti-Washington faction led by Alderman Edward Vrdolyak, chairman of the Democratic Party of Cook County. With a working majority in the council, the mayor was able to push through legislation and get approval of appointments that previously had been blocked by the old 29–21 council majority. The new appointments gave him control of the patronage-heavy Chicago Park District and brought the resignation of a vocal political enemy of the mayor, Parks Superintendent Edmund Kelley.

Not all the mayor's proposals found acceptance in the newly aligned council, where the mayor can decide a tie vote. A controversial gay-rights ordinance that was backed by Washington was defeated soundly after Joseph Cardinal Bernardin, archbishop of the Roman Catholic Archdiocese of Chicago, spoke out against it. Many black aldermen who had always supported Washington bolted from the mayor on that issue.

Also, the mayor's proposal for a $79 million property-tax increase to balance the city's $2 billion annual budget ran into aldermanic opposition. After the mayor threatened to lay off 11,000 city workers, a fourth of the city's employees, the tax increase was passed in late September.

Politics. In what shaped up to an issue in which Chicagoans divided along racial lines, foes of Mayor Washington, the city's first black mayor, moved to block his reelection in 1987 by making the mayoral election nonpartisan. A petition signed by more than 200,000 Chicago voters asked that a binding referendum be placed on the November 1986 ballot. If approved by voters, the measure would have removed party primaries and made the election a race between the top two vote-getters in a nonpartisan primary. The measure received the support of Cook County prosecutor Richard M. Daley, the son of former Mayor Daley and himself an aspirant for Mayor, and most white voters. The mayor, who favored a nonpartisan mayor's race while an Illinois state legislator, branded the referendum drive as racially motivated.

In a move that even Washington's foes conceded was brilliant, the mayor's supporters in the city council preempted that referendum by placing three other referendums on the November ballot, the maximum allowed by law. Chicago election officials ruled that with the referendum ballot already filled, there was no room for the referendum that was sought by 200,000 voters.

In late November two city aldermen and five other persons were indicted on charges of corruption, fraud, extortion, and illegal arms dealings after an undercover investigation into municipal government by the Federal Bureau of Investigation (FBI). The indictments were expected to have an effect on mayoral elections in spring 1987. Former Mayor Jane Byrne emerged in 1986 as Mayor Washington's strongest challenger.

ROBERT ENSTAD, *"Chicago Tribune"*

CHILE

Increasing international pressure on Chile to improve its human-rights record and the attempted assassination of Augusto Pinochet Ugarte in September and subsequent crackdown on the opposition highlighted the year.

Assassination Attempt and Aftermath. General Pinochet narrowly escaped assassination on September 7 while returning to Santiago from his weekend home at El Melocontón. Five of his bodyguards were killed and eleven wounded in the attack on his six-car motorcade, but Pinochet suffered only a slightly cut hand. This was the first reported attempt on Pinochet's life since he overthrew Salvador Allende Gossens on Sept. 11, 1973. None of the estimated 12 to 15 attackers were killed or captured and only one suspect was named. Responsibility for the attack was claimed by the Manuel Rodríquez Patriotic Front.

Chile's ruling four-man junta then decreed a 90-day state of siege, banned six opposition magazines, expelled three French priests, and jailed at least 44 dissident leaders. In addition four persons, including José Carrasco Tapia, foreign editor of the banned magazine *Análisis* and head of the Chilean journalists' federation, were dragged from their homes by armed men in civilian clothes. They were found dead over the next four days in apparent right-wing reprisals for the attack on Pinochet.

One army general who publicly condemned the Carrasco murder, Luís Danús, military governor of the southern region of Magallanes, was replaced when annual promotions and assignments were announced on October 9. The move was one of a series of retirements and promotions that strengthened Pinochet's control of the army.

Other Developments. The regime's credibility was seriously undermined after uniformed men set fire to two persons during a July strike. One of the victims, 19-year-old Rodrigo Rojas de Negri, was born in Chile but had lived in Washington, DC, since 1976, when his mother had been released from jail and exiled. Among those attending his funeral was Harry G. Barnes, Jr., U.S. ambassador to Chile.

The July 2–3 strike had been called by the Civic Assembly, a recently formed coalition of 18 professional guilds, unions, and student groups which hoped that its action would force Pinochet to change his plans to extend his government beyond 1989. The Chilean constitution, rewritten by the military in 1980, provides for a presidential plebiscite in 1989 in which voters will vote only "yes" or "no" to a single candidate chosen by the ruling junta. Most analysts believe Pinochet plans to be the nominee for an eight-year term.

In mid-July 30 of Chile's 31 Roman Catholic bishops issued a report which indirectly blamed much of Chile's continuing violence on Pinochet. Many observers believe that Chilean navy, air force, and national police officers are worried about possible long-term damage to the image and power of the military if military rule is prolonged beyond 1989.

During Army Day ceremonies on September 19, Pinochet referred several times to the discovery of 80 tons of arms in August as further evidence of the efforts of Marxist-Leninist guerrillas linked to the Soviet Union and Cuba to "impose a war without boundaries" and "distort the truth about Chile."

Economic Matters. In September the Central Bank estimated the foreign trade surplus at $1.32 billion, compared with $759 million in 1985 and $356 million in 1984. It also expected the nation's gross domestic product (GDP) to grow at 5% annually, compared with the 1.9% reported in the second half of 1985 and the 6.3% registered in 1984. Gemines, a private firm, estimated the trade surplus at only $960 million and annual GDP growth for the next three years at only 3.5%.

On September 11, Pinochet decreed an increase in the minimum wage to the equivalent of $50 per month and an 8.8% increase in state pensions. Budget director Jorge Selume said the most likely source of funding for the increase would be foreign borrowing.

Chile's ability to repay and restructure its $21 billion foreign debt was hurt by low copper prices, which fluctuated between 61 and 64 cents a pound during most of 1986. Government budget figures were based on an average 1986 price of 69.6 cents and a 1987 price of 74.7 cents. In November, despite objections by human-rights groups, some members of U.S. Congress, and numerous member nations, the World Bank approved a $250 million loan.

Foreign Affairs. On March 14 the United States voted for a United Nations resolution similar to one it had proposed that urged Chile to halt torture, investigate alleged human-rights abuses, end internal exile, and permit Chileans in exile abroad to return home. The Reagan administration also sent Deputy Assistant Secretary of State Robert Gelbard and Deputy Assistant Secretary of Defense Nestor Sanchez to Chile to urge Pinochet to step down in 1989. During his October visit Sanchez also met with Major General Danús and Bishop Tomás González, one of the most outspoken critics of Pinochet within the Church.

Arturo Fontaine Aldunate, Chile's ambassador to Argentina, met with Argentine foreign ministry officials in March to reiterate that Chile had no part in a spy network said to have been operating at Argentina's Mar del Plata submarine base for at least two years. That same month Brazilian foreign ministry officials took the unusual step of announcing that relations between Brazil and Chile were "excellent" after several prominent newspapers had reported that Brazilian President José Sarney wanted relations between the two nations restricted to an "indispensable minimum level." Other newspaper articles alleged that $1 billion of Brazilian-built tanks, rocket launchers, and airplanes had been sold to Chile directly or through Colombian intermediaries. Officials denied the sales were taking place.

Amnesty International and other human-rights organizations were unsuccessful in preventing the participation of the four-masted

---

CHILE • Information Highlights

Official Name: Republic of Chile.
Location: Southwestern coast of South America.
Area: 292,257 sq mi (756 845 km²).
Population (mid-1986 est.): 12,300,000.
Chief Cities (June 30, 1985): Santiago, the capital, 4,318,305 (including suburbs); Viña del Mar, 315,947.
Government: *Head of state and government,* Gen. Augusto Pinochet Ugarte, president (took power Sept. 1973). *Legislature*—Congress (dissolved Sept. 1973).
Monetary Unit: Peso (196.04 pesos equal U.S.$1, official rate Oct. 22, 1986).
Economic Index (Santiago, 1985): *Consumer Prices* (1980 = 100), all items, 262.3; food, 231.3.
Foreign Trade (1985 U.S.$): *Imports,* $2,867,000,000; *exports,* $3,797,000,000.

Chilean training vessel *Esmeralda* in Operation Sail, the parade of tall ships in New York harbor during the July 4 Liberty Weekend celebrations.

Fifteen foreign ambassadors, mostly from Western Europe, boycotted ceremonies commemorating the 13th anniversary of the September 1973 coup and the Army Day ceremonies later that month. Nearly all foreign representatives, however, attended the funeral Mass for the bodyguards killed in the attempted ambush of Pinochet and a September 18 Mass celebrating 176 years of independence.

NEALE J. PEARSON
Texas Tech University

President Augusto Pinochet and a host of domestic and foreign officials attended funeral services for five military guards killed in a September 7 assassination attempt against the Chilean leader. Pinochet escaped with only a grazed hand.

上海光輝服装厂

© Hiroji Kubota/Magnum

Western-style clothing on display at the Shanghai trade fair typifies the fundamental changes taking place in China.

CHINA, PEOPLE'S REPUBLIC OF

The principal tasks set for 1986 by the government and the Chinese Communist Party were to consolidate the unexpectedly large economic gains of the preceding year and to guard against the undermining of the program of reform by those taking advantage of the new freedoms to further their own personal interests through corruption.

Politics. Opposition to corruption was the topic of a meeting of some 8,000 party, government, and army leaders held in early January 1986. Absent from the meeting was Chen Yun, the head of the Central Discipline Inspection Commission. Chen had taken public issue with the liberal reforms of Deng Xiaoping, the nation's supreme leader, at a party meeting six months earlier. Supervision of the campaign against corruption was placed in the hands of a new group of younger officials, leading some to suggest a maneuver on Deng's part around Chen's opposition.

The 82-year-old Deng absented himself from public view during the winter months to demonstrate, he said, that the ongoing pursuit of his policies does not depend on his personal intervention and in order to give younger leaders more responsibility. His first public appearance of the year came at the Fourth Session of the Sixth National People's Congress (NPC), which met March 24–April 12 to review prog-

ress in economic and political reform and to consider the Seventh Five-Year Plan. Premier Zhao Ziyang discussed the problem of the excessive rate of economic growth in 1985, attributing it to overinvestment in fixed assets, excessive growth in consumption funds, and lax controls over imports. The NPC, China's nominal parliament, also adopted a series of general provisions to serve as the basis for a new system of civil law.

The year 1986 marked the completion of a four-year program of reform of the state structure and a three-year "consolidation" of the Chinese Communist Party. These programs resulted in a significant reduction in the size of government and party bureaucracies, the replacement of aging and ill-trained cadres with younger and technically more proficient replacements, and the implementation of a regular system of recruitment and retirement. Looking ahead, the Central Party School held a seminar during the summer of 1986. Initiated at Deng's suggestion, the seminar investigated ways in which the Chinese political system could implement a rule of law that would be insulated from the radical shifts in ideology and policy attributed in the past to the contending views of individual leaders. The seminar initiated a process of fundamental reform of the role and structure of the party and its relationship to the government. The process was scheduled to culminate in the party's 13th Congress in fall 1987.

The 12th Central Committee met in plenary session in mid-September to tackle the difficult problems of waning political commitment and an increase in corruption in China today, especially among the younger generation. The plenum adopted a resolution called "Guiding Principles for Building a Socialist Society with an Advanced Culture and Ideology," which, for the most part, avoided the facile explanation of the past for such decline in commitment and discipline—the influence of the bourgeois West. The resolution called for the development of education as a foundation for a new ethical and ideological structure. At the same time, however, it spoke of the need to preserve the service-oriented ethic and the ideological framework of the past. "It is wrong," the resolution concluded, "to regard Marxism as a rigid dogma. It is also wrong to negate its basic tenets, view it as an outmoded theory, and blindly worship bourgeois philosophies and social doctrines."

Economy. Efforts on the economic front were designed to slow and stabilize economic growth and to correct China's serious trade deficit. Preliminary figures for 1986 suggested that progress was made toward the achievement of both goals. The growth in industrial output for the year was projected at 5–6%, down from 23% in 1985. Growth in the state sector for the first two quarters was 4.9%, while growth in the collective and private sectors, which reached 60% in the first half of 1985, was up only 19% for the comparable period in 1986. Grain output, down in 1985 by 7% from its 1984 record of 407.1 million tons, was projected to reach 400 million tons by year's end.

Although the trade deficit for the first half of the year stood at $6.4 billion, the *yuan* was devalued by approximately 15% in July to increase Chinese exports. Petroleum accounted for about one quarter of China's export earnings in 1985, with nearly half of the oil going to Japanese buyers. Although oil exports were increased in 1986 to help offset very substantial imports from Japan, low oil prices offset some

of the effect of this move. Nonetheless, the 1986 deficit was expected to be smaller than the $10 billion figure registered in 1985.

Sino-U.S. trade reached a level of $8 billion in 1985, up 25% from the preceding year. By 1986 more than 250 American firms had offices in China, and U.S. investment there totaled more than $1.4 billion. In response to American complaints, the Chinese government took a number of steps to make more flexible its policies and regulations regarding the repatriation of profits in joint ventures with foreign firms.

In July, China submitted its application to join the General Agreement on Tariffs and Trade (GATT), the 91-member international organization on which it has sat as an observer since 1983. Although Cuba and six Eastern European states are "non-market economy" members of the organization, China applied as a "developing economy."

Two measures designed to increase industrial productivity were implemented during the year. One of the measures, included in the package of urban reforms announced in the fall of 1984, was the substitution of state loans and corporate taxes for the subsidies and profit transfers typical of the state-owned sector in the past. A corollary of this reform called for enterprises unable to make a profit even after seeking new lines of output to declare themselves bankrupt. A substantial number of enterprises appeared likely to be affected by this measure. It was estimated that up to 20% of state-owned enterprises were operating in the red, with total annual losses exceeding two billion *yuan* ($540 million).

The first firm to declare itself bankrupt was an instrument factory in the northeastern city of Shenyang during August. The fact that the plant had 30 managers for only 72 workers may have explained its financial difficulties. Despite this precedent, the Standing Committee of the State Council rejected for a second time in Sep-

© Forest Anderson/Gamma-Liaison

Once considered "bourgeois" and "decadent," beauty parlors in Beijing, left, *and elsewhere now do a lively business.*

tember a draft law on bankruptcies, sending it back for a third revision. Of particular concern was the fate of workers displaced from jobs by the closing of failed enterprises.

A second provision of the urban economic reforms was the breaking of what the Chinese call the "iron rice bowl." Workers in state-owned enterprises have enjoyed a system of tenure that made it almost impossible for managers to fire even the least productive workers. Since 1979 about 3.6 million workers have been hired on a contract basis. After a three- to six-month probation period, they are given fixed-term contracts, renewal of which is based on productivity. Now, as of October 1986, all new workers in state enterprises were to be hired under the contract system. The effect of this reform on overall productivity was likely to be slow, however, since the remaining 95% of the work force, hired before the reform was begun, still had their iron rice bowls intact.

Rural reform, meanwhile, began to show significant results. Initiated eight years earlier, the "responsibility system" of individual family farming under contract and the system of "specialized households," designed to diversify crops and augment services, have contributed to an annual growth rate that has reached 15% per year since 1984. Average per capita income in the countryside more than doubled during the period of 1978–84 and reached 400 *yuan* ($108) in 1986.

An even more important socioeconomic change was taking place with the very rapid expansion of rural industries. Growing at a rate of more than 50% from 1984 to 1986, rural industries now constitute about 17% of industrial production. It was estimated that they would attract more than 100 million workers, or 30% of the rural work force, over the next three years. This, in turn, will result in a very substantial growth in rural towns and cities.

In spring 1986 the Great Wall Industry Corporation, an agency of the Ministry of Astronautics, signed two contracts for the launching of foreign communications satellites aboard Chinese rockets. The first agreement was with the Swedish Space Corporation, and the second was with Teresat Incorporated of Houston, TX. The latter contract, which provides for two launchings—the first in late 1987, the second six months later—calls for the full transfer of the technology involved in the satellites being launched. The Chinese anticipated being able to conduct 10 to 12 launches per year from a site in southern Sichuan Province. They are offering the service at rates 10–15% below those formerly charged by the U.S. National Aeronautics and Space Administration (NASA) and currently charged by the European Ariane program. In June the Hughes Aircraft Company announced that it had proposed a joint venture under which Chinese rockets would be launched from a base in Hawaii.

And in late September, further testifying to the sweeping changes in Deng's China, the nation's first stock market since the 1949 Communist takeover was opened on an experimental basis in Shanghai.

Society. Somewhat unexpectedly, it was a year of student activism on Chinese university campuses. In January some 3,000 students marched in Urumchi, the capital of the Xinjiang Autonomous Region, to demonstrate their opposition to nuclear weapons testing there. In April two history majors at a university in Beijing were arrested for forming an illegal political organization known as the "Young Marxist Faction." Their object in doing so was to carry on the protest, begun in the fall of 1985, against the "economic invasion" of China by Japan.

In late May at Tianjin University, another outburst involved more than 400 students pro-

© New China/Gamma-Liaison

China's leader Deng Xiaoping (left) *stayed out of public view during the first months of the year, reappearing at the National People's Congress in late March. Two weeks later, he took part in a tree-planting ceremony in a Beijing park. Deng, 82, hinted at retirement.*

During a six-day visit in mid-October, the first by a British monarch, Queen Elizabeth II met with Chinese leaders and took in some of the sights, including the ancient terra-cotta warriors in Xian.

© T. Graham/Sygma

testing a party being held by a group of 40 African students and their guests. The African students were moved by university authorities into local hotels and later to Beijing to avoid clashes on the campus. In 1986 there were approximately 1,600 African students in China, most of whom where studying on scholarships provided by the Chinese government. Many took part in counterdemonstrations in Nanjing and Shanghai, and in early June about 200 carried out a protest march on the offices of the State Education Commission in Beijing, protesting what they described as racist treatment.

In mid-December students demonstrated in Wuhan, Shanghai, and Beijing, calling for the introduction of democratic reforms in the Chinese political system. As many as 50,000 participated in the Shanghai demonstrations, causing city officials to declare the protest illegal. Many students were arrested.

A revival of the slogan, "Let a hundred flowers bloom, let a hundred schools of thought contend" in the late spring was met with mixed reactions. First heard in 1957 and followed closely by a sweeping anti-rightist campaign, the slogan evoked memories of brutal suppression on the part of citizens who had responded to its call for an airing of critical views. The new use of the phrase, Beijing said, was designed to encourage intellectual debate in the sciences, seen as a prerequisite to technological advancement. There is no possibility, said officials, of a repetition of the crackdown of 1957–58.

Job assignments for Chinese college graduates have, until recently, been carried out by the central government in consultation with the student and his or her university faculty and administration. The advantage to the student was the security of a guaranteed position; the disadvantage was that the student frequently had little say in determining the nature or location of the assignment. In 1985 an experiment was launched whereby only 23% of graduating seniors were placed by the state, the others negotiating directly with potential employers. When, as might have been predicted, certain key positions went unfilled because they were geographically or economically less attractive, the placement system was reinstituted for all but about 30% of 1986 graduates. Students being prepared for careers in such key professions as teaching and medicine seemed unlikely to be freed of the state placement system for the foreseeable future.

In 1986 there were about 30,000 Chinese students and scholars studying abroad. Of this number, approximately 16,000 were in the United States, half of them supported by the Chinese government and half by relatives, friends, or scholarships from American colleges and universities. A point of concern for the Chinese government was the fact that, given the very different standard of living and the high quality of academic facilities in the United States, many of these Chinese students and scholars would choose to remain there. Beijing also was concerned that the growing number of Chinese students pursuing graduate degrees in the United States were being trained in fields that would prove irrelevant to China's level of economic, scientific, and technological development. Accordingly, new regulations were being devised under which Chinese students must begin their graduate work in the growing number of master's degree programs available in Chinese universities. They would then be permitted to go abroad for further graduate study, whenever possible in joint degree programs under which their work would be supervised and evaluated by both Chinese and foreign faculty members. Their doctoral degrees would be awarded by their home university in China.

An increasing number of Chinese cities have been opened to foreign travelers, and still other areas can be visited by those seeking permission in advance. The fact that travel to some areas of China is still restricted was brought forcefully to the attention of the outside world with the detention of *New York Times* correspondent John Burns in July. Burns was held for six days on charges of having illegally entered a restricted military area in south-central China while traveling by motorcycle with an American and a Chinese companion. Following his release, Burns was expelled from the country.

Foreign Relations. Soviet General Secretary Mikhail Gorbachev, speaking in Vladisvostok in late July, announced measures designed to encourage Beijing to move toward a rapprochement with Moscow. He promised a withdrawal of Soviet forces from Afghanistan and Mongolia, thereby responding in part to two of the three "obstacles" the Chinese say have stood in the way of improved Sino-Soviet relations. Deng Xiaoping made use of American television to respond to Gorbachev's initiative. Interviewed on the program *Sixty Minutes,* Deng said that, despite his age and semiretirement, he would be happy to meet with General Secretary Gorbachev anywhere once the Soviet Union agreed to remove the "main obstacles" and encourage Vietnam to withdraw its troops from Cambodia.

Deng used the same forum to remind his American listeners that the 1979 Taiwan Relations Act (establishing unofficial U.S. relations with that island nation and providing continued economic ties and some security assurances) constitutes an "enormous obstacle" to the further development of Sino-U.S. relations. Of particular concern to Beijing was Washington's decision to license the transfer by U.S. firms to Taiwan of technology that will allow the manufacture of an advanced fighter aircraft. The Chinese contended that this decision violated the spirit, if not the letter, of the Sino-U.S. joint communiqué of August 1982. Washington contended that the communiqué dealt only with the transfer of hardware, not of technology.

Meanwhile, steps begun as early as 1973 to foster military cooperation between the United States and China began to bear fruit. Negotiations between Washington and Beijing for the sale of military hardware to China resulted in the signing of agreements on sales of helicopters, boat engines, artillery ammunition manufacturing equipment, and avionics equipment for Chinese high-altitude interceptor aircraft. A proposal initially advanced by U.S. Secretary of Defense Caspar Weinberger in Beijing in 1983 resulted in a November port visit by three U.S. Navy vessels to Qingdao in Shandong Province. They were the first American warships to visit China since 1949.

China's relations with Japan were adversely affected once again by China's objections to a history textbook proposed for adoption in Japanese schools. The text, which had been rewritten twice in response to Chinese criticisms, portrays Japan's actions in China during World War II in what the Chinese find to be too favorable a light. Japanese Prime Minister Yasuhiro Nakasone ordered a further review of the text in July.

Negotiations between China and Portugal over the future of the colony of Macau began in June, and an agreement was reached in October. The colony, which lies at the mouth of the Pearl River opposite Hong Kong, was initially settled by the Portuguese in 1557. The October agreement calls for the transfer of sovereignty by the year 2000, three years after British sovereignty over Hong Kong reverts to China. A working group similar to that set up under the Sino-British agreement on Hong Kong was formed to work out the details of Macau's future administration.

The Chinese entertained a number of important foreign guests during the year, including Polish leader Wojciech Jaruzelski, East German party leader Erich Honecker, Canada's Prime Minister Brian Mulroney, South African Bishop Desmond Tutu, Great Britain's Queen Elizabeth II, and Japan's Prime Minister Nakasone.

See also TAIWAN.

JOHN BRYAN STARR
Yale-China Association

CHINA · Information Highlights

Official Name: People's Republic of China.
Location: Central-eastern Asia.
Area: 3,706,564 sq mi (9 600 000 km²).
Population (mid-1986 est.): 1,050,000,000.
Chief Cities (1982 census): Beijing (Peking), the capital, 9,230,687; Shanghai, 11,859,748; Tianjin, 7,764,141.
Government: *Head of state,* Li Xiannian, president (took office June 1983). *Heads of government,* Zhao Ziyang, premier (took office Sept. 1980); Deng Xiaoping, chairman, Central Military Commission. *Legislature* (unicameral)—National People's Congress.
Monetary Unit: Yuan (3.704 yuan equal U.S.$1, August 1986).
Gross National Product (1985 est.): $343,000,000,000.
Foreign Trade (1985 U.S.$): *Imports,* $40,354,000,000; *exports,* $26,478,000,000.

© R. Thompson/Photo Trends

Downtown development continued apace in U.S cities. The Javits Convention Center opened on New York's west side.

CITIES AND URBAN AFFAIRS

In the United States, 1986 was a significant year in the ongoing urban accommodation to President Ronald Reagan's "New Federalism," as major finance programs were ended or amended, creative managerial adjustments were pursued, and new challenges and opportunities arose. The year was spiced by major scandals in several cities and some interesting election referenda. Such persistent urban issues as housing, the homeless, and economic development were joined by such emerging suburban issues as unplanned growth and congestion.

Finance. After a decline from $69 billion to $17 billion in federal funding for U.S. cities since 1980, the Congress in 1986 terminated the one program that city officials had considered sacred since its inception in 1972—the $4.2 billion-a-year general revenue sharing program. Under revenue sharing, a form of unrestricted federal subsidy, more than $83 billion had been allocated to more than 39,000 municipalities, townships, and counties. For 80% of the smaller jurisdictions, revenue sharing was the only form of federal aid; for most jurisdictions the demise of the program would mean service cutbacks and new or higher local taxes. However, since revenue sharing constituted only 2.5% of local revenue overall (but a significant 6% in larger cities), communities were expected to cope more or less effectively with the loss. Some communities have demonstrated imagination and acumen in implementing such strategies as privatization of services (*see* page 554), salaries pegged to performance, increased user fees, and joint purchasing.

The Tax Reform Act of 1986 added another burden on local finances by severely restricting the kinds and amounts of municipal revenue bonds, and making the interest on them subject to federal taxes. (*See also* special report, page 508.) Since revenue bonds have become an increasingly popular method for financing local capital projects ($198 billion in 1985), the restrictions will cause either the cancellation or postponement of public construction projects, or increase their cost.

Under consideration at year's end was a controversial proposal that would dramatically alter the financial responsibility for public assistance within the federal system and, in the process, add to the financial woes of local jurisdictions. The so-called Evans-Robb commission proposal would have the federal government assume 90% of the cost of Medicaid and Aid to Families with Dependent Children (AFDC), the two largest programs whose costs are now divided between the federal government and the states. In exchange, most federal aid programs would become the financial responsibility of state and local governments. Municipal leaders feared that the swap would not be "fiscally neutral" and that the states could not cover their losses.

Corruption and Scandal. As if the fiscal assault were not bad enough, scandals bound to reduce public confidence in local officials shook the cities of New York and Chicago in related incidents concerning lucrative parking meter collection contracts. In New York, Queens Borough President Donald Manes committed suicide following the disclosure of corruption, and Bronx Democratic leader Stanley Friedman, among others, was convicted of racketeering. In Chicago seven officials, including two aldermen allied with Mayor Harold Washington, were indicted. In Philadelphia, still recovering from the MOVE bombing of 1985, two judges and a host of union officials were indicted for bribery, and a city councilman was indicted for election fraud and extortion. Boston police officers were investigated for an alleged protection racket in connection with liquor licenses. And in Omaha, Mayor Michael Boyle fought a recall election over charges of administrative impropriety.

Issues, Referenda, Regulation. While the year was dominated by financial adjustment and a surge in municipal scandals, more traditional urban issues also attracted attention. Mayors and managers were troubled that federal support for highways and mass transit expired. Portland, OR, did open its 15-mi (24-km) MAX system, and Sacramento, San Jose, and Los Angeles had "light rail" projects near completion. Congress passed, but the president vetoed, an $8.5 billion clean water bill for the upgrading of local treatment facilities. There was mounting concern for the growing population of urban homeless and for the efficacy of the new voucher program for housing low- and moderate-income families. Local officials for the first time urged strong federal action against drug abuse.

In November elections, San Francisco became the first city to approve equal pay for jobs of comparable worth among municipal employees. Boston voters overwhelmingly rejected a referendum which would have carved out a predominantly black city to be named after South African black leader Nelson Mandela.

The U.S. Supreme Court placed another potential burden on local governments when it ruled that they may be liable, under some circumstances, for the actions of their officials. The decision was said to expose cities and counties to more frequent lawsuits.

Downtown development and suburban "megacenters" showed continued growth, despite clear signs of commercial overbuilding and suburban highway "gridlock." Proposals to tap urban revitalization for neighborhood investment through "linked" and "negotiated" development, and "incentive zoning," became more widespread. But new tax laws and a soft market were expected to slow development. Voters in San Francisco and Los Angeles voted construction limits on commercial projects. According to a new study, the recent rate of development in the United States would have to be reduced by half through 1995 to bring supply in line with demand.

The U.S. Census Bureau reported that the "rural renaissance" of the late 1970s and early 1980s has stalled and that the trend toward metropolitan growth (and/or a slower rate of decline) since 1984 is significant.

LOUIS MASOTTI, *Northwestern University*

COINS AND COIN COLLECTING

On Oct. 18, 1985, U.S. Secretary of the Treasury James A. Baker III struck the first U.S. coin bearing a likeness of the Statue of Liberty—a $5 gold piece designed by Chief Engraver of the U.S. Mint Elizabeth Jones to commemorate the 100th anniversary of the statue. Also produced in honor of the centennial were silver $1 coins and copper-nickel 50¢ pieces. The dollar coin, depicting Ellis Island, was designed by Mint Engravers John Mercanti and Matthew Peloso, while the half dollar, created by Edgar Steever and Sherl Winter, also of the Mint, honors those who immigrated to America's shores. Surcharges from the sale of the coins were earmarked for restoration of the Statue of Liberty and Ellis Island. The centennial observation spawned many private numismatic issues, as well as a silver 100-franc coin produced by the French government, whose gift of the famed statue was unveiled in New York Harbor in October 1886.

Treasury officials announced in March 1986 that beginning in 1987 Federal Reserve notes will carry microprinting and imbedded security threads, representing the first major change in national currency in nearly 60 years. The redesign comes after several years of debate and research on counterfeiting deterrents. Both new and existing notes will be legal tender and will circulate simultaneously; old bills will be removed from circulation in the normal course of currency processing.

Canada also initiated changes in its paper money, introducing a new series of bank notes depicting Canadian birds. The notes are the same size and color and printed on the same paper as current issues.

The United States joined the ranks of Canada, Australia, and South Africa with the passage of the Gold Bullion Coin Act in 1985, which provides for the minting of four gold coins in denominations of $50, $25, $10, and $5. Chosen for the obverse of the coins was a modified version of the $20 gold piece designed by Augustus Saint-Gaudens during Theodore Roosevelt's administration. The $50 coin, the first of the series to be released, debuted in the fall of 1986. It features a family of eagles on the reverse, executed by Miley Busiek. Also released was a silver $1 coin, which employs on the obverse the Walking Liberty design originally conceived by Adolph Weinman for the half dollar of 1916-47. The reverse features a heraldic eagle designed by John Mercanti.

The British Royal Mint marked 1,100 years of continuous minting in 1986. The institution began operations in London in 886 with the production of crude, hand-struck silver pennies for Alfred the Great. Today, its modern facility in Llantrisant, Wales, strikes coins for more than 67 countries.

BARBARA J. GREGORY, *"The Numismatist"*

COLOMBIA

Elections for the congress and the presidency in 1986 confirmed continuing Liberal party dominance of Colombian politics. Virgilio Barco, the official Liberal candidate, won the presidency easily over his Conservative and leftist opponents, and the Liberal party extended its control over the Colombian Senate and Chamber of Deputies. For the first time since the early 1970s, a leftist alternative to the two major parties—Liberals and Conservatives, which have dominated Colombian politics since the late 19th century—made its appearance. The *Union Patriotica* (Patriotic Union, or UP) made a respectable showing in both the congressional and presidential elections and later was certified as an official political party.

Violence continued to mount during 1986, with the 1984 truce agreement between the government and the guerrillas in tatters. The week-long visit of Pope John Paul II in early July made little or no dent in the continuing struggle between the army and various guerrilla groups. Despite continued inflation and consequent softening of the peso, the Colombian economy performed better than most Latin American economies during the year.

Politics. The congressional elections, held on March 9, were billed as a four-way contest among the Liberals, Conservatives, a dissident Liberal faction under Luis Carlos Galan, and the newly-formed UP. The UP is a coalition of the old-line Communist party and the political wing of the Colombian Revolutionary Armed Forces (FARC), the nation's oldest and largest guerrilla organization. The elections resulted in a resounding victory for the Liberals, who won 48.2% of the vote and 60 of the 114 seats in the Senate. In the Chamber of Deputies, the Liberals won 100 of the 199 seats being contested. President Belisario Betancur's Conservative Party, with 37% of the vote, won 45 Senate and 82 Chamber seats. UP gained 1 Senate seat and 10 Chamber seats with 1.4% of the vote. The dissident Liberals did not nearly meet their preelection expectations, gaining only 8% of the vote and controlling 8 seats in the Senate and 7 in the Chamber.

Galan, who had hoped to make a run for the presidency, subsequently withdrew from the race, leaving Liberal candidate Barco, Conservative Alvaro Gomez Hurtado, and UP candidate Jaime Pardo to battle it out. As expected, Barco won an easy victory in the May 25 balloting with 4.1 million votes, or 58% of the total. Gomez garnered 36%, and Pardo received 4% of the total. Pardo's showing was gratifying to UP partisans, as the party almost tripled its March totals. One result of the elections was the replacement of Gomez by former President Misael Pastrana Borrero as head of the Conservative party. Barco was sworn in on August 7, promising to continue the government's dialogue with the guerrillas and to combat poverty and unemployment. In a break with a precedent followed since 1958, Barco named no Conservatives to his cabinet.

The virtual war between the army and the guerrillas continued during 1986. The M-19, responsible for the November 1985 attack on the Palace of Justice in Bogotá, continued its attacks against the military and police. Only the FARC continued to honor the peace accords worked out previously. An Amnesty International report in August asserted that more than 600 people had died at the hands of the Colombian police and army during the first six months of 1986.

Economy. Despite falling coffee prices, which hit a low of $1.70 (U.S.) per pound in July, the Colombian economy performed well. The value of the peso declined against the U.S. dollar at an annual rate of 30%, but the government estimated an inflation rate of no more than 22% for the year. Unemployment continued at 14%, but the government hoped to reduce it by at least 1% by year's end. Colombia became an oil exporter for the first time since 1974, producing 400,000 barrels per day and exporting 180,000 barrels. Gross domestic product was expected to grow by 6% in 1986.

Foreign Affairs. Two potentially major issues surfaced in Colombian foreign policy during 1986. Flower growers in the United States accused Colombia of dumping cut flowers in U.S. markets. By year's end the issue had not been resolved. And relations between Colombia and Nicaragua became strained in April, when Nicaragua's Foreign Minister Miguel D'Escoto claimed that the treaty giving Colombia sovereignty over the San Andres and Providencia islands in the Caribbean near the Nicaraguan coast was invalid. Colombia promptly reasserted its claim to sovereignty over the islands, a popular vacation spot for people on the mainland.

ERNEST A. DUFF
Randolph-Macon Women's College

COLOMBIA • Information Highlights

Official Name: Republic of Colombia.
Location: Northwest South America.
Area: 439,735 sq mi (1 138 914 km²).
Population (mid-1986 est.): 30,000,000.
Chief City (1985 est.): Bogotá, the capital, 4,584,000.
Government: *Head of state and government,* Virgilio Barco Vargas, president (took office Aug. 1986). *Legislature*—Parliament; Senate and House of Representatives.
Monetary Unit: Peso (207.00 pesos equal U.S.$1, Oct. 10, 1986).
Gross National Product (1985 U.S. $): $29,000,000,000.
Economic Index (Bogotá, 1985): *Consumer Prices* (1980 = 100), all items, 279.0; food, 287.5.
Foreign Trade (1984 U.S.$): *Imports,* $4,052,000,000; *exports,* $3,462,000,000.

COLORADO

Colorado's weakening economy dominated both local news coverage and the state's political debate in 1986. The election was unusually wide open because of the retirement of Colorado's two best known political figures—Democrats Gov. Richard D. Lamm and U.S. Sen. Gary Hart.

State Elections. Lamm's 12 years as governor set a longevity record for a Colorado chief executive. But Republicans controlled the state Senate for Lamm's entire tenure and the state House of Representatives for the final ten years. While Lamm won national attention for his views on such issues as medical care and immigration, his messages evoked little response from his own legislature. His strongest theme was the need for Colorado to rationally manage growth, but so few of his proposals in that area became law that growth management was still a key issue in 1986.

The gubernatorial race was won by Democratic State Treasurer Roy R. Romer, who defeated Republican state Senate President Ted L. Strickland by a margin of 615,833 to 434,134. While Romer shares many of Lamm's views about how growth should be managed, he spent most of the campaign talking about how best to stimulate the state's lagging economy. A successful businessman, he pledged to push economic development, including a new airport in the Denver area and a state convention center to boost tourism.

Romer's landslide helped the Democrats pick up six seats in the state legislature. Republicans would still control the Senate (25–10) and the House (40–25), but the Democratic gains broke a Republican majority which had allowed the GOP to overturn Lamm's vetoes at will and gave Romer a stronger negotiating position with the legislature's GOP majority.

Democrat Gail Schoettler won Romer's old job as state treasurer, while Republican Secretary of State Natalie Meyer and Republican Attorney General Duane Woodard posted impressive reelection victories. A tax-cutting measure also on the ballot was defeated.

Economy. Ruben Valdez, director of the state Department of Labor and Employment, reported that the state's unemployment rate had reached 7% in July, compared with 6.9% for the nation. He said this "marked the first time in modern memory that the jobless rate in Colorado has surpassed that of the nation." Unemployment jumped to 7.5% in September, after 3,700 Coloradans lost their jobs when Denver-based Frontier Airlines declared bankruptcy. Many of those employees later found jobs with Continental Airlines, which took over many of Frontier's planes and routes.

National Races. Both major candidates seeking to succeed Senator Hart, who was expected to try for the 1988 Democratic presidential nomination, used the mounting unemployment statistics to bolster their campaigns. For eight years Republican Ken Kramer had represented the fifth congressional district, where much research on the Strategic Defense Initiative (SDI) is conducted. Kramer, an avid SDI backer, argued that the space-based defense program would be a boon to Colorado's economy. Democrat Timothy E. Wirth, who had represented the suburban second district for 12 years, declared that improving Colorado's educational system would spawn a more balanced and enduring prosperity than would military contracts. Voters narrowly handed the Senate seat to Wirth.

Democrats entered the election trailing the Republicans 4-2 in U.S. House of Representatives seats but ended up splitting the delegation. Ben Nighthorse Campbell defeated one-term Republican incumbent Michael L. Strang in the sprawling third district. Campbell will become the only American Indian in Congress and just the eighth ever to serve in that body. David E. Skaggs kept Wirth's old second district in Democratic hands by defeating Republican Michael Norton. Joel M. Hefly similarly kept Kramer's old fifth district in the GOP column by defeating Democrat Bill Story. In the other Congressional races, three entrenched incumbents—Democrat Patricia Schroeder and Republicans Hank Brown and Daniel Schaefer—easily turned back underfinanced challengers.

Other. On January 21, over Congressional objections, the now defunct U.S. Synthetic Fuels Corporation approved a $327 million loan guarantee to help restart Union Oil Company's Parachute Creek oil shale extraction project. In February heavy rains and unseasonably warm weather led to numerous avalanches in Colorado. Also in 1986, *The Denver Post* won a Pulitzer Prize for journalism for its study of missing children.

BOB EWEGEN, *"The Denver Post"*

COLORADO • Information Highlights

Area: 104,091 sq mi (269 596 km²).

Population (1985 est.): 3,231,000.

Chief Cities (July 1, 1984 est.): Denver, the capital, 504,588; Colorado Springs, 247,739; Aurora, 194,772; Lakewood, 121,114.

Government (1986): *Chief Officers*—governor, Richard D. Lamm (D); lt. gov., Nancy Dick (D). *General Assembly*—Senate, 35 members; House of Representatives, 65 members.

State Finances (fiscal year 1985): *Revenue,* $5,298,000,000; *expenditure,* $4,817,000,000.

Personal Income (1985): $47,859,000,000; per capita, $14,812.

Labor Force (June 1986): *Civilian labor force,* 1,716,600; *unemployed,* 117,500 (6.8% of total force).

Education: *Enrollment* (fall 1984)—public elementary schools, 376,216; public secondary, 169,211; colleges and universities, 161,314. *Public school expenditures,* (1983–84), $1,643,000,000 ($3,261 per pupil).

COMMUNICATION TECHNOLOGY

During 1986, fiber optic (lightwave) communication systems continued to demonstrate their superiority over other transmission systems as a medium with capacity for unlimited growth and with advantages of lower cost, greater reliability, and freedom from electromagnetic interference. Applications ranged from short data links within a building to major intercity networks and to intercontinental transoceanic cable sytems.

Moving toward the Integrated Services Digital Network (ISDN) of the 1990s, end-to-end digital communications included applications updating Private Branch Exchanges (PBXs) and extended to entire systems, in which data signals, video, and voice could be transmitted over a single wide-band high-speed channel. New international standards ensure that the services will work satisfactorily.

An evolving trend—the close union of computer logic and memory with communication facilities, tied together by sophisticated programs for performing functions previously limited to human abilities—became evident in 1986. Applications of speech recognition, speech synthesis, machine vision, conversion of the printed word to spoken sounds and to electrical signals, and the use of mechanical sensors to control the motor activity of industrial robots were made in manufacturing, business, and educational areas.

Transmission and Switching. Transatlantic and transpacific lightwave glass-fiber cables are being planned and constructed for service in 1988 and 1989. The newest of these cables will have a capacity of 40,000 simultaneous telephone conversations or an equivalent amount of data, video, or facsimile information sent at a rate of 246 million bits per second. Wide-band digital signals in the form of laser-generated pulses of light are carried over two pairs of hair-thin ultrapure glass fibers laid along the ocean floor.

In 1986, AT&T completed the first phase of the U.S. government's Defense Commercial Telecommunications Network (DCTN), designed for a variety of voice, data, and video services over a single digital network. The Department of Defense and other government agencies will be served at 150 locations throughout the country. Using a combination of terrestrial and satellite transmission links, the network route will total 85,000 mi (136 790 km). Teleconferencing capability is provided at all locations, and digital encryption will ensure privacy.

The New York City Teleport, which includes small earth stations, a network of lightwave cables, and high-speed electronic switching equipment, started commercial operation. It is intended to provide convenient and economical access to digital satellite and fiber optic transmission capabilities for large nearby businesses. It is expected that it will be a model for clustered communication facilities to be located in close proximity to other large cities.

Early in the year, the largest 5ESS (#5 Electronic Switching System) built to date was installed in Dallas, TX. It can serve up to 100,000 lines and is capable of handling as many as 300,000 calls in one hour. The system replaced three switching machines.

Communication Services. Greater convenience, speed, and safety were added to the AT&T Cellular Mobile Radio telephone system with the first application of dial-by-voice. A person's name spoken into the car phone is examined automatically for its voice-print features, compared in a bank of different prints stored in a computer, and converted to the correct number which is then dialed by the machine. As many as 20 individual numbers can be stored in the system's memory. The voice-prints are made in accordance with the driver's individual pronunciation of each name on the list, as previously recorded.

Major improvements were made in the technology of machine vision, in which computers and communications are closely allied. In conjunction with other machines, popularly termed robots, vision systems are being used for assembly, inspection, repair, and maintenance in such highly automated industries as automobile manufacture. In most of such applications, as in the detection of flaws and the examination of surface contours, the machines are far superior to human faculties.

Research on neural networks is being conducted at AT&T Bell Laboratories to learn more about biological computation and information processing in single nerve cells and simple organisms. Using mathematical models and computers, a simulated 900–neuron network was designed, and experimental electrical circuits were built to demonstrate the way that nerve cells interact to solve problems. Such basic studies are fundamental to an orderly understanding of what is needed for artificial intelligence machines and for the design of more powerful computers.

The French government conducted a large-scale trial of videophones installed in thousands of homes in Biarritz. The videophones were connected by fiber optic lightwave communication systems to one another and to a varied selection of information systems available to every participant. Each installation had a television screen, a TV camera, and control equipment with access to 12 TV channels, 2,000 videocassettes, news service, financial information, catalogs, documents, and colored pictures. The fact that users could call and see one another by videophone was a popular feature. At government expense, several thousand homes were equipped with videophones in

A desktop publisher checks and corrects the proofs of a computer-generated ad. Recent developments in computers and peripheral equipment have revolutionized publishing.

1986, with expectations that more than 3 million households would be connected to the system by 1989. The estimated cost is $10 billion.

Electronic Publishing. Personal computers and peripheral equipment that can create typeset quality text and pictures ready for reproduction and printing are now available. With printers and the necessary software, complicated documents with many different type faces can be composed, edited, and printed economically. IBM and Apple Computer are among those companies entering this rapidly growing activity.

In 1986, the Institute of Electrical and Electronics Engineers (IEEE) initiated a project that will make its technical publications available to anyone on demand. A personal computer and a modem (modulator-demodulator) constitute the terminal equipment. The storage and retrieval system will provide electronic mail, conference capabilities, and access to IEEE technical information files. It is expected to take about five years to fully implement the system.

Microelectronics and Microprocessors. The first photon switch, a device which may become the primary building block of a totally new kind of computer or communication switching machine, has been made at AT&T Bell Laboratories. In its fabrication, 2,500 ultra-thin alternating layers of gallium arsenide and aluminum gallium arsenide are deposited on a chip 200 micrometers square (200 millionths of a meter, or about 0.008 inches). The new switch, actuated by photons of light, opens up possibilities for an optical computer that can carry on a large number of parallel operations at the same time and consequently will be much faster in operation than the current electronic computers, which work in a serial fashion.

During the year, the megabit memory chip found applications in computers built by IBM and several Japanese manufacturers. The device can store 1,048,576 bits of data on a slice of silicon less than 3/8 inches or .95 cm square. This amount of information is equivalent to the contents of 100 double-spaced typewritten pages. The megabit chip will replace the 256,000 bit (256K) unit, which had been the largest available memory.

More efficient and compact microprocessors are being made for use in communications apparatus and in small computers. The 32-bit microprocessor became available to equipment manufacturers in 1986. The microprocessor chip contains more than 275,000 transistors and can handle more than 4 million instructions at a rate of 16 million operations per second. This is about three times faster than the 16-bit microprocessors used in current central processing units.

Software. A new method for solving complex linear programming problems, such as those met in planning communication networks, was devised by N. K. Karmarkar of AT&T Bell Laboratories. Faster than conventional linear programming by a factor of more than ten, it permits real-time network planning for minimum overall cost subject to practical constraints such as demand to be met, capacity limits, time when facilities can be installed, technologies to be used, and a large number of other critical factors. These problems can contain more than 500,000 variables and tens of thousands of constraints. As one example of its capability, a particular planning problem which took 15 hours of computing time by conventional methods was solved in less than 4 minutes by the Karmarkar algorithm.

M. D. FAGEN
Formerly AT&T Bell Laboratories

COMPUTERS

In spite of a sluggish economy, 1986 was a surprisingly good year for much of the computer industry. Earnings and sales were respectable, although they certainly did not equal the breakneck growth of the early 1980s.

For many, 1986 will best be remembered as "the year of the clones," as IBM's top-selling personal computer (PC) faced stiff competition from a raft of less costly compatibles (computers able to run software designed for use on the IBM PC). IBM, hoping to retain major corporate customers, unveiled the PC/XT Model 286, a much faster version of its PC/XT.

More Powerful Chips. At least one third of the PCs used in the United States run on microprocessors developed by Intel Corporation. In June, Intel began shipping its 80386 microprocessor, a 32-bit chip containing some 275,000 transistors and circuits. The 80386, the first 32-bit chip compatible with the MS-DOS operating system used in the IBM PC, is expected to become the brains of the next generation of IBM and IBM-compatible PCs.

In April, IBM became the first computer manufacturer to use a megabit memory chip in a commercial product. The chip, which can hold more than one million bits of data, is being used in IBM's Sierra series of mainframe computers.

Computers of the future may be optical, using light pulses to operate at speeds thousands or even millions of times faster than today's electronic computers. In June, AT&T Bell Laboratories announced that its researchers had built the first photonic switching chip, which may become the primary building block of an experimental optical computer. The chip contains four switches that are turned on and off by light beams, much in the way that electronic transistors are turned on and off by electrical charges. It is built from alternating layers of gallium arsenide and aluminum gallium arsenide.

Researchers also hope to use gallium arsenide to make chips for electronic computers. The chemical conducts electricity five times faster than silicon, the material traditionally used, but it is costly, brittle, and retains heat. Researchers at the University of Illinois have developed a hybrid chip made of alternating layers of gallium arsenide and silicon, thus combining the best qualities of each.

Software. Desktop publishing became the "hot" computer application. An electronic publishing system allows a person to combine text and graphics to produce finished copy for books, magazines, newsletters, and other publications. The copy can be sent electronically to an office printer or to an outside typesetter. Desktop systems generally consist of a PC and a laser printer, and can produce near-typeset quality at a fraction of the usual cost.

In an effort to compete with desktop publishing software, many word processing programs are incorporating page composition features. This may satisfy the needs of some users, but word processing programs are based on character processing rather than on graphics and thus do not include font generation and other graphics features found in desktop publishing programs.

A number of companies introduced artificial intelligence (AI) programs that imitate the decision-making processes of human experts. These so-called expert systems embody the accumulated experience and reasoning strategies of human authorities on a given subject. For instance, Palladian Software introduced Financial Advisor, a program designed to help executives make capital budgeting decisions. The program contains knowledge gathered from more than 30 experts in finance, business strategy, manufacturing, and AI. It also contains economics formulas and summaries of U.S. tax laws and Securities and Exchange Commission rulings. General Electric introduced an expert system that enables manufacturers of injection-molded plastic parts to diagnose and solve problems affecting production and quality.

AI technology also is being merged with existing products, such as spreadsheet and database management programs, to make them "smarter"—that is, more powerful and easier to use. And several dozen companies are selling development programs that help users design their own expert systems.

Currently, most expert systems are run on mini or mainframe computers. Few are available for PCs because the machines are not powerful enough to handle these programs.

Privacy Threat. A report issued by the congressional Office of Technology Assessment (OTA) warned that "the widespread and still growing use of computerized databases, electronic record searches and matches, and computer networking is leading rapidly to the creation of a de facto national database containing substantial personal information on most Americans." The OTA pointed out that while technological developments have improved government efficiency and law-enforcement investigations, the opportunities for inappropriate, unauthorized, and illegal access to personal information also have increased.

Keeping data secure on personal computers is also a problem, particularly as local area networks proliferate. In October the Computer Fraud and Abuse Act of 1986 was enacted, making it a felony to commit certain acts of fraud or theft related to computer trespass. The new law also makes it a felony for anyone to cause more than $1,000 in damages by maliciously trespassing in private computers in another state or into computers owned by the federal government, banks, or security dealers.

JENNY TESAR, *Free-lance Science Writer*

Artificial Intelligence

Imagine a computer that can diagnose illnesses, create legal documents, judge financial risks, advise farmers how to market grain, or communicate with people in their own language. Until recently, this was the stuff of fiction. Now, "smart" computers have entered offices and factories, where they are being used to solve common workday problems.

Giving computers the ability to simulate human reasoning is the objective of a branch of computer science known as *artificial intelligence,* or AI. The first important advances in AI occurred during the 1950s and 1960s, including the development of LISP (List Processing), the language most commonly used in AI programming. Experimental expert systems (programs that emulate the reasoning of human experts) were developed at a number of research institutions during the 1970s, and by 1980 applications companies were being formed. By 1986 complete expert systems were coming onto the market, and analysts were predicting that the AI market would reach $4 billion by 1990.

No one claims that AI systems are intrinsically "intelligent," that they can think or learn in the same manner as human beings. But many AI researchers believe that it is just a matter of time before machines are developed that can simulate human speech, perform complex functions and make reasoned judgments. Programs to create such computers are under way in the United States, Japan, Great Britain, and a consortium of European nations.

Operation and Design. Conventional computers are designed to do one basic job: process numerical data. AI systems can comprehend words and other symbols as well as numbers. Like people, they can compare facts and rules to make deductive responses.

Simulating how people do things and mimicking human reasoning require vastly more computer power and memory than are available in conventional computers. As a result, computer engineers are developing microprocessors (the "brains" of computers) that are much faster and have memory capacities hundreds of times greater than those now found in computers.

They also are working on a radically new type of computer architecture. A conventional computer contains a single microprocessor. The computer works serially, performing one task at a time; a program specifies precisely how the tasks are to be performed. Future AI systems probably will be parallel-processing machines in which hundreds of thousands of microprocessors are linked together, allowing them to perform separate parts of a job. A program will tell the computer what to do rather than how to do it.

Applications. The areas of AI research that hold the most immediate promise are expert systems, natural language, and machine vision. *Expert systems,* also called knowledge-based systems, combine textbook knowledge with the rules of thumb that experts use to solve problems. Such programs usually focus on narrow fields, such as drafting a will or restarting a stalled oil drill. For example, General Electric has developed a system that incorporates the knowledge of the firm's most experienced specialist in diesel locomotive repair. The system is used by maintenance workers in remote areas to fix mechanical problems. It is almost as effective and much cheaper than flying the human expert to the site.

Natural language systems are programs that enable computers to communicate in English or other natural languages. The ultimate goal is to develop systems that allow people to enter requests using whatever words and phrases they desire; the computer would understand the requests and respond accordingly. Present systems have limited capabilities. Those that can be taught to recognize the voice of a specific individual may recognize sentences composed from a vocabulary of up to 5,000 words that has been programmed into the systems. Speaker-independent systems pose a greater challenge because of the variations in people's pronunciation, inflection, and sentence structure. Current systems can only recognize short commands given in a very limited vocabulary.

Machine vision systems create physical representations of what the machines "see" and then interpret and use that data. For example, researchers at Carnegie-Mellon University have developed an autonomous vehicle called the Terregator which uses vision and sonar guidance systems to follow a path, such as a line on a sidewalk or a track through a mine tunnel. In 1986, TRW Inc. introduced a special-purpose computer designed to help a conventional computer recognize images. The system can be used, for example, to make visual quality checks in factories. It is a "neural-net" computer, simulating the interconnections among the billions of neurons in the human brain. With 250,000 processors and 5.5 million connections among them, it is surprisingly capable. Much more sophisticated systems, containing up to 100 million processors, are on the drawing boards.

JENNY TESAR

CONNECTICUT

Democratic Gov. William A. O'Neill was reelected to a second full term Nov. 4, 1986, easily defeating his Republican opponent, veteran State Rep. Julia D. Belaga. The election campaign was lackluster, with no major issues raised.

The voters also reelected U.S. Sen. Christopher J. Dodd, who overwhelmed Republican Roger W. Eddy, a farmer and former state senator. The Democrats recaptured control of the state Senate and the state House of Representatives by substantial margins. The Republicans had gained control of the General Assembly in the 1984 landslide victory of President Ronald W. Reagan. The six incumbents of the state's U.S. House of Representatives delegation were reelected, maintaining the even split between Democrats and Republicans, 3–3.

If O'Neill, 56, serves out his full term, which runs until January 1991, he will become the longest-sitting governor since Jonathan Trumbull II, who left office in 1809. O'Neill became governor on Dec. 31, 1980, when, as lieutenant governor, he succeeded Ella T. Grasso, when she resigned because of illness. He was elected to his first four-year term in 1982.

In other balloting, voters approved removal of party levers from voting machines. The party lever had been viewed by many as an anachronism belonging to the era of machine politics.

Legislation. The 1986 session of the General Assembly set another budget mark, approving record spending programs of $4.85 billion. The legislature also took steps to curb rising consumer insurance costs and to enhance the availability of insurance coverage by enacting changes in civil liability laws. The changes limit attorney fees, allow awards to be paid over a period of years instead of in a lump sum, and make defendants liable only for their share of the blame.

Education and Business. Benno C. Schmidt, Jr., former dean of the Columbia Law School, was inaugurated in September as the 20th president of Yale University. He succeeded A. Bartlett Giamatti, who had served since 1978 and who had resigned, effective in June. Giamatti became president of baseball's National League in December (*see* BIOGRAPHY).

Harry J. Gray, chairman of United Technologies Corp., Hartford, relinquished his chief executive officer's duties to President Robert F. Daniell early in 1986 and later said he would retire as chairman of the board of directors at the end of the year.

The Jackson Newspapers sold the *Register* and the *Journal Courier,* daily newspapers in New Haven, to Ingersoll Publications. Ingersoll announced that it would change the *Register* from an afternoon publication to an all-day

---

CONNECTICUT • Information Highlights
Area: 5,018 sq mi (12 997 km²).
Population (1985 est.): 3,174,000.
Chief Cities (July 1, 1984 est.): Hartford, the capital, 135,720; Bridgeport, 142,140; New Haven, 124,188; Waterbury, 102,861.
Government (1986): *Chief Officers*—governor, William A. O'Neill (D); lt. gov., Joseph J. Fauliso (D). *General Assembly*—Senate, 36 members; House of Representatives, 151 members.
State Finances (fiscal year 1985): *Revenue,* $6,268,000,000; *expenditure,* $5,429,000,000.
Personal Income (1985): $57,408,000,000; per capita, $18,089.
Labor Force (June 1986): *Civilian labor force,* 1,765,100; *unemployed,* 65,700 (3.7% of total force).
Education: *Enrollment* (fall 1984)—public elementary schools, 323,391; public secondary, 144,754; colleges and universities, 159,348. *Public school expenditures* (1983–84), $1,821,000,000 ($4,036 per pupil).

---

paper and would end publication of the *Journal Courier.*

Labor. A 56-day strike of 10,000 employees against the Southern New England Telecommunications Corp., the state's major telephone utility, ended November 7 when members of the Connecticut Union of Telephone Workers accepted a three-year contract.

ROBERT F. MURPHY
"The Hartford Courant"

CONSUMER AFFAIRS

"Change is the essence of the consumer movement. In broad terms, the consumer movement's mission must be to redress the fundamental imbalances in society. Therefore, all consumer organizations are in the influence business." Those words of Bill Roberts, deputy director of the Consumers' Association of the United Kingdom, emphasize the important role consumer organizations have played, are playing, and should play in the future of consumer affairs.

In many respects 1986 was a rather quiet year for consumer affairs. Inflation during the year hovered around 2% in the United States. The price of a single product, gasoline, played a very significant role in keeping inflation down. In some areas unleaded gasoline was selling as low as 65.9¢ per gallon compared with about $1.21 a year earlier.

Federal Consumer Activity. The new tax reform act, enacted in 1986, did not deal directly with consumer affairs, but its implementation will have a major impact on how much disposable personal income consumers will have to spend; what they will spend it on; and how they will invest their savings. (*See* page 508.)

A number of new commissioners were appointed to the Consumer Product Safety Commission (CPSC) and the Federal Trade Commission (FTC). In general these appoint-

U.S. Attorney General Edwin Meese (center) examines consumer products prior to a hearing of a Senate subcommittee on product liability reform proposals. Robert Pritzker (right), who was to head a new advisory committee on liability reform, and Wisconsin's Sen. Robert Kasten, a Republican, look on.

AP/Wide World

ments were looked upon with disfavor by consumer advocacy groups, but were approved by the Senate.

The proposed budget, presented by the President's Office of Management and Budget (OMB) for fiscal year 1987, revealed little change in the budgets for the Food and Drug Administration (FDA), the FTC, and the Consumer Information Center (CIC), but the budget request for the U.S. Office of Consumer Affairs (OCA) was reduced 80%, from almost $2,000,000 to $400,000. In addition the proposed 1987 budget for the CPSC was $33,000,000, 4.2% lower than the 1986 budget. The budget Congress finally approved granted OCA $1,750,000, a cut of only 8%. The CPSC was granted $34,100,000, a 1% cut.

A 1986 U.S. Supreme Court ruling will have an effect on the kinds of advertising coming from the business community. In a 5 to 4 ruling the court sharply limited First Amendment protection for commercial speech (advertising). The court ruled that government may sometimes ban truthful advertising in the interest of regulating products and services that are legal to sell but considered undesirable. The decision upheld Puerto Rico's tight restrictions on local advertising of casino gambling.

The question of whether deregulation of the airlines is a blessing or not was raised during 1986, as two additional airlines had serious financial problems. Frontier went bankrupt, and World Airways discontinued all its regularly scheduled flights and went entirely into the charter business. These changes, along with a number of airline mergers, were creating new problems for consumers.

Interest Rates. The decline in interest rates was having a favorable effect on home purchases. Some rates had declined as much as 25%, spurring both home building and home buying (see also HOUSING). The impact of sharp declines in interest rates was most evident in new car sales. General Motors shocked the market with its 2.9% rate on its 1986 models. Ford quickly followed with a 2.9%, while Chrysler dropped its rate to 2.4%, and American Motors went to zero interest rate. These sharp reductions in interest rates were due to the excessive inventory of new 1986 cars just at the time the 1987 models were about to be introduced. For persons not taking advantage of the low interest rates, the automobile companies were offering rebates of up to $1,500. (See also AUTOMOBILES.)

Rigidity in interest rates continued though on credit-card purchases. Although interest rates in general were declining and some banks lowered interest rates on credit-card purchases, there seemed to be little pressure on banks to lower such rates overall. Consequently the U.S. Congress began considering legislation to limit such charges. Rates vary from state to state and from bank to bank, but the general level of rates was still about 18% in 1986.

Consumers Union. The year marked the 50th anniversary of Consumers Union of the United States, the publishers of Consumer Reports, the only national product-testing and rating magazine. With a 1986 circulation of almost 3.5 million, the magazine continued to be held in high esteem because of its credibility.

STEWART M. LEE, Geneva College

CRIME

After a three-year decline, the number of major crimes reported to the police in the United States during 1985 rose 4%, according to the Federal Bureau of Investigation (FBI). Murder and nonnegligent manslaughter increased 1.5%, forcible rape was up by 4%, robbery climbed 3%, and the number of aggravated assaults rose by 5.5%. Overall, violent crime was up by 5%, while crimes against property increased by 4%. In the latter category, burglary was up 3%, larceny-theft up 5%, motor-vehicle theft up 7%, and arson up 3%.

Explanations for the rise included possible increases in drug use and concomitant criminal activity, as well as apathy in the wake of the previous three-year decline. "People just did not seem as concerned about the preventive measures that might have assisted in crime being reduced," said Jerald Vaughn, executive director of the International Association of Chiefs of Police. Brian Forst, director of research for the Police Foundation, suggested that the increase might have been the result of a growing willingness among victims to notify the police, perhaps because of the expanded use of foot patrols. FBI Director William Webster took a more guarded position. Explanations for crime fluctuations, he said, are "often questionable and certainly controversial."

The rise in crime, according to the FBI report, was disproportionately distributed by national region. No increase appeared in the Midwest, but the crime level rose 9% in the South, 5% in the West, and 2% in the Northeast. The FBI statistics showed Detroit replacing Gary, IN, as the city with the nation's highest murder rate—58 per 100,000 population. Next in line were St. Louis, MO; Newark, NJ; Birmingham, AL; and Miami, FL.

Handguns were the weapons most often used in homicides, accounting for 7,548 of the 17,545 killings. The Washington Report of Handgun Control, issued in 1986, showed the rate of handgun murders in the United States to be 77 times higher than that in the seven other countries studied. The U.S. rate was 5.06 per 100,000 population. The others were: Great Britain (.014), Japan (.066), Sweden (.217), Switzerland (.375), Australia (.027), Israel (.590), and Canada (.034).

Gun Control. In spring 1986, the U.S. Congress passed and President Ronald Reagan signed a bill significantly weakening the landmark 1968 Gun Control Act. The new measure, called the Firearm Owners Protection Act, made it easier to buy and sell rifles and handguns and to transport them across state lines. It represented the first major loosening of firearms curbs contained in the 1968 law.

Victimization Survey. As was the case in a number of earlier years, the U.S. Bureau of Justice Statistics survey on household crime victimization did not tell the same story as the FBI figures. The survey found that crimes against individuals and households had decreased 1.9% during 1985, reaching a 13-year low of 34.9 million—or about one quarter of American households. Most of the decrease was the result of an estimated 6% decline in the number of households victimized by personal theft. The bureau suggested that the downward trend was partially due to population movement away from cities to suburban areas, where crime rates tend to be lower. Michael Rand, author of the report, also speculated that tougher sentencing laws and increased neighborhood crime-prevention activity may have contributed to the drop.

Burglary. Attention during the year focused on tactics that could be useful to reduce burglary rates. Americans have reported particular fear of having their privacy invaded, their lives threatened, and their property stolen by burglars. Studies have shown that, to an overwhelming degree, experienced burglars go to great lengths to avoid confrontation with household members because being recognized greatly increases the risk of apprehension. However, research also indicates that the use of sophisticated security measures is unlikely to be of much help in deterring burglary. Typically, it was reported, burglars select their target based on the assessment of likely rewards and environment risks, most notably whether the house is occupied and whether it is readily visible to neighbors. Security measures (called "target hardening") are not likely to deter them once they pick a target, since most of these measures can easily be overcome.

Sarah Brady, the wife of James Brady, the White House press secretary left paralyzed in the 1981 assassination attempt against President Reagan, lobbied unsuccessfully against the loosening of federal gun control legislation.
AP/Wide World

Other research work summarized in government reports during 1986 suggests that victims of burglary often have security measures as good as households in the vicinity that are not victimized. Burglars often are able to enter houses because doors or windows are left open. And, for example, they can sometimes tell if a house is not occupied during the summer if the windows are shut but the air conditioning is not running. Neighborhood watch programs tend to reduce burglaries when first inaugurated but often peter out as participants, usually enrolled because of a particularly heinous offense in the neighborhood, become bored by unproductive surveillance of the streets. Police patrols were said to be completely ineffective in controling burglary. An urban police officer, research indicated, is apt to be within 100 yards of a burglary once every eight years, and even then he or she probably would not observe the crime because the intruder would not be visible from the patrol car.

Organized Crime. The President's Commission on Organized Crime in a March report identified drug trafficking as "the most serious organized crime problem in the world today." Such trafficking was said to account for about 38% of all organized crime activity in the United States and to generate illegal profits of $110 billion. The commission pointed out that the supply of cocaine in the United States originates exclusively in South America, most particularly in Peru, Bolivia, Colombia, and Ecuador. Colombians were said to control an estimated 75% of the U.S. supply. Cocaine, the commission declared, is smuggled into the United States by American citizens acting as mercenary pilots who lease planes and hire flight crews. The commission was "emphatic in its position that legalization of drugs use is not a viable option." It saw the newly created National Drug Enforcement Policy Board as presenting "a rare, possibly even unique, opportunity" to bring focus and coordination to the federal campaign against drug trafficking.

New York City in the fall was the scene of two of the most significant trials in the history of U.S. organized crime. The highly publicized cases, following a four-year series of indictments affecting 17 of the 24 Mafia families in the United States, struck at four of New York's five mob clans—which are the largest and most influential in the country. In Manhattan federal court, prosecutors pleaded their case against the reputed heads of three families—Anthony Salerno of the Genovese clan, Anthony Corallo of the Lucchese, and Carmine Persico of the Colombo—and five other members. The trial ended in November with all defendants convicted of operating a "commission" that ruled the Mafia as a criminal organization throughout the United States. In Brooklyn, members of what is reputed to be the most powerful U.S. Mafia family of all, the Gambinos, including boss John Gotti, also went on trial, but no verdict had been rendered by year's end. In both trials, charges were based on alleged violations of the 1970 Racketeer Influenced and Corrupt Organizations Act (RICO), which makes the very existence of such organized crime rings illegal.

Career Criminals. A 1986 report by the Bureau of Justice Statistics indicated that almost half of the inmates released from state prisons will return within 20 years, and that 60% of these repeaters will be back by the end of the third year. Another report recommended the establishment of special police squads to concentrate on career criminals. A special project in Washington, DC, targets persons believed to commit at least five serious crimes a week; their names are obtained from arrest records, warrant lists, and informants' tips. Officers participating in the Repeat Offender Project wear street clothes, drive shabby cars, and use tight surveillance schemes and sting tactics to catch offenders.

ATM Crimes. The close relationship between new technological developments and new forms of crime is vividly illustrated by the profusion of robbery offenses directed against clients who withdraw money from the automatic teller machines (ATMs) at banks throughout the country. Robbers know that their victims will have cash after they use the machines, that they are often unaccompanied, and that they often obtain their money in the twilight or dark after work. In 1986 victims of

Luciano Liggio, the alleged boss of the Sicilian Mafia, was one of 474 defendants to stand trial in Palermo, Italy. It was the largest trial of Mafia suspects in history.
AP/Wide World

CRIME / SPECIAL REPORT

Product Tampering

Product tampering, the lacing of store-shelf goods with lethal substances, has emerged as a new form of terrorism in the United States. First and most frequently carried out on non-prescription medications, product tampering has spread to other products as well. In February 1986, a woman in Yonkers, NY, died after taking a capsule of Extra-Strength Tylenol painkiller that had been contaminated with potassium cyanide. In June, a woman and a man living 5 miles (8 km) apart in Auburn, WA, a suburb of Seattle, were killed when they took Extra-Strength Excedrin capsules containing cyanide. And in September, a man in Runnemede, NJ, died from cyanide that had been inserted in a packet of Lipton's Cup-A-Soup.

The four deaths in 1986 were the first known fatal cases of product tampering since 1982, when seven Chicago-area residents died from poisoned Tylenol capsules. Other cases, however, might well have escaped detection, since screenings for toxic substances are not routinely conducted during autopsies. The Auburn poisonings, for instance, came to light only when an alert medical examiner detected the characteristic almond scent of cyanide during routine tests on the deceased's body. Only then were screenings done on other persons who had recently died, leading to the discovery of the second victim.

As of late 1986, none of the drug-tampering murders had yet been solved, despite a $1 million reward by the Proprietary Association, a trade group representing nonprescription drug manufacturers. The association also set up a 24-hour hot line (1-800-222-3081) for anyone who might have information about the crimes.

Johnson & Johnson, the manufacturer of Extra-Strength Tylenol, and Bristol-Myers, which produces Extra-Strength Excedrin, both ended the sale of all their over-the-counter drugs in capsule form. Other pharmaceutical companies, however, continued to market nonprescription capsules. Drugs in capsule form are popular because they are easier to swallow and generally taste better than drugs packaged in other ways. Annual sales of over-the-counter capsule drugs total $1.5 billion.

Several capsule products have been reissued in the form of "caplets," tablets shaped like capsules and coated for easy swallowing. Others have been rendered more secure by adding a band of gelatin around the capsule waist, where the top and bottom overlap, making the capsule difficult to open without leaving a mark.

Such measures, however, are only partial deterrents. "Given sufficient resources, skill,

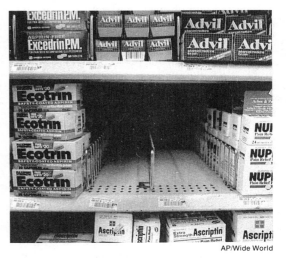

AP/Wide World

Various cases of tampering with nonprescription drugs have caused officials to remove them from store shelves.

and determination, the criminal can beat any safety measure known today," admitted an official of the Warner-Lambert pharmaceutical company. Authorities also note that the removal of drug capsules from store shelves might solve only a small part of a potentially large threat. "We haven't found any tamper-proof dosage form," said Jack Martin, the associate commissioner of public affairs for the U.S. Food and Drug Administration. "If you take capsules off the market, they'll just go to the next thing."

Such foreboding was fueled by at least two false alarms—and one fatal case—during the summer. In July, an anonymous phone caller, using a tape-recorded message, claimed to have laced three boxes of Jell-O with cyanide and placed them on store shelves in the Detroit and Chicago areas. In New York, a caller claimed to have tampered with soda bottles. Then in September came the fatal chicken-noodle Cup-A-Soup case in New Jersey. One government official portrayed the threat of general product tampering in particularly ominous terms: "How do you guard against a lethal chemical being injected into an apple in a supermarket?"

One solution being advanced is to make cyanide more difficult to obtain. Presently, the poison can be purchased with surprising ease. A magazine, for example, sells cyanide by mail-order, advertising it for people who might want to commit suicide in the event of a nuclear holocaust.

GILBERT GEIS

ATM robbery instituted a string of suits against banks, and several state legislators considered bills to force banks to increase security precautions around the machines. U.S. federal law already limits customer liability to $50 for unauthorized withdrawals, and courts have ruled that use of an ATM card by force or trickery constitutes an unauthorized withdrawal.

Insider Trading. The exploitation of information acquired from persons privy to likely stock price fluctuations was the most prominent form of white-collar crime during the year. Dennis B. Levine, a 33-year-old investment banker, was making $1 million a year and had $10 million in the bank when authorities arrested him for insider trading. Levine allegedly had swapped secrets with other brokers and established foreign bank accounts to hide his profits. Levine, who on July 5 pleaded guilty to four felony charges, was one of eight major insider-trading law violators whom *Business Week* called "young men of advantage busily turning opportunity into misfortune."

The investigation of Levine by the U.S. Securities and Exchange Commission (SEC) led to a formal complaint against Ivan F. Boesky, a major Wall Street arbitrageur. According to the complaint, Levine had provided Boesky with nonpublic information about pending corporate takeovers in exchange for a percentage of the profits from any stock purchase made on his recommendation. On November 14, Boeksy agreed to pay $100 million in fines and the return of illicit profits. He also would be barred for life from further securities trading and agreed to plead guilty to one criminal charge. The SEC regards insider trading as grossly unfair to the investing public because someone with privileged access to important knowledge exploits that advantage by buying or selling in public markets.

Crime in the News. On April 11, in one of the bloodiest shootouts in the history of the FBI, two federal agents were killed and five wounded as two suspected armed robbers opened fire in a residential neighborhood in Miami, FL.

On August 20, a total of 14 persons were shot to death inside the post office at Edmund, OK, by Patrick Henry Sherrill, a disgruntled letter carrier. Sherrill, a former marine, then killed himself. It was the third largest number of persons killed in a one-day massacre in the past 40 years in the United States.

A search for Michael W. Jackson occupied more than 100 police officers and federal agents during the fall. Jackson, a former convict and mental patient, was wanted for two and perhaps three murders, five abductions, and at least seven automobile thefts. Jackson's mother had asked the police to commit her son, a man with a long record of violent crime, after he broke two of her ribs with a bear hug. In October, police located Jackson in a barn just west of Wright City, MO. The suspect killed himself before he could be apprehended.

See also Drugs and Alcohol; Law; Prisons.

Gilbert Geis
University of California, Irvine

AP/Wide World

Post office employees in Edmund, OK, mourned the deaths of 14 of their coworkers in a rampage by a disgruntled letter carrier August 20.

AP/Wide World

President Fidel Castro (left) announced a major Communist Party shake-up in February. His brother, Defense Minister Gen. Raúl Castro (right), remained firmly entrenched, and Mrs. Raúl Castro was named to the Politburo.

CUBA

For the government of Cuba, domestically and internationally, 1986 was a disappointing year. The Communist regime, which had hoped for an improvement in the economy and thus in the nation's international standing, conceded that economic and social problems had worsened. President Fidel Castro repeatedly denounced these failings, saying that they existed at all levels of the administration, as well as in the Cuban society at large. He maintained that the very fabric of the country's structure was seriously affected by the growing number of "social vices," including crime, corruption of officials, and juvenile delinquency, all of which he had declared eradicated only two years before.

Begun late in 1985, a purge of top Cuban leadership—albeit below the level of President Castro and his brother, Gen. Raúl Castro, the minister of defense and officially designated presidential successor—was intensified. Despite the purge the Communist regime continued to be firmly entrenched, as was the personal power of President Castro, who turned 60 in August.

Politics. The Third Congress of the Communist Party of Cuba was held in Havana, February 4–7. In an unprecedented shake-up, about one third of the 225-member Central Committee and ten of the 24 members of the Politburo were replaced. Among the latter were the powerful Interior Minister Ramiro Valdés, Minister of Transportation Guillermo García, and Minister of Health Sergio del Valle. Vilma Espín, the wife of Gen. Raúl Castro, became the first woman to be named a full member of the Politburo.

Economy. At the Congress, Castro also unveiled goals for the 1986–1990 economic plan. The new five-year plan would emphasize maximum production of goods for export, reduced imports from Western countries, and further integration with the Soviet-bloc economies. Speaking in July about the plan, President Castro said: "It will be one of the most difficult five-year periods. Some resources are now in shorter supply than ever. The financial problems are very big, especially those related to convertible currency."

As part of the economic reorganization, the much touted free markets, where farmers could sell their produce directly to the public at unregulated prices, were taken over by the state. Direct sales of housing, allowed since 1984, were prohibited. And labor by individual artisans was curtailed. Cuts also were made in productivity bonuses for workers, and all Cubans were urged to donate "voluntary" labor to the state.

The 1985–86 sugar harvest output was only 6.75 million tons, about one million less than in the preceding year. With a sharp decline in Soviet oil subsidies (Cuba previously had received about 40% of its foreign exchange from the resale of Soviet crude) Havana in May ceased making payments on most of its $3.5 billion foreign debt, seeking to renegotiate the terms and obtain a six-year grace period. Cuba also owed about $18 billion to the Soviet Union and Eastern bloc countries. Soviet aid in 1986 was estimated at $4 billion. During a February visit to Moscow, at which he met the new Soviet leader, Mikhail Gorbachev, President Cas-

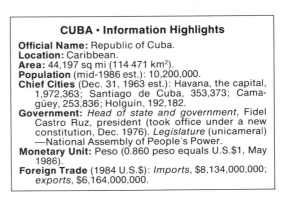

CUBA • Information Highlights

Official Name: Republic of Cuba.
Location: Caribbean.
Area: 44,197 sq mi (114 471 km²).
Population (mid-1986 est.): 10,200,000.
Chief Cities (Dec. 31, 1963 est.): Havana, the capital, 1,972,363; Santiago de Cuba, 353,373; Camagüey, 253,836; Holguín, 192,182.
Government: *Head of state and government,* Fidel Castro Ruz, president (took office under a new constitution, Dec. 1976). *Legislature* (unicameral) —National Assembly of People's Power.
Monetary Unit: Peso (0.860 peso equals U.S.$1, May 1986).
Foreign Trade (1984 U.S.$): *Imports,* $8,134,000,000; *exports,* $6,164,000,000.

tro was assured of continued although reportedly reduced Soviet assistance.

Foreign Affairs. Twenty-five years after the Bay of Pigs invasion, Cuban-U.S. relations were as tense as ever. In July the two sides met in Mexico City to revive a 1984 immigration agreement, under which Cuba was to accept 2,700 of the so-called "Mariel Criminals" (Cuban émigrés being held in U.S. prisons) and the United States was to admit annually 20,000 Cubans eligible for emigration as relatives of Cuban-born American citizens. But the talks broke down over a Cuban request for a clear AM radio frequency to broadcast propaganda to the United States to compensate for the broadcasts of the U.S.-sponsored Radio Martí. On August 22, U.S. President Ronald Reagan cut off virtually all Cuban emigration to the United States by halting the issuance of entry permits to Cubans in third countries—such as Mexico, Panama, and Spain—as well as to those whose visa priorities had been legally approved. Later in the year the order was partially rescinded. At the same time Washington imposed additional controls on U.S. trade with Cuba in an effort to seal its economic blockade.

The stringent immigration measures by Washington prevented about 1,500 Cuban political prisoners and their families from coming to the United States, even though Cuba was willing to let them leave. In August, after intense pressure from the American Catholic bishops and Cuban exile groups, 69 released prisoners were flown from Havana to Miami.

More annoying to Washington than Castro's refusal to take back the Mariel criminals was his increased support, both military and economic, to Nicaragua. However, Havana officials said that the number of Cuban military advisers in Nicaragua actually declined because the Sandinistas were learning to cope on their own with the "contra" guerrillas.

President Castro suffered a diplomatic defeat in Harare, Zimbabwe, where he traveled in September to attend the Eighth Summit Conference of the Nonaligned Movement and failed in his efforts to have Nicaragua chosen as the next leader of that organization. In July the Havana government reestablished diplomatic relations with Brazil, severed 22 years earlier.

GEORGE VOLSKY, *University of Miami*

CYPRUS

Cyprus in 1986 remained a divided island, as it had been since 1974, when a Turkish military action split the country into two de facto zones. The northern zone, now inhabited basically by Turkish Cypriots, was unilaterally declared the Turkish Republic of Northern Cyprus in 1983. The southern zone, inhabited by Greek Cypriots, remains under the recognized government of Spyros Kyprianou.

CYPRUS · Information Highlights

Official Name: Republic of Cyprus.
Location: Eastern Mediterranean.
Area: 3,572 sq mi (9 251 km²).
Population (mid-1986 est.): 700,000.
Chief Cities (1982 est.): Nicosia, the capital, 149,100; Limassol, 107,200.
Government: *Head of state and government,* Spyros Kyprianou, president (took office Aug. 1977). *Legislature*—House of Representatives.
Monetary Unit: Pound (0.506 pound equals U.S.$1, June 1986).
Gross Domestic Product (1983 U.S.$): $2,100,000,000.
Economic Index (1985): *Consumer Prices* (1980 = 100), all items, 137.8; food, 142.6.
Foreign Trade (1985 U.S.$): *Imports,* $1,247,000,000; *exports,* $479,000,000.

UN Efforts. During the year United Nations Secretary-General Javier Pérez de Cuéllar renewed his efforts to bring together the Greek Cypriots and Turkish Cypriots. On March 29 he presented a draft plan that called for a single federal republic with two autonomous states. The Turkish Cypriots agreed to the draft, but the Greek Cypriots did not because, among other things, there was no insistence on a timetable for the withdrawal of Turkish forces.

Although President Kyprianou disliked the draft plan, he took pains to express his overall belief that the UN remains useful in trying to solve the Cyprus imbroglio. Toward the end of the year, in a message to Pérez de Cuéllar on the occasion of the UN's 41st anniversary, Kyprianou reiterated Cyprus' reliance on the UN and called for the implementation of previous UN resolutions which the Greek Cypriots considered advantageous.

Ozal Visit. To bolster the Turkish Cypriots and their president, Rauf Denktas, the prime minister of Turkey, Turgut Ozal, visited the Turkish Cypriot zone July 2–4. Large demonstrations in the Greek Cypriot zone temporarily obstructed his access, and in retaliation Denktas formally closed off all check-points from the Turkish Cypriot side from July 4 to 12. The blockade was implemented even against UN peacekeeping troops, which had been stationed on the island since 1964, and the closing was seen as a decided threat against their continued viable presence. Denktas called his retaliation a demonstration of the strength of his regime, both to the Greek Cypriot leadership and to outsiders who had considered the Ozal visit a provocation. He also called for negotiations on Pérez de Cuéllar's March initiative.

Economy. The United States continued to give economic aid to Cyprus, as it had since the 1974 invasion, even though the economy of the Greek Cypriot area had improved dramatically, sometimes spectacularly, since that time. In October 1986, U.S. President Ronald Reagan signed a continuing resolution of Congress granting Cyprus $15 million in economic assistance, to be used for humanitarian purposes.

Cyprus and the Karachi Hijacking. Palestinian terrorists who seized a Pan American Airways jumbo jet at Karachi, Pakistan, on September 5 demanded to be flown to Cyprus, where they hoped to secure the release of imprisoned comrades. They were apparently referring to two Arabs and a Briton imprisoned at Larnaca for the killing of three Israelis on a yacht in 1985. The Cyprus government indicated that it would not allow the plane to land, and Pakistani security forces stormed the craft in Karachi. In November, Cypriot officials announced that an escape plot had been foiled in the area of the Larnaca prison where the three prisoners were being held.

Akrotiri Attack. On August 3 a sudden armed attack on the sovereign British Akrotiri air base in southwestern Cyprus was carried out by unknown and uncaptured perpetrators. Later it was claimed that the attack was a retaliation for Great Britain's help to the United States in its April bombing of Libya. The base, strategically important in the eastern Mediterranean, had remained under full British sovereignty when Cyprus became independent.

GEORGE J. MARCOPOULOS, *Tufts University*

CZECHOSLOVAKIA

The two main events in Czechoslovakia during 1986 were the 17th Congress of the ruling Communist Party of Czechoslovakia (KSČ) and the elections of representative assemblies on all levels of government.

Party and Government. Meeting in Prague from March 24 to 28, the 17th party congress was a virtual carbon copy of the 16th congress in 1981. Gustáv Husák again was unanimously reelected general-secretary, as were all members of the Presidium and Central Committee. The only notable difference from 1981 was the absence of the top Soviet party leader, as General Secretary Mikhail Gorbachev was represented by another Politburo member.

Similarly, the quinquennial elections for the Federal Assembly, the Czech and Slovak National Councils, and the three levels of local government committees, held May 23–24, were replicas of the 1981 voting. All candidates were chosen by the Communist-controlled National Front, and all were reelected by majorities that exceeded 99%. The composition of the new federal cabinet, as well as the cabinets of the Czech and Slovak republics, remained virtually unchanged.

Economy. In 1986, the first year of the Eighth Five-Year Plan, Czechoslovakia's economy encountered much the same problems as in previous years. While increasing in quantity, production tended to lag in quality, assortment, and technical sophistication. Compared with the first half of 1985, gross national income rose 3.2%, industrial production 3.2%, construction 3.4%, labor productivity 2.6% in industry and 2.9% in construction, investments 3.0%, food production 0.8%, retail trade 2.9%, foreign trade 2.2%, and wages 2.8%. But technical development was 4.5% short of the target; 21.4% of enterprises failed to meet gross production goals; the majority of quality indicators remained unfulfilled; and the annual plan for the construction of apartments was only 32% implemented in the first six months.

Foreign Relations. Among the foreign dignitaries who made official visits in 1986 were the president of Austria; the prime ministers of India and Hungary; the chief commander of the Warsaw Pact forces; and the foreign ministers of West Germany, Tunisia, Venezuela, Turkey, and Iran. In March, President Husák headed the KSČ delegation at the Soviet Communist Party Congress in Moscow. In May he journeyed to Poland, where he signed an agreement on economic and scientific-technical cooperation until the year 2000. In May in Prague, he discussed a similar pact with Hungarian Premier György Lázár. Negotiations were initiated the same month on scientific-technical cooperation with China. And in September, Czechoslovak Premier Lubomir Strougal traveled to Canada to discuss the expansion of political, economic, and cultural relations.

One visitor from abroad whose presence the regime did not like was tennis star Martina Navratilova, who went to Prague representing the United States—to which she defected in 1975 —in Federation Cup competition.

Human Rights. Although spokesmen of the Charter 77 human-rights movement noted that repression was not as severe as it had been earlier in the decade, the improvement was only marginal. Typical of the continued persecution of dissidents was the arrest in September of the leaders of the jazz section of the Union of Musicians and the padlocking of the section's office for the publishing of a newsletter on contemporary culture.

EDWARD TABORSKY
The University of Texas at Austin

CZECHOSLOVAKIA • Information Highlights

Official Name: Czechoslovak Socialist Republic.
Location: East-central Europe.
Area: 49,371 sq mi (127 870 km²).
Population (mid-1986 est.): 15,500,000.
Chief Cities (Jan. 1, 1984 est.): Prague, the capital, 1,186,253; Bratislava, 401,383; Brno, 380,871.
Government: *Head of state,* Gustáv Husák, president (took office 1975). *Head of government,* Lubomír Strougal, premier (took office 1970). *Communist party,* general secretary, Gustáv Husák (took office 1969). *Legislature*—Federal Assembly.
Monetary Unit: Koruna (10.80 koruny equal U.S.$1, June 1986).
Economic Indexes (1985): *Consumer Prices* (1980 = 100), all items, 110.4; food, 113.7. *Industrial Production* (1985, 1980 = 100), 115.
Foreign Trade (1985 U.S.$): *Imports,* $17,548,-000,000; *exports,* $17,474,000,000.

DANCE

An unusually large number of dance companies from other countries performed in the United States during 1986. The foreign impact was the strongest in a decade—manifested chiefly through the high quality of major European ballet companies that had not performed stateside for more than 20 or 30 years. The Paris Opéra Ballet, the Kirov Ballet, the Sadler's Wells Royal Ballet, and the Central Ballet of China attracted packed houses and the most interest. In addition to ballet, Spanish flamenco, Soviet folk dances, and European experimental choreographers contributed to the international flavor of the U.S. season.

Ballet. A new generation of outstanding French dancers created a sensation, beginning with the joint Paris Opéra Ballet-American Ballet Theatre gala that was part of the Statue of Liberty Centennial celebration in New York City in July. It was the Paris company's first U.S. appearance since its American debut in 1948. Patrick Dupond and Sylvie Guillem brought the audience to its feet.

A similar reaction greeted the Paris troupe's subsequent run at New York's Metropolitan Opera House. Memories of the poorly received 1948 season were superseded by the brilliance of a company revived by its current director, Rudolf Nureyev. The French classical style, stressing clarity and precision, was transmitted with exciting energy. The repertory included George Balanchine's *Le Palais de Cristal* ("Symphony in C"), Serge Lifar's *Les Mirages*, Francine Lancelot's *Lulli: Quelques Pas Graves de Baptiste*, and excerpts from *Raymonda*. There was some criticism of Nureyev's version of *Swan Lake* (the swans were indoors to suggest that they were a projection of the hero's mind) and his ballet *Washington Square* (which turned Henry James's novel into a social comment on American history). Yet there was general agreement that the 48-year-old Nureyev, who danced in many of the ballets, had also provided a glittering showcase for several rising French stars.

The Kirov Ballet from Leningrad, absent from the United States since 1964, performed in Los Angeles, Philadelphia, Trenton (NJ), and Wolf Trap Park in Virginia. The superb corps demonstrated the Kirov's celebrated purity of classical style in *Swan Lake* and *La Bayadère*. There were no dancers of the caliber of Nureyev and Mikhail Baryshnikov, both of whom had defected from the Kirov, but ballerinas like Olga Chenchikova, a strong technician, and Altynai Asylmuratova, with her passionate presence, were outstanding. Oleg Vinogradov, the Kirov director, included his own ballet, *The Knight in the Tiger's Skin*, on the Canadian leg of the tour.

The Sleeping Beauty became identified with Britain's Royal Ballet after Margot Fonteyn triumphed with it in the company's American debut in 1949. Two years later the company's junior affiliate, the Sadler's Wells Theatre Ballet, came to New York. Now reorganized as the Sadler's Wells Royal Ballet, it scored its own triumph with Peter Wright's innovative and visually dazzling production of a new *Sleeping Beauty*. David Bintley, a young choreographer, made a better impression with *Flowers of the Forest* than with another ballet, *Choros*.

The Central Ballet of China, an outgrowth of a dance academy founded in Beijing (Peking) in 1954, was guided by Soviet teachers during its early years. The Soviet training was evident during the company's first visit to the United States, a two-month, 11-city tour in spring 1986. At the same time the Chinese troupe conveyed its adaptability to different styles in *Variations for Four* by the British choreographer Anton Dolin and in *Three Preludes* by Ben Stevenson, director of the Houston Ballet. The company also performed Act II of *Swan Lake* and excerpts based on two Chinese stories, *The New Year's Sacrifice* and *The Maid of the Sea*.

The National Ballet of Canada came from Toronto to present what was arguably the season's best ballet. *Alice,* choreographed by Glen Tetley to a score by David Del Tredici, persuasively explored the relationship between Lewis Carroll and Alice Liddell, for whom *Alice in Wonderland* was written.

Other foreign ballet troupes were not as successful in either repertory or standards of dancing but created interest on other grounds. American debuts came from Chile's Ballet de Santiago with *Rosalinda*, the Scottish Ballet with *La Sylphide* and works by Peter Darrell, and the junior group of the Netherlands Dance Theater. The Stuttgart Ballet presented John Neumeier's *Streetcar Named Desire* in Washington.

Among major American companies, the Joffrey Ballet attracted attention with *The Heart of the Matter,* a mixture of drama and abstraction that commented on male-female relations; James Kudelka, a Canadian choreographer, set his slightly sinister ballet to Prokofiev's Piano Concerto No. 2 in G Minor. Other Joffrey premieres were Gerald Arpino's *Birthday Variations,* Laura Dean's *Force Field,* Mark Morris' *Esteemed Guests,* and Mark Haim's *The Gardens of Boboli.*

Dean, Morris, and Haim are all modern dancers. The increasing use of modern-dance choreographers in ballet companies also was visible at the American Ballet Theatre in David Gordon's *Murder* and Karole Armitage's *The Mollino Room.* Along more conventional lines, John Taras choreographed *Francesca da Rimini,* and Kenneth MacMillan created *Requiem,* inspired by Andrew Lloyd Webber's music and performed with vocalists on stage.

The New York City Ballet's Peter Martins also used a singer—Frederica von Stade in the

© Jack Vartoogian

Leslie Caron joined Baryshnikov and Nureyev (right) *in a special gala in honor of the Statue of Liberty centennial.*

first performance—for his new *Songs of the Auvergne*. The sentimentality of the ballet seemed contagious, as evidenced in two Jerome Robbins premieres, the Stravinsky *Piccolo Balletto* and *Quiet City*. The latter, to Aaron Copland's score, was dedicated to Joseph Duell, a principal dancer in the City Ballet who committed suicide in February. The company also presented a new production of *Swan Lake*, with the swans in black tutus and, for the first time since 1960, revived the solo George Balanchine had created for Paul Taylor in *Episodes*.

Other. Foreign companies outside the ballet world also attracted full houses in the United States. Flamenco Puro, a group of exuberant gypsy performers from Spain, became a hit on Broadway. The Moiseyev Dance Company's return to the United States after 12 years was marred by a tear-gas attack at the Metropolitan Opera House, but Igor Moiseyev's theatricalized folk dances from the Soviet Union proved as popular as ever.

Europe provided the outstanding new face on the experimental dance scene. Anne Teresa de Keersmaeker from Belgium showed that the use of repetition could be mixed with emotion in *Rosas Danst Rosas*. Her debut was the highlight of the Brooklyn Academy of Music's Next Wave Festival, which also included the debut of Michael Clark, a British punk-style choreographer whose pieces were poorly received.

An American, Lar Lubovitch, shot to the front ranks of modern dance with *Concerto Six Twenty-Two*, a highly inventive work to Mozart that featured a male duet between its two festive ensemble sections.

Modern dance's senior choreographers were represented by Martha Graham's especially successful season, which included some rare revivals. Among these were the 1929 *Heretic*, a powerful and stark work, the comic 1939 *Every Soul Is a Circus*, and *Denishawn Solos*, a theatrical suite of solos by Miss Graham and her teachers, Ruth St. Denis and Ted Shawn. New Graham works, *Temptations of the Moon*, to music by Bartok, and *Tangled Night*, to Klaus Egge, showed Miss Graham successfully experimenting with fresh movement images.

Paul Taylor created a spoof, *Ab Ovo Usque ad Mala (From Soup to Nuts)* and a serious work to Bach, *A Musical Offering*. Merce Cunningham's premieres were *Grange Eve* and *Roaratorio*. Alvin Ailey's *Survivors* was a tribute to the South African black activists Nelson and Winnie Mandela, while his *Witness* and *Caverna Magica* were more abstract.

Modern dance premieres also included Lucinda Childs' *Portraits in Reflection;* Erick Hawkins' *Ahab* and *Today, with Dragon;* Alwin Nikolais' *Velocities;* and Murray Louis' *The Disenchantment of Pierrot*.

Other dance-related news of 1986 included publication of Gelsey Kirkland's book, *Dancing on my Grave*, which was critical of the ballet world and which became a best-seller.

Key figures died in 1986: Lucia Chase, the founding patron and longtime director of the American Ballet Theatre; Erik Bruhn, the Danish star and ballet director; Robert Helpmann, the British star and choreographer; Serge Lifar, longtime director of the Paris Opéra Ballet; and Dorothy Alexander, founder of the National Association for Regional Ballet.

The Capezio Award and Kennedy Center Honors went to Antony Tudor, and the Samuel H. Scripps-American Dance Festival Award went to Katherine Dunham.

ANNA KISSELGOFF, *"The New York Times"*

DELAWARE

Elections and the raising of a sunken 18th-century British ship were major events in the public life of Delaware in 1986.

Political Developments. Delaware's lone member of the U.S. House of Representatives, Democrat Thomas R. Carper, was the leading victor in the state's 1986 election. Carper, seeking his third term in Congress, overwhelmed his Republican opponent, Thomas Neuberger, with 66% of the vote. In general the electorate supported incumbent officeholders. The state House of Representatives will remain under Republican control by the same margin (22 to 19) as prior to the election. The state Senate, long controlled by the Democrats, also retained its preelection status of 13 to 8. Few significant issues emerged in the campaign. Many candidates ran with no opposition, and voter turnout was one of the lowest in history.

The only significant change in political control occurred in Sussex County, where domination of the county council shifted from Democratic to Republican hands. This county, because of its ocean beaches and inland bays, has undergone rapid development and population growth, with a resulting influence on the voting habits of its residents. Delaware's other two counties (Kent and New Castle) remained under the control of Democrats.

Two of Delaware's top political leaders emerged as presidential aspirants in 1986. Former Gov. and U.S. Rep. Pierre S. duPont IV became the first Republican to announce his candidacy for the GOP nomination in 1988. DuPont, a fiscal conservative, is credited with promoting economic prosperity in the state while he was governor. At the other end of the political spectrum, Delaware's liberal Democratic senator, Joseph Biden, is considered to

be one of the top contenders for the 1988 Democratic presidential nomination. Although he had not declared his plans as 1986 ended, Biden will become more visible as he takes over the chairmanship of the Senate Judiciary Committee in January 1987.

Economy. As of September 1986, Delaware's seasonally adjusted rate of unemployment stood at 4.5%, compared with the national average of 6.9%. The strongest areas of job growth occurred in the finance, insurance, and real-estate industries, which increased by 2,300 jobs or 12.2% in 1985–86. Manufacturing, on the other hand, continued to decline. In 1986 construction began on the Christiana Gateway project in central Wilmington, which will provide office space for many of Delaware's new financial institutions.

Legislative Session. For the third year in a row, Delawareans received a cut in their income taxes—9% across the board. The gross receipts tax also was lowered, while 2 cents per

AP/Wide World

Salvagers and archaeologists examine the hull of the HMS "DeBraak," an 18th-century warship raised from the Chesapeake Bay near Lewes, DE, in August. The town planned to build a museum for the ship's remains.

gallon was added to the gasoline tax. Teachers received a substantial pay increase, and a new classification, training, and pay plan for civil-service workers was adopted. The Housing Development Fund that provides money for construction and rehabilitation of low and moderate income housing was increased by $2.5 million dollars.

The Environment. Hazardous waste clean up, water supply, and coastal-area protection remained major environmental concerns. Legal, technical, and financial hurdles continued to slow the progress toward remedying problems caused by old landfills containing hazardous materials. Water was in short supply as the late summer and fall drought made mandatory water restrictions necessary for the second year in a row.

The DeBraak. A major archaeological event occurred along Delaware's coastline in 1986 with the raising of the 18th-century British two-masted brig, HMS *DeBraak*. The hull of the *DeBraak*, which sank in the Delaware Bay off Lewes, Delaware, in 1798, was salvaged in August. A museum will be built in Lewes to house the ship.

JEROME R. LEWIS, *University of Delaware*

DENMARK

The year 1986 began with a struggle over the "reform package" adopted by representatives of the European Community (EC) at Luxembourg in December 1985. An EC member since 1972, Denmark has benefited greatly from increased agricultural exports to other Common Market countries; nevertheless, many Danes, especially the opposition Social Democrats, were uneasy about the reforms, which increased EC control over member nations in environmental matters—an area in which Denmark's laws are stricter than those of some of its neighbors. Though endorsed by the cabinet of Prime Minister Poul Schlüter, the package was rejected by the Folketing (parliament) on January 21. Schlüter then appealed to the voters in a referendum (February 27) which overturned the Folketing's decision, thus ensuring Denmark's continued adherence to the EC.

The large number of immigrants that have entered Denmark in recent years, many of them refugees from the war-torn Middle East attracted by Denmark's liberal asylum law, also was a major national concern in 1986. In October, the government proposed an amendment to the law designed to restrict the flow of immigration.

U.S. Bases in Greenland. In July, Greenland's peace movement, Sorsunnata (No War) demanded the creation of a special control commission to supervise activities at U.S. bases on the island. New installations were planned for 1987, and it was feared that these would be elements of the U.S. Strategic Defense Initiative ("Star Wars") project. Greenland's provincial government, however, decided that it would be sufficient if its chairman, Jonathan Motzfeldt, were periodically advised of changes in the situation at U.S. bases.

In August, the United States and Denmark signed an agreement which reduced by half the size of the Thule Air Force Base in northern Greenland; one change foreseen as a result of the agreement was closer contact between the U.S. military and the local population.

South African Policy. At the semiannual meeting of Scandinavian foreign ministers held in Copenhagen in August, Denmark and its Nordic partners agreed on a common policy toward South Africa, including the imposition of economic sanctions against that country in retaliation for its discrimination against blacks. At a meeting of EC foreign ministers in Brussels the following month, the Danish representative, Uffe Ellemann-Jensen, joined the Netherlands and Ireland in pressing for stronger anti-South African sanctions that were eventually adopted by the Community.

Cultural Affairs. The signing of a protocol by Denmark and Iceland in August ended a 40-year controversy over a collection of medieval Icelandic manuscripts held in Denmark but claimed by Iceland, which became an independent republic in 1944. Some of the disputed material already had been returned to Iceland; the remainder was handed over after a ceremony at Thingvellir, the meeting place of the medieval Icelandic parliament.

April 1 marked the death of Erik Bruhn, one of Denmark's outstanding figures in the field of dance, at the age of 57. Trained in the Royal Danish Ballet, he was a principal dancer with the American Ballet Theatre from 1953 to 1972. As a choreographer, he was director of the Royal Swedish Ballet from 1967 to 1972 and of the National Ballet of Canada from 1983.

ERIK J. FRIIS
"The Scandinavian-American Bulletin"

DENMARK • Information Highlights

Official Name: Kingdom of Denmark.
Location: Northwest Europe.
Area: 16,632 sq mi (43 076 km²).
Population (mid-1986 est.): 5,100,000.
Chief Cities (Jan. 1, 1983 est.): Copenhagen, the capital, 1,372,019; Århus, 182,645; Odense, 137,606.
Government: *Head of state,* Margrethe II, queen (acceded Jan. 1972). *Head of government,* Poul Schlüter, prime minister (took office Sept. 1982). *Legislature* (unicameral)—Folketing.
Monetary Unit: Krone (7.4445 kroner equal U.S.$1, Oct. 17, 1986).
Gross National Product (1984 U.S.$): $52,400,-000,000.
Economic Indexes (1984): *Consumer Prices* (1980 = 100), all items, 146.3; food, 147.7. *Industrial Production* (1980 = 100), 122.
Foreign Trade (1985 U.S.$): *Imports,* $18,429,-000,000; *exports,* $16,699,000,000.

DRUGS AND ALCOHOL

The death of 22-year-old University of Maryland basketball star Len Bias on June 19, 1986, of cardiac arrest due to cocaine intoxication had ramifications far beyond the College Park, MD, campus. Bias' death—along with the cocaine-induced death of pro football player Don Rogers of the Cleveland Browns on June 27—focused national attention on drug use in general, and on cocaine and its derivative "crack" in particular.

In the weeks following Bias' and Rogers' deaths, President Ronald Reagan spoke out strongly and repeatedly against drug abuse, the Pentagon sent Army troops for the first time to a foreign country (Bolivia) to help wipe out drug-processing facilities, and local, state, and national politicians campaigned against drug use. The drug problem, House Speaker Thomas P. O'Neill, Jr. (D-MA) said on September 10, was "the No. 1 issue in the nation."

Although accurate statistics are virtually impossible to obtain, surveys indicated that while drug use in general probably has declined in recent years, cocaine use has reached unprecedented proportions, especially among young Americans. The National Institute on Drug Abuse (NIDA) believes that about 5 million Americans regularly use cocaine and that 20 to 24 million have tried the drug. The U.S. Drug Enforcement Administration estimated that cocaine use rose 11% from 1983 to 1984. Estimates of the social costs of all drug abuse range from $100 billion to $230 billion annually.

The evidence indicates that the use of such illicit drugs as marijuana, amphetamines, tranquilizers, LSD, and methaqualone has declined significantly in recent years. Nevertheless, drug use remains high, especially among young people. About 42% of college students, for example, reported using marijuana in 1985, according to an NIDA-sponsored study conducted at the University of Michigan.

DRUGS AND ALCOHOL / SPECIAL REPORT

Drug Testing

Steve Kelley/© 1986 San Diego Union-Copley News Service

Nineteen eighty-six was the year in which drug testing of job applicants and employees became a requirement at thousands of American workplaces. It was also the year in which testing workers for drugs emerged as a major legal and social issue, one that promised to remain a live controversy for years to come.

The surge had been building for several years. Between 1982 and 1985, concern over the growth of drug-related safety and integrity problems at the workplace already had led some key employers to install testing programs. Among them were the military services, some federal and state law enforcement agen-

cies, and such specially affected industries as nuclear power and transportation.

Then came the explosion of drug testing activities in 1986. President Ronald Reagan directed that civilian federal workers engaged in "sensitive" tasks (about 1.1 million) be randomly tested for drug use. Almost half the *Fortune 500* companies were said to be moving into testing programs. Many cities, counties, and states began testing police, firefighters, guards, school-bus drivers, and even teachers.

Why the Surge? Since government and private studies agreed that there had been no significant jump in general-population or employee drug use in 1985–86, what caused the 1986 surge in workplace testing? Four factors seem to have come together. First was the emergence of the powerful cocaine derivative "crack" and the media's dramatization of its "epidemic" potential. Second was publicity over drug use in professional and college sports, and the tragic death of University of Maryland basketball star Len Bias. Third was the publication of figures showing the soaring costs of drug abuse at U.S. workplaces at a time of sharp overseas competition. Losses were estimated at $100 billion a year.

The fourth factor was a conclusion reached by President Reagan's Commission on Organized Crime in early 1986, picked up as a central policy by the Reagan administration and finally expanded into a bipartisan theme in the November 1986 elections: that the time had

Cocaine. NIDA's annual survey of college-student drug usage, which was released July 7, reported that cocaine use has increased in recent years. University of Michigan researcher Lloyd D. Johnston, who directed the study, called cocaine use the nation's "most serious [drug] problem."

Cocaine, the drug that took center stage in 1986, is a white powder derived from the coca leaf. Cocaine is grown and processed in large quantities in Bolivia, Peru, Ecuador, and Columbia and shipped illicitly into the United States. Cocaine, once considered so expensive that only upper-income groups could afford it, "is [now] used in all age groups, by all races, both sexes, and at all income levels," Edgar H. Adams, director of NIDA's division of epidemiology and statistical analysis, said June 21.

The type of cocaine known as crack or "rock" is a purified, concentrated, highly addictive solid form of the drug. Crack, which users smoke rather than inhale through the nostrils like cocaine, also is relatively inexpensive. Crack first became popular in New York, Los Angeles, and Miami in 1985, but since then has spread throughout the country.

Because of its low price—as low as $10 per dose—crack appeals primarily to lower-income groups. Police officials have reported significant increases in violent crime in the mostly poor and middle-class urban neighborhoods where crack use is widespread. New York City set up a special anti-crack police unit in May consisting of 101 experienced officers; in August, 100 more officers joined the unit. Officials in Broward County, FL, north of Miami, reported that crime increased 11% during the first six months of the year, a rise police believe was due to the rapid spread of crack.

Crack is not solely a problem among the young and poor. The highly addictive substance also appeals to higher-income, college-educated professionals. "There is a gross distortion about crack, that it is just a teenage

come to attack the "demand" side of drug traffic, not just the "supply" side.

By fall 1986 surveys showed that 75% of the public rated drug use in the nation as "very serious"; 69% favored periodic drug-testing at their own workplaces. For individual occupations, testing of police was favored by 85%; airline pilots by 84%; government workers by 72%; and general employees by 50%.

Social and Legal Issues. While general public support for workplace testing crystallized in 1986, just how such programs should be designed generated sharp debate. The central clash was between advocates of broad testing (the Reagan administration, many state and local agencies, and many private employers) and those urging narrow testing (labor unions, civil-liberties groups, and many medical/professional experts). Four main issues were involved:

1. *Who should be tested?* Broad-testing advocates want all job applicants to be tested, as well as all employees whose jobs involve safety or the integrity of the enterprise. Narrow-testing advocates want testing to be limited to those whose impaired performance would directly pose safety threats.

2. *What is the proper test standard?* Narrow-testing advocates want only impaired condition on work time to be measured, so that off-the-job use of recreational drugs is not punished. Broad-test advocates believe that detection of proscribed drugs identifies an applicant or employee against whom an employer should be allowed to take action.

3. *What tests are acceptable?* Test critics say that urine-sample tests violate due process because they can produce "false positives" and because the observation of urination (to avoid tampering) is a "shocking" violation of privacy rights. Test supporters assert that proper lab procedures and use of a second confirmatory test produces "98–99% accuracy" and that supervisory surveillance is an "unpleasantness" justified by the threat to workplace safety.

4. *What happens to those who flunk?* Narrow-test supporters say that firing workers found to have used drugs (but who are not impaired on the job) is fundamentally unfair and could create an "unemployable class" of hundreds of thousands; they insist that employers provide rehabilitation programs. Broad-testing advocates also support employee assistance programs but argue that firing employees who violate a no-drugs policy should be the employer's right.

Standards and the Future. While private employers may require drug tests unless forbidden by state or federal law, government employers are bound by constitutional standards. Some 80% of the lawsuits challenging random mass screening of government employees in 1986 produced decisions striking down such programs as intrusions on privacy and dignity not based on reasonable suspicion of impairment. In the future, legislation and appellate court rulings will spell out in detail which employees can be tested, how, and with what safeguards. As in other areas of social policy, the American tradition seeks a balance between individual rights and prohibitory enforcement. Working out the delicate balance in workplace drug-testing already has begun, but it will take years of experience to refine.

ALAN F. WESTIN

problem and that it is a problem of the poor," said Arnold Washton, director of research for the National Cocaine Hotline. "We are seeing business executives who have switched from cocaine powder to crack, and it hasn't turned out well for them."

NIDA officials announced on July 10 that the number of cocaine-related deaths and emergency-room visits had increased significantly in the previous five years. Data reported by medical examiners in 25 metropolitan areas showed that cocaine-related deaths rose from 185 in 1981 to 613 in 1985. As was the case with Bias and Rogers, many of the deaths were due to heart problems resulting from cocaine use. Health officials believe, however, that the actual number of cocaine-related deaths was much higher. This is because in many cases medical examiners ascribe the cause of a cocaine-related death to some other condition.

As for emergency-room visits, reports from 700 hospitals across the United States showed that the number of cocaine-related visits increased from some 3,500 in 1981 to about 10,000 in 1985. "These are trends and not actual total numbers" for all the emergency rooms in the nation, said Dr. Donald I. Macdonald, administrator of the Alcohol, Drug Abuse, and Mental Health Administration. "We're in a terrible situation with cocaine."

Government Action. President Reagan came to office with a promise to curb drug abuse and drug smuggling. The president increased spending on a wide range of antidrug programs, and in February 1982 he set up a special South Florida Task Force under Vice-President George Bush to fight drug smuggling from South America. Statistics indicated that the program helped cut back drug shipments to the United States, but the explosion of concern about cocaine in the summer months of 1986 prompted a reassessment of the administration's $1.7-billion-per-year antidrug "war."

During the first week of August, President Reagan gave three speeches on drugs. The president, in announcing stepped-up measures to combat illegal drug use, said he was going to "use the full power of the presidency" to fight drug trafficking and usage. The centerpiece of the program, the president said, would be a voluntary drug-testing effort for federal employees. He and Vice-President Bush underwent drug tests by urinalysis. Also in August, Attorney General Edwin Meese III announced the formation of Operation Alliance, a new, widescale drug-enforcement program that would operate on the Mexican border.

The president and his wife Nancy Reagan—who as first lady has spent a good deal of time working against drug abuse—gave an unprecedented joint national television address on September 14 on the subject of drug abuse. In the 20-minute speech, the president called for a "national crusade" against the "cancer of drugs." The following day, President Reagan unveiled his new drug-fighting program, which included an executive order instituting mandatory drug-testing for federal workers in positions such as law enforcement and others "requiring a high degree of trust and confidence," and a $900-million legislative package which, among other things, called for increased penalties for drug offenses and an educational program aimed at preventing drug use among schoolchildren.

The House of Representatives had approved a sweeping new anti-drug bill September 11 by an overwhelming 392-16 vote. By mid-September the Senate began considering similar legislation. The final omnibus bill, which cleared Congress on October 17 and was signed into law by President Reagan on October 27, authorized $1.7 billion in new funds for drug interdiction, law enforcement, education, treatment, and rehabilitation. It also stiffened penalties for federal drug crimes and gave the president authority to order trade sanctions against nations that do not cooperate with U.S. anti-drug efforts.

The federal government's stepped-up anti-drug efforts produced promising results. More than 6,000 lbs (2 700 kg) of cocaine—about a month's supply for the entire nation—was seized in 15 states in a three-week period in August, and Bolivian authorities reported that the combined U.S.-Bolivian military raids against cocaine processing plants, which began July 18, greatly diminished that nation's illegal cocaine industry. In Florida in October, federal agents seized 4,620 lbs (2 096 kg) of cocaine, the largest confiscation of that drug in U.S. history. Despite such successes, many law-enforcement officials believed that little real progress had been made.

Alcohol. Ironically, the vast publicity given to the drug problem overshadowed concerns about alcohol consumption, which continues to be among the most serious American health problems. In recent years there has been a decline in per capita consumption of alcohol, and drinking has dropped among all age groups. But the NIDA-sponsored college-student survey indicated that the number of college students who had used alcohol rose from 90% in 1984 to 92% in 1985.

Surveys conducted by the National Institute on Alcohol Abuse and Alcoholism continue to indicate that alcohol abuse is not uncommon among high-school students, and health experts believe that perhaps one third of all American adults drink to excess.

Of the approximately 43,800 Americans killed in traffic accidents in 1985, more than 51% lost their lives in accidents in which alcohol was involved, according to the National Highway Traffic Safety Administration.

MARC LEEPSON
"American Politics" Magazine

ECUADOR

The major problem facing Ecuador during 1986 was the drastic decrease in the price of petroleum, which provided more than two thirds of the country's export revenue.

Economic Crisis. The Ecuadorans increased their oil production in an attempt to offset the price fall, and President León Febres-Cordero visited the United States in January to arrange loans for his government. In May, Ecuador became the first oil exporting country to get direct financial aid from the United States, in a "bridge financing" loan of $150 million.

In August the government reached agreements with its creditors to overhaul the country's $5.5 billion private foreign debt and reduce interest payments. Payment was spread over twelve years. At the same time the International Monetary Fund signed a standby agreement for $70 million, which opened the way for substantial additional private bank loans.

In mid-August the government also announced a new economic program, combining austerity and "free-market" measures. It limited Central Bank control of foreign exchange to oil revenues, foreign credits, and foreign currency used for public sector imports. Also, the exchange rate was left free to fluctuate with market pressures, starting with a 35% devaluation of the sucre. Export taxes and interest ceilings were eliminated, and import tariffs reduced. These measures provoked considerable opposition from both industrialists and organized labor.

Political Developments. President Febres-Cordero also was faced with serious political problems in 1986. Early in March the Air Force Commander, Gen. Frank Vargas Pazos, barricaded himself in a base near Quito when the government tried to make him step down. He eventually surrendered, but only after Minister of Defense Luis Pineiros, whose dismissal he demanded, had resigned. A few days later Vargas seized another air base, demanding Febres-

AP/Wide World

During a January trip to Washington, Ecuador's President León Febres-Cordero (far left) was hailed by President Reagan as an "articulate champion of free enterprise."

Cordero's resignation. He was captured when army troops overran the base.

The president proposed to Congress a constitutional amendment that would have allowed independent candidates to run for Congress. When the legislators rejected it, he appealed to the people in a referendum (June 1986). The voters, too, opposed the amendment by a margin of 58%. At the same time forces allied with Febres-Cordero were defeated in parliamentary elections, depriving him of a majority. After these elections the president reorganized his cabinet, replacing 8 of the 14 ministers.

The government also faced problems with guerrilla groups. In May guerrillas seized Enrique Echevarria, a member of the Constitutional Tribunal, but he was freed three days later, when police and soldiers stormed a house where he was being held.

In June, Amnesty International accused Ecuadoran police of using torture against political prisoners. The government denied all such charges.

ROBERT J. ALEXANDER
Rutgers University

ECUADOR • Information Highlights

Official Name: Republic of Ecuador.
Location: Northwest South America.
Area: 109,483 sq mi (283 561 km²).
Population (mid-1986 est.): 9,600,000.
Chief Cities (1982 census): Quito, the capital, 866,472; Guayaquil, 1,199,344; Cuenca, 152,406.
Government: *Head of state and government,* León Febres-Cordero Ribadeneyra, president (took office August 1984). *Legislature* (unicameral)— Chamber of Representatives.
Monetary Unit: Sucre (143 sucres equal U.S.$1, financial rate, Oct. 17, 1986).
Gross National Product (1984 U.S.$): $9,900,-000,000.
Economic Index (1985): *Consumer Prices* (1980 = 100), all items, 324.8; food, 414.4.
Foreign Trade (1985 U.S.$): *Imports,* $1,674,000,000; *exports,* $2,780,000,000.

EDUCATION

U.S. education in 1986 was spotlighted in a hard-hitting "second wave" of reports which, like *A Nation at Risk* in 1983, called for radical change in the nation's schools. Reports by the Holmes Group, Carnegie Forum, National Governors' Association, and other organizations indicated a national consensus that restructuring and enhancing the teaching profession are fundamental to school reform. Polls indicated that student drug abuse was the public's main concern, with Congress and the administration mounting campaigns against the problem. Illiteracy remained another area of concern, with remedial efforts proliferating at the local level. Supreme Court decisions, a widely publicized trial, and the 350th anniversary of Harvard University were among the other highlights of the year.

Educators and students, along with the rest of the nation, grieved the death of Christa McAuliffe—the 37-year-old social-studies teacher from Concord, NH, selected in 1985 to be the "first private-citizen passenger in the history of space flight"—in the explosion of the space shuttle *Challenger* on Jan. 28, 1986 (*see* feature article, page 36).

In other countries, a Kremlin decree laid plans to reform and modernize higher education in the Soviet Union; Britain's House of Commons by one vote prohibited caning in state schools; and government spending cuts caused many British scholars and scientists to seek better conditions abroad.

Holmes Group/Carnegie Forum Reports. Two important 1986 school-reform reports showed a growing national consensus for a radical restructuring of U.S. schools: *Tomorrow's Teachers,* issued in April by the Holmes Group, and *A Nation Prepared: Teachers for the 21st Century,* released May 16 by the Carnegie Forum on Education and the Economy. The Holmes Group, representing the most prestigious research university deans of education, is concerned with strengthening and professionalizing teaching. The Carnegie Forum includes leaders of government, business, and industry, and is concerned with school reform, including teacher education and status.

The conclusions of the two reports are strikingly similar. Both noted inadequacies in teacher preparation, their low salaries and status, the growing teacher shortage, and the tendency to lower standards when teachers are desperately needed. The Holmes Group suggested a "differentiated profession," with escalating salary scales: beginning instructors, middle professional teachers, and the top 20% career professionals. The Carnegie Forum suggested a National Board for Professional Teaching Standards to organize a career ladder: licensed teachers at $15,000 for ten months, certified teachers, advanced certified teachers, and "lead" teachers earning $72,000 for 12 months, who will direct other teachers and run schools. Both groups would replace the requirement of an undergraduate education degree with that of a bachelor's degree in an arts or science specialty. Teaching candidates would then receive a fifth or even sixth year of supervised "clinical" and "intern" training in an actual school setting.

Carnegie Forum member Albert Shanker, president of the American Federation of Teachers, approved the report, but member Mary Futrell, president of the National Education Association, had reservations about the "lead" teacher idea, fearing that, as in the case of merit pay, administrators would reward only complying teachers. Some school administrators questioned the report's assumption that teacher committees can run schools, when evidence shows that strong principals make strong schools. The latter is a position shared by U.S. Secretary of Education William J. Bennett, who otherwise praised the report. The Carnegie Forum's controversial "market approach" suggested that lead teachers might move their expertise from school to school and that students could enter schools of their choice. Opponents saw in this a similarity to President Ronald Reagan's voucher plan, which would allow parents to enroll their children in schools of their choice, private or public. Futrell and others see the "market approach" as creating elite schools at the expense of public schools.

Other critics of the report contended that its plan for raising teacher-education requirements would hurt minorities because fewer minority students are graduating from college, and teacher-training institutions are less able to prepare disadvantaged students for teaching careers. Still others wondered whether the states would relinquish their historic role of certifying teachers. The Carnegie Forum report expressed hope that they would voluntarily accept the new teacher-certification requirements set by a proposed National Board for Professional Teaching Standards. Finally, objection was raised about the cost of implementing all the reforms, estimated at $50 billion over ten years. Educational spending would be linked to overall economic growth, and some observers questioned how the plan might fare if the economy worsened.

On September 4, the Carnegie Forum named a panel to establish the National Board for Professional Teaching Standards by 1987. Start-up funds already had been pledged, and Stanford University was given $817,000 to study criteria for creating an effective and efficient teaching profession. Despite criticism, many hailed the Carnegie Forum report as potentially important as the 1910 Carnegie Report which revolutionized medical education in the United States and Canada.

Vicki Frost meets with reporters outside a federal courthouse in Greenville, TN. Mrs. Frost and other parents were suing a Tennessee school board over textbooks they considered offensive to their religious beliefs. In October a federal court ruled in favor of the Christian fundamentalists.

AP/Wide World

Governor's Report. On August 23, the National Governors' Association report, *Time for Results: The Governors' 1991 Report on Education,* affirmed most of the Holmes Group and Carnegie Forum recommendations. The governors also called for more early childhood classes for the disadvantaged, state takeover of "bankrupt" school districts that repeatedly fail to meet standards, allowing high-school juniors and seniors to take selected courses in their state public colleges and universities (as begun in Minnesota in 1986), and more parental choice of public schools for their children. Critics charged that the last recommendation would create elite schools and questioned how "bankruptcy" would be determined.

Higher Education Report. A major report on undergraduate higher education from the Carnegie Foundation for the Advancement of Teaching came out November 1. The report, entitled *College: The Undergraduate Experience in America,* called for more coherent curriculums, more emphasis on teaching, improved campus life, and greater college/university public accountability. It also recommended dropping standardized admissions tests as a requirement.

Elementary Education Report. Secretary Bennett in September issued his own report, *First Lessons: A Report on Elementary Education in America.* According to his findings, 9-to-13-year-olds today read better than did their peers in the 1970s. The problem, Bennett contended, begins in about the fourth grade, when critical thinking should be developing. The sec-retary laid much of the blame on elementary schools, charging that they have taken the "story" out of history, trivialized art and music, neglected geography and civics, and taken the joy out of science. He urged more parental involvement, more homework, less teacher paperwork, alternative methods of elementary-teacher training, and a longer school day.

While welcoming the focus on elementary education, some members of the educational community objected to Bennett's criticism of elementary curricula as outside the federal purview. Others blamed him for approving Reagan-administration spending cuts, which badly affected public education.

What Works. Earlier, on March 4, Secretary Bennett presented an Education Department report, titled *What Works: Research about Learning and Teaching,* to President Reagan. Its 41 prescriptions for school improvement emphasized school discipline, a rigorous curriculum, regular homework, higher teacher expectations, and more attention to history, math, and other basic subjects.

Drugs and Gallup Poll. According to the 18th annual Gallup Poll, released August 29, drugs topped school discipline as the public's main educational concern. The authorization of $1.05 billion by the House Education Committee in August set in motion a major national anti-drug education campaign. The funding would be disbursed over three years to counter student drug abuse. Then in September, President Reagan announced a sweeping anti-drug plan for the coming years. "Education is too

U.S. Public and Private Schools

	1986–87	1985–86
Enrollment		
Kindergarten through Grade 8	31,600,000	31,200,000
High school	13,700,000	13,900,000
Higher education	12,164,000	12,247,000
Total	57,464,000	57,347,000
Number of Teachers		
Elementary and secondary	2,500,000	2,500,000
Higher	700,000	700,000
Total	3,200,000	3,200,000
Graduates		
Public and private high school	2,650,000	2,600,000
Bachelor's degrees	950,000	945,000
First professional degrees	78,000	74,000
Master's degrees	276,000	290,000
Doctor's degrees	33,700	33,000
Expenditures		
Public elementary-secondary school	$156,000,000,000	$147,600,000,000
Private elementary-secondary	14,000,000,000	13,200,000,000
Public higher	70,700,000,000	66,600,000,000
Private higher	38,100,000,000	36,000,000,000
Total	$278,800,000,000	$263,400,000,000

vital,'' said the president and Mrs. Reagan in their appeal to the nation, ''to be corrupted by drugs.''

Meanwhile, in the final hours of the 1986 session, Congress enacted a major drug bill, increasing penalties for federal drug crimes and providing $1.76 billion for enforcement, education, and treatment programs. (See also DRUGS AND ALCOHOL).

Other poll findings: the public opposes using tax money for private schools, 65% to 27%; 46% of those polled supported school vouchers (a drop from 51% in 1983); and more than 68% favored tougher school standards.

Illiteracy. According to a new government study on literacy, reported in May 1986, approximately 1 of every 8 Americans cannot read. A basic literacy test was administered by the Bureau of the Census to 3,400 randomly selected citizens age 20 and over. Some 13% failed the test, able to answer only 20 or fewer of the 26 simple multiple-choice questions. In addition, 20% of persons originally offered refused to take the test, most for fear of revealing their illiteracy. According to the study, the majority of nonreaders are under age 50, and many have high-school diplomas. Not established by the survey was the number of Americans who, while technically literate, cannot read well enough to perform such everyday tasks as writing a check or addressing an envelope. Meanwhile, as of 1986, 33 states had established formal literacy councils. Remedial programs by local volunteer groups and educational institutions also were on the rise.

Supreme Court Rulings. On May 19 the U.S. Supreme Court voted, 5–4, to reverse a lower court's approval of a Michigan school district affirmative-action plan that resulted in white teachers being laid off before black teachers with less seniority (*Wygant v. Jackson Board of Education*).

In another school-related case, the court on July 7 upheld, 7–2, the suspension of a Piscataway, WA, high-school senior for using ''vulgar and offensive language'' in a school assembly talk (*Bethel School District v. Fraser*). The justices held that the school's disciplinary rules had been adequate warning for the suspension.

Tennessee Trial. In a highly publicized civil case that reached federal court in July 1986, seven religious fundamentalist families, backed by powerful national lobbies, sued a local Tennessee school board over textbooks they deemed offensive to their religious beliefs. The case began in November 1983, when one of the plaintiffs pulled her daughter from a class in which the textbooks were being used and began teaching the girl herself in the school library. The woman was arrested for trespassing but won a judgment for false arrest. With that ruling on appeal, several parents also filed a suit against the county, alleging that a series of books being used in the schools violated their 1st Amendment right to freedom of religious exercise; they demanded the right to alternative textbooks. In October the court ruled in their favor. The federal judge stated that the students could not be forcibly exposed to material violating their religious beliefs.

Also during the year, in Alabama federal court, some 600 fundamentalist parents, students, and teachers took action to remove all traces of ''secular humanism'' from the state public-school curriculum. No decision was reached by year's end.

Harvard Anniversary and Higher Education. Harvard University, which had produced 29 Nobel laureates, 27 Pulitzer-Prize winners, and six U.S. presidents, celebrated its 350th anniversary with ceremonies, receptions, and other special events September 4–7 (see PEOPLE, PLACES, AND THINGS, page 83).

Harvard, the nation's oldest university, as well as U.S. higher education in general, have undergone radical change and growth over the centuries. In the first years after Harvard's founding, any of its handful of students (all male) might have paid one year's tuition with a shank of mutton; today Harvard undergraduates pay $16,145 a year for tuition, room, and board. The average cost at four-year public colleges and universities nationwide was $4,587 in 1986, a 7% rise over 1985. The 3,340 colleges and universities in the United States today turn out 1.4 million graduates a year.

The Harvard celebration was marred only by students protesting Harvard's $400 million investment in companies doing business with South Africa. Similar anti-investment protests occurred nationally throughout 1986, with students of Dartmouth College building shanties to illustrate South African black deprivation.

EDUCATION / SPECIAL REPORT

Early Schooling

U.S. public schools have a new rallying cry: "The sooner the better."

After nearly a decade in which improvement efforts focused on high schools, educators now are turning their attention to younger children—including those still in the crib. "The issue is no longer whether we will serve younger children," says Charles Slater, the superintendent of schools in Brookline, MA. "The only question is how we will do it."

The Trend. According to the Bureau of the Census, the percentage of 3- and 4-year-olds in formal day-care and educational programs nearly doubled from 1970 to 1983, from 21% (1.5 million) to 38% (2.6 million). During the same period, enrollment of five-year-olds, mostly in kindergartens, rose from 69% to 85% of the total number. As of the 1986–87 school year, every state provided money to local school districts for kindergartens. Three states —Delaware, Florida, and Kentucky—made it mandatory.

Some schools are starting even earlier. In 1984, the Missouri legislature began requiring districts to provide developmental, language, hearing, and other types of screening of 1- and 2-year-olds and to offer parent education for families with children up to 3 years old. The project is based on the educational theories of Burton White, director of the Center for Parent Education in Newton, MA. White maintains that fundamental learning patterns are established by the age of three.

The Missouri legislators acted after researchers found that three-year-olds whose parents were involved in a pilot project "consistently scored significantly higher on all measures of intelligence, achievement, auditory comprehension, verbal ability, and language ability than did comparison children."

Public elementary schools also are getting into the day-care business. Several years ago the New Orleans school system began what it calls the Adept Child Care Enrichment Program. Under the scheme, many primary schools stay open from 7 A.M. to 6 P.M. Parents pay $20–$65 a month for the before- and after-school services, which are nonacademic in nature and range from visits by artists to instruction in yoga and other activities.

The surge of interest in early childhood education reflects a variety of social changes, beginning with the growing number of working mothers. Today about half of all mothers with children one year old or younger are working, nearly three quarters of them full-time.

Benefits. Recent research has shown that preschool programs can lead to significant long-term benefits, especially for disadvantaged children. For two decades, researchers from the High/Scope Foundation have been tracking 123 children from impoverished backgrounds with below average IQs who, in the 1960s, took part in the Perry Preschool Project in Ypsilanti, MI. The researchers reported that alumni of the program graduated from high school and went on to jobs or further education at nearly twice the rate of nonparticipants. The program, they concluded, had given the youngsters a greater sense of confidence and control of their environment.

The High/Scope researchers also analyzed school, police, and welfare records and found that graduates had fewer arrests, detentions, and teenage pregnancies. They calculated that the program, which cost nearly $5,000 per child in 1981 dollars, saved Ypsilanti more than $7,000 per child because the children required fewer remedial teaching and other social services.

Conflicting Views. The trend toward early childhood education also has sparked controversy. A principal issue is whether services to 3- and 4-year-old children should be thought of as an upward extension of the home and family, or as a downward extension of formal schooling.

Those who take the former view believe that preschoolers should be in day-care centers and nursery schools where there is a calm, homelike environment and where the emphasis is on giving children the freedom to grow at their own pace and develop social skills. Such centers can be run by day-care workers. They fear that professional teachers will impose their rigid structures on younger and younger children. Michael Olenick, a doctoral candidate at UCLA, examined 100 randomly selected local child-care programs and concluded that the teaching in at least one quarter was of the "sit down, shut up, and count to 100" variety.

Others, however, argue that schools constitute the only pervasive means of delivering the preschool services for which today's parents are clamoring. They contend that professional teachers are fully capable of meeting the needs of younger children.

"Everyone agrees that kindergarten should not be a mini-first grade and that 4-year-olds have different needs than 5-year-olds," says William Cieslukowski, a Connecticut principal who is active in the National Association of Elementary School Principals. "All we need is a little time to train our leaders."

EDWARD B. FISKE

When conservative students destroyed the shanties, clashes broke out between students and police. Similar protests and confrontations spread to other campuses.

International

USSR. In June, as part of the modernization drive of General Secretary Mikhail Gorbachev, the Soviet government issued a decree calling for sweeping reform of higher education. To overhaul the nation's 895 institutions of higher education (enrollment, 5.3 million), the decree called for broader-based education to replace traditional narrow specialties, elimination of duplicate programs, closer university-industry ties, reduced class size, more independent research, more optional courses, and less bureaucratic control.

South African Black Schools. With the rallying cry "Liberation now, education later," segregated black high-school students in the Republic of South Africa have led antiapartheid protests since September 1984, making their schools centers of extremism. Many have renamed their schools "Nelson Mandela High," after their long-jailed leader, or "Communism High," to irritate the white government. Police have tried with little success to clean off the spray-painted names. When the third term of the 1986 school year began in August, armed troops stood guard at centers of student protest. Students were required to carry and show identity cards—a government measure to identify troublemakers—and had to reregister or be suspended. Up to 300,000, or 10% of the black student population, failed to register. "No teaching is taking place," said one black leader. Observers believe that the breakdown of black education means that many blacks will reach adulthood without necessary job skills, and that mounting frustrations will make them even more radical.

Great Britain. Corporal punishment, mainly by caning, long a British school practice, was finally abolished in a narrow House of Commons vote, 231–230, on July 22. Previously a local option, caning had not been used in 25% of state schools in England and Wales, and about 90% of state schools in Scotland. The vote brought Great Britain in line with the rest of Europe.

Cuts in university support have contributed to a steady drain on scientific manpower in Great Britain; each year, more than 1,000 British scientists and engineers enter the United States alone. Many others go to West Germany and France. The lure is higher salaries and better research facilities. "Morale is destroyed by absence of career prospects," said the head of Save British Science, a newly formed professors' lobby.

FRANKLIN PARKER
Northern Arizona University, Flagstaff

Some black students in South Africa returned to school in September following a boycott to protest government policy.

AP/Wide World

EGYPT

Continued economic deterioration, explosive population growth, and widespread political unrest characterized the Egyptian domestic scene during 1986. Successes in foreign affairs included improving relations with Israel.

Domestic Affairs. Egypt's population, which reached 50 million in 1986, continued to increase by one million every ten months. With decreasing farmland, urban population expanded at an unprecedented rate—an increase of 1.5 million in Cairo since 1983. Per capita income declined to $500 per year, and 40% of the population lived below poverty. By July there was a threat of food shortages in the cities despite expenditures of one third of the annual government budget to subsidize low food prices, particularly for bread. More than half the country's food was imported.

According to the International Monetary Fund, Egypt's foreign debt exceeded $38 billion by the end of the year. The budget deficit had doubled since 1983 to a quarter of the gross national product (GNP), with no prospects for improvement because of the economic recession that struck the Persian Gulf. As a result, tens of thousands of Egyptian workers returned from that region, adding to the growing ranks of unemployed and cutting by one third the $3.5 billion sent home by workers in 1984–85.

Deterioration of world markets diminished Egypt's petroleum sales, which had provided half its exports and 20% of the state budget. Income from the Suez Canal also decreased due to decline in oil-tanker shipments. Tourism, the fourth major source of foreign income, was cut because of riots in the capital.

The most serious threat to government stability occurred in February when up to 17,000 young security police draftees rampaged in Cairo for several days protesting against enforced extension of their service. The rioting was quelled by the army with tanks and machine guns; several days of curfew were imposed, and schools and universities were closed. More than 100 people were killed and some 700 wounded in the riots. Hotels and nightclubs were destroyed, and property damages were estimated to be at least $150 million.

Antigovernment protests of Islamic fundamentalists continued with violent clashes against the police in Aswan during April. Throughout the year there were mass trials of Islamic fundamentalists, Communists, and the February police rioters. As a result of the February riots, Egypt's interior minister was dismissed; in April the People's Assembly extended the emergency laws in force since President Anwar el-Sadat's 1981 assassination.

During October there were by-elections for 70 members of the 210 seat Shura Council, an advisory body established by President Sadat in 1980. Egypt's five opposition parties boycotted the election in protest against new laws that required candidates to obtain at least 20% of the votes for a Council seat, and awarding all seats in a province to a party obtaining more than 50% of the votes. Thus, President Hosni Mubarak's ruling National Democratic Party won 97.95% of the ballots cast and all 70 seats.

In November, President Mubarak dismissed Prime Minister Ali Lutfi because of his failure to straighten out Egypt's economic woes. He was replaced by Atef Sedki, an economist.

Foreign Affairs. The deteriorating economy led to a thaw in relations with the Soviet Union, expressed in a new Egyptian-Soviet economic and commercial cooperation agreement and the first visit in 12 years to Cairo by a Soviet trade union delegation. Despite U.S. failure to increase its more than $2 billion in economic assistance, Egypt joined the United States in the sixth set of joint military maneuvers since the 1980 "Bright Star" operation.

Relations with Israel improved despite the assassination of an Israeli embassy employee, the third such attack on Israeli officials by an antigovernment terrorist faction since 1980. After 20 months of bitter negotiations, the dispute between Egypt and Israel over the tiny Taba sliver of land on the Sinai border between the two countries was resolved. In September they agreed to submit the dispute to international arbitration, clearing the way for the first summit meeting between Egypt and Israel since 1981. Israeli Prime Minister Shimon Peres and Egyptian President Mubarak met in Alexandria on September 11 and 12. The summit concluded with a joint declaration marking "A new era in bilateral relations. . . ." A new Egyptian ambassador was named to replace the one withdrawn since 1982 in protest against Israel's invasion of Lebanon.

Mubarak also continued his parleys with Jordan's King Hussein and PLO leaders intended to further the Middle East peace process.

DON PERETZ
State University of New York, Binghamton

EGYPT · Information Highlights

Official Name: Arab Republic of Egypt.
Location: Northeastern Africa.
Area: 386,660 sq mi (1 001 449 km²).
Population (mid-1986 est.): 50,500,000.
Capital: Cairo.
Government: *Head of state,* Mohammed Hosni Mubarak, president (took office Oct. 1981). *Head of government,* Atef Sedki, prime minister (took office November 1986). *Legislature* (unicameral)— People's Assembly.
Monetary Unit: Pound (1.36 pounds equal U.S.$1, commercial rate, Oct. 17, 1986).
Gross National Product (1984 U.S.$): $39,700,-000,000.
Economic Index (1984): *Consumer Prices* (1980 = 100), all items, 172.3; food, 180.6.
Foreign Trade (1985 U.S.$): *Imports,* $9,962,000,000; *exports,* $3,714,000,000.

ENERGY

An abundant oil supply and consequent low oil prices and a major disaster at the Chernobyl nuclear reactor number 4 near Kiev in the USSR dominated the headlines in the energy field in 1986. The latter disaster was of such magnitude that it caused many persons to question once again the wisdom of nuclear energy. Accordingly, the International Atomic Energy Agency held a major conference in Vienna in August to discuss the causes and effects of the disaster. The symposium concluded with a 13-point program to improve the safety of nuclear power. The recommendations included more frequent international inspections of nuclear plants as well as the establishment of international standards on the training of nuclear plant operators (*see* special report, page 218).

The low price of oil had a domino effect on the prices of competing energy sources (*see* special report, page 283). Prices for natural gas and coal declined and, in a few instances, electric utilities also reduced their rates. Although these developments had the effect of eliminating the supply and price of energy as areas of major public concern in the United States, Congress did consider various legislation in the energy area. But final action was limited.

Oil. As 1986 began, the Organization of the Petroleum Exporting Countries' (OPEC) benchmark price for oil was $28 per barrel, a level that had been maintained by Saudi Arabia reducing its production from a high of 10 million barrels per day in 1980 to a low of 2.5 million barrels per day in 1985. A 50% price drop occurred early in 1986 when Saudi Arabia increased its production to 4.5 million barrels, later 5.5 million barrels, per day. Some observers referred to this price break as the "third oil crisis." Any large, sudden change in price—up or down—they argued, has serious widespread effects. Americans generally think of energy crises as resulting from sudden increases in price similar to those that followed the OPEC oil embargo in 1973 and the Iranian revolution of 1979. From the point of view of such oil-producing countries as Mexico and Nigeria—as well as U.S. states that rely heavily on petroleum and petroleum-related industries—the drop in price was a major crisis.

For most Americans the consequences in the short term were very positive, as gasoline prices dropped by one third in many areas of the country. The price reductions contributed significantly to the nation's low rate of inflation, and the nation spent $20 to $25 billion less on imported oil than in 1985.

For those regions of the United States heavily dependent on the oil industry—such as Louisiana, Oklahoma, and Texas—the economic consequences were severe. Unemployment rose; bank failures increased; and state governments found themselves facing large deficits because of reduced tax revenues. The effect on the U.S. oil industry was evidenced by a 60% drop in the number of oil drilling rigs in operation between September 1985 and September 1986. A substantial number of the nation's producing oil wells became uneconomical. Energy analysts predicted that a $14–$15 per-barrel price would result in the nation losing 10% of its production capacity, as a growing number of wells become uneconomical and are taken out of production.

Continuing conservation efforts by the U.S. public resulted in a consumption decline of 1% for all other forms of energy. Oil consumption, responding to lower prices, ran counter to that trend, increasing by more than 3%. The quantity of oil being imported increased by 20%.

In light of the low prices and the plentiful supply, OPEC tried several times to agree on a new pricing and production system. Finally at a July-early August meeting, OPEC agreed to cut its combined oil production by more than three million barrels per day for two months. News of the agreement caused oil prices to increase by as much as 50%. In essence the pact returned OPEC nations to 1985 production quotas—16.8 million barrels per day.

Following a subsequent 17-day OPEC meeting in October, at which price-raising production limits were endorsed through to the year's end, Saudi Arabia's King Fahd dismissed Sheik Ahmed Zaki Yamani as his petroleum and mineral resources minister. During two decades as head of the Saudi energy ministry, Yamani had become OPEC's chief strategist, gained the nickname of "Mr. Oil," and was one of the most powerful men in the world. It was believed that the king had come to disagree with Yamani's policy of pumping Saudi oil as fast as possible when there already was an oil glut. Hisham Nazer was appointed temporarily to the post.

Meeting again from December 11 to 20 in Geneva, the OPEC ministers agreed to cut the cartel's combined oil production by about one million barrels per day, effective Jan. 1, 1987. And, rather than allow market forces to determine prices, the ministers also agreed on a fixed average price—$18 per barrel—beginning Feb. 1, 1987. Nazer reportedly played a key role in hammering out the agreement.

Congressional Action. At the same time that the OPEC meetings were being held in Geneva and elsewhere, debate over various energy proposals was occurring in the halls of the U.S. Congress. Representatives of the oil industry and congressmen from oil-producing states sought help from Congress for their troubled constituents. A number of traditional tax advantages enjoyed by the oil industry became a focus of major controversy as Congress struggled to carry out a comprehensive overhaul of the nation's tax system. The initial reform proposals called for eliminating all industry-specific tax breaks. The oil industry, however, was able to retain some preferential treatment in the final compromise legislation.

The windfall profits tax had been enacted in 1980 when oil prices were near their peak following the Iranian revolution. For some oil, as much as 70% of the difference between the regulated prices of the 1970s and market prices was taken in taxes. Given the strikingly different circumstances existing in 1986, many in Congress believed this was an undue burden on the industry and that the tax should be eliminated. Congress ended its 1986 session without so acting, however.

In addition the U.S. industry and its congressional supporters vigorously advocated establishment of a new tax on imported oil. The industry argued that taxes on imported oil should be set high enough to establish a U.S. price floor in the range of $20 per barrel. The import tax was said to be necessary to maintain a viable domestic oil industry. In addition, tax advocates argued that these revenues would reduce the size of the federal deficit. The Reagan administration demonstrated little support for the import tax, and the measure did not pass.

An abundant supply of natural gas and soft prices increased the pressure on Congress to act on two legislative changes that had been advocated for several years. The first involved a proposal for repeal of the Fuel Use Act passed in 1978. That legislation had resulted from a severe gas shortage during the winter of 1976–77 and banned the construction of new electric generation facilities fueled by natural gas. With gas in abundant supply, representatives of the gas and electric industries, supported by the Reagan administration, argued unsuccessfully that the ban should be eliminated. The Reagan administration also introduced legislation to deregulate totally the price of natural gas. In 1978 the Congress had deregulated roughly half of the nation's natural gas. At that time the arguments against total deregulation were that it would lead to a rapid increase in gas prices. With gas prices declining in 1986, the administration argued that there was little justification for continued price regulation. Congress refused to agree.

In 1976 the Congress had passed legislation which governed the leasing of coal on federally owned lands. One part of that legislation required that the lease owners develop and produce the coal reserves within prescribed periods of time. In 1976 it was expected that the total quantities of energy used in the United States would be much larger than turned out to be the case. Owners of federal leases now argue that there is no market for their coal and that they should be relieved of the requirement for developing and producing coal within fixed periods of time. No action was taken on the issue.

In light of the Chernobyl disaster, congressional action on nuclear power was destined to be highly acrimonious. The primary focus of that acrimony was the need by Congress to extend the Price Anderson Act. That legislation, initially passed in 1957 and extended for ten years in 1975, established the limits of industry liability from any nuclear accident. Price Anderson was passed when the nuclear industry found itself unable to obtain unlimited liability coverage from private insurance companies. The legislation as amended in 1975 limited the industry's liability to $640 million for a single accident and committed the government to cover the difference between the amount of insurance available from private companies and the liability limit. The major focus of the controversy over renewing the Price Anderson Act revolved around a proposal to levy a tax on each kilowatt hour of electricity generated by nuclear plants. That tax would essentially be an insurance premium which the federal government charged the industry for providing liability coverage. Congress adjourned without taking final action on renewing the act which expires on Aug. 1, 1987. However, operating utilities would remain protected from damage claims under existing terms of the act, and new nuclear generating plants would not be able to obtain limitations on liability.

Nuclear waste disposal became a major political issue late in the year. Under a congressionally mandated program, the Department of Energy has been carrying on a long-term study aimed at identifying permanent disposal sites for nuclear wastes. The Department of Energy indicated late in the year that it was no longer considering disposal sites in the eastern United States and would focus its attention on those located in the West. The explanation for that decision was that the broad based and intense opposition to sites in the East made it unlikely that they could ever be used. When this decision became publicly known, congressmen from the western states with sites under investigation indicated they would never agree to disposal in their states. The intensity of this controversy once again underlined the highly charged character of the waste disposal issue. The nation has been searching for an acceptable permanent disposal method for nuclear wastes for more than 20 years. Events during 1986 suggest that there is a long distance to go before this issue is resolved.

As 1986 drew to a close, some experts were warning that with the oil industry so unstable and the coal and nuclear-power industries the foci of controversy, another energy crisis could be around the corner. If so, definite action by the new Congress would be required. It also was accepted that although "Mr. Oil" might be away from the scene, OPEC would remain as important as ever.

DON E. KASH, *The University of Oklahoma*

The Chernobyl Accident

Shortly after 1:00 A.M. (Moscow time) on April 26, 1986, Chernobyl nuclear reactor number 4, located in a reactor complex not far from Kiev in the Soviet Ukraine, exploded and caught fire. The result was by far the worst accident in reactor history. The accident came to light a few days later when a radioactive cloud was detected in Sweden. A massive release of radioactive contamination led to the death of at least 31 plant workers, the evacuation of an estimated 135,000 people from the region adjacent to the plant, and considerable radiation in Europe. The reactor, a type RBMK-1000 capable of producing 1000 megawatts of electricity, is one of the largest, most modern, and most prevalent power reactors in the Soviet Union. In 1980, RBMK-1000 reactors produced 65% of all the nuclear electricity in the USSR.

The worst previous nuclear accident was the 1979 meltdown of the Three Mile Island (TMI) reactor near Harrisburg, PA, in which about 70% of the uranium oxide in the core melted. The reactor was destroyed; clean up will cost more than $1 billion. Fortunately the massive TMI containment vessel prevented the release of large amounts of radioactivity into the environment. Soviet reactors have only limited containment. When something goes wrong with a Soviet reactor, it is more likely that radioactive debris will be released.

Virtually all commercial power reactors rely on the energy released by the thermal fission of the uranium isotope U-235. The term "thermal" means that the energetic neutrons released when U-235 nucleus fissions are slowed down (thermalized) by scattering from other nuclei. In most U.S. and European power reactors thermalization is done by scattering the neutrons from the protons in water. The water serves two purposes: to slow the neutrons and to produce steam to turn a turbine. In the Chernobyl reactor water is used as a coolant, but graphite (carbon) is used to slow down the neutrons. Differences in engineering probably make the Soviet reactor less forgiving of error than Western designs.

By late 1986, the Chernobyl accident appeared to have been due largely to operator error. The accident took place during testing at very low power. The operators had intentionally deactivated a number of safety systems in order to simplify their tests. When the water around some of the fuel rods flashed to steam the normal safety systems failed to respond. Overheating ensued.

The fuel rods in both Western reactors and the Chernobyl reactor are made of uranium oxide pellets contained in a zirconium alloy tube. The uranium oxide is able to withstand very high temperatures, but the zirconium is not. If the zirconium gets too hot it begins to react with the surrounding water coolant. The reaction converts the zirconium to zirconium oxide, a powdery material, and releases hydrogen. A hydrogen explosion at TMI was contained. At Chernobyl it is likely that overheating led to an explosion and hydrogen production. The containment vessel was breached and more explosions occurred. The graphite caught fire, and burned for weeks. Eventually the reactor was enclosed in a mound of concrete.

While the proximate cause of the Chernobyl reactor accident may have been operator error, the full explanation will not be known for some time, if ever. One reason is that the USSR was very slow to release information about the accident. The second reason for reserving judgment is U.S. history regarding the TMI accident. Early reports from TMI made it appear that the accident resulted from operator error. The reactor operators made many mistakes, including shutting off the emergency cooling pumps that would have prevented the overheating that occurred. It was pointed out that if the operators had *done nothing,* no accident would have occurred. It was only after investigations that flaws in the reactor design and in the instructions given by the vendor to the operators were recognized. By late 1986, it was premature to make a final judgment on the real cause of the Chernobyl accident.

Fallout. Uranium bombarded by neutrons can either fission (split into two lighter nuclei and release several neutrons) or it can be transmuted into a heavier isotope of uranium. There are many fission products, some of them highly radioactive. Decay of transmuted uranium leads to radioactive isotopes of plutonium, americium, and other heavy elements.

Radioactive decay releases ionizing alpha, beta, and gamma radiation. This causes disruption of cellular function and genetic damage. At high dose levels death rapidly ensues. Low dose levels decrease resistance to disease, damage organs, increase the probability of developing cancer, and produce damage to the genes that shows up as abnormalities in offspring. The effects are complex and subtle. Some experts argue that at low enough exposures there is no effect from radiation (the "threshold hypothesis"). Others assert that there is no evidence for this, and that any exposure to radiation is cause for concern.

The rupture of the Chernobyl containment released enormous quantities of radioactive

The actual cause and overall effect of a devastating fire and explosion on April 26, 1986, at the Chernobyl nuclear reactor number 4 in the town of Pripyat, about 60 mi (100 km) north of Kiev in the Soviet Ukraine, may never be known.

Tass from Soviet

fission products into the biosphere (an estimated 50-100 million curies). (Curies are the official measurement for radioactivity.) Most of the radioactivity was deposited near the reactor, creating extremely high levels of radioactivity. In the Kiev region a large amount of food had to be destroyed. In part of Europe some crops also were ruined. Little fallout was carried to the United States, so there was far more anxiety about the accident in Europe.

Isotopes emitted as fine particles or as gas were carried downwind. As they moved, some dropped out or were precipitated by rain. Short-lived isotopes decayed significantly. Far downwind, a few isotopes are the dominant health hazards. Iodine-131 has a half-life (the time required for spontaneous decay of half the nuclei) of eight days. Iodine is concentrated in the thyroid gland. High doses can lead to damage to this gland (hypothyroidism). Because of the short half-life, Iodine-131 is a problem for only a few weeks after release. Cesium-134 has a half-life of 2.3 years and cesium-137 has a half-life of 30 years. Cesium tends to concentrate in muscles.

Strontium-90 has a half-life of 28 years and is chemically similar to calcium. It concentrates in bone, leading to risk to bone marrow. Cesium-134 and cesium-137 on grass eaten by cows are concentrated in the milk. Cobalt-60 (half-life 5.3 years) plays a biochemical role in vitamin B-12. Isotopes with long half-lives remain problems for long times. If radiation levels are high, it may be necessary to physically remove or cover top soil or other contaminated material (e.g., children's sandboxes), destroy crops, or take other corrective steps.

Radioactivity exposure is measured in rads (radiation absorbed dose). One rad corresponds to the deposition of 10 microjoules of energy per gram of absorbing material. When a human is exposed to 400 rads in a short time,

there is a 50% change of death occurring within one month. We are all exposed to about 0.2 rads per year or 200 millirads/year. About half of this is due to natural sources (cosmic rays, radioactivity in rocks and soil) and half to artificial sources (primarily medical X rays).

Often the measurement for radioactivity, curies, are expressed per unit mass. For example, following the Chernobyl accident the Austrian government announced that milk containing more than 5 nCi/liter (nanocuries per liter) radioactivity could not be sold. This value was exceeded (though not by a great deal) in some areas, and milk had to be dumped. There was little consistency about the levels of radioactivity considered dangerous. The varying standards made it hard for citizens to know what to do. Fortunately the radioactivity levels soon declined, and by midsummer there was no longer reason for major concern in Western Europe. The situation in the Ukraine, some western Soviet bloc countries, and Scandinavia was much worse. In Scandinavia, reindeer ate contaminated moss which made their meat radioactive and inedible. This seriously injured the economy and culture of the Scandinavian Eskimos.

Relations between the radioactivity level in food and the dose to body organs are complex. They depend on the isotope, its decay products, the half-life, the biological half-life, and the organ where the isotope is concentrated. For example, iodine-131 concentrates in the thyroid gland, and one nanocurie gives a dose of about 28 millirem in a child. The conversion factors for other isotopes vary considerably. Standards for contamination are based on the idea that the additional exposure should be a small fraction of background radiation.

One can estimate the average total radiation dose due to consumption of food and water, and from exposure to radioactivity deposited on the ground. The cumulative dose due to Chernobyl for an average Bavarian (southern German) was estimated at 70–150 millirem for children, and 50–110 millirem for adults. These doses are comparable to those received in one year under normal conditions. The West German government estimated this exposure would increase the risk of cancer by about 0.01%. This number may be interpreted in two ways. On the one hand the increase is so small that it cannot be detected in epidemiological studies. On the other hand, since about 20% of the population normally dies of cancer, in a population of 60 million people one would expect 12 million cancer deaths. If the risk increases by 0.01%, then 1,200 additional deaths would occur.

The situation is far worse in the Soviet Union. Preliminary estimates indicate the accident will result in 6,500–45,000 additional cancer deaths in the eastern part of the Soviet Union, largely as a result of radiation from cesium-137. The increase in cancer rates was estimated at about 0.4%. Because the percentage increases are small, however, it will probably not be possible to associate any particular cancer death with Chernobyl.

The Reactor Industry. The Chernobyl accident will not mean the end of the reactor business. Nuclear energy now is supplying a significant part of the electrical energy in many nations, and the economic costs of shutting down all of the reactors would not be politically acceptable. At the end of 1985 the United Nations' International Atomic Energy Agency recorded 374 power reactors in 26 countries around the world. (There are also many research and military reactors.) The total output of these reactors is 248,000 megawatts (248 gigawatts), and they produce about 15% of the world's electricity.

France is the leading user of nuclear electricity. In fact, 65% of France's electricity is nuclear. Other leaders are: Belgium 60% nuclear electricity; Sweden 50%; Finland 38%; Switzerland 40%; West Germany 30%; Japan 22%; Spain and Britain 20%; the United States 15%; the Soviet Union 14%. In most of these countries, additional reactors are under construction or in advanced stages of planning. Consequently the worldwide production of nuclear fueled electricity will increase.

Escalating costs and the effectiveness of energy conservation lead to a poor prognosis for nuclear power in the United States. In the 1960s and early 1970s, utilities believed reactors would provide cheap electricity, and ordered many. By the mid-1970s, cost overruns occurred, and plant cancellations became commonplace. The problems were exacerbated by the accident at Three Mile Island, which brought the owners, General Public Utilities Corporation, to the brink of bankruptcy (from which it recovered). Utility companies and the financial community came to realize that reactors are expensive and risky investments. Another critical event was the bankruptcy of the Washington Public Power Supply System (WPPSS), a public organization set up to build reactors in the Pacific Northwest to produce electricity for sale to utilities. WPPSS discovered it could not pay for the reactors it had ordered and defaulted on its loans, leading to the largest bankuptcy in the history of public corporations.

The second reason for the collapse of the U.S. reactor industry is the dramatic effectiveness of energy conservation. Prior to the 1973 OPEC (Organization of the Petroleum Exporting Countries) oil embargo, U.S. electricity use was growing by 8% yearly. This meant that the total electricity system (generation, transmission, and distribution systems) had to double every nine years. Rapidly increasing energy prices combined with massive inflation in the construction industries led consumers to take energy conservation and alternative energy systems seriously. By the mid 1980s, electricity growth had dropped to about 2% per year, and there was an oversupply of generating capacity in most parts of the nation. Many of the utilities which now foresee a need for more electricity are opting to purchase small plants or to buy their power from independent suppliers who can generate cheaply from cogeneration systems, wind, or small scale hydropower.

A few more reactors will become operational in the United States, but it is unlikely that any new orders for power reactors will be placed in the United States in the 20th century. The stagnation of the U.S. reactor industry turned out to have little to do with safety. It resulted from changing economics and poor planning and management within the electric utility industry, the industry suppliers, and the government regulatory bureaucracy.

In the aftermath of Chernobyl the Soviet reactor industry is experiencing severe shakeups. Confidence is not what it was in 1983 when B. A. Semenov, the head of the Soviet Department of Nuclear Energy and Safety, wrote that the cooling system of the RBMK-1000 reactor is designed so that "a serious loss-of-coolant accident is practically impossible." In the reactor industry, as in most industries dealing with complex socio-technological systems, the practically impossible sometimes occurs. Though lives are lost, experience is gained, and the risk of future accidents is reduced. Whether the risks of nuclear electricity are worth the benefits is an issue society has not yet resolved.

PAUL P. CRAIG

ENGINEERING, CIVIL

All Americans could inspect the handiwork of civil engineers in 1986, as the United States showed off the newly refurbished Statue of Liberty in extravagant centennial celebrations July 3-6.

The Statue of Liberty-Ellis Island Foundation raised about $280 million to rehabilitate the statue; the island and pedestal on which it sits; and nearby Ellis Island, the immigrant processing center through which millions entered the United States. The work was conducted by a team of engineers and craftsmen from the United States and France, the country that donated the statue to the United States. (*See* feature article, page 61.)

Channel Tunnel. At the same time, another team of French engineers was collaborating with the British on a project that has been dreamed of since before the statue's birth in 1886: France and Great Britain agreed to connect themselves with a tunnel under the English Channel.

The project, as envisioned in its most recent incarnation, actually will be two 24-ft (7.3-m) diameter train tunnels running 31 mi (50 km) from Folkestone, England, to Calais, France. A 15-ft (4.6-m) service tunnel would run between them. The entire project is expected to cost between $3.7 billion and $6.6 billion. Construction of the Chunnel, as it is called, is expected to start in mid-1987, with railroad service scheduled to begin during the spring of 1993.

Tall Stories. The skyscraper also entered its second century in 1986. Marking this stage in the skyscraper's evolution were proposals for no less than three new contenders for the title of the world's tallest building. In New York City, developer Donald Trump announced plans to build a 150-story skyscraper along with eight other high rises on Manhattan's Upper West Side. At 1,670 ft (509 m), the main structure would be 216 ft (66 m) taller than the 1,454-ft (443-m) Sears Tower in Chicago, currently the tallest building on earth. Plans are to complete the $4 billion complex by 1996, but community opposition could stall the project indefinitely.

In Phoenix, AZ, developer George Schriqui was proceeding, though behind schedule, on a 1,692-ft (516-m) building. While in Atlanta, GA, developers Thomas Crowder and Walter Young expected to break ground in 1987 on a 2,015-ft (614-m) structure.

Environmental Engineering. Although civil engineers are well known for their work with tunnels, tall buildings, and other structures, the single fastest growing segment of the field is the one they are least known for: environmental engineering.

The problem of cleaning up after himself is a problem that increasingly is daunting man. In 1986, the Environmental Protection Agency (EPA) expanded its list of sites so polluted that they qualify for Superfund cleanup funds by 170, to 703. The agency also suggested that an additional 45 sites be added to the list, bringing the number of proposed sites to 185. From the list's inception in 1981, through 1986, only eight sites in the entire United States have been deemed sufficiently cleaned up to warrant removal from the list.

Thousands more sites not covered by Superfund are spreading across the United States. One is the Rocky Mountain Arsenal, located 9 mi (14 km) northeast of downtown Denver, CO. Throughout World War II, the government manufactured a variety of toxic and incendiary munitions at the arsenal. After the war, many obsolete explosives were either detonated or burned on the site, nerve agents were made and filled, and the area has been used for the neutralization and incineration of chemical warfare materials. Private industry also has leased parts of the Colorado site for the manufacture of such chemicals as pesticides and herbicides.

For much of its history, industrial wastes were routinely discharged on the site. In the early 1970s, contaminants were found to be migrating off of the site via the area's groundwater. Simply cleaning up the contaminants is no easy chore, in part, because of the sheer size of the arsenal. It occupies more than 17,000 acres (6 883 ha). Until technologies can be devised to clean up the mess, engineers have installed an ingenious system of barriers and wells to intercept the groundwater before it leaves the arsenal, remove the contaminants from it with carbon filters, and pump it back into the ground.

Engineers are getting closer to more permanent cleanup methods. At one site in Verona, MO, researchers from the EPA used a mobile incinerator to destroy dioxin contaminated soil for the first time. Under carefully controlled conditions, the soil was heated to 1,800°F (980°C). At this temperature the dioxin was stripped from the soil and forced into another chamber where it was burned at 2,000°F (1 100°C). In this heat, the dioxin molecules broke apart into carbon, oxygen, chlorine, and hydrogen. When cooled, however, the elements did not join back into dioxin. Instead, they reform into a clean vapor and slightly salty water.

In cases of chemical spills, engineers have found that microbes in the soil will often break down into the contaminants. One promising area of research has been in the development of ways to modify the nutrients, oxygen and water contents, pH and temperature of the soils to help the bacteria, help the engineers, do their work.

HOWARD SMALLOWITZ
"Civil Engineering" Magazine

Research published in 1986 identified a distinct global warming trend in the last 100 years, attributed to the "greenhouse effect"—the trapping in of heat by gases released into the atmosphere. Scientists have warned that a rise in average temperature of only a few degrees would begin to melt the polar ice-caps, raising ocean levels and flooding coastal cities.

© J. Guichard/Sygma

ENVIRONMENT

Several landmark events catapulted environmental issues into the news during 1986. The rupture and meltdown of a reactor at the Chernobyl nuclear power station in the Soviet Ukraine garnered the most global attention (*see* special report, page 218). Potentially more serious, however, were the discoveries of changes in earth's stratospheric-ozone layer— changes that dramatically heightened concern over how industrial societies are controlling their production of atmosphere-altering pollutants. On the U.S. front, strides were made toward tightening environmental regulations.

Ozone and Ozone Holes. For the first time, scientists in 1986 were able to confirm what had been strongly suspected for many years: that the global distribution of stratospheric ozone (O_3) is declining. It is this stratospheric layer that shields life on earth from much of the biologically harmful solar ultraviolet light. In June, atmospheric scientist Donald F. Health of the National Aeronautics and Space Administration (NASA) Goddard Space Flight Center in Greenbelt, MD, reported that new satellite measurements indicate "a real global-scale decrease, although we don't know what the physical mechanism is." Data by scientists at the Oregon Graduate Center in Beaverton showed that atmospheric concentrations of six of the most significant long-lived ozone-destroying pollutants appear to have increased over the past ten years. For instance, levels of the chlorofluorocarbons (or Freons) CFC-11 and CFC-12 have more than doubled.

Moreover, the current growth rate in emissions of CFC-11 and CFC-12 throughout the world poses serious health risks—not just for future generations but also for those alive today, according to the draft version of a new report by the U.S. Environmental Protection Agency (EPA). Released in November, the draft said that even halving the growth of these

CFC emissions could cause 60% more skin cancers and 60,000 additional cases of cataracts in the United States alone. Thinning stratospheric ozone also would lead to more global warming. Even more provocatively, new U.S. research presented at a November United Nations ozone workshop in Amsterdam predicted that decreasing stratospheric ozone would also dramatically increase the production of both photochemical smog and acid-rain precursors in the air near the earth's surface.

Early in 1986, Richard Stolarksi and his coworkers at the Goddard Center shocked the atmospheric science community with their finding that a circular patch of the stratospheric-ozone layer—centered over Antarctica —undergoes dramatic seasonal variation. Ozone concentrations in this "hole" drop by almost 50% starting in mid-August, the end of the dark Antarctic winter; by November each year, the hole is gone. And since 1978, according to the data, the hole has been getting bigger.

Four U.S. research teams headed to the Antarctic in late August 1986 to watch a hole form. On October 20 they announced their first experimental observations. The hole forms in just 20 to 30 days. It starts at high altitudes, about 12 mi (19 km), and gradually penetrates down to about 7.5 mi (12 km) above earth's surface. Although the scientists were able to observe a number of chemical processes at work, the precise cause and overall significance of the hole remained open to speculation.

Such findings were instrumental in convincing members of a U.S. CFC-manufacturers and -users association, the Alliance for Responsible CFC Policy, to volunteer support in September for a "reasonable global limit" on the future rate of growth in CFC production. Previously, the group had fought all global CFC controls. Its new announcement was deemed important because CFCs were still widely used as refrigerants and for the production of insulating foam materials. (In the late 1970s, the United States had banned nonessential uses of CFCs, as for aerosol spray propellants.) And on November 5, the U.S. State Department proposed even more drastic action: "a near-term freeze" on the future growth of the most ozone-threatening CFCs, with the intent of eventually phasing out these chemicals altogether.

Ozone in Smog. Ironically, while concentrations of ozone are declining in the stratosphere, they are growing in the lower atmosphere—especially in the breathable air of major metropolitan cities. That comes as bad news, since ozone is the major irritant in smog and can harm the lungs of persons with emphysema, asthma, and chronic respiratory problems. New research cited in an ozone study released in June by the EPA indicated that even healthy people, especially those who exercise heavily outdoors, may suffer adverse respiratory effects from smog-ozone levels at or below those allowed by EPA regulations. In 1986, more than one in three Americans lived in areas that failed to meet EPA's ozone standard.

Global Warming. For years scientists have warned of the dire environmental changes that could occur if atmospheric levels of certain "greenhouse gases" are allowed to rise. The presence of such gases—many of them combustion pollutants, like carbon dioxide and nitrous oxide—allow incoming solar radiation to pass through and heat earth's surface. But the longer wavelengths of the energy reradiated back from the earth's surface into space can be trapped by these gases, much in the way a greenhouse-window traps in solar heat. A rise in global temperature of only a few degrees would begin to melt the polar ice-caps, raising ocean levels and flooding coastal cities. In addition, the weather needed to grow such vital grains as corn and wheat would shift to higher latitudes—and less productive soils. According to new data published in 1986—global temperature readings spanning the last 100 years—

such a warming trend indeed has already begun. As reported in the British journal *Nature*, "results show little trend in the 19th century, marked warming to 1940, relatively steady conditions to the mid-1970s, and a subsequent rapid warming." Measured global warming over the 100 years was slightly more than 0.5°C.

Dioxin. Since 1984 teams of researchers from the United States, Canada, and Europe have been accumulating evidence that all members of industrialized societies carry background traces of dioxin contamination in their bodies. According to the EPA, dioxin is "one of the most perplexing and potentially dangerous chemicals ever to pollute the environment." Dioxins can be generated by the incineration of many products and are trace contaminants in certain antiseptics, wood preservatives, bactericides, and herbicides—including the Agent Orange defoliant used extensively during the Vietnam War.

At a September 1986 symposium on dioxins and related chemicals at Fukuoka, Japan, researchers from the State University of New York (SUNY) and the University of Rochester (NY) reported finding that trace amounts of toxic dioxins also contaminate the breast milk of North American women. According to one of the researchers, the data suggest that "babies nursing in the United States for one year are getting more dioxins in their body than any of our government agencies recommend for a life-time exposure."

Vietnamese research presented at the Fukuoka meeting showed that Vietnamese populations with wartime exposure to Agent Orange "had a [four-fold] higher risk of developing primary liver cancer" than unexposed persons.

While several studies presented at the Japanese meeting reported no evidence of elevated cancer risk among persons who might have received high exposures to dioxins, a study pub-

© A. Tannenbaum/Sygma

Soil contaminated by radon gas is removed from a neighborhood in Montclair, NJ. The gas, which carries a high risk of lung cancer, has been discovered in high concentrations along the East Coast. In 1986, the U.S. Environmental Protection Agency set a cautionary safety standard— four picocuries per liter of air— for the presence of radon gas in residences.

lished in the British medical journal *Lancet* did. It reported an excess of soft-tissue sarcomas (a type of cancer) among persons who had received heavy dioxin exposure in a 1976 chemical plant explosion in Sevesco, Italy.

Acid Rain. In March the U.S. National Academy of Sciences (NAS) issued a report laying to rest any question about the contribution of acid precipitation to fishless, acid lakes. Though growing numbers of scientists believed that acid rain was responsible for the killing of aquatic life in lakes in the northeastern United States and in Europe, other explanations for the acidification also had been advanced. But the new NAS study, drawing on the fossil record of lake-water pH levels over hundreds of years, said that in several of the cases studied, no alternative mechanism could explain the buildup of water acidity and the increasing sulfur-dioxide emissions from fossil-fuel combustion and related acidification of precipitation.

The EPA's first systematic acid-rain study of Eastern U.S. lakes, unveiled by the National Wildlife Federation in August, found more than 9,000 lakes sensitive to acid rain; more than 2,400 of them already were acidic.

Both reports lent support to a federal proposal for controlling acidifying emissions. Issued in January by President Ronald Reagan's special envoy, former Secretary of Transportation Drew Lewis, and by William G. Davis, former premier of Ontario, Canada, the proposal recommended a five-year, $5 billion U.S. program to reduce sulfur emissions using "coal cleaning" technologies.

And while the acidification of the environment has been most closely scrutinized in Europe and North America, scientists at the Research Institute of Environmental Chemistry in Beijing reported acid rain is a serious and growing problem in China as well. Already half of all rain south of the Yangtze River has a pH of less than 5.6. (Anything less than 7 is acidic.)

Lead. Jan. 1, 1986, was the deadline for U.S. gasoline producers to complete their 91% reduction in the amount of lead permitted in gasoline—to 0.1 grams per gallon (0.026 g/liter). According to a 1986 report by the President's Council on Environmental Quality, the new standard was expected to reduce by at least 172,000 per year the number of U.S. children with high blood-lead levels. But that estimate was based on the assumption that more than 25 micrograms of lead per deciliter of blood is potentially toxic in children.

There was a growing scientific consensus that the toxicity level should be placed much lower. This was based on a number of new studies that showed adverse health effects— from reduced height and IQ scores in children, to elevated blood pressure in adults—among persons who had more than 10 micrograms.

In mid-November the EPA announced that it was considering a proposal to reduce the level of lead that it would allow in public drinking water, from 50 parts per billion to 20 parts per billion. Among the reasons it gave was a recommendation by its clean air science advisory committee that anything more than 10 micrograms of lead per deciliter be considered potentially toxic. The proposed reduction of 30 parts per billion would yield an estimated $800 million in largely health-related benefits, or seven times the projected cost of achieving the reduction. However, the agency noted, new data also showed that an estimated 40 million U.S. residents were drinking water with lead that exceeds the proposed standard.

Not everyone was satisfied with EPA's proposal. According to Ellen Silbergeld, a lead toxicologist with the Environmental Defense Fund (EDF) in Washington, DC, and a member of EPA's science advisory committee on lead in drinking water, the reduction would not provide a "margin of safety." In fact, she said, if one accepts that any body burden of lead above 10 micrograms per deciliter of blood is toxic, then more than 88% of all U.S. children and more than 75% of all U.S. adults carry unacceptable body burdens of lead.

And the problem is likely to become worse, Silbergeld believes, as the incidence of acid rain increases. An EDF study showed that as the acidity of drinking water in one New York City supply system increased, so did the quantity of lead that it leached from water pipes.

Drinking Water Legislation. On June 19, President Reagan signed into law the first piece of major U.S. environmental legislation of 1986 —amendments to the Safe Drinking Water Act of 1974. In the previous 12 years under that law, the EPA had set content limits for only 23 contaminants—a record that such critics as Sen. Dave Durenberger (R-MN), called "miserable, discouraging [and] disturbing." The new amendments not only require EPA to set limits within three years for another 83 contaminants, but also allow for civil lawsuits to compel EPA to implement those standards if the agency begins slipping behind its congressionally set timetable.

Superfund. Despite his concern over its $9 billion price tag, President Reagan on October 17 signed into law a bill to continue the so-called Superfund program for cleaning up hazardous waste sites in the United States. The final legislation, which emerged after more than five months of discussions between House and Senate negotiators, expanded the size of the program more than five-fold, for the first time established minimum standards for cleanup, and recommended that $500 million be used to initiate a program to clean up leaking underground storage tanks. It also required EPA to compile a list of the 275 substances most common to Superfund sites that pose the greatest threat to health.

JANET RALOFF, *"Science News"*

ESPIONAGE

Two well-publicized espionage cases in 1986 affected American-Soviet relations at the highest levels of government, for a while threatening prospects for a planned summit conference. The United States and the USSR also engaged in a series of diplomatic expulsions on spy charges.

The Daniloff-Zakharov Affair. On August 23, Gennadi F. Zakharov, A Soviet physicist employed by a United Nations agency, was seized on a New York City subway platform by agents of the Federal Bureau of Investigation (FBI) after he allegedly tried to buy secret documents relating to U.S. defense contracts. One week later, in a Moscow park, Nicholas Daniloff (*see* BIOGRAPHY), a Moscow correspondent for the American magazine *U.S. News & World Report,* was arrested by agents of the Committee for State Security (KGB) after being handed an envelope by an acquaintance, Mikhail Luzin, who said that it contained newspaper clippings. When opened, the envelope was found to contain two allegedly secret maps, but Daniloff protested that he had been set up by the KGB.

President Ronald Reagan wrote to Mikhail Gorbachev, general secretary of the Soviet Communist Party, claiming that Daniloff was not a spy and demanding his release. Gorbachev responded that Daniloff had been caught "red-handed" and would be placed on trial. Under these circumstances hopes for a summit meeting between the two leaders appeared to be dashed. Although Reagan insisted that no swap was involved, the situation was resolved when Daniloff was allowed to leave the USSR on September 29 without a trial. On the following day Zakharov left the United States after pleading no contest and receiving a court sentence of five years' probation. At the same time two prominent Soviet dissidents, physicist Yuri Orlov and his wife, also were allowed to leave the USSR. Two weeks later, Reagan and Gorbachev met in Iceland.

Tit-for-Tat Expulsions. Early in the year the United States ordered the USSR to reduce the number of staff members in its United Nations mission. On September 28 the United States charged that 25 members of the mission had engaged in espionage and ordered them to leave the country. On October 8 the USSR then expelled five American diplomats on the same charges. The United States retaliated on October 21 by ordering the expulsion of 55 Soviet diplomats, the largest single such expulsion of Soviet personnel. The USSR again replied by expelling five more U.S. diplomats and also prohibiting Soviet citizens from working at the U.S. Embassy in Moscow. The United States then ended the sequence of expulsions, claiming that Soviet espionage in the United States has been "decapitated."

AP/Wide World

Gennadi Zakharov, a Soviet employee of the UN, was arrested in New York on charges of spying on August 23. He was freed in a U.S.-Soviet exchange on September 30.

Covert Activities. Some light was thrown on the murky world of private undercover operations when, on October 5, a C-123 transport plane was shot down over Nicaragua. A captured American survivor, Eugene Hasenfus, admitted taking part in running supplies to the U.S.-backed "contras" fighting Nicaragua's Sandinista regime. In early interviews he suggested that these activities had a covert connection with an American airline, Southern Air, and with two Cuban-Americans who once had worked for the Central Intelligence Agency (CIA). Vice-President George Bush admitted having met one of these men, but he denied any knowledge of the Nicaragua flights, as did Southern Air, the CIA, and officials of the Reagan administration.

When Hasenfus went on trial in Nicaragua, however, he stated under oath that he was not certain who his true employers were. On November 15 he was found guilty of crimes against the state and was given the maximum sentence of 30 years. He was released in December in what Managua termed a gesture of peace to the United States.

In December the Sandinistas arrested another American, Sam Nesley Hall, and charged him with espionage for carrying maps of the area where Hasenfus was imprisoned.

Case Endings. The final sentence in the 1985 spy scandal involving retired Navy warrant officer John Walker, his brother Arthur, son Michael, and friend Jerry Whitworth was delivered on August 28, when Whitworth was given a term of 365 years in prison. The evidence against all four men showed that they had stolen important classified information from the Navy and that John Walker had passed it on to Soviet agents, although Whitworth's lawyers tried to present their client as having acted under the delusion that the secrets were being sold to Israel.

Aftereffects also were felt from another 1985 case, that of KGB officer Vitaly Yurchenko, who apparently had defected to the West but later escaped again to the USSR. Former National Security Agency analyst Ronald W. Pelton, who had been exposed by Yurchenko, was given a life sentence in December for conspiracy, espionage, and disclosing classified information to Soviet agents. Edward Howard, a former CIA operative also identified by Yurchenko, evaded FBI surveillance and escaped to the USSR. There he is believed to have warned the KGB about Adolf Tolchaev, a Soviet research institute worker who was found guilty of spying for the United States and executed in October.

Israel-Related Events. Jonathan J. Pollard, a former intelligence analyst for the Navy, and his wife pleaded guilty on June 4 to spying for Israel. The main charge was that Pollard reported on U.S. missile systems that could be sold to Iran. The Israeli government denied any involvement, and later in the year the Mossad, Israel's version of the CIA, also denied kidnapping disaffected Israeli scientist Mordechai Vanunu on British soil. Vanunu had told the *Sunday Times* of London that Israel operated a secret atomic weapons factory in the desert, and on October 5 the newspaper published the story in what experts considered convincing detail. Vanunu then disappeared.

Sting Operations. FBI agents made several arrests of persons who had believed they were offering secrets to the USSR for money. In March, Randy M. Jeffries, a messenger, was sentenced on this charge, and Robert D. Haguewood, a Navy petty officer, was indicted for offering to sell Navy secrets. In August, Airman 1st Class Bruce Ott was convicted on charges relating to the sale of information on spy aircraft, and in October former Air Force staff sergeant Allen J. Davies was arrested for trying to pass on secret data about Air Force reconnaissance programs.

A more high-level sting operation ended on June 20, when Soviet Air Force Col. Vladimir N. Izmailov was ordered expelled from the United States. He had been apprehended by FBI agents as he tried to retrieve secret documents planted by an American officer posing as a traitor.

Other Spy Stories. In February retired CIA analyst Larry Wu-Tai Chin was convicted of spying for China for 30 years. Chin claimed he was on a personal mission to reconcile China and the United States, but the People's Republic denied any involvement. On February 21, Chin was found hanging in his cell.

On June 19, Richard Miller, the only FBI agent ever charged with espionage, was convicted after an earlier trial had ended in a deadlocked jury. Miller's claim that he actually had been trying to infiltrate the Soviet intelligence service was endorsed by Soviet emigré Svetlana Ogorodnikov and her husband, who earlier had pleaded guilty to lesser spy charges.

British Mole? Rumors had been heard for some time that the late Sir Roger Hollis, who from 1956 to 1965 headed M15, Britain's equivalent to the FBI, had been a double agent, or mole, for the USSR. In an apparent legal maneuver to prevent publication of a book by a former M15 member, the British government declared Hollis guilty.

VINCENT BURANELLI
Coauthor, "Spy/Counterspy"

ETHIOPIA

The famine that had afflicted Ethiopia for two years was brought more under control in 1986 as a result of food aid from the West and the end of drought conditions. In other areas, the government took tentative steps to acquire economic and development aid from the Western world and drafted a new constitution, and a number of high-ranking officials defected to the West.

The Famine. The population "at risk" from starvation declined from nearly 11 million to 6.5 million in 1986. This significant improvement can be attributed to the onset of a normal rainy season, the hundreds of millions of dollars in food aid that poured into the country during 1985–86, and the resettlement program in which 510,287 families were moved from the arid north to the southwest. In addition, the "villagization" program relocated more than 3 million peasants from the interior to centralized villages; plans call for the eventual relocation of more than 30 million people.

International Affairs. Although closely allied militarily and politically with the Soviet Union, the Ethiopian government, urgently in need of economic and development assistance, moved to improve its relations with the West. It began compensating the United States for property it nationalized after coming to power, and allowed the U.S. Information Agency (USIA) to reopen its offices. In addition, Ethiopia's head of state Mengistu Haile-Mariam began negotiations with Mohamed Siad Barre, the pro-Western president of Somalia, in an effort to resolve disputes between the two countries, and concluded an agreement with Italy by which the Italian government is to contribute $220 million to the villagization project. In October, however, Foreign Minister Goshu Wolde, one of the chief proponents of rapprochement with the West, resigned.

Constitution and Defections. In late 1985 the government announced that it was preparing a new draft constitution; Ethiopia has been without a constitution since the revolution of 1974. The clauses of the proposed constitution were discussed by the various political structures in Ethiopia in late 1986.

ETHIOPIA • Information Highlights

Official Name: Socialist Ethiopia.
Location: Eastern Africa.
Area: 471,776 sq mi (1 221 900 km²).
Population (mid-1986 est.): 43,900,000.
Chief Cities (July 1980): Addis Ababa, the capital, 1,277,159; Asmara, 424,532; Dire Dawa, 82,024.
Government: *Head of state and government,* Mengistu Haile-Mariam, chairman of the Provisional Military Administrative Council (took office Feb. 1977).
Monetary Unit: Birr (2.07 birr equal U.S.$1, June 1986).
Gross Domestic Product (1983–84 U.S. $): $5,000,000,000.
Economic Index (Addis Ababa, 1984): *Consumer Prices* (1980 = 100), all items, 121.0; food, 124.0.
Foreign Trade (1984 U.S.$): *Imports,* $942,000,000; *exports,* $417,000,000.

In addition to Foreign Minister Wolde, three other Ethiopian officials—Dawit Wolde Giorgis, commissioner of relief and rehabilitation; his deputy, Berhanne Deressa; and Getachew Kibret, Ethiopian ambassador to France —resigned and sought asylum in the United States or Western Europe during 1985 and 1986. All four expressed disillusion with Mengistu's Communist regime, which Dawit blamed for the famine, and whose primary purpose, according to Berhanne Deressa, was "implanting a foreign ideology and an alien socio-political system" in Ethiopia.

Refugees and Dissidents. According to the United Nations High Commissioner for Refugees, in 1986 about one million Ethiopian refugees were living in Sudan, about 550,000 were in Somalia, and 16,700 were in Djibouti. This extraordinary movement of people out of the country is related to a variety of factors, chiefly the famine, dislocation caused by civil war in the Eritrea and Tigre regions, and political opposition to the government. According to the *International Herald Tribune* (Aug. 19, 1986), the U.S. Central Intelligence Agency has channeled hundreds of thousands of dollars to Ethiopian dissidents inside and outside Ethiopia over a period of several years.

The Ethiopian Jews who were secretly flown from the Sudan to Israel in 1985 have been resettled in that country. About 12,000 of them have been placed in absorption centers where they are being acculturated to Israeli society.

PETER SCHWAB
State University of New York at Purchase

ETHNIC GROUPS

U.S. minority groups spent much of 1986 defending ground gained over the past two decades, and with only mixed success. Civil-rights leaders expressed consternation as the Reagan administration challenged the viability of federal programs they had struggled to put in place to help minorities, including affirmative action in hiring and firing. Welfare reform and the funding of federal social-service programs are among the several battlegrounds. The federal Civil Rights Commission came under political attack for allegedly backsliding on racial issues, and its budget for fiscal 1987 was reduced from $12 million to $7.5 million.

Blacks. Affirmative action, one of the most significant achievements of civil-rights efforts, was refined by the Supreme Court. In the term ending in June, the court upheld employers' decisions to give preference to minorities in hiring but balked at giving the same preference in layoffs. The latter policy, it was ruled, would impose too harsh a penalty on whites who had more seniority than black coworkers.

Busing, another symbol of the civil-rights movement, received a blow when the Supreme Court declined to review cases from Norfolk, VA, and Oklahoma City, OK. The refusal sent a clear signal that a city can end a busing program once its schools are integrated, although black parents and civil-rights leaders had challenged the two cities on the basis that classrooms would become resegregated under the new ways of assigning students to schools.

Long-established leaders of the civil-rights movement came under fire themselves from some in the black community. Growing numbers of black scholars argued that programs designed to aid minorities have backfired, leading beneficiaries into dependency on federal assistance. The scholars said that the wage gap between blacks and whites is growing, and in fact a publication released by the Census Bureau in July revealed that blacks have accumulated ten times less wealth than have whites.

On election day 1986, Atlanta City Councilman John Lewis, who defeated Julian Bond, a fellow black and civil-rights activist, in a widely publicized primary, was elected to the U.S. House of Representatives in Georgia's fifth district; Democrat Mike Espy became the first black since Reconstruction to be elected to the House from Mississippi; William Lucas, a black former Democrat who became a Republican, was unsuccessful in his bid to win the governorship of Michigan; and Mayor Tom Bradley of Los Angeles lost his California gubernatorial race.

Hispanics. One issue of prime concern to Hispanics, immigration reform, was approved by Congress in October after years of wrangling. The Hispanic population did not, as in the past, uniformly oppose the action. As some members of Congress noted, their Hispanic constituents had urged the government to stem the flow of illegal aliens from south of the border on the grounds that the newcomers were taking away jobs by working for less money. The new law grants legal status to illegal aliens who can prove they were in the United States prior to January 1982.

One provision of the new law, however, continues to trouble Hispanics, because it punishes employers who hire illegal aliens. The fear is that Hispanics will have more difficulty finding jobs because of employer leeriness over hiring Hispanic-looking persons, because the employer would be subject to fines or a jail sentence should the employee turn out to be an illegal alien. Farming interests, which rely heavily on migrant labor, are somewhat protected by a special provision in the new law. (*See also* REFUGEES AND IMMIGRATION.)

Elections in November saw Bob Martinez become Florida's first Hispanic governor, and former migrant worker Raul Gonzalez became the first Hispanic to win statewide office when he was elected to the Texas supreme court. In California, on the other hand, voters endorsed a referendum making English the state's official language. Many Hispanics had fought the measure, branding it as xenophobic and as the first step in dismantling dual-language services such as bilingual education.

Asian Americans. The 5.1 million Asian Americans have the highest median income of any ethnic group in the United States, and their scholastic achievements are well documented. A growing number of Asian American leaders, however, assert that the view of this population as a "model minority" is a myth that needs debunking. Although second- and third-generation Asian Americans have become knitted into the fabric of U.S. society, say those leaders, recent immigrants from Vietnam, Cambodia, and Laos are still at loose ends. Further, the "model minority" reputation has had negative consequences. Racial tension and attacks on Asians are on the rise, prompting the Civil Rights Commission to hold hearings on anti-Asian violence.

The leaders in this ethnic group cite a number of reasons for such problems. First, the Asian population has become more visible with the recent influx of refugees from Southeast Asia. Asian Americans also have become scapegoats for people who resent the economic successes of Far Eastern nations. Finally, fear that Asian Americans will "take over" segments of the U.S. economy is fueling a backlash. As a result Asians are forming networks, such as the Coalition Against Anti-Asian Violence in New York, to educate the public, work with police, and respond to the needs of victims.

Japanese Americans continued their efforts to win compensation from the U.S. government for hardships suffered during World War II, when 110,000 of them were interned in relocation camps. The Supreme Court has agreed to decide whether or not surviving former detainees may sue the government for billions of dollars in lost property. Civil-rights violations are not in themselves a basis for filing suit, according to an earlier ruling by a lower court.

Philippine Americans closely watched events taking place in their homeland, as President Ferdinand Marcos was ousted and Corazon Aquino swept into office. In California, home to half the Philippine American population, loyalties were divided. Even so, thousands turned out to welcome the new president when a U.S. tour in September brought her to San Francisco.

Native Americans. American Indian tribes, aware that the flow of federal dollars to their reservations is slowing down, are turning increasingly to the private sector in search of tribal revenues. Most enterprises are modest, such as the new plant on Oregon's Warm Springs Reservation to manufacture Western-style shirts. Another new source of revenue is becoming more popular and at the same time more controversial—gambling on the reservations. About 80 of the 288 Indian tribes have opened casinos or bingo parlors in an attempt to attract tourist dollars. The rights of tribes to operate such establishments, however, are colliding with the rights of states to regulate gambling within their borders. States are concerned that Indian bingo will be infiltrated by organized-crime syndicates. The Supreme Court, in a case between California and two Indian "rancherias," agreed to decide whether a state, a tribe, or the federal government has the authority to regulate gambling on Indian reservations.

A century-old land dispute between the Navajo nation and the Hopi tribe in Arizona remained unresolved, despite Congress's intention that the conflict be settled by the summer of 1986. In 1974, the U.S. Congress had ordered about 10,000 Navajos, whose families had lived on Hopi land for generations, to move elsewhere by July 7, 1986. Hundreds of Navajos, however, refused to go, citing their ties to the land and decrying mass relocation as a violation of international law. Some elders threatened to fire upon any U.S. marshall or national guardsman who tried to move them, but the deadline came and went without a showdown. After that, the Bureau of Indian Affairs in effect postponed the relocation, at least until the federal government could meet its responsibility of providing housing and other amenities for the displaced Navajo families.

In Alaska, native organizations were trying to ensure that Indians, Eskimos, and Aleuts do not lose their aboriginal homelands, which are held as assets of 12 native-owned corporations. By 1991, Congress would permit native shareholders to sell their corporate stocks, sparking concern that the corporations (and the land) will fall into nonnative hands. Congress tried, but failed, to amend the law, and the issue was expected to come to a head in 1987.

CHERYL SULLIVAN
"The Christian Science Monitor"

EUROPE

Confidence in the West European economy was restored in 1986. The European Community (EC) showed further signs of renewed vigor as it welcomed Spain and Portugal as its 11th and 12th members. But the West European countries made little progress in coordinating their efforts against terrorism. They also remained just critical spectators as the two superpowers failed to reach an arms agreement.

Economic Revival. After a decade of economic depression initiated by dramatic rises in oil prices by the Organization of the Petroleum Exporting Countries (OPEC), West Europe enjoyed a mild but encouraging revival in 1986. Inflation, which fell to 2.8%, seemed under control. The rate of growth rose to 3%. High unemployment—a serious problem—appeared likely to drop by about 1.8% overall, although not in such strained economies as Britain's.

Owing to world conservation measures and lack of coordination of pricing and production among OPEC members, the price of oil fell rapidly early in 1986. As the purchaser of one third of all oil sold internationally, the 12 EC members were major gainers from the availability of cheap energy. This situation was expected to raise the EC growth rate as much as 1% per year and contribute to lowering inflation.

The reduction in the value of the U.S. dollar by 26% since early 1985 did not immediately reduce American purchases of European exports, but it boosted European receipts for goods already ordered. The falling dollar also induced American investors to purchase stocks and bonds in strong European currencies, and thereby pushed European bond and stock markets to record highs.

A further factor in the recovery was the success of governmental austerity policies undertaken earlier in the 1980s to combat inflation and unemployment. By devaluing the currency and controlling wage increases, for example, the Belgian government succeeded in halving inflation and ending its balance of payments deficit. The government of Christian Democrat Ruud Lubbers in the Netherlands stabilized the economy by reducing public sector spending in such areas as education and social security, while promising to lower unemployment by retraining programs and a reduction of the workweek to 36 hours.

The results of efforts of conservative governments to reduce the role of the state in economic administration by selling off nationalized companies were less easily assessed. British Prime Minister Margaret Thatcher took the lead. Since taking office in 1979, her government had sold off more than $11 billion worth of state-owned companies by 1986. In Italy, Socialist Premier Bettino Craxi reduced the vast losses of the Institute for Industrial Reconstruction, a state-owned complex of companies, by selling $3 billion of its holdings and cutting its work force by almost 50,000.

The sharpest change of policy occurred in France, where Socialist President François Mitterrand was compelled to appoint the right-wing Gaullist Jacques Chirac as premier after Chirac's two-party coalition defeated the Socialists in national elections in March. Chirac introduced a program for privatization of 65 state-owned companies, including several nationalized after World War II and others, among them several banks, taken over during the early years of the Mitterrand presidency. The sale of three major companies in chemicals, banking, and insurance was expected to realize $4.6 billion in 1987.

The EC. Membership in the European Community was clearly beneficial to its three new-

Syndication International from Photo Trends

France's President Mitterrand and Great Britain's Prime Minister Thatcher signed an agreement in February for the construction of a rail tunnel connecting the two countries under the English Channel. The "Chunnel," which Mitterrand called "the biggest construction project of the century," was to be completed by 1993.

est members: Greece, which joined in 1981, and Spain and Portugal, admitted on Jan. 1, 1986. Greece, faced with an inflation rate that reached 25% in 1985 and with stagnating production, turned to the EC for a two-year loan of $17.5 billion, promising in return a 15% devaluation of its currency and the end of indexing of wages to inflation.

Portugal, which expected to receive $270 million in transfers from the Community in 1986, began immediately to coordinate efforts of public agencies and private business to ensure that use of funds for EC-approved infrastructural investments would not be squandered by inefficient management. Spanish business prepared enthusiastically for new export opportunities within the Community, not least in neighboring Portugal, even though the conditions of entry prescribed a transition period of ten years before Spain would be fully integrated within the Common Market. Spain could, however, make its weight felt at once in Community policymaking, since it had been assigned 60 members in the European Parliament, the majority of them in the Socialist group; 2 members of the EC Commission, 1 judge in the European Court of Justice, and, perhaps most important, 8 votes in the Council of Ministers (compared with the ten votes of such larger members as Germany and France). Spain's presence in the Council not only strengthened the Mediterranean representation but also lessened the ability of the four largest states (Britain, France, Germany, and Italy) to dominate EC policy.

In December 1985 in Milan the council of heads of state or government approved changes in the EC constitutional mechanism that had been proposed earlier, and sent them on to the national parliaments for approval. These changes included majority voting in the Council of Ministers in some areas where unanimity had been required, an increase in the powers of the European Parliament, and measures for coordinating members' foreign policies.

At the December 1986 Council of Ministers meeting, the 12 leaders recognized that the EC was near bankruptcy and faced problems with trading partners, especially on food. But the difficult financial problems never made it on the agenda, and the group focused on more easily settled matters.

At year's end the United States announced plans for a 200% duty on gin, brandy, white wine, assorted cheeses, and various other foods imported from Western Europe. The Reagan administration said the move came in response to European trade policies that cost U.S. farmers $400 million annually. The Europeans came right back with threats of new barriers against American agricultural products.

Apartheid and Terrorism. Two major problems forced the Community to formulate a common political stance: South African apartheid and the increasing incidence of terrorism. In the face of mounting violence in South Africa, European governments were at first divided, with Britain and West Germany opposed to sanctions and the Dutch actively undertaking them. At the summit meeting in The Hague in June, however, the EC heads of state or government denounced the policies of the South African government and promised assistance to victims of apartheid. In September the Community placed an embargo on South African iron and steel.

Renewed terrorist violence in Europe at first provoked varying national responses. Only Britain actively supported the U.S. air attack on Libya in April as retaliation for Libyan participation in bombing an American-patronized discotheque in West Berlin. Mass demonstrations protesting the attacks occurred in several European cities. Confusion and mistrust of American tactics increased with the revelation that the United States had supplied arms to Iran in hope of receiving aid in freeing U.S. hostages in Lebanon. French Premier Chirac, nevertheless, worked to obtain the release of French hostages by concessions to Iran, and, in September, when bombings in Paris killed 9 people and wounded some 160, he attempted to use direct contacts with Arab governments and perhaps indirect contact with the terrorists to prevent future bombings.

After Britain broke diplomatic ties with Syria on grounds that it had collaborated in an attempt to blow up an Israeli airliner at London airport, the other EC members finally acquiesced in taking common action restricting Syrian diplomatic activity.

East-West Agreements. The threat of nuclear confrontation between the Western and Communist blocs continued to provoke antinuclear protests in Western Europe, especially after the spread to Europe of radioactive fallout from the accident in April at the Chernobyl nuclear plant in Russia demonstrated the dangers of even peaceful nuclear energy. Such parties as the Greens in West Germany used the opportunity to call for the withdrawal of West Germany from NATO and abandonment of the use of nuclear energy.

But most Europeans gained hope from the apparent improvement in relations between the Soviet Union and the United States that began at the meeting of Soviet leader Mikhail Gorbachev and President Reagan in Geneva in November 1985 and appeared to continue in early 1986 with exchange of proposals for large-scale dismantling of nuclear weapons. Hopes were dashed, however, at the second Reagan-Gorbachev meeting in Iceland in October 1986, which produced deadlock over U.S. plans to create a new nuclear defense system, the Strategic Defense Initiative.

E. ROY WILLIS
University of California, Davis

FAMILY

Economic pressures and other factors have brought important changes to family life in the United States, raising new concerns that were strongly evident in 1986. Those concerns included parental leave for working couples, day care, and the role of the father in the family. Some continuing problems—domestic violence and child abuse, abductions, and poverty among children—were also in the news.

Meanwhile, a trend toward childless families continued. In 1985, 29% of married women between the ages of 25 and 29 were childless, compared with 13% in 1960. Behind the trend were late marriages, high divorce rates, and the costs and complexities of raising children. Simultaneously, however, it was revealed that more babies were born in the United States than in any year since the mid-1960s.

Working Parents. A 1985 U.S. congressional study confirmed what many families already knew: average income, adjusted for inflation, has dropped in recent years. Meanwhile, despite declines in interest rates, the costs of owning or renting a home have remained at historic highs. The answer for many families with children has been for both parents to work outside the home. About 60% of mothers were working in 1986, up from about 45% a decade earlier. They included nearly 50% of mothers with children under one year old.

As a result, many parents were beset by competing pressures as they tried to balance job and care-giving duties. One controversial question was whether or not employers should grant leaves of absence for the birth of a child. While many countries have policies requiring such leaves, the United States does not, and state laws vary widely. About 80% of working women are likely to become pregnant during their careers, according to the Bureau of National Affairs (BNA).

Responding to demand, the number of companies providing parental leave quadrupled from 1982 to 1986. But many parents, especially those employed by small companies, still faced the choice of giving up their jobs or leaving a new baby in the care of someone else.

A bill, introduced in the House of Representatives in 1986, would require up to 18 weeks of unpaid parental leave every two years for the birth, adoption, or illness of a child, as well as 26 weeks of leave for any worker who is disabled. Companies would be required to keep health insurance and other benefits in effect and to provide the same or a comparable job when the employee returned to work. The leave provisions apply equally to women and men, avoiding the charges of discrimination that have plagued some state laws providing only for maternity leave.

Opponents of the bill argued that small companies would be unable to afford parental

© Ellis Herwig/Taurus

Parental leave not only for working mothers but for working fathers as well was a topic of concern and debate in the home, the workplace, and the U.S. Congress in 1986.

leaves, and the measure failed to receive full congressional approval in 1986. Meanwhile, Canada proposed a similar bill and began to develop plans for a national day-care system that would be funded by the government.

A BNA study released in 1986 also showed that the United States lagged behind other industrial countries in providing day care. About 2,500 U.S. companies offer some sort of child-care assistance to their employees, ranging from on-site care centers to vouchers that will help pay the bills at centers elsewhere. In some states, companies have started to band together to support day-care facilities. A pilot program in Massachusetts offers state loans to companies that want to set up centers. In San Francisco, a city ordinance passed late in 1985 required developers of downtown offices to provide space or funds for child care.

On the whole, however, day care in the United States remained haphazard in 1986, with many states requiring little training for day-care providers. Concern about the quality of child care led to more extensive training programs in several states, including California and Wisconsin. And a growing number of centers applied for accreditation by the National Association for the Education of Young Children.

The "New Father." Another trend evident in 1986 was the increased role played by fathers in child rearing. In the 1950s, raising children was women's work; fathers were often distant figures whose breadwinning roles excluded them from family life. As women have moved out into the work force, however, fathers have been called on to take up more child-care duties. Many have found they like it—they develop closer relationships with their children. Along with the trend has come a flurry of publications aimed at the father of the 1980s. For example, *fathers,* a magazine that made its debut in 1986, was described by its editor as a "hybrid between a parenting magazine and a men's magazine."

One result of the trend is that many fathers are facing the same conflicts between job and home life familiar to working mothers. According to some sociologists, employers have been slow to recognize the shifting roles—many assume that male executives have wives at home to care for their children. Often, then, a father's decision to become more involved in child raising has led to lower earning power and career expectations.

Balancing the trend to greater paternal involvement in 1986 was the fact that unpaid child support continued to be a major problem. Federal officials estimated that more than $3.5 billion in court-ordered child-support payments was going uncollected annually, with fathers responsible for the payments of 99% of the cases. With stiff federal guidelines behind them, many states began to crack down on the problem. Among their weapons were automatic wage withholding, improved computerized records, and increased cooperation among the states. Texas received a federal grant to develop a prototype computer network that would track child-support evaders nationwide.

Abuse in the Family. Police in a number of communities made headway against another persistent family problem, violence between spouses. Traditionally, the law has taken a hands-off approach to domestic violence, answering complaints but attempting to mediate between the spouses rather than arrest the abuser (in the vast majority of cases, the husband). A 1984 Minneapolis study showed, however, that a night in jail did more to cool domestic tempers than did mediation. Of abusers who were arrested and held overnight in jail, just 19% beat their spouse again within six months, compared with 35% in cases handled by other means. Several cities that have adopted the new approach back it up with prosecution and with counseling for victims. One goal is to convince the victims not to drop charges—a major problem in domestic violence cases.

At the same time, the number of cases of child abuse was reported to be increasing. Figures released in 1986, covering the year 1984, showed 1.5 million reported cases, ten times the number reported in 1963. However, experts were divided over whether the figures showed an actual increase in abuse or merely increased awareness on the part of the public, which led to more (often groundless) reports. One expert estimated that some 65% of reports eventually prove false.

Courts continued to grapple with the problems of prosecuting child-abuse cases, particularly those involving sexual abuse. On the one hand was pressure to ease restrictions on children's testimony, to make it easier for victims to come forward. On the other was concern about protecting the rights of the accused. In cases of intrafamily abuse, experts also debated whether counseling or prosecution was more effective.

The problem of missing and runaway children highlighted dangers outside the home. Estimates of missing children ranged as high as 1.5 million but were challenged widely. Meanwhile, a federal panel advised changing state and local laws to permit the police to detain all runaway and neglected children, to protect them from harm. In a week-long campaign in April, volunteers fingerprinted thousands of children in 2,800 shopping centers in the United States and Canada; the prints would provide identification should a child be abducted.

The volunteers also distributed safety booklets warning families of such dangers as leaving a child unattended while shopping. New books and games for children, warning against accepting rides from strangers and similar risks, also were available during the year. Some experts cautioned, however, that the messages they presented might cause children to become too fearful.

Poverty. A national lobby for children and a Senate panel devoted to children in poverty and impoverished families were proposed in 1986. According to testimony at a July Senate hearing, 21% of children lived in poverty in 1984, including half of those in single-parent homes and two thirds of all black children. Since children in poor families often drop out of school and thus have less earning power themselves, a cycle of poverty is set up. Adding to the problem is the number of teenage pregnancies, estimated at 1.25 million a year.

Internationally, the picture was grimmer. In a 1986 report, the United Nations Children's Fund (UNICEF) estimated that 15 million children under the age of five die each year, many from preventable diseases. Those who survive often suffer from malnutrition. UNICEF and other groups embarked on vigorous campaigns to change that picture, concentrating on immunization and medical treatment. Other programs focused on agricultural education, to allay the grinding poverty faced by children of the Third World.

ELAINE PASCOE, *Free-lance Writer*

Courtesy, Missoni

European designers, attempting to attract the somewhat reluctant 1986 consumer, tried their luck with fantasy and retro-fashion. Included in the effort were colorful knits by Missoni (top), made even more so when combined with patterned stockings; the Ungaro suit (lower right), somewhat reminiscent of another fashion era; and the popular bouffant cocktail dress by Lacroix for Patou (right).

© Niall McInerney

© Daniel Simon/Gamma Liaison

FASHION

Fashion in 1986 developed a split personality. Consumer purchasing reluctance forced stores to keep lean inventories and slowed orders at showrooms everywhere. A declining dollar and fear of terrorist bombings kept buyers away from European showrooms and tourists out of their boutiques. Hoping to encourage business, the fashion community found itself divided between those designers who felt that they should continue the traditional looks associated with their houses, and those who felt that only eccentric or exaggerated styles could stimulate interest and fashion creativity.

The classicists were mainly in the United States and included the designers Calvin Klein and Ralph Lauren. Established European design houses like St. Laurent, Givenchy, and Valentino also continued their tradition of elegant and expensive haute couture.

European Fashion. With the younger designers in Europe, however, fantasy and retro-fashion (fashion suggesting an earlier period)

American designers, feeling safer with the tried and true, opted for the classicist view of fashion in 1986. At left, some Calvin Klein designs offer the quality fabrics and careful tailoring of timeless clothing.

Photograph by Horst

were rampant. In Paris, Thierry Mugler revived the "flower power" 1960s with his rich-hippy looks that included bell-bottomed trousers and psychodelic prints, while Vivienne Woodward in London evoked the "Swinging London" of the same period with her minis and baby doll dresses. Emanuel Ungaro brought back the bustle and the cocoon while Christian Lacroix for Patou brought back the 1950s with umbrella skirts and empire-waisted trapeze dresses.

Jean-Paul Gaultier, meanwhile, drew on current East-West tensions and showed Cossack pants, Commissar uniform-like coats and suits, and scattered Cyrillic lettering over his knits. Even at Chanel, where modern classicism was born, Karl Lagerfeld went fanciful and showed cocktail dresses featuring bouffant skirts.

The Italians continued their tradition of superb tailoring but softened and feminized the mannish cuts, exaggerated shoulders, and dull colorations so prevalent in past seasons. Fuller, more graceful skirts topped by shorter, fitted jackets created more ladylike silhouettes. Even the big-coat, a constant in Milanese collections, was belted or smocked to control the fullness. Their knits, particularly those of the Missoni's and Mariuccia Mandelli for Krizia, remained as graphic and colorful as ever.

U.S. Fashion. On the North American side of the Atlantic, the classic components—skirts, blazers, trousers—exuded luxury. They conjured up an elegant and patrician world that was captured in Ralph Lauren's advertising and at his new New York boutique. Cashmere sweater sets paired with graceful mid-calf skirts eased by pleats or godets were done in jersey or lightweight tweed. Blazers of camel's hair, flannel, or quality worsteds and chesterfield or polo coats in cashmere, alpaca, or melton were the backbone of every collection. Gently tailored and fitted dressmaker suits with their subtle detailing were light years away from those Brooks Brothers clones of past seasons. Dresses featured the princess silhouette in supple jersey, crepe, or lightweight wovens. Suede and polished leathers were a staple for skirts, pants, and jackets; shearling in a new lightweight version took on city elegance in coats and jackets with sophisticated styling.

Special Influences. Snakeskin, lizard, and other reptile and animal skins continued to be popular for accessories and ready-to-wear accents, but the most prestigious and ubiquitous material was crocodile. There were crocodile skirts, jackets, bags, belts, and shoes shown in most collections, and copies were available.

Denim was given couture cachet when Karl Lagerfeld and Fendi featured it in shapely city suits which were decorated with embroidery or stitching and, in the United States, Giorgio Sant'angelo glamorized his denim suit with fancy fringed epaulets and gold beading.

In sportswear, besides the country-manor influence, safari looks inspired by the film *Out of Africa* were prevalent. Slim and full hunting skirts, culottes, walking shorts, and cargo pocketed pants, as well as camp shirts and the familiar belted bush jacket were done in khaki or sand poplin, twill, and chino. Primitive prints based on African tribal patterns were used for casual play clothes.

The increasing interest in bicycling, heightened by American Greg LeMond's win of the Tour de France bicycle race, inspired sportswear designers to incorporate the traditional cycling uniform of tights, thigh-length shorts, and colorful jerseys into exercise gear, loungewear, and especially swimwear.

This was also the year of the "Cola Wars"; Coca-Cola and Pepsi, aggressive and antagonistic rivals, both licensed their names to apparel and accessories manufacturers. The items were marketed for the same youthful consumer that was the target of their advertising efforts.

In accessories, classic Chanel-inspired items were everywhere. Quilted leather bags with chain handles, black-toed pumps, chain necklaces and belts, boater hats, hair bows and signature camellias were copied or adapted to create the tasteful elegance that was currently fashionable. Other timeless status accessories made comebacks, most notably the large alligator tote designed decades ago by Hermès that was popularized by Grace Kelly as well as the famous silk scarves in equestrian prints.

The comeback of the prom and the debutante dance brought with it more demure and innocent evening attire. Full skirted, off-the-shoulder or strapless confections of white or pastel taffeta, tulle, or moiré were popular. The more sophisticated party-goer opted for glamour, whether it was the dressed-down evening elegance of a long cashmere dinner dress or a beaded sweater worn with a full-length panne or velvet skirt. For more spectacular events, ball gowns trimmed with fur or feathers, beaded, sequinned, or embroidered were worn.

Trendy, current, and especially popular with youth were the khaki, bush-country styles popularized by the film "Out of Africa," and the casual, humorous clothing that carried the soft-drinks' motifs.

© James D. Wilson

Courtesy, PEPSI Apparel America

The New Male Seeks the Perfect Look

© Paula Kobylarz

"Mirror, mirror on the wall
Who's the fairest of them all?"

Today, the voice intoning that narcissistic rhyme might well be a baritone. For not since the days of Beau Brummell has the male pursued beauty and style as much as now. Nor, until now, have cosmetic companies and satellite industries provided the opportunities for such indulgence. The traditional feminine arsenal of beauty has been adapted for male use, and skin-care products, anti-aging creams and lotions, cleansing and firming masks, bronzers, sunscreens, hair tints, and styling mousses and gels are all being marketed for an eager and growing clientele. Also in use are specific items such as "Razor-burn Relief" and "Muscle Lotion," for use pre- or après exercise. Men are even pampering themselves with facials, body scrubs, facelifts, pedicures, and permanent waves.

This male-enhancement trend began with the fitness craze. Its motives were health-related, but the results gave men a new pride in their appearance and a desire to enhance and maintain it.

After the pride came the realization that personal and business success were easier to achieve when coupled with a more attractive and youthful appearance. Men came to view this "vanity" not as a vice but as a wise and practical business strategy—an investment in success.

Cosmetic companies that rang up sales of close to $50 million for men's skin-care products alone heartily endorsed this attitude, as did menswear manufacturers whose top-of-the-line fashions and accessories clothed the new male. And salons and department stores, encouraging this trend, set aside areas for male pampering.

Where will it all end? With "his" and "hers" makeup tables, or will the American male level off to a healthy, natural approach to caring for himself? Either way, a new market has been born, and isn't that the American way?

ANN M. ELKINS

Menswear. The menswear event of the year was the 100th anniversary of the tuxedo, created when Griswold Lorillard cut the tails off his dress coat and wore it to the Autumn Ball in Tuxedo, NY. This commemoration set the elitist tone for menswear. Aristocratic and moneyed was the look for both casual and business clothing. It was derived from use of the same luxury fabrics and materials that characterized women's fashions. Classic colors and subtle textures and patterns predominated. While the fit still retained a relaxed ease it was due more to superior tailoring than to the former oversized cut. In casual wear there was a mix of sportswear that combined rustic tweeds with rich leathers and knits.

The right accessories were important elements in achieving the proper look. These were the richly woven silk tie, crocodile belt and shoes, antiqued cuff links, silk pocket square, the lean polished leather attache case, and a simple watch.

ANN M. ELKINS
Fashion Director, "Good Housekeeping"

FINLAND

Finland continued its traditional policy of neutrality in 1986, condemning both international terrorism and the U.S. bombing of Libya in April for its support of terrorist activities.

Foreign Affairs. Early in the year Finland marked the 30th anniversary of its membership in the Nordic Council, an advisory body promoting cooperation among the Scandinavian countries. It continued to encourage the development of high technology not only at home but throughout Europe by its participation in the European Research Agency (Eureka).

Finnish participation in the United Nations Interim Force in Lebanon (UNIFIL) continued. On October 6, Finnish Maj.-Gen. Gustav Hägglund, the UNIFIL commander, called on Israel to withdraw from the western half of its security zone in southern Lebanon to test UNIFIL's ability to prevent Palestinian guerrillas from infiltrating the zone and attacking Israel.

Domestic Affairs. Although the nation's economic growth rate was expected to drop from 2.8% in 1985 to 2% in 1986, the basic overall strength of the Finnish economy encouraged increasing foreign participation in the Finnish stock market. The average price per share rose 65% between mid-1985 and mid-1986. In August the Bank of Finland, the equivalent of the U.S. Federal Reserve Bank, temporarily raised its interest rate to borrowers to 40%.

The Soviet Union remains Finland's leading trading partner, with energy products representing 80% of Soviet exports to Finland. Because trade agreements between the two countries call for a balance between imports and exports, the drop in world oil prices reduced Finnish exports to the Soviet Union.

In June, Oy Wärtsila A.B. and the Valmet Corporation announced the merger of their shipbuilding operations. The merger was expected to result in the layoff of about 4,000 Finnish workers.

In March the central organization of the 250,000-member Finnish Trade Unions called a strike for higher wages, making life difficult for the Finnish people. When thousands of government employees joined the strike in April, 90% of all government offices closed and railroad, airline, and postal-service operations ceased. In mid-May President Mauno Koivisto introduced legislation in parliament to end the strike, which was eventually called off.

In Finland, which borders on the Soviet Union, the disaster at the Chernobyl nuclear reactor in the Soviet Union in April caused a great deal of concern. The government introduced a number of measures to prevent the consumption of food that might have been contaminated by nuclear radiation and joined the other Nordic countries in issuing guidelines on future safety measures for nuclear reactors. It was estimated that Finland lost about $100 million in income from foreign tourists.

Finnish presidential campaigns are usually conducted over a long period of time. The next presidential election would not be held until 1988, but the Center Party announced at midyear that its candidate in 1988 would be the current foreign minister, Paavo Väyrynen.

Finns mourned the death on August 31 of former President Urho K. Kekkonen. He had served as president from 1956 to 1981 (*see* OBITUARIES).

ERIK J. FRIIS
"The Scandinavian-American Bulletin"

FINLAND • Information Highlights

Official Name: Republic of Finland.
Location: Northern Europe.
Area: 130,159 sq mi (337 113 km²).
Population (mid-1986 est.): 4,900,000.
Chief Cities (Dec. 31, 1984): Helsinki, the capital, 484,263; Tampere, 168,150.
Government: *Head of state,* Mauno Koivisto, president (took office Jan. 27, 1982). *Head of government,* Kalevi Sorsa, prime minister (took office February 1982). *Legislature* (unicameral)—Eduskunta.
Monetary Unit: Markka (4.835 markkaa equal U.S.$1, Oct. 17, 1986).
Gross National Product: (1984 U.S.$): $50,100,-000,000.
Economic Indexes (1985): *Consumer Prices* (1980 = 100), all items, 150.6; food, 157.2. *Industrial Production* (1980 = 100), 116.
Foreign Trade (1985 U.S.$): *Imports,* $13,215,-000,000; *exports,* $13,616,000,000.

FISHERIES

Until a few years ago per capita consumption of fishery products in the United States seemed stagnant at about 10 pounds (4.5 kg) a year, but this trend changed as Americans became more concerned with health and nutrition. Annual per capita consumption now hovers near 15 pounds (6.8 kg), and the official 1985 figure of 14.5 pounds (6.6 kg) represented an unprecedented increase of .8 pound (.36 kg) over the previous year.

The more nutrition research findings that are reported, the better fishery products fare. Recent studies have vindicated those parents of a couple of generations ago who forced their children to take cod-liver oil. These studies have shown that the "good" polyunsaturated Omega-3 fatty acids found in some fish moderate the production of eicosanoids by "bad" Omega-6 polyunsaturated fats. Although eicosanoids are required for proper functioning of the body's natural signaling process, there is evidence that too many of them can cause heart attack and cancer.

The coast-to-coast demand for Louisiana's 200-year-old Cajun and Creole cuisines, which rely heavily on seafood, has been remarkable. The phenomenon is all the more amazing for having sprung from a single dish—New Orleans chef Paul Prudhomme's blackened redfish. In 1983 a redfish catch of 210,000 pounds (95 256 kg) from U.S. waters in the Gulf of Mexico was enough to supply the demand. By July 1986, 10 million pounds (4.5 million kg) had been landed, and by late August the National Marine Fisheries Service was asking the secretary of commerce to ban commercial fishing of the species in federal Gulf waters until 1988.

In spite of the increased demand for seafood, the production sector of the U.S. fishing industry has remained depressed. Most domestic demand now is met by imports, which in 1985 accounted for a record-breaking 64.4% of the 9.2 billion pounds (4.1 billion kg) of edible fishery products consumed and 58.4% of the total edible and industrial products. Domestic production reached its all-time high in 1980, with almost 6.5 billion pounds (2.9 billion kg) of combined edible and industrial landings. Total 1985 landings of less than 6.3 billion pounds (2.86 billion kg) were the lowest since 1981.

U.S. producers complain that their inability to compete with cheap imports—particularly from Canada, where commercial fishing is government subsidized—is a basic cause of their woes, but there are other factors. The development of condominiums and sea walls along coastal waters has made some prime breeding waters uninhabitable. The fishing fleet was over-built, and the explosive increase in insurance costs has left many boats fishing without insurance. Boat-building has suffered severely, and a number of yards have shut down.

WILLIAM A. SARRATT, *"The Fish Boat"*

FLORIDA

The explosion of the space shuttle *Challenger* just after liftoff from Kennedy Space Center on January 28 cast a dark cloud over the first half of 1986 in Florida. Investigation into the disaster revealed a need for design changes in the shuttle's booster rockets, and future launches were put off until early 1988. (*See* feature article, page 36.) But despite the setback to the space program, the year was one of continued growth and change for Florida.

Elections. In November, after some vicious campaigning, Floridians elected a new U.S. senator and a new governor. Democratic Gov. Bob Graham defeated incumbent Republican Sen. Paula Hawkins by a wide margin in the Senate race. Bob Martinez, mayor of Tampa, became Florida's first Republican to be elected governor in 20 years by soundly defeating Democrat Steve Pajcic, a former state representative from Jacksonville.

Two of the hotter issues placed before voters in referendums were a proposal to permit

---

```
FLORIDA · Information Highlights

Area: 58,664 sq mi (151 939 km²).
Population (1985 est.): 11,366,000.
Chief Cities (July 1, 1984 est.): Tallahassee, the capi-
    tal, 112,258; Jacksonville, 577,971; Miami,
    372,634; Tampa, 275,479; St. Petersburg, 241,294.
Government (1986): Chief Officers—governor, D.
    Robert Graham (D); lt. gov., Wayne Mixson (D).
    Legislature—Senate, 40 members; House of Rep-
    resentatives, 120 members.
State Finances (fiscal year 1985): Revenue,
    $13,798,000,000; expenditure, $12,854,000,000.
Personal Income (1985): $156,184,000,000; per cap-
    ita, $13,742.
Labor Force (June 1986): Civilian labor force,
    5,655,500; unemployed, 342,100 (6.0% of total
    force).
Education: Enrollment (fall 1984)—public elemen-
    tary schools, 1,061,736; public secondary,
    462,371; colleges and universities, 451,392. Pub-
    lic school expenditures (1983–84), $4,401,000,000
    ($3,201 per pupil).
```

casino gambling, which was turned down by a wide margin (as it was in 1978), and one for a state lottery, which was approved resoundingly.

Legislation. In an effort to cut down on highway fatalities, the 1986 legislature passed a mandatory seat-belt law; warnings were given to violators until January 1987, when penalties were to be imposed. Several counties also passed open-container ordinances aimed at taking alcoholic beverages out of the hands of motorists, at least while driving.

The state legislature also approved several measures, including insurance-rate cuts and caps on liability awards, designed to reduce the skyrocketing cost of commercial liability insurance. The state's cigarette tax was increased, and property taxes and tuition for state university students were raised to boost school funding. Another new law required the clean-up of leaking underground gasoline storage tanks. A

Democratic Gov. Bob Graham spent more than $5.5 million in a successful campaign for the U.S. Senate. He outpolled the incumbent, Paula Hawkins, by more than 330,000 votes.

AP/Wide World

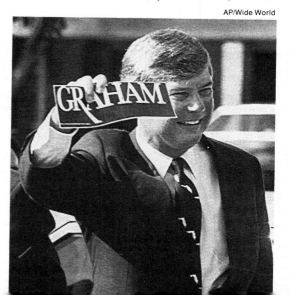

Former Tampa Mayor Bob Martinez (second from right) became Florida's first Hispanic governor and its first Republican governor in 16 years. He defeated Steve Pajcic.

AP/Wide World

"whistleblower" law protected employees of government agencies and contractors from reprisals should they report wrongdoing on the part of their employers.

Economy. The Sunshine State's economy was pronounced fit despite the troubles of several major employers, including Eastern Airlines, which was taken over by Texas Air, and IBM, which contended with slumping personal computer sales. The citrus crop—threatened by disease at home and by competition abroad—was spared the type of harsh winter weather that had decimated crops in 1984 and 1985. Retail citrus prices were low throughout the year. The hurricane season was one of the lightest in years, sparing the state serious storm damage.

Various studies showed Florida growing at a phenomenal rate, with jobs increasing at nearly three times the national level in the first half of the 1980s. The problems that come with growth continued, too. Crime was on the upswing in 1986, and police agencies said that one major culprit was crack, a smokable form of cocaine. Deaths from crack were up, reportedly averaging ten a month. Fast-growing cities such as Orlando wrestled with problems in housing and transportation. Miami's first Cuban-born mayor, Xavier Suarez, sought cooperation among the city's many ethnic groups in his first full year in office.

Environment. A master land-use plan to control development in the ecologically sensitive Florida Keys was adopted despite some resistance. A congressional move to protect more of the Everglades was delayed for at least a year, but the state government joined with a coalition of environmental groups in proposing a series of measures to restore and protect the swamp. The plans included unleashing the channeled Kissimmee River north of Lake Okeechobee, reflooding drained farmland, and rerouting proposed highways, at an estimated cost of $300 million. Conflict arose between property owners in some of the affected areas and environmentalists who saw the swamp as vital to the state's water supply. Meanwhile, federal and state agencies cooperated in efforts to correct algae blooms in Lake Okeechobee, a prime source of drinking water for central Florida.

Whales beached themselves on both coasts during the year, near Key West and Naples. Efforts to keep them alive failed, as they had in previous beachings, and marine experts could not agree on why the whales had lost direction.

GREG MELIKOV
State News Desk, "Miami Herald"

FOOD

The food industries of the United States, Canada, and other major exporters faced problems in 1986, as increased agricultural production coincided with reduced foreign markets. Falling prices for grains and other commodities deepened the financial crisis of small farms and forced agribusinesses and farm cooperatives to sell off assets. In the southeastern United States, extended drought conditions caused hundreds of millions of dollars in food crop and livestock losses. Food production and supply continued to show modest improvement in sub-Saharan Africa, though famine was still widespread.

World Food Production. The total world output of grains and oilseeds was expected to reach an all-time high in 1986, even though stocks of nearly every major food category were already high from the record production levels of the previous year. In 1985 total world food production increased an estimated 2%. U.S. output was about the same as in 1984, while food production in both Eastern and

Western Europe was about 2% below the record 1984 amount. Soviet production remained at about the same level, while China's output dropped slightly after increasing more than 10% for three consecutive years. The United States, Western Europe, USSR, and China all were expected to show growth in 1986.

The composition of food production worldwide has been in the process of change over the past 35 years. Usage of cereals, oilseeds, and meats has increased significantly, while the use of root crops and dairy products has declined. Currently it is estimated that animal products constitute about 15% of the global average caloric intake, with meat products accounting for 7%; milk products, 4%; fats and oils, 2%; and eggs and fish, about 1%. People in North America and Europe ingest about 30% of their total calories from animal products, compared with 8% for Africans and 6% for South, East, and Southeast Asians, excluding Japan and China.

Sub-Saharan Food Production. After several years of drought and civil strife, food production in Africa south of the Sahara Desert reached a new high in 1985, with further increases expected in 1986. Sub-Sahara Africa's combined output of wheat, rice, and coarse grains totaled about 60 million metric tons in 1985. This was one third above the 1984 harvest and 13% more than the 1981 to 1983 average. However, the recovery from the 1984 famine in many of the countries was not complete. In Ethiopia, Angola, and Mozambique, food emergencies continued. Although Ethiopian cereal grain production increased 10% in 1985, it was still less than the 1981 to 1983 average. In Sudan, Chad, and other Sahelian countries, cereal grain production improved, but local food shortages continued in many areas of these countries.

U.S. Food Supply. Production increases for individual U.S. commodities showed wide variation in 1985, with distinct differences also expected in 1986. Commercial production of red meats (beef, veal, pork, and lamb) rose marginally (+0.36%) in 1985, while output of poultry meats (broilers and turkeys) increased 5%. Combined grain (wheat, rice, and corn) production was approximately 11.8% higher than the 1984 total, with actual declines anticipated for 1986. Figures for 1985 showed declines in U.S. production of fruit and vegetable crops, attributed mainly to bad weather conditions and reduced plantings. Florida's citrus crop rebounded somewhat in 1986 after three years of freeze damage. Commercial vegetable production decreased about 3% in 1985 because of reduced plantings.

Consumer Food Prices. The U.S. Consumer Price Index for food for the first nine months of 1986 registered a 2.6% increase over 1985, while 1985's index averaged 2.7% above the 1984 index. A summer drought in the southern United States during 1986 brought on higher prices for poultry, eggs, and many fruits and vegetables.

The general inflation rate for 1985 had been about 4%. In individual commodities for the same period, cattle prices were depressed, and supplies of beef were relatively large, causing beef prices to edge downward for much of the year. Pork prices remained about even with those of 1984. Although poultry supplies were higher in 1985, consumer demand was strong, and poultry prices averaged only about 1% lower in 1985 than in 1984. Retail prices for cereals and bakery products increased about 3.5%, reflecting increased marketing costs. Fresh fruit prices were up about 11% during 1985, while vegetable prices were down 5%.

U.S. Food Industry. Because of economic difficulties in American agriculture, many jobs related to the agricultural sector were lost. These included nearly 83,000 in food processing plants and an additional 26,000 in the area of food storage. On the plus side, poultry processing plants increased their employment by 24,000, and makers of pasta, cheese, breakfast cereal, chocolate, cookies, crackers, and sausage increased employment by 15,000.

The microwave oven remained one of the fastest selling home appliances in the United States, a fact, it has been suggested, that reflects the surging demand for convenience foods. As a result major food processors were developing a line of prepackaged foods, designed specifically for microwave cooking. A good example was the introduction of a prepackaged microwave pizza by Pillsbury. The pizza is enclosed in a special package that contains a "susceptor" in the packaging material that absorbs microwave energy and raises the temperature sufficiently to cause browning of the pizza crust. Additional microwave cooking items included quick frozen vegetables, meat entrées, and complete dinners.

Another line of products that has gained acceptability nationwide is imitation processed meat products, prepared from deboned and shredded poultry meat. Included among these are chicken and turkey frankfurters, turkey ham, chicken and turkey bologna, and a list of about 50 other types of meat products. In 1985 chicken and turkey frankfurters accounted for about 20% of the total frankfurter market. From a nutritional viewpoint, the chicken frankfurter contains much less fat, cholesterol, and calories than beef or pork frankfurters.

In packaging, the American Can Company introduced a light, shatter-resistant, squeezable plastic bottle, called the Gamma bottle, that is both moisture and oxygen impermeable.

In July the Food and Drug Administration banned the use of sulfite preservatives in fresh vegetables and fruits. Sulfites had been linked to 13 deaths and many illnesses.

DAVID A. EVANS
University of Massachusetts

A conservative victory in legislative elections March 15 led to the naming of Jacques Chirac, left— the mayor of Paris and leader of the neo-Gaullist Rassemblement pour la République—as prime minister. His swearing in March 20 marked the beginning of a power-sharing arrangement with Socialist President François Mitterrand.

© Serblat-Keystone Paris/Picture Group

FRANCE

France's political life in 1986 was dominated by a power-sharing arrangement, known as "cohabitation," between conservative Prime Minister Jacques Chirac and Socialist President François Mitterrand. Foreign policy was aimed at maintaining a strong French position in Lebanon and improving relations with Syria and Iran, which was linked to a key domestic priority: avoiding new waves of terrorism at home.

Politics. With parliamentary elections approaching in March, the first weeks of 1986 were marked by intense campaigning in which leftists defended their record since their tumultuous victory five years earlier. But polls showed that the Socialist government of Prime Minister Laurent Fabius would probably lose its majority in the National Assembly.

"Socialism has been a failure," asserted the first sentence of the joint platform of the two main opposition parties, the Gaullist Rally for the Republic (RPR) and the centrist Union for French Democracy (UDF). Defending the record, Finance Minister Pierre Bérégovoy announced in January that inflation had slowed to a rate of 4.7%, the lowest in 20 years. He said the government would achieve a 2.5% rate in 1986, amid accelerating government-sponsored efforts to deregulate the French economy.

Conservative politicians, led by Paris Mayor Jacques Chirac (*see* BIOGRAPHY), insisted on the need for law and order and for crackdowns on immigrants; they emphasized the record unemployment rate of about 10.5%.

On March 15 the key allied conservative parties, led by the RPR, won a narrower-than-expected victory against the Socialists, gaining control of 286 seats. This was three short of an absolute majority of 289 deputies in the 577-member chamber. The Socialists wound up with 212 seats, thus remaining France's largest party. The extreme-right National Front and the Communists each elected 35 supporters.

The conservative victory meant that for the first time since the Fifth Republic was established in 1958, a president and prime minister from opposing political camps would govern together. Mitterrand, whose seven-year term ends in 1988, offered the premiership to Chirac, who accepted formally on March 20 and immediately formed a new government, representing a conservative, RPR-led coalition. Édouard Balladur was named minister for the economy, finance, and privatization. Jean-Bernard Raimond became foreign minister, while André Giraud was given the ministry of defense.

Chirac on March 20 announced plans to lift remaining price controls and privatize leading industrial companies and banks nationalized by the Socialists. He also pledged to restore parliamentary majority voting (instead of the proportional system) and to strengthen internal security.

On the day Chirac took office, a bomb exploded in a crowded Paris shopping arcade, killing 2 people and wounding 28. By late November, following other terrorist attacks, the death toll was 11, with more than 160 persons wounded.

Paris was rocked by terrorist bombings throughout the year. On July 11 police inspector Marcel Basdevant was killed in a bombing at a downtown police annex, left. The domestic left-wing terrorist group Direct Action claimed credit. Arab groups claimed responsibility for a host of other attacks.

© J. Pavlovsky/Sygma

In his first major policy statement, Chirac told the National Assembly on April 9 that unemployment was the major problem facing the country, and he presented a program that stressed reform and more freedom for business. He confirmed that privatization of 65 industrial and insurance companies, banks, and financial groups would be implemented over five years. He said the government would work to shift responsibility from the state to the individual. He also emphasized that the criminal law on terrorism would be amended and a minimum 30-year prison sentence introduced for capital crimes. He called for stricter measures to expel foreigners and for increased powers for the police.

The government's proposal to return France to majority voting was narrowly approved by the National Assembly on May 23. In a major victory for employer associations, a law was passed on June 8 allowing companies to lay off workers without having to seek approval from government labor authorities. The immigration bill also was approved—against strong leftist opposition—providing for tightened conditions for long-term stays in France and easier expulsion of foreign immigrants.

Distancing himself early on from the government, Mitterrand told the National Assembly that it "had the task of determining and conducting the policies of the nation" but would be answerable "to all French citizens." As Chirac's coalition pushed his program through parliament, Mitterrand spoke out against some initiatives but accepted others.

Following two weeks of student protests, Chirac on December 5 announced that the government would withdraw a university reform bill. The measure would have increased modest fees and given universities the right to issue their own diplomas. As the violent demonstrations were unfolding, Mitterrand had urged

Chirac to drop the plan, enhancing the president's prestige, polls showed.

Economy. France entered 1986 with a declining inflation rate, the notable bright spot in the economy. The government announced on January 21 that the 1985 trade deficit had fallen only slightly from 1984, to 24 billion francs (about $3.5 billion) primarily because of an upsurge in imports of capital goods. Expectations were that trade would remain in deficit until early 1987.

Growth of the economy remained moderate throughout 1986, rising to about 2.3% at year's end, compared with 1.1% for 1985. Most analysts agreed that the government would not attain its 1987 goal of 2.8% growth.

Partly to improve France's competitiveness, the new Chirac government on April 6 agreed to devalue the franc as part of a realignment of currencies in the European Monetary System. During a meeting of Common Market finance ministers in the Netherlands, the franc was devalued by 3%, following unsuccessful efforts by French Finance Minister Balladur to obtain an 8% cut. Balladur told newsmen that the move was a "precondition" for a package of fiscal reforms and austerity measures, which he announced hours later in Paris. As part of the realignment, West Germany and the Netherlands raised their currencies by 3%.

The Balladur reform measures, which were implemented in a 1986 supplementary budget announced April 16, contained a cut in business taxes, plans to sell shares in partially state-owned companies, changes in taxation on the French bond market, and a major job-creation program for youth. Spending in the 1987 budget, Balladur said, would for the first time in 30 years rise less swiftly than prices, with the planned budget deficit projected at 2.5% of gross domestic product (GDP), compared with 2.9% in 1986.

French banks on April 17 continued a gradual trend in lowering interest rates by cutting their base lending rate to 10.1% from 10.5%. Less than a month later, Chirac pledged the government to remove all remaining exchange controls by the end of the year, which he termed "something of a revolution." However, Yvon Gattaz, president of the National Council of French Employers, termed the economic situation in France "alarming." He called for more vigorous cuts in interest rates, taxes, and social charges.

Tensions and disputes marked some major Franco-U.S. investment projects. A notable instance involved stalled negotiations between Walt Disney Company and the French government for building a $2.2 billion theme park near Paris. The main obstacles were legal, including a demand by Disney that any disputes be resolved by international arbitration. French authorities insisted that future disputes be resolved in the local courts. An agreement was expected early in 1987.

Several large state-owned French companies completed substantial investments in the United States during 1986. Rhône-Poulenc, a chemical manufacturer, announced on November 14 that it was acquiring the agricultural chemical business of Union Carbide Corporation for between $540 and $580 million. Compagnie Générale d'Électricité (CGE), France's largest telecommunications company, said in late November that it had assured financing for acquisition of ITT Corporation's interests in Europe. CGE had agreed earlier to pay ITT $1.5 billion; the French company would become the second-largest maker of telecommunications equipment after AT&T.

The murder by terrorists of Georges Besse, chairman of Renault, on November 17 raised questions about the future of the ailing state-owned automaker. A Paris newsletter reported that Renault had begun making profits in September. The company lost 10.93 billion francs (about $1.6 billion) in 1985 and had been expected to lose about half that amount in 1986. The revised loss for 1986 was estimated between 2.5 and 5 billion francs (about $350–$700 million); there was widespread consensus that Besse's successor would have to accelerate cost-cutting drastically—notably in labor—and possibly sell Renault's 46.1% shareholding in American Motors, the U.S. car manufacturer. Raymond Levy, a French steel executive, was named the new chairman on December 16.

Foreign Affairs. Foreshadowing tensions with Washington, the Socialist government on January 8 said it wanted to first study President Ronald Reagan's announcement that the U.S. administration was imposing economic sanctions against Libya. Washington had appealed for allied support, but similarly cool reactions came initially from Britain, West Germany, the Netherlands, and Japan. The allies, notably France, argued that sanctions would be ineffective.

Meantime, despite the growing stresses over direct sanctions, Defense Minister Paul Quiles said February 17 that France was deploying a "deterrent force" in Chad in response to an attack against government forces by Libyan-backed Chadian rebels. Although the "deterrent force" was modest in strength, 1,500 French paratroopers in the neighboring Central African Republic were placed on alert. This represented the fourth time that France had intervened militarily in its former colony since Chad achieved independence in 1960.

The Libyan government had accused Mitterrand of being "a pawn" of Reagan, but Chadian President Hissène Habré on February 25 charged that Libya's "expansionist aims" were responsible for his country's continuing civil strife. Washington strongly approved the French move.

Amid growing speculation about impending U.S. military action against Libya, American warplanes on April 14 bombed Tripoli and

© Witt/Gamma-Liaison

President François Mitterrand (second from left) strolls in Moscow with Soviet General Secretary Mikhail Gorbachev during a four-day visit in July. Arms control and U.S.-Soviet relations were the central topics of discussion.

Benghazi. That triggered a major diplomatic incident that continued to strain French-U.S. relations in subsequent months. Reagan's representatives, UN Ambassador Vernon Walters, had met with Mitterrand and Chirac in Paris on April 13. But they jointly refused him permission for overflight by U.S. bombers. As anti-French sentiment erupted in the United States, both Chirac and Mitterrand remained silent. French officials confirmed the refusal, saying it had been a joint decision under the cohabitation power-sharing arrangement. Valéry Giscard d'Estaing, former president and head of the UDF, reflected large segments of opinion, however, when he said that the raid was justified and France should have been more cooperative.

French officials, speaking privately, said the refusal stemmed from Chirac's attempt to build a Middle Eastern policy and from fear for the safety of French hostages in Lebanon. They emphasized that Reagan had avoided prior consultations. Soon, however, the Chirac government began taking a tougher anti-Libyan stance, along with other European Community (EC) governments, which feared terrorist reprisals following the raid. France expelled four unidentified Libyans April 18. Several days later, Chirac pledged to cooperate with Washington in fighting international terrorism.

This shift greatly contributed to the successful outcome of the annual economic summit meeting of the seven main industrialized democracies held in Tokyo May 4–6. In sharp contrast to the 1985 Bonn summit, at which Mitterrand and Reagan clashed, France supported the final communiqué, which denounced terrorism and singled out Libya. It was the first time Mitterrand had agreed to allow a summit in which he participated to address a major noneconomic issue. He was accompanied by Chirac.

France announced July 7 that it and New Zealand had agreed to settle their differences over France's role in the 1985 maiming and sinking in Auckland harbor of the *Rainbow Warrior*, a boat operated by the Greenpeace environmentalist protest group. With UN Secretary-General Javier Pérez de Cuéllar mediating, the accord stipulated that the two French agents imprisoned for the bombing, Maj. Alain Mafard and Capt. Dominique Prieur, would leave New Zealand but would have to spend three years at France's military garrison on the Pacific atoll of Hao. In return, France agreed to pay New Zealand $7 million in damages and to apologize in writing.

Mitterrand concluded a four-day visit to the USSR on July 10 by telling a news conference in Moscow that he considered Soviet leader Mikhail Gorbachev a "man of his time," and he characterized recent Soviet arms proposals as "fairly sensational." The French president reiterated France's refusal to include its independent nuclear striking force in any U.S.-Soviet arms negotiations.

Although Mitterrand repeatedly affirmed that he had prime constitutional responsibility for foreign affairs and defense, practical responsibility gradually shifted to Chirac and the government, particularly regarding the Middle East. On October 8, Chirac said the government had no proof that a foreign government was behind the wave of terrorist attacks in Paris. His statement contrasted sharply with assertions by French officials and allies that Syria and Iran may have supported the terrorists.

Chirac repeatedly denied that France was negotiating with any government supporting terrorism, notably for the release of at least seven French hostages being held in Lebanon. But French officials acknowledged that the government was seeking to improve its relations with both Syria and Iran. Revelations that the Reagan administration also had been dealing with Iran over American hostages—in fact, had been selling arms—greatly strengthened Chirac's hand.

In a spectacular move on November 11, two French hostages were flown to Paris after being freed in Damascus by kidnappers who had held them in Lebanon. Then on December 24, in a Christmas eve "gesture of peace" by pro-Iranian Shiite Muslim extremists there, another French hostage was released. As the year ended, however, at least four more remained in Lebanon, including two diplomats.

On November 17, the foreign ministry announced that France and Iran had signed an agreement under which France would pay Iran $300 million as the first step in ending a seven-year-old financial dispute. The payment represented a share of a $1 billion loan made by the Shah of Iran to France, which has strained ties between the two countries since the Shah's overthrow in 1979.

AXEL KRAUSE
"International Herald Tribune," Paris

FRANCE • Information Highlights

Official Name: French Republic.
Location: Western Europe.
Area: 211,207 sq mi (547 026 km²).
Population (mid-1986 est.): 55,400,000.
Chief City (1982 est.): Paris, the capital, 8,706,963.
Government: *Head of state,* François Mitterrand, president (took office May 1981). *Chief minister,* Jacques Chirac, prime minister (took office March 1986). *Legislature*—Parliament: Senate and National Assembly.
Monetary Unit: Franc (4.96465 francs equal U.S. $1, Dec. 16, 1986).
Gross Domestic Product (1984 U.S.$): $490,-000,000,000.
Economic Indexes (1985): *Consumer Prices* (1980 = 100), all items, 158.0; food, 158.9. *Industrial Production* (Jan. 1986, 1980 = 100), 101.
Foreign Trade (1985 U.S.$): *Imports,* $107,809,-000,000; *exports,* $97,726,000,000.

GARDENING AND HORTICULTURE

The number one problem facing U.S. gardeners and agriculturists in 1986 continued to be insufficient rainfall and extreme heat in many parts of the nation. The Southeast and Midwest suffered extensively from insufficient rainfall and prolonged periods with temperatures of 100°F (37.7°C) or higher during the summer. Billions of dollars in damage to agriculture resulted.

National Garden Week. Gardening received national recognition when President Ronald Reagan signed a proclamation authorizing National Garden Week, April 13–19, 1986. The commemoration, conceived by Doug Oliphant, past president of the National Garden Bureau, took five years and the efforts of more than 16 horticultural organizations to accomplish. Its purpose was to recognize the numerous contributions of America's gardeners. Later the president signed legislation establishing the rose as the national flower (*see* page 80).

Researcher Honored. The New York State Nurserymen's Association and the New York State Department of Agriculture and Markets presented the 1986 Gold Medal of Horticulture to Dr. Arthur Bing, professor emeritus of floriculture and ornamental horticulture at Cornell University. The award was presented in August at the New York State Fair, Syracuse, NY. Dr. Bing received the award for his outstanding research in weed control for greenhouse, nursery, turf, and landscape use. Dr. Bing's studies have provided the basis for Cornell's recommendations for weed control in both commercial and residential applications.

New Trial Category. All-America Selections (AAS) announced for 1986 the addition of a new category, Bedding Plant Flower Trials. The trial will test the performance of bedding plants in both the greenhouse and outdoors, and only those plants that score high in both categories will be eligible for an AAS bedding plant award.

Award Winners. The first shrub rose ever to receive the All-America Rose Selection Award (AARS) was announced for 1987 to be "Bonica," introduced by Conard-Pyle Co., West Grove, PA. "Bonica," an everblooming shrub rose, presents a mass of pastel pink with as many as 20 blossoms per cluster. The most outstanding characteristic of "Bonica" is its proven hardiness in winter weather from Minnesota to Massachusetts, as well as its ability to tolerate heat in the Gulf Coast.

The only AARS 1987 award winner hybrid tea was "Sheer Bliss." Hybridized by William A. Warriner of Tustin, CA, "Sheer Bliss" produces a 4 to 5 inch (10 to 12.7 cm) creamy white center blushed with soft pink blossoms with a very strong, sweet fragrance. "New Year," a grandiflora, received the 1987 AARS award for its strikingly different Spanish-orange color, 3-inch (7.6-cm) blossoms with excellent form and lasting quality. "New Year" was hybridized by Sam McGredy IV of Auckland, New Zealand, and showed above-average disease resistance and continuous bloom.

All-America Selections (AAS) 1987 winners for flowers and vegetables included five introductions. Petunia F, "Purple Pirouette," bred by Pan American Seed Co., begins a new bicolor class of double petunias with fully double grandiflora blossoms. "Purple Pirouette" is the first double petunia with blossoms of pure white border and a velvety purple center measuring 3½ to 4 inches (9 to 10 cm) when mature. Snapdragon F, "Princess White with Purple Eye," the totally new bicolor, semidwarf, 14 to 16 inches (35.6 to 40.6 cm) high, bred by Takii and Company, Ltd., received recognition for its striking color combination and abundance of flower spikes all season long. The third AAS flower winner Sanvitalia "Mandarin Orange" (Creeping Zinnia) is the first orange flowering sanvitilia in the world, according to AAS. Introduced by K. Sahin Zaden, "Mandarin Orange" produces 1 inch (2.5 cm) semidouble blossoms with a dark center, similar to a sunflower, on a plant with a spread of 12 to 15 inches (30 to 38 cm). AAS 1987 vegetable winners were Basil "Purple Ruffles" and Pumpkin "Autumn Gold."

The Dallas fern, produced by Casa Flora, Dallas, TX, was introduced in 1986. The new foliage plant requires only low light and can thrive in low humidity. It looks similar to the Boston fern but is compact in growth, measuring 16 to 18 inches (40.6 to 45.7 cm) across and 8 to 10 inches (20 to 25.4 cm) tall.

RALPH L. SNODSMITH
Ornamental Horticulturist

The new Dallas fern (Nepholepis exaltata dallasii) *is a compact foliage plant that thrives in indoor conditons.*

© Jaime L. West for Casa Flora, Dallas

The Cut-Flowers Boom

© Thomas S. England

One of the quiet trends among U.S. consumers in recent years has been a blossoming of the fresh flower market. According to the industry's Floral Index, total U.S. sales grew from $640 million in 1958 to $4.3 billion in 1984, with $7.0 billion projected for 1986. With domestic supplies bolstered by record imports, prices have fallen and popular varieties have become available year-round. The American public has indulged its taste in cut flowers as never before. And, says Alvi O. Voigt, professor of agricultural economics at Penn State University, "this is no fad."

The big change has been the availability of fresh flowers in a new array of retail outlets. Besides traditional florist shops, they have been appearing in supermarkets, department stores, discount chains, shopping malls, and, following the European tradition, on street corners. In 1986, according to one survey, half of all U.S. supermarkets were selling flowers at least periodically. The Cincinnati-based Kroger chain, for example, had flower departments in 60% of its 1,351 stores. Safeway had self-service flower sections in all of its 1,963 stores.

Despite this shift, traditional florists also have enjoyed the boom. The number of retail florist shops in the United States increased from an estimated 19,000 in 1958 to more than 32,000 in 1984. Revenues for Florists' Trans-world Delivery (FTD) have risen more than 10% annually, reaching $551 million in 1985.

The 1985 Floral Marketing Report of the Society of American Florists identified several factors that have contributed to the increased consumer sales. It suggested that the old "floral mystique"—flowers are bought only for someone else and only for a special occasion or reason—has been dispelled. Now consumers purchase flowers for "self use" and for their own "household use." Today any time is the perfect time for the fresh flower. Dealers have identified other new trends. A California retailer sees more and more "ladies buying flowers for their men." A New York florist sees the floral explosion "creating a demand for single flowers and arrangements designed with a looseness relating to today's life-style."

In terms of supply, imports have played a key role. From 1975 to 1985, according to U.S. government statistics, imports of cut flowers increased from $19.8 million to $220.9 million; the latter figure represented 37% of the domestic wholesale market. Dutch exports—of tulips, freesias, lilies, and others—alone accounted for 24.8% of U.S. sales in 1985. Other countries that share in the U.S. market include Colombia, Israel, Italy, Brazil, and the nations of the Caribbean region.

RALPH L. SNODSMITH

GENETICS

Our ability to perceive the form of an object depends on special rod-shaped cells in the retina of the eyes, while our ability to detect colors is determined by special cone-shaped cells. There are three types of cone cells, each sensitive to one of the primary colors (red, green, blue).

In 1986, Dr. Jeremy Nathans and his coworkers at the Stanford University School of Medicine showed that the gene for form-detection is located on human chromosome #3, whereas the gene for blue-color detection is on chromosome #7. Although it has been known for a long time that the genes for red-color and green-color detection are located on the human X-chromosome, these investigators discovered that there was only one gene for red-color detection but that there were two genes for green-color detection. Whether a particular cone cell becomes sensitive to red, green, or blue depends on which of the genes is active in the cell. The investigators also found that the respective genes for red-color or green-color detection were missing (deleted) from the X-chromosomes of those individuals who lack either ability (red-green color blindness).

Deletions as well as duplications of genes result from the exchange of unequal lengths of chromosome sections. Unequal exchanges of chromosome sections can occur between members of a chromosome pair during the process of sperm or egg production. Once these rare events have occurred, the altered chromosome will be passed on to future generations.

Inheritance of Obesity. Dr. A. J. Stunkard of the University of Pennsylvania and other colleagues compared the weights of 540 adults who had been adopted as children with the weights of both their biologic and adoptive parents. It was found that there was a strong correlation between the adult weights of adoptees and their biologic parents, but no such relationship was found between the adoptees and their adoptive parents. It was further found that one could identify with a good deal of assurance those who were at risk of becoming obese. Namely, 80% of the offspring of two obese parents become obese as compared with no more than 14% of the offspring of two parents of normal weight. The investigators concluded that genetic influences have an important role in determining human weight whereas the family environment alone has little apparent effect.

Forensic DNA. In crimes where there has been a violent struggle between assailant and victim, the attacker is able, all too often, to leave the scene of the crime before being apprehended. If this occurs, it may be very difficult for the victim to subsequently identify the assailant. However, identification of the attacker can still be possible if bloodstains or semen stains on clothing, vaginal swabs taken after a rape, or hair roots are available for analysis. Unfortunately, in some cases, the results of such forensic tests can be inconclusive.

In 1986, Dr. Peter Gill and his associates at the Home Office Forensic Science Service, England, reported on their use of DNA extracted from bloodstains, semen stains, and hair roots. They found that upon subjecting DNA from various sources to special enzymatic treatment and electrophoresis, a pattern of distribution of DNA segments (DNA "fingerprints") emerged that was specific to the individual who provided the sample. Clearcut DNA fingerprints were obtained from bloodstains that were four years old. In addition, sperm nuclei could be separated from vaginal cellular debris on a vaginal swab, making the subsequent identification of a rape suspect possible.

Resistance to a Microbial Insecticide. In an attempt to preserve stored grain from infestation by insects, some farmers have been spraying their storage facilities with the bacterium *Bacillus thuringiensis.* This organism produces spores containing an endotoxin. When an insect ingests the spores, the endotoxin is released into the insect's digestive tract, killing it.

One of the major pests of stored grain is the Indian meal moth *Plodia interpunctella,* whose larvae feed on the grain. Recently, Dr. W. H. McGaughey of the U.S. Department of Agriculture took moth larvae from a laboratory stock that was susceptible to the endotoxin and grew larvae on grain to which had been added enough endotoxin to kill half of them. The survivors were used as the parents of the next generation, and the procedure was repeated for nine generations. At that time, the larvae were exposed to various concentrations of endotoxin and were found to be 100 times more resistant to its killing effect than the laboratory strain. It also was found that resistance to the endotoxin was inherited as a recessive trait. In further studies, it was discovered that *P. interpunctella* larvae collected from grain stores which had been sprayed with *B. thuringiensis* were more resistant to the bacterial endotoxin than larvae from untreated bins.

Ethics. For an ever increasing number of genetic diseases that appear later in life, the individuals at risk can be identified years before there are any manifestations of the particular disorder. This advance in genetic testing has raised such questions as: Is an adoptive parent entitled to have a child being considered for adoption tested for genetic disease? Is an employer entitled to have a would be employee tested? Is a life insurance company entitled to have a policy applicant tested? These issues now are being debated and will have to be settled to govern the rights of individuals to privacy in such matters.

LOUIS LEVINE, *City College of New York*

GEOLOGY

During 1986 geoscientists studied unusual volcanic and seismic events, made several significant fossil finds, and continued to puzzle over the causes of mass extinctions.

Volcanic Activity. Although fewer in number than in 1985, volcanic phenomena and seismic activity remained newsworthy. Of special interest was the catastrophic gaseous eruption on the floor of Cameroon's Lake Nios. On August 21, Nios, which partially fills the crater of one of Cameroon's many extinct volcanoes, released a cloud of poisonous gas that burst through the lake's bottom sediments and shot skyward. As the deadly mixture of carbon dioxide and hydrogen sulfide swept over the land, it killed some 1,700 people and devastated herds of livestock. Scientists did not agree on the exact cause of the unusual phenomenon. Some geologists believed that a landslide, possibly triggered by an earthquake, disturbed the bottom sediment and released the gas. Others suggested that renewed volcanic activity beneath the crater may have caused toxic gases in the rocks beneath the lake to break through the water and spurt skyward. However, biologists theorized that the gas was generated by the decay of organic matter on the lake bottom. This produced a giant bubble that eventually exploded. And it was also suggested that temperature changes may have been the cause.

Other volcanic eruptions of note were the March and April outbursts of Alaska's Augustine Volcano at the tip of the Alaska Peninsula; the November eruptions, accompanied by earthquakes, of Mount Mihara in Japan; and the latest current activity, which began in July, of Kilauea Volcano in Hawaii. In early January a submarine eruption produced a new volcanic island in the Pacific Ocean near Iwo Jima, Japan.

Seismic Events. Although not considered "earthquake country," the states of Pennsylvania, Ohio, West Virginia, Indiana, Illinois, Michigan, New York, and Wisconsin were shaken by a strong temblor on January 31. Centered 30 miles (48 km) northeast of Cleveland, the quake measured 5.0 on the Richter scale and was felt in Barrie, Ontario. The sporadic renewal of seismic activity in the eastern United States has led seismologists to speculate on the possibility of more and larger quakes, perhaps on the scale of the "superquake" that destroyed much of Charleston, SC, in 1886. Seismologists also are reviewing the status of the New Madrid Fault, a subsurface fracture that extends 120 miles (190 km) from northeast Arkansas to southern Illinois.

Meanwhile, a 6.1-magnitude temblor rocked parts of California, Nevada, and Utah on July 21. Its epicenter was 12 miles (19 km) northwest of Palm Springs. Other strong California earthquakes in April and July spurred renewed speculation as to when the San Andreas Fault will spawn the next 1906-type "killer" quake. On September 13 a 6.2 quake killed at least 17 people near Kalamata, Greece, and on August 30, a 6.5 quake hit Romania and the Soviet Union, killing one person, injuring hundreds, and damaging 2,300 buildings. The most devastating of all was a quake measuring 5.4, followed by another of 4.5, that struck San Salvador, the capital of El Salvador, on October 10 and killed 1,500.

Paleontology. Vertebrate paleontologists reported new finds of great significance. Remains believed to be those of the oldest known bird were found in a quarry in Texas. Named *Protoavis* ("first bird") and possessing both avian and reptilian characteristics, this primitive crow-sized bird is some 75 million years older than *Archaeopteryx,* the famous fossil bird found in Bavaria in 1861. In northwestern Colorado, 230 million-year-old footprints found near Dinosaur National Monument are believed to be the oldest dinosaur tracks yet discovered. Meanwhile, bones of what may be the world's largest dinosaur were found in 150 million-year-old Jurassic strata in New Mexico. Dubbed *Seismosaurus* (or "earth shaker"), this supergiant was probably 100–120 ft (30–37 m) long and 18 ft (5.5m) tall at the shoulder, and weighed 80–100 tons.

The discovery of a 2.5 million-year-old cranium in northern Kenya may change the structure of the human family tree. The so-called "black skull" casts doubt on the belief that humans evolved from the earliest known species of *Australopithecus* and upsets the accepted view of australopithecine evolution.

Fossil remains of the oldest undisputed primate were collected in Wyoming. These teeth and jaw fragments belonged to *Cantius torresi,* a squirrel-like animal that lived more than 53 million years ago and could be the oldest ancestor of humans. Scientists also found new species among the earth's oldest fossils. They appear to be slimy green algae that suggest photosynthesis started 700 million years earlier than previously believed. The new find supports earlier research that the oldest known organisms inhabited our planet more than 3.5 billion years ago.

Extinction Debate Update. Controversy continued over the cause of the five major mass extinctions that have punctuated biological evolution. New studies of the Cretaceous-Tertiary boundary in Canada reveal coincident anomalies in the abundance of iridium in plant spores. Of special interest is the persistence across this boundary of the most climatically sensitive plant groups. This suggests that if the paleoclimate did change at the end of Cretaceous time, it changed only briefly.

New studies indicate that an extinction during the Ordovician Period (440 million years ago) reduced the diversity of families on earth by 20%, with an especially heavy impact on marine invertebrates. Later, at the end of Permian time (245 million years ago), as many as 96% of marine invertebrate species may have been wiped out in a mass extinction. Studies of the iridium content of certain Ordovician and Permian rocks suggest that these extinctions were not related to the impact of a terrestrial object, as some scientists have contended. Recent research also reveals that only 1–5 species of the 30 known species of dinosaurs could have been extinguished by an asteroid impact, and that the last dinosaurs apparently became extinct 40,000 years after the postulated impact 65 million years ago. A new theory proposed that the assumed terrestrial object fell into the Bering Sea between Alaska and Siberia.

WILLIAM H. MATTHEWS III
Lamar University

GEORGIA

For Georgians in 1986, only a long drought diverted attention from politics and economics.

Weather. The drought, accompanied by scorching temperatures, almost reached crisis proportions. Outdoor water use was restricted; federal aid was requested; and farmers got emergency shipments of hay from the Midwest. (*See* AGRICULTURE.)

Elections. The fall political activity began with a close run-off election between two civil-rights veterans, State Sen. Julian Bond and Atlanta City Councilman John Lewis, for the Democratic nomination for the U.S. congressional seat in the fifth district. In a dramatic upset victory Lewis, backed 4–1 by the white electorate, defeated Bond, who was supported by such black leaders as Atlanta Mayor Andrew Young. Lewis later defeated his Republican opponent, Portia Scott, to become one of two black U.S. congressmen from the South.

The big event of the general election was Wyche Fowler's surprise defeat of Republican incumbent Mack Mattingly in the U.S. Senate race. Fowler, previously the fifth district congressman, eliminated former presidential aide Hamilton Jordan in the primary and went on to defeat an opponent who outspent him by $2 million and for whom President Ronald Reagan personally campaigned. The defeat of Georgia's first Republican senator since Reconstruction dampened hopes for a two-party state, especially since the Democrats retained control of the General Assembly and Democratic Gov. Joe Frank Harris won reelection.

Economics. Georgia continued to prosper, ranking fifth nationally in job growth and in the formation and expansion of new business. In the previous four years, Georgia added 425,000 new jobs and increased its average hourly wage by 19%. A record 226 new businesses located in Atlanta in 1985, and the metro area employment rate increased by 6.5%. Gwinnett County was the fastest-growing county in the United States for the second consecutive year.

While newcomers entered Georgia, an "old" Atlanta company celebrated its 100th birthday. An estimated 13,000 people representing 120 nations helped fete the centennial of the Coca-Cola Co.

Legislature. The General Assembly approved a $5.3 billion budget and an ethics law covering state officials, but it effectively killed several key bills when it adjourned. One of those was a tort reform measure that would have restricted the reporting of injury by victims in damage suits as a way to retard increases in liability-insurance premiums. Other failed legislation included a bill to require notification of parents of minors seeking abortions and a bill requiring physicians to report all cases of AIDS to state health officials.

Kemp Trial. An assistant professor of remedial English at the University of Georgia focused national attention on the state and on issues surrounding college athletics. Jan Kemp won a $2.5 million award after alleging she had been fired because she protested preferential treatment for student athletes. The trial and accompanying publicity led to an investigation of athletic-academic relations at the university; the creation of a no pass, no play study committee; and the resignation of Fred Davidson, university president.

Carter Presidential Center. Jimmy Carter and Ronald Reagan met in Atlanta on Carter's 62d birthday to dedicate the Carter Library and Presidential Center. Some 300 demonstrators at the ceremony protested the construction of an expensive parkway through historic neighborhoods as part of the $27 million complex, which includes a Japanese garden, a policy center, and two foundation offices. (*See* page 78.)

KAY BECK, *Georgia State University*

GEORGIA • Information Highlights

Area: 58,910 sq mi (152 576 km²).

Population (1985 est.): 5,976,000.

Chief Cities (July 1, 1984 est.): Atlanta, the capital, 426,090; Columbus, 174,824; Savannah, 145,014.

Government (1986): *Chief Officers—*governor, Joe Frank Harris (D); lt. gov., Zell Miller (D). *General Assembly—*Senate, 56 members; House of Representatives, 180 members.

State Finances (fiscal year 1985): *Revenue,* $8,760,000,000; *expenditure,* $7,618,000,000.

Personal Income (1985): $74,960,000,000; per capita, $12,543.

Labor Force (June 1986): *Civilian labor force,* 2,999,100; *unemployed,* 181,700 (6.1% of total force).

Education: *Enrollment* (fall 1984)—public elementary schools, 745,837; public secondary, 316,478; colleges and universities, 196,826. *Public school expenditures* (1983–84), $2,341,000,000 ($2,322 per pupil).

Economics and defense dominated talks between West German President Kohl (left) and France's President Mitterrand.

GERMANY

On Aug. 13, 1986, the leaders of the two German states, the Federal Republic of Germany or West Germany (FRG) and the German Democratic Republic or East Germany (GDR), were in Berlin to mark the 25th anniversary of the Berlin Wall. In West Berlin, Chancellor Helmut Kohl of the Federal Republic, echoing the statements of his predecessors and other Western leaders of the past quarter century, condemned the barrier as "the most visible expression of the moral difference between a free democracy and totalitarian communism." Less than two miles away in East Berlin, Erich Honecker, leader of the GDR's ruling Communist Party, commemorated the construction of the "anti-fascist protective rampart" as a heroic act which saved the young East German state from an impending NATO invasion.

The Cold War rhetoric of the two leaders notwithstanding, relations between the German states in 1986 continued to improve. In May the first-ever cultural and educational exchange agreement between the two states was signed. In September the GDR announced that refugees, mainly from Third World countries, attempting to enter West Berlin by using East Berlin's airport as a transit point would no longer be allowed to do so unless they possessed a valid entry visa for West Germany or some other country of destination. (The issue had been a source of disagreement for several years. By allowing the transit, Bonn main-

tained, the GDR had been contributing to West Germany's growing refugee problem.) Shortly after the East German announcement on refugees, the two states concluded negotiations on an environmental agreement under which the Federal Republic will pay about $150 million to help clean up industrial pollution in the GDR. Talks also began for a major agreement on technical and scientific cooperation which would provide the GDR access to advanced technology. And 1986 saw the first "sister city" agreement between the two states, as the FRG's Saarlouis became the "sister" of the GDR's Eisenhüttenstadt.

Federal Republic of Germany (West Germany)

In 1986 politics in West Germany were dominated by campaigning and preparations for the Jan. 25, 1987, national elections. In March the Kohl government passed legislation which the trade unions and the opposition Social Democrats charged was designed to weaken the unions' capacity to strike. Widely interpreted as an electoral concession to business interests, the measure changed the provisions under which striking workers could receive unemployment compensation; workers idled by strikes at other plants in the same industry will not receive benefits. The trade unions bitterly opposed the legislation, claiming that it would reduce their sway with employers, and they organized mass protest demonstrations throughout the country.

Early in 1986, Chancellor Kohl's popularity dropped when prosecutors in Bonn and his home state (the Rhineland-Palatinate) opened formal investigations into charges, filed by a leading figure in the Green party, that the chancellor had given false testimony to two parliamentary committees investigating the fund-raising practices of Kohl's party, the Christian Democratic Union (CDU). Kohl was the first chancellor to be the subject of such investigations. In May, however, both probes ended, and the complaints were dismissed for lack of evidence.

As it prepared for the 1987 election, the junior partner in Chancellor Kohl's coalition, the Free Democratic Party (FDP), emphasized its differences with the CDU—a standard procedure at election time. In domestic affairs the FDP claimed the lion's share of credit for the improved economic situation. In foreign policy, Foreign Minister Hans-Dietrich Genscher of the FDP became the main critic in the government of Bonn's participation in the U.S. Strategic Defense Initiative (SDI, or "Star Wars").

The opposition Social Democrats (SPD) began the year with high hopes for returning to power after the 1987 election. Their new leader, Johannes Rau, was, according to most polls, more highly rated than the chancellor, and Rau's middle-of-the-road image was attracting new support to his party. But in June the SPD failed to unseat the CDU government at a key state election in Lower Saxony. Then at the SPD's preelection party congress in August, the Social Democrats passed resolutions calling for the repudiation of West Germany's agreement with the United States for cooperation on SDI research, and for the withdrawal of NATO's U.S.-made medium-range nuclear missiles. While the party's left wing failed to adopt a resolution which would have required Rau as chancellor to remove the U.S. missiles during his first six months in office, the overall impact of the defense resolutions was to weaken Rau's centrist image. The SPD also repudiated its earlier support for atomic energy and pledged to shut down the FRG's 20 nuclear plants within ten years. A few weeks after the conference, at an important state election in Bavaria, the SPD received only 27.5% of the vote, its poorest performance in 40 years. The Bavarian result reflected voter dissatisfaction with the leftward course of the party.

As they prepared to face the electorate, Rau and the SPD also had to decide how to deal with the Green party, which many voters see as an extreme left faction. Rau promised that he would not allow himself "to be elected with the votes of the Greens," and the SPD claimed that it would govern alone after the elections. But to govern alone the SPD would have to receive an absolute majority of votes, something it has never come close to achieving at the national level. The CDU and FDP, therefore, attempted to undermine Rau's pledge by stressing that the SPD must have Green support to govern. The choice, they said, would be between Kohl's center coalition or "Red-Green chaos."

For the Greens themselves, 1986 also was a difficult year. As the only party consistently opposed to nuclear energy, the Greens expected a political windfall from the April nuclear accident at Chernobyl (*see* special report, page 218). And indeed in the weeks following the disaster, Green support in the polls jumped from 6% to 12%. But Chernobyl also brought the "Fundamentalists," or radical wing of the party, back into control. At its May convention the party called for West Germany's withdrawal from NATO, unilateral demilitarization of the Federal Republic, and the immediate shutdown and dismantling of all nuclear plants. These radical policy positions cost the party about as much support as it had gained from the Soviet accident. Nonetheless the Greens, who received a surprising 7.5% at the October Bavarian election, expected to win enough votes in 1987 to return to the Bundestag.

Economy. With a real increase in gross national product (GNP) of about 3.5%, West Germany in 1986 achieved its fourth consecutive year of economic growth. Consumer prices actually dropped by one half of a percent, giving the FRG its lowest inflation rate in 34 years. The country's trade balance showed a strong surplus of almost $35 billion. More importantly for the Kohl government, unemployment finally started a slow decline, ending the year at about 8%. By midyear factory production was at 85% of capacity, the highest level since 1979. However, in such industries as automobiles and machine tools, production was unable to keep up with demand. The retooling of the country's industrial plant with computers and robots proceeded at a faster pace than in any other Western European country.

WEST GERMANY • Information Highlights

Official Name: Federal Republic of Germany.
Location: North-central Europe.
Area: 95,976 sq mi (248 577 km²).
Population (mid-1986 est.): 60,700,000.
Chief Cities (June 30, 1983): Bonn, the capital, 291,700; West Berlin, 1,851,800; Hamburg, 1,600,300; Munich, 1,277,000.
Government: *Head of state,* Richard von Weizsäcker, president (took office July 1, 1984). *Head of government,* Helmut Kohl, chancellor (took office Oct. 1982). *Legislature*—Parliament: Bundesrat and Bundestag.
Monetary Unit: Deutsche mark (1.9750 D. marks equal U.S.$1, Oct. 17, 1986).
Gross National Product (1984 U.S.$): $616,100,-000,000.
Economic Indexes (1985): *Consumer Prices* (1980 = 100), all items, 121.0; food, 117.0. *Industrial Production* (1980 = 100), 98.
Foreign Trade (1985 U.S.$): *Imports,* $157,645,-000,000; *exports,* $183,406,000,000.

The government's economic policies continued to emphasize deficit reductions and only modest increases in spending for social programs. Privatization plans also continued in 1986, as the government sold its remaining shares in the Volkswagen corporation and in VEBA, the largest energy company in West Germany.

Foreign Policy. The Kohl government, the most pro-U.S. regime in Bonn since the 1950s, concluded an agreement with Washington in March for participation in the SDI program. Several German companies received some of the largest SDI research contracts awarded to foreign firms.

On the other hand, the Kohl regime gave only limited backing to the Reagan administration's actions toward Libya, an important West German trading partner. It opposed any economic sanctions against that country and expressed misgivings about the U.S. air strike in April, while still acknowledging its understanding of Washington's position. The U.S. ambassador in Bonn, Richard Burt, termed this reaction "half-hearted." Polls showed that about 75% of the West German public opposed the attack. During the year Bonn also resisted U.S. pressure to lower West Germany's inter-

During a four-day trip to West Germany in late January, then Israeli Prime Minister Shimon Peres made a solemn visit to the Nazi concentration camp at Bergen-Belsen.

© P. Piel/Gamma-Liaison

est rates and to increase government spending in order to stimulate growth in other Western economies. And during his October visit to Washington, in the wake of the U.S.-Soviet mini-summit in Iceland, Chancellor Kohl expressed West Germany's concern over any agreement that might remove medium-range nuclear missiles from Europe. Kohl emphasized that West Germany would be left vulnerable to Soviet short-range weapons or to conventional Warsaw Pact forces.

Nicaragua was another source of German-U.S. differences in 1986. Responding to calls by the Sandinista regime for European volunteers to aid in the struggle against the U.S.-supported "contra" rebels, more than 1,000 West German leftists through 1986 had gone to Nicaragua to work in agriculture, construction, and education, but not, apparently, to engage in combat. In April eight German nationals were kidnapped by contras in southern Nicaragua. The rebels claimed that the Germans were armed and part of a Sandinista militia unit. As negotiations for their release dragged on, legislators from several parties in Bonn complained that U.S.-subsidized "terrorists" were holding Germans while Washington was demanding that Bonn crack down on Libyan-supported terrorists. When the Germans finally were released after 25 days, even officials within the Kohl government complained that the Reagan administration could have acted sooner on their behalf.

West Germany's relations with the Soviet Union improved in 1986. Since the deployment of the NATO missiles in 1983, Moscow had attempted to isolate the Bonn government from its Western allies. Shortly after coming to power in 1985, Soviet General Secretary Mikhail Gorbachev traveled to France and Great Britain, but not to West Germany. In July 1986, however, German Foreign Minister Genscher traveled to Moscow, where he had extensive talks with the Soviet leader. An agreement on scientific and technical cooperation, delayed since the mid-1970s, was signed, and negotiations began for a new cultural exchange agreement.

Terrorism. Attacks by terrorist groups in West Germany increased in 1986. In July the Red Army Faction (RAF), the successor to the Baader-Meinhof band of the 1970s, claimed responsibility for the car-bombing death of an official of the giant Siemens company who was in charge of the firm's nuclear power program. A letter found near the bombing site said that the official had been murdered because he was a proponent of nuclear energy and a collaborator in the Star Wars program. In September a bomb exploded outside the Cologne offices of West Germany's counterintelligence agency, wounding a passing motorist. In October a senior official of the Foreign Ministry was shot and killed outside his home in Bonn, and again the RAF claimed responsibility. The bombing of an IBM research facility in Heidelberg in November also was attributed to that organization. Security officials estimated that the RAF has 25–30 hard-core members, about 200 "militants" who engage primarily in bombings of offices and defense installations, and some 2,000 sympathizers who distribute the group's propaganda and provide logistical support.

Environment. The Chernobyl nuclear accident had major repercussions in the Federal Republic. Although the fallout damage was relatively minor, state and national governments banned the sale of many agricultural products and cautioned residents to avoid taking walks in forests or allowing children to visit playgrounds for fear of contamination from radioactive material on trees and in sandboxes. The government compensated vegetable and dairy farmers for their lost sales.

The accident had a far greater impact on public opinion toward nuclear power. By May opposition to any further construction of nuclear power plants in the country had grown to 83%, up from 52% in 1982. In June massive and sometimes violent antinuclear protests took place in West Berlin, Hamburg, and Schleswig-Holstein, and at a reprocessing plant under construction in Bavaria. Police clashed with protestors in the ensuing violence, which resulted in some 100 casualties and 200 arrests.

Chancellor Kohl continued to support nuclear power—which accounts for about 30% of the nation's electricity production—but, following the Chernobyl incident, he shifted responsibility for nuclear and environmental matters from the Interior Ministry to a new Ministry for the Environment and Reactor Safety.

Minorities. While West Germany's 4.3 million foreign residents remained the country's major social problem, there were signs in 1986 that tolerance was increasing among the native population. Several polls showed that German acceptance of foreign workers' life styles and understanding for the particular housing and educational problems of foreigners had grown in the past decade. Another indicator of change was the extraordinary success of a book, *Ganz Unten* ("At the Very Bottom"), by journalist Günter Wallraff, who disguised himself as a Turkish worker and spent several months in various towns and cities working at low-level jobs. His chronicle of discrimination, humiliation, and the indifference of authorities and institutions sold more than 3 million copies by the end of the year, making it West Germany's biggest best-seller of the postwar period.

German Democratic Republic (East Germany)

The most important political event of 1986 in East Germany was the 11th Party Congress of the ruling Communist (Socialist Unity) party in April. The attendance of Soviet leader Gorbachev, who sent only deputies to similar meetings in Bulgaria and Czechoslovakia, underscored the importance of the GDR to the Soviet Union. The congress reelected Erich Honecker to another five-year term as general secretary of the party and approved plans to modernize the economy—the most prosperous in Eastern Europe—through the introduction of high-tech computerized production methods.

Economy. Despite confident official pronouncements at the party congress, East Germany faces some major economic problems if it is to continue as a model Communist state and retain its position as one of the world's top ten industrialized nations. Many of its industrial plants are aging and unproductive. Investments in new plants, equipment, and research have steadily declined, from 23% of GNP in 1975 to 15% in 1986. The country's telephone system, roads, and railway networks are woefully underdeveloped by Western standards. Per capita productivity (industrial and agricultural) is about 50% lower than in West Germany.

The East German economy is especially weak in the high-tech areas of microelectronics, computers, and robotics. The electronic and computer components of the nation's most sophisticated machinery are imported from Western Europe and Japan. This dependence on foreign technology reduces the profits of many GDR exports. Because of the GDR's outdated technology, none of the products of its fledgling computer industry can be sold in the competitive Western market. Only the protected markets of other Communist countries are available for East German high-tech exports. Technologically, the GDR today is perhaps 4–7 years behind the leading industrialized nations of the West. Much of the problem may lie in the nation's planned econ-

---

EAST GERMANY • Information Highlights

Official Name: German Democratic Republic.
Location: North-central Europe.
Area: 41,768 sq mi (108 178 km²).
Population (mid-1986 est.): 16,700,000.
Chief Cities (June 30, 1983): East Berlin, the capital, 1,185,500; Leipzig, 559,000; Dresden, 522,500.
Government: *Head of state,* Erich Honecker, chairman of the Council of State. *Head of government,* Willi Stoph, chairman of the Council of Ministers. General Secretary of the Socialist Unity (Communist) Party, Erich Honecker (took office 1971). *Legislature* (unicameral)—Volkskammer (People's Chamber).
Monetary Unit: DDR mark (2.38 DDR marks equal U.S.$1, June 1986).
Gross National Product (1984 U.S.$): $163,700,-000,000.
Economic Index (1985): *Industrial Production* (1980 = 100), 122.
Foreign Trade (1985 U.S.$): *Imports,* $25,268,-000,000; *exports,* $25,684,000,000.

omy, which emphasizes sheer output of goods without competition, thereby discouraging research and innovation.

Energy and the Environment. In spite of the Chernobyl accident, which was belatedly reported in the GDR media, the government went forward with plans to expand its nuclear power capacity by importing additional reactors from the Soviet Union. Nuclear power presently accounts for about 10% of the country's electricity production, with the figure expected to increase to 30% by the year 2000. There is little alternative. Oil shipments from the Soviet Union have declined, and the GDR lacks the foreign currency to increase purchases from the Middle East. East Germany's major energy source is domestic brown coal, or lignite, but mining has damaged the environment. Whole villages have been leveled in mining areas, and groundwater has been polluted. Moreover, the burning of brown coal also contaminates the air. In the industrialized areas of Halle and Leipzig, the average life-expectancy is six years less than the national average.

Foreign Policy. The GDR in 1986 formally restored relations with the People's Republic of China; ties had been broken since the early 1960s. In October, General Secretary Honecker made a six-day official visit to China, the first by any East European Communist leader in some two decades. Apparently with Soviet approval, East Germany sought to expand its economic ties to the Chinese. The GDR hoped to improve its balance of trade by exporting machine tools and other basic industrial equipment. During 1986 trade between the two states increased by an estimated 50%, to almost $3 billion.

West Berlin

After several years of political stability and steady economic improvement, West Berlin in 1986 was convulsed by a major political scandal and a large influx of Third World refugees. Late in 1985 a Christian Democratic official had been arrested for accepting bribes from building contractors—an impropriety invited by the shortage of building sites, by the generous subsidies for development, and by the extensive controls and regulations of local government. The investigation was widened by a special prosecution unit, and by mid-1986 leading CDU members of the government, including the interior senator and Lord Mayor Eberhard Diepgen, had been implicated in the affair. Diepgen admitted that, before becoming mayor, he had accepted about $35,000 in campaign contributions from one of the builders. In April three members of the city government, including the senators for building and the environment, resigned.

Adding to the city's woes in 1986 was a flood of refugees from the Third World. By midyear some 42,000 Iranians, Ghanians, Lebanese, Palestinians, and others fleeing war and poverty had entered the city. The total for all of 1986 was expected to reach up to 100,000, a 45% increase from 1985.

West Berlin's economy, however, continued to improve in 1986. Unemployment declined, and new high-tech industries showed impressive growth. Several state-of-the-art factories being built for electronic components and industrial process systems were expected to bring 20,000 new jobs by 1995.

DAVID P. CONRADT, *University of Florida*

© Forrest Anderson/Gamma-Liaison

Seeking stronger economic ties, East Germany's Erich Honecker made an official state visit to China in October. It was the first visit to that country by an East European Communist leader in nearly two decades.

GREAT BRITAIN

Seldom has Britain's attachment to its closest historic allies been so sorely tested as it was in 1986. The U.S. attack on Libya in April from British air bases and Britain's rift with the Commonwealth over South Africa were among the controversial challenges that arose in two of Britain's three most important areas of geopolitical influence.

These challenges were reminders that despite its declining influences over the years, Britain had a preeminent role to play in international affairs. In addition, as the longest serving leader of the Western alliance, Prime Minister Margaret Thatcher has acquired a respected reputation as an international stateswoman. For example, on the vexed issue of South African sanctions, U.S. President Ronald Reagan tended to follow the lead of Mrs. Thatcher because of Britain's historic role as former colonial master and largest single investor in southern Africa.

As the United States' most important and dependable Western ally, Britain also played a special role in 1986 in superpower diplomacy, acting as a conduit in the arms-control area between the United States and the Soviet Union. To some extent, too, Britain also was called upon by its European partners to express European concerns to the United States on Washington's strategic policies.

Meanwhile, Britain's links to its third key regional grouping, the European Community (EC), were enhanced by its elevation to the presidency of the 12-nation European Council.

International Affairs

Europe. Britain's commitment to Europe was exemplified in a January 20 agreement between Prime Minister Thatcher and President François Mitterrand of France to build a tunnel beneath the English Channel. Initially it would be a rail-only link (*see* ENGINEERING). That symbolic and practical gesture to bridge the historic divide with the rest of Europe did not automatically make Britain see eye to eye with its European partners. Conflicts arose over the different responses within the European Community to the "Hindawi bomb plot."

In October, Nezar Hindawi, a Jordanian-born Palestinian, was found guilty and sentenced to 45 years in prison for concealing a time bomb in the luggage of his unsuspecting girlfriend. The device was timed to go off when a plane load of passengers took off from London's Heathrow Airport en route to Tel Aviv in mid-April.

The case caused outrage in Britain, and London broke diplomatic relations with Syria over the incident. But Britain was deeply disappointed that Europe initially took only mini-

© Peter Turner/Black Star

Prince Andrew and Sarah Ferguson wave to well-wishers after their wedding July 23. The Westminster Abbey ceremony was seen by a worldwide TV audience of 300 million.

mal action at the EC foreign ministers' meeting in Luxembourg on October 27 after Britain had produced "incontrovertible evidence" of Syrian complicity in the affair. Subsequently, however, all of the EC members, except Greece, agreed to take measures against Syria, including a ban on the sale of new arms. (*See also* TERRORISM.)

South Africa and the Commonwealth. While Britain was determined to act firmly on terrorism, its reluctance to adopt stronger economic measures against South Africa brought it into collision with the Commonwealth, a unique association of former British colonies that embraces a quarter of the world's population. Britain's rejection of concerted Commonwealth action to bring pressure on the Pretoria government to reform its apartheid policies totally isolated it from the rest of its 48 Commonwealth partners.

Britain defended its action by reasserting its traditional belief that sanctions, whether against the Soviet Union on Afghanistan or

Seven Commonwealth heads of state met in London, August 2–5, to discuss sanctions against South Africa. Only Britain's Margaret Thatcher (front, left) resisted. Other attendees were (counterclockwise from left): India's Rajiv Gandhi, Canada's Brian Mulroney, Commonwealth Secretary General Sir Sridrath Ramphal, Australia's Robert Hawke, Zimbabwe's Robert Mugabe, Zambia's Kenneth D. Kaunda, and the Bahamas' Lynden Pindling.

© Roger Hutchins/Camera Press from Photo Trends

against South Africa on its race policies, do not work. But critics suspected that Britain, as an important trade partner of South Africa, also was motivated by economic self-interest. Anti-British reaction manifested itself in a boycott by more than half the Commonwealth countries at the Commonwealth Games in Edinburgh, Scotland, in late July. There were fears that Britain's stand on sanctions could break up the Commonwealth. The dispute even strained relations between Prime Minister Margaret Thatcher and Queen Elizabeth II.

As head of government, the prime minister exercises executive power. As head of state, the monarch has no power and is obliged to keep out of the political arena. But the monarch does wield considerable influence, particularly as head of the Commonwealth, to which Queen Elizabeth II is deeply attached. It was in her latter capacity that Buckingham Palace let it be known that the queen was concerned about the implications of Mrs. Thatcher's policy for Commonwealth unity. Such disagreements did not deter the prime minister, even though public opinion rallied in support of the queen. It was an indication of the broad support that the Royal Family enjoys in Britain. The appeal of royalty was evident on July 23, when millions of enthusiastic viewers watched the "wedding of the year." This was the wedding of Prince Andrew, younger brother of Prince Charles and fourth in line to the British throne, to a commoner, Sarah Ferguson.

The United States. A potentially more damaging development for Mrs. Thatcher was a growing impression that Britain was becoming too subservient to U.S. policy and influence. It was brought home dramatically during the U.S. raid on Libya, launched from British bases. It was to surface again over the future of Britain's struggling and sole surviving helicopter company, Westland, and the country's ailing motor-vehicle industry.

Militarily, British involvement in the Libyan attack was not strictly necessary. But it was politically useful to the United States to demonstrate that its actions had the support of at least one major nation of the North Atlantic Treaty Organization (NATO). Only Britain among the European NATO allies gave the United States unqualified backing.

While Mrs. Thatcher was greeted as a hero in the United States, her stand was opposed by a clear two thirds of the British public. The Libyan raid was to be only one of a series of setbacks for the British government in which a U.S. connection was an important aspect.

The Westland affair, producing eventually a U.S. financial solution to the problems of the insolvent Westland helicopter company in the west of England, was to pose the most serious challenge yet to the prime minister's long political career. The controversy also resulted in the resignation of two senior Cabinet ministers —Michael Heseltine, the secretary of state for defense, and Leon Brittan, the trade and industry secretary. Heseltine, who had supported a European-based rescue of Westland, resigned suddenly on January 9. He charged Mrs. Thatcher and Brittan with intervening to support a rescue proposal by Sikorsky Aircraft division of the United Technologies Corporation of the United States and Fiat S.p.A. of Italy in spite of the government's stated policy of nonintervention. Subsequently, Mrs. Thatcher's judgment and authority were called into question when she admitted knowing of the leaking of a confidential letter written by Sir Patrick Mayhew, the solicitor general, to Heseltine. The letter, released without the solicitor general's prior knowledge or approval, was leaked to discredit Heseltine. In the letter Mayhew said that earlier correspondence from Heseltine to the European consortium regarding Westland contained "material inaccuracies."

Although the leak emanated from the Department of Trade and Industry, forcing Brittan to resign, it was inspired from within the prime minister's own office at 10 Downing Street. Heseltine backed the European consortium because he believed in strengthening the European pillar of NATO to balance American dominance in Europe.

The American factor was even more crucial in the government's plans for restructuring the British motor industry. Jaguar, the British auto company which had been returned to the private sector, was thriving on strong export demand from the United States. Yet the rest of Britain's heavily state-subsidized motor industry faced weak consumer demand at home and saturated markets in Europe. To prop up the financially troubled industry, the government called in the two U.S. automobile giants, Ford and General Motors. When word got out that Ford and Austin Rover were locked in secret talks, negotiations were called off. By now there was growing concern that the country was no longer in control of its economic destiny.

Reports that negotiations were also under way for a proposed General Motors takeover of both Leyland Trucks and Land Rover, a prestigious status symbol, touched a particularly sensitive nerve. The idea of selling off such a cherished national institution as Land Rover to a U.S. corporation brought consternation within the Conservative Party. The government, again under political pressure, was forced to retreat. This time, it withdrew the sale of Land Rover, which had been the principal inducement to General Motors.

In another development involving a U.S. corporation, the Thatcher government announced late in the year that Britain would purchase U.S. AWACS from the Boeing Company, thereby rejecting its own Nimrod aircraft.

Domestic Affairs

The Political Scene. The Westland and Land Rover crises took their toll on the government. For the first time the political pendulum, which had swung sharply rightward at the 1983 general elections, began to move noticeably toward the left. The 1983 balloting had not only returned the ruling Conservative Party with an overwhelming majority, it also had left the badly defeated Labour Party demoralized and divided. But the dramatic events of 1986, coupled with an apparent shift in the public's perception of what the government's priorities should be, brought about a reversal in the fortunes of Britain's two major political parties.

To some extent the Labour Party, with its somewhat diluted commitment to socialism, had capitalized on the Conservative Party's misfortunes. At the same time Labour's newfound strength had a momentum of its own. In Neil Kinnock, Labour now had a younger, more modern leader with considerable television appeal. The 44-year-old leader gave the party a more dynamic and up-to-date image. As a tactician Kinnock imposed stricter party discipline on the rank and file and enhanced the party's electoral appeal by moving it toward the political center, expelling the Militant Tendency, a Trotskyite faction that had dominated the Liverpool City Council.

Meanwhile the public, after seven years of continuous Tory rule, showed signs of getting bored with Thatcherism. As the Conservative Party lurched from one crisis to another, its popularity drained to the Labour and Alliance (Liberal and Social Democratic) parties.

The Economy. The Thatcher Cabinet became increasingly frustrated that the government's message was not getting across to the public.

Under Conservative rule, Britain, which once had been regarded as the "sick man of Europe" had propelled itself to the top of the Common Market's economic growth league. Britain also was growing at a faster pace than the United States. And for 1987 the London Business School forecast a 3% growth rate for Britain. Even more salutary to the government's overall economic goals was the fall in inflation to roughly 3% in 1986. This represented the lowest inflation level in Britain in more than 20 years.

The Conservatives also were moving ahead on another favorite campaign pledge: cutting taxes. In the government's budget for fiscal 1986–87, Chancellor of the Exchequer Nigel Lawson announced a reduction in income tax by one penny in the pound to 29 pence. Later in the autumn he reaffirmed his hope that the standard rate of income tax would be lowered to 25 pence in the pound. The decline in North Sea oil revenues necessarily limited the chancellor's scope for tax cuts. At the same time Treasury coffers were being filled from the sale of state assets.

This so-called privatization program was condemned by the Earl of Stockton, Harold Macmillan, who likened the process to selling off the family silver. (The former Conservative prime minister died on December 29.) For the Thatcher government, it represented a fundamental ideological doctrine. At the national level it was rolling back the frontiers of the state. At the individual level it was fulfilling Mrs. Thatcher's hopes of transforming Britain into a share-owning democracy. Studies showed that the idea was catching on.

When the Conservatives first came into power in 1979, only 6% of the people owned stocks and shares in Britain. By 1986 that figure had virtually tripled to 17%. One of the largest ever share flotations in the world, the sale of

British Gas in December raised the figure still higher. (*See also* page 554.)

Social Problems. While the government seem determined to reshape the ideological landscape, it had less success in convincing the public that lower inflation, curbs on public expenditure, and cuts in taxes were necessarily the right priorities. Opinion polls showed that the public appeared less interested in tax cuts than in raising levels of public expenditure to improve health, social services, and education, even if it meant increasing taxes.

The government, which was already sensitive to record high unemployment running close to the 3.5 million mark, was facing demands right across the board from trade unions to industrialists for a major public works program to bring down unemployment. The stubbornly high unemployment figures were the government's most pressing economic and political problem. It highlighted more than anything the growing divide between an affluent south and an economically stagnant north. Soaring property values in the south made it virtually impossible for people in the north, where salaries were lower, to transfer their place of work. By autumn 1986 house prices in the south were 2½ times those in the north. Similar disparities were found in the rental market.

The most damaging criticism made against the Thatcher government in public surveys was that under the Conservatives, the rich had become richer, and the poor poorer. During the seven years of Conservative rule, the number of people living at, or near, the poverty line jumped from 11.5 million to 16.3 million—nearly one third of the population.

Political Conventions. It was against this backdrop that Britain's political party conference season began in September. The party conferences were to mark a dramatic watershed in British politics. It also signaled the Conservative Party's return to public favor after months of disapproval. The transformation came on the issue of defense.

At their conventions all three opposition parties became preoccupied with defense. This had special significance for the Conservatives. First, it pushed unemployment, education, health, and social services—areas in which the government was vulnerable—into the background. Secondly, it played up what has traditionally been a winning card for the Conservatives. The Conservatives sweeping election win in 1983 is almost entirely attributed to the government's victorious handling of the Falklands War.

Defense was to be the overriding issue for the Alliance parties' steep drop in public support after the 1986 party conference in September. The Alliance's difficulties over defense arose over the inability of the Social Democrats (pronuclear) and the Liberals (antinuclear) to reconcile their differences and come up with a uniform defense policy.

No such splits tore the Labour Party. But its decision at its October conference in Blackpool to go nonnuclear for the first time represented a stark break with Labour's previous defense policy. Labour not only voted for the removal of all U.S. nuclear weapons and bases from Britain, it also rejected the U.S. nuclear umbrella. The decision spelled the end of 40 years of bipartisan defense policy in British politics. By the end of the conference, only the Conservatives were committed to Trident, Britain's new and more powerful independent nuclear deterrent. Trident, to be ushered in during the 1990s, was to replace Polaris, Britain's existing and aging deterrent.

Northern Ireland. The issue of Northern Ireland, particularly sensitive in 1985, was to pass almost unnoticed at the 1986 party confer-

AP/Wide World

Under 44-year-old Neal Kinnock (second from right), the Labour Party won new support with a more moderate, better organized image. At the close of the party conference in October, Kinnock predicted that Labour would "win the next general election outright."

GREAT BRITAIN · Information Highlights

Official Name: United Kingdom of Great Britain and Northern Ireland.
Location: Island, western Europe.
Area: 94,200 sq mi (243 977 km²).
Population (mid-1986 est.): 56,600,000.
Chief Cities (mid-1984 est.): London, the capital, 6,756,000; Birmingham, 1,009,400; Glasgow, 744,000; Leeds, 712,200; Sheffield, 540,500.
Government: *Head of state,* Elizabeth II, queen (acceded Feb. 1952). *Head of government,* Margaret Thatcher, prime minister and First Lord of the Treasury (took office May 1979). *Legislature* —Parliament: House of Lords and House of Commons.
Monetary Unit: Pound (0.6986 pound equals U.S.$1, Oct. 17, 1986).
Gross National Product (1984): $426,300,000,000.
Economic Indexes (1985): *Consumer Prices* (1980 = 100), all items, 141.5; food, 131.4. *Industrial Production* (1980 = 100), 108.
Foreign Trade (1985 U.S.$): *Imports,* $109,269,000,000; *exports,* $101,332,000,000.

ences. It was not even on the Conservative Party's agenda. The omission demonstrated the wide acceptance of the 1985 Anglo-Irish Agreement by all four political parties.

Northern Ireland Protestants, who make up 60% of the province's population, remained implacably opposed to a deal that gave the Republic of Ireland a say in their own affairs. When peaceful protests and a referendum failed to move the British government to nullify or change, frustrated militants in the province vented their anger on the homes of police officers. More than 100 homes were either vandalized or burned down, forcing police families to flee. This insidious new development in Northern Ireland politics ended almost as soon as it began. At 1986's end the agreement remained intact, but unrelenting Protestant opposition was stalling progress. Meanwhile in July the U.S. Senate had ratified a new extradition treaty with Britain. The agreement facilitated the extradition from the United States of members of the outlawed Irish Republican Army (IRA) accused of terrorist acts.

Other News. Revolutionary changes in the financial and newspaper worlds competed with the political headlines in 1986. The "Big Bang" of October 27 saw the Stock Exchange opened up to international competition. The immediate impact of the deregulation of British stocks and government securities was diminished when the computers initially crashed because the electronic trading system could not cope with the demands. The year 1986 also marked the long-awaited technological revolution in Britain's national newspapers when publishers, frustrated by the restrictive manning practices of the unions and outdated machinery, fled Fleet Street to set up shop in brand new modern printing plants. Eddie Shah paved the way when on March 4 he published *Today,* Britain's first nonunion, fully computerized newspaper. The bitter union dispute that accompanied Rupert Murdoch's move to the district of Wapping to publish *The Times* and three other newspapers pointed up in the midst of technological change long-standing animosities between unions and management.

DAVID WINDER, *British Isles Correspondent*
"The Christian Science Monitor"

The Arts

The main problem for the British arts in 1986 was the adjustment in funding necessitated by the abolition of the metropolitan county councils of London, Manchester, and elsewhere. The national Arts Council, awarded an additional £25 million (about $35 million) to cover the problem, challenged local borough councils to contribute their share.

Theater. The year saw many new plays: David Hare's *The Bay at Nice* and *Wrecked Eggs,* Alan Bennett's *Kafka Dick,* Trevor Griffith's *Real Dreams,* and Pam Gems' *The Danton Affair.* Alan Ayckbourn's *A Woman in Mind* arrived in London to unanimous acclaim as a "savage tragicomedy" and gave Julia Mackenzie a huge part as a wife driven mad by the emotional poverty of her relationships.

In Britain going to the theater is more popular than football, and one third of all adults went to a play or musical at least once in 1986. Sparkling performances show why. The National Theatre started off 1986 with Ian McKellan and a uniformly excellent cast in *The Cherry Orchard* and ended with Anthony Hopkins playing *King Lear* and Maggie Smith in a new play by Stephen Poliakoff, *Coming in to Land.* At the Royal Shakespeare Company (RSC) in Stratford, Jeremy Irons played *Richard II,* while Jonathan Pryce tackled *Macbeth.* The RSC's hit was undoubtedly *Les Liaisons Dangereuses,* an adaptation by Christopher Hampton of the Laclos classic novel, with Alan Rickman as the dissolute Vicomte de Valmont.

In May, a new theater-in-the-round was opened in Stratford; the Swan is an addition to the RSC complex dedicated to the works of Shakespeare's contemporaries. The Swan opened with *The Two Noble Kinsmen* by Shakespeare and Fletcher, followed by *The Rover,* written in 1677 by Aphra Behn.

Outside the major national companies there were excellent performances from Vanessa Redgrave and Timothy Dalton in *Antony and Cleopatra,* from Glenda Jackson and Joan Plowright in *The House of Bernarda Alba,* and from Paul Scofield in *I'm Not Rappaport.*

Light entertainment was not neglected. In the fall, 14 musicals were running in London, including *Chess* from Tim Rice, Benny Andersson, and Björn Ulvaeus, and *Phantom of the Opera* from Andrew Lloyd Webber.

Music. A rich musical year included many festivals, a number emphasizing modern music. The Bath Festival focused on contemporary French music. The Almeida Festival in London's Islington, devised by Pierre Audi, featured modern Spanish and Japanese music. Classical festivals included Edinburgh, Aldeburgh, Buxton, and Glyndebourne, where Verdi's *Simon Boccanegra* was conducted by Bernard Haitink and directed by Sir Peter Hall.

The new musical work that attracted the greatest attention was Harrison Birtwistle's opera *The Mask of Orpheus*, performed by the English National Opera and welcomed as "a work of immense power and fascination" by the critic of *The Times*.

Among performers, Barry Douglas, a musician almost unknown to the record-buying public, stood out by winning the Tschaikovsky Piano Competition in Moscow. Simon Rattle, resident conductor of the City of Birmingham Symphony Orchestra, continued to bring his orchestra to a level of brilliance that would attract funds to hire more musicians and build a new concert hall.

Britain's regions fought the musical dominance of London and sometimes won. In a variable year at Covent Garden, which saw Sir Colin Davis relinquish the post of musical director after 15 years, one of the successes was an imported *Ring* from the Welsh National Opera. Earlier in the season, the Cardiff-based company had attracted Peter Stein from Berlin for a strong *Otello*.

Fine Arts. The death of Henry Moore at 88 ended a lifetime of prolific and monumental works of art. London enjoyed exhibitions from other leading figures of the 20th century, including Oskar Kokoschka at the Tate Gallery.

The Royal Academy had an interesting year, starting off with the Victorian sculptor Sir Alfred Gilbert, popularly known for his statue of Eros in Piccadilly Circus, and ending with perhaps the year's best exhibition, on the architecture of Norman Foster, Richard Rogers, and James Stirling. Foster's Hong Kong and Shanghai bank building and Stirling's Staatsgalerie Museum in Stuttgart were prominently documented. Rogers' "London as It Could Be" featured a stunning silver-painted model for a pedestrian and monorail bridge over the Thames.

Dance. Visitors during 1986 included the Bolshoi and the national companies of China and Japan. Ballet Rambert celebrated its 60th birthday with six new works, including *Mercure* by Ian Spink. The Royal Ballet's fall season opened, under new director Anthony Dowell, with the first London performance of *Galanteries* by David Bintley, now appointed resident choreographer. Bintley's new three-act ballet, *The Snow Queen*, was first seen in Birmingham, then at Covent Garden.

Film and Television. Roland Joffe's *The Mission*, with Jeremy Irons and Robert De Niro, was awarded the Palme d'Or at the Cannes Film Festival. *Mona Lisa*, directed by Neil Jordan, provided Bob Hoskins with a share of the Best Actor prize at the same festival. Among other notable films were Merchant-Ivory's *A Room with a View*, Derek Jarman's *Caravaggio*, and Julien Temple's *Absolute Beginners*. Television provided Alan Bennett's play, *The Insurance Man*, and the series *Man and Music*, a survey of nine centuries of musical invention.

MAUREEN GREEN, *Free-lance Writer, London*

Harrison Birtwistle's "The Mask of Orpheus," performed by the English National Opera, won critical acclaim.

© Dominic Photography

GREECE

Greece during 1986 was beset by economic problems, which the government of Prime Minister Andreas Papandreou and his Panhellenic Socialist Movement (PASOK) tried to alleviate through austerity measures. In October, PASOK did poorly in municipal elections that increased the prestige of the conservative New Democracy Party, the chief parliamentary opposition, and its leader Constantine Mitsotakis.

Elections. Municipal elections were held in Greece on October 12, with runoffs on October 19. PASOK-backed candidates won only 146 of the 303 large municipalities at stake, compared with the 1982 elections, in which they had won 167 of the 276 municipalities at stake. The Greek Communist Party won 53 cities, ten more than before. New Democracy-backed candidates increased their hold from 49 cities in 1982 to 78, including the three largest: Athens, Piraeus, and Salonika. Among the more than 5,000 smaller communities, PASOK came out ahead, but the conservatives won some 500 communities that had previously been under socialist control. These elections did not change Papandreou's 160-seat majority in the Greek Parliament of 300, where New Democracy held 110 seats.

Economy and Tourism. Stringent economic measures such as limiting wage increases, started by the Papandreou government in October 1985, were continued into 1986. The prime minister was under great pressure from his fellow European Community (EC) members as well as from the International Monetary Fund (IMF) to improve Greece's economy. Economic problems included unemployment, high inflation, and a balance of payments deficit. The austerity measures were resented by many Greeks; consequently, criticisms of Papandreou and PASOK increased. Many strikes hit the country, including a short one by Greek diplomatic staffs at home and abroad. To add to the economic woes, shipping, an important element in the economy, was adversely affected by worldwide problems. Also, some Greek exports had difficulty competing with exports of countries with much more technologically sophisticated manufacturing systems.

A bomb explosion April 2 on TWA flight 840 bound from Rome to Athens took the lives of four Americans. This tragedy, along with random bombings in Athens during the year, underlined the problems of international terrorism and raised questions about the safety of travel in Greece. Although large numbers of tourists visited Greece in 1986, few Americans did, and this had a disastrous impact on the Greek tourist industry. Questions about security at the Athens airport and possible problems with terrorism seem to have been the concerns that kept many Americans away, despite efforts by the Greek government to emphasize that measures had been taken to keep the country safe. There was evidence, however, that anti-American utterances over the years by Papandreou, who once had been a U.S. citizen, may have influenced some Americans.

Foreign Relations. U.S. Secretary of State George P. Shultz visited Athens in March. A few days before his arrival a statue of President Harry S. Truman was damaged severely by a bomb explosion. It had been a gift to the people of Greece in 1963 from the American Hellenic Educational Progressive Association (AHEPA) in recognition of the Truman Doctrine and U.S. assistance that helped the Greek government crush a leftist civil war in the 1940s. The Athens City Council, dominated by PASOK supporters, and then Mayor Dimitris Beis (who later lost the October election) refused to re-erect the statue on the same site. Prime Minister Papandreou promised that the statue would be repaired and given a place of honor again.

There were, however, other strains with the United States during the year, particularly when Papandreou openly criticized aspects of American foreign policy.

In April 1986, Papandreou condemned the United States for bombing Libya, and he refused to put into effect sanctions against Libya that had been voted by the EC. Later, however, he did decrease the Libyan diplomatic presence at Athens. In late May, Syrian President Hafez al-Assad paid a three-day visit to Greece, where he was warmly received by Papandreou. After Great Britain broke relations with Syria in October, Papandreou and his government avoided any condemnation of Syria. On November 10 the Greek government refused to join the 11 other members of the EC in sanctions against Syria.

Royal Birth. Queen Anne-Marie, wife of deposed Greek King Constantine II, gave birth to the couple's fifth child, a son, on April 26, 1986, in London. The infant prince was baptized Philippos (Philip) on July 10 at London's

---

GREECE · Information Highlights

Official Name: Hellenic Republic.
Location: Southwestern Europe.
Area: 50,944 sq mi (131 944 km²).
Population (mid-1986 est.): 10,000,000.
Chief Cities (1981 census): Athens, the capital, 885,737; Salonika, 406,413; Piraeus, 196,389.
Government: *Head of state,* Christos Sartzetakis, president (took office March 1985). *Head of government,* Andreas Papandreou, prime minister (took office Oct. 1981). *Legislature*—Parliament.
Monetary Unit: Drachma (133.0 drachmas equal U.S.$1, Oct. 17, 1986).
Gross National Product (1984 U.S.$): $33,500,-000,000.
Economic Indexes (1985): *Consumer Prices* (1980 = 100), all items, 255.7; food, 262.8. *Industrial Production* (1980 = 100), 100.
Foreign Trade (1985 U.S.$): *Imports,* $10,139,-000,000; *exports,* $4,542,000,000.

St. Sophia Greek Orthodox Cathedral. God-parents included King Juan Carlos of Spain, the Princess of Wales, and Prince Philip, duke of Edinburgh, whose father Prince Andrew of Greece was a great uncle of King Constantine II.

Disaster and Obituaries. A major earthquake on September 13 and subsequent aftershocks caused a loss of life and destroyed great parts of the southern port city of Kalamata and nearby villages.

Greek politician Panayotis Kanellopoulos, age 83, died on September 11. The military had expelled him after 18 days as prime minister in 1967 and established a dictatorship that lasted until 1974. Lady Amalia Fleming, Greek widow of Britain's Sir Alexander Fleming, the discoverer of penicillin, died on February 26 at age 73. Active in the World War II resistance, she later opposed the military dictatorship. At the time of her death she was a PASOK deputy in Parliament.

GEORGE J. MARCOPOULOS, *Tufts University*

Rivers of lava continued to flow from Hawaii's Kilauea Volcano, destroying forestland and private homes. One molten flow reached the sea, but new streams fanned out.

AP/Wide World

HAWAII • Information Highlights

Area: 6,471 sq mi (16 759 km²).
Population (1985 est.): 1,054,000.
Chief Cities (1980 census): Honolulu, the capital, 365,048; Pearl City, 42,575; Kailua, 35,812; Hilo, 35,269.
Government (1986): *Chief Officers*—governor, John D. Waihee III (D); lt. gov., Benjamin J. Gayetano (D). *Legislature*—Senate, 25 members; House of Representatives, 51 members.
State Finances (fiscal year 1985): *Revenue,* $2,677,000,000; *expenditure,* $2,539,000,000.
Personal Income (1985): $14,558,000,000; per capita, $13,814.
Labor Force (June 1986): *Civilian labor force,* 502,300; *unemployed,* 27,800 (5.5% of total force).
Education: *Enrollment* (fall 1984)—public elementary schools, 111,650; public secondary, 52,210; colleges and universities, 49,937. *Public school expenditures* (1983–84), $596,000,000 ($3,982 per pupil).

HAWAII

Hawaii's voters kept the Democratic Party in power in most statewide elections in 1986.

Elections. U.S. Sen. Daniel K. Inouye (D) was reelected handily to his fifth term in Washington, keeping his unblemished record for never losing an election. U.S. Rep. Daniel K. Akaka (D) also won reelection, but Rep. Cecil Heftel, who resigned in July to run for the governorship, lost in the Democratic primary to Lt. Gov. John D. Waihee III, who went on to defeat Republican D.G. (Andy) Anderson in the November balloting. Former state Sen. Benjamin J. Gayetano (D) was elected lieutenant governor.

In a special election to fill Heftel's remaining term as Hawaii's U.S. representative from the first district, the voters picked former state Sen. Neil Abercrombie (D) in a five-way race. However, Patricia Saiki (R), who finished second in the special election, was elected in November to the full two-year term beginning January 1987, becoming Hawaii's first Republican in Congress since the retirement of former U.S. Sen. Hiram L. Fong in January 1977.

The state legislature remained solidly Democratic, with 20 Democrats and 5 Republicans in the Senate and 40 Democrats and 11 Republicans in the House. The Honolulu City Council also remained in the hands of the Democrats, with only one Republican on the nine-member body. Mayor Frank F. Fasi (R) was not up for reelection in 1986.

On the island of Maui, Republican Mayor Hannibal Tavares won reelection, but the Democrats retained control of the County Council. The Democrats also control the islands of Kauai and Hawaii, holding the mayor's posts and a majority of the councils on those islands. Voters on Hawaii rejected a proposal that would have banned nuclear ships or power plants on the island. Opponents of the measure said it was unconstitutional.

The Economy. Concern over Hawaii's tight budget persuaded lawmakers in 1986 to levy a hotel-room tax in hopes of augmenting the state's tax coffers. They were overjoyed when, instead of a drop in tourists, there was an increase of 15% in visitor arrivals in the first nine months of 1986, despite the tax.

Polls during the 1986 political campaign showed that jobs were the major concern of Hawaii's citizens. Although unemployment reached its lowest point in several years (4.5% in September), the job count also declined (to a 484,500 civilian labor force).

Exile. Hawaii became home to a third ruler-in-exile in the post-World War II era with the arrival in February of deposed President Ferdinand Marcos of the Philippines. Earlier exiles were President Syngman Rhee of South Korea and Cambodian leader Lon Nol, neither of whom ever returned to his homeland. None of the earlier exiles had to endure the bitter legal battles that marked the Marcos era in Hawaii, however. Nor were they subjected to the harassment, catcalls, and vandalism that marked the stay of Marcos and his family.

Volcano. An eruption of a different sort continued on the island of Hawaii, 200 mi (320 km) from Honolulu, where lava still flowed down the slopes of Kilauea crater. The eruption began in 1983 and damaged private property as well as valuable stands of hardwood trees in Hawaii Volcanoes National Park, and endangered access to scenic Kalapana beach highway. There was no loss of life, but some ten houses were set on fire by the lava flows in late November and early December.

CHARLES H. TURNER
Free-lance Writer, Honolulu

HONG KONG

Focal issues in 1986 were the drafting of the Basic Law and construction of the Daya Bay nuclear-power project. Queen Elizabeth II and Prince Philip stopped in Hong Kong in October after their first state visit to China.

Basic Law. A Basic Law Drafting Committee (BLDC) was set up to write the Basic Law, the constitution of the future special administrative region (SAR) of Hong Kong after it becomes part of China in 1997. The BLDC consists of 36 members from China and 23 members from Hong Kong. The Basic Law Consultative Committee (BLCC), an advisory body of 180 mostly Hong Kong residents, is meant to represent the 5.5 million people of Hong Kong. Members of both committees, however, were virtually appointed by the Chinese government.

There was apprehension that the BLDC and the BLCC would gradually undermine the power of Hong Kong's highest policy-making body, the Executive Council, and its lawmaking advisory body, the Legislative Council. A few outspoken BLDC members criticized the draft of the Basic Law, made public in April; they wanted it to state the relationship between the Chinese constitution and the Basic Law, as well as the concept of residual power for the SAR. Many Hong Kong residents still question China's promises of permitting democracy after 1997.

Daya Bay Project. After the Chernobyl nuclear disaster in the USSR, Hong Kong residents expressed concern about the safety of the $27 billion nuclear plant under construction at Daya Bay, 31 mi (50 km) east of Hong Kong. In August the Hong Kong government sent delegations to Europe, the United States, and Japan for expert advice on the project, jointly owned by the Chinese Guangdong Nuclear Investment Co. (75%) and the Hong Kong Nuclear Investment Co. (25%). Throughout the year, antinuclear activists lobbied China to shelve the project.

Economy. Exports increased by 8%, imports by 9%, and re-exports by 1% during the first six months of 1986, compared with the same period of 1985. The unified Stock Exchange of Hong Kong Ltd., formed from four existing exchanges, opened for trading on April 2, designated as the base day of the new Hong Kong Index set at 1,000. On August 18, the Hong Kong index reached a high of 1,221.71. The Hong Kong dollar stabilized in the foreign-exchange market because of its linkage with the U.S. dollar.

Tourism, Hong Kong's third-largest foreign exchange earner, generated income of $1.9 billion in 1985, up 5.5% from the previous year. Hong Kong became a member of the General Agreement on Tariffs and Trade (GATT) in April.

Construction began late in the year on the Tate's Cairn road tunnel linking Sha Tin with East Kowloon and on the second cross-harbor tunnel between Quarry Bay and Cha Kwo Ling. A planning committee began looking for a site for Hong Kong's third university, which is expected to open around 1994.

Relations with China. Hong Kong provided 80% of the total foreign investment in China during the 1979–85 period. A bridge and link road at Lok Ma Chau, begun in June, will offer the third vehicular crossing between Hong Kong and China. Dragonair, a new Hong Kong-based airline, was licensed to operate scheduled service between Hong Kong and eight Chinese cities.

Hong Kong was the meeting place for aviation officials from China and Taiwan, who, on May 17, held the first-ever direct talks between the two governments. They discussed a Taiwan-owned cargo aircraft that had been diverted to Canton.

DAVID CHUENYAN LAI
University of Victoria, British Columbia

HOUSING

The year 1986 was a good one for U.S. housing. Construction remained strong; prices increased moderately, and mortgage finance remained affordable. In 1986 housing starts ran at an annual rate of approximately 1.85 million units, up from 1.74 units in 1985. Fixed interest rates for mortgages edged up slightly, averaging between 9.5 and 10%. (Adjustable rate mortgages are generally 1.5 percentage points below those carrying the fixed rate.) Calculations of "real" mortgage costs, adjusted for inflation, showed mortgage rates increasing from 3.75% at the beginning of 1984 to 5.5% in the third quarter of 1986. Affordable housing remains a major problem for many Americans.

While housing starts were higher in 1986 than in 1985, a projected boom of 2 million or more units did not materialize. Major reasons for the lower performance, as against expectations, seemed to be the relatively high real cost of mortgage money and the fears of tax reform. The median price of a new home in June 1986 was $89,600, a 3.8% increase over the $86,300 median price tag of a year earlier. The median resale price of a used home was $82,300 up 7.6% from the previous year.

The most popular form of housing on the market was the moderately priced single-family detached house. Lower priced condominium units and mobile homes as well as expensive homes did not move as well as in previous years. There were also dramatic regional differences in the housing market. Some of the strongest housing markets were in the Northeast. Areas dependent on energy and agriculture were weak.

Tax Reform. The Tax Reform Act of 1986 makes investment in rental housing less attractive and therefore is likely to mean the construction of fewer units available for rent. Representatives of the housing industry have estimated as much as a 50% decline in the construction of rental units in the first year after the new tax law becomes effective. Other estimates point to a possible 20% rise in the price of rental housing between 1986–90. This will happen because the new legislation limits tax shelters, including changes in the deductibility of interest and taxes, and the lengthening of depreciation schedules. The tax rate on capital gains also will increase under the new tax law. Owner-occupied housing will still enjoy the deductibility of interest and taxes, but tax brackets will be lowered, making those deductions relatively less valuable.

Prior to the 1986 tax act, investors were able to shelter large amounts of their total income from taxes by investing in limited partnerships, which in turn owned housing and other urban-development projects. Paper losses were created through the use of accelerated depreciation schedules. These losses were then deducted against the investors total income, including income from the investor's primary job. Under the new tax act losses cannot be deducted from income of the investor's primary job. The new law also stretches depreciation schedules from 19 to 27½ years for rental housing.

Recreational Housing. Initial proposals by the Reagan administration, eliminating the deductibility of interest and taxes on second homes, were not included in the tax bill as enacted. The proposal for changing deductibility provisions for the second home produced substantial confusion and softening in this market. Once the final provisions of the tax act became apparent, second homes became an area for renewed interest. While deductions for the first and second homes will not be as valuable after 1986, they will remain a way for many people to shelter income from taxes.

Refinancing. With mortgage rates dropping the pace of mortgage refinancing began to quicken in 1986. Between 1980 and 1985 mortgage-interest rates averaged about 13%. The rule of thumb in mortgage financing is that a 2% or greater spread in mortgage rates makes refinancing advantageous. Business for lending institutions boomed as many mortgage holders began to fall into the category where mortgage refinancing was valuable.

International Developments. In Great Britain, the government of Prime Minister Margaret Thatcher continued its policy of moving the housing market away from its dependence on the government. Public housing in Britain is provided to low and moderate income families at a rent level fixed as a percentage of income. Traditionally, private rental housing had never been encouraged, and home ownership was considered possible only for the wealthy and upper-middle income classes. Since 1979 the Thatcher government has tried with some success to alter this pattern. The construction of new council housing units has been curtailed, while existing units are being sold to their tenants. The private rental housing market is now being stimulated. Estimates indicate that by 1986, owner-occupied housing had reached 64% of the housing stock. (In 1975 such housing was 55% and in 1914 it had stood at 10%.) Publicly owned housing, which accounted for 29% of the housing market in 1975, now accounts for only about 25%. Rental housing had dropped from approximately 90% of the housing stock in 1914 to 12% today. The rate of decline, however, of the private rental market has slowed since 1975.

In Canada, as in Britain and the United States, the trend has been in the direction of home ownership, rehabilitation of existing housing stock, and aid to the poor and working class households without making government the landlord. In the Montreal region, for example, the proportion of family households owning their homes has more than doubled since 1951. Tax incentives and other forms of economic stimuli have given the home owner a significant advantage over the renter.

In Canada forms of home ownership which achieve certain social objectives—aid to the poor, elderly, and handicapped—without direct government ownership now are emphasized. These include housing owned by nonprofit organizations, housing coops, condominiums, and undivided co-ownerships (a share of the building, not the individual unit, is owned). The newer forms of ownership are causing a wider divergence in housing types.

The American-style suburban single-family house is growing in popularity in Japan. The number of American-style homes, while still small in terms of total number of units, grew by 25% in the fiscal year which ended March 1986. The American home is attractive because of its increased space for home-oriented leisure time activities, its style of bedrooms and bathrooms, and its insulation system.

JEROME R. LEWIS, *University of Delaware*

HUNGARY

In 1986, Hungary's successful experiment with economic innovation and political liberalization continued, but not without difficulties.

Economic and Political Affairs. In December 1985 the published guidelines for the Seventh Five-Year Plan (1986–90) placed emphasis on increasing productive efficiency through technological modernization and maximizing exports over imports. Cooperation with the Soviet Union and the other East European countries was labeled the "decisive factor" in Hungary's international economic relations. The government announced that Hungary would spend more than $100 million to improve the quality of basic research in the country's universities and scientific institutes.

In January 1986 the tax structure was revised to benefit people with low incomes and to raise taxes on business profits. Taxes on joint ventures with Western companies were sharply reduced, however. Price increases were instituted for a broad range of consumer items, from fruit and telephone calls to refrigerators and autos. The "private work partnerships," which allow employees to use factory equipment after hours for private ventures, were criticized for diminishing normal labor productivity. Problems familiar in the West, such as job-loss anxiety, bankruptcy, and fraudulent use of company assets, were increasing in Hungary's market-oriented society.

Political dissenters grew bolder in 1986. In February members of the "Danube Circle," a group of dissident Hungarian environmentalists and scholars, joined with Austrian and West German colleagues in a march to oppose construction of the Gabčikovo-Nagymáros hydroelectric dam complex on the Danube. Most of the cost of the project is to be paid by a consortium of Austrian banks, and 70% of the construction work is to be done by Austrian companies. In March several hundred people marched in celebration of the Hungarian revolution of 1848–49. On the 30th anniversary of the Hungarian revolution of 1956 (October 23), 54 Hungarians, joined by Poles, Czechs, and East Germans, signed a public declaration praising the uprising as "a common heritage and inspiration."

In early 1986 it was estimated that between 100 and 200 conscientious objectors to military service were currently imprisoned. And the government issued a decree extending legal and police measures, particularly surveillance, against those "displaying an attitude harmful to the internal order or security of the Hungarian People's Republic." Nevertheless, in March the Central Committee of the Hungarian Socialist Workers' (Communist) Party (HSWP) endorsed a proposal to limit the length of time in office of political and other public leaders.

Gen. István Olah, the minister of defense who died on Dec. 15, 1985, was succeeded by his deputy, Lt. Gen. Ferenc Karpati. Lászlo Cardinal Lekai, the Roman Catholic archbishop of Esztergom and primate of Hungary, died on June 20, 1986.

Foreign Affairs. In June 1986, Soviet leader Mikhail Gorbachev, allegedly interested in Hungary's economic reforms, visited the country. In late 1985 and throughout 1986 agreements increasing economic, technological, and cultural ties were signed with Romania, East Germany, Japan, China, and Angola. Hungary and Austria signed the first reported environmental agreement between East and West European countries, to exchange information and expertise on nuclear plants.

JOSEPH FREDERICK ZACEK
State University of New York at Albany

HUNGARY • Information Highlights

Official Name: Hungarian People's Republic.
Location: East-central Europe.
Area: 35,919 sq mi (93,030 km²).
Population (mid-1986 est.): 10,600,000.
Chief Cities (Jan. 1, 1985): Budapest, the capital, 2,071,484; Miskolc, 211,645; Debrecen, 208,891.
Government: *Head of state,* Pál Losonczi, president of the presidential council (took office April 1967). *Head of government,* György Lázár, premier of the council of ministers (took office 1975). Secretary general of the Hungarian Socialist Workers' Party, János Kádár (took office 1956). *Legislature* (unicameral)—National Assembly.
Monetary Unit: Forint (45.788 forints equal U.S.$1, June 1986).
Economic Indexes (1985): *Consumer Prices* (1980 = 100), all items, 139.1; food, 136.0. *Industrial Production* (1980 = 100), 110.
Foreign Trade (1985 U.S.$): *Imports,* $8,228,000,000; *exports,* $8,542,000,000.

International attention focused on Iceland in October 1986 as U.S. President Reagan and Soviet General Secretary Gorbachev held a hastily scheduled summit in Reykjavik, the nation's capital. Hofdi House, left, a 75-year-old mansion overlooking Reykjavik Bay, was the site of the talks between the two leaders.

AP/Wide World

ICELAND

The Progressive-Independence Party centrist-right coalition government headed by Steingrímur Hermannsson remained in power in 1986. Municipal elections and opinion polls, however, showed a marked increase in support for the Social Democratic Party.

The meeting between U.S. President Reagan and Soviet leader Gorbachev in Reykjavík in October was announced with only ten days notice, and caused a rush to organize facilities and accommodations for the 3,500 foreign personnel and reporters.

Prime Minister Hermannsson made an official visit to China in October, and discussed with Chinese leaders possible cooperation in the fields of geothermal energy and fisheries.

The state monopoly on radio and TV broadcasting was abolished in January, and two new broadcasting companies began operations.

Reykjavík celebrated its 200th anniversary and the University of Iceland its 75th.

ICELAND • Information Highlights

Official Name: Republic of Iceland.
Location: North Atlantic Ocean.
Area: 39,708 sq mi (102 845 km²).
Population (mid-1986 est.): 200,000.
Chief Cities (Dec. 1, 1985): Reykjavík, the capital, 89,868; Kópavogur, 14,631; Akureyri, 13,766.
Government: *Head of state,* Vigdís Finnbogadóttir, president (took office Aug. 1980). *Head of government,* Steingrímur Hermannsson, prime minister (took office May 1983). *Legislature*—Althing: Upper House and Lower House.
Monetary Unit: Króna (41.21 krónur equal U.S.$1, June 1986).
Gross National Product (1986 est. U.S.$): $3,474,-000,000.
Foreign Trade (1985 U.S.$): *Imports,* $904,000,000; *exports,* $814,000,000.

Economy. Various factors combined to make 1986 a prosperous year for Iceland. Economic growth exceeded expectations, with gross domestic product (GDP) increasing by an estimated 5% and national income by about 7%. Interest rates, previously set by the Central Bank, were deregulated. Following an important wage settlement in February the cost of living index fell in March (by 1.53%) for the first time in 15 years. The government undertook to maintain a stable nominal exchange rate of the krona, and inflation fell to about 11% for the year (from 36% in 1985). Real-interest rates improved to about 3% (from −1% in 1985). This, combined with increased purchasing power and a rise of 8% per capita in real earnings, meant that bank deposits grew considerably. The housing-loan scheme was restructured, and large sums were raised, without taking foreign loans, by the union pension funds' purchase of Treasury bonds. Foreign debts comprised 51.5% of GDP, a slight decrease since 1985. Unemployment remained negligible at 0.7%.

The state-owned Fisheries Bank declared a loss of $10.5 million on dealings with the Hafskip shipping company (liquidated in November 1985). Banking reforms were planned, and a solution to the bank's problems was sought. Legislation permitted foreign banks to open offices for consultancy in Iceland, and the possibility of allowing foreign investors a limited share in banks was discussed.

Talks were held with the British-based company Rio Tinto Zinc on the possible establishment of a silicon metal smelter in Iceland.

A dispute over the U.S. monopoly on cargo freighting to the U.S.-manned Iceland Defence Force was settled when the United States agreed to share freighting with Iceland.

Fisheries. Catch figures seemed set to outstrip 1985's record 1.68 million tons, with a higher proportion of more valuable species. There was a shift in sales volume away from the United States to Europe, due mainly to the depreciation of the dollar, and exports of fresh fish to Europe increased.

Whaling. Limited catches, authorized by the International Whaling Commission for research, were halted in July after the United States disputed the legality of proposed exports of whale meat and threatened to impose economic sanctions against Iceland. A compromise was reached in August when Iceland agreed to 50% of the whale meat being consumed locally. In November saboteurs from the conservationist organization Sea Shepherd sank two whaling ships in Reykjavík harbor and wrecked the control room of the whaling station.

ANNE COSSER
Free-lance Journalist, Reykjavík

IDAHO

Idaho law enforcement officials were kept busy in 1986 investigating racially motivated bombings in Coeur d'Alene and searching for self-styled mountain man Claude Dallas, who escaped from the Idaho State prison.

The first in a series of bombings in Coeur d'Alene went off on September 15 at the home of the head of the Kootenai County Task Force on Human Relations. On the morning of September 29, three more bombs exploded in the downtown area, while a fourth was defused. Early in October, Edward Hawley and Robert Pires were arraigned and charged with the bombings, which David Dorr was charged with aiding and abetting. Dorr is a former security chief of the neo-Nazi group Aryan Nations, based in Hayden Lake. Hawley and Pires allegedly have connections to the same group.

Dallas, serving a 30-year manslaughter sentence for the 1981 slayings of two Idaho Fish and Game Department officials, escaped on March 30. The search for him continued in the months that followed.

Legislature. Forced to cover a $20 million shortfall for fiscal 1986 and to avert a shortfall for fiscal 1987, the legislature passed a temporary 1% increase in the sales tax. The increase (to 5%) was slated to expire at the end of June 1987. Despite a projected $75 million in revenue generated by this measure, most state agencies' fiscal 1987 budgets showed no increase over the previous year. State employees were denied raises for the second consecutive year.

Pressure from the federal government in the form of a threat to withhold matching federal highway funds from states with drinking ages lower than 21 once again failed to influence the

---

IDAHO • Information Highlights

Area: 83,564 sq mi (216 432 km²).
Population (1985 est.): 1,005,000.
Chief Cities (1980 census): Boise, the capital (July 1, 1984 est.), 107,188; Pocatello, 46,340; Idaho Falls, 39,590.
Government (1986): *Chief Officers*—governor, John V. Evans (D); lt. gov., David H. Leroy (R). *Legislature*—Senate, 42 members; House of Representatives, 84 members.
State Finances (fiscal year 1985): *Revenue,* $1,610,000,000; *expenditure,* $1,440,000,000.
Personal Income (1985): $11,173,000,000; per capita, $11,120.
Labor Force (June 1986): *Civilian labor force,* 489,600; *unemployed,* 38,300 (7.8% of total force).
Education: *Enrollment* (fall 1984)—public elementary schools, 148,937; public secondary, 59,143; colleges and universities, 42,668. *Public school expenditures* (1983–84), $435,000,000 ($2,198 per pupil).

---

legislature. A bill to raise the drinking age from 19 to 21 passed the House but died in committee in the Senate.

Election Results. Statewide races for the U.S. Senate, governor, and lieutenant governor were all close. In the Senate race, incumbent Republican Steve Symms turned back a challenge by Democratic Gov. John Evans, winning 52% of the vote. In the gubernatorial race, former Democratic Governor and U.S. Interior Secretary Cecil Andrus squeaked by Republican Lt. Gov. David Leroy. Andrus won by only a plurality, and his election may well have turned on the presence of independent candidate James A. Miller, who won 1% of the vote. In the lieutenant governor's race, Republican C. L. ("Butch") Otter eked out a victory over Democrat Marjorie Ruth Moon.

First congressional district U.S. Rep. Larry Craig, a Republican, easily defeated challenger Bill Currie. In the second district, Democratic incumbent Richard Stallings held onto his seat over Republican challenger Mel Richardson.

By netting two seats in the state Senate, Democrats regained the ability to sustain a gubernatorial veto. Nonetheless, Republicans retained an edge in the Senate of 26 seats to 16 for the Democrats. Republicans won 64 House seats to 20 for the Democrats.

Major initiatives included passage of a state lottery and a proposal to reduce the size of the legislature. Voters also approved a referendum on the prohibition of compulsory union membership enacted by the legislature in 1985.

M. C. HENBERG, *University of Idaho*

ILLINOIS

Republican Gov. James R. Thompson defeated challenger Adlai E. Stevenson III by more than 400,000 votes to win an unprecedented fourth term in November 1986. Thompson was first elected in 1976 and has served longer than any other governor in Illinois history.

The Gubernatorial Campaign. Stevenson, the son of former Gov. Adlai Stevenson II, who twice lost the presidency to Dwight D. Eisenhower, tried to capitalize on Thompson's longevity in office and blamed him for Illinois' loss of hundreds of thousands of jobs and its decline as a major industrial state. Thompson in turn attacked what he called Stevenson's lackluster record as U.S. senator from Illinois. And the governor, remembering that Stevenson had nearly beaten him in 1982, fought the campaign as though he were the underdog.

Stevenson had been embarrassed in the March Democratic primary when two supporters of political extremist Lyndon LaRouche (*see* BIOGRAPHY) won spots on the Democratic slate for lieutenant governor and secretary of state. Not wishing to be associated with LaRouche, he resigned from the Democratic ticket and ran as an independent. This cost him the votes of thousands of persons who, out of habit, traditionally vote a straight Democratic ticket.

Other Contests. In other election results, Illinois Sen. Alan Dixon (D) swamped his Republican challenger, state Rep. Judy Koehler, by nearly one million votes to retain his reputation as Illinois' most enduring and popular politician. And in Cook County, which includes most of metropolitan Chicago, Republican James O'Grady, a former Chicago police superintendent, ended Democrat Richard Elrod's 16-year reign in the sheriff's office. O'Grady, the first Republican to be elected to a county-wide office in ten years, made corruption in the sheriff's office under Elrod the major issue in the campaign. His margin of victory over Elrod was only 45,000 votes out of 1.34 million cast in the race.

Floods. Record rainfall in the Chicago area in September sent the Des Plaines and Fox rivers overflowing their banks, bringing the most costly floods in Illinois history. Parts of Cook, Lake, and McHenry counties were declared federal disaster areas as property damage reached an estimated $40 million.

"Economically, this is the worst flood we've ever experienced in Illinois," said a spokesman for the Illinois Emergency Services and Disaster Agency. About 3,500 families were forced from their homes as the Des Plaines reached a 100-year flood level. Only 12% of the people flooded out were said to have been covered by insurance.

Corruption and Organized Crime. Operation Greylord, the ongoing federal investigation of corruption in the Cook County Circuit Court, continued to claim crooked judges, lawyers, policemen, and others in 1986. Of 53 persons charged since the investigation first surfaced in 1983, 30 persons—including six Cook County judges—have been convicted of wrongdoing.

One former judge, Reginald Holzer, was sentenced to 18 years in prison in May as "retribution" for using his position to extort $200,000 from lawyers and others who appeared in his courtroom. In passing sentence, U.S. District Judge Prentice Marshall told Holzer: "I am convinced, sir, that the community in this area and the members of this community are entitled to some degree of retribution. That is the purpose of this sentence, and I make no bones about it."

Organized Crime. Anthony Spilotro, 48, a Las Vegas crime syndicate figure from Chicago, and his brother Michael, 41, were kidnapped in Chicago in June and later found murdered in Indiana. Authorities believe the two were beaten before being buried alive in a shallow grave in a wildlife preserve near the Illinois-Indiana state line. The freshly dug grave was discovered by a farmer spreading fertilizer. The murders occurred only a few days before Anthony Spilotro, who once boasted he would some day head the crime syndicate in Chicago, was to go on trial in Las Vegas on racketeering charges.

Economy. Illinois continued to lose manufacturing jobs to other states and to suffer from a high level of unemployment. In October the jobless level stood at 7.5%, a half of one percentage point above the national average. Still, a record number of 5,270,000 persons were employed in the state that month as more jobs were being found in the service industries.

During the election campaign, Governor Thompson took credit for bringing a new Chrysler-Mitsubishi auto plant to the Bloomington-Normal area. Those jobs would probably be offset, however, by the phaseout of the General Motors stamping plant in Willow Springs that employs 2,900. GM announced the shutdown as part of a plan to phase out 29,000 workers in four Midwest states over the next three years.

ROBERT ENSTAD, *"Chicago Tribune"*

ILLINOIS • Information Highlights

Area: 56,345 sq mi (145 934 km²).
Population (1985 est.): 11,535,000.
Chief Cities (July 1, 1984 est.): Springfield, the capital, 101,570; Chicago, 2,992,472; Rockford, 136,531.
Government (1986): *Chief Officers*—governor, James R. Thompson (R); lt. gov., George H. Ryan (R). *General Assembly*—Senate, 59 members; House of Representatives, 118 members.
State Finances (fiscal year 1985): *Revenue,* $17,573,000,000; *expenditure,* $16,491,000,000.
Personal Income (1985): $169,999,000,000; per capita, $14,738.
Labor Force (June 1986): *Civilian labor force,* 5,813,400; *unemployed,* 489,200 (8.4% of total force).
Education: *Enrollment* (fall 1984)—public elementary schools, 1,254,477; public secondary, 579,878; colleges and universities, 678,689. *Public school expenditures* (1983–84), $5,470,000,000 ($3,397 per pupil).

Prime Minister Rajiv Gandhi and wife Sonia attend an October 2 prayer session marking the 117th birthday of the late Mohandas K. Gandhi. Shortly thereafter, a lone gunman made an unsuccessful attempt against the prime minister's life.

INDIA

Communal and other forms of violence—the worst since independence—marked the internal scene in India in 1986. The Punjab continued to be a particularly disturbed area, and a Sikh extremist made an unsuccessful assassination attempt against Prime Minister Rajiv Gandhi in New Delhi. Faced with growing criticism at home, Gandhi took several steps to strengthen his government and revitalize his Congress (I) party. He was particularly active in foreign affairs, making numerous trips abroad and participating in several international meetings, including the eighth summit of the Nonaligned Movement in Harare, Zimbabwe. The economic situation was relatively favorable, in spite of a massive trade deficit and rising debt service payments.

Domestic Affairs. In an address to the first session of Parliament on February 20, President Zail Singh described the ongoing strife in India. "Communalism continues to pose a serious threat to national unity," he said. "It is being reinforced by religious fundamentalism and fanaticism." The remaining months of the year confirmed his observations repeatedly. As in the previous two years, the Sikh-majority state of Punjab was the center of the worst communal violence, involving conflicts between not only Sikhs and Hindus but also moderate and militant Sikhs.

The new surge of unrest was triggered by several events in January. The first was the handing down of death sentences to three Sikhs who had been on trial for the assassination of Prime Minister Indira Gandhi in October 1984. Tensions were heightened further by a delay in one of the key provisions of the July 1985 peace accord—making the city of Chandigarh, the shared capital of Punjab and Haryana states, the exclusive capital of Punjab.

Killings in Punjab as a result of the continuing violence exceeded 500 during the year. Claims by the Indian government that the violence was on the wane were refuted by another major outbreak in December, triggered by the killing of 22 people, mostly Hindus, by Sikh terrorists and spreading to New Delhi in the form of anti-Sikh violence. Complicating the situation were charges by the Indian government that Pakistan was stirring unrest in Punjab and supporting demands by Sikh extremists for a separate state of Khalistan. New Delhi's plan to establish a 5-km (3-mi) wide "security belt" along the Pakistan border, to be controlled by the Indian Army, was opposed by almost all Punjabis, including Chief Minister Surgit Singh Barnala.

The violence in Punjab soon spilled over to other regions. On August 10 in Pune, in the state of Maharashtra, young Sikhs murdered retired Army Chief of Staff Gen. Arun Vaidya, who had been in charge of army operations during the bloody assault on the Golden Temple in 1984. A Sikh terrorist group calling itself the Khalistan Commando Force took responsibility for the action.

The attempted assassination of Prime Minister Gandhi on October 2 in New Delhi was another consequence of the bitterness and militancy of Sikh extremists. The would-be assas-

In late March, with Sikh extremists intensifying their attacks against Hindus, a curfew was imposed in Amritsar, above, and other Punjab cities. Meanwhile in New Delhi, below, thousands of Hindus protested Sikh terrorism.

sin apparently had no links with any terrorist organizations, but he was a Sikh who blamed the prime minister for anti-Sikh violence.

Other centers of violence in 1986 were Gujarat and Kashmir, where friction between Hindus and Muslims frequently led to bloody clashes. And in the northern part of West Bengal, in the tea-growing areas around Darjeeling, some 30 people were killed during demonstrations by members of the dominant ethnic group, the Gurkhas, in support of a separate state. Prime Minister Gandhi infuriated the Communist leaders of West Bengal by stating that he did not regard the Gurkhaland movement as a threat to India's national unity.

Major protests against price increases on petroleum and other oil products were staged in New Delhi and other major cities in February. Several thousand demonstrators, including more than 100 members of the Indian Parliament, were arrested.

Prime Minister Gandhi made three major changes in his cabinet and shook up the top leadership of the Congress (I). In January he appointed Commerce Minister Arjun Singh to the new post of vice-president of the Congress (I). And two other cabinet members, Labor Minister T. Anjiah and Oil Minister Naval Kishore Sharma, were reassigned to positions of general secretary in the party. On May 12, Gandhi himself took over the defense ministry, moving incumbent minister V. P. Singh to the post of minister of finance. And Minister of Agriculture Buta Singh became the new minister of home affairs. The latter appointment aroused particular interest because Buta Singh is a Sikh and as home minister would be directly responsible for the maintenance of internal law and order. Gandhi also dismissed B. R. Bhagat as minister of external affairs, replacing him with P. Shiv Shankar.

On October 22 three new ministers of cabinet rank were appointed: Arjun Singh, who returned to the cabinet after a brief tenure as vice-president of the party (communications), Bhajan Lal, a former chief minister of Haryana (environment and forests), and J. Vengal Rao (industry). P. Shiv Shankar was moved to the commerce ministry, and was succeeded as minister of external affairs by N.D. Tiwari. On November 12 the executive president of the Congress (I), Kamlapati Tripathi, and other top leaders resigned, paving the way for a thoroughgoing reorganization of the party.

On March 8 the Congress (I) withdrew its support of the National Conference government in Muslim-dominated Jammu and Kashmir, and that northwestern border state was placed under governor's rule. The political situation remained troubled, however, and on September 7 president's rule—direct rule by the central government—was proclaimed. On November 6 a National Conference-Congress

(I) coalition government, with Farooq Abdullah as chief minister, was formed.

In August the northeastern tribal Union Territory of Mizoram became the 23rd state in the Indian Union. A coalition ministry headed by Laldenga, the leader of the Mizo National Front, was installed.

Economy. In his address to Parliament on February 20, President Zail Singh commented at length on major trends in the nation's economy. He referred to the successful launching of the Seventh Five-Year Plan, which "is cast in a longer term perspective of eradication of poverty and building a strong, self-reliant and modern economy." He reported "vigorous implementation of antipoverty programs," "steady progress" in agriculture, a 6.3% growth rate in industrial production, "a buoyant investment climate," and an unprecedented increase in both direct and indirect tax collection. He stressed the need for "steadily rising levels of public investment," the reduction of costs and prices of "final products and services," and an improvement in the balance of payments position.

Prominent features of the general budget for fiscal 1986–87, presented to Parliament five days later by then Finance Minister Vishwanath Pratap Singh, included a quantum leap of 65% in expenditures for antipoverty programs, measures to strengthen the public sector, and a substantial boost in allocations for the Seventh Five-Year Plan. The antipoverty programs included increased support for the national rural development program and the national rural employment program, and a new housing scheme for scheduled castes and tribes. Broad objectives were to promote greater self-reliance and to provide relief to the ordinary citizen. Despite a tax increase, the budget estimated an overall deficit of some 40 billion rupees (about $3.1 billion). An overall economic growth rate of 4.5% was expected.

In June the Aid India Consortium agreed on commitments to India of $4.5 billion for fiscal 1986–87, an increase of 16% over 1985–86.

In its annual report, released in September, the Reserve Bank of India presented a generally favorable picture of the state of the economy. It referred specifically to a steady decline in the rate of inflation, an increase in food grain production to an estimated 150 million tons (a record), and a higher level of savings. In spite of a massive trade deficit, one of the most worrisome features of the economy, the Reserve Bank reported a "reasonably comfortable" level of foreign exchange reserves. And it forecast an even better economic performance in 1986–87.

Nevertheless, India still faced the problem of finding the resources to finance the heavy investments necessary to achieve even minimal development objectives. Impressive as India's development effort has been, its goals of "distributive justice" and the abolition of poverty were still far from realization. That fact was acknowledged by President Singh in his Independence Day message in mid-August.

Foreign Affairs. Prime Minister Gandhi made official visits to the Maldives in February, to four "front-line" African nations—Zambia, Zimbabwe, Angola, and Tanzania—in May, to Mauritius in July, to Czechoslovakia in August, and to Indonesia, Australia, New Zealand, and Thailand in October. In March he traveled to Sweden for the funeral of Prime Minister Olof Palme. And in August he made a nine-day trip that included visits to Great Britain, Mexico, and Czechoslovakia; the return trip included an unscheduled stop in Moscow, necessitated by engine trouble on his aircraft. While in Great Britain, Gandhi joined six other Commonwealth heads of government in trying (unsuccessfully) to persuade British Prime Minister Margaret Thatcher to go along with their strong sanctions against South Africa. Gandhi resisted demands that India pull out of the Commonwealth because of Thatcher's stand, but in July, India did join other Commonwealth states in boycotting the Commonwealth Games in Edinburgh, Scotland.

On his August tour, Gandhi met in Ixtapa, Mexico, with five other foreign leaders—President Miguel de la Madrid of Mexico, President

Visiting in February, Pope John Paul II met with the Hindu Srimad Swaminathan and other religious leaders.

AP/Wide World

Raúl Alfonsín of Argentina, Prime Minister Ingvar Carlsson of Sweden (Palme's successor), Prime Minister Andreas Papandreou of Greece, and former President Julius Nyerere of Tanzania—who sponsored the so-called Five Continent Peace Initiative. After a two-day meeting, the group reiterated its pleas to the superpowers to halt nuclear testing.

In September, Prime Minister Gandhi traveled to Harare, Zimbabwe, for the annual summit of the Nonaligned Movement, of which he was serving as chairman. After delivering a report on the activities of the movement during the previous year, he turned over the leadership to the president of the host country, Zimbabwe's Robert Mugabe.

On November 16–17 the second summit meeting of the South Asian Association for Regional Cooperation (SAARC), attended by heads of state or government of the seven South Asian states, was held in Bangalore. In a "Bangalore Declaration," the leaders expressed their consensus on a great variety of international issues, but did not refer to intraregional issues in dispute. Rajiv Gandhi succeeded President Ershad of Bangladesh as chairman of SAARC.

An unusually large number of world leaders also visited India during the year. In addition to those associated with the Five Continent Peace Initiative and SAARC, the visitors included the chancellor of West Germany, the presidents of the Seychelles and Nicaragua, the prime ministers of Turkey, Yugoslavia, Italy, and Zambia, the king of Jordan, the general secretary of the Soviet Communist Party, and Pope John Paul II and the Archbishop of Canterbury. The visits of the two religious leaders were kept low-key, as might be expected in a non-Christian land. India and the USSR signed several agreements, mostly involving economic cooperation, during General Secretary Mikhail Gorbachev's visit November 25–28. It was Gorbachev's first trip to an Asian nation since he became general secretary.

The discernible improvement in Indo-Pakistani relations in the wake of amicable meetings between Prime Minister Gandhi and President Zia ul-Haq in 1985 continued briefly into 1986. On January 10, in Islamabad, the finance ministers of the two countries signed an important bilateral economic agreement, which included a provision for the resumption of private trade. At about the same time, the countries' defense secretaries were reported to be working on a peace accord to end two years of clashes in the disputed Siachen Glacier region of Kashmir. But relations soon deteriorated, mainly because of the growing violence in Punjab, Kashmir, and elsewhere in India; Pakistani criticisms of India's handling of these problems; and India's allegations that Pakistan was giving assistance to Sikh extremists and other dissidents. A scheduled meeting of the Indo-Pakistan Joint Commission and a scheduled visit to Islamabad by India's foreign minister were postponed indefinitely, and plans for a visit by Prime Minister Gandhi to Pakistan in April were shelved. The Islamabad government objected to India's alleged sympathy for opposition leader Benazir Bhutto and to Indian criticisms of Pakistan's handling of a hijack situation at Karachi airport in September (see PAKISTAN). Prime Minister Gandhi was outspoken in his criticism of the Pakistani regime, but he had friendly meetings with President Zia at the Nonaligned and SAARC summits.

At the Harare gathering, Gandhi expressed exasperation with the leaders of Sri Lanka, saying he could not be sure whether they really wanted India's assistance in seeking a peaceful resolution of their civil conflict—a conflict which Sri Lanka's President Junius Jayewardene warned might destroy his country unless substantial outside help was immediately forthcoming (see SRI LANKA). During the course of the year, Gandhi all but suspended his assistance efforts. On the whole, despite repeated expressions of good will and a mutual desire to see an end to Sri Lanka's internal crisis, relations between New Delhi and Colombo were frustrated by repeated mutual criticisms.

Indo-U.S. relations were marked by two interesting developments: the announcement that India might buy some 400 engines from the General Electric Company for its first indigenous light combat aircraft, and a marked increase in bilateral high-tech trade. In April, Prime Minister Gandhi expressed harsh criticism of the U.S. bombing of Libya. In September, Pratap Kishan Kaul, a senior civil servant, presented his credentials as India's new ambassador to the United States, succeeding K. S. Bajpai.

NORMAN D. PALMER
Professor Emeritus
University of Pennsylvania

INDIA • Information Highlights

Official Name: Republic of India.
Location: South Asia.
Area: 1,269,340 sq mi (3 287 590 km²).
Population (mid-1986 est.): 785,000,000.
Chief Cities (1981 census): New Delhi, the capital, 5,157,270; Bombay, 8,243,405; Calcutta, 3,288,148.
Government: *Head of state,* Zail Singh, president (took office July 1982). *Head of government,* Rajiv Gandhi, prime minister (took office Oct. 31, 1984). *Legislature*—Parliament: Rajya Sabha (Council of States) and Lok Sabha (House of the People).
Monetary Unit: Rupee (12.8200 rupees equal U.S.$1, Oct. 17, 1986).
Gross National Product (fiscal 1984–85 U.S.$): $193,000,000,000.
Economic Indexes (1985): *Consumer Prices* (1980 = 100), all items, 155.9; food, 154.2. *Industrial Production* (1980 = 100), 136.
Foreign Trade (1985 U.S. $): *Imports,* $14,204,-000,000; *exports,* $7,631,000,000.

INDIANA

Indiana participated in the nationwide Democratic resurgence in the 1986 off-year elections, but Republicans managed enough significant wins to enable both parties to claim victory. The General Assembly's 30-day, alternate-year, short session saw major shifts in policy on two long-debated issues.

Elections. Democrats made considerable gains in national, state, and local elections. Incumbent Republican J. Danforth Quayle overwhelmed challenger Jill Long in the race for the U.S. Senate. All contested state offices remained in Republican hands except that of secretary of state, where Democrat B. Evan Bayh, son of former U.S. Sen. Birch E. Bayh, defeated Republican Robert Bowen, son of former Gov. Otis R. Bowen, (who had become U.S. secretary of Health and Human Services on Dec. 20, 1985). Bayh's victory may have long-range significance for the Democratic Party in Indiana.

Republicans maintained control of both houses of the state legislature, although by much slimmer margins. Particularly important were the Democratic gains in the lower house, where the Republican edge slipped from 61–39 to 52–48, and the defeat of powerful House Speaker J. Roberts Dailey. Republicans Gov. Robert D. Orr and Lt. Gov. John Mutz did not face reelection in 1986.

Six of Indiana's ten seats in the U.S. House of Representatives went to Democrats and three to Republicans. The third district race, centering around South Bend, remained undecided late in the year. Incumbent Republican John P. Hiler's 66-vote lead over Thomas W. Ward assuredly would occasion a recount, which could not be completed until at least January 1987. Indiana's traditional fiscal conservatism defeated two proposed constitutional amendments. One would have allowed the legislature to use the state's common-school fund for any purpose with no restrictions other than

AP/Wide World

Indianapolis' Union Station, built in 1853, underwent a $60-million restoration. The former railroad depot was reopened as a shopping, dining, and entertainment center.

federal regulations. The other would have approved the investment of state retirement funds in corporate stock.

Legislature. In a major departure from tradition, the General Assembly approved a proposed constitutional amendment that would repeal the state's ban on lotteries and parimutuel betting. The bitterly debated and often defeated lottery bill must still be passed by another legislative session and face a statewide referendum before it can become law, but the legislative about-face appeared to reflect the mood of the voters.

In landmark legislation that also seemed a response to public pressure, the General Assembly set in motion a two-year program to shift control of the state's license branches from the party of the governor to a bipartisan commission. Beginning July 1, 1988, the state rather than political parties will employ all license branch managers and workers, whose heretofore undisclosed salaries will be made public. Political parties will thus lose direct control over a major source of patronage.

INDIANA • Information Highlights

Area: 36,185 sq mi (93 720 km²).

Population (1985 est.): 5,499,000.

Chief Cities (July 1, 1984 est.): Indianapolis, the capital, 710,280; Fort Wayne, 165,416; Gary, 143,096.

Government (1986): *Chief Officers*—governor, Robert D. Orr (R); lt. gov., John M. Mutz (R). *General Assembly*—Senate, 50 members; House of Representatives, 100 members.

State Finances (fiscal year 1985): *Revenue,* $7,917,000,000; *expenditure,* $7,084,000,000.

Personal Income (1985): $68,442,000,000; per capita, $12,446.

Labor Force (June 1986): *Civilian labor force,* 2,783,400; *unemployed,* 183,700 (6.6% of total force).

Education: *Enrollment* (fall 1984)—public elementary schools, 661,779; public secondary, 310,880; colleges and universities, 250,567. *Public school expenditures* (1983–84), $2,399,000,000 ($2,730 per pupil).

To avoid the controversial recount procedure that threw the closely contested 1984 eighth district race into the U.S. House of Representatives for solution, the legislature established a bipartisan recount commission to conduct recounts in any disputed election involving more than one county. The General Assembly also established a state pool from which cities, counties, townships, and school corporations can buy liability insurance and shifted the administration of welfare programs and hospital care from counties to the State Department of Public Welfare. Despite strong pressure from Governor Orr, the legislature refused to pass a bill making the office of State Superintendent of Public Instruction appointive rather than elective, reinforcing Indiana's traditional belief that state officeholders should be accountable to the people. Also defeated was a bill repealing mandatory seat-belt use.

Other. In June the U.S. Supreme Court held that the 1981 gerrymandering of Indiana legislative districts did not exceed constitutional limits. In August the Department of Justice dropped its challenge to an affirmative action consent decree covering Indianapolis city workers.

Restoration of Union Station in Indianapolis was completed as part of the city's downtown redevelopment plan. The restored railroad depot opened as a shopping and entertainment center in late April.

LORNA LUTES SYLVESTER, *Indiana University*

INDONESIA

In 1986 a steep drop in world oil prices had a negative effect on Indonesia's economy, which is heavily dependent on exports of petroleum. For the first time in nearly two decades, the Suharto government announced substantial budget cuts and postponed all new development projects. It also devalued the rupiah by 45%, the fifth such devaluation since Suharto came to power in 1965.

Analysts estimated that, with a projected growth rate of 1.3% rather than the planned 5%, more than 30% of the 1.8 million new workers entering the labor market during 1986 would not find jobs. In a nation whose overall unemployment rate is sometimes rated as high as 35% (officially, between 2 and 6%), the figures were discouraging. The prospect of 8 million young adults, many of whom are jobless, voting for the first time in the elections scheduled for 1987 had many government officials worried.

Indonesia, nevertheless, received praise from such institutions as the World Bank, the International Monetary Fund, and the Intergovernmental Group on Indonesia, for its conservative management and financial planning. The nation maintains a $10.7 billion foreign ex-

change reserve, and has invested its oil profits more wisely than many other nations with similar resources. The World Bank suggested that the government give small private industry more freedom and take further steps to remove hindrances to the export trade, but also noted positive achievements such as a 3 million ton rice surplus and a rise in non-oil exports.

Foreign Affairs. Foreign Minister Kusumaatmadja continued his attempts to arrange a better relationship between Vietnam and the Association of Southeast Asian Nations (ASEAN), of which Indonesia is a member. Tension with the United States was relieved when a bill which would have reduced Indonesia's textile exports failed to pass in the U.S. Congress. Relations with Australia, however, worsened markedly because of an article in the Sydney press that criticized the financial and political dealings of Suharto and his relatives. The Indonesian government reacted by announcing that visas would be required for Australian tourists, but the regulation was soon rescinded.

The Role of the Army. The rioting that had disturbed the country in 1984 and 1985 subsided, and as the elections approached, public attention turned toward issues raised by military participation in political life. Commander-in-chief L. B. Murdani reiterated his belief that the armed forces were in no position to rule Indonesia, but he also affirmed that the military had no intention of surrendering the "dual function" inherited from the revolutionary period, combining military and political activities. Alleged government interference in local elections, in which military men have been placed despite the outcome of popular vote, has raised questions about the current system. The recent reorganization of the armed forces has also drawn critics' fire because, along with streamlining and economizing, it provided for expanded training and responsibilities for military men in "socio-political affairs."

WILLIAM H. FREDERICK, *Ohio University*

INDONESIA • Information Highlights

Official Name: Republic of Indonesia.
Location: Southeast Asia.
Area: 782,659 sq mi (2 027 087 km²).
Population (mid-1986 est.): 168,400,000.
Chief Cities (Dec. 31, 1983 est.): Jakarta, the capital, 7,636,000; Surabaya, 2,289,000; Medan, 1,966,000; Bandung, 1,602,000.
Government: *Head of state and government,* Suharto, president (took office for fourth five-year term March 1983). *Legislature* (unicameral)—People's Consultative Assembly.
Monetary Unit: Rupiah (1,630.0 rupiahs equal U.S.$1, Oct. 17, 1986).
Gross National Product (1985 U.S.$): $90,300,-000,000.
Economic Index (1985): *Consumer Prices* (1980 = 100), all items, 158.9; food, 149.3.
Foreign Trade (1984 U.S.$): *Imports,* $13,882,-000,000; *exports,* $21,888,000,000.

Using the most up-to-date equipment available, a technician adds color to a vintage Shirley Temple film. The coloring of classic black-and-white motion pictures stirred controversy within the industry and with many movie fans.

AP/Wide World

INDUSTRIAL REVIEW

Mature industrial nations collectively had modest growth in industrial output for 1986. Newly industrialized countries, on the other hand, experienced a surge in their factory output, as their goods enjoyed a brisk demand in dollar markets.

The United States

The year 1986 was marked by heightened concern about the competitiveness of U.S. manufacturing industries in world markets. Bringing urgency to the concern was the realization that high technology (high tech)—the very sector that had been regarded as the key to a renewal of American manufacturing—was very much at risk. The issue was outlined sharply by a dramatic swing in trade of products turned out by high-tech industries, including computers, scientific instruments, aircraft, and specialty chemicals. Such industries incur heavy research and development expenditures.

From a high-tech trade surplus of $27 billion in 1980, enough to outweigh the $13 billion trade deficit in nonhigh-tech manufactures, the U.S. edge steadily eroded until the high-tech trade surplus dropped to $4 billion in 1985. The remainder of manufacturers ran a deficit of $117 billion. The first half of 1986 saw continuing deterioration, as U.S. high-tech exports amounted to $35.2 billion and imports of high-tech goods totaled $36.5 billion revealing a $1.3 billion deficit.

A study for the Joint Economic Committee of the U.S. Congress puts the first full-year high-tech trade deficit at about $2 billion. For much of this deterioration the study looked be-

yond the usual explanations such as the strength of the dollar and adverse macroeconomic conditions.

According to the study, one way U.S.-based high-tech firms have responded to the deteriorating competitiveness of the United States as a place for production and engineering has been to relocate facilities to, and hire workers from, low-labor-cost countries. There is a distinction between the comparative advantage of the United States as a geographic place of production and the competitiveness of U.S.-based firms in a global context. A complex international division of activity is emerging as evidence suggests that in some high-technology sectors the U.S. technical and engineering work force may have lost its competitiveness. The study raised the question of whether U.S. firms' individual measures to maintain their competitiveness against their foreign-based competitors are, in the long run, of benefit to the U.S. economy overall.

Mature Industries. For motor vehicles, the 1986-model year set a sales record of 15.9 million cars and trucks, with imports accounting for 25% of the total. The number of domestic 1986-model cars produced was 8,059,000, down 3.9% from 1985. The number of domestic 1986-model trucks produced rose 1.7% to 3.9 million, boosted by an enthusiastic demand by consumers for light-duty trucks.

The U.S. steel industry, reflecting massive overcapacity and a sharp decline in the importance of the metal in the U.S. economy, experienced a long strike against a major company without much of a disturbance. The fact that the company, the largest steel firm in the country, changed its name from U.S. Steel to USX Corporation underscores the growing trend to reduce steel-making capacity and to diversify. Shipments of steel mill products dropped 5% in 1986, after declining 0.9% in 1985. And 20 million tons of the estimated 69 million in 1986 came from abroad. Raw steel poured in 1986 came to 84 million tons, a 5% drop.

Coal production, after reaching a peak of 896 million tons in 1984, dropped 1% in 1985, and rose a bit less than 1% in 1986 to 894 million tons. As oil prices dropped to a seven-year low in 1986, the U.S. petroleum industry cut the number of working oil and gas rigs at year-end 1986 in half from the nearly 2,000 at work at year-end 1985. To keep up revenues and to meet increased demand, the industry raised output a shade above the 3.3 billion barrels produced in 1985.

New Products. For consumers, 1986 brought a new camera from Polaroid, the Spectra. Its prints compare to 35-mm quality, and sales of about 500,000 were estimated for the year. Computer users' interest was aroused by three personal computer manufacturers who introduced machines based on the 32-bit Intel 80386 microprocessor. And South Korea had reason to celebrate the introduction of its Hyundai Excel automobile into the U.S. market in February 1986 at prices listed as low as $4,995. Sales in 1986 came to about 160,000, making it the best performance for a first-time import.

Production. U.S. industrial production in 1986 increased barely 1%, nudging the Federal Reserve Board Index of Quantity Output to 125 (1977-100). In 1985 the gain was 2%.

Manufacturing industries registered a 2% increase, after posting a 2.5% gain in 1985. Output of consumer goods advanced 3.3%, following a 1.9% increase. Production of defense equipment rose 5.5%, compared with a 9.1% growth in 1985. Business-equipment production declined 0.6%, after rising 4.2%.

Output of final products rose only 0.8%, compared with a 3% increase in 1985. Intermediate products showed a 4.7% growth, after rising 4.8%. Output of materials dropped 0.5%, following no change in 1985. Production of products in general posted a 1.9% gain, compared with 3.3% in the previous year.

Factory use edged down to 79.7% of capacity from 80.1% in 1985. Capacity utilization in the materials industries was 78.4% in 1986, compared with 80.2%. Primary-processing industries had a rate of 83.3%, up from 82.1% in 1985. Advanced-processing industries utilized 78.2% of their capacity, compared with 79.2%. However, all industries continued to increase their capacity to produce. Compared with a 3% increase in manufacturing capacity in 1985, the 2.6% increase in 1986 was remarkable in view of the sluggish rate of production.

Utilities had a 1.4% reduction in their output, after a 1.1% gain; mining output dropped 8.6%, following a 2.1% decline. Oil and gas extraction plunged 10.9%, after dropping 2.7%.

Industries showing production gains outnumbered those showing losses, as several turned around. Thus, the output of structural clay products rose 12.3%, after a 2.6% decline. Textile-mill products posted a gain of 9.6%, following a 0.9% reduction. Paperboard containers advanced 7.1%, compared with a 1% loss. Petroleum products were up 6.7%, following a dip of 0.7%. Pulp and paper production rose 5.5%, after declining 2.1%. Pressed and blown glass was up 5.9%, following a 1.8% retrenchment. TV and radio output rose 2.4%, following a 9.4% fall. Electrical equipment declined 0.6%, after dropping 7.1%. Ships and boats gained 3.4%, after declining 0.6%. Consumer-instrument products gained 1.8%, following a 2.7% decline. Apparel production rose 2%, after a 1.8% cutback. Beverages gained 2.7%, following a 0.2% decline.

Aircraft and parts production shot up 12%, improving on a 10% rise. Soaps and toiletries gained 10.8%, after increasing 9.4%. Synthetic materials rose 8.8%, following a 6.5% increase. Lumber and wood products were up 7.6%, after rising 3.9%. Household furniture gained 3.1%, on top of a 0.9% increase. Fixtures and office furniture output increased 4.6%, after gaining 7.3%. Converted paper products advanced 8.7%, following a 3.9% advance. Metal-working machinery gained 4.6%, following a 4.6% gain. Household appliances were up 8.1%, on top of 0.5%. Output of trucks and buses rolled up a 3.3% increase, after registering a 9.1% gain. Railroad equipment was up 3.5%, topping a 13.2% jump in 1985. Rubber and plastic products gained 3.8%, after increasing 2.4%. Printing and publishing output rose 5.8%, on top of 5.1%. Drugs and medicines gained 5.5%, after a 6.0% increase. Paint production was up 2.9%, improving on the 6.8% increase of the preceding year. Cement production gained 4.3%, following a 1.7% increase. Concrete products were up 2.8%, after increasing 2.7%. Metal cans racked up a 5.6% increase, following a 3.4% advance. Hardware output quickened to 1.8% from 0.4%. Output of communications equipment rose only 0.5%, compared with an 8.1% jump. Structural-metal-products production slowed to a 0.2% increase from 7.9%. Output of fasteners dropped to a 0.7% advance from a 5.3% rate of growth in 1985. Instrument production increased 4.4% in 1986, compared with a 2.2% rise.

Production losses were heavy for agricultural chemicals, down 10.8%, after a 2.2% drop in 1985. Basic chemicals edged down 0.2%, following a 1.7% loss. Iron and steel production fell 11.2%, after a 3.7% decline. Nonferrous metals output slipped 0.1% after rising 0.4% in 1985. Farm equipment and engines fell 3.8%, following a drop of 7.8%. Construction equipment declined 5.3%, after falling 4.9%. Office and computing equipment, after posting a 5.7% gain in 1985, dropped 4.5% in 1986. Copiers

The Plastics Revolution

Once synonymous with tawdry, second-rate merchandise, plastics have become the darlings of high technology—and of consumers. The United States now produces more than 21 million metric tons of plastics annually, and uses more plastics than steel, aluminum, and copper combined. The future will see even greater use of these once-maligned substances.

More than 10,000 varieties of plastics are available, with a broad range of properties. Plastics can be engineered to be incredibly strong or very brittle, stiff or pliable, fragile or indestructible. They can be electrical conductors or insulators. They can be formed into sheets much thinner than paper, fibers of any length, tubes wide or narrow.

Because of their versatility, plastics are replacing steel, aluminum, glass, paper, and other materials in every kind of product imaginable. Plastics are used to make clothing, bicycles, cookware, ski poles, tennis rackets, roller skates, grocery bags, paints, house siding and plumbing, and artificial hearts and other replacement parts for human bodies.

The first high-volume plastic-bodied car, General Motors' Fiero, was introduced in 1984. Other cars have all plastic bumpers; a plastic engine has found its way into race cars; and Volkswagen is developing a plastic fuel tank. It is just a matter of time before an all-plastic car rolls off the assembly line. Plastic planes may not be far behind. Boeing is developing a jetliner that will make extensive use of plastics. Even the wings may be plastic.

Important Advantages. Unlike plastics of old, many of today's plastics are not cheap. Some are actually more expensive to produce than the metals they replace. The plastics used to package soft drinks are an example. Despite the initial cost advantages of glass, however, plastics are grabbing an ever-larger percentage of the soft-drink packaging market. The breakability of glass creates safety and housekeeping problems for supermarkets. And glass weighs significantly more than plastic, resulting in higher shipping costs.

Plastics are corrosion-proof and resist denting and abrasion. This makes them ideal for auto bodies, hot water heaters, camera and watch bodies, and fishing rods. Plastic sprocket gears are replacing steel gears in many applications because of their excellent resistance to corrosion, abrasion, and aging, and because they result in a significant reduction of noise.

The ability to easily mold plastics into any desired shape enables manufacturers to re-

Nonbreakable and very lightweight plastics have had a major effect on today's bottling industry.

place multipiece metal parts with a single plastic part. This eliminates assembly problems and greatly reduces tooling and labor costs.

To give products a number of desirable characteristics, a process called barrier coextrusion is increasingly being used. In this process, plastics with different properties are layered into a single sheet. One layer may provide strength, another flexibility, another shape. A new squeezable ketchup bottle consists of six layers of plastic, each designed to do a different job.

New and Improved. New varieties of plastics are continually being introduced, as researchers try to expand their uses and solve some of the problems associated with these materials. For instance, some new plastics contain flame retardants, to decrease the hazards created when plastics burn. Others contain antioxidants, to decrease the susceptibility of plastics to oxidation and hence improve the shelf life of foods stored in plastic containers. Researchers also hope to develop plastics that are biodegradable. This would help solve the solid-waste and litter problems caused by the wide use of today's plastics.

JENNY TESAR

lost 2.4%, after increasing 1.7%. Industrial machinery was down 1.8%, after a production decline of 0.6%. Electronic components output fell 5.7%, following a drop of 7.9%. Motor-vehicles and parts production edged down 1.3%, after gaining 6.7%. Tires dropped 3.7%, after declining 3.0%. Output of tobacco products declined 2.5%, following a 0.5% cut. Leather and leather products fell 10%, after posting a 10.4% loss in 1985.

American business spent $381 billion for new plant and equipment in 1986, about 1.7% less than in 1985. Manufacturing industries cut 6%, after increasing capital spending by 10.6% in 1985. The largest reduction was by non-electrical machinery producers, almost 14%, following a 3.7% increase in 1985. Motor-vehicle manufacturers reduced outlays by 0.4%, after boosting expenditures by 30.6% in 1985. Steel industry cut spending by 16.5%, after a 16.5% increase. Stone, clay, and glass industry recorded a 8.6% drop, following a 10.1% increase. Aircraft-industry outlays grew 8.4%, reversing a cut of 3.3%. Fabricated-metals manufacturers raised spending by 13.4%, on top of a 3.9% gain in 1985. All told, durable-goods producers reduced capital spending by 4.5%, compared with a 10.6% increase in 1985.

Nondurable goods industries reduced outlays by 6.7% in 1986, compared with a 10.5% increase in 1985. The sharpest reduction was by petroleum, down 30%, as against a 4.6% increase. Textiles cut by 7%, following a 7.6% drop. Food producers expanded their spending by 1% after a 17.1% increase. Chemicals recorded a 4% increase, following a 7.3% increase in 1985. The paper industry raised capital spending by 3.5% on top of a 19.2% jump in the preceding year.

Scrambling to stay in business, manufacturers were taking a fresh look at factory automation. Flexible manufacturing systems is the latest concept now seen as the answer to meet the demand for a variety of new products, produced in small batches. The idea is to configure machine tools and materials-handling equipment—under computer control—so that they can be reprogrammed easily and quickly from making one product to producing another.

Employment. Factory jobs have been declining since the middle of 1984. In 1986 alone, 180,000 were lost. By year's-end, after four years of general economic expansion, only 44% of the manufacturing employment lost during the 1981–82 recession had been regained. Some 150,000 mining jobs were lost in 1986.

Manufacturing employed just a shade more than 19 million workers at year-end 1986, two thirds of them were production workers and the remainder were professional, managerial, technical, and clerical employees. Producers of durable goods employed some 11 million, accounting for 59% of total manufacturing. The largest employer was the electrical and elec-tronic equipment industry with 2.2 million, followed by nonelectrical machinery (2 million), transportation equipment (1.2 million), fabricated metal products (1.4 million), primary metals (750,000), lumber and wood products (738,000), instruments (709,000), stone-clay-glass (589,000), furniture and fixtures (500,000), and miscellaneous manufacturing (365,000).

Nondurables producers employed 7.9 million. The largest employer was food and kindred products with 1.6 million, followed by printing and publishing (1.5 million), apparel (1.1 million), rubber and plastics (813,000), textile mill products (715,000), paper and allied products (695,000), petroleum and coal products (161,000), leather and leather products (151,000), and tobacco manufacturers (61,000).

Productivity. Manufacturing sector's productivity rose 4.4% in 1985, with durable-goods producers registering a 6.8% gain and nondurables manufacturers posting an increase of 0.7%. Through the first three quarters of 1986, productivity in the manufacturing sector rose at an annual rate of 3%, with durable goods posting a 2.3% increase and nondurable-goods manufacturers stepping up the rate of productivity improvement to 5%.

International

Industrial production in major industrial countries slowed in 1986. Countries belonging to the Organization for Economic Cooperation and Development (OECD) posted a production gain of less than 2% in 1986, down from the nearly 3% increase recorded for 1985.

Preliminary estimates put the increase in industrial production at no change in Japan, compared with a 5% increase in 1985. The slowdown reflected the appreciation of the yen against the dollar. West Germany posted a 3% increase, a slowdown from the 5% increase in 1985. After a fractional decline in 1985, France raised its factory production by 2%. Italy's growth quickened to nearly 5% after a sluggish 1% advance. United Kingdom, after increasing production by nearly 5%, slowed to an advance of about 2%. Belgium stepped up its gain to 3%, double the rate of gain in 1985. Spain gained 3%, after a 1% increase. Australia's production gain slowed to 2% from a 3% increase in 1985. Denmark, after posting a 3% gain for 1985, racked up a 5% increase for 1986. The Netherlands recorded a 2% gain for 1986, after an increase of nearly 3% in 1985.

Manufacturing output in newly industrialized countries picked up considerably in 1986. After a sluggish 1% increase in 1985, Taiwan surged with a 9% increase in 1986. Cashing in on its automotive success in North America, South Korea's factory output surged 13% in 1986, almost tripling its rate of manufacturing growth in 1985.

AGO AMBRE, *U.S. Department of Commerce*

With more consumers seeking assistance for their home decorating problems, department stores are establishing or expanding their design services.

Courtesy of J.C. Penney

INTERIOR DESIGN

Interior design moved ahead on several fronts during 1986. On the one hand, the American Society of Interior Designers (ASID), the field's major trade group, initiated a drive for licensing of designers in each state. On the other, the general public was given greater access to decorating services at the retail level, as many furniture retailers emphasized free decorating services.

Licensing. ASID's fight for title registration would tend to restrict access to interior-design services by discouraging entry into the field; yet consumers have begun requesting more design help, creating a need for more decorators. The apparent dichotomy is resolved by the fact that the trade group seeks only to limit use of the term interior designer, thus institutionalizing a two-tier system of interior designers. One tier would specialize in work requiring large expenditures; the other would primarily help clients with home decorating.

ASID's model legislation would apply only to those calling themselves interior designers. To become a licensed designer would require a degree from an interior-design program, plus several years of experience before taking a two-day competency examination. Alabama, Connecticut, and Louisiana have passed laws establishing title registration for designers. Such legislation was considered in New York, Florida, Minnesota, Oklahoma, and the District of Columbia, and steps for similar action were taken in other states as well.

Decorating Services. Overall demographic trends in the United States also have affected the field of interior design. A study by ASID found, for example, that a broader range of clients seeks help with their design questions than in the past. In addition to older affluent couples, formerly the primary users of design services, younger and less affluent families, including two-income professional couples, and singles now are using decorating services.

The living room remains the most frequently professionally decorated room. The ASID study found that an average of $15,584 was spent on the living room. Other rooms being redecorated frequently include bedrooms and bathrooms, which often are reworked as luxurious retreats. Exercise equipment and whirlpool bathtubs are part of the redesign. Confirming this trend, several manufacturers of bath fixtures enjoyed a large sales increase in luxury items.

More consumers have been consulting the design department of department and furniture stores. The Chicago department store, Marshall Field's, for example, has recorded an annual increase in design sales for 12 years. Even large national chains, such as J.C. Penney, Sears, and Spiegel, have begun providing limited decorating guidance, particularly in selection of window treatments and upholstery fabrics.

Design styles more frequently requested by clients of designers surveyed by ASID were traditional, contemporary, and eclectic. In the Northeast there were more calls for contemporary and eclectic styles. Country French was most popular in the West; American country in the North Central region.

Individuals generally opted for more formal decorating styles, continuing and accentuating a trend that has been noted for at least three years. In decorator showhouses and store model rooms across the United States (both excellent barometers of decorating tastes), 19th century fabrics were increasingly shown.

Decorators have begun applying wood moldings to contemporary rooms that were built without ornamentation. At the windows are multilayered treatments that include elaborate trimmings of braid and tassels. The greater use of accessories (begun with the country look) was noted in influential decorating magazines as well as in showhouses created by some of the nation's best known decorators.

BARBARA MAYER, *The Associated Press*

INTERNATIONAL TRADE AND FINANCE

In several ways 1986 proved an economic disappointment. By fall, International Monetary Fund (IMF) economists and many others had marked down their year-end forecasts for the non-Communist industrial nations. With some pickup in the second half, they anticipated growth in this economically powerful group to run approximately 2.75%. The developing countries also grew somewhat slower than anticipated, running abut 2.5%. Their export earnings showed sluggish growth, and their foreign debt problem was far from solved.

In the world's largest economy, the United States, the deficits grew rather than shrank. The budget deficit for fiscal 1986 amounted to $220.7 billion, surpassing the previous record of $211.93 billion in fiscal 1985. The trade deficit showed some improvement in the second half, but it still ran close to $140 billion, well up from the $124 billion in 1985.

Already by the end of 1986, the United States had become the world's largest debtor nation. The net U.S. debt had reached $107 billion at the end of 1985, and C. Fred Bergsten, the director of the Institute for International Economics in Washington, warned that the figure could rise to $500 billion by 1989 and more than $1 trillion by the early 1990s.

In Western Europe economists still complained of "structural rigidities" that prevented flexibility in the labor market. Government welfare regulations or trade unions have made it difficult for businesses to expand or shrink rapidly as the market dictates. As a result businesses are often reluctant to hire new workers, and the unemployment rate in 1986 averaged close to 11%.

Nonetheless, the world did rack up some clear economic achievements in 1986. The recovery in the United States entered its fifth year, with most economists expecting it to last at least well into 1987. The expansion was already one of the longer-lived of the post-World War II era. Similarly, recovery continued in Western Europe and Japan, though at a decidedly slower pace in that island nation. Japanese export volume declined, as the value of the yen rose 55.57% against the U.S. dollar; the latter development followed in the 12 months after the September 1985 decision of the Group of Five (France, Great Britain, Japan, the United States, and West Germany) to push down the value of the dollar.

Other good news in 1986 was a decline in interest rates and inflation in the United States. A dramatic plunge in the price of oil during the first half of the year—to as low as $7 per barrel in the summer—helped keep the rise in the consumer price index to approximately 2%.

After lengthy meetings the member nations of the Organization of the Petroleum Exporting Countries (OPEC) agreed in August to limit production, pushing prices closer to $14. At the end of October, the ouster in Saudi Arabia of longtime Oil Minister Ahmed Zaki Yamani led to speculation that the Saudis would attempt to push the price of petroleum higher still.

The rate of inflation in the industrial countries, measured by the so-called deflator for national output, was just more than 3% in 1986, the lowest figure in 20 years. Meanwhile, international interest rates dropped 2% in 1986, falling more than 6% below the 1982 level. The decline in interest rates was especially important to Third World debtor nations: each percentage point decline saved them some $3.75 billion in annual net interest payments.

Business profits were up almost everywhere in the industrial world, and there was even a greater prospect for reducing government deficits. In the United States the Gramm-Rudman balanced budget legislation, passed by Congress in December 1985, though later found unconstitutional in part by the U.S. Supreme Court, was at least prompting some restraint on government spending. Growth in expenditures during fiscal 1986 amounted to about 4%, down from 12% in fiscal 1985. In West Germany and Japan, and to a lesser extent in Canada, France, and Great Britain, fiscal deficits actually declined.

One issue much discussed in 1986 was the international coordination of domestic economic policies. In late February a majority of four on the seven-member U.S. Federal Reserve Board defied Chairman Paul A. Volcker by seeking a reduction in the interest discount rate charged to financial institutions for loans. Volcker persuaded the board to compromise, suggesting that the decision be held up until he was able to coordinate a joint interest-rate reduction with West Germany and Japan. He succeeded in that goal early in March.

However, neither West Germany nor Japan wanted to see their currencies strengthen any further on the foreign exchange market against the U.S. dollar. Their export industries were already grumbling about difficulties in meeting the competition on international markets. The two nations therefore resisted additional coordinated interest-rate drops and believed it was unnecessary to stimulate their economies further. The United States had hoped for faster economic growth by its key economic allies so they would suck in more imports.

Summit. The 12th annual economic summit of major industrialized democracies, held in Tokyo, May 4–7, actually focused more on political issues than on economic issues. The seven national leaders issued a joint statement that condemned terrorism, singling out Libya as a key target for antiterrorist measures, and called for an international convention requiring the exchange of information on nuclear accidents and emergencies. In economic matters Japan's Prime Minister Yasuhiro Nakasone had hoped for some hint from the United States that the dollar had fallen far enough, which would have helped him meet the attacks from aggrieved exporters at home. He did not get his wish. U.S. Treasury Secretary James A. Baker emphasized the need for greater economic coordination, particularly on fiscal policy, urging the industrial powers to set "indicators" for such things as inflation, interest rates, growth, unemployment, budget deficits, current account and trade balances, monetary growth, and exchange rates. Whenever a country goes off course, according to Baker's plan, the group would recommend remedial measures. But none of the other participants wanted foreign countries poking their noses into domestic economic questions. Eventually the seven nations did agree vaguely on the need for greater coordination, but putting that wish into practice would not be easy. The seven planned further discussion of the indicators with the help of the IMF, but such talks would be toothless unless the indicators are actionable.

The United States did make more kindly hints about the yen just before Japanese elections in July, and Prime Minister Nakasone's party scored a majority victory. The Japanese-U.S. dispute on the value of the yen took another turn at the end of October, when Japan took modest measures to stimulate its own economy while the United States promised to refrain from further efforts to boost the yen. Japan reduced its discount rate from 3.5% to 3.0% and strengthened its commitment to previously unveiled plans to spur its economy

through new spending and tax-revision programs. In return the Reagan administration pledged to stop urging foreign-currency traders to push up the value of the yen. Secretary Baker and Japanese Finance Minister Kiichi Miyazawa issued a joint statement saying that the yen-dollar exchange rate had shifted enough and "is now broadly consistent with the present underlying fundamentals." However, there were signs that the United States would have liked the Japanese to boost their economy harder.

Also at the Tokyo summit the Group of Five decided to enlarge itself to include Canada and Italy at times. Those two nations had been left out of the September 1985 meeting, to their political discomforture.

Japanese Finance. Japan's growing financial clout was more fully recognized in 1986. The nation invested some $80 billion in world financial markets in the year ending March 31, 1986, and additional large sums flowed abroad during the remainder of the calendar year. Japan thus became the second largest financial power in the world, passing Great Britain. Indeed, in the United States, Japanese money was the key marginal supplier of capital to a nonfinancial market absorbing some $800 billion, filling the gap left by the relatively low savings rate. In 1986 the Japanese had some 40 banks, as well as their major brokerage houses, operating in the United States. Sam Nakagama, a Wall Street economist, estimated that Japan will have a net-asset position of some $410 billion by 1990.

Japanese direct investment abroad in plant and equipment also has been growing rapidly. It is now the third largest in the world after the

AP/Wide World

On the Tokyo Foreign Exchange, the value of the U.S. dollar fell by more than 55% from 1985 levels. During the summer, yen were traded at 150–155 per dollar, the lowest in the postwar era.

United States and Britain. One Japanese government study estimated that the nation's direct overseas investment will reach $300 billion by the year 2000. (*See also* JAPAN.)

Trade. Meeting in Punta del Este, Uruguay, from September 15 to 20, some 74 ministers from nations subscribing to the General Agreement on Tariffs and Trade (GATT) managed to launch a new round of talks aimed at reducing world trade barriers. The discussions were scheduled to last four years, though many observers expected them to take longer, and they promised to be the most complex and ambitious of the several GATT rounds in the postwar years. The joint declaration at Punta del Este called for a standstill and rollback on trade restrictive or trade distortive measures. The ministers also agreed to negotiate trade in services for the first time, though this will occur outside the GATT framework. Also included in negotiations for the first time was agriculture, a politically sensitive matter in most countries.

As the *Christian Science Monitor* commented editorially: "The news out of Punta del Este, Uruguay, indicates that the global community is not coming unraveled. It also reminds us that the forces for economic cooperation outweigh calls for the type of go-it-alone divisiveness of the late 1920s and early '30s that helped spur global economic chaos."

During much of the year, however, the trade news was less happy from the standpoint of free trade. The Arrangement Regarding International Trade in Textiles, generally known as the Multifibre Arrangement, was extended on July 31 to the same date in 1991. It will enable the industrial countries to continue limiting the textile imports of the developing countries, and indeed will tighten the controls in some areas.

In addition the year saw new protectionist measures put into place or debated throughout the world. The United States, for example, began subsidizing its farm exports to compete more effectively with the subsidized exports of the European Community (EC). Australia, Argentina, Canada, and other grain exporters were caught in the cross fire. The United States levied a 35% duty on Canadian red cedar shakes and shingles in the spring, and Canada promptly retaliated with higher tariffs on some products of interest to the United States. In October the United States imposed a 15% duty on softwood lumber imports from Canada after a preliminary ruling that they were being subsidized primarily through low fees on government-owned timber. The United States and Japan also agreed on a deal calling for Japanese computer chip manufacturers to stop selling in the United States at prices below a fair market price ("dumping") and for Japan to buy more U.S. chips.

More positively, President Ronald Reagan successfully vetoed a bill that would have rolled back imports of textiles and shoes, and other serious protectionist measures died in Congress. All in all, according to IMF and GATT estimates, world trade continued to grow in volume by more than 4% in 1986, compared with a 3% gain in 1985.

Debt. The year 1986 also saw some signs of progress in dealing with the $1 trillion in external debts being carried by the less developed countries. Commercial bankers were considering Ecuador, Colombia, and Uruguay as possible candidates for further loans because of their economic reforms and belt tightening. There was even talk that Brazil, with a trade surplus of some $13 billion in 1986, might get some voluntary loans in 1987.

Mexico, whose problems were intensified by the drop in oil prices, was the country which made bankers the most nervous. At the joint annual meeting of the IMF and World Bank in Washington, DC, in September, Mexico and bank negotiators agreed in principle on an additional $6 billion in loans to help get Mexico through 1987. As the year moved toward a conclusion, however, the details were still being worked out. From the standpoint of U.S. Treasury Secretary Baker, the Mexican loan was to be the first fruit of his initiative at the 1985 IMF-World Bank, where he proposed fresh loans to the debtor nations to help them grow faster in return for economic reforms. In 1986 the non-oil developing nations were growing at a modest average rate of 3.5% despite a net outflow of financial resources.

Bankers were in better shape to take the loan losses of developing countries. In the United States, for example, loans to these countries amounted to 125% of their capital by late 1986, compared with nearly 200% in 1982. Banks in Europe and Canada generally were in even better financial condition in this regard.

The "Big Bang." On October 27, in a move referred to as the "Big Bang," fixed minimum commissions were discontinued on the London Stock Exchange. Actually the deregulation of the London securities and banking business had been going on for some three years, leading to great turmoil, fresh competition, an increase in merger activity, and an incursion of foreign financial firms.

In the meantime international capital markets continued to grow. By the end of the third quarter, they had raised $242 billion, compared with $284 billion for all of 1985.

Commodity Prices. Reflecting continued weakness in the price of commodities, including oil into the summer of 1986, the terms of trade for developing countries (what they pay for imports, versus what they get for exports) declined 16% through the fall. As the year was coming to an end, however, there were some signs of a turnaround.

DAVID R. FRANCIS
"The Christian Science Monitor"

The Effects of Cheap Oil

© E.A. Harris/Rothco

The slump in world oil prices that began at the end of 1985 continued through 1986, with prices reaching their lowest levels in the first half of the year and recovering moderately in the latter half. OPEC (the Organization of the Petroleum Exporting Countries) struggled throughout the year to stabilize prices, but with uneven results. Faced with spot market quotes of less than $10 per barrel in April and May—less than a quarter of the historic high of $42 per barrel in 1981—OPEC members met in June seeking agreement on production controls to shore up prices, but they failed to settle on a strategy. Agreement finally was reached in August to limit total OPEC output to 14.8 million barrels per day, nearly 3 million barrels below July levels. In October the agreement was extended through the end of 1986. OPEC's stated aim was to raise prices by $4 to $5 per barrel, but during the second half of 1986 prices generally ranged between $13 and $16.

The oil price slump was triggered by a Saudi Arabian decision to increase production above its OPEC quota. The Saudi Arabian quota of 4.35 million barrels per day was far below the country's production capacity. By exceeding OPEC limits, the Saudis sought to flood the market and push prices down to drive marginal producers out of business. But the sharp decline went beyond Saudi expectations and in October 1986, King Fahd of Saudi Arabia dismissed his oil minister, Ahmed Zaki Ya-

mani. Subsequently the OPEC countries—with the exception of Iraq—agreed on reduced production quotas. Prices quickly rose to more than $16 per barrel, but many analysts doubted the rise could be sustained.

International Impact. The effect on the world economy of cheaper oil prices has been mixed. In general the price slump has brought lower inflation, reduced interest rates, and stronger economic growth to oil-importing countries, and economic difficulties to oil exporters. However, there have been some significant deviations from the overall trend.

Oil-exporting countries generally may be divided into two groups: those for which falling oil prices necessitate a period of belt-tightening and those for which the declines mean economic disaster unless outside help is forthcoming. In the first group are the oil giants of the Persian Gulf, which built huge foreign exchange reserves when prices were high and whose relatively small populations can be supported with lower export earnings. Also in this group are countries with diversified economies to which oil exports are important but not critical. Norway, Great Britain, Canada, and the Soviet Union are in this category.

The oil-exporting countries most severely hurt are those with large populations, heavy foreign debt burdens, and a disproportionate dependence on oil exports for foreign exchange earnings. Mexico, which receives 70%

of its export income and more than 40% of its fiscal revenues from oil and has a foreign debt of $100 billion, is the foremost example. In 1986, according to official projections, Mexico's oil income was less than half the $13.3 billion earned in 1985, which has driven the economy into recession, raised inflation to perhaps 100% or more, nearly doubled the federal budget deficit, and forced Mexico to seek massive new loans from creditors.

In July, Mexico reached a landmark $1.6 billion standby agreement with the International Monetary Fund (IMF) which, for the first time, tied Mexico's debt repayment schedule to its oil export earnings. The agreement includes a $500 million contingency fund to supplement investment if economic recovery fails to materialize and a provision for automatic additional financing if oil prices fall below $9 per barrel. If prices rise above $14 per barrel, Mexico is automatically required to scale down its borrowing requests. The agreement contemplates a total loan package of $12 billion in 1986 and 1987, with half coming from the IMF, the World Bank, and the Inter-American Development Bank, and the rest from private banks.

The Mexican arrangement could set a precedent for creating a linkage between export earnings and the payment of external debt. Argentina sought similar concessions from the IMF, basing its payment schedule on the country's grain export earnings, and several other oil-exporting countries could benefit from a trade-debt link. Nigeria, for one, has a total foreign debt of nearly $20 billion, with scheduled interest and principal payments in 1986 of $4.8 billion. Oil accounts for 94% of Nigeria's export income; during the period of peak oil prices, oil brought in about $7 billion a year, a figure that was cut in half in 1986. Algeria, which depends on oil and gas for virtually all its export income, is similarly hard-pressed, as are Venezuela, Ecuador, and Trinidad and Tobago in the Western Hemisphere. In Southeast Asia, Indonesia and Malaysia must contend not only with low oil prices but with weak markets for other commodities as well.

Boon for Importers. The industrialized countries and a few oil-importing developing countries, such as Brazil, reaped major benefits from lower oil prices in 1986. In the case of Brazil the country's oil import bill shrunk to nearly $2 billion, compared with $5.6 billion in 1985. As a result Brazil enjoyed a merchandise trade surplus of $12 billion during the year and registered economic growth of 6%. Brazil also was aided by the oil-related decline in interest rates on its foreign debt.

The oil-price slump showed signs during the year of spurring faster economic growth in the industrialized countries. In the United States federal officials predicted a 1986 growth rate of 4%, well above the 2.2% rate of the previous year. In Western Europe economists foresaw 3.5% growth, a full percentage point above the December 1985 forecast by the Organization for Economic Cooperation and Development (OECD). In both Europe and North America stock markets soared to record levels on the upbeat economic forecasts.

Differential Effects. In the United States the overall rosy economic picture was moderated by differences in regional and sectoral outlooks. While gasoline prices were down everywhere and the fuel-consuming states in the Northeast could look forward to lower heating bills during the winter, gloom settled over such oil-producing states as Texas, Oklahoma, Louisiana, and Alaska, where economic growth had begun to slow even before the collapse of oil prices. By one estimate every one dollar decline in the price of oil cost Texas 25,000 jobs, $3 billion per year in purchasing power, and $100 million in state and local tax revenues. In the oil states the decline in drilling activity, the capping of small "stripper" wells, and layoffs by the big oil companies sent shock waves through the economy. Two economists at Southern Methodist University in Dallas foresaw a long-term decline in the U.S. oil industry. "It is unlikely that the oil industry will disappear completely from the American industrial landscape," they wrote, "but it will continue to shrink in size and importance. . . ."

In addition to the stress in oil-producing states, the U.S. banking industry felt the impact of cheaper oil. Federal banking regulators identified 536 banks that had 25% or more of their capital, $61 billion in all, committed to oil and gas loans. The failure in July of the First National Bank and Trust Company of Oklahoma City, the second largest bank failure in U.S. history, was attributed to energy-related lending problems.

OPEC's Future. Industry analysts warned that the oil glut could be quickly reversed if the industrialized countries are lulled into a false sense of security about the longer-term energy future. Among the signs of complacency cited by experts were the termination of the U.S. government's synthetic fuels program, the dramatic slowdown in oil exploration in the United States, the relaxing of federal standards for automobile fuel efficiency, and a sharp rise in oil imports (20% more in 1986 than in 1985). A report by the U.S. Department of Energy suggested that higher prices are "inevitable" within the next decade. If the Energy Department is correct cheap oil may be a sometime thing. The foundations of a new energy crisis and a return of market domination by OPEC may already be in place.

See also ENERGY.

RICHARD C. SCHROEDER

AP/Wide World

Fred Grandy (R), formerly "Gopher" on TV's "The Love Boat," was elected to the U.S. House from Iowa's sixth district.

Iowa

A major reorganization of the state government and ticket-splitting in the November election were topics of interest in 1986.

Legislation. The legislature enacted more than 200 bills in 1986. Probably the most important single bill enacted was a reorganization of the state's administrative structure recommended by Gov. Terry E. Branstad. The number of state departments and agencies was reduced from 68 to 24, resulting in a staff reduction of more than 1,000. The total saving from the new administrative structure was estimated to be more than $5 million.

In another major change, the state will get out of the retail liquor business in 1987, although it will remain the only wholesale liquor dealer in the state. The drinking age was raised to 21 from 19. Other new laws mandated the use of seat belts, reduced the fine for speeding on the state's highways, and lowered to .10% the blood-alcohol level required for convictions of drunken driving.

The state's share of public-school financing was increased by $400 million. All public elementary and secondary schools were required to begin classes after Labor Day in 1986 in a measure intended to promote tourism.

The $10 million from state lottery proceeds earmarked for a world trade center was reallocated to local development projects. For the beleaguered farm community, two major measures were passed making it more difficult for the Farm Credit System to take land from financially strapped farmers. A farm mediation plan providing better legal assistance for farmers also was approved.

A $2.2 billion budget, recommended by Governor Branstad, was passed by the General Assembly with few exceptions. No major state taxes were enacted, although many legislators were convinced that the budget would not be balanced by the end of the fiscal year.

Elections. Republican Charles Grassley became the first U.S. senator from Iowa in 20 years to be returned for a second term. Incumbent U.S. Congressman Jim Leach (R), Thomas J. Tauke (R), Neal Smith (D), and James R. Lightfoot (R) won reelection. David Nagel became the first Democrat to win in the third district in 50 years, and newcomer Fred Grandy (R), an actor on the television program *The Love Boat*, replaced retiring Democrat Berkley Bedell.

Republican Governor Branstad defeated challenger Lowell Junkins, but Democrat JoAnn Zimmerman became the first woman to be elected lieutenant governor of Iowa. Democrats also captured the offices of secretary of state and secretary of agriculture, and Democratic incumbents won reelection as attorney

---

IOWA • Information Highlights

Area: 56,275 sq mi (145 753 km²).
Population (1985 est.): 2,884,000.
Chief Cities (July 1, 1984 est.): Des Moines, the capital, 190,832; Cedar Rapids, 108,669; Davenport, 102,129; Sioux City (1980 census), 82,003.
Government (1986): *Chief Officers*—governor, Terry E. Branstad (R); lt. gov., Robert T. Anderson (D). *General Assembly*—Senate, 50 members; House of Representatives, 100 members.
State Finances (fiscal year 1985): *Revenue,* $4,697,000,000; *expenditure,* $4,630,000,000.
Personal Income (1985): $36,315,000,000; per capita, $12,594.
Labor Force (June 1986): *Civilian labor force,* 1,456,700; *unemployed,* 94,600 (6.5% of total force).
Education: *Enrollment* (fall 1984))—public elementary schools, 328,835; public secondary, 162,176; colleges and universities, 152,897. *Public school expenditures* (1983–84), $1,500,000,000 ($3,212 per pupil).

general and state treasurer. The Democrats retained control of both houses of the General Assembly.

Voters also approved a constitutional amendment allowing state statutes to become law without first being published in newspapers.

Other. In 1986, Iowa farmers enrolled 91.1% of their corn base acres in the set-aside program, an all-time record that reduced the total corn crop. Nearly 1.75 million acres (710,000 ha) were taken out of corn production.

Federal census bureau estimates showed that Iowa's population declined by more than 11,000 since the 1980 census.

Dog-racing tracks opened in Council Bluffs and Waterloo in 1986, bringing to three the number of dog tracks in operation in the state.

RUSSELL M. ROSS, *University of Iowa*

IRAN

Despite the continued official position demanding total defeat of Iraq, indications of internal differences within the Iranian government over the Gulf War began to emerge during 1986. A more moderate faction seemed willing to discuss compromise solutions and to seek an improvement of relations with other Middle Eastern and Western nations. Differences over domestic and other foreign policies also surfaced. Nevertheless, Iran initiated major military campaigns during 1986, penetrating Iraq at several strategic points.

War with Iraq. During February, Iran captured the southern Iraqi port of Fao and nearly reached the border of Kuwait, inflicting heavy casualties on the enemy. Victories also were scored in the central sector, where Mehran was recaptured from Iraq, and in the north, where Iranian forces joined Iraqi Kurdish rebels to threaten Iraq's Mosul oil fields. Iranian casualties continued to escalate, reaching more than 250,000 dead and 500,000 wounded, according

to U.S. official estimates. Despite Iraq's superiority in aircraft and ground equipment, Iran held a great advantage in manpower. Supporting official declarations that it was about to embark on a "final campaign" to crush Iraq, Iran massed 650,000 troops along the border, but no such offensive was forthcoming.

Domestic Affairs. Differences over war strategies and internal affairs were revealed in a power struggle between a faction associated with Ayatollah Hussein Ali Montazeri, designated in November 1985 as the eventual successor to Ayatollah Ruhollah Khomeini, and a moderate faction led by Speaker of the Parliament Hojatolislam Hashemi Rafsanjani. A loyal follower of Khomeini, Montazeri is perceived as a hard-liner on foreign policy and a liberal in domestic affairs. He advocates the exporting of Iran's Islamic revolution and has met frequently with visiting Shiite leaders to arrange monetary and military assistance. Montazeri also supports unrestrained war against Iraq. In domestic affairs, he has taken a stand against state control of the economy and has been critical of many economic and social changes advocated by young militants of the Islamic Republican Party. He supports private property as essential to economic development and calls for an end to persecution of liberal and moderate critics of government programs.

Montazeri has given discreet support to Mehdi Bazargan, a secular moderate who in 1979 became the first prime minister of the republic but was soon driven from power by Islamic militants. Bazargan is the leader of the Iranian Liberation Movement (ILP), an association of liberals that was tolerated until 1986. The ILP was to have resumed some of its public activities during the spring, but at a May 15 ceremony commemorating the movement's 25th anniversary, nine of its leaders, including Bazargan, were kidnapped and held for several hours; neither the Interior Ministry nor the police intervened.

In October, in another attempt to undercut Montazeri, his close associate and relative, Mehdi Hashemi, the head of the Bureau for Liberation Movements Abroad, was arrested on charges of treason, murder, kidnapping, and illegal possession of weapons. Although no formal political opposition parties were permitted, growing disaffection with government policies began to emerge openly during 1986. In July for example, physicians and other health care workers staged the nation's first strike since the 1979 revolution, protesting the arrest of the president of the Iranian Medical Association and his replacement with a government appointee.

On the economic front, Iran's problems were greatly intensified by a decline in oil revenue, the result of new OPEC (Organization of the Petroleum Exporting Countries) production

---

IRAN • Information Highlights

Official Name: Islamic Republic of Iran.
Location: Southwest Asia.
Area: 636,293 sq mi (1 648 000 km²).
Population (mid-1986 est.): 46,600,000.
Chief City (1982 est.): Tehran, the capital, 5,734,199.
Government: *Supreme faqih*, Ayatollah Ruhollah Khomeini, *Head of state,* Ali Khamenei, president (took office Oct. 1981). *Head of government,* Mir Hosein Musavi-Khamenei, prime minister (took office Oct. 1981). *Legislature* (unicameral)—Islamic Consultative Assembly.
Monetary Unit: Rial (78.799 rials equal U.S.$1, June 1986).
Gross National Product (1984 U.S.$): $80,400,-000,000.
Economic Index (1985): *Consumer Prices* (1980 = 100), all items, 207.4; food, 205.8.
Foreign Trade (1984 U.S.$): *Imports,* (est.) $16,500,000,000; *exports,* $13,979,000,000.

AP/Wide World

Ayatollah Hussein Ali Montazeri, the designated successor to Ayatollah Khomeini, was said to be in a power struggle with the more moderate Hojatolislam Hashemi Rafsanjani.

quotas, the sharp drop in world market prices, and Iraqi attacks on oil installations. (Oil accounts for some 95% of Iran's foreign currency earnings.) During January the national electricity network suffered a 40% drop in power because of gas shortages. In March economic observers reported that unemployment reached 15%.

Foreign Affairs. The opponents of Montazeri's hard-line foreign policy included advocates of negotiations with the United States and France on economic and military support. In November it was revealed that U.S. officials had traveled to Iran for secret negotiations, that the United States had sold and transferred several arms shipments to Tehran, and that the release of a U.S. hostage by pro-Iranian militants in Lebanon may have been tied to the deal. U.S. President Ronald Reagan defended the sales as an effort to strengthen ties with Iranian moderates, hasten the end of the Gulf War, and possibly gain the release of hostages. He announced, however, that no further arms would be sent.

Similar negotiations were held with France during May and June, in which Iranian officials made three essential demands: repayment of a $1 billion loan made by the late shah; expulsion from France of Iranian dissidents; and a pledge from Paris not to sign new arms sales contracts with Iraq. All three demands apparently were met, and on June 20 two French hostages in Lebanon were set free. Two others were released in November and a third in a Christmas "gesture of peace."

Attempts also were made during 1986 to ease growing strains with Syria, still one of the few Arab countries to support Iran in the Gulf War. The strained relations had developed after Syria reneged on payment of a $1.5 billion debt for oil shipments received over several years. In April the fourth tripartite meeting of Syrian, Libyan, and Iranian foreign ministers

was held in Tehran in an effort to mend deteriorating relations.

At OPEC meetings in Geneva during August, October, and December, Iranian representatives agreed to oil production quotas aimed at raising prices. Iranian representatives also held discussions with Saudi Arabia and the United Arab Emirates on a "regional security arrangement."

DON PERETZ
State University of New York, Binghamton

IRAQ

The war initiated by Iraq's invasion of Iran in September 1980 continued to overshadow both domestic and foreign affairs during 1986. By the end of the year, U.S. officials estimated Iraq's casualties at more than 100,000 dead and nearly 500,000 wounded. Falling oil prices and escalating war costs further undermined the economy and increased domestic political unrest.

War with Iran. During February, Iraq suffered a major reverse when it lost its southern oil port, Fao (Faw), and Oum el-Rasas Island during a new Iranian offensive. Although Fao was no longer of economic importance because of extensive destruction early in the war, the offensive was a psychological blow for it enabled Iran's troops almost to reach the border of Kuwait and resulted in heavy Iraqi casualties.

Although Iraq later recaptured Oum el-Rasas Island, and Mehran and four other Iranian towns in the central front, Iran penetrated northern Kurdish regions close to Iraq's Mosul oil fields. Despite Iran's buildup of large forces along the border and threats of a "final offensive" to overthrow Iraqi President Saddam Hussein, Iraq continued to maintain its superiority in mechanized and air forces. Western observers reported that Iraq's frontline troops seemed well equipped, well trained, and well led.

Iraq and Iran exchanged charges that each was using illegal chemical weapons against the other. In March, however, a team of UN-appointed experts accused Iraq of using chemical weapons "on many occasions." Both mustard and nerve gas were used against Iranian forces, according to the report issued under the name of UN Secretary-General Javier Pérez de Cuéllar.

Animosity between Iraq and Iran flared in the Organization of the Petroleum Exporting Countries (OPEC) meeting in Geneva in October when Iraq supported Kuwait's demands, against Iran, for a substantial increase in Kuwait's quota of oil production. Iraq demanded that its OPEC allotment of 1.2 million barrels per day be raised to match Iran's quota of 2.3 million barrels. In a compromise, Iraq was ex-

IRAQ • Information Highlights

Official Name: Republic of Iraq.
Location: Southwest Asia.
Area: 167,924 sq mi (434 924 km²).
Population (mid-1986 est.): 16,000,000.
Chief City (1981 est.): Baghdad, the capital, 3,400,000.
Government: *Head of state and government,* Saddam Husayn, president (took office July 1979).
Monetary Unit: Dinar (0.311 dinar equals U.S.$1, June 1986).
Gross National Product (1984 U.S.$): $27,000,-000,000.
Foreign Trade (1985 est. U.S.$): *Imports,* $11,500,000,000; *exports,* $11,700,000,000.

cluded from the agreed production quotas and is free to continue producing up to 2 million barrels per day.

Domestic Affairs. Although Iraq's oil revenues were twice those of Iran, and Baghdad continued to receive economic assistance from Saudi Arabia and Kuwait, its economy suffered setbacks. Iraq failed to meet a repayment of a $500 million foreign bank loan due in September, inflation continued to push prices higher, and the austerity measures taken by the government to offset loss of oil revenues began to erode living standards.

Continued escalation of war casualties and the need to maintain a million-strong standing army led in June to a three-month draft of some 60,000 university students between the ages of 18 and 25 and of their professors under 45 years of age. Some observers reported that such unpopular war measures led to unrest in the army and among civilians, resulting in summary execution of officers held responsible for the rout at Fao and of others who were planning a military coup.

In March, Iranian women marked the 2,000th day of the Iran-Iraq war. Although Iraq has more aircraft and ground equipment than Iran, the latter has a bigger military force.

AP/Wide World

To buttress his political position, President Hussein convened an extraordinary session of the Baath Party's National Congress during July, at which he obtained positions in the Revolutionary Command for six of his closest associates. These included a cousin, Ali Hassan el-Majid, who also holds the key post of chief of internal security. The July conference also sacked an important leader of the Baath, Naim Haddad, president of the National Assembly. Haddad, one of the few Shiite Muslim Iraqi leaders (most are Sunni Muslim), had been deprived of one major post after another since 1982. Although Haddad remained head of the National Progressive Front—a political alliance of the Baath, the Communist Party, and the Kurdish Democratic Party—a leftist Lebanese newspaper reported that he was killed in September. The July conference also reelected Saddam Hussein secretary-general of the Baath Party and established a new party administration of 17 members.

Foreign Affairs. During 1986 President Hussein attempted to improve diplomatic relations on several fronts. Ties with Jordan were strengthened by visits to Baghdad by King Hussein of Jordan during March and May. Although the Jordanian monarchy and the Iraqi republic had been hostile since the 1958 Iraqi revolution, the threat of an Iranian victory in the Gulf war brought the king and the Baathist president together. King Hussein was reported to be an intermediary between Iraq and Syria, which sided with Iran in the war. Although both Syria and Iraq were ruled by Baathist socialist regimes, Western diplomats reported that King Hussein's efforts to reconcile the two countries were not successful.

While attempting to improve relations with the West, Iraq maintained its cooperation with the Soviet Union dating back to the first Soviet-Iraqi contract in 1958. In May the Permanent Iraqi-Soviet Economic, Scientific, and Technical Cooperation Commission held its 16th annual session in Baghdad. The volume of trade between the two countries has increased ninefold, to about $1 billion, since the 1982 treaty of friendship and cooperation between Baghdad and Moscow.

To maintain relatively good relations with France, Hussein in March agreed to release two anti-regime Iraqis. The French, who earlier, under Iranian pressure, had sent them to Iraq, requested that they be permitted to return.

In November, following disclosure of secret U.S. arms deliveries to Iran with the assistance of Israel, the Iraqi ambassador in Washington stated that for years Iraq had complained to U.S. officials that Israel was sending military equipment to Iran. The United States, he said, had simply relayed Israeli denials to Iraq.

DON PERETZ
State University of New York, Binghamton

IRELAND

After signing the Anglo-Irish Agreement on Nov. 15, 1985, and winning its approval in the Irish Parliament later that month, Ireland's Prime Minister Garret FitzGerald in 1986 had to cope with economic recession and the defeat of a proposal to legalize divorce.

Anglo-Irish Agreement. Designed to give the Irish government a consultative role in the administration of the six northern counties, the Anglo-Irish Agreement created an Intergovernmental Conference under which representatives of both countries would meet regularly to discuss matters of mutual interest. From December 1985 to the end of 1986, the Conference met almost a dozen times in Belfast, Dublin, and London. The British and Irish delegates addressed such issues as the impartial enforcement of the law in the north by the Royal Ulster Constabulary and the British Army, cross-border security, financial subsidies to trade and industry, and schemes to promote better relations between the Protestant and Roman Catholic communities. Although the Agreement provoked much hostility from the Sinn Fein party and the Irish Republican Army (IRA) as well as militant Protestant Unionists, most moderates hoped the accord would improve conditions in the north and relations between Great Britain and Ireland.

In a momentous policy shift in November, Gerry Adams, the president of Sinn Fein, the political arm of the Provisional IRA, persuaded a majority of his followers to end the party's 65-year boycott of the Dail. Sinn Fein candidates thus would seek parliamentary seats in the next general election and perhaps someday hold the balance between the major parties.

Economy. The budget presented to the Dail on January 29 by Minister of Finance Alan Dukes proposed to lower the national deficit to 7.4% of the gross national product (GNP) by cutting government expenditure (by 55 million Irish pounds or about $70 million) and by raising indirect taxes. Dukes also yielded to public pressure by reducing to 10% the Value Added Tax (VAT) for restaurant meals and other personal services. Criticized for austerity measures and facing an unemployment rate of 17%, the government hoped to revive the economy and thereby enhance its appeal to voters. But the raising of the central bank's prime lending rate by 3% (on February 4), the replacement of Dukes as finance minister by John Bruton (February 13), and the devaluation of the Irish pound, or punt, by 8% (August 2) did little to end the prolonged recession. In response to the declining value of the British pound and the U.S. dollar, the coalition cabinet of Fine Gael and Labour decided to devalue the punt in order to make Irish exports more attractive to overseas buyers, especially those in Great Britain and the United States.

Government. Besides the change at the Ministry of Finance, the cabinet shuffle of February 13 also saw Dukes move to the Ministry of Justice, succeeding Michael Noonan, who took over Industry and Commerce. On February 24 in Strasbourg, France, Dukes signed the European Convention on the Suppression of Terrorism.

In a June 26 referendum, Irish voters soundly defeated a proposed amendment to end the constitutional ban on divorce. Although FitzGerald had staked much of his political credit on the reform, almost 64% of the voters supported the Catholic hierarchy's objections to any liberalizing of the law against divorce. The referendum made clear that most Irish people followed Pope John Paul II's conservative theology in matters of morality as well as faith.

For Prime Minister FitzGerald, the outcome was also a major political setback. His coalition government narrowly won a vote of confidence on October 23, but the prime minister would face another key test in January 1987, when he submits a new budget, as well as with national parliamentary elections later that year.

Crime. Two prominent crimes kept the police preoccupied during the spring. On April 8, three armed men kidnapped the wife of wealthy Dublin banker John Guinness and demanded a ransom of 2 million pounds ($2.6 million). The kidnappers left enough clues to enable the police to discover their hideout. After a short siege on April 16, the men released Mrs. Guinness unharmed and surrendered. Then, on May 21, a gang of thieves broke into historic Russborough House south of Dublin before dawn and stole 17 paintings valued at more than 30 million pounds (about $37 million) and including works by Vermeer, Rubens, and Goya. The police found seven of the paintings the next day but could not trace the others.

L. PERRY CURTIS, JR. *Brown University*

IRELAND • Information Highlights

Official Name: Ireland (Eire).
Location: Island in the eastern North Atlantic Ocean.
Area: 27,136 sq mi (70 282 km²).
Population (mid-1986 est.): 3,600,000.
Chief Cities (1981 census): Dublin, the capital, 525,882; Cork, 149,792; Limerick, 75,520.
Government: *Head of state,* Patrick J. Hillery, president (took office Dec. 1976). *Head of government,* Garret FitzGerald, prime minister (took office Dec. 1982). *Legislature*—Parliament: House of Representatives (Dail Eireann) and Senate (Seanad Eireann).
Monetary Unit: Pound (0.7257 pound equals U.S.$1, Oct. 17, 1986).
Gross National Product (1984 U.S.$): $16,000,000,000.
Economic Indexes (1985): *Consumer Prices* (1980 = 100), all items, 178.3; food, 160.2. *Industrial Production* (1980 = 100), 125.
Foreign Trade (1985 U.S.$): *Imports,* $10,028,000,000; *exports,* $10,360,000,000.

In the prime minister's office in Jerusalem, October 17, Prime Minister Shimon Peres (left) and Foreign Minister Yitzhak Shamir sign a memorandum formalizing their job switch.

AP/Wide World

ISRAEL

The transition of power under the terms of the 1984 national unity agreement was the central development of 1986 in Israeli domestic affairs, while on the foreign front there were several diplomatic breakthroughs but little fundamental change in the nation's standing.

Domestic Affairs. Despite several periods of uncertainty, Prime Minister Shimon Peres of the center-left Labor Party and Foreign Minister Yitzhak Shamir of the right-wing Likud bloc swapped positions in October, as stipulated in the power-sharing agreement of 1984. Under that unique arrangement, each party would have an equal number of cabinet positions in a unity government, and each party leader would serve as premier for 25 months.

From the beginning, few expected the coalition to last, and during 1986 it was threatened by at least two major challenges. One was the so-called Shin Bet affair, in which the Shamir government of 1984 was accused of suppressing evidence that the Israeli secret service, Shin Bet, had killed two Arab terrorists who had been taken into custody after attacking an Israeli bus and that Shamir had forbidden the attorney general to prosecute the case. Those who opposed a new investigation and prosecutions argued that important national security procedures would be jeopardized, but Attorney General Yitzhak Zamir and several other officials resigned in protest. The crisis deepened in May, when the chief of Shin Bet resigned in return for immunity from prosecution. Shamir and Peres differed on how the case should be handled, but the situation eased during the summer, when the coalition cabinet voted against establishing a state commission of inquiry and when the Israeli Supreme Court upheld the granting of immunity.

The other major challenge to the national unity government was more purely political. It was widely thought that Prime Minister Peres would look for opportunities to call an early election, and several such situations did arise. In March, for example, the national convention of the Herut party—the core of the Likud bloc—was suspended because of internal rifts which appeared unresolvable; at the last minute, compromises were reached. More generally, Peres himself had several key successes in foreign affairs and proved to be an unexpectedly popular leader. Unfortunately for him, his popularity did not carry over to the party, and on October 10 he resigned the premiership; Shamir was sworn in ten days later.

That the national unity coalition hung together was also due in part to the strong public conviction that its breakup might have the grave effect of ending the shared responsibility essential to implementing the economic stabilization program. After triple-digit inflation the previous year, the bipartisan program did succeed in reducing the rate to approximately 30% in 1986 through strict wage and price controls. On the other hand the government was able to agree on only a few of the large budget cuts which many considered an equally vital element of economic recovery. Those that it did agree to make were primarily in the areas of subsidies of basic commodities and some of the social services—which contributed to a lowering of the real standard of living for many Israelis. The austerity measures and the perception that wage controls were being enforced more rigorously than price controls led to strikes.

Israel's national trade deficit was reduced slightly during the year, but the economy remained in need of vast U.S. aid. The tourist industry fell off sharply because of fears of international terrorism, and that decline was only partially offset by the drop in oil prices. The economic difficulties were among the reasons for the record low number of new Israeli immigrants and the sizable number of emigrants.

Public confidence in the financial system was shaken by the April 20 report of a public commission investigating the bank shares collapse of 1983. The report of the Beijsky Commission confirmed allegations that the heads of some of Israel's largest commercial institutions had caused the crash through systematic manipulation of stocks. While no formal prosecutions were recommended, several of the bank chiefs resigned.

One of the nation's continuing domestic problems was the growing conflict between secular and ultra-Orthodox Jewish Israelis. Among the issues that led to violence during 1986 were Orthodox demands for stricter Sabbath observance; limitations on "provocative" billboard advertisements; the cancellation of daylight savings time, which was said to make religious observance more difficult; and budgetary changes. The government resisted most of these demands, but tensions remained high.

In November the government announced that it was holding Mordechai Vanunu, a disenchanted former nuclear technician whose detailed description of Israeli atomic weapons development appeared in the *London Sunday Times*.

Foreign Affairs. The year saw several potentially important successes in foreign affairs, but little real progress was made in solving some of the nation's fundamental problems. Among the successes were the extensions of formal recognition by Spain, the Ivory Coast, and Cameroon. The latter two represented the continuation of the slow process of restoration of relations with African states that had broken ties after the Yom Kippur War of 1973.

Another noteworthy diplomatic development, albeit fruitless, was a meeting in Helsinki between representatives of Israel and the Soviet Union to discuss the possible resumption of consular links. It was the first formal contact between the two countries since the Six-Day War of 1967. After the unsuccessful talks, however, Moscow announced that it planned no further discussions on the issue.

In the Middle East itself, relations with two moderate Arab states took turns for the better. In July, Prime Minister Peres traveled to Morocco for two days of secret talks with King Hassan II, who apparently hoped to generate momentum for a new Middle East peace effort. The surprise meeting marked the first visit by an Israeli leader to an Arab nation other than Egypt since Israel's independence in 1948. Little came of the summit, however, except for bitter recriminations against Hassan by the Arab "rejectionist" states.

The other moderate Arab state with which Israel managed to improve relations was Egypt. In early August the two nations reached agreement on an arbitration formula to settle their longstanding dispute over Taba, a sliver of land in the Sinai. The agreement opened the way for a summit meeting September 11–12 in Alexandria, Egypt, between Peres and Egypt's President Hosni Mubarak. It was the first summit between the two nations since 1981.

Meanwhile, troubles continued on the border with Lebanon. Although one of the successes of the national unity government had been the withdrawal of Israeli troops from Lebanon in 1985 and the establishment of a "security zone" in southern Lebanon, the arrangement proved insufficient to prevent completely the renewed infiltration of Palestinian guerrillas into southern Lebanon and some renewed shelling of settlements in northern Israel. Shiite Muslim militants also launched attacks in the security zone on Israeli forces and the Israeli-supported South Lebanon Army.

The issues of the West Bank and Gaza strip also moved no closer to solution. Militant Palestinians in both areas were able to maintain their influence through such actions as the murder of an Arab mayor who had accepted appointment by Israel. The Israeli government responded with new measures to suppress the most radical expressions of Palestinian nationalism. Again there were incidents of violence between Arab residents and Jewish settlers on the West Bank.

On the negotiating front there was also little progress in resolving the Palestinian issue. Israel made a number of attempts to bring Jordan into talks to find a formula for the future of the territories, but King Hussein was not amenable. U.S. officials again made several trips to the Middle East to move the parties toward direct talks, but the Reagan administration put forth no new substantive proposals.

On February 11, Israel gave a joyous welcome to freed Soviet dissident Anatoly Shcharansky (*see* BIOGRAPHY), but officials emphasized that there had been no change in Soviet policy on Jewish emigration.

See also MIDDLE EAST; RELIGION—Judaism; TERRORISM.

WALTER F. WEIKER, *Rutgers University*

ISRAEL • Information Highlights

Official Name: State of Israel.
Location: Southwest Asia.
Area: 8,000 sq mi (20 720 km²).
Population (mid-1986 est.): 4,200,000.
Chief Cities (June 4, 1983 est.): Jerusalem, the capital, 428,668 (including East Jerusalem); Tel Aviv-Jaffa, 327,625; Haifa, 235,775.
Government: *Head of state,* Chaim Herzog, president (took office May 1983). *Head of government,* Shimon Peres, prime minister (took office Sept. 14, 1984). *Legislature* (unicameral)—Knesset.
Monetary Unit: Shekel (1.4743 shekels equal U.S.$1, Oct. 17, 1986).
Gross National Product (1985 U.S.$): $25,900,-000,000.
Economic Indexes (1985): *Consumer Prices* (1980 = 100), all items, 22,497.0; food, 21,703.0. *Industrial Production* (1984; 1980 = 100), 116.
Foreign Trade (1985 U.S.$): *Imports* $8,096,000,000; *exports,* $6,086,000,000.

ITALY

Despite his popularity, Socialist Premier Bettino Craxi was unable to control his five-party coalition in Parliament in 1986. He resigned in June but formed a new government after accepting a power-sharing arrangement with the Christian Democratic Party. Craxi continued his efforts to improve the economy and crack down on terrorism and the Mafia. Italy's relationship with Libya deteriorated.

Domestic Affairs

By surmounting the 1985 crisis over the Palestinian hijacking of the Italian cruise ship *Achille Lauro,* Craxi's coalition government (Socialists, Christian Democrats, Social-Democrats, Republicans, and Liberals) established a longevity record for a post-World War II Italian government. Since becoming premier on Aug. 4, 1983, Craxi had brought Italy's economic growth rate up to a respectable 2% to 3% a year. Inflation fell from 15% to 6%, thanks to changes in the system of wage indexing, and unemployment (13%) and the huge budget deficit (16% of the gross domestic product) at least remained stable. Italy's impressive growth was aided by an American-led boom. The Milan stock exchange flourished in 1986 as a host of new investors discovered the chances for big profits.

Government and Politics. Ciriaco De Mita, the leader of the Christian Democrats, feuded openly with Craxi. De Mita insisted that the Christian Democrats, as Italy's largest party, were entitled to the premiership, a post they had monopolized for most of the postwar period. He hoped to regain leadership of the government well before the parliamentary elections scheduled for June 1988.

The first opportunity to test the relative strength of the parties in 1986 was provided by the June 22 election for the Sicilian regional assembly. The Christian Democrats, traditionally the strongest party in conservative Sicily, had been tarnished by their links to the Mafia. De Mita therefore presented a fresh slate of candidates and campaigned vigorously for them. Craxi campaigned for the Socialists. The five parties composing the national coalition government won two thirds of the total vote. The opposition Communist Party, with 19.4% of the vote, lost a percentage point and saw its seats in the 90-member regional assembly reduced from 20 to 19. The Christian Democrats lost 2 of their 38 seats but remained in first place with 38.8% of the popular vote. Craxi was unable to transform his personal popularity into electoral gains; his Socialist Party retained the 14 seats they had held previously. No one was happy with the results.

On June 27, Craxi's coalition government resigned when it was defeated 293 to 266 in a secret ballot in Parliament on a local finance bill. This meant that 70 to 80 deputies from the government's majority had defected. The defectors, known as "snipers," came mainly from the ranks of the Christian Democrats but included members of all the coalition parties. Some of the Socialist defectors may have thought they were doing Craxi a favor by bringing his confrontation with De Mita to a head. What made the defeat especially bitter for Craxi was that his government had won a confidence motion by 338 to 230 votes only minutes earlier.

Craxi accepted President Francesco Cossiga's invitation to serve as caretaker premier until a new government could be formed. The crisis lasted a month before Cossiga asked Craxi on July 22 to try to form a new government.

Craxi decided at this point to accept a compromise he had rejected a month earlier. In an unusual and formal bargain, he resumed the premiership until March 1987, when the Socialist Party congress was scheduled to meet. At that time he would hand over the premiership to the Christian Democrats, who would hold it until the 1988 parliamentary elections while Craxi devoted himself to energizing his party. On this basis a new government of the same five parties was sworn in on August 1. De Mita called the crisis "the most difficult" the 40-year-old republic had ever experienced.

Terrorism. The brutal massacre by Palestinian terrorists at Rome's Leonardo da Vinci Airport on Dec. 27, 1985, caused Italy to augment its security system. Yet many tourists remained frightened, and Americans, in particular, stayed away in 1986. Although the Red Brigades and other domestic terrorists had been largely suppressed by the authorities, the intractable problem of Palestinian terrorism continued unabated. Numerous major trials took place in 1986.

In June the second trial of members of the Palestine Liberation Front who had hijacked the *Achille Lauro* got underway in a Genoa courtroom that was fortified like a bunker. Fifteen Palestinians had been indicted, but only five were in custody. The other ten, including Abul Abbas, the alleged mastermind of the operation who had been allowed to leave Italy in October 1985 after U.S. planes had forced him down in Sicily, were tried in absentia. On July 10 a jury convicted 11 of the group on charges of "carrying out a kidnap with terrorist intent, leading to the death of a hostage [the American Leon Klinghoffer]." Three of the absentees, including Abul Abbas, received life sentences. Eight other defendants were given sentences ranging from 15 to 30 years. Four were acquitted for lack of evidence.

In May, 20 persons were indicted for the 1980 bombing of the Bologna railway station that caused heavy casualties. This group was

Prime Minister Craxi leaves the presidential palace after submitting his resignation. He later formed a new cabinet.

allegedly composed of right-wing activists under control of a faction in the Italian secret service.

In mid-June a trial began for 174 members of the left-wing Red Brigades charged with various acts of violence dating back to 1978.

After three years of investigation, a monster trial of 474 mafiosi accused of drug trafficking and 90 murders got underway in Palermo in February. The complicated trial, involving hundreds of lawyers, was expected to continue well into 1987. Much of the prosecution's evidence was provided by star witnesses Tommaso Buscetta and Salvatore Contorno, high-ranking informers who were allowed to live in the United States under a witness protection plan. The alleged Mafia ''boss of bosses'' in Sicily, Luciano Liggio, testified that he had been asked to support a military coup in Italy in the early 1970s.

The ten-month trial in Rome of 7 men (4 Turks and 3 Bulgarians) charged with conspiring to murder Pope John Paul II in May 1981 came to an end on March 29, 1986. All won qualified acquittal on the main charges. Mehmet Ali Agca, the Turk who had fired the shots in 1981 and remained in prison under a life sentence, had alleged that there was a Turkish-Bulgarian conspiracy behind the assassination attempt. But his later outbursts, retractions,

and counter-retractions turned the trial into a near farce. The long trial failed to show that the Bulgarian security service had ordered the assassination attempt or, indeed, had any connection with the plotters. It also failed to address the question that lay behind the alleged Bulgarian connection—whether the idea had originated with the Soviet KGB.

Michele Sindona, a Sicilian-American financier who was adviser to a Vatican bank and already faced prison terms in the United States and Italy for bank fraud, was convicted in Milan on March 18 of contracting with a U.S. gangster for the murder of a Milan lawyer in 1979. He was also shown to have ties with the Mafia and the secret P2 Masonic Lodge, which had recently been declared a subversive organization by Parliament. Sindona received a life sentence but died in prison three days later after swallowing cyanide in his coffee.

Foreign Relations

Libya's place in Italy's decade-long policy of conciliating the Arab world had survived a number of threats, including Muammar Qaddafi's 1981 threat to bomb NATO missiles in Sicily. At the start of 1986, Italy was Libya's biggest trading partner. Libya owned about 15% of the giant Italian automobile manufacturer, Fiat, and some 8,000 Italian workers resided in Libya. After Qaddafi characterized the December 1985 massacre at the Rome airport as "heroic operations," however, relations between the two countries deteriorated fitfully. Craxi quickly responded that "ones who judge the massacre as a 'heroic operation' reveal all their fanaticism and bloody attitudes," but he was not inclined to follow suit when U.S. President Ronald Reagan broke all economic ties with Libya on January 7. Instead, Craxi asked for an emergency meeting of the ministers of the European Community (EC). "When it comes to Libya, Italian and U.S. interests are very different," he explained.

Craxi was also critical of U.S. naval attacks against a Libyan missile site and patrol vessels in the disputed Gulf of Sidra on March 24. "Italy does not want wars on its doorstep," he told Parliament. At the same time Craxi strongly criticized Libya for claiming jurisdiction over the clearly "international waters" of the Gulf of Sidra and characterized as "absolutely unacceptable" Qaddafi's threats to retaliate against NATO bases in Italy. Craxi pointed out that the U.S. operation took place "outside the framework of NATO" and was thus "exclusively the responsibility of the government of the United States." At the regular meeting of the NATO council in Brussels on March 26, Italy took the lead in identifying the dangers raised by the U.S. naval exercises.

The next day, however, as U.S. Secretary of State George Shultz was about to arrive in Rome, Craxi moderated his tone. Aide Antonio Badini explained that "the most important part of what Craxi did was the tough decision he took to condemn Libya and defend the Americans on their rights in the situation." Italy's exposure in the conflict and "domestic politics" made it necessary for Craxi to link his support of the United States with some criticism of the naval maneuvers.

A new crisis erupted on April 14, when U.S. planes bombed Libyan targets in Tripoli and Benghazi in retaliation for Libyan support of international terrorism. The bombing occurred only hours after Reagan's special envoy, Vernon A. Walters, conferred with Craxi, who warned him that U.S. military action might undermine the consensus that had emerged that same day at a meeting of EC foreign ministers. The ministers had decided to cut the size of Libyan embassies in Europe and restrict the movements of Libyan diplomats.

On April 15, Craxi told Parliament that the U.S. attack on Libya could cause "a further explosion of fanaticism and extremism." He went on to complain that "the position adopted by Europe was ignored" by the United States. His tone changed later in the day when he learned that Libyan patrol boats had fired missiles at U.S. Coast Guard installations on the Italian island of Lampedusa. The missiles ex-

ploded harmlessly into the sea. Craxi declared on April 19 that Italy would respond with "severity" to any new Libyan attacks on Italian territory, although he rejected any economic sanctions against Libya, citing Italy's range of economic interests there. Subsequently Italy, complying with the EC ministers' decision, ordered Libya to cut its diplomatic staff in Italy by ten. Other Libyans were expelled later.

At the Tokyo summit of industrial powers in May, President Reagan suggested that Italy "review" its purchases of Libyan oil and look for other suppliers. Although Craxi demurred at first, he later quietly ordered the state-controlled oil company to reduce its purchases from Libya. By June the number of Italian workers in Libya had been cut to 3,000.

On June 24, Italy's interior minister and the U.S. attorney general signed an agreement to pool their intelligence resources in the fight against international terrorism. This agreement expanded a 1984 accord against drug trafficking and organized crime.

On September 23, Libya decided to sell its 15.19% share of Fiat stock for $3.15 billion (seven times what it paid for it in 1976). Libya apparently needed cash because of the slump in world oil prices. The sale freed Fiat of a partner that had proved an embarrassment to it and to the Italian government and had prevented Fiat from obtaining contracts for work on the U.S. Strategic Defense Initiative (SDI). Four days earlier the Pentagon had announced a new agreement with Italy which opened the way for Italian companies like Fiat to seek grants for SDI research.

Italian leaders were shocked that President Reagan, at his October summit with Soviet leader Mikhail Gorbachev in Iceland, almost agreed to dismantle Western Europe's nuclear defenses without consulting his NATO partners. They were further annoyed when it was revealed that the Reagan administration, which had admonished Europeans not to deal with terrorist states, had itself sold arms to Iran.

CHARLES F. DELZELL, *Vanderbilt University*

ITALY • Information Highlights

Official Name: Italian Republic.
Location: Southern Europe.
Area: 116,302 sq mi (301 223 km²).
Population (mid-1986 est.): 57,200,000.
Chief Cities (Dec. 31, 1983): Rome, the capital, 2,830,650; Milan, 1,561,438; Naples, 1,208,545.
Government: *Head of state,* Francesco Cossiga, president (took office July 1985). *Head of government,* Bettino Craxi, prime minister (sworn in Aug. 4, 1983). *Legislature*—Parliament: Senate and Chamber of Deputies.
Monetary Unit: Lira (1,376.5 lire equal U.S.$1, Nov. 25, 1986).
Economic Indexes (1985): *Consumer Prices* (1980 = 100) all items, 190.3; food, 180.3. *Industrial Production* (1980 = 100), 97.
Foreign Trade (1985 U.S.$): *Imports,* $90,994,-000,000; *exports,* $78,957,000,000.

At his official residence in Tokyo, Prime Minister Yasuhiro Naka-sone catches up on the latest pre-election news as the polls opened July 6. His Liberal-Democratic Party scored strong victories in both houses of parliament.

AP/Wide World

JAPAN

As Japan prepared for the seventh annual summit conference of major industrial democracies in May (the second hosted in Tokyo), the nation found itself in an almost embarrassingly strong position. Japan accounted for 10% of global economic production. By the end of 1985, official and private assets held abroad exceeded liabilities by $129.8 billion, making Japan the world's premier exporter of capital. About one third of Japan's gross holdings abroad were in securities; 86% of foreign investments were in U.S. bonds. In April the level of reserves—gold, convertible currencies, and special drawing rights (SDRs)—totaled $31.1 billion. The sharp rise in foreign holdings resulted from a trade surplus and an appreciation in the value of the yen. In 1985, Japan's trade surplus with the United States reached one third of the total U.S. trade deficit. As a result, trade issues dominated U.S.-Japan relations.

At home Prime Minister Yasuhiro Nakasone and his ruling Liberal-Democratic Party (LDP) scored a dramatic victory in July elections to select members of both houses of the Diet (parliament). Strong factions within the LDP, however, maneuvered toward the day when Nakasone would no longer serve as president of the party and prime minister.

Domestic Affairs

While the nation enjoyed its status as a modern industrial power, the Japanese still found time to celebrate the 60th anniversary of Emperor Hirohito's accession to the Chrysan-

themum Throne, the world's oldest imperial line. Hirohito at 85 was in good health, and the 52-year-old Crown Prince Akihito continued his long wait for succession. Next in line was Akihito's elder son, Prince Hiro, 26, who returned from two years of study at Oxford University in Great Britain.

Party Politics. In October 1985, Prime Minister Nakasone was at the halfway point of a second two-year term as president of the LDP. Party rules forbade a third term, and Nakasone stated that he would abide by these regulations. In a government reshuffle on Dec. 28, 1985, he had retained key cabinet members and party officials. Masaharu Gotoda, a close associate of former Prime Minister Kakuei Tanaka, took the key post of chief cabinet secretary. Foreign Minister Shintaro Abe and Finance Minister Noboru Takeshita were reappointed, and a former foreign minister, Kiichi Miyazawa, became chairman of the LDP executive council. Abe, Takeshita, and Miyazawa had become known as the three "new leaders" of the LDP, identified as possible successors to the prime minister.

When the 104th Diet convened in December 1985, the LDP—with its New Liberal Club (NLC) allies—controlled 262 seats in the (lower) House of Representatives and 139 seats in the (upper) House of Councillors. The Japan Socialist Party (JSP), with 112 seats in the lower house and 42 seats in the upper house, represented the chief opposition. Other parties included the Clean Government Party (Komeito), the Democratic Socialist Party (DSP), and the Japan Communist Party (JCP).

In 1985 the Supreme Court had ruled that the 1983 general election results were unconstitutional. Although it did not set aside the results, the court did demand a new public election law. On the last day of its session, May 22, 1986, the Diet increased the total number of seats in the lower house by one (to 512), subtracted one seat from each of the seven least populated districts, and added one seat to each of the eight densest districts.

On June 2, Prime Minister Nakasone dissolved the lower house only hours after an extraordinary session was convened. He thus cleared the way for a general election on July 6, to be held simultaneously with scheduled voting for the upper house. In a public opinion survey conducted in April, more than half the Japanese polled registered support of Nakasone; 38% indicated that they approved of the prime minister's foreign policy.

In the election, the LDP took 300 seats in the lower house, 50 more than it won in 1983. In addition, the LDP got the support of four members of the Diet who had run as independents, and another five in August, when the splinter NLC decided to rejoin the party. The opposition JSP, because of declining labor union support, suffered a crushing defeat. As a result, lower house seats were distributed as follows: LDP 309; JSP 85; Komeito 56; DSP 26; JCP 26; and independents 10 (total 512). In the upper house, where half the 252 seats were up for election, the LDP controlled 142 of the total seats.

On April 29, Japan celebrated the 85th brithday of the Emperor Hirohito and held special ceremonies to mark his 60th year on the throne. Empress Nagako is at his left.

AP/Wide World

Even as the Diet reelected Prime Minister Nakasone on July 22, his party was struggling with the issue of the presidential term, which was scheduled to expire October 30. Within the LDP, Naksone had the direct support of a faction of 83 Diet members. Abe had succeeded to the leadership of an 82-member faction long headed by former Prime Minister Takeo Fukuda; Miyazawa chaired an 88-member faction identified with former Prime Minister Zenko Suzuki; and Takeshita maneuvered to succeed former Prime Minister Tanaka as head of the largest faction, 138 members. After the LDP's startling election victory, the three "new leaders" bided their time.

The prime minister took the initiative by making sweeping changes in his cabinet. He neutralized Miyazawa, who had opposed Nakasone's austere budgets, by appointing him to the post of finance minister. Takeshita and Abe assumed key positions in the LDP, from which they continued to bid for succession. The prime minister eliminated the post of LDP vice-president, held by Susumu Nikaido, who seemed to be waging a losing battle with Takeshita for leadership of the powerful Tanaka faction. Shin Kanemaru (Tanaka faction) was appointed to the seldom-filled position of deputy prime minister. In all, some 20 cabinet portfolios and the major party posts were allocated on the basis of factional strength.

On September 11, some 422 LDP members of the Diet formally approved a one-year extension of Nakasone's term as party president. This would, as the prime minister put it, give him "time to enact administrative reforms," such as holding down expenditures, privatizing public corporations, and opening Japan's markets to imports.

Immediately after the July election, in which the JSP had suffered a disastrous loss of 27 seats in the lower house, veteran party chairman Masashi Ishibashi announced his intention to retire. He was succeeded by the vice chair, Takako Doi, who became the first woman to head a major political party in Japan.

Economy. The Economic Planning Agency (EPA) reported that Japan's gross national product (GNP) increased by 4.2% (exactly the rate the government had predicted) in fiscal 1985 (ended March 30, 1986). Total output was estimated at 289.4 trillion yen (about $1.626 trillion U.S.). Hurt by a decline in exports, the rate of growth had actually fallen 0.5% in the last quarter (January-March). Growth remained sluggish at 0.9% in the first quarter of fiscal 1986, but the EPA nonetheless predicted a 4% growth rate for the year.

Japan's labor force totaled 59.4 million in July, according to the management and Coordination Agency, with a record unemployment rate of 2.9%. The inflation rate, however, remained modest (2% in 1985), and the average savings per household (about $28,660) exceeded the average annual household income for the first time. Japanese women, especially housewives, were caught up in what the press called an "investment fever."

In 1986 the most serious maladjustments resulted from a 30% appreciation in the value of the yen. Between September 1985 and August 1986, the foreign exchange rate fell from 237 yen per U.S. dollar to a record low of 153, despite the Bank of Japan's intervention in support of the dollar. According to Tokyo Shoko Research, the strong yen played a part in more than 100 bankruptcies, mainly in businesses linked to exports.

In April the Diet approved the Nakasone government's characteristically austere budget. Expenditures increased only 3%, to a total of 54.1 trillion yen (about $302 billion). On April 8, however, on the eve of a meeting with U.S. President Ronald Reagan in Washington, the prime minister unveiled a comprehensive package of measures designed to stimulate demand, ease the effects of the appreciation of the yen, and increase imports. And on September 19 the government approved a 3.6 trillion yen ($20.2 billion) supplementary budget to stem growing unemployment and to expand domestic demand. Meanwhile, between January and October, Japan's central bank lowered the discount rate four times, eventually to 3%, also to stimulate demand.

Social Issues. Both because of pressure from abroad and the sluggish economy at home, the government's aims were to expand domestic demand, increase imports, and thus reduce friction arising from Japan's towering trade surplus. Official steps were in accord with a report submitted to the government in April, urging a restructuring of Japanese society. A 17-member panel headed by former Bank of Japan Governor Haruo Maekawa recommended that the nation overhaul its export-oriented economy and adopt measures giving the public shorter working hours and an opportunity to move out of their "miserable homes." In addition a major overhaul of the nation's tax system was announced late in the year (*see* TAXATION).

According to the Ministry of Health and Welfare, by the year 2000, 15.6% of the population will be 65 years of age or older; by 2015 some 21% will be among the elderly. The aging of Japan presented to the government yet another policy problem inherent in a developed and mature society.

Foreign Affairs

In July the Foreign Ministry released its 1986 Diplomatic Blue Book, which endorsed the findings of the Maekawa commission in calling for a reduction of Japan's dependence on exports. The nation's commitment to the Japan-U.S. security treaty was reaffirmed, but Japan would not seek to become a "military power which poses a threat to its neighbors." Paradoxically, Japan was being regarded as very much of an economic threat, even to its allies.

Finance and Trade. In April the Bank of Japan announced that the net outflow of capital was averaging $7 billion per month, putting Japan ahead of Great Britain as the world's largest net creditor nation. The Finance Ministry estimated that holdings of foreign securities rose 66.4% in 1985, to a total of $145.8 billion. As the central bank bought dollars to slow the yen's surge, foreign-exchange reserves reached a seven-year high. On April 11 the International Monetary Fund (IMF) put Japan on notice that the yen could be expected to reach even higher levels.

One indication of the nation's economic strength was the emergence of Dai Ichi Kangyo, Ltd. as the world's largest banking concern (measured in total assets), surpassing Citibank. In fact, six of the world's ten largest financial institutions in 1986 were located in Japan. The nation's overseas holdings were being fed by a towering current account surplus, which reached $55.1 billion in fiscal 1985. The Finance Ministry estimated that the overall trade surplus reached a record high of $34.2 billion in the first half of 1986.

U.S. Relations. The effects of the surplus were most keenly felt in the markets of Japan's chief ally. In 1985, the U.S. trade deficit with Japan totaled $49.7 billion (up from $36.8 billion in 1984), a gap representing one third the total U.S. trade deficit. In 1985, Japan purchased an estimated one fourth of all bonds issued by the U.S. Treasury.

The American business community in Japan maintained that real progress had been made in 1985 toward opening Japanese markets to imports from the United States, particularly in the areas of pharmaceuticals, telecommunications, electronics, and forest products. At meetings in Washington and Camp David, MD, April 13–14, just prior to the summit in Tokyo, Prime Minister Nakasone discussed trade issues with President Reagan and promised to allow increased imports. The U.S. leader praised Nakasone for the (Maekawa) plan to restructure Japan's economy. Back home, however, Nakasone informed the Diet that the plan did not constitute "policy."

Moreover, negotiations over trade in semiconductors became an acrimonious issue during the year. In January and in March the U.S. Trade Commission ruled that Japanese electronics manufacturers were dumping memory chips—i.e., selling them at below cost. Finally, on July 31, the two nations agreed to a comprehensive pact which provided a price structure and the dropping of two antidumping cases.

Japan and the United States also faced problems in the area of joint security. On September 9, the Japanese cabinet formally agreed to participate in the U.S. Strategic Defense Initiative (SDI), insisting that the step did not violate a 1969 Diet resolution banning military use of space. On earth, however, some 8,000 demonstrators opposed the August 24 port call of the U.S. battleship *New Jersey* at Sasebo. In Zushi, near the U.S. naval base at Yokosuka, voters recalled their assembly for approving a large housing complex for Americans. On Miyake Island, the site of a new landing strip for U.S. naval fliers, residents recalled two assemblymen for their approval of the plan.

Tokyo Summit. The leaders of the seven advanced industrial democracies (Japan, United States, Great Britain, France, West Germany, Canada, and Italy) met in Tokyo for their annual summit conference May 4–6. As chairman, Prime Minister Nakasone summed up the meetings as a reaffirmation of "mutual understanding and trust among us." The most significant decision of the summit was to create a new instrument, "the Group of Seven," charged with cooperation toward compatible domestic policies and equilibrium in the various currencies.

Despite minor demonstrations by Japanese radical groups, the Japanese government joined with the six other powers in denouncing world terrorism. Some Japanese criticized Nakasone's decision to adhere to the U.S. insistence on singling out Libya as a "unique threat."

Soviet Relations. On October 13, Prime Minister Nakasone expressed his regret at the lack of agreement at the superpower summit talks in Reykjavik, Iceland. Meanwhile, he awaited further word regarding a proposed visit to Japan by Soviet General Secretary Mikhail Gorbachev. On July 28 in Vladivostok, the Soviet leader had called for an Asian and Pacific security conference and had hinted that he would visit Tokyo "in the near future."

In January, Eduard Shevardnadze spent five days in Tokyo, the first visit by a Soviet foreign minister in a decade. Foreign Minister Abe made a three-day visit to Moscow in June, and his successor, Tadashi Kuranari, met with Shevardnadze at the United Nations in late September. Although the Soviets agreed to resume negotiations toward a peace treaty, they maintained a rigid stance on an outstanding boundary issue: Soviet troops were engaged in a military buildup on what Japanese called "the northern territories," a group of islands off Hokkaido historically regarded by Tokyo as within Japanese jurisdiction.

Northeast Asia. On April 12, China's Foreign Minister Wu Xueqian visited Tokyo, where he received Prime Minister Nakasone's pledge to aid Beijing in its current development program. Nakasone, in turn, visited China November 8–9. Part of his three-day visit was devoted to a report on the dismissal of a controversial member of his cabinet, Masayuki

Fujio. As education minister, Fujio had granted an interview to a popular journal in which he asserted that Japan's role in the 1937 so-called "Rape of Nanjing" had been justified as an act of war. He was also critical of China's Tokyo Tribunal, which, after World War II, had tried Japanese war criminals.

Fujio's public remarks had caused a furor in South Korea as well. Seoul delivered a formal protest to Tokyo, specifically objecting to the minister's opinion that Koreans had been partly responsible for the 1910 seizure of the peninsula. On September 20, while in Seoul to attend opening ceremonies of the 10th Asian Games, Nakasone apologized to President Chun Doo Hwan for the Fujio incident.

Southeast Asia. On February 27, Motoo Shiina and Hiroshi Oki of the International Bureau of the LDP carried Prime Minister Nakasone's message of support to President Corazon Aquino and other leaders of the new Philippine government. Japan remained the second largest provider, following the United States, of economic assistance to the Philippines. Mrs. Aquino visited Japan in November.

Addressing a meeting of the Association of Southeast Asian Nations (ASEAN) June 26 in Manila, Foreign Minister Abe pledged to establish a "creative partnership" between Japan and the region. In 1985 the ASEAN group had a $9 billion trade surplus with Japan.

South Africa. On September 19, Japan announced a package of limited sanctions against South Africa, including a ban on imports of pig iron and steel. Chief Cabinet Secretary Gotoda expressed hope that the gesture might foster an "environment" for direct negotiations between South Africa and outlawed rebel forces.

Royal Visit. Japanese had an opportunity to express adulation for foreign royalty as well as for their own emperor in 1986, as Britain's Prince Charles and Diana, princess of Wales, paid an official visit May 8–13.

ARDATH W. BURKS, *Rutgers University*

JAPAN • Information Highlights

Official Name: Japan.
Location: East Asia.
Area: 143,750 sq mi (372 313 km²).
Population (mid-1986 est.): 121,500,000.
Chief Cities (Oct. 1, 1984 est): Tokyo, the capital, 8,351,893; Yokohama, 2,773,674; Osaka, 2,648,180; Nagoya, 2,087,902.
Government: *Head of state,* Hirohito, emperor (acceded Dec. 1926). *Head of government,* Yasuhiro Nakasone, prime minister (took office Nov. 1982). *Legislature*—Diet: House of Councillors and House of Representatives.
Monetary Unit: Yen (160.2 yen equal U.S.$1, Nov. 12, 1986).
Gross National Product (1985 U.S.$): $879,000,-000,000.
Economic Indexes (1985): *Consumer Prices* (1980 = 100), all items, 114.4; food, 114.4. *Industrial Production* (1980 = 100), 122.
Foreign Trade (1985 U.S.$): *Imports,* $129,480,-000,000; *exports,* $175,683,000,000.

JORDAN

Two major developments dominated the year in Jordan. The first concerned the break-off of joint Jordanian-Palestine Liberation Organization (PLO) efforts to pursue the Middle East peace process—the break-off culminating in the closing down of PLO offices in Jordan and the ousting of prominent PLO figures from Jordan. The second was the crackdown on all political opposition groups (except for the Muslim Brothers) in the wake of violent clashes between students and police at Yarmuk University.

Jordanian-PLO Split. The Jordanian-PLO accord of Feb. 11, 1985, was suspended when King Hussein announced on Feb. 19, 1986, that the yearlong attempts by Jordan and the PLO to reach agreement on how to advance the peace efforts had ended. According to Hussein, Yasir Arafat, the PLO leader, had "broken his word" after Hussein had persuaded the United States to make a commitment to invite the PLO as a full participant in the proposed international conference dealing with the Arab-Israeli conflict if the PLO would recognize and accept UN Resolution 242 of November 1967 (acknowledging Israel's right to exist). It appeared that PLO leaders had insisted on a U.S. statement recognizing the legitimate rights of the Palestinian people, including their right of self-determination within the framework of the confederation of Jordan and Palestine (East and West Bank), which was stipulated in the accord of Feb. 11, 1985.

The U.S. proposal (conveyed to the PLO by King Hussein in early February 1986), which called for convening the international conference on the basis of UN Resolution 242 and "the guaranteeing of the legitimate rights of the Palestinian people," was rejected by Arafat as insufficient. Consequently, Hussein saw no choice but to end the political coordination with the PLO. This unilateral decision by Jordan was played down by the PLO, which had hoped that the February 1985 accord would survive, and perhaps be revived—or at least that the presence of PLO officials in Jordan would not be affected by Hussein's decision.

The PLO's hopes were dashed, however, when its relations with Jordan deteriorated (just as Jordan's relations with Syria had improved). On July 7, 1986, the Jordanian government closed down 25 PLO offices that had been opened since 1982, including Arafat's headquarters. Khalil al-Wazir (Abu Jihad), the number-three top leader of the PLO, as well as other political and military commanders of the PLO were asked to leave Jordanian territories. Jordan justified this action on the grounds that the PLO's political campaign against Jordan was contrary to the spirit of cooperation that had characterized Jordanian-PLO relations when the PLO officials were allowed, in late

---

JORDAN • Information Highlights

Official Name: Hashemite Kingdom of Jordan.
Location: Southwest Asia.
Area: 37,737 sq mi (97 740 km^2), includes West Bank.
Population (mid-1986 est.): 3,700,000.
Chief Cities (Dec. 1983): Amman, the capital, 744,000; Zarqa, 255,000; Irbid, 131,200.
Government: *Head of state,* Hussein I, king (acceded Aug. 1952). *Head of government,* Zayd al-Rifa'i, prime minister (appointed April 4, 1985). *Legislature*—Parliament: House of Representatives and Senate.
Monetary Unit: Dinar (0.33900 dinar equals U.S.$1, Oct. 19, 1986).
Economic Index (1985): *Consumer Prices* (1980 = 100), all items, 131.1; food, 121.0.
Foreign Trade (1985 U.S.$): *Imports,* $2,656,000,000; *exports,* $838,000,000.

1982, to operate again in Jordan. Nevertheless, Jordan reiterated its long-standing commitment to the view that the PLO is the sole legitimate representative of the Palestinian people and vowed that Jordan would not make a deal with local Palestinian leaders of the West Bank and the Gaza Strip at the expense of the PLO.

Crackdown on Opposition. On May 15, 1986, clashes took place between students and security forces on the campus of Yarmuk University in Irbid that resulted in the shooting of at least three students and the arrest of many others. Although the causes of the riots were ostensibly a tuition hike and the expulsion of 32 students who had participated in earlier demonstrations, the disturbances had serious consequences in terms of the political activities of the opposition groups.

Jordanian Prime Minister Zayd al-Rifa'i, who was in charge of reforming the educational system in the wake of the riots at Yarmuk University, had claimed that Arafat's Al Fatah organization was responsible for fomenting trouble at the university. Al-Rifa'i also linked the closing down of the PLO offices to the riots in Irbid and to the PLO's role in the by-election of June 1986 in the Irbid constituency.

By the summer of 1986, members of leftist parties and leading intellectuals had been imprisoned without trial. On July 7, 1986, 15 professors and six members of the staff of Yarmuk University were dismissed without recourse to legal procedures. Representatives of Amnesty International were refused entry to Jordan to investigate allegations of violations of human rights by the Jordanian authorities.

Reaction to U.S. Arms Deals. Jordanian officials regarded the late 1986 revelations of secret U.S.-Iran arms deals with dismay. A friend of the United States as well as a supporter of Iraq in the Iran-Iraq war, Hussein (and other centrist Arab leaders) felt betrayed by the U.S. actions. Early in 1987, President Reagan sent Assistant Secretary of State for Middle Eastern Affairs Richard W. Murphy to meet with Hussein in the first of a round of visits to U.S. allies in the region.

MARIUS DEEB, *Georgetown University*

Sen. Robert Dole (right) easily won a fourth term on November 4. However, with the Democrats regaining control of the Senate, Kansas' senior senator would be forced to give up his post as majority leader. The current minority leader, Sen. Robert Byrd of West Virginia (left), would take over that role.

KANSAS

Sagging farming and oil sectors continued to plague Kansas in 1986, and heavy rains in mid-October caused flooding and delayed the fall harvest. Voters elected a new governor and decided the fate of seven constitutional amendments.

Elections. Since Gov. John Carlin had served the maximum of two four-year terms, Kansans were assured a new governor would take office in January 1987. In a hotly contested Republican primary, House Speaker Michael Hayden defeated six other candidates to face Lt. Gov. Thomas R. Docking in the general election. After a campaign that focused on personalities rather than issues, Hayden won the governorship by a narrow margin. U.S. Sen. Robert Dole was reelected overwhelmingly. All five incumbent U.S. Representatives—Pat Roberts (R), James Slattery (D), Jan Meyers (R), Dan Glickman (D), and Bob Whittaker (R) —also won reelection.

Kansans also decided the merits of five constitutional amendments in the general election. A proposal to give the state legislature more control over the state board of education was defeated, but an amendment calling for the classification of property for taxation purposes was approved. Constitutional amendments supporting the sale of liquor by the drink, parimutuel wagering, and a state-operated lottery were approved. (For the first three years, 60% of lottery proceeds would be devoted to economic development.) In the August primary, voters had approved two additional amendments. One allows the state to invest idle funds in local public works projects and the other gives local governments the authority to grant property tax exemptions for up to ten years for new manufacturing, warehouses, or research and development.

Agriculture. The 1986 wheat crop totaled 326.4 million bushels, a decrease of 25% from 1985 and the smallest crop since 1981. The overall yield of 32 bushels per acre was down 6 bushels from 1985. The crop was grown on 10.2 million acres (4.1 million ha), about 11% less than 1985. Planting was delayed due to heavy rains in October 1985, and a cold November stunted growth. Warm weather in March and April hastened development, however, leading to a completion of harvest by July 13, the earliest date since 1974. Production was hampered by diseases, and the fall harvest was delayed by heavy rains in early October.

Legislation. In addition to passing the seven proposed constitutional amendments, the legislature approved a one-cent increase in the

---

KANSAS • Information Highlights

Area: 82,277 sq mi (213 098 km²).

Population (1985 est.): 2,450,000.

Chief Cities (July 1, 1984 est.): Topeka, the capital, 118,945; Wichita, 283,496; Kansas City, 160,468.

Government (1986): *Chief Officers*—governor, John Carlin (D); lt. gov., Thomas R. Docking (D). *Legislature*—Senate, 40 members; House of Representatives, 125 members.

State Finances (fiscal year 1985): *Revenue,* $3,714,000,000; *expenditure,* $3,248,000,000.

Personal Income (1985): $33,755,000,000; per capita, $13,775.

Labor Force (June 1986): *Civilian labor force,* 1,261,800; *unemployed,* 65,200 (5.2% of total force).

Education: *Enrollment* (fall 1984)—public elementary schools, 282,182; public secondary, 123,165; colleges and universities, 141,359. *Public school expenditures* (1983–84), $1,221,000,000 ($3,361 per pupil).

state sales tax that went into effect on July 1, 1986. It was estimated that the increase would generate an additional $182.5 million in revenue for the state in its first year. Several bills were passed to promote economic development and encourage new businesses to locate in Kansas. Several measures designed to aid the farm economy also passed, including one allowing district courts to give farmers up to a three-year moratorium on foreclosure, another cutting interest rates on farm operating loans, and a third to keep rural banks open by allowing them to lease repossessed land for up to ten years rather than sell in a depressed market.

Fall Floods. In early October, 8–9 inches (203–229 mm) of rain fell in a 24-hour period in southeast Kansas, causing heavy flooding and an estimated $12.8 million of damage to public property in 12 counties. National Guard troops were activated to help flood victims.

PATRICIA A. MICHAELIS
Kansas State Historical Society

KENTUCKY

Major emphasis was placed on efforts to attract new businesses to Kentucky and to improve the quality of education at all levels in the state during 1986. There was growing awareness that educational advances were essential to make Kentucky competitive economically.

Toyota in the Bluegrass. The Toyota company began construction of an $800 million car assembly plant in Scott County, near Lexington. The plant was expected to employ some 3,000 workers and to attract related industries to central Kentucky.

Gov. Martha Layne Collins, whose political position was strengthened by her success in attracting Toyota to Kentucky, made several visits to Japan in a continuing effort to bring businesses to the state and to open up more markets in Japan for Kentucky products. The Collins administration offered Toyota a package of benefits estimated at $125 million to lure it to the state, and this price tag became a controversial issue in the months that followed. The state legislature, after considerable debate, approved the package as part of the biennial budget for 1986–88.

Educational Reform and Funding. The issue of educational reform and funding continued to be high on the legislature's agenda in 1986. The biennial budget incorporated an increased spending program for primary and secondary education that the legislature had designed during a special session in 1985. After several years of limited gains, higher education received a major increase in funding, permitting higher salaries, a construction program, and the establishment of several "centers of excellence" in the state universities.

KENTUCKY · Information Highlights

Area: 40,410 sq mi (104 660 km²).
Population (1985 est.): 3,726,000.
Chief Cities (July 1, 1984 est.): Frankfort, the capital (1980 census), 25,973; Louisville, 289,843; Lexington-Fayette, 210,150.
Government (1986): *Chief Officers*—governor, Martha Layne Collins (D); lt. gov., Steven L. Beshear (D). *General Assembly*—Senate, 38 members; House of Representatives, 100 members.
State Finances (fiscal year 1985): *Revenue,* $6,178,000,000; *expenditure,* $5,447,000,000.
Personal Income (1985): $40,328,000,000; per capita, $10,824.
Labor Force (June 1986): *Civilian labor force,* 1,702,300; *unemployed,* 151,200 (8.9% of total force).
Education: *Enrollment* (fall 1984)—public elementary schools, 451,111; public secondary, 193,310; colleges and universities, 141,724. *Public school expenditures* (1983–84), $1,493,000,000 ($2,550 per pupil).

Other Legislative Issues. The 1986 session of the General Assembly also adopted a five-cent per gallon increase in the gasoline tax, a step that it had refused to take when the tax increase was first proposed by the governor in 1985. The relatively low price of gasoline and the urgent need for highway improvements were expected to make the new tax more pal-

In May, Kentucky's Gov. Martha Layne Collins joined officials of the Toyota Motor Company in breaking ground for the company's new assembly plant near Lexington.

AP/Wide World

atable to the public. The legislature struggled with the issue of health-care funding, particularly for people not covered by insurance, but left the problem unresolved.

Politics. Governor Collins suffered a setback in the November election when the voters rejected a constitutional amendment for which she had campaigned actively: a proposal to make the superintendent of public instruction an appointed rather than an elected official. Kentuckians reelected Democratic Sen. Wendell Ford with 74% of the vote, the largest percentage ever won by a senatorial candidate in a contested race. With relatively low voter turnout, the Democrats retained large majorities in the state legislature.

By the end of the year, the major focus of political attention had become the 1987 gubernatorial election. The campaign for the Democratic primary, scheduled for May, was well under way. State law bars Governor Collins from serving two consecutive terms.

The legislature voted to restore Kentucky's presidential primary and to schedule it in 1988 to coincide with the date chosen by other Southern and border states for a "super primary."

MALCOLM E. JEWELL
University of Kentucky

KENYA

A much improved economy and rumblings of political unrest highlighted 1986 in Kenya.

Record Crops. It was a boom year for the Kenyan economy. A drought in Brazil increased demand for Kenya's premium arabica coffee, which enjoyed record production thanks to favorable weather. Good growing conditions also led to record harvests of maize and tea and an outstanding year for the other major crops, cotton and pyrethrum. There was a maize surplus of 1.5 million metric tons (1.7 million tons), but insufficient storage cost Kenya some of the surplus. Also, the good harvest allowed some prosperous farmers to buy

more land, forcing others off their farms and into the growing ranks of the urban unemployed.

Other Economic Factors. Tourism prospered in 1986, due partly to the success of the 1985 motion picture *Out of Africa*. The award-winning film was shot on location in Kenya and enticed many to visit the country.

The favorable economic picture permitted Kenya to service its foreign debt without further borrowing, while lower oil prices greatly eased the country's foreign exchange problems. As a result, less foreign aid, from fewer donor countries, was needed. Aid was used conservatively, supporting the consolidation of ongoing projects and permitting the privatization of some state-owned businesses.

Population Problems. The other side of Kenya's development was continued rapid population growth. In 1986 the population grew by 4%, exactly matching the projected increase in the gross national product. Kenyan women averaged eight children each. Population growth consumed surplus capital that might have been put back into the economy and increased the pressures on scarce arable land.

Political Unrest. Low-level but persistent opposition to President Daniel arap Moi continued in 1986. The most serious involved a mysterious group called *Mwakenya*, which left anti-Moi propaganda in streets and offices throughout Nairobi. The government attempted to suppress the material and prohibited any mention of it in newspapers. About 40 Kenyans, most of them university lecturers or recent graduates, were jailed in 1986 as suspected members of *Mwakenya*.

Little was known about *Mwakenya*, but it appeared to be a Kikuyu-based movement. The Kikuyu, the ethnic group of the late President Jomo Kenyatta, had long resented its declining political influence under Moi, a non-Kikuyu. Information suggested that the shadowy group was an outgrowth of the leftist Kikuyu December 12 Movement, which many blame for the bloody coup attempt of August 1982.

By year's end it appeared that Moi's power was increasing. Parliament unanimously approved an amendment removing tenure from the powerful positions of attorney general and auditor general. Tenure had been given to both posts to remove them from the political sphere. Now they would be under the president's jurisdiction.

Foreign Affairs. Moi was among seven heads of state to attend a regional summit at Entebbe, Uganda, on March 20. The participants pledged assistance in the reconstruction of Uganda and agreed to cooperate on regional security issues. In June, Moi and Tanzanian President Ali Hassan Mwinyi agreed to establish a permanent joint commission to coordinate cooperation between their countries.

ROBERT GARFIELD, *DePaul University*

KENYA • Information Highlights

Official Name: Republic of Kenya.
Location: East Coast of Africa.
Area: 224,960 sq mi (582 646 km²).
Population (mid-1986 est.): 21,000,000.
Chief Cities (1979 census): Nairobi, the capital, 827,775; Mombasa, 341,148.
Government: *Head of state and government,* Daniel T. arap Moi, president (took office Oct. 1978). *Legislature* (unicameral)—National Assembly, 170 members.
Monetary Unit: Kenya shilling (16.336 shillings equal U.S.$1, June 1986).
Gross Domestic Product (1985): $4,500,000,000.
Economic Index (1985): *Consumer Prices,* (Nairobi, 1980 = 100), all items, 199.8; food, 184.3.
Foreign Trade (1984 U.S.$): *Imports,* $1,437,000,000; *exports,* $958,000,000.

In September, President Chun Doo Hwan inspected Seoul's Kimpo International Airport after a bomb explosion left at least five persons dead and more than 30 injured. Officials blamed North Korea for the attack, charging that the North was trying to sabotage the forthcoming Asian Games.

AP/Wide World

KOREA

Both South and North Korea experienced tensions in anticipation of political successions in the near future.

Republic of Korea (South Korea)

President Chun Doo Hwan is committed to stepping down in 1988, and political interest focuses on the identity of his successor and on the method of electing the successor.

Politics and Government. The opposition to President Chun's government centers on the New Korea Democratic Party (NKDP), which has been demanding a constitutional revision to permit direct (rather than indirect, as at present) election of the next president. This is unacceptable to the ruling Democratic Justice Party (DJP), which appears determined to retain power and to fear that a direct election might be won by NKDP leader Kim Dae Jung, currently barred from formal political activity under a 1980 conviction for sedition. Chun's military-dominated DJP establishment, which effectively rules the country, deeply distrusts Kim as leftist and ambitious. The DJP asserts that a direct election would create instability on which North Korea might seek to capitalize, perhaps even through an invasion.

Both the government and the opposition were profoundly interested in the fall of President Ferdinand Marcos of the Philippines in February—not so much by the fall itself as by the withdrawal of U.S. support from Marcos because he reportedly had tried to rig an election. Might the United States do the same to the DJP if it seemed to manipulate the 1988 election? On February 24, President Chun gave approval in principle to constitutional revision (he mentioned the possibility of a shift from a presidential to a parliamentary form of government), but not until after the inauguration of his successor, whom he presumably hoped to handpick, in 1988. Dissatisfied, the opposition continued to collect signatures on a petition for a direct presidential election.

In March more militant elements (Christian church leaders, radical students, labor unionists) took a hand. For six weeks beginning March 23, there were turbulent and often violent demonstrations and rallies in the major cities, apart from Seoul; they were run jointly by the NKDP and the militants, a type of cooperation very disturbing to the DJP.

Subsequently, on April 30, President Chun conceded the possibility of constitutional revision before 1988, if the major parties could agree. Since the DJP (the majority party in the National Assembly) was still strongly committed to indirect election of the president, this concession must have seemed safe to Chun.

In June the National Assembly set up a special committee to consider constitutional revision. The DJP's draft called for a parliamentary system with a ceremonial president and a governing premier elected by the National Assembly, in which the DJP clearly expected to retain a majority. The NKDP's draft envisaged direct popular election of the president, who would continue to be the chief executive, and it abolished a provision of the existing constitution under which the plurality or majority party in parliament (i.e., the DJP) gets enough bonus seats to ensure its control.

In July the DJP accepted the principle of election rather than appointment of local officials in the future and launched a campaign to recruit new members and broaden its popular base, which has been rather small. Its leadership was somewhat reshuffled on August 23, although the chairmanship was retained by for-

303

mer Gen. Roh Tae-woo, a likely successor to Chun Doo Hwan. Three days later, President Chun reshuffled the cabinet to ensure its complete loyalty to himself; Lho Shin-yong remained prime minister.

At the end of August, Kim Young-sam, one of the NKDP's key leaders, said that if no agreement on constitutional revision had been reached by the end of September, his party would launch a "struggle for democracy side by side with the people."

Meanwhile, student demonstrations, including a violent rally in Seoul on July 19, had begun. Some of them (such as the seizure of the U.S. cultural center in Pusan on May 21) had an anti-American aspect, since many militants view the United States as propping up the government and also as trying to dominate the South Korean economy.

From the end of September the NKDP boycotted the constitutional revision process within the National Assembly, although contacts of other kinds between the two sides continued. There was no change in basic positions. In October the NKDP demanded a referendum on the form of the new constitutional structure (rather than on a completed draft constitution); the DJP rejected this idea.

The Asian Games (or Asiad), which were held in Seoul from September 20 to October 5, were obviously intended by the government both as a rehearsal for the 1988 Olympics and as a device for enhancing South Korea's prestige abroad and quieting opposition at home. The latter purpose was incompletely served: the government found it necessary to close five universities in Seoul during the games.

The government and the DJP showed an increasing tendency to characterize opposition activities as, in some fashion, aiding North Korea, which the opposition generally denied. President Chun reportedly threatened a reimposition of martial law if disorder got worse. The establishment insisted that anticommunism (that is, the struggle against North Korea)

must take precedence over work for unification of the Koreas; some of the opposition maintained the reverse priority. For stating the latter view, an NKDP member of the National Assembly, Yoo Sung Hwan, was arrested on October 17 under the National Security Law; the Assembly approved his arrest by a straight party vote. At the end of October large student demonstrations, met by strong police counteraction, occurred in Seoul.

On November 5, Kim Dae Jung announced that he would not seek the presidency if the government accepted direct presidential elections. The DJP promptly ridiculed Kim Dae Jung's action as insincere.

Economic Developments. In 1985 the South Korean economy had experienced its worst year since disastrous 1980. In 1986 the economy, including exports, began to pick up; the first half of the year registered a 10.9% growth rate. The explanation seemed to be what the South Koreans called the "three lows": lower oil costs, lower international interest rates, and the lower value of the U.S. dollar (to which the South Korean currency is informally linked) in relation to the yen.

Numerous problems remained, however. The overstrained banking system, central to corporate finance, badly needed liberalization, but the government was reluctant to relax its control. A huge foreign debt, approaching $48 billion, overhung the entire economy. South Korean construction workers continued to return from the Middle East, often with no new jobs in sight. Protectionism and the threat of it abroad, especially in the United States, created a serious problem for business confidence. Labor unions were growing increasingly dissatisfied with their wages and working conditions.

The South Korean nuclear power program, undeterred by the accidental disaster at the Soviet plant in Chernobyl, pressed ahead with plans for two new units beyond the five already operational and the four others under construction. Expectations were that the energy supply would be increased in the near future by liquefied natural gas from Indonesia and crude oil from Alaska.

The South Korean market remained relatively closed to foreign goods and investment, with a notable exception for Japan. As a concession to U.S. pressures, foreign (mainly American) cigarettes were allowed to go on sale in September. South Korean exports did rather well in competition with Japanese exports, which tended to grow more expensive due to such factors as upscaling and the appreciation of the yen. South Korea continued to have a trade deficit with Japan, but it ran a surplus with the United States.

Some of the frictions in South Korean-U.S. relations were economic in nature. Seoul rejected an American request to revalue the won (upward). American acquiescence in Korean

---

SOUTH KOREA • Information Highlights

Official Name: Republic of Korea.
Location: Northeastern Asia.
Area: 38,031 sq mi (98 500 km²).
Population (mid-1986 est.): 43,300,000.
Chief City (Oct. 1985 est.): Seoul, the capital, 9,798,057.
Government: *Head of state,* Chun Doo Hwan, president (formally inaugurated March 1981). *Head of government,* Lho Shin Yong, prime minister (appointed Feb. 1985). *Legislature*—National Assembly.
Monetary Unit: Won (872.0 won equal U.S.$1, Oct. 19, 1986).
Gross National Product (1984, 1984 prices): $90,100,000,000.
Economic Indexes (1985): *Consumer Prices* (1980 = 100), all items, 141.0; food, 139.4. *Industrial Production* (1980 = 100), 158.
Foreign Trade (1985 U.S.$): *Imports,* $31,136,-000,000; *exports,* $30,283,000,000.

Air's desire to fly into Chicago was not forthcoming. The United States was not enthusiastic about South Korea's wish to export arms, many of which would have components of American design, to the Third World, in competition with U.S. weapons. In August the United States imposed a ceiling of 0.8% on the annual growth rate of textiles imported from South Korea. Despite some progress the United States still regarded the South Korean market as unduly closed and as insufficiently protective of certain foreign property rights (copyrights, patents, etc.).

In September the government announced the introduction in 1988–89 of a package of social-welfare legislation (minimum wage, pensions, health insurance).

International Relations. The government was relieved—and the opposition angered and disappointed—when U.S. Secretary of State George Shultz, visiting Seoul in May, dismissed any analogy between the South Korean and Philippine political situations and expressed the usual official U.S. support for the South Korean government's professed desire for a peaceful transition to democracy.

Another important visitor to South Korea, Prime Minister Lee Kuan Yew of Singapore, arrived in May, mainly in the hope of persuading his hosts to buy more goods to help the ailing Singaporean economy.

A controversy in South Korean-Japanese relations dating from 1982 flared up again in the summer of 1986. Officially authorized Japanese textbooks had been whitewashing the behavior of pre-World War II Japan toward Korea (and China) and creating profound resentment in those countries. During a visit to Seoul for the opening of the Asian Games, Japanese Prime Minister Yasuhiro Nakasone apologized for the textbooks and then fired his Education Minister Masayuki Fujio, who had made remarks considered insulting by the South Koreans.

Democratic People's Republic of Korea (North Korea)

Under its tight authoritarian surface, North Korea was clearly undergoing a planned transition from the rule of Kim Il Sung to that of his son Kim Jong Il.

Domestic Affairs. After their escape to U.S. custody in March, a South Korean couple—film director Shin Sang Ok and actress Choi En Hui—who had been kidnapped eight years earlier at Kim Jong Il's orders and taken to North Korea to make films, revealed some interesting glimpses of politics and policy-making in Pyongyang. According to them the younger Kim (age 47) was in more-or-less complete charge, except for the most important questions of policy. The elder Kim (74) would very much like to see the unification of the Koreas before his death. Defense Minister O Jin U reportedly has boasted that he could, and would like to, conquer South Korea in a week. The North Korean leadership expected serious political disorders in South Korea, perhaps in 1988, and hoped to be able to take advantage of them. It was held likely that at some point Kim Jong Il would encounter serious opposition to his assumption of his father's power.

In late December the Supreme People's Assembly (parliament) reelected Kim to another presidential term, named Li Gun Mo as premier, and presented a new seven-year economic plan. The latter seeks to solve the nation's food, housing, and clothing shortages.

The North Korean economy has been in serious trouble for some time as a result of such factors as overcentralization, lack of incentives, overborrowing from abroad, and a high military budget (10% of gross national product, or GNP). An apparent effort, on a small scale, to imitate China's "open" policy by encouraging foreign trade and investment has largely been a failure.

A nuclear-power installation is under construction at Yong Byon, near the Yellow Sea coast. It is unclear whether this has military potential, as is feared in South Korea.

An important speech by Soviet leader Mikhail Gorbachev at Vladivostok on July 28 indicated his strong interest in stability and trade in the Western Pacific—and accordingly no real support for North Korea's campaign of pressure on the South. Evidently troubled by

North Korea's President Kim Il Sung (right) *welcomed Mongolia's Jambyn Batmonh to Pyongyang in November. Kim's appearance dispelled rumors that he had been killed.*

AP/Wide World

this, Kim Il Sung made one of his infrequent visits to Moscow in late October. An element of urgency was suggested by the facts that he flew both ways, despite his known strong dislike of air travel, and that no specific agenda or outcome of the trip was announced.

In the light of the dramatic but murky ensuing events, it is likely that Kim agreed, reluctantly, to conform to Gorbachev's dovish line, perhaps in the hope of Soviet acquiescence in Kim's plan to be succeeded by his son. If so, it is also likely that the hawkish Defense Minister O Jin U protested, and in mid-November he either attempted a coup or was himself violently purged in order to prevent him from staging one. In any event, despite initial South Korean government reports that he had been killed, Kim Il Sung remained in control, and as far as outsiders could determine, his succession plan continued in effect.

International Relations. On Dec. 5, 1985, North Korea signed the Treaty on the Non-Proliferation of Nuclear Weapons, thereby opening its nuclear facilities to inspection by the International Atomic Energy Agency, at least in theory.

A general improvement in North Korea's relations with its Soviet ally that had begun in about 1981 continued in 1986. This trend tended to balance, consciously or otherwise, a growing unofficial relationship between South Korea and North Korea's other ally, China. Moscow supplied some fairly advanced military equipment, including MiG-23 jet fighters, presumably intended to cope with the F-16s beginning to be transferred to South Korea by the United States. In return the Soviet Union got (in 1985) overflight rights for its reconnaissance aircraft across North Korea and port-call privileges for its naval vessels at Wonsan (east coast) and Nampo (west coast).

North Korea boycotted the Asian Games in Seoul, after failing in an effort to cosponsor them (that is, to host some of the events in Pyongyang).

China, clearly worried (despite occasional statements to the contrary) about Soviet-North Korean relations, continued to woo Pyongyang, but its cards were largely political and inadequate to counter the growth of Soviet influence. It was practically certain that, as for some time past, neither Communist great power wanted North Korea to attack the South again.

North Korea continued fairly active in arms sales and military aid to the Third World, especially to such radical regimes as the Iranian. In March the North Korean military mission withdrew from Zimbabwe, where it had been the cause of considerable trouble and violence.

The Two Koreas

The year was a tense one in North-South relations; Pyongyang threatened to disrupt the Asian Games in Seoul, as well as the 1988 Olympic Games there.

The Military Balance. At the present time North Korea holds an edge in offensive air and ground power, though a rough balance is maintained by the U.S. military presence (including the Second Division) in the South. North Korea has a higher military budget in terms of percentage of GNP (10%); the South spends about 6% on defense, but because of its much larger GNP it has a larger defense budget in absolute terms (about $5 billion).

North Korea has about two thirds of its forces deployed in tactical formations near the Demilitarized Zone. It is able to attack at any time, but it would encounter a stout defense, and probably retaliation against its own territory as well. North Korea claims to be diverting 150,000 men from the armed forces to economic pursuits.

At the time the Asian Games opened, the United States deployed a sizable naval task force in Korean waters in order to deter any possible overt moves by North Korea to disrupt the games.

Political Contacts. Essentially, both sides—waiting for the political transitions about to occur in each capital—were frozen in their positions toward one another. The North has proposed three-way political talks (the two Koreas and the United States) on unification; President Chun advocates instead a summit conference between him and Kim Il Sung.

In January the North suspended the three types of bilateral talks or contacts that have been in progress intermittently since the early 1970s: talks between the two Red Cross societies (mainly on family reunions), economic talks, and talks between delegations from the two parliaments. The reason given was the holding of regular joint U.S.-South Korean military exercises, known as Team Spirit. The South promptly began to demand a resumption of these contacts, but without effect.

HAROLD C. HINTON
The George Washington University

NORTH KOREA • Information Highlights

Official Name: Democratic People's Republic of Korea.
Location: Northeastern Asia.
Area: 46,768 sq mi (121 129 km²).
Population (mid-1986 est.): 20,500,000.
Chief Cities (July 1980 est.): Pyongyang, the capital, 1,445,000; Hamhung, 780,000.
Government: *Head of state,* Kim Il Sung, president (nominally since Dec. 1972; actually in power since May 1948). *Head of government,* Li Gun Mo, premier (appointed December 1986). *Legislature* (unicameral)—Supreme People's Assembly. The Korea Workers' (Communist) Party: General Secretary, Kim Il-sŏng.
Gross National Product (1984 U.S.$): $23,000,-000,000.

The United Steelworkers of America marked its 50th anniversary at its convention in Las Vegas in August. The steelworkers and the USX Corporation (formerly U.S. Steel) were engaged in one of the major labor disputes of 1986.

AP/Wide World

LABOR

The U.S. labor force could find both good news and bad news in the nation's economy in 1986, but persistent unemployment continued to dominate many free-world labor developments. As a result, unions in most countries were on the defensive during the year.

United States

Janet Norwood, commissioner of the Bureau of Labor Statistics (BLS), provided Congress's Joint Economic Committee with a mixture of good and bad news about the U.S. labor situation in 1986. On the positive side the nation's economy continued to demonstrate what Norwood called an "absolutely phenomenal" power to create jobs, so that in August the number of employed persons (not counting the military) surpassed 110 million for the first time—a growth of 2.3 million in 12 months. On the negative side the number of unemployed remained at more than 8 million for almost the whole year. Thus the civilian unemployment rate hovered around 7%, an only slightly better percentage than in 1985.

The total labor force (military included)—that is, the total of all those working or looking for work—topped 120 million for the first time in October. In other words nearly two out of three persons 16 years of age or older were in the labor force. The importance of women in this total continued to increase in 1986, with one third of all mothers who had children under six years of age holding full-time jobs. Women comprised 44% of the labor force, and they accounted for 53% of the growth of the labor force during the year.

Adult women as a group and adult men as a group had almost identical jobless rates of just about 6%, but unemployment otherwise was not distributed equally in the population. Among adults (20 years and older), black males fared the worst with an unemployment rate of 14% or higher. White women fared the best, at about 5%. Across the country, unemployment ranged from the highs of Louisiana, Mississippi, and West Virginia (11% and higher) to the low of New Hampshire (3% and lower). On the average, 1 out of 10 of the 17 million unskilled and semiskilled blue-collar workers were unemployed, compared with the 1 out of 40 among the 27 million managers and professionals. Largely because many states have tightened eligibility requirements, the percentage of unemployed persons collecting unemployment compensation dipped to 28% in September, compared with 67% in 1975.

Deindustrialization. The trend toward so-called deindustrialization in the U.S. job market continued. Although some economists pointed out that U.S. manufacturing is far from dead, since it employs more than 19 million persons, that was also the employment level 20 years earlier. By contrast the booming service sector—including hotel, restaurant, transportation, retail, and other services—has nearly doubled its employment figure since 1966 to more than 76 million persons, and it now accounts for three out of four employees on nonagricultural payrolls. In 1986 alone, the service sector increased by 2.4 million, whereas employment in the manufacturing sector decreased by 100,000.

The change has particularly affected large corporations. Thus General Motors, the nation's largest company, decided to close 11 of its older plants and to eliminate 29,000 jobs, plus a 25% cut elsewhere in salaried jobs.

Productivity. Labor productivity, measured by volume of output per hour of work, stayed almost level for farm and nonfarm businesses. Productivity for businesses outside farming approximated the 0.5% annual increase of 1985. By contrast the productivity of manufacturing workers grew by almost 2.5%. The biggest gains came in the "smokestack" industries. Workers in a modern steel mill took 7.5 man-hours to make a ton of steel, as compared with the 8 hours required for a Japanese worker and the 10.5 hours a U.S. worker needed in 1982.

Earnings. Average weekly earnings of non-supervisory workers in all nonfarm businesses in October were $306.40, as compared with $301.54 a year earlier. After adjustment for increases in the Consumer Price Index (CPI), the earnings increase in real terms came to 0.4%. For manufacturing businesses alone the average weekly earnings were $396.01, compared with $390.05 a year earlier—a 0.3% increase in real terms. These figures do not include benefits. According to a study by Business International, the average hourly total compensation in manufacturing came to $13.29. Only two other countries had higher rates: Switzerland, at $14.01, and West Germany, at $13.85.

Family income rose, thanks largely to working wives. In the third quarter of the year, average total weekly income of families with wage earners was $551, compared with $520 a year earlier—which, with a CPI raise of 1.6%, came to a nominal increase of 6%.

Work Stoppages. There were few strikes and lockouts as compared with the years before 1980, but the number increased compared to 1985. By the end of October, 65 major work stoppages—those involving at least 1,000 workers—had occurred, compared with 54 in all 1985 and an average of 235 each year in the 1970s. One of the most serious disputes in years affected the steel industry. USX Corporation, the largest steel producer in the nation, was shut down on August 1 by what the company called a strike and the union called a lockout.

Unions. The AFL-CIO policy of encouraging smaller affiliates to combine with larger ones gained ground. The United Furniture Workers of America (20,000 members) agreed to merge with the International Union of Electronic Workers (175,000), and the Telegraph Workers (4,000) and the International Typographical Union (70,000) both agreed to merge with the Communications Workers of America (700,000). After these mergers the AFL-CIO still had 89 affiliates, 39 of them with memberships of less than 50,000.

In actions promoting greater coordination among affiliates, the AFL-CIO set up a special reduced-interest-rate, credit-card plan and a discount legal-service plan for its regular members and a new category of "associate" members (those not covered by collective-bargaining contracts). It also adopted an internal

mechanism to minimize rivalry among its affiliates in organizing the same group of workers. In mobilizing support for the United Steelworkers in its dispute with USX, the AFL-CIO established a solidarity committee that was unusual for being chaired by Textile and Clothing Union president Murray Finley, rather than by a Steelworker representative.

The nation's largest union, the International Brotherhood of Teamsters, which is not an AFL-CIO affiliate, reelected Jackie Presser to a five-year term as president just days after he was indicted by a federal grand jury on charges of siphoning $700,000 in a payroll-padding scheme in his Cleveland local.

Legislation. Congress made it illegal to retire workers because of age alone, mandatory retirement at 70 having previously been allowed in the private sector. Congress also subjected employers to fines and jail sentences should they knowingly and persistently hire illegal aliens, but it prohibited private employers from discriminating against legal aliens merely because they are not citizens.

Despite widespread concern over loss of jobs due to foreign competition, however, Congress got nowhere on controversial trade bills. A comprehensive trade law did pass the House by a veto-proof margin, but it languished in a Senate committee. One of its provisions would limit access to the U.S. market to those countries that recognize minimum labor standards. A coalition of labor, religious, and academic leaders was formed in November to press the next Congress to adopt this requirement.

Elections. Two out of three candidates who were backed by the AFL-CIO's Committee on Political Education (COPE) were victorious in the November elections. Out of 32 COPE-endorsed gubernatorial candidates, 18 were elected. In the House of Representatives, 239 of the 362 Democrats and all nine of the Republican candidates who ran with COPE backing won. Labor's biggest victory came in the Senate, where the Democrats scored a net gain of eight seats to take control of the new Senate with a 55-45 margin. Out of 27 candidates endorsed by COPE, all Democrats, 19 of them won.

The outcome of an Idaho referendum held on November 4, however, was highly disappointing to the unions. Despite a major campaign by labor, voters approved the retention

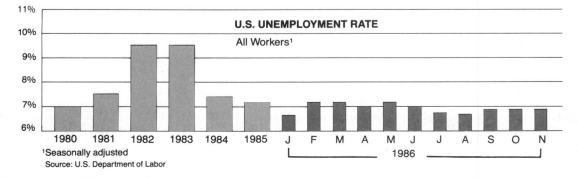

U.S. UNEMPLOYMENT RATE

All Workers[1]

1980 1981 1982 1983 1984 1985 J F M A M J J A S O N

[1]Seasonally adjusted

1986

Source: U.S. Department of Labor

of Idaho's "right to work" law, which labor calls a "compulsory open show" law because it prohibits agreements that make union membership a condition of employment.

Canada

As in the United States, the economy of Canada has produced a prolonged growth in employment. The average number of persons working there during the first three quarters of 1986 was more than 3% above the number for the same period in 1985. Joblessness continued to decline from a peak of 12% in 1983, and it fluctuated between 9% and 10% in 1986.

Wage rates rose between 2% and 3%, roughly half the pace of 1985. Prices (as measured by the CPI) rose at a corresponding rate, partly because of higher price tags on imports caused by depreciation of the Canadian dollar.

Canadian union membership stood at 3.73 million, a 1.7% increase in a year. Because of an increase in the labor force, however, union membership actually declined from 39% to 37.7% of nonagricultural wage and salary workers.

The Canadian Labour Congress (CLC), which with 2,164,000 members is by far the largest national center, elected its former secretary-treasurer Shirley Carr as its new president. Carr, who came from the Canadian Union of Public Employees, became the first woman ever to head the national trade union center of an industrialized nation. Her predecessor, Dennis McDermott of the Auto Workers, was named ambassador to Ireland.

The International Woodworkers of America, which unites 70,000 lumber workers in the United States and Canada, was to be divided into two national organizations in early 1987. The Canadian section, which represents about two thirds of the union membership, decided at a special convention in British Columbia to set up its own national Union.

International

Unemployment. Although the 1986 U.S. unemployment rate of about 7% was high compared with the 3.8% of 20 years earlier, it was low compared to the pattern in most industrialized nations. In Western Europe, 19 million men and women—more than 11% of the total labor force—were jobless. Great Britain, France, Italy, Spain, Portugal, Belgium, the Netherlands, and Ireland all endured unemployment rates of 10% or higher, on up to Spain's 22%.

Partly because of unemployment and partly because nearly two million Turks already live within their areas, the 12 nations of the European Community (EC) backed off from the Community's 1963 commitment to open its frontiers to Turkish migrant workers. Reactions against foreign workers also took other forms. In France, for example, which has an unemployment rate of 11% (the EC average), the government decided to place restrictions on the rights of its large immigrant population.

West Germany, with a booming industry, coasted along on a relatively favorable jobless rate of less than 8%. Sweden did even better, continuing to enjoy low unemployment—with a rate just under 3% in 1986—partly because of what the Swedes call "work sharing." That is, taking vacations, holidays, maternity and paternity leaves, part-time work, and other time-off periods into account, the Swedish labor force has a work week that averages only about 28 hours—probably the world's shortest.

Japan also had a low unemployment rate of slightly less than 3% for the year, but even this stirred widespread concern. For one, it was regarded as a bad omen that in July the number

Shirley Carr, a former stenographer, succeeded Dennis McDermott (left) as president of the Canadian Labour Congress.

of unemployed males rose for the first time to above 1 million, because of layoffs in manufacturing industries facing competition from South Korea, Taiwan, and elsewhere. For another, according to a U.S. BLS study, Japan has substantial "hidden" unemployment in the form of people who want jobs but have given up on finding them. According to the study, such uncounted joblessness probably has increased.

Union Headaches. Because of unemployment, unions almost everywhere were on the defensive in 1986. In many countries total union membership decreased or remained stagnant. Even in economies showing growth, negotiations with public or private employers often produced slim gains. Another reason for this trend was that the service sector, where unions are usually weak, continued to grow in importance, whereas the manufacturing sector, where unions are relatively strong, declined.

In Britain, however, where almost half of the work force is still unionized (compared with only one fifth in the United States and France, and one third in Japan and West Germany), workers averaged pay increases of 7.5% against a price rise of 3%—the largest real wage increase in any large Western nation. In Australia, by contrast, economic conditions and a social contract between the unions and the Labor government caused a drop in real wages for the third straight year.

In West Germany, despite a modest jobless rate, the labor movement was in difficulty because of a scandal in its huge housing conglomerate, Neue Heimat, set up as a "common good" organization. Gross failings in management created both a multibillion dollar debt and continual bad publicity, to the detriment of labor leaders as well as to their close allies in the Social Democratic Party, which was preparing for the general election in January 1987.

In many countries unions faced government initiatives toward privatization, by which certain government-owned operations such as banks or telecommunications are shifted to private status. In Japan, for example, the public-sector rail unions declared their opposition to Prime Minister Nakasone's plans to privatize the Japan National Railways—a move expected to lead to the firing of a third of the JNR's work force of 300,000 persons in 1987.

Solidarity. Speaking in Warsaw in July to the congress of Poland's Communist Party, Soviet leader Mikhail Gorbachev made clear that Moscow would not tolerate the existence of a mass workers' organization such as Solidarity in Eastern Europe. Solidarity was the independent labor organization in Poland that grew to 10 million members before the Polish government suppressed it in 1980–81. A month before the congress, the government announced the arrest of 31-year-old Zbigniew Bujaw, who had run Solidarity's underground section for nearly five years. Even with Bujaw, however, the Sol-

idarity underground survives and has a thriving information and publishing network. In November the International Confederation of Free Trade Unions (ICFTU) and the World Confederation of Labor (WCL), both headquartered in Brussels, accepted the affiliation of Solidarity. Poland's officially established replacement for Solidarity, a Communist Party organization that confiscated Solidarity's funds and property, is an affiliate of the World Federation of Trade Unions (WFTU), which is headquartered in Prague, Czechoslovakia.

WFTU. For the World Federation of Trade Unions (WFTU), 1986 was a big year, because 1,000 participants from every continent gathered in East Berlin in September for the Communist organization's 11th international congress. There the WFTU represented itself as the instrument of the world's workers struggling for peace and disarmament against oppressive capitalism and imperialism. The WFTU claimed that its affiliates had a total membership of 296 million in 154 nations, but the center of its strength is actually in the USSR, where the All-Soviet Central Council of Trade Unions has 130 million members—all enrolled by government compulsion.

In its campaign to win support in the Third World, the WFTU paid the way to East Berlin for an estimated 500 observers and delegates from Asia, Africa, Latin America, and the Pacific region. The Congress reelected a Sudanese, Ibrahim Zakaria, as its general secretary. Sandar Gaspar of Hungary serves as the WFTU president, and Soviet appointees are key members of the Prague secretariat.

The AFL-CIO, an ICFTU affiliate, reaffirmed its criticism of the WFTU for its "slavish adherence to the Moscow line"—for example, its defense of the Soviet invasion of Afghanistan, its "relentless attacks" on Israel, and its rejection of Solidarity and embrace of the government-controlled unions of Poland.

International Labor Organization. In Geneva in November, the International Labor Organization (ILO)—a United Nations agency and a unique one, since it is comprised of government, employer, and worker representatives—received word that the Polish government was reconsidering its 1984 decision to withdraw from the organization. In that year, a special ILO commission had charged Warsaw with violating ILO conventions by suppressing the worker's right to organize and bargain.

Although the ILO puts pressure on governments to protect worker rights, a country's absence from the ILO denotes some loss of status in the international community. Thus non-ILO member South Korea in October sponsored a labor meeting in Seoul that was attended by top Labor Ministry officials from 19 Asian and African countries, and lobbied for their support of its application to join the organization.

Robert A. Senser, *Free-lance Labor Writer*

LAOS

Laos entered its second decade of Communist rule without internal political competition or significant economic growth. The major participants in Laotian affairs during 1986 remained the ruling Lao People's Revolutionary Party (LPRP), Chairman Kaysone Phomvihan, the neighboring country of Vietnam, and the unsettled Laotian people.

The LPRP remained firmly in power, reflecting, among other things, its skill in not pressing Marxist policies too heavily on a still highly traditional population. The Communist regime of neighboring Vietnam maintained considerable control in alliance with the LPRP, keeping at least 40,000 troops in Laos. Prince Souphanouvong, who led the Communists to power in Laos in 1975, resigned as president for health reasons in late October.

Many of the Lao people, meanwhile, continued to show different political sympathies. More than one tenth of the country's population has left the land since the Communists came to power in 1975. At the end of 1986, more than 91,000 Laotians were still in refugee camps in neighboring Thailand. Thousands more, unsympathetic to the Vientiane regime, were being held in prisons inside Laos.

Economy. Within the party leadership there was recurring debate over the extent of change that was needed in the country's economic policies. The differences reflected a division between orthodox Marxists and those advocating the type of reform elements implemented in Vietnam. At midyear, heads of government departments were told of a new national economic policy, but the details were not made public. The shift, according to the government, instituted a "new economic mechanism" and a system of "collective mastership," but neither of these terms was explained. From available evidence, the new policy appeared to be less a substantive change of direction than a reorganization of procedures and practices (as in government accounting methods) and an attempt to involve workers in new functions.

Foreign Relations. Laotian foreign relations focused on persisting cooperation with Vietnam and strained ties with Thailand, its neighbor to the west. In June, troops from Laos entered Thailand and killed 35 Laotian refugees, and in September the Thai reportedly were considering the forced repatriation of more than 1,000 Laotian refugees in exchange for Thai soldiers detained in Laos since the Indochina war.

RICHARD BUTWELL
California State University, Dominguez Hills

LATIN AMERICA

Latin America as a whole in 1986 remained locked in the grip of a recession that began five years earlier and showed only faint signs of easing. There were individual exceptions to the general trend, notably Brazil, which enjoyed an economic growth rate of 6–7% and posted a balance of trade surplus in excess of $12 billion. But in general, according to the Inter-American Development Bank (IDB), "Latin America's recession is lengthening dangerously and the region's debt problem continues to be a serious one."

Aside from Brazil, most of the region showed relatively stagnant growth in 1986, with such countries as Chile, Colombia, and Peru increasing their per capita gross domestic products (GDPs) by only about 2% and at least half the countries showing declines. The countries most severly hit by recession were Ecuador, Mexico, Trinidad and Tobago, and Venezuela, all exporters of petroleum. By the end of the year, Latin America's per capita GDP was 9% below the level of 1980.

In the estimation of the IDB, "There is little hope of Latin America emerging from the recession until it can stop transferring resources abroad as it has had to do for four consecutive years, a reversal of the long-term trend when foreign capital was used to augment domestic savings." From 1982, the IDB said, the net transfer of Latin American resources abroad totaled nearly $100 billion. The region's external debt exceeded $370 billion in 1986, and, according to studies by the World Bank, interest and amortization payments represented 25–30% of earnings from exports of goods and services. A massive flight of domestic private capital to safe havens overseas, which reached a cumulative total of $123 billion in 1986, further exacerbated the problem.

Trade. From 1980 to 1985, the volume of Latin America's exports expanded significantly. The rise of 7.2% per year compared with an annual increase in total world trade of only 2.1%. At the same time, however, the region's imports declined sharply. In 1985, according to the IDB, Latin America's import volume was 37% lower than in 1981, and was even below the level of 1975.

The rise in exports, coupled with the fall in imports, has produced annual trade surpluses for many countries of the region, much of which has been applied to servicing the debt. In 1985 the region as a whole registered an

---

LAOS • Information Highlights

Official Name: Lao People's Democratic Republic.
Location: Southeast Asia.
Area: 91,430 sq mi (236 804 km²).
Population (mid-1986 est.): 3,700,000.
Government: *Head of state:* Phoumi Vongvichit, temporary president; *Head of government,* Kaysone Phomvihan, chairman. *Legislature* (unicameral)—National Congress of People's Representatives.

$18.8 billion merchandise trade surplus with the United States. The positive effect of the surpluses, however, has been weakened by the continuing decline in the unit value of the region's exports. In 1985 the prices commanded by Latin American exports fell 6.6%, after declining by an annual average of 4.6% in the four preceding years.

The critical importance of these figures lies in the fact that exports in 1985 provided 95.5% of Latin America's total foreign exchange earnings, while in the prerecession years the comparable figure was 70%. The resulting scarcity of foreign exchange has forced most countries of the region sharply to reduce investment in their domestic economies. Real gross domestic investment in 1985 was 27% less than it was in 1980; investment accounted for 25.5% of the GDP in 1980, but for less than 18% in both 1984 and 1985. Economists say that the decline in investment activities and the shrinkage of imports, particularly imports of capital goods, have grave medium- and long-term implications for the Latin American economies.

To reverse the trend, Latin American governments have been pressing for closer linkage between export earnings and debt repayment schedules. A July 1986 agreement between Mexico and the IMF provides for adjustment of Mexico's repayment schedule according to increases or decreases in the price of oil, the country's principal export. Argentina was seeking similar arrangements with the IMF based on the price of its grain exports.

At the meeting of the General Agreement on Tariffs and Trade (GATT) in Punta del Este, Uruguay, in September, the Latin American bloc supported a proposal for closer coordination between the GATT and the IMF, and for debt-payment adjustments tied to foreign-exchange earnings from exports. In October, the 25 member countries of the Latin American Economic System (SELA) endorsed the GATT proposal, declaring "The external debt cannot be repaid under present conditions."

Population. Economic hardships, intensified by rising population pressures, sent an increasing tide of migrants northward to the United States in 1986. According to estimates by the United Nations, the region's population of just more than 400 million will reach 546 million by the year 2000 and 779 million by 2025. The UN predicts that the Latin American population will stabilize by the end of the 21st century, but not before there are 1.2 billion people in the region.

Terrorism. Depressed economic conditions were also partly responsible for a rise in terrorist activities in several Latin American countries during 1986. In some instances, terrorist groups were linked to drug trafficking organizations. In other cases, terrorism was the product of internecine warfare between government forces and insurgents.

Terrorist violence rose in Colombia during the year, with at least 186 terrorist-related kidnappings recorded in the first nine months. Left-wing guerrillas attacked a presidential motorcade in Chile, killing five guards and wounding ten others; President Augusto Pinochet escaped with minor cuts. Chilean forces also seized a cache of 70 tons of weapons, valued at $10 million, which government officials said had been sent from Cuba to insurgent groups.

In Peru, the far-left *Sendero Luminoso* (Shining Path) guerrillas continued their violent attacks on public utilities and buildings and clashed frequently with the Peruvian Army.

International Organizations. The Inter-American Investment Corporation, an affiliate of the IDB, began operations in September. The new entity will aid small- and medium-sized businesses in the region.

The Organization of American States (OAS), at its annual General Assembly in Guatemala in November, approved the creation of an Inter-American Drug Control Commission to combat drug abuse and trafficking throughout the hemisphere.

RICHARD C. SCHROEDER, *"Visión" Magazine*

Six Latin leaders met in Colombia for the inauguration of President Virgilio Barco: (l-r) El Salvador's José Napoleón Duarte; Venezuela's Jaime Lusinchi; Barco; Costa Rica's Oscar Arias; Honduras' José Azcona; Argentina's Raúl Alfonsín.

AP/Wide World

AP/Wide World

With William Rehnquist taking over as chief justice and Antonin Scalia becoming an associate justice, a new chapter in U.S. Supreme Court history begins. The nine members of the new court are (l-r): Sandra Day O'Connor, Lewis Powell, Thurgood Marshall, William Brennan, W. Rehnquist, Byron White, Harry Blackmun, John Paul Stevens, and A. Scalia.

LAW

An era in U.S. Supreme Court history came to a close in 1986, as Chief Justice Warren E. Burger, in a surprise announcement, retired to devote full time to heading a commission planning the celebration of the bicentennial of the U.S. Constitution in 1987. To succeed Burger, President Ronald Reagan selected Associate Justice William H. Rehnquist as the nation's 16th chief justice (*see* BIOGRAPHY). And the newest member of the court, like Burger and Rehnquist a staunch conservative, is Antonin Scalia who was a federal-appeals-court judge in Washington, DC (*see* BIOGRAPHY).

The last days of Burger's tenure produced a flurry of important decisions, highlighting a 1985–86 term in which the court buttressed the fight for equality by racial minorities and women but dealt homosexuals a major legal defeat. The court also struck down a key portion of the new federal law mandating automatic reductions in the federal deficit. And it was a bad year for the Reagan administration's social agenda, as the court reaffirmed abortion rights and again refused to allow organized prayer in public schools. In the lower courts, spy cases again were big news stories.

An extraordinary impeachment proceeding in Congress cast a shadow over the federal judiciary in 1986. The House of Representatives impeached Harry E. Claiborne, and the Senate found him guilty of "high crimes and misdemeanors" and ordered him to give up his federal judgeship in Nevada. Claiborne already was serving a two-year prison sentence for tax evasion but had refused to resign.

In international law, a ruling by the World Court on the conflict of Nicaragua and U.S. ratification of a United Nations treaty outlawing genocide were major events of the year.

United States

Supreme Court. In a year of historic transition, the U.S. Supreme Court demonstrated that its moderate members continue to control the balance of power, as they had so often during Burger's 17 years as chief justice. The key swing votes were, predictably, Justice Lewis F. Powell and, startlingly, Justice Sandra Day O'Connor.

O'Connor, President Reagan's first appointee to the court, and Powell dissented fewer times than any other justice. Each was in the minority in only 14 of the court's 147 signed decisions. Of 38 cases decided by 5–4 votes, Powell and O'Connor were in the majority in 28. Those statistics underscore the uncertainty of President Reagan's ultimate ideological impact on the court. O'Connor, who generally had been viewed as a reliable conservative vote, moved discernibly toward the middle in 1986. The addition of Scalia for the departing Burger is not expected to alter the ideological composition of the court. But Powell, 79, back on the bench after prostate cancer surgery the year before, is one of four justices age 78 or older. The others are Justices Thurgood Marshall, 78, and William J. Brennan, 80, the Liberal anchors of the court, and Harry A. Blackmun, 78, a more dependable ally of the Liberals than ever before.

Perhaps the most controversial case of the 1985–86 term was the court's ruling that states do not violate constitutionally protected privacy rights by outlawing private homosexual conduct between consenting adults (*Bowers v. Hardwick*). While there are rarely enforced antisodomy laws in 24 states and the District of Columbia, the ruling was expected to have wider impact. Homosexual-rights advocates said it could impair their efforts in fighting discrimination in jobs, parental custody, housing,

313

The Burger Court

AP/Wide World

Warren E. Burger served as chief justice of the U.S. Supreme Court from June 23, 1969, to Sept. 26, 1986.

When President Richard Nixon in 1969 appointed Warren E. Burger to be the 15th chief justice of the United States, many believed it heralded the dismantling of the liberal, activist rulings of the court under Burger's predecessor, Earl Warren. Those expectations were never realized.

During his 17-year tenure as chief justice, Burger proved to be a tough "law and order" judge, making important contributions to whittling away or circumscribing previous decisions favoring criminal suspects. But in numerous other areas, the Burger court broke new ground in behalf of civil rights and equality, personal privacy, religious freedom, and separation of government power between the executive and legislative branches. In case after case, the true balance of power rested with moderate justices—not with either the court's liberals or with Burger and his main conservative ally, William H. Rehnquist, picked by President Reagan to be the next chief justice.

While there is no apparent dominant theme of the court's Burger years, the main legacy left by the man may be his dedication to court reform and efficient administration. Legal experts praised Burger for proposals to ease the burden on the nation's court system and to im-

prove the quality of lawyers. But the chief justice's dream of a new national appeals court to ease the high court's overload did not become a reality during Burger's tenure. The proposal was pending in Congress in 1986.

Justice Burger said he frequently worked more than 80 hours a week, and in announcing, on June 17, 1986, his surprise retirement said he wanted to devote full time to heading a commission planning the celebration of the 200th anniversary of the Constitution in 1987.

Perhaps the most controversial ruling of the Burger years is the 1973 decision, in *Roe v. Wade,* legalizing abortions nationwide. The court held then and has reaffirmed twice since a woman's privacy right to abortion. Burger voted in 1973 with the majority, although in 1986 he joined the dissenters.

No justice in history has written more than Burger about the separation of powers between the branches of government. That included his opinion in 1986 when the court struck down a key portion of the law mandating a balanced federal budget by fiscal year 1991. Burger also authored decisions in which the court established busing as a tool for racial desegregation of public schools, expanded public access to the nation's courts, and enhanced women's protection against sexual discrimination.

In 1974, the court helped precipitate Nixon's resignation, ordering him to surrender White House tape recordings and papers for use as evidence in the trial of presidential aides accused of covering up the Watergate scandal. Burger wrote the opinion. Burger also was the author of a 1973 decision defining obscenity that is still in force today. The standard states: material may be banned if it appeals to a morbid interest in sex with patently offensive depictions or descriptions of sexual conduct, and on the whole has no serious literary, artistic, political, or scientific value.

The retired chief justice also wrote the court's landmark three-part standard in the area of separation of church and state. The court said a governmental practice is valid if it has a nonreligious purpose, its primary effect does not advance or inhibit religion, and it does not foster excessive governmental entanglement with religion.

Burger, a Minnesotan, earned his law degree at night while working days in an insurance office. With his deep baritone and full head of white hair, he looked and sounded the part of a chief justice. He announced his retirement at age 78.

JIM RUBIN

and other areas. They noted that the ruling came at a particularly troubled time for gay rights because of the highly publicized epidemic of Acquired Immune Deficiency Syndrome (AIDS).

The court took a different approach in upholding a woman's privacy right to have an abortion. Reaffirming its 1973 ruling legalizing abortion, the court ruled that states may not use abortion regulations to intimidate women into giving birth (*Thornburgh v. American College of Obstetricians and Gynecologists*).

The court upheld two affirmative-action plans and struck down a third. The three decisons amounted to a major victory for civil-rights forces and a defeat for the Reagan administration's position that such special preferences should be limited to actual victims of discrimination. In one case, the court held that federal judges may approve race-conscious plans agreed to by public employers who admit past discrimination against the minority group (*Local 93 of International Association of Firefighters v. Cleveland*). In a companion ruling, the court upheld quotas for a private employer's hiring and promotions or for a union's membership if there is proof of "egregious" past discrimination by the employer or union (*Local 28 of Sheet Metal Workers International Association v. EEOC*). But the justices also held that courts generally may not insulate recent gains by minorities and women by approving plans that would first lay off white men with more seniority (*Wygant v. Jackson Board of Education*).

In a victory for women's rights advocates, the court said that on-the-job sexual harassment is illegal even if the victim suffers no economic harm, and employers who are not aware of sexual harassment by a supervisor may still be held liable (*Meritor Savings Bank v. Vinson*).

In a major ruling on the separation of powers between the legislative and executive branches, the court struck down a key portion of the Gramm-Rudman-Hollings Act aimed at balancing the federal budget by 1991 (*Bowsher v. Synar*). The law's mechanism for automatic spending cuts unconstitutionally assigned executive-branch duties to an officer of the legislative branch, the justices said.

Four other rulings also will have significant impact on government and politics. The court ruled that gerrymandering, the long-standing art of drawing election district lines for partisan advantage, may be unconstitutional even when the created districts are equally populated and satisfy the one-person, one-vote rule (*Davis v. Bandemer*). State and local governments may not withdraw their employees from the federal pension system created by Social Security, the court ruled (*Bowen v. Public Agencies*). Also, the court held that municipalities can be held legally accountable for the conduct of their employees when such conduct reflects official policy, even if the wrongdoing happens only once (*Pembauer v. Cincinnati*). And the justices allowed cities to impose rent controls even when the regulations are not authorized explicitly by state law (*Fisher v. Berkeley*).

In the area of religious freedom, the court said that the armed services may ban the wearing of yarmulkes by Orthodox Jews while they are on duty (*Goldman v. Weinberger*). It said the government may force someone to obtain a Social Security number even if doing so violates that person's religious beliefs (*Bowen v. Roy*). And, the justices said, state aid to a blind student enrolled in a Bible school does not violate the constitutionally required separation of church and state (*Witters v. Washington Department of Services for the Blind*).

In another setback for the Reagan administration, the court struck down so-called "Baby Doe" federal regulations aimed at pressuring doctors and hospitals to preserve the lives of severely handicapped infants (*Bowen v. American Hospital Assocation*).

In cases involving free expression, the court ruled that public school administrators may take disciplinary action, including suspension, against students for using "vulgar and offensive" language (*Bethel School District v. Fraser*). And it upheld Puerto Rico's ban on gambling-casino advertising aimed at the island's residents (*Posados v. Tourism Co.*).

In two free-press cases, the court held that private individuals who sue news organizations for libel have the burden of proving that the allegedly libelous statements are false "on matters of public concern" (*Philadelphia Newspapers v. Hepps*), and that judges may throw out public figures' libel lawsuits before they reach a jury if "clear and convincing" proof of malice is lacking (*Anderson v. Liberty Lobby*).

On the subject of race, the court made it easier under a federal-voting-rights law for blacks to challenge redistricting plans that dilute their voting strength (*Thornburgh v. Gingles*). Also, the court ruled that prosecutors never may exclude potential jurors in criminal cases because of their race (*Batson v. Kentucky*). And the justices said that murder defendants facing possible death sentences must, upon conviction, be allowed to ask potential jurors about their racial views (*Turner v. Murray*).

On another death-penalty matter, the court held that insane murderers may not be executed, even if they were sane when they committed their crimes and became unbalanced on death row (*Ford v. Wainwright*). The court also ruled that capital-punishment opponents may be excluded as jurors in capital trials, even if that results in "conviction-prone" juries (*Lockhart v. McCree*).

In the area of law enforcement, court authorities do not need court warrants to conduct searches from airplanes for marijuana fields or other illegal activity (*California v. Ciraolo*). The justices also determined that police do not have to cooperate, and even may use deception, in dealing with lawyers seeking to reach criminal suspects when the attorneys have not been hired by the suspects personally (*Moran v. Burbine*). Also, the court said that lawyers representing criminal defendants do not violate their clients' rights by insisting that they testify truthfully when taking the witness stand (*Nix v. Whiteside*). Finally, the court ruled that the presence of armed and uniformed state troopers sitting directly behind a defendant at the trial does not violate the suspect's rights (*Holbrook v. Massachusetts Correctional Institution.*).

Local Justice. Spy trials attracted headlines around the United States in 1986. In a federal courtroom in Los Angeles, Richard W. Miller became the first FBI agent ever to be convicted of espionage. He was sentenced to two life terms plus 50 years in prison for conspiring with his lover and her husband to pass classified documents to the Soviet Union.

In San Francisco, former Navy radioman Jerry Whitworth was convicted as a member of John Walker's Soviet-run spy ring in what the Navy said was the worst breach of U.S. military secrets since World War II. Whitworth, of Davis, CA, was the last member of the Walker spy ring to be tried. Walker, 48, of Norfolk, VA, pleaded guilty in 1985 to spying for the

Stephen Bingham hugs his wife after being acquitted of murder and conspiracy charges stemming from an attempted escape from San Quentin (CA) Prison in 1971.

AP/Wide World

Soviet Union for 17 years. Whitworth, 47, was sentenced to 365 years in prison with no chance of parole for at least 60 years for selling vital code and communications secrets for $322,000 to the spy ring run by Walker.

Another FBI agent, Robert S. Friedrick, also was in trouble with the law. Friedrick, former head of the FBI's organized-crime squad in Cleveland, was accused of making false statements to the Justice Department concerning Teamsters President Jackie Presser. Friedrick allegedly tried to head off Presser's indictment and allegedly lied to a superior in saying that he authorized Presser to make illegal payments to people who did no work. The Friedrick trial got under way in Washington, DC, in December 1986. Presser was charged with racketeering, embezzling union funds, and filing false reports to the federal government.

Former U.S. Secretary of Labor Raymond J. Donovan went on trial in New York City with nine others on charges stemming from a subway-construction project run by Donovan's former company, Schiavone Construction Co. of New Jersey. Company officials were accused of overstating payments to a subcontracting firm owned by New York State Sen. Joseph Caliber and William Maselli, a reputed mobster.

Also in New York, the state's top court ordered Bernhard Goetz to stand trial on charges of attempted murder and assault in the 1984 shootings of four youths on a Manhattan subway. The New York Court of Appeals reinstated charges thrown out by lower courts.

In San Francisco, Stephen M. Bingham, a former poverty lawyer and civil-rights worker, was acquitted of murder and conspiracy charges stemming from an attempted escape from San Quentin Prison in California on Aug. 21, 1971. Six people died in the incident, including convict and writer George Jackson. Two other inmates and three guards also died in the attempted break. Bingham, 44 at the time of his 1986 trial, was accused of smuggling a pistol into San Quentin in 1971. He disappeared after the violence and spent 13 years as a fugitive before surrendering in 1984.

In a federal courtroom in Concord, NH, *Hustler* magazine lost a $2 million libel verdict to rival *Penthouse* magazine executive Kathy Keeton. She alleged that she had been libeled by publication of defamatory material in *Hustler* over an 11-year period beginning in 1975.

In widely publicized federal court cases in Tennessee and Alabama, fundamentalist parents challenged the content of textbooks they said promote anti-Christian themes. The parents said that textbooks promoting "secular humanism" are being used. In the Church Hill, TN, case, the court ruled in favor of the fundamentalists in October. No verdict was rendered in the Mobile, AL, suit by year's end.

JIM RUBIN, *The Associated Press*

Pornography

Some hailed it as a return to strong moral values, others decried it as a swing toward repression and censorship. Either way, the year 1986 saw clear signs of a new spirit of militancy against the commerce of pornography, however defined. Retail chains across the United States removed sexually explicit magazines from their shelves. Efforts were under way in more than a dozen states to restrict the sale of explicit publications and video programming (although voters in Maine rejected an antipornography referendum). Local governments everywhere passed strict ordinances against the pornography trade. In February the U.S. Supreme Court gave cities and towns broad authority to use zoning laws to dictate the location of theaters that show X-rated movies. And, at the very heart of the issue, crystallizing the movement as well as the debate, was the final report of the U.S. Attorney General's Commission on Pornography.

After a year of investigation, the 11-member commission, headed by Henry E. Hudson, U.S. attorney for the Eastern District of Virginia, turned over its 1,960-page, two-volume report to U.S. Attorney General Edwin Meese in July. Calling for tough new measures, the panel advocated longer jail sentences for convicted pornographers, especially in cases involving child pornography, and favored stricter controls over what it regarded as pornographic cable television programs. Among its specific recommendations was congressional action requiring convicted pornographers to forfeit profits and property involved in the production or distribution of obscene materials.

Underlying the recommendations was the commission's finding that "substantial exposure to sexually violent materials . . . bears a causal relationship to antisocial acts of violence." This finding was diametrically opposed to that of the 1970 President's Commission on Pornography, which had recommended repeal of all legislation prohibiting the sale of sexual material to consenting adults. The current commission said that the "enormous technological changes" in the past 16 years had made the previous report "starkly obsolete."

The 1986 report also condemned "sexually degrading" material, maintaining that it, too, was related to sexual assaults. This finding, however, was reached with "less confidence" than that regarding portrayals of sexual violence and was said to be "more in the way of an assumption." Present statutes outlawing pornography were declared adequate, though the commission favored new statutes outlawing "dial-a-porn" telephone services and making possession of "kiddie-porn" materials a felony. What was unsatisfactory, the commission maintained, was the level of effort devoted by law enforcement agencies to the suppression of pornographic materials.

Finally, the commission advocated that local religious and civic groups picket, protest, and take other actions to disrupt the sale of materials which they find objectionable.

The various findings and recommendations of the commission were generally supported by conservatives, some very strongly. The Rev. Jerry Falwell, president of the Liberty Foundation, for example, extolled the work: "I believe that it is a good and healthy report that places the United States government clearly in concert with grass roots America," he said.

Others were less taken with the recommendations. Two of the commission's 11 members —Judith V. Becker, a Columbia University psychologist, and Ellen Levine, editor of *Woman's Day* magazine—formally dissented from the conclusion relating pornography to sexual violence. The dissenters insisted that the one-year timetable for the project and the $500,000 budget were insufficient to judge the complex relationship between pornography and violence. Other critics pointed to the advocacy of citizen action as a threat to the 1st Amendment.

Indeed the commission was involved in controversy even before its report was issued. Retail stores throughout the country, including those in the 7-Eleven and Rite Aid chains, received letters from the commission saying that they would be named in the final report for involvement in "the sale or distribution of pornography" unless they could offer an explanation for merchandising such magazines as *Playboy, Penthouse,* and *Hustler.* The stores withdrew the magazine from their shelves, but a federal district judge subsequently ordered the commission to send out new letters retracting its implied threat.

That the commission's conclusions meshed with the current views of the American people, and perhaps also influenced such views, was demonstrated by a Gallup Poll conducted two days after the report was released. The poll found that 72% of Americans favor a ban in their communities on the sale or rental of videocassettes showing sexual violence, while 74% would ban theaters showing movies that depict sexual violence. Twenty percent of the respondents favored a ban on magazines that depict nudity, while 42% would ban theaters showing X-rated movies. Each of these figures had risen 6%–10% from a 1985 poll.

GILBERT GEIS

Juvenile Justice

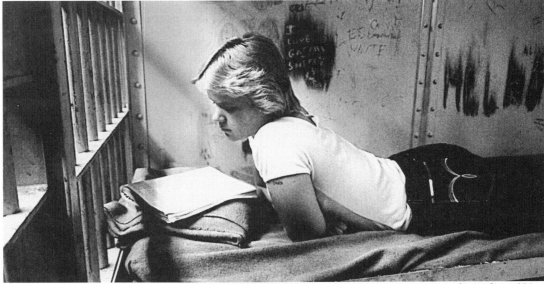

© Stephen Shames/Visions

Up to 500,000 youthful offenders are held in adult jails and police-station lockups each year in the United States.

The treatment of youthful offenders by the U.S. criminal justice system has long been a source of controversy. In 1986, however, the debate reached a new level of intensity over the application of the death penalty and reports of widespread confinement of juveniles in adult jails. A new book, meanwhile, set off vigorous discussion of the role of heredity in criminal behavior. And in Washington, the U.S. Office of Juvenile Justice and Delinquency Prevention was another focus of debate.

Death Penalty. On Jan. 10, 1986, James Terry Roach, 25, was executed by electrocution at the South Carolina state penitentiary in Columbia. Roach had been convicted of the rape and murder of two teenage girls in 1977, when he was 17 years old. He became the first person in more than two decades to be executed for a juvenile offense without having waived his right to appeal. His death set off heated debate over the propriety of capital punishment for individuals who commit serious crimes before they reach adulthood.

According to Federal Bureau of Investigation (FBI) statistics, 1,311 juveniles (under age 18) in the United States were arrested for murder in 1985. While that still represented less than 10% of all homicide arrests in the nation, each case again raised the dilemma of appropriate punishment. In a study for the U.S.

Justice Department, a special commission recommended that convicted killers age 14 or under be held in a juvenile facility for at least seven years, while those 15 and over be treated as adult offenders. According to the FBI statistics, most of the 1,311 juveniles arrested for murder in 1985 were 16 or 17 years old.

Of the 37 U.S. states with death penalty laws, 30 allow for the execution of juveniles. Some set a minimum age. In Indiana, children ten years old can be sentenced to death. At the time of Roach's execution, there were 32 other persons on death row for crimes they committed as minors. In July 1986, 16-year-old Paula Cooper became the youngest person to be sentenced to death since the U.S. Supreme Court reinstituted capital punishment in July 1976.

Those who favor the imposition of the death penalty point to the sometimes shockingly violent nature of the crimes. Opponents argue that minors have less capacity than adults to grasp the seriousness of their acts, less understanding of the death penalty as a sanction (thereby making it ineffective as a deterrent), and greater potential for rehabilitation. In addition, they contend, some of the young people on death row may have suffered from physical or psychological disabilities, or been convicted by racially biased juries.

In a 1982 case *(Eddings v. Oklahoma),* the U.S. Supreme Court considered the imposition of the death penalty on a defendant who had been 16 at the time of the crime. But the justices reversed and remanded the case to state court on the grounds that the minor's turbulent family history had not been considered at his sentencing. Ultimately the Supreme Court may render a decision on the constitutionality, or lack of it, of juvenile execution.

Incarceration and Detention. Since 1974, U.S. federal law has prohibited the jailing of minors with adult inmates; most states have similar statutes. In many places, however, the laws go unenforced, as law enforcement officials use the local jail or police-station lockup out of convenience, tradition, or the lack of less punitive alternatives.

It has been estimated that as many as 500,000 juveniles are held in adult jails and police-station lockups each year. Although most of them are charged with only minor offenses, some suffer physical or psychological abuse— or worse. Recent years have seen the rape of a 15-year-old girl by a deputy jailer in Ohio, the sexual assault of an 11-year-old boy by inmates at a Washington, DC, lockup, and the murder of a 17-year-old boy by other inmates in Idaho. In Arizona, California, and Kentucky, children in jail have committed suicide.

The problem is perhaps most serious in California, where up to 100,000 minors may be held in adult jails each year. Beginning in 1985, however, the Youth Law Center in San Francisco brought several successful lawsuits to stop the jailing of children in the state. The litigation and resulting public attention prompted the California legislature to pass a law restricting the use of jails for minors. Similar moves had been made in Pennsylvania, Virginia, and North Carolina.

Even within the juvenile justice system itself, the response to wayward children increasingly has been incarceration or detention. The National Council on Crime and Delinquency and the Hubert Humphrey Institute of Public Affairs at the University of Minnesota report that, even though the U.S. youth population and the number of juvenile arrests have declined over the past decade, more minors are being institutionalized and with longer commitments. In excess of 400,000 children are locked up in juvenile pretrial detention centers each year, and more than 60,000 are committed after trial to state training schools. One trend remains constant: minority youth are incarcerated at a rate three to four times higher than that of white youth.

Heredity and Crime. Professors Richard J. Hernstein and James Q. Wilson of Harvard University ignited a new round of the "nature versus nurture" debate with the publication of their book, *Crime and Human Nature* (1985). Hernstein and Wilson argue the thesis that biological as well as environmental factors are responsible for delinquency and that intelligence and temperament—which have a "heritable base"—have a particular influence on criminal behavior.

The authors speculate that people of low intelligence may have difficulty grasping the consequences of their acts or understanding codes of behavior. Young people of low intelligence may experience difficulties in school, leading to anger, frustration, and antisocial behavior. They may also find it more difficult to express themselves verbally and may resort to other means, such as violence. Such other traits as impulsiveness, insensitivity to social mores, lack of deep emotional attachment to others, and an appetite for danger may also predispose a person to a life of crime.

Hernstein's and Wilson's attempt to reconcile the findings of biology, developmental psychology, and criminology was applauded by some but vigorously attacked by others. Critics accused them of biological determinism and questioned their assumptions of the heritability of intelligence and temperament. At the very least, their work generated fresh discussion of a centuries-old question that lies at the heart of the juvenile justice system.

Public Policy and the Administration. In recent years, advocates of juvenile justice reform have voiced criticism of certain policy and administrative positions of the U.S. Office of Juvenile Justice and Delinquency Prevention (OJJDP). Alfred S. Regnery, who resigned in June 1986 after three and a half years as administrator of OJJDP, had stirred controversy in some quarters for supporting capital punishment of serious juvenile offenders and for claiming that few minors, if any, are held in adult jails. Amid the debate over such issues, Regnery supported efforts by the Reagan administration to abolish the OJJDP.

Meanwhile a panel of ten scholars and lawyers recommended in August that state legislatures adopt fixed penalties for juveniles convicted of crimes. The recommendation followed a two-year, $1 million study that was financed by the OJJDP. Under the plan, punishment would be determined by a point system that would consider the seriousness of the offense as well as the age and background of the offender. Supporters of the proposal believe that the plan would end disparities in sentences administered to juvenile offenders. On the other hand, the plan's opponents express fear that it would lead to longer terms of incarceration generally and add to the burdens of already crowded juvenile correctional institutions.

MARK I. SOLER

International Law

The International Court of Justice at The Hague on June 27 found the United States guilty of violating international norms by supporting the "contra" rebels in Nicaragua. The 15-judge panel, known as the World Court, ordered Washington to halt the arming and training of the insurgents and to negotiate with the Sandinista government appropriate reparations for damages caused by the attacks. The United States rejected the jurisdiction of the court and the validity of its judgments on 15 specific counts, maintaining that U.S. actions in Central America were "entirely consistent with international law."

Nicaragua had brought the case to the judicial arm of the United Nations in 1984, after disclosures that the U.S. Central Intelligence Agency (CIA) had directed the mining of its ports. Three days before the filing, however, Washington announced that it was temporarily withdrawing from World Court jurisdiction over cases involving Central America. It claimed that U.S. actions were based on "collective self-defense" against Nicaraguan backing of leftist guerrillas in the region. The court reaffirmed its jurisdiction in the case, and in January 1985 the United States announced that it would boycott the proceedings. Then in October 1985, Washington declared that it was ending its acceptance of the World Court's compulsory jurisdiction in all political cases.

In its 142-page majority opinion—from which the U.S., British, and Japanese judges generally dissented—the court dismissed the American arguments, holding that U.S. training, arming, and financing of the rebels, as well as its overflights and trade embargo against Nicaragua, all were violations of treaty obligations or customary international law. The court, however, has no enforcement power, even for mandatory judgments, beyond those the UN Security Council might provide. Twice during the year the United States vetoed Nicaraguan resolutions in the UN Security Council calling on the United States to abide by the court decision. On November 3 a similar resolution was adopted by the General Assembly (94 to 3, with 47 abstentions), but Assembly resolutions are not binding. Also during the year Nicaragua brought its claim for $370 million in damages before U.S. courts. And in a separate case, brought before the World Court on July 28, Nicaragua charged that rebel attacks from Costa Rica and Honduras obliged those countries to pay reparations and prevent the contras from using such sanctuaries.

In a landmark but largely symbolic action, the U.S. Senate on February 19 voted, 83-11, to ratify the UN International Convention on the Prevention and Punishment of the Crime of Genocide. President Harry Truman had signed the pact in 1948, and 96 other countries had ratified it, but the treaty had remained mired in the Senate for nearly 37 years. It was finally presented for a floor vote after the addition of "reservation" amendments that curbed the jurisdiction of the World Court in cases involving the United States.

A panel of five World Court judges, considering a border dispute between the African nations of Burkina Faso and Mali, issued a temporary restraining order in January 1986 demanding that both sides halt their skirmishing. The panel heard oral arguments in June.

In another legal dispute involving the United States, the Reagan administration announced on March 7 that it was ordering the Soviet Union to reduce its UN Mission staff in New York from 275 to a maximum of 170, in stages, by April 1988. The reason, said Washington, was to cut down on "wrongful acts" by Soviet personnel, "including espionage." Soviet officials challenged the legality of the order under the 1946 Headquarters Agreement, which governs relations between the UN and its host country, arguing that the Americans had no right to determine unilaterally what size mission is appropriate. UN officials disputed the legality of the unilateral U.S. action but urged an amicable settlement through negotiations. In September, just before the first required cutback to 218, Washington submitted a list of 25 specific individuals who must leave the country. The deadline was extended until mid-October, but when no agreement was reached at the U.S.-Soviet mini-summit in Reykjavik, Iceland, the Soviets were forced to leave. A series of diplomatic expulsions by both sides followed in quick succession.

More successful international negotiation followed the nuclear accident that released a huge radiation cloud from the Chernobyl nuclear power station in the Ukraine on April 26. Just five months later, 94 members of the International Atomic Energy Agency, meeting in Vienna, approved international conventions requiring nations to inform each other immediately of a nuclear accident if radiation is released across borders, and to help any country in which such a disaster takes place. The pact on early notification was signed by 51 states and went into force on October 27.

In other developments, governments agreed to extend the Convention on the Law of Treaties to those international instruments to which one or more international organizations (such as the UN) is a party. The International Law Commission reached agreement on the text of a treaty to ensure the sanctity of diplomatic pouches and couriers. And on September 5 a preparatory commission drawing up rules for deep-seabed mining under the Law of the Sea (LOS) Treaty achieved a breakthrough agreement on procedures under which investors will be able to file for undersea mining sites.

MICHAEL J. BERLIN, *"The Washington Post"*

AP/Wide World

Sectarian violence continued to plague Lebanon. Car bombings struck densely populated areas of Beirut in late July.

LEBANON

During 1986 Lebanon remained a major stage for the playing out of the Arab-Israeli conflict; it was also the springboard for state-sponsored terrorism operating with impunity on Lebanese soil. Domestically, President Amin Gemayel gained support as he defied Syria by rejecting the Tripartite Agreement of Dec. 28, 1985. He also received overwhelming Arab support abroad. Lebanon suffered economically as the value of its currency declined sharply.

Domestic Political Developments. The rejection of the Tripartite Agreement of Dec. 28, 1985—an accord between leaders of Lebanon's major rival militia forces designed to end years of fighting—by President Gemayel in mid-January 1986 was the first step in a course that eventually bolstered the Lebanese president. Because the Tripartite Agreement would have eliminated the independent role of the Lebanese army in favor of the Syrian army, President Gemayel was backed in his stand by the Lebanese army. He also visited Arab states— Morocco in February, Tunisia in May, and the United Arab Emirates, Bahrain, Oman, Kuwait, and Qatar in June 1986. President Hosni Mubarak of Egypt publically supported the Lebanese president and called for a "hands-off Lebanon" policy, which clearly implied the withdrawal of all non-Lebanese forces, including the Syrian troops, from Lebanese territories.

As legitimate Lebanese authority, as represented by the presidency, has grown stronger, Syrian policy toward Lebanon has become more aggressive and conflictive. Syria has put pressure on Lebanese Prime Minister Rashid Karami and other cabinet members to boycott the president. A series of car bombings in East Beirut and West Beirut occurred in late July, creating a climate of distrust when Gemayel was on the verge of announcing, on August 1, a new initiative with respect to national reconciliation and political reform.

Syrian President Hafez-al Assad had already taken advantage of the secret U.S. arms shipments to Iran and conciliatory U.S. overtures to Syria (a visit by the director of the Central Intelligence Agency, for instance) to expand the deployment of Syrian troops. He dispatched troops on July 4 ostensibly to mediate the armed conflict between the Shiite Muslim movement called Amal and the Palestine Liberation Organization (PLO) in West Beirut. In fact, however, this move was part and parcel of Assad's objective of returning to areas of Lebanon from which his forces had been expelled during the period 1978–82.

Fitting, perhaps, in this context was the abortive attempt by Elie Hobeika, former commander of the Christian militia, called the Lebanese Forces, who has worked closely with the Syrians since his ouster from his post on Jan. 15, 1986, to storm East Beirut on Sept. 27, 1986, and occupy the main radio-broadcasting station. Syria had hoped that, had Hobeika's raid been successful, it would then be asked to deploy its troops in East Beirut.

While mediators were trying (beginning in December 1986) to arrange a meeting between Presidents Assad and Gemayel, one of the leading critics of the Syrian role in Lebanon,

321

Daoud Daoud, the leader of the Shiite Amal militia in southern Lebanon, declared in May that there was no possibility of a security agreement with Israel. Yet, in the tangle of Middle East affairs, the Amal also was at odds with Yasir Arafat's Palestine Liberation Organization.

AP/Wide World

former President Camille Chamoun, was the target of an unsuccessful assassination by means of a car bomb on Jan. 7, 1987. It appeared that Syria, contrary to some views, was little inclined to resolving the conflict in Lebanon—let alone to leaving the country.

The Amal-PLO Conflict. There has long been tension between the Palestinians in Lebanon and the Shiite Amal movement. But the conflict between them during May and June 1986, which was confined to Beirut, and the more violent clashes beginning in October, which included the Palestinian camps in southern Lebanon, were prompted by Syria and Yasir Arafat's Palestine Liberation Organization (PLO).

Syria's objectives in fomenting this conflict are basically threefold. First, the factor of timing: the outbreak in May was related to the discovery of Syrian involvement in an attempt to blow up an Israeli El Al airliner en route from London to Tel Aviv on April 17, which led Britain to break off diplomatic relations with Syria on Oct. 24, 1986. The second objective is to deter an Israeli attack, for the Amal-Palestinian camps war is meant to send the message to Israel that Syria is obligingly destroying potential PLO bases in Lebanon. Third, the continued conflict is in itself vital for Syria's dominant role, making it possible for Syria as well as Iran to use Lebanon as a base for terrorist operations.

It is clear, from the parties allowed by Syria to mediate between Amal and the Palestinians, that Assad has no intention of resolving this conflict. Libya has attempted to act as a mediator, but Libya cannot function in the role because one of the parties to the conflict, Amal,

accuses Libya of responsibility for the disappearance of its founder, Imam Musa al-Sadr, while on a visit to Libya in 1978. The other would-be mediator has been Iran, which cannot play the role effectively either, because Iran supports Amal's rival among the Shiites of Lebanon, the Party of God (*Hizballah*).

In addition, the other party to the conflict—the PLO—is viewed with disdain by the Iranians on ideological grounds as well as because the PLO's leader Arafat has his headquarters in Iraq, the archenemy of Iran. The PLO's principal interest in fighting Amal, and in safeguarding its camps in Beirut and southern Lebanon, is to increase its options. PLO guerrillas were expelled from Jordan and Tunisia in 1986 and have bases only in Iraq and North Yemen.

Terrorism and Western Hostages. Terrorism again loomed large in 1986. With respect to Western hostages, it became obvious that the organizations in Lebanon—such as the Islamic Jihad Organization and Revolutionary Justice Organization and even the Palestinian Fath-Revolutionary Council (the Abu Nidal organization)—that have been engaged in kidnapping citizens of the United States, France, and Britain have the parameters of their actions determined by either Syria or Iran or by both.

The claim that Syria and Iran have no role in taking hostages has been perpetuated, but various deals—in particular the selling of U.S. arms to Iran—have shown the hollowness of such a claim. Two U.S. hostages, the Rev. Lawrence Jenco and David Jacobsen, were released on July 26 and November 2, respectively, after seven secret arms shipments were sent to Iran between November 1985 and October 1986. The Islamic Jihad Organization, which held these hostages, is the covert arm of the pro-Iranian *Hizballah,* which has its headquarters in the Syrian-controlled regions of Lebanon. In other words, these organizations operate in Lebanon under Syrian sufferance (which is not surprising, since Iran has no common borders with Lebanon, and only through Syrian acquiescence can Iran exert influence over these organizations). Syria is Iran's major ally, while Syria without Iran would be less effective in influencing the Persian Gulf states, which fear Iranian expansionism.

Thus, militant Shiite organizations such as *Hizballah* in its various forms serve the interests of both Iran and Syria in covert activities. Terrorism in Lebanon, in particular the taking of Western hostages, has been encouraged and sponsored by states such as Iran and Syria, which have utilized it since 1983 to achieve such foreign policy objectives as driving Western powers from Lebanon. Syria and Iran, through Lebanese surrogates, have capitalized on terrorism to change the policies of France with respect to giving refuge to Iranian opposition leaders and providing support for the Lebanese state. Attacks in 1986 on the French contingent of the UN peacekeeping forces in southern Lebanon had the same goals. On the other hand, the release of five French citizens by the Revolutionary Justice Organization (two on June 20, two on November 10, and one on December 24) resulted in a change in French policy with respect to both Iran's and Syria's roles in Lebanon.

There were, however, four Frenchmen still in captivity and five Americans still in captivity at the end of 1986 (two Americans, Terry Anderson and Thomas Sutherland, were kidnapped on March 16 and June 9, 1985, respectively; three were kidnapped after six shipments of U.S. arms had been sent to Iran —Frank Reed, kidnapped on Sept. 9; Joseph Cicippio, on Sept. 12; and Edwin Tracy, on Oct. 21, 1986). This fact shows clearly that U.S. and French policies in dealing with Iran and Syria are counterproductive, as they have led to additional kidnappings and have given the impression that terrorism works in the interest of those who practice state-sponsored terrorism.

Unfortunately, Lebanon has been victimized by a small number of militants working with Syria, Iran, and Libya (two Britons and one American were executed in Lebanon on April 17, 1986, in reaction to the U.S. military raid on Libya on April 15) to keep the country in a state of conflict. This enables them to engage in terrorism with impunity. Only the pacification of Lebanon and the withdrawal of Syrian troops and the Iranian Revolutionary Guard, which has been the backbone of *Hizballah,* would drastically reduce the covert terrorist operations of both the *Hizballah* and the Abu Nidal militant organizations.

AP/Wide World

Police guard the American University of Beirut, which considered closing unless security conditions improve.

Economy. Because of the continued state of conflict and the political uncertainty that engulfs the country, the value of the Lebanese pound declined to 86 pounds per U.S. dollar by the end of December 1986. This represented less than one fourth of the pound's value in December 1985 (18.4 pounds per U.S. dollar). Lebanon relies heavily on imports and trade; consequently, it faces tremendous hardships from the plummeting pound—compounded by skyrocketing inflation and massive unemployment.

MARIUS DEEB, *Georgetown University*

LEBANON • Information Highlights

Official Name: Republic of Lebanon.
Location: Southwest Asia.
Area: 4,000 sq mi (10 360 km²).
Population (mid-1986 est.): 2,700,000.
Chief Cities (1980 est.): Beirut, the capital, 702,000; Tripoli, 175,000.
Government: *Head of state,* Amin Gemayel, president (took office Sept. 1982). *Head of government,* Rashid Karami, prime minister (took office May 1984). *Legislature* (unicameral)—National Assembly.
Monetary Unit: Lebanese pound (86.000 pounds equal U.S.$1, Dec. 31, 1986).
Foreign Trade (1984 U.S.$): *Imports,* $2,700,000,000; *exports,* $595,000,000.

LIBRARIES

Budget reductions and access to government information were two areas of prime concern to American librarians in 1986. The release in July of the report of the Attorney General's Commission on Pornography also was of interest to librarians. (*See* special report, page 317.)

Librarians were pleased in April when the U.S. Congress failed to go along with Reagan administration plans to cut back federal funds for libraries. Nevertheless the 1985 Gramm-Rudman-Hollings balanced budget act hit hard at libraries, especially the Library of Congress. Several persons were evicted from the Library of Congress for staging a sit-down to protest shorter library hours brought about by financial restrictions. A Federal District Court later ruled that the library acted wrongly when it evicted the protesters. On the state level, library budgets generally fared according to the economy of the state.

The 1966 Freedom of Information Act (FOIA) frees government records and materials to public scrutiny. Librarians have championed the act and opposed efforts to curtail it. In 1986 attention was centered on Circular-A 130, which was written by the Office of Management and Budget (OMB) as a means of complying with the federal Paperwork Reduction Act. Librarians saw the measure as simply a means of curtailing access to government information and opposed it. They were particularly disturbed by the fact that in 1986 the U.S. State Department was answering only 30% of its FOIA requests. Meanwhile, the White House continued to push privatization, the turning over of government operations to private interests. In fact, the Government Printing Office was so busy putting out printing contracts with private concerns that it had to open a third satellite office in San Diego. Librarians consider privatization another threat to access to government information.

Buildings. The surge of new library construction and renovation noted in 1985 continued, as did a steady outlay for the removal of asbestos from older library buildings. New main libraries opened in Miami and Orlando, FL; Gasden and Birmingham, AL; Indianapolis, IN; and Pasadena, CA. A massive, statewide library building program was underway in Illinois. The $22.9 million Arthur S. Sackler Center for Health Communications, including a four-level library, was dedicated at Tufts University, and Harvard University's new automated book storage building was opened.

The Los Angeles Public Library was devastated in April, just as its Hollywood Branch was reopening after an earlier fire.

President Reagan signed legislation limiting the size and cost of presidential libraries (after his). The Carter Presidential Center, including the Jimmy Carter presidential library, in Atlanta was dedicated on October 1 (*see also* PEOPLE, PLACES, AND THINGS, page 78).

Preservation. Concern for the preservation of library materials gained momentum in 1986. State and regional preservation facilities were discussed. Hopes for mass deacidification of the millions of books now disintegrating on library shelves were set back when a pilot plant operated by the Library of Congress had to be blown up after it suffered unexplained fires and explosions. Nonacid paper in books is becoming more common, and a new paper pulping process was reported. The discovery raised hopes that permanent, nonacid paper could be made even more economically.

Programs. The appetite of public library patrons for videotapes continued unabated, with libraries reporting both collections and circulation growing by leaps and bounds. Libraries and librarians generally showed a new interest in serving rural and aged populations, providing legal and medical information to the public, and improving reference services.

Automation continued to spread rapidly, even to small libraries, now that microcomputer-based systems are both inexpensive and reliable. Rising telecommunications costs, however, spurred interest in alternatives to phone lines.

Associations. The American Library Association (ALA) held its 105th annual conference in New York City, June 28–July 3. Concern about the problems of government dominated the conference at which Regina Minudai, director of the Berkeley (CA) Public Library, took over as ALA president. A total of 1,094 delegates attended the 1986 conference of the Canadian Library Association (CLA) in Quebec City June 19–24. "Information—People Still Count" was the conference's theme. Ken Jensen of the Regina (Sask.) Public Library was inaugurated as CLA's president for the forthcoming year.

KARL NYREN, *"Library Journal"*

LIBRARY AWARDS OF 1986

Beta Phi Mu Award for distinguished service to education for librarianship: Agnes Lytton Reagan, retired professor of library science, University of Texas-Austin

Randolph J. Caldecott Medal for the most distinguished picture book for children: Chris Van Allsburg, *The Polar Express*

Melvil Dewey Award for recent creative professional achievement of a high order: Richard De Gennaro, director of libraries, University of Pennsylvania

Grolier Foundation Award for unusual contribution to the stimulation and guidance of reading by children and young people: Isabel Schon, professor of library science, Arizona State University

Joseph W. Lippincott Award for distinguished service to the profession of librarianship: Elizabeth W. Stone, dean emeritus, School of Library and Information Sciences, Catholic University

John Newbery Medal for the most distinguished contribution to literature for children: Patricia MacLachlan, *Sarah, Plain and Tall*

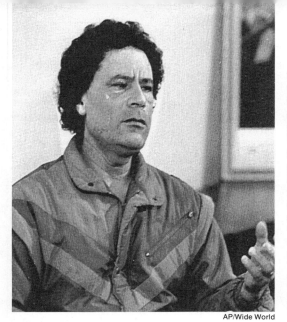

AP/Wide World

Rarely seen publicly after the U.S. bombing in April, Libya's Muammar Qaddafi returned to the limelight on September 1 to mark the 17th anniversary of his coming to power.

LIBYA

Allegations by the United States that Libya sponsored terrorist attacks on American citizens precipitated the most serious confrontations between the two countries since Muammar el-Qaddafi came to power in 1969. The 1986 crisis escalated from sanctions to military action, with the United States gaining little support for its actions from its allies. The confrontation overshadowed other important matters, including economic problems and diplomatic realignments.

Economic and Political Sanctions. The year opened with the United States alleging that Libya had aided terrorists under the command of a shadowy figure, Abu Nidal, to carry out attacks at the Rome and Vienna airports on Dec. 27, 1985—a charge Libya denied. The Reagan administration's tough public stand on terrorism spawned rumors of an impending U.S. military foray against Libya. But in light of the impossibility of locating those responsible for the outrages, and fearful that an attack would jeopardize the safety of Americans living in Libya, U.S. officials decided instead to impose a series of sanctions on the Qaddafi regime.

In an Executive Order issued January 7, President Ronald Reagan prohibited virtually all trade between Libya and the United States and ordered the approximately 1,500 Americans in Libya to leave by the end of the month. On the following day, he ordered Libyan government assets in the United States, estimated at some $2.5 billion, frozen. The president also appealed to Western European governments and Japan to join the United States in isolating Libya.

Reaction in foreign capitals was generally unfavorable. Few European leaders believed the sanctions would curb international terrorism, but concern that they might cause greater economic hardships in their own countries than in Libya also diminished enthusiasm for them. U.S. restrictions on trade with Libya had already reduced economic ties between the two countries to a minimum. As recently as 1984, however, members of the European Community had imported some $6 billion of Libyan oil and natural gas, while exporting some $4 billion of merchandise to Libya. Thus, sanctions would fall more heavily on the Europeans than on American businessmen. Despite its efforts to create a united front against Libya, the United States was able to extract little more than a commitment that its allies would not undercut its efforts by taking over jobs and contracts vacated by Americans.

Hopes that sanctions would create economic hardships in the form of shortages for the general public and an inability, owing to the withdrawal of American technicians, to lift and market Libyan oil, failed to materialize. Indeed, the five American oil companies in Libya had argued that too hasty a departure would saddle them with excessive losses and present the Libyans with a billion-dollar windfall of equipment and other assets. In response, Washington modified its restrictions and allowed the companies to continue limited operations in Libya until the end of June.

Condemnations of the sanctions came from the Arab League and the Organization of the Islamic Conference, as well as from virtually every Arab state, China, and the Soviet Union. When aircraft from the U.S. Sixth Fleet began operating near Libya as part of a "war of nerves" designed to keep Qaddafi off balance regarding future American intentions, the USSR increased its naval forces in the Mediterranean in order to monitor more closely U.S. activities and provide intelligence to Libya.

Confrontation in the Gulf of Sidra. These U.S. naval maneuvers occurred without incident, but in late March American and Libyan forces clashed in the Gulf of Sidra. Libya's claim to this body of water had for some time been a matter of contention between the two nations. The United States maintained that only waters within 12 mi (19 km) of the coast could be construed as Libyan territorial waters. Libya, however, claimed that the entire gulf, up to a line drawn roughly across its mouth, was part of its internal waters. To underscore the American position, ships and planes from the Sixth Fleet frequently entered the gulf, and, in 1981, U.S. planes had shot down Libyan aircraft that had challenged them.

The American decision to send combat planes on training exercises over the Gulf of Sidra did not, therefore, represent a new policy. Since January, however, Qaddafi had warned the Sixth Fleet not to cross what he labeled "the line of death" marking the northern limits of Libyan claims. The size of the fleet assembled in late March—three aircraft carriers and 27 support vessels, constituting perhaps the largest U.S. flotilla since World War II—and the timing of the maneuvers, therefore, virtually ensured a confrontation. On March 24, coastal missile batteries fired on U.S. planes flying over Libyan-claimed waters. The aircraft sustained no damage, but in a series of counterattacks over the next two days American planes destroyed the missile base and sank two Libyan patrol boats said to be menacing American vessels.

As with the imposition of sanctions, the administration won strong public backing at home. Only a minority of Americans expressed concern that the United States had deliberately provoked the encounter, or deplored the ensuing resort to violence. Similarly, a few legislators observed that the president should have consulted with Congress, in accordance with the War Powers Act, before committing U.S. forces to what was almost certain to be a combat mission.

Overseas, reactions were less enthusiastic. Only Great Britain and Israel unequivocally endorsed the American actions, with most Western European states expressing varying degrees of dismay. Although all recognized the U.S. position regarding the Gulf of Sidra, many believed the World Court, or some other international forum, would have been a more appropriate scene for asserting it.

Condemnations came quickly from throughout the Arab world, although the Arab League declined a Libyan request to impose sanctions on the United States. The USSR, despite its criticisms of Washington, made no effort to encourage Libya or to provide it with additional weaponry. The administration apparently took the ambivalent response of the Europeans, the Arab League, and the Soviet Union as tacit indications that none was averse to Libya's being disciplined.

The Bombing of Tripoli and Benghazi. The widespread fear that the Libyan-U.S. confrontation would trigger reprisals was realized almost immediately. In the following week, a TWA jetliner exploded en route from Rome to Athens and a bomb went off in a West Berlin disco frequented by U.S. servicemen. American officials could establish no direct link between Libya and the TWA blast, but they did claim there was conclusive evidence tying Qaddafi and the Libyan People's Bureau (embassy) in East Berlin to the nightclub attack.

The United States began a concerted campaign, led by Gen. Vernon Walters, U.S. ambassador to the United Nations, to have its allies impose stiff sanctions on Libya. Walters visited Western European capitals to try to persuade leaders to do this and also to seek support for a possible U.S. military strike against Libya. European Community foreign ministers, meeting on April 14, agreed to restrict the number and limit the movements of Libyan diplomats, whom the United States accused of abetting terrorists. They declined, however, to accede to an American request to expel the Libyans altogether.

Early in the morning of April 15 (Libya time), U.S. Air Force F-111 bombers from bases in the United Kingdom and U.S. Navy A-6 bombers and A-7 and F-18 fighters from

U.S. Defense Secretary Weinberger points to a map while discussing the U.S.-Libya confrontation in the Gulf of Sidra.

AP/Wide World

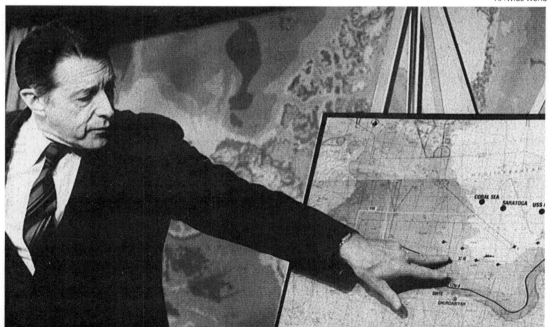

U.S. Ambassador Vernon Walters tells the UN Security Council that the U.S. bombing of Libya was an act of self-defense.

aircraft carriers in the Mediterranean conducted bombing raids on targets in Tripoli and Benghazi described as part of Libya's terrorist infrastructure. In addition to the intended targets, however, the attack also damaged residential neighborhoods. Estimates of casualties varied widely, but at least 20 Libyan civilians perished in the raid, as did two U.S. servicemen whose plane was lost.

Officially, the United States justified the raid as retaliation for the Berlin bombing. The administration continued to insist it could link that incident directly to Libya, but it refused, on security grounds, to make concrete evidence public. World reaction to the attack followed the pattern established by earlier Libyan-U.S. confrontations: very strong support from the American public; some reservations among members of Congress irritated that the president had consulted with them only after a decision on the bombing had already been made; and bitter criticism abroad.

In Europe, only Britain had cooperated in the raid. Other countries, notably France, had declined involvement and denied overflight rights to U.S. planes en route to or from Libya. The Soviet Union voiced strong criticisms, even though its forces in the Mediterranean had done nothing to warn the Libyans of the impending attack or to try to avert it. Throughout the Third World, and especially in Arab and Muslim countries, denunciations of the United States and Britain were rampant. The shooting of an American official in Sudan, the execution of two Britons and an American kidnapped in Lebanon, and the firebombing of a U.S. Marine compound in Tunis were all part of a wave of anti-American and anti-British violence following the attacks. More peaceful anti-American demonstrations occurred in many European cities.

The raid was seen in many countries as an American attempt to remove Qaddafi, either by killing him in the bombing or by instigating a general uprising against him in its wake. Expectations that the Libyan leader would be discredited backfired, however, and he emerged in many quarters with his prestige enhanced. In the Libyan army, which had long been a source of opposition to Qaddafi because of his attempts to supplant professional soldiers with a mass militia, and which some U.S. planners hoped would mutiny after the attack, the bombing generally instilled a spirit of solidarity and support for the regime.

After the raid the European Community implemented the stricter regulations concerning Libyan diplomats agreed to just before the bombing. Almost every Western European country ordered reductions in the size of Libyan People's Bureau staffs, and Britain expelled several hundred Libyan civilians undergoing technical training there. Libya, in turn, expelled a number of European workers. At the Tokyo summit of the major industrialized democracies in early May, the participants adopted a resolution condemning Libya as a sponsor of international terrorism, although the document fell short of imposing other sanctions sought by the United States.

The "Disinformation" Campaign. Qaddafi's public appearances after the bombing were limited, and he was reportedly badly shaken by the incident. During the summer, two U.S. aircraft carriers remained in the central Mediterranean, and, beginning in July, naval aircraft resumed flights near the Gulf of Sidra. The Reagan administration continued to accuse Libya of promoting terrorist attacks that, it suggested, might lead to additional military strikes. More subtly, American officials hinted that the United States might work to destabilize Qaddafi's government or help anti-Qaddafi exiles to do so. In August the *Wall Street Journal* described the two countries as on a "collision course." General Walters once again toured the European capitals promoting sanctions and calling on the allies to cut air traffic with Libya and embargo Libyan oil, but without success.

In October, however, an investigative report in the *Washington Post* revealed that American intelligence reports throughout the summer had indicated that Qaddafi had refrained from any involvement in terrorist plots. It further revealed that the administration had authorized the CIA to plant misleading stories in the foreign press (which U.S. papers learned of and assumed to be true) about American assessments of Libyan activities and probable American responses. The naval maneuvers, hints of covert activity, and General Walter's mission all gave credence to such reports. Washington hoped the stories would unsettle Qaddafi, perhaps leading him to do something that would justify another attack or perhaps generating enough popular discontent in Libya to spark a rebellion. While neither outcome resulted, the damage to the administration's credibility was severe.

Aftermath. By year's end it remained to be seen whether the U.S. approach to Libya had succeeded in curbing terrorism, but it was certain that relations with the allies and the Arab world had been strained. The American failure to produce incontrovertible evidence linking Libya to either the Rome and Vienna airport massacres or the Berlin disco bombing left other nations hesitant to take as hard a line as the United States. American allies were also reluctant to endorse proposed sanctions that would have had a major impact on their economies but would hardly have affected the United States, particularly since U.S. oil companies continued to profit from their Libyan oil companies until the end of June (and even later, after their wholly owned foreign subsidiaries took over).

Aircraft hijackings and other forms of terrorism did not end with the bombings of Tripoli and Benghazi. Indeed, the bombings triggered a spate of such incidents. The air raids may have been satisfying to many Americans who needed assurances that random terrorism would lead to some form of retribution, but the unwillingness of other nations to invoke the military option in other instances—as when autumn trials in Europe implicated Syria as a sponsor of terrorism—suggested that grave doubts about that form of retaliation persisted.

Other Developments. The Libyan-U.S. confrontation assumed such epic proportions that it eclipsed other important events, including some closely connected with it. Even before the imposition of economic sanctions, Libya was experiencing an economic crisis, attributable primarily to declining oil revenues. This resulted in severe shortages of consumer goods, but also underscored the potential liabilities of Libya's very substantial foreign debt. Such a situation played into the hands of the regime's opposition, which had been active both within the country and outside it.

Important shifts in Libyan relations with Arab and African states also took place during 1986. Sudan, one of Libya's most vocal critics until the overthrow of Jaafar al-Nemery in 1985, became a beneficiary of Libyan economic and military aid. In return for a commitment to prevent Libyan dissidents from operating freely in Sudan, Libya terminated its support for Sudanese opposition forces in the south and provided weapons to help government troops contain the rebellion there.

Agreements between Libya and others of its neighbors, however, fell on hard times. The unity accord with Morocco, in effect since 1984, floundered in the aftermath of Israeli Prime Minister Shimon Peres' visit to Morocco in July. After more than a month of Qaddafi's vehement denunciations of Morocco's King Hassan, the latter terminated the treaty in a move the Libyan government claimed was illegal and refused to acknowledge.

In the fall, the long-standing Libyan role in Chad also appeared to be weakening. Goukouni Oueddi, whom Libya had backed in Chad's civil war, fell out with Qaddafi and was arrested in Tripoli. Most of his troops joined the army of his former opponent, Hissein Habré, in an effort to drive the estimated 7,000 Libyan forces occupying northern Chad out of the country. Late in December fighting flared as Goukouni's guerrillas devastated a Libyan armored column after Libyans had bombed the guerrillas. The United States joined France in sending emergency military equipment to Chad.

KENNETH J. PERKINS
University of South Carolina

LIBYA • Information Highlights

Official Name: Socialist People's Libyan Arab Jamahiriya ("state of the masses").
Location: North Africa.
Area: 679,359 sq mi (1 759 540 km²).
Population (mid-1986 est.): 3,900,000.
Chief Cities (1980 est.): Tripoli, the capital, 1,223,000; Benghazi, 530,000.
Government: *Head of state,* Muammar el-Qaddafi (took office 1969). *Legislature*—General People's Congress (met initially Nov. 1976).
Monetary Unit: Dinar (0.296 dinar equals U.S. $1, Feb. 1986).
Gross Domestic Product (1985 est. U.S.$): $26,900,000,000.
Foreign Trade (1985 U.S.$): *Imports,* $7,000,000,000; *exports,* $10,841,000,000.

Wole Soyinka, a Nigerian best known for his plays and political activism, was the first African to be awarded the Nobel Prize for Literature.

J. Langevin/Sygma

LITERATURE

Without any discernible decline in the volume or quality of literary output—indeed with landmark works appearing in virtually every language, form, and tradition—attention in the world of letters seemed to focus more on institutions than on books themselves in 1986. The International PEN Congress was a clamorous affair that made front pages. The Swedish Academy made history by awarding the Nobel Prize for Literature to an African writer. And the United States designated its first official poet laureate.

PEN Congress. The 48th annual International PEN Congress, held in New York City from January 12 to 17, was the largest—and loudest—in the organization's history. (Founded in 1921, PEN is a worldwide organization of some 10,000 novelists, poets, playwrights, essayists, and editors.) Its 1986 conference, attended by some 800 members from more than 45 countries, was to address a plainly political theme: "The Writer's Imagination and the Imagination of the State." The controversy developed when novelist Norman Mailer, the congress chairman and president of American PEN, invited U.S. Secretary of State George Shultz to deliver the conference's opening address. The invitation, made without notification to the PEN board of directors, set off a shrill and indignant protest. In speeches, published articles, a signed petition, and impromptu debates, scores of attendees decried the appearance of any government official—especially an American one—at the gathering. Other PEN members responded vigorously to the attacks on U.S. policy. Then, in a separate issue raised during the final sessions, a caucus of women members protested the small number of females on the congress' panels—a charge that set off more heated debate. All in all, the proceedings proved as plainly political as the designated theme.

Nobelist. Wole Soyinka, the 52-year-old Nigerian playwright, poet, novelist, and political polemicist, became the first African writer in the 85-year history of the award to win the Nobel Prize for Literature. Soyinka, according to the Swedish Academy, "in a wide cultural perspective and with poetical overtones fashions the drama of existence." A member of the Yoruba tribe—whose spirits and myths appear in many of his writings—Soyinka was educated in England and, after his return to Nigeria in 1960, was imprisoned several times—once for 22 months—for alleged political subversion. He writes in English, and his many works include the childhood memoir *Aké: The Years of Childhood* (1981), the prison memoir *The Man Died* (1972), and such plays as *Dance of the Forests* (1960), *Kongi's Harvest* (1965), and *Death and the King's Horsemen* (1975).

U.S. Poet Laureate. Filling a position created by an act of Congress in 1985, 80-year-old Robert Penn Warren was named the first official U.S. poet laureate in February 1986. Librarian of Congress Daniel J. Boorstin, who made the selection, cited Warren for "his feelings for the promise and the frustrations of American life" and for depicting in his work "the comic, the violent, and the tawdry as well as the great and heroic." The Kentucky-born author has won the Pulitzer Prize three times —once for fiction (*All the King's Men,* 1947) and twice for poetry (*Promises,* 1957; *Now and Then,* 1979). His most recent collection is titled *New and Selected Poems, 1923–1985.* In his new (part-time) role as poet laureate, which he officially began in October 1986, Warren's chief responsibilities are to deliver a lecture and a public reading each year, to advise the Library of Congress on its literary programs, and to recommend the new poets recorded in the Library of Congress archive.

American Literature

The works of an emerging group of American writers—including Ann Beattie, Raymond Carver, Frederick Barthelme, David Leavitt, Bobbie Ann Mason, and others—have given rise to a lively debate among literary critics. Their ironic, sometimes cryptic tales, which brilliantly capture the rootlessness and idosyncracies of modern life, have been acclaimed both for their vitality and their technical virtuosity. Yet a number of critics in 1986 began to complain that American literature was becoming too spare, understated, and minimalistic. Madison Bell's article in *Harper's* magazine, "Less is Less: The Diminishing Short Story," attacked several of these emerging authors for their short, elliptical, and acutely but narrowly observed stories. Michiko Kakutani and Ben Yagoda in *The New York Times Book Review* and Jack Killey in *The Nation* voiced similar criticisms. And Sven Birkerts in *The New Republic* particularly cited the teacher and editor Gordon Lish for creating a school of writing in which "disembodied characters . . . move about in a generic sort of present."

Short Stories. The excitement and controversy that short stories continue to generate in American literature was confirmed by the attention paid to *20 under 30: Best Stories by America's New Young Writers,* an anthology edited by Debra Sparks. Whatever the objections of some critics, the writers represented in the collection seemed accomplished beyond their years. Some, like Leavitt, Lorrie Moore, and Susan Minot, had highly praised first novels appear in 1986 (*see* list, page 333). Jesse Lee Kercheval won the Associated Writing Program Award for her own short-story collection.

Another charge against contemporary American literature, that authors are unaware of the political complexities of other countries, was contradicted by a number of works. Peter Meinke's Flannery O'Connor Award-winning collection of stories, *The Piano Tuner,* deals with the sad ironies of life in Africa and Poland, and Norman Rush's moving first book, *Whites,* is about the daily misunderstandings between the races in Africa. (Among novels, Denis Johnson's tragic *The Stars at Noon* eloquently expresses the anguish of Central America.)

Another criticism is that contemporary writing is dominated by depictions of the aimless lives of urban semi-sophisticates. But successful works dealing with these themes, such as Beattie's *Where You'll Find Me* and Tama Janowitz's *Slaves of New York,* represented but one of the many strands of fiction about city life. Hubert Selby's *Song of the Silent Show* presents a more dangerous urban vision, while Harvey Swados' *Nights in the Garden of Brooklyn* presents a warmer view.

But all of America still contributes to the literary landscape. The poet Tess Gallagher's first fiction collection, *The Lover of Horses,* centers on the dramas of small-town life. Russel Banks' *Success Stories* takes place mainly in Florida. Ellen Gilchrist's *Drunk With Love* ranges from New Orleans to California. Thomas McGuane's *To Skin a Cat* shows his love of the West, and Mary Ward Brown's *Tongues of Flame* explores racial relations in the South.

Novels. Southern writers continued to make a major contribution to American literature. Once dominated by William Faulkner and the various modes of Southern Gothic, today's Southern novelists are not so easily categorized.

Reynolds Price's *Kate Vaiden* concerns the way in which each generation must suffer for the sins of its forebears. Kate Vaiden's unhappy mother was killed by Kate's father, who then committed suicide. Kate must carve out a life of her own, but to do so she abandons her own child. But Kate's story is of survival, not destruction, and Price seems to imply that Kate's unnatural act might break a tragic cycle.

In *A Summons to Memphis,* his first novel since *A Woman of Means* in 1950, master storyteller Peter Taylor also writes of the traditional South. His knowledge of cultural nuance and the significance of lives held together by manners lets us understand the constrictions which informed that world.

Michael Malone's *Handling Sin* presents a South as raucous as Peter Taylor's is genteel. Malone's novel tells of a man's wild journey from North Carolina to New Orleans in search of his eccentric father. The Don Quixote-like protagonist runs into characters who, bizarre as they are, seem genuine parts of the Southern landscape. But under the wild comedy and the outrageous literary allusions, Malone slyly raises serious moral issues. Even more episodic is T.R. Pearson's *Off For the Sweet Hereafter,* which is reminiscent of Mark Twain's grotesquely funny and simultaneously sad stories of odd characters and accidents.

In Mary Lee Settle's *Celebration,* the respected author of the Beulah Quintet leaves the South for London, where her heroine becomes involved in a strange world of international exiles, expatriates, eccentrics, and spies, many of whom have their own complex stories.

Perhaps the most controversial novel of the year was Ernest Hemingway's *The Garden of Eden.* Hemingway began the book in 1946 and wrestled with it up to the time of his death in 1961, producing a number of incomplete manuscripts. This version, edited by Tom Jenks, contains one third of the original material. The story of a man's relationship to two women, it explores the definitions and boundaries of sexual identity in a way not usually associated with Hemingway. The controversy, however, lies not in the subject matter, but in the ethics of publishing an author's unfinished work.

John Updike's *Roger's Version* elusively echoes Hawthorne's *The Scarlet Letter* in the story of a chillingly uncharitable theologian who fantasizes about his wife's affair with a sincerely religious young man who believes he can prove the existence of God by computer calculations.

Donald Barthelme takes up the problem of human happiness with paradox and wit in *Paradise*. An architect, finding himself living with three lingerie models, discovers that the stereotypes of fantasy are as inescapable as they are unfulfilling. Although Barthelme playfully fragments the conventional forms of fiction, he ponders the same moral issues addressed by our most serious writers.

Poetry. The importance of poetry in American life was recognized by Robert Penn Warren's appointment as the nation's first poet laureate. The many fine books of poetry appearing in 1986 reflected a healthy diversity of styles and subject matter.

Mary Swander's *Driving the Body Back* seemed to signal a resurgence of interest in narrative poetry. The nine eloquently simple poems tell, through the voices of the people involved, tales of the lives and deaths of several generations of an American farm family. Ai's *Sin* also avoids the autobiographical mode that has tended to dominate lyric poetry. The author speaks in the first person, but through it becomes different persons, including Jack Kennedy and Joseph McCarthy.

Christianne Balk's *Bindweed* is a moving sequence of ten sonnets that are both the history of a beautiful relationship and an elegy for a gifted man who died too young. Balk's vivid pictures of Alaskan life are drawn in language

John Updike, above, *produced his twelfth novel, "Roger's Version," which examines the mysteries and intricacies of religious faith, passion and sensuality, and modern science and mathematics. Robert Penn Warren, below, the 80-year-old three-time Pulitzer Prize winner, was named the first official poet laureate of the United States.*

© George W. Mellor

David Eisenhower completed an in-depth history of his grandfather's role as supreme commander of the Allied forces in Europe, "Eisenhower: At War 1943–1945."

both natural and precise. In "The Kitchen Shears Speak," for example, she harks back to Anglo-Saxon riddles, but without a trace of literary preciosity.

Brad Leithauser, on the other hand, is unashamedly artful. In *Cats of the Temple,* he plays language, image, and form against one another in ways that are both delightful and resonant. His poems, too, often have a story line, as in "Two Incidents On and Off Guam," which describes watching a helicopter save two people from drowning.

Poetry is by no means losing its highly personal voice. Marilyn Hacker's *Love, Death, and the Changing of the Seasons* tells, in a series of intimate sonnets, of a year of obsessive love. Kenneth Koch's *On the Edge* consists of two long pieces, the elusive autobiographical title poem and "Impressions of Africa," which creates vivid images of experiences in such diverse countries as Madagascar, Zaire, Senegal, and Kenya.

The most elaborate narrative poem of the year was Vikram Seth's *The Golden Gate,* an entire novel in verse, deploying the complex stanza form of Pushkin's *Eugene Onegin* to satirize life in contemporary California.

Robert Bly's *Selected Poems* draws from his work since the late 1940s. The brief introductions to each section comprise both a spiritual autobiography and a kind of history of almost 40 years of American poetic impulse. Perhaps prophetic is his final essay, "The Prose Poem as an Evolving Form," in which he reflects on Baudelaire's prediction that the prose poem would be the major form of the 20th century. With short stories getting shorter and more poetic, and poems getting longer and more narrative, the prose poem, although it has, as Bly points out, no formal standards, may yet have its day.

The life achievement of the New York poet Edwin Denby, who died in 1983, is recognized in *The Complete Poems,* edited by the poet Ron Padgett. Denby's attention to rhyme and form, rather than self-revelatory confessions, and his gentle ironies and wittily observant images never brought him enormous fame; yet his poetry wears well and might even outlast more fashionable contemporaries.

History and Biography. Several interesting literary biographies appeared in 1986. Arnold Rampersad's *The Life of Langston Hughes, 1902–1941: I, Too, Sing America* and Richard Lingeman's *Theodore Dreiser: At the Gates of the City, 1871–1907* are the first volumes of what will be major studies of the two authors. Dorothy Herrmann's *S.J. Perelman: A Life* reveals the cantankerous side of the humorist. Michael Reynolds' *The Young Hemingway* is a particularly perceptive account of the writer's formative years.

But the most important biography of 1986 is about a relatively unknown figure. Theodore Rosengarten, winner of the 1974 National Book Award for *All God's Dangers: The Life of Nate Shaw,* turned his attention in *Tombee: Portrait of a Cotton Planter* to the inner life of a white Southern slave holder, Thomas B. Chaplin, whose journal is included in the volume.

The approaching bicentennial of the U.S. Constitution began to precipitate books on the period. Michael Kammen's *A Machine That Would Go of Itself: The Constitution in American Culture* concentrates on legal and philosophical issues. Henry Mayer's *A Son of Thunder: Patrick Henry and the American Republic* focuses on a colorful and important personality of the era.

Two beautifully written books dealt with vanishing ways of life. Peter Matthiessen's *Men's Lives* tells of a community of Long Island fishermen whose life-style is being destroyed by urbanization. Barry Lopez's *Arctic Dreams* describes the Eskimos who see their icy surrounding not as a hostile force but as a refuge and home. In their depiction of man's complex and tragic relationship to nature, these works represent the enduring concerns of the best American literature and art.

JEROME STERN, *Florida State University*

AMERICAN LITERATURE: MAJOR WORKS | 1986

NOVELS

Atlas, James, *The Great Pretender*
Auchincloss, Louis, *Diary of a Yuppie*
Barthelme, Donald, *Paradise*
Breslin, Jimmy, *Table Money*
Calisher, Hortense, *The Bobby-Soxer*
Clark, Eleanor, *Camping Out*
Conroy, Pat, *The Prince of Tides*
De Vries, Peter, *Peckham's Marbles*
Erdrich, Louise, *The Beet Queen*
Ford, Richard, *The Sportswriter*
Gardner, John, *Stillness and Shadows*
Gold, Herbert, *A Girl of Forty*
Hemingway, Ernest, *The Garden of Eden*
Hoagland, Edward, *Seven Rivers West*
Howard, Maureen, *Expensive Habits*
Kinsella, W. P., *The Iowa Baseball Confederacy*
Knowles, John, *The Private Life of Axie Reed*
Leavitt, David, *The Lost Language of Cranes*
Leggett, John, *Making Believe*
Major, Clarence, *My Amputations*
Malone, Michael, *Handling Sin*
Merkin, Daphne, *Enchantment*
Miller, Sue, *The Good Mother*
Minot, Susan, *Monkeys*
Moore, Lorrie, *Anagrams*
Oates, Joyce Carol, *Marya: A Life*
Pearson, T. R., *Off For the Sweet Hereafter*
Price, Reynolds, *Kate Vaiden*
Purdy, James, *In the Hollow of His Hand*
Reed, Ishmael, *Reckless Eyeballing*
See, Carolyn, *Golden Days*
Settle, Mary Lee, *Celebration*
Spencer, Scott, *Waking the Dead*
Stone, Robert, *Children of Light*
Taylor, Peter, *A Summons to Memphis*
Theroux, Paul, *O-Zone*
Updike, John, *Roger's Version*
Wolff, Geoffrey, *Providence*
Wolitzer, Meg, *Hidden Pictures*
Yates, Richard, *Cold Spring Harbor*

SHORT STORIES

Abbott, Lee K., *Love is the Crooked Thing*
Banks, Russell, *Success Stories*
Beattie, Ann, *Where You'll Find Me*
Brown, Mary Ward, *Tongues of Flame*
Cameron, Peter, *One Way or Another*
Gallagher, Tess, *The Lover of Horses*
Gilchrist, Ellen, *Drunk With Love*
Gold, Herbert, *Lovers & Cohorts*
Haake, Katharine, *No Reason on Earth*
Janowitz, Tama, *Slaves of New York*
Johnson, Charles, *The Sorcerer's Apprentice*
Kavaler, Rebecca, *Tigers in the Wood*
Kesey, Ken, *Demon Box*
McGuane, Thomas, *To Skin a Cat*
Meinke, Peter, *The Piano Tuner*
Munro, Alice, *The Progress of Love*
Oates, Joyce Carol, *Raven's Way*
Petesch, Natalie L. M., *Wild With All Regret*
Rush, Norman, *Whites*
Selby, Hubert, Jr., *Song of the Silent Snow*
Spark, Debra, ed., *20 Under 30*
Swados, Harvey, *Nights in the Gardens of Brooklyn*
West, Jessamyn, *Collected Stories of Jessamyn West*

POETRY

Ai, *Sin*
Allman, John, *Scenarios For A Mixed Landscape*
Axinn, Donald Everett, *Against Gravity: Poems 1982–85*
Balk, Christianne, *Bindweed*
Berg, Stephen, *In It*
Bly, Robert, *Selected Poems*
Booth, Philip, *Relations: Selected Poems 1950–1985*
Brodsky, Joseph, *Less Than One*
Carver, Raymond, *Ultramarine*
Creeley, Robert, *Memory Gardens*
Denby, Edwin, *The Complete Poems*, ed. Ron Padgett
Digges, Deborah, *Vesper Sparrows*
Dubie, Norman, *The Springhouse*
Feldman, Irving, *All Of Us Here*
Fulton, Alice, *Palladium*
Ginsberg, Allen, *White Shroud: Poems 1980–1985*
Goldbarth, Albert, *Arts & Sciences*

Hacker, Marilyn, *Love, Death, and the Changing of the Seasons*
Hall, Donald, *The Happy Man*
Haxton, Brooks, *Dominion*
Hirsch, Edward, *Wild Gratitude*
Ignatow, David, *New and Collected Poems 1970–1985*
Koch, Kenneth, *On The Edge*
Laughlin, James, *Selected Poems, 1935–1985*
Morris, Herbert, *Dream Palace*
Oliver, Mary, *Dream Work*
Seth, Vikram, *The Golden Gate*
Spires, Elizabeth, *Swan's Island*

CRITICISM AND CULTURE

Barrett, William, *Death of the Soul: From Descartes to the Computer*
Bloom, Alexander, *Prodigal Sons: The New York Intellectuals and Their World*
Braudy, Leo, *The Frenzy of Renown: Fame & Its History*
Bruner, Jerome, *Actual Minds, Possible Worlds*
Burroughs, William S., *The Adding Machine: Collected Essays*
Charyn, Jerome, *Metropolis: New York as Myth, Marketplace, and Magical Land*
Dworkin, Ronald, *Law's Empire*
Ellison, Ralph, *Going to The Territory*
FitzGerald, Frances, *Cities on a Hill: A Journey Through Contemporary American Cultures*
Guralnick, Peter, *Sweet Soul Music: Rhythm and Blues and the Southern Dream of Freedom*
Howe, Irving, *The American Newness: Culture and Politics in the Age of Emerson*
Krupnick, Mark, *Lionel Trilling and the Fate of Cultural Criticism*
Lopez, Barry, *Arctic Dreams: Imagination and Desire in a Northern Landscape*
Matthiessen, Peter, *Men's Lives: The Surfmen and Baymen of the South Fork*
Ostriker, Alicia Suskin, *Stealing the Language: The Emergence of Women's Poetry in America*
Podhoretz, Norman, *The Bloody Crossroads: Where Literature and Politics Meet*
Simpson, Louis, *The Character of the Poet*
Stevens, Ralph, ed., *The Correspondence of Flannery O'Connor and the Brainard Cheneys*
Wilson, Edmund, *The Fifties,* ed. Leon Edel
Wolff, Cynthia Griffin, *Emily Dickinson*

HISTORY AND BIOGRAPHY

Angelou, Maya, *All God's Children Need Traveling Shoes*
Berlin, Ira, and others, eds., *Freedom: A Documentary History of Emancipation, 1861–1867 The Destruction of Slavery*
Critchfield, Richard, *Those Days: An American Album*
Davis, David Brion, *From Homicide to Slavery: Studies in American Culture*
Davis, Kenneth S., *FDR: The New Deal Years, 1933–1937*
Eisenhower, David, *Eisenhower: At War 1943–1945*
Goldberg, Vicki, *Margaret Bourke White*
Handlin, Oscar and Lilian, *Liberty and Power 1600–1760*
Herrmann, Dorothy, *S. J. Perelman: A Life*
Hersh, Seymour, *"The Target is Destroyed": What Really Happened to Flight 007 and What America Knew About It*
Kammen, Michael, *A Machine That Would Go Of Itself: The Constitution in American Culture*
Lifton, Jay, *The Nazi Doctors: Medical Killing and the Psychology of Genocide*
Lingeman, Richard, *Theodore Dreiser: At The Gates of the City, 1871–1907*
Lopez, Barry, *Arctic Dreams*
Mayer, Henry, *A Son of Thunder: Patrick Henry and the American Republic*
Mcneill, William H., *Mythistory and Other Essays*
Myers, Gerald E., *William James: His Life and Thought*
Norrell, Robert J., *Reaping the Whirlwind: The Civil Rights Movement in Tuskegee*
Rampersad, Arnold, *The Life of Langston Hughes. Vol. I: 1902–1941. I, Too, Sing America*
Reynolds, Michael, *The Young Hemingway*
Rosengarten, Theodore, *Tombee: Portrait of a Cotton Planter*
Schlesinger, Arthur M. Jr., *The Cycles of American History*
Sperber, A.M., *Murrow: His Life and Times*
Shelton, Robert, *No Direction Home*
Stout, Harry S., *The New England Soul: Preaching and Religious Culture in Colonial New England*
Truman, Margaret, *Bess W. Truman*
Twombly, Robert, *Louis Sullivan: His Life and Work*
Winslow, Kathryn, *Henry Miller: Full of Life*
Woodward, C. Vann, *The Perils of Writing History*

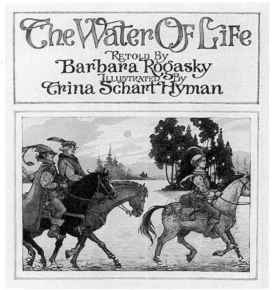

© 1986 by Trina Schart Hyman used by permission from Holiday House

The fairy tale "The Water of Life," retold by Barbara Rogasky, is rich in the traditional elements of folklore.

Children's Literature

The good news in children's books is that more of them are being published than ever before. Several publishers introduced new lines in 1986, and some leading paperback houses brought out their own hardcover lines rather than purchase rights to previously published works. Upscale baby boomers determined to give their children a head start became an increasingly influential market, and many more books for babies and toddlers were published. Series and sets of books proliferated. The paperback romance craze peaked, but there was no dearth of books set against such high-interest backgrounds as television, the fashion industry, and high school.

Awards. Among the waves of ephemeral books were some titles with staying power. In 1986 the prestigious John Newbery Medal, presented annually by the American Library Association (ALA), went to Patricia MacLaughlin for *Sarah, Plain and Tall*. A brief but striking story set in frontier days, the book tells of a young woman who goes west as a mail-order bride and heals an emotionally needy family with her love. The ALA's Randolph Caldecott Medal was awarded to Chris Van Allsburg for *The Polar Express*, a fantasy about a boy's trip to the North Pole to receive Santa's first gift of Christmas.

Recommended Books. Among the best books published in 1986 for babies and toddlers was Tana Hoban's *Red, Blue, Yellow Shoe*, a board book about colors. Also noteworthy was Helen Oxenbury's set of four board books entitled *I See, I Touch, I Hear,* and *I Can*.

Notable picturebooks for slightly older children included Paul Zelinsky's *Rumplestiltskin* and Barbara Rogasky's *The Water of Life*. Both were solid interpretatons of old tales backed with powerful illustrations. Trina Schart Hyman, illustrator of *The Water of Life*, was the Caldecott medalist for 1985 for *Saint George and the Dragon*.

Children in grades 4 to 6 found rich entertainment between the covers of Jane Leslie Conly's fantasy, *Racso and the Rats of NIMH*, a sequel to the Newbery Medal-winning *Mrs. Frisby and the Rats of NIMH*, by Conly's father, Robert C. O'Brien. A different sort of fantasy was E.L. Konigsburg's *Up From Jericho Tel*, a witty, eccentric story of two children who solve a mystery for a ghost named Tallulah.

For junior-high readers (ages 11 to 13), there were several perceptive explorations of young people coming of age. Margaret Willey's *Finding David Dolores* is an intense portrayal of adolescent turmoil in which a girl feuds with her mother and develops an all-consuming interest in a boy she knows only from afar. Cynthia Rylant's *A Fine White Dust* tells of lost innocence in a wrenching story about a boy whose strong religious feelings are betrayed by a traveling tent preacher. In Phyllis Reynolds Naylor's *The Keeper*, a boy struggles to deal with his father's terrifying schizophrenia.

Young adults aged 13 and up found Paula Fox's *The Moonlight Man* a sophisticated portrait of a young woman painfully coming to terms with her alcoholic father. M.E. Kerr's *Night Kites* was a sensitive drama about a boy who learns his older brother is gay and has developed AIDS.

Outstanding nonfiction titles in 1986 included Patricia Lauber's *Volcano*, an elegant photo essay on how Mount St. Helens is healing itself, and astronaut Sally Ride's account of a space-shuttle mission in *To Space and Back*.

The 1986 Caldecott Medal for best picture book for children went to Chris Van Allsburg for "The Polar Express."

Reprinted with permission by Houghton Mifflin Company

SELECTED BOOKS FOR CHILDREN*

Preschool-Age 6
Arnosky, Jim, *Deer at the Brook*
Brett, Jan, *The Twelve Days of Christmas*
Carlstrom, Nancy White, *Jesse Bear, What Will You Wear?*
Chorao, Kay, *The Baby's Good Morning Book*
Hest, Amy, *The Purple Coat*
Hogrogian, Nonny, *Noah's Ark*
Hoquet, Susan Ramsay, *Solomon Grundy*
MacDonald, Suse, *Alphabetics*
Prelutsky, Jack (selector), *Read-Aloud Rhymes*

Ages 7-10
Aliki, *How a Book is Made*
Little, Jean, *Lost and Found*
Menotti, Gian Carlo, *Amahl and the Night Visitors*
Powzyk, Joyce, *Wallaby Creek*
Sewall, Marcia, *The Pilgrims of Plimoth*

Ages 9-12
Alexander, Lloyd, *The Ilyrian Adventure*
Bauer, Marion Dane, *On My Honor*
Froelich, Margaret Walden, *Reasons to Stay*
Haas, Dorothy, *The Secret Life of Dilly McBean*
Hahn, Mary Downing, *Wait Till Helen Comes*
Meltzer, Milton, *Winnie Mandela*
Sachs, Marilyn, *Underdog*
Simon, Seymour, *The Sun*
The Stars
Tayntor, Elizabeth; Erickson, Peter; and Kaufman, Les, *Dive to the Coral Reefs*

Young Teens
Facklam, Marjorie and Howard, *Changes in the Wind*
Fritz, Jean, *Make Way for Sam Houston*
Lasky, Kathryn, *Pageant*
Peck, Richard, *Blossom Culp and the Sleep of Death*
Rostowski, Margaret I., *After the Dancing Days*
Shura, Mary Francis, *The Josie Gambit*
Smith, Doris Buchanan, *Return to Bitter Creek*
Stolz, Mary, *Ivy Larkin*
Voigt, Cynthia, *Come a Stranger*

Young Adults
Bess, Clayton, *Tracks*
Brooks, Bruce, *Midnight Hour Encores*
Graber, Richard, *Doc*
Jones, Diana Wynne, *Howl's Moving Castle*
Macauley, David, *Baaa*
Mahy, Margaret, *The Catalogue of the Universe*
Pei, Lowry, *Family Resemblances*
Works not cited in article.

In a class by itself is Sheila Kitzinger's *Being Born*. This riveting look at life in the womb and birth itself is illustrated with stunning full-color photographs by famed medical photographer Lennart Nilsson.

See also LIBRARIES.

DENISE MURCKO WILMS
Assistant Editor, "Booklist"

Canadian Literature: English

Events and figures in Canada's past interested a number of writers in 1986.

Nonfiction. Several notable new books recalled Canada's role in the two world wars. In *Vimy*, celebrated author Pierre Berton turns back to Canada's greatest military victory, the 1917 capture from the Germans of Vimy Ridge in France. James R. Lamb's *On the Triangle Run* tells how the Canadian Navy in World War II escorted convoys to the mid-Atlantic, where the British Navy took over. And *"They're Still Women After All"—The Second World War and Canadian Womanhood*, by Ruth Roach Pierson with Marjorie Cohen, describes how Canada's women felt about their wartime roles.

War in the West, subtitled *Voices of the 1885 Rebellion*, by Rudy Wiebe and Bob Beal, recounts the unsuccessful uprising of some settlers under Louis Riel. Sherrill MacLaren's *Braehead* is about the Macleods, Crosses, and Drevers, three Scottish families who emigrated to Canada in the early 19th century. Elizabeth Jones's *Gentlemen and Jesuits* describes the French settlement of Port Royal, Nova Scotia. In *We Were the Salt of the Earth*, Victor Howard recalls the Regina riot of July 1, 1935, when relief camp workers clashed with the police. *It Seems Like Only Yesterday—Air Canada: The First Fifty Years*, by Philip Smith, is an interesting chapter in aviation history.

Randall White's *Ontario 1610–1985* is the first of a series of books from the Ontario Heritage Foundation. Eric Downton's *Pacific Challenge: Canada's Future in the New Asia* urges businessmen to wake up to the economic importance of the Pacific Rim. And Carol Giangrande's *Down to Earth: The Crisis in Canadian Farming* looks at Canadian farmers' problems.

Biographies and autobiographies also explored recent Canadian history. Sen. Keith Davey, a leading Liberal Party planner, writes his memoirs in *The Rainmaker*. Ronald Graham's *One-Eyed Kings* is a look at Canada's last four prime ministers: Pierre Trudeau, Joe Clark, John Turner, and incumbent Brian Mulroney. Robert H. Hahn's *None of the Roads Were Paved* tells how his family left a dusty Saskatchewan farm to become the Harmony Kids, a musical troupe who eventually made it to Broadway. *Don Moore, An Autobiography* recounts how the author, a native of Barbados, came to Canada and served the cause of immigrant blacks. Moore wrote his autobiography at the age of 92.

In other nonfiction, Canada's distinguished scholar Northrop Frye contributes *Northrop Frye on Shakespeare*, a masterful examination of the bard's plays. John Caldwell Adam's biography of Canadian poet Sir Charles G. D. Roberts, who died in 1943, is titled *Sir Charles God Damn*, from the nickname given him by people trying to remember the sequence of his middle two initials. Phyllis Grosskurth contributes *Melanie Klein*, the biography of an influential figure in psychoanalysis early in this century. June Callwood's *Emotions* is a clearly written examination of feelings common to all of us.

Poetry. Miriam Waddington's *Collected Poems*, gathered from 11 published volumes,

Keith Davey, a 60-year-old Toronto-born senator, Liberal Party planner, and former commissioner of the Canadian Football League, published his memoirs, "The Rainmaker."

as well as from unpublished works, demonstrates the scope and development of this enduring poet's work. Al Purdy's *Collected Poems: 1956–1986* is another collection by a poet of long standing.

Leonard Cohen's latest is *The Book of Mercy*, and Irving Layton contributes *Dance With Desire*, a collection of love poems written over the last 30 years. Don Coles's *Landslides* is subtitled *Collected Poems 1975–85*. Mary di Michele's *Immune to Gravity* is her fifth volume of poetry. Joy Kogawa's *Woman in the Woods* looks at life as a frightening pilgrimage, and in *Domestic Fuel*, Erin Moure, too, views the world as an unhappy and often violent place. John Newlove's *The Night the Dog Smiled* is a selection of both new and earlier poems. Diana Hertog's latest volume is *Candy from Strangers*, and Paulette Jiles' is *Celestial Navigation*.

Fiction. Scott Symons spent more than ten years writing his latest novel, *Helmet of Flesh*. Both moving and funny, it concerns a prominent man who is married to a lovely wife and has a cherished son but is not happy. His conventional life collapses when he falls in love with a young man and goes to live with him in Morocco. Richard Rohmer's tenth novel, *Starmageddon*, is a thriller set in the year 2000; an American aircraft is shot down when a wrong computer setting steers it into Russian territory, and a "Star Wars" confrontation occurs. Computers also figure in *Dreamland* by Garfield Reeves-Stevens, in which one is pos-

sessed by an evil spirit, with horrifying results. And computer espionage is the topic of David Gurr's *On the Endangered List*.

Robina Salter's first novel, *Hannah*, is about a midwife in a Newfoundland outport. *Crabbe*, by William Bell, concerns a high-school student who escapes to the woods rather than take his final exams. Another story of a young man's problems is *Blaine's Way*, by Monica Hughes. The heroine of Aritha van Herk's *No Fixed Address: An Amorous Journey* travels the prairies selling ladies' panties and conquering men wherever she goes. *Buried on Sunday*, by Edward Phillips, is about a quiet country weekend that becomes anything but quiet. And in Max Braithwaite's *All the Way Home*, a famous playwright returns to his family on the prairies to find that the problems that drove him away almost 50 years before are still there.

Short story collections include Alice Munro's latest, the highly praised *The Progress of Love;* novelist Janette Turner Hospital's *Dislocations*, which is set in Canada, New York, southern India, and elsewhere; and Gordon Green's *The Devil is Innocent*, a group of connected tales about a 13-year-old boy growing up with strict parents in a Baptist home in a rural section of Ontario.

DAVID SAVAGE,
Free-lance Writer, Vancouver, B.C.

English Literature

This was a good year for the English novel. Kingsley Amis published *The Old Devils*, a sly tale of old age in Wales, mocking among other targets the Dylan Thomas industry. The book was judged his best since *Lucky Jim* and inspired Anthony Burgess to comment, "there is one old devil who is writing better than he ever did."

Anthony Burgess himself contributed *The Pianoplayers*, a rackety medley of sexual excesses, and Anthony Powell published *The Fisher King*, his first major novel for ten years. In *A Misalliance*, Anita Brookner continued to examine in stylish detail the world of the lonely and law-abiding in crushing contrast to the adventurous and free. In *Coasting Along*, Lisa St. Aubin de Teran transported her plot to the Italian Riviera. Beryl Bainbridge published *Filthy Lucre*, a novel written in her teenage years, and Piers Paul Read examined the moral predicaments of France during the 1930s in *The Free Frenchman*. A. N. Wilson contributed an elaborate comedy of manners, *Love Unknown*, and Fay Weldon a military satire, *The Shrapnel Academy*. D. M. Thomas completed his trilogy of the Cold War with *Sphinx*, and Julian Barnes added to his reputation with *Staring at the Sun*, which boasted a striking opening.

One of the most highly praised novels of the year was Paul Bailey's *Gabriel's Lament,* a tale of despair in the life of Gabriel, whose mother left home when he was 12 years old, abandoning him to the pretenses of a monstrous father, Oswald, who is unable to face grief and loss straightforwardly. *An Insular Possession* by Timothy Mo was an admired account of the Opium Wars in Canton and Macao, and Canadian Margaret Atwood's *The Handmaid's Tale* was a powerful feminist fable.

Readers who devour accomplished thrillers could not complain about a year that produced *A Perfect Spy* from John Le Carré and *A Taste for Death* from P. D. James.

The shortlist for the 1986 Booker McConnell Prize for fiction proved a strong one, including Kingsley Amis, Margaret Atwood, Paul Bailey, Timothy Mo, Canadian Robertson Davies for *What's Bred in the Bone,* and Kazuo Ishiguro for *An Artist of the Floating World.* The only possible complaint was the omission of Julian Barnes. The winner, announced on October 22, was Kingsley Amis.

Nonfiction. Many interesting works of history, biography, and memoirs also appeared in 1986. Most massive was the seventh volume of Martin Gilbert's life of Winston Churchill, *The Road to Victory,* dealing with the period from Pearl Harbor to the end of World War II, which was acclaimed for its grasp of detail. The life of *Truman* by Roy Jenkins, Britain's former chancellor of the exchequer, was more of a short, elegant essay, but was considered sound in its conclusion, of President Truman's decisions,

that he was as "generally right on the big ones, as he was frequently wrong on the small ones." Among other biographies, Dame Felicitas Corrigan wrote movingly of the scholar Helen Waddell; Richard Perceval Graves, the poet's nephew, published the first volume of a life of Robert Graves; the charming diplomat Duff Cooper was summed up by John Charmley, and the neglected G. K. Chesterton was reassessed by Michael Ffinch.

Of the year's autobiographies, *Growing Up in the Gorbals* by psychologist Ralph Glasser was praised as a vivid account of boyhood in the slums of Glasgow, while *Some Small Harvest* by archaeologist Glyn Daniels described a lifetime as a Cambridge academic, and *Union Man* by Jack Jones related his years in the labor movement. Juliet Huxley, in *Leaves of the Tulip Tree,* revealed the marriage she experienced with Julian Huxley and the intellectual life of the brilliant brothers Julian and Aldous. In *Chronicle of Friendship,* Vera Brittain's diary of 1932–39, edited by Alan Bishop, the personality of the author of *Testament of Youth* was further revealed. *The Pebbled Shore,* the memoirs of the noted biographer Elizabeth Longford, arrived on the scene alongside her granddaughter Flora Fraser's first biography, *Beloved Emma,* a life of Lady Hamilton, illustrating the inherited drive of the generations of Longford writers.

Among literary publications, the second volume of *The Collected Letters of Joseph Conrad* revealed a lonely, melancholy personality. *Beatrix Potter's Journal,* the now uncoded diary kept by the writer from the ages of 14 to 30, filled in fascinating missing years. *Early Verse by Rudyard Kipling 1879–1889,* a series of unpublished, uncollected, and rarely collected poems edited by Andrew Rutherford, and Kipling's *India: Uncollected Sketches* added to the author's known works.

In politics, Conor Cruise O'Brien's history of Zionism, *The Siege,* aroused great interest, and in philosophy two Platonic dialogues by Iris Murdoch, *Acastos,* discussed the problems of art and morality in a classical form.

Poetry. Roy Fuller celebrated his 70th birthday with a new volume, *Consolations,* an exploration of the joys and pains of old age. Elizabeth Jennings pleased her large and loyal following with her *Collected Poems,* and A. S. J. Tessimond, who died a generation ago, received new appreciation with the publication of his *Collected Poems.* Craig Raine published *The Electrification of the Soviet Union,* originally designed as the libretto of a new opera by composer Nigel Osborne for the Glyndebourne Festival Opera. The skillful Wendy Cope, a first-class comic poet, produced a witty first volume, *Making Cocoa for Kingsley Amis,* which ran through several printings and took poetry into circles not always reached.

MAUREEN GREEN, *Free-lance Writer, London*

Kingsley Amis toasts himself after winning the Booker Prize, Britain's top award for fiction. He was honored for "The Old Devils," the tale of an elderly Wales couple.

AP/Wide World

World Literature*

Happily, the harsh squabbles and posturings that dominated the International PEN Congress in New York in early 1986 (*see* LITERATURE introduction, page 329) did not set the tone for the literary year. European and Third World writers alike produced an array of first-rate new works; important foreign writers from less accessible languages gained new readers in translation; and previously unpublished materials by deceased 20th-century classics finally emerged into public view.

German. Particularly strong in breadth and depth were the newest books by leading writers of the German-speaking countries. Günter Grass, one of the most outspoken participants at the PEN meeting, weighed in with *The She-Rat*, a grim but imaginative vision of an imminent apocalypse that will leave rats as the dominant surviving species. Earlier Grass characters, such as Oskar Matzerath and Anna Koljaicek (from *The Tin Drum*), put in cameo appearances, as in a swan song or a summa; the book indeed was rumored to be Grass's last major novelistic effort, as he turns exclusively to his artwork and to global politics. Austrian author Peter Handke's new novel *Die Wiederholung* (the title means both "Repetition" and "Retrieval") also points toward the aftermath of a possible future cataclysm, but reaches that end via more mythic-poetical means, tracing a young writer's 25-year quest for his vanished brother in the Slovene countryside. Handke's

* *Titles translated.*

West German author Günter Grass published "The She-Rat," rumored to be his last major novelistic undertaking.

© Layle Silbert

prolific countryman Thomas Bernhard produced his most comprehensive work yet, the 600-page novel *Extinction*, whose writer-protagonist seeks to obliterate his now-abhorred hometown via literary exaggeration and excess. In East German letters, only *Bronze Age*, five interrelated tales by Hermann Kant featuring his recurrent protagonist, the accountant Farssman, proved noteworthy for its "unique mixture of 19th-century idiom and contemporary cheekiness," as one critic noted. These four works were joined by new novels from West Germany's Max von der Grün and Hermann Lenz and Austria's Gerhard Roth, short-story collections by Luise Rinser and Hermann Burger, poetry volumes by Reiner Kunze and Wolfgang Hilbig, and the latest installment in Thomas Mann's posthumously published diaries.

French and Italian. The year in France was almost as strong as in the Germanic countries. Robert Sabatier completed his best-selling tetralogy with *David and Olivier*, the moving chronicle of an adolescent's explorations in 1930s Montmartre. Jean Cayrol focused on the darker, less congenial world of an orphaned youth's country estate in *The Chestnuts*, a stripped down récit reminiscent of the *nouveau roman* ("New Novel") of three decades ago. Michel Butor, once a leading practitioner of the *nouveau roman*, continued along his own unique literary road with the fifth and final volume of *The Stuff of Dreams*, a fanciful and free-flowing weave of fact and fiction that follows the associative logic of dreams. New fiction also appeared from Julien Green, J.M.G. Le Clézio, and Dominique Fernandez, but of equal note were two voices from earlier times: *Past Definite*, the second volume of Jean Cocteau's diaries, covering the year 1953; and the letters of Max Jacob to a young friend on a wide range of artistic and literary topics.

New releases by two of Italy's finest prose writers, Primo Levi and the late Italo Calvino, highlighted that country's modest literary production in 1986. Levi continued his series of inspired, insightful accounts of his death-camp experiences during World War II with *The Lost and the Saved*. Calvino's posthumous *Under the Jaguar Sun* gathered a series of narrative "exercises," his own structural invention combining indirect narration, a "geometric" framework, fantasy, myth, and tangible sensation.

Spanish and Latin American. Spain's authors continued to mine the fertile field of that country's civil war, as in Francisco Umbral's *Pius XII, the Moorish Escort, and a One-Eyed General*. However, such writers as Gonzalo Torrente Ballester turned to other historical subjects, as in *The Coup in Guadalupe Limón*, about revolutionary upheaval in a New World colony closely resembling Mexico.

In the New World itself, Peru's Mario Vargas Llosa led the way with two new works:

© Giansanti/Sygma

Italy's Primo Levi produced another novel about his concentration camp experiences, "The Lost and the Saved."

Who Killed Palomino Molero?, a cerebral, phantasmagoric, yet politically astute account of the convoluted events surrounding the murder of a young military pilot; and the play *The Vixen*, a study in sordid local realism within an urban setting in northern Peru. Alfredo Bryce Echenique proved again that Peru has more than one writer of talent with his new novel *The Man Who Spoke of Octavia de Cádiz*, a comic turn on the theme of the charming but ne'er-do-well young bohemian. *Quintuplets*, a play by Puerto Rico's Luis Rafael Sánchez, and *Anteparadise*, presenting the excellent poetry of Chile's Raúl Zurita in a bilingual format, also were noteworthy, as were two novels by Brazilian authors: *The Polish Girl*, Dalton Trevisan's first full-length novel, captures the sound and rhythm of modern Brazilian Portuguese and presents one of Brazilian literature's most memorable characters in recent years; *High Art*, a parody of the excesses and unrealities of detective fiction, brought Rubem Fonseca to the attention of American readers.

Eastern and Central European. Russian-language literature in 1986 was ably represented both at home and abroad. Konstantin Simonov, one of the mainstays of Soviet Russian prose in the postwar years, published *Sofia Leonidovna*, a novelette written 26 years earlier about three women in the resistance movement against Nazi occupation forces in 1941. Two other leading Soviet Russian prose writers, the gracefully Jamesian Andrei Bitov and the psy-

chologically astute Yuri Nagibin, were introduced to Western audiences via the translated story collections *Life in Windy Weather* and *The Peak of Success*, respectively. The prominent Russian émigrés Joseph Brodsky and Vladimir Voinovich departed from their usual Augustan poetry and comic fiction to publish volumes of nonfiction prose: Brodsky's essay collection *Less Than One*, on a wide range of writers and topics, and Voinovich's *The Anti-Soviet Soviet Union*, containing wryly moving anecdotes and elaborated reports on everyday facets of Soviet and émigré life.

Eastern European writers produced several important books. The 1984 Nobel laureate, the late Czech poet Jaroslav Seifert, was made more widely accessible to non-Czech readers through the publication of the 194-page *Selected Poems*, with translations by Ewald Osers and George Gibian. The eminent Czech playwright Václav Havel set the scholar-hero of his drama *Largo desolato* against the infernal machinations of state authorities and the pressures of friends and colleagues. First-time novelist Jan Pelc created the year's biggest sensation with *It Could Be Worse*, an innovative and scatological novel centered on the lowest milieu of contemporary Czech society in all its squalor and nihilism—presumably illuminating the deficiencies of the current political system. On a loftier plane, the 1980 Nobel recipient, Polish-born Czesław Miłosz, issued a new volume of his verse in translation, *Unattainable Earth*, in which he moves away from the largely historical themes of his earlier work and into the realms of metaphysics and ontology.

Caribbean and African. In the Caribbean, the outstanding poet-playwright Derek Walcott again led the way, following the previous year's enormously successful *Collected Poems* with *Three Plays*. The best of the three, *Beef, No Chicken*, is a farcical diagnosis of the corruption, "commodification," and total lack of nostalgia that characterizes the modernization of the West Indies. Ronald Dathorne of Guyana explores the nature of emerging political leadership in the Caribbean in his novel *Dele's Child*, finding mostly bald ambition and venality.

From Africa came several works of note, including *The Scaffold* by the South African writer Edward Lurie, who uses the cynical conversion of a welfare complex for "coloreds" into a monstrous "hypermarket" as a concrete emblem of apartheid's destructive nature. In *Mating Birds*, the exiled black South African writer Lewis Nkosi produced a more muted and agonizing narrative on the same subject, using the metaphor of forbidden yet irresistible sexual attraction between a black man and a white woman to expose the anguish generated by the sociopolitical circumstances. Kenya's Ngugi wa Thiong'o bade "farewell to English as a vehicle for [his] writings" in *De-*

colonising the Mind, a collection of essays and lectures on issues in fiction, theater, criticism, and the teaching of literature. Algeria's Ali Ghanem produced *The Seven-Headed Serpent,* the picaresque odyssey of a young Berber orphan from his mountain village, through the liberation war, to university study in France, to success and recognition in film. Other prominent African Francophone publications in 1986 included *Birth at Dawn* by Algeria's Driss Chraïbi, *The Child of Sand* by Morocco's Tahar Ben Jelloun, and the first English translation from the work of the Ivory Coast novelist Bernard Dadié, *The City Where No One Dies.*

Near Eastern. Egyptian writers dominated the year's production from the Near East, led by the most-translated and most highly skilled Arabic prose writer, Naguib Mahfouz. Two Mahfouz novels were added to the growing list of his books available in English: *Autumn Quail,* the 1962 tragedy of a government official in King Farouk's regime who is purged following the revolution; and *Wedding Song,* a story of sordid intrigue and hatred within the Egyptian theater world. Naawal el-Saadawi produced a much-discussed novel as well, *Two Women in One,* whose teenage heroine is gradually pushed into violent rebellion against social conventions and the political order. In *The Net,* Sherif Hetata offers a searing commentary on the changes wrought on Egyptian society during the Anwar el-Sadat era. Yaakov Shabtai's *Past Continuous,* issued almost simultaneously in Hebrew and English, highlighted the year in Israeli literature with its complexly structured evocation of the dynamism that characterizes modern-day urban Israeli life and the concomitant clash of generations and values. *Istanbul My Love* by Nedim Gürsel, which appeared a year earlier in French, was the most important of Turkey's many fine new publica-

Polish-born Ruth Prawer Jhabvala, who is married to an Indian, brought together 15 stories for "Out of India."

tions in 1986, a collection of 18 interrelated stories that—despite the title—are set in a number of world capitals and explore the themes of alienation and solitude. Across the Bosporus, the 1979 Nobel laureate Odysseus Elytis' Greek poetry of the last seven years was rendered into English by Olga Broumas in *What I Love,* half of which is occupied by the book-length 1983 poem *Maria Nephele.*

Asian and Pacific. Lastly, the year brought the first publication and/or translation of a number of fine recent works by writers from Asia and the Pacific region. *The Uncollected Stories of Christina Stead* rounded off the late Australian author's successful career with several unexpected treasures. The half-aboriginal writer B. Wongar followed his earlier successes with the novel *Karan,* characterized by critics as "a powerful tale of a [tribal] culture on the brink of extinction. . . . " *The Birth and Death of the Miracle Man,* a collection of stories by the Samoan writer Albert Wendt, tracks several intriguing and complex island figures whose tales offer a highly original tapestry of their Pacific community as a microcosm of the modern world.

Japan's Kenzaburō Ōe, whose work continues to find a wide audience in the West, published *A Story of M/T and the Mysteries of the Forest,* a Utopian novel that evokes both the mythological power of the Matriarch and Trickster figures and the mystical life forces that lie hidden in nature and humankind, even in present-day Japanese society. Wholly different in tone and manner is Saiichi Maruya's prizewinning *Singular Rebellion,* a clever and light-footed comic novel that is as insightful about Japanese ways as it is humorous in satirizing them. *The Shōwa Anthology* offers 21 stories dating from 1926 by writers both famous in the West (Ōe, Kawabata, Endō, Abe) and previously unfamiliar to Western readers (Jun Ishikawa, Toshio Shimao, Junzo Shono).

The first translation of two major works from the late 1930s plus one completely new novel stood out in the Chinese literary year. Xiao Hong's accomplished and compelling 1936 novel *Market Street* recounts the poverty, hardship, and Confucian misogyny that the author encountered at the start of her abbreviated career. Cao Yu's skillful 1940 play *Peking Man* offers hope for better times in its portrait of the decline of the traditional family and the awakening humanitarian ideals of the younger generation. And in *The Butcher's Wife,* the young Taiwanese novelist Li Ang reports the harrowing, factually based story of a young peasant woman who, brutalized by her pig-butcher husband and by a male-dominated superstitious society, is driven to madness and ultimately to murder; despite the stark prose and macabre subject matter, the work was praised as the finest example of Chinese fiction in recent years.

WILLIAM RIGGAN, *"World Literature Today"*

LONDON

On March 31, 1986, the Greater London Council (GLC) ceased to exist, and London was without its own governing body for the first time since 1889. To the strains of Haydn's *Farewell Symphony* at a candlelit ceremony at the Royal Festival Hall, Ken Livingstone, the leader of the GLC, blew out all the candles, plunging the auditorium into a symbolic moment of darkness. As a result of one of the most curious and controversial acts on the part of Prime Minister Margaret Thatcher's national government, London and six other cities are to be governed without elected authorities.

Final passage of the Local Government Act means that the main functions of the GLC—including planning, housing, traffic, parks, firefighting, and waste disposal—now are to be divided among 80 different central appointees and local councils. So complex has been the transfer of power that the original reason for the GLC's abolition—to save money—now is considered impossible to evaluate.

The London Residuary Body, headed by Sir Godfrey Taylor, faces the task of tying up the remaining loose ends. Among the unsolved problems is the future of County Hall, a protected building of architectural merit, which had housed the GLC's 21,500 employees, but which now stands empty on the opposite bank of the Thames from the Houses of Parliament.

The Greater London Council leaves a notable legacy in such creations as the Green Belt, land purchased to prevent the urban sprawl of the capital from covering southeast England, and the Thames Barrier, which saved a geologically sinking London from flooding.

Another question for the future, since both the Labour Party and the SDP Liberal Alliance envisage the creation of a new, most probably smaller and more central elected authority to govern London, is what that authority should be and what it should cover. As one Conservative Greater London councillor, Robert Mitchell, wrote, "Almost all GLC members would have welcomed reform. But they consider abolition disastrous for London. . . . I feel sure we'll be back."

London's appearance was altered in 1986 by the addition of two important new buildings. In the City, the new, high-tech headquarters of Lloyd's of London, the famous insurance company was opened. Its design by Richard Rogers, famed for Paris's Pompidou Center, was admired by many and criticized equally. On an even more crucial site facing Westminster Abbey, the new Queen Elizabeth II Conference Centre was designed by the architects Powell, Moya, and Partners to blend in discreetly while not being overawed by its famous neighbor. Diplomatic and commercial events will be held in the Centre.

MAUREEN GREEN, *Free-lance Writer, London*

LOS ANGELES

A tragic fire, a conflict over the fair selection of council members, and the reopening of the famed Pasadena Playhouse were some of the highlights of 1986 in Los Angeles. Meanwhile the city's Democratic mayor, Tom Bradley, staged an unsuccessful campaign to unseat the incumbent governor, George Deukmejian (*see* CALIFORNIA).

Library Fire. A devastating fire struck the city's central library on April 28. The $20 million blaze destroyed or damaged 45% of the holdings. The 60-year-old building, which had been scheduled for renovation and expansion, was regarded as an architectural gem and is a designated historical landmark. Its basic structure withstood the heat and many of the water-damaged volumes were saved, but only through hard work by an army of volunteers. In early September, a second arson fire added to the damage, particularly in the fine-arts collection.

City Council. Although the city's Hispanic population is about 27% of the total, it has been without a Hispanic council member since 1962. As a result, the Department of Justice filed a suit in late 1985 charging violation of the Civil Rights Act and asking for a court order to alter the boundaries of the 15 council districts to make easier the election of Hispanics. Two weeks after the suit was filed a Hispanic, Richard Alatorre, was elected to fill a vacancy, but the districting issue remained. In September 1986, a federal judge accepted a redistricting plan, which was designed to increase Hispanic representation on the Council from one to two.

Playhouse. A refurbished Pasadena Playhouse, long a training ground for actors, was reopened on April 19. The company had filed for bankruptcy and closed in 1969. The building itself was declared a historic site in 1976, but its reopening had to await large contributions.

Planning and Renewal. The federal government, over the opposition of the Reagan administration and after a long dispute, signed a contract to pay about 50% of the cost of the first segment of a subway for the city. The 4.4-mi (7-km) downtown portion will cost about $1.25 billion.

After a yearlong search, Mayor Bradley appointed Kenneth C. Topping as city planning director, replacing Calvin Hamilton who had served for 20 years. Topping had headed planning in San Bernardino County.

The city's Community Development Agency approved a huge 51% increase in its budget, mostly in order to deal with the needs of the central library, expansion of the convention center downtown, and the renovation of the Crenshaw shopping center, one of the nation's first.

CHARLES R. ADRIAN
University of California, Riverside

341

LOUISIANA

The governor's acquittal on federal racketeering charges, continuing state financial crises, and a hotly contested race for the U.S. Senate made headlines in Louisiana in 1986.

Edwards' Acquittal. After a hung jury resulted in a mistrial for Gov. Edwin W. Edwards in December 1985, the governor and four co-defendants were found not guilty of racketeering and fraud in May 1986, ending 19 months of uncertainty that had begun with his indictment in September 1984.

The U.S. Justice Department had charged that Edwards and others had conspired illegally to obtain and sell state hospital approvals, which entitle developers to substantial federal reimbursement for project costs. As governor, prosecutors said, he imposed a moratorium on approval of new hospitals but allowed and fostered the approval of health-care projects by his partners.

Three of eight defendants were acquitted in the first trial. Among the five found not guilty in the retrial was the governor's brother, Marion D. Edwards.

Plans to Run Again. In spite of the acquittal opinion polls showed the governor's popularity had dropped to all-time lows. But late in the year he announced his intention to seek another term in the 1987 gubernatorial race. Edwards had served as governor from 1972 to 1980, and again ran successfully in 1983. He said it was the upset victory of his fellow Democrat, Congressman John Breaux, over Republican W. Henson Moore for the Senate seat being vacated by Russell B. Long that persuaded him to seek a fourth term. According to the governor the coalition that allowed Breaux to defeat Moore—a combination of blacks, labor, and other traditionally Democratic voters—would carry him to victory in the 1987 gubernatorial race, despite his current low approval rating of 22% in the polls.

Election Results. Moore, a U.S. congressman from Baton Rouge, had been a strong early favorite in the Senate race and had hoped to become Louisiana's first Republican senator since Reconstruction. He had been expected to win the state's unusual open primary, which forces candidates of all parties to run together, but the entrance of many minor candidates spread the vote around and, while Moore led in the primary, he did not have the majority needed to win. Apparent Republican attempts to purge the voter rolls of black voters hurt Moore in the runoff, and Breaux won comfortably with 54% of the total vote and 95% of the black vote.

In the races for Louisiana's eight House seats, the Republicans gained one spot, bringing the party's state total to three. Republican Clyde Holloway of Forest Hill narrowly defeated Democrat Faye Williams of Alexandria, who would have been Louisiana's first black female member of Congress. That race was for the seat formerly held by the late Gillis Long. In the race to fill Breaux's old seat, Jimmy Hayes of Lafayette defeated fellow Democrat Margaret Lowenthal of Lake Charles. Democrats Lindy Boggs, W.J. (Billy) Tauzin, Buddy Roemer, and Jerry Huckaby either faced no opposition or were easily reelected in the first primary. Republican Bob Livingston was reelected without opposition, and Republican Richard Baker of Baton Rouge won a first primary victory to fill Moore's old seat.

In a March runoff election for the office of mayor of New Orleans, Sidney Barthelemy defeated William Jefferson. Both candidates are black Democrats.

Economy. Politics offered only a brief respite from the state's financial woes, which seemed to go from one crisis to another. The continuing slump in oil prices hurt the state by causing high unemployment in the oil fields and decreasing state revenues from petroleum taxes. The legislature had apparently wiped out an $800 million fiscal 1986–87 deficit by adopting almost $600 million in spending cuts and raising revenues of $236 million, with most of the revenues coming from the abolition of state sales tax exemptions on food and medicines.

Hundreds of state employees lost their jobs, and substantial cuts were made in education, health and social services, public safety, corrections and courts, highway programs, and state aid to local governments. State historical sites were closed because of staff layoffs.

In spite of the cuts, continued declines in state revenues left the deficit at $370 million. In a special session at year's end, legislators continued their strong opposition to Edwards' proposal for casino gambling and a state lottery but gave the governor unprecedented power to make spending cuts on his own.

JOSEPH W. DARBY III
"The Times-Picayune/States-Item"

LOUISIANA • Information Highlights

Area: 47,752 sq mi (123 677 km²).
Population (1985 est.): 4,481,000.
Chief Cities (July 1, 1984 est.): Baton Rouge, the capital, 368,571; New Orleans, 559,101; Shreveport, 219,996; Houma, 101,998.
Government (1986): *Chief Officers*—governor, Edwin W. Edwards (D); lt. gov., Robert L. Freeman (D). *Legislature*—Senate, 39 members; House of Representatives, 105 members.
State Finances (fiscal year 1985): *Revenue,* $8,156,000,000; *expenditure,* $7,581,000,000.
Personal Income (1985): $50,513,000,000; per capita, $11,274.
Labor Force (June 1986): *Civilian labor force,* 1,993,900; *unemployed,* 271,200 (13.6% of total force).
Education: *Enrollment* (fall 1984)—public elementary schools, 578,911; public secondary, 222,030; colleges and universities, 177,176. *Public school expenditures* (1983-84), $1,970,000,000 ($2,802 per pupil).

MAINE

Maine's two-term, first-district congressman, John R. McKernan, Jr., became the state's first Republican to be elected governor since 1962.

Election Results. With 40% of the 424,653 votes cast, McKernan beat the Democratic candidate, Attorney General James Tierney, by a 10% margin. Two Independents, former GOP state Sen. Sherry Huber and Portland businessman John E. Menario, split the balance with 15% each.

The outgoing Democrat, Gov. Joseph E. Brennan, won McKernan's vacated congressional seat in a race against first-time Republican candidate H. Rollin Ives. Brennan, who had served his constitutionally limited two four-year terms as governor, left the governorship after presiding over almost a decade of unprecedented Maine economic prosperity. Why this record failed to translate into a Democratic gubernatorial victory is a question state pundits were trying to answer as the year came to a close.

Second-district GOP incumbent Rep. Olympia Snowe was a landslide winner over Richard Charette, a newcomer to Maine politics. The Republican victory did not include either body of the Maine legislature; the new governor will work with both a House and Senate that have hefty Democratic majorities, even though the GOP picked up five new state Senate seats.

While the Maine Democrats held on to their majorities, U.S. Sen. George J. Mitchell (D-ME) had reason to celebrate in Washington. As the national chairman of the Democratic Senatorial Campaign Committee, Mitchell was credited by his peers for the work he did to restore a Democratic majority in the Senate.

Maine citizens set an example for the nation when more than 56% of the registered voters went to the polls on November 4; the national average was 37%.

MAINE • Information Highlights

Area: 33,265 sq mi (86 156 km²).
Population (1985 est.): 1,164,000.
Chief Cities (1980 census): Augusta, the capital, 21,819; Portland, 61,572; Lewiston, 40,481; Bangor, 31,643.
Government (1986): *Chief Officer*—governor, Joseph E. Brennan (D). *Legislature*—Senate, 33 members; House of Representatives, 151 members.
State Finances (fiscal year 1985): *Revenue,* $2,137,000,000; *expenditure,* $1,948,000,000.
Personal Income (1985): $13,835,000,000; per capita, $11,887.
Labor Force (June 1986): *Civilian labor force,* 572,300; *unemployed,* 28,000 (4.9% of total force).
Education: *Enrollment* (fall 1984)—public elementary schools, 141,975; public secondary, 65,361; colleges and universities, 52,201. *Public school expenditures* (1983-84), $549,000,000 ($2,813 per pupil).

Economic Developments. The state's new governor would take office at a time when the data indicates that Maine will continue to enjoy economic vitality and moderate growth. "Our projections indicate this trend will continue at least until 1995," said economic analyst Richard Sherwood of the State Planning Office. "Unemployment is well below the national average, with a rate of 5% for the state, and less than 3% in the greater Portland area," he said.

Maine's population continued to grow at a yearly rate of about 1%, which translates to a net gain of 7,500 new residents. This swelling populace, most of it in the state's southernmost counties, did not, however, include enough baseball fans to support the Maine Guides, the state's only professional baseball team, which had been given such an enthusiastic welcome in 1983 at a brand new ballpark in Old Orchard Beach. With the franchise sold pending a court decision, the future of the national pastime in Maine was gloomy.

Joining the Guides on the downside of the year's developments was the news that the Great Northern Paper Company, which was feeling the effects of increasing foreign competition, would lay off some 200 workers at its Millinocket plant during 1987. However, with the increase in electronics manufacturing, continued growth in the tourist industry, the rising demand for service personnel, and escalating land values, economists said that the overall stability and vitality of Maine's job markets would not be affected.

JOHN N. COLE, *"Maine Times"*

MALAYSIA

Despite tumult on the political scene, the ruling National Front coalition won solid victories in August state and national elections.

Politics. Under pressure from government leaders, the Malaysian Chinese Association (MCA) held party elections. Tan Koon Swan won a clear victory as president, but his arrest in Singapore for stock manipulation, plus criticism of National Front policies toward non-Malays, resulted in poor election showings by the MCA and other Chinese parties in the National Front and substantial gains by the opposition Democratic Action Party (DAP) in non-Malay areas. In August, when Tan received a jail sentence in Singapore, the MCA accepted his resignation. Ling Liong Sik was named as Tan's successor.

Leading the National Front was the United Malays National Organization (UMNO), which won all but one of the national seats it contested. The National Front retained two-thirds majorities in the 11 states holding simultaneous elections. Most leaders of the Pan Malaysian Islamic Party (PAS), the major opposition to the UMNO for Malay votes, were defeated.

In February, Musa Hitam resigned as deputy prime minister, charging that he lacked the support of Prime Minister Mahathir bin Mohamad. Although Musa remained in the UMNO, Mahathir supporters easily retained control in party elections. Veteran UMNO power broker Ghafar Baba succeeded Musa as deputy prime minister, while former Islamic youth leader and Minister of Agriculture Anwar Ibrahim was promoted to head the powerful education ministry.

The United Sabah Party (PBS), which had narrowly won control of the Sabah state government in 1985, dissolved the government in February as party defections threatened its majority. Leaders of the opposition Berjaya and United Sabah National Organization (USNO) parties were blamed for March riots over claims that the government did not protect Islamic interests; many of the rioters proved to be illegal Filipino immigrants. An April High Court decision rejected opposition claims to control of the state. The PBS, led by founder and chief minister Joseph Pairin Kitingan, easily won a two-thirds legislative majority in May elections. The National Front then finally agreed to admit PBS. USNO was readmitted, while Berjaya quit the coalition.

Economics. The 1986–90 Five-Year Plan, which called for fostering development through the private sector, predicted an average 5% annual growth. Slumping commodity prices, especially for petroleum, later led the government to reduce its growth predictions for fiscal 1986–87. To counter a stagnating economy and attract more foreign investment, the long-

standing domestic and ethnic ownership requirements of the government's New Economic Policy were relaxed. The soaring value of the yen seriously affected Malaysia's debt and caused the government to seek concessions from Japan.

Other Matters. The government released a report charging officials of the Bank Bumiputra with corruption and mismanagement, including bad loans to companies in Hong Kong. No specific charges were brought against the officials, however.

Articles in the *Asian Wall Street Journal* questioning the financial dealings of Finance Minister Daim Zainuddin led to the September expulsion of two *Journal* correspondents and a three-month ban on the sale of the publication. The ban and expulsion orders were lifted in mid-November.

K. MULLINER, *Ohio University*

MALAYSIA • Information Highlights

Official Name: Malaysia.
Location: Southeast Asia.
Area: 129,286 sq mi (334 851 km²).
Population (mid-1986 est.): 15,800,000.
Chief City (1980 census): Kuala Lumpur, the capital, 937,875.
Government: *Head of state,* Mahmood Iskandar Ibni Sultan Ismail (elected Feb. 9, 1984). *Head of government,* Mahathir bin Mohamad, prime minister (took office July 1981). *Legislature*—Parliament: Dewan Negara (Senate) and Dewan Ra'ayat (House of Representatives).
Monetary Unit: Ringgit (Malaysian dollar) (2.625 ringgits equal U.S.$1, June 1986).
Economic Index (1985): *Consumer Prices* (1980 = 100), all items, 125.5; food, 123.1.

Malaysia's Prime Minister Mahathir bin Mohamad led the National Front to victories in national and state elections.

AP/Wide World

MANITOBA

Political developments dominated the news in Manitoba during 1986.

Elections. On March 18 the New Democratic Party (NDP) led by Howard Pawley won the closest election in Manitoba's history, with less than a 1% lead over the Progressive Conservatives (PCs). Two splinter conservative groups got 3%, so the combined conservative vote was slightly higher than that of the NDP. In terms of legislative seats, the NDP's majority was cut to three. The provincial Liberals, under Sharon Carstairs, a 43-year-old former schoolteacher who was chosen party leader in 1984, doubled their percentage of the vote from the previous election, going from 7% to 14%. Carstairs won the first Liberal seat in a provincial general election in Western Canada since 1978.

In mid-1983 the New Democratic government had backed a constitutional provision guaranteeing the use of French in parts of the provincial civil service. Reaction against this proposal had caused opinion polls to register the lowest standing ever shown for an incumbent Manitoba government. During the next 2½ years, Pawley's government adopted a conscious policy of avoiding controversy on virtually every issue, thus depriving the opposition Conservatives of any easy way to attack it. Premier Pawley's methods paid off, though some of his supporters preferred a more interventionist attitude, especially in social policy.

During the 1986 election campaign the major parties avoided speaking about linguistic problems where possible. This drove some conservative voters to support more openly anti-French groups, such as the Confederation of Regions (COR), which did well in several rural constituencies. Only 7 of 57 legislative seats changed hands in the election, with the PCs picking up five from the NDP, while losing one to the NDP and one to the Liberals. Ironi-

cally, one of the PC gains came in Springfield, where the incumbent New Democrat, Andy Anstett, had been a major force in toning down the anti-NDP feeling over the French issue. He was defeated by a francophone PC candidate, which was also ironic since the PCs had been opponents of French language services.

Municipal elections held throughout Manitoba in October saw Russell Doern, a former NDP cabinet minister who had broken with his party over French services, finish a relatively close second against the well-established mayor of Winnipeg, Bill Norrie. Some observers felt that Doern's showing reflected continued anxiety over the language question, even though it was not an issue in the municipal elections.

Hydropower. In February, Premier Pawley and Energy and Mines Minister Wilson Parasiuk announced a C$4.3 billion sale of hydroelectric power to a group of U.S. utilities. According to Parasiuk, 50% of the profits from the sale would go toward maintaining low electricity rates in Manitoba. In his Speech from the Throne on May 8, the premier announced the creation of a Manitoba Energy Foundation to act as a form of heritage fund for such profits. Officials believe that Manitoba's surplus power situation should encourage new industry in the province and lead to an export boon. In an unrelated development Parasiuk resigned from the cabinet in May amid charges of impropriety and conflict of interest.

Unemployment. Unemployment in Manitoba declined in 1986. From a seasonally adjusted rate of 8.1% in January, unemployment in the province dropped to 6.6% in September. This compared with a national average of 9.8% and 9.5% in January and September, respectively.

MICHAEL KINNEAR
The University of Manitoba

MANITOBA · Information Highlights

Area: 250,946 sq mi (649 950 km²).

Population (Jan. 1986 est.): 1,075,400.

Chief Cities (1981 census): Winnipeg, the capital, 564,473; Brandon, 36,242; Thompson, 14,288.

Government (1986): *Chief Officers*—lt. gov., Pearl McGonigal; premier, Howard Pawley (New Democratic Party). *Legislature*—Legislative Assembly, 57 members.

Provincial Finances (1986–87 fiscal year budget): *Revenues,* $3,401,000,000; *expenditures,* $3,900,-000,000.

Personal Income (average weekly earnings, May 1986): $399.92.

Labor Force (July 1986, seasonally adjusted: *Employed* workers, 15 years of age and over, 532,000; *Unemployed,* 41,000 (7.7%).

Education (1986–87): *Enrollment*—elementary and secondary schools, 218,880 pupils; postsecondary—universities, 19,750; community colleges, 3,970.

(All monetary figures are in Canadian dollars.)

MARYLAND

William Donald Schaefer, a Democrat who had been mayor of Baltimore for 15 years, was elected governor by a four-to-one landslide in the 1986 elections, setting a state record for the largest margin of victory in a governor's race in the 20th century. Democratic Congresswoman Barbara Mikulski defeated Linda Chavez, a former aide to President Reagan, to capture for her party the Senate seat being vacated by retiring Sen. Charles Mathias, a Republican. The voters returned three Democrats and a Republican to the U.S. House of Representatives and elected one Republican and three Democrats in districts where incumbents were not running.

Baltimore Clipper Tragedy. The *Pride of Baltimore,* a 136-ft-(41-m-) long wooden sailing ship that served the city as a goodwill ambas-

MARYLAND • Information Highlights

Area: 10,460 sq mi (27 092 km²).
Population (1985 est.): 4,392,000.
Chief Cities (1980 census): Annapolis, the capital, 31,740; Baltimore (July 1, 1984 est.), 763,570; Rockville, 43,811.
Government (1986): *Chief Officers*—governor, Harry R. Hughes (D); lt. gov., J. Joseph Curran, Jr. (D). *General Assembly*—Senate, 47 members; House of Delegates, 141 members.
State Finances (fiscal year 1985): *Revenue,* $8,221,000,000; *expenditure,* $7,365,000,000.
Personal Income (1985): $69,680,000,000; per capita $15,864.
Labor Force (June 1986): *Civilian labor force,* 2,362,200; *unemployed,* 92,400 (3.9% of total force).
Education: *Enrollment* (fall 1984)—public elementary schools, 446,244; public secondary, 227,596; colleges and universities, 231,649. *Public school expenditures* (1983–84), $2,305,000,000 ($3,720 per pupil).

sador on trips throughout the world, rolled over and sank May 14 in a fierce storm north of Puerto Rico. The captain and 3 of the other 11 crew members died: 2 women and 6 men squeezed into a life raft and drifted in the Atlantic Ocean for five days before being picked up by a Norwegian freighter. The city-owned reproduction of a 19th century Baltimore clipper had been hand built in 1976–77 and had sailed more than 135,000 mi (217 256 km) to promote the city in U.S. and foreign ports. By October plans were being formulated to build another *Pride of Baltimore,* a larger, safer, more stable vessel that would, of necessity, sacrifice some of the original *Pride*'s authenticity for technological advances.

Old Court Scandals. Jeffrey A. Levitt, the former president of the defunct Old Court Savings and Loan Association, pleaded guilty to embezzlement and theft of $14.7 million and promised to repay the funds. On July 2 he was sentenced to 30 years in prison and ordered to pay a $12,000 fine for his part in the collapse of the thrift, which shook the state's savings and loan industry to its roots in 1985 and brought to light serious weaknesses in several other thrifts. The Internal Revenue Service (IRS) said Levitt owed some $1.67 million in back income taxes, and it confiscated a great deal of his wife's personal property, including real estate, cars, and objects of art.

By the end of 1986 only about half the Old Court depositors whose funds were frozen when the institution went into bankruptcy had been repaid. The General Assembly instituted programs to encourage strong savings institutions to absorb weak ones and to prevent the sorts of mismanagement that were revealed by the Old Court scandal. Allegations that Gov. Harry R. Hughes had been told of trouble developing in the savings and loan industry and had ignored the warning were considered a factor in his failure to gain his party's nomination to the U.S. Senate.

Other. A few months after the General Assembly enacted a $350,000 limit on "pain and suffering" awards in an attempt to hold down the rising cost of insurance, the company that insures most Maryland physicians raised its premiums an average of 50%, on top of a 29% increase in 1985. Medical Mutual Liability Insurance Society of Maryland, a not-for-profit company owned by policyholders, reported it had paid out more for malpractice claims in the first seven months of the year than in all of 1985.

The oldest newspaper in Baltimore, the *News American,* published its final edition on May 27, after its owner, the Hearst Corporation, was unable to find a buyer for the financially ailing daily. The following day, the Los Angeles-based Times Mirror Company, announced its $600 million purchase of the A.S. Abell Company, owner of the *Baltimore Sun* and *Evening Sun,* as well as local radio and TV stations.

The U.S. Congress transferred ownerships of two Virginia airports—Washington National and Dulles International airports—from federal ownership to a regional authority that is controlled by Virginia representatives. The state of Maryland had argued that the move would result in unfair competition for Baltimore-Washington International Airport.

The National Association for the Advancement of Colored People moved its headquarters from Brooklyn, NY, to Baltimore.

PEGGY CUNNINGHAM
"Insight Magazine"

MASSACHUSETTS

An unusual statewide election spelled more trouble for the beleaguered Massachusetts Republican Party, and controversies rocked the state's higher education system.

Elections. Despite President Reagan's victory in the state in 1984, no Republican has been elected to statewide office since 1970, when Francis W. Sargent was chosen governor. In 1986, Massachusetts looked even more like a "one party" state. Michael S. Dukakis, who was elected governor in 1974 and again in 1982, was a strong favorite for a third term. The contest among possible Republican challengers was halfhearted, with a young party activist, Gregory S. Hyatt, emerging in the lead at midyear. Charges of improper behavior, however, sent Hyatt's candidacy into eclipse, and Republican state leaders turned to a veteran legislator, state Rep. Royall H. Switzler of Wellesley. To the shock of the party faithful, after accepting the offer to run, Switzler announced that he had made untrue statements about his military record, falsely claiming combat service in Vietnam. After many days of agonizing consultation, Switzler withdrew his candidacy. As summer neared an end and the election loomed ahead, a businessman, George Kariotis, was persuaded to run. The final result was a predictable landslide for Dukakis, who won two thirds of the vote and was mentioned as a possible contender for national office after his strong showing.

Other statewide contests went to the Democrats as well. The lieutenant governor's spot was easily won by Evelyn Murphy, who became the first woman elected to statewide office.

The race for the congressional seat in the eighth district being vacated by retiring U.S. House Speaker Thomas P. O'Neill, Jr., was the subject of a great deal of political activity and considerable national attention. This was due in part to the candidacy of Joseph P. Kennedy II, son of the late Sen. Robert F. Kennedy. In the September primary Kennedy won out over a large field of opponents. In November, Kennedy easily defeated Republican Clark Abt to win the seat once held by his uncle, President John F. Kennedy.

The election also featured a number of closely fought referendum questions. Voters defeated proposals to regulate state-funded abortions and to permit state aid to private schools. The defeats were seen as a setback to the attempts of the powerful Catholic Church, which had lobbied hard for the proposals, to influence questions of public policy. Voters approved a measure limiting increases in state spending to the overall rate of economic growth and a measure repealing a mandatory auto seat-belt law, passed in 1985.

Education. Higher education is a major industry in Massachusetts, where the state college system is overshadowed by a large number of private institutions. The often-troubled state college system was dealt two blows during the year. In June the board of regents of higher education voted to name state Rep. James G. Collins (D) as chancellor, passing over candidates recommended by a search committee. The move was widely interpreted as an attempt to keep strong political links to the college system. The action angered Governor Dukakis,

MASSACHUSETTS • Information Highlights
Area: 8,284 sq mi (21 456 km²).
Population (1985 est.): 5,822,000.
Chief Cities (July 1, 1984 est.): Boston, the capital, 570,719; Worcester, 159,843; Springfield, 150,454.
Government (1986): *Chief Officer*—governor, Michael S. Dukakis (D). *Legislature*—Senate 40 members; House of Representatives, 160 members.
State Finances (fiscal year 1985): *Revenue,* $11,485,000,000; *expenditure,* $11,028,000,000.
Personal Income (1985): $95,361,000,000; per capita, $16,380.
Labor Force (June 1986): *Civilian labor force,* 3,075,000; *unemployed,* 113,900 (3.7% of total force).
Education: *Enrollment* (fall 1984)—public elementary schools, 566,028; public secondary, 293,363; colleges and universities, 421,175. *Public school expenditures* (1983–84), $2,979,000,000 ($3,739 per pupil).

who on August 1 appointed three new regents to replace Collins supporters whose terms had expired. The reconstituted board then removed Collins and began again the search for a new chancellor, but the actions left angry feelings on all sides and a cloudy future ahead.

Earlier in the year the state college system was rocked by charges that the president of Westfield State College, Francis J. Pilecki, had sexually assaulted a number of male students and that state officials had approved a $10,000 settlement with one of the students. Pilecki resigned his post to face criminal charges. As the case dragged on, public skepticism about the higher education system in the state increased.

Economy. The state's economic surge continued throughout the year. Unemployment, which stood at 3.9% at the start of 1986, rose only slightly to 4.3% by the end of the third quarter. The real-estate market—both commercial and residential—continued to boom, creating concerns about rising prices and the lack of affordable housing for low- and middle-income people. Industrial production, long a weak link, also gained during the year.

HARVEY BOULAY
Rogerson House

AP/Wide World

Joseph P. Kennedy II followed in his family's footsteps and staged a successful campaign for the U.S. House of Representatives. In winning the seat vacated by the retiring House Speaker Thomas P. O'Neill, the eldest son of the late Robert F. and Ethel (third from left) Kennedy spent more than $1.5 million.

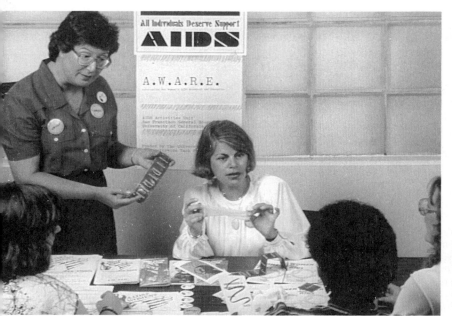

Judith Cohen (center) is codirector of the Association for Women's AIDS Research and Education (AWARE), which is based in San Francisco. Educating the public about the deadly disease was a prime objective of health officials in 1986.

© James D. Wilson, "Newsweek"

MEDICINE AND HEALTH

Americans are healthier and living longer than ever before according to a government report issued in early 1986. A man who was 45 years old in 1983 could expect to live to the age of 74.7; his female counterpart could expect to live to 80.4. Gains have had their price, however. Per capita spending on health reached $1,580 in 1984—three times the amount spent ten years earlier. Medical costs continued to increase more rapidly than consumer prices in general, accounting for a record 10.6% of the U.S. gross national product.

During 1986 promising gains were made in understanding Alzheimer's disease and in identifying genes involved in cancer and muscular dystrophy. But the year's medical headlines were dominated by two scourges: AIDS and addiction to crack, an extremely potent form of cocaine (see DRUGS AND ALCOHOL).

AIDS. All known cases of Acquired Immune Deficiency Syndrome (AIDS) in the United States have been caused by a so-called retrovirus identified in 1984. During 1986 scientists identified two other retroviruses that cause AIDS in humans, plus a closely related virus that does not appear to cause the disease.

By late 1986 more than 27,000 cases of AIDS had been reported in the United States. There was increasing concern over the probable spread of the deadly disease into the general population from the present high-risk groups (primarily homosexual men and intravenous drug abusers), although experts disagreed over how rapidly and to what extent this might occur. The Public Health Service esti-

mated that by 1991 there could be a tenfold increase in the number of AIDS cases and deaths, with about 9% of those cases occurring among heterosexual men and women. Because there appears to be an average time lag of five years between infection with the AIDS virus and the onset of the disease, most of the people who will develop AIDS by 1991 are believed to be already infected with the virus.

The National Academy of Sciences urged a $2 billion-a-year educational and research program to combat AIDS, saying this "is a small fraction of the billions of dollars for care that the epidemic is sure to cost, especially if it is not rapidly curbed." Surgeon General C. Everett Koop recommended strong sex-education programs in homes and schools to inform children about how AIDS can and cannot be spread.

Many public-health officials believe that vaccination is the only way to stop the spread of AIDS. A potential AIDS vaccine has been developed by researchers at the National Institutes of Health (NIH) and at Oncogen, a biotechnology firm in Seattle. Oncogen tested the vaccine on monkeys and chimpanzees, reporting that the animals showed evidence of developing protective antibodies and cellular immunity—two essential types of immunity against viral invasion. Trials of the vaccine on high-risk human volunteers were expected to begin in 1987.

Researchers at the University of California at Davis reported success in using a vaccine to suppress an AIDS-like virus in monkeys. Twelve monkeys were injected with a lethal dose of the simian virus. After one year, none of the six vaccinated monkeys showed any signs of infection; of the six monkeys that had not been vaccinated, three were dead and the remainder showed signs of exposure to the disease.

Vaccination would protect only people who do not have AIDS. For those with the disease, hopes of survival depend on the development of a drug that will slow or reverse the disease's progress. In September, following reports that the experimental drug azidothymidine (AZT) cut death rates markedly among some AIDS patients, the government announced that the drug would be made more widely available. Officials stressed, however, that AZT is not a cure and that its long-term effects remain unknown.

Medical Genetics. The development of a possible vaccine against AIDS and the discovery of a hitherto unknown gene in the AIDS virus were but two advances during 1986 in the increasingly important fields of medical genetics and biotechnology. In July the U.S. Food and Drug Administration (FDA) approved commercial production of the first genetically altered vaccine for humans—a vaccine designed to protect people against infection by the hepatitis B virus, which causes an incurable and sometimes fatal liver disease.

A team of Harvard scientists discovered the gene that causes Duchenne's muscular dystrophy, an illness that weakens muscles and is eventually fatal. A team headed by Dr. Robert A. Weinberg of the Massachusetts Institute of Technology identified a gene that they believe prevents retinoblastoma, a rare form of cancer of the eye. Discovery of these genes may lead to treatments for the disease.

Cancer. Since interferon, a hormone-like protein produced by the body in response to infection, was discovered in 1957, there has been hope that it would prove to be an effective agent in the fight against cancer. With the development of gene splicing, scientists have been able to produce sufficient quantities of the substance to study its effects on patients suffering from various illnesses. Experiments with patients suffering from cancer have produced mixed results; the most promise has been shown among those with a rare form of malignancy called hairy cell leukemia. In June the FDA approved two preparations of interferon to treat hairy cell leukemia—the first time that the genetically produced drug became available by prescription in the United States.

According to the National Cancer Institute "there now is scientific consensus that about 80% of cancer cases appear to be linked to the way people live their lives." The role of diet is particularly important, especially for cancers of the colon and rectum, stomach, breast, prostate, endometrium, and perhaps lungs. A study by scientists at the Johns Hopkins School of Hygiene and Public Health indicated that beta-carotene and vitamin E, nutrients found in vegetables and grains, appear to reduce the risk of lung cancer.

More than 500,000 new cases of skin cancer are diagnosed each year in the United States, making it the most common of all cancers. The incidence of melanoma, the most virulent form of skin cancer, has doubled since 1970, reaching an estimated 23,000 new cases and 5,600 deaths in 1986. The Skin Cancer Foundation and dermatologists point out that the increase has resulted from Americans' love affair with tanning. They urge people to decrease the time they spend in the sun and to use sunscreens to protect against the sun's harmful radiation. They also caution against the use of tanning booths, most of which use ultraviolet-A (UVA) radiation, which penetrates more deeply into the skin than does ultraviolet-B radiation, causing changes in blood vessels and premature aging. Scientists at Argonne National Laboratory have shown that molecules in skin cells can absorb UVA radiation and pass the energy along in a form that can damage DNA, resulting in mutations that can lead to cancer. In September an FDA warning went into effect asserting that suntanning devices may pose a serious health threat.

A study of people suffering from pancreatic cancer revealed that cigarette smoking was associated with a five- to sixfold increased risk of developing the disease. A National Academy of Sciences report released in November stated that environmental tobacco smoke—that is, smoke from other people's cigarettes—clearly increases health risks for children and non-smoking spouses of cigarette smokers.

A study based on an analysis of more than 9,000 women concluded that longtime use of birth-control pills does not increase a woman's risk of breast cancer, even if she has a family history of the disease. Another study estimated that diagnostic X-rays may cause 1,000 cancer cases annually—about 1% of all leukemia and breast cancer cases in the United States.

The Common Cold. Rhinoviruses, the largest single group of cold-causing viruses, account for 30% to 50% of all colds. In January researchers in the United States and Australia reported that the use of an interferon nasal spray can prevent the spread of rhinovirus infections in families after one member of a family shows signs of a cold. Families that used the drug had 40% fewer colds than families using a placebo. This was the first time that a drug was shown to be effective in halting the spread of the common cold. However, the current cost of interferon limits the drug's practical use.

When rhinoviruses enter a person's nose, they attach to special receptors on the surface of nasal cells. They then insert their genetic material into the cells and begin to reproduce. In an experiment at the University of Virginia School of Medicine, volunteers were given nose drops containing special antibodies designed to attach to the same receptors that the viruses use. This subsequently blocked the entrance of rhinoviruses into the nasal cells, and the volunteers had less severe colds than did people who received placebos.

Another approach to designing a drug that will cure the common cold was being pursued by researchers at Purdue University. They have pinpointed the site on a rhinovirus where antiviral compounds bind and work to thwart reproduction. The compounds prevent the outside shell of the virus from breaking apart and releasing ribonucleic acid (RNA). "Without RNA to direct the synthesis of more viral proteins, the virus cannot replicate itself and cause infection," explained Michael G. Rossmann, head of the research group.

Alzheimer's Disease. New hope was raised in the battle against Alzheimer's disease, the leading cause of senility among elderly Americans. Drs. Peter Davies and Benjamin Wolozin, researchers at New York City's Albert Einstein College of Medicine, found that the brains of Alzheimer's victims contain large amounts of a protein that is not found in the brains of healthy people. Later in the year they announced that they had developed an experimental test to detect the protein in cerebrospinal fluid. The test may make it possible to diagnose Alzheimer's during its early stages.

In a study conducted by researchers working in Pasadena, CA, an experimental drug, tetrahydroaminoacridine (THA), significantly improved the memories of a small group of senile people and temporarily reduced other symptoms of the disease. The researchers found "no serious side effects attributable to THA" and noted that when the drug was withdrawn the patients' symptoms of senility returned.

Heart Disease. Heart and circulatory diseases, the nation's main cause of death, cost Americans an estimated $78.6 billion in 1986 according to the American Heart Association. A major cause of these diseases is hardening of the arteries, or atherosclerosis, which has been closely related to high levels of cholesterol in the blood—which, in turn, have been related to poor dietary habits that include the excessive intake of saturated fats and cholesterol. In the United States, these poor habits begin early in life. Approximately 30% of America's children have cholesterol levels considered to be abnormally high. Yet a study of 3,000 children conducted by the American Health Foundation showed that even modest dietary changes combined with exercise can significantly reduce cholesterol levels.

In August the American Heart Association announced that it had revised its influential dietary guidelines. The new guidelines recommend that total fat intake be limited to 30% of the calories consumed daily. Currently, about 40% of the calories consumed by the average American comes from fats. No more than 10% of total calories should be saturated fats, and cholesterol intake should not exceed 300 milligrams per day—about the amount in one egg.

The value of checking and controlling cholesterol levels beginning in childhood was reinforced by Dr. William P. Newman III of Louisiana State University Medical Center, who found that teenagers who have high blood cholesterol levels exhibit early stages of ath-

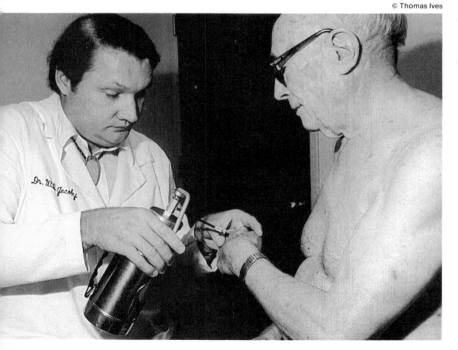

© Thomas Ives

A dermatologist sprays liquid nitrogen on the skin of a patient to remove a precancerous growth. Early detection is of major importance in treating skin cancer, a disease that reportedly affects 1 in 7 Americans.

erosclerosis. These youths are likely to have fatty streaks of cholesterol in their blood vessels. The streaks gradually become plaque that hardens the artery walls and narrows the channels through which blood flows.

Although the buildup of plaque can be slowed by diet, drugs, and exercise, until recently there had been no known way to get rid of plaque that already had formed. But a new blood-cleansing treatment called LDL-pheresis shows promise of reversing atherosclerosis. LDL stands for low-density lipoproteins, particles in blood plasma that are believed to deposit the cholesterol on the artery walls. LDL-pheresis is much like kidney dialysis. A patient's blood flows from the body through a device that removes LDL particles from the plasma; the cleansed blood is then returned to the patient.

The two longest-surviving recipients of permanent artificial hearts died during 1986. William J. Schroeder, who survived 620 days on the device, died on August 6. Murray P. Haydon, who lived for 488 days, died on June 20. At year's end no one else was living on a permanent artificial heart, but the device continued to be used as a temporary measure to keep critically ill patients alive until a human heart donor can be found.

Organ Transplants. In September, U.S. Secretary of Health and Human Services Otis R. Bowen announced the establishment of a single national network to match donated human organs for transplanting to recipients. "This . . . will improve access to donor organs and ensure fairness in the allocation of organs," he said. The issue of fairness was raised in June when one baby in need of a heart transplant was bypassed in favor of a more-publicized infant. The baby finally received a transplant, but the incident focused attention not only on troubling ethical issues but also on the scarcity of organs. According to Bowen some 10,000 Americans are awaiting donor organs. To increase the supply, 27 states have passed laws requiring hospital officials to remind relatives of brain-dead individuals that organs are badly needed.

In June the FDA approved the first therapeutic use within the human body of a monoclonal antibody, a substance produced by fusing and cloning cells in a laboratory. The product is designed to reverse acute kidney transplant rejections, which affect about 60% of the 7,000 Americans who annually receive such transplants.

Endometriosis. Endometriosis, the abnormal growth of tissue lining the uterus, afflicts as many as 10 million American women and is a major cause of infertility. It is sometimes called the "career woman's disease" because it often strikes women in their 20s and 30s. Harvard researchers reported that women with heavier, longer, or more frequent menstrual periods are more susceptible to endometriosis. They also noted that rigorous exercise, which previously had been shown to decrease menstrual flow, seems to decrease risks of getting the disease.

Contraception. In January, G. D. Searle & Company, the last major manufacturer of intrauterine contraceptive devices (IUDs), announced that it was discontinuing the sale of the devices in the United States because of "unwarranted product litigation" and the difficulty of obtaining liability insurance. The firm's IUDs, like others that previously had been withdrawn from the market, were the subject of hundreds of lawsuits brought by women who charged that the devices caused pelvic infections, fertility problems, and other injuries.

Product-liability fears have also slowed contraceptive research, though several dozen methods are in some stage of research or development. Perhaps the closest to FDA approval in 1986 was Norplant, a string of tiny capsules containing a hormone that inhibits ovulation. The capsules are implanted under the skin of the arm and gradually release the hormone over a period of up to five years. If a woman wishes to become pregnant, the capsules can be removed; fertility returns almost immediately. Norplant is available in many European countries and was undergoing the last phase of clinical trials in the United States in 1986.

JENNY TESAR, *Medicine and Science Writer*

Dentistry

During the past twenty years, there has been a 50% decrease in tooth decay among Americans, thanks to fluoridation and improved oral hygiene. New research promises to lead to a continued decrease, not only among the young but among adults whose fear of pain have made them reluctant to visit dentists.

Alternative to Drilling. An amino-acid-based solution developed by orthodontist Joseph Kronman and root-canal specialist Melvin Goldman holds particular appeal for the millions of people who postpone dental treatment because of their fear of the dentist drill. Marketed under the trade name Caridex, the solution breaks down decay but not healthy tooth enamel. It allows the dentist to flush out the decay, thereby greatly reducing the need of drilling and the use of anesthetics. (Some drilling is still needed to attach a filling to the excavated tooth.)

Replacement Therapy. More than 1,000 different types of bacteria live in a person's mouth. Some cause tooth decay and periodontal disease. Others are antagonistic to the pathogens, inhibiting their growth. At the Forsyth Dental Center in Boston, dentist Jeffery D. Hillman has created a mutant strain of bacteria that is more successful at colonizing the mouth than are certain cavity-causing bacteria. The mutants produce a particularly powerful variant of the protein bacteriocin, which stops the growth of closely related strains that generate large amounts of the acid that decay teeth. When introduced into the mouth the mutants replace the pathogens, thereby helping to prevent tooth decay. Further work may soon make such replacement therapy a practical reality.

Infected Toothbrushes. The American Dental Association recommends switching to a new toothbrush every three or four months. But Dr. Thomas Glass, an oral pathologist at Oklahoma University School of Dentistry reports that a brush can accumulate a large bacterial population within 17 to 35 days. He recommends changing brushes at least once a month—and more frequently among people who suffer from respiratory, periodontal, and other oral diseases. He and his associate, May Lare, found that patients suffering from mouth infections experienced significant improvement when they changed brushes every two weeks.

Sensitive Teeth. University of Iowa researchers found that Scotchbond, a substance developed to bond white fillings to teeth, provides long-term relief to people whose teeth are exceptionally sensitive to hot or cold foods and beverages. A single coating of the adhesive brings immediate relief and, for the great majority of people, prevents sensitivity for six months or more.

JENNY TESAR

Mental Health

In June 1986, the National Institute of Mental Health (NIMH) observed the 40th anniversary of the signing by President Harry Truman of the National Mental Health Act which made NIMH the federal agency responsible for improving the mental health of all Americans. The observance took the form of a two-day scientific seminar, at which a number of renowned mental-health researchers recounted advances made during the four decades since 1946.

NIMH has actively encouraged interdisciplinary cross-fertilization, and the confluence of discoveries from previously unrelated research areas has contributed appreciably to our growing understanding of normal and abnormal behavior. Due in part to NIMH research-training support the fields themselves have blended. Where once there were psychologists, psychiatrists, neurologists, biologists, and pharmacologists, there are now neuroscientists, psychoimmunologists, psychopharmacologists, biopsychologists, and neuroendocrinologists, often working together in the same laboratory.

Depression. NIMH has found that either of two forms of psychotherapy—cognitive/behavior therapy and interpersonal therapy—is as effective as standard drug usage in treating depression. The NIMH Depression Collaborative Study is the first multisite study to test two forms of psychotherapy with use of a tricyclic antidepressant in treating depression.

Because 9.4 million Americans suffer depression during a six-month period, and about 80 million Americans have used some form of psychotherapy, the results of the study have attracted wide interest. The $10 million study, which began in 1980, involved 239 moderately to severely depressed patients treated at three sites—George Washington University, the University of Pittsburgh, and the University of Oklahoma. The study excluded manic-depressive and psychotic-depressive patients.

Patients, randomly assigned to four groups, received 16 weeks of one of these treatments: cognitive/behavior therapy, interpersonal therapy, antidepressant imipramine with 30 minutes of supportive therapy, or a pill-placebo with 30 minutes of supportive therapy. Patients are being followed for 18 months after the initial treament. Researchers hope the study will be a step along the way predicting which type of depression will respond better to one of these treatments. Final results from the study were expected in late 1986.

In another area of work in depression, NIMH has developed a national education program, the Depression Awareness, Recognition, and Treatment program, to improve the identification, assessment, treatment, and clinical management of depressive disorders through a campaign outreach to three major audiences—primary-care providers, mental-health specialists, and the general public.

Schizophrenia. The year 1986 saw the beginning of the largest study of schizophrenia treatment ever undertaken. The $5 million study would be focused on patients at five major treatment centers across the United States, involving about 60 professional workers on multidisciplinary teams, 540 selected subjects and their families, and will extend to 1990. It will examine use of standard dose neuroleptic medication, reduced dosage, and targeted dosage in separate groups of patients whose treatment will be combined with family management. Impetus of the study comes from the fact that major treatment for schizophrenia, the use of anti-psychotic drugs, causes neurological side effects such as tardive dyskinesia and, in high dosages, may render patients less accessible to treatment. Because talking therapies have not proved successful in most cases of schizophrenia, therapists are looking to reduce drug dosage, and to maintain a balance between reducing symtoms on the one hand and not inducing relapse on the other.

See also feature article, PHOBIAS, page 67.

SHERVERT H. FRAZIER, M.D.
Director, National Institute of Mental Health

© Tom Smart/Gamma-Liaison

Above average rainfall caused the Great Salt Lake in Utah to reach record levels. Salt Lake City battled flooding.

METEOROLOGY

Meteorologists in 1986 observed an ozone "hole" in the Antarctic stratosphere that might be related to global atmospheric changes. Other major phenomena under study included the possibility of global warming, the effects of acid rain, and the nuclear winter theory.

Ozone Hole. The ozone layer about 15 mi (24 km) above the earth serves as a protective screen against much of the sun's harmful ultraviolet radiation. Scientists from the British Antarctic Survey first reported in 1985 that a region of this layer above Antarctica had a remarkably low concentration of ozone. Study of records has since revealed that over the past several years the "hole" has appeared and expanded each September and October, then closed up again. Since the late 1960s the amount of ozone in the hole may apparently have decreased by about 50%, but on the other hand the 1986 concentration at the center of the hole was about the same as in 1984.

Concern over the phenomenon relates to whether it is temporary and perhaps natural, or whether it is instead a precursor to further deterioration of the ozone layer as a result of human activities—in particular, the introduction of chlorofluorocarbons (CFCs) and other gases into the atmosphere. CFCs are used in spray cans, refrigerators, air conditioners, foam rubber, and industrial solvents. A U.S. research team that went to Antarctica in August to study the hole further confirmed its existence but was unable to establish its cause. Leading candidates among possible natural causes are changing winds that redistribute the

ozone, and sunspot effects. The answer may be a complex combination of these and other mechanisms.

Global Warming. Concern is also growing that introduction of carbon dioxide, CFCs, and other gases into the atmosphere, along with activities such as deforestation, could cause the global climate to warm significantly in the 21st century and lead to a rise in sea level. Scientists are studying current climate patterns for indications that the warming is under way, as suggested by data on global surface temperatures that do show a warming trend. The most recent Antarctic research, however, has shown that the ice cover on the whole is increasing and is therefore acting to lower the sea level rather than raise it.

Acid Rain. Most scientists agree that sulfur-containing emissions from smokestacks are major contributors to the so-called acid rain that is damaging forests and polluting lakes in many areas. Despite pressure from Canada and from U.S. environmentalists, however, the Reagan administration in 1986 agreed only to support research into emission-control technology. An attempt in Congress to require restrictions on factory emissions emerged from subcommittee but was not passed. Late in 1986 the Environmental Protection Agency (EPA), which has the authority to mandate such restrictions, was appealing a federal court order to obey the law and require installation of any of the proven, but expensive, methods to reduce emissions.

Nuclear Winter. A report issued by the Scientific Committee on Protection of the Environment strengthened the scientific case for the nuclear winter theory and provided a detailed ecological assessment of the effects of such a catastrophe. The result of a two-year effort by 300 scientists from more than 30 countries, the report described the possible climatic results of the materials thrown into the atmosphere should even a portion of the world's nuclear arsenal be detonated. Several hundred million persons could die from the direct effects of nuclear war, but several billion more could die from starvation when food production and distribution ceased during an extended period of intense cloud cover and freezing temperatures. A small-scale test of the nuclear winter theory also was conducted in California in December, when scientists studied the atmospheric effects of an intentional brush fire covering several hundred acres. Results of this test were expected by early 1987.

El Niño Prediction. During some years, weakened trade winds change the pattern of Pacific Ocean currents, including the El Niño current off the coast of Peru. If the so-called El Niño event is a severe one, as in 1982–83, the resulting climatic effects can be drastic and widespread. On March 13, scientists from Columbia University's Lamont-Doherty Geological Observatory issued a forecast of such an event for the winter of 1986–87. The forecast was made possible by advances in computer modeling of the atmosphere and ocean in the tropical Pacific region that, for the first time, incorporated essential aspects of the ocean-atmosphere interaction. On the same day, the Climate Analysis Center of the National Oceanic and Atmospheric Administration (NOAA) issued a more mildly worded statement on the possibility of an El Niño. By the year's end evidence existed that an event was in progress, but one of a mild nature that could simply be called a "Pacific warming."

Aviation Aids. Wind shear has caused many aviation accidents during takeoff and landing, and installation of the NEXRAD radar system is essential for a ground-based means of avoiding wind shear. The federal government has delayed funding the system, however, so the Federal Aviation Administration and NASA embarked on a five-year program to produce a system that will work in the cockpit, alerting a pilot that the plane is approaching a wind-shear situation and providing instructions as to how to avoid it. A current program by the Department of Transportation is also training pilots to deal with wind shear, using simulators.

Icing is another disruptive phenomenon for pilots, and one of the most dangerous. The U.S. government has embarked on a research effort to improve the forecasting and detection of icing and the design of aircraft to prevent it. Meanwhile, a current research effort at Denver's airport demonstrated the ability to identify, remotely, 90% of the icing conditions reported by pilots within 10 mi (16 km) of the airport, and 77% of such conditions up to 50 mi (80 km) away.

Other Forecasting News. In 1985, a federal judge awarded $1,250,000 against NOAA's National Weather Service (NWS) after three fishermen died near Boston as a result of relying on a weather forecast that did not include a quickly developing storm. In 1986 a three-judge panel of the U.S. Court of Appeals unanimously overturned the award, ruling that the NWS was doing the best job it could and was not to be held responsible if some forecasts proved wrong.

At NOAA's National Meteorological Center, a second Cyber 205 supercomputer was installed for making numerical weather forecasts. The added computer makes possible an accelerated research program, particularly on the problem of medium-range forecasts (one to three weeks).

Following the nuclear reactor disaster at Chernobyl in the USSR (*see* page 218), U.S. computer models were able to forecast the paths of the clouds of radioactive materials released into the atmosphere. They also predicted the resulting concentrations of radioactivity in nearby European countries.

In Europe, the Eumetsat meteorological organization was established by 16 participating nations. Eumetsat, which will operate and distribute data from Europe's Meteosat weather satellite system, has headquarters in Darmstadt, West Germany.

Weather Highlights. The devastating drought in Africa's Sahel region ended as normal rainfall returned. At the same time, southern Brazil, Paraguay, and northeastern Argentina experienced the worst drought in more than 100 years. A record drought also hit the southeastern United States, from Delaware through Mississippi. As a result of less than 70% of normal rainfall during the spring and summer, the area experienced failing crops and low reservoirs. In the center of the region the rainfall was 40% of normal, the least recorded in a century. In July record temperatures of more than 100° F (38° C) baked the region, but in August normal precipitation returned.

The Great Salt Lake and Great Lakes rose to record levels due to above-normal rainfall in those regions during recent years. In 1985–86 the Great Salt Lake rose 10 ft (3 m) and caused millions of dollars worth of damage. Aerial surveys were assisting in the planning of efforts to drain some of this water into the desert.

Only four hurricanes occurred in the Atlantic Ocean, or half the normal number. Study of 1985 records showed that on September 22 of that year, a buoy located 200 mi (320 km) east of Cape Hatteras measured a wave of over 46 ft (13 m) high as Hurricane Gloria passed to the west. This was the highest wave ever measured by an Atlantic buoy.

ALAN ROBOCK, *University of Maryland*

MEXICO

Mexico's economic crisis deepened when oil prices tumbled in the first quarter of the year. The economy was thrown into a deep recession while the government had to cut public spending further to meet creditors' demands. Controversial elections in Chihuahua state erupted in strong antigovernment protests. Relations with the United States became bitter when prominent U.S. officials severely criticized both high Mexican government officials and the government itself.

Politics. In July, Mexicans elected a number of state governors and legislatures as well as municipal officials, but attention was focused on the state of Chihuahua, which has seen an upsurge of strength from the chief opposition party, the National Action Party (PAN in Spanish). The government and its party, the Institutional Revolutionary Party (PRI), poured money and personnel into the state to counter the possibility of a PAN gubernatorial victory.

PAN offered Francisco Barrio Terrazas, mayor of Ciudad Juárez, as its candidate for the governorship. PRI, however, broke precedent by running Fernando Baeza Meléndez, a former PAN supporter and wealthy businessman as its candidate, thus regaining some of the private enterprise support lost when Mexican banks were nationalized in September 1982. Gerrymandering of polling places, the presence of troops, and the printing of extra ballots seemed to indicate that the government was determined to maintain control of Chihuahua at any cost. A Gallup poll a few weeks before the election indicated that PRI would obtain 58% of the vote.

PRI claimed a landslide victory in all but one mayor's race, but PAN members accused the government of fraud and demonstrated for weeks in an effort to change the results. Election results are not announced until one week after the election takes place, giving the government ample time to alter the true results and opposition parties time to try to intimidate the government. PAN members closed international bridges to the United States, led antigovernment demonstrations, and rioted in some places.

The Chihuahua electoral controversy stirred Mexican politics for almost two months. Chihuahua businessmen, suffering economic losses, especially from tourism in Ciudad Juárez, protested PAN's tactics. President Miguel de la Madrid, seeking to calm the situation, ordered the government ministry to conduct an exhaustive analysis of the elections. As expected the ministry's report vindicated the government's claim of a PRI landslide. Almost simultaneously with de la Madrid's action, three Catholic bishops in Chihuahua state urged the annulment of the elections, asserting they were fraudulent. The government quickly

© Tony O'Brien/Picture Group

The government's Institutional Revolutionary Party (PRI) campaigned heavily in Chihuahua and claimed a landslide victory in July elections. The opposition charged fraud.

reminded them that the Church is forbidden to participate in politics. After the Chihuahua electoral college certified that PRI got 60% of the votes to PAN's 35%, PAN appealed to the Mexican Supreme Court to overturn the elections, an action it refused to take. In late August six PAN leaders sought political asylum in the United States but were refused. The Mexican government did recognize a mayoralty victory each for PAN and the People's Socialist Party. In his State of the Union address, President de la Madrid stressed that all of the elections held during 1986 were conducted legally and fairly.

The government could not afford to allow PAN to gain control of Chihuahua. Mexico's largest state, it produces 10% of the gross domestic product and borders the United States. Mexico has long feared that its border states would become too Americanized and slip out of Mexico City's orbit. In addition a PAN victory in light of the current economic crisis might encourage other states to select opposition parties to rule them. Much of Mexico's more than six decades of political stability is the result of one-party rule, and the government's tactics in the elections demonstrated its determination to retain control.

Economy. The precipitous drop in petroleum prices in the first quarter of the year sent the economy into a severe downward spiral.

AP/Wide World

In an address to the UN General Assembly on September 24, Mexico's President Miguel de la Madrid called on industrialized nations to restructure Third World debts.

Lost petroleum export income reduced the gross national product (GNP) by 6% as oil earnings dropped to less than half what they were the year before. The balance of trade declined 65%. Oil exports represented 70% of all export income and 45% of government revenue. The peso tumbled some 60% by midsummer. Net tourism revenue declined 3.3%. Inflation continued to rage, and experts expected the rate to approach 90% for the year. The nation's industrial production continued to decline.

There were a few bright spots. By September the agricultural and forestry sector increased production by 2.2%. For the same period the fish harvest grew 12.7%. Oil prices showed some sign of rising slightly.

Economic Policy. De la Madrid continued to reduce the government's role in the economy in an effort to meet the demands of the International Monetary Fund (IMF). Government expenditures were reduced to 22% of the gross domestic product (GDP), and the budgetary deficit was reduced to 4% of the GDP. Tariffs were reduced, with the highest rate cut in half to 50%. In July, Mexico joined the General Agreement on Trade and Tariffs (GATT), thus substantially weakening Mexico's historic protectionist policies. In the agreement, however, special protection was given to agriculture. The process of privatizing government enterprises continued. The national bank made more credit available to private enterprise. Foreign investment rules were relaxed to allow 51% foreign ownership on a case-by-case basis. Interest rates were raised on government bonds to attract more capital and to discourage capital flight.

To help offset government revenues lost with the oil price drop, an income tax surcharge was added to middle- and high-income groups. The price of gasoline, a government monopoly, was increased dramatically. The cost of other government products and services were raised less substantially and were offset, in part, by a 65% increase in the minimum wage.

Debt Crisis. After months of negotiation, Mexico and the IMF reached a new agreement on the servicing of Mexico's $98 billion foreign debt and continued IMF assistance to Mexico. Instead of the usual austerity requirements, the IMF yielded to Mexican threats to halt interest payments and tie future debt payments to Mexico's oil export income. The agreement, signed in October, called for the IMF and private banks to lend Mexico $12 billion over 18 months, to lower the interest rate slightly, and to reschedule $53 billion of the old debt. In addition Mexico would suspend payments on the principal of the old debt until 1993, use $8–10 billion as interest payments, and devote the remainder of the new money to stimulating non-oil exports and investing in economic infrastructure projects. Earlier in the year the IMF, the World Bank, and the Inter-American Development Bank had agreed to loan Mexico a total of $3.54 billion.

Foreign Affairs. Relations with the United States remained strained even though Washington supported Mexico's efforts to handle its debt crisis. The torture in August of Drug Enforcement agent Victor Cortez in Guadalajara was revealed while President de la Madrid was visiting President Ronald Reagan in Washington. The United States expressed outrage that Cortez was assaulted by Mexican police. When, by November, Mexico had taken few steps to discipline the perpetrators, Mexico was in danger of being put on the list of nations with serious human-rights violations, an action which would deny it U.S. aid. The case of the 1985 torture-murder of Enrique Camarena still had not been resolved to the satisfaction of the United States.

Accusations by members of the Reagan administration that President de la Madrid's relatives were involved in the production of narcotics was seen by many Mexicans as an attempt to undermine the Mexican government. In May, hearings before the U.S. Senate Foreign Relations subcommittee on Western Hemisphere affairs, chaired by Sen. Jesse Helms, prompted a strong diplomatic protest by Mexico. At the hearings U.S. federal officials severely criticized Mexico's handling of illegal immigration, the drug traffic, and governmental corruption. The mid-May resignation of outspoken U.S. Ambassador John Gavin was greeted with pleasure by Mexico not

MEXICO · Information Highlights

Official Name: United Mexican States.
Location: Southern North America.
Area: 761,601 sq mi (1 972 547 km²).
Population (mid-1986 est.): 81,700,000.
Chief Cities (1979 est.): Mexico City, the capital (1980 census), 9,377,300; Guadalajara, 1,906,145; Monterrey, 1,064,629.
Government: *Head of state and government,* Miguel de la Madrid Hurtado, president (took office Dec. 1982). *Legislature*—National Congress: Senate and Federal Chamber of Deputies.
Monetary Unit: Peso (795 pesos equal U.S.$1, floating rate, Oct. 19, 1986).
Gross Domestic Product (1984 U.S.$): $176,000,000,000.
Economic Indexes (1985): *Consumer Prices* (1980 = 100), all items, 1,071.5; food, 1,034.7. *Industrial Production* (1980 = 100), 107.
Foreign Trade (1985 U.S.$): *Imports,* $13,995,000,000; *exports,* $21,821,000,000.

only because his public criticisms of Mexico would cease but also because his departure suggested that the Reagan administration was not trying to destabilize the nation. Charles J. Pilliod, former chairman of Goodyear Tire and Rubber Co., was named to the post.

On the positive side Mexico and the United States reached a new agreement to stop the production of narcotics in Mexico and their export to the United States. The United States promised an additional $266 million to aid the Mexican anti-drug efforts. The United States worked closely with Mexico as the latter sought to refinance its foreign debt.

Presidents de la Madrid and Reagan met twice during 1986, discussing illegal immigration, drug traffic, financial and trade issues, and the Central American crisis. As a leader of the Contadora group, Mexico continued to oppose U.S. support of the "contras" in Nicaragua and to call for a negotiated settlement in Central America. On other fronts Mexico continued to seek friendship, trade, and aid from other nations. The leaders of Argentina, Greece, India, Tanzania, and Sweden met in Mexico with President de la Madrid for a Peace and Disarmament Conference. Guatemala and Mexico reached agreement on the return home of Guatemalan refugees who had fled to Mexico to escape persecution by previous Guatemalan regimes.

DONALD J. MABRY
Mississippi State University

MICHIGAN

The reelection of Gov. James J. Blanchard, cutbacks by General Motors Corporation, and the sale of Detroit's largest newspaper claimed major attention in Michigan during 1986.

Elections. Governor Blanchard, a Democrat, was reelected over Republican William Lucas in a two to one victory, dashing Lucas'

hope of becoming the nation's first elected black governor. Blanchard's winning margin (68.2%) was the largest since Republican Fred W. Green beat Democrat William A. Comstock for governor in 1928 with 69.9% of the vote. The Republicans retained their 20–18 majority in the state Senate, but the Democrats increased their 57–53 House majority to 64–46.

Economy. General Motors sent shock waves through the state by announcing plans to shut down six Michigan plants, moves expected to have a devastating impact on Flint, and also to hurt Detroit and Pontiac. Economists estimated that suppliers and others would lose three jobs for each of the 17,450 GM workers facing layoffs in Michigan over the next three years.

Although half the job losses were to occur in Pontiac and Detroit, Flint faced the most serious consequences. Economists estimated that half the earnings of Flint businesses are linked to the manufacture of durable goods, much higher than many other cities with more diversified economies. The company announced the closings after reporting a third quarter loss of $338.5 million. GM Chairman Roger Smith said the cutbacks would save the company $500 million a year.

Gannett Co., Inc. purchased the Evening News Association, publisher of *The Detroit News,* for $717 million effective February 18, ending 112 years of family ownership of the *News* by the descendants of James E. Scripps, who founded the paper.

The *News* and the competing *Detroit Free Press,* a Knight-Ridder Inc. publication, sub-

Michigan Gov. James J. Blanchard toasts supporters of his successful campaign for reelection. The 44-year-old Democrat was returned to office with 68.2% of the vote.

AP/Wide World

Some 7,000 Detroit municipal employees went on strike July 16, demanding a 26% pay raise over three years. The new three-year pact, agreed to August 4, called for 8%.

AP/Wide World

sequently requested approval of the U.S. Justice Department to form a Joint Operating Agreement under a federal law exempting some newspaper mergers from antitrust measures. The *Free Press* filed as a failing newspaper, claiming a projected $12 million loss in 1986. Under a Joint Operating Agreement, business operations of the two newspapers would be merged in an effort to cut operating expenses and guarantee profits; editorial functions would remain separate.

Storms. Devastating rains which started September 10 lashed central Michigan, forcing thousands to abandon their homes, washing away roads, bridges, and 11 dams, and swamping crops at harvest time. Rain continued to fall for 26 consecutive days in some places, and six deaths were attributed to the storms. Seeking financial assistance from the federal government, Governor Blanchard said Michigan suffered at least $323 million in losses during the initial 24 hours of rain. But farm losses alone, estimated at $118 million when the governor asked for aid, later were placed at $240 million after rain prevented the harvest of the surviving crops. Eventually 30 counties were declared disaster areas, making them eligible for a variety of state and federal relief measures.

Detroit. Work on a $200 million expansion of Detroit's Cobo Hall, the city's convention center, began late in 1985. The expansion is to add 350,000 sq ft (32 515 m²) to the facility and move it from 12th to 7th place in size among the nation's convention facilities.

Parks Controversy. The American Civil Liberties Union and the NAACP challenged an ordinance passed by Dearborn voters in November 1985, which restricted use of city parks to residents. The two groups contended that the ordinance was motivated by racial prejudice and would result in blacks being illegally

searched and detained. Supporters insisted it was designed to halt overcrowding of parks. On September 29, Wayne County Circuit Judge Marvin R. Stempien held the law to be invalid because it discriminated against blacks, and enforcement would have violated constitutional protection against illegal search and seizure.

Mansour Resignation. Agnes M. Mansour, a former Roman Catholic nun, resigned November 10 as state welfare director, ending a stormy four-year tenure that included a face-off with Pope John Paul II over the abortion issue. Shortly after she assumed office, the Vatican had ordered her to choose between her 30 years of religious life and the state job of running the Department of Social Services. Mansour, who said she personally opposes abortions but refused to oppose state funding of abortions for the poor, chose the state job.

CHARLES W. THEISEN, *"The Detroit News"*

MICHIGAN • Information Highlights

Area: 58,527 sq mi (151 586 km²).
Population (1985 est.): 9,088,000.
Chief Cities (July 1, 1984 est.): Lansing, the capital, 127,972; Detroit, 1,088,973; Grand Rapids, 183,000; Warren, 152,035; Flint, 149,007; Sterling Heights, 109,440.
Government (1986); *Chief Officers*—governor, James J. Blanchard (D); lt. gov., Martha W. Griffiths (D). *Legislature*—Senate, 38 members; House of Representatives, 110 members.
State Finances (fiscal year 1985): *Revenue,* $17,262,000,000; *expenditure,* $15,634,000,000.
Personal Income (1985): $123,673,000,000; per capita, $13,608.
Labor Force (June 1986): *Civilian labor force,* 4,422,000; unemployed, 415,400 (9.4% of total force).
Education: *Enrollment* (fall 1984)—public elementary schools, 1,117,814; public secondary, 589,168; colleges and universities, 507,293. *Public school expenditures* (1983–84), $5,200,000,000 ($3,208 per pupil).

MICROBIOLOGY

It is necessary to include foods containing ascorbic acid (vitamin C) in one's diet if the disease scurvy is to be avoided and general good health is to be maintained. Vitamin C has enjoyed considerable popularity as a diet supplement. In fact 30 million kg (66 million lbs) of the vitamin are used worldwide each year. Most vitamin C is produced industrially through a lengthy and expensive process.

In 1986, Dr. Stephen Anderson at Genentech, together with his colleagues at other institutions, reported on their use of recombinant DNA technology to produce an engineered bacterium that could carry out all but the last step of vitamin C production. It has been known for some time that the species *Erwinia herbicola* naturally converts glucose to the compound 2,5-diketo-D-gluconic acid (2,5-DKG), using a series of enzymatic steps. It also has been known that members of the genus *Corynebacterium* can convert 2,5-DKG to the compound 2-keto-L-gulonic acid (2-KLG) through a single enzymatic step.

In constructing the recombinant bacterium, the gene needed for the conversion of 2,5-DKG to 2-KLG was removed from the *Corynebacterium* strain and transferred to *E. herbicola*. This altered bacterium is able to synthesize 2-KLG from glucose. The conversion of 2-KLG to ascorbic acid requires only a simple reaction, catalyzed by either an acid or a base. Thus there now is the application of recombinant DNA technology to an industrial process for the production of a vitamin.

Alcohol from Lactose. In cheese making, the milk protein casein is coagulated by the enzyme rennin to form the curd, and the remaining liquid whey portion is generally discarded. Whey, which is formed in large amounts, contains the sugar lactose which is a potential resource for alcohol production. For the conversion of lactose to alcohol, the organism of choice is the yeast *Saccharomyces cerevisiae* because it has long been used by the brewing industry, and procedures for its use in commercial-scale production are highly developed. Unfortunately, the commonly available form of this species cannot be used because it lacks a lactose permease system that is needed to transport the sugar across its cell membrane and, in addition, it lacks the enzyme beta-galactosidase. This enzyme hydrolyzes lactose to glucose and galactose which are the basic substrates for alcohol production. However, other species of yeasts are able to split lactose into glucose and galactose and are able to produce alcohol, but they do so inefficiently.

In 1986, Drs. K. Sreekrishna and R. C. Dickson of the University of Kentucky reported on their success in transferring a gene for the lactose permease system and a gene for the enzyme beta-galactosidase from the yeast *Kluyveromyces lactis* to *S. cerevisiae*. There now is the potential for developing an efficient alcohol-producing process from whey, long considered a waste-product of cheese production.

Genetically Altered Microbes. The continuing controversy over field tests of genetically altered microbes appears to be approaching a resolution. A 1986 report of the U.S. Office of Science and Technology Policy recommended that the testing of genetically engineered products be supervised as follows: the Environmental Protection Agency (EPA) will handle microbial products; the U.S. Department of Agriculture (USDA) will regulate animal vaccines and genetically engineered plants; and the Food and Drug Administration (FDA) will have responsibility for pharmaceuticals and human vaccines.

On May 13, 1986, EPA granted permits to Drs. S. Lindow and N. Panopoulos of the University of California to test a genetically altered strain of *Pseudomonas syringae* on potatoes. The commonly found bacteria of this species secrete a protein that initiates the formation of ice crystals. In the modified strain, the gene that codes for the protein has been deleted. By spraying the potato plants with the altered bacteria so that the commonly found bacteria cannot establish themselves on the plants, it is hoped that the plants will be protected from frost. This will save many crops that now are lost when there are sharp drops in temperature.

AIDS Update. By the end of 1986, the number of U.S. cases of AIDS (Acquired Immune Deficiency Syndrome) passed 35,000, of whom half had died. The first AIDS cases in the United States were reported in 1981, and the number has about doubled each year. The U.S. Public Health Service has predicted that by the end of 1991 there will be a cumulative total of 270,000 cases in the United States and 179,000 deaths. As of late 1986, no one had been known to recover permanently from the disease. It takes an average of four years for an infected person to develop the disease and most die within two years after the condition becomes established.

On the hopeful side, Dr. P. S. Sarin at the National Cancer Institute and his colleagues at other institutions found that an antiserum prepared against a hormone (thymosin alpha-one) was effective in blocking the replication of the AIDS virus when it was growing in a cell culture line. An analysis of the amino acid composition of the hormone and the protein coat of the virus showed that certain sections of both amino acid sequences were extremely similar. This discovery raises the possibility of using that particular amino acid sequence in the preparation of a vaccine against the AIDS virus. (*See also* MEDICINE AND HEALTH.)

LOUIS LEVINE
City College of New York

AP/Wide World

Egypt's President Hosni Mubarak (left) and Israeli Prime Minister Shimon Peres met in September in Alexandria. A joint communiqué, issued at the end of the two-day summit, declared 1987 a year for serious peace negotiations.

MIDDLE EAST

Change, or at least the possibility of change, was the watchword in the Middle East in 1986. Though real peace seemed perhaps as distant as ever, tentative moves or definite steps indicated the possibility of significant transformations in a number of situations that had been frozen in immobility for years.

A number of these changes had to do with the success of Israel in breaking down the wall of international hostility that had surrounded it. These successes resulted in large measure from the diplomatic skill of Israel's Prime Minister Shimon Peres. Peres held the premiership from September 1984 to October 1986 under an unusual power-sharing agreement that created a coalition between his Labor Alignment and Yitzhak Shamir's rightist Likud bloc, an agreement which granted each man 25 months as prime minister. Under the terms of this agreement, Peres resigned and yielded his place to Shamir on October 20. Even if much of the credit had to go to Peres, his diplomatic moves were facilitated by the decline in oil prices, which diminished the diplomatic clout of the Arab oil states and the previous reluctance to adopt policies that might offend them.

Perhaps the most interesting of these novel steps was the visit of Peres to Morocco for a two-day summit, July 23–24, with King Hassan II. The summit, held in Ifrane, marked the first public visit by an Israeli leader to an Arab nation other than Egypt since the foundation of the state of Israel in 1948. As for results, however, there was more symbolism than substance in the meeting, and the event brought no direct progress toward breaking Middle East

deadlocks. Peres would neither agree to recognize the Palestine Liberation Organization (PLO) nor to withdraw from the Left Bank territories occupied since 1967. But, as the king said, "We did not meet to negotiate or to find a solution, but to explore the possibilities." Peres also acknowledged that few immediate results were to be expected from the talks. King Hassan was widely criticized in the Arab world for having met with Peres. The Moroccan embassy in Beirut was stormed and sacked, and Hassan resigned his chairmanship of the Arab League conference.

Spain established official ties with Israel in January, and the Ivory Coast reestablished links in February. Plans were announced for Israel and Poland to open low-level representation in each other's capitals. And in August, Peres made a successful state visit to Cameroon to celebrate the reestablishment of diplomatic relations with that African state.

The first Egyptian-Israeli summit meeting in five years was held September 11–12, when Peres and Egypt's President Hosni Mubarak met in Alexandria. The meeting was made possible by an August 12 agreement that created a procedure for settling the chronic territorial dispute over Taba on the Gulf of Aqaba. The main topic of discussion in Alexandria was the future of the Palestinians.

The USSR and Israel. Another diplomatic novelty among these Israeli gambits was the August 18 meeting in Helsinki between Israeli and Soviet representatives. It was the first direct official contact between the two countries since the Soviet Union, like many others, broke off diplomatic relations in 1967. (The breach, however, was never total. Contact had been maintained through that diplomatic innovation of the late 1960s, "interests sections" located in the embassies of third countries. The Soviets had maintained low-level representation through the Finnish embassy in Tel Aviv; the Israelis had established a section at the Dutch embassy in Moscow.) Normalized relations with Israel would mark a major shift for the Kremlin, since Soviet policy in the Middle East for two decades had featured a close alignment with, and support of, the anti-Israeli states of Iraq and, later, Syria. The Helsinki meetings, however, led to little. Scheduled to be held over two days, the discussions in fact terminated after only 90 minutes and were not resumed. An Israeli spokesman described them as "candid and correct"—candid being a diplomatic code word used for meetings that reveal a serious difference of view. Nevertheless, Shamir, then Israel's foreign secretary, said that other meetings might follow, leading to closer relations, "something we want."

Jordan. Of perhaps greater importance to Israel, because closer to home, were indications that Jordan was drawing closer to face-to-face negotiations. On October 7, Prime Minister Peres told the Knesset (Israeli parliament) that the United States was acting as a go-between in talks between Jerusalem and Amman that might pave the way to direct dealings.

Indeed, the policies of Jordan have been the most flexible, and therefore the most interesting, of those of any state in the region. Although Jordan is a parliamentary monarchy, its policies are very much the personal creation of King Hussein and his immediate circle. Though an Arab state, Jordan has practiced an unannounced policy of live-and-let-live with neighboring Israel, which permits considerable traffic between Jordan and the West Bank as well as other kinds of implicit cooperation. The Jordanian king has striven for many years to find a solution for Arab-Israeli problems, but his capacity to do this is limited by, among other things, Jordan's small size, population, and power.

In another attempt at peacemaking in the Middle East, the mediation of King Hussein led to the promise of a meeting on July 13 between representatives of Syria and Iraq (both Baathist states but chronically on bad terms). The proposed meeting, however, was canceled.

Hussein-Arafat Break. In 1986 Jordanian policy did take a significant turn. During the previous two years, King Hussein had made efforts in several meetings with PLO leader Yasir Arafat to work out an agreed negotiating position for dealings with Israel. The most recent of these meetings had occurred in late January. But in a striking development on February 19, Hussein abandoned such efforts, accusing Arafat of bad faith for reneging on earlier undertakings to accept UN Resolutions 242 and 338 as the basis for a settlement.

(These stipulate that Israel should return occupied Arab lands in return for recognition by the Arab states within "secure and recognized" borders.)

Jordan's freedom to initiate new peace policies presumably is curbed by the 1974 Arab League decision that the PLO is the sole legitimate representative of the Palestinians and by the fact that any direct attack on this principle by Amman would jeopardize the $100-million-per-year subsidy that Jordan receives from the Arab League. Nevertheless, the vigor with which the Jordanian king denounced the PLO on February 19, as well as a number of trends in his policy, made it clear that there was a growing rivalry between Jordan and the PLO for the loyalty of the West-Bank Palestinians. Jordan on July 7 ordered the closing of all 25 offices of Arafat's El Fatah, the largest faction within the PLO, and the next day expelled Khalil Wazir, a key Arafat aide. In the second half of the year, Jordan pursued a proposed $750 million, five-year development plan for the West Bank, but it had little success in interesting the wealthier Arab states to provide financing. It was also reported in November that Israel and Jordan had been secretly discussing a joint venture to develop the rich shale-oil deposits in the Negev, the desert shared by the two countries. Israel apparently has developed a new process that greatly reduces the cost of generating electricity from shale oil.

Lebanon. If some novelties did appear in 1986, it was also true that in the Middle East some things seem never to change. Among these tragic situations was the civil war in Lebanon, now in its 11th year with—despite innumerable "cease-fires"—no real resolution in sight. The principal clashes in 1986 were between Syria's moderate Shiite Muslim allies and fundamentalist groups supported by the clerical regime of Iran. Syria sought a multiparty solution in Lebanon that would preserve the essentials of a secular state, whereas Iran aimed at creating another extremist Islamic nation.

Syria. In the Middle East's market of power and influence, the stock of Syria slumped in 1986. Not only did it lose the control over the Lebanon situation that it appeared to possess the previous year, but it also was beset by a multitude of problems both domestic and foreign. These, in the eyes of some observers, imperiled the regime of President Hafez al-Assad, which had been in power since 1970—a long period of stability by previous Syrian standards. During 1986 Syria's currency was shaky, its relationship with Iran was viewed askance by other Arab states, and it was implicated in acts of international terrorism.

Iran-Iraq War. Another sadly persistent Mideast phenomenon was the war between Iran and Iraq, which passed into its seventh year in September but has been called, with

Loutof Allah Haydar (center), Syria's ambassador to Britain, met newsmen outside the Syrian embassy in London following Britain's diplomatic break with Damascus in October.

some justice, "the forgotten war." The fighting in 1986 was widely perceived as having tilted slightly in favor of Iran, which made its first significant penetration of Iraqi territory in February with the capture of Faw, an abandoned oil terminal in the Gulf. An attempted Iraqi counterstroke, the capture in May of Mehran on the central front, was reversed by Iran's recapture in July. Iraq continued to enjoy a great superiority in air power, which it used more extensively in 1986 to raid Iranian oil terminals and cities; in December there was an apparently damaging raid on the capital city of Tehran. Still, the scale of aerial bombardment was more reminiscent of World War I than of World War II.

From midsummer on, Iran put out reports of an impending decisive offensive. In early December it sent a new contingent of 100,000 to the front, but by year's end the promised big push still had not been delivered. Nevertheless, doubts about Iraq's long-term prospects in the war were enough to cause some perceptible thoughts among the oil-rich Gulf states about the desirability of hedging bets against an Iranian victory.

Early in December the Soviet Union and Iran signed an economic agreement aimed at increasing cooperation in commerce, banking, transportation, fisheries, and technology.

Terrorism. Much activity in and concerning the Middle East arose in connection with the baffling question of terrorism and how to counter it. Major events with regard to this question had to do with three states in particular: Libya, Syria, and Iran.

The U.S. desire to inflict some telling blow against Libya's Muammar el-Qaddafi was strengthened by terrorist attacks on Dec. 27, 1985, at Rome and Vienna airports, in which 19 people, five of them Americans, were killed. Libya was believed to be linked to the incidents. In January the United States imposed a trade embargo on Libya, and in March a U.S. armada made a "freedom of navigation" cruise in the Gulf of Sidra (claimed by Libya as territorial waters) during which there were minor military confrontations. Finally, after evidence emerged linking Libya to a bombing at a West Berlin disco in which a U.S. serviceman was killed, the United States on April 14 launched an air attack on targets in Libya. The British government of Prime Minister Margaret Thatcher was the only U.S. ally that gave wholehearted approval; indeed, it facilitated the mission by providing use of British airfields for U.S. fighter planes. Despite the widespread doubts, there did seem to be a decline in terrorist activity during the rest of the year.

Britain was particularly concerned with Syrian-sponsored terrorism. On October 24 the Thatcher government broke diplomatic relations with Damascus, closing down the Syrian embassy in London. The move was a consequence of "conclusive evidence of Syrian official involvement" in the abortive attempt on April 17 to blow up an Israeli airliner en route from London to Tel Aviv. Nezar Hindawi, a Palestinian found guilty at the Old Bailey of planting a bomb in the suitcase of his unwitting Irish girlfriend and sentenced to 45 years in prison, had traveled on a Syrian passport, and his visa application had been supported by the Syrian foreign ministry. British actions against Syria were denounced by the Soviet Union but supported by the United States and Canada and, after some hesitation, by Britain's European partners.

U.S. policy toward terrorism took on a more convoluted and inconsistent look as a result of revelations that began surfacing in November and went on unfolding in unlovely complexity. While the Reagan administration had been pressuring its allies to treat Iran as a pariah and had been enforcing a U.S. trade embargo against Iran, it now appeared that for some 15 months elements in the U.S. government had been engaged in an elaborate clandestine operation: contact had been made with "moderate" elements in Iran, quantities of arms had been sold to Iran as an inducement to free certain hostages, and proceeds of the sales had been funneled to "contra" rebels in Nicaragua. The eventual impact on U.S. politics and policies was still unclear, but it seemed likely to be a complicating or even crippling factor for the Reagan administration.

See also articles on individual countries.

ARTHUR CAMPBELL TURNER
University of California, Riverside

MILITARY AFFAIRS

Much of the emphasis in military affairs during 1986 was focused on the Strategic Defense Initiative (SDI), the U.S. plan for a space-based defense system to repel nuclear ballistic missile attack. Nowhere was the influence of SDI more evident than at the October mini-summit in Reykjavik, Iceland, where U.S. President Ronald Reagan and Soviet General Secretary Mikhail Gorbachev were unable to reach far-reaching arms control agreements because of differences over limitations on SDI testing and development. (*See* ARMS CONTROL.)

As the year drew to a close, the revelation that the United States had secretly sold weapons to Iran and that the profits from such sales were being diverted to Nicaraguan "contra" rebels fighting the Sandinista regime was a focus of attention in world military circles. (*See* special report, page 365.)

SDI Debate. During the year the Pentagon periodically showcased SDI experiments in which one of the exotic weapons being researched would demonstrate a lethal capacity against various kinds of targets. One $150 million exercise featured two payloads fired into space which stalked each other until ordered to collide in a demonstration of "kinetic kill" technology. The director of the SDI program, Lt. Gen. James Abrahamson, pointed to the success of the experiment as evidence that an antimissile defense is closer to reality than many believe. Opponents of SDI argued that success in destroying one object in a scientific experiment was a far cry from shooting down thousands of warheads amid 100,000 decoys in the chaos of a 30-minute space battle.

As research continued on various lasers, particle beam weapons, and kinetic kill vehicles, attention was focusing on what many thought would be the toughest technical facet of the entire SDI project—developing adequate computer software, i.e., the written instructions that direct the SDI computers to assimilate information about a missile attack so that defensive forces can be directed against the incoming missiles, decoys, and warheads. SDI critics and advocates both agree that writing the SDI software will be a formidable undertaking. The former note that it is inevitable for "bugs" to creep into the system and seriously erode the ability of SDI to perform adequately during an attack. They also contend that complete "de-bugging" of a system as large and complex as the SDI will not be likely. Advocates of SDI retort that the entire SDI system can be broken down into component parts comprised of sensors, computers, and weapons, and that these smaller aggregations of equipment can be integrated parts of a larger whole.

In the fall, Sen. William Proxmire (D-WI) released the results of a survey conducted by a Cornell University research team regarding the views held by members of the National Academy of Science who work in the basic fields most important to SDI, such as physics, chemistry, mathematics, and engineering. Of the 451 scientists who responded to the survey, 87% stated they considered it improbable that an SDI project could be tested sufficiently to provide confidence that it would operate as intended in a full-scale attack. According to Proxmire, "What the best scientific minds in this country are [saying] is that Star Wars won't work and it's a waste of money."

Part of the Pentagon's arguments in favor of conducting SDI research is based on the belief of Secretary of Defense Caspar Weinberger that the Soviets may be gaining a lead over the United States in SDI-type research. According to the Pentagon's publication *Soviet Military Power, 1986,* "The USSR's laser program is much larger than U.S. efforts and involves over 10,000 scientists and engineers and more than a half-dozen major research and development facilities and test ranges. . . . A laser weapons program of the magnitude of the Soviet Union's effort would cost roughly $1 billion per year in the United States."

Other Strategic Weapons. As U.S. and Soviet negotiators discussed the possibility of deep cuts in ICBMs (intercontinental ballistic missiles) a paradoxical situation developed: the cuts in the large nuclear missiles might shift the emphasis to other means of nuclear weapons delivery. "Airbreathers," for example, are vehicles, such as planes and cruise missiles, that operate only in the atmosphere. SDI would not be as effective against these as they would against ICBMs, thus possibly forcing the Soviets to turn to them as an alternative means of delivering nuclear weapons.

Military Accidents. During 1986 both superpowers suffered accidents involving sophisticated military equipment. Neither incident was fully explained by Washington or Moscow.

In July a mysterious U.S. aircraft crashed and burned in the Sequoia National Forest near the border of Nevada and California. The area was immediately sealed off by armed Air Force guards, and the Pentagon refused to divulge any details except that the pilot was attached to the 4450 Tactical Group at Nellis Air Force Base in Nevada. A number of reports appeared in the press speculating that the downed craft was a secret fighter plane employing what is called "stealth" technology. This form of high technology is generally believed to include the use of advanced materials, aerodynamic designs, and possibly electronic techniques to make the plane difficult for radar or infrared sensors to detect and track. Some press reports even identified the plane as an F-19, a craft the Pentagon denies even exists. Later in the year, reports surfaced that the Soviet Union also was working on stealth technology.

In October a Soviet nuclear-powered submarine carrying nuclear-tipped ballistic missiles was rocked by an explosion 500 mi (800 km) east of Bermuda in the western Atlantic. According to a spokesman for the U.S. Joint Chiefs of Staff, liquid fuel propellent in one of the submarine's missiles caught fire and exploded. The submarine surfaced quickly and was placed in tow by a Soviet merchant vessel in the area. After efforts to save the stricken submarine were abandoned, the crew was evacuated and the craft sank.

Because of the depth of water in which the submarine came to rest, U.S. government sources stated that there would be no radiation danger from the nuclear warheads on board; the warheads would be crushed by the water pressure in ways which would preclude an explosion. The U.S. Navy also asserted that the nuclear reactor which powered the craft would not be a radiation danger because it was housed in a heavy metal vault within the submarine, and that saltwater erosion of the reactor's protective shield would take a very long time. This was the fourth known sinking of a Soviet submarine; three were nuclear-powered.

U.S. Defense Budget. The year 1986 was one in which the U.S. Congress, including the Republican-controlled Senate, showed increasing resistance to the full military funding requested by President Reagan. After a month of wrangling over separate House and Senate versions, a conference committee hammered out a final funding bill for $291.8 billion. The president had requested $320 billion.

The White House did prove successful in securing the deletion of a number of arms control provisions which Democrats had attempted to add to the budget bill. Among the provisions dropped from the final version were the freezing of SDI funding, the banning of underground nuclear testing until the Soviets break their self-imposed moratorium on such tests, the halting of antisatellite systems (ASATs) testing, and an effort to halt the production of new chemical weapons. Wording in the original bill requiring the president to comply with the unratified SALT II treaty was changed to a request that the president comply.

Late in the year, the U.S. Air Force announced that it had selected the General Dynamics F-16 as the basic air defense fighter jet for the current period. At the same time it stated that Lockheed and Northrop corporations each would be commissioned to construct a prototype supersonic jet for use early in the 21st century. The Air Force would decide in approximately four years which one of the prototypes would be adopted as the Advanced Tactical Fighter. The total price for the new craft, including costs of research and development, was estimated at $40 billion.

International Politics and U.S. Deployment. In widely scattered parts of the globe, political developments threatened to undercut long-standing U.S. defense programs and alliances.

Among such NATO (North Atlantic Treaty Organization) countries as Great Britain, West Germany, Denmark, and the Netherlands, various socialist political parties mounted a growing attack on the role of nuclear weapons in NATO defense plans. Perhaps the most serious erosion of U.S. and NATO strategy could come from the British Labour Party, should it replace the Conservative government of Prime Minister Margaret Thatcher. According to the party program, a future Labour government would cancel the projected addition of new Trident SLBMs (submarine-launched ballistic missiles) to Royal Navy submarines and would dismantle Britain's existing SLBM force. Labour politicians also called for the closing of the naval base at Holy Loch, Scotland, used by U.S. nuclear submarines; for the removal of U.S. cruise missiles from Britain; and for the removal of nuclear weapons from the U.S. F-111 fighter-bombers stationed in England.

In West Germany, the Social Democratic Party (SPD) supported two propositions that disturbed NATO officials. One was the renunciation of any "first use" of nuclear weapons by NATO, a position that contradicts NATO's long-standing policy of attempting to compensate for the numerical superiority of the Warsaw Pact nations with the threat of nuclear weapons. And NATO leaders also were disturbed by the SPD's issuance of a joint appeal, with the East German Communist Party, for a nuclear-free zone in central Europe. Critics maintained that such a proposal would provide support to Soviet efforts to remove NATO nuclear forces and would restore the advantage of the Soviets' larger number of conventional forces. Socialist parties in the Netherlands and Denmark also were critical of NATO's reliance on nuclear weapons.

In the Philippines, the replacement of the Ferdinand Marcos government with that of Corazon Aquino also raised the possibility of trouble for U.S. military bases, such as the naval installation at Subic Bay. The new Philippine president came under pressure from some supporters to renegotiate the rights currently enjoyed by the U.S. forces.

Also in the Pacific, the action taken by the government of New Zealand in 1985 to ban visits to that country by U.S. naval ships equipped with nuclear power reactors remained in effect. In response, the United States in 1986 suspended its security obligations to New Zealand under the ANZUS (Australia, New Zealand, U.S.) Treaty. The action effectively cut off intelligence information from the United States to New Zealand, canceled joint training activities, and slowed the supply of spare parts for American-made equipment.

ROBERT M. LAWRENCE
Colorado State University

MILITARY AFFAIRS / SPECIAL REPORT

The Weapons Market

From Central America to Afghanistan and the Middle East, troops on both sides of any conventional armed conflict may employ weapons from the same ultimate sources. The United States, Soviet Union, Western European nations, and Israel are among the world's leading exporters of conventional arms. Right: The Honduran army displays a cache of weapons captured from Nicaraguan forces.

AP/Wide World

Although the media headlines tend to concentrate on such nuclear weapon delivery systems as ICBMs, SLBMs, and Stealth bombers, and more recently on the exotic beam weapons proposed for the Strategic Defense Initiative (Star Wars), all of the persons killed in the world's conflicts since World War II have been killed by conventional weapons. Many of these weapons are high technology products that were developed by the most advanced nations. Such weapons find their way into the hands of a wide variety of users, from Afghan tribesmen fighting against the more than 100,000 Soviet troops in their land to guerrillas in El Salvador labeled as Communist by the U.S. government. Perhaps the most ubiquitous weapon being used around the world today is the Soviet-designed AK-47 assault rifle. It is joined by the American M-1 and M-16, the Israeli Uzi, the Chinese-made Type 56 Kalashnikov that was copied from the original Russian model, and other rapid firing guns that serve as submachine guns. This type of weapon has even found its way into the movies and television as heroes blast their way in "Rambo" style toward Hollywood's version of the better world.

While several organizations attempt to monitor the production, sales, and distribution of conventional weapons, much less is known about them than the weapons of mass destruction that are monitored carefully by the superpowers and others. One explanation for the lack of information and statistics regarding the conventional weapons market is that a large number of weapons are bought and sold in what amounts to a worldwide black market in arms. Associated with the secret dealings in weapons is the mercenary soldier who is available for hire to fight for various causes. While the mercenary may fight in support of ideological objectives, he or she often fights for money or adventure. In the United States such persons even have a magazine that caters to some of their interests. Published in Boulder, CO, *Soldier of Fortune* is subtitled The Journal of Professional Adventurers.

In addition to information provided by the different governments concerning weapons manufacturing and sales abroad, there are three particular sources of information that are useful in assessing the world's market in arms. One source is the United Nations which publishes weapons data from time to time. The International Institute for Strategic Studies, in London, publishes each year *The Military Balance,* which contains information on the conventional weapons found in national arsenals. The Stockholm International Peace Research Institute annually publishes *World Armaments and Disarmament.* Americans interested in data about their government's supply of weapons to other nations should read the hearings and reports printed by the Foreign Affairs Committee of the U.S. House of Representatives and the Foreign Relations Committee of the U.S. Senate. Typically the Soviet Union and other Communist nations are reluctant to publish detailed information about their arms sales to each other or to Third World nations.

The Sellers. It generally is believed that the United States is the leading exporter of conventional weapons. Many of the U.S. weapons sales and transfers occur as part of Washington's security and economic assistance program, which includes foreign military sales, international military education and training, and military assistance programs. The rationale for the large exporting of U.S. weapons traditionally has been twofold. The major reason for arms exportation is given as the government's belief that the spread of Communism—as in Central America—is prevented by assisting to arm potential targets of both external and internal Communist activity. Another reason supporting arms exports is the idea that in certain regions of the world, most notably the Middle East, U.S. interests or the cause of peace itself are served by maintaining a military balance (or altering it) between actual or potential adversaries. Indeed, when it was disclosed in fall 1986 that the United States had been secretly selling arms to Iran and transferring the proceeds to Nicaraguan "contra" rebels, both of these arguments were used to defend the decision.

Opponents, however, criticize weapons exports on several grounds. First, some believe that the Communist threat is overstated and does not justify the magnitude of counter-arms-support by the United States and other countries. Other critics, particularly of weapons exports to Third World countries, argue that instead of building stability, U.S. arms sales are actually disruptive of economic and social progress. As for the Iran-contra affair, Reagan administration critics maintained that, in any case, the substantive policy issues were far outweighed by the clandestine nature of the deal. (See UNITED STATES.)

Although information is difficult to obtain, it is believed in the West that the Soviet Union is the second largest exporter of arms, both to other Communist nations and to countries in the Third World. The rationale for the Soviet arms-sales effort is thought to be pursuit of ideological objectives and the need to earn hard currency which is in short supply in the Soviet Union. Other major arms exporting nations are France, Great Britain, West Germany, the People's Republic of China, and Spain. Among the smaller nations, Israel is a leading arms merchant. Those nations seeking to sell arms abroad have found their most lucrative market in the Middle East, where the Israeli-Arab rivalry and the war between Iran and Iraq have stimulated arms sales.

The Buyers. According to U.S. government statistics, the principal purchasers of U.S. conventional arms are Washington's principal Far-East ally, Japan, and three Middle East nations —Israel, Egypt, and Saudi Arabia. Many of the remaining arms sales are made to members of the North Atlantic Treaty Organization (NATO). A potentially large market for U.S. weapons is the People's Republic of China (PRC) which is seeking advanced military equipment in order to counter the massive Soviet armed presence on its borders. However, at the present time, political considerations in both nations generally limit sales of military equipment to such nonlethal items as light planes, helicopters, and certain electronic components. A complicating factor regarding increased sales of military equipment to the PRC is the fact that the United States also sells to the rival Chinese government based on the island of Taiwan.

The bulk of arms exports from the other Western nations go to Middle Eastern and Latin American nations and to India. Arms exports from the Soviet Union and other Communist nations of Eastern Europe flow to Middle Eastern nations, other countries that appear to be sympathetic to the Communist brand of ideology supported by Moscow, and India. According to data collected by the Stockholm International Peace Research Institute, the six leading Third World countries for arms imports are Egypt, Syria, Iraq, India, Libya, and Saudi Arabia.

The Weapons. In addition to the automatic rifles mentioned previously, the arms trade involves many types of weapons, including some of the most sophisticated jet aircraft in the world. For example, the list of exported arms from both Communist and non-Communist nations to the Third World includes heavy and medium tanks, armored personnel carriers (APC), artillery pieces, surface-to-surface (SSM) missiles, surface-to-air (SAM) missiles, patrol boats and destroyers, submarines, helicopters, transport planes, and fighters and fighter/bombers. The latest compilation of arms sales in the Stockholm International Peace Research Institute yearbook contains 65 pages of weapons and equipment known to have been purchased in international trade. Among the most advanced weapons are such jet aircraft as the Soviet-built MiG-23, MiG-25, MiG-29; F-15s and F-16s from the United States; and the French Mirage-2000.

Future Trends. At the close of 1986 several trends were discernible in the world-arms market which should continue for at least several years. One was the dramatic decline in the price of oil charged by members of the Organization of the Petroleum Exporting Countries (OPEC). Since the OPEC nations are typically Third World nations, and are often Middle East countries, the buying power of these traditional purchasers of arms has been reduced and may remain so until the worldwide glut of oil disappears. Another trend was the wider use of the offset agreement. In this type of arrangement, the selling nation assists the buyer to offset the cost of the weapons to be purchased. The latter can be done by joint production of the weapon, by letting the purchaser subcontract for components and spare parts for the weapon, and by the seller importing various products or commodities from the purchaser.

ROBERT M. LAWRENCE

MINNESOTA

A comeback by the Democratic-Farmer-Labor Party (DFL), continued distress for farmers and miners, the merger of Northwest and Republic airlines, and a settlement of the meatpacking strike at Hormel highlighted the year.

Elections. The DFL moved to reclaim its longtime political dominance in November by reelecting Gov. Rudy Perpich who withstood a serious primary challenge from St. Paul Mayor George Latimer and won 57% over conservative former state legislator Cal Ludeman's 43%. The DFL also won all but one of the other statewide offices, recaptured control of the state House of Representatives, and increased its already large majority in the state Senate.

The state's incumbent U.S. congressmen (5 DFL, 3 Republican) were all reelected, but Vin Weber, a leader among young Republican conservatives, was almost unseated and the DFL contested Arlan Stangeland's narrow victory.

Agriculture, Economy, and Labor. Yields in corn, soybeans, and wheat—the state's leading crops—were at near record levels, increasing oversupplies and further depressing already low prices. Further contractions in iron-ore mining deepened the depression in the Iron Range. Employment in mining dropped from a peak of 14,000 in 1978 to less than 4,000 in 1986. The LTV Corporation and Armco's First Taconite Company declared bankruptcy, resulting in a shutdown of Reserve Mining plants in Silver Bay and Babbitt.

The two major Minnesota-based airlines, Northwest and Republic, merged in 1986. The merger created an uncertain future for many employees in the Twin Cities area.

A bitter 18-month strike at Hormel's Austin plant was settled after the International Food and Commercial Workers Union placed the leadership of Local P9 under receivership. A suit by the local against the international was dismissed.

Redevelopment Progress. Major physical development in the Twin Cities metropolitan area continued. In Minneapolis ground was broken for a 70-story Norwest Bank Building. In St. Paul construction of the Minnesota World Trade Center moved toward completion in 1987, and in suburban Bloomington a controversial mega-mall was proceeding.

The Legislature. The 1986 legislative session ended with a razor-tight balance of the budget. Having depleted a $450 million reserve, however, the state still faced a likely scramble over spending and tax policies. The legislature's June 1985 decision to transfer almost all of the state treasurer's duties to the finance department was ruled unconstitutional by the state Supreme Court in 1986. Treasurer Robert Mattson was defeated for reelection in the DFL primary.

MINNESOTA · Information Highlights

Area: 84,402 sq mi (218 601 km^2).
Population (1985 est.): 4,193,000.
Chief Cities (July 1, 1984 est.): St. Paul, the capital, 265,903; Minneapolis, 358,335; Duluth (1980 census), 92,811.
Government (1986): *Chief Officers*—governor, Rudy Perpich (DFL); lt. gov., Marlene Johnson (DFL). *Legislature*—Senate, 67 members; House of Representatives, 134 members.
State Finances (fiscal year 1985): *Revenue,* $9,378,000,000; *expenditure,* $8,121,000,000.
Personal Income (1985): $59,068,000,000; per capita, $14,087.
Labor Force (June 1986): *Civilian labor force,* 2,287,900; *unemployed,* 113,800 (5% of total force).
Education: *Enrollment* (fall 1984)—public elementary schools, 464,107; public secondary, 237,590; colleges and universities, 221,162. *Public school expenditures* (1983–84), $2,234,000,000 ($3,378 per pupil).

A protracted legislative struggle over what business claimed were excessive worker benefits ended in a compromise only to be vetoed by Governor Perpich, setting the stage for a new struggle in 1987.

University Reform. The University of Minnesota launched a comprehensive effort to reduce undergraduate enrollment and improve graduate instruction. Undergraduate enrollment there for fall 1986 was up sharply, however, as it was at colleges throughout the state.

Pipeline Disaster. An explosion and fires resulting from a leak in a gasoline pipeline in suburban Mounds View caused two deaths and prompted a flurry of state and federal investigations into pipeline safety. Reactivation of the Twin Cities-Duluth pipeline was delayed as authorities studied new safety regulations.

ARTHUR NAFTALIN, *University of Minnesota*

MISSISSIPPI

The election of the state's first black U.S. Congressman in more than a century and the removal of a 96-year constitutional prohibition against serving successive gubernatorial terms were events that made Mississippi headlines in 1986. Other news items of particular interest included a legislative session that began with a flurry of accomplishment and ended in deadlock and an economy that continued to give a lackluster performance.

Congressional Elections. In a contest targeted by both national parties, 32-year-old black attorney Mike Espy (D) won 52% of the vote to unseat second district Rep. Webb Franklin (R). While voting in this black-majority Delta district (53% of the voting-age population) was split along racial lines, Espy's focus on unemployment and the farm crisis attracted sufficient white support to give him a victory. Incumbent congressman in the state's remaining districts were returned to office, one Dem-

Mike Espy, a 33-year-old lawyer from Yazoo City, became Mississippi's first black congressman since Reconstruction, defeating two-term Republican Webb Franklin in the state's second district.

AP/Wide World

ocrat without opposition, and two Democrats and one Republican with large majorities.

Constitutional Change. In June voters ratified a provision easing the property tax burden on homeowners but rejected a measure that would have moderated conflict-of-interest provisions applying to public officials. In November they gave overwhelming approval to amendments allowing both the governor and the state treasurer to succeed themselves. They also approved provisions creating an educational trust fund, safeguarding public employees' retirement funds, and extending leases on Sixteenth Section school lands.

The Legislature. Within days of its January 7 opening, the 1986 legislature fully funded public education, including teacher pay raises and statewide kindergartens. Dwindling revenues, the impact of the federal deficit reduction

law, and a refusal to increase taxes later resulted in 1987 budget slashes for other state agencies. Higher education was particularly hard hit by the cut, which averaged 15%. A stalemate between the legislature and the governor left the state highway department unfunded when the session ended on April 11. A three-day special session was held in May to resolve the funding crisis.

Noteworthy accomplishments of the regular session included repeal of the state's Sunday closing laws, enactment of an election reform package, passage of a uniform school law, and authorization for statewide and interstate banking.

The Economy. Low oil prices and farm problems continued to affect the economy. Employment levels rose during the year but did not keep pace with growth in the labor force. As a result Mississippi's unemployment rate was nearly twice that of the national average. July's level of 13% was one of the highest in the nation.

Other Items. U.S. District Judge Walter L. Nixon, Jr., was convicted February 9 on two counts of perjury. A November 4 Hinds County Circuit Court decision stripped the office of lieutenant governor of its longstanding authority to name legislative committees and to assign bills. The ruling was appealed to the state Supreme Court, but a decision had not been issued at year's end.

More than 500 persons were evacuated from their homes near Collins, and a stretch of U.S. Highway 49 was closed to traffic for several days, when tank cars containing chlorine gas derailed September 7.

DANA B. BRAMMER
The University of Mississippi

MISSISSIPPI • Information Highlights

Area: 47,689 sq mi (123 515 km²).

Population (1985 est.): 2,613,000.

Chief Cities (1980 census): Jackson, the capital (July 1, 1984 est.), 208,810; Biloxi, 49,311; Meridian, 46,577.

Government (1986): *Chief Officers*—governor, William A. Allain (D); lt. gov., Brad Dye (D). *Legislature*—Senate, 52 members; House of Representatives, 122 members.

State Finances (fiscal year 1985): *Revenue,* $3,923,000,000; *expenditure,* $3,561,000,000.

Personal Income (1985): $24,004,000,000; per capita, $9,187.

Labor Force (June 1986): *Civilian labor force,* 1,170,500; *unemployed,* 146,900 (12.6% of total force).

Education: *Enrollment* (fall 1984)—public elementary schools, 325,454; public secondary, 140,604; colleges and universities, 101,180. *Public school expenditures* (1983–84), $858,000,000 ($1,962 per pupil).

Christopher S. Bond and his wife and son greet supporters after he won the GOP nomination for the U.S. Senate in August. The former governor went on to victory in November, defeating Lt. Gov. Harriett Woods (D).

AP/Wide World

MISSOURI

In the words of retiring U.S. Sen. Thomas F. Eagleton (D), the 1986 election "wiped out" the Democratic Party in Missouri. As a result of the November 4 vote both Senate seats, every statewide office except that of lieutenant governor, and 4 of the 9 seats in the U.S. House of Representatives would be controlled by Republicans. Although both houses of the Missouri legislature remained Democratic, there were no visible Democratic candidates waiting in the wings.

The Woods-Bond Campaign. Lt. Gov. Harriett Woods (D), who lost her second bid for the Senate to former Gov. Christopher S. Bond (R), was less pessimistic. "Tomorrow is another day," she told her supporters as she promised to continue the fight and "eventually we'll win."

The Bond-Woods campaign was the most expensive canvass in Missouri history, with Bond spending an estimated $5 million and Woods approximately $4 million. However, money alone was not the explanation of the outcome. Woods' campaign suffered from a combination of difficulties which began four years earlier when she defied the old guard in her party and entered the race against incumbent Sen. John Danforth (R). She came within an eyelash of beating him, but the professionals in the party did not forgive this "upstart" who did not "play by the rules."

Worse was the fact that she failed to compensate for her lack of backing from the regulars with her own organization. Her campaign suffered from confusion and lack of direction. Responding to flack over a TV commercial in June, she fired her media consultant despite the fact that he was one of the leading Democrats in the country in that business.

In contrast Bond left few tools unused. He was on good terms with Republican stalwarts throughout the state because for the last decade he had worked for many candidates and had helped to raise money for the party. He echoed the Reagan line on both foreign and domestic issues, and both the president and Vice-President George Bush made several appearances in Missouri on Bond's behalf.

The Economy. Regardless of Republican electoral success, the party's program of low taxes and junkets to persuade Far Eastern firms to locate in Missouri failed to solve the state's growing economic problems. Farm foreclosures and rural business failures continued. Automobile production declined as General Motors announced the closing of one large plant and laid off more than 1,000 workers at another. The Kroger Company discontinued its last Missouri grocery store, and Ozark Airlines ceased operation. Monsanto, long a Missouri stalwart, eliminated a large number of positions including those of some top chemists. Another indication of chronic recession in the state's largest city was the demise of the *St. Louis Globe-Democrat*, after several years' struggle to keep the paper alive.

Weather. Temperatures in Missouri averaged above normal in each of ten months, but August proved one of the coolest in the 20th century. Until September, precipitation lagged behind normal. Then a deluge of rain resulted in the worst flooding in the history of central and eastern Missouri.

RUTH W. TOWNE
Northeast Missouri State University

MISSOURI • Information Highlights

Area: 69,697 sq mi (180 516 km²).

Population (1985 est.): 5,029,000.

Chief Cities (July 1, 1984 est.): Jefferson City, the capital (1980 census), 33,619; Kansas City, 443,075; St. Louis, 429,296; Springfield, 136,939; Independence, 112,121.

Government (1986): *Chief Officers*—governor, John Ashcroft (R); lt. gov., Harriett Woods (D). *General Assembly*—Senate, 34 members; House of Representatives, 163 members.

State Finances (fiscal year 1985): *Revenue,* $6,682,000,000; *expenditure,* $5,817,000,000.

Personal Income (1985): $66,605,000,000; per capita, $13,244.

Labor Force (June 1986): *Civilian labor force,* 2,561,800; *unemployed,* 151,800 (5.9% of total force).

Education: *Enrollment* (fall 1984)—public elementary schools, 545,062; public secondary, 248,731; colleges and universities, 241,146. *Public school expenditures* (1983–84), $1,850,000,000 ($2,600 per pupil).

MONTANA

Montanans voted in 1986 to limit, but not to eliminate their property taxes.

A grassroots constitutional initiative that would have eliminated property taxes and required a vote to raise or initiate any other form of tax was defeated 44% to 56% in the November balloting. A second tax proposal on the same ballot easily won approval of voters. A constitutional initiative to cap property taxes at their 1986 level and require the Montana legislature to find new sources of revenue to replace any drop in the statewide portion of the property tax passed 55% to 45%. Montanans also voted for an initiative to create a state lottery, but killed a ballot measure that would have ended state control of milk prices.

The voters gave the Democrats control of the Montana House of Representatives, but elected an equal number of Republican and Democratic state senators. Republican Ronald

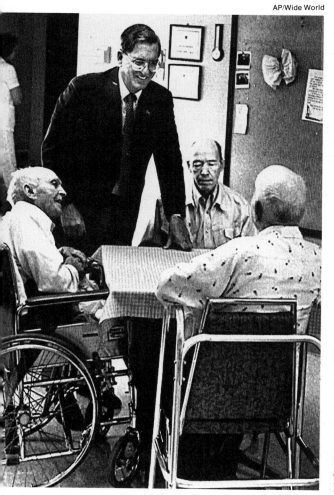

Montana Gov. Ted Schwinden gives residents of a nursing home in Choteau an opportunity to air their concerns.

AP/Wide World

MONTANA · Information Highlights

Area: 147,046 sq mi (380 848 km²).
Population (1985 est.): 826,000.
Chief Cities (1980 census): Helena, the capital, 23,938; Billings, 66,798; Great Falls, 56,725.
Government (1986): *Chief Officers*—governor, Ted Schwinden (D); lt. gov., George Turman (D). *Legislature*—Senate, 50 members; House of Representatives, 100 members.
State Finances (fiscal year 1985): *Revenue,* $1,738,000,000; *expenditure,* $1,557,000,000.
Personal Income (1985): $9,067,000,000; per capita, $10,974.
Labor Force (June 1986): *Civilian labor force,* 423,100; *unemployed,* 30,500 (7.2% of total force).
Education: *Enrollment* (fall 1984)—public elementary schools, 108,796; public secondary, 45,616; colleges and universities, 35,958. *Public school expenditures* (1983–84), $504,000,000 ($3,631 per pupil).

Marlenee and Democrat Patrick Williams easily won reelection to their seats in the U.S. House of Representatives.

Legislation. The Montana legislature met in two special sessions during 1986, both aimed at reducing the anticipated state-budget deficit and adjusting the state's business climate to encourage growth of the economy and tax base.

A six-day session that opened March 4 was prompted when the state Supreme Court overturned legislation that would have limited the amount of welfare that young and able-bodied Montanans could have collected. The biennial state budget was drafted in 1985 with the assumption that the state's welfare costs would drop under the new law. The legislature failed to approve a referendum to reinstate the welfare limit, however. It also killed other proposals, including ones to cut railroad and airline taxes and create a state office to mediate agricultural financing problems.

The second special session was called on June 16 to plug an anticipated $83 million shortage in the state budget. A general downturn in the state's economy, led by slumping oil production and prices, was blamed for the shortage. The legislature responded by transferring money to the state general fund from such accounts as those used to build highways. The lawmakers also ordered an across-the-board 5% spending cut, froze salaries, and cancelled a promised increase in state help to schools.

Burlington Northern Cutbacks. Montana experienced a serious economic blow when the Burlington Northern Railroad closed its locomotive repair shops in Livingston on February 4. On June 1 the railroad also eliminated its white-collar jobs in Billings and closed its division offices.

Property Reappraisal. Even before the ballot initiatives were drafted, property taxes were among the biggest concerns of Montanans. Early in the year, the state reappraised all property, which resulted in the doubling of the taxable value of most property. The state compensated for the increase by halfing the rate at which most property is taxed. The process still resulted in some tax increases and prompted hundreds of homeowners to crowd into every county courthouse in the state to file formal protest to both the reappraisal and their taxes. The protests tied up millions of dollars in tax money that could not be spent until the disputes were settled.

ROBERT C. GIBSON
"The Billings Gazette"

MOROCCO

As the conflict in the Western Sahara entered its tenth year, Moroccan forces remained militarily dominant, but the opposition Polisario Front, backed by Algeria, continued its guerrilla war. Algerian and Polisario sources asserted that more than 300 Moroccan soldiers were killed in battles between January and June. Although Polisario's claims of military successes may have been exaggerated, Morocco clearly was being hurt by the war's economic burden.

Foreign Affairs. Morocco's biggest losses to Polisario were in the diplomatic arena. In December 1985 the United Nations adopted an Algerian-backed resolution calling on Morocco to negotiate with Polisario, which King Hassan II refused to do. Meanwhile, international recognition of Polisario's demand for Saharan independence increased.

Morocco was pressured further by tension between Libya and the United States. The Arab-African Union, which Morocco and Libya formed in 1984, resulted in deepening cooperation between the two countries until spring 1986. At that time King Hassan gave priority to his U.S. ties, as demonstrated when U.S. CIA Director William Casey and U.S. Ambassador to the UN Vernon Walters were

honored guests at ceremonies in March to celebrate the king's 25 years on the throne.

The U.S. attack on Tripoli in April also reduced Morocco's enthusiasm for the union with Libya, and a final blow was struck when King Hassan met with Israeli Prime Minister Shimon Peres in July. Like other recent Moroccan-Israeli contacts, Hassan met Peres largely to demonstrate to the United States that he is a valuable Arab ally. His timing also reflected a desire for U.S. help in negotiations with the International Monetary Fund (IMF). Libya and other radical Arab states vigorously denounced the Hassan-Peres meeting, and late in August, Morocco withdrew from the Arab-African Union.

Disturbances in Spain's North African enclaves, Ceuta and Melilla, complicated relations with Madrid and were a source of concern. Spanish efforts to regularize the status of Moroccans living in the enclaves led to friction early in the year. In February it was agreed that qualifying Moroccans should be given residence permits, but the uncertainty remained and new clashes took place in June.

Economy and Politics. Economic difficulties eased slightly. Particularly helpful were plentiful rains, which led to an excellent harvest and reduced the need to import foodstuffs. Also important were increased tourism revenues and the declining price of oil, normally an expensive import.

A three-year-old program of austerity and economic reform also had an impact. In September 1985 the government reduced subsidies on basic commodities, and in 1986 it sought to limit expenditures generally. Economic reforms, many introduced in response to pressure from the IMF, included a reduction in import restrictions and state-run economic ventures and efforts to expand the private sector.

As a result the 1986 current accounts deficit was expected to be about $600 million, compared with almost $1 billion in 1985. Nevertheless, Morocco's huge foreign debt continued to mount, albeit at a slower rate, reaching approximately $13.5 billion by the end of the year. Unable to pay for imports and meet debt service obligations, the country faced a mounting financial crisis. Pressure was temporarily relieved in August, when the IMF praised Morocco's economic policies and agreed to renegotiate its debt.

Continuity marked the domestic political scene in 1986, and opposition movements found few opportunities to challenge the government. In January and February, several dozen leftists were sent to prison for antistate activities. In the latter month, Amnesty International accused Morocco of torturing political prisoners, although in June the king pardoned 101 political detainees as a gesture of good will.

MARK TESSLER, *University of Wisconsin*

MOROCCO · Information Highlights

Official Name: Kingdom of Morocco.
Location: Northwest Africa.
Area: 172,413 sq mi (446 550 km²).
Population (mid-1986 est.): 23,700,000.
Chief Cities (1982 census): Rabat, the capital, 518,616; Casablanca, 2,139,204; Fès, 448,823; Marrakech, 439,728.
Government: *Head of state,* Hassan II, king (acceded 1961). *Head of government,* Mohamed Karim Lamrani, prime minister (took office Nov. 1983). *Legislature* (unicameral)—Chamber of Representatives.
Monetary Unit: Dirham (9.114 dirhams equal U.S.$1, June 1986).
Gross Domestic Product (1984 U.S.$): $11,900,-000,000.
Economic Indexes (1984): *Consumer Prices* (1980 = 100), all items, 148.5; food, 153.6. *Industrial Production* (1984, 1980 = 100), 108.
Foreign Trade (1985 U.S.$): *Imports,* $3,849,000,000; *exports,* $2,165,000,000.

In "The Mission," Jeremy Irons (center) portrays an 18th-century Jesuit priest who heads a Latin American mission.

MOTION PICTURES

Hollywood's slavish quest for teenage audiences was strikingly diminished in 1986. While young audiences targeted by market research were still considered key prospects, producers showed that they were willing to make and distribute more demanding adult fare. The typical teen fluff was by and large channeled into the summer vacation months.

Wide varieties of relatively sophisticated dramas and comedies from major studios and independents were released, with a particularly heavy crush during the latter part of the year in time to compete for the holiday business. The films often met with contradictory responses from critics, but it was significant that risks were being taken on mature ventures.

Drama. *The Mission*, scripted by Robert Bolt and directed by Roland Joffé, was a particularly prestigious epic that won the top award at the Cannes Film Festival. It starred Robert De Niro and Jeremy Irons as missionaries protecting Indians from being enslaved in 18th-century Latin America. Also ambitious was the adaptation of Paul Theroux's novel *Mosquito Coast*, directed by Peter Weir, which gave Harrison Ford his most challenging role yet as a survivalist who takes his family on a grueling, dangerous jungle adventure. Another book by Theroux was also adapted for the screen; his *Half Moon Street* starred Sigourney Weaver as an academic caught up in Mideast intrigue when she moonlights as an escort girl.

Writer-director Oliver Stone's *Platoon*, based on his own experiences, was a searing,

often brutal examination of what it was like to be an American soldier in the Vietnam War. Martin Scorsese succeeded in making an engrossing sequel to *The Hustler* (1961); *The Color of Money* picks up the trail of pool shark Fast Eddie Felson, played by Paul Newman, 25 years later as he teaches the tricks of the trade to Tom Cruise as his protégé. Tom Hanks, who built his reputation as a lightweight actor in youth films, starred in two dramas: *Nothing in Common*, in which he played an advertising executive at odds with Jackie Gleason, cast as his difficult father, and *Every Time We Say Goodbye*, a World War II romance set in Jerusalem. In *Streets of Gold* Klaus Maria Brandauer distinguished himself playing a Russian exile in New York.

Jane Fonda starred as an alcoholic actress who wakes up with a dead body in bed and wonders what really happened in *The Morning After*, a mystery thriller directed by Sidney Lumet. William Hurt and Marlee Matlin were paired in an adaptation of Mark Medoff's play *Children of a Lesser God*, an intensely emotional love story of a teacher and a young, reclusive deaf woman. *The Name of the Rose* starred Sean Connery and F. Murray Abraham in the adaptation of Umberto Eco's intricate ecclesiastical murder thriller set in the Middle Ages. *Native Son*, Richard Wright's classic novel about race relations, reached the screen with Victor Love in the key role of Bigger Thomas.

Marsha Norman's taut play *'night Mother*, about a woman who announces to her mother that she is about to commit suicide, became a film with Sissy Spacek squaring off against

Anne Bancroft. David Lynch stirred controversy with *Blue Velvet,* an unsettling excursion into sex and violence behind the facade of small town tranquillity.

Comedies. Movies aimed at the funnybone turned out to be more ambitious than usual. Woody Allen's *Hannah and Her Sisters,* starring Dianne Wiest, Barbara Hershey, and Mia Farrow, as well as Allen himself, dealt sensitively with relationships and career aspirations while producing laughs. *A Room With a View,* another result of the longtime collaboration between producer Ismail Merchant and director James Ivory, was a funny, classy adaptation of E. M. Forster's novel about an English girl's romantic adventure in Italy. *Crimes of the Heart,* scripted by Beth Henley from her play, was one of the year's most awaited comedies, cast with Diane Keaton, Sissy Spacek, and Jessica Lange as Henley's colorful sisters. Francis Coppola's *Peggy Sue Got Married,* with Kathleen Turner in the title role, went beyond laughter to examine whether someone traveling back in time might make the same choices in life. Blake Edwards' *That's Life,* in effect an elaborate home movie, used comedy as its format, but seriously considered the fear of dying and the need to count one's blessings.

Spike Lee, working on a shoestring budget of under $200,000, wrote and directed the unusual *She's Gotta Have It,* a comic but incisive look at the romantic escapades of a spirited young black woman. Jim Jarmusch, who established himself as a talented, offbeat director with *Stranger Than Paradise* (1984), returned with the artistically striking *Down By Law,* a quirky comedy about three losers who break out of jail in Louisiana. Jonathan Demme made a demanding, contemporary screwball comedy, *Something Wild,* with Jeff Daniels as a yuppie executive whose life is turned upside down when he is seduced by a strange, exotic woman, played by Melanie Griffith. Steve Miner's *Soul Man* became controversial for treading on race relations, with its story of a white student who pretends to be black to get a scholarship to Harvard Law School.

To be sure, some of the holiday-season attractions at year's end aimed more broadly with less difficult themes. *The Three Amigos,* in the persons of Steve Martin, Chevy Chase, and Martin Short, was a comedy romp catering to a young audience. *Star Trek IV: The Voyage Home,* geared to the "Trekkie" faithful, nevertheless took the novel approach of setting nearly two thirds of the customarily futuristic saga in present-day San Francisco as part of a time-travel yarn. *Little Shop of Horrors,* starring Steve Martin and Rick Moranis, reprised the free-wheeling stage musical.

Summer Hits. Among the movies released during the summer and generally geared to the youthful audience, was the box office winner, *Top Gun.* The Navy-pilot action adventure starred Tom Cruise and featured dogfights with the latest hardware in the skies. Runner-up in the summer sweepstakes, *The Karate Kid Part*

Gamma-Liaison

© Ron Phillips/Sygma

Two of the year's important films, "Hannah and Her Sisters" (above) and "The Color of Money," were the works of top directors Woody Allen and Martin Scorsese, respectively. Allen (above left) also starred in his film of complex family relationships, along with Mia Farrow, who of late seems to have become his favorite leading lady. Scorsese in "Money" teamed one of filmdom's most enduring stars, Paul Newman (far left), with the exciting young actor Tom Cruise, fresh from his "Top Gun" triumph, in this sequel to "The Hustler."

In "Nothing in Common," Jackie Gleason (left) *and Tom Hanks play an estranged father and son who learn to care again.*

MOTION PICTURES | 1986

ABOUT LAST NIGHT. . . . Director, Edward Zwick; screenplay by Tim Kazurinsky and Denise DeClue. With Rob Lowe, Demi Moore, Jim Belushi, Elizabeth Perkins.

ALIENS. Written and directed by James Cameron. With Sigourney Weaver.

AN AMERICAN TAIL. Director, Don Bluth; screenplay by Judy Freudberg and Tony Geiss. (Animated)

BACK TO SCHOOL. Director, Alan Metter; screenplay by Steven Kampmann, Will Porter, Peter Torokvei, Harold Ramis. With Rodney Dangerfield.

BLUE VELVET. Written and directed by David Lynch. With Isabella Rossellini, Dennis Hopper, Laura Dern, Kyle MacLachlan.

THE BOY WHO COULD FLY. Written and directed by Nick Castle. With Bonnie Bedelia, Lucy Deakins, Jay Underwood, Fred Gwynne, Colleen Dewhurst.

BRIGHTON BEACH MEMOIRS. Director, Gene Saks; screenplay by Neil Simon, based on his play. With Jonathan Silverman, Blythe Danner, Bob Dishy, Judith Ivey.

CHILDREN OF A LESSER GOD. Director, Randa Haines; screenplay by Hesper Anderson and Mark Medoff, based on a play by Mr. Medoff. With William Hurt, Marlee Matlin, Piper Laurie, Philip Bosco.

CLOCKWISE. Director, Christopher Morahan; screenplay by Michael Frayn. With John Cleese, Alison Steadman.

COBRA. Director, George P. Cosmatos; screenplay by Sylvester Stallone, based on the novel *Fair Game* by Paula Gosling. With Sylvester Stallone.

THE COLOR OF MONEY. Director, Martin Scorsese; screenplay by Richard Price, based on the novel by Walter Tevis. With Paul Newman, Tom Cruise.

CRIMES OF THE HEART. Director, Bruce Beresford; screenplay by Beth Henley, based on her play. With Sissy Spacek, Diane Keaton, Jessica Lange.

CROCODILE DUNDEE. Director, Peter Faiman; screenplay by Paul Hogan, Ken Shadie, and John Cornell. With Paul Hogan, Linda Kozlowski.

DANCING IN THE DARK. Written and directed by Leon Marr, from a novel by Joan Barfoot. With Martha Henry.

THE DECLINE OF THE AMERICAN EMPIRE. Written and directed by Denys Arcand. With Dominique Michel, Dorothée Berryman, Louise Portal.

DESERT BLOOM. Written and directed by Eugene Corr. With Jon Voight, JoBeth Williams, Ellen Barkin, Annabeth Gish.

DOWN AND OUT IN BEVERLY HILLS. Director, Paul Mazursky; screenplay by Mr. Mazursky, Leon Capetanos. With Nick Nolte, Richard Dreyfus, Bette Midler.

DOWN BY LAW. Written and directed by Jim Jarmusch. With Tom Waits, John Lurie, Roberto Benigni, Billie Neal, Ellen Barkin.

EXTREMITIES. Director, Robert M. Young; screenplay by William Mastrosimone, based on his play. With Farrah Fawcett, James Russo.

FERRIS BUELLER'S DAY OFF. Written and directed by John Hughes. With Matthew Broderick.

52 PICK-UP. Director, John Frankenheimer; screenplay by Elmore Leonard and John Steppling. With Roy Scheider, Ann-Margret.

THE FLY. Director, David Cronenberg; screenplay by Charles Edward Pogue and Mr. Cronenberg from a story by George Langelaan. With Jeff Goldblum.

GINGER AND FRED. Director, Federico Fellini; screenplay by Mr. Fellini, Tonino Guerra, Tullio Pinelli. With Giulietta Masina, Marcello Mastroianni.

THE GOLDEN CHILD. Director, Michael Ritchie; screenplay by Dennis Feldman. With Eddie Murphy.

A GREAT WALL. Director, Peter Wang; screenplay by Mr. Wang, with Shirley Sun. With Peter Wang.

HALF MOON STREET. Director, Bob Swaim; screenplay by Mr. Swaim and Edward Behr. With Sigourney Weaver, Michael Caine.

HANNAH AND HER SISTERS. Written and directed by Woody Allen. With Woody Allen, Mia Farrow, Michael Caine, Barbara Hershey, Dianne Wiest.

HEARTBREAK RIDGE. Director, Clint Eastwood; screenplay by James Carabatsos. With Clint Eastwood, Marsha Mason.

HEARTBURN. Director, Mike Nichols; screenplay by Nora Ephron. With Meryl Streep, Jack Nicholson.

HOWARD THE DUCK. Director, Willard Huyck; screenplay by Mr. Huyck, Gloria Katz. With Lea Thompson.

THE JOURNEY OF NATTY GANN. Director, Jeremy Kagan; screenplay by Jeanne Rosenberg. With Meredith Salenger.

JUMPIN' JACK FLASH. Director, Penny Marshall; screenplay by David H. Franzoni, J.W. Melville, Patricia Irving, Christopher Thompson. With Whoopi Goldberg.

THE KARATE KID PART II. Director, John G. Avildsen; screenplay by Robert Mark Kamen. With Noriyuki (Pat) Morita, Ralph Macchio.

LEGAL EAGLES. Director, Ivan Reitman; screenplay by Jim Cash and Jack Epps, Jr. With Robert Redford, Debra Winger, Daryl Hannah.

LETTER TO BREZHNEV. Director, Chris Bernard; screenplay by Frank Clarke. With Margi Clarke, Alexandra Pigg, Peter Firth, Alfred Molina.

LITTLE SHOP OF HORRORS. Director, Frank Oz; screenplay by Howard Ashman. With Rick Moranis, Ellen Greene, Steve Martin.

A MAN AND A WOMAN: 20 YEARS LATER. Written and directed by Claude Lelouch. With Anouk Aimée, Jean-Louis Trintignant.

THE MANHATTAN PROJECT. Director, Marshall Brickman; screenplay by Mr. Brickman and Thomas Baum. With John Lithgow, Christopher Collet, Jill Eikenberry.

MANHUNTER. Written and directed by Michael Mann. With William L. Petersen.

MEN. . . . Written and directed by Doris Dorrie. With Julius Armbrust, Ulrike Kriener, Uwe Oschsenknecht.

MÉNAGE. Written and directed by Bertrand Blier. With Gerard Depardieu, Michel Blanc, Miou-Miou.

THE MISSION. Director, Roland Joffé; screenplay by Robert Bolt. With Robert De Niro, Jeremy Irons.

MONA LISA. Director, Neil Jordan; screenplay by Mr. Jordan and David Leland. With Bob Hoskins, Cathy Tyson.

THE MORNING AFTER. Director, Sidney Lumet; screenplay by James Hicks. With Jane Fonda, Jeff Bridges.

MOSQUITO COAST. Director, Peter Weir; screenplay by Paul Schrader, from the Paul Theroux novel. With Harrison Ford, Helen Mirren, River Phoenix.

MY BEAUTIFUL LAUNDRETTE. Director, Stephen Frears; screenplay by Hanif Kureishi. With Daniel Day Lewis, Saeed Jaffrey, Gordon Warnecke, Shirley Anne Field.

THE NAME OF THE ROSE. Director, Jean-Jacques Annaud; screenplay by Andrew Birkin, Gerald Brach, Howard Franklin, Alain Godard. With Sean Connery, F. Murray Abraham.

NATIVE SON. Director, Jerrold Freedman; screenplay by Richard Wesley, based on the novel by Richard Wright. With Victor Love, Elizabeth McGovern, Akosua Busia, Oprah Winfrey.

'NIGHT, MOTHER. Director, Tom Moore; screenplay by Marsha Norman. With Sissy Spacek, Anne Bancroft.

9½ WEEKS. Director, Adrian Lyne; screenplay by Patricia Knop, Zalman King, and Sarah Kernochan. With Mickey Rourke, Kim Basinger.

NOBODY'S FOOL. Director, Evelyn Purcell; screenplay by Beth Henley. With Rosanna Arquette, Eric Roberts.

NO MERCY. Director, Richard Pearce; screenplay by James Carabatsos. With Richard Gere, Kim Basinger.

NO SURRENDER. Director, Peter Smith; screenplay by Alan Bleasdale. With Ray McAnally, James Ellis, Joanne Whalley, Bernard Hill, Mark Mulholland.

NOTHING IN COMMON. Director, Garry Marshall; screenplay by Rick Podell and Michael Preminger. With Tom Hanks, Jackie Gleason, Eva Marie Saint.

OTELLO. (Screen version of Verdi's opera) Director, Franco Zeffirelli. With Placido Domingo.

PEGGY SUE GOT MARRIED. Director, Francis Coppola; screenplay by Jerry Leichtling and Arlene Sarner. With Kathleen Turner, Nicolas Cage.

PIRATES. Director, Roman Polanski; screenplay by Gerard Brach and Mr. Polanski. With Walter Matthau.

PLATOON. Written and directed by Oliver Stone. With Charlie Sheen, Tom Berenger, Willem Dafoe.

POWER. Director, Sidney Lumet; screenplay by David Himmelstein. With Richard Gere, Julie Christie, Gene Hackman, Kate Capshaw.

PRETTY IN PINK. Director, Howard Deutch; screenplay by John Hughes. With Molly Ringwald, Harry Dean Stanton.

A ROOM WITH A VIEW. Director, James Ivory; screenplay by Ruth Prawer Jhabvala, based on the novel by E. M. Forster. With Maggie Smith, Julian Sands, Helena Bonham Carter.

'ROUND MIDNIGHT. Director, Bernard Tavernier; screenplay by Mr. Tavernier and David Rayfiel. With Dexter Gordon.

RUTHLESS PEOPLE. Directors, Jim Abrahams, David Zucker, and Jerry Zucker; screenplay by Dale Launer. With Danny DeVito, Bette Midler.

SHE'S GOTTA HAVE IT. Written and directed by Spike Lee. With Tracy Camila Johns, Spike Lee.

SID AND NANCY. Director, Alex Cox; screenplay by Mr. Cox and Abbe Wool. With Gary Oldham, Chloe Webb.

SMOOTH TALK. Director, Joyce Chopra; screenplay by Tom Cole. With Treat Williams, Laura Dern, Mary Kay Place.

SOMETHING WILD. Director, Jonathan Demme; screenplay by E. Max Frye. With Jeff Daniels, Melanie Griffith.

SOUL MAN. Director, Steve Miner; screenplay by Carol Black. With C. Thomas Howell.

STAR TREK IV: THE VOYAGE HOME. Director, Leonard Nimoy; screenplay by Steve Meerson, Peter Krikes, Harve Bennett, Nicholas Meyer. With William Shatner, Leonard Nimoy.

STEAMING. Director, Joseph Losey; screenplay by Patricia Losey. With Vanessa Redgrave, Sarah Miles.

STREETS OF GOLD. Director, Joe Roth; screenplay by Heywood Gould, Richard Price, and Tom Cole. With Klaus Maria Brandauer.

SUMMER. Written and directed by Eric Rohmer. With Marie Rivière.

SWEET LIBERTY. Written and directed by Alan Alda. With Alan Alda, Michael Caine.

TAI-PAN. Director, Daryl Duke; screenplay by John Briley and Stanley Mann, based on the novel by James Clavell. With Bryan Brown, Joan Chen.

THAT'S LIFE! Director, Blake Edwards; screenplay by Mr. Edwards and Milton Wexler. With Jack Lemmon, Julie Andrews.

THÉRÈSE. Written and directed by Alain Cavalier. With Catherine Mouchet.

THREE AMIGOS. Director, John Landis; screenplay by Steve Martin, Lorne Michaels, Randy Newman. With Mr. Martin, Chevy Chase, Martin Short.

TOP GUN. Director, Tony Scott; screenplay by Jim Cash, Jack Epps, Jr. With Tom Cruise, Kelly McGillis.

TOUGH GUYS. Director, Jeff Kanew; screenplay by James Orr and Jim Cruickshank. With Burt Lancaster, Kirk Douglas.

TROUBLE IN MIND. Written and directed by Alan Rudolph; with Kris Kristofferson, Keith Carradine, Lori Singer.

TRUE STORIES. Director, David Byrne; screenplay by Stephen Tobolowsky, Beth Henley, David Byrne. With David Byrne, John Goodman, Swoosie Kurtz.

TURTLE DIARY. Director, John Irvin; screenplay by Harold Pinter, adapted from the novel by Russell Hoban. With Glenda Jackson, Ben Kingsley.

VAGABOND. Written and directed by Agnes Varda. With Sandrine Bonnaire.

VIOLETS ARE BLUE. Director, Jack Fisk; screenplay by Naomi Foner. With Sissy Spacek, Kevin Kline.

WILDCATS. Director, Michael Ritchie; screenplay by Ezra Sacks. With Goldie Hawn, Swoosie Kurtz.

Gamma-Liaison

Robert Redford and Debra Winger are two Manhattan lawyers in "Legal Eagles," a sophisticated mystery-thriller with a decidedly light touch. The two stars show their comedic deftness as they spar with each other in the courtroom and ultimately join forces to solve a murder mystery and to fall in love.

II, again featured Ralph Macchio and Noriyuki (Pat) Morita. Not far behind was *Back to School*, an outrageous farce with Rodney Dangerfield as a businessman who goes to college along with his son. *Aliens*, the sequel to the hugely successful *Alien* (1979), brought back Sigourney Weaver in a tough action role that earned her the nickname Rambolina, and *Ferris Bueller's Day Off* presented Matthew Broderick as a wily high-school truant.

The biggest flops of the summer included the expensive fiasco *Howard the Duck*, puppeteer Jim Henson's fantasy *Labyrinth*, and the Sean Penn-Madonna dud, *Shanghai Surprise*. Indicative of the financial bonanza mentality that grips Hollywood was the response to *Cobra*, the violent film starring Sylvester Stallone. Even though it grossed almost $50 million by Labor Day, it was judged a flop because it was not doing the astronomical business projected on the basis of Stallone's mega-hit *Rambo*.

From Abroad. New stirrings in the cinema of Canada and England, provocative work from France and Italy, and a surprise hit from Australia provided lively and diverse fare for audiences seeking the unusual. French-Canadian director Denys Arcand wrote and filmed *The Decline of the American Empire*, a movie dissecting the personal lives of a group of male and female university professors with candor, wit, and intellectual sophistication. Another Canadian film *Dancing In The Dark* starred Martha Henry in a shattering performance as a woman whose supposedly ideal life as a traditional housewife crumbles.

British cinema also gave evidence of new life. *My Beautiful Laundrette* was acclaimed for its look at Pakistanis struggling to climb the economic ladder in London. *Letter to Brezhnev*, made in Liverpool, was a frisky romantic story about two working class women trying to give more meaning to their drab lives. Another film shot in Liverpool was *No Surrender*, a bizarre mix of comedy and violence pertaining to the Irish conflict. *Turtle Diary*, with Ben Kingsley and Glenda Jackson, was a compelling, wistful drama about kindred spirits conspiring to set giant turtles free from an aquarium and return them to the sea. Bob Hoskins gave a memorable performance as a former convict in love with a call girl in *Mona Lisa*.

France's Bertrand Tavernier made one of the best films ever about jazz. *'Round Midnight* followed the touching friendship of an American musician and his French admirer during the 1950s. Jean-Jacques Beineix, previously acclaimed for *Diva* (1982), was back with *Betty Blue*, the story of a tragic love between a writer and an alluring but psychotic woman. Another arresting film from France was *Ménage*, Bertrand Blier's risque comedy starring Gerard Depardieu, Miou-Miou, and Michel Blanc as an unlikely threesome. Agnes Varda's *Vagabond* was a realistic, uncompromising look at the alienation of a young woman dropout. Italy's master director Federico Fellini used television as a metaphor for satirizing society's crassness in *Ginger and Fred*, teaming Marcello Mastroianni and Giulietta Masina as two aging vaudevillians.

The box office shocker was *Crocodile Dundee*, a film from Australia starring comedian Paul Hogan. Its gross revenue as the end of the year neared had risen to some $60 million in the United States alone, an unheard of figure for an Australian import.

Color War. No movie controversy has aroused the artistic community in recent years as much as the burgeoning practice of adding color through computer technology to old black and white films to increase television and videocassette sales. Organizations and individuals passionately have opposed colorization on the ground that it crassly alters the creative work of others. To color such films, the argument went, would be like deciding a work by a master painter would look better if doctored. Among films designated for such transformation were such classics as *Casablanca, The Maltese Falcon,* and *Citizen Kane.* Statements of opposition came from the Director's Guild of America, the American Film Institute, and the National Council on the Arts, as well as from various union groups and leading directors. Only moral outrage stood any chance of impeding the process. In general the owners of the films legally could do what they choose.

Monopoly. A major economic development in the motion-picture industry was the growing acquisition of theaters by the companies that make and distribute movies. The Cannon Group, in addition to its expanding concentration of theater holdings in Europe, bought the Commonwealth chain of 425 screens in the Midwest. The 360-screen Mann theaters chain was purchased by Gulf and Western, the parent company of Paramount. Tri-Star announced acquisition of the 250-screen Loews chain.

Concern mounted among independent theater owners that they would have trouble booking films because the movie companies might favor their own showplaces. But Jack Valenti, president of the Motion Picture Association of America, asserted that the purchases are good for the movie business because they show that there is faith in the cinema's future.

Doubts about that future continued to persist with the proliferation of videocassette players and the purchase and rental of cassettes. A study commissioned by Columbia Pictures cited a total rental of 58.4 million cassettes during August and September of 1985 by 10–19 year-olds, more than eight times the figure for 1983. According to an Arbitron poll, 38% of all homes with television sets now have videocassette players.

WILLIAM WOLF, *Gannett News Service*

© Henry Grossman

At Avery Fisher Hall in New York, Leonard Bernstein conducted the Israel Philharmonic in his own new "Jubilee Games."

MUSIC

A unique recognition of American music occurred when, for the first time in U.S. history, a comprehensive survey of its music and musicians was available in a single reference work, the four-volume *New Grove Dictionary of American Music,* published on November 3. The fields of concert, traditional, folk, and popular music were covered with 1,000 entries on composers, 2,500 entries on performers of classical and popular music, and scholarly articles on genre subjects. A five-year project, the new dictionary incorporates the work of 1,000 specialist contributors.

Classical

Another unusual event of the year, which resulted from a new cultural-exchange agreement between the United States and the Soviet Union signed at the Geneva summit in November 1985, was the sensational performance and reception of pianist Vladimir Horowitz at age 81 in Moscow on April 20. It marked his return to his native country after an absence of 61 years. Playing Scarlatti, Mozart, Liszt, Schumann, Chopin, and most importantly Rachmaninoff and Scriabin, Horowitz overwhelmed the audience of 1,400 officials and diplomats and 600 members of the general public. The event, televised in Western Europe and the United States, was emotional and greeted by thunderous applause and cheers; it moved many in Horowitz' audience to tears. Soviet artists performing in the United States on the cultural agreement included the Kirov Ballet, with its musical director Yuri Temirkanov conducting the New York Philharmonic on January 8, and the Moscow State Symphony, conducted by Yevgeny Svetlanov in New York's Avery Fisher Hall on October 18.

New Music. Festivals were especially active in performance of large new works. Festival Miami presented by the University of Miami, offered the premiere of Elliott Carter's String Quartet No. 4 (September 17) and in other concerts during October, works by Jacob Druckman, Silvestre Revueltas, and Donald Erb. The Music of the Americas Festival at Indiana State University, Terre Haute, featured works by Timothy Kramer, Bernard Rands, and John Adams, among others, as well as composers from South America and Canada. The Omaha Symphony's Contemporary Music Festival, May 18–22, performed works by seven composers-in-residence—John Adams, James Hobbs, Dexter Morrill, Ned Rorem, Joan Tower, David Ward-Steinman, and David White. The Fromm Week of New Music at the Aspen (CO) Festival offered pieces by Paul Lansky, Rand Steiger, Daniel Asia, Steven Mackey, Stephen Mosko, and Faye-Ellen Silverman.

The New York Philharmonic's Horizons Festival of seven programs at Avery Fisher Hall in May and June began with older theatrical works by György Ligeti—*Aventures/Nouvelle Aventures* (1971) and excerpts from *Le Grand Macabre* (1977), staged by Ian Strasfogel. Horizons ranged through works in a variety of idioms to the final concert of large works by John Corigliano, Bernard Rands, and Jacob Druckman.

Jacob Druckman's *Athanor* was introduced by the New York Philharmonic, Zubin Mehta conducting, on May 8. On September 13, Leonard Bernstein led the Israel Philharmonic in Avery Fisher Hall in his own new *Jubilee Games.* The work is a departure for him in that in it he gives the performers a certain freedom of pitch choice and also incorporates an electronic playback device. Works by composers-in-residence with major orchestras received premieres; among them were Charles Wuorinen's *The Golden Dance,* by the San Francisco Symphony, September 10, and Tobias Picker's Symphony No. 2, *Aussohnung,* by the Houston Symphony, October 25.

The American premiere of three scenes from Olivier Messiaen's five-hour opera *St. Francis of Assisi* (1983) was performed by the Boston Symphony, with soloists and chorus, Seiji Ozawa conducting, in Boston, April 10.

Opera. A major opera company was born, and Los Angeles' musical aspirations of more than 30 years were realized when the Los Angeles Music Center Opera produced its first three operas in the Dorothy Chandler Pavilion on October 7, 8, and 9. The company made its debut with a new Günther Schneider-Siemmsen production of Verdi's *Otello,* directed by Götz Friedrich. *Madama Butterfly* followed, and then came Strauss' *Salome,* di-

rected by Peter Hall, with his wife, Maria Ewing, in the title role. The production featured striking designs by John Bury. On November 4 in the Wiltern Theater, the new company presented Handel's *Alcina.*

New operas receiving premieres in the United States for the most part were conservative and unremarkable in their music, even when the librettos and conceptions seemed bold. Anthony Davis' *X (The Life and Times of Malcolm X),* given its first performance by the New York City Opera on September 28, focused on words and ideology in the operatic treatment of the life of the assassinated black separatist leader. The musical thrust was primarily rhythmic, the singing predominantly incantational. William Mayer's *A Death in the Family* (1983), given its second production by the Opera Theater of St. Louis on June 4, was based on James Agee's novel of the same name and Tad Mosel's play *All the Way Home.* It treated episodes but not often the powerful essences of these sources, with the music drawing freely on folk and spiritual music and jazz.

The Guilt of Lillian Sloan, a new opera by William Neil, the Chicago Lyric Opera's composer-in-residence, was introduced in a performance by that company's American Artists' wing at Northwestern University on June 6. The libretto by Frank Galati deals with a celebrated British murder trial of the 1920s. Lee Hoiby's *The Tempest,* to Marc Shulgasser's li-

The Los Angeles Music Center Opera made its debut with three productions, including "Madama Butterfly," in October.

© Frederick Ohringer

© Joan Marcus

Gian Carlo Menotti's new opera, "Goya," with Placido Domingo, was given its premiere by the Washington (DC) Opera.

bretto on Shakespeare's play, was given its premiere by the Des Moines (IA) Metro Opera, June 21. The spirit Ariel was made the main and highly coloratura character in a musical, lyrical, and decidedly romantic setting. Gian Carlo Menotti's opera *Goya,* based on the painter's life, with Placido Domingo in the title role, was given its premiere by the Washington (DC) Opera on November 15. The premiere was accompanied by a month-long series of related events in the capital city that concluded with a national PBS telecast of the opera on November 28.

The American premiere of British composer Peter Maxwell Davies' *Taverner,* on events in the life of the Tudor composer John Taverner, was given by the Opera Company of Boston, Sarah Caldwell conducting and directing, on March 9. *The King Goes Forth to France* (1984), by the Finnish composer Aulis Sallinen, received its American premiere July 26, during the Santa Fe (NM) Opera's 30th anniversary season. The opera, which drew mixed critical reviews, depicts an English king fleeing the second Ice Age by crossing the channel to France and is an antiwar allegory.

The main exploratory thrust in opera repertory continued to be historical in the rediscovery of older works. The San Francisco Opera opened its season September 5 with the first American performance of Verdi's *Don Carlos* in its original French and in a five-act version combining the best of Verdi's earliest material with his 1884 revision. On September 14 the same company's revival of Janáček's *Jenufa* in Czech used the composer's original score of 1904, which proved superior and more

characteristic of the composer than Karel Kovařovic's traditionally employed 1916 reorchestration. Other revivals and restorations of note included Rossini's *The Journey to Rheims,* lost since its first production of 1825. The opera, its score reconstructed, was well received at its American premiere, June 12, by the Opera Theater of St. Louis.

One new production cycle of Wagner's *Der Ring des Nibelungen* was completed on the West Coast in August, and another was begun promptly on the East Coast. To its *Die Walküre,* new in 1985, the Seattle Opera added the other three operas of the tetralogy in August. The mixture of 19th- and 20th-century design ideas for deliberate anachronistic effect was widely criticized, while the Seattle Opera performances were praised. As the first work of its new *Ring,* the Metropolitan Opera opened its season September 22 with *Die Walküre.* In this case the performances, under the conduction of James Levine and staging by Otto Schenk, were sharply reviewed, while Günther Schneider-Siemssen's sets were found attractive in an old-fashioned way.

In July, Birgit Nilsson, 68, one of the great Wagnerian sopranos of all time, announced her retirement from public singing 40 years after first joining the Stockholm Opera. Milan's Teatro alla Scala brought a company of 350 to Vancouver, B.C., to give six performances of Verdi's *I Lombardi* and two performances of Verdi's *Requiem* between August 24 and September 4 at the World Festival given as part of Expo 86 (*see* CANADA—The Arts).

Symphony. A rash of operating crises, mostly financial, afflicted orchestras in the intermediate category, including those in Buffalo, Columbus, Denver, Honolulu, Houston, New Orleans, Oakland, Omaha, Oregon, Phoenix, San Diego, San Jose, Seattle, Springfield (MA), and Tulsa. Two orchestras were out on strike—the Honolulu Symphony over wages and the Columbus (OH) Symphony in a contract dispute over personnel and artistic issues. Most of the other orchestras' difficulties stemmed from cumulative and current operating deficits. These were met by cutbacks in performance weeks and players' wages and increased efforts in fund-raising and ticket sales. On September 12 the Oakland Symphony became the first American symphony in modern times to declare bankruptcy.

Lorin Maazel was appointed music director of the Pittsburgh Symphony, which he had served as music consultant since 1984. Dennis Russell Davies, principal conductor of the Saratoga Performing Arts Center and director of the Stuttgart Opera and the Cabrillo Music Festival (CA), was appointed music director of the city of Bonn, West Germany, in February, to take effect in 1987.

Festivals. Honoring the 100th anniversary of Franz Liszt's death (July 31), festivals took place worldwide, in Austria, East Germany, Sweden, and the United States—Princeton, NJ; Miami (in November); and Washington, DC. The Franz Liszt Centennial Celebration in the U.S. capital, June 22–29, offered performances and lectures by eminent Liszt musicians and scholars in the Smithsonian Institution, Kennedy Center, Washington Cathedral, and St. Matthew's Cathedral. The

Aspen (CO) Music Festival also honored the centennial by adopting as its 1986 theme, "Liszt and His Descendants," and offering music by composers of Hungarian origin, including Liszt's contemporaries Ferenc Erkel and Mihály Mosonyi, as well as Ernst Dohnányi, Zoltán Kodály, and Béla Bartók, and the living composers Sándor Balassa, András Szöllösy, and György Ligeti.

Awards. Marian Anderson, 84, and Aaron Copland, 85, were among nine American cultural figures given the National Medal of Arts by President Ronald Reagan on July 14. MacArthur Foundation Awards were given to composers George Perle, 71, $300,000; Milton Babbitt, 70, $300,000; and Charles Wuorinen, 48, $236,000; the awards are spread out over five years. Perle had been awarded the 1986 Pulitzer Prize in music for his *Wind Quintet IV*. On October 26 the Kennedy Center Friedheim Award was shared by Bernard Rands, for his suite, *Le Tambourin* (1984), and Richard Wernick, for his Violin Concerto (1986), each receiving $3,000. The Franciscan String Quartet, in residence at Yale University, won the second Banff (Alberta, Canada) International String Quartet Competition which carried an award of $15,000, a valuable set of matched bows, and a period of residency at the Banff Centre. Charles Neidich was the winner of the Walter W. Naumburg clarinet competition, February 11. Clarinetist Richard Stoltzman received the Avery Fisher Artist Program award of $25,000 on March 1.

ROBERT COMMANDAY
Music Critic, "San Francisco Chronicle"

Pianist Earl Wild gave a series of all-Liszt performances to mark the 100th anniversary of the composer's death.

M.L. Falcone, Public Relations

The respected jazz pianist Chick Corea (second from the right), who once headed the group Return to Forever, moved in new directions during 1986 as his new group, Elektric Band, made an impact on the jazz scene.

© Glenn Wexler Studio

Jazz

The direction and creative verve of jazz in 1986 was evident in the new recordings and new groups on the year's jazz scene.

Chick Corea's new group, Elektric Band, with bassist John Patitucci and drummer Dave Weckl, marked Corea's first time as leader of a jazz-pop fusion group. Corea contends that listeners under 45 who grew up with Elvis and the Beatles can "palate the music" because it comes from electric instruments. Red Alert, trumpeter Red Rodney's new group, added fusion funk to its mainstream repertoire by using electronics to color Rodney's trumpet sounds. The jazz sextet O.T.B. (Out of the Blue) offered on their critically acclaimed first release, *O.T.B.*, an original blend of jazz, rock, and be-bop solo playing. Drawing on the bossanova-jazz style of the past, the new Brazilian group Azymuth gleaned from be-bop rock and the samba a unique sound and rhythm called *samba doido,* or crazy samba.

One of the most important new releases of 1986 was the album *Song X,* featuring the united talents of young fusion-rock guitarist Pat Metheny and established composer and alto-sax player Ornette Coleman. Other "five star" albums of the year included Henry Threadgill's *Subject to Change, Black Codes (from the Underground)* from Wynton Marsalis, *Buddy DeFranco Presents John Denman, Lost in the Stars: The Music of Kurt Weill* (by various artists), Eddie Daniels' *Breakthrough,* and Freddie Hubbard and Woody Shaw's *Double Take.* Important collection releases included *The Complete Black Lion and Vogue Recordings of Thelonious Monk, The Complete Candid Recordings of Charles Mingus,* and *Billie Holliday on Verve, 1946–1959.*

Two important big bands surfaced in 1986. The Orange, Then Blue 12-piece cooperative chamber jazz orchestra is made up mainly of graduates from the New England Conservatory's third-stream department. The exciting Marshall Vente/Project 9+ group featured on their album *Alison's Backyard* the writing of Vente and the fine solo work of saxophonists Bill Sears and Jim Massoth, trumpeter Art Davis, guitarist Frank Dawson, and vocalist Anna Dawson.

In 1986 the National Jazz Service Organization (NJSO), under the leadership of president David Baker and executive director Eunice J. Lockhart-Moss, instituted a technical assistance program for jazz artists and organizations. Founded in 1984, NJSO has provided in excess of $85,000 to more than 75 artists and groups. The organization, whose board members include many important musicians, plans a program for 1987 called New Perspectives on Jazz.

The 1986 jazz education scene was a hotbed of activity, with a number of artists changing academic venues or entering the education scene for the first time. Important new books on jazz included a four-volume discography on Dizzy Gillespie, Roger Wernboe's discography on Lee Morgan, a biography of Chet Baker and *Good Morning Blues,* Count Basie's autobiography as told to Albert Murray.

Awards. The 34th annual *Down Beat* International Critics Poll winners included: Gil Evans—Hall of Fame; James Newton's *The African Flower*—record of the year; Count Basie—big band; Art Blakey's Jazz Messengers—acoustic group; Miles Davis—electric group; Carla Bley—composer; Lester Bowie—trumpet; Jimmy Knepper—trombone; Steve Lacy—soprano sax; Ornette Coleman—alto sax; Charlie Haden—bass; Steve Swallow—electric bass; Max Roach—drums; Sonny Rollins—tenor sax; Pepper Adams—baritone sax; Cecil Taylor—acoustic piano; Chick Corea—electric piano; John Scofield—guitar; Joe Williams—male singer; Sarah Vaughan—female singer; and Manhattan Transfer—vocal group.

DOMINIC SPERA, *Indiana University*

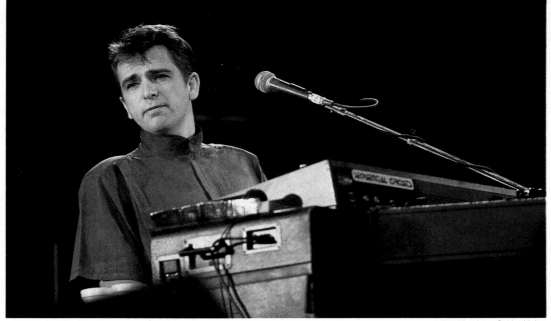

© Nick Elgar/Lynn Goldsmith Inc.

Peter Gabriel, formerly of the group Genesis, made it big in 1986 with a top-selling album, "So," and a hit single, "Sledgehammer." Gabriel also got wide exposure in the Conspiracy of Hope benefit tour for Amnesty International.

Popular

Popular musicians shifted their attention away from international charity and toward personal reassessment in 1986. The music reflected a reintegration of once-popular styles, as performers reevaluated their goals and their relationship to the past.

Inspired by the enormous scope and heartfelt sentiment of the anti-hunger crusade that culminated in 1985's Live Aid concert and the ubiquitous *We Are the World* (single, album, and video), artists were committed to more political causes in 1986. Organizer Bob Geldof's second attempt at a mega-event, the Hands Across America poverty benefit, lacked the spontaneity of Live Aid. But the Conspiracy of Hope tour to benefit Amnesty International performed to sold-out audiences in 11 cities. Peter Gabriel and Canadian Bryan Adams, who drew enormous crowds on separate tours of their own, joined Miles Davis, U2, Jackson Browne, Lou Reed, and others. A highlight of the Amnesty tour was an appearance in New Jersey by the popular Latin *salsa* artist Rubén Blades, who in 1986 also played opposite Richard Pryor in the film *Critical Condition*.

Gabriel, formerly of Genesis, was one of the year's big names, with a hit album *(So)* and a hit single *(Sledgehammer)*. Even without him, however, his former band also scored major successes, with the LP and single *Invisible Touch*. Another big name was the multitalented David Byrne of Talking Heads, who directed and acted as narrator in the motion picture release *True Stories*, whose musical cornerstone was the Heads' hit *Wild Wild Life*.

Once written off as a Bruce Springsteen imitator, John Cougar Mellencamp finally came into his own. His triple-platinum 1985 album *Scarecrow* was a leading seller through much of 1986. Mellencamp drives home his simple appeal as a patriotic, small-town, midwestern rock 'n' roller by questioning what he perceives as his country's crisis of values. The artist's formative role in the Farm Aid benefit concerts, in their second year, underscored this quest. Country songwriter Steve Earle appeals to a similar audience in his accomplished debut *Guitar Town*. Bryan Adams *(Reckless)* reduces this formula to the basics, as he belts out updated love songs inspired by his favorite rock 'n' roll heroes of the 1950s. And Bob Dylan teamed with Tom Petty and the Heartbreakers for his biggest tour ever.

The difference between nostalgia and respect for the past was articulated by 200 artists, writers, musicologists, and business people who elected the first ten inductees of the Rock 'n' Roll Hall of Fame: Chuck Berry, James Brown, Ray Charles, Sam Cooke, Fats Domino, the Everly Brothers, Buddy Holly, Jerry Lee Lewis, Little Richard, and Elvis Presley. The hall is planned as part of a new Cleveland museum featuring extensive audiovisual archives, scheduled to open in 1989. Inductees will be added annually.

Black music's answer to nostalgia was *retronuevo,* a term coined by the music historian and critic Nelson George, author of the excellent new Motown Records history *Where Did Our Love Go? Retronuevo* refers to a style that fuses gospel, jazz, and pop, modernized by fresh arrangements and instrumentation. Whitney Houston, who swept the Grammies with her hit debut album *Houston,* almost single-handedly brought back romantic ballad singing; Detroit native Anita Baker, a 28-year-old pop-soul contralto, sang up a storm—or "quiet storm," as radio stations dubbed playlists that integrate Sarah Vaughan and Nancy Wilson, for example, with Baker, Houston, Luther Vandross, and Freddie Jackson.

New Edition, a quartet of rapping kids from Roxbury, MA, a poor neighborhood outside Boston, turned in glistening performances on the huge smash *All for Love,* produced by Jimmy Jam and Terry Lewis, who also handled Janet Jackson's hit LP *Control.* The younger sister of Michael Jackson, Janet Jackson evokes the dilemmas and aspirations of black teenage girls everywhere with her sassy wit and provocative beat. Other applauded new-comers and relative unknowns were Peter Case, the Del Lords, the Bodeans, Husker Du, and Mofunso in rock; Dwight Yoakum and Nancy Griffith in country; Tramaine Hawkins in gospel; the Pet Shop Boys, Gwen Guthrie, and the Timex Social Club in dance music; and Run-D.M.C., and LL Cool J in rap.

Such seasoned professionals as the Rolling Stones *(Dirty Work),* Billy Joel *(The Bridge),* Jeffrey Osborne *(Emotional),* Paul Simon *(Graceland),* Elvis Costello *(King of America),* and Lou Reed *(Mistrial),* all turned out superior new works. Prince pleased younger fans with *Kiss,* one of the year's top singles. Madonna stirred new controversy with *Papa Don't Preach,* a song heralded by the antiabortion movement; and the maturity of her vocal style on the album *True Blue* changed the minds of many former detractors. Unfortunately, anticipated follow-ups to earlier smashes by superstars Tina Turner *(Break Every Rule)* and Lionel Richie *(Dancing on the Ceiling)* were disappointing. And Paul McCartney's long-awaited new LP, *Press to Play,* failed to catch on.

The British rock scene slowed to almost a halt. Stevie Winwood's comeback LP, *Back in the High Life,* met with the warmest reception, and the beloved Elton John returned to adoring crowds. Except for the continued rise of Sade and the Smiths, however, only the debut of the Pet Shop Boys, originally recorded in 1984, showed promising signs of new blood.

Outside of the music from *The Mystery of Edwin Drood* and the smash comedy *Me and My Girl,* the Broadway harvest was relatively meager in 1986. But country music suffered the worst decline; new traditionalists the Judds and Reba McIntyre, as well as new artists Earle and Yoakum, who both play to rock audiences, were perceived as possible antidotes to the ailing Nashville sound.

See also RECORDINGS.

GEORGIA CHRISTGAU
Free-lance Writer

Rock 'n' roller John Cougar Mellencamp, below left, *came into his own; his 1985 LP "Scarecrow" remained high on the charts.* Whitney Houston, below right, *brought back the romantic ballad and swept the Grammies with her debut album.*

Photos © Nick Elgar/Lynn Goldsmith Inc.

Nebraska gubernatorial candidate Kay Orr meets a young supporter while awaiting the results of the Republican primary in May. Orr won the party nod and went on to defeat Democrat Helen Boosalis in November. It was the first time in U.S. history that two women faced each other as major-party nominees for a governorship.

AP/Wide World

NEBRASKA

Agricultural depression, related economic problems, and the election of a new governor dominated Nebraska news in 1986.

Agriculture and the Economy. Despite two years of record and near-record crops, low prices and heavy indebtedness kept many farmers on the verge of disaster, and repercussions from the agricultural depression were felt throughout the state. Bankruptcy cases hit an all-time high of 3,006 in 1985, and that record had been exceeded by late October 1986.

Predominantly rural counties continued to lose population. Taxable income in rural areas has decreased to the point that more than half the state's individual income taxes come from Omaha and Lincoln, and case loads in federal poverty programs have grown more rapidly in rural than in urban areas. The value of Nebraska farmland dropped by 17.6% in the year ending April 1, 1986, which means a corresponding reduction in county revenues from property taxes.

NEBRASKA • Information Highlights

Area: 77,355 sq mi (200 350 km²).

Population (1985 est.): 1,606,000.

Chief Cities (July 1, 1984 est.): Lincoln, the capital, 180,378; Omaha, 332,237; Grand Island (1980 census), 33,180.

Government (1986): *Chief Officers*—governor, J. Robert Kerrey (D); lt. gov., Donald F. McGinley (D). *Legislature* (unicameral)—49 members (nonpartisan).

State Finances (fiscal year 1985): *Revenue,* $2,144,000,000; *expenditure,* $2,137,000,000.

Personal Income (1985): $21,323,000,000; per capita, $13,281.

Labor Force (June 1986): *Civilian labor force,* 839,700; *unemployed,* 38,100 (4.5% of total force).

Education: *Enrollment* (fall 1984)—public elementary schools, 184,618; public secondary, 80,981; colleges and universities, 97,769. *Public school expenditures* (1983–84), $740,000,000 ($2,927 per pupil).

The Governor's Race. Nebraska's most dramatic event in 1986 was the gubernatorial election. Gov. Robert Kerrey, the popular Democratic incumbent, announced in October 1985 that he would not seek a second term. That announcement led to heavy speculation about Kerrey's future plans and also attracted a field of seven Democratic and eight Republican gubernatorial candidates to the May primary elections.

Republican Kay Orr, who had served as state treasurer, and Democrat Helen Boosalis, former mayor of Lincoln, were nominated. National attention quickly focused on the fact that, for the first time in U.S. political history, both of a state's major party candidates for governor were women.

A hard-fought campaign brought national figures, including President Reagan, into the state, but the outcome remained too close to call in the preelection polls. Kay Orr won, becoming Nebraska's first woman governor and the nation's first Republican woman governor. Republicans retained the other state offices, and in a referendum a 1985 law to consolidate school districts and increase state aid to schools was repealed by a substantial margin. In another referendum a 1985 law mandating use of seat belts was repealed by a margin of a bare one tenth of one percent.

The Legislature. In its 1986 session the Nebraska unicameral legislature passed laws to permit grandparents to go to court in certain cases to obtain visitation rights to their grandchildren; to outlaw paramilitary training camps; to give local governments control over liquor licenses; to eliminate alienation of affection suits; to deregulate telephone companies; and to protect farmers from losing all of their land in foreclosure actions. Critics of this last law argued that it prevented farmers from obtaining credit, and a special session in November amended it.

Football. Economic anxieties did not, however, dampen the traditional enthusiasm for University of Nebraska football. As in preceding years, early victories excited hopes of a national championship, but losses to Colorado and Oklahoma doomed Husker hopes.

WILLIAM E. CHRISTENSEN
Midland Lutheran College

NETHERLANDS

Prime Minister Rudolf (Ruud) F. M. Lubbers, facing what polls had predicted would be a narrow defeat, carried his Christian Democrat-Liberal (conservative) coalition to victory May 21 in the Netherlands' first parliamentary elections since 1982.

Election Results. The Christian Democrats' victory was attributed largely to Lubbers' political skills and voter acceptance of his tough, often unpopular, program to stimulate the economy; the party's campaign slogan had been "Let Lubbers finish the job." Government policies directed toward reduction of public expenditure and improvement of economic conditions were further confirmed by the elections of deputies to the Second Chamber, the principal house of the Dutch parliament (States General).

The governing coalition maintained its majority of 81 seats out of a total of 150, although with a strong shift in favor of the Christian Democrats, who gained 9 seats for a total of 54, while the Liberals dropped the same number of seats for a total of 27. Labor increased its representation from 47 to 52, but remained in opposition. The minor leftist parties lost 2 seats, going from 14 to 12, with the badly split Communist Party losing its parliamentary representation completely. Following the voting the leadership of both the Liberal and the Labor parties changed hands, with a shift in Labor to a less ideological orientation.

Budget. The Christian Democrat-Liberal coalition formed a new government on July 14 to continue its program of steady cutting of government expenditure, with strikes and other protests—mainly against cuts in welfare benefits—generally ineffectual. Drastic reorganization was undertaken in education, from kindergartens to universities, with consolidation and reduction of programs.

The 1987 budget, presented September 16, called not only for reduced government spending, but also for tax increases. Both measures were designed to offset a fall in oil and natural gas revenues. Spending would be reduced to 166.9 billion guilders (about $72.1 billion), from 168.2 billion guilders ($72.6 billion) in 1985. Taxes would be raised on energy products and capital gains, and the value-added tax (VAT) would go up from 18% to 20%, to raise an expected 6.8 billion guilders ($2.9 billion) in new

---

NETHERLANDS • Information Highlights

Official Name: Kingdom of the Netherlands.
Location: Northwestern Europe.
Area: 15,770 sq mi (40 844 km²).
Population (mid-1986 est.): 14,500,000.
Chief Cities (Jan. 1, 1985 est.): Amsterdam, the capital, 675,579; Rotterdam, 571,081; The Hague, the seat of government, 443,456.
Government: *Head of state,* Beatrix, queen (acceded April 30, 1980). *Head of government,* Ruud Lubbers, prime minister (took office Nov. 1982). *Legislature*—States General: First Chamber and Second Chamber.
Monetary Unit: Guilder (2.475 guilders equal U.S.$1, June 1986).
Economic Index (1985): *Consumer Prices* (1980 = 100), all items, 122.7; food, 117.8.
Foreign Trade (1985 U.S.$): *Imports,* $65,218,-000,000; *exports,* $68,282,000,000.

---

revenue. The opposition Labor Party criticized the budget for giving too little attention to unemployment, which at more than 15% remained one of the highest rates in Europe.

Nuclear Affairs. Nuclear power issues proved less than decisive in the elections, even after the accident at Chernobyl in the Soviet Union. Prime Minister Lubbers had been committed to a major expansion of nuclear power in the Netherlands by the end of the century, but after Chernobyl, plans to build two already approved plants were suspended until the full effects of the accident could be assessed. And the government's "safety first" policy to contain public alarm about Chernobyl was markedly effective.

The controversial decision made in 1985 in the face of massive protest demonstrations to accept installation on Dutch territory of U.S. cruise missiles carrying nuclear warheads also failed to affect the election outcome. Lubbers' compromise measure on the issue had been passed in February by a parliamentary vote of 79 to 70, ending a six-year debate over the missiles, which are now scheduled to be in place by 1988. The Netherlands thus became the last of the northern European NATO members to accept deployment.

The Sea. The historic Dutch battle with the sea saw two victories in 1986. The new lands regained over the decades from the Ijssel Meer (the former Zuider Zee) were established as a separate province, called Flevoland, in January. And on October 4, Queen Beatrix officially opened the final dam in the Delta Works, the immense project designed to protect the provinces of Zeeland and Holland from a repetition of the disastrous flood of 1953. The new storm surge barrier across the Eastern Sheldt River estuary is the most technologically advanced weapon ever in the 900 years the Dutch have been fighting the sea. The barrier's 62 huge sliding steel gates normally remain open, but they can be rapidly closed if high water threatens. (*See also* page 79.)

HERBERT H. ROWEN, *Rutgers University*

A $300 million showcase addition to McCarran International Airport in Las Vegas, dedicated in October 1985, was a source of controversy as airlines contended that they were being asked to pick up the cost by paying higher user fees.

AP/Wide World

NEVADA

The race for the seat of retiring U.S. Sen. Paul Laxalt and a spotty performance by the gambling industry were highlights of 1986.

Elections. Despite three visits to the state by President Reagan and all-out campaigning by the popular incumbent, the Republicans failed to retain Laxalt's seat. Two-term Democratic Congressman Harry M. Reid used a 24% margin in his home county of Clark (Las Vegas and vicinity) to gain a 6% statewide victory over Jim Santini, a former four-term Democratic congressman who had turned Republican in 1985. As Santini had been the handpicked choice of Laxalt and Frank Fahrenkopf (the Nevadan who chairs the Republican National Committee), his defeat appeared to deal a severe blow to Laxalt's presidential ambitions. Democratic State Sen. James Bilbray won a bitter battle with fellow Sen. Bob Ryan for Reid's House seat, while Republican Rep. Barbara Vucanovich won a third term by defeating Reno Mayor Peter Sferrazza.

With 72% of the vote, Democratic Gov. Richard H. Bryan won a record landslide victory over state Treasurer Patty Cafferata, the daughter of Representative Vucanovich. Clark County District Attorney Bob Miller, a Democrat, was elected lieutenant governor in a race that received unusual attention because of the possibility that Governor Bryan would challenge U.S. Sen. Chic Hecht in 1988. University of Nevada Regent Frankie Sue Del Papa became the first woman elected secretary of state in Nevada history.

A unified Democratic Party picked up 12 seats to regain control of the state Assembly, while Republicans took control of the upper house for the first time in 22 years. This marked the first time since 1883 that both houses had changed hands simultaneously. Voters also approved a $31 million bond issue to allow the state to purchase environmentally sensitive land in the Lake Tahoe area.

Economy. State gaming revenue for the 1985–86 fiscal year increased by 5.3% over the previous year. Revenue from the casinos in northern Nevada actually decreased for the 1986 calendar year, however, giving rise to speculation that the California lottery was hurting the Reno-Lake Tahoe-Carson City area. Statewide sales tax revenue for fiscal 1986 was up about 6%, but total revenue for the last half of 1986 was well below the anticipated 7% increase included in the state's budget.

Other. Environmentalists, led by Harry Reid, gained congressional approval for a national park in the state; 77,000 acres (31 185 ha) were allotted to created Great Basin National Park in northeastern Nevada.

In May the federal government announced that Yucca Mountain, Nevada, was one of three sites under final consideration as the nation's first permanent repository for high-level nuclear wastes. Governor Bryan immediately filed lawsuits challenging the decision. Nevada

---

NEVADA · Information Highlights

Area: 110,561 sq mi (286 352 km²).
Population (1985 est.): 936,000.
Chief Cities (July 1, 1984 est.): Carson City, the capital (1980 census), 32,022; Las Vegas, 183,227; Reno, 105,615.
Government (1986): *Chief Officers—*governor, Richard H. Bryan (D); lt. gov., Robert A. Cashell (R). *Legislature—*Senate, 21 members; Assembly, 42 members.
State Finances (fiscal year 1985): *Revenue,* $1,909,000,000; *expenditure,* $1,643,000,000.
Personal Income (1985): $13,560,000,000; per capita, $14,488.
Labor Force (June 1986): *Civilian labor force,* 524,300; *unemployed,* 31,200 (5.9% of total force).
Education: *Enrollment* (fall 1984)—public elementary schools, 104,089; public secondary, 47,544; colleges and universities, 43,656. *Public school expenditures* (1983–84), $401,000,000 ($2,861 per pupil).

also sued the federal government in a challenge to the nation's 55 miles-per-hour speed limit.

Harry E. Claiborne, chief judge for the U.S. district court of Nevada, became the first federal official impeached and convicted by Congress in 50 years. Claiborne, convicted of tax evasion in 1984, had refused to resign.

DON W. DRIGGS
University of Nevada, Reno

NEW BRUNSWICK

The related and ever-controversial issues of language rights and French-English equality were much in the news during 1986. And the political pot continued to boil as New Brunswickers patiently waited for Premier Richard Hatfield, a Conservative, to call a provincial election.

Language Report. On June 19, Premier Hatfield tabled the long-awaited report of the Advisory Committee on Official Languages. The report recommended, among other things, twin unilingual English and French work units in government departments, affirmative action programs to promote French-speaking civil servants, a linguistic rights commission, and a policy to make the membership of local boards reflect their areas' linguistic make-up.

After unveiling the report in the legislature, Hatfield then rejected most of its proposals. This provoked Aurele Thériault, secretary-general of the New Brunswick Acadian Society, to comment bitterly that the government had decided to "ignore" a process that had cost it more than C$1 million.

The advisory committee's report came one day after the New Brunswick Society of Acadians released its own study calling for even more radical measures. The society, main lobby group for the province's 255,000-strong French community, advocated separate French and English public administrations, including a separate French ministry of education, hospital system, and judiciary.

Tabloid is Born. The first edition of a new French-language daily newspaper to serve New Brunswick's Acadian community rolled off the presses in Moncton on August 11. The tabloid, *Le Matin,* is intended to help fill the void left when Moncton's *L'Évangeline* folded four years earlier. Editor Charles D'Amour said he was aiming at a daily circulation of 20,000–25,000.

Near-balanced Budget. The budget presented to the legislature on April 22 by Finance Minister John Baxter projected a razor-thin deficit of C$7.3 million on spending of C$3.1 billion. The deficit just three years earlier was $203 million. "We have achieved stability in our financial affairs," Baxter told the House. There were no major tax increases or tax breaks.

NEW BRUNSWICK • Information Highlights

Area: 28,355 sq mi (73 440 km²).
Population (Jan. 1986 est.): 720,300.
Chief Cities (1981 census): Fredericton, the capital, 43,723; Saint John, 80,521; Moncton, 54,743.
Government (1986): *Chief Officers*—lt. gov., George Stanley; premier, Richard B. Hatfield (Progressive Conservative). *Legislature*—Legislative Assembly, 58 members.
Provincial Finances (1986–87 fiscal year budget): *Revenues,* $3,092,700,000; *expenditures,* $3,100,-000,000.
Personal Income (average weekly earnings, May 1986): $395.01.
Labor Force (July 1986, seasonally adjusted): *Employed* workers, 15 years of age and over, 309,000; *Unemployed,* 46,000 (14.9%).
Education (1986–87): *Enrollment*—elementary and secondary schools, 141,300 pupils; postsecondary—universities, 15,380; community colleges, 2,470.
(All monetary figures are in Canadian dollars.)

Only two weeks before the budget presentation, the government offered a basket of pre-election goodies. The Speech from the Throne, opening the spring legislative session, promised new help for home-builders, an increased minimum wage, and an equal-opportunities program for female civil servants. There were also plums for farmers, senior citizens, and other groups.

Election Tune-up. The Liberals prepared for the approaching provincial election by taking the Edmundston constituency away from the Tories in a February 10 by-election. Their candidate, Roland Beaulieu, won with 3,849 votes to 2,048 for Charles Fournier of the Tories.

Protests. A decision by federally owned Canadian National Railways to close its Moncton shops provoked angry demonstrations by the hundreds of workers whose jobs would be eliminated. Prime Minister Brian Mulroney was the target of one noisy protest, staged by about 200 workers in Fredericton on August 25. Eight days later about 1,200 workers and supporters vented their spleen at federal Transport Minister John Crosbie when he visited Moncton.

JOHN BEST, *"Canada World News"*

NEWFOUNDLAND

The economic strains of the recent past continued to affect Newfoundland in 1986, long after central Canada had regained lost ground. The unemployment rate neared or exceeded 20% throughout the first nine months.

Labor Problems. Government general service workers went on strike twice. The issue was wage parity and a 1983 amendment to the Public Service Collective Bargaining Act that withholds the right to strike from "essential" public employees. The government, unwilling to negotiate during an illegal strike, worked out an end to the month-long dispute in March,

NEWFOUNDLAND · Information Highlights

Area: 156,649 sq mi (405 720 km²).
Population (Jan. 1986 est.): 580,700.
Chief Cities (1981 census): St. John's, the capital, 83,770; Corner Brook, 24,339.
Government (1986): *Chief Officers*—lt. gov., W. Anthony Paddon; premier, A. Brian Peckford (Progressive Conservative). *Legislature*—Legislative Assembly, 52 members.
Provincial Finances (1985–86 fiscal year budget): *Revenues*, $2,377,000,000; *expenditures*, $2,450,-000,000.
Personal Income (average weekly earnings, May 1986): $402.24.
Labor Force (July 1986, seasonally adjusted: *Employed* workers, 15 years of age and over, 232,000; *Unemployed*, 51,000 (22.0%).
Education (1986–87): *Enrollment*—elementary and secondary schools, 140,000 pupils; postsecondary—universities, 11,550; community colleges, 3,020.
(All monetary figures are in Canadian dollars.)

only to see it break out again in September. Some 5,500 workers were involved. The union finally went back to work following intervention by a group of church representatives.

In October a provincial Royal Commission on Unemployment, after a two-year study, recommended new approaches to rural economic development and improved education as a start to relieve some of the problems, especially for young Newfoundlanders.

Railway Service. The continued operation of the financially troubled Canadian National Railways Freight line in Newfoundland drew public controversy in June. The federal government offered a choice: either give up the railway entirely and use the $40 million subsidy for different transportation purposes or continue railway operations with little hope of new money. The provincial authorities opted for the railway. Ottawa responded with $36 million to upgrade the system, but gave notice that in the future market forces would determine operations.

Fishing Industry. In April, Newfoundland fisheries were hurt when the United States imposed a 5.8% duty on the import of whole fresh groundfish to protect its own fishing industry.

The following month Canadian fisheries inspectors boarded two Spanish trawlers off the coast of Newfoundland. The Spanish vessels, which had allegedly been fishing illegally in Canadian waters, then tried to escape across the Atlantic with the inspectors still on board. Halted by a Canadian patrol boat, they were escorted back to St. John's, where their captains were taken into custody. The Canadian and Spanish governments announced plans to form a commission to resolve disputes over fishing rights.

Toward the end of the year two major offshore fishing companies, National Sea and Fisheries Products International, announced profits ($10 and $12 million, respectively) for the first time since 1980.

Budget. The provincial budget, brought down in March, increased the debt to more than $4.2 billion and allowed spending to rise by 6.8%. In general the reaction to the proposal was lukewarm. The provincial government relies heavily on transfers from the federal level, and the decrease in transfers was affecting the delivery of services—especially in health and education.

Air Tragedy. On Dec. 12, 1985, an Arrow Air DC-8 jetliner with an eight-man crew and 248 passengers crashed on takeoff after a refueling stop at Gander. All aboard were killed. The passengers were U.S. military personnel returning from peace-keeping duties in Egypt.

SUSAN MCCORQUODALE
Memorial University of Newfoundland

NEW HAMPSHIRE

The year began with great anticipation that turned quickly to shock and sorrow on January 28, when Christa McAuliffe and six other crew members perished in the *Challenger* space shuttle tragedy. McAuliffe, a 37-year-old high-school social-studies teacher from Concord, NH, had been selected in 1985 to be the first "citizen observer" to ride the space shuttle. The accident caused a sense of shared grief throughout the state.

Environment. Nuclear power and nuclear waste made headlines throughout the year. In late January the U.S. Department of Energy announced that a site in southern New Hampshire was one of 12 being considered for the disposal of nuclear waste. There was immediate protest about the site's unsuitability. During town meetings in March, citizens of 114 towns debated the issue; opinion was overwhelmingly against the site. The controversy dragged on until late May, when the federal government "indefinitely postponed" plans to build a second nuclear waste site in an Eastern state.

Not so easily resolved was the ongoing saga of the Seabrook nuclear power plant. Although Unit I was complete, it could not generate power until emergency evacuation procedures for towns within a 10-mi (16-km) radius of the facility were approved. Some of these towns are in Massachusetts, where Gov. Michael Dukakis has refused to approve such plans. The utilities that own Seabrook have received permission to load nuclear fuel, but the date for power generation remained uncertain. Cost overruns at the facility continued, with Unit I projected to cost more than $5 billion, compared with an original estimate of $900 million for two reactors. Unresolved was how the construction costs would affect the price of electricity; all agree that it would rise.

A lawsuit brought by New Hampshire and six other New England states seeking federal

AP/Wide World

Christa McAuliffe, the 37-year-old high-school social-studies teacher—to have been the first private citizen to fly in space —was buried near her home in Concord, NH.

action to curb acid rain was dismissed in September.

Elections. Compared to environmental issues, the midterm election seemed a mild affair with predictable outcomes. Republicans swept all of the key contests and retained control of all sectors of the state government.

Both incumbent Republican Congressmen Robert Smith and Judd Gregg won reelection, as did Sen. Warren B. Rudman, whose challenger was former Massachusetts Gov. Endicott Peabody. Gov. John Sununu received 54% of the vote to defeat Democrat Paul McEachern. Sununu's margin was less than many had predicted because of his strong support for Seabrook; McEachern had pledged to keep it from generating power. The record low turnout —only 46.6% of registered voters—was disturbing.

Economy. The state's economy continued to boom in 1986. Unemployment remained consistently at record low levels—September's

2.6% rate marked the 13th consecutive month that New Hampshire had the lowest unemployment rate in the nation. This has created a dilemma for employers, who are having great difficulty finding enough workers. Residential and commercial construction continued at record levels. Representative of the trend was the opening in Nashua of Pheasant Lane Mall, the state's largest, with 150 stores.

Sherman Adams. New Hampshirites mourned the death on October 27 of Sherman Adams, a former governor of the state and special assistant to President Eisenhower (*see* OBITUARIES).

WILLIAM L. TAYLOR, *Plymouth State College*

NEW JERSEY

Economic and environmental concerns and partisan quarrels in the legislature held center stage in New Jersey in 1986.

Economics. Prosperity continued in most regions of the state, from the aging cities on the west bank of the Hudson River to the high-tech corridor between New Brunswick and Princeton. In Jersey City and Hoboken, the conversion of rental apartments into condominiums continued, as did further construction on multipurpose communities like Newport City and Port Liberté. A similar revitalization was planned for the decaying areas of downtown Newark. In late October a major obstacle to development along the Hudson was removed when plans were announced for a mass-transit system linking all cities from Bayonne to Fort Lee. The long-delayed opening of Interstate 78 was expected to spur growth in the west-central part of the state, while Newark International Airport continued to expand as a major passenger hub. More than 28 million people flew into or out of the facility in 1985, a 20% increase over the year before. Most of the upturn was due to People Express, headquartered at Newark since 1981. The financial problems of that carrier, which Texas Air agreed to purchase in September, seemed unlikely to reverse the trend.

Despite the positive economic climate, there were grounds for apprehension about how deep-seated the prosperity was, and whether it would be undercut by reductions in federal spending. The $9.3 million state budget approved in early summer carried a small surplus but failed to compensate cities for vast cutbacks in federal aid. Condominium conversion raised questions about the scarcity of housing for low-income people forced out of their old apartments, while coastal development continued to arouse environmental concerns.

The New Jersey Turnpike. The proposed $2.2 billion project to widen the turnpike to 12 lanes from Ridgefield Park to Jamesburg

---

NEW HAMPSHIRE • Information Highlights

Area: 9,279 sq mi (24 032 km²).
Population (1985 est.): 998,000.
Chief Cities (1980 census): Concord, the capital, 30,400; Manchester, 90,936; Nashua, 67,865.
Government (1986): *Chief Officer*—governor, John H. Sununu (R). *General Court*—Senate, 24 members; House of Representatives, 400 members.
State Finances (fiscal year 1985): *Revenue,* $1,361,000,000; *expenditure,* $1,195,000,000.
Personal Income (1985): $14,931,000,000; per capita, $14,964.
Labor Force (June 1986): *Civilian labor force,* 571,700; *unemployed,* 18,300 (3.2% of total force).
Education: *Enrollment* (fall 1984)—public elementary schools, 105,525; public secondary, 50,621; colleges and universities, 52,283. *Public school expenditures* (1983–84), $401,000,000 ($2,796 per pupil).

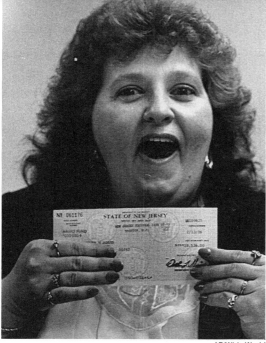

AP/Wide World

Convenience store manager Evelyn Marie Adams, 32, believes in miracles. In February she won $3.9 million in the New Jersey Lottery. In 1985 she had won $1.5 million.

aroused controversy. Environmental groups said the New Jersey Turnpike Authority had paid insufficient attention to the ecological impact of its plan and questioned whether the widening was necessary at all. In more congested areas, particularly around Newark and Elizabeth, opposition stemmed from concern for homeowners and businesses along the route who would be forced to move. After the city of Elizabeth threatened a lawsuit to block the project, a compromise limited the expansion to ten lanes. Some opponents were still dissatisfied, arguing that construction would unnecessarily inconvenience many motorists.

Environment. In May the Environmental Protection Agency denied a permit to allow experimental burning of toxic waste aboard an incinerator ship off the New Jersey coast. In November voters approved the sale of bonds to pay for the cleanup of toxic wastes.

Politics. Gov. Thomas H. Kean remained popular after his landslide reelection victory in 1985. Since he had shown that a Republican could win a large following among minorities and organized labor, Kean was much sought after at party rallies around the country. Democratic Sen. Bill Bradley also gained national prominence for his role in shaping the 1986 federal tax-reform legislation.

The legislature was divided between a Republican Assembly and a Democratic Senate. Kean proposed a number of constitutional revisions in January, especially the creation of the office of lieutenant governor and provision for the initiative and referendum. Both proposals, billed as moves to give voters greater control over the governmental process, were strongly opposed in the Senate. The two houses also disagreed over a bill to make liability insurance easier to purchase and another to reduce penalties for hosts accused of serving their guests too much to drink.

Although there were no statewide elections in 1986, a number of local contests were important. In the spring, Newark Councilman Sharpe James defeated incumbent fellow Democrat Kenneth Gibson in the city mayoralty race, while the fall election for Essex County Executive resulted in defeat for Democratic incumbent Peter Shapiro, his party's nominee for governor in 1985. The 1986 congressional races produced no changes in the New Jersey delegation: all eight Democratic and six Republican incumbents were reelected.

HERMANN K. PLATT
St. Peter's College

NEW MEXICO

A fiscal crisis, a gubernatorial race, and educational reform were key issues in 1986.

Politics. Gov. Toney Anaya (D) was ineligible for a third term. Democratic gubernatorial candidate Ray Powell tried to distance himself from the controversial Anaya, whose financial dealings were under federal investigation. Nevertheless, he was defeated by Republican Garrey Carruthers in a state where registered Democrats outnumber Republicans by nearly two to one. Campaign issues included honesty in government, state finances, public education, the environment, and crime. In November, Anaya, an opponent of capital punishment, commuted the sentences of the five inmates on death row to life imprisonment.

Voters in New Mexico's three congressional districts returned incumbents Manuel Lujan, Jr. (R), Joseph R. Skeen (R), and Bill Richardson (D). The Democrats expanded their majority in the lower house of the state legislature; the upper house was evenly divided, 21–21.

Education. The legislature enacted a controversial reform of public education which provided a $2,200 raise for all elementary and secondary school teachers, stiffened teacher certification requirements, specified new requirements for high-school graduation, and set the number of minutes per week to be devoted to certain subjects. In higher education a special state commission recommended more local funding of the state's community colleges, a reduction of most graduate programs at three of the six state universities, and the elimination of remedial programs at the universities.

Economy. Falling gas and oil prices injured the state's economy, especially since state revenue depends heavily on severance taxes from the sale of gas and oil and on money from the leasing of state gas and oil lands. The continuing slump in the agricultural and mining industries also had an impact. The shortfall in the state budget was projected at more than $100 million. Governor Anaya called a special legislative session in June to confront the fiscal crisis. Measures enacted to balance the state budget (required by the state constitution) included the repeal of $52 million in food and medical rebates for state citizens and a 2% cut in spending for state government and public and higher education. In February the legislature had approved sales and income tax increases designed to raise $150 million.

Indian Affairs. On the Navajo Reservation, part of which is in New Mexico, America's largest Indian tribe voted for a new tribal chairman. Peter MacDonald, chairman from 1970 to 1982, narrowly defeated incumbent Peterson Zah. Because some 7% of New Mexicans are Indians and about 8% of the state's area is in Indian reservations, continuing conflicts between Indians and the state and federal governments were important to all residents. (*See also* ETHNIC GROUPS.)   •

NEW MEXICO • Information Highlights

Area: 121,593 sq mi (314 925 km²).
Population (1985 est.): 1,450,000.
Chief Cities (1980 census): Santa Fe, the capital, 48,953; Albuquerque (July 1, 1984 est.): 350,575; Las Cruces, 45,086.
Government (1986): *Chief Officers*—governor, Toney Anaya (D); lt. gov., Mike Runnels (D). *Legislature*—Senate, 42 members; House of Representatives, 70 members.
State Finances (fiscal year 1985): *Revenue,* $3,579,000,000; *expenditure,* $3,041,000,000.
Personal Income (1985): $15,828,000,000; per capita, $10,914.
Labor Force (June 1986): *Civilian labor force,* 686,300; *unemployed,* 66,300 (9.7% of total force).
Education: *Enrollment* (fall 1984)—public elementary schools, 194,928; public secondary, 77,550; colleges and universities, 68,295. *Public school expenditures* (1983–84), $749,000,000 ($2,921 per pupil).

The Art World. Georgia O'Keeffe, who had lived and painted in northern New Mexico from 1929, died in March (*see* OBITUARIES). The Museum of New Mexico in Santa Fe exhibited two rare buffalo-hide paintings depicting Spanish encounters with the Indians in 1714 and 1720. A museum official noted that the paintings ". . . may represent the earliest known depiction of a documented historical event in what is today the United States."

MICHAEL L. OLSEN
New Mexico Highlands University

NEW YORK

Solidifying his position as a potential presidential candidate, Gov. Mario Cuomo (D) swept to a stunning reelection victory in 1986, breaking most of the state's records.

After months of tantalizing the public about whether he would run for reelection as governor or run for president, Cuomo announced his decision in May, but he refused to rule out the possibility of a national race as well. Around the country, national Democrats eyed Cuomo as a potential candidate in 1988.

The election year in New York—all 211 state legislative seats were up for grabs as well as the statewide offices—proved an incentive for agreements on several major issues that had proved elusive in previous years. From a public power bill to a measure providing access to the courts for victims of toxic poisoning, incumbents made sure they had a lot of accomplishments to tell the voters about. And the state's $41.7 billion budget, the first prepared under a healthy economy and with few fiscal restraints, contained a lot of popular programs, from more money for mass transit and highways to record spending for education. But the November election also was marked by one of the lowest turnouts in modern times, about 52% of the registered voters.

Elections. Cuomo, running with his handpicked candidate for lieutenant governor, former U.S. Rep. Stan Lundine, from Jamestown, won with 65% of the vote, breaking a record set by Grover Cleveland in 1882. Cuomo defeated Westchester County Executive Andrew O'Rourke, the Republican candidate, after a lackluster campaign marked mostly by finger-pointing and personal attacks. Perhaps the most talked about issue in the campaign was whether or not the two would debate; they did meet face-to-face once.

Three other incumbents—U.S. Sen. Alfonse D'Amato, a Long Island Republican; Attorney General Robert Abrams, a New York City Democrat; and Comptroller Edward V. Regan, a Westchester Republican—also won easy reelection victories. In the legislature, the balance of power remained identical. Democrats control the Assembly by a margin of 94 to

New York Gov. Mario Cuomo (right) won reelection and was seen as a potential presidential candidate in '88. For New York City Mayor Ed Koch (left), 1986 was a "terrible year."

© Vic DeLucia/NYT Pictures

56, while Republicans rule the Senate by a 35 to 26 split.

Insurance. The increasing difficulty of finding affordable insurance resulted in three major new laws, dubbed the "trifecta" by legislative leaders. One, sought for many years by victims of diseases such as asbestosis and daughters of women who took the hormone DES, allows such victims access to the courts for the first time by changing the law so that they have time to sue after they discover the illness rather than for a period of time after they are exposed to the drug. Another bill made changes to try to make liability insurance more affordable and available to municipalities. And a third measure changed certain ways that malpractice insurance is written in order to try to keep down skyrocketing premiums for doctors.

Energy. The fate of both the Long Island Lighting Co. and its Shoreham nuclear plant

continued to dominate energy issues. In a step toward a move that would be the largest public takeover of a private utility, Cuomo signed a bill that created a Long Island Power Authority. The new authority, which would come into existence Jan. 15, 1987, was authorized to begin negotiations to take over the Long Island utility. State and LILCO officials met in an attempt to work out an agreement, which Cuomo said must include the utility's agreement not to operate Shoreham as a nuclear facility.

Legislation. Lawmakers enacted a major housing initiative, using future profits from Battery Park City Authority, a luxury development at the tip of Manhattan, to finance $400 million worth of low- and moderate-income housing in New York City. The state budget included a $95 million program to provide local school districts with money to enhance teachers' salaries. The state also approved an Organized Crime Control Act, creating a new crime of racketeering. And voters approved a $1.45 billion environmental bond act to help clean up toxic waste sites and purchase environmentally sensitive land.

MIRIAM PAWEL
Albany Bureau Chief, "Newsday"

NEW YORK · Information Highlights

Area: 49,108 sq mi (127 189 km²).
Population (1985 est.): 17,783,000.
Chief Cities (July 1, 1984 est.): Albany, the capital, 100,048; New York, 7,164,742; Buffalo, 338,982; Rochester, 242,562; Yonkers, 191,234; Syracuse, 164,219.
Government (1986): *Chief Officers*—governor, Mario M. Cuomo (D); lt. gov., vacant. *Legislature*—Senate, 61 members; Assembly, 150 members.
State Finances (fiscal year 1985): *Revenue,* $46,762,000,000; *expenditure,* $40,106,000,000.
Personal Income (1985): $285,419,000,000; per capita, $16,050.
Labor Force (June 1986): *Civilian labor force,* 8,489,500; *unemployed,* 507,800 (6.0% of total force).
Education: *Enrollment* (fall 1984)—public elementary schools, 1,714,219; public secondary, 933,592; colleges and universities, 1,000,098; *Public school expenditures* (1983–84), $11,302,-000,000 ($4,783 per pupil).

NEW YORK CITY

New York City's worst municipal scandal in decades rocked Mayor Edward I. Koch's administration with charges of bribery and corruption in 1986. The affair, dominating the news much of the year, spawned the suicide of a borough president and a skein of resignations, dismissals, investigations, and trials. The city's war on another menace—the highly addictive, smokable form of cocaine known as crack—

shared other major headlines with sensational crimes and trials, an ongoing struggle with the crippling effects of AIDS, racial tension in the borough of Queens, and a summer of alarm over an old urban evil: children falling out of windows. But an improving city economy, a World Series triumph by the Mets, the gala unveiling of a refurbished Statue of Liberty, and a spectacular Liberty Weekend provided upbeat notes in the year's chronicles.

Scandal. As 1986 began Mayor Koch was sworn in for a third term that was expected to be little more than a modest reprise for the colorful mayor, who had brought the city out of fiscal crisis and seemed to be coasting on his wit and new fame as an author. But within weeks, scandal broke with an unlikely twist: Queens Borough President Donald R. Manes was found in his car, dazed and bleeding from mysterious wrist and ankle cuts. Unable to substantiate his tale of abduction and assault by strangers, the police concluded the cuts were self-inflicted. But why would Manes want to kill himself?

Answers soon emerged in corruption charges. Manes and others had allegedly turned the city's Parking Violations Bureau into a racketeering enterprise, taking bribes from companies in exchange for lucrative contracts to collect parking fines for the city. Manes, dubbed a "crook" by Koch, resigned in February and killed himself in March. Almost daily revelations from federal and state investigations ensued. Charges were made against former officials of the Parking Violations Bureau, the Taxi and Limousine Commission, the Health and Hospitals Corporation, and other agencies. Bronx Democratic leader Stanley M. Friedman was accused of taking bribes and luring the city into a $22 million contract with a company in which he had a secret interest. His trial in the fall was moved to New Haven, CT, which had not been saturated with publicity. On November 25, Friedman and three other defendants were found guilty.

Koch canceled tainted contracts, shuffled personnel, and changed city business and investigating practices. There was no suggestion that he was personally involved in wrongdoing, and the public seemed to accept his assertion that he had no way of even knowing about the corruption.

In November the city's police department also was rocked by scandal, as 12 current or former officers of the 77th Precinct in Brooklyn were arrested and charged with a variety of crimes, including stealing and selling drugs.

Economy, Development, and City Policy. The city's economic news was mostly heartening. The $2 billion plan to renew tawdry Times Square won six legal challenges. Gimbel's flagship store on Herald Square closed, ending the legendary Miracle-on-34th-Street competition with Macy's, but the new Jacob K. Javits Convention Center opened on the West Side. Tourism was up, and while stock markets climbed to record highs on Wall Street, inflation in the city was at a 22-year low.

Subway, bus, and rail-commuter fares went up Jan. 1, 1986, with no visible improvement in service. But new fare tokens were introduced to catch cheaters, transit officials contended there was less graffiti, and, with capital improvements in progress, Mayor Koch contended that the rattling subways were poised for a great leap forward.

In new promulgations, the city adopted a homosexual rights bill, banned smoking in city buildings, and began making computerized welfare payments to 500,000 households directly through banks, making welfare checks a thing of the past.

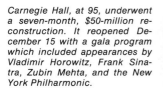
Carnegie Hall, at 95, underwent a seven-month, $50-million reconstruction. It reopened December 15 with a gala program which included appearances by Vladimir Horowitz, Frank Sinatra, Zubin Mehta, and the New York Philharmonic.

Drugs and Crime. The epidemic of the cocaine derivative crack produced overflowing treatment centers, a surge in drug-related crime, a crisis in the courts, and countless personal tragedies. Crack overtook heroin as the city's number one drug problem. But raids and round-ups were mounted, often in hideaways reminiscent of old-time opium dens. There were calls for harsh new drug penalties, extra judges and treatment facilities were found, companies tested employees for drugs, and anti-drug activism rose dramatically.

In the Howard Beach section of Queens late in the year, three black men were assaulted by a group of white youths, and one victim was killed by a car while fleeing the attack. In the controversial aftermath, tensions increased as New York's black community criticized the police and district attorney for their handling of the matter.

Other crimes and court cases captured headlines. The face of a 25-year-old model was disfigured in a razor attack by two men allegedly hired by her landlord. A deranged man with a sword went berserk on a Staten Island ferry boat in July, killing two passengers and wounding nine. And in a highly publicized case in August, an 18-year-old woman was killed in Central Park; a prep-school graduate whom she had met in an East Side bar was charged with her murder.

John Gotti, reputed head of the nation's largest organized crime group, and seven other defendants were found guilty of federal racketeering charges in November. And in December the trial of alleged subway gunman Bernhard Goetz got under way.

Health and Safety. Cases of acquired immune deficiency syndrome (AIDS) continued on the rise, but a new drug, azidothymidine, or AZT, offered hope to some. Six children with AIDS or an AIDS-related viral complex attended public schools, and courses on AIDS were given in the high schools to minimize confusion and fear.

Children falling out of the windows of tenements and housing projects raised alarm. By late summer, 10 had been killed and 81 injured. City officials said that most were cases of neglect by parents or by landlords responsible for putting in window guards.

Other. In sports, the Mets, looking like the Yankees of old, beat the Boston Red Sox in a breathtaking come-from-behind World Series, and in football the Giants rolled through their best season in many years.

Liberty Weekend—a five-day extravaganza of festivals, fireworks, and nautical events centered on the unveiling of the renovated Statue of Liberty—came off without a hitch in early July and let New York show off for millions of visitors and television viewers.

ROBERT D. MCFADDEN
"The New York Times"

NEW ZEALAND

The shaky state of the economy and a series of domestic political developments captured New Zealanders' attention during 1986.

The Economy. A midyear report by the Organization for Economic Cooperation and Development (OECD) on New Zealand's immediate prospects made gloomy reading. It forecast a shrinkage in growth to 1% of the gross domestic product (GDP) in 1986 and stagnation in 1987, and expected inflation, which was 13.2% for the year ending March 1986, to stay around 12.5%. The anticipated unemployment level of 4.75% of the work force had actually reached 5.3% in September, being materially affected by the dramatic closure of two large export meat works. By October the sliding New Zealand dollar had not made much impact on export expansion.

The July budget was an anticlimax, as the crucial new tax measure had already been announced. To complement the introduction of the 10% goods and services (value-added) tax in October, the income tax scale was simplified and reduced. The cost of petroleum was cut by 6 cents per liter, and many business-tax loopholes were closed. Two figures causing alarm were the deficit of $2.45 billion and the nation's total overseas debt of $27 billion.

Foreign Issues. The dispute with the United States over the visits of U.S. nuclear-armed warships remained in stalemate. A stir was caused by the report of the Defence Committee of Enquiry, which showed that by a margin of 52% to 44% New Zealanders were prepared to accept such visits if they were needed to keep the ANZUS (Australia, New Zealand, United States) defense pact afloat. The report urged that defense spending be maintained and that bilateral military relations with Australia be strengthened.

In July settlement of the 1985 sinking of the Greenpeace protest ship *Rainbow Warrior* was reached with France through UN arbitration. The French agents responsible were released by New Zealand to serve three years on a remote French Pacific atoll, and New Zealand received an unqualified, formal apology and U.S. $7 million in compensation.

Domestic Politics. Fluctuating opinion polls tended to give a slight edge to the governing Labour Party, although at one point it reached 52%, equal to the highest level of support recorded since the inception of polls in 1970. In March, Jim McLay, the leader of the National Party opposition, was replaced by his deputy, 50-year-old dairy farmer Jim Bolger. On the same day the free-market New Zealand Party voted to dissolve and merge with National. Later, the long-standing leader of the Democrat (formerly Social Credit) Party, Bruce Beetham, was deposed by Neil Morrison, a member of Parliament.

NEW ZEALAND · Information Highlights

Official Name: New Zealand.
Location: Southwest Pacific Ocean.
Area: 103,736 sq mi (268 676 km²).
Population (1986): 3,281,000.
Chief Cities (March 31, 1985 est.): Wellington, the capital, 342,500; Auckland (1986), 877,000; Christ-Church, 323,500; Hamilton, 170,100.
Government: *Head of state,* Elizabeth II, queen, represented by Archbishop Sir Paul Reeves, governor-general (took office Nov. 1985). *Head of government,* David Lange, prime minister (took office July 26, 1984). *Legislature* (unicameral)—House of Representatives.
Monetary Unit: New Zealand dollar (1.9646 N.Z. dollars equal U.S.$1, Oct. 27, 1986).
Gross Domestic Product (year ending March 1985): $21,700,000,000.
Economic Index (1985): *Consumer Prices* (1980 = 100), all items, 176.3; food, 166.0.
Foreign Trade (1985 U.S.$): *Imports,* $6,080,000,000; *exports,* $5,736,000,000.

Domestic Events. Radical changes in the structure of the state sector were initiated. Trading departments will be converted into corporations; charging for services will become standard; and monopolies will be surrendered.

In July, Parliament passed the Homosexual Law Reform Act by 49 votes to 44. The measure decriminalizes homosexual acts between consenting males over the age of 16 years.

On the religious front, Brian Davis, bishop of Waikato, was chosen as archbishop of New Zealand, the titular head of the nation's 800,000 Anglicans. In November, Pope John Paul II made the first-ever papal visit to the country.

Concern about the declining strength of the world-famous geyser at Whakarewarewa, in the heart of the Rotorua geothermal zone, led the government to introduce tough new conservation restrictions on the use of geothermal energy.

GRAHAM BUSH, *University of Auckland*

NIGERIA

The first anniversary of the coup that brought Maj. Gen. Ibrahim Babangida to power witnessed improvement in Nigeria's economy and increasing political stability.

Economic Developments. A decrease in oil revenues combined with corruption and mismanagement to produce a debt in excess of $23 billion by the time of the overthrow of the civilian government of Shehu Shagari in December 1983. The succeeding military regime of Gen. Muhammad Buhari made little progress in checking spending, inflation, and rescheduling of debts. The International Monetary Fund (IMF) demanded harsh economic remedies.

President Babangida put many of the IMF recommendations into effect, including surcharges on wages, ending petroleum subsidies, and diverting money to rural development. The World Bank then agreed to a $675 million loan for export and trade promotion and planned to increase project lending to $950 million annually. A debt service moratorium agreed upon in April 1986 by commercial bank creditors was extended for 90 days in September, and a long-term rescheduling of the country's debt substantially reduced its yearly payments. Nigerian representatives in Europe obtained additional credits of more than $600 million from the commercial banks for 1986. These factors, combined with stabilized production and improved world prices for petroleum, gave Babangida's government some relief from the pressures that had brought the downfall of the previous regimes.

Internal Developments. Babangida attempted to mollify the opposition by releasing persons detained for political reasons by the Buhari regime. In January more than 100 prisoners were set free. Former President Shagari and his deputy, Alex Ekwueme, after 30 months in detention, were tried before a special court in July which found them innocent of participating in the widespread corruption of the Shagari government. They were permanently banned from political activity or holding political office, joining 50 others, including 11 former state governors, who earlier had been banned for life. Another of those released was the musician Fela Anikulopo-Kuti. Many Nigerians disagreed with the government's amnesty policy, claiming that little had been done to check corruption or punish those guilty of skimming an estimated $1 million per day during the Shagari regime. Some of the most dissatisfied were students whose demonstrations at Ahmadu Bello University brought on clashes with the police. The campus disturbances in July quickly spread throughout the country, and an estimated 40 students were killed before the government closed 20 colleges. An earlier and potentially more dangerous threat to Babangida's control was the coup attempt by high ranking officers the previous December. The coup failed, and subsequently ten leaders, including Babangida's close associate, the poet, Gen. Maman Vatsa, were executed. A further ex-

NIGERIA · Information Highlights

Official Name: Federal Republic of Nigeria.
Location: West Africa.
Area: 356,667 sq mi (923 768 km²).
Population (mid-1986 est.): 105,400,000.
Chief City (1983 est.): Lagos, the capital, 1,097,000.
Government: *Head of state and government,* Maj. Gen. Ibrahim Babangida, president, federal military government (took office Aug. 27, 1985). *Legislature*—Armed Forces Ruling Council; National Council of Ministers and National Council of States.
Monetary Unit: Naira (1.062 naira equals U.S.$1, May 1986).
Economic Index (1985): *Consumer Prices* (1980 = 100), all items, 236.2; food, 251.3.
Foreign Trade (1984 U.S.$): *Imports,* $9,392,000,000; *exports,* $14,124,000,000.

ample of tension at high levels was the major reshuffling of the governors of the states in August.

Foreign Policy. Babangida's policies continued those of his predecessor—support of the Economic Community of West African States (ECOWAS), opposition to the South African regime, attempts at closer relations with the creditor nations of Western Europe and the United States, and improving relations with Nigeria's neighbors by reopening the borders closed earlier by Buhari.

HARRY A. GAILEY, *San Jose State University*

NORTH CAROLINA

Weather and politics provided the big news in North Carolina in 1986.

Weather. The hottest July on record—24 days of 90°F (32.2°C) or above—aggravated a debilitating drought in central and western North Carolina. August rains only temporarily broke the dry spell, and by December some communities still had water restrictions. Charlotte had 41% below normal annual rainfall.

Politics. In a May referendum, voters opposed the siting of a high-level nuclear waste dump in North Carolina and rejected a Democratic-backed proposal to shift state and local elections to odd-numbered years.

In November, the drought, falling farm prices, layoffs in the textile industry, and the reversal of protectionist stands by the two political parties contributed to the first Democratic victory in a dozen years in a U.S. Senate race in the state. Terry Sanford, a former governor and former president of Duke University, ousted Republican James T. Broyhill, who had

been appointed by Gov. James G. Martin (R) after the suicide of paraplegic Sen. John East. Democrats also picked up two congressional seats, shifting the delegation to eight Democrats and three Republicans. At the local level, Republicans showed surprising strength, increasing their hold on county commissions to 30 and on county sheriffs to 19. Their loss of state legislative seats was held to five.

The retirement of Joseph Branch resulted in a partisan campaign for chief justice when Governor Martin, breaking a tradition established during decades of Democratic hegemony, passed over senior Associate Justice James G. Exum and appointed Rhoda B. Billings to the top spot. Exum then resigned, ran for the post, and won it back for the Democrats.

Economy and the Environment. Troubles in both the textile industry and agriculture kept statewide unemployment at about 5%. There was substantial growth in nonmanufacturing jobs, and the trend toward fewer but larger farms continued.

Despite resistance by state officials, North Carolina was adjudged the most appropriate location for a proposed low-level regional hazardous waste depository for the Southeast. Carolina Power and Light Company's Shearon Harris nuclear plant in Wake County was licensed.

Education. Charlotte businessman Clemmie Dixon Spangler, Jr., succeeded the retiring William C. Friday as president of the 16-campus University of North Carolina. Shaw University, the state's oldest black college, narrowly escaped closing following the disclosure of critical financial problems.

Names in the News. Robert J. Brown, a black High Point businessman, was dropped

Former Gov. Terry Sanford became the first North Carolina Democrat in 12 years to win a U.S. Senate seat. He defeated Sen. James Broyhill, 52%-48%.

NORTH CAROLINA · Information Highlights
Area: 52,669 sq mi (136 413 km²).
Population (1985 est.): 6,255,000.
Chief Cities (July 1, 1984 est.): Raleigh, the capital, 169,331; Charlotte, 330,838; Greensboro, 159,314; Winston-Salem, 143,366; Durham, 101,997.
Government (1986): *Chief Officers*—governor, James G. Martin (R); lt. gov., Robert B. Jordan (D). *General Assembly*—Senate, 50 members; House of Representatives, 120 members.
State Finances (fiscal year 1985): *Revenue,* ($9,879,000,000; *expenditure,* $8,492,000,000.
Personal Income (1985): $72,670,000,000; per capita, $11,617.
Labor Force (June 1986): *Civilian labor force,* 3,206,000; *unemployed,* 176,400 (5.5% of total force).
Education: *Enrollment* (fall 1984)—public elementary schools, 755,313; public secondary, 333,411; colleges and universities, 327,288. *Public school expenditures* (1983–84), $2,507,000,000 ($2,447 per pupil).

from consideration as U.S. ambassador to South Africa after questions were raised about his business dealings.

Astronaut Michael J. Smith of Beaufort died in the January 28 explosion of the *Challenger* space shuttle. Other North Carolinians who died in 1986 included Dan K. Moore, a former governor and state Supreme Court justice, singer Kate Smith (*see* OBITUARIES), and educator and former Wake Forest University president Harold W. Tribble.

H. G. JONES
University of North Carolina at Chapel Hill

NORTH DAKOTA

Democrats gained full control of North Dakota's three-member U.S. congressional delegation in 1986. Problems in the agricultural sector continued, and the federal government foreclosed on a pioneering energy plant.

Politics. In the U.S. Senate race, State Tax Commissioner Kent Conrad, a Democrat, focused his campaign on farm problems and defeated incumbent Sen. Mark Andrews by less than 1% of the total vote. Democratic Rep. Byron Dorgan won a fourth term, resoundingly defeating challenger Syver Vinje. Voters turned down two initiated measures that had enjoyed solid support in early opinion polls—a measure to establish a state lottery and a proposal to allow most businesses to operate on Sunday afternoons. Opponents painted the initiatives as threats to the quality of life.

Agriculture. Diseases and poor late-season growing weather sharply cut what was expected to be another record harvest. The spring wheat harvest of about 192 million bushels was down 9% from the 1985 record-setting crop. Durum production, estimated at 76 million bushels in late October, was down 20%. The winter wheat harvest was estimated at 124 mil-

lion bushels, down 12%, while the barley harvest was expected to total 176 million bushels, down 5%.

Water. After decades of conflict, supporters and opponents of the Garrison Diversion Project finally hammered out a compromise that led to congressional reauthorization of the massive diversion of the Missouri River. The revised plan shifts the focus of Garrison away from irrigation and emphasizes water delivery to city and rural water systems. The plan also included precedent-setting penalties for farmers who use Garrison water to grow crops already in surplus and established a trust fund to purchase endangered wetlands in the area. The House and Senate appropriated $33 million for work on the revamped project in fiscal 1987.

Energy. The federal government finally foreclosed on the Great Plains Coal Gasification Plant, the nation's first such installation of commercial size and a central element in the U.S. synthetic fuels program. The Department of Energy (DOE) had taken operational control of the facility in 1985 after its owners defaulted on $1.5 billion in government-guaranteed construction loans. DOE officials said they would operate the plant, located near Beulah, while seeking a private buyer.

Education. Due to declining state revenues, the State Board of Higher Education agreed to cut the budgets of its colleges and universities by 4% for 1986–87.

Crime. A pipe bomb exploded at the U.S. Post Office in Fargo on August 18, slightly injuring four postal workers. A second bomb, in a package addressed to federal District Judge Paul Benson, was discovered two days later. By mid-November, no arrests had been made.

In the state's biggest murder trial ever, one defendant was found guilty of first degree murder, another of second degree murder, and 11 others of assault on May 21 in connection with the beating death of former Devils Lake policeman Jerome Edward Peltier.

JIM NEUMANN, *"The Forum," Fargo*

NORTH DAKOTA · Information Highlights
Area: 70,702 sq mi (183 119 km²).
Population (1985 est.): 685,000.
Chief Cities (1980 census): Bismarck, the capital, 44,485; Fargo, 61,383; Grand Forks, 43,765; Minot, 32,843.
Government (1986): *Chief Officers*—governor, George A. Sinner (D); lt. gov., Ruth Meiers (D). *Legislative Assembly*—Senate, 53 members; House of Representatives, 106 members.
State Finances (fiscal year 1985): *Revenue,* $1,651,000,000; *expenditure,* $1,541,000,000.
Personal Income (1985): $8,255,000,000; per capita, $12,052.
Labor Force (June 1986): *Civilian labor force,* 353,700; *unemployed,* 22,400 (6.3% of total force).
Education: *Enrollment* (fall 1984)—public elementary schools, 83,635; public secondary, 35,076; colleges and universities, 37,939. *Public school expenditures* (1983–84), $336,000,000 ($2,969 per pupil).

NORTHWEST TERRITORIES

Persistent low prices for base metals, a sharp fall in the price of oil, and a decline in international fur prices combined to create a downturn in the economy of the Northwest Territories (NWT) in 1986.

Economy. Oil and gas exploration in the Beaufort sea-Mackenzie delta area was most severely affected. Exploration bases near Tuktoyaktuk operated by Dome Petroleum, Esso Resources, and Gulf Canada were closed, and the offshore drilling rigs and other equipment were placed in storage or moved out of the region. Plans for further development were postponed until oil prices stabilize at higher levels. The Canada Tungsten Mine ceased operations in October and Pine Point Mines (lead and zinc) experienced cutbacks. There was a modest recovery in gold prices.

There was a concerted effort by the territorial and federal governments and the private sector to develop short-term economic development programs for the hardest hit regions and longer term plans to diversify, particularly in renewable resources fields, light industry, and such service areas as tourism.

Expo. The participation of the Northwest Territories in Expo 86, the world's fair in Vancouver, B.C., was considered to be a great success by people throughout the NWT and many other countries. The NWT pavilion was judged to be the best of the Canadian pavilions and one of the top five at Expo. Indications were that a large increase in tourism to NWT would result as a consequence of its participation in the fair. (*See also* CANADA—Expo 86.)

Education. Among important legislation passed in 1986 was the Arctic Colleges Act, establishing a college system in the NWT to deliver adult and postsecondary education. The Arctic College now has campuses in Fort Smith in the West and Frobisher Bay on Baffin Island, and plans to establish a campus in Inuvik.

ROSS M. HARVEY
Culture and Communications
Government of the Northwest Territories

NORTHWEST TERRITORIES
• Information Highlights

Area: 1,304,903 sq mi (3 379 700 km²).
Population (Jan. 1986 est.): 50,900.
Chief Cities (June 1985 est.): Yellowknife, the capital, 11,077; Inuvik, 3,166; Hay River, 3,142.
Government (1986): *Chief Officers*—commissioner, John H. Parker; government leader, Nick Sibbeston. *Legislature*—Legislative Assembly, 24 elected members.
Public Finances (1985–86 fiscal year): Revenues, $633,931,000; expenditures, $611,866,000.
Personal Income (average weekly earnings, May 1986): $568.78.
Education (1986–87): *Enrollment*—public and secondary schools, 13,630 pupils. *Public school expenditures* (1985–86), $117,468,000.
(All monetary figures in Canadian dollars.)

NORWAY

The world oil price collapse created grave difficulties for Norway's petroleum-dependent economy in 1986, sharply reducing tax take from offshore oil and gas and converting a 1985 payments surplus to a forecast 1986 deficit.

Government. Indirectly, the country's economic problems led to a change of government early in the year. A Labor administration took over from the Conservative-led coalition headed by Kåre Willoch, after the Storting (parliament) rejected a proposed package of belt-tightening measures, including an increase in the tax on gasoline. The rightist Progress Party, whose two representatives had held the balance of power in the Storting since 1985, played a crucial role in Willoch's defeat when it refused to approve the gas-tax increase. Willoch would not amend his proposals and made the Progress Party's approval an issue of confidence, thus effectively offering the government's resignation.

Gro Harlem Brundtland became the new prime minister on May 2; she had held the same position in the final months of the last Labor administration, in 1981. Another Labor veteran, Knut Frydenlund, returned to his former job as minister of foreign affairs.

The Economy. Norway's economic difficulties also contributed to a run on the Norwegian krone (Nkr) in May. One of the first acts of the new finance minister, Gunnar Berge, was, therefore, to order a 12% devaluation of the currency. He followed this with an even tougher crisis program than the one the Storting had rejected only weeks earlier. But this time, although the Conservatives and the Progress Party opposed most of the financial package, the Christian Democratic and Center parties were willing to support it with some modifications.

Brundtland's government hoped to secure similar support for its draft 1987 budget, tabled on October 6, which included strongly criti-

---

NORWAY • Information Highlights

Official Name: Kingdom of Norway.
Location: Northern Europe.
Area: 125,181 sq mi (324 219 km²).
Population (mid-1986 est.): 4,200,000.
Chief Cities (Jan. 1, 1985): Oslo, the capital, 447,351; Bergen, 207,231; Irondheim, 134,093.
Government: *Head of state,* Olav V, king (acceded Sept. 1957). *Head of government,* Gro Harlem Brundtland, prime minister (took office May 2, 1986). *Legislature*—Storting: Lagting and Odelsting.
Monetary Unit: Krone (7.287 kroner equal U.S.$1, Oct. 19, 1986).
Gross National Product (1984 U.S.$): $53,150,-000,000.
Economic Indexes (1985): *Consumer Prices* (1980 = 100), all items, 154.1; food, 164.3. *Industrial Production* (1980 = 100), 119.
Foreign Trade (1985 U.S.$): *Imports,* $15,558,-000,000; *exports,* $19,941,000,000.

cized plans for a reform of the tax system. By Budget Day the nation's economic situation was worse than it had been when Willoch's coalition resigned, partly as a result of the numerous inflationary wage deals struck before the change of government.

Oil and Gas. Despite a long work stoppage by offshore oil and gas production workers in the spring, Norway's total oil and gas output in 1986 was expected to be much higher than a year earlier: 68 million tons of oil equivalent compared with 63.2 million tons in 1985.

In June a tentative $60 billion, 27-year gas purchase agreement between Statoil, the Norwegian national oil company, and a consortium of European companies was concluded. The agreement would pave the way for development of the giant Troll and Sleipner fields beneath the North Sea. A new gas pipeline—Zeepipe—is planned to carry some of the gas from those fields to the European market, coming ashore in Zeebrugge, Belgium.

The new government actively supported efforts by OPEC to stabilize oil prices at what Oslo called a "reasonable" level. In the fall the new oil minister, Arne Øien, ordered a 10% cut in Norwegian crude oil exports for November and December, to be achieved by stockpiling the state's royalty crude. Øien said he would consider further measures if OPEC curbed its output, possibly including mandatory cuts in Norwegian production in 1987.

Fallout. In some parts of Norway radioactive fallout from the Chernobyl nuclear plant explosion in the USSR seriously polluted fish in mountain lakes and rivers, livestock, and crops of wild berries and cultivated fruit and vegetables. The government compensated sheep farmers and Lapp reindeer herders who had to destroy or hold back from slaughter large numbers of their animals because radioactivity levels exceeded the official limit of 600 becquerels per kilo.

THOR GJESTER
Free-lance Writer

NOVA SCOTIA

The year 1986 brought Nova Scotians a new high-tech manufacturing firm, oil and gas discoveries on the Scotian shelf, higher costs for electricity, and sluggish economic growth.

Legislation and Government. The government of Premier John Buchanan introduced 127 bills, of which 103 became law in 1986. The enacted laws included major pension reforms, an overhaul of the 60 year old Forest Act, "Right to Farm" legislation that protects farmers from nuisance suits by neighbors, and environmental measures designed to control the use of pesticides. In the meantime the opposition parties challenged the government in lively question periods on various public issues such as patronage, environmental bungling, and fraudulent expense accounts of a cabinet minister, Billy Joe MacLean. On the industrial front the government induced Litton Systems to locate in Halifax an $18 million plant to manufacture radar systems and repair military aircraft for the Canadian armed forces. The Aerotech Business Park, where Litton and Pratt & Whitney of Canada are now building plants, is being developed as a future site for locating other high-tech firms.

Economy. The virtual abandonment of offshore oil and gas exploration caused a marked slowdown in Nova Scotia's economy. The provincial unemployment rate of 12.9% in September, though lower than the August figure, was still higher than the national average of 9.5%. Additional signs of sluggishness were apparent from dwindling wages and salaries, falling housing starts, declining business investment and a 19% drop in coal production over the first half of 1986. Balancing this, however, was increased activity in fishing, farming, and manufacturing, which stemmed the tide of a serious economic decline. Output in the food and beverage, fish processing, and pulp and paper industries rose; the farming sector recorded a modest 1.7% gain in total receipts.

Energy. Significant deposits of petroleum and natural gas were found on the Scotian shelf in 1986. The oil companies, before leaving the province, identified four gas discoveries, two oil finds, and only one dry hole; Shell Canada Resources also struck oil on the shelf at Panuke Wildcat well. Ironically these discoveries came at a time when low oil and gas prices were forcing a virtual shutdown of the offshore exploration business. At the same time Nova Scotians were forced to pay higher electric rates because the provincial government eliminated a C$36 million annual subsidy to the Nova Scotia Power Corporation.

R. P. SETH
Mount Saint Vincent University, Halifax

NOVA SCOTIA · Information Highlights

Area: 21,425 sq mi (55 490 km²).

Population (Jan. 1986 est.): 883,000.

Chief cities (1981 census): Halifax, the capital, 114,594; Dartmouth, 62,277; Sydney, 29,444.

Government (1986): *Chief Officers*—lt. gov., Alan R. Abraham; premier, John Buchanan (Progressive Conservative). *Legislature*—Legislative Assembly, 52 members.

Provincial Finances (1986–87 fiscal year budget): *Revenues,* $3,267,100,000; *expenditures,* $3,500,-000,000.

Personal Income (average weekly earnings, May 1986): $389.44.

Labor Force (July 1986, seasonally adjusted: *Employed* workers, 15 years of age and over, 396,000; *Unemployed,* 54,000 (13.6%).

Education (1986–87): *Enrollment*—elementary and secondary schools, 174,840 pupils; postsecondary—universities, 24,050; community colleges, 2,980.

(All monetary figures are in Canadian dollars.)

OBITUARIES[1]

UPI/Bettmann Newsphotos

O'KEEFFE, Georgia

U.S. artist: b. near Sun Prairie, WI, Nov. 15, 1887; d. Santa Fe, NM, March 6, 1986.

With limpid colors and lines at once delicate and forceful, Georgia O'Keeffe interpreted the natural world in a way that made her a crucial figure in the development of modern painting. No less than her art, her strong personality brought her to the fore of what had for many years been a man's field.

O'Keeffe took her subjects from the world around her—flowers, leaves, rock formations, shells—and pared them down to elemental purity. In the 1920s and 1930s, while living in New York with her husband, the photographer Alfred Stieglitz, the Manhattan skyline was a favorite theme. Later, after her husband's death and a move to the edge of the New Mex-

AP/Wide World

CAGNEY, James

American actor: b. New York City, July 17, 1899; d. near Millbrook, NY, March 30, 1986.

Whether as hoodlum, hero, or hoofer, James Cagney brought an electrifying presence to the screen that is still cherished by a new generation viewing his classics on television, videocassette, or in movie house revivals. The raw energy and force of personality that he infused into each role became his trademark.

As he rose to fame in the 1930s, the scrappy, cocksure manner, the body language, and the distinctive voice became familiar to millions the world over. He brought to his performances the kind of spunk that had been nurtured in the tough street life he experienced while growing up in poverty in New York City.

Cecil Beaton/Photo Trends

WINDSOR, Duchess of

American-born wife of Great Britain's Duke of Windsor, the former King Edward VIII: b. Blue Ridge Summit, PA, June 19, 1896; d. Paris, France, April 24, 1986.

With the death of the Duchess of Windsor, the personal love story of the former king of Great Britain, Edward VIII, and Wallis Simpson, the twice-divorced American, came fully to a close. Their relationship, advanced by the December 1936 abdication of the throne by Edward, had all the elements of high romance—a strikingly attractive and clever woman, a playful prince, glamorous settings, great riches, and powerful forces capable of separating the pair.

The Duchess's ascent to the heady and, by some standards, scandalous position of being

[1] Arranged chronologically by death date

ico desert, powerful landscapes and sun-bleached bones appeared in her work. Her paintings spanned a wide range of styles but always retained a stamp of individuality.

Background. O'Keeffe, who grew up on a wheat farm, decided on her career at an early age and studied art in Chicago and New York. In 1912, she took a job teaching art in Texas. Four years later, a friend showed a group of her drawings and watercolors to Stieglitz, who is said to have remarked, "At last, a woman on paper!" He promptly put them on exhibit in his New York gallery, where they caused a stir.

Incensed at some of the comments sparked by her works, O'Keeffe arrived from Texas to upbraid Stieglitz for exhibiting the paintings without her permission. Instead, he persuaded her to give up her teaching job, move to New York, and devote herself to painting full-time. In 1924 they married; she joined him in running the gallery, which was a center for New York's

avant-garde. Some of what became her most famous works were shown there, while her husband's more than 500 photographs of her have been called the greatest love poem in the history of photography. Outspoken and often whimsical, O'Keeffe maintained her independence.

After Stieglitz died in 1946, O'Keeffe moved to an adobe house near Abiquiu, NM. Her work reached full flower in this setting.

A retrospective exhibit of her work at New York's Whitney Museum of American Art in 1970 led to her rediscovery by the New York art world, which lauded her ability to absorb new developments pioneered by European artists while retaining a distinctly American voice. The exhibit was followed by an autobiography and an award-winning documentary. Her many awards included the Medal of Freedom (1977) and the National Medal of Arts (1985).

ELAINE PASCOE

Background. Cagney's Irish father, a saloon keeper, died in the 1918 flu epidemic. His mother, of Norwegian descent, raised her family of five. Cagney first struggled with odd jobs, then learned to dance and went into Vaudeville. While in the chorus of a 1920 Broadway musical, he met Frances Willard (Willie) Vernon, whom he married in 1922 and who survived him. They became touring stage partners. Trying Hollywood, Cagney began to get movie parts. In 1931 he made his breakthrough as the tough-talking gangster in *Public Enemy,* which set the tone for a new genre of gangland movies.

Cagney's favorite of his long line of films was *Yankee Doodle Dandy,* in which he portrayed Broadway songwriter and showman George M. Cohan. It won him his only Oscar. His many skillful performances included the

gangster role in *Angels with Dirty Faces,* an espionage agent in *13 Rue Madeleine,* and the psychotic killer in *White Heat.* He retired in 1961 after a stirring performance in Billy Wilder's satire of Cold War relations, *One, Two, Three.* Cagney, who lived with his wife on a farm in Dutchess County, NY, was lured out of retirement to play a New York police chief in *Ragtime,* and for a last hurrah as a former boxing champ in the TV drama *Terrible Joe Moran.*

In interviews through the years, the veteran actor emphasized personal values and ethics he held dearly whether in his work or family relationships. (His brother, William Cagney, was his business manager, and his late sister, Jeanne Cagney, an actress, appeared in several movies with him).

WILLIAM WOLF

---

the woman for whom a king gave up his throne began in 1930 when the still-married Mrs. Simpson and Edward became friends. Their attachment deepened, and in 1936 Edward decided to give up the throne rather than the woman he loved. He suggested a morganatic marriage in which the wife and children are not privy to royal titles or privilege, but Prime Minister Stanley Baldwin insisted that such an arrangement would not receive public support. Following the abdication, Edward was given the title of Duke of Windsor. On June 3, 1937, the couple were married in France. They spent much of their lives there from then on. The Duchess was never granted royal rank.

Background. Bessie Wallis Warfield came from a background of long-established American families. Her father died five months after her birth, and she and her mother lived in a sort of genteel poverty for some years. Wallis went

to Arundell, a girl's school in Baltimore that was paid for by a prosperous uncle, and in 1912 she entered Oldfields, a finishing school. She was presented to society in 1914.

Her first marriage at age 20 to Earl Winfield Spencer, Jr., a naval aviator, lasted until 1927. In 1928 she married Ernest Simpson. The Simpsons settled in England and began an association in international social circles.

Following their marriage, the Duke and Duchess led an almost completely social existence except for the years that the Duke served as governor of the Bahamas (1940–45). The Duchess, often named to the list of best-dressed women, maintained a sense of style all of her life.

After a private funeral service at St. George Chapel in Windsor, the Duchess was buried next to her husband near Windsor Castle.

SAUNDRA FRANCE

AP/Wide World

GOODMAN, Benny

U.S. jazz musician: b. Chicago, May 30, 1909: d. New York City, June 13, 1986.

During a long and illustrious career, Benny Goodman, the "King of Swing," set a number of precedents. In 1935 he fronted the first major integrated jazz group, a trio with Goodman on clarinet, Teddy Wilson on piano, and Gene Krupa on drums. This trio was the nucleus of the Goodman quartet and sextet. These groups became the first small combos to be established within a big band. In 1938, Goodman introduced jazz to Carnegie Hall; in 1962 he conducted the first jazz band tour of the USSR. An esteemed jazz clarinetist, he also enjoyed simultaneous success as a classical soloist.

Background. When Goodman was ten, a local Chicago synagogue loaned him a clarinet

AP/Wide World

SMITH, Kate

U.S. singer: b. Greenville, VA, May 1, 1909; d. Raleigh, NC, June 17, 1986.

When President Franklin Roosevelt introduced Kate Smith to King George VI in 1939, he said: "This is Kate Smith. Miss Smith is America."

Kate Smith was one of the most popular American singers of the 20th century. She cheered her radio audiences through the Depression and roused their patriotism with *God Bless America*, the Irving Berlin song that she made into an unofficial national anthem. During World War II, she sold record numbers of war bonds.

Never formally trained as a singer, Kate Smith possessed a naturally rich contralto voice that sold millions of copies of the popular

Harris & Ewing/Photo Trends

RICKOVER, Hyman G.

U.S. Navy admiral: b. Makow, Russia, Jan. 27, 1900; d. Arlington, VA, July 8, 1986.

Since the launching of the *Nautilus*, the world's first nuclear powered submarine, the name Hyman Rickover has been synonymous with the words—U.S. nuclear Navy. A former secretary of the Navy, Dan Kimball, described Admiral Rickover's contribution to naval advancement as "the most important piece of development work in the history of the Navy."

During his 63 years as a naval officer, Admiral Rickover built a reputation which transcended his successful effort to introduce nuclear propulsion to submarines, and later to surface ships such as the largest aircraft carriers in the U.S., or any other, fleet. For example, he was responsible for developing the

and provided him with music lessons. At 14, he was making $48 per week in a local band. In 1926, Ben Pollack formed his own band and called Goodman to join it. After three years, Benny left the band to do free-lance work on radio and records, earning $350 to $400 per week. In 1933 jazz activist John Hammond asked Goodman to organize a big jazz band for several recordings to be released in England. Later with the Depression in full swing and Goodman's income down, Hammond again helped Goodman organize a band, this time for the Billy Rose Music Hall. When the music hall management changed, the band was fired. However, during their vaudeville music hall experience, the Goodman band auditioned successfully for the *Let's Dance* radio program and soon became the show's major band.

In 1934, Fletcher Henderson had given and sold to Goodman arrangements that had been played by the Henderson band. Such tunes as *King Porter Stomp, Blue Skies,* and *Sometimes I'm Happy* helped make the Goodman band the most popular band in the country. After the *Let's Dance* program went off the air, the band played a short-lived, two week Roosevelt Grill job. The band's subsequent tour of the West Coast also was unsuccessful. On the last date of the tour, however, Goodman brought out his favorite Henderson arrangements, and the audience roared with delight. The swing era had arrived.

In 1940, Eddie Sauter took over as Goodman's arranger for bands that boasted Stan Getz, Billy Butterfield, and other greats. Critics agree that these 1940 bands were his best. After an attempt at bebop in 1950, Goodman continued until his death to play the music he had helped establish.

DOMINIC SPERA

---

songs she recorded during her long career. Her radio shows in the 1930s and 1940s and television appearances in the 1950s generated some 25 million fan letters from audiences who responded to her down-to-earth warmth and cheerful optimism.

Background. Kathryn Elizabeth Smith made her first public appearance as a singer at the age of four, singing hymns in a church choir. At eight, she entertained World War I troops in Washington, DC. Although her family wanted her to become a nurse, Kate was determined on a singing career, and at 17, with no formal training, she made her debut in *Honeymoon Lane,* a musical that opened on Broadway in September 1926.

Although she was a success in musicals, because of her size Kate Smith was always cast in a comic role as a fat girl, a humiliation that affected her offstage, if not in public. But in 1930 she met Ted Collins, an artists' representative, who urged her to go into radio. She made her first broadcast on May 1, 1931, introducing the song that became her theme, *When the Moon Comes Over the Mountain.* The show was an immediate success, and Kate Smith's partnership with Ted Collins lasted until his death in 1964. In 1938, Kate Smith began a daytime radio program of commentary on current events. In 1950 she branched out into television with *The Kate Smith Hour,* which ran until 1954. She continued to make guest appearances on television and in 1963 made her concert debut at Carnegie hall.

Although she and Ted Collins were often thought to be married, Kate Smith remained unmarried. Her life story was told in two books, *Living in a Great Big Way* (1938) and *Upon My Lips a Song* (1960).

LINDA TRIEGEL

---

first civil, nuclear-power plant at Shippingport, PA, which provides electricity to the Pittsburgh area. Later in life, Admiral Rickover expressed criticism of the educational system. He advocated the revamping of public education with an emphasis on the sciences. Following his retirement from the Navy, Rickover established a foundation, now known as the Center for Excellence in Education, to implement his vision.

Background. When he was four years old Admiral Rickover emigrated to the United States with his parents and other Jewish refugees. The family settled in Chicago. A 1922 graduate of the Naval Academy, the future admiral earned a master's degree in electrical engineering from Columbia University.

Despite rising to admiral rank, Rickover had a stormy career in the Navy. In the early 1950s he was passed over twice for promotion from captain to rear admiral. However, the interest shown in Captain Rickover's situation by the press and important politicians caused the Navy to reconsider and to promote him. During his naval career, Admiral Rickover was known for both positive and negative traits. Some admired him for persistence in the face of bureaucratic obstinacy. Others found him to be headstrong and arrogant.

Secretary of the Navy John F. Lehman ordered Rickover retired against his desires in 1982. Then in 1985, Secretary Lehman criticized the admiral for accepting gifts from the General Dynamics Corp., a defense contractor. Rickover denied any wrongdoing.

In July 1984 the Navy conferred an unusual honor on a living person. It commissioned a nuclear powered attack submarine the *Hyman G. Rickover.*

ROBERT M. LAWRENCE

AP/Wide World

HARRIMAN, W(illiam) Averell

U.S. public official: b. New York City, Nov. 15, 1891; d. Yorktown Heights, NY, July 26, 1986.

An American patrician born to great wealth, Averell Harriman—an ardent convert to the Democratic Party in 1928—devoted himself for decades to public service. He was an adviser to four Democratic presidents (Roosevelt, Truman, Kennedy, and Johnson) and emissary to the world's leaders. President John Kennedy remarked once that, with the possible exception of John Quincy Adams, Harriman had held "as many important jobs as any American in our history."

Background. The son of railroad magnate Edward H. Harriman and an heir to an estimated $100 million fortune, William Averell

UPI/Bettmann Newsphotos

MOORE, Henry Spencer

British sculptor: b. Castleford, England, July 30, 1898; d. Much Hadham, England, Aug. 31, 1986.

Henry Moore made an indelible mark on 20th-century art with sculptures that gained almost universal popularity. His large carvings and castings, with their characteristic smooth, organic contours and sense of weight and mass, adorn parks and public spaces at museums and corporate headquarters around the world. Smaller works and drawings are prized by collectors.

Moore drew inspiration from many traditions—primitive art; the Renaissance works of Michelangelo and others; and modern masters. He once remarked that Paul Cézanne's painting *Large Bathers,* with its rounded, sculptural

AP/Wide World

GRANT, Cary

American actor: b. Bristol, England, Jan. 18, 1904; d. Davenport, IA, Nov. 29, 1986.

Alexander Archibald Leach came to the United States in 1920 with a troupe of acrobats. He stayed to become Cary Grant, Hollywood's stellar example of the handsome and debonair leading man, and a box-office favorite for more than 30 years.

Although Cary Grant appeared in popular adventure stories like *Gunga Din* (1939) and dramas like *None But the Lonely Heart* (for which he was nominated for an Academy Award in 1944), he was best known to moviegoers for the romantic comedies he made with such leading ladies as Katharine Hepburn and Irene Dunne, and for the Alfred Hitchcock thrillers later in his career in which he played

Harriman attended Groton School and was graduated from Yale University in 1913. Within two years he was vice-president of his father's Union Pacific Railroad. His other business activities included investment banking and a major shipping venture. He served as an administrator (1934–35) in the National Recovery Administration.

In 1941 President Franklin Roosevelt sent Harriman to expedite lend-lease assistance in England, where he developed close working relations with Prime Minister Winston Churchill. He also undertook two important missions to Moscow before service (1943–46) as ambassador there and as participant in various major wartime conferences. From war's end, Harriman counseled a policy of strength, firmness, and patience toward the USSR.

Briefly U.S. ambassador to London in 1946, Harriman was then secretary of commerce (1946–48), President Truman's special representative to coordinate the Marshall Plan (1948–50), Truman's special assistant (1950–51), and director of the Mutual Security Agency (1951–53).

Harriman was elected governor of New York in 1954 but lost his reelection bid overwhelmingly to Nelson Rockefeller in 1958. In 1961–62—President Kennedy having named him ambassador at large and then an assistant secretary of state—he helped negotiate an end to the conflict in Laos. As under secretary for political affairs, he negotiated the limited nuclear test ban treaty of 1963. Again ambassador at large under President Johnson, he conducted the Paris peace negotiations with North Vietnam in 1968–69.

Harriman's survivors include his third wife, Pamela, a former daughter-in-law of Churchill.

WESLEY F. STROMBECK

---

forms, was "for me, like Chartres Cathedral." The female figure—often reclining—was the subject of much of his work. He often said that sculpture should be displayed outdoors, in natural settings.

Background. One of eight children of a mining engineer, Henry Spencer Moore grew up in the Yorkshire coal-mining town of Castleford. Although he was drawn to sculpture as a youth, he trained as a teacher and served in France during World War I. Veteran's benefits allowed him to enroll at Leeds School of Art, and he went on to London's Royal College of Art.

After years of study in England and abroad, Moore had his first one-man show and obtained his first public commission at the age of 30. Soon after, he married Irina Radetzky, a student at the Royal College of Art. He taught at the Chelsea School of Art until 1939 and, as an official war artist during World War II, produced some of his best-known drawings—a series showing Londoners in underground bomb shelters during the blitz.

These drawings, along with a Madonna and Child carved for a church in Nottingham, England, and a 1941 retrospective of his work at a museum near Leeds, brought Moore a wider audience. In 1946 the Museum of Modern Art in New York City held a Moore retrospective that marked the start of his long popularity in the United States. Over the years, Moore works were requested for the Karlskirche in Vienna, Lincoln Center in New York City, the National Gallery in West Berlin, and the East Wing at the National Gallery of Art in Washington, DC, among others.

Moore's awards and honors included the British Order of Merit. Since World War II he lived in a farmhouse near Much Hadham.

ELAINE PASCOE

---

much the same parts opposite Ingrid Bergman, Joan Fontaine, and Grace Kelly. His performances, in the words of the film critic Vincent Canby, "were as complex as the internal rhyme schemes of a Cole Porter lyric—and seemed as effortless." They were cumulatively awarded an honorary Academy Award.

Background. The son of a garment presser in Bristol, England, Archie Leach began haunting local theaters at 12, and at age 13 he joined the Bob Pender acrobatic troupe, which taught him comedy. When the troupe went home after its New York engagement in 1920, Leach stayed behind and worked as a Coney Island stiltwalker, among other jobs, before landing a leading role in the operetta *Golden Dawn* in 1927. In 1932 he went to Hollywood and made a screen test. Paramount Studios immediately hired him, changed his name, and began building him to be a rival to Gary Cooper.

Instead, he consciously studied the elegant style of Noel Coward. Combined with his training in knockabout comedy, this produced the Cary Grant persona that first emerged in 1935 in *Sylvia Scarlett* and was quickly confirmed in such now-classic film comedies as *Topper, The Awful Truth, Bringing Up Baby, Holiday, His Girl Friday,* and *The Philadelphia Story.* He made a total of 72 films between 1932 and 1965.

Unlike many younger actors, Cary Grant portrayed the man every man aspired to be and every woman wanted to love. This personality remained essentially the same in each film. "I pretended to be somebody I wanted to be," Grant himself said, "and I finally became that person. Or he became me."

Cary Grant was survived by his fifth wife, Barbara Harris, whom he married in 1981, and his daughter by the actress Dyan Cannon.

LINDA TRIEGEL

The following is a selected list of prominent persons who died during 1986.
Articles on major figures appear in the preceding pages.

Adams, (Llewellyn) Sherman (87), chief White House assistant (1953–58) under President Dwight Eisenhower and governor of New Hampshire (1949–53). He resigned from his White House position when a controversy arose over his having accepted gifts from a longtime friend, Bernard Goldfine, a New England textile manufacturer. In 1966 Adams opened a successful ski resort on Loon Mountain in New Hampshire: d. Hanover, NH, Oct. 27.

Adams, Pepper (Park) (55), jazz musician; played baritone saxophone and clarinet: d. Brooklyn, NY, Sept. 10.

Addabbo, Joseph (61), U.S. representative (D-NY, 1961–86): d. Washington, DC, April 10.

Agnew, Sir Geoffrey (78), British art dealer. A former chairman of the family firm of Thomas Agnew and Sons, he was considered the dean of London art dealers: d. London, Nov. 22.

Alcott, John (55), British-born cinematographer; best known for his work on the color films of director Stanley Kubrick: d. southern France, July 28.

Alda, Robert (born Alphonse D'Abruzzo) (72), stage, film, and television actor; appeared in the famed Broadway musical *Guys and Dolls* (1950), for which he won a Tony Award. He also appeared in films and on television, and early in his career was in radio and burlesque: d. Los Angeles, CA, May 3.

Alessandri Rodríguez, Jorge (90), president of Chile (1958–64): d. Santiago, Chile, Aug. 31.

Alexander, Dorothy (82), founder of the Atlanta Ballet (1929); was a pioneering figure in the American regional ballet movement: d. Atlanta, GA, Nov. 17.

Almond, James Lindsay, Jr. (87), Democratic governor of Virginia (1958–62); he also served in the U.S. House of Representatives from 1947 to 1949 and as the attorney general of Virginia. In that capacity he pleaded the states-rights doctrine before the U.S. Supreme Court in *Brown v. Board of Education,* but later as governor he made some moves toward school integration: d. Richmond, VA, April 14.

Arbuzov, Aleksei (77), Soviet playwright; sometimes criticized in the USSR for not always adhering to the party line with regard to play writing: d. April 20.

Arlen, Harold (born Hyman Arluck) (81), composer; wrote such songs as *Get Happy, Stormy Weather, Over the Rainbow,* and *That Old Black Magic.* He won an Academy Award in 1939 for *Over the Rainbow:* d. New York City, April 23.

Armstrong, Herbert W. (93), religious evangelist and broadcaster; he was the founder and pastor general of the Worldwide Church of God: d. Pasadena, CA, Jan. 16.

Arnaz, Desi (69), Cuban-born actor, musician, producer, and an important figure in the earlier years of television. He and Lucille Ball, his wife from 1940 to 1960, created the television comedy *I Love Lucy* (1951–56), which became one of the most successful series ever. That success allowed them to create a show business empire through Desilu Productions. After his divorce from Miss Ball, Arnaz sold his stock in Desilu to her and retired. He did take some interest in show business, thereafter, and created pilots for several different television series. Earlier in his career he appeared on Broadway and in films: d. Del Mar, CA, Dec. 2.

Baddeley, Hermione (79), British actress; well known as the maid in the television series *Maude:* d. Los Angeles, Aug. 19.

Baker, Ella (83), civil-rights activist and a major force in that movement during the 1950s and 1960s: d. New York City, Dec. 13.

Baldwin, Raymond Earl (93), Republican governor of Connecticut (1939–41, 1943–46), U.S. senator (1947–49), and chief justice of the state's highest court (1959–63): d. Fairfield, CT, Oct. 4.

Barrett, William E. (85), author; known especially for the novels *The Left Hand of God* (1951) and *The Lilies of the Field* (1962), both later made into films. He also wrote short stories and biographies: d. Denver, CO, Sept. 14.

Bayar, Celâl (103), president of Turkey from 1950 until he was deposed by a military coup in 1960. As a member of the Grand National Assembly, he helped found the Turkish Republic: d. Istanbul, Turkey, Aug. 22.

Beauvoir, Simone de (78), French writer; most famous for *The Second Sex* (1949), her nonfiction account of the status of women which made her a theorist of feminism and a heroine of the women's movement. She was an important member of the French existentialist movement as well as a lifelong companion of the philosopher Jean-Paul Sartre. A leading leftist, she engaged in acts of political protest from time to time: d. Paris, April 14.

Behrens, William (63), U.S. Navy admiral and a submariner and sea scientist; he was one of the Navy's most decorated officers. After retirement from the Navy in 1974 he became director of the Florida Institute of Oceanography in 1978: d. St. Petersburg,FL, Jan. 21.

Bernardi, Herschel (62), actor, best known for his role as Tevye in the stage musical *Fiddler on the Roof.* He appeared in the role after it was created on Broadway by Zero Mostel, followed by Luther Adler: d. Los Angeles, CA, May 9.

Bernhardt, Clyde (80), jazz trombonist and singer: d. Newark, NJ, May 20.

Berry, George Packer (87), bacteriologist and virologist; was dean of the Harvard University Medical School (1949–66): d. Princeton, NJ, Oct. 5.

Bestall, Alfred (Edmeades) (93), British cartoonist; he was for 30 years (1935–65) the illustrator of the Rupert Bear stories in the *Daily Express:* d. Jan. 15.

Beuys, Joseph (64), West German sculptor and teacher at the Academy of Arts in Düsseldorf, West Germany. He also helped found West Germany's Green Party: d. Düsseldorf, West Germany, Jan. 23.

Bias, Len (Leonard) (22), basketball player; All America from the University of Maryland. He had been selected by the Boston Celtics in the professional draft of college players held two days prior to his death, which was considered drug-related: d. Riverdale, MD, June 19.

Bingham, Jonathan (72), U.S. representative (D-NY, 1965–83): d. New York City, July 3.

Bohlen und Halbach, Arndt von (48), last descendant of the German Krupp industrial dynasty: d. Munich, May 8.

Borges, Jorge Luis (86), Argentine writer of short stories, poetry, and essays. Considered one of Latin America's greatest writers, he explored in his work the human psyche and the fantastic within the seemingly commonplace. He was a lover and master of the short-story genre, and his fame rests most on the result of his short-story writing. In addition to writing, Borges was director of the National Library in Buenos Aires and a professor: d. Geneva, Switzerland, June 14.

Borglum, Lincoln (73), stonecarver; spent more than ten years helping his father, Gutzon Borglum, carve the four presidents' faces on Mount Rushmore. He completed the work after the death of his father: d. Corpus Christi, TX, Jan. 27.

Bowles, Chester (85), statesman and businessman. After graduation from Yale in 1924 he began working for an advertising agency and soon thereafter started his own firm, retiring a multimillionaire in 1941 at the age of 40. Thereafter, during World War II, he worked for the War Production Board and in 1946 became director of the Office of Economic Stabilization. A Democrat, he was elected governor of Connecticut in 1948.

Sherman Adams
AP/Wide World

Desi Arnaz
AP/Wide World

Simone de Beauvoir
AP/Wide World

Jorge Luis Borges
UPI/Bettmann Newsphotos

UPI/Bettmann Newsphotos   AP/Wide World   AP/Wide World   AP/Wide World

Lucia Chase   *James Eastland*   *Perry Ellis*   *Hank Greenberg*

From 1951 to 1953 he was ambassador to India and Nepal. He was a member of the House of Representatives from 1959 to 1961 and was President John Kennedy's undersecretary of state in 1961. He was again appointed ambassador to India in late 1961, a post in which he remained until 1969: d. Essex, CT, May 25.

Braine, John (Gerard) (64), British novelist and playwright; part of Britain's "angry young men" generation of the 1950s, a group of writers disenchanted with the traditional British class system. He is well known for his first novel, *Room at the Top* (1957; film 1959): d. London, Oct. 28.

Bricker, John (92), U.S. senator (R-OH, 1947–59); he also served as governor of Ohio (1939–45) and in 1944 was a vice-presidential candidate on the Republican ticket of presidential candidate Thomas E. Dewey: d. Columbus, OH, March 22.

Brown, Harrison (69), atomic scientist; played a key role in producing plutonium for the first atomic bombs. He later worked toward the prevention of further nuclear development: d. Albuquerque, NM, Dec. 8.

Bruhn, Erik (57), Danish-born ballet dancer; artistic director of the National Ballet of Canada from 1983. Bruhn was a leading dancer with the American Ballet Theatre in New York, beginning in 1953. Prior to that time he had been with the Royal Danish Ballet, and he continued to make appearances with that company, becoming its director in 1967 while still at the height of his dancing career. He retired from leading ballet roles in 1972. As a choreographer he was faithful, but offered some variations to the classic ballets: d. Toronto, Canada, April 1.

Bubbles, John (born John William Sublett) (84), inventor of the rhythm style of tap dancing, he was a member of Buck and Bubbles, a celebrated dance team in vaudeville. He originated the role of "Sportin' Life" in *Porgy and Bess:* d. Los Angeles, CA, May 18.

Caesar, Adolph (52), actor; starred in the stage and film versions of *A Soldier's Story,* for which he received an Oscar nomination: d. Los Angeles, CA, March 6.

Canfield, Cass (88), publisher; associated with Harper and Row (formerly Harper and Brothers) for more than 60 years. He joined the company in 1924, was president (1931–45), chairman of the board (1945–55), and chairman of the executive committee (1955–67). He became house senior editor in 1967. He was director of the company until 1967 and became an honorary director in 1969. He wrote several books as well, including *Up and Down and Around* (1971), *The Iron Will of Jefferson Davis* (1978), *Outrageous Fortunes* (1981), and *The Six* (1983): d. New York City, March 27.

Carmichael, John P. (83), sportswriter for the *Chicago Daily News* for some 40 years. His "Barber Shop" sports column was one of the best known in the United States: d. Chicago, June 6.

Carrillo, Flores Antonio (76), Mexican statesman; was treasury secretary (1952–58), ambassador to the United States (1955–64), foreign minister (1964–70), and ambassador to the USSR (1980–81): d. Mexico City, Mexico, March 20.

Cash, Norman D. (51), first baseman for the Detroit Tigers (1960–74) and the American League batting champion in 1961: d. (drowned) northern Lake Michigan, Oct. 12.

Cecil, Lord (Edward Christian) David (Gascoyne) (83), British literary historian and biographer; known for his biography of Lord Melbourne, a prime minister during the reign of Queen Victoria. He was Goldsmith's professor of English literature at Oxford University (1948–69): d. Jan. 1.

Cehanovsky, George (94), Russian-born baritone; associated with the Metropolitan Opera for 60 years: d. New York City, March 25.

Chase, Lucia (88), founder of American Ballet Theatre. Though her first love was acting she seriously studied ballet with Mikhail Mordkin, a former member of the Bolshoi Ballet, and in

1937 made her dancing debut with his ballet company. In 1940, Ballet Theatre (later known as American Ballet Theatre) made its debut at Rockefeller Center. Miss Chase danced with the company and gave it considerable financial support. In 1945 she became codirector of the company, along with Oliver Smith, a post that she held until 1980: d. New York City, Jan. 9.

Chase, William Curtis (91), U.S. Army major-general; in World War II he was a leader of American forces reentering Manila and those entering Tokyo. He later was a military adviser to Chiang Kai-shek: d. suburban Houston, TX, Aug. 21.

Chenoweth, J. Edgar (88), U.S. representative (R-CO, 1941–49, 1951–65): d. Trinidad, CO, Jan. 2.

Childress, Alvin (78), actor; played Amos in the television version of *Amos 'n' Andy* that was popular in the 1950s: d. Inglewood, CA, April 19.

Christiansen, Jack (57), pro-football player and National Football League coach. A defensive back with the Detroit Lions, he played on their championship teams in 1952, 1953, and 1957. He was elected to the Football Hall of Fame in 1970. He was head coach for the San Francisco 49ers (1963–67) and at Stanford University (1972–76): d. Palo Alto, CA, June 29.

Ciardi, John (69), poet, essayist, and translator. The author of some 40 books of poetry and criticism, he taught at Rutgers University and at Harvard and was a poetry editor (1956–72) of the *Saturday Review* magazine. He was highly acclaimed for his translation of Dante's *Inferno:* d. Edison, NJ, March 30.

Clancy, King (Francis Michael) (83), Canadian hockey player; for over 50 years he was a defenseman, coach, and vice-president of the Toronto Maple Leafs. He became a member of the Hockey Hall of Fame in 1958: d. Toronto, Nov. 10.

Coatsworth, Elizabeth (93), author of poetry, children's stories, novels, short stories, and essays. She received the 1931 Newbery Medal for her children's book, *The Cat Who Went to Heaven* (1930): d. Nobleboro, ME, Aug. 31.

Cohen, Myron (83), Polish-born nightclub comedian; famed for his use of dialect. He worked mainly with a Yiddish accent, but sometimes did Irish and Italian dialects as well: d. Nyack, NY, March 10.

Cohn, Roy (59), defense lawyer; gained fame as the chief counsel for Joseph R. McCarthy's Senate investigations in the 1950s into Communist influence in American life. He left Washington in 1954 to practice law in New York. He early found himself in conflict with the Internal Revenue Service and had his taxes audited for 20 years in a row. He also was tried and acquitted three times for conspiracy, bribery, and fraud. Other troubles stemmed from legal dealings that many considered shady; among these cases were four that finally led to his disbarment shortly before his death: d. Bethesda, MD, Aug. 2.

Colonna, Jerry (born Gerardo Luigi) (82), comic actor; his trade marks were big rolling eyes, walrus mustache, and bellowing voice. He appeared in such films as *Road to Singapore* and *Road to Rio* with Bob Hope and made 12 overseas trips with Mr. Hope to entertain U.S. troops: d. Woodland Hills, CA, Nov. 21.

Coluche (born Michel Colucci) (41), French comedian; known for his outrageous and irreverent humor. In 1981 he ran for president of France: d. near Grass in southern France, June 19.

Cook, Bill (89–90?), Canadian hockey player; elected to the Hockey Hall of Fame in 1952. He was once regarded as the best right winger to play in the National Hockey League and was with the New York Rangers for 12 years. He retired after the 1936–37 opening season: d. Kingston, Ontario, May 5.

Cooper, Lady Diana (born Diana Manners) (93), British aristocrat; known for her eccentricities. She was active in British social circles and was friendly with royalty. Her three-volume autobiography began appearing in the late 1950s: d. London, June 16.

Charles Halleck

Jacob Javits

Photos, AP/Wide World

Crawford, Broderick (74), actor; won an Academy Award for the film *All the King's Men*. He later starred in the television series *Highway Patrol:* d. Rancho Mirage, CA, April 26.

Crawford, Cheryl (84), theatrical producer and cofounder of New York's Group Theater and the Actors Studio. In 1937 she became an independent producer. Her many successes include Broadway productions of four Tennessee Williams plays, including *The Rose Tattoo* and *Sweet Bird of Youth:* d. New York City, Oct. 7.

Crothers, Scatman (Benjamin Sherman) (76), actor; well known to television viewers as Louie, the garbage collector, on *Chico and the Man:* d. Van Nuys, CA, Nov. 22.

Crowley, James H. (83), football player and coach; was a member of Notre Dame University's undefeated 1924 football team and a member of the famed "Four Horsemen" of that team: d. Scranton, PA, Jan. 15.

Cunningham, Winfield (86), U.S. Navy admiral; was commander of the U.S. forces on Wake Island when it was attacked by the Japanese soon after the attack on Pearl Harbor. He retired from the Navy in 1950: d. Memphis, TN, March 3.

Da Silva, Howard (76), stage, screen, and television actor; was also a theatrical director and producer. In his 50 years in show business he appeared in the Broadway musicals *Oklahoma, Fiorello!*, and *1776* and in 40 films: d. Ossining, NY, Feb. 16.

Dassault, Marcel (born Marcel Bloch) (94), French aircraft manufacturer. His company, built up rapidly after World War I, was nationalized twice by the French government and in 1967 merged with Breguet Aviation. In addition to aircraft manufacturing he was involved in publishing ventures, made several films, and since 1951 was a member of the French parliament almost without interruption: d. Paris, April 18.

Davis, Eddie (Lockjaw) (65), jazz musician; played tenor saxophone; best known for his stints with Count Basie: d. Culver City, CA, Nov. 3.

Defferre, Gaston (75), Socialist mayor of Marseilles (1944, 1945, 1953–86); he was a lawyer and a leader in the French Resistance in World War II. He twice ran for the French presidency and served as minister of the interior (1981–84) under President François Mitterrand: d. Marseilles, France, May 7.

DiMaggio, Vincent (74), baseball player; played ten seasons (1937–46) in the National League with five different teams. He was the older brother of the baseball players Joe and Dom DiMaggio: d. Los Angeles, CA, Oct. 3.

Ding Ling (born Jiang Bingzhi) (82), Chinese writer; one of her country's foremost writers. She wrote about 300 novels, short stories, plays, and essays, and was a champion of women's rights. Her best known novel is *The Sun Shines Over the Sanggan River* (1949): d. Beijing, March 4.

Dionne, Elzire (77), mother of the famous Dionne quintuplets that were born in Canada in 1934: d. North Bay, Ontario, Nov. 22.

Doisy, Edward, Sr. (92), biochemist; he shared the 1943 Nobel Prize in Physiology and Medicine for isolating vitamin K and two female hormones, estrone and estradiol: d. St. Louis, MO, Oct. 23.

Dougherty, John J. (78), American Catholic priest; was host of *The Catholic Hour* on radio and television in the 1940s and 1950s: d. Teaneck, NJ, March 20.

Douglas, Thomas Clement (81), Canadian political leader; set up the first Socialist government in North America as premier of Saskatchewan (1944–61). He became the first national leader of the New Democratic Party and sat in Parliament (1962–68, 1969–79): d. Ottawa, Canada, Feb. 24.

East, John P. (55), U.S. senator (R-NC, 1981–86): d. (found dead, an apparent suicide) Greenville, NC, June 29.

Eastland, James O. (81), U.S. senator (D-MS, 1942–79): d. Greenwood, MS, Feb. 19.

Eliade, Mircea (79), Romanian-born writer and scholar of religion. He was a professor at the University of Chicago (1956–

85) and was considered one of the world's foremost interpreters of spiritual myths and symbolism: d. Chicago, April 22.

Ellin, Stanley (69), mystery writer and a former president of the Mystery Writers of America: d. Brooklyn, NY, July 31.

Ellis, Perry (46), fashion designer; a top designer of sportswear: d. New York City, May 30.

Ellsworth, Harris (86), U.S. representative (R-OR, 1943–57): d. Albuquerque, NM, Feb. 7.

Erickson, Leif (born William Wycliff Anderson) (74), stage, movie, and television actor; perhaps best known for his role in the television series *High Chaparral* (1967–71): d. Pensacola, FL, Jan. 29.

Fernández, Emilio (82), Mexican actor, screenwriter, and director. His films of the 1940s drew attention to the Mexican cinema. He also worked in the Hollywood films *The Wild Bunch* and *Under the Volcano:* d. Mexico City, Aug. 6.

Finch, Charles C. (59), Democratic governor of Mississippi (1976–80): d. Batesville, MS, April 22.

Fleming, Lady Amalia (73), Greek-born widow of the British scientist, Sir Alexander Fleming, who discovered penicillin; a physician; and a political activist in her own right. She was a member of the Greek parliament (1977–86) and of the European parliament; was active in the Greek resistance movement during World War II: d. Athens, Feb. 26.

Flesch, Rudolf (75), authority on literacy and clear writing; his books include *The Art of Plain Talk* and *Why Johnny Can't Read:* d. Dobbs Ferry, NY, Oct. 5.

Fournier, Pierre (79), French cellist; known for his wide repertory: d. Geneva, Switzerland, Jan. 8.

Gabel, Martin (73), actor and director; particularly known as a stage actor. He was an original member of Orson Welles' Mercury Theater and also a producer. One of his successes in that capacity was the Broadway play *Life with Father*, which set a record for longest-running play. He worked in films, on radio and television, and, with his wife, Arlene Francis, appeared as a television panelist: d. New York City, May 22.

Garcia, Mike (62), baseball pitcher for the Cleveland Indians for 14 seasons: d. Fairview Park, OH, Jan. 13.

Garmatz, Edward A. (83), U.S. representative (D-MD, 1947–73): d. Baltimore, MD, July 22.

Genet, Jean (75), French playwright, poet, and novelist. An illegitimate child abandoned by his mother, he grew up with foster parents in the country. As a boy he was accused by his foster mother of being a thief, a label he subsequently embraced. He spent some years in a reformatory and during World War II spent time in jail. In the late 1940s he began to write plays. Soon his work attracted the French literati, including Jean-Paul Sartre, who in 1952 published *Saint Genet: Actor and Martyr*. At one point this group helped to gain him a pardon from another imprisonment for theft. His plays include several important contributions to the experimental theater of the mid-20th century: d. Paris, April 15.

Gennadios, Bishop of Paphos (93), Cypriot Orthodox church leader, defrocked in 1973; supported the Greek Cypriot guerrilla movement: d. Nicosia, Cyprus, March 27.

Gerstenmaier, Eugen Karl Albrecht (79), West German political leader of the Christian Democrats; was president of the lower house of parliament from 1954 to 1969. He was jailed during World War II for a 1944 attempt to assassinate Hitler: d. Oberwinter, West Germany, March 13.

Gilmore, Virginia (born Sherman Poole) (66), stage and film actress; was the wife of actor Yul Brynner from 1944 to 1960: d. Santa Barbara, CA, March 28.

Glubb, Sir John (88), commander of the Arab Legion; he was the legendary Glubb Pasha who helped build Jordan's Arab Legion. He spent 36 years among the Arabs. In 1956 he was dismissed as chief of staff of the Legion by Jordan's King Hussein: d. Sussex, England, March 17.

Goldstein, Rabbi Israel (89), leading figure in the U.S. Zionist movement: d. Tel Aviv, Israel, April 11.

Greeley, Dana McLean (77), first president of the Unitarian Universalist Association (1961–69): d. Concord, MA, June 13.

Greenbaum, Dorothea (92), American sculptor: d. Princeton, NJ, April 6.

Greenberg, Henry Benjamin (Hank) (75), baseball player. After a brief stint with the Detroit Tigers in 1930 he joined the club in 1933 and played for 12 seasons. He led the American League in home runs five times and in runs-batted-in four times and retired in 1947 after one season with the Pittsburgh Pirates. He later was a general manager of the Cleveland Indians and vice-president and general manager of the Chicago White Sox. He was the American League's most valuable player in 1935 and 1940 and was elected to the Baseball Hall of Fame in 1956: d. Beverly Hills, CA, Sept. 4.

Gross, Paul (91), chemist and educator; began his teaching career in 1919 at Trinity College in Durham, NC, which became the beginnings of Duke University in 1924. He retired from Duke in 1965. A specialist in physical inorganic and fluorine chemistry, he was chairman of the committee that wrote the 1961 report for the U.S. surgeon general on environmental health problems: d. Durham, NC, May 4.

Grotberg, John E. (61), U.S. representative (R-IL, 1985–86): d. St. Charles, IL, Nov. 15.

Grumiaux, Arthur (65), Belgian violinist; known for his recordings and concerts. He often performed with pianist Clara Haskil: d. Brussels, Oct. 16.

Halleck, Charles (85), U.S. representative (R-IN, 1935–69). A conservative member of the House, Halleck surprised his colleagues in 1963 by aiding in the passage of the civil-rights bill. During his tenure he was both majority and minority leader of the House. He was considered as a vice-presidential candidate but was never selected. He became a familiar figure to the public when he and Sen. Everett Dirksen of Illinois had a regularly scheduled television news conference that became known as "the Ev and Charles Show": d. Lafayette, IN, March 3.

Halop, Florence (63), actress; known for her portrayal of the bailiff on the television series *Night Court.* From 1952 to 1956 she played Elena Verdugo's mother on the television series *Meet Millie:* d. Los Angeles, CA, July 15.

Haughton, Billy (62), harness-racing driver and trainer; he was a member of that sport's Hall of Fame. He was the winner of 4,910 races and $40.2 million in purses. He died following a July 5 racing accident at Yonkers Raceway: d. Valhalla, NY, July 15.

Hayden, Sterling (born Sterling Relyea Walter) (70), actor, writer, and sailor; his film credits include *The Asphalt Jungle, Dr. Strangelove,* and *The Godfather.* Although he made more than 50 movies, his major love was the sea as was evident in his 1963 autobiography, *Wanderer,* and his novel of the sea, *Voyage:* d. Sausalito, CA, May 23.

Haydon, Murray P. (59), artificial-heart recipient. The third person ever to receive an artificial heart, he lived for 16 months and two days after the device was implanted: d. Louisville, KY, June 19.

Head, Bessie (born Bessie Emery) (48), South African writer who lived in Botswana; she wrote the novels *Maru* (1971) and *A Question of Power* (1974): d. Botswana, April 17.

Heidt, Horace (85), American bandleader of a group called the Musical Knights that appeared on radio in the 1930s and 1940s. He also starred on the show *Pot O'Gold,* which began in 1941, and was prominent in the early days of television: d. Los Angeles, Dec. 1.

Helpmann, Sir Robert (77), Australian dancer, choreographer, actor, and director. Between 1933 and 1950 he was with Britain's Sadler's Wells Ballet (now the Royal Ballet). He also had a career in films (*The Red Shoes,* 1948); on the stage, appearing with the Old Vic Company; and as a director of operas and plays. He was codirector of the Australian Ballet (1965–74) and from 1974 to 1976 was its sole director: d. Sydney, Australia, Sept. 28.

Hemingway, Mary Welsh (78), foreign correspondent during World War II and the widow of novelist Ernest Hemingway. After his death in 1961, she continued to write for magazines and completed her autobiography *How It Was* (1976): d. New York City, Nov. 26.

Herbert, Frank (65), writer of science fiction; well known for the best selling *Dune* and for the "Dune" series of books: d. Madison, WI, Feb. 11.

Herzog, Paul M. (80), lawyer, educator, and chairman of the National Labor Relations Board (NLRB) under President Harry Truman: d. New York City, Nov. 23.

Hicks, James L. (70), journalist; was the first black American accredited to cover the United Nations, the first black member of the State Department Correspondents Association, and the first black sent to cover the Korean War: d. New York City, Jan. 19.

Hijikata, Tatsumi (57), Japanese choreographer, director, and teacher; known as the father of Butoh, a Japanese theater-dance form: d. Tokyo, Japan, Jan. 21.

Hobson, Laura Z. (85), writer; well known for her 1947 novel *Gentleman's Agreement:* d. New York City, Feb. 28.

Hoffmann, Banesh (79), British-born mathematician and physicist; he collaborated with Albert Einstein in the 1930s and published a biography of Einstein in 1972. He also wrote *The Tyranny of Testing:* d. New York City, Aug. 5.

Hubbard, L. Ron (74), founder of the Church of Scientology (1954): d. near San Luis Obispo, CA, Jan. 24.

Huie, William Bradford (76), writer; was a newspaperman in Birmingham, AL, and an editor of the literary magazine, *The American Mercury.* He wrote a series of books about the South of the 1960s as well as *The Execution of Private Slovik, The Revolt of Mamie Stover,* and *The Americanization of Emily:* d. Guntersville, AL, Nov. 22.

Isherwood, Christopher (81), British-born writer; well known for his short-story collection *Goodbye to Berlin* and the book *The Last of Mr. Norris* that were the bases of *I Am a Camera* (the play and movie) and the musical *Cabaret.* Isherwood also wrote plays; a biographical book about his parents, *Kathleen and Frank* (1977); and collaborated on several books on the religion Vedanta: d. Santa Monica, CA, Jan. 4.

Isley, O'Kelly (48), rhythm and blues singer; performed with the Isley Brothers for some 25 years: d. Englewood, NJ, April 1.

Jacuzzi, Candido (83), inventor of the whirlpool bath (in 1949): d. Scottsdale, AZ, Oct. 7.

Jameson, Storm (95), British writer; wrote more than 50 books and was a leading supporter of refugee writers: d. Cambridge, England, Sept. 30.

Jarvis, Gregory B., *see* page 41.

Jarvis, Howard (83), California businessman; led a 1978 California referendum against rising property rates: d. Los Angeles, CA, Aug. 12.

Javits, Jacob (81), U.S. senator (R-NY, 1957–81). A liberal Republican, Javits considered his major legislative achievements to be the War Powers Act, limiting the ability of the president to make war without the consent of Congress; the Erisa Act, which sought to guarantee private pensions; and the National Endowment for the Arts and Humanities. Prior to becoming a senator, he served four terms in the U.S. House of Representatives (1947–55) and was New York state's attorney general: d. West Palm Beach, FL, March 7.

Jessup, Philip C. (89), justice on the International Court of Justice (1960–69) and a member of the U.S. delegation to the United Nations (1948–52): d. Newtown, PA, Jan. 31.

Jones, Thad (63), jazz trumpeter and cornetist: d. Copenhagen, Denmark, Aug. 20.

Kanellopoulos, Panayotis (83), Greek prime minister briefly in 1945 and again in 1967, when his caretaker government was overthrown in a coup: d. Athens, Sept. 11.

Kantorovich, Leonid V. (74), Soviet economist and mathematician; shared the Nobel Prize in Economics in 1975: d. Moscow, April 7.

Kaplan, Lazare (102), diamond dealer; known worldwide, he was the man who cut the 726 carat Jonker diamond in 1936: d. Sullivan County, NY, Feb. 12.

Katayev, Valentin (89), Soviet novelist and playwright: d. Moscow, April 12.

Kekkonen, Urho (85), president of Finland (1956–81). As president he followed a post-World-War-II policy developed under his predecessor Juho Paasikivi of neutrality and of friendship with the USSR. He also helped to safeguard trade with the West. He was chosen in a normal election only once, in 1956; after that, opposition parties did not place strong candidates against him for fear of what the Soviets might do. He resigned because of ill health in 1981: d. Helsinki, Aug. 31.

Kirstein, George G. (76), publisher and principal owner of the *Nation* magazine (1955–65): d. Mamaroneck, NY, April 3.

Klopfer, Donald (84), publisher; cofounder with Bennett Cerf of Random House in 1927. He was the company's chairman (1970–75): d. New York City, May 30.

Knight, Ted (born Tadeus Wladyslaw Konopka) (62), actor, well known as the egotistical TV news anchorman in *The Mary Tyler Moore Show* (1970–77). He later starred in his own series *Too Close for Comfort* (1980–83): d. Pacific Palisades, CA, Aug. 26.

Koch, Erich (90), governor of East Prussia during World War II and a Nazi war criminal: d. Barczewo Prison, Poland, Nov. 12.

Kraft, Joseph (61), journalist; was a widely syndicated liberal columnist and the author of books and articles on national and foreign affairs: d. Washington, DC, Jan. 10.

Kraus, Lili (83), Hungarian-born pianist; particularly admired for her talents regarding the music of Mozart: d. Asheville, NC, Nov. 6.

Krishnamurti, Jiddu (90), Indian religious philosopher and teacher. He was the author of 40 books, and his teaching was based on self-reliance and self-knowledge: d. Ojai, CA, Feb. 17.

Lanchester, Elsa (84), stage and screen actress; known best for her offbeat, sometimes comic roles like that of the monster's wife in *The Bride of Frankenstein* (1935). She was married to the actor Charles Laughton until his death in 1962, and she

Ted Knight
Elsa Lanchester
Photos, AP/Wide World

had sometimes performed with him: d. Woodland Hills, CA, Dec. 26.

Landgrebe, Earl F. (70), U.S. representative (R-IN, 1969–75): d. Valparaiso, IN, June 29.

Lartigue, Jacques-Henri (92), French photographer and painter; known for his views of the "belle époque": d. Nice, Sept. 12.

Layne, Bobby (59), football quarterback; a legend at the University of Texas, he went on to play for the Detroit Lions and Pittsburgh Steelers and was elected to the Pro Football Hall of Fame in 1967: d. Lubbock, TX, Dec. 1.

Le Duan (78), secretary general of the Vietnamese Communist Party; he managed the collective leadership after the death of Ho Chi Minh in 1969: d. Hanoi, July 10.

Lee, Russell (83), photographer; known for his portraits of Depression-era migrant workers, postwar coal miners, and industrial scenes: d. Austin, TX, Aug. 28.

Le Luron, Thierry (34), French satirist and impersonator: d. Paris, Nov. 13.

Lennon, Alton Asa (80), U.S. representative (D-NC, 1957–73); had been appointed to the U.S. Senate in 1953, but he was defeated in the 1954 primary when he attempted to be elected to the seat: d. Cape Fear, NC, Dec. 28.

Lerner, Alan J. (67), lyricist and playwright; famed for his works created in association with the composer Frederick Loewe that included the Broadway musicals *Brigadoon* (1947), *Paint Your Wagon* (1951), *My Fair Lady* (1956), and *Camelot* (1960). (All were also made into films.) They also worked together on a musical made directly for the screen, *Gigi* (1958). After Loewe's retirement, Lerner, who had worked on his own in the films *Royal Wedding* and *An American in Paris*, created a few more musicals. The most successful of these was *On a Clear Day You Can See Forever* (stage, 1965; film, 1970): d. New York City, June 14.

Lifar, Serge (81), dancer and choreographer; was ballet master of the Paris Opera Ballet (1929–45, 1947–58). He published more than 25 books of dance theory: d. Lausanne, Switzerland, Dec. 15.

Lipinski, Edward (97), Polish economist; in 1976 he founded the Committee for Workers' Self-Defense (KOR), credited as forerunner of Solidarity: d. Warsaw, July 13.

Lipmann, Fritz A. (87), German-born biochemist; shared a Nobel Prize in Physiology or Medicine in 1953 for the discovery of coenzyme A: d. Poughkeepsie, NY, July 24.

Liu Bocheng (94), Chinese military strategist; General Liu fought in the 1911 revolution that overthrew China's last emperor. In 1926 he joined the Communist Party and later was involved in the Long March of the 1930s. Under Mao he held a variety of government positions: d. Beijing, Oct. 7.

Lockhart, Carl (Spider) (43), pro-football defensive back for the New York Giants (1965–76): d. Hackensack, NJ, July 8.

Loewy, Raymond (92), French-born industrial designer; known as the "father of streamlining": d. Monte Carlo, Monaco, July 14.

Love, Bessie (born Juanita Horton) (87), actress; her career spanned from the era of silent movies to that of television. Her films include *Intolerance* (1916), *Isadora* (1968), *Sunday, Bloody Sunday* (1971), and *Ragtime* (1980): d. London, April 26.

Lovett, Robert A. (90), U.S. secretary of defense (1951–53); had also served as under secretary of state in the late 1940s. A Republican, he was an investment banker by profession: d. Locust Valley, NY, May 7.

Lowrey, Harry (Peanuts) (67), baseball outfielder and coach. In his 13 years in the major leagues, he played with the Chicago Cubs, the Cincinnati Reds, the St. Louis Cardinals, and the Philadelphia Phillies, before retiring from playing in 1955. He coached in the major leagues for another 17 years: d. Inglewood, CA, July 2.

Alan Jay Lerner

AP/Wide World

Harold Macmillan

UPI/Bettmann Newsphotos

Lyons, Theodore Amar (Ted) (85), baseball player; he was a pitcher for the Chicago White Sox for 21 years and in 1955 was elected to the Baseball Hall of Fame: d. Sulphur, LA, July 25.

MacDonald, John D. (70), mystery novelist; he produced some 70 books, of which 21 were of the highly successful Travis McGee series: d. Milwaukee, WI, Dec. 28.

Machel, Samora M. (53), president of Mozambique (1975–86). He joined the Mozambique Liberation Front (Frelimo) and waged guerrilla warfare to gain his country's independence from Portugal: d. South Africa, Oct. 19.

Mack, Peter Francis, Jr. (69), U.S. representative (D-IL, 1949–63): d. Washington, DC, July 4.

Macmillan, Harold (Earl of Stockton) (92), British prime minister (1957–63); was made an earl in 1984. A Conservative, Macmillan was known for his skill at compromise, and he often spoke of his policies as "the middle way." During his tenure he accepted Egyptian control of the Suez Canal, after an abortive attack on Egypt in 1956 while he was chancellor of the exchequer. He also saw and expressed the need for independence of Britain's African colonies. He resigned in 1963 following a scandal involving his secretary of state for war, John Profumo. A book-publishing heir, he was educated at Eton and Oxford and saw military action during World War I. He served his country as defense minister and foreign minister in 1954 and 1955: d. Birch Grove, Sussex, England, Dec. 29.

MacRae, Gordon (64), singer and actor; starred in the musical films *Oklahoma* (1955) and *Carousel* (1956) and in four musicals with Doris Day: d. Lincoln, NE, Jan. 24.

Malamud, Bernard (71), novelist and short-story writer; known for his ability to create stories that were almost like fables. His work showed regard for Jewish tradition, but he did not consider himself only a Jewish writer. His first novel was *The Natural* (1952), which was released in 1984 as a movie. Perhaps his most acclaimed novel was *The Assistant* (1957). He won a Pulitzer Prize and two National Book Awards: d. New York City, March 18.

Malone, Dumas (94), historian; regarded as the foremost authority on Thomas Jefferson. He wrote the six-volume *Jefferson and His Time*, (completed in 1981): d. Charlottesville, VA, Dec. 27.

Manuel, Richard (40), rock singer and pianist; was with the rock group The Band: d. Winter Park, FL, March 4.

Marjolin, Robert (74), French economist; was secretary general of the Organization for European Economic Cooperation (1948–55) and vice-president of the Commission of the European Economic Community (1958–67): d. Paris, April 15.

Markham, Beryl (83), British aviation pioneer; was the first person to fly solo across the Atlantic from east to west (1936). Her 1942 memoir, *West with the Night*, reissued in the 1980s, told of her upbringing in Kenya and of her historic flight: d. Nairobi, Kenya, Aug. 3.

Matthews, Marjorie (69), bishop of the United Methodist Church (1980–84), the first woman so elected: d. Grand Rapids, MI, July 1.

McAuliffe, Sharon Christa, see page 41.

McConnell, John Paul (78), Air Force chief of staff (1965–69) and vice commander of the Strategic Air Command: d. Bethesda, MD, Nov. 21.

McGrath, Christopher C. (84), judge, U.S. representative (D-NY, 1949–53), and surrogate of the Bronx, NY: d. New York City, July 7.

McKenna, Siobhan (63 or 64?), Irish actress; skilled in performances in Gaelic, particularly her own translation of George Bernard Shaw's *Saint Joan*, first performed in 1951. She later did the same role in English: d. Dublin, Nov. 16.

McNair, Ronald E., see page 41.

Menard, Henry William (65), marine geologist; made discoveries on the Pacific Ocean floor that were crucial to the development of the plate tectonics theory: d. La Jolla, CA, Feb. 9.

Merkel, Una (82), actress; made a successful transition from silent to talking films. She was nominated for an Academy Award for *Summer and Smoke* (1961). She won a Tony Award in 1956 for her performance on Broadway in *The Ponder Heart*: d. Los Angeles, Jan. 2.

Milland, Ray (born Reginald Truscott-Jones) (81?), actor; most famous for his Academy-Award-winning role in *The Lost Weekend* (1945). All together he made 120 movies: d. Torrance, CA, March 10.

Miller, Frank (73), cellist; was principal cellist of the Chicago Symphony Orchestra (1959–84) and the NBC Symphony Orchestra (1939–54): d. Skokie, IL, Jan. 6.

Miller, Merle (67), novelist and biographer; wrote best-selling oral biographies of presidents Harry Truman and Lyndon Johnson and recently had completed a biography of Dwight Eisenhower. In 1971 he wrote an essay in the *New York Times Magazine*, "What It Means to Be a Homosexual," which stirred much discussion: d. Danbury, CT, June 10.

Minnelli, Vincente (76), film director. One of the greatest directors of film musicals, he won an Academy Award in 1958 for the film *Gigi*, which also was awarded an Oscar for best pic-

AP/Wide World

Culver

Olof Palme

Marlin Perkins

ture. His *An American in Paris* (1951) also received an Oscar for best picture. Other notable film musicals that he directed include *The Band Wagon* (1953) and two with his former wife, the late Judy Garland: *Meet Me in St. Louis* (1944) and *The Pirate* (1948). (His daughter with Miss Garland is the actress Liza Minnelli.) Besides musicals, he directed the dramas *The Bad and the Beautiful* (1952) and *Lust for Life* (1956) and the comedy *Father of the Bride* (1950). Prior to his career in Hollywood, he directed three successful Broadway shows: d. Los Angeles, CA, July 25.

Molotov, Vyacheslav M. (96), Soviet leader; one of Stalin's closest aides. For about 35 years he was near the top of the Soviet hierarchy—as a party secretary (1921–30), as prime minister (1930–41), and as a first deputy prime minister (1941–57). He served concurrently as foreign minister (1939–49, 1953–56). He was ousted from the Communist Party in 1962 but was reinstated in 1984 during Konstantin Chernenko's tenure: d. USSR, Nov. 8.

Moore, Don W. (81), U.S. writer; for 20 years, beginning in 1934, he wrote the *Flash Gordon* comic strip: d. Venice, FL, April 7.

Morgan, Russell H. (75), radiologist and dean emeritus of Johns Hopkins School of Medicine; a pioneer in his field who perfected methods of improving X-ray images for diagnostic purposes in the 1960s: d. Baltimore, MD, Feb. 24.

Mulliken, Robert Sanderson (90), chemist and physicist; his 1928 molecular orbit theory provided a link between the atom and the molecule by showing how electrons behave when atoms combine to form molecules. He received the Nobel Prize in Chemistry in 1966: d. Arlington, VA, Oct. 31.

Multer, Abraham (85), U.S. representative (D-NY, 1947–67). He later was a New York state Supreme Court judge: d. Hartford, CT, Nov. 4.

Myrdal, Alva (84), Swedish diplomat, cabinet member (1962–73), and cowinner of the Nobel Peace Prize in 1982 for her efforts toward world disarmament. Her books include *The Crisis in the Population Question* (1934), written with her husband, the economist and sociologist Gunnar Myrdal, and *The Game of Disarmament* (1976): d. Stockholm, Sweden, Feb. 1.

Nakian, Reuben (89), sculptor; most famous for his heroic sculptures, often drawn from Greek and Roman mythology: d. Stamford, CT, Dec. 4.

Narain, Raj (69), Indian Socialist leader; had been elected to India's upper house of Parliament in 1966: d. New Delhi, India, Dec. 30.

Neagle, Dame Anna (born Florence Marjorie Robinson) (81), British stage and film actress; she was a leading film actress in the 1930s and 1940s, appearing usually in romantic comedies or costume biographies. She was married for many years to the director Herbert Wilcox with whom she frequently worked. Between 1965 and 1971 she appeared on stage in 2,062 performances of *Charlie Girl*: d. Surrey, England, June 3.

Nelson, George H. (77), architect, furniture designer, editor, and writer; was influential in industrial design: d. New York City, March 5.

Nyswander, Marie (67), psychiatrist; was one of the first in her profession to treat drug addiction as a medical problem. She helped develop the methadone maintenance treatment method for heroin addiction: d. New York City, April 20.

O'Brian, George M. (69), U.S. representative (R-IL, 1973–86): d. Bethesda, MD, July 17.

Onizuka, Ellison S., *see* page 41.

Orton, Vrest (89), author and founder of the Vermont Country Store in Weston, VT. He worked for H. L. Mencken on *The American Mercury* and wrote *Dreiserana* (1929), about the author Theodore Dreiser; *Vermont Afternoons with Robert Frost; And So Goes Vermont;* and several other books. He founded the country store in 1946 and wrote a mail-order

catalogue, which today is greatly expanded: d. Springfield, VT, Dec. 2.

Pakhomova, Lyudmila (39), ice skater who with her husband Aleksandr Gorshkov won six world championships for the USSR and captured the first Olympic gold medal awarded in the sport in Innsbruck in 1976: d. Moscow, May 17.

Palme, Olof (59), prime minister of Sweden (1969–76, 1982–86) and chairman of the Social Democratic Party. He was from an upper-class family, but became a Socialist and was considered perhaps the most left-wing of the Western leaders. He spoke out in opposition to American involvement in Vietnam, for nuclear disarmament and a nuclear-free Europe, and he unsuccessfully sought a solution to the Iran-Iraq border war. He was assassinated after leaving a movie theater in Stockholm: d. Stockholm, Sweden, Feb. 28.

Palmer, Lilli (born Lillie Marie Peiser) (71), actress; appeared on stage, in films, and on television, frequently with her first husband, Rex Harrison. They appeared together in the stage version of *Bell, Book, and Candle* on Broadway in 1950 and were in the film *The Four Poster* (1952). She later wrote her autobiography and five novels: d. Los Angeles, CA, Jan. 27.

Papanin, Ivan (91), Soviet polar explorer; commanded the Soviet's first ice-floe station in 1937–38: d. Moscow, Jan. 30.

Pears, Sir Peter (75), British tenor; had a close collaboration with the composer Benjamin Britten, who wrote all of his major tenor roles and most of his solo vocal works for Pears: d. Aldeburgh, England, April 3.

Perkins, R. Marlin (81), zoologist; became well known for his television appearances in *Zoo Parade* in the 1950s and then, beginning in 1963 for 23 years, as the host of *Wild Kingdom:* d. St. Louis, MO, June 14.

Picasso, Jacqueline (60), second wife of artist Pablo Picasso and the prime inspiration for his later work: d. Mougins, France, Oct. 15.

Plante, Joseph Jacques Omer (57), Canadian hockey player; one of the great goaltenders of the National Hockey League: d. Geneva, Switzerland, Feb. 26.

Pollard, Frederick Douglas (Fritz) (92), football coach and player; was the only black head football coach of a National Football League team. After a college football career at Brown University, he became a running back with the Akron Pros of the American Football Association, which became the NFL in June 1922. In 1920 he took over many of the coaching responsibilities of the Akron Pros, but he was not listed as a head coach until the 1923 season with the Hammond Pros of Indiana: d. Silver Spring, MD, May 11.

Prebisch, Raúl (85), Argentine economist; considered the Third World's leading economist in the 1960s: d. Santiago, Chile, April 29.

Preminger, Otto (79), director and producer; known for such films as *Laura, The Moon Is Blue, The Man with the Golden Arm, Anatomy of a Murder,* and *Exodus.* He also directed for the stage and acted in four films: d. New York City, April 23.

Pritzker, Abram Nicholas (90), Chicago entrepreneur; founded a vast business empire that included the Hyatt Hotel chain, Braniff Airlines, and *McCall's* magazine. He was also a philanthropist: d. Chicago, IL, Feb. 8.

Rainwater, James (68), professor emeritus of physics at Columbia University. He shared the Nobel Prize in Physics in 1975 for his work in analyzing the structure of atomic nuclei: d. Yonkers, NY, May 31.

Ram, Jagjivan (78), Indian political figure; he was born into an Untouchable family and became a champion of India's Untouchables. Between 1946 and 1963 he held a series of important cabinet posts, including the labor, transport, railways, and communications portfolios. In 1967 he was named agriculture minister and he served as defense minister (1970–74, 1977–79): d. New Delhi, India, July 6.

Reed, Donna (born Donna Belle Mullenger) (64), actress; often played the "nice girl" in movies of the 1940s. She was cast against type in *From Here to Eternity* and won an Oscar. Another of her important films was *It's a Wonderful Life.* On television she was successful in *The Donna Reed Show* and appeared briefly in *Dallas:* d. Beverly Hills, CA, Jan. 14.

Resnik, Judith A., *see* page 41.

Reynolds, Tommy (69), clarinetist and band leader of the 1940s: d. New York City, Sept. 30.

Ritz, Harry (born Harry Joachim) (78), comedian; a member of the Ritz Brothers comedy team that began in 1925 as vaudeville precision dancers: d. San Diego, CA, March 29.

Rudenko, Lyudmila (81), Soviet chess champion; was the first women's world chess champion: d. Leningrad, March 2.

Ruffing, Charles (Red) (81), baseball pitcher; his major league career covered 22 seasons, including 15 with the New York Yankees: d. Mayfield, OH, Feb. 17.

Rulfo, Juan (67), Mexican novelist; one of the creators of the school of "magic realism" that influenced several Latin American writers. He was best known for his book *Pedro Páramo* (1955): d. Mexico City, Mex., Jan. 7.

Russell, Dillon (Curly) (69), jazz bassist, known as a leading bebop musician: d. New York City, July 3.

Donna Reed

Photos, AP/Wide World

Rudy Vallee

Santmyer, Helen Hooven (90), educator and novelist; became known quite late in her life when her book . . . *And Ladies of the Club* became a best-seller in 1984: d. Xenia, OH, Feb. 21.

Saunders, Allen (86), drama critic and linguist; creator of the *Steve Roper* comic strip and writer for the *Mary Worth* comic strip: d. Maumee, OH, Jan. 28.

Schaefer, Walter V. (81), Illinois state Supreme Court judge (1951–76); regarded as one of the most distinguished state jurists cf the 20th century: d. Lake Forest, IL, June 13.

Scholz, Jackson (89), runner; in 1924 in the Paris Olympics he earned a gold medal for the United States in the 200-meter run, but lost to Britain's Harold Abrahams in the 100-meter run. The contest between the two was depicted in the film *Chariots of Fire*: d. Delray Beach, FL, Oct. 26.

Schroeder, William (54), second of the five patients who received the Jarvik-7 artificial heart; Schroeder lived 620 days on the device, the longest of any recipient: d. Louisville, KY, Aug. 6.

Scobee, Francis R., see page 40.

Seifert, Jaroslav (84), Czechoslovak poet; was the winner of the Nobel Prize for Literature in 1984: d. Prague, Czechoslovakia, Jan. 10.

Semyonov, Nikolai (90), Soviet scientist; shared the 1956 Nobel Prize in Chemistry for his work in exploring chemical chain reactions: d. Sept. 25.

Sherer, Albert W., Jr. (70), career diplomat; specialized in Eastern Europe. He wrote the draft of the human-rights provisions of the Helsinki accords of 1975: d. Chicago, IL, Dec. 27.

Lord Shinwell (Emanuel) (101), British politician; served for 40 years until 1970 in the House of Commons. He then entered the House of Lords as a life peer: d. London, May 8.

Sindona, Michele (65), Italian financier; once served as an adviser to the Vatican, during which time it lost millions of dollars. At the time of his death he was under a 25-year sentence (imposed in 1980) for fraud in the United States for his role in the 1974 failure of the Franklin National Bank. In 1986 he was sentenced to life imprisonment for contracting a murder: d. Voghera, Italy, March 22.

Six, Robert F. (79), founder of Continental Airlines and a commercial aviation pioneer; he served as head of Continental Airlines for 46 years until his retirement in 1982: d. Beverly Hills, CA, Oct. 6.

Smith, Al (84), cartoonist; created the *Mutt and Jeff* comic strip: d. Rutland, VT, Nov. 24.

Smith, Frances Scott (Scottie) (64), writer and only child of the writers F. Scott Fitzgerald and his wife Zelda: d. Montgomery, AL, June 18.

Smith, Jerry (43), pro football player; a receiver for the Washington Redskins (1965–77): d. Silver Spring, MD, Oct. 15.

Smith, Michael J., see page 40.

Steiner, Ralph (87), photographer and cinematographer: d. Hanover, NH, July 13.

Stoessel, Walter J., Jr. (66), career diplomat; served in the USSR and in Poland. He was appointed deputy secretary of state in 1982, the only career diplomat in 30 years to attain that position: d. Washington, DC, Dec. 9.

Sweet, Blanche (90), film actress of the silent movie era: d. New York City, Sept. 6.

Szent-Gyorgyi, Albert (93), biochemist; won the 1937 Nobel Prize in Physiology or Medicine for his isolation of vitamin C. In 1954 he received an Albert Lasker Award for his research in heart muscle contraction, including his discovery of actomyosin: d. Woods Hole, MA, Oct. 22.

Tarkovsky, Andrei (54), Russian director whose films were often criticized and banned in the USSR and applauded in the West. His *Ivan Rublev*, completed in 1966, was considered a masterpiece, and his last film, *The Sacrifice*, won a Cannes festival award in 1986: d. Paris, Dec. 29.

Taussig, Helen (87), pediatrician with Johns Hopkins University; founder of pediatric cardiology and a codeveloper of the first successful "blue baby" operation: d. West Chester, PA, May 20.

Tenzing Norkay (or Norgay) (72), Nepalese-born mountain guide of the Sherpa tribe who, along with New Zealand's Sir Edmund Hillary, became the first to climb Mount Everest on May 29, 1953: d. Darjeeling, India, May 9.

Throckmorton, John L. (72), U.S. Army general; was deputy commander of U.S. forces in Vietnam from 1964 to 1965 and was commanding general of the Third Army from 1967 to 1969: d. Washington, DC, Feb. 11.

Tierno Galván, Enrique (67), Spanish Socialist intellectual and mayor of Madrid (1979–86); was a leader in the transitional period to democracy following the rule of Franco: d. Madrid, Spain, Jan. 20.

Ullman, Al (Albert C.) (72), U.S. representative (D-OR, 1957–81): d. Bethesda, MD, Oct. 11.

Vallee, Rudy (born Hubert Prior Vallee) (84), singer, saxophone player, and film and stage actor; extremely popular in the 1930s and 1940s. Also a radio and nightclub star, he made famous the songs *My Time Is Your Time*, *The Whiffenpoof Song*, and *I'm Just a Vagabond Lover*, as well as *The Maine Stein Song* and *Say It Isn't So*. During the 1960s he had Broadway and film success in *How to Succeed in Business Without Really Trying*: d. North Hollywood, CA, July 3.

Van Dyke, Willard (79), photographer, documentary filmmaker; two of his films, *The River* and *The City*, were considered classics: d. Jackson, TN, Jan. 23.

Van Zandt, James E. (87), U.S. representative (R-PA, 1939–43, 1947–63): d. Arlington, VA, Jan. 6.

Veeck, Bill (71), colorful and innovative former baseball club owner of the Cleveland Indians, the St. Louis Browns, and the Chicago White Sox, and operator of Suffolk Downs racetrack near Boston: d. Chicago, IL, Jan. 2.

Wallis, Hal B. (88), motion-picture producer. Among his important films are *Little Caesar* (1930), *The Maltese Falcon* (1941), *Casablanca* (1942), *Come Back Little Sheba* (1952), and *True Grit* (1969): d. Rancho Mirage, CA, Oct. 5.

Wedel, Cynthia Clark (77), first woman to become president of the National Council of Churches (1969–72); she later headed the World Council of Churches (1975–83): d. Alexandria, VA, Aug. 24.

White, Theodore (71), writer and journalist; best known for his "Making of the President" books about the U.S. presidential campaigns of 1960, 1964, 1968, and 1972, of which *The Making of the President 1960* won him national fame and a Pulitzer Prize. He followed these books with *Breach of Faith* (1975), his memoir *In Search of History* (1978), and *America in Search of Itself* (1982). Early in his career he was a foreign correspondent, and from his experience in covering war and famine in China, he coauthored the well-received 1946 book, *Thunder Out of China*: d. New York City, May 15.

Williams, Kim (62), radio personality on Public Radio's *All Things Considered* for ten years: d. Missoula, MT, Aug. 6.

Williams, William B. (born William Breitbard) (62), New York City radio personality for more than 40 years. d. New York City, Aug. 3.

Wilson, John (84), trial lawyer; defended White House aides H. R. Haldeman and John D. Ehrlichman in the Watergate hearings of 1973–74: d. Washington, DC, May 18.

Wilson, Teddy (Theodore) (73), jazz pianist; New Britain, CT, July 31.

Wood, Robert (61), president of CBS television network (1969–76): d. Santa Monica, CA, May 20.

Wu, John C. H. (86), Chinese diplomat, scholar, and international law authority; he was the principal author of the Nationalist Constitution adopted in 1946. After the Communist takeover in China, he settled in the United States. He went to Taiwan in 1967. In 1957 he was appointed judge of the Permanent Court of Arbitration at The Hague by Nationalist President Chiang Kai-shek: d. Taipei, Taiwan, Feb. 5.

Wynn, Keenan (70), actor; played in more than 200 movies and 250 television shows. His films include *Kiss Me Kate* and *Dr. Strangelove*: d. Brentwood, CA, Oct. 14.

Wyzanski, Charles E., Jr. (80), judge of the Federal District Court in Massachusetts (1941–86). He was also a judge of the International Administrative Court in Geneva 1950–55: d. Boston, MA, Sept. 3.

Yamasaki, Minoru (73), Japanese-American architect; designed New York's World Trade Center: d. Detroit, MI, Feb. 6.

Ye Jianying (90), Chinese Communist army officer; Marshal Ye was head of state in China (1978–83) and earlier had been defense minister (1975–78): d. Beijing, Oct. 22.

Youde, Sir Edward (62), British diplomat; governor and commander in chief of Hong Kong from May 1982: d. Beijing, Dec. 4.

Zacharias, Jerrold R. (81), atomic physicist; he reshaped the teaching of physics for high school students. Earlier, he designed the first atomic clock: d. Belmont, MA, July 16.

Zorin, Valerian A. (84), Soviet foreign ministry official for 45 years; was a Soviet delegate to the United Nations (1952–53, 1960–62): d. Jan. 14.

OCEANOGRAPHY

The key words in current oceanographic activity are climate and environment. Both are part of the continuing concern for the Pacific Ocean circulation system now known as ENSO (El Niño/Southern Oscillation). Already completed in 1986 was the first year of a ten-year program by ocean and atmospheric scientists worldwide—known as the Tropical Ocean and Global Atmosphere Program (TOGA)—to collect data on the genesis of El Niño. Scientists from France, Australia, Chile, Peru, the People's Republic of China, and the United States, among others, are involved. The program is part of the World Climate Research Program of the World Meteorological Organization and the International Council of Scientific Unions to determine the predictability of the earth's climate and the extent of human influence on it. All data collected during the TOGA program will go to world data centers maintained by both the United States and the Soviet Union, providing access for scientists everywhere.

An ENSO system changes conditions in both the atmosphere and ocean. In a normal season, the winds blow steadily across the tropical Pacific toward Asia, pushing warm surface winds before them. Updrafts cause high rainfall near Asia, while the cold waters off Ecuador and Peru support dense schools of fish. During an El Niño, a pressure shift (or Southern Oscillation) causes the easterly winds to weaken, with new updrafts forming storms in abnormal locations. Rainfall patterns change around much of the globe, and deepening warm water near South America results in extensive fish kills. The ENSO of 1982-83 was the most severe on record and may even have affected mid-latitude weather systems near the United States. In March 1986 early evaluations from computer modeling warned of a warming trend in the eastern Equatorial Pacific, but conditions returned to near normal in later months. Continuing data analysis and interpretations will help refine prediction methods. Under development, for example, is a new technique for examining subsurface changes by sound-wave profiles.

The Equatorial Pacific Ocean Climate Studies (EPOCS) program, part of the U.S. effort for TOGA, seeks to simulate and predict tropical ocean and atmosphere conditions. The meteorological part of the project aims to identify the onset signals of Southern Oscillation and to describe the atmospheric processes involved in surface sea temperature changes. The oceanographic component of the study focuses on the surface system of equatorial currents, countercurrents, and associated undercurrents, along with an evaluation of the extent to which weather conditions exert a forcing effect at a distance remote from the actual weather changes.

In the Atlantic, the 1986 project GALE (Genesis of Atlantic Lows Experiment) was the largest field survey of winter storms ever conducted. Its purpose was to follow the air and ocean motions that result in the formation of strong middle-scale weather systems, which cover a few hundred miles and last up to one day, as opposed to the larger systems already being followed in routine weather analysis. Caught between the Appalachian Mountains and the offshore Gulf Stream, which releases much energy and moisture to the overlying colder atmosphere, such systems may grow rapidly near the Carolina coast south of Cape Hatteras. The Canadian Atlantic Storms Program (CASP) extended the survey to more northern regions. Preliminary results emphasize the effect of the Gulf Stream on the lower 2 km (1.2 mi) of the atmosphere. The Experiment on Rapidly Intensifying Cyclones in the Atlantic (ERICA) was planned for the winter of 1989 to determine the minimum set of observations necessary for accurate forecasts of such intense storm development at sea.

Recent geological studies have continued to give details of sea-floor activity. Evidence from recently detected shallow intraplate earthquakes along the Solomon and Hebrides Island arc in the western Pacific is believed to define a new convergent plate boundary and an incipient oceanic trench in Micronesia. Small overlapping offsets on the East Pacific Rise have been interpreted as the result of independent episodes of magma eruption, causing symmetric growth and the movement of one portion of the ridge away from the line of adjacent segments. Drill cores from the central Pacific have been used to date and classify crustal layers and to correlate seismic reflections marking the boundaries between layers of different rock types over a wide area.

Joides Resolution, the drill ship for the Ocean Drilling Program (ODP), was deployed in the Atlantic Ocean during 1986, with drill sites in Baffin Bay and the Labrador Sea, the Norwegian Sea, the mid-Atlantic ridge, the Mediterranean, and the coast of northwest Africa. ODP is funded by the United States, Canada, France, Japan, and West Germany. At a site on the Mid-Atlantic ridge, a television camera provided details of a submarine hydrothermal vent system with a singular biological community of small mobile organisms—shrimp-like crustacea of various sizes—much different from the sedentary fauna in Pacific vents. Cores from three locations in Baffin Bay above the Arctic Circle—the most northerly data yet obtained—retrieved almost 1 mi (1.6 km) of sediment and rock samples from depths up to 1 147 m (3,500 ft) beneath the sea floor. The cores confirmed that formation of the Labrador Sea began about 85 million years ago.

DAVID A. McGILL
U.S. Coast Guard Academy

AP/Wide World

Ohio Gov. Richard Celeste has a taste of a Democratic "victory cake" on Election Day. Celeste easily defeated his four-term Republican predecessor, James Rhodes.

OHIO • Information Highlights

Area: 41,330 sq mi (107 044 km²).
Population (1985 est.): 10,744,000.
Chief Cities (July 1, 1984 est.): Columbus, the capital, 566,114; Cleveland, 546,543; Cincinnati, 370,481; Toledo, 343,939; Akron, 226,877; Dayton, 181,159.
Chief Government (1986): *Chief Officers*—governor, Richard F. Celeste (D); lt. gov., vacant. *General Assembly*—Senate, 33 members; House of Representatives, 99 members.
State Finances (fiscal year 1985): *Revenue,* $21,242,000,000; *expenditure,* $17,568,000,000.
Personal Income (1985): $142,110,000,000; per capita, $13,226.
Labor Force (June 1986): *Civilian labor force,* 5,259,300; *unemployed,* 457,400 (8.7% of total force).
Education: *Enrollment* (fall 1984)—public elementary schools, 1,220,019; public secondary, 585,421; colleges and universities, 514,745. *Public school expenditures* (1983–84), $5,150,000,000 ($3,042 per pupil).

OHIO

An earthquake, the likely end of the long political career of former Gov. James Rhodes, and major manufacturers' problems engaged Ohioans' attention in 1986.

The Election. The November election ended Rhodes' hope of serving a fifth four-year term as governor. Richard F. Celeste of Cleveland, Democratic governor since 1983, defeated the former governor by a 61–39% margin in a light (53%) turnout. Among the major issues was Rhodes' age, 77. Rhodes in a November 2 televised debate had criticized Celeste's cabinet choices, and the governor had said that Rhodes had left the state in bad financial condition.

In 1978 Rhodes had defeated Celeste, then Ohio's lieutenant governor. Under Ohio law a governor may succeed himself only once, so a new state leader will be picked in 1992. The Republicans maintained their 18–15 majority in the Ohio Senate, and the Democrats will continue to rule the House, 60–39.

Ohio Supreme Court Chief Justice Frank D. Celebrezze of Cleveland was defeated by Franklin County (Columbus) Appeals Court Judge Thomas J. Moyer. Cleveland's *Plain Dealer* and other newspapers had revealed that two union locals with crime connections had donated to Celebrezze's campaign fund.

Two former Cleveland mayors were also-rans: Dennis Kucinich dropped out of the gubernatorial race in favor of Celeste, and Carl B. Stokes, first black mayor of a major U.S. city, failed to win a common pleas judgeship. He continued as a Cleveland municipal judge.

Nuclear Controversy. On January 31 an earthquake measuring 5.5 on the Richter scale shook Lake County, 10 mi (16 km) from a new $5 billion nuclear power plant at Perry. Following the quake, opposition to the facility by antinuclear groups increased. Centerior Energy Corporation, which operates the plant, stated that it had suffered no damage and discounted the danger of a nuclear accident.

The Nuclear Regulatory Commission granted Centerior a full-power license on November 7, but a U.S. Court of Appeals in Cincinnati was asked to rule on a State of Ohio suit involving questions about the plant's safety. Centerior's other nuclear plant, near Toledo, began start-up operations in late December after repairs of equipment which failed in 1985.

Employment. The bankruptcy of LTV Corporation (Republic Steel); General Motors' plan to close two outmoded plants near Cincinnati, with the loss of 6,500 jobs; and the closing of much of the steel-making capacity of the Youngstown and Cleveland areas cast shadows over the state's economic picture. Nevertheless unemployment figures held level in late 1986, and more than a score of Japanese-owned factories have opened, seven in 1985.

Rail Plan. In August an Ohio High-Speed Rail Authority began to investigate the possibility of developing 140-minute passenger service between Cincinnati and Cleveland via Columbus, at speeds up to 170 miles per hour. The estimated cost would be $2.1 billion, but prospects for financing dimmed when federal authorities questioned whether bond proposals were legal under the new tax laws.

Population. The Census Bureau reported 41 of Ohio's 88 counties lost population between 1980 and 1985. In 1980–1984 the state's total fell 0.4% to 10,752,000 from 10,798,000.

Education. Cleveland's troubled Board of Education had its third superintendent in 18 months when Alfred D. Tutela assumed the post. He had been interim chief after the Jan. 26, 1985, suicide of Frederick D. Holliday, but was passed over with the appointment eight months later of Ronald A. Boyd, who came from a California school post. Boyd conflicted with board members on appointments, desegregation programs, and school budgets.

JOHN F. HUTH, JR., *Former Reporter*
"The Plain Dealer," Cleveland

OKLAHOMA

In the 1986 elections the Republicans captured the governorship, but the Democrats retained control of the state legislature.

Election Results. In the U.S. senatorial race, incumbent Republican Don Nickles defeated seven-term first district Democratic Congressman James R. Jones by a 54–46 margin in the most costly contest (more than $5 million) in state history.

Republican James M. Inhofe, former Tulsa mayor, won the congressional seat vacated by Jones. Democratic incumbents Mike Synar, Wes Watkins, and Dave McCurdy returned to Congress with easy victories. Glenn English went unopposed. Mickey Edwards (R) retained his seat.

Republican Henry Bellmon, who was governor of Oklahoma from 1963 to 1967 and a U.S. senator from 1969 to 1981, was returned to the governorship. He polled 47% of the vote, narrowly defeating Democratic newcomer David Walters and two independents. Robert S. Kerr III (D), namesake and grandson of the former U.S. senator, won the lieutenant governor's race defeating Tim Leonard (R), state Senate minority leader.

Legislature. The legislature met for the constitutional 90-legislative-day limit, adjourning June 13 after a 26-hour marathon session. A $2.2 billion budget was approved, $345 million below 1985. Lower revenues in sales, income, and gross production taxes led to an average 13.4% slash in appropriations to agencies. Education, health and human services, and corrections received less than average cuts.

A presidential primary was adopted to replace the caucus system in choosing delegates to national party conventions. Reform legislation was passed to streamline the workers compensation court, place a ceiling on punitive damages in civil suits (tort liability), and establish an ethics commission.

An executive branch reorganization bill passed, creating a cabinet system under the governor. By executive order almost 300 state agencies, boards, and commissions were assigned to 15 cabinet secretaries appointed by Gov. George Nigh.

The Economy. The state's economy continued to tailspin. Tax increases enacted in 1985 failed to produce sufficient revenues and, as a result, state services were further reduced.

Individual and business bankruptcies continued to increase. Wheat and beef prices declined, but oil prices rallied after hitting a low of $9.75 per barrel. Unemployment increased to 8.6%, and construction and building permits were down. Bank failures continued; 35 had failed since 1982. First National Bank and Trust (Oklahoma City), the state's second largest, closed in July.

Public trust authorities were authorized to help finance development efforts. The Oklahoma Industrial Finance Authority loan program was expanded to promote financing of small and medium sized businesses. A new state office to promote international trade was established in London. The decision to locate a Hitachi plant in Norman was cited as evidence of success in attracting Japanese firms. State leaders espoused the need to diversify the economy to provide a transition from agricultural and oil production dependency.

Floods. Heavy rains in September and October led to an estimated $140 million damage. Twenty-eight counties were declared disaster areas. The state's highways, roads, and bridges were seriously damaged.

JOHN W. WOOD, *University of Oklahoma*

ONTARIO

A buoyant provincial economy in 1986 provided an auspicious background for Premier David Peterson's new minority Liberal government to begin implementation of its electoral platform.

Government and Legislation. Despite the opposition of teachers and some church groups, legislation for full funding of Roman Catholic high schools was introduced after a 3–2 decision in the Ontario Supreme Court upheld its constitutionality. But the issue is not closed; an appeal to the Supreme Court of Canada was pending late in the year.

A major plank of the Liberal platform had been a promise to prohibit doctors from extra-billing—charging their patients more than the rates allowed by the provincial health-insurance plan. After attempts to negotiate an agreement with the Ontario Medical Association failed, the government introduced legislation in June, spurring a series of one-day work stoppages by doctors which escalated into a full-scale strike. Some doctors were unhappy with the militancy of the Medical Association, however, and a series of rotating strikes found scant support outside Toronto and fizzled by August.

Premier Peterson found the implementation of other election promises even more troublesome. The proposal to legalize the sale of Ontario wine and beer in grocery stores ran into considerable opposition from both the Conservatives and the New Democratic Party (NDP). Proposals requiring equal pay for work of equal value and an extension of rent controls—both essential items in the pact between the Liberals and the NDP which brought the government to power in 1985—proved a severe test of the Liberal-NDP alliance. Measures were introduced to require equal pay for equal work in the public sector. The NDP wants the legislation ex-

tended to the economy in general, which the government is reluctant to do because of strong opposition from small businesses. And the premier threatened to withdraw Bill 51, which he saw as a fair compromise between builders and renters, if there were any drastic opposition amendments.

The Speech from the Throne in April, outlining government policy, promised to make the educational system more responsive to the needs of business by stressing science and engineering. Provincial Treasurer Robert Nixon also indicated that more money would be spent on the universities, after years of neglect which has seen their funding shrink drastically. The increased funding was announced in November.

The government was embarrassed when two cabinet ministers were forced to resign after charges of conflict of interest. A legislative committee was set up to investigate, and Premier Peterson came under heavy criticism for failing to enforce adequate guidelines for his cabinet. The decision to complete the Darlington Nuclear power station at a cost of C$4 billion provoked relatively little criticism, unlike a decision to give the retiring clerk of the provincial legislature a settlement worth about $2 million, which occasioned outcries from all sides.

Treasurer Nixon, in his May budget, foresaw a growth rate of 4.2% and a drop in unemployment to 6.9%. With the economy buoyant, there were no tax increases other than a 4¢ hike on a pack of cigarettes. Spending would be up 7.4% to $31.5 billion, with expected income of $29.96 billion and a deficit of $1.54 billion, a reduction from 1985. A total of $850 million was promised for additional hospital construction over an unspecified period.

The Economy. Economic news continued to be good, particularly from the auto industry which unveiled expansion plans. In February, American Motors announced a new plant to build Renault cars, and in March, General Motors indicated it planned a new $2 billion plant in Oshawa. Using new technology based on the Japanese model for car construction, this plant would be the second largest in North America. In August, GM and Suzuki announced a $500 million plant for Ingersoll (aided by provincial funds) to produce 200,000 cars a year.

PETER J. KING
Carlton University

ONTARIO · Information Highlights

Area: 412,580 sq mi (1 068 580 km²).
Population (Jan. 1986 est.): 9,139,800.
Chief Cities (1981 census): Toronto, the provincial capital, 599,217; Ottawa, the federal capital, 295,163; North York, 559,521; Mississauga, 315,056; Hamilton, 306,434; London, 254,280.
Government (1986): *Chief Officers*—lt. gov., Lincoln Alexander; premier, David Peterson (Liberal). *Legislature*—Legislative Assembly, 125 members.
Provincial Finances (1986–87 fiscal year budget): *Revenues,* $29,960,000,000; *expenditures,* $31,500,000,000.
Personal Income (average weekly earnings, May 1986): $439.29.
Labor Force (July 1986, seasonally adjusted: *Employed* workers, 15 years of age and over, 4,872,000; *Unemployed,* 349,000 (7.2%).
Education (1986–87): *Enrollment*—elementary and secondary schools, 1,852,300 pupils; postsecondary—universities, 183,200; community colleges, 91,900.
(All monetary figures are in Canadian dollars).

OREGON

During 1986 the Oregon economy began a modest recovery from the recession of recent years.

Economy. Unemployment declined; jobs in the service sector grew by 4% and were expected to maintain that growth through 1987. Commercial salmon fishermen enjoyed the

Nine climbers were killed on Oregon's Mt. Hood after being caught in a mid-May snowstorm. Rescue workers, left, found two other climbers still alive in an ice cave. Both survived.

AP/Wide World

largest catches of recent years. The manufacturing sector made little progress, however, and more layoffs were expected in the high-tech area as the worldwide slump in that industry continued. The Frederick and Nelson department store chain laid off 240 when stores in Portland and Salem were closed. Wood products mill closures slowed; several mills, closed in previous years, reopened under new ownership, but offered appreciably lower hourly wages.

Education. The state government furnishes only about one third of the costs of local schools; the balance must come from local property taxes. Many school district tax bases are seriously antiquated, and in 1986 there appeared to be a growing resentment that state mandated educational programs must be financed by the local communities. Eleven of 23 school levees appearing on November ballots were rejected. Only nine of 56 requests for modern tax bases were passed. It was likely that a number of school districts would run out of operating funds in early 1987, forcing the closure of schools. Enrollment in state colleges and universities showed modest increases for the third consecutive year.

Elections. Oregon's congressional delegation was little changed by the November elections. All incumbents seeking reelection were successful. Peter DeFazio, Democrat, and former aide to Congressman Jim Weaver, won the seat vacated by Weaver in the fourth district. Winning reelection were Republicans Denny Smith and Robert Smith and Democrats Les AuCoin and Ron Wyden. Sen. Bob Packwood, Republican, won reelection, but both he and Sen. Mark Hatfield will be stripped of the influential committee chairmanships they held because of the Senate's shift to a Democratic majority.

Former Portland mayor and secretary of transportation in the Carter administration Neil Goldschmidt won the race for governor against Republican Norma Paulus. The Democrats retained majorities in both houses of the Oregon legislature. A total of 16 measures, 12 referred

by initiative, appeared on the ballots. Among the losers were measures that sought to limit property taxes, institute a sales tax, increase the state income tax, legalize the cultivation and possession of marijuana for personal use, stop state funding of abortions, and close the state's only nuclear power plant. Winning were measures that would require the secretary of state to live in Salem, require voters to have registered at least 20 days prior to an election, and put in place a crime victims' "Bill of Rights."

Other. In July, eight months after Indian Guru Bhagwan Shree Rajneesh closed down his controversial Oregon commune and returned to India, his former secretary, Ma Anand Sheela, and two codefendants pleaded guilty to eight federal and state charges including a conspiracy to poison the people of The Dalles, a town near the commune. Sheela was sentenced to 20 years in prison and fined $400,000. By late 1986 the commune, Rancho Rajneesh, was abandoned and for sale, and the village of Rajneesh Puram had been renamed Antelope.

L. CARL AND JOANN BRANDHORST
Western Oregon State College

OREGON • Information Highlights

Area: 97,073 sq mi (251 419 km²).
Population (1985 est.): 2,687,000.
Chief Cities (July 1, 1984 est.): Salem, the capital (1980 census), 89,233; Portland, 365,861; Eugene, 101,602.
Government (1986): *Chief Officers*—governor, Victor Atiyeh (R); secretary of state, Barbara Roberts (D); *Legislative Assembly*—Senate, 30 members; House of Representatives, 60 members.
State Finances (fiscal year 1985): *Revenue,* $5,337,000,000; *expenditure,* $4,812,000,000.
Personal Income (1985): $33,921,000,000, per capita, $12,622.
Labor Force (June 1986): *Civilian labor force,* 1,359,100; *unemployed,* 121,400 (8.9% of total force).
Education: *Enrollment* (fall 1984)—public elementary schools, 305,628; public secondary, 141,256; colleges and universities, 137,967. *Public school expenditures* (1983–84), $1,561,000,000 ($3,771 per pupil).

OTTAWA

Ottawa, the Canadian capital, failed to share the prosperity enjoyed by the rest of the province of Ontario in 1986. Hard hit by the federal hiring freeze, with public workers declared in surplus and part-time and contract work curtailed, Ottawa saw housing starts and real-estate sales down, office construction tailed off, and a vacancy rate of more than 8%. Hotel, service, and computer-support industries were especially vulnerable. Welfare recipients increased by 14% over 1985, the second highest rate in the province. And the situation was expected to continue. Mayor Jim Durrell said the city cannot survive as just a government town and must look to other sources of employment, especially the tourist industry.

A spill of coal-tar polluting the Rideau River became the source of an acrimonious dispute between the national capital region and the province. The spill resulted from excavations for a transit station being built by the region on a former gasworks site. At issue was who was responsible for the spill and who would pay for its cleanup. At one point, Ministry of the Environment officials raided the regional government offices and seized documents.

Environmental issues were also a major source of debate within the city itself. Strong opposition developed to federal government plans to locate the new U.S. embassy, as part of a new "embassy row", on the Mile Circle, an area of parkland in an exclusive Ottawa neighborhood. Area residents were upset by the loss of the open space and fearful of terrorist attacks. In another matter, public opposition was successful in forcing the city council to reverse a decision to allow a high-rise development in the city's old Byward Market area.

A large part of the downtown area was without electricity for three days in August, following a fire in a distribution substation. Government offices had to close, and stores and hotels were unable to function. Losses were estimated in the millions of dollars.

Winterlude, the city's February carnival, was particularly successful in 1986. With his new emphasis on tourism, Mayor Durrell hoped to attract the Commonwealth Games in 1994.

PETER J. KING, *Carleton University*

PAKISTAN

Pakistan's fledgling civilian government survived major political challenges in 1986. The economy showed strong growth, but international pressures continued to cause concern.

Politics. With the lifting of martial law on Dec. 30, 1985, by President and Army Chief of Staff Mohammad Zia ul-Haq, Pakistan's military courts were disbanded, and constitutional civil-rights provisions were restored. During the months that followed, Prime Minister Mohammad Khan Junejo strengthened his political position by reestablishing legal political parties, beginning with his own Pakistan Muslim League (PML). He and his party tightened their grip at both the provincial and national levels by forcing the resignation of Sind assembly speaker Abdullah Hussain Haroon in April and that of National Assembly speaker Syed Fakhar Imam in May. Both were ousted for permitting discussion of motions that questioned PML actions.

The major challenge to the government came from Benazir Bhutto, the 33-year-old leader of the Pakistan People's Party (PPP), who was greeted by crowds of cheering supporters when she returned to Pakistan from exile on April 10. The daughter of former Prime Minister Zulfikar Ali Bhutto, whom Zia overthrew in 1977 and had executed in 1979, she soon launched a nonviolent movement to force the resignations of Zia and Junejo and the holding of new parliamentary elections. Following antigovernment demonstrations on July 5, the ninth anniversary of the military takeover, a third phase of protest was scheduled for Pakistan's Independence Day, August 14. Junejo imposed a ban on political rallies and arrested many opposition leaders, including Bhutto, in a pre-Independence Day sweep. Violent protests erupted, particularly in Sind. After police fired on demonstrators, killing several, the protests quickly collapsed. On September 8, Bhutto was released.

Bhutto's public prominence, her reluctance to share leadership, and her failure to mount sustained, effective opposition, all contributed to growing alienation and fragmentation within her own PPP and the 11-party Movement for the Restoration of Democracy (MRD)—of which the PPP is a member. Disaffected PPP members formed a new party, the National People's Party. Another new party, the Awami National Party (ANP), was created by the merger of four leftist components of the MRD.

The hijacking of a U.S. jetliner in Karachi on September 5 ended in a violent bloodbath. The surviving hijackers were captured by Pakistani commandos after the shooting ended, but Pakistan was harshly criticized for its handling of the affair.

A major domestic crisis broke out in mid-December, when ethnic violence between Pathans and Muhajirs erupted in Karachi. At least 150 persons were killed and hundreds more injured in two days of fighting. In the wake of the outburst, which included widespread arson and looting, the Pakistani cabinet resigned on December 20. The government had been strongly criticized for failing to halt the increase in ethnic tension. Prime Minister Junejo, who remained in office, announced that he would name a new government shortly.

Pakistan's opposition leader Benazir Bhutto is escorted by her lawyer as she is released from prison. The 33-year-old daughter of the former Prime Minister Zulfikar Ali Bhutto spent nearly one month in jail for defying a government ban against political rallies.

AP/Wide World

The Economy. Pakistan continues to approach the threshold which separates poor from middle-income countries. The economy maintained the strong performance it has enjoyed for the past decade. The gross domestic product (GDP) grew by 7.5%, well above the expected 6.5%. Agriculture was up by 6.5%, manufacturing by 8.2%, and exports by 21%. Cotton production rose from 5.9 million bales to a record 7.1 million bales, and the wheat harvest increased by more than 15%. Inflation was held to 5.2%, the lowest rate in more than a decade. Worker remittances, which increased about 5% to $2.5 billion, were expected to decline in the coming year because of reduced demand for foreign workers in the oil-rich nations of the Persian Gulf. External debt and the balance-of-payments deficit rose in 1986.

Government expenditures on education, health, and rural development increased sharply but remained among the lowest in the developing world. The government continued to emphasize private sector development, including the privatization of six previously nationalized companies. The public sector share of industrial investment was reduced.

Foreign Affairs. Tensions between Pakistan and neighboring Afghanistan and India continued. Despite a symbolic Soviet withdrawal of 8,000 troops from Afghanistan, a negotiated settlement of the Afghan conflict remained stymied by disagreement between Pakistan and the USSR over the timetable for the withdrawal of the approximately 100,000 Soviet soldiers remaining in Afghanistan. Following repeated border violations and bombing of Afghan refugee settlements in Pakistan, Pakistani fighters shot down an Afghan aircraft in May.

Talks with India on the disputed Siachen Glacier in Kashmir failed to reach any conclusive agreement. But in late December the two nations agreed to greater coordination of border security forces to stop Sikh extremists from using Pakistani territory to launch attacks on India.

Prime Minister Junejo visited Turkey, West Germany, and the United States in July. Pakistan and the United States reached agreement on a $4.02-billion, six-year extension of their current military and economic assistance program, scheduled to end in October 1987.

Pakistan continued to seek, with at least some modest success in 1986, security despite major threats on its borders, autonomy despite considerable dependence upon external assistance, and political stability despite enduring internal divisions and animosities.

WILLIAM L. RICHTER, *Kansas State University*

PAKISTAN • Information Highlights

Official Name: Islamic Republic of Pakistan.
Location: South Asia.
Area: 310,403 sq mi (803 943 km²).
Population (mid-1986 est.): 101,900,000.
Chief Cities (1981 census): Islamabad, the capital, 201,000; Karachi, 5,103,000.
Government: *Head of state,* Mohammed Zia ul-Haq, president (took power July 5, 1977). *Head of government,* Mohammed Khan Junejo, prime minister (installed April 10, 1985). *Legislature*—Parliament: Senate and National Assembly.
Monetary Unit: Rupee (17.10 rupees equal U.S.$1, Oct. 19, 1986).
Gross National Product (1985 est. U.S.$): $31,-000,000,000.
Economic Index (1984): *Consumer Prices* (1980 = 100), all items, 113.2; food, 113.3.
Foreign Trade (1985 U.S.$): *Imports,* $5,892,000,000; *exports,* $2,719,000,000.

419

PARAGUAY

In August 1986, Gen. Alfredo Stroessner, 74, ended speculation over his continuation in the presidency of Paraguay beyond 1988, announcing that he would seek an eighth consecutive term. Opposition to the dictatorship was more open and widespread in 1986 than at any other time during Stroessner's prolonged rule.

Unrest. Encouraged by the downfall of military dictators elsewhere, Stroessner's opponents within the ruling Colorado Party had made known their preference for a civilian replacement. A rash of protests began early in the year. Acuerdo Nacional (AN), an opposition coalition of four parties, held a demonstration in Asunción on February 14, attended by 15,000 supporters who demanded an end to the state of siege under which General Stroessner had ruled since 1954. AN also called for a constituent assembly, signalized the plight of political prisoners, and condemned censorship.

Other demonstrations were staged by the Authentic Radical Liberal Party (PLRA), physicians and hospital staff workers, university students, priests, nuns, and laborers. To these manifestations of opposition, officials responded with tear gas, truncheons, cattle prods, and fire hoses. Pro-government demonstrations were organized, and paramilitary forces twice attacked the offices of Radio Nandutí, a station that aired interviews with prominent leaders.

In a belated democratic overture the Stroessner government allowed some prominent exiles to return: among them were the famed novelist, Augusto Roa Bastos, and Luis Resck, the founder of the Christian Democratic Party.

Economy. The government's reluctant decision to devalue the guaraní in August represented a step toward economic recovery. Argentina had threatened to halt construction of the binational Yacyretá hydroelectric project if Paraguay failed to devalue.

Soybean and cotton exports fell to $102 million between January and June. They had reached $190 million the previous year. Losses in export revenues were attributed to weather conditions as well as declining world prices. Development-minded industrialists feared that debt service ($270 million) would exceed export income in 1986. An economic strategy was initiated in January for reducing dips in revenue caused by persistent contraband activity. The strategy included a liberalization of the law on investments.

A billion-dollar scandal at the central bank was uncovered in December 1985, resulting in the arrest of 14 businessmen, and 15 bank officials, including the bank president, César Romero Acosta. They were accused of illegally exporting millions of dollars.

Foreign Relations. At the end of 1985, Clyde Taylor, a career diplomat, assumed the post of U.S. ambassador to the Asunción regime. His agenda included support for a dialogue between the government and its opponents, and extended to administrative corruption and contraband activity. Taylor's meetings in January with opposition forces were criticized by members of the cabinet, and daily attacks on his activities, which were termed interference in Paraguayan internal affairs, appeared in the state-controlled media.

LARRY L. PIPPIN
University of the Pacific

PENNSYLVANIA

The election so dominated the political agenda that 1986 seemed in other respects a quiet year in Pennsylvania.

Election. The battle to succeed Republican Gov. Richard L. Thornburgh, prohibited from seeking a third term by the state's constitution, features two of Pennsylvania's most distinguished political names from the 1960s and 1970s: Scranton and Casey. Lt. Gov. William W. Scranton III, son of a former governor, opposed former Democratic state auditor Robert P. Casey. Negative advertising marked the campaign, including a Scranton advertisement accusing Casey of malfeasance in public office, and a Casey ad accusing Scranton of following transcendental meditation guru Maharishi Mahesh Yogi. In a victory credited to the impact of the "guru ad" late in the campaign, Casey captured the governorship with 51% of the vote.

Perhaps the biggest political upset of the year was the victory of Democratic Congressman Bob Edgar over state auditor Don Bailey for the Democratic nomination to run against moderate incumbent Republican Sen. Arlen Specter. Edgar was supported by a coalition of environmental and nuclear-weapons-freeze proponents. In the general election Specter easily beat back Edgar with 57% of the vote. Earlier, in spite of much encouragement from conservative Republicans, Governor Thorn-

Some 15,000 municipal workers, including garbage collectors, in Philadelphia went on strike July 1. They heeded a court back-to-work order July 22, but only after Mayor Wilson Goode threatened to fire them. The new two-year contract, calling for a 10% pay raise, was seen as a political victory for the mayor.

AP/Wide World

burgh announced that he would not challenge Specter for the Republican nomination.

In the battles for Congress and the state legislature, incumbents did extraordinarily well. Although every incumbent running for Congress won, the Republicans did manage to pick up the seat vacated by Congressman Edgar to raise their total to 11 of the 23-member delegation in Washington. The Democrats narrowed the Republicans' control of the state Senate to a 26–24 margin by winning the one race in which an incumbent lost. Guy M. Kratzer, who was originally elected as a Republican but left the caucus after a drunk-driving conviction, lost his reelection bid as an independent. He finished third behind the major party nominees. In the races for the state House of Representatives, the Democrats maintained their narrow control by a 103–100 margin. The absence of major new campaign themes made the 1986 elections an affirmation of the status quo.

Labor. The October state unemployment percentage dropped to 6.4%, the lowest since July 1979.

Two strikes received major attention. In Philadelphia, blue-collar workers of the American Federation of State, County, and Municipal Employees Union, which includes garbage collectors, struck July 1 to July 22. A back-to-work order was issued because of the "clear and present danger to health and safety." Two days after workers voted to end the strike, the city and the union agreed on a 10% salary increase over two years.

The second major strike was between the United Steelworkers Union and USX Corporation. On the expiration deadline of the old contract, union workers voted to extend the old contract and to continue labor negotiations. The company refused. The United Steelworkers claimed the work stoppage was a lockout, not a strike. On August 21 the Department of Labor and Industry sided with the union,

which entitled the 6,200 workers to unemployment benefits averaging $192 per week.

Law. The U.S. Supreme Court struck down a Pennsylvania abortion law on grounds that it was an unconstitutional restraint against abortion. The 5–4 ruling voided the law, which required among other things that a doctor provide a woman with information before performing an abortion—including probable characteristics of the fetus at that stage and a list of social services available for care of a baby.

MOVE Aftermath. In 1986 the follow-up story to the MOVE siege in Philadelphia continued to make headlines. A commission appointed by Mayor W. Wilson Goode (D) concluded that Goode had been "grossly negligent" in failing to stop the firebombing and fatal police showdown with the radical MOVE members on May 12, 1985. The panel blamed the resulting 11 deaths on the city's fire commissioner William C. Richmond and former police commissioner Gregore J. Sambor, con-

---

PENNSYLVANIA • Information Highlights

Area: 45,308 sq mi (117 348 km²).
Population (1985 est.): 11,853,000.
Chief Cities (July 1, 1984 est.): Harrisburg, the capital (1980 census), 53,264; Philadelphia, 1,646,713; Pittsburgh, 402,583; Erie, 117,461.; Allentown, 103,899.
Government (1986): *Chief Officers*—governor, Richard L. Thornburgh (R); lt. gov., William W. Scranton III. *Legislature*—Senate, 50 members; House of Representatives, 203 members.
State Finances (fiscal year 1985): *Revenue,* $20,337,000,000; *expenditure,* $18,067,000,000.
Personal Income (1985): $159,276,000,000; per capita, $13,437.
Labor Force (June 1986): *Civilian labor force,* 5,676,400; *unemployed;* 416,600 (7.3% of total force).
Education: *Enrollment* (fall 1984)—public elementary schools, 1,102,776; public secondary, 599,104; colleges and universities, 533,198. *Public school expenditures* (1983–84), $5,875,000,000 ($3,725 per pupil).

cluding that the explosives used were "excessive and life-threatening." Blame also fell on the adult MOVE members.

ROBERT O'CONNOR
The Pennsylvania State University

PERU

Despite public shock over the killing of hundreds of jailed leftists in June prison uprisings, unsuccessful efforts to contain the guerrilla movement, and an improving but still weak economy, President Alan García Pérez enjoyed strong popular support during 1986.

Prison Assaults. Troops of the Republican Guard launched military assaults June 18–20 on three prisons—Lurigancho, El Frontón, and Santa Barbara—where inmates belonging to the Sendero Luminoso (Shining Path) rebel group were staging simultaneous mutinies. Authorities put the death toll at 156, but other sources estimated casualties in excess of 400. President García initially defended the use of force to restore order, but he called for an investigation after evidence became public that at least 100 prisoners were executed after surrendering. The head of the Republican Guard was dismissed, and 100 guardsmen were put under barracks arrest. The uprisings were believed to have been organized to taint the image of García on the eve of the Congress of the Socialist International, held in Lima in June.

Guerrillas and the Government. The García regime was unable to make much headway against terrorist attacks by the Shining Path or the urban-based Tupac Amarú (MRTA), which announced the end of a one-year truce in early August by seizing two radio stations in Cuzco. By mid-1986 more than 7,000 peasants, rebels, security forces, and government officials had been killed since the Shining Path began its revolt in 1980. In February, after a spate of terrorist bombings, the regime declared a state of emergency in Lima and elsewhere. The emergency was extended in late March and early June, but the violence continued. The tourist industry suffered a blow when trains carrying tourists to the Incan ruins at Machu Picchu were bombed.

In an effort to improve security against terrorist violence and kidnappings, as well as to reduce corruption linked to the cocaine trade, national police forces were reorganized into 12 regional groups in August. In a landmark human-rights case the previous month, a court sentenced 11 police officers to prison for the 1983 murder of 34 Indian peasants.

According to a popularity poll in August, President García enjoyed a 76% approval rating. He appeared to win a vote of confidence in November municipal elections, as his left-of-center American Popular Revolutionary Alliance scored a solid victory.

Economy. The government's major economic achievement was to reduce inflation from more than 180% the previous year to approximately 60% in 1986. Economic growth, meanwhile, was expected to reach 6.5%, the highest since 1974. On July 28, the first anniversary of his inauguration, President García announced several measures to achieve stability and continued growth. Foreign companies were not allowed to send dividends, profits, royalties, or debt payments abroad for two years. And the Peruvian government would stick to its policy of paying no more than 10% of its export earnings toward its foreign debt of $13.8 billion. The latter strategy, however, led the International Monetary Fund (IMF) in August to declare Peru ineligible for new credits. And declining prices for oil, silver, and zinc caused a drop in export income.

Foreign Affairs. During visits to Argentina, Uruguay, and Costa Rica, President García engaged in intensive talks on the Latin American debt problem and peace in Central America. While in Buenos Aires in March, García surprised his hosts by publicly declaring that Peru would break relations with any foreign power that invaded Nicaragua.

At the Eighth Nonaligned Summit in Harare, Zimbabwe, in September, President García sought support for Peru's debt position and promoted Lima as the site for the 1989 summit, but he returned home empty-handed.

Natural Disasters. An estimated 350,000 people in southeastern Peru were left homeless in January and February, when Lake Titicaca rose from heavy rains and caused the nation's worst flooding in this century. Then in early April, at least 16 persons were killed, 170 persons injured, and 2,000 homes destroyed in an earthquake that hit Cuzco and 30 other towns in the Inca Valley.

NEALE J. PEARSON, *Texas Tech University*

PERU • Information Highlights

Official Name: Republic of Peru.
Location: West Coast of South America.
Area: 496,222 sq mi (1 285 216 km²).
Population (mid-1986 est.): 20,200,000.
Chief Cities (mid-1985 est.): Lima, the capital, 5,008,400; Arequipa, 531,829; Callao, 515,200.
Government: *Head of state,* Alan García Pérez, president (took office July 28, 1985). *Head of government,* Luis Juan Alva Castro, prime minister (took office July 1985). *Legislature*—Congress: Senate and Chamber of Deputies.
Monetary Unit: inti (14.50 intis equal U.S.$1, official rate, Oct. 19, 1986).
Gross National Product (1984 U.S.$): $17,000,-000,000.
Economic Index (Lima, 1985): *Consumer Prices* (1980 = 100), all items, 3,371; food, (Aug. 1986), 6,164.3.
Foreign Trade (1985 U.S.$): *Imports,* $1,838,000,000; *exports,* $2,952,000,000.

PHILIPPINES. *See feature article, page 26.*

PHOTOGRAPHY

While product introductions were perhaps less revolutionary than during the previous year, the field of photography was still highly active in 1986. Improvements in equipment—both hardware and software—continued to be made, and there was a growing sophistication in the fine-art and publishing aspects of the medium. Video maintained a strong presence, and interesting new developments occurred in instant-print technology.

Hardware and Software. Following the introduction of the auto-focusing (AF), auto-everything 35mm single-lens reflex (SLR) Minolta Maxxum 7000 in 1985 came new entries into the AF SLR market: the Nikon N2020 and Minolta's own 5000, a simplified version of its big sister. By the end of the year, the Olympus OM77 also became available.

In the meantime, a wave of Maxxum-compatible accessories from independent companies were due to arrive, though among the lens makers—Tamron, Tokina, Cosina, and Kobori—none had as yet been given permission to make Maxxum lenses under its tradename.

Among lenses in general, zooms continued to boom, with new molding techniques and the increasing use of plastics in barrels making for some exciting lenses at lower prices.

On the flash scene, "dedication" continued to be the word of the day as manufacturers created units compatible with the unique auto-focusing systems of specific cameras; they are also smaller yet more powerful than ever before. Semiprofessional handle-mounting flash units were in great evidence, as was a flash unit made especially for the Maxxums.

Among the compact non-SLR 35s, three trends emerged: amphibious and/or waterproof models, wide-angle and telephoto capabilities in the same camera, and the use of lithium batteries for quick flash recycling. And most of the new models had auto-focusing. For the first time in 16 years, the Eastman Kodak Company was selling 35mm cameras in the United States —the VR 35 models K 12 and K 10.

Canon made available its RC-701, the first electronic still camera that uses floppy disks; the body was priced at $2,595, with the SV 11-66mm f/1.2 lens at $695 or the 50-150mm f/2.8 at $795. And camcorders—combining video cameras and recorders—have proliferated. Kodak brought out its Modular Video System (MVS), consisting of a small 8mm camera and equally small recorder, which can be locked together to form a compact camcorder or be used in traditional two-piece fashion, connected by a cable. And Sony's was the first video camera to approach the compactness and ease of use of super-8 movie equipment, with its 4¼x4¼x8½-inch (107x109x215mm), 3-lb (1.4 kg) unit.

In instant-picture photography, Kodak was judged in court to have infringed on seven Polaroid patents and received an injunction to cease production of its instant cameras and films. Polaroid, now the sole maker of instant cameras, came out with a new camera and system—the Spectra. Ten years in development, it represents a radical departure from the SX-70/660 folding camera in that it contains a new lens, picture format, film, viewfinder, and control console. The Spectra camera, a non-SLR auto-focus, auto-exposure unit with override for exposure control, is about the size of a jewelry box when closed and gains only about an inch in height when opened for picture-taking. Its three-element, 125mm lens system, patented under the name Quintec, has ten-zone

Courtesy of the New Orleans Museum of Art

The show "Ilse Bing: Three Decades of Photography," shown at New York's International Center of Photography and in Europe, paid overdue tribute to a gifted German photographer. Her "Self-Portrait With Leica in Mirror," right, was taken in a Paris hotel room in 1931.

focusing from 2 ft (.6 m) to infinity. The film, ten-pack Spectra Instant Print material with the quality of 35mm color, has a speed of approximately ISO 600 and a new rectangular picture format, a larger picture size with white borders, and improved sharpness and color rendition due to new dye materials and coupler technology and thinner emulsion coat.

In darkroom technology, a new crop of chemicals, papers, and processing gear indicate significant interest in both black and white and color. And in the film arena, improvements were made in Kodak and Fuji color negative film, now called Kodacolor VR-G and Fuji Super HR 100 and 400. 3M was selling its updated line of color print and slide films, including the new HR 400, under the Scotch label. And Agfa brought out a new entry, Maxi 24 + 3 (three more shots) color-print film with improved emulsion speed; officially labeled XR100, it is actually an ISO 160 film.

Exhibitions and Publications. There was much activity at the Museum of Modern Art (MoMA) in New York. The contemporary room in the photography collection galleries was entirely reinstalled to emphasize lesser known and younger artists, as well as work never before seen. Special attention also is given to the important developments of recent years—more artists working in color, using larger formats, arranging set-ups, and combining text with images. Springs Industries gave a three-year grant to support MoMA's New Photography Series #2 and awarded $14,000 to preserve the final work of Garry Winogrand, who died in 1984 leaving 2,500 rolls of unprocessed film.

On the West Coast, major shows included "Supreme Instants: The Photography of Edward Weston," which began its two-year tour at the San Francisco Museum of Art. The 250-print exhibition, including some seldom-seen color as well as letters and pages from his diary, marks the 100th anniversary of Weston's birth. Another show in his honor was mounted at the Art Institute of Chicago. In Los Angeles, the J. Paul Getty Museum presented its first photography show ever, focusing on the Victorian portraitist Julia Margaret Cameron. Called "The Whisper of the Muse," the exhibition was selected from among the 225 prints acquired by the museum since 1984. And at the enlarged International Museum of Photography in Rochester, NY, the year's major offering was "This Edifice Is Colossal," a show of 19th-century architectural photography.

Two radically different conceptions of the photography medium were strongly in evidence during the year. The journalistic approach was represented in a major show for Alfred Eisenstaedt, the 88-year-old *Life* magazine photographer whose retrospective at the International Center of Photography (ICP) in New York City marked the 12th anniversary of that institution.

A Laura Gilpin retrospective at the Amon Carter Museum in Fort Worth, TX, honored a long-neglected American photographer. Her "Navajo Covered Wagon," above, was shot in 1934 and is indicative of her photos of Pueblo and Navajo Indians. The show was viewed in five cities.

Also shown there was "Idas y Chaos: Trends in Spanish Photography, 1920–1945," the first major showing of Spanish photography in the United States.

The other "school," emphasizing the medium's fictional possibilities, was represented by an exhibition of Joel-Peter Witkin's surrealistic monster in a hellish world, shown at the Brooklyn (NY) Museum. Reflecting a similarly flexible, often misleading approach, was a show at the Queens (NY) Museum called "The Real Big Picture," including 50 works by 50 photographers.

In photography publishing, noteworthy events included the publication of *Robert Frank, New York to Nova Scotia* and a new edition of Frank's *The Americans*, originally published in 1959. Other noteworthy new books were *Lucien Clergue*, a 35-year retrospective; a biography of Margaret Bourke-White, written by Vicki Goldberg; and Ralph Steiner's upbeat *In Pursuit of Clouds: Images and Metaphors*. Steiner, 87, who worked in the medium for six decades—as an advertising photographer, filmmaker, and photographer of commonplace objects in urban society—died in July. Steiner was regarded as the last of the American modernist photographers.

BARBARA L. LOBRON
Writer, Editor, Photographer

PHYSICS

With the discovery of the W and Z particles in 1983 and the top quark in 1984, the electroweak theory seemed confirmed. The intermediate vector bosons (W^+, W^-, and $Z°$) transfer the force for the weak interaction, just as the photon does for the electromagnetic interaction. There are six quarks, with such unusual properties as fractional electric charge. For example, two up quarks and one down quark form a proton. Following the successful unification of the electromagnetic and weak interactions, new principles are needed to unite the many "fundamental" particles or quarks.

One intriguing approach—called supersymmetry—starts with the observation that the fundamental particles—quarks and leptons (such as electrons and neutrinos)—have half integral spin (fermions) while the particles that transfer the forces (such as photons, Zs and Ws) have integral spin (bosons). Supersymmetry assumes that every particle will have a superpartner, named by adding the prefix s- to the fermion name, or the suffix -ino to the boson name. For example, the superpartner of the spin ½ electron is the spin 0 selectron, while the partner of the spin 1 photon is the spin ½ photino. New experiments planned at the Stanford (CA) Linear Accelerator Center (SLAC), the European Center for Nuclear Research (CERN) in Geneva, and the Fermi National Accelerator (Fermilab) near Chicago should observe the hypothetical sleptons and squarks or determine that the masses are beyond the energy range of any existing accelerator.

Superconducting Super Collider. The standard model for fundamental particles and their interactions leaves many basic properties unexplained. Nonaccelerator studies of neutrino mass or searches for magnetic monopoles and proton decay are extremely valuable. However, the particle physicists claim that the best approach for studying fundamental particles and their interactions is a higher energy accelerator. The proposed Superconducting Super Collider (SSC) would be the biggest and most expensive accelerator ever built. The design calls for two colliding beams of protons of 20 TeV each (1 TeV $= 10^{12}$ eV). Even with superconducting high field magnets the circumference of the beam's orbit would be 62 mi (100 km). The cost has been estimated at more than $5 billion. Requirements include a level site, with uniform geology; mild climate and low vibration; as well as large quantities of fresh water and electric power. More than half of the states are preparing to bid for construction of the SSC. However, its critics fear such a major project would have serious negative impact on the rest of science.

Anomalous Positron Peaks. One of the major goals of heavy ion physics has been to create nuclei far beyond those presently existing in nature. Such superheavy elements would have exotic properties. Quantum electrodynamics predicts that for a nucleus with high enough charge (Z about 173), a vacancy in the lowest electron orbit would be filled by creating an electron-positron pair from the vacuum. Since the electron is captured, the emission of a low energy positron with definite energy would be the signature of this unusual event. No superheavy nucleus has been observed, but scattering of heavy ions is used to simulate those conditions for a very short time.

Such experiments as uranium on uranium are performed at the Gesellschaft für Schwerionenforschung (GSI) in Darmstadt, West Germany. Low energy positrons have been observed for a number of reactions where the total charge (Z of target plus projectile) was more than 180. A narrow, fixed energy positron peak is observed. At first it was thought the predicted spontaneous positron production (sparking of the vacuum) had been observed. The narrowness of the peak implied a relatively long lifetime for the composite system, which could be accounted for by a giant metastable nuclear system. However, the energy of the positron peak should change rapidly with Z, and the observed positron peak has a fixed energy. Several groups pointed out that this could be the signature of a new particle. Whether the positrons signal a new particle, new nuclear structure, or other unexpected effects should be answered by new experiments and analysis.

Quantum Interference in Disordered Metals. A well known but exotic quantum interference effect has been observed in ordinary matter. When an electron beam is split coherently, travels different paths, and then recombines, the beams exhibit interference effects. If the two partial beams pass around a confined magnetic field, then the interference will depend on the strength of the magnetic field, although the magnetic field is zero everywhere the electron travels. The phase of the electron is shifted by the magnetic vector potential. This surprising result was first predicted by Yakir Aharonov and David Bohm in 1959 and has been observed many times.

Recent experiments at IBM have studied the effect in small gold rings surrounding a strong magnetic field. The experiment was performed at low temperatures, but the system was not superconducting. Striking oscillations in the magnetoresistance of the ring were observed, confirming the existence of the Aharonov-Bohm effect in ordinary gold. The ring had a typical diameter of 0.5 microns, with a width of the metal about one tenth the diameter. Although small, these dimensions are comparable to microelectronic device sizes. Therefore this quantum interference effect may have major technological applications.

GARY MITCHELL
North Carolina State University

On June 29, 1986, President and First Secretary Gen. Wojciech Jaruzelski opened the 10th Congress of the ruling Polish United Workers Party (PZPR) with a four-hour address. The general's overall position was strengthened as a result of the five-day congress.

AP/Wide World

POLAND

The year in Poland was marked by changes in the party and government, continuing economic difficulties, and, paradoxically, the arrest of several key figures in the dissident movement, and an amnesty for political prisoners.

Party and Government. The ruling Polish United Workers Party (PZPR) underwent some major personnel and institutional changes during the year. The party held its 10th Congress, its first since July 1981, in Warsaw from June 29 to July 3. Some 1,700 delegates and guests, including Soviet General Secretary Mikhail Gorbachev, attended the proceedings. President and First Secretary Gen. Wojciech Jaruzelski opened the congress with a four-hour keynote address in which he took credit for increasing domestic stability and "progressing decomposition and social isolation of anti-state groups," presumably a reference to Solidarity. Jaruzelski promised a sweeping amnesty for political prisoners (and common criminals) and voiced an interest in improving relations with Poland's Roman Catholic Church. He warned, however, that "we shall expect and demand respect for the constitution and the laws." The party leaders also appealed for economic austerity and greater efficiency in Polish industrial enterprises. Among the remedies he proposed were cutbacks in wages, in subsidies to various social programs, and in the size of the state bureaucracy.

Most of the Politburo and Central Committee members who had been elected during the reformist period of 1981, the heyday of Solidarity, were dropped. The policy-making Politburo was expanded from 13 to 15 members, with seven members dismissed and nine added. New members included such apparent Jaruzelski loyalists as Gen. Czeslaw Kiszczak, who became minister of internal affairs; Gen. Florian Siwicki, minister of defense; Gen. Jozef Baryla, party ideologist; Marian Orzechowski,

minister of foreign affairs; and Alfred Miodowicz, head of the legally recognized trade unions. The Central Committee of the party was expanded from 214 to 230 members, with only 57 holdovers from the 1981 body. Among those ousted were Stanislaw Kania, whom Jaruzelski had replaced as party leader in 1981, and Stefan Olszowski, a former minister of foreign affairs and an alleged rival of Jaruzelski.

The reformist rules adopted in 1981, which had allowed the party congress to choose the Politburo and the Secretariat in addition to the Central Committee, now were repealed. The choices henceforth would be made by the Central Committee on the customary "recommendation" of the party leader. The PZPR thus returned to its previous, Soviet style of internal organization.

One of the highlights of the congress was the June 30 speech by Gorbachev, who lavished praise on Jaruzelski for his "outstanding leadership." Gorbachev also intimated that the Soviet Union had been prepared to intervene in Poland in 1981 if the party's rule had been further endangered by the opposition.

Information published in official organs during April indicated that the PZPR was facing serious difficulty in attracting Polish youth to the cause of Communism. Less than 8% (160,000) of the party's 2.1 million members were less than 30 years old.

Economy. At the beginning of 1986, according to data published by Western banking sources, Poland, with a $30 billion debt, ranked seventh among the world's principal debtor nations.

In mid-March the regime announced a new round of price increases on food stuffs and liquor, with some items going up by as much as 11%. Inflation early in the year was reported to be about 15% above 1985 levels. The March price increases brought scattered protest demonstrations, and the smuggling of consumer goods from the West remained fairly widespread.

Poland's debt problems led to cutbacks in purchases of vital industrial products from abroad. This, in turn, led to increased shortages, longer consumer lines, hoarding, and black-marketeering. Solidarity sources claimed the cost of living had risen about 90% in the last four years and demanded sharp increases for Poland's lowest paid workers. Even the official union federation (OPZZ) advocated a doubling of the lowest wages at its November congress in Warsaw.

Regime vs. Solidarity. In late January the government announced that it would prosecute Lech Walesa, the founder of Solidarity, on charges of slandering state officials. Walesa had questioned publicly the government's figures on voter turnout in the June 1985 parliamentary elections. The United States condemned the decision to prosecute Walesa. Somewhat surprisingly the state prosecutor dropped the charges in mid-February, after Walesa declared in court that he "had not intended to slander anybody." In early March, however, five other dissidents were put on trial for alleged attempts to defame the regime and incite public unrest. And in late May the government announced that it would try a recently captured Solidarity activist, Czeslaw Bielecki, for attempting to overthrow the regime.

Then on May 31, Polish police captured fugitive Solidarity leader Zbigniew Bujak, the most wanted political dissident in Poland since the imposition of martial law in 1981. A government spokesman charged that Bujak had connections to the U.S.-supported Radio Free Europe in Munich, West Germany. Other official spokesmen linked Bujak to Western intelligence organizations. The announcement of the capture led to widespread demonstrations and altercations with police throughout Poland. Walesa condemned the regime for its "lawlessness" and called on Solidarity supporters to continue their struggle. In mid-June, Anna Walentynowicz, sometimes called the "first lady of Solidarity," was arrested for "causing public unrest." Her firing as a crane operator in August 1980 at the Gdansk shipyard had led to the strike which sparked the establishment of Solidarity.

Amnesty. The party began to implement its amnesty program soon after the July congress. (The announcement of the amnesty had been accompanied by a stern warning that violators of the law would be arrested again.) In early September the regime announced that 100 political prisoners had been released since July. Two weeks later the government claimed to have "emptied its jails." Among those released were such prominent oppositionists as Wladyslaw Frasyniuk, Henryk Wujec, and Leszek Moczulski; Bujak was released after only four months of detainment. By the expiration of the amnesty on September 15, a total of 225 political prisoners was said to have been let go,

along with some 20,000 common criminals out of a total prison population of about 100,000.

Meanwhile, in late August, Lech Walesa called for dialogue between the government and opposition on ways to solve Poland's economic, social, and political problems. The following month he formed an 11-member Solidarity group in Gdansk to seek talks with the government. Bujak organized a similar group in Warsaw, claiming that henceforth the union leadership would operate in the open. Walesa indicated that Solidarity would defy the ban on its activities, arguing that they were sanctioned by the Polish Constitution; Solidarity's cause was supported by the Roman Catholic bishops. In October, Walesa was summoned to defend his actions and warned of "legal consequences" if he persisted.

Anniversaries. Nationwide observances were held on August 31 to mark the sixth anniversary of the founding of Solidarity. The most significant gathering occurred in Warsaw, where more than 10,000 persons attended an outdoor Mass. Police patrols, helicopters, and water cannons were in evidence in most of the larger cities, and substantial numbers of people were detained.

October 19 marked the second anniversary of the murder by secret police of Father Jerzy Popieluszko, a Catholic priest who had supported Solidarity. Walesa declared Popieluszko's death "a permanent element in the history of the Christian Polish nation." The government, on the other hand, observed the day by reducing the jail terms of two of the three policemen who had been convicted of the murder.

Chernobyl. The accident at the Chernobyl nuclear power plant in the Soviet Ukraine in late April (*see* special report, page 218) took place a mere 260 mi (420 km) from Poland's eastern border and had untold economic and health effects. With radiation in milk exceeding emergency levels, the government banned the

---

POLAND • Information Highlights

Official Name: Polish People's Republic.
Location: Eastern Europe.
Area: 120,700 sq mi (312 612 km²).
Population (mid-1986 est.): 37,500,000.
Chief Cities (Dec. 31, 1984): Warsaw, the capital, 1,649,000; Lodz, 849,400; Cracow, 740,300.
Government: *Head of state,* Gen. Wojciech Jaruzelski, chairman of the Council of National Defense and chairman of the Council of State (took office Nov. 6, 1985) and first secretary of the Polish United Workers' Party (took office Oct. 1981). *Head of government,* Zbigniew Messner, chairman of the Council of Ministers (took office Nov. 6, 1985). *Legislature* (unicameral)—Sejm.
Monetary Unit: Zloty (163.000 zlotys equal U.S.$1, June 1986).
Gross National Product (1984, 1984 U.S.$): $228,500,000,000.
Economic Indexes (1985): *Consumer Prices* (1980 = 100), all items, 393.4; food, 449.7. *Industrial Production* (1980 = 100), 99.
Foreign Trade (1985 U.S.$): *Imports,* $10,761,- 000,000; *exports,* $11,447,000,000.

sale of milk from grass-fed cows and distributed powdered milk for consumption by children under age three. It also restricted the sale of fresh vegetables and required all children to take doses of iodine to prevent thyroid cancer. According to unofficial reports, however, radiation levels were higher, lasted longer, and contaminated a greater variety of consumables than the government was willing to admit.

Church-State Relations. The Polish Catholic Church, led by Josef Cardinal Glemp, continued to exert pressure on the regime to liberalize its policy toward political dissidents and encouraged Walesa in his efforts to obtain legal status for Solidarity. In September the church abandoned its aid foundation for farmers, which had been financed by donations from abroad. According to church sources, the regime had been trying to control the funds.

The regime did show signs of a conciliatory attitude toward the church. At the party congress Jaruzelski referred to Pope John Paul II as a "supporter of world peace." And it did sound out the opposition on a proposal to allow moderate Catholic elements limited membership on local government councils.

Foreign Affairs. In mid-February, General Jaruzelski attended and addressed the 27th Congress of the Soviet Communist Party in Moscow, where he accused "Western imperialists" of trying to "break up the Polish state."

Some help for Poland's foreign debt problem came in the spring. On May 31, after a six-year campaign by Warsaw officials, the International Monetary Fund voted to admit Poland as a member. On June 9, Great Britain agreed to extend $31 million in credit, the first British loan to Poland since 1981. And on June 12, Western creditor banks agreed to a rescheduling of about $2 billion in Polish loan payments due in 1986 and 1987.

In late September, General Jaruzelski visited China for talks with Deng Xiaoping. His visit was widely interpreted as a resumption of relations between the Communist parties of the two countries, which had been severed since the 1960s when Poland sided with Moscow in the Sino-Soviet split.

ALEXANDER J. GROTH
University of California, Davis

POLAR RESEARCH

Antarctic. During the Antarctic summer from September 1985 to February 1986, 360 U.S. researchers conducted 87 scientific projects, and a satellite link was established between the United States and the McMurdo and South Pole stations.

Research conducted along the Transantarctic Mountains near the 99-mi (160-km) Beardmore Glacier suggests that geologists may have to revise current theories that Antarctica's ice sheets have remained in place over the past 15 million years. Discoveries of plant and animal fossils now suggest that an extensive forest flourished only about 400 mi (640 km) from the South Pole as recently as 3 million years ago. Microscopic fossils further suggest that open water existed across the continent as recently as 2.5 million years ago, as does the discovery by an Australian team of a fossilized dolphin—the only vertebrate fossil found in Antarctica less than 35 million years old. In the Transantarctic Mountains, U.S. scientists also found fossils, up to 225 million years old, of four unknown amphibian and reptile species, and an Argentinian team working on James Ross Island found the fossil remains of a 70-million-year-old dinosaur, a new plant-eating species.

In June, U.S. and British workers announced that the ozone layer over Antarctica had decreased by 40% since 1975. Ozone, a form of oxygen, is concentrated in a layer about 15 mi (24 km) above the earth and is essential to life because it screens out most of the sun's harmful ultraviolet radiation. The depletion process, not yet understood, may be part of a natural cycle, but it has aroused concern because of suggestions that it may be linked to human activities such as the release of chlorofluorocarbons into the atmosphere. (*See* ENVIRONMENT.)

In August biologists studying Antarctic sea-ice algae and bacteria announced the isolation of an enzyme that acts on molecules such as the nucleic acid DNA. Because it is 50 times more potent in the reshaping of such molecules than are commonly used enzymes, it may become of great importance in genetic engineering. Researchers also found an "antifreeze" protein in tissues of Antarctic cod that helps explain how such animals can live in freezing waters.

Biologists working near the Antarctic Peninsula found that the crustaceans called krill—an essential part of the ocean food chain—are not nearly as plentiful and prolific as had been thought.

The Soviet Union's Dryzhnaya 1 research station and two other unoccupied stations were lost during their unoccupied period during 1986 when a chunk of ice about 120-mi (190-km) long broke off from the Filchner Ice Shelf along the Weddell Sea.

Arctic. In 1986 the Arctic research projects supported by the National Science Foundation included 28 in geology, glaciology, and biology.

In May, Alaska's Hubbard Glacier advanced so rapidly that it blocked Russell Fiord, creating a lake that rose to 83 ft (25 m) above sea level. Scientists rushed to save marine mammals trapped in the lake, but in October the ice dam broke and released the animals.

WINIFRED REUNING
National Science Foundation

Mario Soares, a former Socialist prime minister, was elected Portugal's first civilian president in 60 years. Soares inherited an improving economy and the challenges of Portugal's new membership in the European Community.

AP/Wide World

PORTUGAL

Portugal's January 1 entry into the European Community (EC) linked the country's destiny to the rest of Europe and provided an opportunity to spur an economy that had floundered in the early 1980s.

Politics and Government. No sooner had Prime Minister Aníbal Cavaco Silva, a Social Democrat, settled into office in November 1985 than five candidates launched presidential bids. In the initial balloting on January 26, conservative Diogo Freitas do Amaral received 46.30% of the vote. The leader among his three leftist rivals (the Communist candidate withdrew at the last minute) was former Socialist Prime Minister Mário Soares (25.44%), who was strongly opposed by both outgoing President Antonio Ramalho Eanes and Communist leader Alvaro Cunhal. To the amazement of many observers, Soares received 51% of the vote in the February 16 runoff. On March 9 he became Portugal's first civilian president since 1926, thanks to an effective campaign highlighted by television appearances emphasizing his courageous opposition to both the protracted right-wing dictatorship and the leftist radicals who came to power in the wake of the 1974 democratic revolution. The Socialist Party threw its full weight behind its leader, and the Communists also lined up solidly behind Soares in the second round to avert a conservative victory. Finally, Soares, who had worked tirelessly to involve his nation in European affairs, seemed the right choice for president as Portugal entered the EC.

Economy. The austerity plan implemented by Soares in 1983, when he was prime minister, combined with cheaper oil prices and EC aid to give Portugal a 4% growth rate for 1985—one of Europe's highest. Meanwhile inflation, which had soared above 20% for more than a decade, declined to 12%. Even though the rigorous restraints imposed by Soares had inflicted hardships on workers, they helped produce a current account surplus of more than $400 million for 1985 and a favorable refinancing of some external debt by international bankers whose confidence in Portugal rose with the application of stringent economic policies.

Cavaco Silva acknowledged Soares' contributions to stabilizing the economy but faulted him for applying shock therapy too long and too severely and then failing to take adequate steps to spark recovery. Cavaco Silva has insisted that the key to sustaining growth lies in shifting priorities from curbing credit and demand to spurring productive investment and combating inflation. The centerpiece of his strategy is modernizing and enlarging Portuguese industries to meet the challenge of EC competition.

The treaty governing EC membership provides for transfer payments to Portugal, whose

---

PORTUGAL • Information Highlights

Official Name: Portuguese Republic.
Location: Southwestern Europe.
Area: 35,553 sq mi (92 082 km²).
Population (mid-1986 est.): 10,100,000.
Chief Cities (1981 census): Lisbon, the capital, 807,937; Oporto, 327,368; Amadora, 95,518.
Government: *Head of state,* Alberto Mário Soares, president (took office March 1986). *Head of government,* Aníbal Cavaco Silva, prime minister (took office November 1985). *Legislature* (unicameral)—Assembly of the Republic.
Monetary Unit: Escudo (144.0 escudos equal U.S.$1, Oct. 19, 1986).
Gross National Product (1984 U.S.$): $19,200,-000,000.
Economic Indexes (1985): *Consumer Prices* (1980 = 100), all items, 284.0; food, 287.0. *Industrial Production* (1980 = 100), 111.
Foreign Trade (1985 U.S.$): *Imports,* $7,652,000,000; *exports,* $5,685,000,000.

per capita income is barely 25% of the EC average. In May the EC Commission authorized $207 million in social aid for such purposes as training unemployed teenagers in a country where the 1985 jobless rate was 11%. As of mid-1986, Portugal had also received $269 million from a separate category of regional development funds for disadvantaged areas. Of even greater financial significance is the assistance to be provided to industries unable to compete, as customs barriers are gradually dismantled. The amount and beneficiaries of such monies await the outcome of EC-Portuguese negotiations on a plan for regional development.

On June 26, Cavaco Silva displayed his tough leadership on economic issues by demanding a confidence vote after the opposition thwarted his legislation to make it easier for employers to dismiss workers. He won the showdown with a 15-vote majority, due to unanimous support from his own Social Democrats, belated backing from the Central Democratic party, and abstentions by the 44 deputies of the Democratic Renewal Party (PRD). Neither the PRD nor the Socialists (who joined the Communists in condemning the labor bill) boasted effective leadership during the legislative confrontation.

To stay in power once the opposition coalesces, Cavaco Silva will have to combine assertiveness on meticulously chosen issues with a willingness to bargain and compromise on others. Both he and Soares face the challenge of converting their proud nation from an undeveloped backwater of Western Europe into a modern EC state.

GEORGE W. GRAYSON
College of William and Mary

POSTAL SERVICE

The year 1986 saw the United States Postal Service (USPS) through three postmasters general (PMG), a major scandal, and the fourth operating surplus in five years.

Behind these developments has been the unexpectedly firm guidance of a revitalized nine-member Board of Governors, chaired sinced early 1984 by John R. McKean, head of a California accounting firm. Under his leadership there has been a reversal of the situation of a decade or so during which the board was criticized as mainly reactive to its chief executive officer, the PMG.

On Jan. 6, 1986, the board fired PMG Paul N. Carlin, who had held the job barely a year. Carlin had faced the prospect of the first USPS deficit in three years. A 16-year veteran of the USPS, Carlin began to reorganize the system to reduce costs. He was helped by a modest rate increase in February 1985. As a result the fiscal year (FY) 1985 was held to $251 million, half that anticipated earlier.

Nevertheless, disappointed that Carlin's reorganization had been limited to the central office, the board felt the need for a more forceful management. On Jan. 7, 1986, the board replaced Carlin with Albert V. Casey, 65, former chairman and chief executive officer of American Airlines and by reputation a tough manager.

Casey quickly appointed several study groups to review USPS affairs. In April he effected a massive decentralization of operations in an agency long viewed as overly controlled from the top. Several members of the top headquarters staff also were released. The object, he said, was "to build local control and flexibility." In May, Casey stressed a commitment to maximum automation and introduced International Priority Air Mail, designed to compete for overseas bulk mail. He also was able to reduce overtime considerably. Mail volume continued to rise, and in June he announced that the USPS was in the black for FY 1986.

Meanwhile, Casey and the Board of Governors were embarrassed by the first major USPS scandal since the Reform Act of 1970. On May 30, 1986, Peter E. Voss, vice chairman of the board, pleaded guilty to three felony counts, two for receiving bribes and one for embezzlement. To complicate matters, chairman McKean was investigated for a connection to the firm allegedly favored improperly by Voss. At the same time former PMG Carlin sued the board, accusing it of having fired him because he tried to stop the improper contracting procedures that had been the downfall of Voss. McKean's investigation was dropped and thus far the courts have upheld the authority of the board to discharge the PMG for any or no reason. Voss' sentencing was delayed during further investigation, but on Oct. 24, 1986, he was committed to four years in prison and fined $11,000. He also must repay nearly $44,000 which he embezzled by collecting first class air fares when he actually traveled coach.

Casey early made it clear that he did not expect to remain PMG long—"If I'm really good," he said, "six months; if I'm poor, nine months." He kept his word, advising the board he would retire in August. On August 6 board chairman McKean announced the selection of Preston Robert Tisch to succeed Casey on August 15 as the 68th PMG. Tisch, 60, had been president and chief operating officer of Loews Corporation. In his retiring report Casey indicated that the USPS would show a surplus of more than $300 million for FY 1986, based on a record volume of 146 million.

Canada. There were few changes in the Canadian postal system during 1986. However, Canada Post Corporation, which was formed in 1981, continued its economy efforts. It closed its FY 1986 (ending March 31) with a deficit of only $184 million, nearly half that for FY 1985.

PAUL P. VAN RIPER, *Texas A&M University*

Joe Ghiz (right), the Liberal Party leader of Prince Edward Island since 1981, meets the press after becoming provincial premier. His party defeated the Conservatives in elections in April. The flamboyant Ghiz, who holds a master's degree from Harvard Law School, is known for his commitment to family values and to the rural life-style esteemed by his constituents.

© Canapress Photo

PRINCE EDWARD ISLAND

In 1986 political power swung back to the Liberals on Prince Edward Island (P.E.I.) as the result of a provincial election. The province lost a radar factory it had been promised, and new proposals were made for a fixed crossing between P.E.I. and the mainland.

The Liberal Victory. A revitalized Liberal Party under Joe Ghiz ended seven years of Conservative rule on April 21, sweeping the Tories out of office—and Premier Jim Lee out of his Legislative Assembly seat—in a provincial general election. Eleven days later, Ghiz was sworn in as premier at the head of an 11-member cabinet. The Liberals won 21, the Tories 11, of the 32 Assembly seats, reversing the results of the last election in 1982. Two other cabinet ministers, in addition to Lee, suffered personal defeat.

Joe Ghiz, 42, is a Harvard-educated lawyer and son of a Lebanese corner-store grocer in Charlottetown. He credited a combination of popular dissatisfaction with the former government and his own party's "positive program" for the election outcome.

Litton's Withdrawal. Three months after the election, Litton Systems Canada Ltd. announced that it would build an $18 million radar plant near Halifax, N.S., rather than on P.E.I. as had been arranged. The reason given was Premier Ghiz's refusal to give Litton $9 million in grants promised by the previous Conservative government unless the company pledged to stay on the island at least five years. Ghiz remarked that his government wanted jobs, but not at any price.

Litton's original commitment to a P.E.I. site was tied to a Canadian defense contract which was confirmed by the Conservative government in Ottawa just days before the election. Liberal spokesmen charged that it was a case of one Tory government doing what it could to keep another Tory government in office.

New Crossing. Interest in a bridge or tunnel to the mainland—long a dream of many islanders—quickened with the unveiling of a stream of new construction proposals. At least three companies and consortiums were publicly competing for a federal contract to carry out a feasibility study, but by late 1986 the government had not yet formally committed itself to a fixed crossing. The project could cost about $500 million.

Veterinary College. The Atlantic Veterinary College, Canada's first and only such school, opened to its first 50 students in early September. The $14 million facility, located on the University of Prince Edward Island campus in Charlottetown, is financed jointly by the federal government and the four Atlantic provinces.

The lead-up to the opening was marred by controversy over the college's policy of charging students from outside the Atlantic provinces a higher tuition than Atlantic-area students. The school undertook to review the policy.

JOHN BEST, *"Canada World News"*

PRINCE EDWARD ISLAND
• Information Highlights

Area: 2,185 sq. mi (5 660 km²).
Population (Jan. 1986 est.): 127,900.
Chief Cities (1981 census): Charlottetown, the capital, 15,282; Summerside, 7,828.
Government (1986): *Chief Officers*—lt. gov., Lloyd G. MacPhail; premier, Joe Ghiz (Liberal). *Legislature*—Legislative Assembly, 32 members.
Provincial Finances (1986–87 fiscal year budget): *Revenues,* $491,700,000; *expenditures,* $538,-100,000.
Personal Income (average weekly earnings, May 1986): $350.58.
Labor Force (July 1986, seasonally adjusted): *Employed* workers, 15 years of age and over, 59,000; *Unemployed,* 8,000 (13.9%).
Education (1986–87): *Enrollment*—elementary and secondary schools, 24,955 pupils; postsecondary—universities, 1,830, community colleges, 960.
(All monetary figures are in Canadian dollars.)

PRISONS

The number of people behind bars in the United States, from county jail to death row, continued to increase dramatically in 1986. The construction of new prison facilities produced heavy economic burdens, and the danger of AIDS within the correctional system troubled both the keepers and the kept. With the majority of the nation's jails and prisons filled beyond legal capacity, tensions remained high and violence erupted periodically.

Violence. Public awareness of prison violence is generally limited to media accounts of dramatic uprisings or riots, but the day in, day out tensions, often accompanied by sporadic violence, continued throughout the year. On New Year's Day, prisoners at the West Virginia Penitentiary in Moundsville took control of an entire wing and held 15 guards hostage for two days. An agreement between prisoners and correction officials finally was signed on live television, and the hostages, many showing bruises and other signs of rough treatment, were released. The 120-year-old fortress-like structure had been under court order to reduce overcrowding and correct a variety of other problems. Officials agreed to address the grievances brought by the inmates, but before control was restored, three inmates had been killed and extensive damage to the building and its contents was reported. In July the prison complex at Lorton, VA, where offenders from Washington, DC, are held, was almost destroyed in a fiery riot. More than 500 prisoners had to be transferred to federal facilities around the country and to state prisons in Virginia, Maryland, and Delaware. Proposals to build a new prison inside the city remained unpopular with many residents and met with resistance from members of the city council. Reports from several states suggested that day-to-day fighting, stabbings, and homosexual rape within the prisons were becoming more and more widespread.

Record Costs. In 1986, U.S. federal and state governments appropriated more than $3 billion for new prison construction. The outlays were expected to provide a total of 59,000 new beds (an average of nearly $50,000 per bed) and signaled the beginning of a long-term commitment by the public sector to staff and support the facilities at ever-escalating costs. Of the 1986 outlays, however, the federal government appropriated less than $200 million; Ohio allocated $575 million, and California more than $300 million. Proposals from the private sector (*see* special report, page 554) continued to emerge, and many governments looked to other solutions to offset the severe overcrowding. New York City, for example, with its jails filled beyond capacity and under court order to remedy the situation, announced emergency plans to construct prison facilities several hundred miles away near the Canadian border and to refurbish two abandoned Staten Island ferryboats as floating jails.

AIDS Behind Bars. The complex problems of AIDS (Acquired Immune Deficiency Syndrome) are compounded in the prison environment. With a high proportion of AIDS risk groups, especially intravenous drug users, and with homosexual rape reportedly on the rise, prisons are especially vulnerable to the fears and realities of AIDS. A study sponsored by the National Institute of Justice and the American Correctional Association confirmed the presence of the disease in almost half of U.S. federal and state prisons as well as 22 of the 33 large city and county jails surveyed. Although there was no direct evidence of the AIDS virus having been transmitted within correctional institutions, and although the two primary means of AIDS transmission—homosexual activity and intravenous drug use—are prohibited in jails and prisons, the report noted that "logic and common sense suggest that, even in the best-managed correctional facilities, there may be at least some transmission of the infection occurring among inmates."

Prison officials throughout the United States have responded to the problem in a variety of ways but have found themselves challenged by legal and management difficulties. A few states—Nevada, Colorado, Iowa, and Missouri—began implementing mass screening of inmates, but most correctional officials moved forward cautiously, citing the serious legal and ethical issues involved in mandatory testing.

Meanwhile, the growing fear of AIDS was manifested in the threat of job actions by prison staffs and of legal actions by prison inmates. Moreover, because correctional inmates are ineligible for Medicaid and certain other forms of reimbursement, the costs of medical care and associated services already were adding serious budget liabilities to an overstrained system.

Death Penalty. By October 1986, the number of persons on death row in the United States rose to 1,788—compared with 1,540 at the end of the previous year. The pace of executions also quickened, with the number expected to approach 25 before year's end. Texas, with 230 men and three women on death row, gave lethal injections to three inmates within one week in August. Florida, leading all states with 248 inmates on death row, created a special office with a staff of more than 20 and a 1986–87 budget of $859,000 to provide legal representation for death row inmates. In October, the U.S. Supreme Court began hearing the case of *McClesky v. Kemp,* in which it was argued that the death penalty is imposed on blacks disproportionately in cases involving white victims.

DONALD GOODMAN
John Jay College of Criminal Justice

PRIZES AND AWARDS

NOBEL PRIZES[1]

Chemistry: Dudley R. Herschbach, Harvard University; Yuan T. Lee, University of California, Berkeley; John C. Polanyi, University of Toronto; "for helping to create the first detailed understanding of chemical reactions, replacing a traditional frozen picture with a way of seeing the intimate interplay of energy that transforms one kind of matter into another."

Economics: James M. Buchanan, George Mason University (VA); cited as "the leading researcher in a fast-growing field of potential significance known as 'public choice theory.'"

Literature: Wole Soyinka, Nigerian playwright and poet. (*See* page 329.)

Peace Prize ($270,000): Elie Wiesel, cited as "a messenger of mankind . . . His message is one of peace, atonement, and human dignity. His belief that the forces fighting evil in the world can be victorious is a hard-won belief." (*See* page 84.)

Physics: Ernst Ruska, Fritz Haber Institute, Max Planck Society, West Berlin, for his invention of the electron microscope in 1931; Gerd Binning and Heinrich Rohrer, both of the IBM Research Laboratory, Zurich, Switzerland, for inventing "a device that can map surfaces in terms of their individual atoms."

Physiology or Medicine: Rita Levi-Montalcini, Institute of Cell Biology, Rome, and Stanley Cohen, Vanderbilt University, (TN); cited for opening "new fields of widespread importance to basic science. As a direct consequence we may increase our understanding of many disease states such as developmental malformations, degenerative changes in senile dementia, delayed wound healing and tumor diseases."

[1] about $290,000 in each category

ART

American Academy and Institute of Arts and Letters Awards
Academy-Institute Awards ($5,000 ea.): art—Pat Adams, Gregory Botts, Lois Dodd, Paul Georges, Lowell Reiland; music—Martin Boykan, Martin Brody, Wayne Peterson, Sheila Silver

Nathan and Lillian Berliawsky Award ($5,000): The Composers' Conference and Chamber Music Center (Wellesley College)

Walter Hinrichson Award: Richard Wilson

Charles Ives Fellowship ($10,000): Eric David Chasalow

Charles Ives Scholarships ($5,000 ea.): Robert Kyr, James Legg, Glenn Lieberman, Paul Moravec, Martin A. Matalon, Frank A. Ticheli

Goddard Lieberson Fellowship ($10,000 ea.): Susan Blaustein, Andrew Mead

Richard and Hinda Rosenthal Foundation Award ($5,000): Richard Ryan

American Institute of Architects Honor Awards: (*See* ARCHITECTURE.)

Capezio Dance Award: Antony Tudor

John F. Kennedy Center Honors for career achievement in the performing arts: Lucille Ball, Ray Charles, Hume Cronyn, Yehudi Menuhin, Jessica Tandy, Antony Tudor

National Academy of Recording Arts and Sciences Grammy Awards for excellence in phonograph records
Album of the year: *No Jacket Required*, Phil Collins (singer and producer), Hugh Padgham (producer)
Classical album: *Berlioz: Requiem*, Atlanta Symphony Orchestra, Robert Shaw, conductor; Robert Woods, producer
Country music song: *Highwayman*, Jimmy L. Webb (songwriter)
Jazz vocal performance, female: Cleo Laine, *Cleo at Carnegie*
New artist: Sade
Record of the year: *We Are the World*, USA for Africa, Quincy Jones (producer)
Song of the year: *We Are the World*, Michael Jackson and Lionel Richie (songwriters)

National Medal of Arts: Marian Anderson, Frank Capra, Aaron Copland, Willem de Kooning, Agnes de Mille, Eva Le Gallienne, Alan Lomax, Lewis Mumford, Eudora Welty

Pritzker Prize ($100,000): Gottfried Boehm

Pulitzer Prize for Music: George Perle, *Wind Quintet IV*

Samuel H. Scripps American Dance Festival Award ($25,000): Katherine Dunham

JOURNALISM

Maria Moors Cabot Prizes ($1,000 ea.): *Rio Negro* of General Roca, Argentina, and its editor Julio Raúl Rajneri; *El Mundo* of Medellín, Colombia, and its editor, Dario Arizmendi Posada; Alfonso Chardy, *The Miami Herald*; Gavin Scott, South American bureau chief, *Time* magazine and the Time-Life News Service.

National Magazine Awards
Articles in the public interest: *Science 85*
Design: *Time*
Essays and criticism: *The Sciences*
Fiction: *The Georgia Review*
General excellence awards: *New England Monthly, Contact, Discover, Money*
Personal service: *Farm Journal*
Photography: *Vogue*

Overseas Press Club Awards
Book on foreign affairs: Joseph Lelyveld, *Move Your Shadow: South Africa, Black and White*
Business or economic news reporting from abroad: (magazines and books, $500)—Michael Meyer and team, *Newsweek*, "Here Comes Korea, Inc."; (newspapers and wire services, $1,000)—E. S. Browning, *The Wall Street Journal*, "Japan's Trade Issues and Tensions"
Cartoon on foreign affairs ($150): Tony Auth, *Philadelphia Inquirer*, "Editorial Cartoons"
Daily newspaper or wire service interpretation on foreign affairs ($1,000): Joseph C. Harsch, *The Christian Science Monitor* for "selected commentary"
Daily newspaper or wire service reporting from abroad ($1,000): Joseph B. Treaster, *The New York Times*, "Volcano Disaster in Colombia"
Magazine story on foreign affairs: Robert J. Rosenthal, *Philadelphia Inquirer Sunday Magazine*, "South Africa: The Fires of Revolution"
Magazine reporting from abroad ($500): Henry S. Stokes, *Harper's Magazine*, "Lost Samurai"
Photographic reporting from abroad: (magazines and books, $500)—David Hume Kennerly, *Time*, "Behind Closed Doors"; (newspapers and wire services)—David Carl Turnley, *Detroit Free Press*, "South Africa: Living Under Apartheid"
Radio interpretation of foreign affairs ($1,000): Karen Burnes, ABC Entertainment Network, "Reporter's Journal: Ethiopia"
Radio spot news from abroad: Philip Till, NBC Radio Network, "Coverage of TWA Flight 847"
Television interpretation or documentary on foreign affairs: Ted Koppel, Richard N. Kaplan, *ABC News Nightline* for "South Africa series"
Television spot news reporting from abroad: Bill Moyers, *CBS Evening News with Dan Rather*, "Africa: Struggle for Survival"
Robert Capa Gold Medal: Peter Magubane, *Time*, "Cry for Justice: Cry for Peace"
Madeline Dane Ross Award ($1,000): Kristin Helmore, *The Christian Science Monitor*, "The Neglected Resource: Women in the Developing World"

George Polk Memorial Awards
Business reporting: *The Boston Globe*
Career award: George Tames, *The New York Times*
Criticism: Arthur C. Danto, *The Nation*
Foreign reporting: Alan Cowell, *The New York Times*
International reporting: Pete Carey, Katherine Ellison, Lewis M. Simons, *San Jose Mercury News*
Local reporting: Stan Jones, *Fairbanks Daily News-Miner*
Local television reporting: Vic Lee, Craig Franklin, Brian McTigue, KRON-TV, San Francisco
Medical reporting: Lawrence K. Altman, *The New York Times*
Metropolitan reporting: Jimmy Breslin, *The (NY) Daily News*
National reporting: Diana Griego, Louis Kilzer, *The Denver Post*
Network television reporting: Ted Koppel, Richard N. Kaplan, ABC News
Political reporting: Frank Greve, Knight-Ridder Newspapers
Radio reporting: Peter Laufer, NBC Radio News

Pulitzer Prizes
  Commentary: Jimmy Breslin, *The* (New York) *Daily News*
  Criticism: Donal Henahan, *The New York Times*
  Editorial cartooning: Jules Feiffer, *The Village Voice*
  Editorial writing: Jack Fuller, *The Chicago Tribune*
  Explanatory journalism: *The New York Times*
  Feature photography: Tom Gralish, *The Philadelphia Inquirer*
  Feature writing: John Camp, *The St. Paul Pioneer Press and Dispatch*
  General news reporting: Edna Buchanan, *The Miami Herald*
  International reporting: Lewis M. Simons, Pete Carey, Katherine Ellison, *The San Jose Mercury News*
  Investigative reporting: Jeffrey A. Marx, Michael M. York, *The Lexington (KY) Herald-Leader*
  National reporting: Craig Flournoy, George Rodrigue, *The Dallas Morning News;* Arthur Howe, *The Philadelphia Inquirer*
  Public service: *The Denver Post*
  Specialized reporting: Andrew Schneider, Mary Pat Flaherty, *The Pittsburgh Press*
  Spot news photography: Michel duCille, Carol Guzy, *The Miami Herald*

LITERATURE

American Academy and Institute of Arts and Letters Awards
  Academy-Institute Awards ($5,000 ea.): Russell Banks, Frederick Busch, Robert A. Caro, Robert Kelly, Barry Lopez, David Mamet, Marsha Norman, Lore Segal
  The American Academy in Rome Fellowship in Literature: Richard Kenney
  Award of Merit Medal for Poetry ($5,000): Kenneth Koch
  Witter Bynner Prize for Poetry ($1,500): C. D. Wright
  E. M. Forster Award ($5,000): Julian Barnes
  Sue Kaufman Prize for First Fiction ($2,500): Cecile Pineda
  Richard and Hinda Rosenthal Foundation Award ($5,000): Richard Powers
  Jean Stein Award ($5,000): Gregory Corso
  Harold D. Vursell Memorial Award ($5,000): Gretel Ehrlich
  Morton Dauwen Zabel Award ($2,500): Philip Whalen
American Book Awards ($10,000 ea.)
  Fiction: E. L. Doctorow, *World's Fair*
  Nonfiction: Barry Lopez, *Artic Dreams*
Bancroft Prizes ($4,000 ea.): Kenneth T. Jackson, *Crabgrass Frontier: The Suburbanization of the United States;* Jacqueline Jones, *Labor of Love, Labor of Sorrow: Black Women, Work, and the Family from Slavery to the Present*
Canada's Governor-General Literary Awards ($5,000 ea.)
  English-language awards
    Drama—George Walker, *Criminals in Love*
    Fiction—Margaret Atwood, *The Handmaid's Tale*
    Nonfiction—Ramsay Cook, *The Regenerators*
    Poetry—Fred Wah, *Waiting for Saskatchewan*
  French-language awards
    Drama—Maryse Pelletier, *Duo pour voix obstinées*
    Fiction—Fernard Ouellette, *Lucie qu un midi en novembre*
    Nonfiction—François Ricard, *La littérature contre elle-même*
    Poetry—André Roy, *Action Writing*
Robert F. Kennedy Book Awards: J. Anthony Lukas, *Common Ground;* Robert J. Norrell, *Reaping the Whirlwind*
Ruth Lilly Poetry Prize ($25,000): Adrienne Rich
Mystery Writers of America/Edgar Allan Poe Awards
  Best novel: L. R. Wright, *The Suspect*
  Best critical/biographical work: Peter Lewis, *John Le Carré*
  Grand master award for lifetime achievement: Ed McBain
National Book Critics Circle Awards
  Biography/autobiography: Leon Edel, *Henry James: A Life*
  Criticism: William Gass, *Habitations of the Word*
  Fiction: Anne Tyler, *The Accidental Tourist*
  Nonfiction: J. Anthony Lukas, *Common Ground*
  Poetry: Louis Glück, *The Triumph of Achilles*
Neustadt International Prize for Literature ($25,000): Max Frisch
PEN Literary Awards
  Faulkner Award ($5,000): Peter Taylor, *The Old Forest and Other Stories*
  Ernest Hemingway Foundation Award ($7,500): Alan V. Hewat, *Lady's Time*

Translation prize for poetry ($1,000): Dennis Tedlock, for *Popol Vuh: The Mayan Book of the Dawn of Life*
Translation prize for prose ($1,000): Barbara Bray, for *L'Amant (The Lover)* by Marguerite Duras
Pulitzer Prizes
  Biography: Elizabeth Frank, *Louise Bogan: A Portrait*
  Fiction: Larry McMurtry, *Lonesome Dove*
  General nonfiction (shared): Joseph Lelyveld, *Move Your Shadow: South Africa, Black and White;* J. Anthony Lukas, *Common Ground*
  History: Dr. Walter A. McDougall, . . . *the Heavens and the Earth: A Political History of the Space Age*
  Poetry: Henry Taylor, *The Flying Change*
Rea Award for the Short Story ($25,000): Cynthia Ozick
Ritz Paris Hemingway Award ($50,000): Marguerite Duras, *L'Amant (The Lovers)*
Whiting Writers Awards ($25,000 ea.): Hayden Carruth, August Wilson, John Ash, Kent Haruf, Denis Johnson, Darryl Pinckney, Padgett Powell, Mona Simpson, Frank Stewart, Ruth Stone

MOTION PICTURES

Academy of Motion Picture Arts and Sciences ("Oscar") Awards
  Actor—leading: William Hurt, *Kiss of the Spider Woman*
  Actor—supporting: Don Ameche, *Cocoon*
  Actress—leading: Geraldine Page, *The Trip to Bountiful*
  Actress—supporting: Anjelica Huston, *Prizzi's Honor*
  Cinematography: David Watkin, *Out of Africa*
  Costume design: Emi Wada, *Ran*
  Director: Sydney Pollack, *Out of Africa*
  Film: *Out of Africa*
  Foreign-language film: *The Official Story* (Argentina)
  Music—original score: John Barry, *Out of Africa*
  Music—song: Lionel Richie, *Say You, Say Me*
  Screenplay—original: William Kelley, Pamela Wallace, Earl W. Wallace, *Witness*
  Screenplay—adaptation: Kurt Luedtke, *Out of Africa*
  Jean Hersholt Humanitarian Award: Charles (Buddy) Rogers
  Honorary Awards: Paul Newman, Alex North
American Film Institute's Life Achievement Award: Billy Wilder
Cannes Film Festival Awards
  Golden Palm Award (best film): *The Mission* (Britain)
  Special Jury Grand Prize: *The Sacrifice* (Sweden)
  Jury Prize: *Thérèse* (France)
  Best actor—(shared) Michel Blanc, *Tenue de Soirée* (Evening Wear); Bob Hoskins, *Mona Lisa*
  Best actress—(shared) Barbara Sukowa, *Rosa Luxembourg;* Fernanda Torres, *Eu Sei que vou te Amar* (Speak to Me of Love)
  Best director: Martin Scorsese, *After Hours*

PUBLIC SERVICE

American Institute for Public Service Jefferson Awards
  National awards ($5,000 ea.): George Shultz, H. Ross Perot, Eugene Lang, Robert Hayes
  Local awards ($1,000 ea.): Sonya and Tanya Witt, Therese Dozier, Philip Viall, Fannie Royston, Ruby Calloway
Congressional Gold Medal: Aaron Copland
Charles A. Dana Foundation's Awards for pioneering achievements in health and education
  $50,000 awards: Nancy Reagan; Donald A. Henderson; Thomas R. Dawber and William B. Kannel (shared); Samuel S. Butcher, Dana W. Mayo, and Ronald M. Pike (shared)
  $10,000 awards: Margaret L. A. MacVicar; Andrew S. Dibner and Susan S. Dibner (shared)
Robert F. Kennedy Human Rights Award ($40,000): Adam Michnik, Zbigniew Bujak
Franklin D. Roosevelt Freedom Medals: Bernard Cardinal Alfrink, Bradford Morse, Olof Palme (posthumously), Sandro Pertini, El País (Spain daily newspaper)
Templeton Prize for Progress in Religion ($250,000): James I. McCord, Princeton Theological Seminary
Harry S. Truman Public Service Award: Congressman Thomas P. O'Neill
U.S. Presidential Medal of Freedom (awarded by President Ronald Reagan on May 12, 1986): Walter H. Annenberg, Earl (Red) Blaik, Barry Goldwater, Helen Hayes, Matthew B. Ridgeway, Vermont Royster, Albert B. Sabin; (awarded by President Reagan on July 28): Vladimir Horowitz

SCIENCE

Bristol-Myers Award for distinguished achievement in cancer research ($50,000): Susumu Tonegawa, Massachusetts Institute of Technology, Cambridge, MA

Enrico Fermi Award ($100,000 ea.): Ernest D. Courant, Brookhaven National Laboratory, Upton, NY; M. Stanley Livingston (posthumously)

General Motors Cancer Research Foundation Awards ($130,000 ea.): Harold zur Hausen, German Cancer Center, Heidelberg, Germany; Donald Pinkel, M.D. Anderson Hospital and Tumor Institute, Houston, TX; Phillip Allen Sharp, Massachusetts Institute of Technology, Cambridge, MA

Louisa Gross Horwitz Prize for research in biology or biochemistry ($22,000 shared): Erwin Neher, Bert Sakmann, both of the Department of Membrane Biophysics, Max Planck Institute for Biophysical Chemistry, Göttingen, West Germany

Albert Lasker Medical Research Awards ($15,000 ea.): Stanley Cohen, Vanderbilt University; Myron Essex, Harvard University; Robert C. Gallo, National Cancer Institute; Rita Levi-Montalcini, Institute of Cell Biology (Rome); Ma Haide, Ministry of Health, People's Republic of China; Luc Montagnier, Pasteur Institute (Paris)

National Medal of Science (presented by President Ronald Reagan on March 12, 1986): Solomon J. Buchsbaum, Stanley Cohen, Horace R. Crane, Herman Feshbach, Harry B. Gray, Donald A. Henderson, Robert Hofstadter, Peter D. Lax, Yuan Tseh Lee, Hans W. Liepmann, Tung Yen Lin, Carl S. Marvel, Vernon B. Mountcastle, Bernard M. Oliver, George E. Palade, Herbert A. Simon, Joan Argetsinger Steitz, Frank H. Westheimer, Chen Ning Yang, and Antoni Zygmund

National Medal of Technology (presented by President Ronald Reagan on March 12, 1986): Bernard Gordon, Reynold B. Johnson, William C. Norris, Frank N. Piasecki, Stanley D. Stookey, and Francis VerSnyder

TELEVISION AND RADIO

Academy of Television Arts and Sciences ("Emmy") Awards
Actor—comedy series: Michael J. Fox, *Family Ties* (NBC)
Actor—drama series: William Daniels, *St. Elsewhere* (NBC)
Actor—miniseries or a special: Dustin Hoffman, *Death of a Salesman* (CBS)
Actress—comedy series: Betty White, *The Golden Girls* (NBC)
Actress—drama series: Sharon Gless, *Cagney and Lacey* (CBS)
Actress—miniseries or a special: Marlo Thomas, *Nobody's Child* (CBS)
Animated program: *Garfield's Halloween Adventure* (CBS)
Children's program: "Anne of Green Gables," *Wonderwork* (PBS)
Cinematography—series: John McPherson, "The Mission," *Amazing Stories* (NBC)
Cinematography—miniseries or a special: Sherwood Woody Omens, *An Early Frost* (NBC)
Classical program in the performing arts: *Wolf Trap Presents the Kirov: Swan Lake* (PBS)
Comedy series: *The Golden Girls* (NBC)
Drama series: *Cagney and Lacey* (CBS)
Informational series: "Laurence Olivier—A Life," *Great Performances* (PBS) and *Planet Earth* (PBS) Informational special: *W. C. Fields Straight Up* (PBS)
Miniseries: *Peter the Great* (NBC)
Special drama: "Love Is Never Silent," *Hallmark Hall of Fame* (NBC)
Supporting actor—comedy series: John Larroquette, *Night Court* (NBC)
Supporting actor—drama series: John Karlen, *Cagney and Lacey* (CBS)
Supporting actor—miniseries or a special: John Malkovich, *Death of a Salesman* (CBS)
Supporting actress—comedy series: Rhea Perlman, *Cheers* (NBC)
Supporting actress—drama series: Bonnie Bartlett, *St. Elsewhere* (NBC)
Supporting actress—miniseries or a special: Colleen Dewhurst, *Between Two Women* (ABC)
Variety, music, or comedy program: *The Kennedy Center Honors: A Celebration of the Performing Arts* (CBS)

Humanitas Prizes
Long-form category ($25,000): Vickie Patik, *Do You Remember Love?*
One-hour category ($15,000): Richard Eisele, "Ordinary Hero," *Cagney and Lacey*
One-half-hour category ($10,000): John Markus, episode of *The Cosby Show*
Children's live-action program ($10,000): Josef Anderson, Fern Field, Anson Williams, *No Greater Gift* (ABC afternoon special)
News or documentary award (no monetary award): *CBS Reports: The Vanishing Family—Crisis in Black America*

George Foster Peabody Awards
Radio: *Breakdown and Back* (independently produced documentary); CBS News, *The Number Man—Bach at Three Hundred: Liberation Remembered* (independently produced); WGBH Radio, Boston, for overall programming and its leadership in state-of-the-art broadcasting; WHAS Radio, Louisville, KY, *Down and Outside on the Streets in Louisville*
Television: CBS Entertainment and Dave Bell Productions, *Do You Remember Love;* CBS News, *Whose America Is It?;* Central Independent Television and WETA-TV, Washington, *The Skin Horse;* Columbia University Graduate School of Journalism, *Seminars on Media and Society; The Final Chapter?* (documentary); *Frontline,* "Crisis in Central America"; The Harvey Milk Film Project, Inc., WNET/13, *The Times of Harvey Milk;* KDKA-TV, Pittsburgh, PA, *Second Chance;* KDTV-TV, San Francisco, for coverage during the two major Mexico City earthquakes and for raising considerable funds for disaster relief; KGO-TV, San Francisco, *The American West: Steinbeck Country;* Lincoln Center for the Performing Arts, NY, *Live from Lincoln Center;* MacNeil/Lehrer Newshour, *Apartheid's People;* NBC News, *Vietnam Ten Years After;* NBC Television, *An Early Frost;* Spinning Reels and Home Box Office, *Braingames;* WBBM-TV, Chicago, *Armed and Dangerous;* WCCO-TV, Minneapolis, MN, for a five-month investigation by its I-Team, exposing abuses in the home health care industry in Minnesota; WBZ-TV, Boston, *Tender Places;* WSMV-TV, Nashville, TN, *A Higher Standard;* Johnny Carson, *Tonight Show with Johnny Carson;* Lawrence Fraiberg; Bob Geldof and Live Aid for his personal commitment to helping alleviate hunger in the world

THEATER

Susan Smith Blackburn Prize ($3,500): Anne Devlin, *Ourselves Alone*

New York Drama Critics Circle Awards
Best new play: *Lie of the Mind,* by Sam Shepard
Foreign play: *Benefactors,* by Michael Frayn
Musical: no award
Special citation: Lily Tomlin, Jane Wagner, *The Search for Signs of Intelligent Life in the Universe*

Antoinette Perry ("Tony") Awards
Actor—drama: Judd Hirsch, *I'm Not Rappaport*
Actor—musical: George Rose, *The Mystery of Edwin Drood*
Actress—drama: Lily Tomlin, *The Search for Signs of Intelligent Life in the Universe*
Actress—musical: Bernadette Peters, *Song and Dance*
Choreography: Bob Fosse, *Big Deal*
Director—drama: Jerry Zaks, *The House of Blue Leaves*
Director—musical: Wilford Leach, *The Mystery of Edwin Drood*
Featured actor—drama: John Mahoney, *The House of Blue Leaves*
Featured actor—musical: Michael Rupert, *Sweet Charity*
Featured actress—drama: Swoosie Kurtz, *The House of Blue Leaves*
Featured actress—musical: Bebe Neuwirth, *Sweet Charity*
Musical: *The Mystery of Edwin Drood,* adapted by Rupert Holmes
Musical—book: Rupert Holmes, *The Mystery of Edwin Drood*
Musical—score: Rupert Holmes, *The Mystery of Edwin Drood*
Play: *I'm Not Rappaport* by Herb Gardner
Reproduction of a play or musical: *Sweet Charity*
Special awards: The American Repertory Theatre, Cambridge, MA

Pulitzer Prize for Drama: no award

PUBLISHING

Industry statistics for all segments of U.S. publishing were expected to be good in 1986, although not quite as good as in 1985. For the next decade, all signs pointed to continued and steady expansion. Population will grow, as will household formation, school enrollments, disposable income, and levels of education. Investors in 1986 continued to put a high value on publishing stocks.

The industry continued to utilize new technologies, both for production and distribution and for new products—audio and video products by book publishers, data transmission services by newspapers and magazines.

The "merger mania" of 1985 slowed to some extent but did not cease. In 1986 newspaper chains owned nearly 70% of all daily newspapers and about 80% of circulation. The traditional newspaper and magazine companies continued to expand aggressively into the telecommunications market. Some forecasters predicted that a handful of large media conglomerates will control a sizable share of all publishing and telecommunications media by the end of the century.

Publishers continued to fight for the protection of the 1st Amendment in the face of attempts by various groups to impose censorship on the sale and availability of books and magazines in local communities (*see* special report, page 317).

Books. The U.S. book publishing industry enjoyed record dollar-volume sales in 1986, but with fewer and fewer large companies leading the way. Employment in the industry as a whole, including bookstores, was well above the 1980 level—up by about 11,000, to 75,000.

In 1985, led by more aggressive marketing, bookstores accounted for 30% of all book sales, compared with 20% a decade earlier. Sales also increased in college stores, while book clubs and mail order sales tended to decline. Mass-market paperbacks continued to hold more than a quarter of the market, with technical and professional books steadily taking a greater share of sales. No significant increases were expected in publishers' costs during the next five years.

Through the mid-1990s growth in shipments was projected at about 4% per year. The growing educational market, which expects to have four million more children in elementary school in 1990, will probably be served by publishers with combinations of textbooks, instructional materials, and software.

Book buying by adults remained steady in 1985, but a Gallup survey showed that young adults (aged 18 to 24) were buying fewer books. New trends included children's books that "tell kids all about the cold, cruel world," as one report described it. Among these were stories that described the end of the world as a result of nuclear war, as well as others about divorced parents and fathers who lost their jobs.

The best-sellers continued to sell in inordinately high numbers. Aided by aggressive merchandising, about 40 hardcover titles in 1985 sold more than 250,000 copies; almost half of these went over the 400,000 market. A dozen hardcover titles in the mass market hit more than 500,000, and five went over the one million mark.

In January, North American hardback and paperback rights for the latest novel by James Clavell, *Whirlwind,* were sold for a record $5 million to William Morrow & Co. and Avon Books, respectively.

Financially the major book publishers did well in 1986, and stock market investors recognized that fact. *Publishers Weekly,* the major book publishing trade magazine, launched a new index based on the market value of stocks of nine major publishing firms (Addison-Wesley, Grolier, Gulf & Western, Harcourt Brace Jovanovich, Harper & Row, Houghton Mifflin, Macmillan, McGraw-Hill, and Wiley and Sons). For the first quarter, the index rose 14.2%, compared with 17.6% for the Dow Jones industrial stock index.

Major book publishing corporations continued to make acquisitions in 1986. Gulf & Western acquired Silver Burdett for $125 million, while Harper & Row bought the publishing assets of Winston-Seabury Press from CBS, Inc. Macmillan purchased several small companies, including some college textbook lists. Other acquisitions included the purchase of Congdon & Weed assets by Contemporary Books, and Praeger Publishers by Greenwood Press.

The number of international publishing companies with book publishing interests in the United States also increased during the year. Among these were the Wolters Samson Group of the Netherlands, which acquired Raven Press; Verlagsgruppe George von Holtzbrinck of West Germany, which purchased Holt General Books; Reed Publishing which bought R. R. Bowker Company; and the Rupert Murdoch group, which made Salem House its first U.S. book acquisition. And in the largest deal of the year, agreed to in October, the West German communications giant Bertelsmann acquired Doubleday for $475 million. Bertelsmann thus became the second largest U.S. book publisher, after Simon & Schuster.

New technology—including word-processing equipment, electronic graphics and facsimile transmission between printers and publishers—continued to enhance the publishing process. In 1986 a computer-assisted publishing system was installed at a major book publishing house, the J.B. Lippincott division of Harper & Row, for the first time. Supplied by Penta Systems International, the system automates the editing and publishing process, reducing the time needed to process a manuscript to the final printed form.

And new technologies also represented new markets for publishers. Sales of spoken-word audios were expected to double in 1986, to $500 million. Warner Audio Publishing marketed more than 300 titles in bookstores, drugstores, and discount stores. Several publishers, including Bantam and William Morrow, announced new audio ventures for top-selling authors. Prism Entertainment launched an ambitious video program with 30 titles in music, sports, children's movies, and other entertainment fields. By the end of 1985, Western Publishing had sold more than 2.5 million videos in its Golden Books Video Series.

Magazines. The magazine segment of the publishing industry remained in good health during 1986, although growth did slow. One study of the communications industry in the first half of the 1980s showed that magazine publishers had done better than any other segment in terms of operating income margins and return on assets, but not in terms of compound revenue growth (ranked sixth or seventh). The study included newspapers, broadcasting, cable and pay television, business information services, book publishing, entertainment programming, recorded music, and advertising. Experts forecast moderate revenue and circulation growth (2–4% after inflation) for magazines for several years to come.

Magazines appeared to be doing better than newspapers in the competition for advertising dollars. In 1985 advertising revenues were up about 8%. Magazines gained a competitive advantage in 1985–86 when television rates for advertisers increased. At the same time magazines continued to market themselves to advertisers as a channel to affluent readers, with the ability to reach a selective market through more specialized publications.

The greatest increases in magazine circulation during 1985 came from business and professional publications. Circulation declines were experienced by many general-interest magazines, newsweeklies, and regional magazines, although subscription prices tended to increase.

The largest circulation increases for consumer magazines during the second half of 1985 were recorded by *Gourmet, The Star, New Woman, Country Living, Rolling Stone, Cosmopolitan, Money, Ladies Home Journal, National Geographic,* and *Vanity Fair.* Other gainers included *Art & Antiques, inCider, The Artist's Magazine* and *Milwaukee Magazine.*

The newsweeklies were either flat or declined slightly. Most men's magazines recorded circulation declines. Business magazines, on the other hand, fared well as a group. The gainers included *Financial World, Venture, Inc., Business Week, Fortune,* and *Forbes.* Food magazines represented another

AP/Wide World

Jean Auel's third novel, "The Mammoth Hunters," had a record first printing of 1 million copies. Her first two books had sold some 7.5 million copies as of early 1986.

strong category, as did some computer magazines. Several of the health magazines also showed gains. The "shelter" magazines, however, had a mixed record: *Country Home* and *House & Garden* both were up, *House Beautiful* was down, and *Better Homes and Gardens* was flat.

In 1985 there was a net addition of nearly 300 magazines published in the United States. Many of the new entries were special-interest consumer magazines in such fields as health, hobby, travel and leisure, entertainment, and sports. In the business publication area the gains were made by regional, electronics, and communications publications.

Among new electronic formats, magazine publishers were most heavily involved in database publishing, although some were producing programs for radio and television. Many also were involved in on-line data transmission and computer software products.

Takeovers in the U.S. magazine industry in 1984–85 were valued at more than $1 billion. Most of the purchasers were large media companies seeking to expand through the acquisition of well-established magazines. The invasion of the industry by foreign investors, principally from Canada and Great Britain, also continued.

Growth in foreign markets continued at a slower rate—4% in 1985, compared with an average of nearly 12% in the previous eight or nine years. The slowdown was caused by the strength of the U.S. dollar, as well as the spending practice of licensing U.S. magazines to foreign companies.

Newspapers Senior executives of major publicly held newspaper companies expected no more than "moderate" growth in 1986.

Moreover, they said, fewer newspapers would be acquired because of the high sale prices of recent purchases. Instead, the direction of acquisition was headed toward broadcasting, with a declining interest in cable television and the development of videotex. More attention would be paid, the executives said, to improving the operating efficiency of their existing newspaper holdings, as well as increasing market penetration and developing special and zoned sections.

The trend toward acquisitions in broadcasting rather than publishing was dramatically illustrated by Capital Cities Communications' friendly takeover of American Broadcasting Companies (ABC), which was completed in January 1986. But the year did see the sale and purchase of several major dailies. The Gannett Company, the largest U.S. newspaper group, acquired the *Louisville Courier-Journal* and *Louisville Times* for a reported $300 million. The *Chicago Sun-Times* was sold to an investor group for $145 million. And the Times Mirror Company, the nation's sixth largest chain (by circulation) made two major deals: it bought the *Baltimore Sun* and *Baltimore Evening Sun* for $600 million, and it sold the *Dallas Times Herald* for $110 million to the Media News Group. Other companies also were involved in takeovers—both hostile and friendly—and newspaper groups hastened to erect defenses against unwelcome takeovers. Among the papers to cease publication in 1986 were the *Baltimore News American* and the *Columbus (OH) Citizen-Journal*.

While overall newspaper advertising revenues did not grow as fast as they once did, gains continued to be made—4% (in constant dollars) in 1985 and an estimated 2% in 1986. Annual increases of 2–3% were forecast for the next five-year period. By the end of the decade, however, on-line computer information services are expected to begin cutting into newspaper revenues from local advertising. And already, with such other ad media as television and direct mail providing stiffer competition for the advertising dollar, the newspaper share of national ad spending was declining.

Nevertheless total daily newspaper circulation climbed again in 1985, with major-market dailies leading the way. Many former evening newspapers continued the trend toward morning publication. While newspapers are not expected to increase their penetration of the market (currently about 68%) for the rest of the decade, they are expected to target readers with high disposable incomes and to raise prices. Weekly papers did not fare as well as dailies, with the number of publications declining and circulation continuing to fall at a rate of about 1 million per year. To hold on to its competitive position, the newspaper industry overall continued to invest about $1 billion a year.

Meanwhile, the credibility of newspapers continued to be a much-discussed topic at major trade association meetings and journalism conclaves. As one researcher said, credibility "is not a fad, but a cornerstone of the franchise of newspapers." In an address to a group of editors, an esteemed elder statesman of the newspaper industry was much blunter: "You're in trouble, a lot deeper than this credibility study shows," he said. "If the public won't be on your side, we're going to have a terrible time keeping a free press." He begged editors to practice accountability and decide what ethics to apply.

Other issues of concern to the newspaper community included the "chilling effect" of libel suits and the salaries of young reporters. Salary studies were sparked by reports from college educators that students were choosing to enter fields other than newspapers because of the low starting pay scale. A study by one national newspaper association reported that begining salaries at newspapers outside the major metropolitan areas ranged between $10,500 and $11,500, several thousand dollars below starting salaries of teachers and other professionals in similar communities.

ELIZABETH S. YAMASHITA
University of Oklahoma

On May 27, the Hearst Corporation published the final edition of the "Baltimore News American," Maryland's oldest daily newspaper. Circulation had dropped from 210,000 to 101,000 since the early 1970s.

PUERTO RICO

Government and business leaders in Puerto Rico breathed a sigh of relief that the new U.S. tax reform law spared Section 936 of the Internal Revenue Code, which they consider the principal incentive for attracting badly needed industry to the island.

The officials had feared that Congress, in its zeal to close loopholes in the tax laws, would phase out the tax benefits provided to U.S. corporations operating in Puerto Rico. Under Section 936, U.S. firms setting up on the island receive close to 100% tax exemption and take home profits tax free after investing them for a time in the local economy. But Congress made only two relatively minor changes in the tax law as it affects the island: a 10% minimum tax in effect for three years and royalty payments for 936 firms that use the cost-sharing method of accounting.

Economy. There was good news on the job front. Unemployment dropped to 17% in October, the lowest jobless rate in six years, and a full 3 percentage points lower than 1985, when more than 20% of the labor force constantly could not find work. For the first time ever, more than 800,000 islanders held jobs.

The administration of Gov. Rafael Hernández Colón also enacted a number of tax laws meant to further boost the economy. The maximum income-tax rate for individuals was lowered to 50%; inheritance taxes on Puerto Rican holdings were virtually eliminated; and the tax rate on interest and dividend income was lowered. Also, inflation stayed below 2%, while the island's economy has been growing at a slightly higher rate than the sluggish U.S. economy.

The one major setback to the economy was the continuing impact of a court order obtained by the Environmental Protection Agency (EPA) that banned sewer hookups in 91 of the island's deteriorated waste-water treatment plants. The ban prevented in 1986 desperately needed housing construction and other building projects. The EPA cracked down because of what it said was 20 years of poor performance by the Commonwealth Aqueduct and Sewer Authority. In an attempt to remedy the situation, the Hernández Colón administration earmarked more than $1.1 billion for a four-year crash program to upgrade the island's sewerage system.

Other News. The EPA and the commonwealth government also continued to lock horns over just how serious was the mercury contamination that caused the evacuation of a working-class housing development, Christian City, in the southeast coast town of Humacao. Commonwealth officials insisted during Puerto Rico Senate hearings in July that some 300 families were moved out in March 1985 because of imminent danger to their health. But the EPA

PUERTO RICO • Information Highlights

Area: 3,515 sq mi (9 104 km²).
Population (mid-1986 est.): 3,300,000
Chief Cities (1980 census): San Juan, the capital, 434,849; Bayamon, 196,206; Ponce, 189,046.
Government (1986): *Chief Officer*—governor, Rafael Hernández Colón (Popular Democratic Party). *Legislature*—Senate, 27 members; House of Representatives, 51 members.

asserted the government had overreacted and that mercury traces found in the soil and in urine samples of some residents were too slight to cause physical harm. Nevertheless, comprehensive tests of the area's soil, water, and fish were being carried out for the EPA.

In a sensational murder trial that captured headlines for months, Lydia Echevarria, one of the island's most popular actresses, was convicted by a jury in April of slaying her estranged husband, TV personality Luis Vigoreaux. She was sentenced to 208 years in prison.

On December 31, a fire at San Juan's Dupont Plaza Hotel killed 96 people.

ROBERT FRIEDMAN, *"The San Juan Star"*

QUEBEC

Constitutional and language issues have a way of dominating the Quebec political agenda. In this respect 1986 was a very typical year.

The Constitution. Canada's Prime Minister Brian Mulroney and Quebec Premier Robert Bourassa both espoused the goal of bringing Quebec into the federal constitution. Alone of Canada's ten provinces, Quebec rejected the constitution when it was drawn up in 1981.

The political foundation for a rapprochement appeared to be well laid in 1985 when Bourassa's pro-federalist Liberal Party ousted the separatist-leaning Parti Québécois (PQ) in a provincial election. In 1986, nevertheless, it became clear that progress will not necessarily be easy and automatic. In the area of language, 1986 was notable for a softening of provincial laws curbing the use of English.

On April 2, Bourassa expressed hope that Quebec and the rest of Canada would reach a constitutional accord during Mulroney's present term of office, expected to last until 1988. "We would like to sign an agreement before the next federal election," he said in a radio interview. Three months later, Mulroney announced that he had established a cabinet committee to pursue an accord.

Then on August 12, meeting in Edmonton, Alberta, all ten premiers issued a statement giving top constitutional priority to bringing about Quebec's "full and active participation" in the Canadian federation. A number of premiers, however, publicly opposed Quebec's demands, including a veto over future consti-

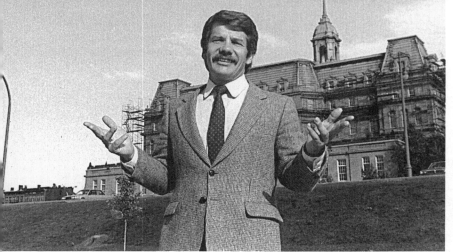

Jean Doré, a 41-year-old labor lawyer, was elected mayor of Montreal on November 9. With a campaign that appealed to renters and low wage earners, Doré defeated the chosen successor of the popular Jean Drapeau, who retired after 29 years in office. Doré's Montreal Citizens Movement virtually swept the City Council.

© Daniel Auclair/Alpha Diffusion

tutional change. A Mulroney-Bourassa meeting in September did not advance matters very far, and in the speech from the throne on October 1, the Mulroney government was noncommittal.

Exemption Lifted. Quebec will no longer systematically exempt its laws from the Canadian Charter of Rights and Freedoms, Quebec's Intergovernmental Affairs Minister Gil Rémillard said March 2. "We want Quebecers to enjoy the same protection of their fundamental rights as other Canadians." The Bourassa government took action at about the same time to stop launching prosecutions for the display of English-language commercial signs. A Quebec law making such signs illegal had been successfully challenged in the courts.

Language-of-Education. Quebec's Education Minister Claude Ryan said April 22 that provincial law would be changed to allow children of Canadians educated in English anywhere in Canada to be educated in English in Quebec. This would make official what the province had been practicing since 1984, when the Supreme Court of Canada declared invalid a provision of Quebec Bill 101 limiting English education to children whose parents were educated in English in Quebec.

Francophone Summit. A meeting of leaders and representatives of French speaking nations near Paris in February was marred by a dispute between the Canadian and Quebec delegations. At the close of the conference February 19, Prime Minister Mulroney issued a warning that the federal government cannot, "and never will," share its jurisdiction over foreign relations. The tiff began two days earlier when Bourassa unexpectedly proposed to the Paris conference a "new Marshall Plan" to distribute European food surpluses to the Third World. Under a federal-Quebec agreement, the premier can intervene on global economic questions that arise at Francophone summits only with the "specific agreement" of the prime minister.

Politics. The Parti Québécois leadership left a two-day national council meeting in Quebec City on June 8 brimming with confidence that the party was finally back on its feet six months after its shattering defeat in the 1985 provincial election. The 250 delegates decided to remain committed to the long-term goal of Quebec independence.

Premier Bourassa regained a seat in the National Assembly on January 20, easily defeating nine other candidates in a by-election in the Montreal area riding of St. Laurent. Bourassa failed to get elected in Bertrand riding in 1985. Jean Drapeau, the long-time mayor of Montreal, retired at the end of his term in November. His chosen successor, Claude Dupras, was easily defeated in November 9 elections by Jean Doré of the Montreal Citizens Movement.

Spending Cuts. The government went on a cost-cutting spree March 25, chopping $1 billion from a wide variety of services. Five weeks later, on May 1, it presented a budget which projected a deficit of C$2.89 billion for 1986–87, down $26 million from the previous year. Some taxes were increased, and some exemptions were abolished.

JOHN BEST, *Chief, "Canada World News"*

QUEBEC · Information Highlights

Area: 594,857 sq mi (1 540 680 km²).
Population (Jan. 1986 est.): 6,609,700.
Chief Cities (1981 census): Quebec, the capital, 166,474; Montreal, 980,354; Laval, 268,335; Longueuil, 124,320.
Government (1986): *Chief Officers*—lt. gov., Gilles Lamontagne; premier, Robert Bourassa (Liberal). *Legislature*—National Assembly, 122 members.
Provincial Finances (1986–87 fiscal year budget): *Revenues,* $25,510,000,000; *expenditures,* $28,400,000,000.
Personal Income (average weekly earnings, May 1986): $416.50.
Labor Force (July 1986, seasonally adjusted: *Employed* workers, 15 years of age and over, 3,182,000; *Unemployed,* 366,000 (11.5%).
Education (1986–87): *Enrollment*—elementary and secondary schools, 1,157,700 pupils; postsecondary—universities, 117,300; community colleges, 161,400.
(All monetary figures are in Canadian dollars.)

RECORDINGS

The music of the Sixties joined the music of the Eighties among the popular new recordings of the year. Among contemporaries, Whitney Houston *(Houston)*, Janet Jackson *(Control)*, Peter Gabriel *(So)*, Patti LaBelle *(Winner in You)*, John Cougar Mellencamp *(Scarecrow,* 1985), and Dire Straits *(Brothers in Arms,* 1985) had some of the year's top-selling albums. *Houston* became the first debut album ever to sell more than 6 million copies. Janet Jackson, 20, the younger sister of Michael Jackson, became the third youngest artist ever to have a number one LP. Bruce Springsteen released a five-album boxed set culled from ten years of live performances.

As for oldies, the Beatles' single *Twist and Shout* made the Top 40 playlist 23 years after its original issue. Atlantic Records released *The History of Atlantic Rhythm & Blues,* a seven double-LP anthology of that label's pioneering work in r&b. *Motown Remembers Marvin Gaye* fashioned 1960s' outtakes into a fitting tribute. Polygram added LPs to its faithful restoration of Hank Williams recordings. And there was a surfeit of jazz reissues by Fantasy, Blue Note, Mosaic, and other labels.

In the classical sphere, there was a host of releases to mark the 100th anniversary of the death of the composer-pianist Franz Liszt. Old Broadway fare was also back in vogue, as Leonard Bernstein scored with a popular remake of *West Side Story* and the London Symphony Orchestra presented a new recording of *South Pacific.* And it was a strong year for movie soundtrack sales. The music from *Top Gun* shot that album to number one. By midyear, record companies had released an unprecedented eight soundtracks. Part of the success of movie soundtracks lay in the trend toward three-way promotional blitzes by recording, film, and home-video interests.

Compact Discs. The market for compact disc (CD) recordings continued to boom, with sales volume far exceeding the $320 million registered in 1985. The sale of CD players was expected to double by year-end 1986, reaching 1.6 million units. As indications of the growing popularity of the CD format, Schwann's quarterly *Compact Disc Catalogue* was made a monthly; the first Canadian CD plant, built by Praxis Technologies, opened to an immediate two-year backlog of orders; and the U.S. recording companies Telarc and Delos converted almost exclusively to the CD format.

CD sales were strongest in pop music, where mainstream product is generally released in three formats (record, tape, and CD). In other genres, CD offerings are narrower in range. Reissues seem especially appropriate for CD, and with back catalogues mounting, sales should increase steadily. For the time being, at least, cassettes are still selling at a much faster rate. Finally, 1986 saw the introduction of yet another new format—digital audio tape (DAT), which offers the same noise-free sound as the CD but also has a recording capability.

Video. Following the recent trend, several of the year's pop-music favorites—the likes of Mr. Mister, the Hooters, Arcadia, and others —got their big boosts from exposure in music videos. But MTV, the 24-hour music video cable television station that popularized the form, experienced its own growing pains during 1986. Encountering its first substantial competition from excellent local music video programs, MTV demanded exclusivity rights from most major labels to air promotional clips. But prohibitive production costs, routinely figured into marketing budgets, finally caused some artists and labels to balk. Consequently, it was no longer de rigueur for every vinyl release to be accompanied by a video. British rock talent Joe Jackson even wrote an editorial for the trade magazine *Billboard* in which he disassociated himself from the video medium.

Meanwhile, the more than $6 billion home video industry was booming. A free fall in prerecorded videocassette prices boosted sales, and rentals also remained strong. Low prices also brought hundreds of new specialized videocassettes, with an emphasis on "how-tos."

Censorship? Hard rock remained the object of criticism for its lyrical content, deemed by some as inappropriate for young listeners. The evangelist Jimmy Swaggart preached a sermon condemning Walmart, a 900-store mass-market retail chain, as a corrupter of youth for selling rock recordings and related items. Walmart subsequently pulled its hard-rock and heavy-metal albums, as well as 32 teenage magazines. But some in the music community retaliated against the movement. Quiet Riot, one of the many popular acts that regularly sells out auditoriums to avid fans, fought back with a video *The Wild and the Young,* which depicts rock censorship as a restriction imposed by a police state. And members of the music-business community formed Recording Retailers Opposing Censorship.

Record Industry Investigation. In spring 1986, U.S. Sen. Albert Gore, Jr. (D-TN) announced that the Senate Permanent Subcommittee on Investigations was launching a probe of independent record promoters. The committee was to investigate allegations that the promoters routinely pay off radio station executives—in cash and drugs—to get air time for particular records. In the wake of allegations of wrongdoing, most major record companies—including CBS, Warner, RCA/Ariola, Capitol-EMI, and MCA—announced that they would suspend or halt the use of independent promoters. They denied any knowledge of illegal activities and expressed concern over negative images of the industry.

GEORGIA CHRISTGAU, *Free-lance Writer*

REFUGEES AND IMMIGRATION

The mass movement of people across international boundaries continued with increasing frequency during 1986. The world's refugee population was estimated to exceed 13 million, with the number of people displaced within their own country probably even greater.

Long-Standing Problems. In 1986 the world refugee situation was characterized by interminable refugee-producing problems and long, debilitating stays in camps for refugees. The major refugee problems in South and Southeast Asia, Central America, and the Horn of Africa all began six or more years before, and long-term political solutions to regional conflicts remained as elusive as ever. Eleven years after changes in government, "boat people" continued to flee Vietnam, and "land people" continued to escape from Laos and Cambodia. Many of the 150,000 refugees who remained in holding centers in Southeast Asia and the 250,000 Cambodians and Vietnamese who remained in squalid camps along the Thai-Cambodian border had left their own countries years before. Nearly 10,000 boat people in Hong Kong—63% of whom had already spent more than three years in closed camps behind barbed wire—anxiously awaited resettlement overseas. In Pakistan and Iran, most of the 4 million Afghan refugees who resided in camps along the militarized border had been there since 1980. Somalia had an estimated 700,000 refugees from Ethiopia in camps. The latter four programs cost the Office of the United Nations High Commissioner for Refugees (UNHCR) $150 million during 1986.

In addition to these problem areas, there continued to be burgeoning refugee populations in the Sudan, Ethiopia, Central America, southern Africa, and elsewhere. Nor was there anything to suggest that the trend would be reversed in the immediate future, particularly in the developing countries. Population growth, economic stagnation, political instability, the ever-growing arms trade, and increased militarism and ethnic conflict all signaled greater mass movements of population in the years to come. In the West, government attitudes toward refugees became increasingly hard and restrictive during 1986, as visa requirements and other deterrents were imposed to stem the tide of asylum-seekers. An agreement between the East and West German governments virtually closed Berlin as an entry point for Third World refugees, who had been flooding in at an unmanageable rate.

U.S. Refugee Policy. The United States continued to be one of the most generous contributors to international emergency refugee relief efforts. Although refugee resettlement in the United States was down by two thirds since 1979 and 1980, admission numbers remained at significant levels. The U.S. admission quota for refugees worldwide in 1986 was 67,000. As in previous years, however, the United States discriminated heavily in favor of refugees fleeing Communist regimes and against those fleeing authoritarian, right-wing regimes with ties to Washington. Of the 67,000 places in 1986, 55,000 were reserved for refugees fleeing Communist governments in the Soviet Union, Eastern Europe, and Indochina, with 3,000 for refugees from Latin America and the Caribbean, 6,000 from the Middle East, and 3,000 from Africa. Many of the Middle Eastern slots were reserved for Afghans seeking shelter from Soviet military attacks, and most of the Latin American and Caribbean slots were reserved for Cubans.

U.S. asylum policy followed a similar pattern. In 1986 the Department of Justice drafted new procedures that made it easier for citizens of Poland, Nicaragua, and other Communist or leftist countries to gain asylum in the United States. The new rules established a presumption that asylum-seekers fleeing "totalitarian" regimes had a "well-founded fear of persecution," thereby meeting statutory requirements. At midyear about 60% of Nicaraguan applicants had been granted political asylum, contrasting sharply with the rates for Salvadorans (9%), Guatemalans (3%), and Haitians (3%). The policy represented a significant departure from the Refugee Act of 1980, which adopted an ideologically neutral standard for asylum, consistent with international law.

Other developments indicated a trend toward restrictionism. The U.S. Coast Guard interdicted vessels carrying Haitians on the high seas, gave them summary hearings on board, and returned them to Haiti. Large numbers of asylum-seekers were detained for long periods in prisons across the country. In April, the Immigration and Naturalization Service (INS) opened a remote detention center in Oakdale, LA, designed to detain 1,000 or more undocumented aliens. The Congress failed to pass a bill providing for a temporary stay of deportation for Salvadorans in the United States. Instead, the INS deported Salvadorans back to El Salvador at the rate of 500 per month. Religious and lay activists continued to offer sanctuary to illegal aliens from El Salvador and Guatemala. In May eight sanctuary workers were convicted in Arizona for such activity.

Immigration. In its final days, the 99th U.S. Congress passed a landmark immigration bill to curtail the influx of illegal aliens. Under the new law, called the Immigration Reform and Control Act of 1986, the hiring of illegal aliens is punishable by a fine of $250 to $10,000 per alien. At the same time, however, the legislation offered legal status, or amnesty, to the millions of illegal aliens who have lived continuously in the United States since before Jan. 1, 1982.

GIL LOESCHER, *University of Notre Dame*

RELIGION

Dr. James I. McCord, 66-year-old Presbyterian theologian, was awarded the 1986 Templeton Prize for Progress in Religion. Dr. McCord, the founder and current chancellor of the Center for Theological Inquiry in Princeton (NJ) and a former president of the Princeton Theological Seminary, was honored for his efforts as a leader of religious education.

According to statistics released by the National Council of Churches in June, total U.S. church membership, from 219 religious denominations reporting, was 142,172,138 in 1984; enrollment in U.S. seminaries declined to 52,794 students in 1985; and the number of women attending divinity schools was continuing to grow.

The year 1986 was an active one for dialogue between religious leaders. For example, during a ten-day trip to India in February, Pope John Paul II not only met with a group of non-Christian religious leaders of Tamil Nadu but also with the Dalai Lama of Tibet, the exiled Buddhist leader, and Dr. Robert Runcie, the archbishop of Canterbury, who also was visiting the Asian nation. On October 27, leaders of 12 religions gathered in Assisi, Italy, to join the pope in a "World Day of Prayer for Peace."

Far Eastern

Mahikari is one of Japan's new religions that emerged in the aftermath of World War II. Representatives of the Japanese government, the prefectures and major cities of Japan, and many foreign countries attended the Autumn Grand Ceremony held at the Main World Shrine in Takayama in 1986. The ceremony marked the growth and significance of this new tradition.

Mahikari is a Japanese word for Divine True Light, and refers to a form of cosmic energy available for the purification and restoration of creation. The religion features a method, called Mahikari no Waza, which radiates energy through the hands. Effects are thought to cure disease and illness, restore mechanical malfunctions, and prepare its members for the Holy Century which is to follow the present age of crisis. Mahikari was founded in 1959 by Kòtama Okada, whose daughter is the current spiritual head. Oshienushisama, as she is called, is honored and revered as a divine personage.

The World Shrine in Takayama symbolizes Mahikari as a religion that seeks to be a unifying tradition for all of humanity. However, Buddhist, Shinto, and folk elements are the most evident ingredients in Mahikari.

In the fall of 1985, theologians and religion scholars, representing indigenous churches of South and Southeast Asia, met at the Nanzan Institute for Religion and Culture in Nagoya, Japan, to make final preparation for a visit to China. The group was somewhat resigned to a limited introduction to important sites and religious leaders in China. Instead they were amicably received and came away with the hope of future collaboration and exchange with Chinese scholars, representing Taoist, Buddhist, and Islamic traditions.

In commemoration of the 80th birthday of Heinrich Dumoulin, internationally known scholar of Buddhism and pioneer of Buddhist-Christian dialogue, a special symposium was held in November 1985 at the Institute of Oriental Religions in Tokyo. Professors Dumoulin and Koshiro Tamaki delivered lectures.

In Hong Kong, leaders of Buddhism, Confucianism, Islam, Roman Catholicism, Taoism, and Protestantism continued to meet two or three times annually at the Tao Fong Shan Ecumenical Center to address community problems and issue a joint "pastoral letter" to all citizens on the Chinese New Year.

RICHARD E. WENTZ
Arizona State University

Islam

The Organization of the Islamic Conference, representing 46 countries whose populations are predominantly Muslim or include substantial Muslim minorities, worked actively during 1986 to protect the religious, political, and cultural interests of its members. In several large Muslim countries, organizations seeking to implement Islamic legal systems gained in popularity. In a few nations with Muslim minorities, tensions arose from Muslim efforts to safeguard traditional institutions and practices from state control.

The Islamic Conference condemned the U.S. decision in January to sever ties with Libya, characterizing the action as a threat to all Muslim countries. Of particular concern to the organization was the tendency of the United States and other Western nations to make sweeping generalizations linking Islam and terrorism. Such accusations contributed to a climate of hostility toward Muslims, which resulted in attacks on mosques, Islamic social organizations, and Muslim individuals in the United States and elsewhere. Concern over reports of vandalism and alleged Israeli interference at mosques in East Jerusalem prompted the al-Quds (Jerusalem) Committee of the Islamic Conference to launch an international appeal to protect these holy places.

A series of disorders throughout Egypt in 1986 was linked by some observers to a resurgence of Islam. At a number of Egyptian universities, conservative Muslim student organizations won campus elections and inaugurated efforts to compel university administrators to adopt conservative policies.

In Sudan, spring elections brought to power the country's first freely elected government in more than 15 years but failed to heal the serious breach between the Muslim northern portion of the country and the pagan and Christian south. The new government moderated the application of the *sharia* (Islamic law), which had been made the law of the land in 1983, but it refused to suspend the *sharia* altogether, as southern opponents of the regime desired.

Elsewhere in Africa, Nigeria, another country whose population is divided between Muslims and non-Muslims, joined the Islamic Conference. The decision angered many of Nigeria's 40 million non-Muslims, who would have preferred not to have the state affiliate with an international sectarian body.

In India, which is about 10% Islamic, a 1986 law exempted Muslims from paying alimony to divorced wives. Many non-Muslim Indians objected to this preferential treatment, but Muslims argued that earlier government rulings requiring the payments violated their religious traditions. Some outbreaks of intercommunal violence ensued in areas of mixed Muslim and non-Muslim populations. Conditions were aggravated by the recent upsurge in militancy among some Hindus, the religious majority.

Disturbances also occurred in the Philippines and Bulgaria, both states in which Muslim minorities sought to preserve their individuality in the face of non-Muslim governments. In Bulgaria this involved efforts by the government to assimilate citizens of Turkish ancestry by obliterating their cultural links with the Muslim world. Efforts to have such persons abandon their Turkish names in favor of Christian ones met with particularly stiff resistance.

In the Philippines, Muslims on the island of Mindanao continued to voice longstanding demands for autonomy. President Corazon Aquino showed more willingness to meet and negotiate with Muslim leaders than had former President Ferdinand Marcos, but little progress was made.

KENNETH J. PERKINS
University of South Carolina

Judaism

For world Jewry, 1986 saw the unfolding of several historic developments. In February, the Soviet Union released the long-imprisoned Jewish dissident Anatoly Shcharansky, and the U.S. Senate ratified a long-debated United Nations treaty outlawing genocide. In March, the Nazi past of former UN Secretary-General Kurt Waldheim was disclosed, and the state of Georgia issued a posthumous pardon for Leo Frank. In April, John Paul II made the first known papal visit to a Jewish synagogue. In

AP/Wide World

Sephardic Chief Rabbi Mordechai Eliyahu (left) joined Istanbul's head rabbi, David Asseo, at the funeral for victims of a terrorist attack on an Instanbul synagogue.

June, religious strife erupted in Israel. In September, Arab terrorists staged a massacre in an Istanbul synagogue, and a retired Ohio autoworker was indicted in Israel for Nazi war crimes. In October, the USSR also allowed David Goldfarb, a world famous Jewish geneticist, and his wife to emigrate to the United States. Also in October, in perhaps the most symbolically significant event of the year for world Jewry, Elie Wiesel, the Romanian-born Holocaust survivor, author, and promoter of human rights, was named the winner of the Nobel Peace Prize (*see* page 84).

The release of 38-year-old Anatoly (Natan) Shcharansky after a nine-year ordeal in the Soviet Gulag brought to a close one of the world's most publicized human-rights cases (*see also* BIOGRAPHY). In Germany, where he was released in an East-West spy swap February 11, Shcharansky was reunited after 12 years with his wife Avital, whose untiring efforts had drawn international attention to his struggle. The Shcharanskys left immediately for Israel, where they received a joyous welcome.

Jewish groups hailed the February 19 U.S. Senate vote ratifying, 83–11, the UN genocide convention 38 years after it was signed by President Harry Truman. The treaty defines genocide as any act committed with the intent to destroy or harm national, ethnic, racial, or religious groups.

Secret wartime documents released by the World Jewish Congress connecting former UN Secretary-General Waldheim to Nazi atrocities sent shock waves through the Jewish community. Worldwide consternation was amplified by Waldheim's victory in Austria's June presidential election (*see also* BIOGRAPHY). At the inauguration ceremonies in Vienna, Rabbi Avraham Weiss of New York and Nazi-hunter Beate Klarsfeld of Paris led a 24-hour candlelight vigil, and a group of prominent intellectuals calling themselves "New Austria" held public protests.

The pardon of Leo Frank laid to rest a 73-year-old murder conviction that had been passed in an atmosphere of anti-Semitic frenzy in rural Georgia. In 1913 the young Atlanta Jew, despite evidence of his innocence, was convicted of the murder of a 13-year-old girl and lynched by a mob. Petitions by Jewish groups based on eyewitness testimony finally resulted in the March 11, 1986, decision by the Georgia Board of Pardons.

The historic visit of Pope John Paul II to Rome's main synagogue on April 13 was seen by Jewish and Catholic leaders as a step toward Vatican recognition of the State of Israel. Another landmark on the road to Catholic-Jewish reconciliation was the distribution throughout Latin America of a Spanish version of an interreligious prayer service commemorating the victims of the Holocaust.

Conflict between ultraorthodox and secular Jews in Israel reached an unprecedented level in June. Secular extremists vandalized Tel Aviv synagogues in retaliation for the defacement or burning down of Jerusalem bus shelters by ultraorthodox Jews who objected to advertisements for women's swimsuits. Prime Minister Shimon Peres delivered an impassioned plea to stem the tide of religious strife.

The Arab terrorist massacre of 21 Jews during September 6 Sabbath services at Istanbul's largest synagogue horrified the public and revived memories of the Holocaust. Jews throughout the world held memorial services for the victims, and Jewish leaders called for an all-out campaign against terrorism.

Another reminder of the Holocaust was the indictment in Israel of accused Nazi war criminal Ivan Demjanjuk, who had been extradited from the United States in February. Demjanjuk had been nicknamed "Ivan the Terrible" by inmates of Treblinka death camp, where he allegedly operated the gas chambers. He was charged with the murder and torture of 900,000 Jews. His trial began in November.

To mark the centennial of New York's Yeshiva University, the U.S. Postal Service issued a postage stamp honoring Dr. Bernard Revel, a Talmudic scholar and the first president of that Jewish institution.

LIVIA E. BITTON-JACKSON
Herbert H. Lehman College, CUNY

Orthodox Eastern

The main problem confronting Orthodoxy remained that of the division of the Orthodox churches in Western Europe, America, and Australia in ethnic jurisdictions. Facing the issue, Patriarch Ignatius IV of Antioch wrote a letter to Metropolitan Theodosius of the Orthodox Church in America (OCA) calling for concrete action toward the establishment of a fully unified Orthodox church in the Western Hemisphere, beginning with cooperation between the Antiochian archdiocese and the autocephalous OCA. Meanwhile meetings of preconciliar commissions to organize a Great and Holy Synod of all Orthodox churches were held in Geneva, Switzerland. However, the convening of such a gathering in the near future remained unlikely due to political divisions within the Orthodox churches.

Orthodox leaders responded to a statement on Baptism, Eucharist, and Ministry by the Faith and Order Commission of the World Council of Churches (WCC). While generally positive about the document, the leaders called for a rite of Chrismation (a distinct act of conferring the gift of the Holy Spirit at the time of baptism) and an exclusively male presbyterate and episcopate for sacramental sharing among Christian churches.

Orthodox-Roman Catholic relations remained cordial on the level of episcopal visitations, but disputes over a Vatican exhibition of icons from a dissident Orthodox body in Macedonia disrupted the official Roman Catholic-Orthodox Consultation in Bari, Italy, in May. Less than half of the Orthodox representatives at the meeting remained to its end.

USSR and Eastern Europe. The Orthodox Church in the USSR continued plans for the celebration of the millenium of christianity in Russia in 1988. Such dissidents as Gleb Yakunin and Alexander Ogorodnikov remained imprisoned. John Meyendorff, dean of St. Vladimir's Seminary in New York, and Leonid Kishkovsky of the external affairs department of OCA, were denied visas to enter the USSR to attend official church meetings. Meyendorff was even attacked on Soviet television.

Metropolitan Theodosius of the OCA received an official visit from Metropolitan Dorotheos, primate of the Orthodox Church of Czechoslovakia. He also visited the Orthodox Churches of Czechoslovakia and Poland.

Evangelical Orthodox. In September the Evangelical Orthodox Church, a denomination founded in the 1970s by former leaders of the Campus Crusade for Christ, headed by Bishop Peter Gillquist, took action to enter the Orthodox Church. The body, numbering some 3,000 members in the United States and Canada, expected to be officially received by Metropolitan Philip of the Antiochian Orthodox Archdiocese.

THOMAS HOPKO, *St. Vladimir's Seminary*

The Mormons and the Mormon Church

Ezra Taft Benson, the Mormon Church president, greets members at the faith's 156th general conference April 6.

Recent growth in membership, a new president, the murders of two persons involved in authenticating controversial letters about church founder Joseph Smith, and the construction of a center for academic study in Jerusalem caused an unusual amount of attention to focus on the Church of Jesus Christ of Latter-day Saints (LDS), commonly known as the Mormons, in 1986.

The Mormon church was established in the early 19th century in Palmyra, NY. The church has its foundations in revelations from God to Joseph Smith, Jr., through the Angel Moroni in written scripture which contains the "fullness of the everlasting Gospel. . . . " These revelations, compiled as the *Book of Mormon,* are accepted by the faithful as a divine record, and the believers look to its pages for inspiration, religious doctrine, and the mysteries of life. The revelations to Joseph Smith, Jr., came in the form of golden plates, the authenticity of which was attested to by a number of witnesses. Joseph Smith, Jr., assumed the leadership of the church as "seer, a translator, a prophet, and apostle of Jesus Christ, and elder of the church through the will of God the Father, and the grace of your Lord."

Membership. The church was formally established on April 6, 1830, with only six members. Within a month, membership had grown

to 40. Conversion and missionary activities increased the church faithful to 1,000 persons by the next spring. In spite of persecutions and governmental interference over a variety of issues, the church has grown substantially in membership (*see* accompanying table). Extensive missionary activity—more than 30,000 missionaries are currently serving in 188 missions in the United States and abroad—contributed to the growth.

Congregations of the church are currently organized in 95 countries and 20 territories, colonies, and possessions. Forty temples are now in operation in the United States and 21 other countries, with 7 more under construction. In addition, facilities of the Church Educational System have an enrollment in excess of 411,000 students. The largest and best-known is Brigham Young University (BYU) in Provo, Utah.

Church Assets. The financial foundation of the church is derived primarily from the tithes and offerings from its membership. Faithful church members give 10% of their incomes as tithing to the church, contribute monthly fast offerings, and make additional contributions for construction and maintenance of facilities. The church also has income-producing properties, including life-insurance companies; television and radio stations; the *Deseret*

News, Salt Lake City's evening newspaper; hotels; Zions Security Corporation, which operates commercial properties owned by the church. The church does not own nor, according to its authorities, does it seek controlling interest in any major national company. It is not considered a function of the church to operate for financial profit. Many critics of the church and numerous publications, including the 1985 book *The Mormon Corporate Empire* by John Heinerman and Anson Shupe, hold otherwise. However, other outside researchers believe that the "great financial empire" of the LDS church would begin to fall on its face within 30 days if the tithing income were cut off. Church assets also include an extensive welfare-services program and the world's largest system of genealogical libraries.

Church Leadership. Each LDS president is believed to have inherited the mantle of authority of Joseph Smith, Jr., as prophet, seer, and revelator. The president holds the office for life, and his doctrinal decisions are accepted as the will of God. Ezra Taft Benson, who served as President Eisenhower's secretary of agriculture, became president following the death of President Spencer W. Kimball on Nov. 5, 1985. President Benson, in his initial statement to church members, vowed to continue the threefold mission of the church: to preach the gospel, to perfect the saints, and to redeem the dead. One of his first goals is to encourage inactive and critical members to return to full and active support of the teachings of the church.

In September 1986, President Benson, a firm believer that the U.S. Constitution was divinely inspired, publicly expressed his convictions that the principles and precepts of the Constitution as expounded by the Founding Fathers have been eroded. He urged church members to become involved in civic affairs, and to elect "good, wise, and honest" men and women as a means of preserving the Constitution. He described the current situation as follows: "For the past two centuries, those who do not prize freedom have chipped away at every major cause of our [the U.S.] Constitution until today we face a crisis of great dimensions." And, accordingly, the U.S. is approaching the time prophesied by Joseph Smith, Jr., that "when the Constitution is upon the brink of ruin . . . [the Mormons] shall bear the Constitution away from the verge of destruction." Thus, the divinely inspired Constitution "will be saved by the citizens [Mormons] . . . who love and cherish freedom."

Recent Issues. The discovery and attempted sale of documents that purport to contradict the account of the original revelation to Joseph Smith, Jr., made the headlines in 1985–86. The most controversial document was the so-called "Salamander Letter," written in 1830 by Martin Harris, which describes how a spirit transformed itself into a white salamander and struck Smith as he tried to recover the golden plates. The documents have been called forgeries by church authorities. However, after a young Mormon, Mark Hofmann, sold the "Salamander Letter" in 1984 to a Mormon stockbroker, Steven F. Christensen, who in turn donated the letter to the church, Christensen and the wife of a business associate were killed on Oct. 15, 1985, in separate bomb explosions in Salt Lake City. A day later, Hofmann was injured accidently in a similar blast. Evidence gathered by the police resulted in the arrest and charges against Mark Hofmann on two counts of first-degree murder and 28 other charges of fraud, theft by deception, and bomb-making. By late 1986, Hofmann had yet to come to trial, and an attempt by the prosecution to consolidate the charges into one trial was denied by Third District Judge Kenneth A. Rigtrup. Judge Rigtrup was scheduled to preside over the trial involving murder charges and theft by deception, beginning March 2, 1987. Three other Third District judges have been assigned to preside over a trial involving the other counts later in 1987.

For many years, the church has conducted Study Abroad programs in a number of international locations. Considered academic programs by the church, they are reportedly not designed or used for proselyting activities. Such a program has been functioning in Israel since 1968. After considerable public planning, the church decided to construct a BYU "annex" in Jerusalem for academic programs, which would include study of both the ancient and modern civilizations in the region. The procedure for the construction of the annex raised strong protest within the Israeli Knesset (parliament) and among Zionists on the grounds that the purpose of the facility was to convert Jews to Mormonism. This conflict was alleviated in May 1986 when a letter, signed by 154 members of the U.S. Congress, was sent to every member of the Knesset calling for an end to the opposition to the construction of the BYU's Jerusalem Center for Near Eastern Studies. On the same day, Yitzhak Zamir, Israel's attorney general, issued a detailed opinion that no irregularities or illegalities existed. Construction of the facility, with Israeli approval, is proceeding.

LORENZO K. KIMBALL

	Membership	*U.S.*	*%*	*Non U.S.*	*%*
1930	670,000	549,400	82	120,600	18
1960	1,693,200	1,523,900	90	169,300	10
1970	2,930,800	2,315,300	79	615,500	21
1980	5,919,900	3,855,900	65	2,064,000	35
1986	6,000,000	3,900,000	65	2,100,000	35

Protestantism

Ordination of women was a divisive issue for the worldwide Anglican communion in 1986, both in its internal and ecumenical relationships. The 28 Anglican primates called for further consultation before any Anglican church moves to consecrate a woman as a bishop. Such action was endorsed in principle by the General Synod of the Anglican Church of Canada and the church's newly elected archbishop, Michael Geoffrey Peers, who succeeded Edward W. Scott. The Church of England's General Synod referred ordination of women to the denomination's House of Bishops for further study. Pope John Paul II and Johannes Cardinal Willebrands, head of the Vatican Secretariat for Christian Unity, warned that the issue of women priests was becoming a serious obstacle to unity talks between Catholics and Anglicans.

The Roman Catholic Church in Scotland agreed to take part in discussions with mainstream Protestant churches for the first time since the Reformation. The World Evangelical Fellowship approved a ''Contemporary Evangelical Perspective on Roman Catholicism'' at its Eighth General Assembly in Singapore. A representative of the Anglican-Roman Catholic International Commission announced an agreement on salvation by faith, which had divided Protestantism and Roman Catholicism since the Reformation.

Lutheranism. The sometimes rocky road toward Lutheran unity continued in 1986 among three U.S. denominations. At separate national conventions in August the American Lutheran Church (ALC), the Association of Evangelical Lutheran Churches (AELC), and the Lutheran Church in America (LCA) officially approved a plan to merge into one body, the 5.3-million-member Evangelical Lutheran Church in America. The merger would be submitted to congregations of the American Lutheran Church for final approval in 1987.

The Rev. Daniel Solberg of Alison Park, PA, became the second Pennsylvania minister to be defrocked by the LCA for his involvement in a group that held protests to dramatize the plight of unemployed workers in the Pittsburgh area. (The Rev. D. Douglas Roth of Clairton, PA, had been defrocked for similar cause in 1985.) Solberg disrupted the LCA's convention in Milwaukee to read a statement denouncing the Lutheran merger.

The Presbyterian Church (U.S.A.) voted to recognize the ministries and sacraments of the three merging Lutheran denominations, a step that was reciprocated by the ALC and AELC. The head of the Anglican communion, Archbishop Robert Runcie of Canterbury, exchanged Communion with Lutheran Church in America Bishop James R. Crumley, Jr., at the LCA convention.

Leaders and Meetings. The Lutheran Church-Missouri Synod reaffirmed its traditional opposition to women pastors and re-elected the Rev. Ralph A. Bohlmann to a third term as president, rebuffing a right-wing challenge. The Rev. Benjamin M. Weir, who was released in 1985 after 16 months of captivity in Lebanon by Shiite Muslims, was elected moderator of the Presbyterian Church (U.S.A.).

The strife-torn Southern Baptist Convention (SBC) elected another fundamentalist president. The Rev. Adrian Rogers of Memphis, who had served as president from 1979 to 1980, defeated the Rev. Winfred Moore of Amarillo, TX, considered a theological ''moderate.'' A federal judge in Atlanta refused to hear a complaint brought by three Southern Baptist laypersons against the denomination over rulings made at the 1985 SBC convention, saying that civil tribunals have no power to resolve such church disputes.

Eva Burrows of Australia was elected general commissioner of the worldwide Salvation Army. At age 56, she was the youngest person and only the second woman to be elected general. The Army's first woman leader, Evangeline Booth, the daughter of Salvation Army founder William Booth, served from 1934 to 1939. In one of her first official actions, Burrows named Commissioner Andrew S. Miller of Atlanta as U.S. national commander.

Bishops of the United Methodist Church issued what they called ''a clear and unconditional 'no' to nuclear weapons'' in a four-page pastoral letter that was approved unanimously. The church's hymnal revision commission voted to delete *Onward Christian Soldiers* and the *Battle Hymn of the Republic* from a revised edition because of their militaristic language, but reversed the decision after receiving thousands of letters of protest.

Politics. The movement among mainline churches to offer sanctuary to illegal aliens from Central America continued despite the convictions of eight religious workers on charges of conspiring to smuggle them into the United States.

Mainline Protestants also continued to protest the apartheid system in South Africa. Several denominational and parachurch organizations took steps to divest their holdings in U.S. corporations doing business there, and the United Methodist Pension Board was a target of protests for its refusal to totally divest such holdings. Nobel laureate Desmond Tutu was installed as archbishop of Cape Town and head of South Africa's Anglican Church.

In Greece, an appeals court overturned the convictions of three evangelical Christians who were charged with violating the country's anti-proselytizing law. In Egypt, ten former Muslims who had converted to Christianity were arrested, but four of them were later released.

DARRELL J. TURNER, *Religious News Service*

© Patrick Durand/Sygma

© Donatello Brogioni/Sygma

© Nick Arroyo/Atlanta Newspapers

Some 1986 Religion Highlights: *On September 7, Nobel laureate Desmond M. Tutu (top, second from right) became the first black to be installed as archbishop of Cape Town and head of South Africa's Anglican Church. Twenty-two Anglican bishops, including the Archbishop of Canterbury, Robert Runcie (third from right), attended the service. In June, Adrian Rogers (above) of Memphis, TN, was elected president of the Southern Baptist Convention. In April, Pope John Paul II paid a historic visit to Rome's central synagogue. The pontiff and Rome's chief rabbi, Elio Toaff (extreme right), embraced, read psalms, and exchanged gifts.*

AP/Wide World

The Rev. Charles E. Curran of Catholic University of America was told by the Vatican that his liberal views on sexual issues would prevent him from teaching theology.

Roman Catholicism

Widening theological dissent worldwide, but especially in the United States, led to the surfacing in 1986 of a strongly conservative crackdown by the Vatican in matters of doctrine and the teaching authority of the Roman Catholic Church. The year also was marked by a continuing flurry of pastoral visits by Pope John Paul II, including trips to India, Latin America, France, and other parts of the world. During the year preparations were made for two major events in 1987—a papal trip to the United States and a world Synod of Bishops in Rome that would deal with the roles of the emerging Catholic laity.

The pope himself wrestled with a wide variety of thorny questions, ranging from internal church problems to church-state tensions in Nicaragua, the Philippines, Brazil, and Indonesia, and condemnations of human-rights abuses in South Africa, the Middle East, Central America, and Northern Ireland.

The Vatican issued new guidelines on the controversial question of "liberation theology," acknowledging that the church must work to aid the poor and the oppressed while striving for a "conversion of hearts." Pope John Paul issued the fifth encyclical of his papacy. Titled *Dominum et Vivificantem* ("The Lord and Giver of Life"), the encyclical focuses on the Holy Spirit and is strongly critical of Marxism and other forms of philosophical materialism.

After 18 months in captivity in Lebanon, Servite Father Lawrence Martin Jenco, an American who headed the Catholic Relief Services office in West Beirut, was freed by Muslim extremists in July 1986.

U.S. News. In what promises to grow into a long-term, complex controversy, the Vatican removed the teaching credentials of a popular moral theologian, Father Charles Curran, who was a tenured professor of moral theology at the Catholic University of America in Washington, DC. The priest refused to change his dissenting views on several moral issues dealing primarily with human sexuality and what Curran termed "noninfallible church teaching."

In an unprecedented move, the Vatican required Archbishop Raymond G. Hunthausen of Seattle, WA, to transfer to his auxiliary bishop authority over several areas of church discipline. The archbishop had been the subject of a two-year Vatican investigation. During 1986, the Vatican also continued to put pressure on more than 20 nuns who signed a controversial ad in *The New York Times* that claimed the church offered an alternative teaching on abortion. During the year, most of the sisters reached an understanding with Vatican authority.

The American bishops culminated a five-year development of a pastoral letter on the economy, approving the third and final draft at their November meeting. The pastoral, "Economic Justice for All," was the second such effort in three years that used widespread consultation to gather data from various sectors of the church and society. The bishops also set up a special ad hoc committee to study the question of nuclear deterrence. In a 1983 pastoral on war and peace, the bishops said that deterrence could only be justified if the United States was actively working for nuclear disarmament.

The U.S. bishops took strong positions against American aid to the "contra" rebels in Nicaragua, and on behalf of economic sanctions against the apartheid regime in South Africa. Like most of the global church, the bishops supported the popular revolution in the Philippines that toppled the regime of Ferdinand Marcos in favor of Corazon Aquino.

The year also saw increased attention by all sectors of the church to the "explosion" of lay ministries, as well as continuing declines in clergy numbers.

ROBERT L. JOHNSTON
Editor, "The Chicago Catholic"

RELIGION / SPECIAL REPORT

The Television Factor

In the United States, a nation that is pervasively religious and pervaded by television, it was inevitable that religion would become a factor in television. What was not predictable was the radical change in religious-program sponsorship that began building in the 1950s and took hold in the 1970s. Control has shifted from national agencies of so-called mainline denominations toward independent broadcasters overwhelmingly drawn from the Evangelical movement and its interrelated subcategories, Fundamentalism and Pentecostalism. (Confusingly, many Evangelicals who support the independent broadcasters belong to the mainline church bodies.)

This shift both reflects a changing balance of power in American religion and, in turn, enhances the cultural influence of conservative Protestants. In addition, the broadcasters have a broad effect on the agenda and the public perception of Evangelicalism. Certain prominent preachers have stirred great controversy with their increasing involvement in politics, beginning with the 1980 presidential campaign.

The History. Early radio religion, and then television, was monopolized by doctrinally bland Protestant, Catholic, and Jewish programs produced by the networks for the older religious establishment and carried on free public service time by their affiliated stations. Independent programs, with doctrinally conservative Bible preaching and appeals for commitment to Jesus Christ, had to scramble for access, and to purchase their time.

Difficulties in purchasing radio time caused 50 conservative agencies to form a trade association, National Religious Broadcasters (NRB), in 1944, as an affiliate of the National Association of Evangelicals. The access issue helped to unify the newly energized Evangelical movement. The medium of radio remains the backbone of evangelistic broadcasting, despite the attention TV preachers receive.

Independent pioneers on television included the revivalist Billy Graham, Evangelicalism's prime post-World War II leader; Rex Humbard, whose Akron church was conceived as a broadcast studio; and Oral Roberts of Tulsa, whose healing revivals caused a sensation when they were filmed for television. As recently as 1959, the independent religious broadcasters filled only half of religious air time. Today they have a near-monopoly. NRB lists a constituency of 2,296 organizations, including program producers, 1,134 radio stations, 200 local TV stations, and several nationwide cable TV networks. The biggest of these enterprises is the Christian Broadcasting

Network (CBN) of Virginia Beach. This cable-based network is run by the Rev. Marion Gordon ("Pat") Robertson, a 56-year-old Pentecostal-style Southern Baptist who in 1986 announced that he was withdrawing as host of *The 700 Club* because of the demands of political travel. He would continue as a commentator on the program.

Today's TV Evangelist. Ben Armstrong, executive director of NRB, estimates that annual spending for religious radio and TV time alone amounts to $1 billion, possibly $2 billion. It is, however, a field of boom and bust, with continual crisis appeals for funds necessitated by the high costs of television and the preachers' empire-building. Scandals or questions about use of money arise periodically. Many of the better-known TV evangelists have launched ancillary institutions, such as universities or Bible colleges (Robertson; Jerry Falwell of Lynchburg, VA; Roberts; Jimmy Swaggart of Baton Rouge), a theme park with luxury hotel (Jim Bakker of Charlotte, NC), and a medical center (Roberts).

In 1986, TV evangelist Pat Robertson tested the waters for a run for the GOP presidential nomination in 1988.

Courtesy of the Christian Broadcasting Network Inc.

Television evangelist Jimmy Swaggart, 50-year-old Pentecostal preacher and Gospel singer, maintains the old tent revival style at his 7,000-seat Family Worship Center outside Baton Rouge, LA.

A controversial 1985 Nielsen survey comissioned by Robertson reported that 21% of U.S. households have at least minimum six-minute exposure to religious television in a week, and 40% of them (projected to equal 61 million adults) in a month's time. The same survey showed that the stars with the biggest per-month exposure are: Robertson (whose *700 Club* gets daily exposure); Swaggart; Robert Schuller of Garden Grove, CA; Bakker (also broadcasting daily); Roberts; and Falwell. Of these leaders, the only non-Pentecostals are Schuller, whose lavish Crystal Cathedral is nominally part of the Reformed Church in America, and Falwell, a Baptist Fundamentalist who is well-known for his founding role in the political "new religious right." (Billy Graham achieves top ratings, but his prime-time specials appear only intermittently.)

American TV religion is a distinctly Protestant affair. The nation's largest church, the Roman Catholic, has not had a major TV personality since the heyday of Bishop Fulton J. Sheen's weekly prime-time lectures in 1952–57. (Sheen's air time was not provided free or bought by the church, but purchased by a commercial sponsor.) The only denominational project of note is the American Christian Television System (ACTS) of the Southern Baptist Convention, an Evangelical group that is the nation's largest Protestant body. ACTS, which cost $20 million in its first two years, has run behind income projections and as of 1986 was available 24 hours daily to a modest 4 million homes via 225 cable systems, and on seven low-power stations.

Success and Criticism. Among the many explanations for the inroads made by the independent religious broadcasters are: the expansion of nonnetwork stations and cable outlets; the interest of stations in raising profits by selling time while mainline church leaders insisted on the stations' duty to grant free time; the mainliners' aversion to the independent's tactic of appealing on the air for money to keep broadcasts going; the 1960 decision of the Federal Communications Commission that purchased-time religion was equal to free programs in tallying "public service" time; availability of cheap videotaping production; audience preferences; and the commitment of conservatives to media evangelism. Another aspect, no doubt, was the rise of conservative Protestantism and simultaneous decline of mainline churches. Due to that decline, by the 1980s the relatively liberal groups affiliated with the National Council of Churches accounted for less than 50% of U.S. Protestants.

The fear of critics that TV programs siphon off dollars and attendance from conventional churches is groundless, according to a University of Pennsylvania/Gallup study issued in 1984. Attacks on the new leaders in religious television often revolve around secular political matters, but other qualms are raised. TV religion's relentless fund-raising gives faith a commercial aura. Television's emphasis on emotion, visual impact, and images of success concerns religious analysts who fear that the TV style is subtly reshaping the content of American Christianity.

RICHARD N. OSTLING

Japanese-made imitations of brand-name handbags, as well as watches and other goods, proliferated through black-market distribution in 1986. The situation warranted the attention of the European Community, which raised the problem of counterfeiting with Japan, a move that resulted in increased vigilance on the part of Japanese police to crack down on the offenders.

AP/Wide World

RETAILING

U.S. retailing in 1986 was dominated by major consolidations and divestitures, more focused merchandising, and efforts to realize greater value from real estate. Analysts called those trends signals of a maturing industry.

The year's biggest development was undoubtedly the merger of May Department Stores and Associated Dry Goods Corporation, with May the survivor of a $10 billion retail complex. Allied Stores Corporation, another large retailer, became the target of a hostile takeover by Campeau Corporation, a Canadian real-estate development company. In an attempt to ward off the takeover, Allied tentatively agreed to accept another offer. However, Campeau persisted and in November reached agreement with Allied regarding the takeover.

Mergers in the form of leveraged buyouts, in which management and outside investors make a bid for the company, involved two of the largest retailers. As a result, R. H. Macy & Company and Safeway Stores, America's largest supermarket chain, were acquired from their shareholders and were changed from public to private firms.

The bell tolled, however, for two well-known retailers because of persistent unprofitability. B.A.T. Industries, the British conglomerate, sold its 36 Gimbel department stores after acquiring them in 1974. Gimbel sites in New York, Philadelphia, Pittsburgh, and Milwaukee were occupied by other retailers, and Gimbels departed after 140 years. And Amcena Corporation, the American arm for the Brenninkmeyer interests in Europe, decided to terminate the Ohrbach's apparel stores.

These moves were explained by Fred A. Wintzer, Jr., an analyst for Alex Brown & Son, Baltimore. "Retailers face an environment of slower growth, market saturation, intense competition, fragmented specialized consumer markets, rising resource costs, and accelerating technological advancements," he said.

The 17 John Wanamaker stores were put on the block by Carter Hawley Hale Stores, which deemed their growth rate insufficient. But the Dayton Hudson Corporation said it was selling its 775-store B. Dalton book chain because it wanted to concentrate on bigger stores. Despite the sale of that specialized business, the specialty-store concept became a principal trend in 1986. The opportunity for more flexibility and better economic performance was behind the lure of the smaller, more concentrated store.

Bloomingdale's opened the first two of a projected chain of airport stores, one being "Bloomie's Express," at Kennedy International Airport in New York. Carson Pirie Scott, Chicago, said it soon would introduce its first separate "corporate level" store for career women in downtown Washington. F. W. Woolworth opened many small stores based on top-performing counters in its variety stores. And Montgomery Ward used the specialty approach in its existing stores, and also opened separate units.

Reflecting a real-estate fever, Alexander's Inc. planned to redevelop its Manhattan flagship store into a multipurpose tower. And B. Altman, which had been taken over by a real-estate group, began to halve the size of its Fifth Avenue store and to replace the emptied five floors with offices.

ISADORE BARMASH, "The New York Times"

The tall ships were in Newport for celebrations marking the 350th anniversary of the founding of Rhode Island by Roger Williams. The ships then made their way to New York for Fourth of July festivities.

AP/Wide World

RHODE ISLAND

Rhode Island marked its 350th anniversary in 1986. Throughout the year parades, balls, concerts, and local festivals celebrated the state's three-and-a-half centuries. Among other events in this turbulent year were a constitutional convention and a series of scandals and investigations that involved some of the state's most prominent individuals and institutions.

Impeachment. The first Supreme Court impeachment proceeding in the state's history began January 9 with a bipartisan House resolution to impeach Chief Justice Joseph A. Bevilacqua, accused of links with organized crime. Former U.S. Attorney General Benjamin R. Civiletti was chosen to carry on an inquiry into the justice's conduct for the House Judiciary Committee. Weeks of closed-door investigation culminated in the start of open committee hearings May 14. Two weeks later Bevilacqua submitted his resignation, effective June 30.

Constitutional Convention. On January 6 the state convened its second unlimited constitutional convention since the framing of the present 1842 constitution. Its committees soon began work on numerous proposed amendments. By mid-June, 25 had been adopted by the convention. Of these, 18 were approved by voters in November.

General Assembly. The annual session began on January 7 and, slowed somewhat by the impeachment proceedings, did not complete its normal work until the end of June. As had been true in 1985, relations between the Democratic Assembly leadership and the Republican governor were fairly smooth.

Adoption of the 1987 budget caused little controversy, though proposed pay raises for state general officers produced a brief flurry of partisan wrangling before they were approved. Legislation was passed to implement a solid waste incineration scheme adopted in 1985; another effort was made to deal with teacher strikes through mandatory mediation legislation; smoking in the workplace was regulated; and a package of child-care bills was passed.

Economy. From an economic standpoint the state had a very good year. The unemployment rate remained below the national average throughout the year. The business climate had improved measurably. In November, Electric Boat, the submarine manufacturer, reportedly had 500 jobs paying $10 per hour on average that it could not fill.

Election. November 4 saw Gov. Edward D. DiPrete (R) easily defeat Bruce Sundlun (D); Lt. Gov. Richard A. Licht (D) narrowly win over Secretary of State Susan L. Farmer (R); and relative unknown James E. O'Neil (D)

RHODE ISLAND · Information Highlights

Area: 1,212 sq mi (3 140 km²).
Population (1985 est.): 968,000.
Chief Cities (1980 census): Providence, the capital (July 1, 1984 est.), 154,148; Warwick, 87,123.
Government (1986): *Chief Officers*—governor, Edward D. DiPrete (R); lt. gov., Richard A. Licht (D). *General Assembly*—Senate, 50 members; House of Representatives, 100 members.
State Finances (fiscal year 1985): *Revenue,* $2,129,000,000; *expenditure,* $2,010,000,000.
Personal Income (1985): $13,465,000,000; per capita, $13,906.
Labor Force (June 1986): *Civilian labor force,* 510,400; *unemployed,* 18,600 (3.6% of total force).
Education: *Enrollment* (fall 1984)—public elementary schools, 89,372; public secondary, 44,662; colleges and universities, 69,927. *Public school expenditures* (1983–84), $456,000,000 ($3,720 per pupil).

edge out Attorney General Arlene Violet (R) in a surprise upset. Democrats Roger N. Begin (incumbent) and Kathleen S. Connell had little trouble in their runs for general treasurer and secretary of state, respectively. U.S. Representatives Fernand J. St. Germain (D) and Claudine Schneider (R) both defeated challengers.

Scandals. In April the Fleet National Bank, the state's largest, was indicted in connection with alleged illegalities at a state agency that grants low-interest mortgages.

In November, Rhode Island began investigations of its attorney general's office for possible misconduct, including altering transcripts of taped testimony. The attorney general is the state's chief prosecutor.

ELMER E. CORNWELL, JR.
Brown University

ROMANIA

Problems in Romania's energy sector during the past several years, caused by chronic drought, unusually severe winter weather, and shortfalls in the production of coal and oil, climaxed in late 1985.

Energy Crisis. In October 1985 the Executive Political Committee (EPC) of the Romanian Communist Party (RCP) declared a state of emergency. A "militarized work regime" was begun in the power-producing system, with military personnel moving into major enterprises to ensure an uninterrupted supply of electricity. The government enacted drastic curbs on energy consumption and made efforts to stimulate greater production. Coal miners were required to work around-the-clock; factory shifts were rescheduled to avoid periods of high energy consumption; while offices, shops, and service establishments were permitted to operate only during the daylight hours.

At the same time the government, determined to repay Romania's entire foreign debt (perhaps as much as $12 billion) by 1990, cut imports and maximized exports. This, coupled with the energy crisis, caused a serious shortage of foodstuffs. In late 1985 and early 1986, Romanian security forces were said to have quelled popular unrest in rural areas. Neighboring Yugoslavia reported increased numbers of Romanians crossing over the border.

Other Domestic Developments. The state plan and budget for 1986 were approved by the Grand National Assembly in December 1985. National income was expected to rise by 10–12%, industrial production by 8–9%, consumer goods production by 7–8%, agricultural production by 6–7%, and foreign trade by 12–15%. Effective Jan. 1, 1986, child benefits to families were increased, and taxes were raised for childless couples, in an attempt to stimulate the Romanian birthrate.

In August 1986 Foreign Minister Ilie Vaduva, a trained economist, replaced Vasile Pungan as minister of foreign trade; he was succeeded as foreign minister by Ioan Totu, and Finance Minister Petre Gigea was replaced by Alexandru Babe.

Foreign Relations. Romania's Communist regime continued to come under fire from U.S. critics, including members of Congress, who charged it with violations of human rights, persecution of a number of evangelical sects, and repression of its national minorities, particularly ethnic Hungarians living in Transylvania. In December 1985, U.S. Secretary of State George Shultz warned Romanian leader Nicolae Ceauşescu that his country was in danger of losing its Most Favored Nation trade status. The two nations agreed to set up high-level machinery in Washington and Bucharest to deal directly with charges of rights violations as they arise. In February 1986, Romania permitted a sizable number of dissidents and would-be-emigrants to leave the country. But Romanian police were alleged to have staged raids to confiscate copies of a memorandum protesting the mistreatment of the Hungarian minority in Romania, which had been submitted to the European Cultural Forum held in Budapest in October–November 1985.

Romania's relations with other members of the Warsaw Pact and the Council for Mutual Economic Assistance (CMEA) also continued to be unstable. At a December 1985 meeting of CMEA in Warsaw, Ceauşescu declared his dissatisfaction with the poor implementation of agreements to supply Romania with energy and raw materials, particularly oil and iron ore from the Soviet Union. The Romanian leader, who has long advocated that the Warsaw Pact countries cut military expenditures, called a December referendum in Romania on his plan to reduce the country's arms, troops, and military spending by 5%. Voters favored the plan unanimously.

JOSEPH FREDERICK ZACEK
The State University of New York at Albany

ROMANIA • Information Highlights

Official Name: Socialist Republic of Romania.
Location: Southeastern Europe.
Area: 91,698 sq mi (237 499 km²).
Population (mid-1986 est.): 22,800,000.
Chief Cities (1984 est.): Bucharest, the capital, 2,197,702, including suburbs; Braşov, 334,992; Cluj-Napoca, 299,786.
Government: *Head of state,* Nicolae Ceauşescu, president (took office 1967) and secretary-general of the Communist Party (1965). *Head of government,* Constantin Dăscălescu, prime minister (took office May 1982). *Legislature* (unicameral) —Grand National Assembly.
Monetary Unit: Leu (17.410 lei equal U.S.$1, June 1986).
Gross National Product (1984, 1984 U.S.$): $117,600,000,000.
Foreign Trade (1984 U.S.$): *Imports,* $10,300,000,-000; *exports,* $12,600,000,000.

SASKATCHEWAN

Saskatchewanians enjoy politics. It was fortunate, then, that 1986 featured a provincial election, for the fiscal and resource pictures were fairly gloomy.

General Election. Elections for the 64-seat provincial legislature were held on October 20. The governing Progressive Conservatives (PCs) and Premier Grant Devine won but with their total number of seats reduced from 49 (at dissolution) to 38. The official opposition New Democratic Party (NDP), under Alan Blakeney, corrected the lopsided nature of the previous assembly by growing from 9 to 25 seats. Liberal Party leader Ralph Goodale won the first Liberal seat since the 1978 election erased all Liberal representation.

The campaign revealed a curious blend of old and new. Premier Devine pictured the PC in its by-now familiar futuristic image of innovation and diversification with his "Saskatchewan, Builds" package. But he outraged his NDP opponents by portraying himself as the philosophic heir of the highly respected populist NDP leader, the late Tommy Douglas. The NDP advanced familiar themes in its call for fair taxation and higher employment, the latter to be fueled in large part by public projects. Yet it seemed to echo the recent PCs by promising a generous long-term housing and mortgage program. As in the 1960s, Liberals called for fiscal restraint and castigated other parties for expensive promises.

The campaign and election featured several firsts in Saskatchewan's history. The three party leaders participated in the first televised election debate. Devine's was the first Conservative government to be reelected for a second consecutive term. It was the first time in provincial history that the party coming first in the popular vote lost the election. The breakdown was NDP, 45.2%; PC, 44.6%; Liberals, 10.0%; and others, 0.2%, leading to calls for proportional representation reform.

Fiscal and Economic Issues. In the cabinet shuffle of Dec. 16, 1985, Minister of Finance Bob Andrew was replaced by the more traditional Gary Lane. He based his March 26 budget on old-fashioned electoral considerations, announcing C$3,000 grants for first-time purchasers of new homes, matching funds for a voluntary Saskatchewan Pension Plan aimed at the self-employed and homemakers, and large increases in agriculture and health spending. The $3.747 billion budget included the forecast of a $389 million deficit for 1986–87 (this government's fifth such deficit), which would push the accumulated deficit to more than $1.9 billion, the highest in provincial history. It might have been even higher, Lane conceded, had not the government created the Saskatchewan Property Management Corporation and Saskatchewan Agriculture and Commercial Equity

---

SASKATCHEWAN • Information Highlights

Area: 251,865 sq mi (652 330 km²).
Population (Jan. 1986 est.): 1,019,600.
Chief Cities (1981 census): Regina, the capital, 162,613; Saskatoon, 154,210; Moose Jaw, 33,941.
Government (1986): *Chief Officers*—lt. gov., F. W. Johnson; premier, Grant Devine (Progressive Conservative). *Legislature*—Legislative Assembly, 64 members.
Provincial Finances (1986–87 fiscal year budget): *Revenues*, $3,358,000,000; *expenditures*, $3,747,-000,000.
Personal Income (average weekly earnings, May 1986): $401.48.
Labor Force (July 1986, seasonally adjusted: *Employed* workers, 15 years of age and over, 496,000; *Unemployed*, 39,000 (7.9%).
Education (1986–87): *Enrollment*—elementary and secondary schools, 215,340 pupils; postsecondary—universities, 19,020, community colleges, 3,340.
(All monetary figures are in Canadian dollars.)

Corporation. Ironically, the deficit issue was to be important but not central in the October election.

Resources. The resources picture was not good. Grain prices dipped in the face of a U.S.-European Community subsidy war, and hopes for a high-quality crop were tempered by rain and frost in early autumn. Oil prices were depressed due to the worldwide glut, but the province contributed to a $650 million heavy-oil upgrader project in Regina. According to the *Globe and Mail* (Oct. 6, 1986), Saskatchewan farm income had declined by 46% since 1981, oil drilling by 95% in the previous 12 months, and potash prices by 45% since 1979. Saskatchewan, however, is no stranger to resource fluctuations. In "Next Year Country," optimism persists.

CHRISTOPHER DUNN
University of Saskatchewan

SAUDI ARABIA

In a key policy reversal, Saudi Arabia in mid-1986, in cooperation with the Organization of the Petroleum Exporting Countries (OPEC), began to limit its production of oil so as to drive up world prices. And in a move that stunned the international market, King Fahd in late October abruptly dismissed longtime Oil Minister Sheik Ahmed Zaki Yamani.

Oil and Finance. In late 1985, after oil production had fallen to a 20-year low of 2 million barrels per day and with the budget deficit climbing to about $9 billion for the fiscal year, Saudi Arabia announced that it would break with OPEC policy and increase its petroleum output. The Saudis claimed that the other OPEC countries had abandoned production quotas and official price agreements, leaving Saudi Arabia to shoulder the burden of revenue losses. Thus, seeking to reduce the world market share of non-OPEC countries and to cause

Saudi Oil Minister Sheik Ahmed Zaki Yamani (right) confers with his Kuwaiti counterpart, Ali Khalifa al-Sabah before the opening of an OPEC conference in Geneva in October. Later that month, Yamani was dismissed from his position.

AP/Wide World

a price war that would force OPEC to agree on a new pricing and production system, the Saudis continued to raise production into 1986. As of January the nation was pumping 4 million barrels per day, and by the summer it was averaging nearly 5.5 million barrels per day. World oil prices fell to a six-year low in January ($7 per barrel of benchmark crude). (*See* special report, page 283.)

Nevertheless, in its April and June meetings, OPEC refused to accept the Saudi plan. It was not until August 4 that all OPEC members agreed to cut total production by 3 million barrels per day, effective from September 1 to October 31. Saudi Arabia agreed to produce no more than 4.35 million barrels per day. The temporary agreement did bring an increase in prices, but there was no clear system of enforcing the quotas. In October, Saudi Arabia tried to persuade the rest of OPEC to adopt a permanent plan, but Yamani accepted a compromise extension of the August agreement through the end of the year.

Eight days later, however, on October 30, Yamani was dismissed from the post he had held for 24 years. No reason was given for the action, but analysts suspected that there had been a rift with King Fahd over oil-pricing policy. Hisham Nazer, the minister of planning, was named to the post temporarily.

At a ten-day OPEC meeting in December, Nazer was a key figure in negotiating an agreement to cut total production by about one million barrels per day and institute a fixed average price of $18 per barrel. For Saudi Arabia, the quota and fixed price represented a reversal of Yamani's ''price-war'' strategy.

The uncertainty in oil policy affected virtually every aspect of the Saudi economy. The government never issued a budget for the fiscal year that began in March. Instead, it simply limited spending to the levels of the previous year, and it devalued the riyal in June. Although some government ministries were slow in making payments to foreign contractors, bright spots in the economy included the first full year of petrochemical production at the new industrial cities of Jubail and Yanbu.

Government and Military. Except for the dismissal of Yamani, the economic recession brought about no major changes in the Saudi government. King Fahd continued to dominate all aspects of policy-making, and nothing further was done on a constitution or the formation of a consultative council.

New developments included an increase in spending for the Eastern Province, the home of the dissatisfied Shiite minority. Government hospitals added special sections for drug rehabilitation. The government began to allow advertising on Saudi television, although tobacco ads were forbidden by the Muslim ulema (a body of mullahs, or clerics).

On February 17, Saudi Arabia finalized a deal with Great Britain for the purchase of warplanes valued at some $7 billion. In March the Saudis requested the right to buy U.S. Stinger antiaircraft missiles, Sidewinder air-to-air missiles, and Harpoon antiship missiles to add to those already purchased in 1984. The Reagan

---

SAUDI ARABIA • Information Highlights

Official Name: Kingdom of Saudi Arabia.
Location: Arabian peninsula in southwest Asia.
Area: 829,996 sq mi (2 149 690 km²).
Population (mid-1986 est.): 11,500,000.
Capital (1981 est.): Riyadh, 1,000,000.
Government: *Head of state and government,* Fahd bin 'Abd al-'Aziz Al Sa'ud, king and prime minister (acceded June 1982).
Monetary Unit: Riyal (3.7400 riyals equal U.S.$1, Oct. 19, 1986).
Gross Domestic Product (fiscal year 1984 est. U.S.$): $108,000,000,000.
Economic Index (1985): *Consumer Prices* (1980 = 100), all items, 99.6; food, 103.3.
Foreign Trade (1984 U.S.$): *Imports,* $33,696,000,000; *exports,* $36,834,000,000.

administration favored the sale, but in early May both houses of the U.S. Congress voted to block it. President Ronald Reagan vetoed the Congressional action but deleted the Stinger missiles from the sales package. The Senate narrowly upheld his veto on June 5, and the sale to the Saudis could go through.

Foreign Affairs. Saudi Arabia in 1986 continued its traditional role as mediator of Middle East disputes, helping to improve relations between Jordan and Syria, and Bahrain and Qatar. However, attempted Saudi mediation of the Iran-Iraq war produced no results. Riyadh continued to provide economic aid to Iraq, and Saudi ships in the Persian Gulf came under increasing attack by Iran during the spring.

U.S. Vice-President George Bush visited Riyadh for three days in early April, expressing concern to King Fahd about the low cost of oil and the threat that it posed to the U.S. domestic oil industry. The king urged Washington to support stabilization of world prices.

On April 15, Saudi Arabia joined most of the other Arab states in condemning the U.S. bombing attack on Libya. However, relations between Washington and Riyadh remained warm and close through the end of the year.

WILLIAM OCHSENWALD
Virginia Polytechnic Institute

SINGAPORE

Singapore's continuing economic slump led to a probing reassessment of economic strategy in 1986 and prompted Prime Minister Lee Kuan Yew to consider delaying his retirement, which had been announced for 1988.

Economics. Singapore, long considered one of Asia's economic miracles, saw its growth rate plunge from more than 10% a year to negative figures after nearly two decades of spectacular growth. This economic slide stimulated a searching examination of government economic policies. Lee Hsien Loong, the son of the prime minister, was named acting minister for trade and industry in February. He chaired a select panel which issued an outline for future development focusing on tax reductions and investment incentives. Many of the panel's recommendations were incorporated in modified form into the 1986 budget, as was increased spending for capital projects. As high labor costs contributed to Singapore's increasing lack of competitiveness in world markets, a general wage freeze was also imposed. While still weak, particularly in traditional sectors, the economy showed some signs of recovery in the second half of the year.

The late 1985 collapse of one of Singapore's largest business concerns, Pan-Electric Industries, Ltd., forced a temporary suspension of stock trading and currency transactions. Some major brokerage firms were forced to close

when they were unable to meet their obligations from futures trading in Pan-Electric stock. Stricter stock market regulations were introduced to guard against similar manipulations in the future and to restore confidence in Singapore as a financial center.

Structural defects were blamed for the March collapse of the New World Hotel, which left 33 persons dead. Nevertheless, the collapse tarnished the nation's image as a safe city at a time when lagging tourist trade was contributing to economic problems.

Politics. Prime Minister Lee Kuan Yew said he might remain in office past his 65th birthday to help with the economic recovery.

The legal and parliamentary battles between the dominant People's Action Party and one of the only two opposition members in parliament, J.B. Jayaretnam of the Workers' Party, ended with a November court decision. Jayaretnam was fined and jailed for one month for making a false declaration, bringing automatic expulsion from parliament. Chiam See Tong, the other opposition member of parliament, faced a serious division in his Singapore Democratic Party as three of its top leaders left to form the new Singapore Solidarity Party.

International. Philippine President Corazon Aquino visited Singapore in August on her first trip out of the country since coming to power.

Delays in Singapore's signing of the Convention on International Trade in Endangered Species led the United States to impose a two-week prohibition in September on the import of tropical fish from Singapore because of inadequate certification. Singapore is the world's largest exporter of tropical fish, and the United States is among its major customers.

In the first action under an August law aimed at foreign publications, the distribution of *Time* magazine was curtailed after it declined to print in full a letter from a government spokesperson. As *Time* prints a regional edition in Singapore, this was the first test of the law's effect on the government's effort to make Singapore a printing and information center.

K. MULLINER, *Ohio University*

SINGAPORE • Information Highlights

Official Name: Republic of Singapore.
Location: Southeast Asia.
Area: 239 sq mi (618 km²).
Population (mid-1986 est.): 2,600,000.
Capital: Singapore City.
Government: *Head of state,* Wee Kim Wee, president (took office September 1985). *Head of government,* Lee Kuan Yew, prime minister (took office 1959). *Legislature* (unicameral)—Parliament.
Monetary Unit: Singapore dollar (2.170 S. dollars equal U.S. $1, Oct. 19, 1986).
Gross Domestic Product (1985 U.S.$): $17,600,-000,000.
Economic Index (1985): *Consumer Prices* (1980 = 100), all items, 117.3; food, 115.8.
Foreign Trade (1985 U.S.$): *Imports,* $26,189,-000,000; *exports,* $23,756,000,000.

Ada Alexander runs a summer food program for children in Philadelphia. According to the Census Bureau, some 20% of U.S. children live in poverty.

AP/Wide World

SOCIAL WELFARE

While the United States appeared relatively untouched by some of the severe economic difficulties affecting many areas of the world in 1986, it still had to try to deal with a number of significant social-welfare problems.

International

Rains, record harvests, and mass infusions of aid from Western countries brought profound relief to famine-stricken Africa for the first time in two years. Even so, most African countries had significant problems in 1986, including declining agricultural output, rising foreign debt, and unchecked population growth. The UN General Assembly, from May 27 to June 1, held an unprecedented special session on Africa's economic problems. The session ended with an agreement calling for African governments to make major economic reforms and for Western nations to provide some $80 billion in aid over five years.

The drop in world oil prices to six-year lows caused economic and social disruptions in many nations, including Great Britain. In January the British jobless rate reached an all-time high of 13.2%, with some 3.2 million persons out of work. The nation's unemployment rate remained high throughout the year.

Enormous foreign debt adversely affected life in many developing nations. Inflation in Brazil for the first six months of the year rose at the (annual) rate of nearly 300%, as the nation struggled with more than $105 billion in foreign debt. In an effort to end the inflationary spiral, Brazilian President José Sarney in February instituted a price freeze, a rise in the minimum wage from $44 to $58 a month, and other measures. Neighboring Argentina also experienced triple-digit annual inflation rates in 1986.

United States

In a year of general economic and social well-being, the United States continued to experience significant social-welfare problems. The official poverty rate, announced by the Census Bureau on August 26, stood at 14% of the total population. Some 33.1 million Americans were found to fit the official definition of poverty, which is an annual cash income of less than $10,989 for a family of four. Of the nation's children, 20% lived in poverty, and throughout the year the unemployment rate hovered around 7%. More than 8 million Americans were without jobs. In addition, more than 2 million full-time workers earned less than the poverty-level wage.

Blacks continued to bear a disproportionate share of the poverty burden. More than 30% of black Americans, or some 8.9 million persons, lived in families with incomes below the poverty line, and 50% of all black children (as compared with 17% of white children) lived in poverty. The black unemployment rate of about 14% was more than double the unemployment percentage of the white population, and more than 40% of black teenagers were unemployed. The median income for black American families was not quite $17,000, which was $12,000 less than the median figure for white families.

Homeless Persons. Homeless persons have always been part of the American scene, but beginning in the early 1980s a series of circumstances brought about a significant increase in the number of persons who had hit the bottom rung of the poverty ladder and wound up penniless and homeless. First came the movement, beginning in the 1960s, to release large numbers of mental patients from institutions. Second, persons working with the homeless said that the problems of the mentally disabled homeless had been worsened by cutbacks made by the Reagan administration in federal social services programs. A third underlying cause of the seeming rise in the number of homeless persons was the deteriorating supply of housing for the poor, especially in urban areas. These three factors, and a continued relatively high unemployment rate, brought about a fundamental change in the makeup of the nation's homeless population. In the past the typical homeless person might be considered a white, middle-aged, male alcoholic, but by 1986 there were significantly more women, children, and minorities in the numbers of homeless Americans.

The exact number was exceedingly difficult to measure. A study conducted by the National Coalition for the Homeless and released in October estimated that there were between 2 million and 3 million homeless persons nationwide. The Community for Creative Non-Violence—a Washington, DC, advocacy group that works with the homeless—put the figure even higher, at 3.5 million. The federal government's estimates of the homeless population, on the other hand, were much lower. Two years previously, for example, the Department of Housing and Urban Development (HUD) had released a survey that estimated the number of homeless at less than 350,000.

More locally, social-service workers reported increases in homeless populations in many areas of the country. In New York City, for example, officials planned on sheltering up to 10,000 homeless individuals and about 5,000 family groups. In October the city's mayor, Edward Koch, announced a $100 million program to build 20 new shelters that could house 7,000 people. In St. Louis the homeless population was estimated at from 10,000 to 15,000 in the summer—a 100% increase over the previous summer. Other local estimates of homelessness included 4,000 to 7,000 such persons in Newark, NJ, 10,000 to 25,000 in Houston, 13,000 in Philadelphia, 40,000 in Los Angeles, and some 2,000 even in affluent Santa Barbara, CA.

The Problem of Hunger. Paralleling the seemingly growing problem of the homeless was that of the hungry. A survey released on May 21 by the Physicians' Task Force on Hunger in America and by Harvard University's School of Public Health estimated that some 20 million Americans suffered periodically from hunger during any given month. The survey also blamed the Reagan administration for trimming the number of poor persons eligible for federal nutritional assistance programs, including food stamps. This survey, combined with reports by church groups, charitable organizations, and city and county officials of long lines of persons at soup kitchens and food pantries, indicated that hunger was a significant problem in the United States.

Reagan administration officials and others, however, said that reports of hunger in America were exaggerated. Administration officials asserted that the multibillion-dollar federal outlays going to food-assistance programs (such as food stamps and various child-nutrition programs) were working well, and that people who crowded into food kitchens across the country were not necessarily destitute but instead simply wanted to take advantage of free meals. On the day the Physicians' Task Force report was made public, President Reagan told a group of high school students at the White House, "I don't believe that there is anyone going hungry in America simply by reason of denial or lack of ability to feed them. . . . It is by people not knowing where or how to get help."

Welfare Reform. The debate over what the federal role in welfare should be accelerated in 1986. In his annual State of the Union address to Congress, February 6, President Reagan called for a review of the nation's welfare system. The president said that he was seeking to redefine the government's role, stating that "We must revise or replace programs enacted in the name of compassion that degrade the moral worth of work, encourage family breakups, and drive entire communities into a bleak and heartless dependency." He asked his Domestic Policy Council, a cabinet-level group headed by Attorney General Edwin Meese 3d, to report to him with "a strategy for immediate action to meet the financial, educational, social, and safety concerns of poor families."

By late November the council had received the results of three study groups that it had set up to make welfare-reform recommendations. According to press reports, the recommendations did not call for a sweeping revision of the nation's welfare system. In addition, with the Democrats in control of the House of Representatives and the Senate for the first time during the Reagan administration, prospects for congressional passage of significant welfare reform in 1987 appeared unlikely.

The reports of the study groups were all made public. One group, under the direction of Assistant Attorney General Charles J. Cooper, focused on the federal-state relationship and called for the states to take on a larger share of the welfare burden. The second group, a 22-member intergovernmental task force headed by Under Secretary of Education Gary Bauer and focusing on family issues, concluded that welfare "contributes to the failure to form the family in the first place" and that the "easy availability of welfare in all of its forms has become a powerful force for destruction of family life through perpetuation of the welfare culture." The group called for single mothers under 21 to be denied federally subsidized housing as well as basic cash payments under the Aid to Families with Dependent Children (AFDC) program, because according to the report these restrictions would be a means of discouraging "teen-agers tempted to promiscuity." The third group, under the direction of Charles D. Hobbs, head of the White House Office of Policy Development, had the mandate of reviewing all public-assistance programs. Hobbs' group did not recommend an overall streamlining of the welfare process. Instead it called for the establishment of 10 to 12 small demonstration projects in a handful of states. The projects, which would concentrate on getting welfare recipients on paying jobs, would be run by private organizations.

In that respect critics and supporters of welfare changes found common ground. Everyone agreed that the goal of reform was to help recipients end their dependence on public assistance and find gainful employment. Disagreement continued, however, over how best to put welfare recipients into job-training programs and eventually into paying jobs. Democrats in Congress, for example, pushed for continued high federal involvement in providing welfare funds and job-training programs; whereas the Reagan administration advocated turning more of the public assistance burden over to the states.

One major stumbling block in welfare reform is the fact that a large percentage of those receiving assistance are single women with young children. It is extremely difficult to provide these women with both training programs and affordable child care. The situation is best illustrated by the scope of the AFDC program, a $14 billion-per-year effort that is financed jointly by the states and the federal government. AFDC is intended to support children 18 years old and younger who live with an economically disadvantaged single parent. In the overwhelming majority of these cases, the children live with divorced, separated, or unwed mothers.

AFDC state benefits vary. A family of four in Texas, for example, receives only $221 per month in AFDC grants. In Ohio, that same family would be eligible to receive $374 per month. Congressional Democrats—including Rep. Harold Ford of Tennessee, who chairs the House Ways and Means subcommittee on public assistance, and Sen. Daniel Patrick Moynihan of New York, the Senate's leading welfare expert—proposed standardizing AFDC benefits nationwide and increasing federal support for various job-training programs for welfare recipients. Several states proposed other types of AFDC reforms. These included a proposal by Washington's Gov. W. Booth Gardner (D) that would eliminate AFDC entirely and instead use federal and state AFDC funds to finance a new plan. This plan, which was called the Family Independence Model, would (among other proposals) provide cash incentives for welfare recipients who were able to find work, help absent fathers to find employment and thus to contribute to the family's well-being, and create thousands of jobs in volunteer and nonprofit agencies and state government offices for parents in the AFDC program.

Private Relief Efforts. While federal and state officials continued to argue the merits of governmental assistance, private individuals donated approximately $8.8 billion to human-service charitable groups in 1985, according to the American Association of Fund-Raising Counsel. In 1986 the Hands Across America campaign in which more than five million Americans (including President Reagan and his family) linked hands on May 25, distributed more than $575,000 to food banks, homeless shelters, and other groups in November. (This was, however, far below the original goal of the organizers.) A comedians' telethon called Comic Relief raised some $3 million for the homeless and hungry, and USA for Africa, the 1985 campaign formed by rock musicians to raise funds for famine relief in Africa, donated $200,000 to anti-hunger and anti-homeless U.S. groups in 1986.

MARC LEEPSON
"American Politics" Magazine

Advocates for the homeless erected a statue on the grounds of the U.S. Capitol in late November to remind Congress of the plight of street people. An inscription on the base read "And Still There Is No Room At The Inn." Capitol regulations required the statue to be removed after 24 hours.

©Louise Gubb/JB Pictures

Winnie Mandela, wife of jailed opposition leader Nelson Mandela, continued to defy the white minority government.

SOUTH AFRICA

The cycle of black resistance and white repression in South Africa continued throughout 1986 with widespread violence, sporadic labor unrest and school boycotts. While many black townships remained ungovernable, the government seemed to have reestablished superficial control late in the year through the use of extreme force.

The state of the economy, reflecting South Africa's current political instability, remained uncertain. The financial rand (the restricted form of currency quoted at a lower rate than the commercial rand and used for exporting capital) fell by more than 35% during the course of the year. The real-estate market, another key economic indicator, fell by at least 20% in Johannesburg. Inflation, fueled by the weakness of the rand, was running at an annual rate of 17%. Gold exports, however, were expected to give the country a current-account surplus of more than $3 billion.

State of Emergency. In what some considered the most serious breach of civil liberties in the country's history, the imposition of a nationwide state of emergency on June 12 announced to the world that neither international criticism nor escalating black violence at home would be allowed to determine government policy. The declaration of this second, and more draconian, state of emergency was aimed in the short term at preempting plans by

government opponents to commemorate the tenth anniversary of the Soweto uprising. South African police immediately arrested leaders of unions, township organizations, and others from the United Democratic Front (UDF), the Azanian People's Organization (AZAPO), and even several entire church congregations while attending services. The Institute of Race Relations estimated that at least 3,000 people were arrested in the first days after the emergency. From the declaration of the emergency in June to the end of the year, hundreds of people were killed, most of them black, and approximately 22,000 black labor, political, and religious leaders were detained. It thus became apparent that, in the long term, the government hoped to restore law and order through widespread arrest and detention.

Reform in the Midst of Repression. At the beginning of the year, President Pieter W. Botha announced that South Africa had "outgrown the outdated concept of apartheid." Three months later, on April 23, the government published a white paper on urbanization that called for the repeal of 34 laws and proclamations which, for more than 60 years, had restricted the rights of blacks to live and work in white areas. On July 1, Parliament passed the Restoration of South African Citizenship Act, which ostensibly restored citizenship to the nation's millions of dispossessed blacks. Upon closer scrutiny, however, only an estimated 1.7 million out of a total of 9 million independent homeland citizens were eligible to regain their citizenship, and then only after written application. Also on July 1, Parliament passed the Abolition of Influx Control Act, which was to have restored freedom of movement to black South Africans, many of whom had been arrested in the past for violations of the notorious pass laws. With the abolition of the influx-control laws, new freedom of movement was extended to black South African citizens only, while the remaining millions of blacks were likely to be even worse off, since their movement, residence, and employment henceforth would be governed by the harsher restrictions of the Alien Act.

Right-Wing Opposition. Faced with continuing upheaval and uncertainty, increasing numbers of whites turned toward such right-wing political groups as the Conservative Party and the Herstigte Nasionale Party (HNP). An even more extreme right-wing reactionary group, the Afrikaner Resistance Movement (Afrikaner Weerstandbewiging, or AWB), also increased its popular support in 1986, primarily in the rural areas of the Transvaal and Orange Free State and among working-class Afrikaners. The AWB capitalized on white fears with a blatant appeal to white racism and a call for the reestablishment of the independent Boer Republics of the 19th century. Eugene Terre Blanche, the leader of the AWB, appealed to members of the organization, whom he saw as "true freedom fighters," to defend the heritage and the future of the Afrikaner *volk* (people, nation). While the National Party remained firmly in control of the white parliament and no general election was scheduled until 1989, the radical right, with apparently increasing support, could well be a force to be reckoned with in the future.

Kwa-Natal Option. At talks initiated in March by Mangosuthu Gatsha Buthelezi, the chief minister of Kwazulu (a Bantu homeland) and the Natal provincial government and other civic leaders, the possibility of regional power-sharing between blacks and whites was discussed. Conservative white groups and most blacks declined to participate; the national government only sent observers. Nevertheless, the so-called "Kwa-Natal Option" was regarded by some as a viable model for an integrated form of regional government within a larger federal system. After nine months of negotiations, representatives of 38 interest groups recommended the establishment of a multiracial government of Natal to be elected on a one-person, one-vote basis. The agreement provided for a two-chamber legislature, the first of which would be elected by universal suffrage, the second consisting of representatives from English, Afrikaans, African, and Asian groups. It also proposed an independent judiciary and a bill of rights. Pretoria's Minister for Home Affairs Stoffel Botha publicly rejected the power-sharing proposal, although there was some speculation that the government might yet decide to hold a referendum on the issue.

Opposition Leader Resigns. On February 7, during the opening debate of the parliamentary session, the leader of the Progressive Federal Party (PFP), Frederik van Zyl Slabbert, resigned because he saw the white political system as irrelevant to what was really happening in South Africa. In a speech to Parliament, Slabbert challenged the basis of the government's reformist policy, declaring that "the dismantling of apartheid has nothing to do with negotiation. Apartheid is not up for negotiation, it has to go completely. . . . [R]eform or constitutional change will never be successful as long as this government insists that it takes place on the basis of compulsory group membership."

Commonwealth Eminent Persons Group. The so-called Eminent Persons Group (EPG) created by the secretariat of the British Commonwealth traveled to South Africa in May to investigate political conditions on behalf of other Commonwealth nations. The group, led by former Australian Prime Minister Malcolm Fraser, intended to meet with the widest range of political leaders in order to assess the possibility of a negotiated settlement. The EPG cut short its visit and left abruptly following attacks by South African troops against representatives of the African National Congress (ANC) in neighboring Botswana, Zimbabwe, and Zambia on May 19. The EPG concluded that the only way to hasten the end of apartheid without violence was for Commonwealth nations to exert increased political and economic pressure on the Pretoria regime.

Sanctions. External pressures increased significantly during 1986, culminating in the imposition of economic and political sanctions by many countries, including members of the Commonwealth, the European Community (EC), the United States, and Japan. While Great Britain and the United States initially resisted imposing sanctions, pressure from other members of the Commonwealth on the one hand and from the U.S. Congress on the other, forced Britain's Prime Minister Thatcher and U.S. President Reagan to acquiesce.

On October 2 the Republican-controlled U.S. Senate voted, 78-21, to override President Reagan's veto for legislation imposing sanctions against South Africa. Earlier the House of Representatives had supported the sanctions measure by a vote of 313-83. The law banned all new public and private loans and investments, except for the reinvestment of profits, short-term credits, and the rescheduling of existing debts. The importation of South African iron, steel, arms, ammunition, military vehicles, farm products, uranium, coal, and textiles all were prohibited, as was the export of U.S. petroleum, munitions, nuclear technology, and

In Kwanobuhle, a black township in eastern Cape Province, a memorial service was held on March 21, the first anniversary of the killing by police of 19 black marchers. Growing unrest during the first months of 1986 led the Pretoria government to declare a state of emergency on June 12.

© W. Campbell/Sygma

computer hardware and software, specifically to the South African military and police. In addition, the U.S. landing rights of South African Airways and a 1946 bilateral tax treaty both were terminated. The legislation imposed penalties ranging from $50,000 in fines and imprisonment for individual violations, to $1 million for corporate violators.

Earlier, on September 16 foreign ministers of the 12 EC nations had agreed to a somewhat weaker package of sanctions that banned imports of South African iron, steel, and gold coins and prohibited new investment there. Britain went along with the measures.

On October 25, Third World and Soviet bloc countries successfully led a move to expel the South African delegation from an International Red Cross Conference at Geneva, further isolating South Africa and, for the first time, threatening the organization's historic neutrality.

Late in the year, General Motors, IBM, Coca-Cola, and other major U.S. corporations announced that they would terminate operations in South Africa, apparently in response to the uncertainties—and criticism—of doing business there.

ANC Strategy. While the ANC remains committed to violent opposition, including the most recent trend of bombing "soft (civilian) targets," its multiple strategy for liberation also includes links with such internal South African organizations as the UDF and various labor unions and the pursuit of diplomatic initiatives and opportunities. In August at Lusaka, Zambia, three senior members of the ANC met with the U.S. ambassador, the first official meeting of its kind. Earlier, U.S. Secretary of State George Shultz, in testimony to the Senate Foreign Relations Committee, said that because the ANC was "an important part of the political equation in South Africa," both the United States and the ANC needed to hear "authoritative statements of each others' policies and interests." Subsequent meetings with the ANC and the Pan Africanist Congress (PAC) reaffirmed the U.S. interest in establishing linkages with the African nationalists, although Secretary Shultz emphasized that the United States "recognized no single group as the primary vehicle for black aspirations." There were also meetings between the leader of the ANC, Oliver Tambo, and representatives of the British Foreign Office. Such activities accorded the ANC an official international legitimacy as one of the primary actors in South African politics.

While throughout the year there were rumors that jailed ANC leader Nelson Mandela would be released, the government feared that because of his enormous popularity it would be unable to control the popular uprising that likely would follow. As a result, the opposition's most popular leader—and symbol of the anti-apartheid movement—spent his 23rd year in prison in 1986. His wife, Winnie Mandela, continued to work for his release and to speak out against the Pretoria government.

Archbishop Tutu. On September 7, the 1984 Nobel Peace Prize winner Bishop Desmond M. Tutu was installed as the first black archbishop of the Anglican Church in South Africa by the Archbishop of Canterbury, the Most Rev. Robert Runcie. Guests at the installation included Winnie Mandela; Coretta Scott King, widow of the late U.S. civil-rights leader Martin Luther

King, Jr.; Mayor Coleman Young of Detroit; and Bishop John T. Walker, the Episcopal bishop of Washington, D.C. No South African government officials were invited to the installation, and none of the ceremonies were shown on state controlled television.

Cabinet Changes. On December 1 four new cabinet ministers and 12 deputy ministers were sworn into office in Pretoria. Alwyn Schlebusch, the former vice-president and chairman of the President's Council, was appointed minister in the Office of the State President. Adriaan Vlok, who had been deputy minister of both defense and law and order, became the new minister of law and order. Two ministers who had played a prominent role in enforcing the state of emergency were dropped from the cabinet—Minister of Law and Order Louis Le Grange, who became speaker of the white Parliament, and Louis Nel, the former deputy minister for information. The changes seemed unlikely to result in significant new policy directions; the government hoped that the replacement of these two ministers by younger and lesser-known politicians might give a new image to the two controversial ministries.

Press Censorship. On December 11 the government introduced new restrictions on news reporting, resulting in nearly total censorship on black political activities. Foreign and South African reporters were forbidden to publish unauthorized accounts of violence, the conditions of persons under detention, boycotts, "restricted" meetings, and the like. Under the regulations, legislators may oppose and question the government within the privileged confines of the parliaments, but what they say may be considered subversive outside of the legislatures and may not be published without approval. All previous restrictions on the press,

such as television coverage of protest and violence, remained in effect. The regulations also severely curtailed editorial comment and public discussion of these and other proscribed activities. Violations are punishable by fines or imprisonment. The government's expectation was that if it were able to stop the flow of news about South Africa's political crisis, it might be able to diminish the impact of the news and discourage opponents from engaging in political activities.

Additional regulations, aimed at further constraining such opposition groups as the UDF, expanded the definition of subversion to make it illegal for individuals or groups to promote boycotts or other opposition activities.

PATRICK O'MEARA AND
N. BRIAN WINCHESTER
Indiana University

SOUTH AFRICA • Information highlights

Official Name: Republic of South Africa.
Location: Southern tip of Africa.
Area: 471,443 sq mi (1 221 037 km²).
Population (mid-1986 est.): 33,200,000.
Chief Cities (1980 census): Pretoria, the administrative capital, 528,407; Cape Town, the legislative capital, 213,830; Johannesburg, 1,536,457; Durban, 505,963.
Government: *Head of state and government,* Pieter Willem Botha, state president (took office Sept. 1984). *Legislature*—Parliament (tricameral): House of Assembly, House of Representatives (Coloured), and House of Delegates (Indians).
Monetary Unit: Rand (2.23710 rands equal U.S. $1, Oct. 19, 1986).
Gross Domestic Product (1984 U.S.$): $73,000,-000,000.
Economic Index (1985): *Consumer Prices* (1980 = 100), all items, 192.5; food, 188.4.
Foreign Trade (1984 U.S.$): *Imports,* $10,309,-000,000; *exports,* excluding exports of gold, $9,390,000,000.

© P. Habans/Sygma

President P.W. Botha met in February with representatives of the Zion Christian Church, South Africa's largest black religious group, but his government offered few reforms of the apartheid system during the course of the year. Indeed, as international pressure increased, new repressive measures, such as strict press censorship, were instituted.

Charleston Place, a new $78 million hotel and retail complex, spurred further development in the downtown area.

SOUTH CAROLINA

Elections, a drought and heat wave, and continuing improvements in education were among the developments in the state in 1986.

Politics. Independent voting marked the 1986 election. U.S. Sen. Ernest F. Hollings, a Democrat, easily won reelection. Also reelected were incumbent Congressmen Floyd Spence (R), Butler Derrick (D), John M. Spratt, Jr. (D), and Robin Tallon (D). Rep. Carroll A. Campbell, Jr., narrowly defeated Democratic Lt.-Gov. Michael R. Daniel in the gubernatorial race, and Rep. Thomas F. Hartnett lost his bid for lieutenant governor to Democrat Nick A. Theodore. The House seats vacated by Campbell and Hartnett were won by Elizabeth J. Patterson (D) and Arthur Ravenel, Jr. (R), for a net Democratic gain of one seat. Republicans made only minor gains in the lower house of the state legislature, where significant changes in leadership occurred in 1986. Speaker Emeritus Solomon Blatt, who had served for 53 years, died in May, and Speaker Ramon Schwartz, Jr., retired in October.

The Legislature. A $3 billion budget was enacted but later reduced by 2.9% due to declining state revenues. A new Omnibus Crime Act designed to reduce prison overcrowding while stiffening penalties for violent criminals also was enacted. Other new legislation included a modernization of the probate code, authorization for living wills, the elimination of exemptions for jury service, measures limiting lawsuits and damages against the state and local governments, a clarification of landlord-tenant rights, the consolidation of the state's two adoption agencies, and a workfare program. Actions were taken to punish violators of pollution laws; voting hours were extended; and residents were allowed to vote by mail.

Education. The increased funding and upgraded standards provided by the 1984 Public Educational Improvement Act continued to benefit public education. Students earned higher scores on state-administered tests, the dropout rate declined to 4%, attendance reached 97%, and 43% of high-school graduates enrolled in college. Scores on the Scholastic Aptitude Tests (SATs) were up 11 points. Teacher salaries met the southeastern average, and improved standards for teacher training

---

SOUTH CAROLINA • Information Highlights

Area: 31,113 sq mi (80 582 km²).

Population (1985 est.): 3,347,000.

Chief Cities (1980 census): Columbia, the capital (July 1, 1982 est.), 101,457; Charleston, 69,510; Greenville, 58,242.

Government (1986): *Chief Officers*—governor, Richard W. Riley (D); lt. gov., Michael R. Daniel (D). *General Assembly*—Senate, 46 members; House of Representatives, 124 members.

State Finances (fiscal year 1985): *Revenue,* $5,825,000,000; *expenditure,* $4,400,000,000.

Personal Income (1985): $35,434,000,000; per capita, $10,586.

Labor Force (June 1986): *Civilian labor force,* 1,636,200; *unemployed,* 109,300 (6.7% of total force).

Education: *Enrollment* (fall 1984)—public elementary schools, 422,417; public secondary, 180,301; colleges and universities, 131,902. *Public school expenditures* (1983–84), $1,255,000,000 ($2,255 per pupil).

in colleges were effected. In higher education, tuition increased; funds were acquired to complete the new engineering center at the University of South Carolina; and a center to study national school dropouts was established at Clemson University.

Economy. The state experienced the worst drought and heat wave of the 20th century, resulting in major reductions in yields for most crops. Tobacco output held, and fresh peach production was good but below normal. The poultry industry experienced significant gains. Farmers planted less, but most held on to their farms.

Unemployment dropped to 6%, but the number of jobs did not increase materially. The major industrial development was the location of the $80 million Mack Truck assembly plant and supporting industries in Fairfield County. The rate of decline in the textile industry stabilized, and several South Carolina banks merged with out-of-state institutions. The largest newspaper in the state, the *Columbia State/Record,* was sold to the Knight-Ridder chain.

Urban. In Columbia, which celebrated its bicentennial in 1986, the Vietnam Monument and Memorial Park opened and a number of scenic improvements were made in the downtown area. The Charleston Spoleto Festival successfully concluded its tenth year.

ROBERT H. STOUDEMIRE
University of South Carolina

SOUTH DAKOTA

Economic distress was a factor in almost every major development in South Dakota in 1986. A rural depression brought the resurgence of the Democratic Party and inspired legislation to aid recovery, and the Sioux Indians experienced their most severe unemployment since the 1920s.

Elections. In the 1986 Senate race, with strong voter turnout, Democratic Congressman Tom Daschle defeated incumbent Republican James Abdnor. In June, Abdnor had won a narrow victory over Gov. William Janklow in the Republican primary. State legislator Tim Johnson (D) won over Dale Bell (R) to take Daschle's seat in the U.S. House of Representatives. Democrats gained seats in the state legislature. Yet Republicans retained control of both houses, and George Mickelson (R) defeated Lars Herseth (D) for governor. Both candidates were the sons of former governors. In a referendum, a state lottery was approved.

Legislation. The $845 million General Appropriations Act allocated the largest amounts to education, economic capital assistance, water development projects, and a new rural renaissance program. The renaissance program provided minimum wage payments to those driven from farms or ranches in economic col-

lapse, for retraining in accredited programs. By November more than 1,000 had enrolled. Other legislation authorized construction of a heritage center in Pierre and a compact with Arizona and California for low-level radioactive waste disposal.

Economy. Farmers and ranchers watched land prices plummet, and many fell into bankruptcy. Financial consultants said economic cycles and lowered federal price supports were partly to blame. But they fixed more blame on loan officers who had extended credit without cash-flow analyses, and on operators who had borrowed and spent freely. Some observers predicted that a fourth of the state's agricultural producers would fail. Business closures, lowered sales-tax receipts, and small-town recessions were statewide effects of the agrarian recession. Unemployment increased in transportation, manufacturing, and commerce, but there were moderate improvements in tourism and employment in education, government, and service industries.

Indian Affairs. Reservation residents suffered most as the unemployment rate in every tribe exceeded 80%. Turmoil in tribal politics was one result. Another was increased tension in Indian-white relations. With tax revenues, jobs, cultural interests, and constitutional freedom at stake, Indians and non-Indians faced each other in negotiations regarding tribal jurisdiction within original reservation borders. Major points of contention included the possession of Lake Andes by the Yankton Tribe and control of hunting and fishing licensing. Without clear precedents, judges and attorneys floundered in confusion. Incidents of racial abuse and several murders were attributed in part to the unresolved question of tribal authority.

Increasing numbers of reservation residents sought relief by migrating to towns and cities. Estimates of Indian population exceeded 7,000 in Rapid City and 2,000 in Sioux Falls.

HERBERT T. HOOVER
The University of South Dakota

SOUTH DAKOTA • Information Highlights

Area: 77,116 sq mi (199 730 km²).
Population (1985 est.): 708,000.
Chief Cities (1980 census): Pierre, the capital, 11,973; Sioux Falls, 81,343; Rapid City, 46,492.
Government (1986): *Chief Officers*—governor, William J. Janklow (R); lt. gov., Lowell C. Hansen II (R). *Legislature*—Senate, 35 members; House of Representatives, 70 members.
State Finances (fiscal year 1985): *Revenue,* $1,082,000,000; *expenditure,* $1,005,000,000.
Personal Income (1985): $7,903,000,000; per capita, $11,161.
Labor Force (June 1986): *Civilian labor force,* 366,400; *unemployed,* 15,300 (4.2% of total force).
Education: *Enrollment* (fall 1984)—public elementary schools, 86,724; public secondary, 36,590; colleges and universities, 32,772. *Public school expenditures* (1983–84), $308,000,000 ($2,640 per pupil).

SPACE EXPLORATION

Manned space exploration suffered a major catastrophe in 1986 with the destruction of the U.S. space shuttle *Challenger* and the tragic loss of its crew. The subsequent grounding of the shuttle fleet resulted in delays in the launching of several major satellite missions planned for 1986. (*See* feature article, page 36.) The Soviet Union launched a new space station, Mir, and occupied the complex for 71 days. In unmanned space research, Voyager 2 flew past the planet Uranus (*see* page 469), and an armada of spacecraft from several nations encountered Halley's comet (*see* page 122).

Manned Space Flight. One successful U.S. space shuttle mission was flown in 1986, prior to the *Challenger* accident on January 28. STS-24 (Space Transportation System Mission 24), *Columbia*'s seventh flight, was launched from Kennedy Space Center, FL, on January 12. The crew of seven included mission commander Robert L. Gibson, Charles F. Bolden, Jr., George D. Nelson, Steven A. Hawley, Franklin R. Chang-Diaz, Robert J. Cenker, and flight observer Rep. C. William (Bill) Nelson (D-FL). The crew deployed an RCA Satcom K-1 communications satellite, conducted materials experiments, and obtained images of Halley's comet and infrared imagery of atmospheric spectra. The shuttle landed at night January 18 at Edwards Air Force Base, CA.

Soviet manned flight efforts continued at a rapid pace. A new, modular space station called Mir ("Peace") was launched, unmanned, on February 19, to supplant the aging Salyut 7 space complex. The new station is 13.8 ft (4.2 m) in diameter and 44 ft (13.4 m) long and is intended to be the central part of a permanently manned Soviet space complex in the future. On March 13, Soyuz T-15 was launched, with cosmonauts Leonid Kizim and Vladimir Solovyev aboard, to dock with Mir and activate the station. On March 21 and April 25, two unmanned Progress cargo vehicles, each carrying 4,000 lb (1 820 kg) of fuel, instruments, and provisions, docked with Mir. Both Progress vehicles were sent on a destructive reentry path into the earth's atmosphere.

On May 5 the Soyuz T-15 cosmonauts flew their craft from Mir to the Salyut 7 space complex, about 1,850 mi (3 000 km) away. They reactivated the station, which had been uninhabited since November 1985, and began a series of experiments that the previous crew had not completed. On May 28 and again on May 31, Kizim and Solovyev performed four-hour spacewalks, during which they practiced procedures for the assembly of large structures in space. They also retrieved samples of materials that had been exposed to space for extended periods, as well as the Soviet/French dust experiment that had collected particles from Comet Giacobini-Zinner when the station passed through the comet's orbit in October 1985. On June 25, after 50 days in Salyut 7, the cosmonauts returned to Mir, and on July 16, after 125 days in space, they returned to earth.

On May 21, a new version of the Soyuz cosmonaut transport vehicle, Soyuz TM, was launched unmanned from the Tyuratam Cosmodrome and docked automatically with Mir. The purpose of the mission was to test the upgraded spacecraft and verify new docking pro-

The new Soviet modular space station Mir ("Peace") was completed, launched, and activated in space by March 1986.

Uranus

For two centuries, the planet Uranus had appeared as a tiny blue-green dot in even the world's largest telescopes. But on Jan. 24, 1986, the U.S. Voyager 2 spacecraft streaked 51,000 mi (82 000 km) above the Uranian cloudtops and forever changed our view of the mysterious planet.

During its historic flyby, Voyager radioed to earth 4,300 photographs and countless other data on the Uranian system. It found ten new moons and several new rings, discovered a bizarre terrain, and spotted a peculiar "electroglow" on the planet's day side. Hours before its closest approach, Voyager crossed Uranus' bow-shock—the point where supersonic winds of charged solar particles bend around the planet's magnetic field.

The photos revealed Uranus' atmosphere as a bland aquamarine disk without the colorful belts, zones, and storms of Jupiter and Saturn. But computer image-enhancement techniques revealed subtle features, including a reddish "smog" high above the planet's south pole. Successive images showed atmospheric wind shears traveling opposite standard predictions at more than 200 mph (320 km/h).

Of the five previously known Uranian moons, Oberon and Umbriel appear to have the oldest cratered surfaces. The largest, Titania, has an extensive series of fault valleys with light, frostlike patterns running next to long cracks. Ariel is crisscrossed by jagged valleys and faults created by the stretching of its icy crust. Miranda, only 300 mi (480 km) in diameter, is the smallest and innermost of the major Uranian moons—and the most bizarre. Its terrain is a peculiar hybrid of sinuous fault valleys, parallel ridges, impact craters, mountains, and towering cliffs.

Voyager found ten new satellites. Most are tiny, with the smallest only 30 mi (48 km) in diameter. Six may even be fragments of a larger moon that once broke up. Two others, named 1986U7 and 1986U8, flank the planet's "epsilon" ring and control its structure. Such "shepherding" satellites were not found near other Uranian rings, perhaps because they are too small and dark.

As Voyager streaked through the planet's ring plane at 49,000 mph (78 400 km/h), it snapped pictures from all angles and studied the nine rings discovered from earth in 1977. By watching how bright the stars flickered behind them, Voyager revealed the patchiness of the main rings and discovered several ring fragments. It also discovered two new complete rings and found the epsilon ring to con-

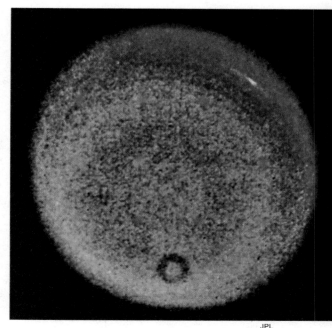

JPL

False-color photo of Uranus radioed by Voyager 2 shows a discrete cloud seen as a bright spot near the planet's limb. Donut-shaped features (bottom) are shadows cast by dust in the camera's optics.

tain dense areas less than 100 ft (30 m) thick and 1 mi (1.6 km) apart. Like the other rings, epsilon is composed of boulders blacker than coal.

Once behind the planet, Voyager sent its radio signals back to earth through the Uranian atmosphere. Scintillations in the signal revealed cloud structures in Uranus' stratosphere and upper troposphere, a multilayered ionosphere, and a hydrogen corona. Atmospheric temperature readings were about 365°F (185°C) below zero.

On Uranus' night side, aurorae forming a glowing oval 15°–20° across were found over the planet's magnetic pole. On the daylight side, a sheen of ultraviolet radiation was seen. Such emissions also have been seen on Jupiter and Saturn, but the energy source of these "electroglows" remains a mystery.

Voyager 2, launched in August 1977, now heads toward an encounter with the planet Neptune scheduled to occur in August 1989. Meanwhile, data from Uranus are still being analyzed and are providing a solid foundation for understanding the mysterious green planet for the first time.

DENNIS L. MAMMANA

cedures. Soyuz TM returned to earth on May 30. Development of the Soviet shuttle orbiter also continued, with the initiation of approach and landing tests early in the year. As observed by spacecraft, a new 15,000-ft (4 570-m) shuttle-recovery runway has been completed at Tyuratam Cosmodrome.

Space Station. Developers defined the initial orbital configuration for the U.S./International space station, currently scheduled for launch in the 1994–1996 time period. The station will consist of two pressurized modules aligned in parallel and connected by airlocks and tunnels. The modules, each 13.8 ft (4.2 m) in diameter and 45 ft (13.7 m) long, are to be located at the center of a long truss structure with solar panels mounted at either end. One module will be developed by the European Space Agency (ESA). Japan and Canada also are participating in development of the station.

Scientific Satellites. On January 24 the U.S. Voyager 2 spacecraft passed through the orbital plane of the ring and satellite system of the planet Uranus, and in March an armada of five European, Soviet, and Japanese spacecraft flew by Halley's comet. The Soviet Vega 1 and Vega 2 probes encountered Halley on March 6 and 9 at distances of 5,520 mi (8 890 km) and 4,990 mi (8 030 km), respectively, providing navigation data that enabled precise targeting of ESA's Giotto spacecraft for its high-speed encounter with Halley on March 14 at a distance of 365 mi (590 km). The Japanese spacecraft Suisei and Sakigake crossed Halley's orbit on March 8 and 11 at distances of 93,000 mi (150 400 km) and 4.4 million mi (7 million km), respectively, acquiring data on the interaction of the comet with the solar wind.

Of the two geodetic satellites launched during the year, the Soviet Union's is to obtain accurate measurements of the gravitational field. The other, Japan's Ajisi laser satellite, precisely locates points on the earth's surface.

Application Satellites. The French SPOT-1, an earth resources satellite, and Sweden's Viking, a scientific satellite, were launched piggyback from Kourou, French Guiana, by an Ariane 1 booster on February 22. SPOT's nearly polar orbit enables panchromatic imagery to be acquired of any area on the earth every 26 days at a resolution of 33 ft (10 m), and three-band multispectral imagery to be obtained at a resolution of 66 ft (20 m). The imagery is used in agricultural, forestry, geologic, hydrologic, and land-use applications. Meanwhile the U.S. Landsat 5 earth resources satellite continued its data acquisition of selected land and water areas worldwide in seven spectral bands at a resolution of 92 ft (28 m). The Soviet Union also launched its seventh sunsynchronous remote sensing satellite, Cosmos 1757, on June 11, to provide multispectral imagery at a resolution of about 98 ft (30 m). China launched its eighth film-return-type land

resources survey satellite October 6 and recovered the film canister five days later.

The high-altitude weather observation capability of the United States suffered a serious blow on May 3, when the failure of a Delta launch vehicle shortly after lift-off resulted in the loss of the GEOS-G spacecraft. The single geostationary weather satellite remaining, GEOS-6, provides coverage over North America but cannot observe important weatherforming areas far off the continental coasts. On the other hand, the low-altitude, polar-orbiting meteorological satellite system was restored to full capability in September with the launch of NOAA-10.

The Soviet Union orbited a Meteor satellite on May 27 to augment its four-spacecraft Meteor 2 low-altitude meteorological system. The satellites provide cloud-cover information and atmospheric data, along with multispectral imagery of selected land areas.

Communications Satellites. Of the 14 communications satellites launched in 1986, ten were placed in geosynchronous orbit. The only communication satellite orbited by the United States was the RCA Satcom K-1 deployed by the shuttle *Columbia* in January. Europe's Ariane 3 booster placed two communications satellites in geosynchronous orbit, a U.S. Spacenet G Star 2 and a Brasilsat S-2. China successfully launched its second geosynchronous satellite on a CZ-3 booster on February 1, and Japan used an N-2 booster on February 12 to launch a BS-2B direct-broadcast television satellite into a geosynchronous orbit to replace the failed BS-2A.

The Soviet Union launched nine communications satellites. A replacement spacecraft was orbited for the USSR's three-satellite, low-orbit, global communications system; two Molniya spacecraft were added to the elliptical-orbit domestic communications network; and six geostationary satellites were launched.

Booster Problems. With the shuttle fleet grounded, American space efforts were further plagued by a series of rocket failures, including that of the Delta in May, the explosion of a Titan 34D shortly after liftoff on April 18, and the destruction of an Aries sounding rocket on August 23. Following the *Challenger* disaster, U.S. launch attempts did not succeed until a military test in September that used a Delta rocket. In the meantime, the Ariane 2 rocket developed for ESA was also experiencing a nine-month delay following a failed attempt to launch an Intelsat 5 satellite on May 30.

In response several nations had plans under way for fleets of expendable rockets. On August 13, Japan successfully test-launched its new H-1 booster. China took advantage of Western rocket failures during the year by arranging to orbit a number of small satellites for several nations, including the United States.

WILLIAM L. PIOTROWSKI

SPAIN

Entry into the European Community (EC) on Jan. 1, 1986, moved Spain from the fringes to the mainstream of Western Europe, and midyear parliamentary elections strengthened the nation's 11-year-old democracy.

Politics and Government. Prime Minister Felipe González, who gave impulse to his country's integration into Western Europe, won an impressive victory in June 22 national elections. Some observers believed that persisting economic problems, exemplified by a 22% unemployment rate, would pose electoral difficulties for González's Socialist Workers' Party (PSOE), which in the 1982 parliamentary contests captured 46% of the vote and 202 seats in the 350-member Chamber of Deputies. Criticism of the 44-year-old González also focused on his alleged arrogance and manipulation of the state-owned television network.

Although voter turnout fell by 10% from the 1982 total, to 70%, the PSOE emerged from the balloting with 44% of the popular vote and a working majority of 184 legislative seats. The party benefited from González's remarkable popularity, the widespread perception of improving economic conditions, a weak opposition, and the momentum gained when the Socialist government won an absolute majority (52.5%) in a March 12 referendum on the question of Spain's continued membership in the North Atlantic Treaty Organization (NATO). Before that vote, González warned that ending the nation's four-year participation in the defense pact would represent a trend toward "backwardness, poverty, unemployment, and third-worldism."

The conservative Popular Coalition presented the stiffest challenge to the PSOE in the parliamentary election. Led by Manuel Fraga Iribarne, the Popular Coalition embraced Fraga's own Popular Alliance, as well as the Christian Democrats and free-trade Liberals. Even with a well-financed campaign that championed cutting government spending, reducing taxes, and privatizing industry, the right-wing bloc garnered only 26% of the vote—up from 25% in 1982—while losing one seat to wind up with 105. The coalition's failure to make substantial gains raised doubts about the continuation of Fraga as leader of the conservative forces.

Finishing third in the voting was the Democratic and Social Center (CSD), which obtained 9% of the ballots cast and increased its representation from 2 to 19 seats. Led by former Prime Minister Adolfo Suárez, the ideologically eclectic CSD advocated substantial public investment in industry to generate jobs, removal of U.S. troops from Spain, and improved ties with Latin America and other Third World regions.

The Communist-dominated United Left secured seven seats, while the remainder of the votes went to regional parties—the most important of which were the Catalan Nationalists (18 seats), the Basque Nationalists (6), and the Basque separatist ETA (5).

The Socialists won 124 of the 208 seats contested in the voting for the Spanish Senate, and also emerged as the leading party in the November election in the Basque region.

Economy. Prime Minister González, who won election in 1982 under the slogan "Socialism Means Freedom," downplayed the PSOE's traditional enthusiasm for widespread planning and state ownership of key industries. Instead, he evinced pragmatism in closing, consolidating, or selling inefficient state firms, while encouraging the private sector to invest in electronics, office equipment, defense systems, and other "growth" industries.

Cheap oil and lower commodity prices spurred exports, as Spain ran a $4.3 billion current account surplus from January through August. Meanwhile, industrial output climbed 10% over 1985, and the gross national product grew 2.5% amid an 8% inflation rate.

Entry into the EC coupled with the government's courting of the business community enhanced investor confidence, as reflected in a 97% upswing in the value of shares traded on the Madrid Stock Exchange between January and September.

The confidence of the Spanish people received another boost in October 1986, when Barcelona was chosen as a site for the 1992 summer Olympic Games. Regarding the selection as international recognition of the country's rapid progress from dictatorship to democracy, González foresaw the games as a "leap forward for Spain's projection in the world." The Barcelona games were expected to spark tougher measures against ETA terrorists, who had killed more than 500 people over 18 years, including 11 civil guards in July.

GEORGE W. GRAYSON
College of William & Mary

SPAIN • Information Highlights

Official Name: Spanish State.
Location: Iberian Peninsula in southwestern Europe.
Area: 194,897 sq mi (504 782 km²).
Population (mid-1986 est.): 38,800,000.
Chief Cities (1982 est.): Madrid, the capital, 3,271,834; Barcelona, 1,720,998; Valencia, 770,277.
Government: *Head of state,* Juan Carlos I, king (took office Nov. 1975). *Head of government,* Felipe González Márquez, prime minister (took office Dec. 1982). *Legislature*—Cortés Generales: Senate and Congress of Deputies.
Monetary Unit: Peseta (131.34 pesetas equal U.S.$1, Oct. 19, 1986).
Gross National Product (1984 U.S.$): $160,400,-000,000.
Economic Indexes (1985): *Consumer Prices* (1980 = 100), all items, 178.0; food, 178.3. *Industrial Production* (1984, 1980 = 100), 101.
Foreign Trade (1985 U.S.$): *Imports,* $29,992,-000,000; *exports,* $24,301,000,000.

SPORTS

AP/Wide World

At 46, Jack Nicklaus became the oldest player to win the Masters. It was "The Bear's" 20th major tournament win.

An Overview

For a while it looked like 1965 all over again. The Boston Celtics won the NBA championship, and the Montreal Canadiens won the Stanley Cup. Jack Nicklaus captured the Masters Golf Tournament, and Willie Shoemaker rode another winner in the Kentucky Derby. Yet the more things stayed the same, the more things changed. One need not have looked very closely to notice that the 1986 sports year was manifestly not the 1965 sports year. In 1986 the excitement and drama of sport itself seemed to take second place to issues and problems that barely existed in 1965.

Drugs. The long-festering problem of drugs in sports manifested itself in the most tragic and compelling events to date. On June 19, only two days after being chosen by the Celtics in the NBA college draft, University of Maryland basketball star Len Bias died from an overdose of cocaine. Only eight days after that, Cleveland Browns defensive back Don Rogers died of a fatal dose of the same drug. He was to have been married the next morning.

The highly publicized deaths of Bias and Rogers helped fuel a rising national concern over the pervasiveness of drug use in American life. The redeeming feature of their loss was precisely this consciousness-raising, as well as

At 54, Willie Shoemaker became the oldest jockey to win the Kentucky Derby, driving home 17–1 longshot Ferdinand. Buffalo Bills' quarterback Jim Kelly was one of several former USFL stars who became "impact players" in the NFL.

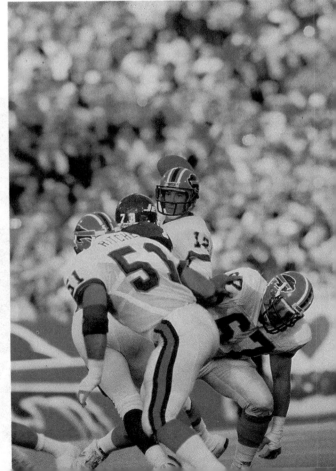

impetus for new antidrug measures in the sports world and throughout American society. The NCAA, for example, implemented drug testing for athletes participating in some 74 postseason championships and 19 football bowl games. (*See also* DRUGS AND ALCOHOL.)

Academic Standards. The death of Len Bias underscored another festering problem in college sports—academic abuse in the enrollment and advancement of student-athletes. Bias, it turned out, like many other top college athletes, was far from qualifying for an academic degree despite attending the University of Maryland for four years. According to one survey, only 27% of U.S. college basketball players and 30% of college football players have graduated in recent years; for black athletes, the rate is about 20%. Worth literally millions of dollars in television revenues, ticket sales, and other income for their schools, the college athlete typically receives favored treatment in the admission process and academic advancement. With only a tiny fraction succeeding as professional athletes, many are woefully underprepared for other careers.

The problem, of course, was well known before the Bias incident. In February, a federal jury in Atlanta ruled that a University of Georgia instructor had been fired illegally in retaliation for opposing preferential treatment for athletes. Jan Kemp was awarded more than $2.5 million for lost wages, mental anguish, and punitive damages.

Around the World: *From Flushing, NY, to Mexico City to the French countryside, the world's top athletes won prestigious events the old-fashioned way. Martina Navratilova (above, right) won her third U.S. Open tennis championship, but only after surviving three match points against West Germany's young Steffi Graf in the semifinals. Diego Maradona (right, holding cup) and the Argentine national soccer team were the best of the best in the month-long World Cup tournament, defeating West Germany, 3–2, in a hard-fought final. And Greg LeMond of the United States (below, left) became the first non-European ever to win the 2,500-mile (4 000-km) Tour de France bicycle race.*

Beginning in fall 1986, a new rule concerning academic standards was implemented for NCAA Divison I schools. In order to compete, first-year athletes must have earned a "C" average in basic high-school courses and scored a specified number of points on standard college admissions tests. The new rule was criticized by some black educators as racially discriminatory.

Demise of the USFL. One off-the-field development that did stir memories of the mid-1960s was a determination of the fate of the United States Football League (USFL). Unlike the old American Football League (AFL), however, whose merger with the established National Football League (NFL) was agreed upon in 1966, the USFL was forced to suspend play—probably forever. The knockout blow was a token damage award of $1, trebled to $3, for one antitrust violation by the NFL. The highly publicized suit by the USFL, held in a New York City federal court, claimed $1.7 billion in damages for the NFL's alleged monopoly of major network television coverage and other efforts to drive the USFL out of business. For the money-losing upstart league, which perhaps had been hoping to force a merger, the July 29 verdict was sudden-death. A week later, the eight remaining USFL franchise owners voted to call off the 1986 fall season. Players were released from their contracts and free to negotiate with NFL teams. The likes of Herschel Walker, Jim Kelly, Kelvin Bryant, and other top stars had little trouble hooking on with new employers, but scores of other players were left on the sidelines.

JEFFREY H. HACKER

Festivals: *The XIII Commonwealth Games opened July 25 at Edinburgh's Meadowbank Stadium (above), but 31 nations boycotted the ten-day event over Britain's rejection of economic sanctions against South Africa. Overcoming political differences was the purpose of the first Goodwill Games, a 70-nation competition in Moscow, July 4–20. The event was conceived and sponsored by U.S. broadcasting maverick Ted Turner. Soviet pole vaulter Sergei Bubka (below) leaped a world-record 19'8½" (6.01 m).*

Auto Racing

Alain Prost of France successfully defended his Formula One world driving championship by winning the season-ending Australian Grand Prix and edging out Great Britain's Nigel Mansell by two points. It was the fourth straight year in which Prost finished first or second. Mansell, who led the standings for most of the season, needed only a third-place finish in Australia to take the title but blew a tire.

The CART-PPG Indy Car series also went down to its final event before the champion was determined. By winning the Nissan Indy Challenge at Miami, FL, 33-year-old Bobby Rahal of Dublin, OH, overcame the challenge of Michael Andretti of Nazareth, PA. Rahal posted six victories in the 17-race series, including the prestigious Indianapolis 500, and earned a CART record purse of $1,457,049. Andretti, the 24-year-old son of former Indianapolis and Formula One champion Mario Andretti, was trying to become the youngest champion in CART's history. The younger Andretti had trailed Rahal by three points entering the final event, but mechanical problems forced him out of the race. Rahal's victory in the Indy 500 marked the closest three-car finish in that race's history, as the first three cars finished within 1.881 seconds of each other.

Dale Earnhardt of Kannapolis, NC, won NASCAR'S Winston Cup stock-car championship with 4,468 points, clinching the honor with one race left on the schedule. Defending champion Darrell Waltrip finished with 2,180, edging Tim Richmond by six points for second place. Richmond posted a season-high seven victories, while Earnhardt had four wins.

STAN SUTTON, *Louisville Courier-Journal*

AUTO RACING
Major Race Winners, 1986

Indianapolis 500: Bobby Rahal
Michigan 500: Johnny Rutherford
Pocono 500: Mario Andretti
Daytona 500: Geoff Bodine

1986 Champions

World Championship: Alain Prost (France)
CART: Bobby Rahal
NASCAR: Dale Earnhardt

Grand Prix for
Formula One Cars, 1986

Australian: Alain Prost (France)
Austrian: Prost
Belgian: Nigel Mansell (Great Britain)
Brazilian: Nelson Piquet (Brazil)
British: Mansell
Canadian: Mansell
Detroit: Ayrton Senna (Brazil)
French: Mansell
German: Piquet
Hungarian: Senna
Italian: Piquet
Mexican: Gerhard Berger (Austria)
Monaco: Prost
Portuguese: Mansell
San Marino: Prost
Spanish: Senna

Baseball

The 1986 major league baseball season will be remembered as the Year of the New York Mets. In their 25th anniversary season, the Mets paralyzed their opposition by leading the National League (NL) in batting average, runs scored, and earned run average, then capitalized on rivals' mistakes in postseason play to win their first world championship since 1969.

Play-Offs and World Series. After capturing the NL Eastern Division title by 21½ games, a divisional-play record, the Mets confronted the Houston Astros in the League Championship Series (LCS). Strikeout king Mike Scott pitched two complete-game victories for the Astros, but New York took advantage of a shaky Houston relief corps—winning three times with uprisings in the last inning—to take the series, four games to two. The last game, played in Houston, lasted a play-off record 16 innings, with the Mets scoring three runs and the Astros two in the final frame of a 7–6 thriller. The drama of that contest was matched only by Game 3 at New York, in which the Mets' Len Dykstra hit a two-run, ninth-inning homer that gave the New Yorkers a 6–5 win.

There was also high drama in the American League (AL) play-off between the Boston Red Sox and California Angels. The Angels, losers of two previous LCS encounters, took a commanding 3–1 lead in the best-of-seven series when they erased a 3–0 Boston advantage in the ninth inning of Game 4 and won, 4–3, in 11 innings. The next day California held a 5–2 lead with two outs and two strikes in the ninth inning, but two-run homers by Don Baylor and Dave Henderson put the Red Sox ahead. The Angels tied it, then lost, 7–6, in 11 innings. When the series returned to Boston, the Red Sox won the final two games, 10–4 and 8–1, to earn their first AL pennant in 11 years.

The Red Sox, who had not won a World Series since 1918, got off to a strong start against the Mets, winning Games 1 and 2, both at New York's Shea Stadium, by scores of 1–0 and 9–3. Only once before—in 1985—had a team lost the first two games at home and rebounded to win a World Series.

Playing on enemy turf in Boston's Fenway Park, the Mets got two home runs each from Gary Carter and Len Dykstra to win Games 3 and 4, 7–1 and 6–2. But Game 1 winner Bruce Hurst came back to take Game 5, 4–2, and give the Red Sox a lead of three games to two as the series returned to New York. When Boston's bullpen failed in the late innings of Games 6 and 7, the Mets rallied for 6–5 and 8–5 victories. The 6–5 win in Game 6 consumed 10 innings and climaxed with a three-run rally that began with two outs, nobody on base, and two strikes on the batter. Two subsequent hitters also had two strikes on them before the Mets tied the score.

A seventh-inning solo home run by New York Mets third baseman Ray Knight, above, broke a 3-3 tie in Game 7 of the World Series. The Mets went on to win the game, 8-5, and Knight was named the series MVP. Boston Red Sox fireballer Roger Clemens, right, won the American League Cy Young and MVP awards but managed only two no-decisions in the October Classic.

New York third baseman Ray Knight, whose seventh-inning home run was the decisive blow in Game 7—and only the second home run to decide a World Series—was named most valuable player (MVP) of the series. He hit .391 and knocked in five runs during the seven-game October Classic, the first to be played completely at night.

Regular Season. With 108 victories during the 162-game schedule, the Mets tied the 1975 Cincinnati Reds for most wins under the divisional format, which began in 1969. Four New York starting pitchers, led by newcomer Bob Ojeda (18–5), won at least 15 games, while relievers Roger McDowell and Jesse Orosco became the second bullpen tandem to exceed 20 saves each.

Met sluggers Gary Carter, Keith Hernandez, and Darryl Strawberry were selected to start in the July 15 All-Star Game in Houston, but the American League won, 3–2, as Boston fireballer Roger Clemens became the first pitcher since 1980 to hurl three perfect innings in All-Star play. Clemens, with a record 20-strikeout game against Seattle on April 29 and a season-opening 14-game winning streak en route to a 24–4 record, was named the All-Star Game MVP, the American League MVP, and the AL Cy Young Award winner.

Mike Scott, the Cy Young winner in the NL, went 18–10 for Houston and struck out 306 batters, the most in the majors. Scott's best game was a 2–0 no-hitter against the San Francisco Giants in Houston on September 25. The win gave the Astros—who have never won a pennant—their first NL West title since 1980. Fernando Valenzuela of the Los Angeles Dodgers led the league with 21 victories and 20 complete games; San Francisco's Mike Krukow (20–9) was the NL's only other 20-game winner. American Leaguers who joined Clemens at the 20-victory level were Jack Morris of Detroit and Teddy Higuera of Milwaukee.

A former starter, lefthander Dave Righetti of the New York Yankees, saved a record 46 games, one more than former record-holders Bruce Sutter (1984) and Dan Quisenberry (1983). Former Righetti teammate Joe Cowley, now with the Chicago White Sox, hurled a 7–1 no-hitter against the Angels on September 19. Earlier in the season Cowley started a game by striking out the first seven Texas Ranger hitters. Texas rookies Dale Mohorcic and Pete Incaviglia also entered the record book. Mohorcic pitched in 13 straight games, tying Mike Marshall's 1974 mark, while Incaviglia struck out 185 times, an AL record that missed the major-league futility standard by four.

Incaviglia, who also had 30 homers and 88 runs batted in (RBIs), was one of several slugging rookies who starred in the American League. Rookie of the Year Jose Canseco of the Oakland Athletics hit 33 homers and knocked in 117 runs, four less than major-league leader Joe Carter of Cleveland. California's Wally Joyner knocked in 100 runs, helping Angel fans forget that he replaced seven-time batting king Rod Carew at first base. And in Chicago, White Sox centerfielder John Cangelosi stole 50 bases, a record for American League freshmen.

Another rookie record was established by St. Louis relief specialist Todd Worrell, who saved 36 games. Worrell won NL rookie honors, succeeding teammate Vince Coleman, whose 107 steals led both leagues in 1986. Rickey Henderson of the New York Yankees topped the AL for the seventh straight season with 87 stolen bases. Another speed merchant, Tim Raines of the Montreal Expos, won his first batting title with a .334 mark, two points ahead of Dodger Steve Sax, whose 25-game hitting streak was the longest of the season. Wade Boggs (*see* BIOGRAPHY) of Boston won his third AL title with a .357 mark after waging a down-the-stretch fight with Don Mattingly (*see* BIOGRAPHY) of the New York Yankees. The home-run champions were Toronto's Jesse Barfield, the only man in the majors to hit 40, and Philadelphia's Mike Schmidt, who led the NL with 37 home runs and 119 RBIs. Schmidt, winning his eighth home-run title and fourth RBI crown, was named National League MVP for the third time. No player has ever won the coveted trophy more often.

While Schmidt will cherish the memories of his fine 1986 season, the Baltimore Orioles will not. They finished last for the first time since their 1954 transfer from St. Louis. On the other hand, the San Francisco Giants became the first team in this century to go from 100 losses one year to a winning record the next. All 26 teams drew at least 1 million fans, a major-league first that was a preseason goal of Commissioner Peter V. Ueberroth.

The commissioner declared the game drug-free after penalizing more than a dozen players with previous records of drug abuse. A. Bartlett Giamatti, formerly the president of Yale University, was elected president of the National League (*see* BIOGRAPHY).

Three players were inducted into the Hall of Fame in Cooperstown, NY, on August 3: former Giant slugger Willie McCovey, the 16th man enshrined in his first year of eligibility, along with Veterans Committee choices Ernie

Lombardi, a catcher in the 1930s and 1940s primarily with the Cincinnati Reds and New York Giants, and Bobby Doerr, a 14-year second baseman for the Red Sox beginning in 1937.

DAN SCHLOSSBERG, *Baseball Writer*

BASEBALL

Professional—Major Leagues
Final Standings, 1986

AMERICAN LEAGUE

Eastern Division	W	L	Pct.	Western Division	W	L	Pct.
Boston	95	66	.590	California	92	70	.568
New York	90	72	.556	Texas	87	75	.537
Detroit	87	75	.537	Kansas City	76	86	.469
Toronto	86	76	.531	Oakland	76	86	.469
Cleveland	84	78	.519	Chicago	72	90	.444
Milwaukee	77	84	.478	Minnesota	71	91	.438
Baltimore	73	89	.451	Seattle	67	95	.414

NATIONAL LEAGUE

Eastern Division	W	L	Pct.	Western Division	W	L	Pct.
New York	108	54	.667	Houston	96	66	.593
Philadelphia	86	75	.534	Cincinnati	86	76	.531
St. Louis	79	82	.491	San Francisco	83	79	.512
Montreal	78	83	.484	San Diego	74	88	.457
Chicago	70	90	.438	Los Angeles	73	89	.451
Pittsburgh	64	98	.395	Atlanta	72	89	.447

Play-offs—American League: Boston defeated California, 4 games to 3; National League: New York defeated Houston, 4 games to 2.

World Series—New York defeated Boston, 4 games to 3. First Game (Shea Stadium, New York, Oct. 18, attendance 55,076): Boston 1, New York 0; Second Game (Shea Stadium, Oct. 19, attendance 55,063): Boston 9, New York 3; Third Game (Fenway Park, Boston, Oct. 21, attendance 33,595): New York 7, Boston 1; Fourth Game (Fenway Park, Oct. 22, attendance 33,920): New York 6, Boston 2; Fifth Game (Fenway Park, Oct. 23, attendance 34,010): Boston 4, New York 2; Sixth Game (Shea Stadium, Oct. 25, attendance 55,078): New York 6, Boston 5; Seventh Game (Shea Stadium, Oct. 27, attendance 55,032): New York 8, Boston 5.

All-Star Game (Astrodome, Houston, July 15, attendance 45,774): American League 3, National League 2.

Most Valuable Players—American League: Roger Clemens, Boston; National League: Mike Schmidt, Philadelphia.

Cy Young Memorial Awards (outstanding pitchers)—American League: Roger Clemens, Boston; National League: Mike Scott, Houston.

Managers of the Year—American League: John McNamara, Boston; National League: Hal Lanier, Houston.

Rookies of the Year—American League: Jose Canseco, Oakland; National League: Todd Worrell, St. Louis.

Leading Hitters—(Percentage) American League: Wade Boggs, Boston, .357; National League: Tim Raines, Montreal, .334. (Runs Batted In) American League: Joe Carter, Cleveland, 121; National League: Mike Schmidt, Philadelphia, 119. (Home Runs) American League: Jesse Barfield, Toronto, 40; National League: Schmidt, 37. (Hits) American League: Don Mattingly, New York, 238; National League: Tony Gwynn, San Diego, 211. (Runs) American League: Rickey Henderson, New York, 130; National League: Gwynn and Von Hayes, Philadelphia, 107.

Leading Pitchers—(Earned Run Average) American League: Roger Clemens, Boston, 2.48; National League: Mike Scott, Houston, 2.22. (Victories) American League: Clemens, 24; National League: Fernando Valenzuela, Los Angeles, 21. (Strikeouts) American League: Mike Langston, Seattle, 245; National League: Scott, 306. (Shutouts) American League: Jack Morris, Detroit, 6; National League: Scott and Bob Knepper, Houston, 5. (Saves) American League: Dave Righetti, New York, 46; National League: Todd Worrell, St. Louis, 36.

Stolen Bases—American League: Rickey Henderson, New York, 87; National League: Vince Coleman, St. Louis, 107.

Professional—Minor Leagues, Class AAA
American Association: Indianapolis
International League: Richmond
Pacific Coast League: Las Vegas

Amateur
NCAA: Arizona
Little League World Series: Tainan City, Taiwan

The Celtics won another NBA title—their 16th—and forward Larry Bird (33) won another MVP—his third in a row.

BASKETBALL

The Boston Celtics climaxed one of the most remarkable seasons in National Basketball Association (NBA) history by beating the Houston Rockets, four games to two, in the 1985–86 championship round of the league play-offs. The Celtics compiled the fourth best regular-season record (67–15) in NBA history and then won their second title in three years.

After carrying the No. 1 ranking into the 48th National Collegiate Athletic Association (NCAA) men's championship, Duke University fell one game short of winning the title. In the title match, the Blue Devils fell to the Louisville Cardinals, 72–69. The Ohio State Buckeyes won the National Invitation Tournament (NIT). And undefeated Texas took the women's NCAA tournament.

The World Basketball Championships concluded in Madrid, Spain, in July. For the first time since 1954, the United States captured the title. The U.S. men's team defeated the Soviet Union, 87–85, in the finals.

The Professional Season

The NBA continued its surge in popularity, setting a total attendance record for the third straight year while also enjoying a 7% ratings increase for the seven regular-season games broadcast over the CBS television network. The league's bright outlook continued into the play-offs, where two of the six final-round games were ranked in the weekly top-10 ratings of all prime-time TV shows. The rating for the title series was the highest in NBA history.

Boston was the league's dominant team from the first days of the season. By the end of the campaign, they had won a record 31 straight games on their home court. Their total of 67 regular-season victories was only two shy

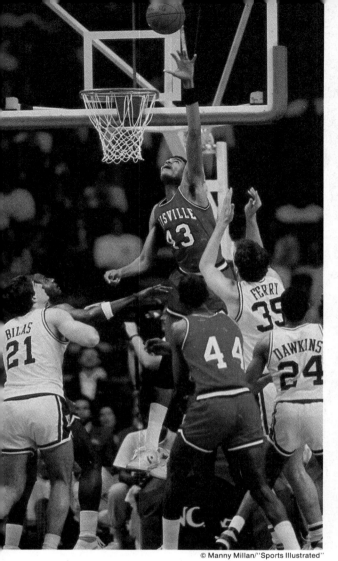

© Manny Millan/''Sports Illustrated''

Freshman center Pervis Ellison was the dominant force as Louisville defeated Duke, 72–69, in the NCAA finals.

The Hawks completed the regular season with 16 more victories than in 1984–85. One of the league's most positive developments took place in Sacramento, where the former Kansas City Kings spent their first season. The Kings played before sellout crowds at home, even though they could manage only a 37–45 record. Attendance in Chicago and throughout the league suffered when the Bulls' Michael Jordan, one of the NBA's most exciting players, was injured early in the season and did not return to full strength until the play-offs.

Larry Bird, the Celtics' star forward, became only the third player in NBA history to win the most valuable player (MVP) award three years in a row. Bird, considered one of the best players of all time, placed fourth in scoring (25.8 points per game), seventh in rebounding (9.8), first in free-throw percentage (.896), and ninth in steals (2.02). Dominique Wilkins of Atlanta, an exciting player who specializes in dunks, captured his first scoring championship (30.3), while Detroit's Bill Laimbeer was a surprise winner of the rebounding title (13.1). The leading shot blocker was Washington Bullets' center Manute Bol (4.96). A native of the Sudan, the 7'6" Bol was the NBA's tallest player and one of its most successful rookies. But it was another impressive center, Patrick Ewing of the New York Knicks, who was named rookie of the year. Ewing had been the first pick in the 1985 draft and was expected to lead the Knicks to a strong season, but New York's play-off chances were erased by a series of crippling injuries. Magic Johnson of the Lakers edged out his friend, Isiah Thomas of the Detroit Pistons, for the assist title (12.6 to 10.8).

All season long it was anticipated that the final round of the play-offs would pit Boston and Los Angeles for the third straight year. Those expectations held up through the early days of the play-offs, as the Lakers ousted San Antonio (3 games to 0) and Dallas (4–2), while the Celts were beating Chicago (3–0) and Atlanta (4–1). Boston won the Eastern Conference title with a 4–0 sweep of Milwaukee, but the Lakers ran into the peaking Rockets. Houston defeated Los Angeles in five close games to advance to the finals. The Rockets' final victory over Los Angeles was sealed when 7'4" forward-center Ralph Sampson, who teamed with Olajuwon to form the team's ''Twin Towers,'' tossed in a miraculous turnaround shot at the buzzer.

Boston, coached by K.C. Jones, was heavily favored to beat Houston, one of the league's youngest teams. The Celtics played true to their favorite's role in Game 1, overwhelming the Rockets, 112–100, on Memorial Day in Boston Garden. Things looked even bleaker for Houston after Game 2, in which Bird took control during the third quarter and led the Celtics to an easy 117–95 victory.

of the league record and five more than that of the next-best team in 1985–86, the Los Angeles Lakers. The defending champion Lakers were plagued by injuries and inconsistency, and they never played up to the standard of the 1984–85 club. But they still won the Pacific Division championship by 22 games, led once more by center Kareem Abdul-Jabbar, now 38 and again a member of the all-NBA team. Houston, which had been considered at least a year away from being a true championship contender, took the Midwest Division title with a fine 51–31 record. Houston center Akeem Olajuwon, in only his second pro season, finished strong and may have been the best at his position by season's end.

The Central Division championship went to the Milwaukee Bucks (57–25), who overcame a strong challenge by vastly improved Atlanta.

The Celts seemed on the verge of running away with the series when they took an eight-point lead with three minutes left in Game 3, played in Houston. But the Rockets, led by Olajuwon and Sampson, came back to win the contest, 106–104. Game 4 was the best of the series, a close, hard-fought affair that the Celtics won, 106–103, when reserve center Bill Walton put in a rebound shot with 99 seconds remaining.

PROFESSIONAL BASKETBALL

National Basketball Association
(Final Standings, 1985–86)

Eastern Conference

Atlantic Division	W	L	Pct.
*Boston	67	15	.817
*Philadelphia	54	28	.659
*New Jersey	39	43	.476
*Washington	39	43	.476
New York	23	59	.280
Central Division			
*Milwaukee	57	25	.695
*Atlanta	50	32	.610
*Detroit	46	36	.561
*Chicago	30	52	.366
Cleveland	29	53	.354
Indiana	26	56	.317

Western Conference

Midwest Division	W	L	Pct.
*Houston	51	31	.622
*Denver	47	35	.573
*Dallas	44	38	.537
*Utah	42	40	.512
*Sacramento	37	45	.451
*San Antonio	35	47	.427
Pacific Division			
*L.A. Lakers	62	20	.756
*Portland	40	42	.488
L.A. Clippers	32	50	.390
Phoenix	32	50	.390
Seattle	31	51	.378
Golden State	30	52	.366

*Made play-offs

Play-Offs
Eastern Conference

First Round	Atlanta	3 games	Detroit	1
	Boston	3 games	Chicago	0
	Milwaukee	3 games	New Jersey	0
	Philadelphia	3 games	Washington	2
Second Round	Boston	4 games	Atlanta	1
	Milwaukee	4 games	Philadelphia	3
Finals	Boston	4 games	Milwaukee	0

Western Conference

First Round	Dallas	3 games	Utah	1
	Denver	3 games	Portland	1
	Houston	3 games	Sacramento	0
	Los Angeles	3 games	San Antonio	0
Second Round	Houston	4 games	Denver	2
	Los Angeles	4 games	Dallas	2
Finals	Houston	4 games	Los Angeles	1
Championship	Boston	4 games	Houston	2
All-Star Game	East 139, West 132			

Individual Honors

Most Valuable Player: Larry Bird, Boston
Most Valuable Player (play-offs): Larry Bird
Most Valuable Player (all-star game): Isiah Thomas, Detroit
Rookie of the Year: Patrick Ewing, New York
Coach of the Year: Mike Fratello, Atlanta
Leading Scorer: Dominique Wilkins, Atlanta, 30.3 points per game
Leader in Assists: Earvin (Magic) Johnson, Los Angeles Lakers, 12.6 per game
Leading Rebounder: Bill Laimbeer, Detroit, 13.1 per game
Leader in Field Goal Percentage: Steve Johnson, San Antonio, .632

Needing one more victory to clinch the series, Boston hoped to take Game 5 in Houston and return home as champions. Instead, Houston, paced by Olajuwon's 32 points and 14 rebounds, won easily, 111–96. The contest was marred by a fight involving Sampson and Celtic guard Jerry Sichting. Sampson was thrown out of the game, which ignited the Rockets.

Back in Boston for Game 6, the Celtics wrapped up their record 16th NBA championship with a convincing 114–97 victory. Bird, who earned play-off MVP honors, gave his most impressive performance, scoring 29 points, grabbing 11 rebounds, and handing out 12 assists. The Rockets managed to shoot only 43% against a very strong Boston defense. Celtic forward Kevin McHale led all scorers in the finals with a 25.8 average.

The College Season

Unlike the NBA campaign, the 1985–86 college basketball season was not dominated by a single team. Instead, it was largely dominated by a league, the Atlantic Coast Conference. The ACC, long one of the top conferences in the nation, had perhaps its best year ever. At some points during the season, three ACC schools (North Carolina, Duke, and Georgia Tech) were ranked among the country's top four teams in the weekly wire service polls. The North Carolina Tarheels were considered No. 1 during the first part of the season, but Duke eventually took over the top spot and stayed there until the final minutes of the NCAA tournament.

Besides the trio of ACC teams, the nation's strongest squads included Kansas, Syracuse, St. John's, North Carolina State, Kentucky, Indiana, Georgetown, Michigan, Notre Dame, Navy, Nevada-Las Vegas, and Memphis State. And then, of course, there was Louisville. The Cardinals, who got off to a slow start and were not considered to be that strong by the end of December, went on to become national champions. Other than the ACC, the year's strongest conferences were the Big Ten, with Michigan and Indiana, and the Big East, which had been so dominant during 1984–85.

Among individual players, the top performer was St. John's center Walter Berry, who won most of the player-of-the-year awards and was largely responsible for his team's unexpectedly successful season. Other standouts included Duke guard Johnny Dawkins, Maryland forward Len Bias, North Carolina center Brad Daugherty, Georgia Tech guard Mark Price, Michigan State guard Scott Skiles, Kansas forward Greg Manning, Kentucky center Kenny Walker, Miami (Ohio) forward Ron Harper, Syracuse guard Dwayne Washington, Virginia Tech guard Dell Curry, Navy center David Robinson, and Indiana guard Steve Alford.

As the NCAA tournament got under way, Duke was the nation's top-ranked team. Playing in the East Region, the Blue Devils were also the No. 1 seed in the tournament. Major challenges were expected to come from the other regional top seeds—St. John's (West), Kentucky (Southeast), and Kansas (Midwest).

Duke had little trouble advancing to the Final Four, breezing through the East Regional and knocking off surprising Navy in the regional championship game. Kansas also lived up to its billing, taking the Midwest Regional. The Jayhawks did have to struggle, however, beating Michigan State in overtime (with the help of a faulty game clock) and only narrowly defeating North Carolina State in the regional final. St. John's and Kentucky were not so fortunate. The Redmen lost in the second round to Auburn, and the Wildcats were upset in the Southeast Regional final by unranked LSU, which had barely earned a bid to the tournament. Before the final four teams were determined, other upsets had been recorded by the likes of Cleveland State and Arkansas-Little Rock.

In the Final Four at Dallas, LSU's Cinderella ride ended against Louisville, which routed the Tigers, 88–77, with a fine second-half performance. LSU, which started four former guards and standout forward John Williams, was directed by Coach Dale Brown, who had his players believing in miracles. But the Cardinals played so well that suddenly they were considered strong contenders for the the championship, even though they were starting a freshman, Pervis Ellison, at center and a sophomore, Herbert Crook, at forward.

The featured game of the Final Four was the other semifinal, between Duke and Kansas, who had been ranked No. 1 and 2, respectively. This unofficial national championship game lived up to expectations, with Duke securing a 71–67 win on a layup by freshman Danny Ferry with only 22 seconds remaining.

In the championship game, the freshman Ellison played like a veteran for Louisville. He scored 25 points, grabbed 11 rebounds, and blocked 2 shots to earn the game's MVP award. In this closely matched contest, Ellison was the difference, giving the Cardinals an edge in the middle. Louisville was a marvelous team to watch, with plenty of quickness and shooting skill to go along with a large amount of sheer athletic ability. The Cardinals did not play particularly well in the first half, but Duke's poor execution prevented the Blue Devils from taking advantage. In the second half, with Duke's star guard Johnny Dawkins going 15 minutes without a field goal, Louisville jumped on the Blue Devils' poor 40% shooting to pull away for a 72–69 win.

In the finals of the NIT, played at New York's Madison Square Garden, Ohio State defeated Wyoming, 73–63. The Buckeye victory was a sort of going-away present for Coach Eldon Miller, whose dismissal, effective at the end of the season, had already been announced.

In women's NCAA competition, Texas proved too strong for the rest of the field. The Lady Longhorns completed a 34–0 season, ranking them as one of the best women's teams of all time, by defeating USC, 97–81, in the tournament finals at Lexington, KY. Clarissa Davis won the tournament MVP award, while USC's Cheryl Miller (the star of the 1984 U.S. Olympic team) was named women's player of the year.

Despite the ever-growing popularity of college basketball and despite all the excitements of top-quality competition, the year's most publicized story took place after the season and once again raised questions about the role of athletics and the status of athletes on college campuses. On June 19, only two days after being chosen second in the NBA draft by the champion Boston Celtics, University of Maryland All-American Les Bias collapsed suddenly in his dormitory room and died. On June 24, the Maryland state medical examiner ruled that the 22-year-old ACC player of the year had died of cocaine intoxication. The incident touched off new calls for a crackdown on drugs in collegiate and professional sports, as well as in the nation as a whole.

PAUL ATTNER, *"The Sporting News"*

COLLEGE BASKETBALL

Conference Champions*

Atlantic Coast: Duke
Atlantic-10: St. Joseph's
Big East: St. John's
Big Eight: Kansas
Big Sky: Montana State
Big Ten: Michigan
Colonial Athletic: Navy
East Coast: Drexel
ECAC Metro: Marist
ECAC North Atlantic: Northeastern
Ivy League: Brown
Metro: Louisville
Metro Atlantic Athletic: Fairfield
Mid-American: Ball State
Mid-Continent: Cleveland State
Mid-Eastern Athletic: North Carolina AT&T
Midwestern Collegiate: Xavier
Missouri Valley: Tulsa
Ohio Valley: Akron
Pacific Coast Athletic: Nevada-Las Vegas
Pacific-10: Arizona
Southeastern: Kentucky
Southern: Davidson
Southland: Northeast Louisiana
Southwest: Texas Tech
Southwestern Athletic: Mississippi Valley State
Sun Belt: Jacksonville
Trans America Athletic: Arkansas-Little Rock
West Coast Athletic: Pepperdine
Western Athletic: Texas-El Paso
    * Based on postseason conference
    tournaments, where applicable

Tournaments

NCAA: Louisville
NIT: Ohio State
NCAA Div. II: Sacred Heart
NCAA Div. III: Potsdam State
NAIA: David Lipscomb
NCAA (women's): Texas

Boxing

Unbeaten 20-year-old Mike Tyson of Catskill, NY, became the youngest boxer ever to win a heavyweight championship when he scored a second-round technical knockout over Trevor Berbick in their scheduled 12-round World Boxing Council (WBC) title match in Las Vegas on November 22. It was Tyson's 28th straight victory, 26 of them by knockout. Having turned 20 on June 30, Tyson thus broke the record for youngest heavyweight champion, previously held by Floyd Patterson, who was 21 years, 11 months old when he knocked out Archie Moore to win the crown in November 1956. Tyson was trained by the late Cus D'Amato, who also trained Patterson.

The Tyson-Berbick bout was part of a Home Box Office (HBO) cable-television series aimed at unifying the heavyweight title. Tyson's victory put him in line to fight the winner of the December 12 scheduled match between World Boxing Association (WBA) champion Tim Witherspoon and challenger Tony Tubbs. At the last minute, however, Tubbs pulled out of the fight and was replaced by James ("Bonecrusher") Smith. In a major upset at New York's Madison Square Garden, Smith became the WBA champion with a first-round knockout.

Smith's triumph marked the fourth time in 1986 that a heavyweight title changed hands. In January, Witherspoon dethroned Tubbs for the WBA title, scoring a 15-round majority decision in Atlanta. In March, Berbick, a Jamaican who lives in Florida, became the WBC champion with a 12-round unanimous decision over Pinklon Thomas in Las Vegas. Then in November, Tyson defeated Berbick.

The only heavyweight crown that did not change hands in 1986 was that of the International Boxing Federation (IBF). Michael Spinks, who had dethroned previously undefeated Larry Holmes as the IBF titleholder in September 1985, successfully defended the championship twice during 1986. Both fights were part of the HBO series. In April, Spinks, 29, won a hard-fought, 15-round split decision in a Las Vegas rematch with Holmes. The 36-year-old former champion, who fought with a broken right thumb from the third round on, later announced his retirement. In September, Spinks impressed again with a fourth-round knockout of Norway's Steffen Tangsted, the European champion, in another Las Vegas title defense.

In other weight divisions, 31-year-old undisputed middleweight champion Marvelous Marvin Hagler, regarded by many as the finest fighter in the sport, retained his title with an 11th round knockout of Uganda's John ("The Beast") Mugabe in Las Vegas. The defense was Hagler's 12th straight, leaving him only three short of the middleweight record.

Among the surprises during the year was the loss suffered by previously undefeated welterweight champion Donald Curry of the United States, often billed as "the best fighter pound for pound" in boxing. Curry was stopped in the sixth round by Great Britain's Lloyd Honeyghan in Atlantic City, NJ, in September. Earlier in the year, Curry had given credence to his billing with a second-round knockout of Panama's Eduardo Rodriguez.

Barry McGuigan of Northern Ireland was another popular champion to fall by the wayside during the year. The WBA featherweight titleholder was upset in June by the American Stevie Cruz, who scored a 15-round unanimous decision in Las Vegas. In February, McGuigan had successfully defended his title in a Dublin ring with a 14th-round knockout of Danilo Cabrera of the Dominican Republic.

Early in February, Marvin Johnson became the first fighter to win the light-heavyweight title three times when he stopped Leslie Stewart in the seventh round to capture the WBA crown at Market Square Arena in Indianapolis.

In the exciting lightweight division, undefeated WBC champion Hector ("Macho") Camacho kept his title with a split-decision over former champion Edwin Rosario in June. In October, Camacho won a unanimous decision over Uganda's Cornelius Boza-Edwards, and on the same card Rosario took the WBA title with a knockout of Livingstone Bramble.

GEORGE DE GREGORIO, *"The New York Times"*

World Boxing Champions*

Heavyweight—James Smith, United States (1986), World Boxing Association (WBA); Mike Tyson, United States (1986), World Boxing Council (WBC); Michael Spinks, United States (1984), International Boxing Federation (IBF).

Cruiserweight—Evander Holyfield, United States (1986), WBA; Carlos DeLeon, Puerto Rico (1986), WBC; Ricky Parkey, United States (1986), IBF.

Light Heavyweight—Marvin Johnson, United States (1986), WBA; Dennis Andries, Great Britain (1986), WBC; Bobby Czyz, United States (1986), IBF.

Middleweight—Marvelous Marvin Hagler, United States (1980), WBA, WBC, and IBF.

Junior Middleweight—Mike McCallum, Jamaica (1984), WBA; Duane Thomas, United States (1986), WBC; Buster Drayton, United States (1986), IBF.

Welterweight—Lloyd Honeyghan, Great Britain (1986), WBA, WBC, and IBF.

Junior Welterweight—Patrizio Oliva, Italy (1986), WBA; Tsuyoshi Hamada, Japan (1986), WBC; Joe Manley, United States (1985), IBF.

Lightweight—Edwin Rosario, Puerto Rico (1986), WBA; Hector Camacho, United States (1985), WBC; Greg Haugen, United States (1986), IBF.

Junior Lightweight—Brian Mitchell, South Africa (1986), WBA; Julio Cesar Chavez, Mexico (1984), WBC; Barry Michael, Australia (1986), IBF.

Featherweight—Steve Cruz, United States (1986), WBA; Azumah Nelson, Ghana (1984), WBC; Antonio Rivera, Puerto Rico (1986), IBF.

Junior Featherweight—Samart Payardoon, Thailand (1986), WBC; WBA, IBF vacant.

Bantamweight—Bernardo Pinango, Venezuela (1986), WBA; Miguel Lora, Colombia (1985), WBC; Jeff Fenech, Australia (1985), IBF.

Junior Bantamweight—Khaosai Galaxy, Thailand (1984), WBA; Gilberto Roman, Mexico (1986), WBC; Elly Pical, Indonesia (1985), IBF.

Flyweight—Hilario Zapata, Panama (1985), WBA; Sol Chitalada, Thailand (1984), WBC; Hisup Shin, South Korea (1986), IBF.

Junior Flyweight—Yoo Myong Moo, South Korea (1985), WBA; Chang Chong Koo, South Korea (1983), WBC; Jumhwan Choi, South Korea (1986), IBF.

* As of Dec. 31, 1986; year of achieving title in parentheses.

Football

Following the trends in professional baseball and basketball, the National Football League in 1986–87 crowned a new champion, the New York Giants. Not since the Pittsburgh Steelers in 1980 has any team managed to retain its NFL title. The Chicago Bears, winners of Super Bowl XX, compiled a 1986 regular-season record of 14–2—tied with the Giants for best in the league—but fell in their first play-off game.

Super XXI, played before a crowd of 101,063 at the Rose Bowl in Pasadena, CA, pitted two teams that relied heavily on their defenses: the Giants, who succeeded the Bears as champions of the National Football Conference (NFC), and the Denver Broncos, champions of the American Football Conference (AFC). Nevertheless, Super Bowl XXI turned out to be a high-scoring affair. After a tightly contested first half that left the Broncos with a 10–9 halftime lead, the Giants dominated the second half and defeated Denver, 39–20. Giants quarterback Phil Simms completed a total of 22 of 25 passes, including three for touchdowns, and was voted the game's most valuable player. According to Giants Coach Bill Parcells, Simms played the game of his career.

The year in professional football also included the demise of the financially troubled United States Football League (USFL), *see* page 474. In the Canadian Football League (CFL), the Hamilton Tiger-Cats won their first Grey Cup since 1972 by defeating the heavily favored Edmonton Eskimos, 39–15, at Vancouver's B.C. Place Stadium.

In the U.S. collegiate ranks, the Nittany Lions of Penn State emerged as unofficial national champions after upsetting the top-ranked Miami Hurricanes, 14–10, in the Fiesta Bowl. Miami quarterback Vinny Testaverde was a landslide winner in balloting for the Heisman Trophy.

National Football League

In quest of their first Super Bowl appearance, the Giants lost their season-opening contest (to the Dallas Cowboys) but suffered only one other setback (to the Seattle Seahawks) en route to an NFC Eastern Division title and a home-field advantage in the play-offs. The success of the team was attributable largely to its defense, headed by linebacker Lawrence Taylor, everybody's choice for NFL player of the year; other defensive standouts were linebackers Harry Carson and Carl Banks, end Leonard Marshall, and nose tackle Jim Burt. Offensively the charge was led by running back Joe Morris, whose 1,516 yards were second-highest in the NFL and set a new team record; quarterback Phil Simms; and all-pro tight end Mark Bavaro. Sean Landeta, another all-pro, was the NFC's top punter (44.8-yard average).

The other play-off teams in the NFC were the Central Division champion Bears, who boasted the league's stingiest defense (187 points) and its all-time leading rusher, Walter Payton (1,333 yards in 1986, 16,193 yards career); the Western Division champion San Francisco 49ers (10–5–1), led by quarterback Joe Montana, who came back from early-season back surgery, and all-pro receiver Jerry

Giants running back Joe Morris (20) eluded the Redskins for 87 yards and a touchdown in the NFC championship game—a 17–0 victory by the New Yorkers. Morris' 1,516 rushing yards in the regular season were the second highest in the NFL and the most ever by a Giant.

In Cleveland's frigid Municipal Stadium, Denver Bronco kicker Rich Karlis toed a 33-yard field goal in overtime to give his team a 23–20 triumph in the AFC championship game.

AP/Wide World

Rice; and the two "wild card" entries, the Washington Redskins (12–4) and Los Angeles Rams (10–6). The Dallas Cowboys (7–9), despite the addition of former USFL star running back Herschel Walker (*see* BIOGRAPHY), failed to make the play-offs for only the third time in 20 years.

Washington was impressive in its first two post-season matchups, defeating the Rams, 19–7, in the wild card game and then upsetting the Bears, 27–13, at Chicago's Soldier Field. The Bears, who had suffered a series of injuries at quarterback during the year, pinned their hopes in that game on back-up Doug Flutie, a former Heisman Trophy winner and USFL performer whose mid-season acquisition had been a source of dispute among the quarrelsome defending champions. The Giants, meanwhile, fired on all cylinders in their first play-off contest, thrashing San Francisco, 49–3. Then in the NFC championship game, played at wind-swept Giants Stadium (East Rutherford, NJ), the home team treated its fans to a 17–0 shutout of the Redskins. It was the Giants' third victory of the season against Washington.

The upshot of competition in the AFC was a changing of the guard. Denver (11–5), which had not even reached the play-offs in 1985, won its first six games in 1986 and went on to capture the Western Division title. The perennially powerful L.A. Raiders (8–8) and San Diego Chargers (4–12) did not qualify for post-season play. Like the Giants, the Broncos drew their momentum from the defense; end Rulon Jones and linebacker Karl Mecklenburg, both Pro Bowl selections, were standouts. Offensively, Denver relied on the arm of quarterback John Elway and on the running of Sammy Winder, whose 14 touchdowns led the AFC.

The Cleveland Browns (12–4) qualified for the play-offs by winning the AFC Central Division title, and the defending conference champion New England Patriots (11–5) took the Eastern Division crown. Another perennial power, the Miami Dolphins (8–8) failed to earn a post-season berth. The up-and-down New York Jets (10–6) and the Kansas City Chiefs (10–6) squeaked into the play-offs as wild cards.

Coming off five straight losses, the Jets rebounded for a 35–15 victory over the Chiefs in the wild-card round. The following week, however, the New Yorkers squandered a 10-point lead in the fourth quarter and fell to Cleveland, 23–20, in double overtime; Browns quarterback Bernie Kosar passed for a play-off record 489 yards. In the other conference semifinal, Elway triggered the Broncos to a 22–17 victory over the Patriots. The AFC championship game, played in Cleveland, was another thriller. In the final minutes of the fourth quarter, Elway engineered a 98-yard drive that tied the score at 20. Then in overtime, the Denver defense held, its offense drove again, and Rich Karlis ended the deadlock with a 33-yard field goal. The Broncos moved on to Pasadena.

Among the NFL's other outstanding individual performers in 1986 were running backs Eric Dickerson of the Rams, who led the league with 1,821 rushing yards, and Curt Warner of the Seahawks, who led the AFC with 1,481.

The Dolphins' Dan Marino was the top-rated quarterback in the AFC, while the Vikings' Tommy Kramer headed the list in the NFC. Patriots kicker Tony Franklin was the NFL scoring champion with 140 points, while Redskin running back George Rogers led the league with 18 touchdowns. Todd Christensen of the Raiders caught 95 passes. Ronnie Lott of the 49ers had 10 interceptions. Lawrence Taylor of the Giants had 20½ sacks. And Rohn Stark of the Colts averaged 45.2 yards per punt.

Seattle wide receiver Steve Largent broke the NFL record (128) for most consecutive games with a pass reception and registered his record eighth 1,000-yard season. San Diego pass catcher Charlie Joiner surpassed Don

PROFESSIONAL FOOTBALL

National Football League

Final Standings

NATIONAL CONFERENCE

Eastern Division	W	L	T	Pct.	Points For	Points Against
N.Y. Giants	14	2	0	.875	371	236
Washington	12	4	0	.750	368	296
Dallas	7	9	0	.438	346	337
Philadelphia	5	10	1	.344	256	312
St. Louis	4	11	1	.281	218	351
Central Division						
Chicago	14	2	0	.875	352	187
Minnesota	9	7	0	.563	398	273
Detroit	5	11	0	.313	277	326
Green Bay	4	12	0	.250	254	418
Tampa Bay	2	14	0	.125	239	473
Western Division						
San Francisco	10	5	1	.656	374	247
L.A. Rams	10	6	0	.625	309	267
Atlanta	7	8	1	.469	280	280
New Orleans	7	9	0	.438	288	287

PLAY-OFFS

Washington 19, L.A. Rams 7
Washington 27, Chicago 13
N.Y. Giants 49; San Francisco 3
N.Y. Giants 17, Washington 0

AMERICAN CONFERENCE

Eastern Division	W	L	T	Pct.	Points For	Points Against
New England	11	5	0	.688	412	307
N.Y. Jets	10	6	0	.625	364	386
Miami	8	8	0	.500	430	405
Buffalo	4	12	0	.250	287	348
Indianapolis	3	13	0	.188	229	400
Central Division						
Cleveland	12	4	0	.750	391	310
Cincinnati	10	6	0	.625	409	394
Pittsburgh	6	10	0	.375	307	336
Houston	5	11	0	.313	274	329
Western Division						
Denver	11	5	0	.688	378	327
Kansas City	10	6	0	.625	358	326
Seattle	10	6	0	.625	366	293
L.A. Raiders	8	8	0	.500	323	346
San Diego	4	12	0	.250	335	396

PLAY-OFFS

N.Y. Jets 35, Kansas City 15
Cleveland 23, N.Y. Jets 20
Denver 22, New England 17
Denver 23, Cleveland 20

SUPER BOWL XXI: N.Y. Giants 39, Denver 20

Maynard's career record of 11,834 receiving yards. Dave Jennings of the Jets became the all-time leader in punts, with more than 1,085.

Among the year's notable trends was the longer duration of games. Part of the reason was the league's new "replay rule," by which referees could consult television instant replay footage to verify disputed calls. Fans generally liked the new rule, but most agreed that refinements—especially faster rulings—were needed.

A more disturbing trend was an apparent increase in game violence. In the most glaring incident, Bears' quarterback Jim McMahon was slammed to the ground in a game against the Green Bay Packers, well after the play had ended. McMahon was sidelined for the rest of the season with a shoulder injury.

The year's inductees into the Pro Football Hall of Fame were running back Paul Hornung, quarterback Fran Tarkenton, defensive back Ken Houston, linebacker Willie Lanier, and the multidimensional Doak Walker.

The College Season

Amid new calls for a post-season tournament to decide the official National Collegiate Athletic Association (NCAA) football championship, the traditional bowl format produced a clear-cut national champion in 1986–87. By defeating the top-ranked and previously undefeated (11–0) Miami Hurricanes in the Fiesta Bowl, 14–10, the Penn State Nittany Lions, ranked number 2 and also undefeated, laid legitimate claim to the national collegiate title. The matchup of the top two teams and the excitement of the contest itself only added fuel to the movement for a tournament system.

Miami was the heavy favorite going into the Fiesta Bowl, played in Tempe, AZ, on Jan. 2, 1987. The Hurricanes had occupied the top spot in the polls since September, when they beat the then-number-1 Oklahoma Sooners, 28–16. In that game as throughout the season, the Miami offense was ignited by quarterback Vinny Testaverde, the consensus selection as collegiate player of the year. The Miami offense finished the season second in the nation (to Oklahoma) in scoring (38.2 points per game to 42.4). The Hurricane defense also was one of the strongest in the country and included two All-Americas, tackle Jerome Brown and safety Bennie Blades.

Joe Paterno's Penn State squad, meanwhile, ground out victory after victory, but several were close, low-scoring affairs. Defense was the name of the game for the Nittany Lions, who yielded only 11.2 points and 69.7 yards rushing per game (both third-best in the nation). The defense was anchored by All-America linebacker Shane Conlan. Running back D. J. Dozier was the chief offensive threat.

COLLEGE FOOTBALL

Conference Champions	Atlantic Coast—Clemson Big Eight—Oklahoma Big Ten—Michigan, Ohio State (tie) Ivy League—Pennsylvania Mid-American—Miami (OH) Pacific Coast—San Jose State Pacific Ten—Arizona State Southeastern—Louisiana State Southland—Arkansas State Southwest—Texas A&M Western Athletic—San Diego State
NCAA Champions	Division I-AA—Georgia Southern Division II—North Dakota State Division III—Augustana
NAIA Champions	Division I—Carson-Newman (TN) Division II—Linfield (OR)
Individual Honors	Heisman Trophy—Vinny Testaverde, Miami Lombardi Award—Cornelius Bennett, Alabama Outland Trophy—Jason Buck, Brigham Young

Major Bowl Games

All-American Bowl (Birmingham, AL, Dec. 31)—Florida State 27, Indiana 13
Aloha Bowl (Honolulu, Dec. 27)—Arizona 30, North Carolina 21
Bluebonnet Bowl (Houston, Dec. 31)—Baylor 21, Colorado 9
California Bowl (Fresno, Dec. 13)—San Jose State 37, Miami (OH) 7
Cotton Bowl (Dallas, Jan. 1)—Ohio State 28, Texas A&M 12
Fiesta Bowl (Tempe, AZ, Jan. 2)—Penn State 14, Miami 10
Florida Citrus Bowl (Orlando, Jan. 1)—Auburn 16, Southern California 7
Freedom Bowl (Anaheim, CA, Dec. 30)—UCLA 31, Brigham Young 10
Gator Bowl (Jacksonville, FL, Dec. 27)—Clemson 27, Stanford 21
Hall of Fame Bowl (Tampa, FL, Dec. 23)—Boston College 27, Georgia 24
Holiday Bowl (San Diego, CA, Dec. 30)—Iowa 39, San Diego State 38
Independence Bowl (Shreveport, LA, Dec. 20)—Mississippi 20, Texas Tech 17
Liberty Bowl (Memphis, TN, Dec. 29)—Tennessee 21, Minnesota 14
Orange Bowl (Miami, Jan. 1)—Oklahoma 42, Arkansas 8
Peach Bowl (Atlanta, Dec. 31)—Virginia Tech 25, North Carolina State 24
Rose Bowl (Pasadena, CA, Jan. 1)—Arizona State 22, Michigan 15
Sugar Bowl (New Orleans, Jan. 1)—Nebraska 30, Louisiana State 15
Sun Bowl (El Paso, TX, Dec. 25)—Alabama 28, Washington 6

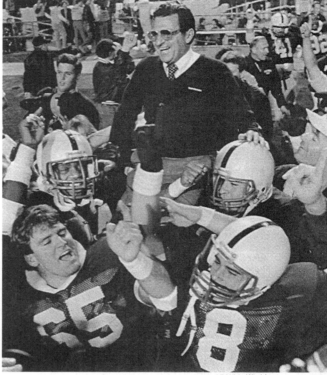

AP/Wide World

Joe Paterno, the widely respected coach of Penn State, guided his team to an undefeated regular season for the sixth time, then earned his second national championship.

The Penn State defense was at its best against the high-powered Miami offense in the Fiesta Bowl, intercepting five Testaverde passes and sacking the Heisman Trophy winner four times. Still, the Nittany Lions needed to come from behind to win. After a 7–7 tie at halftime and a scoreless third quarter, Miami kicked a field goal with about 12 minutes remaining. After Conlan's second interception, Penn State took the lead with 8:13 left on a six-yard TD run by Dozier, who gained 99 yards on the evening. Miami made one final drive, but its hopes ended on another interception.

In another post-season matchup, the Oklahoma Sooners (11–1) laid final claim to the number 3 ranking with a 42–8 trouncing of Arkansas (9–3) in the Orange Bowl. In addition to scoring the most points in the country during the year, the Sooners gained the most yards rushing (404.7 per game) and allowed the fewest yards rushing (60.7) as well as passing (108.9). The Sooner defense was headed by zany, outspoken All-America linebacker Brian Bosworth. "The Boz" finished fourth in the Heisman Trophy balloting, but he was barred from the Orange Bowl after testing positive for steroid use.

In the Rose Bowl, the Pac-Ten champion Arizona State Sun Devils (10–1–1) defeated the Big Ten representative, Michigan (11–2), 22–15. Arizona State ranked fourth in the final Associated Press poll. Michigan, led by Jim Harbaugh, who finished third in the Heisman vote and was second in quarterback rating, ranked eighth. The Wolverines' cochampion in the Big Ten, number-7 Ohio State (10–3), beat Texas A&M (9–3) in the Cotton Bowl, 28–12. And Nebraska (10–2), the nation's number-5 team, beat number-10 Louisiana State (9–3) in the Sugar Bowl, 30–15. AP's other top-10 teams included number-6 Auburn (10–2) and number-9 Alabama (10–3).

Brigham Young defensive tackle Jason Buck and Alabama linebacker Cornelius Bennett were named as recipients of the Outland Trophy and Lombardi Award, respectively, as the nation's top college linemen. Temple running back Paul Palmer led the nation in rushing with 1,866 yards and finished second in the Heisman Trophy balloting.

Among NCAA Division I-A records set in 1986 were 10,623 career passing yards by Kevin Sweeney of Fresno State; 262 career pass receptions by Templeton; 80 career field goals by Jeff Jaeger of Washington; and 135 consecutive extra points by Van Tifflin of Alabama and Tim Lashar of Oklahoma.

JEFFREY H. HACKER

Golf

Greg Norman and Pat Bradley marched through spectacular seasons on the Professional Golfers' Association (PGA) and Ladies Professional Golf Association (LPGA) tours, respectively, in 1986.

For Norman, the year was one of frustrations as well as successes. The powerful Australian led or was tied for the lead after the third round of all four major championships. But he won only one, a five-shot victory in the British Open. "The Shark" also won two tournaments and a record $653,296 on the U.S. tour, despite missing the last nine events in order to play overseas. There he won eight tournaments, to raise his worldwide winnings to $1.8 million.

Norman played a key role in a marvelous year for the major men's tournaments. Nostalgia buffs were caught up in 46-year-old Jack Nicklaus' final-round 65, as he came from behind to win his sixth Masters title by a stroke over Norman and Tom Kite. When Norman faltered on the last day of the U.S. Open, veteran Raymond Floyd was there to take command with a four-under-par 66 and a two-shot victory; at 43, Floyd became that tournament's oldest winner. In the PGA Championship, Norman frittered away a four-shot lead over the last eight holes and lost when Bob Tway holed a spectacular bunker shot on the 18th. It was the fourth victory of the year for Tway, a 27-year-old, second-year player. Tway eventually lost the money title to Norman by just $516 but was named the PGA Player of the Year. He also won the tour's Vantage Cup Series, worth $500,000. Scott Hoch, although winless on tour, won the Vardon Trophy for low scoring average at 70.08, the best in five years.

In LPGA play, Bradley abolished her reputation as a runner-up. (In 12 years on the tour, she had won 16 tournaments while finishing second 36 times.) In 1986 she won a total of five events, including three of the four women's majors—the Nabisco Dinah Shore, the LPGA Championship, and the du Maurier Classic. She also established a single-season money record ($492,021), won the Vare Trophy for low scoring average (71.1), captured the LPGA-Mazda Series, and was named the Rolex Player of the Year. The only major to escape Bradley was the U.S. Open, won by Jane Geddes in a playoff over Sally Little.

On the Senior PGA Tour, it was the year of the 50-year-old rookie. Bruce Crampton, the winner of 15 PGA tour events and two Vardon Trophies from 1961 through 1975, won seven tournaments in his first full season as a senior and banked $454,299, the most ever for a senior player. Dale Douglass, who became eligible in March, won the U.S. Senior Open and three other tournaments. Chi Chi Rodriquez and Gary Player won three tournaments apiece.

LARRY DENNIS, *Free-lance Golf Writer*

Golf

PGA 1986 Tournament Winners

MONY Tournament of Champions: Calvin Peete (267)
Bob Hope Chrysler Classic: Donnie Hammond (335)
Phoenix Open: Hal Sutton (267)
AT&T Pebble Beach National Pro-Am: Fuzzy Zoeller (205)
Shearson Lehman Brothers Andy Williams Open: Bob Tway (204)
Hawaiian Open: Corey Pavin (272)
Los Angeles Open: Doug Tewell (270)
Honda Classic: Kenny Knox (287)
Doral-Eastern Open: Andy Bean (276)
Hertz Bay Hill Classic: Dan Forsman (202)
USF&G Classic: Calvin Peete (269)
Tournament Players Championship: John Mahaffey (275)
Greater Greensboro Open: Sandy Lyle (275)
Masters: Jack Nicklaus (279)
Sea Pines Heritage Classic: Fuzzy Zoeller (276)
Houston Open: Curtis Strange (274)
Panasonic Las Vegas Invitational: Greg Norman (333)
Byron Nelson Classic: Andy Bean (269)
Colonial National Invitation: Dan Pohl (205)
Memorial Tournament: Hal Sutton (271)
Kemper Open: Greg Norman (277)
Manufacturers Hanover Westchester Classic: Bob Tway (272)
U.S. Open: Raymond Floyd (279)
Georgia-Pacific Atlanta Classic: Bob Tway (269)
Canadian Open: Bob Murphy (280)
Canon-Sammy Davis, Jr. Greater Hartford Open: Mac O'Grady (269)
Anheuser-Busch Classic: Fuzzy Zoeller (274)
Hardee's Golf Classic: Mark Wiebe (268)
Buick Open: Ben Crenshaw (270)
Western Open: Tom Kite (286)
PGA Championship: Bob Tway (276)
The International: Ken Green (12 points)
NEC World Series of Golf: Dan Pohl (277)
Federal Express St. Jude Memphis Classic: Mike Hulbert (280)
B.C. Open: Rick Fehr (267)
Bank of Boston Classic: Gene Sauers (274)
Greater Milwaukee Open: Corey Pavin (272)
Southwest Golf Classic: Mark Calcavecchia (275)
Southern Open: Fred Wadsworth (269)
Walt Disney World/Oldsmobile Golf Classic: Raymond Floyd (275)
Vantage Championship: Ben Crenshaw (196)
Tallahassee Open: Mark Hayes (273)
Seiko-Tucson Match Play Championship: Jim Thorpe

LPGA 1986 Tournament Winners

Mazda Classic: Val Skinner (280)
Elizabeth Arden Classic: Ayako Okamoto (280)
Sarasota Classic: Patty Sheehan (279)
Standard Register/Samaritan Turquoise Classic: Mary Beth Zimmerman (278)
Uniden LPGA Invitational: Mary Beth Zimmerman (281)
Women's Kemper Open: Juli Inkster (276)
GNA/Glendale Federal Classic: Chris Johnson (212)
Circle K Tucson Open: Penny Pulz (276)
Nabisco Dinah Shore: Pat Bradley (280)
Kyocera Inamori Classic: Patty Sheehan (278)
S&H Golf Classic: Pat Bradley (272)
United Virginia Bank Golf Classic: Muffin Spencer-Devlin (214)
Chrysler-Plymouth Classic: Becky Pearson (212)
LPGA Corning Classic: Laurie Rinker (278)
LPGA Championship: Pat Bradley (277)
McDonald's Championship: Juli Inkster (281)
Lady Keystone Open: Juli Inkster (210)
Rochester International: Judy Dickinson (281)
Mayflower Classic: Sandra Palmer (278)
Mazda Hall of Fame Championship: Amy Alcott (284)
U.S. Women's Open: Jane Geddes (287)
Boston Five Classic: Jane Geddes (281)
du Maurier Classic: Pat Bradley (276)
LPGA National Pro-Am: Amy Alcott (283)
Henredon Classic: Betsy King (277)
Nestlé World Championship: Pat Bradley (279)
MasterCard International Pro-Am: Cindy Mackey (276)
Atlantic City LPGA Classic: Juli Inkster (209)
Rail Charity Classic: Betsy King (205)
Cellular One/Ping Golf Championship: Ayako Okamoto (207)
Safeco Classic: Judy Dickinson (274)
Konica San Jose Classic: Patty Sheehan (212)

Other Tournaments

British Open: Greg Norman (280)
World Match Play: Greg Norman
U.S. Senior Open: Dale Douglass (279)
General Foods PGA Seniors Championship: Gary Player (281)
Senior Tournament Players Championship: Chi Chi Rodriquez (206)
U.S. Men's Amateur: Buddy Alexander
U.S. Women's Amateur: Kay Cockerill
U.S. Men's Public Links: Bill Mayfair
U.S. Women's Public Links: Cindy Schreyer
Mid-Amateur: Bill Loeffler
U.S. Senior Men's Amateur: Bo Williams
U.S. Senior Women's Amateur: Constance Guthrie
U.S. Junior Boys: Brian Montgomery
U.S. Junior Girls: Pat Hurst
Curtis Cup: Great Britain-Ireland 13, United States 5
NCAA Men: Individual—Scott Verplank; Team—Wake Forest
NCAA Women: Individual—Page Dunlap; Team—Florida
Women's World Amateur Team: Spain
Men's World Amateur Team: Canada

Snow Chief, with Alex Solis aboard, captured the 111th running of the Preakness by four lengths. He covered the 1³⁄₁₆-mi track in 1:54.8. The black colt won six of nine races during 1986, and his earnings, $1,875,200, were the most for a thoroughbred.

AP/Wide World

Horse Racing

Lady's Secret, a four-year-old daughter of Secretariat, won 10 of 15 races and was named Horse of the Year in 1986. Trained by D. Wayne Lukas, Lady's Secret won such races as the Breeders' Cup Distaff, the Whitney Handicap, the Maskette, the Ruffian Handicap, the Beldame Stakes, and the Shuvee Handicap and piled up total earnings of $1,871,053.

Manila, a grass specialist trained by LeRoy Jolley, triumphed in eight of ten races during the year. The three-year-old son of Lyphard won the Breeders' Cup Turf.

Woody Stephens sent out Danzig Connection to win the Belmont Stakes, marking the fifth straight year that the Hall of Fame trainer succeeded in this 1½-mile race.

Ferdinand, ridden by 54-year-old Bill Shoemaker and trained by Charlie Whittingham, captured the Kentucky Derby. Whittingham also won the Budweiser-Arlington Million with Estrapade, a six-year-old mare who became the first female to triumph in this race.

Snow Chief won the Florida Derby, the Santa Anita Derby, the Preakness, and the Jersey Derby. This son of Reflected Glory had a total of six victories in nine starts and earnings of $1,875,200, the most for a thoroughbred.

Skywalker, ridden by Laffit Pincay, Jr., won the Breeders' Cup Classic. Pincay also won the Breeders' Cup Juvenile, piloting Capote. A son of Seattle Slew, Capote won three of four races and was voted the two-year-old male champion of 1986. Brave Raj, trained by Mel Stute, ruled as the two-year-old filly champion with six victories in nine starts.

Harness Racing. Forrest Skipper, a four-year-old pacer who won all 15 of his starts and earned $637,675, was honored as Harness Horse of the Year. Among his victories was the Breeders' Crown's $301,350 race for aged pacing horses. Jate Lobell, a two-year-old pacer, also was unbeaten in 15 starts in 1986.

Driver Michel Lachance set a world record for wins in a single season with 770; the old record was 707.

Harness racing was saddened by the death of Billy Haughton, the best known and most accomplished driver in the sport. Haughton, 62, who amassed 4,910 career victories, died from injuries suffered in a spill on July 5 at Yonkers (NY) Raceway.

JIM BOLUS, *Louisville, KY*

HORSE RACING

Major North American Thoroughbred Races

Beldame Stakes: Lady's Secret, $316,250 (money distributed)
Belmont Stakes: Danzig Connection, $564,400
Breeders' Cup Classic: Skywalker, $3,000,000
Breeders' Cup Distaff: Lady's Secret, $1,000,000
Breeders' Cup Juvenile: Capote, $1,000,000
Breeders' Cup Juvenile Fillies: Brave Raj, $1,000,000
Breeders' Cup Mile: Last Tycoon, $950,000
Breeders' Cup Sprint: Smile, $1,000,000
Breeders' Cup Turf: Manila, $2,000,000
Budweiser-Arlington Million: Estrapade, $1,000,000
Hollywood Invitational: Flying Pidgeon, $300,000
Hollywood Futurity: Temperate Sil, $1,000,000
Florida Derby: Snow Chief, $500,000
Jockey Club Gold Cup: Creme Fraiche, $850,500
Kentucky Derby: Ferdinand, $784,400
Man o' War Stakes: Dance of Life, $340,000
Marlboro Cup: Turkoman, $500,000
Maskette: Lady's Secret, $137,600
Preakness: Snow Chief, $534,400
Rothmans International: Southjet, $702,500
Ruffian Handicap: Lady's Secret, $280,400
Santa Anita Handicap: Greinton, $1,139,500
Spinster: Top Corsage, $234,450
Suburban Handicap: Roo Art, $329,500
Travers: Wise Times, $344,500
Turf Classic: Manila, $705,250
Woodward: Precisionist, $332,000

Major North American Harness Races

Cane Pace: Barberry Spur, $542,764
Governor's Cup: Redskin, $1,513,500
Hambletonian: Nuclear Kosmos, $1,172,082
Hambletonian Oaks: JEF's Spice, $397,000
Jugette: Anniecrombie, $208,300
Kentucky Futurity: Sugarcane Hanover, $160,530
Kentucky Pacing Derby: Jate Lobell, $434,570
Little Brown Jug: Barberry Spur, $407,684
Meadowlands Pace: Laughs, $1,025,500
Merrie Annabelle: Armbro Fling, $594,250
Messenger: Amity Chef, $333,762
Peter Haughton Memorial: Ditka Hanover, $879,250
Sweetheart Pace: Nadia Lobell, $915,500
Woodrow Wilson Pace: Cullin Hanover, $1,561,500

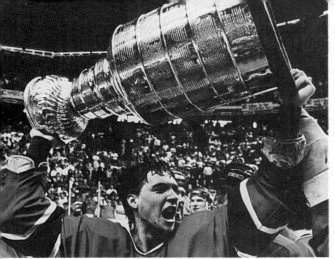

"The Calgary Herald" from Canapress

Rookie goaltender Patrick Roy, age 20, carried the load in Montreal's quest for a 23rd Stanley Cup championship.

Ice Hockey

In the National Hockey League (NHL), 1985–86 was the Year of the Upset, as the main contenders tumbled one after another to apparent pretenders in the race for the Stanley Cup. In the end, the Montreal Canadiens—who had the league's seventh best record during the regular season—won the Cup with a four-games-to-one victory over the Calgary Flames—who had the sixth best record. The reign of the defending champion Edmonton Oilers ended after two seasons when they fell early in postseason play.

Regular Season. Oiler center Wayne Gretzky was named the league's most valuable player (MVP) for the seventh straight year and won the league scoring title for the sixth straight year. His total of 215 points smashed his own single-season mark of 212, set in 1981–82. It was the fourth time "The Great One" scaled the 200-point plateau; no one else in the game's history has even reached 160 points in one campaign. Gretzky was so dominant that he could have gone the entire season without a goal and still won the scoring crown easily. He compiled a total of 163 assists, while Pittsburgh center Mario Lemieux finished second in total points with 141. Oiler teammates Paul Coffey (138) and Jari Kurri (131) were third and fourth in final scoring. Kurri led the NHL in goals with 68. Coffey broke Bobby Orr's record for most goals by a defenseman in a single season, hitting for 48. A total of 13 players had 100 or more points during the regular season. Among them was Minnesota center Neal Broten, whose 105 points made him the highest-scoring American-born player in any season. Only six players scored 50 or more goals in 1985–86, down from nine the year before. New York Islander winger Mike Bossy, who finished second to Kurri with 61, had his ninth straight 50-plus season. Philadelphia's Tim Kerr (58),

Edmonton's Glenn Anderson (54), Quebec's Michel Goulet (53), and Gretzky (52) were the only others to score 50. The only major career milestone was recorded by Los Angeles center Marcel Dionne, who moved past Phil Esposito into second place on the all-time scoring list with 1,599 points.

Finishing the regular season with 119 points and losing just five times in conference play, the Edmonton Oilers were easy winners in the Smythe Division. Philadelphia (110 points) topped the Patrick Division. Quebec (92) took the Adams title. And Chicago (86) headed the Norris.

Play-offs. At age 20, Montreal's rookie goaltender Patrick Roy became the youngest winner of the Conn Smythe Trophy as the MVP of the play-offs. In 20 games he had a microscopic 1.92 goals-against average and tied the Oilers' Grant Fuhr and the Islanders' Billy Smith for most wins (15) in a play-off year. Roy proved to be the decisive factor in the Canadiens' drive to their 23rd NHL championship.

The defending champion Oilers were eliminated from the play-offs in the Smythe Division final, losing to the Calgary Flames in an exciting seven-game series. Edmonton lost the final contest, 3–2, when defenseman Steve Smith accidentally shot the puck past goalie Grant Fuhr and into his own goal. To reach the Smythe Divison championship, Edmonton had defeated Vancouver, and Calgary had beaten Winnipeg.

The Oilers were not the only powerhouse to fall from grace. The Philadelphia Flyers, who had the second best record in the league, were upset by the New York Rangers in five games in the first round of the Patrick Division play-offs. The Rangers then went on to surprise the Washington Capitals—who had the third best regular-season record—in the division final.

The Quebec Nordiques, fourth overall, were humbled in three straight by the Hartford Whalers in the preliminary round of the Adams play-offs. The Canadiens, meanwhile, blasted Boston three in a row and then escaped with a seventh-game win over the Whalers for the division title.

In the Norris Division, the Toronto Maple Leafs kept up the bizarre upset ritual, beating Chicago in three straight. St. Louis got past Minnesota in five games before subduing Toronto in seven close contests for the Norris crown.

The Flames (sixth overall in the league) were the highest-ranked team in the final four, followed by Montreal (seventh), St. Louis (12th), and the Rangers (14th). The Canadiens got past the Rangers in five games in the Wales Conference final, as Roy deflated the New Yorkers with superb goaltending. The Flames, meanwhile, had to go seven games against the hard-working Blues in the Campbell Conference final.

The Cup final was the first in 19 years that involved two Canadian teams. It also matched two rookie goaltenders—Montreal's Roy and Calgary's Mike Vernon.

Calgary took the opener on home ice, breaking through Roy's mystique for a 5–2 win. The Flames scored four times on Roy (the

ICE HOCKEY

National Hockey League
(Final Standings, 1985–86)

Wales Conference

Patrick Division	W	L	T	Pts.	Goals For	Goals Against
*Philadelphia	53	23	4	110	335	241
*Washington	50	23	7	107	315	272
*N.Y. Islanders	39	29	12	90	327	284
*N.Y. Rangers	36	38	6	78	280	276
Pittsburgh	34	38	8	76	313	305
New Jersey	28	49	3	59	301	374

Adams Division	W	L	T	Pts.	For	Against
*Quebec	43	31	6	92	330	289
*Montreal	40	33	7	87	330	280
*Boston	37	31	12	86	311	288
*Hartford	40	36	4	84	332	302
Buffalo	37	37	6	80	296	281

Campbell Conference

Norris Division	W	L	T	Pts.	For	Against
*Chicago	39	33	8	86	351	350
*Minnesota	38	33	9	85	327	305
*St. Louis	37	34	9	83	302	291
*Toronto	25	48	7	57	311	386
Detroit	17	57	6	40	266	415

Smythe Division	W	L	T	Pts.	For	Against
*Edmonton	56	17	7	119	426	310
*Calgary	40	31	9	89	354	315
*Winnipeg	26	47	7	59	295	372
*Vancouver	23	44	13	59	282	333
Los Angeles	23	49	8	54	284	389

*Made play-offs

Stanley Cup Play-Offs
Wales Conference

First Round	Hartford	3 games	Quebec	0
	Montreal	3 games	Boston	0
	N.Y. Rangers	3 games	Philadelphia	2
	Washington	3 games	N.Y. Islanders	0
Semifinals	Montreal	4 games	Hartford	3
	N.Y. Rangers	4 games	Washington	2
Finals	Montreal	4 games	N.Y. Rangers	1

Campbell Conference

First Round	Calgary	3 games	Winnipeg	0
	Edmonton	3 games	Vancouver	1
	St. Louis	3 games	Minnesota	2
	Toronto	3 games	Chicago	0
Semifinals	Calgary	4 games	Edmonton	3
	St. Louis	4 games	Toronto	3
Finals	Calgary	4 games	St. Louis	3

Championship

Montreal	4 games	Calgary	1

Individual Honors

Hart Trophy (most valuable player): Wayne Gretzky, Edmonton
Ross Trophy (leading scorer): Wayne Gretzky
Vezina Trophy (top goaltender): John Vanbiesbrouck, N.Y. Rangers
Norris Trophy (best defenseman): Paul Coffey, Edmonton
Selke Award (best defense forward): Troy Murray, Chicago
Calder Trophy (rookie of the year): Gary Suter, Calgary
Lady Byng Trophy (sportsmanship): Mike Bossy, N.Y. Islanders
Conn Smythe Trophy (most valuable in play-offs): Patrick Roy, Montreal
Adam Trophy (coach of the year): Glen Sather, Edmonton

All-Star Game

Wales Conference 4, Campbell Conference 3
Most Valuable Player: Grant Fuhr, Edmonton

NCAA: Michigan State

fifth going into an empty net), the most the Montreal goalie gave up in any play-off game. In Game 2, however, the Canadiens bounced back with a 3–2 victory in overtime. Brian Skrudland knocked the puck past Vernon only nine seconds into the extra period. It was the fastest overtime goal in NHL play-off history.

The Canadiens got stronger as the series wore on and won the next three contests. In Game 3, played at Montreal, they scored three times in a 68-second span during the first period and went on to a 5–3 victory. Game 4 was a hard-fought contest that remained 0–0 into the third period. Montreal's Claude Lemieux proved to be the hero, scoring the game's only goal midway through the final frame. The only downer was a post-game brawl that led NHL President John Ziegler to levy a league-record $42,000 in fines.

Montreal wrapped up its 23rd Stanley Cup title with a nail-biting 4–3 victory in Game 5. Lemieux, the runner-up to Roy for the Conn Smythe Trophy, assisted on the first two Montreal goals. Leading 2–1 going into the final period, the Canadiens seemed to lock things up with quick scores by Rick Green and Bobby Smith at the ten-minute mark. But Calgary came back with scores by Steve Bozek and Joe Mullen late in the game, creating an exciting finish. Only a miraculous save by Roy with 14 seconds left ensured the Montreal victory.

Other. The Soviet Union won the World Hockey Championship for a record 20th time, defeating Sweden, 3–2, in the title contest.

Michigan State won the National Collegiate Athletic Association (NCAA) Division I hockey tournament with a 6–5 victory over Harvard in the championship match.

JIM MATHESON, *"Edmonton Journal"*

Ice Skating

Debi Thomas and Brian Boitano, both Californians, became the new world figure skating champions in 1986, dethroning two powerful Eastern-bloc skaters who had been favored to retain their crowns at the Geneva championships in March.

The 18-year-old Thomas, from San Jose, CA, became the first black American to capture both the world and U.S. championships. A premedical student at Stanford University, Thomas dazzled the judges with a versatile and creative performance to take the title from Katarina Witt of East Germany, a two-time champion and the 1984 Olympic gold medalist.

Thomas actually placed second in the final free-skating program to Witt, who stumbled during the short program the previous day and was fourth entering the final. But Witt's flawless free-skating performance was not enough to catch the American, who was in first place after the short program. Third place overall

AP/Wide World

Debi Thomas took a break from her pre-med studies to claim the U.S. and World figure skating championships.

Skiing

In a World Cup season in which the weather played havoc with the schedule, Marc Girardelli of Luxembourg took the men's overall title for the second straight year, and Maria Walliser of Switzerland prevailed among the women.

The 22-year-old Girardelli clinched the title on March 21 at Bromont, Quebec, in the final slalom of the season. Girardelli led Switzerland's Pirmin Zurbriggen, 294–276, going into the race and needed to finish only among the top 15 to take the crown. Girardelli skied fearlessly but fell 20 seconds from the end of his second run. Zurbriggen, the 1984 champion and runner-up to Girardelli in 1985, registered the fastest time in the second heat but still came out .45 seconds behind Bojan Krizaj of Yugoslavia. Thus, Girardelli prevailed, 294–284.

The U.S. men's team was plagued by injuries and fared poorly. In the overall category, their best showing was 39th, by Doug Lewis.

The men's slalom title was won by Rok Petrovic of Yugoslavia with 125 points. Ingemar Stenmark of Sweden, a former champion, finished in a three-way tie for second with Krizaj and Paul Frommelt of Liechtenstein. The 30-year-old Stenmark lifted his career total of World Cup victories to 86. He was edged out for the giant slalom title, 97–96, by Joel Gaspoz of Switzerland. Peter Wirnsberger of Austria was the downhill champion with 120 points, holding off Switzerland's Peter Mueller.

Walliser led the Swiss women's assault, capturing overall honors with 287 points. She was followed by teammates Erika Hess and Vreni Schneider. Walliser was also the downhill champion, with Schneider taking the giant slalom. Roswitha Steiner of Austria took the honors in the slalom, averting a Swiss sweep; Hess was second in the event. Pam Fletcher finished eighth in the downhill, the best U.S. placing in any discipline, men or women.

In team standings, Switzerland won the women's Nations Cup with 1,530 points and Austria won the men's with 1,294. The overall title, combining men and women, went to Switzerland with 2,817.

In the World Cup Nordic events, Matti Nykaenen of Finland won the jumping; Hermann Weinbuch of West Germany took the combined; Gunde Svan of Sweden won men's cross-country skiing; and Marjo Matikainen of Finland took women's cross-country skiing.

In the U.S. Alpine championships, Tiger Shaw won the men's overall and giant slalom titles; Henrik Smith-Meyer of Norway took the slalom and Lewis won the downhill. Among the women, Beth Madsen won the overall and giant slalom crowns; Tamara McKinney captured the slalom and Hilary Lyndh took the downhill.

GEORGE DE GREGORIO

went to Tiffany Chin, another Californian, who was the 1985 U.S. national champion.

The 22-year-old Boitano, from Sunnyvale, CA, was fourth entering the final and put on a dramatic free-skating performance to Gershwin and blues music. He completed the event's only triple-axel in dethroning Alexandr Fadeyev of the Soviet Union, who fell once, faltered on three triple-jumps, and finished third overall. Second place went to Brian Orser of Canada, who also tumbled on a triple-axel jump and faltered on another. Orser scored 5.4 factored-placement points, the same as Boitano, but the Californian had 6 of 9 top scores in the long program to take the title.

The world pairs championship went to Sergei Grinkov and Ekaterina Gordeeva of the Soviet Union. Another Soviet team, Andrei Bukin and Natalya Bestemianova, retained the ice dancing crown.

In the U.S. championships, held at Uniondale, NY, in February, Boitano retained his men's title and Thomas dethroned Chin for the women's title. Caryn Kadavy was runner-up to Thomas, with Chin third. Gillian Wachsman and Todd Waggoner took the pairs competition, and Donald Adair and Renee Roca claimed the ice dancing title.

GEORGE DE GREGORIO

Soccer

Soccer in 1986 was inevitably dominated by the 13th World Cup tournament, whose 24-team finals were played in June. Held in the intense heat and at the often vertiginous altitude of Mexico, the 52-match finals, played in nine cities, were viewed by an estimated nine billion television spectators in 156 countries. In the championship contest, held at Azteca Stadium in Mexico City, Argentina defeated West Germany, 3–2, to capture its second World Cup in the last three tournaments. (It also won in 1978.) Diego Maradona, Argentina's exciting 5'5" (1.65 m) midfielder, was far and away the salient player of the entire competition.

The 1986 World Cup produced a handful of outstanding games and some marvelous performances, as well as several controversial aspects. Among the most memorable contests was France's quarterfinal defeat of Brazil, 5–4, in an overtime penalty-kick shootout. Two other quarterfinal matches—West Germany's 4–1 triumph over Mexico, and Belgium's 5–4 defeat of Spain—also were decided on penalty kicks. The newly instituted system of deciding the winner of tie games on the basis of a penalty-kick shootout (after overtime play) was widely criticized as arbitrary.

The penalty shootout was just one of the controversial features of the expanded 24-team format. (Previously, only 16 teams competed in the final tournament.) By the new system, the 24 teams were divided into six groups (A–F), each of which played a round-robin schedule. The top 16 teams then advanced to a second-round elimination. The prolonged tournament, compounded by the heat and altitude of Mexico in June (with games scheduled at midday to meet the demands of European television) greatly increased the physical burden on the players. The penalty shootout was adopted as a time saver. And, perhaps most controversially of all, teams that finished third in their group, often with dismally inadequate records, could proceed to the next round. Uruguay, for example, which had not won a game in its group, advanced to a second round game against Argentina. With a mixture of cynical fouling, time wasting, and shrewd defensive tactics—as it had employed throughout first-round competition—Uruguay kept the contest close, losing 1–0. FIFA, the organizing body for international soccer, had already issued a serious warning to the Uruguayan squad for its dangerous style of play.

By contrast, the play of Argentina's Maradona was a brilliant highlight of the 1986 World Cup—though it, too, was not without controversy. In an emotional second-round match against England, Maradona scored his team's first goal apparently by punching the ball past the goaltender. Later in the game, however, Maradona scored perhaps the most spectacular goal of the tournament, dribbling half the length of the field and beating four defenders. Argentina won, 2–1. Then in the semifinals against Belgium, the Argentine team captain scored two more astonishing goals, capping a 2–0 shutout. Maradona scored a total of five goals in the tournament and assisted on numerous others with key passes. England's Gary Lineker, however, was the overall leading scorer with six goals.

And there were other outstanding team and individual performances. Denmark, which played superbly in round-robin competition (as did the Soviet Union), was defeated by Spain, 5–1, in the second round; Emilio Butragueno tied a World Cup record by scoring four goals in the game. France, which had scored second-round victories over defending champion Italy, 2–0, and a powerful Brazilian team (the 5–4 shootout), took third place in the tournament by defeating surprising Belgium, 4–2 in overtime. West Germany, itself surprising, advanced to the championship match with a 1–0 win over Morocco—the first African team ever to reach the second round—the 4–1 shootout victory over Mexico, and a 2–0 shutout of France.

The Argentina-West Germany championship game was close and hard-fought. The West Germans, coached by former captain Franz Beckenbaur, marked Maradona so closely that he played something of a secondary role. But that gave his teammates more space in which to maneuver. Argentina scored first on a header by José Luis Brown, off a free kick by Jorge Luis Burruchaga. Then in the second half, with only 35 minutes left to play, Jorge Valdano made it 2–0. But the staunch Germans struck back with two goals. Only minutes later, however, the irrepressible Maradona struck a perfect pass to the sprinting Burruchaga, who shot the winning goal.

Other Competition. The European Cup tournament was severely diminished by the absence of English teams, who had been banned because violence by Liverpool fans had led to the deaths of 39 spectators at the 1985 final. The 1986 championship match, held in Seville, Spain, was won by Romania's army team, Steaua Bucharest, which defeated Barcelona on penalty kicks. Much the most exciting European team, however, was the Soviet Union's Dynamo Kiev, which defeated Spain's Atletico Madrid for the European Cupwinners' Cup in Lyon, France. Liverpool defeated crosstown rival Everton, 3–1, for the English Cup.

In the United States, professional outdoor soccer gave no signs of life after the 1985 demise of the North American Soccer League (NASL). The Major Indoor Soccer League (MISL), however, continued to flourish. The San Diego Sockers captured their fifth straight indoor title.

BRIAN GLANVILLE, *"Sunday Times," London*

Swimming

The big splash in swimming in 1986 was made by women from East Germany, who thoroughly dominated the world championships at Madrid in August, winning 13 of 16 events and setting five world marks. American swimmers fared poorly in Spain, turning in their worst performance ever in a major championship. For the first time since the 1956 Olympics, U.S. men failed to qualify for the finals of an event, missing in both the 100-meter breaststroke and the 200-m butterfly. When it was all over, the United States had won five of 26 individual events and two of six relays.

The East German record assault was led by 18-year-old Kristin Otto, who took the 100-m freestyle in a world-record time of 54.73 seconds, bettering the mark of 54.79 by countrywoman Barbara Krause at the 1980 Olympics. Otto set the record as a member of the 400-m freestyle relay team, whose clocking of 3:40.57 erased the 3:42.41 mark of a 1984 East German foursome (on which Otto swam the leadoff leg). The East Germans also set a world mark of 7:59.33 in the women's 800-m freestyle relay, bettering the 1983 record of 8:02.27.

Other individual world records set by East Germans at the Madrid meet were by Sylvia Gerasch, whose 1:08.11 in the 100-m breaststroke bettered her own mark of 1:08.29 in the Moscow Olympics; and Silke Hoerner, who surpassed Gerasch's mark of 2:28.20 in the 200-m breaststroke with a clocking of 2:27.40.

Tamara Costache of Romania lowered the 50-m freestyle record four times during the year—to 25.50 seconds, 25.34, 25.31, and 25.28. Betsy Mitchell, an American, broke the 200-m backstroke mark with a time of 2:08.60 in June at Orlando, FL, erasing the four-year-old mark of 2:09.91 by Cornelia Sirch. And yet another East German, Heike Friedrich, timed 1:57.55 in the 200-m freestyle, erasing the old record of 1:57.75 by Otto in 1984.

Among the men, Matt Biondi of the United States continued to excel in the freestyle sprints, setting world marks in the 50-m (22.33) and 100-m (48.74) events. Another American, Pablo Morales, set a world record in the 100-m butterfly, 52.84. Olympic champion Michael Gross of West Germany lowered his own 200-m butterfly standard to 1:56.24. Alex Baumann of Canada equaled his mark of 2:01.42 in the 200-m individual medley. And Vladimir Salnikov of the USSR broke his own mark in the 800-m freestyle with a time of 7:50.64 at the Goodwill Games in Moscow in July.

In diving, Greg Louganis swept the one-meter, three-meter, and platform events at the U.S. championships for the fifth straight time, raising his total of national titles to 40. In April he swept all three events in the indoor championships for the fourth time.

GEORGE DE GREGORIO

Tennis

Martina Navratilova, Ivan Lendl, and Chris Evert Lloyd continued as dominant figures in professional tennis during 1986, while the precocious West German, 18-year-old Boris Becker, once more regarded Wimbledon Centre Court as his own backyard, repeating as the men's champion of the game's oldest tournament.

Because of a change in dates, from December 1986 to January 1987, the Australian Open was not played during the year. The number of major tournaments thus was limited to three: Wimbledon, the U.S. Open, and the French Open. A Czechoslovak-born pair, U.S. naturalized citizen Navratilova and U.S. resident Lendl, each took two of the major singles titles. Navratilova won her seventh Winbledon and third U.S. Open crowns. Lendl won his second French and U.S. titles. Both Navratilova and Lendl appeared in all three finals. At Wimbledon, Lendl could not keep up with the high-velocity serving of the powerful Becker, falling 6–4, 6–3, 7–5. Navratilova, for the second successive year, was the victim of Evert Lloyd in the finals of the French Open in Paris, 2–6, 6–3, 6–3.

The red clay of Paris has been the most hospitable footing for Evert Lloyd, who registered a record seventh French Open title, one more than Bjorn Borg, and extended another even more remarkable record. The victory assured Evert Lloyd of at least one major championship for the 13th consecutive year. By winning six tournaments altogether, Evert Lloyd also increased her all-time record to a total of 148. Navratilova was high for the season, however, with 14 tournament victories and $1,905,841 in prize money, a category in which she led the women.

In both the Wimbledon and U.S. Open finals, Navratilova beat Czechs who had done her the favor of ousting Evert Lloyd in semifinal play. In London, Navratilova defeated Hana Mandlikova, 7–6 (7–1), 6–3, and in New York she beat Helena Sukova, 6–3, 6–2. In her own semifinal at the U.S., Navratilova rescued three match points in a gripping, 6–1, 6–7 (3–7), 7–6 (10–8) victory over 17-year-old West German Steffi Graf, who signaled impending danger for the women at the top by winning eight tournaments.

Evert Lloyd's French win was her 18th major singles title, third on the all-time roll behind Margaret Smith Court's 24 and Helen Wills Moody's 19. The versatile Navratilova also won the three major doubles during the year: the French with Hungarian Andrea Temesvari, and Wimbledon and the U.S. with American Pam Shriver. Thus she climbed to second place in total career grand slam championships with 42, surpassing Billie Jean King's 39 but behind Court's record total of 62.

Ivan Lendl was the undisputed number one player on the men's professional tennis tour in 1986. The 26-year-old Czech native won two of the year's three major tournaments, the French Open and U.S. Open.

AP/Wide World

Lendl, who beat unseeded finalists in two major tournaments—Sweden's Mikael Pernfors, 6–3, 6–2, 6–4 at the French Open and Czechoslovakia's Miloslav Mecir, 6–4, 6–2, 6–0 at the U.S. Open—remained number one on the computer. His $1,987,537 in prize money for the year was the most on the men's tour. His nine tournament victories gave him a career total of 62.

John McEnroe, the American whom Lendl had deposed in 1985, took a seven-month leave from the circuit, returning in August. His three tournament victories raised his career total to 70, keeping him second on the all-time list behind Jimmy Connors' 105.

Swedes were the national force on the men's side, accounting for 15 tournament victories and gaining a fourth straight Davis Cup final. However, their two-year hold on the Cup was broken by Australia, 3–2, in Melbourne.

Returning to her native Czechoslovakia for the first time since her 1975 defection, Navratilova was well received in Prague, where she, Evert Lloyd, and Pam Shriver, and Zina Garrison, wrested the Federation Cup from the host country, 3–0.

The Grand Prix Masters for men and the Virginia Slims Championships for women were held at New York's Madison Square Garden twice during 1986. Lendl and Navratilova rounded the year by winning both events— Lendl in January and December, Navratilova in March and November.

BUD COLLINS, *"The Boston Globe"*

TENNIS

Davis Cup: Australia
Federation Cup: United States
Wightman Cup: United States

Major Tournaments

Grand Prix Masters (January 1986)—men's singles: Ivan Lendl (Czechoslovakia); men's doubles: Stefan Edberg (Sweden) and Anders Jarryd (Sweden). (December 1986)—men's singles: Ivan Lendl (Czechoslovakia); men's doubles—Stefan Edberg (Sweden) and Anders Jarryd (Sweden).

Virginia Slims (March 1986)—women's singles: Martina Navratilova; women's doubles—Hana Mandlikova (Czechoslovakia) and Wendy Turnbull (Australia). (November 1986)—women's singles: Martina Navratilova; women's doubles—Martina Navratilova and Pam Shriver.

World Championship Tennis—Anders Jarryd (Sweden).

U.S. Open Clay Courts—men's singles: Andres Gomez (Ecuador); men's doubles: Hans Gildemeister (Chile) and Andres Gomez; women's singles: Steffi Graf (West Germany); women's doubles: Steffi Graf and Gabriela Sabatini (Argentina).

Italian Open—men's singles: Ivan Lendl (Czechoslovakia); men's doubles: Guy Forget (France) and Yannick Noah (France).

French Open—men's singles: Ivan Lendl (Czechoslovakia); men's doubles: John Fitzgerald (Australia) and Tomas Smid (Czechoslovakia); women's singles: Chris Evert Lloyd; women's doubles: Martina Navratilova and Andrea Temesvari (Hungary); mixed doubles: Ken Flach and Kathy Jordan.

Wimbledon—men's singles: Boris Becker (West Germany); men's doubles: Joakim Nystrom (Sweden) and Mats Wilander (Sweden); women's singles: Martina Navratilova; women's doubles: Navratilova and Pam Shriver; mixed doubles: Ken Flach and Kathy Jordan.

Canadian Open—men's singles: Boris Becker (West Germany); men's doubles: Chip Hooper and Mike Leach; women's singles: Helena Sukova (Czechoslovakia); women's doubles: Zina Garrison and Gabriela Sabatini (Argentina).

U.S. Open—men's singles: Ivan Lendl (Czechoslovakia); men's doubles: Andres Gomez (Ecuador) and Slobodan Zivojinovic (Yugoslavia); women's singles: Martina Navratilova; women's doubles: Navratilova and Pam Shriver; mixed doubles: Sergio Casal (Spain) and Raffaella Reggi (Italy); men's 35 singles: Tom Gullikson; junior boys singles: Javier Sanchez (Spain); junior girls singles: Elly Hakami.

NCAA (Division I)—men's singles: Dan Goldie, Stanford; men's team: Stanford; women's singles: Patti Fendick, Stanford; women's team: Stanford.

N.B. All players are from the United States, unless otherwise noted.

Yordanka Donkova of Bulgaria set a world's record in the women's 100-m hurdles three times within three weeks during the summer, finally lowering the mark to 12.29 seconds.

AP/Wide World

Track and Field

World records were set or tied in a total of 14 track and field events (outdoors) during 1986, four by men and ten by women.

Among the men, new standards were established by two Soviet and two East German athletes. The 22-year-old Sergei Bubka of the USSR, the dominant figure in the pole vault in recent years, broke his own world mark with a vault of 19′ 8½″ (6.01 m) at the Goodwill Games in Moscow on July 8. Countryman Yuri Syedikh broke his own world record in the hammer throw twice, registering 284′ 4″ (86.66 m) on June 22 and 284′ 7″ (86.74 m) at the European Track and Field Championships in Stuttgart, West Germany, on August 30. The East Germans Udo Beyer and Jurgen Schult both set new world standards in throwing events. Beyer put the shot 74′ 3½″ (22.64 m) in East Berlin on August 20. Schult turned in a discus throw of 243′ 0″ (74.08 m) in Neubrandenburg, East Germany, on June 6.

In women's competition, Heike Drechsler was the star of the European Championships. The 21-year-old East German won the long jump with a mark of 24′ 5½″ (7.45 m), which equaled her record-setting leap of June 21. And she took the 200-m sprint with a time of 21.71 seconds, which tied her own time on June 29 and that of Marita Koch in 1979 for the world record. Marina Stepanova of the Soviet Union established a new standard in the women's 400-m hurdles at Stuttgart, coming in at 53.32 seconds, but she eclipsed that mark with a time of 52.94 in a September meet in the Soviet Union. And Fatima Whitbread of Great Britain set yet another world record at the European Championships with a javelin throw of 254′ 1″ (77.44 m).

Yordanka Donkova and Stefka Kostadinova of Bulgaria each broke or tied world records more than once in their respective events. Donkova set the standard in the 100-m hurdles three times within three weeks during the summer. On August 17, in a preliminary heat in Cologne, West Germany, she was timed in 12.34 seconds. In the finals the same day, she recorded 12.29. And on September 7 she clocked 12.26. Kostadinova, a high jumper, figured in the record twice within seven days. On May 25 in Sofia, she tied the world mark with a jump of 6′ 9½″ (2.07 m). And on May 31 in Vienna, she took sole possession of the record with a jump of 6′ 9¾″ (2.08 m).

Jackie Joyner of the United States twice put together world-record point totals in the women's heptathlon. On July 6–7 at the Goodwill Games, she compiled 7,148 points, breaking the previous record of 6,867. And on August 1–2, she extended the record to 7,161.

Olympic gold medalist Maricica Puica of Romania lowered the standard for the 2,000 meters with a time of 5 minutes, 28.69 seconds in London in July. But the outstanding women's distance runner of the year clearly was Norway's Ingrid Kristiansen. On August 5 in Stockholm, she set a world record in the 5,000 meters with a time of 14 minutes, 37.33 seconds. And in July at Oslo, she bettered her own world mark in the 10,000 with a clocking of 30:13.74.

Kristiansen also won the women's division of the Boston Marathon in April; Rob de Castella of Australia won the men's. In the New York City Marathon in November, Grete Waitz of Norway won the women's division for the eighth time in nine appearances; the men's title went to Gianni Poli of Italy.

GEORGE DE GREGORIO

SPORTS SUMMARIES[1]

ARCHERY—U.S. Champions: men: Rich McKinney, Gilbert, AZ; women: Debra Ochs, Howell, MI.

BADMINTON—U.S. Champions: men: Chris Jogis, Tempe, AZ; women: Nina Polk, Phoenix, AZ.

BIATHLON—U.S. Champions: men: 10 km: Raymond Dombrovsky, Seattle, WA; 20 km: Dombrovsky; women: 5 km: Pam Nordheim, Helena, MT; 10 km: Anna Sonnerup, Hanover, NH.

BILLIARDS—World Champions: men: Nick Varner, Owensboro, KY; women: Loree Jon Jones, Hillsboro, NJ.

BOBSLEDDING—U.S. Champions: two-man: Elmer Zahurak, Stowe, OH, and Gene Janeco, Huntington Beach, CA; four-man: Zahurak, Janeco, Jim King, Magadore, OH, and Wayne DeAtley, Virginia Beach, VA.

BOWLING—Professional Bowlers Association: U.S. Open: Steve Cook, Roseville, CA; Firestone Tournament of Champions: Marshall Holman, Medford, OR; National Champion: Tom Crites, Tampa, FL. **American Bowling Congress:** regular division: singles: Jeff Mackey, Mexico, MO; doubles: Don Cook and Bob Larson, Milwaukee; all-events: Ed Marzka, Detroit; team: Faball Enterprises 1; masters division: singles: Mark Fahy, Chicago. **Women's International Bowling Congress:** singles: Dana Stewart, Morgan Hill, CA; doubles: Sally Gates, Palmdale, CA, and Marilyn Frazier, Lancaster, CA; all-events: (tie) Robin Romeo, Van Nuys, CA, and Maria Lewis, Manteca, CA; team: Sillia's Pro Shop, Cleveland.

CANOEING—U.S. Champions (flatwater): men's kayak: 500 m: Norman Bellingham, Rockville, MD; 1,000 m: Greg Barton, Homer, MI; 10,000 m: Barton; women's kayak: 500 m: Sheila Conover, Newport Beach, CA; men's canoe: 500 m: Jim Terrell, Milford, OH; 1,000 m: Bruce Merritt, Ridge, MD.

CROSS COUNTRY—World Champions: men: John Ngugi, Kenya; women: Zola Budd, Great Britain. **U.S. Champions:** men: Pat Porter, Alamosa, CO; women: Lesley Welch: Lynn, MA. **NCAA:** men: Aaron Ramirez, Arizona; team: Arkansas; women: A. Chalmers, Northern Arizona; team: Texas.

CURLING—World Champions: men: Eddie Luckowich, Canada; women: Marilyn Darte, Canada. **U.S. Champions:** men: Steve Brown, Madison, WI; women: Geri Tilden, St. Paul, MN.

CYCLING—Tour de France: Greg LeMond, United States. **World Pro Champions:** men: road: Moreno Argentin, Italy. **World Amateur Champions:** men: road: Hwe Ampler, East Germany; sprint: Michael Hueber, East Germany; women: road: Jeannie Longo, France; sprint: C. Rothenburger, East Germany; pursuit: Longo.

DOG SHOWS—Westminster: best-in-show: Ch. Marjetta National Acclaim, pointer owned by Isabel Robson, Glenmore, PA, and Michael Zollo, Bernardsville, NJ.

FENCING—U.S. Champions: men: foil: Michael Marx, Portland, OR; épée: Lee Shelley, Hackensack, NJ; saber: Peter Westbrook, New York City; women: foil: Caitlin Bilodeau, Concord, MA; épée: Vincent Bradford, Austin, TX. **U.S. Collegiate:** men: foil: Adam Feldman, Penn State; épée: Chris O'Loughlin, Pennsylvania; saber: Michael Lofton, NYU; team: Notre Dame; women: individual: Molly Sullivan, Notre Dame; team: Pennsylvania.

FIELD HOCKEY—NCAA (women): Iowa.

GYMNASTICS—U.S. Gymnastics Federation Champions: men's all-around: Tim Daggett, Los Angeles; women's all-around: Jennifer Sey, Allentown, PA; rhythmic: Marina Kunyavsky, Los Angeles. **NCAA:** men's team: Arizona State; women's team: Utah.

HANDBALL—U.S. Handball Association Champions (four-wall): men: Naty Alvarado, Hesperia, CA; collegiate team: Memphis State; women: Glorian Motal, Martinez, CA.

HORSE SHOWS—World Cup: Leslie Lenehan, Westport, CT, riding McLain. **U.S. Equestrian Team:** dressage: Tom Valter, Rancho Palos Verdes, CA, riding Tudor; three-day event (spring): James Wofford, Upperville, PA, riding The Optimist; three-day event (fall): Bruce Davidson, Unionville, PA, riding Noah; show jumping: Katie Monahan, Middleburgh, VA, riding Bean Bag.

JUDO—U.S. Champions: men: 60-kg class: Fred Glock, Colorado Springs; 65-kg: Douglas Tono, Chicago; 71-kg: Nicholas Yonezuka, Cranford, NJ; 78-kg: Brett Barron, Burlingame, CA; 86-kg: Kenny Patteson, Los Angeles; 95-kg: Robert Berland, Wilmette, IL; over 95-kg: Douglas Nelson, Englewood, NJ; open: Damon Keeve, San Francisco; women: 48-kg: Darlene Anaya, Albuquerque, NM; 52-kg: Mary Lewis, Albany, NY; 56-kg: Eve Arnoff, Hartsdale, NY; 61-kg: Lynn Roethke, North Troy, NY; 66-kg: Christine Penick, San Jose, CA; 72-kg: Diana Bridges, Colorado Springs; over 72-kg: Corinne Shigemoto, San Jose, CA; open: Shigemoto.

LACROSSE—NCAA: men: Division I: North Carolina; Division III: Hobart; women: Division I: Maryland; Division III: Ursinus.

LUGE—U.S. Champions: men: Miroslav Zajonc, Annapolis, MD; women: Erica Terwillegar, Lake Placid, NY; doubles: Zajonc and Tim Nardiello, Lake Placid, NY.

MODERN PENTATHLON—World Champions: men: Massulo Carlo, Italy; women: Irina Kisseleva, USSR. **U.S. Champions:** men: Blair Driggs, Phoenix, AZ; women: Kim Dunlop, Tallahassee, FL.

PADDLEBALL—U.S. Champions: (four-wall): men's open: Mark Kozub, Livonia, MI; women's open: Carla Teare, Flint, MI.

POLO—International Gold Cup: White Birch Farms, CT. **World Cup:** White Birch Farms.

RACQUETBALL—U.S. Champions: men: singles: Ed Andrews, Huntington Beach, CA; doubles: Doug Ganim, Columbus, OH, and Dan Obremski, Pittsburgh; women: singles: C. Baxter, Lewiston, PA; doubles: Mona Mook and Trina Rasmussan, Sacramento, CA. **U.S. Pro Champions:** men: Marty Yellen, Southfield, MI; women: Lynn Adams, Costa Mesa, AZ.

ROWING—World Open Champions: men: single sculls: West Germany; double sculls: Italy; quadruple sculls: USSR; pair without coxswain: USSR; pair with coxswain: Great Britain; straight four: United States; four with coxswain: East Germany; eight: Australia; women: single sculls: East Germany; double sculls: East Germany; quadruple sculls: East Germany; pair without coxswain: Romania; four with coxswain: Romania; eight: USSR. **U.S Collegiate Champions:** men: Wisconsin; women: Wisconsin.

RUGBY—U.S. Champions: Old Blues, Berkeley, CA.

SHOOTING—Olympic Style Champions: men: air rifle: Robert Froth, Colorado Springs; small-bore rifle, three positions: Froth; skeet: Matthew Dryke, Ft. Benning, GA; trap: Daniel Carlisle, Corona, CA; free pistol: Don Nygord, La Crescenta, CA; air pistol: Ben Amonette, Radford, VA; women: air rifle: Elaine Proffitt, Colorado Springs; small-bore rifle, three positions: Pat Spurgin, Billings, MT; skeet: C. Schiller, College Station, TX; trap: A. Grosch, Eden Prairie, MN; sport pistol: Ruby Fox, Parker, AZ; air pistol: Judith Kemp, Anaheim, CA.

SOFTBALL—U.S. Champions: men: major fast pitch: Pay 'n Pack, Bellevue, WA; class-A fast pitch: Tubbs and Sons Electric, Manteca, CA; major slow pitch: Non-Ferrous Metals, Cleveland; super division slow pitch: Steele's Sports, Grafton, OH; modified fast pitch: Don Swann Sails, Atlanta; women: major fast pitch: Southern California Invasion, Los Angeles; class-A fast pitch: San Diego Astros; class A slow pitch: Comfort Inn, Raleigh, NC.

SPEED SKATING—U.S. Champions: men: outdoor: Eric Klein, St. Louis; indoor: Brian Arseneau, Chicago; women: outdoor: Deb Perkins, Milwaukee; indoor: Bonnie Blair, Champaign, IL.

SQUASH RACQUETS—World Champions: men: Mario Sanchez, Mexico; women: Alicia McConnell, United States.

SURFING—U.S. Pro Champions: men: Tom Curran, Santa Barbara, CA; women: Freida Zamba, Flagler Beach, FL.

TABLE TENNIS—U.S. Champions: men: Sean O'Neill, Vienna, VA; women: In Sook Bhushan, Aurora, CO.

VOLLEYBALL—World Champions: men: United States. **U.S. Champions:** men: Molten/SSI, Torrance, CA; women: Merrill Lynch, Albuquerque, NM. **NCAA:** men: Pepperdine; women: University of the Pacific.

WATER POLO—World Champions: men: Yugoslavia. women: Australia. **NCAA:** men: Stanford; women: University of the Pacific.

WEIGHTLIFTING—U.S. Weightlifting Federation: men: 52-kg: Steve Womble, Hudson, OH; 56-kg: Gene Galsdorf, Onaga, KS; 60-kg: Brian Miyamoto, Kanehoe, HI; 67.5-kg: Cal Schake, Newport News, VA; 75-kg: Gary Savage, Kansas City; 82.5-kg: Curt White, Ballwin, MO; 90-kg: Mike Cohen, Savannah, GA; 100-kg: Rich Schutz, Mt. Prospect, IL; 110-kg: Mario Martinez, San Francisco; over 110-kg: John Bergman, San Rafael, CA; women: 44-kg: Carol Santandrea, Santa Fe, CA; 52-kg: Danelle Markham, OR; 56-kg: Michelle Evris, Garfield, OH; 60-kg: Colleen Colley, Smyrna, GA; 67.5-kg: Arlys Kovach, Walnut, CA; 75-kg: Jody Anderson, Cypress, TX; 82.5-kg: Carol Cady, Stanford, CA; over 82.5-kg: Annette Bohach, Muskegon Heights, MI.

WRESTLING—NCAA: Division I: Iowa.

YACHTING—U.S. Yacht Racing Union: championship of champions: Paul Foerster, Austin, TX; Mallory Cup (men): Jack Christiansen, Seattle; Adams Trophy (women): Cathy Christman, Charleston, SC.

[1] Sports not covered separately in pages 472–496.

SRI LANKA

Ethnic violence and government counter-measures, features of the troubled Sri Lankan scene since July 1983, escalated markedly in 1986. This situation adversely affected the economy and added to fears for Sri Lanka's future as a united and democratic nation.

Ethnic Violence. Underlying the violence were mounting tensions between the Sinhalese majority and the Tamil minority and between various Tamil guerrilla groups. In January, Tamil militants called off the uneasy truce that had been in effect for seven months. The violence soon escalated to new heights. Hundreds of people were killed in bomb explosions in public places, especially in the northern and northeastern provinces and in Colombo. A highly publicized bombing of a Sri Lankan passenger aircraft at Katanayake Airport on May 3 killed 16 persons, most of them European and Japanese tourists. Government officials alleged that a major Tamil militant group, the Liberation Tigers of Tamil Eelam, was responsible. A few days later President Junius R. Jayewardene said: "The outside world must help now, because this is an international problem.... (A)nother few years of this and we will have bled to death or we will be partitioned like Cyprus." This extraordinary statement called attention to the seriousness of the situation.

Other international dimensions of the Sri Lankan crisis included the alleged links of Tamil guerrilla groups with the Palestine Liberation Organization and other militant groups and the continuing flow of refugees from Sri Lanka. Most of the estimated 130,000 refugees fled to Tamil Nadu in India, but many found their way to other countries, including West Germany and Canada (as was dramatized by the 155 Sri Lankan Tamils found drifting off the coast of Newfoundland in August).

In late July, August, and October, the government and the leading "moderate" Tamil organization, the Tamil United Liberation Front (TULF), held a series of talks in an attempt to find an acceptable formula for ending the crisis. Presumably this would include far-reaching concessions by the government in the direction of autonomy for the Tamil minority areas and an agreement by Tamils to end the violent agitation. Even if such an agreement could be reached, however, there was no certainty that it would be accepted by extremist groups among both Tamils and Sinhalese or that it could be implemented in the face of extremist opposition. Two large-scale Army drives against Tamil militants in October seemed to indicate that the government might seek a military rather than a political "solution."

The Economy. Encouraging economic developments were the decline in the annual rate of inflation to 1.5%, a growth rate of 5%, and a substantial increase in foreign assistance. In general, however, the economic decline of recent years continued, due primarily to the continuing ethnic violence but also to the sharp drop in world prices for tea and coconuts, the major export crops, and a rise in military spending. The Sri Lanka Aid Consortium, chaired by the World Bank, pledged $703 million in aid for the 1987 fiscal year, a substantial increase over fiscal 1986. A World Bank statement praised the government for its economic management of the internal violence and called for the correction of imbalances in the economy. In October, Finance Minister Ronnie De Mel said that Sri Lanka had only a two-month reserve of foreign exchange and that its trade and payment positions were in jeopardy.

Foreign Policy. Attempts to enlist sympathy and support for its efforts to deal with the internal crisis and its economic problems dominated the visits of Sri Lanka's leaders abroad—notably President Jayewardene's visit to the Soviet Union in July and his participation in the second summit meeting of the South Asian Association for Regional Cooperation (SAARC) in India in November and Prime Minister Ranasinghe Premadasa's participation in the nonaligned summit in Zimbabwe in September.

Relations with India continued to be a blend of cooperation and tension. Sri Lanka's leaders realize that a solution to their internal conflict probably cannot be found without India's cooperation, but they feel that India is not "neutral" in this conflict. In September, Indian Prime Minister Rajiv Gandhi spoke out with surprising acerbity on Indian-Sri Lankan relations, stating categorically that "there are no training camps for militants . . . in India" (as Sri Lanka's leaders have frequently alleged). He added that India would withdraw from the peace effort if Sri Lanka did not want its help. Relations between the two countries improved somewhat after the SAARC summit.

NORMAN D. PALMER
University of Pennsylvania

SRI LANKA · Information Highlights

Official Name: Democratic Socialist Republic of Sri Lanka.
Location: South Asia.
Area: 25,332 sq mi (65 610 km²).
Population (mid-1986 est.): 16,600,000.
Chief Cities (1983 est.): Colombo, the capital, 623,000; Dehiwala-Mount Lavinia, 181,000; Jaffna, 128,000; Kandy, 114,000.
Government: *Head of state,* J. R. Jayewardene, president (took office Feb. 1978). *Head of government,* R. Premadasa, prime minister (took office Feb. 1978). *Legislature* (unicameral)—Parliament.
Monetary Unit: Rupee (28.1 rupees equal U.S.$1, July 1986).
Gross Domestic Product (1984 U.S.$): $6,000,000,000.
Economic Index (Colombo, 1985): *Consumer Prices* (1980 = 100), all items, 176.4; food, 176.1.
Foreign Trade (1985 U.S.$): *Imports,* $1,885,000,000; *exports,* $1,251,000,000.

STAMPS AND STAMP COLLECTING

On July 4, 1986, the U.S. Postal Service issued a 22-cent commemorative stamp on the occasion of the celebration of the Statue of Liberty's centennial. A French stamp of similar design was issued in conjunction with the American commemorative, and other nations also joined in to honor the occasion.

Earlier in 1986, on January 23, the U.S. Postal Service (USPS) released a Stamp Collecting booklet in joint issuance with Sweden. A highlight for collectors was "Ameripex 86," the first international stamp show in the United States in ten years, which opened in Rosemont, IL, on May 22. The USPS heralded the event with four miniature sheets of nine stamps featuring past U.S. presidents. There were 35 stamps portraying the presidents and a 36th depicting the White House.

The first commemorative stamp issued in 1986, on January 3, was for the 150th anniversary of Arkansas' statehood. The 150th anniversary of the Republic of Texas also was hailed. The 350th anniversary of the settlement of Rhode Island, the 150th birthday of the Wisconsin Territory, and the 300th anniversary of the settlement of Connecticut were commemorated with 14-cent postcards.

Blocks of four stamps, a favorite with many collectors, were spread throughout 1986. These included 22-cent stamps for Navajo Indian art, Polar explorers, and woodcarved figurines of the 19th century. A 22-cent stamp in the Black Heritage series, honoring Sojourner Truth, was issued February 4, along with one in the Performing Arts series for Duke Ellington. The Great Americans series recognized Jack London, Hugo L. Black, William Jennings Bryan, Belva Ann Lockwood, Margaret Mitchell, Father Edward Flanagan, John Harvard, Paul Dudley White, and Bernard Revel.

Another "Love" stamp, popular for greetings and invitations, was issued early in the year. Others were scheduled for 1987.

Thousands of suggestions for new stamps are submitted to the Postal Service each year. The task of evaluating their merits falls to the Citizens' Stamp Advisory Committee, whose members are chosen by the postmaster general for their expertise in art, history, philately, and other fields. Based on the committee's review, a limited number of subjects are recommended for approval each year.

Stamp dealers and catalog publishers saw a leveling of world prices after several years of downward movement. Some countries showed increases, particularly with older issues.

SYD KRONISH, *The Associated Press*

Selected U.S. Comemorative Stamps, 1986

Subject	Denomination	Date
Arkansas Statehood	22¢	Jan. 3
Jack London	25¢	Jan. 11
Stamp Collecting (book)	22¢	Jan. 23
Love	22¢	Jan. 30
Ameripex 86 (card)	33¢	Feb. 1
Sojourner Truth	22¢	Feb. 4
Hugo L. Black	5¢	Feb. 27
Republic of Texas	22¢	March 2
William J. Bryan	$2.00	March 19
Fish (booklet)	22¢	March 21
Public Hospitals	22¢	April 11
Settling Connecticut	14¢	April 18
Duke Ellington	22¢	April 29
U.S. Presidents	22¢	May 22
Stamp Collecting	14¢	May 23
Francis Vigo	14¢	May 24
Polar Explorers	22¢	May 28
Belva Ann Lockwood	17¢	June 18
Settle Rhode Island	14¢	June 26
Margaret Mitchell	1¢	June 30
Wisconsin Territory	14¢	July 3
Statue of Liberty	22¢	July 4
Father Flanagan	4¢	July 14
John Harvard	56¢	Sept. 3
Navajo Art	22¢	Sept. 4
Dr. Paul White	3¢	Sept. 15
Dr. Bernard Revel	$1.00	Sept. 16
Dog Sled	7.1¢	Sept. 25
T.S. Eliot	22¢	Sept. 26
Woodcarved Figurines	22¢	Oct. 1
Christmas (contemporary)	22¢	Oct. 24
Christmas (traditional)	22¢	Oct. 24
National Guard	14¢	Dec. 12

STOCKS AND BONDS

For the U.S. stock market, 1986 was a year of heady new highs and record-breaking declines, of prosperity tainted by controversy and scandal. Through all of these ups and downs, the bull market that had begun in mid-1982 remained intact as the year drew to a close.

The Dow Jones average of 30 industrials, which had surpassed 1,500 for the first time in 1985, soared to 1,700 in February, 1,800 in March, and 1,900 on July 1. Progress, after that, proved a little harder to attain. Even so, the widely recognized average of many of the nation's most famous corporate names finished the year at 1,895.95, up 349.28 points, or 22.6%, from the end of 1985. Trading volume in the major markets easily surpassed the record levels reached in the preceding year.

All was not euphoria, however, in the trading rooms of Wall Street and in brokerage offices across the country. For one thing the market's advance grew increasingly selective as it progressed. While most of the blue chips thrived, many other stocks languished, notably those of high-technology enterprises and small-growth companies. In the first ten months of the year, while the Dow Jones industrial average rose 21.4%, Value Line's much broader composite index managed a gain of only 7.3%.

Takeovers. Many market observers also were concerned that the idea of investing based on sound economic values was being subverted by new trading tactics employed by investment professionals, and by "takeover mania" that led to wild speculation in stocks of companies reported or rumored to be likely candidates for takeover, restructuring, or liquidation.

One controversy focused on computer-program trading by professionals armed with large sums of money and seeking to profit from temporary disparities between the prices of stock index options and futures contracts, and the individual stocks that make up the indexes. No one complained much when program activity helped propel the market higher early in the year. It was a different story when these transactions contributed to the largest single-day point declines ever posted by the Dow Jones industrial average—61.87 points on July 7, and 86.61 points on September 11.

The takeover game, which involved some very big players, was at the same time being widely decried as a speculative excess that was setting up the market for potential trouble. But beneath the surface of the rumors and maneuvering regarding actual and possible corporate deals, an even more sinister issue was lurking: the illegal use of privileged information by people in powerful positions.

Insider Trading. In May the Securities and Exchange Commission (SEC) accused Dennis B. Levine, an investment banker and managing director at the firm of Drexel Burnham Lambert Inc., of using inside information to turn profits of $12.6 million from various transactions. Levine subsequently pleaded guilty and agreed to cooperate with a government investigation that was expected to lead to even bigger game.

On November 14 the SEC announced that Ivan F. Boesky, known as the "king of the arbitrageurs" investing in takeover stocks, had agreed to pay $100 million to settle government allegations that he had used inside information from Levine in his trading activities. Boesky also was cooperating with the authorities, a strong sign that the case was by no means closed.

Market Response. All these developments were hardly favorable publicity for Wall Street and its markets. Even so, many observers of the investment scene voiced the hope that some good would come of it, if only because the rankling issues of insider abuses and unrestrained greed were being subjected to the harsh light of national attention. Many Wall Streeters were heartened by the market's response to the Boesky disclosures. After a brief decline stock prices staged a rally that carried them close to the highs reached earlier in the year.

Effects of Tax Reform. As 1986 progressed, investors and brokers also had to adjust to the prospect of a complete overhaul of the U.S. tax system. Most analysts agreed that the Tax Reform Act of 1986 would significantly alter the behavior of investors. One of the most important provisions of the law, from the point of view of the investor, decreed an end to the preferential tax treatment of long-term capital gains, which had provided a significant incentive for taxpaying investors to buy stocks. Another provision put limits on the deductibility of many people's contributions to individual retirement accounts, which had been a hot growth product for many financial-services firms, notably the sponsors of mutual funds.

Mutual Funds. Even so, the mutual-fund industry enjoyed another boom year. Through

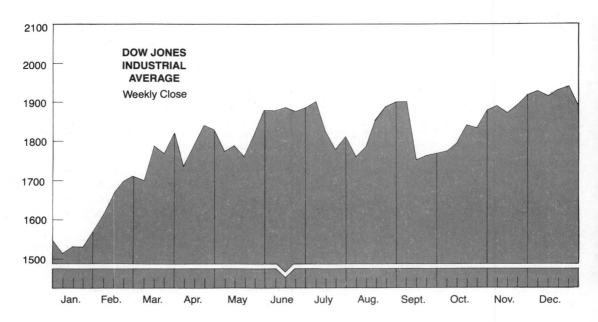

the first nine months, sales of mutual-fund shares, as tallied by the Investment Company Institute, reached $157.5 billion, far surpassing the full year's record of $114.3 billion set in 1985. Among the industry's best sellers for the second consecutive year were international funds investing from a worldwide perspective.

Global Investing. A growing interest in global investing was fueled in part by advances in communications technology, and by regulatory changes that helped make markets in many countries more accessible to foreign investors. The most notable event was ''Big Bang'' day in London's financial district, on October 27, when the British marketplace was introduced to electronic trading, an end to fixed commission rates, and other new, competitive rules. Although the day was marred by computer troubles, almost everyone agreed that it was a historic occasion.

Another straightforward explanation could be found for the keen appetite many Americans felt for overseas investments. While the U.S. market was giving quite a respectable account of itself, markets in many other countries were doing even better. At mid-November, according to the Morgan Stanley Capital International Perspective of Geneva, a world index of nine markets showed a gain for the year of 34.1%, more than twice the U.S. advance of 15.5%. Japan, up 44.3%, led the pack, followed by France, up 44.1%; Australia, up 33.3%; Hong Kong, up 31.6%; Great Britain, up 17.8%; Canada, up 6.0%; and West Germany, up 2.0%. The only one in the minus column was Switzerland, down 1.7%.

CHET CURRIER, *The Associated Press*

SUDAN

The escalation of the civil war in Sudan's three southern provinces was the most troublesome problem facing the new civilian government in Khartoum.

Domestic Affairs. Gen. Abdel Rahman Suwar el Dahab, the leader of the April 1985 coup and chairman of the Transitional Military Council, true to his promise, allowed elections for a civilian government in early April 1986. Voter turnout was excellent in the northern Muslim areas, but in the south significant voting occurred in only a few places. Sidiq el Mahdi, the leader of the Umma Party, once again became prime minister, forming a coalition with his chief rival, Hassan el Turaki of the National Islamic Front. In lieu of a president, a five-man council was designated to act as a collective head of state.

The installation of a freely elected government failed to end hostilities in the Christian and pagan south, where the 20,000-strong Sudan Peoples Liberation Army (SPLA), led by Col. John Garang, controlled much of the territory in Bahr el-Ghazal and Equatoria provinces. The new government moderated application of the Islamic code, which had been made the law of the land in 1983, but refused to suspend it completely. In July, el Mahdi and Garang met for talks in Addis Ababa but failed to settle differences. By autumn government forces controlled only some of the largest towns, and such others as Juba, Wau, and Malakal were under siege.

World attention was focused on Sudan in mid-August, when rebel forces shot down a Sudan Airways plane at Wau, killing 63 passengers. Garang blamed the airline for its support of the government war effort and threatened to destroy any other planes flying in the area. The SPLA also effectively halted relief supplies of grain to hundreds of thousands who faced starvation in the refugee camps and beleaguered cities.

Economy. In addition to the civil war, natural and man-made disasters have plagued Sudan's economy during the 1980s. A combination of bad weather and overgrazing of arable land gradually reduced the production of foodstuffs. For example, production of the major crop, sorghum, fell off from 3.4 million tons in 1981 to slightly more than 1 million tons in 1985. Along with the lack of funds for imports and poor distribution infrastructure, this meant serious food shortages throughout the country, even in Khartoum. Food shipments from relief agencies and credits from the United States and Europe could have averted starvation if conditions had been normal. Even before the April 1985 coup, however, an estimated 750,000 refugees from Ethiopia, Uganda, and Chad had settled into Sudanese refugee camps. Problems in drought-stricken areas were exacerbated when locusts began to ravage crops before harvest.

The International Monetary Fund (IMF) in February declared Sudan ineligible for loans because of its failure to repay $250 million of its estimated $10 billion debt. The U.S. Agency for International Development approved a $25

SUDAN • Information Highlights

Official Name: Republic of the Sudan.
Location: Northeast Africa.
Area: 967,495 sq mi (2 505 813 km²).
Population (mid-1986 est.): 22,900,000.
Chief Cities (1983 census): Khartoum, the capital, 476,218; Omdurman, 526,287; Khartoum North, 341,146.
Government: *Head of state,* Ahmad al-Mirghani, chairman, State Council (took over May 6, 1986). *Head of government,* Sadiq Siddiq al-Mahdi, prime minister (took over May 6, 1986). *Legislature* (unicameral)—National People's Assembly.
Monetary Unit: Pound (2.5 pounds equal U.S.$1, May 1986).
Gross Domestic Product (1984, U.S.$): $7,300,-000,000.
Foreign Trade (1985 U.S.$): *Imports,* $757,000,000; exports, $367,000,000.

million loan for the purchase of 121,000 tons of American wheat and $7.6 million for the transport of grain to Darfur and Kordofan, but these were stopgap measures.

Foreign Affairs. Sudan's long-time harmony with the United States, developed during the rule of former President Jafaar al-Nemery, was seriously threatened by the growing ties between Sudan and Libya. In 1986 there were an estimated 1,000 Libyans based in Sudan, as well as many Palestinian refugees and Syrian advisers. In March the U.S. State Department announced a temporary halt in aid, with the exception of emergency relief. And although the bulk of all relief to Sudan was still coming from the United States, anti-U.S. sentiment swept the country. The American bombing raid on Libya in April brought forth a march of 10,000 protesting students in Khartoum. On April 15, the day after the raid, a U.S. envoy was assassinated in Khartoum. After an attempted storming of the embassy, Washington ordered an evacuation of nonessential staff and dependents of all U.S. personnel.

In August, Prime Minister el-Mahdi visited Tripoli, where he held talks with Qaddafi and signed an agreement for the purchase of Libyan oil. Earlier in the year, Khartoum dissolved its 1982 integration pact with Libya, calling it an undesirable legacy of the Nemery era.

HARRY A. GAILEY
San Jose State University

SWEDEN

One of the most tragic events in the history of Sweden took place in Stockholm on the evening of Feb. 28, 1986, when Prime Minister Olof Palme was assassinated while walking home from a movie theater with his wife Lisbet. It was the first killing of a Swedish leader since King Gustav III in 1792.

On March 10 the Swedish parliament joined a national moment of silence in memory of slain Prime Minister Olof Palme, whose flower-decked seat is in the foreground.

AP/Wide World

SWEDEN • Information Highlights

Official Name: Kingdom of Sweden.
Location: Northern Europe.
Area: 173,731 sq mi (449 964 km²).
Population (mid-1986 est.): 8,400,000.
Chief Cities (Dec. 31, 1984 est.): Stockholm, the capital, 653,455; Göteborg, 424,085; Malmö, 229,107; Uppsala, 152,579.
Government: *Head of state,* Carl XVI Gustaf, king (acceded Sept. 1973). *Head of government,* Ingvar Carlsson, prime minister (elected March 12, 1986). *Legislature* (unicameral)—Riksdag.
Monetary Unit: Krona (6.821 kronor equal U.S.$1, Oct. 19, 1986).
Gross Domestic Product (1984 U.S.$): $96,000,-000,000.
Economic Indexes (1985): *Consumer Prices* (1980 = 100), all items, 153.8; food, 172.9. *Industrial Production* (1980 = 100), 110.
Foreign Trade (1985 U.S.$): *Imports,* $28,497,-000,000; *exports,* $30,504,000,000.

Palme, who had served as chairman of the Social Democratic Party since 1969 and as prime minister from 1969 to 1976 and again from 1982, was shot in the back at close range, and was believed to have died instantly. His wife escaped with only minor injuries. More than 600 foreign dignitaries, including 13 presidents and 16 prime ministers, attended Palme's funeral, and the site of his murder became an informal national shrine. Stockholm police quickly launched the largest manhunt in Swedish history, but Palme's killer had not been identified by year's end. The investigation fueled public frustration and led to bickering between the police and the prosecutor's office.

Government. Ingvar Carlsson was selected as the new leader of the ruling Social Democratic Party on March 3. On March 12 he was elected prime minister by the Riksdag (Parliament). Carlsson, who had been Palme's close political associate and deputy prime minister, was expected to continue the policies of his predecessor. In his address at the October 7 opening of the 1986–87 session of the Riksdag, Carlsson focused on the economy, particularly the fight against inflation, and backed Sweden's policy of neutrality and a strong defense. He also announced the creation of a new ministry of environment and energy.

Conservative Party leader Ulf Adelsohn, who had been disappointed by his party's poor showing in the 1985 elections, announced his resignation on June 4. Carl Bildt, 37, was elected to succeed him on August 23.

Nuclear Issues. Sweden reported high levels of radioactivity after the April accident at the Soviet nuclear power station at Chernobyl. The disaster increased public pressure to find alternatives to nuclear energy, and in October the government introduced a bill in the Riksdag which would establish a legal ban on the construction of new nuclear reactors. All nuclear energy is scheduled to be phased out by 2010 under terms of a 1980 referendum.

In June the Nordic countries issued a joint statement recommending multilateral agreements on safety measures to prevent similar nuclear accidents and calling for international cooperation in the event of such disasters.

Economy. The budget for the fiscal year beginning July 1 was $6.4 billion. According to government projections, the gross domestic product (GDP) was expected to increase by 1.6% in 1986, the inflation rate to drop to 4.2% (compared with 5.7% in 1985), and unemployment to remain at 2.9%.

On September 30, after a breakdown in mediation efforts, workers in municipal, county council, and central government service went on strike. Workers in state-owned and municipal agencies followed. The strike was supported by some 600,000 members of the Municipal Workers' Union, Sweden's largest union, who refused to work overtime, and eventually involved 1.6 million workers. A settlement reached on October 30 granted raises averaging 8.8% for 1986–87. The original demand of the striking workers, that their wages should equal those in private industry, was to be taken up during the 1988 negotiations.

Stockholm Conference. After almost three years of deliberation, the Stockholm conference on security and disarmament in Europe concluded its last session on September 22. A September 19 document listed a series of measures designed to reduce the danger of armed conflict due to misunderstanding or miscalculation. The participating states—the nations of Europe, except Albania, plus the United States and Canada—reaffirmed their determination to continue efforts to reduce military confrontation, enhance security for all, and combat terrorism. They also reaffirmed their commitment to the principles set forth in the 1975 Helsinki declaration.

Myrdal. Swedish diplomat and disarmament advocate Alva Myrdal, winner of the 1982 Nobel Peace Prize, died on February 1 (*see* OBITUARIES).

ERIK J. FRIIS
"The American-Scandinavian Bulletin"

SWITZERLAND

Issues involving Swiss banks, United Nations membership, the armed forces, and education of foreigners were of major concern in Switzerland during 1986.

New Banking Policies. Although Switzerland had confiscated Nazi German assets in Swiss banks after World War II, until recently, Swiss bank accounts had generally been considered inviolable. In 1986, however, the Swiss government ordered the accounts of two ousted political leaders—Ferdinand Marcos of the Philippines and Jean-Claude Duvalier of Haiti—frozen at the request of the Philippine

and Haitian governments. Similarly, in accordance with a 1984 directive from the Swiss federal tribunal, Swiss banking authorities cooperated in February and again in May with the U.S. Securities and Exchange Commission in its successful investigation and prosecution of two major insider trading groups that had been operating illegally in the United States and depositing money in Swiss accounts. In October a bill outlawing insider trading in Switzerland was approved by the Swiss senate.

United Nations Membership Rejected. In a national referendum on March 16, Swiss voters resoundingly defeated a government-supported proposal that Switzerland join the United Nations. The 1,691,428-511,548 vote brought to a close several years of bitter debate and intense lobbying, and reasserted Swiss preference for the traditional policy of "armed neutrality" in international affairs.

Armed Forces Referendum. On September 13 a coalition of pacifists, religious groups, and socialists presented a petition bearing 113,000 signatures requesting the abolition of Switzerland's armed forces. This issue seemed certain to be even more devisive than that of UN membership. Since lengthy parliamentary debate is required prior to a national referendum, the vote is not expected for several years.

Educational Restrictions. Only slightly less controversial was a government proposal on August 31 that enrollment of foreign students at private secondary schools in Switzerland be limited to persons under the age of 16, and at universities to those under the age of 22. Observers saw this as a continuation of the backlash against foreigners residing in Switzerland; the fact that 20,000 persons had sought political asylum in Switzerland in 1985, the largest number since World War II, was also cited as fueling antiforeign sentiment. Implementation of these regulations could signal an end to the Swiss tradition of providing an elite international education for children of the world's wealthiest families.

PAUL C. HELMREICH, *Wheaton College, MA*

SWITZERLAND · Information Highlights

Official Name: Swiss Confederation.
Location: Central Europe.
Area: 15,918 sq mi (41 228 km²).
Population (mid-1986 est.): 6,500,000.
Chief Cities (Jan. 1985 est.): Bern, the capital, 140,612; Zurich, 354,525; Basel, 176,227.
Government: *Head of state,* Alphons Egli, president (took office Jan. 1986). *Legislature*—Council of States and National Council.
Monetary Unit: Franc (1.6180 francs equal U.S.$1, Oct. 19, 1986).
Gross National Product (1984 U.S.$): $96,100,-000,000.
Economic Indexes (1985): *Consumer Prices* (1980 = 100), all items, 123.3; food, 128.9. *Industrial Production* (1980 = 100), 103.
Foreign Trade (1985 U.S.$): *Imports,* $30,818,-000,000; *exports,* $27,485,000,000.

SYRIA

Two key incidents made 1986 a year of great significance for Syria. First, the regime of President Hafez al-Assad, which had been accused of sponsoring international terrorism for more than a decade, was caught red-handed in a plot to blow up an El Al Israel Airlines plane en route from London to Tel Aviv. Second, the Syrian regime, along with certain elements in Iran, was instrumental in revealing the secret U.S. arms deal with Iran, precipitating a political crisis for the Reagan administration.

Terrorism and Foreign Policy. On April 17 at London's Heathrow airport, Jordanian Nezar Hindawi was arrested for allegedly planting a bomb in a bag carried by his unwitting (and pregnant) girlfriend, who was about to board a plane for Israel. Evidence soon emerged that Hindawi had ties with the Syrian Air Force Intelligence Service. Earlier there had been allegations that Syria played a role in the December 1985 terrorist bombings at the Rome and Vienna airports, and in the March 1986 bombing of a West Berlin discotheque, but in none of these cases was the evidence so direct as in the Hindawi case.

President Assad reacted to the situation with a three-pronged policy. First, he sought to improve his international image with trips to Yugoslavia, Jordan (his first visit since 1977), and Greece. His diplomatic efforts in the Middle East also were believed to have an economic motivation. With the nation in difficult straits, Assad apparently hoped that a unified Arab League conference might enable him to get financial support from oil-producing nations. Secondly, President Assad made conciliatory public statements about the December 1985 Tripartite Agreement in Lebanon. And thirdly, a series of car bombings took place in and near the Christian sections of Beirut, and the Syrian-backed Amal militia was unleashed against Palestinian refugee camps in Beirut.

The developments in Lebanon during the year seemed to show that Assad regards the military occupation of that country as vital to his regime. With Egypt's President Hosni Mubarak calling for a hands-off policy in Lebanon, and with Lebanon's President Amin Gemayel bolstering his support with visits to several Arab states, Assad pressured West Beirut politicians to ask for the deployment of Syrian troops.

Meanwhile, as tensions with Israel mounted —for months there were rumors of imminent war—Syria broke ties with Morocco after a July meeting in Fez between Morocco's King Hassan II and Israel's Prime Minister Shimon Peres. The following month, Assad traveled to Libya for talks with Muammar el-Qaddafi.

On October 24 a British court convicted Hindawi. London, citing "conclusive evidence" of his ties to Syria, severed diplomatic relations with Damascus. The European Community (EC) imposed diplomatic sanctions on November 10, followed by the United States four days later. The U.S. sanctions included a ban on the sale of sophisticated technology, including computers and aircraft; an end to the financing of Syrian exports through the U.S. Export-Import Bank; the canceling of a U.S.-Syrian air transport agreement; a reduction in the U.S. embassy staff in Damascus; a prohibition on high-level diplomat visits between the two nations; and a suggestion that U.S. oil companies stop operating in Syria. Again, Assad's reaction was multidimensional. On November 10, the same day the EC voted its sanctions, two French hostages were released from Lebanon. Next, Assad unleashed the Amal militia in southern Lebanon to placate Israel and reaffirmed his role as a mediator by summoning the leaders of various Palestinian and Lebanese factions to Damascus. Most significantly of all, perhaps, Assad allowed a pro-Syrian magazine in Beirut to divulge the secret arms deals between the United States and Iran, which, it was claimed, had been going on for 15 months. The disclosure pointed up a lack of credibility in the U.S. sanctions against Syria, since Washington had been dealing with another state identified as a terrorist sponsor.

Similar events were played out once more before the year came to an end. In late November, a court in West Germany convicted two Palestinians, apparently with ties to Syria, of the March disco bombing in West Berlin. The Bonn government ordered three Syrian diplomats to leave the country and said it would not replace its outgoing ambassador in Damascus.

As a "gesture of peace" in late December, another French hostage was released in Beirut. In 1986 it became clear that Western hostages being held by shadowy groups in Lebanon were simply pawns to be used by Syria and Iran to achieve their foreign policy goals.

MARIUS DEEB, *Georgetown University*

SYRIA • Information Highlights

Official Name: Syrian Arab Republic.

Location: Southwest Asia.

Area: 71,498 sq mi (185 180 km²).

Population (mid-1986 est.): 10,500,000.

Chief Cities (Dec. 1982 est.): Damascus, the capital, (1983 est.) 1,202,000; Aleppo, 905,944; Homs, 414,401.

Government: *Head of state,* Gen. Hafiz al-Assad, president (took office officially March 1971). *Head of government,* 'Abd al-Ra'uf al-Kasm, prime minister (took office Jan. 1980). *Legislature* (unicameral)—People's Council.

Monetary Unit: Pound (3.925 pounds equal U.S.$1, May 1986).

Gross Domestic Product (1983 U.S.$): $19,700,000,000.

Economic Index (1985): *Consumer Prices* (1980 = 100), all items, 184.2; food, 180.6.

Foreign Trade (1985 U.S.$): *Imports,* $3,844,000,000; *exports,* $1,627,000,000.

TAIWAN (Republic of China)

The year on Taiwan was marked by two unprecedented events and an event to honor precedents. In May, Taiwanese officials found themselves engaged, for the first time in 40 years, in negotiations with their Beijing counterparts. Martial law, in effect since 1949, was lifted in October. Later that month, Soong Meiling returned to Taiwan to take part in ceremonies marking the centenary of the birth of her husband, the late Chiang Kai-shek.

Politics. In March the Central Standing Committee of the Kuomintang (KMT, or Nationalist Party) met for the first time since 1984. The aging and ailing President Chiang Ching-kuo appeared to designate Vice-President Lee Teng-hui as his successor in the presidency but failed to indicate who would replace him as party chairman. Effective political power apparently would be distributed among a number of government and party officials. A campaign also was under way to bring in younger officials and more members drawn from the Taiwanese population (the 85% of residents who settled on the island prior to World War II). The four government ministers who were added to the 31-member committee reduced its average age and increased from 12 to 14 the number of Taiwanese members. Vice-President Lee also is Taiwanese.

Two months later the committee appointed a task force to carry out a "comprehensive study" on the rejuvenation of parliament, the formation of new political parties, the lifting of martial law, and the recruitment by popular election of provincial-level authorities. In late September, challenging the 37-year-old ban on the formation of political parties, 135 opposition leaders announced the creation of the Democratic Progressive Party. An overseas branch was formed in the United States, and its founders announced that they intended to defy the government and return to Taiwan in time for legislative elections in early December. The decision to form a new party followed nearly two weeks of demonstrations—believed to be the largest in Taiwan's history—to protest the arrest of five opposition leaders.

In mid-October, on the recommendation of the task force, the KMT agreed to lift martial law and replace it with "national security legislation," and allowed the creation of opposition parties, provided that they swear allegiance to the constitution and follow an anti-communist policy. In mid-November the U.S.-based opposition leaders were denied entry into Taiwan, but in the December 6 balloting candidates of the Democratic Progressive Party took 23% of the vote and won 12 of the 72 contested seats in the 314-seat Legislative Yuan. The KMT received 63% of the vote.

Economy. The estimated growth of the Taiwanese economy in 1986 was 8% (preliminary), compared with 4.7% in 1985. The nation enjoyed a trade surplus of some $13 billion, contributing to foreign exchange reserves expected to reach $32 billion by year's end. Taiwan's balance of payments with the United States showed a surplus of some $12 billion, leading to strenuous efforts on the U.S. side to restore a balance. In May the U.S. House of Representatives passed the Trade Enhancement Act, calling for a 10% annual reduction in the surplus until balance is achieved. In trade negotiations during the summer and fall, the United States pressed for greater access to Taiwan markets for U.S. cigarettes, beer, and wine. Taiwan agreed to change its customs valuation system in order to reduce tariffs on U.S. products and to open markets in banking, insurance, and construction.

Projections by the Council for Economic Development and Planning in March called for an average annual growth rate of 6.5% over the next 14 years, raising the per capita gross national product (GNP) from $3,100 to $13,400, and increasing total two-way trade from $50.7 billion to $290 billion. A National Science and Technology Conference in January called for an increase in investment in scientific and technical research from 0.7% of GNP to 2% over the next seven years.

Foreign Affairs. In May the pilot of a China (Taiwan) Airlines cargo plane forced his co-pilot and navigator to divert the aircraft to Guangzhou (Canton) during a flight from Bangkok to Hong Kong. The pilot, Wang Hsi-chueh, said he was motivated by a desire to be reunited with his elderly father. Unexpectedly, the authorities on Taiwan, presumably with the concurrence of President Chiang, acceded to Beijing's request that negotiations take place between representatives of the government-owned airline and representatives of the CAAC, the flag carrier of the People's Republic. At Taiwan's insistence, however, the talks took place in Hong Kong rather than Beijing. After three days of negotiations, the aircraft,

---

TAIWAN • Information Highlights

Official Name: Republic of China.
Location: Island off the southeastern coast of mainland China.
Area: 12,456 sq mi (32 260 km²).
Population (mid-1986 est.): 19,600,000.
Chief Cities (Dec. 31, 1984): Taipei, the capital, 2,449,702; Kaohsiung, 1,285,132; Taichung, 655,196; Tainan, 631,614.
Government: *Head of state,* Chiang Ching-kuo, president (installed May 1978). *Head of government* Yü Kuo-hua, president, executive yuan (premier) (took office, June 1984). *Legislature* (unicameral) —Legislative Yuan.
Monetary Unit: New Taiwan dollar (36.56 NT dollars equal U.S.$1, Oct. 19, 1986).
Gross National Product (1984 est. U.S.$): $56,600,000,000.
Foreign Trade (1984 est. U.S.$): *Imports,* $21,600,000,000; *exports,* $30,400,000,000.

its cargo, the copilot, and the navigator were returned to Taiwanese custody. While there was speculation that the talks might lead to broader negotiations between Taipei and Beijing, the two governments insisted that nothing more than civil aviation was involved.

On May 28 an Argentine warship opened fire on three Taiwanese fishing vessels within the 200-mile restricted zone claimed by the Buenos Aires government. One vessel was sunk and its crew taken prisoner. Taipei protested the action in the strongest terms.

See also CHINA, PEOPLE'S REPUBLIC OF

JOHN BRYAN STARR
Yale-China Association

> ### TANZANIA • Information Highlights
> **Official Name:** United Republic of Tanzania.
> **Location:** East coast of Africa.
> **Area:** 363,947 sq mi (942 623 km²).
> **Population** (mid-1986 est.): 22,400,000.
> **Chief City** (1980 est.): Dar es Salaam, the capital, 900,000.
> **Government:** *Head of state,* Ali Hassan Mwinyi, president (took office Nov. 1985). *Head of government,* Joseph S. Warioba, prime minister (took office Nov. 1985). *Legislature* (unicameral)—National Assembly, 233 members.
> **Monetary Unit:** Tanzanian shilling (40.343 shillings equal U.S.$1, June 1986).
> **Gross Domestic Product** (1984 U.S.$): $4,200,000,000.
> **Economic Index** (1984): *Consumer Prices* (1970 = 100), all items, 1,035.3; food, 1,222.2.
> **Foreign Trade** (1984 U.S.$): *Imports,* $847,000,000; *exports,* $377,000,000.

TANZANIA

Following the retirement of long-time President Julius K. Nyerere in November 1985, developments in Tanzania in 1986 were marked by continued severe economic problems and increasing debate over the role of socialism in Tanzania.

Political Transition. Nyerere's successor in the peaceful transfer of power, President Ali Hassan Mwinyi, was a compromise candidate for the position, and some see him as a transitional figure who will serve only one five-year term. Nyerere retained the chairmanship of the Chama Cha Mapinduzi, the nation's sole political party, and many expect him to continue to be the real ruler of Tanzania until he gives up the party post at the end of 1987.

Along with other East African nations, Tanzania enjoyed an upswing in tourism. Ngorongoro Crater (below) and nearby Serengeti National Park were popular attractions.

AP/Wide World

Economic Slide. Tanzania's failing economy has shrunk by 6% per year since 1982, while the population has grown by more than 3% annually. Nyerere prevented any real easing of Tanzania's rigidly socialist economic system and blocked agreement with the International Monetary Fund (IMF) for aid in return for reforms. One of Mwinyi's first moves as president was to conclude an agreement with the IMF that gave Tanzania almost $2 billion for debt service and the purchase of raw materials, spare parts, and other needed imports. In exchange, Tanzania agreed to devalue its currency by two thirds and to open some parts of the economy to free market forces. The IMF agreement led to the release of more than $500 million in new and back aid from other sources.

The communal *ujamaa* villages remain the cornerstone of agricultural policy, but several sisal estates were transferred to private ownership as the government moved to encourage large-scale private farming. The availability of consumer goods also increased in an attempt to spur productivity.

The growth of an unofficial economy known as the *ulanguzi* both stemmed from and contributed to Tanzania's economic crisis. Not quite a black market (which also exists), the *ulanguzi* consists of small-scale private enterprise. People generally spend only 40% of their workdays on their jobs and the rest pursuing various sideline businesses; almost every salaried Tanzanian has a piece of land, called a *shamba,* which is used to raise chickens or grow fruits and vegetables. The *ulanguzi* is winked at by the government because it enables workers to survive on low salaries.

Foreign Affairs. The final division of the assets of the long-defunct East African Community took place in July, and the presidents of Tanzania, Kenya, and Uganda have moved to restore regional trade links. Tanzania continued to call for additional international pressure on the white minority regime in South Africa.

ROBERT GARFIELD, *DePaul University*

TAXATION

Tax policy was a major issue in public debates in many countries because of widespread concern over unemployment, slow economic growth, and low investment. The leaders of several major industrial nations advocated measures to broaden the income tax base and reduce rates.

United States

After nearly two years of deliberation the U.S. Congress completed action on one of the most sweeping and comprehensive tax revision bills in the nation's history, and President Ronald Reagan signed it into law on October 22. (*See* special report, page 508.)

Supreme Court. Two of the ten tax cases handed down by the U.S. Supreme Court in 1986 ruled for the government in curtailing the fund-raising ability of nonprofit organizations, whose income is generally tax exempt. Under federal law the "unrelated business income" of such groups is taxable. In *U.S. v. American College of Physicians,* the court ruled that income from advertising in the association's journal, *Annals of Internal Medicine,* does not contribute importantly to the group's educational purpose and is therefore unrelated business income within the meaning of the law. But the court disagreed with the government's additional claim that profits earned from all commercial advertising in such journals are *per se* taxable without a specific analysis of the circumstances. In *U.S. v. American Bar Association,* the court also ruled that a tax-exempt legal professional group must pay unrelated business income tax on profits derived from its group insurance program. That program requires participating members to assign policy dividends to the association, which uses most of the proceeds for educational projects. Members then claim the dividends as a charitable deduction. The court said that this activity represents a "trade or business" subject to the unrelated business income tax. Further the participants may not claim as a charitable deduction any portion of their premium payments recouped as dividends.

In *Sorenson v. Secretary of the Treasury,* the court ruled that the Internal Revenue Service has the authority to intercept and withhold refundable earned-income credits from taxpayers who are delinquent in paying child support. Federal law requires that income tax refunds be withheld from taxpayers delinquent in their child-support payments and be remitted instead to state welfare agencies. The court disagreed with the taxpayer's claim that refunds resulting from the earned income tax credit do not qualify as tax refunds under the law.

In *Exxon v. Hunt* the court held that major portions of a 1977 New Jersey law imposing special taxes on oil and chemical industries are preempted by federal law. The New Jersey law levied a tax on petroleum and certain chemicals to fund the state's efforts to control hazardous substances. The 1980 U.S. "superfund" law, which imposed federal taxes for similar purposes, included a preemption provision which the court interpreted as evidence of congressional concern about the adverse effects of overtaxation on the competitivenesss of the U.S. petrochemical industry. The court's decision means that states can collect a tax on companies subject to the federal superfund law only for purposes not covered by the federal law.

State and Local Taxes. State and local governments collected $370.8 billion in taxes during the 12 months ending June 30, 1986, an increase of $24.2 billion, or 7.0%, over the previous year. The increase a year earlier had been 8.2%. State legislatures in 1986 raised taxes by about $1.6 billion annually on a net basis. Sixteen states increased taxes, largely on general sales and motor fuels, by $2.4 billion. These were partly offset by reductions in personal income taxes in six states, totaling $800 million.

International

Canada. The proposed Canadian federal budget for fiscal 1986–87, presented in February, called for tax increases totaling C$1.5 billion in 1986–87 and $2.4 billion the following year. A 3% surtax was imposed on income taxes, and higher rates were levied on federal sales taxes and on tobacco and alcohol taxes. For corporations the budget announced the first stage of a revision plan, withdrawing some tax reductions and cutting rates. In October the government announced that it would introduce tax reforms similar to those in the United States in order to keep Canadian exports competitive.

Europe. Great Britain's 1986–87 budget, presented in March, called for a modest reduction in income taxes, increases in some commodity taxes, and new savings incentives. France's budget, presented in September, contained tax cuts of about $4.03 billion, split between individuals and industry. Top individual income tax rates would drop from 65% to 60% and the corporate tax rate from 50% to 45%. In August, West Germany revealed plans for substantial changes in the tax code after the 1987 elections, including more than $10 billion in personal and corporate income tax cuts.

Japan. The Japanese government released details of a major tax overhaul program. The plan, which was intended to make Japan's tax system fairer and to stimulate the economy, included reduction in income taxes, the introduction of a value-added sales tax, and the abolition of tax-free savings accounts.

ELSIE M. WATTERS, *Tax Foundation, Inc.*

The Tax Reform Act of 1986

On October 22, U.S. President Ronald Reagan signed into law the Tax Reform Act of 1986, calling it "the most sweeping overhaul of our tax code in our nation's history." The law combines sharp reductions in tax rates with extensive base-broadening provisions that scale back or repeal numerous tax preferences. Although "revenue neutral" in its overall effect, the law significantly modifies tax burdens for different categories of taxpayers. Over the next five years, individual taxes would be reduced by about $120 billion, while corporate taxes would be raised by a similar amount.

The changes introduced in the law reflected a growing public perception that all taxpayers were facing higher marginal rates in order to make up for the revenue lost to numerous special preferences, deductions, and tax shelters used by a relatively small number of taxpayers. A major thrust of the new law was to reduce the importance of tax considerations in economic policy-making and to move away from the use of the tax code to encourage activities deemed socially or economically worthwhile.

While the basic principles that shaped the new law had entered into public debates sporadically for many years, there was until recently no strong political consensus for the drastic changes entailed. The groundwork for revision was laid in 1982 when Sen. Bill Bradley (D-NJ) and Rep. Richard Gephardt (D-MO) introduced the "Fair Tax Act," a so-called flat-tax bill proposing lower tax rates and broader bases. Similar legislative proposals followed in the next two years. The stage was set for the congressional tax reform drive in May 1985, when President Reagan submitted proposals embodying concepts similar to those in the law that was finally enacted.

The odyssey of the bill through Congress was long and arduous, culminating in September 1986 with House and Senate approval of a compromise measure ironing out differences between the bills approved by the two houses. The two bills embraced many of the same concepts but were unlike in many key details. A major difference was that the House favored higher corporate taxes and lower individual taxes than did the Senate. Although tax reform had broad bipartisan support in Congress, the debates over specific issues almost led to stalemate on many occasions. Final passage of the measure was attributable largely to the efforts of three individuals: President Reagan, who made tax reform the top domestic priority for his second term; House Ways and Means Committee Chairman Dan Rostenkowski (D-IL); and Senate Finance Committee Chairman Bob Packwood (R-OR).

Individual Tax Provisions. Rate reductions were a pivotal force in congressional approval of tax revision. For individuals, a new and compressed rate and bracket structure would be phased in. Beginning in 1988, two rates of 15% and 28% will replace 15 rates ranging from 11% to 50% in 1986 (and up to 70% as recently as 1981). The 15% rate will apply to taxable income up to $29,750 for married taxpayers filing jointly, $17,850 for single taxpayers, and $23,900 for heads of households. Above those amounts, which are to be adjusted for inflation beginning in 1989, the 28% rate generally will apply. High income taxpayers, however, will pay marginal rates of up to 33% because the benefits of the 15% rate and the personal exemption will be phased out above specified income levels. In 1987 a blended rate schedule will apply, with five rates ranging from 11% to 38.5%.

Substantial increases in personal exemptions and standard deductions will remove about six million low-income households from the tax rolls and will lower tax burdens for most other taxpayers. The personal exemption will rise from $1,080 in 1986 to $1,900 in 1987, $1,950 in 1988, and $2,000 in 1989; it will be indexed for inflation starting in 1990. Beginning in 1988 the standard deduction, used by the majority of taxpayers, will be $5,000 for married couples, $3,000 for single persons, and $4,400 for heads of households, with inflation adjustments starting in 1989.

Most of the controversy over the bill in Congress involved disputes over ways to make up for some of the revenue lost from the tax-cutting provisions. A major source of new revenue will come from the full taxation of capital gains, which have been taxed at preferential rates since 1921. Previously a 60% exclusion was allowed, and the maximum tax rate was 20%. After 1986 the top capital gains rate is 28%.

One of the most bitterly contested provisions of the new law was the repeal of tax-deductible Individual Retirement Account (IRA) contributions for many taxpayers. Henceforth, the full $2,000 deduction will be available only to workers not covered by a company pension plan or to low- and middle-income workers (married persons with incomes up to $40,000 and single persons with incomes up to $25,000). Smaller deductions will be available for those earning up to $10,000 above those limits. All workers, however, may still make nondeductible IRA contributions and defer tax

Among the tax bill's prime movers in the Senate were (l-r) Finance Committee Chairman Robert Packwood (R-OR); Minority Leader Robert Byrd (D-WV); Russell Long (D-LA), the ranking Democrat on the Finance Committee; and Minority Leader Robert Dole (R-KS).

AP/Wide World

on the earnings until withdrawal. The law also revamps numerous other employee pension plan rules.

Other former exclusions from taxable income that were repealed by the law include special deductions of up to $3,000 for two-earner married couples; income averaging; the dividend exclusion of $200 for married couples and $100 for single persons; and the previously untaxed portion of unemployment compensation benefits. The law also sharply restricts deductions for interest on loans to finance investments and, with certain exceptions, limits business meal and entertainment expense deductions to 80% of the expense.

For taxpayers who itemize deductions, some of the most popular preferences are retained in the new law, but others are dropped or limited. Mortgage interest payments remain fully deductible for first and second homes. The law leaves intact income and property tax deductions, but repeals the general sales tax deduction. Deductions for non-mortgage consumer interest payments, such as those on car loans and credit cards, will be phased out over five years. Medical expense deductions will be limited to amounts above 7.5% of gross (formerly 5%), and charitable contributions by non-itemizers will no longer be deductible. Miscellaneous itemized deductions will be restricted to amounts above 2% of adjusted gross income; and employee business expense deductions will be scaled back.

Another key provision of the law will prevent taxpayers from using paper losses generated by tax shelters to reduce tax. To be phased in over five years, the new rule provides that "passive" losses—those from trade or business activities in which the taxpayer does not play a managerial role—will be deductible only against passive income from similar sources. In addition, the law strengthens the alternative minimum tax for individuals by in-

cluding more tax preferences in the calculations and by raising the rate from 20% to 21%.

Other revenue-raising provisions of the law include taxing the unearned income of children under age 14 at the parents' rate; limiting exclusions for scholarships and fellowships; repealing the political contributions and residential energy credits; and placing new limitations on the amount of tax-exempt bonds that state and local governments may issue to finance private activities.

Corporate Tax Provisions. The five-year increase in corporate tax burdens, as finally approved, fell midway between the amounts in the Senate bill ($100 billion) and the House bill ($140 billion). The $120 billion boost approved by the conferees was almost exactly the same as that proposed by the president.

Effective July 1, 1987, the new law cuts the top corporate income tax rate from 46% to 34%. For small companies, the lower graduated rate structure is retained in modified form.

The largest single corporate tax boost will result from repeal of the investment tax credit of up to 10% on new investment, retroactive to Jan. 1, 1986. The law also trims depreciation write-offs on plant and equipment and makes dozens of changes in accounting rules that will raise taxes for many firms. Corporations also will pay the regular 34% rate on capital gains, instead of the old 28% rate. The new law extends the research and development tax credit for three years, but reduces the rate from 25% to 20%. And a host of changes in international tax rules will mean higher taxes for many companies engaged in multinational business.

Another major change for corporations is the replacement of the previous 15% add-on minimum tax with a stiffer 20% alternative minimum tax to ensure that companies with large incomes will not avoid taxes through a combination of tax incentives.

ELSIE M. WATTERS

Maximilian Schell (left) played the title role in the NBC mini-series "Peter the Great." Sir Laurence Olivier (right) played King William of Orange.

TELEVISION AND RADIO

With declining advertising revenues, big corporate mergers, and bitter leadership shakeups, American television underwent a stormy transformation in 1986. A leaner industry began to emerge by year's end, but its direction was still unclear.

A study by the Television Bureau of Advertising found that average daily TV viewing in 1985 reached an all-time high of seven hours, ten minutes per household. But those viewers and minutes were spread out over an array of networks, channels, and subscription services that continued to expand through 1986. Under a banner headline that declared "It's a Two-and-a-Half TV Network Race: Audience Erosion Poses Problems," *Variety* reported that for the first time since American Broadcasting Companies' (ABC's) struggles of the early 1960s, advertising revenue was so low that in most time slots the third-ranked show in the A.C. Nielsen ratings could not meet its production costs.

With Fox Broadcasting Company declaring itself a new over-the-air national network with ten weekly hours of prime-time programming, four entities were scrambling for dollars that barely supported three. Harvey Shepherd, the Columbia Broadcasting System (CBS) programming chief, stepped down a year after he had lost to NBC the ratings dominance he had enjoyed since 1980, telling *The New York Times* that the pressures were "beyond belief." Meanwhile, the resurgent National Broadcasting Company (NBC), led by *The Cosby Show,* scored its second consecutive win in 1985-86 with a 17.5 Nielsen rating, against CBS' 16.7 and ABC's 14.9.

Critics complained that the most conspicuous victims of the new, straitened era in television (700 layoffs at CBS' broadcast division, for example) were the news departments, which suffered the most traumatic cutbacks. Another symbol of television's financial overextension was Ted Turner, whose Atlanta-based Turner Broadcasting System (TBS) was reported by *Time* magazine to be carrying a $2 billion debt.

There were major corporate and leadership shakeups. ABC was taken over by Capital Cities Communications and continued the elimination of 1,300 jobs. After merging with NBC's parent, RCA, the General Electric Company named one of its officers, Richard C. Wright, to replace NBC Chairman Grant Tinker, who engineered the network's stunning turnaround of 1984-86. William S. Paley, the 84-year-old founder of CBS, returned as active chairman of the network, ousting Thomas H. Wyman, and shared leadership of the troubled organization with its largest shareholder and new chief executive officer, Lowes Corporation Chairman Lawrence A. Tisch.

New Network Series. Two of TV's trend-setting producers, Steve Bochco of *Hill Street Blues* and Michael Mann of *Miami Vice,* created stylish new series for 1986–87. Early indications were that Bochco's well-received NBC portrait of hip young attorneys, *L.A. Law,* would outperform Mann's *Crime Story,* a gritty study of 1950s Chicago cops. Other trend-conscious entries were *Designing Women,* CBS' sitcom about professional women roommates, and vehicles for Ellen Burstyn (ABC) and Elliott Gould (CBS) as heads of nontraditional family groups.

Another new program targeting a young upwardly mobile ("Yuppie") audience nostalgic for the '50s and '60s was ABC News' *Our World,* with the outspoken Linda Ellerbe, which used film archives to chronicle years in the recent past. *The New York Times* called this cheaply produced program a symbol of the new austerity in network news. *World* joined NBC's *1986* and CBS' *West 57th* (heavily criticized for its trendiness in 1985, and revamped) as the new challengers to the perennial news-magazine powers, *60 Minutes* and *20/20.*

At the opposite demographic pole, *Variety* noted that " 'old' is what's new on TV these days." Spurred by the success of *Golden Girls* and Angela Lansbury in *Murder, She Wrote,* the networks introduced vehicles for mature stars. Lucille Ball, 75, returned from a long TV hiatus in ABC's *Life with Lucy* (after the show debuted to scathing criticism, a network spokesman promised that it would be remodeled); Wilford Brimley, 65, played a grandfather on NBC's family drama, *Our House;* Andy Griffith, 60, and Raymond Burr, 69, revisited the tube as lawyers in NBC's series *Matlock* and the TV film, *Perry Mason Returns,* respectively.

Network spokesmen noted that theatrical films were slowly retreating from prime time— 54 were aired in the 1985–86 season, down from 67 the previous year—and that only a handful performed strongly in the ratings. Film "overexposure" on cassettes and pay-cable was one reason cited. Another was the rising popularity of miniseries and TV films.

News and Sports. Network news, after experimenting throughout the early and mid-1980s to adjust to changing tastes, viewer habits, and state-of-the-art technology—first with a computer graphics look, then with a troublesome tier of late-night and off-hour programming—finally reached a reckoning in 1986–87. A major analysis piece in *The New York Times* cited the cancellation of the long-struggling, low-rated *CBS Morning News* as symbolic of the upheaval at CBS News, once unchallenged as the premier news department; the *CBS Evening News* with Dan Rather slipped far enough to allow ABC and NBC to join it in a three-way ratings dogfight. News-staff cuts at all three networks aimed to restore profitability, and *60 Minutes* commentator Andy Rooney used his syndicated newspaper column to attack the new executives who were "company men first, newsmen second."

The decline in overall advertising revenue also reversed the profitability of sports programming. ABC Sports President Dennis Swanson said that network bidding wars had escalated so high that 80% of sports budgets went into purchasing broadcast rights. As a result even such highly rated shows as *Monday Night Football* ran in the red, and it was projected more than a year in advance that broadcasts of the 1988 Calgary Winter Olympics could not break even.

Cable Television. The cable TV industry won a major legal battle when a U.S. federal court overturned a ruling that raised the royalties owed to feature film producers. The film industry vowed to appeal.

Cinemax, the offspring of Home Box Office (HBO), enjoyed a subscription surge on the celebrity of Max Headroom, an aptly named character created by the computer distortion of actor Matt Frewer. A scatter-brained, egotistical TV personality, Max heralded a new age of creative video graphics and satirization of old TV clichés. Comedy on cable, generally, tended to be more sophisticated and risqué than on commercial TV, with Robin Williams and the Second City Television (SCTV) troupe on HBO and Martin Mull on Cinemax.

New speciality program services in 1986 included the Nostalgia Channel, consisting of repeats of favorite shows of the 1950s and '60s and vintage films. In the same vein, the WTBS Superstation offered the complete *Honeymooners* series of the '50s and reunited another beloved cast for *The New Leave It to Beaver.*

The U.S. Senate voted to allow gavel-to-gavel coverage of congressional proceedings on the C-SPAN channel; some critics felt the move would improve public accountability; others said it would encourage showboating.

Katharine Hepburn and Harold Gould starred in "Mrs. Delafield Wants to Marry," a CBS movie about an elderly couple that gets engaged—to the consternation of their families.

AP/Wide World

The **Adventures of Huckleberry Finn**—A four-part *American Playhouse* adaptation of Mark Twain's novel. With Jim Dale, Patrick Day, Samm-Art Williams. PBS, Feb. 10.

The **Africans**—A nine-part series examining 20th-century Africa. PBS, Oct. 9.

All-Star Celebration Honoring Martin Luther King, Jr.—Special from three cities on the occasion of the first federal holiday honoring the civil-rights leader. Host, Stevie Wonder. NBC, Jan. 20.

Anastasia—A two-part drama about Anna Anderson, who claimed to be the daughter of the last czar of Russia. With Amy Irving, Rex Harrison. NBC, Dec. 7.

Anne of Green Gables—A three-part *Wonderworks* adaptation of the L.M. Montgomery novel. With Megan Follows. PBS, Feb. 16.

Barnum—TV movie about the life of showman P.T. Barnum. With Burt Lancaster. CBS, Nov. 30.

Brat Farrar—A three-part *Mystery!* adaptation of Josephine Tey's novel. PBS, Nov. 15.

Choices—Drama on the issue of abortion. With George C. Scott, Jacqueline Bisset, Melissa Gilbert. ABC, Feb. 17.

Comrades—A 12-part series on representative Soviet citizens. PBS, July 3.

Crossings—A three-part miniseries based on a novel by Danielle Steel. With Cheryl Ladd. ABC, Feb. 23.

The **Day the Universe Changed**—A ten-part series on how knowledge has changed civilization. PBS, Oct. 16.

Dead Man's Folly—TV-movie adaptation of an Agatha Christie mystery featuring detective Hercule Poirot. With Peter Ustinov, Jean Stapleton. CBS, Jan. 8.

The **Deliberate Stranger**—A two-part TV-movie based on a factual account of the slaying of suspected serial killer Theodore Bundy. With Mark Harmon. NBC, May 4.

Divorce Wars—A *Frontline* examination of the difficulties resulting from the end of a marriage. PBS, Feb. 25.

Eugene O'Neill—A Glory of Ghosts—Documentary on the *American Masters* series about the author of *Long Day's Journey into Night* and other plays. PBS, Sept. 8.

A **Flash of Green**—An *American Playhouse* adaptation of a John D. MacDonald short story. With Ed Harris. PBS, April 21.

48 Hours on Crack Street—A *CBS News Special* documentary on cocaine dealing in New York City. With Dan Rather. CBS, Sept. 2.

Fresno—A comedy miniseries satirizing the "night-time soaps." With Carol Burnett, Dabney Coleman. CBS, Nov. 16.

George Washington II: The Forging of a Nation—A two-part sequel to the 1984 series, covering Washington's years in office. With Barry Bostwick. CBS, Sept. 21.

Goya—A *Great Performances* telecast of the premiere of a new opera by Gian Carlo Menotti about the Spanish painter. With Plácido Domingo. PBS, Nov. 28.

Help Wanted: Kids—A *Disney Sunday Movie* about a couple who need children quickly to impress the husband's boss. With Bill Hudson, Cindy Williams. ABC, Feb. 2.

Horowitz in Moscow—Concert by Vladimir Horowitz from the classical pianist's native Russia. CBS, April 20.

Is Anybody Out There?—A *Nova* episode pondering the probability of intelligent life elsewhere in the universe. With Lily Tomlin. PBS, Nov. 18.

Jack Paar Comes Home—A program of clips from the *Tonight* show (1957–62), when Jack Paar was host. NBC, Nov. 29.

Jerusalem: Within These Walls—A *National Geographic Special* about the ancient city. PBS, March 12.

Kingdom of the Ice Bear—A three-part *Nature* series exploring Arctic ecosystems. PBS, Feb. 16.

The **Last Frontier**—TV-movie in two parts about an American widow struggling to save her ranch in the Australian Outback. With Linda Evans. CBS, Oct. 5.

Life, Death, and AIDS—Report on the worldwide AIDS epidemic. With Tom Brokaw. NBC, Jan. 21.

Lohengrin—A *Live from the Met* telecast of Wagner's opera. With James Levine conducting. PBS, March 26.

Lord Mountbatten: The Last Viceroy—A six-part *Masterpiece Theatre* dramatization of Philip Ziegler's biography of the last British governor of India. With Nicol Williamson, Janet Suzman. PBS, Jan. 26.

The **Making of a Continent**—A six-part series on the geology of North America. PBS, Dec. 1.

Managing Our Miracles: Health Care in America—A ten-part series examining issues in medicine. PBS, Sept. 30.

Mrs. Delafield Wants to Marry—TV-movie about an older couple whose families object to their engagement. With Katharine Hepburn. CBS, March 30.

Nazi Hunter: The Beate Klarsfeld Story—TV-movie about a German woman's efforts to bring Nazi Klaus Barbie to trial. With Farrah Fawcett, Tom Conti. ABC, Nov. 23.

Nobody's Child—Drama based on the life story of a woman confined for 20 years in a mental institution who becomes a leading mental-health administrator. With Marlo Thomas. CBS, April 6.

Northern Ireland: At the Edge of the Union—Documentary on the strife in Northern Ireland. PBS, Feb. 18.

One River, One Country: The U.S.-Mexico Border—A *CBS Reports* documentary on U.S.-Mexican relations. With Bill Moyers. CBS, Sept. 3.

Paradise Postponed—*Masterpiece Theatre*'s 11-part dramatization of the John Mortimer novel about Britain since World War II. With Peter Egan, Michael Hordern, Paul Shelley, David Threlfall. PBS, Oct. 19.

Peter the Great—A four-part miniseries on the life of Czar Peter I of Russia. With Maximilian Schell, Jan Niklas, Lilli Palmer, Vanessa Redgrave. NBC, Feb. 2.

Phil Donahue Examines the Human Animal—A five-part documentary miniseries about family life and human nature. With Phil Donahue. NBC, Aug. 11.

Planet Earth—A seven-part series presenting a geophysical survey of the earth. Episodes include "The Living Machine," "The Climate Puzzle," "Gifts from the Sea," "Fate of the Earth." PBS, Jan. 22.

The **Price**—A three-part drama about Irish terrorists who kidnap members of a wealthy British family from their Irish estate. With Derek Thompson, Aingeal Grehan, Peter Barkworth, Harriet Walter. PBS, Aug. 17.

Promise—TV-movie about a middle-aged man unexpectedly given the care of his schizophrenic brother. With James Garner, James Woods. CBS, Dec. 14.

Roanoke—A three-part historical drama about the first English settlement in America. PBS, May 26.

The **Roommate**—An *American Playhouse* adaptation of a John Updike story about incompatible college roommates. With Lance Guest, Barry Miller. PBS, Jan. 27.

Shadowlands—A dramatization of the real-life love affair of English author C.S. Lewis and American poet Joy Gresham. With Joss Ackland, Claire Bloom. PBS, Oct. 29.

Shroud for a Nightingale—A five-part *Mystery!* adaptation of P.D. James' thriller. With Roy Marsden. PBS, Oct. 11.

Sins—A three-part miniseries about international intrigue and high fashion. With Joan Collins. CBS, Feb. 2.

The **Story of English**—A nine-part survey of the English language. With Robert MacNeil. PBS, Sept. 15.

That Secret Sunday—TV-movie about four policemen who cause the death of two sisters, and the reporter who investigates the case. With James Farentino. CBS, Nov. 25.

There Must Be a Pony—TV-movie about a faded movie star recovering from a mental breakdown. With Elizabeth Taylor, Robert Wagner. ABC, Oct. 5.

Under Seige—TV-movie about terrorism in the United States. With Peter Strauss, Hal Holbrook. NBC, Feb. 9.

Under the Influence—Drama about alcoholism. With Andy Griffith, Joyce Van Patten. CBS, Sept. 28.

Unknown Chaplin—A three-part series on *American Masters* about the movies' most famous star. PBS, July 14.

Unnatural Causes—Fact-based TV-movie about a Vietnam vet battling the Veterans Administration. With John Ritter, Alfre Woodard. NBC, Nov. 10.

The **Vanishing Family—Crisis in Black America**—A Bill Moyers report on the problems of unwed mothers, absent fathers, unemployment, and poverty in black families. CBS, Jan. 25.

When The Bough Breaks—TV-movie about a child psychologist who helps the police solve a child-molesting case. With Ted Danson. NBC, Oct. 12.

The **West of the Imagination**—A six-part series about the history and artists of the U.S. West. PBS, Sept. 22.

A **Year in the Life**—TV-movie in three parts dramatizing 12 months in the lives of one contemporary American family. With Richard Kiley, Eva Marie Saint. NBC, Dec. 15.

Public Television. The Corporation for Public Broadcasting, the funding parent of the Public Broadcasting Service (PBS), announced that it would investigate the objectivity and balance of PBS programming in the wake of continuing accusations of a leftist bias on the network. The latest controversy in this vein resulted from the National Endowment for the Humanities refusing to be identified as a funding source on the documentary series *The Africans* because it felt the material to be anti-Western. Producers of *Sun City,* in which American pop musicians discussed their boycott of a South African music festival as a gesture against apartheid, claimed that conservative political pressure was behind PBS' refusal to air the documentary. PBS argued that the program was too promotional of the music industry.

Critically acclaimed new programs on PBS during 1986 included the documentary series *The Story of English,* hosted by newsman Robert MacNeil, and *The West of the Imagination,* about the American West.

TV and Public Issues. The question of TV news ethics as it relates to terrorism commanded a full-page report in *Time* magazine. In exchange for an exclusive interview with Abul Abbas, the Palestinian leader involved in the 1985 hijacking of the Italian cruise ship *Achille Lauro,* NBC agreed not to disclose the terrorist's hideout. The arrangement was termed "reprehensible" by the U.S. State Department and condemned by media critics.

The Reagan administration's Meese Commission on Pornography proposed that the Federal Communications Commission adopt stronger measures against allegedly obscene material on cable TV, but the FCC voted to continue its previous standards (*See also* special report, page 317.)

A "drug bust," telecast live during Geraldo Rivera's documentary *The Doping of a Nation* was attacked for sensationalism, particularly after the suspects in question were found innocent. Still, it was the highest-rated syndicated program ever.

Personalities. Nineteen eighty-six was also the year of the talk show sweepstakes, with several new hosts trying to claim Johnny Carson's *Tonight* throne. Carson carried on a bitter newsprint feud with his former stand-in host, Joan Rivers, who launched her own talk show on the new Fox network; a roundup in the newspaper *USA Today* dismissed her and the other new entries—David Brenner, Oprah Winfrey, the columnist Jimmy Breslin, and a returning Dick Cavett—who all got off to slow ratings starts. *Esquire* magazine crowned David Letterman the new talk king because of his fresh, offbeat humor and the affluent Yuppie audience of his *Late Night* (NBC). David Hartman, host of ABC's *Good Morning America* since its 1975 inception, announced that he was leaving the show.

© MacNeil Lehrer Productions

Newsman Robert MacNeil (left) hosted "The Story of English," a nine-part PBS study "about all the different varieties [of the language] and how they came to be."

Radio. The major record companies suspended their dealings with many independent record promoters after a federal grand jury opened an investigation of widespread allegations that the promoters had ties to organized crime and were offering various forms of bribery to win radio airplay for new releases. The scandal was expected to restructure radically the way record companies and radio stations do business.

Oleg Tumanov, a Soviet defector who worked for the Munich, West Germany, station of Radio Liberty, a branch of the U.S. government-funded Radio Free Europe, returned to the USSR after 21 years. In a Moscow news conference he denounced his former employer as a front for covert operations against the Communist bloc.

Radio lost one of its leading personalities with the death of William B. Williams, a disc jockey for 40 years, principally with WNEW in New York. Williams coined the nickname "Chairman of the Board" for Frank Sinatra, whose career he was credited with reviving with constant airplay.

See also PRIZES AND AWARDS.

DAN HULBERT
"The Dallas Times Herald"

The Return of the Game Show

"Wheel of Fortune," the highest rated syndicated program in TV history, led a revival of the half-hour game show.

© John Livzey/DOT

The phenomenal success of *Wheel of Fortune* and its "shirttails-like" ability to provide success for other television shows are somewhat akin to the reinvention of the wheel. So elementary and functional for television revenues is the show that suddenly the game-show genre, once extremely popular with viewers, again is hot. In addition, *Wheel of Fortune,* which usually airs in a time slot traditionally occupied by evening news programs, can influence for good or ill the ratings of these news programs.

The reasons for the popularity of this rather simple word game can be baffling to the uninitiated. The host Pat Sajak is a mild-mannered former weatherman. Vanna White, his pretty sidekick, has the job of turning over letters of the alphabet placed on a big board as they are asked for by the contestants, after a spin of the wheel determines the cash involved. Eventually these letters spell out a phrase, person(s), place(s), event, thing, or other category, allowing a puzzle to be solved and a winner to be named. Whether it is the simplicity of the show that explains its popularity or the welcome respite it offers from the news shows that it rivals, it was in 1986 the highest-rated syndicated show in television history, reaching some 40 million viewers daily.

Wheel of Fortune's tremendous success has positively affected game shows generally. During 1986 two other game shows—*Jeop-

ardy!* and *The New Newlywed Game*—were ranked in the top five on Nielsen's syndicated-shows list. Also, there were 15 other game shows running in syndication and 10 more on the three major networks.

The networks' renewed interest in game shows should be no surprise, considering that such shows have been around since the beginning of television broadcasting. Such early shows as *Break the Bank* and *Strike It Rich* were first on radio. In 1955 another transition to the era of big-money quiz shows in prime time began with *The $64,000 Question.* That show gained tremendous popularity and brought about copycat versions that offered still bigger prizes. Problems arose when, in order to liven the shows, more colorful guests were sought and provided with answers to the questions. In 1958 when a defeated contestant from a show called *Dotto* indicated that the shows were rigged, the scandal that ensued tarnished the image of television itself.

Eventually daytime game shows helped return the genre to respectability. In the 1960s and 1970s such shows as *The Match Game, Hollywood Squares,* and *Password,* among others, gained viewer loyalty. *Wheel of Fortune* itself had been mildly successful on the NBC network for eight years prior to the creation in 1983 of a syndicated version that apparently helped make the show a massive hit.

SAUNDRA FRANCE

TENNESSEE

A lawsuit reminiscent of the 1925 Scopes "monkey trial" and an election that brought a Democrat to the governorship were among events that drew national attention to Tennessee in 1986. The state also suffered from the severe drought that afflicted much of the South.

Politics. In a race closely monitored nationwide, Democrat Ned Ray McWhorter defeated former Republican Gov. Winfield Dunn to succeed Gov. Lamar Alexander. McWhorter ran strong in rural and urban counties of middle and west Tennessee and made serious inroads on Dunn's expected support in predominantly Republican east Tennessee. A longtime speaker of the state House of Representatives, McWhorter had defeated two opponents in the Democratic primary in a $7.6 million campaign filled with charges of back-room deals and vote buying.

Democrats assigned special significance to this victory in a state where a substantial majority of voters profess to be Democrats but have voted Republican in recent years. Republicans have carried Tennessee in seven of the last nine presidential elections and three of the last four for governor. In another contest William H. Boner was returned to Congress from the Nashville district amid reports that he was under investigation by a federal grand jury.

Legislation. Legislation passed during the year included a mandatory seat-belt law and a four-cent increase in the gasoline tax, the latter designed to raise more than $100 million for much-needed improvements to the state's interstate highways and for new connecting routes aimed at attracting industry. Municipalities were to receive a fourth of the increase in the tax. The state's $6.6 billion budget included $1 million to expand Medicaid and Aid to Families with Dependent Children, and salary increases for state employees.

Education. In a nationally spotlighted federal lawsuit in Greenville, seven religious fundamentalist families sued public school officials over the use of what they termed "offensive" textbooks in grades 1–8. Claiming First Amendment rights guaranteeing freedom of religion, the families persuaded U.S. District Judge Thomas Hull to rule that their children could not be required to read books that offend their religious beliefs.

Crops and Weather. Severe drought caused extensive crop damage across the state. Counties in the far west and east were hardest hit, with some experiencing losses as high as 50% in corn, wheat, and soybean crops. Farmers in 40 of the state's 95 counties were declared eligible for federal aid.

"Homecoming '86." The state's tourist trade greatly exceeded expectations as Tennesseans celebrated "Homecoming '86" from Mountain City to Memphis. The program of special

---

TENNESSEE • Information Highlights

Area: 42,144 sq mi (109 152 km²).
Population (1985 est.): 4,762,000.
Chief Cities (July 1, 1984 est.): Nashville-Davidson, the capital, 462,450; Memphis, 648,399; Knoxville, 173,972; Chattanooga, 164,400; Clarksville (1980 census), 54,777.
Government (1986): *Chief Officer*—governor, Lamar Alexander (R). *General Assembly*—Senate, 33 members; House of Representatives, 99 members.
State Finances (fiscal year 1985): *Revenue,* $6,142,000,000; *expenditure,* $5,439,000,000.
Personal Income (1985): $53,540,000,000; per capita, $11,243.
Labor Force (June 1986): *Civilian labor force,* 2,302,100; *unemployed,* 180,300 (7.8% of total force).
Education: *Enrollment* (fall 1984)—public elementary schools, 581,452; public secondary, 235,760; colleges and universities, 194,845. *Public school expenditures* (1983–84), $1,684,000,000 ($2,173 per pupil).

---

events was developed by Governor Alexander and was designed to make Tennesseans more aware of their heritage. It was chaired by Alex Haley of Henning, the nationally acclaimed author of *Roots*.

News Makers. Former Gov. Ray Blanton was released from prison after serving time for extortion, conspiracy, and mail fraud in the issuance of liquor licenses, and was promptly hired by a Nashville radio station as a news commentator. Stanley Cohen of Vanderbilt University and James Buchanan, who was born in Tennessee, won Nobel Prizes in Physiology and Economics, respectively (*see* PRIZES AND AWARDS). Tennessean Kellye Cash was named Miss America.

ROBERT E. CORLEW
Middle Tennessee State University

TERRORISM

The problem of terrorism, and how to combat it, continued to be a major concern for Western governments during 1986. After months of warnings about military retaliation, the United States finally launched a raid against Libya for that country's involvement in the bombing of a club in West Berlin frequented by American servicemen. Other governments also took action against state sponsors of terrorism, including Great Britain's breaking of relations with Syria over an attempt to place a bomb aboard an El Al plane in London, and West Germany's expulsing of a number of Syrian diplomats for involvement in a terrorist incident in West Berlin. Yet it was not only state-sponsored terrorists that were active during 1986. Terrorist groups and individuals aligned with a variety of causes, and using different tactics on a vast array of targets worldwide, assured that the problem of terrorism is unlikely to dissipate in the near future.

Libyans inspect the damage after U.S. warplanes bombed "terrorist-related targets" in Tripoli and Benghazi in April.

Europe. As in previous years Europe was a major region for terrorist activity in 1986. Among the more dramatic incidents was the explosion of a bomb aboard a Trans World Airlines (TWA) jet over Greece on April 2, killing four passengers. However, it was a bombing in a discotheque in West Berlin three days later that proved to be one of the most significant terrorist events of the year. Two U.S. servicemen and a Turkish woman were killed in the attack, and more than 200 people were injured, including several Americans. U.S. intelligence intercepted communications between the Libyan "People's Bureau" (embassy) in East Berlin and Tripoli, providing evidence that the government of Col. Muammar el-Qaddafi was responsible for the attack. Based on this "incontrovertible evidence," U.S. fighter-bombers, taking off from bases in Britain, struck targets in Tripoli and Benghazi.

The raid resulted in a rash of retaliatory terrorist incidents, including the killing of one American and two British hostages in Lebanon, a rocket-propelled grenade attack against the British ambassador's residence in Beirut, and the shooting of a U.S. diplomat in Sudan. An attempt also was made to place a bomb aboard an El Al plane in London. In that incident, in which explosives were placed in the hand baggage of the unsuspecting girlfriend of a Jordanian terrorist, a British court found evidence linking Syrian intelligence to the plot. Britain subsequently broke diplomatic relations with Damascus.

West Germany also took diplomatic action against Syria, expelling three Syrian diplomats and temporarily not replacing its ambassador to Damascus, for Syrian involvement in the bombing of the German-Arab Friendship Society office in West Berlin in March. A Palestinian arrested for the attack stated that the Syrian Embassy in East Berlin had supplied the explosives. In addition to the diplomatic measures,

West Germany suspended $36 million in development aid credits for Syria. In a separate incident a bomb exploded in June at the El Al ticket counter at Madrid's Barajas Airport, injuring several people. Spain also was struck by acts of domestic terrorism, the most serious incident being a July 14 bombing that killed 8 Civil Guards and wounded more than 60 other people. The Basque separatist group ETA claimed responsibility for the attack.

France was especially victimized by terrorism, as a series of bombings rocked Paris. During a two-week period in September, several people were killed and more than 150 injured in five separate incidents, including a bombing outside a crowded clothing store. The Committee of Solidarity for Arab and Middle East Political Prisoners claimed responsibility for the attacks. Left-wing terrorists also were active in France, with the Direct Action group claiming responsibility for the murder of the president of the Renault auto company in November.

The Irish Republican Army continued its campaign of terror in Northern Ireland, with bombings and assassinations taking the lives of a number of British soldiers and policemen. Terrorists in Europe also assassinated Sweden's Prime Minister Olof Palme.

Middle East. Just as the issue of hostages and Iran preoccupied the Carter administration for more than a year, so the issue of secret arms deals to Iran in exchange for the release of American hostages in Lebanon engulfed the Reagan administration in a major controversy at the end of 1986. Pro-Iranian extremists had been holding several hostages from Western nations in Beirut for some time. While a number of hostages were released during 1986—including the Rev. Lawrence Jenco and David Jacobsen, Americans who had been held captive for more than a year—others remained in captivity and additional ones were taken. Among the demands of the group holding the hostages, Islamic Jihad, was the release from Kuwaiti prison of several Shiite terrorists implicated in the blowing up of the U.S. and French embassies in that country in 1983. In an incident that clearly demonstrated the link between political events and terrorism, three employees of the Spanish Embassy in Beirut were kidnapped only hours after Spain established full diplomatic relations with Israel in January. They were released a few weeks later.

Terrorism in the Middle East also included "car bomb wars" between rival factions in Lebanon. Both Christian and Muslim groups used this tactic against each other, with many innocent people killed in the process. In one incident in July, 25 persons were killed and 180 injured in a car bombing in a crowded marketplace in Muslim West Beirut. This was in retaliation for a car bombing the previous day in Christian East Beirut that claimed 31 lives. It was not only in Lebanon that car bomb attacks occurred. In August, 20 persons were killed in Iran when a car bomb exploded in a central square in Tehran.

One of the more grisly terrorist attacks of the year occurred September 6 in Turkey, when two Arab terrorists opened fire on worshipers at Istanbul's main synagogue, killing 21 and themselves. Increased security in Turkey earlier in the year helped avert another major incident, when police arrested two Libyans outside a U.S. officers' club in Ankara. One of the Libyans had a bag containing grenades and other explosives. The importance of good security in the battle against terrorism also was evident in Kuwait, where authorities foiled a plot in April by 12 terrorists to hijack a Kuwaiti Airways plane. Iraqi officials were not as fortunate as one of their planes was hijacked on December 25. Two grenades exploded in mid-flight, causing the plane to crash in Saudi Arabia, killing 62 persons.

As in previous years Israel continued to respond militarily to terrorist attacks against its citizens and officials. On October 15 three grenades were hurled at a group of Israeli soldiers and their families near the Wailing Wall in Jerusalem. One person was killed and 65 others injured in the incident, for which the Palestine Liberation Organization (PLO) claimed responsiblity. The next day Israeli warplanes attacked suspected PLO bases in Lebanon; one of the planes was shot down. Meanwhile, in Cyprus, a British air base came under a mortar and rocket attack in August. A terrorist group called the Unified Nasserite Organization stated that the assault was in retaliation for Britain's support for the U.S. air strike in Libya.

Asia. Terrorism associated with the Sikh separatist campaign in the Punjab region of India escalated during 1986. Militant Sikhs attacked moderate members of their sect as well as Hindus and government officials. More than 500 people were killed during the year. Assassination was a favored tactic of the Sikh extremists. Victims included Lt. Gen. Arun Vaidya, the retired Army chief of staff who led the 1984 assault on the Golden Temple in Amritsar. Prime Minister Rajiv Gandhi was the target of an assassination attempt in October. In addition Sikh extremists twice hijacked buses and shot the Hindus on board. In July, 15 people were executed in this manner, while in November more than 20 people were killed in a similar fashion.

Another country in which terrorism was used in the cause of separatism was Sri Lanka, where Tamil extremists attacked both government and civilian targets. In May a bomb exploded on a plane at Colombo International Airport, killing 21 persons and injuring 40 others. At the same time, however, extremists in the Sinhalese majority, who oppose conces-

Former hostage David Jacobsen (extreme left) is reunited with his family at Wiesbaden Air Force Base in West Germany following his release by pro-Iranian Lebanese kidnappers in November. Jacobsen, the director of the American University Hospital in Beirut, had been a hostage for 17 months.

sions to the Tamils, were suspected of bombing a pro-government rally in September.

Terrorist incidents in Asia also included an airliner hijacking in Pakistan on September 5 that was significant for several reasons. As the first major publicized international hijacking since the U.S. air raid on Libya, it renewed the public's fear of international terrorism. The incident also revealed serious lapses in airport security, as the four Palestinian terrorists were able to gain access to the plane by posing as airport security guards and driving onto the airfield. The escape of the cockpit crew as soon as the hijacking began also was an important development, since it eliminated the possibility of the plane taking off. This did not prevent bloodshed, however, as the hijackers, fearing that a rescue attempt was underway when the lights went out in the plane, began shooting passengers and detonating grenades. Twenty-one persons were killed and more than 40 were injured.

Other major terrorist incidents in Asia included the firing of several rockets at the state guest house in Tokyo during the May economic summit meeting of Western leaders. Although the rockets missed their target, the attack nevertheless demonstrated the increasing sophistication of terrorist tactics. Radical leftist groups were suspected of that incident, as well

At international airports, including Rome's, below, security checks and other protective measures become more prevalent after an increase in the number of terrorist attacks.

© Pierro Guerrini/Gamma-Liaison

as other attacks on the U.S. Embassy, the Imperial Palace, and the official residence of Prime Minister Yasuhiro Nakasone.

Latin America. Several countries in Latin America were victimized by terrorism, as various groups tried to topple existing regimes. In Chile, President Augusto Pinochet narrowly escaped assassination when his motorcade came under a grenade, rocket, and machine-gun attack in September. Several of Pinochet's bodyguards were killed in the assault, for which the Manuel Rodriguez Patriotic Front claimed responsibility.

In Peru, the Maoist Shining Path guerrillas and the Tupac Amaru Revolutionary Movement continued their campaigns of terror in both rural and urban areas. Among the numerous incidents during 1986 were assassinations of police officials and members of President Alan Garcia's APRA party, bombings of APRA offices, cutting of power lines, killings of peasants, the bombing of a tourist train, and a variety of other tactics aimed at creating fear throughout the country. International targets also were hit, including embassies and consulates of several nations and U.S. business offices. The bloodiest incident of the year occurred in June, when more than 150 Shining Path members were killed when government troops quelled riots in three Peruvian prisons. President Garcia admitted that at least 100 of the prisoners were executed after surrendering to authorities.

In other terrorist events in Latin America, the Guatemalan National Revolutionary Unit claimed responsibility for the downing of a helicopter belonging to an American petroleum company, and rebels in Colombia kidnapped several foreigners and bombed foreign businesses.

North America and Africa. Compared with other regions, North America and Africa did not experience a high frequency of terrorist incidents. Among the more significant events in Africa were the shooting down of a civilian airliner by rebels in southern Sudan, an attempt to blow up the U.S. embassy in Togo, and several bombings in South Africa by the African National Congress.

Terrorism in North America included numerous bombings and arson attacks on abortion clinics in the United States, a bombing campaign against U.S. military facilities in Puerto Rico by the nationalist Macheteros group, and several bombings in Idaho by the neo-Nazi Aryan Nations. The United States was also victimized by the contamination of several food and drug products (*see* special report, page 197). Finally, a major terrorist incident was averted when authorities in Canada arrested five Sikhs for plotting to blow up an Air India jet that was to fly out of New York.

JEFFREY D. SIMON
The Rand Corporation

TEXAS

Texas confronted a host of problems as it celebrated its 150th anniversary in 1986 (*see* page 520). With farm prices declining and the domestic oil industry in shambles, the state was forced to raise taxes and cut spending for education and other services.

Politics. Elected governor in 1978 but unseated by Democrat Mark White in 1982, Republican William Clements was elected again as governor of Texas in November 1986. Exceeding his party's fondest hopes, Clements polled 53% of the votes, scoring a stunning victory over White. During a campaign marked by negative advertising on both sides, Clements painted the incumbent White as a reckless spender who would back an individual or corporate income tax to balance the state budget. At one point, down by 17 points in the pre-election polls, White rallied by charging that Clements would slash welfare and education funds, already among the lowest in the nation. (*See also* UNITED STATES—Elections.)

All political factions in Texas were agreed that the gubernatorial race had strong implications for the national presidential contest in 1988. Had he won, Mark White would have been a possible vice-presidential selection on the Democratic ticket. On the other hand, with a Republican governor in his home state of Texas, Vice-President George Bush's prospects for the Republican nomination were markedly improved. Finally, the city of Houston made a strong bid to host the 1988 Democratic national convention.

Economy. With the conclusion of the governor's race, the economy became the principal issue in the state once again. Many farmers faced bankruptcy and mortgage foreclosures multiplied; conditions in the state's vital petroleum industry were equally bad. With the price of oil at a low $15.00 per barrel, State Comptroller Bob Bullock predicted huge deficits when the legislature convenes in January 1987. Real-estate and banking operations also have been caught in the economic slump, and the 1986 unemployment rate was 9%, two points above the national average.

Houston and Dallas, which for so long paced the nation in new construction figures, have been particularly hard hit as unemployment in oil-related industries and personal bankruptcies continued to mount. U.S. Sen. Lloyd Bentsen called for a federally mandated oil-import fee, which would bring the price of oil back to its accustomed range, but prospects for such a solution seemed remote. Hoping to emulate the success of Massachusetts and California, state leaders were trying to attract hi-tech industries to Texas. The city of Austin, benefiting from the research facilities of the University of Texas, was in the vanguard of this movement.

TEXAS · Information Highlights

Area: 266,807 sq mi (691 030 km²).
Population (1985 est.): 16,370,000.
Chief Cities (July 1, 1984 est.): Austin, the capital, 397,001; Houston, 1,705,697; Dallas, 974,234; San Antonio, 842,779; El Paso, 463,809; Fort Worth, 414,562; Corpus Christi, 258,067.
Government (1986): *Chief Officers*—governor, Mark White (D); lt. gov., William P. Hobby (D). *Legislature*—Senate, 31 members; House of Representatives, 150 members.
State Finances (fiscal year 1985): *Revenue,* $21,346,000,000; *expenditure,* $19,074,000,000.
Personal Income (1985): $220,715,000,000; per capita, $13,483.
Labor Force (June 1986): *Civilian labor force,* 8,204,100; *unemployed,* 906,800 (11.1% of total force).
Education: *Enrollment* (fall 1984)—public elementary schools, 2,188,511; public secondary, 851,794; colleges and universities, 769,692. *Public school expenditures* (1983–84), $8,156,000,000 ($2,913 per pupil).

Education. On the public-school level, Governor White's controversial "no pass, no play" rule that students on athletic teams must maintain passing scholastic averages had been in effect for a year. SAT scores had risen slightly, and opposition from athletic officials had diminished somewhat, but Governor-elect Clements indicated he might seek to change the ruling. More than 95% of Texas public-school teachers passed a competency exam on teaching skills, but a residue of bitterness lingers among teachers forced to take the examination.

The special session of the state legislature imposed drastic cuts, averaging 10% on the budgets of all state universities. With perhaps even deeper cuts in the offing, higher education faced a crisis situation. A committee was appointed to make recommendations for the future, and its report would be submitted to the legislature in 1987. Certain to be controversial were possible recommendations that might seek to dismantle the tenure system and that would designate two or three campuses as "research centers" to the exclusion of all others. Tuition at all state universities was increased substantially in 1985, but the possibility of another increase existed.

Sports. Professional teams generally enjoyed an unprecedented degree of success in Texas in 1986. In basketball the Houston Rockets took the Boston Celtics to six games in the NBA championship, and with a young team, the Rockets showed much promise for the future. In baseball, the Houston Astros ultimately lost the National League pennant to the New York Mets. The series was marked by a 16-inning game and by intense fan interest in both cities. Football's Dallas Cowboys, however, finished the season with a 7–9 record and failed to qualify for the play-offs for only the third time in 20 years.

STANLEY F. SIEGEL
University of Houston

Texas at 150

© J.P. Laffont/Sygma

© J.P. Laffont/Sygma

AP/Wide World

Amid severe economic difficulties caused by drastic declines in the price of oil, the "Lone-Star State" put on a yearlong, Texas-size celebration of its 150th anniversary of independence from Mexico. On March 6 in San Antonio, above, the Alamo was remembered in an authentic battle reenactment. On April 6 in Houston, below, independence itself was celebrated with a laser-and-fireworks show that attracted 1 million viewers.

THAILAND

In 1986, Thailand held its third consecutive parliamentary election under the present constitution without a military coup. Prime Minister Prem Tinsulanonda was asked to form a new coalition government, which continued to grope for solutions to the country's main problem, that of slow economic growth.

Politics. Although the July election produced few changes in the leadership or policies of the government, it indicated the growing strength of democratic institutions in Thailand. The election followed constitutional procedures, and the army did not intervene openly, as it often had in the past. More than 3,500 candidates representing 16 parties contested the election. The Democratic Party, Thailand's oldest civilian party, recorded the largest number of votes, and Prem, a retired general with no party affiliation, received a new mandate for his moderate government.

Prem had been forced to call the election when a large number of pro-government members of parliament deserted him over a minor issue (the cost of operating diesel trucks). It was widely reported in Bangkok that the members who deserted the government had been paid to do so by bankers and business leaders opposed to economic austerity measures introduced by Prem's finance minister Sommai Huntrakun. The politically ambitious supreme commander of the armed forces, Gen. Arthit Kamlang-ek, who was being forced into retirement by Prem, may have been secretly in league with those seeking to oust the prime minister. Arthit's successor, army chief of staff Gen. Chaovalit Yongchaiyuth, is a Prem supporter.

The Economy. Thailand has a large, young, and increasingly well-educated and urbanized population. The agricultural sector, whose share of the gross domestic product (GDP) has declined steadily, although it employs two thirds of the labor force, can no longer absorb as many new workers as in the past. Prem's government has promised to give top priority to creating almost one million new jobs a year over the next five years—a rate that would just keep pace with the number of young people entering the job market. The sixth five-year plan, which came into effect in October, calls for expanding and diversifying exports, which account for one half of the GDP. It stresses the importance of more effective management, including the continuing privatization of money-losing state enterprises, and emphasizes urban development.

The government faces many problems in trying to expand the economy at the anticipated 5% annual rate. Thailand's traditional markets in the United States, Japan, and Western Europe are being restricted to protect jobs in those countries, while world prices for many Thai exports, such as tin, rice, and sugar, are weak. The Thai government does not have large resources and must rely on the private sector, which is not very efficient because of monopoly control of some industries. Moreover, almost one third of Thailand's export earnings are now being used just to pay the interest on the country's large foreign debt.

Foreign Affairs. Thailand continued its centuries-old struggle with Vietnam for dominant influence in the two smaller countries that lie between them, Cambodia and Laos. In recent years, in alliance with the other members of the Association of Southeast Asian Nations (ASEAN), the United States, and China, Thailand has attempted to force the withdrawal of the Vietnamese forces that have occupied Cambodia since 1978. With several other nations, it supports a coalition of Communist and non-Communist forces fighting the Vietnamese in Cambodia. During 1986, there was considerable diplomatic activity. Thailand supported a proposal by the resistance groups that would have established an independent Cambodian government that would include the Cambodian resistance forces based in Thailand, as well as the leaders of the pro-Vietnamese regime in Phnom Penh. Vietnamese leaders claimed to share this goal, but they also feared that any government including the Khmer Rouge faction would again fall under the influence of China, Vietnam's main enemy.

In 1986, as in previous years, Thailand hosted thousands of refugees from Cambodia and Laos, as well as smaller numbers from Vietnam and Burma. A refugee population of more than 125,000, plus about 240,000 displaced Cambodians, remained in camps along the Thai border. Three of the 11 refugee camps in Thailand were closed in 1986 in what was seen as an effort to discourage new arrivals and put pressure on other nations to accept more refugees for resettlement.

PETER A. POOLE
Author, "The Vietnamese in Thailand"

THAILAND • Information Highlights

Official Name: Kingdom of Thailand (conventional); Prathet Thai (Thai).
Location: Southeast Asia.
Area: 198,772 sq mi (514 820 km²).
Population (mid-1986 est.): 52,800,000.
Chief City (Dec. 1984 est.): Bangkok, the capital, 5,018,327.
Government: *Head of state,* Bhumibol Adulyadej, king (acceded June 1946). *Head of government,* Gen. Prem Tinsulanonda, prime minister (took office March 1980).
Monetary Unit: Baht (26.30 baht equal U.S.$1, June 1986).
Gross National Product (1984 U.S.$): $52,400,-000,000.
Economic Index (Bangkok, 1985): *Consumer Prices* (1980 = 100), all items, 128.4; food, 116.6.
Foreign Trade (1985 U.S.$): *Imports,* $9,261,000,000; *exports,* $7,119,000,000.

THEATER

In its wrap-up of the 1985–86 theater season, *Variety* magazine announced, "The Fabulous Invalid Is Still Sick." But this kind of dreary diagnosis had become such a commonplace that observers began to turn more of their attention away from the decline and shrinkage of the commercial Broadway theater to the equally notable ascension of nonprofit, off-Broadway, and regional theaters.

If one took this broader view of the American theater scene in 1986, one would have to conclude that, in effect, the glass was half full rather than half empty. Although mass audiences still lagged in their awareness of the artistic prestige of the nonprofit theater and the low artistic stock of Broadway, and although the surge of good new playwrighting of the early 1980s had flattened out, there was a sense of excitement and renewal in such far-flung nonprofit institutions as Joseph Papp's Public Theater in New York; Lloyd Richards' Yale Repertory Theatre in New Haven, CT; Des McAnuff's La Jolla Playhouse in San Diego, CA; and Robert Brustein's American Repertory Theatre in Cambridge, MA.

Broadway. According to *Variety*, the Great White Way's attendance of 6,527,497 in 1985–86 continued a pattern of decline to 40% below the 1980 figure. Ticket prices, up to $47.50 for weekend performances of musicals, had tripled since 1975, and the season's 33 new productions represented barely more than half the volume of a decade earlier.

In interviews with *The Dallas Times Herald*, James Nederlander of Nederlander Productions blamed the scarcity of good new material; Emanuel Azenberg, producer of the most recent Neil Simon hits, blamed high production costs and an archaic marketing system that had failed to capture the television-fed generation of "yuppies"; and producer Elliott Martin (of the *Arsenic and Old Lace* revival) blamed the technical unions in particular but added, "It's greed, greed, all the way up and down the line."

Lowest of all, perhaps, was the artistic state of Broadway. The plays of integrity and substance that did manage to get produced were generally received with only public indifference. For instance there were two superb revivals of Eugene O'Neill masterworks. In *The Iceman Cometh*, actor Jason Robards and director José Quintero recreated the production that established their reputations 30 years before. In the London-launched *Long Day's Journey Into Night*, British director Jonathan Miller raised eyebrows with his speeded-up, conversational version of O'Neill's autobiographical play, and Jack Lemmon impressed all with his long-delayed stage comeback, a shattering portrayal of James Tyrone. Both productions closed early and lost money.

There were other classy casualties of Broadway's mercilessly mercenary system. A surprisingly fresh, contemporary-sounding revival of *Loot*, Joe Orton's dark farce of the early 1960s, transferred from off-Broadway's Manhattan Theatre Club under John Tillinger's sharp direction but died at the Broadway box office. Meeting the same fate was a London revival of Noël Coward's effervescent 1920s society comedy, *Hay Fever*, with Rosemary Harris heading a stellar cast. A moving revival of Athol Fugard's 1961 antiapartheid drama, *The Blood Knot*, was similarly unappreciated. *The Petition*, a new nuclear-debate drama from Britain's Brian Clarke, was generally regarded as weak, except for the juicy roles it offered the venerable husband-wife team of Hume Cronyn and Jessica Tandy; that play, too, was quickly nuked by poor ticket sales.

Benefactors, a subtle and provocative comedy-drama by Michael Frayn about the death of 1960s idealism, brought critical laurels from London and was perhaps the most important and best-received new play of 1985–86. But it managed only a so-so run, that on the star power of Glenn Close and Sam Waterston; Mary Beth Hurt stole many of the acting kudos.

The plays that succeeded commercially were, of course, lighter. Lily Tomlin's one-woman comic tour de force, *The Search for Signs of Intelligent Life in the Universe*, written with Jane Wagner, was a smash hit and brought Tomlin the Antoinette Perry ("Tony") Award for best actress of 1986, John Guare's dark 1971 farce about blue-collar dreamers and losers, *The House of Blue Leaves*, was rediscovered and helped the Lincoln Center Theater Company, under Gregory Mosher, gain an initial footing; the zany but poignant production by Jerry Zaks featured Stockard Channing and Swoosie Kurtz, and transferred to Broadway.

Herb Gardner's *I'm Not Rappaport*, an old-fashioned and saccharine comedy-drama about the relationship between an old black janitor and a crusty Jewish radical, did not receive a strong notice from several major critics, except with regards for the powerful and heartwarming performance by Judd Hirsch. *Rappaport* and Hirsch won Tonys for best play and best actor.

Hirsch, the former star of the TV series *Taxi*, was one of several erstwhile television stars whom some observers worriedly surmised might be necessary to make the theater marketable in the 1980s. Others were Jean Stapleton and Polly Holliday in the vintage black comedy, *Arsenic and Old Lace*, and Marlo Thomas in the banal, sitcom-like contrivance from Andrew Bergman, *Social Security*.

With the exception of *Arsenic*, all of the above-mentioned plays opened before the end of the 1985–86 season in June. The fall of 1986 proved disturbingly barren of new dramatic en-

© Martha Swope

Revealing once again Broadway's debt to Britain were two of the year's strongest musicals—the Tony-award-winning "Mystery of Edwin Drood" (above), adapted from Charles Dickens, and "Me and My Girl," a restored 1937 English musical.

© Alan Berliner

BROADWAY OPENINGS | 1986

MUSICALS

Big Deal, music from various sources; written and directed by Bob Fosse; based on the film *Big Deal on Madonna Street;* with Loretta Devine, Cleavant Derricks; April 10–June 8.

Brigadoon, music by Frederick Loewe, book and lyrics by Alan Jay Lerner; directed by Gerald Freedman; with Richard White, Tony Roberts, Sheryl Woods; March 1–30.

Honky Tonk Nights, music by Michael Valenti, book and lyrics by Ralph Allen and David Campbell; directed and choreographed by Ernest O. Flatt; with Joe Morton, Teresa Burrell, Ira Hawkins; Aug. 7–9.

Into the Light, music by Lee Holdridge, lyrics by John Forster, book by Jeff Tambornino; directed by Michael Maurer; with Dean Jones, Susan Bigelow, Danny Gerard, Alan Mintz; Oct. 22–26.

Jerome Kern Goes to Hollywood, music by Jerome Kern; lyrics by Ira Gershwin, Dorothy Fields, and others; book by Dick Vosburgh; conceived and directed by David Kernan; with Elaine Delmar, Scott Holmes, Liz Robertson, Elisabeth Welch; Jan. 23–Feb. 2.

Me and My Girl, music by Noel Gay, book and lyrics by L. Arthur Rose and Douglas Furber, book revised by Stephen Fry; directed by Mike Ockrent; with Robert Lindsay; Aug. 10–.

Oh, Coward!, words and music by Noel Coward; devised and directed by Roderick Cook; with Roderick Cook, Patrick Quinn, Catherine Cox; Nov. 17–.

Raggedy Ann, music and lyrics by Joe Raposo, book by William Gibson; directed and choreographed by Patricia Birch; with Ivy Austin, Lisa Rieffel, Bob Morrisey, Elizabeth Austin; Oct. 16–19.

Rags, music by Charles Strouse, lyrics by Stephen Schwartz, book by Joseph Stein; directed by Gene Saks; with Teresa Stratas, Larry Kert; Aug. 21–23.

Smile, music by Marvin Hamlisch, book and lyrics by Howard Ashman from the film of the same name; directed by Howard Ashman; with Marsha Waterbury, Jeff McCarthy, Anne Marie Bobby, Jodi Benson; Nov. 24–.

Sweet Charity, music by Cy Coleman, lyrics by Dorothy Fields, book by Neil Simon; directed and choreographed by Bob Fosse; with Debbie Allen; April 27–.

Uptown . . . It's Hot!, created, directed, and choreographed by, and starring Maurice Hines; narration by Jeffrey V. Thompson and Marion Ramsey; Jan. 28–Feb. 16.

PLAYS

Arsenic and Old Lace, by Joseph Kesselring; directed by Brian Murray; with Jean Stapleton, Polly Holliday, Abe Vigoda, Tony Roberts, William Hickey; June 26–.

The Boys in Autumn, by Bernard Sabath; directed by Theodore Mann; with George C. Scott, John Cullum; April 30–June 29.

Broadway Bound, by Neil Simon; directed by Gene Saks; with Jason Alexander, Linda Lavin, Phyllis Newman, Jonathan Silverman, Philip Sterling; Dec. 4–.

The Caretaker, by Harold Pinter; directed by John Malkovich; with Gary Sinise, Jeff Perry, Alan Wilder; Jan. 30–March 9.

Corpse!, by Gerald Moon; directed by John Tillinger; with Keith Baxter, Pauline Flanagan, Milo O'Shea, Scott LaFeber; Jan. 5–April 21.

Cuba and His Teddy Bear, by Reinaldo Povod; directed by Bill Hart; with Robert De Niro, Ralph Macchio, Burt Young; July 16–Sept. 21.

Execution of Justice, written and directed by Emily Mann; with John Spencer, Gerry Mamman, Peter Friedman, Adam Redfield, Mary McDonnell; March 14–24.

The Front Page, by Ben Hecht and Charles MacArthur; directed by Jerry Zaks; with Richard Thomas, John Lithgow, Julie Hagerty; Nov. 23–.

The House of Blue Leaves, by John Guare; directed by Jerry Zaks; with John Mahoney, Swoosie Kurtz, Stockard Channing; April 29–.

Lillian, by William Luce, based on the autobiographical works of Lillian Hellman; directed by Robert Whitehead; with Zoe Caldwell; Jan. 16–Feb. 23.

Long Day's Journey into Night, by Eugene O'Neill; directed by Jonathan Miller; with Jack Lemmon, Bethel Leslie, Kevin Spacey, Peter Gallagher; April 28–June 29.

Loot, by Joe Orton; directed by John Tillinger; with Charles Keating, Alec Baldwin, Zoe Wanamaker, Zeljko Ivanek, Joseph Maher, Nick Ullett; April 7–June 28.

Nicholas Nickleby, based on the book by Charles Dickens, abridged by David Edgar; directed by Trevor Nunn and John Caird; with Michael Siberry, Tony Jay, John Lynch, Simon Templeman; Aug. 20–Oct. 12.

The Petition, by Brian Clark; directed by Peter Hall; with Jessica Tandy, Hume Cronyn; April 24–June 29.

Precious Sons, by George Furth; directed by Norman Rene; with Judith Ivey, Ed Harris; March 20–May 10.

Rowan Atkinson at the Atkinson, by Dick Curtis, Ben Elton, Rowan Atkinson; directed by Mike Ockrent; with Rowan Atkinson, Angus Dearyton; Oct. 14–20.

Social Security, by Andrew Bergman; directed by Mike Nichols; with Ron Silver, Marlo Thomas, Joanna Gleason, Olympia Dukakis; April 17–.

Wild Honey, by Michael Frayn, based on a play by Anton Chekhov; directed by Christopher Morahan; with Ian McKellen, Kathryn Walker, Kate Burton; Dec. 18–.

You Never Can Tell, by George Bernard Shaw; directed by Stephen Porter; with Victor Garber, Philip Bosco, Stephen McHattie, Uta Hagen, Stefan Gierasch, Amanda Plummer; Oct. 9–.

Other Entertainment

Flamenco Puro, Spanish dance review created by Claudio Segovia and Hector Orezzoli; Oct. 15–Nov. 30.

The Flying Karamazov Brothers; April 1–20.

A Little Like Magic, a production by the Famous People Players puppeteers; Oct. 17–Dec. 7.

Mummenschanz, mime revue; June 17–Oct. 26.

---

tries. But George Bernard Shaw's rarely produced comedy, *You Never Can Tell,* brought raves for its old pro, Uta Hagen, and the Lincoln Center revival of the warhorse comedy, *The Front Page,* with John Lithgow and Richard Thomas, finally gave Broadway a glimmer of fun in the late fall. As December approached, Broadway waited hopefully for *Wild Honey,* the new adaptation of Chekhov's *Ivanov* with Ian McKellen repeating his acclaimed London role, and the finale of Neil Simon's autobiographical trilogy, *Broadway Bound,* expected to be as much a bonanza as its predecessors, *Brighton Beach Memoirs* and *Biloxi Blues.*

In a reversal of the most recent trends, the 1985–86 crop of Broadway musicals was even more stunted than that of plays. Rupert Holmes' adaptation of *The Mystery of Edwin Drood* (later renamed *Drood*), a transfer from Papp's New York Shakespeare Festival, had practically no competition for best musical and several other Tony categories. George Rose and Betty Buckley had a field day in this witty production, staged by Wilford Leach as a play-within-a-music-hall with the audience voting among several alternative endings to Charles Dickens' unfinished tale.

A revival of the 1966 hit *Sweet Charity,* with Debbie Allen (former star of the TV series *Fame*) in the role made famous by Gwen Verdon, proved the surprisingly durable freshness of Bob Fosse's choreography. But it shamed Fosse's uninspired, overblown new musical, *Big Deal,* which opened at almost the same time and closed shortly thereafter.

The continued popularity of the long-running musicals—*Cats, 42nd Street, A Chorus Line*—managed to mask the terrible dearth of good new musical product. It was clear that Broadway was sitting on a time bomb if good new shows did not materialize soon.

The litany of flops did not spare some of Broadway's most celebrated talents. *Rags,* a new work about the immigrant experience, tumbled despite its composer, Charles *(Annie)* Strouse; its lyricist, Stephen *(Godspell)* Schwartz; and its author, Joseph *(Fiddler on the Roof)* Stein. *Smile,* based on the 1975 beauty-pageant-debunking movie, had music by Marvin *(Chorus Line)* Hamlisch and a book by Howard *(Little Shop of Horrors)* Ashman, but a "thumbs down" from the *New York Times* made its long-term prospects look dim.

With half of Broadway's 30 houses regularly dark, the late summer of 1986 looked like precisely the wrong time to open the Main Stem's first new theater since the early 1970s. But the setting of the new Marquis Theatre was so opulent—inside the spectacular Marriott Marquis Hotel—and the inaugural production so superb that it made many start humming about Broadway's future. The show, *Me and My Girl,* Noel Gay's long-forgotten 1937 confection about a cocky Cockney torn between love and inheritance, arrived in triumph from London, and star Robert Lindsay drew delirious comparison to such clowns as Buster Keaton and Zero Mostel.

Off Broadway. The problems of soaring costs and depleted writing talent were felt off Broadway as on Broadway, but a loyal audience and hardy core of producing talent still made the smaller houses of New York the best forums for worthwhile and exciting theater.

Kevin Kline performed one of the most acclaimed American Hamlets ever in a Liviu Ciulei staging that was notable for its clarity. *Hamlet* was part of another rich season for Papp's New York Shakespeare Festival and its headquarters, the Public Theater. Also in the Public were two politically provocative new plays: *Map of the World,* by Britain's David Hare, and Wallace Shawn's *Aunt Dan and Lemon.*

Playwrights Horizons, another major source for exciting new plays, offered the sparklingly witty work, *The Perfect Party,* a satire of the beleaguered culture of the Northeastern WASP, by A. R. Gurney, Jr. *A Lie of the Mind,* Sam Shepard's haunting, epic-sized drama about the primal nature of love and the myth of the American West, showed a new warmth and lyricism in the playwright and was regarded as the most important new play of 1985–86. But the compelling production, with Geraldine Page, Harvey Keitel, and Amanda Plummer, could not survive the year at the Promenade Theatre. There were hopes that the Promenade's new tenant in the fall, Simon Gray's *The*

Common Pursuit, a typically subtle play about the death of ideals among the staff of a Cambridge University literary journal, might prove more popular in its New York premiere.

The creeping commercialism that was devastating Broadway was also taking its toll on the artistic seriousness off Broadway, as campy musicals and revues *(Angry Housewives, Have I Got a Girl for You)* and superficial, yuppie-oriented entertainments *(Beehive, Brownstone)* proliferated. Still, off Broadway could be the scene of powerful and uncompromising drama. La Mama, under the iconoclastic direction of Ellen Stewart, observed its 25th anniversary with a revival of its landmark Tom O'Horgan staging, *The Architect and the Emperor of Assyria.* And *Krapp's Last Tape,* a rare public appearance and directorial effort by its legendary 80-year-old author, Samuel Beckett, was a milestone.

Regional Theater. After only two, frustrating years, Washington's Kennedy Center for the Performing Arts shelved its American National Theater (ANC), a program created and funded by congressional charter in 1935 but practically dormant since World War II. Peter Sellars, the wunderkind ANC director, could not win audiences or consistently good notices with his revisionist classics and took an indefinite leave.

Under artistic director Robert Brustein, the American Repertory Theater (ART) continued as a lighthouse for stunning classic and avant-garde works. Robert Wilson, the scenarist-designer whose mysterious, monumental "operas" were acclaimed in some quarters—and condemned in others—as the vanguard of a wholly imagistic, nonverbal movement in theater, had a rare production, based on Euripedes' *Alcestis,* at ART.

Garland Wright, a Texan known for his buoyant, stylish regional stagings of Molière and other classic writers, was named artistic director of the Guthrie of Minneapolis, considered the flagship of regional theaters. At Actors Theatre of Louisville, critical coverage of the Humana Festival of New American Plays, which had been enthusiastic during the late 1970s and early 1980s, fell off sharply in 1986. But the theater unveiled a new program of national interest—*Classics in Context*—an intensive program of coordinated plays, exhibits, lectures, and symposia.

A full-page article in *Time* magazine testified to the new prestige of the San Diego theater scene, centered around the Old Globe and its Shakespeare program, and the young La Jolla Playhouse under the adventurous leadership of Des McAnuff. Elsewhere on the West Coast, the founding artistic director of San Francisco's faltering American Conservatory Theatre, William Ball, stepped down after nearly 30 years.

DAN HULBERT, *"The Dallas Times Herald"*

TRANSPORTATION

Transportation activities in the United States closely paralleled the general economy during 1986, i.e., slow growth but accelerated restructuring between and within the various sectors. The nation's sluggish economic growth and mounting trade deficit had a dramatic impact on the domestic transportation industries. Total freight expenditures declined slightly as a percentage of the gross national product (GNP), a trend that may be attributable more to increased imports than to increased transportation efficiencies.

Even though overall earnings were relatively flat, a surprising number of long- and short-term events revealed the continuing restructuring of the U.S. transportation industry. Merger and acquisition activity increased dramatically during 1986, with trucking firms turning more to the equity markets for financing and the $50-billion-a-year airline industry undergoing radical realignment. Competition remained keen in the air-freight and courier businesses, but consolidation of carriers generally continued in all modes of transportation. Price competition in all of the domestic transportation industries remained intense because of deregulation, excess capacity, and new entrants in the for-hire markets. Consequently, a wave of bankruptcies continued to plague various segments, especially trucking. And layoffs, strikes, and other labor issues figured prominently in the restructuring process.

Airlines. The year 1986 was one of the most turbulent for the U.S. airline industry since deregulation in 1978. Unregulated competition affected everyone from passengers to employees to stockholders. Domestic traffic increased, but so did passenger complaints of flight delays and cancellations. Although no major rate war erupted, price competition remained fierce. Airline earnings were depressed, causing a shakeout of carriers. The number of commuter airlines declined, and the industry as a whole underwent major realignment as the result of bankruptcies, mergers, and acquisitions.

Among the major deals consummated during the year were Northwest Orient's purchase of Republic for $884 million, announced in January; TWA's acquisition of Ozark for $250 million in February; the merger of Delta and Western in an $860 million deal announced in September; and Texas Air's purchase of Eastern for $600 million in July and of People Express for $298 million in September (later reduced to $254 million). People Express faced serious financial difficulties, in large part because of losses registered by Frontier Airlines, which it acquired in November 1985. United agreed to buy Frontier in mid-1986 but could not come to terms with the Air Line Pilots Association over pay for Frontier pilots. And so in late August, Frontier shut down and began bankruptcy proceedings. Texas Air's acquisition of People Express made it the largest U.S. airline and the world's second largest carrier behind the Soviet Aeroflot.

Another post-deregulation trend that continued in 1986 was hub-and-spoke operations. Because this system depends largely on feeder traffic, all major carriers entered marketing agreements with or, as in the case of Delta and Presidential, acquired commuter carriers. Those that made no such arrangements experienced financial problems or departed the for-hire market. American Airlines established a new hub at Nashville, TN, and planned to open another in Raleigh, NC, to compete with Piedmont. United established a new hub at Dulles Airport in Washington, DC. And Delta established one in Cincinnati. In other developments, Eastern started requiring reservations for Boston-New York-Washington shuttle flights, with Pan Am starting shuttle service between New York City and Boston.

U.S. overseas carriers Pan Am, TWA, and American suffered traffic declines on European routes because of fears of terrorism. (*See also* TRAVEL). Pan Am levied a surcharge on international passengers to pay for security measures. In reaching an agreement with the U.S. government over bilateral air rights, Swiss Air consented to discount fares.

Following a string of disastrous accidents in 1985, air safety became a central issue. As the traffic lanes became even more congested, safety measures continued to be a source of controversy between the Federal Aviation Administration (FAA), Air Line Pilots Association, and National Transportation Safety Board. The FAA increased the intensity of its domestic carrier inspections and levied fines against such major airlines as Eastern ($9.5 million), Pan Am ($1.95 million), and American ($1.5 million) for violating federal regulations. The collision of a Mexican jetliner and a small private plane over southern California on August 31, in which 82 people were killed, led the FAA to adopt new regulations concerning the entry of private planes into restricted areas over the nation's 23 busiest airports.

Railroads. U.S. railroad industry earnings were relatively flat during 1986, even though the number of contracts with shippers expanded. And while average return on investment exceeded 5%, the Interstate Commerce Commission declared the industry "revenue inadequate." The granting of rate relief exacerbated the relationship between carriers and captive shippers, as the latter faced higher movement costs. Meanwhile, numerous complaints regarding excessive connecting charges were levied against trunkline carriers by short-line firms, and a major lobbying campaign was mounted to seek relief.

As in the airline industry, major companies faced financial difficulties and merger activity

Employees of Frontier Airlines, right, are glum and the airline's planes at Denver's Stapleton International Airport, above, and elsewhere are grounded as the company shut down and declared bankruptcy in August.

Photos, © Eric Bakke, Photostaff

was heavy. Burlington-Northern and Union Pacific Railroad charged $600 million in writedowns of non-rail assets. Union Pacific completed its merger with Missouri Pacific, but the ICC rejected a proposed merger between the Santa Fe and the Southern Pacific Railroad.

Despite the opposition of truckers and the Teamsters, rail carriers continued the trend toward "intermodalism." During 1986 the Burlington Northern alone acquired six trucklines for their operations, and CCX consummated its purchase of a barge line. Meanwhile, Union Pacific acquired Overnight Transportation, a nonunion motor carrier. Major trunkline carriers continued to abandon trackage, but a number of new short-line carriers, such as Arkansas

Missouri, emerged to provide additional service.

Carrier marketing continued to focus on piggyback, the longhaul movement of certain commodities between major railheads. "Double stacking" of containers by steamship lines represents a new form of competition for the industry, a force that the railroad industry has reacted to by adding more piggyback trains.

In one of the key developments of the year, Congress approved legislation that ended two years of debate over how to return Conrail, the federally owned freight railroad, to the private sector. The Reagan administration favored selling the carrier to Norfolk Southern, but the legislation called for a $2 billion public sale of

Conrail stock. It would be the largest public stock offering in Wall Street history.

A major labor dispute over work rules started with the Gulleford System in New England and soon spread to other lines. To settle the issues, President Ronald Reagan appointed a special emergency board under provisions of the Railroad Labor Act.

Trucking. U.S. motor trucking earnings remained generally flat (less than 8% of return on equity) during 1986, although such companies as Yellow Freight and Consolidated scored impressive increases. The level of concentration among less-than-truckload (LTL) general freight carriers continued, and two major carriers—McLean and Hall's Motor Freight—filed for Chapter 11 bankruptcy protection. As of 1986, a total of 87 LTL carriers had declared bankruptcy since 1980. Unemployment exceeded 126,000 in this segment of the industry, but more than 3,000 new truckload carriers entered the market during 1986. Heavy rate discounting remained pervasive, with several carriers levying charges of price discrimination against major carriers. In response to the discounting, many carriers have combated their cost problems by adopting Employee Stock Ownership Programs (ESOPs). Other notable activities of the year included the spin-off of Sun Carriers, a motor freight company, from Sun Oil Corporation; the continued expansion into Canada of Roadway, Consolidated Freightways, and Yellow Freight; and Roadway's new Roadway Package Express to compete with United Parcel Service.

The major issue of the year for U.S. trucking, however, was insurance. By 1986 several thousand carriers had been forced to depart the for-hire truck market because of their inability to secure or afford adequate insurance. In addition, the ICC every day was revoking carriers' certificates and permits because of lack of insurance. Some carriers turned to foreign captive insurance companies, and the ICC permitted some limited self-insurance. The American Trucking Association (ATA) even considered forming an insurance firm to provide coverage, though it did not pursue the matter to any meaningful extent.

As an amendment to the anti-drug legislation passed in October, Congress approved a requirement that the federal government set national standards for the licensing of commercial truck and bus drivers. The measure calls for states to issue "classified" licenses, specifying the type of vehicle a driver would be eligible to operate, and to require a road test in the same type of vehicle; the legislation also makes it illegal for a driver to hold a commercial license from more than one state.

Earlier in the year, Sen. Robert Packwood (R-OR) introduced legislation to deregulate the trucking industry. To win industry backing, Packwood included an amendment that would have allowed designated western states to give "longer combination vehicles" (LCVs) greater access to interstate highways. However, the bill died in the Senate Commerce Committee.

Maritime Shipping. Plagued by excess capacity and fierce price competition, the international shipping industry faced its worst slump in decades. The United States, which had about 20 general cargo lines in 1970, had only seven in 1986. Among U.S. inland water carriers, a number of barge line operators filed for bankruptcy. Intense competition with rail carriers and low water levels in the Southeast held traffic movements below 1985 totals. Deteriorating demand for shipping by the agricultural sector contributed to the excess capacity and depressed rates.

GRANT M. DAVIS, *University of Arkansas*

A new $320 million light-rail public transit system went into service in Portland, OR, in September. Dubbed MAX (Metropolitan Area Express), the 15-mi (24-km) railway links the city's downtown with its east side.

© Michael C. Hayman/Photo Researchers

Americans tended to travel in their own country in 1986 and enjoy such spots as Mackinac Island, MI, above.

TRAVEL

Americans did an about-face in their travel habits in 1986, and the principal reason was a concern for personal safety. With the threat of attack by political terrorists foremost in their minds, they slammed the brakes on the steady stream of traffic to Europe of the past several years. Instead they opted for destinations perceived as less vulnerable or traveled in their own country.

Americans who did travel overseas reported a noticeable increase in security measures at airports, rail stations, and other public places—and few complained about any inconvenience. Cruise ships instituted more identity checks and screening devices and also, in many cases, restricted or even eliminated shipboard visitors. Another sign of the times was the requirement of visas to visit France starting late in the year after a spate of bombing incidents there—the first such requirement in decades for Americans vacationing in France.

Staying Home. A combination of circumstances helped make 1986 a healthy year for U.S. domestic travel. Along with the fear of terrorism abroad, cheaper gasoline, and less favorable foreign exchange rates, a couple of major tourist events on either coast served as travel magnets. In Vancouver, Canada, Expo 86 exceeded attendance expectations and attracted many U.S. vacationers (*see* special report, page 161). The Pacific Northwest and northern California benefited substantially from Expo-bound traffic, and both Amtrak and the American Automobile Association (AAA) reported increased travel on routes to Vancouver and throughout the West. On the East Coast, the reopening of the renovated Statue of Liberty in New York City seemed to be at least partially responsible for an influx of visitors that raised summer hotel occupancy throughout New York State by 13.7%.

Overall, the AAA reported a 4.3% increase in trip routing requests for the first nine months of the year—6.8% for the third quarter. Amtrak registered a bigger than usual 17% jump in passenger miles and revenue through September, the end of its fiscal year. Fare wars also helped account for a 12% increase in domestic air travel during the first half of the year. Hawaii and Alaska both did exceptionally well in 1986. Still, it was a little hard to characterize the year from the standpoint of domestic travel. While travel was up in general, some parts of the country did remarkably well while others failed to live up to expectations. And while vacation trips during the critical June and July months rose 3.5%, those vacations seemed to be shorter than in past years.

The United States welcomed a projected 8.4 million overseas travelers in 1986, some 11% more than in 1985. Strong sources of overseas visitors were Japan, West Germany, France, and Great Britain. Travel from Canada to the United States was static, however, and travel from Mexico dropped.

Going Abroad. Reversing the strong outward-bound trend of the past several years, overseas travel by Americans dropped by about 10% in 1986—from about 12,700,000 overseas travelers in 1985 to an estimated 11,450,000 in 1986. In contrast, some 14,155,000 Americans visited Canada—a 17% increase. Travel to Mexico dropped by some 10%, with 3,185,000 Americans heading south of the border. The big loser was Europe. Terrorist incidents in Europe in 1985 and 1986 changed Americans' travel patterns dramatically, with airline and travel agents reporting immediate drops in business of 50% and more following the April bombing of a TWA jet, en route from Rome to Athens, and the subsequent U.S. air raid on Libya. Then the Soviet nuclear disaster at Chernobyl further increased travelers' wariness, though its impact on bookings seemed to be shorter-lived.

To lure American travelers back across the Atlantic, airlines offered free car rentals, free domestic air tickets, special prizes, and reassurances of beefed-up security programs. By the latter half of the year, travel by Americans to Europe was approaching more normal levels, but the estimated final tally of 4.8 million fell far short of 1985's record-breaking figure of 6.4 million.

Travel in the opposite direction fared better. Australia and other South Pacific destinations were increasingly popular with Americans. Transpacific travel continued to be spurred on by accelerated trade relations between the United States and Pacific rim nations, and a number of new transpacific air links were introduced. Elsewhere, the Caribbean was the vacation destination of many Americans in 1986.

Cruising. An estimated 2.3 million Americans set sail on cruise ships in 1986—15% more than 1985's record passenger figures. What was new was their choice of destinations, thanks largely to the repositioning of many ships away from the Mediterranean because of the perceived threat of terrorism.

Alaska was the year's cruising success story. Both the transfer of ships from the Mediterranean and the regional draw of Expo 86 helped make this a particularly popular cruise destination for Americans. The east coast of Canada and New England also saw an upswing of cruise activity as cruise lines sought alternative ports. In the South Pacific, cruises scheduled to offer Halley's Comet views were sellouts. China continued to do well, and South America began to emerge as a significant cruise destination. The popular Caribbean cruise circuit became yet more crowded, remaining one place where ship passengers could expect to find bargains as cruise lines sought to fill an abundance of berths.

New ships introduced in 1986 pointed to two opposite trends: the megaship and the intimate luxury cruiser. Among the new ships were Home Lines' *Homeric,* with 1,000-plus passenger capacity; Carnival Cruise Lines' 1,500-passenger *Jubilee;* and, on the other end of the size scale, Windstar Sail Cruises' 150-passenger sail-driven *Wind Star.* A number of new vessels, from small to jumbo, are expected to enter service in 1987 and 1988—including the world's biggest, a 2,500-passenger liner to be operated by Royal Caribbean Cruise Line.

A continuing trend in 1986 was for cruise lines to offer shorter trips, as they tried to reach more first-time cruisers in younger age brackets. Many lines also emphasized health and fitness programs, with extensive fitness facilities becoming standard on new ships.

New Directions. As airline deregulation entered what appeared to be its final shakedown phase and more air carriers consolidated, the super-duper discount fare appeared to be on the decline. Although occasional cut-rate fares could still be found on heavily traveled routes, some domestic air fares were raised during the latter part of 1986.

Travelers also continue to be introduced to the growing uses of modern technology, as more and more computerized information and travel-booking services become available to them. They were able to call up data about weather, flight schedules, hotel-room availability, and special events on monitor screens in airports, hotels, shopping centers, and so on. Some airlines made computerized general travel information and flight facts available to consumers via the buttons on their home phones. And some hotel chains introduced in-room checkout procedures via computers.

The year also saw a stronger wooing of the "senior" travel market. A number of airlines, hotels, and tour companies offered special travel clubs and discounts in an effort to attract passengers over a certain age.

PHYLLIS ELVING, *Free-lance Travel Writer*

AP/Wide World

Cruises to Alaska have become increasingly popular with vacationers. The "Sagafjord," left, was one of several ships to offer such a holiday in 1986.

Air Security and Safety

© F. Duhamel/Sygma

A midair collision over Los Angeles in August 1986, following a spate of accidents the previous year, made aviation safety as much of a concern as security against terrorism for U.S. and world travelers.

On New Year's Day 1986, armored vehicles surrounded London's Heathrow airport while armed troops patrolled the three terminal buildings. The highly visible joint army-police exercise was a show of force to deter terrorism.

The action followed simultaneous attacks less than a week earlier by Arab terrorists at El Al Israel Airlines check-in counters at Rome's Leonardo da Vinci and Vienna's Schwechat airports which left 19 dead and more than 100 wounded. The International Civil Aviation Organization (ICAO) cited 25 incidents of violence at international airports between 1973 and 1985 and an average of 32 hijackings per year over the past decade. The year 1986 saw several more major terrorist attacks on the world's airline network. (See TERRORISM.)

Airline and Airport Security. In response to the increase in such terrorist attacks, airports and airlines have taken increasingly comprehensive protective measures. Evidence of enhanced security could be seen throughout 1986 in the form of armed guards patrolling airport terminals, more thorough hand examination and X-raying of both checked and carry-on luggage, passenger body searches, and in some cases, the holding of cargo for 24 hours.

Armed U.S. air marshals, approved for international flights through bilateral agreements, were sent to potential trouble spots worldwide. U.S. Federal Aviation Administration (FAA) security agents were dispatched to foreign airports to provide technical assistance to U.S. carriers and to airports. The key to airport security became visibility. Would-be terrorists were to be discouraged from perpetrating their crimes by convincing them that their plans would be foiled.

Fear of terrorist activity took its toll on airline passenger traffic from the very beginning of the year. According to a U.S. Travel Data Center survey taken in February 1986, 1.8 million U.S. residents had changed their reservations to foreign countries following the most recent terrorist activity. An estimated 1.4 million had either canceled a foreign trip or changed to a domestic destination.

The net impact in terms of loss to the airlines was estimated to reach $700 million–$1 billion by the end of 1986. The perceived threat of terrorism and the accident at the Soviet nuclear power plant in Chernobyl combined to cause precipitous declines in passenger traffic to Europe.

The airlines became more actively involved in creating a secure environment for their passengers and employees. Pan Am, for instance, formed Alert, a security unit that includes detection experts and equipment to screen passengers, employees, baggage, airport facilities, and aircraft at all Pan Am locations. Alert serves as the primary security arm at the airline's domestic locations and a supplemental service at its overseas terminals, where local authorities have primary responsibility. American Airlines also implemented more stringent security measures for its flights between the United States and Europe, including requiring passport information when making transatlantic reservations, X-ray screening or hand inspection of all checked baggage, use of a questionnaire about baggage at all U.S. cities, and a comprehensive predeparture inspection of all aircraft serving Europe.

A report released in August 1986 by the U.S. House of Representatives Foreign Affairs Committee Task Force on International Terrorism and Diplomatic Security, entitled "The Adequacy of Foreign Airport Security," recommended that foreign carriers serving the United States be required to institute security procedures equivalent to those required of American carriers, thus ensuring a universally high level of security. The committee suggested that the FAA reorganize the security structure to provide more expertise overseas and that the role of air marshals be expanded to give them a greater security role on the ground.

Other proposals included streamlining the gathering and sharing of intelligence on security matters, providing additional security at airports to combat the threat of international terrorism, and reaching more bilateral and multilateral agreements to strengthen airport and aircraft security. Greater emphasis on screening passengers and carry-on baggage also was recommended.

In releasing the report, Committee chairman Dante B. Fascell (D-FL) called for strengthening the role of the ICAO in enforcing security standards for international airports and in developing sanctions against nations that refuse to enforce security or otherwise support terrorism.

Aviation Safety. Unfortunately, terrorism was not the only threat to the safety of the airline passenger in 1986. In the United States the FAA continued its crackdown, begun in 1985, on airline maintenance practices. Yet the FAA itself was under the magnifying glass throughout the year, defending itself against allegations that it was ill-equipped to monitor an industry that has grown in complexity following deregulation.

A report, written by six retired FAA inspectors, conflicted with the official government conclusion that 95% of U.S. airlines met or exceeded federal safety standards at the time of the National Air Transportation Inspection in 1984. According to the 1986 study, one of every three FAA airline inspections unearthed safety discrepancies, and the incidence of serious violations was high.

In May 1986 the FAA countered that it had been conducting an aggressive airline inspection program, having made 17 inspections since January and adding one inspection each month. Yet the U.S. General Accounting Office (GAO) joined critics of the FAA, contending that the agency had been slow in preparing for the changes caused by deregulation, including the increasing numbers of airlines and aircraft. The FAA inspector work force, for example, was reduced by 34% from 1978 to 1983, from more than 2,000 inspectors to 1,332. The result has been an overworked inspector force that is unable to monitor the industry effectively. In one case, an inspector was documented as being responsible for 39 airlines.

U.S. Secretary of Transportation Elizabeth Hanford Dole said she intends to increase the inspector work force by 500 by 1988. Secretary Dole also denied any connection between airline deregulation and a decline in air safety. She said that of the 1,622 persons who died in air crashes in 1985, 70% died while traveling on foreign airlines. Dole described the U.S. accident rate as the lowest in ten years.

The system is getting safer, but is it safe now? Airline pilots—who are as concerned about safety as any passenger, and well qualified to assess the safety of air travel—generally respond that they "wouldn't be up there" if they were not confident of the system's inherent safety. But the August 31 midair collision near Los Angeles of an Aeromexico DC-9 with a Piper Archer focused attention on one area of grave concern to all pilots—private aircraft operating through terminal control areas. In the aftermath of the crash, the FAA passed a series of new regulations for private planes flying over the 23 busiest U.S. airports. It also planned to require more small planes to be equipped with transponders (which signal air-traffic controllers of their altitude) and airlines to be equipped with a device to warn of approaching aircraft.

CECILIA PREBLE

TUNISIA

Political infighting and demonstrations of opposition took place against a backdrop of mounting economic pressure during 1986.

Government and Opposition. The government of President Habib Bourguiba continued its effort to weaken the powerful General Union of Tunisian Workers (UGTT). After closing the UGTT's headquarters and arresting its secretary-general late in 1985, the government revived the union under new leadership. Despite strikes and protests, pro-government factions took charge. Ismail Laraji became the UGTT's new secretary-general, and in June, Bourguiba named him to the political bureau of the ruling Destourian Socialist Party (PSD).

Meanwhile, opposition political parties continued to press their case against the government. These included the Movement of Social Democrats (MDS), the Communist Party, the Progressive Socialist Movement, the Popular Unity Movement (MUP), and the Islamic Tendency Movement (MTI). In a rare show of unity, all five parties in February formed the Committee for Solidarity with UGTT and for the Defense of Democratic Freedom.

MDS leader Ahmed Mestiri was arrested in April and sentenced to four months in prison for organizing a demonstration against the U.S. raid on Libya. The conviction prevented Mestiri from running in future elections, since anyone sentenced to three months in prison may not serve in parliament. In early November, 14 officials of the Progressive Socialist Movement were arrested and sentenced to six months in prison. The most powerful opposition party remained the MTI, which was tolerated but not officially recognized and thus not eligible to participate in elections.

All opposition parties boycotted the National Assembly elections of November 2, and PSD candidates thus captured all 125 seats.

Leadership Changes. By early in the year it had become clear that Prime Minister Mohamed Mzali, Bourguiba's designated successor, had fallen out of favor with the president. Among the apparent reasons for Mzali's disfavor were the nation's economic problems and his advocacy of a dialogue with opposition movements. The first major sign of Mzali's eroding authority came in April, when Bourguiba replaced several of his supporters in the cabinet. Then in July, Mzali himself was replaced as prime minister by Rachid Sfar, who had been the finance minister. That post was filled by Ismail Khelil. Mzali fled the country in September and was tried in absentia for crossing the border illegally.

President Bourguiba, who turned 83, also broke with his son and wife during the year, accusing both of political maneuvering. Habib, Jr., lost his post as special presidential adviser in January; both he and his mother, Wassila,

TUNISIA · Information Highlights

Official Name: Republic of Tunisia.
Location: North Africa.
Area: 63,170 sq mi (163 610 km²).
Population (mid-1986 est.): 7,200,000.
Chief City (1984 census): Tunis, the capital, 1,349,749, district population.
Government: *Head of state*, Habib Bourguiba, president for life (took office 1957). Rachid Sfar, prime minister (took office July 8, 1986). *Legislature* (Unicameral)—National Assembly.
Monetary Unit: Dinar (.786 dinar equals U.S.$1, June 1986).
Gross National Product (1985 U.S.$): $9,300,000,000.
Economic Indexes (1985): *Consumer Prices* (1980 = 100), all items, 117.1; food, 119.8. *Industrial Production* (1983, 1980 = 100), 112.
Foreign Trade (1985 U.S.$): *Imports,* $2,597,000,000; *exports,* $1,627,000,000.

were banished from the presidential palace. Wassila went into exile in the United States, and in August it was announced that the president had divorced her.

Bourguiba's domination of political life was further evidenced at the PSD Party Congress in June. He personally appointed the 90-member Central Committee, which normally is elected, as well as the 20-member Politburo.

Economy. Poor rains increased the need for agricultural imports, and this, along with falling revenues from oil exports and tourism, compounded a serious current-accounts deficit. With Tunisia's foreign debt approaching $5 billion, the International Monetary Fund (IMF) relieved short-term financial pressure by providing a stand-by loan of $240 million in August. At IMF and World Bank urging, the Sfar government proposed austerity measures and economic reforms. The former included a 10% currency devaluation, a $140 million cut in government spending, and gradual removal of price subsidies on basic commodities. Reforms included a reduction in state-directed economic activity and an expansion of the private sector, to be led by agriculture and export industries. These elements were embodied in the 1987–1991 economic development plan, issued late in the year.

MARK TESSLER
University of Wisconsin-Milwaukee

TURKEY

The year 1986 was an active one for Turkey on both the domestic and international scenes.

Internal Developments. One of the year's key trends was the continuing increase in the number of political parties qualified to take part in national elections. Some 12 parties contested parliamentary by-elections in September. The democratic left continued its development following the late 1985 merger of its two major parties, the Populist Party and the Social Dem-

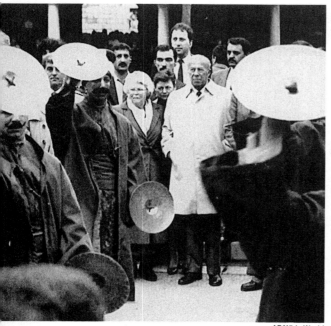

AP/Wide World

A Janissary Band welcomes U.S. Secretary of State and Mrs. George Shultz to Turkey. During the March visit Turkish officials demanded that a new agreement on U.S. military bases be tied to trade and other concessions.

ocrat Party, into the Social Democrat Populist Party. The dissolution of the Nationalist Democracy Party in May left the Motherland Party of Prime Minister Turgut Ozal, with 231 of the 400 seats in parliament, as the only survivor of the three parties that had contested the 1983 general elections. Several new parties emerged on the right, particularly the Truth Path party (which had close ties to former Prime Minister Suleyman Demirel) and the Free Democrat party. The increasing political fragmentation and the reemergence of old political leaders disappointed those who had hoped that the reshaping of the political structure under the 1983 constitution would prevent the instability cited as a major factor in the 1980 military takeover.

Internal security problems remained, although martial law was lifted in all but the five southeastern largely Kurdish-speaking provinces; 11 of the 67 provinces remained under a less severe state of emergency. A number of clashes between government forces and Kurdish separatists took place, and trials of political radicals arrested after the 1980 coup dragged on the military courts.

There was optimism about Turkey's long-range economic prospects despite continuing economic problems. Inflation was still considered the country's most serious problem by the Turkish public, and few believed that the goal of reducing it from 40% in 1985 to 25% in 1986 would be achieved. Exports, particularly to other Middle Eastern countries, continued strong, however, and economic growth continued at about 5%. A number of major new projects, including the construction of a second bridge over the Bosphorus and important additions to energy facilities, were initiated. Turkey's first nuclear power plant is to be built with technical and financial assistance from Canada. Efforts to develop a private capital market were undertaken with the opening of the reorganized Istanbul stock exchange and the public sale of shares in industries and public projects.

The 1985 census results, released in 1986, showed an annual rate of population growth of 2.78% since 1980. This was higher than all but one five-year period since World War II.

Foreign Affairs. President Kenan Evren's official visits included Tunisia, Egypt, Qatar, and Hungary. Prime Minister Ozal traveled to Iran, Great Britain, Iraq, India, Italy, Romania, and the USSR. Heads of state or government visiting Turkey included those of West Germany, Algeria, Sri Lanka, Pakistan, and China. U.S. Secretary of State George Shultz also visited Turkey, and relations between the two nations remained cordial despite their failure to reach accord on the renewal of the agreement under which the United States leases several military bases in Turkey. Their differences centered on Turkish requests for increased military shipments and more liberal import quotas for textiles and steel.

Turkey and Greece remained bitterly at odds over Cyprus despite new efforts by United Nations Secretary-General Javier Pérez de Cuéllar to settle the dispute. Turkey continued its efforts to publicize the suppression of the rights of the Turkish ethnic minority in Bulgaria.

In September two gunmen, suspected to be Arabs, massacred 21 Turkish Jews at the Neve Shalom synagogue in Istanbul. The terrorist attack was condemned in Turkey, where Jews and Muslims have long coexisted peacefully.

TURKEY • Information Highlights

Official Name: Republic of Turkey.
Location: Southeastern Europe and southwestern Asia.
Area: 301,381 sq mi (780 576 km²).
Population (mid-1986 est.): 52,300,000.
Chief Cities (1980 census): Ankara, the capital, 1,877,755; Istanbul, 2,772,708; Izmir, 757,854.
Government: *Head of state,* Gen. Kenan Evren, president (took office Nov. 10, 1982. *Head of government,* Turgut Özal, prime minister (took office Dec. 13, 1983). *Legislature*—Grand National Assembly.
Monetary Unit: Lira (693.7 liras equal U.S. $1, Oct. 19, 1986).
Gross National Product (1984 U.S.$): $50,000,-000,000.
Economic Index (1985): *Consumer Prices* (1980 = 100), all items, 282.6; food, 278.5.
Foreign Trade (1985 U.S.$): *Imports,* $11,120,-000,000; *exports,* $7,918,000,000.

The Council of Europe signified its satisfaction with the restoration of Turkish democracy by electing Turkey to its regular turn as the Council's deputy chairman and later chairman.

WALTER F. WEIKER
Rutgers University

UGANDA

The second dramatic overthrow of the government in less than a year and attempts to restore social and economic order were the highlights of 1986 in Uganda.

The NRA Victory. The military government that overthrew Milton Obote in 1985, led by Gen. Tito Okello, and the National Resistance Army (NRA), led by Yoweri Museveni, signed a cease-fire agreement in December 1985 granting the NRA a substantial role in the government. The agreement, however, never came into effect. The NRA charged that the Okello regime continued to massacre and terrorize opponents and ethnic minorities and resumed hostilities in late January 1986. After a week of bitter fighting, NRA forces entered Kampala in triumph on January 26. Museveni was sworn in as Uganda's ninth head of state on January 29 and claimed control of the entire country by late March.

President Museveni. Yoweri Kaguta Museveni, a member of the Ankole ethnic group of southern Uganda, was born in 1944. He received a degree in economics and political science from the University of Dar es Salaam in Tanzania in 1970 and was a researcher for Milton Obote during the latter's first presidency (1966–71). Museveni went with Obote to Tanzania after Obote was overthrown by Idi Amin Dada. He later traveled to nationalist-held areas of Mozambique during its war against Portugal, where he learned techniques of political organization and guerrilla warfare.

Museveni returned to Uganda after Amin's overthrow in 1979 and served as defense minister in an interim government. After the December 1980 elections, which returned Obote to power but were widely considered fraudulent, Museveni broke with Obote and fled into the bush, where he launched the guerrilla movement later called the NRA and its political arm, the National Resistance Movement (NRM). Over the next five years, as hundreds of thousands of southern Ugandans were uprooted, tortured, and slaughtered by Obote's northern-dominated and ill-disciplined army in a brutal attempt to end the insurgency, support for Museveni and the NRA grew.

Museveni's Policies. Museveni's statements showed him to be a fervent nationalist, strongly anticolonial and vaguely Marxist in his views. He was openly contemptuous of most African leaders, stating that their corruption and/or incompetence had ruined their nations and made Africa an international tragedy.

Museveni named a 36-member National Resistance Council to serve as an interim parliament until the election of a constituent assembly to prepare a new constitution. His cabinet, while dominated by southerners, included representatives of all the old political parties.

Museveni openly favored the cities over rural areas in distributing scarce resources. Subsidies on sugar, fuel, and grain were continued. Coffee farmers, the source of most of Uganda's foreign exchange, still received only a small percentage of the final price for their crop despite a doubling of producer prices. In an attempt to channel spending into areas of greatest need, conserve scarce foreign exchange, and undermine the black market, the government introduced a two-tier exchange rate system similar to one adopted in 1982. Under this system, raw materials and consumer goods could be bought for one fourth the cost of other imports.

Social Reconstruction. Museveni faced the daunting task of restoring the idea and reality of law and order in Uganda after years of bloody brutality. One major priority was getting children back into school; the social anarchy they had known all their lives threatened the future stability of Uganda if peaceful habits could not be reintroduced.

The government confiscated weapons, ammunition, and uniforms wherever found, forbade roadblocks, and attempted to enforce rigorous discipline on its own troops. Scattered armed resistance continued, however, and on top of its other problems the country faced a possible epidemic of AIDS.

Foreign Affairs. At Entebbe in March, the heads of state of six neighboring countries pledged to support Museveni's efforts to unite and rebuild Uganda. Rail-cargo service between Kenya and Uganda resumed after a nine-year hiatus, and the two countries agreed to extend the Mombasa-Nairobi oil pipeline to Uganda. Museveni said he would maintain Uganda's nonaligned policy and appealed for international aid.

ROBERT GARFIELD, *DePaul University*

UGANDA • Information Highlights

Official Name: Republic of Uganda.
Location: Interior of East Africa.
Area: 91,075 sq mi (235 885 km²).
Population: (mid-1986 est.): 15,200,000.
Chief Cities (1980 census): Kampala, the capital, 458,423; Jinja, 45,060.
Government: *Head of state,* Yoweri Museveni, president (Jan. 29, 1986). *Head of government,* Samson Kisekka, prime minister (Jan. 30, 1986). *Legislature* (unicameral)—National Assembly.
Monetary Unit: Uganda shilling (1,400 shillings equal U.S. $1, July 1986).
Foreign Trade (1983–84 U.S.$): *Imports,* $509,000,000; (1984) *exports,* $399,000,000.

General Secretary Gorbachev reports to the Soviet people on the unsuccessful arms control talks in Iceland.

USSR

In the second year of the rule of General Secretary Mikhail Gorbachev, the Soviet Union moved hesitantly toward reform of both its political administration and economy. Although expectations of rapid or fundamental change were not realized, the steady replacement of older officials with younger ones more closely bound to Gorbachev continued through the year. With the new leadership apparently prepared to think through old problems in fresh ways, the image of the Kremlin improved in the West. Gorbachev and Foreign Minister Eduard Shevardnadze hammered away at the need for containing the nuclear arms race and restricting the development of space weapons. But even as the Soviet government encouraged "openness" in domestic discussion and better management of the state machine, the nuclear accident at Chernobyl brutally exposed old habits of state secrecy and deeply rooted inefficiencies and disorganization. Relations between the two superpowers did not realize the promise of the November 1985 Reagan-Gorbachev summit meeting, and little real progress was made in arms control or other major areas of difference. The Iceland summit in October came close to a far-reaching arms limitation agreement but foundered on the issue of a U.S. space-based defense system.

Domestic Affairs.

Party Congress. The Communist Party of the Soviet Union, whose total membership numbered about 18.5 million, held its 27th congress in Moscow from February 25 to March 6. The congress, held every five years, was the first of the Gorbachev era, and hopes for major changes accompanied the estimated 5,000 delegates who attended. General Secretary Gorbachev spoke candidly and forcefully in a five-and-a-half-hour keynote address, attacking the inertia, apathy, and administrative bureaucracy that had developed under previous leadership. He called for a more flexible system of economic management along with greater input from workers, but no gesture was made toward instituting the more radical types of market reforms adopted in Hungary and China.

Using the rhetoric of democracy, Gorbachev also encouraged greater openness and more publicity concerning shortcomings of the system. "Communists want the truth, always and under all circumstances," he said. "Government should not be the privilege of a narrow circle of professionals." A highlight of the ten-day congress was the adoption of a new party program, the first since 1961. Whereas the old rhetoric had called for a rapid transition to pure Communism—the classless, stateless society promised by Karl Marx—the new program spoke more cautiously of the "systematic and all-around improvement of socialism." Socialism was even said to include "genuine democracy—power exercised for the people and by the people." Yet, at the same time, the congress itself was conducted in the same stage-managed fashion as previous party gatherings, and the style—if not the substance—of the discussions differed little from those during the Leonid Brezhnev era. Rather than broaching far-ranging issues of foreign policy, cultural life, or the international Communist movement, speakers at the congress concentrated almost exclusively on problems of economic development. Several officials attacked nonconformists, dissident writers, and even video recorders, which, it was claimed, are used to spread alien ideas, immorality, and a cult of violence. Moscow party boss Boris Yeltsin attacked the special privileges and perks enjoyed by high-ranking officials, but Politburo member and party ideologist Yegor Ligachev took the party newspaper *Pravda* to task for publishing letters that were too critical of such privileges.

Leadership. Formally elected at the party congress, the realigned Politburo, Secretariat, and Central Committee represented further consolidation of the Gorbachev team.

Unlike the entirely septuagenarian Politburo of the later Brezhnev era, the new policy-making body had only five men in their seventies or eighties, eight in their sixties, and six in their fifties (including Gorbachev). In addition to Gorbachev, Shevardnadze, and Ligachev, the 12 full members included: Geidar Aliev, vice-chairman of the Council of Ministers; Vitaly Vorotnikov, prime minister of the Russian Republic; Andrei Gromyko, president; Lev Zaikov, party secretary in charge of economy and defense industry; Dinmukhammed Kunayev, first secretary of the Kazakh Communist Party; Nikolai Ryzhkov, premier; Mikhail Solomentsev, chairman of the Party Control Committee; Viktor Chebrikov, chairman of the KGB; and Vladimir Shcherbitsky, first secretary of the Ukrainian Communist Party. Gone were such Brezhnev favorites and potential Gorbachev rivals as Viktor Grishin, the long-time party boss of Moscow, and Grigory Romanov, his counterpart in Leningrad. In December, Kunayev was removed as head of the Kazakh party and replaced by an ethnic Russian, a move that set off student rioting in the republic capital of Alma-Ata.

The party Secretariat was expanded from 8 to 11 members, as two secretaries left the body and five new ones were added. Among the latter were Anatoly Dobrynin, the former ambassador to the United States, and Aleksandra Biryukhova, the first woman in 25 years to hold a high party office.

The dynamic tone of the new leadership was set in Yeltsin's congress speech, in which he denounced "time-servers in possession of party cards" and admitted that in the past he had "lacked the courage and political experience" to criticize failings of the party.

Economy. The top priority and greatest challenge for General Secretary Gorbachev was to get the stagnant Soviet economy moving again. His principal economic adviser, Abel Aganbegian, is known as a reformer, and in his keynote address at the party congress, Gorbachev called for "radical reform" of the nation's economic management. He favored a radical revision of the pricing system and greater autonomy for local farm and plant managers. The new Five-Year Plan (1986–90) approved at the congress featured the goals of more and better-quality consumer goods.

Nevertheless, Gorbachev promised that there would be no retreat from the principles of "planned economic guidance," and the thrust of reforms in 1986 were toward more efficient allocation of resources, automation, and computerization, rather than widespread implementation of market mechanisms. Some thought was given to small-scale private enterprise in such areas as auto repair and home renovation. With some 17–20 million people involved in illegal private service trades, the regime hoped to create incentives to bring these activities into the legal economy. But resistance to innovation was pervasive, especially from entrenched enterprise managers and bureaucrats used to doing business in the old way of fulfilling plan targets. Gorbachev complained publicly that there are people "among us who have difficulty grasping the word restructuring and sometimes even have difficulty pronouncing it." At the June plenum of the Central Committee, the general secretary asserted that a "fossilized mentality" among managers was blocking modernization, and he called for greater decentralization in the industrial bureaucracy. Measures were taken to give local governments and enterprises greater authority in distributing surplus consumer goods.

Soviet economists also showed greater interest in working with the capitalist world. The USSR asked for observer status at the General Agreement on Tariffs and Trade (GATT) meeting in September. The International Monetary Fund and the World Bank were referred to positively in the Soviet press. And Japanese and Finnish businessmen were invited to consider joint ventures with Soviet enterprises. Gorbachev even spoke about opening up Vladivostok, a city closed to foreigners, and creating a major international seat of trade and culture.

Meanwhile, Gorbachev's ongoing campaigns against alcoholism and for increased labor discipline contributed to some impressive economic and demographic statistics. Industrial output grew 5.6% in the first half of 1986 (compared with the same period in 1985), while labor productivity in industry rose 5.2%. Oil production, however, was still below plan targets, as was the output of the machine tool industry. Although the high prices for wine and vodka were very unpopular, as were the long lines that formed at the reduced number of outlets for alcohol, statistics on infant mortality and life expectancy (which previously had been suppressed) showed improvements. The infant mortality rate had declined markedly from the high point of 1974, and deaths from accidents, poisoning, and injuries had declined by 24% since June 1985.

The weak spot in Soviet economic performance remained agriculture, an area of special interest to Gorbachev. During his short tenure, neither the extraordinarily poor harvest of the last year of Brezhnev's rule (1981) nor the bumper crops of the mid-1970s were repeated. The year 1985 saw a respectable grain harvest of 191.6 million metric tons, but the 1986 harvest was expected to be somewhat smaller.

Chernobyl. The April 26 explosion and fire at the nuclear power plant at Chernobyl in the Ukraine created a serious environmental crisis and political embarrassment for the Soviet Union. The accident in the station's Number 4 reactor spewed a radioactive cloud that spread over the Ukraine and other European nations. An estimated 135,000 people were evacuated from the area of the plant, at least 30 people died, and several hundred were hospitalized. One of the most immediate casualties was the credibility of the Gorbachev regime, which hesitated to release information on the accident for several days. Wild rumors and sensational stories of thousands of deaths filled the Western press, and when Gorbachev finally spoke to the nation in a May 14 televised address, he condemned the "very shameless and malignant lies" of Western governments and media.

After their initial silence the Soviet media were filled with daily reports on the consequences of the accident, on individual and collective heroism, and on the difficulties of quenching the burning reactor. A detailed report was made to an international meeting on atomic energy in Vienna, but very little hard data was given on the levels of radiation released into the atmosphere. Information on the cause and full extent of the accident remained scarce for several months, and only in the summer were the officials responsible for the disaster removed from their positions. (*See also* special report, page 218.)

Culture and Dissent. In late 1985 the controversial Soviet poet Yevgeny Yevtushenko boldly told the Congress of Russian Writers that the new openness advocated by the party leadership required writers to foresake silence. His hope was that "self-flattery will be forever rejected and that nonconcealment will become the norm of civic behavior." At the time the Union of Soviet Writers held its congress in June 1986, Gorbachev met privately with the writers and encouraged them to be even more daring. The poet Andrei Voznesensky demanded the full publication of the works of Boris Pasternak, the 1958 Nobel Prize-winning writer whose novel *Doctor Zhivago* was still banned in the USSR. Conservative members of the literary establishment were attacked, and both Yevtushenko and Voznesensky were elected to the executive bureau of the union.

Radical changes in the system of censorship were undertaken during the year, though the full contours of the reforms were not yet clear. Rumors circulated that Glavlit, the state's principal censorship committee, was to have its role restricted only to military and national-security matters. More visible were the activities of artists and intellectuals seeking to dissipate the stagnant atmosphere of the past. The Union of Cinematographers elected as its leader Elem Klimov, a controversial filmmaker whose film *Agony* (*Rasputin*) had been held back for years by the censors. Klimov immediately set up a committee of filmmakers to review cinematic works that had been rejected by the official State Committee for Cinematography. In the realm of theater, new plays were staged which explored such hitherto forbidden themes as the collectivization of the peasantry, the 1962 Cuban missile crisis, and the evils of Stalinism. An allegorical Georgian film, *Repentance*, dealt with the mysterious and malevolent figure of Beria, one of Stalin's closest associates and the longtime head of the Soviet secret police. Voznesensky published a long poem about Soviet anti-Semitism, and the novelist Anatoly

AP/Wide World

Ailing dissident Yuri Orlov (seated), who had been condemned to internal exile in Siberia, was allowed to leave the Soviet Union on October 5. He was joined on the plane to the United States by journalist Nicholas Daniloff (rear, seated) and industrialist Armand Hammer (shaking hands).

Rybakov received permission to publish a work in which Stalin himself would be a major figure. Works by the long-neglected émigré writer Vladimir Nabokov were printed for the first time in Soviet journals, as was the verse of Nikolai Gumilev, a poet who had been shot as a counterrevolutionary in 1921.

But even as the regime was allowing greater cultural freedom, the problem of human-rights violations and restrictions on emigration continued to haunt the Gorbachev government. The general secretary admitted in an interview with the French press that about 200 persons were being held in prisons for trying to subvert Soviet society. He also refused to allow Andrei Sakharov, the human-rights activist and 1975 Nobel Peace Prize recipient, to emigrate abroad because of his knowledge of state secrets. In December, however, Sakharov and his wife, Elena Bonner, were released from internal exile in the Volga city of Gorky and permitted to return to Moscow. Earlier that month it was learned that another prominent dissident, Anatoly Marchenko, age 48, had died in prison.

In February the Soviet authorities did release Jewish dissident Anatoly Shcharansky in exchange for spies and later allowed members of his family to join him in Israel. Stalin's daughter, Svetlana Alliluyeva, who had returned to the USSR in 1984 after defecting to the West nearly 20 years earlier, was granted a request to leave the Soviet Union with her daughter. The dissidents Yuri Orlov and David Goldfarb, as well as several members of divided families also were permitted to emigrate. In general, the year saw some accommodation by the Soviets on the issue of emigration, though no broad solution to the problem of Jewish "refuseniks" was put forward. But the year did end with some optimism that Soviet policy on human rights would improve under the Gorbachev regime.

Foreign Affairs

Arms Control and U.S. Relations. Following the Geneva summit of November 1985, Gorbachev called for a worldwide ban on nuclear weapons by the year 2000 as well as a three-month extension of the Soviet moratorium on nuclear testing, begun in August. The United States was unenthusiastic about the test ban and continued its own underground testing program. In December, Moscow announced that it would end its moratorium as soon as the United States conducts its first test in 1987.

The Soviets also proposed a reduction in their strategic anti-ballistic missiles if the United States would agree to strengthen the Anti-Ballistic Missile (ABM) Treaty of 1972. Washington, however, called for a revision of the treaty to permit implementation of the U.S. Strategic Defense Initiative, (SDI, or "Star

AP/Wide World

Anatoly F. Dobrynin, the Soviet ambassador to the United States for 24 years, and his wife returned to Moscow in April. Dobrynin, 66, became a member of the Secretariat.

Wars") program. More ominous for the Soviet Union was the confusion over whether the United States intended to abrogate the SALT II agreement of 1979. In May, President Reagan said that the United States would not comply with the limitations established in the treaty if the Soviets continued to violate them. (The Kremlin disclaimed any violations.) In June, Reagan declared that the SALT limitations "no longer exist," but the administration, on the urging of Congress and European allies, continued to observe the treaty. But then in late November, the United States took action to exceed SALT II limits. Gorbachev called the move "a major mistake."

Relations between the superpowers were cool during the first half of the year. Gorbachev told the party congress that a letter from Reagan on the arms question was "swamped in various reservations, linkages, and conditions which in fact block the solution of radical problems of disarmament." In March the United States ordered drastic staff reductions in the Soviet missions to the United Nations. The Soviets protested that move as well as the incursion of two U.S. ships into Soviet waters. A month later, when American planes conducted a bombing raid on Libya in retaliation for international terrorist activity, the Soviets angrily charged Washington with "contempt for international law and morality." In May, Yuri Dubinin, the chief Soviet delegate to the UN, was named to succeed Dobrynin as ambassador to the United States.

In June, with both sides seemingly interested in a second Reagan-Gorbachev summit, more fruitful exchanges on arms control began to take place. Reagan declared that the Soviets were making a "serious effort" to negotiate arms cuts. But in August, when Gorbachev called for a treaty eliminating all nuclear testing, the United States refused, stating that the Soviets had already modernized their nuclear arsenal while the Americans were still in the process of doing so. Plans for the summit were derailed at the end of August, when a Soviet official at the United Nations, Gennadi Zakharov, was arrested for espionage. The Soviets retaliated by arresting U.S. journalist Nicholas Daniloff (*see* BIOGRAPHY) and accusing him of espionage. During the next several weeks, charges and countercharges flew back and forth between Washington and Moscow, and it became clear that no summit could be held as long as this "hostage crisis" remained unresolved. Foreign Minister Shevardnadze visited the United States to speak at the UN in mid-September, and after intense negotiations with U.S. Secretary of State George Shultz, a solution was found: Zakharov and Daniloff were released; the Soviet dissident Yuri Orlov and his wife were allowed to leave the USSR; 25 diplomats at the Soviet UN mission were expelled from the United States; and a Reagan-Gorbachev meeting was scheduled to be held in Reykjavik, Iceland.

For two days, October 11–12, the U.S. president and Soviet general secretary met in closed sessions to discuss arms control. Gorbachev surprised President Reagan with a proposal to cut strategic arms by 50% within five years and to ban deployment of space-based weaponry for ten years. The Americans countered by proposing a complete elimination of all ballistic missiles within ten years. Both sides agreed to eliminate all medium-range nuclear missiles based in Europe. Gorbachev acceded to Reagan's desire to reduce but not

end all nuclear testing and accepted the president's proposal to rid the world of strategic missiles in ten years. But the entire set of agreements collapsed over the SDI issue. Gorbachev called for "strengthening" the ABM Treaty and limiting research on space weapons to the laboratory, while Reagan insisted on continuing research and testing of SDI. The meeting broke up with both sides blaming each other for the failure to reach an accord.

In subsequent weeks, as Soviet-American relations cooled once again, the two sides engaged in an escalating series of diplomatic expulsions. The mutual retaliatory moves culminated with the Kremlin removing all 250 Soviet workers from the U.S. embassy and consulate in Moscow. Shevardnadze and Shultz met in Vienna in early November but made no progress in restoring momentum toward arms control.

Western Europe, Asia, Middle East. The year 1986 saw a clear effort by the Soviet leadership to improve relations with Western Europe. In mid-July, Foreign Minister Shevardnadze visited Great Britain, where he signed three minor diplomatic agreements. The same month, France's President François Mitterrand and West Germany's Foreign Minister Hans-Dietrich Genscher traveled to Moscow for talks with Gorbachev and Shevardnadze.

Gorbachev also signaled a desire for normalized relations with China, but Beijing responded that three main obstacles remained: the Soviet military intervention in Afghanistan, the presence of Soviet troops on the Chinese border, and the Vietnamese occupation of Cambodia. Similarly, the buildup of Soviet troops on the "northern territories," a group of islands off Hokkaido claimed by Japan, barred closer ties with Tokyo. A four-day visit to India by Gorbachev in late November strengthened relations with that country, but no formal strategic or military agreements were reached.

In the Middle East, Syria remained a key Soviet ally, undermining Moscow's overtures to Great Britain and Western Europe (which blamed the Damascus regime for state-sponsored terrorism). Soviet and Israeli representatives met in August for the first time in 19 years to discuss possible resumption of consular ties. But it was as much the issue of Jewish emigration from the USSR as it was disagreement over the Palestinian problem that frustrated diplomatic efforts.

For much of the non-Communist world, the positive aspects of Gorbachev's innovative policies—both domestic and foreign—were tempered by the continuing violations of human rights within the USSR, the Soviet support of radical movements in the Third World, and its continuing military intervention in Afghanistan (*see* AFGHANISTAN).

RONALD GRIGOR SUNY
University of Michigan

USSR · Information Highlights

Official Name: Union of Soviet Socialist Republics.
Location: Eastern Europe and northern Asia.
Area: 8,649,498 sq mi (22 402 200 km²).
Population (mid-1986 est.): 280,000,000.
Chief Cities (Jan. 1, 1985 est.): Moscow, the capital, 8,642,000; Leningrad, 4,867,000; Kiev, 2,448,000.
Government: *Head of state,* Andrei A. Gromyko, chairman of the Presidium of the Supreme Soviet, president (elected July 2, 1985). *Head of government,* Nikolai I. Ryzhkov, chairman of the USSR Council of Ministers (took office Sept. 1985). General secretary of the Communist Party, Mikhail S. Gorbachev (elected March 11, 1985). *Legislature*—Supreme Soviet: Soviet of the Union Soviet of Nationalities.
Monetary Unit: Ruble (0.730 ruble equals U.S.$1, June 1986—noncommercial rate).
Gross National Product (1984, U.S.$): $1,957,600,000.
Economic Indexes (1984): *Consumer Prices* (1980 = 100), all items, 104.2; food, 106.6. *Industrial Production* (1985, 1980 = 100), 119.
Foreign Trade (1985 U.S.$): *Imports,* $82,596,000,000; *exports,* $87,201,000,000.

UNITED NATIONS

One year after celebrating its 40th anniversary with ceremonial homage from kings, presidents, and prime ministers, the United Nations during 1986 faced the worst fiscal and political crisis in its history.

The year began with UN coffers showing a cumulative shortfall of $240 million, the result of political withholdings that stretched back decades, and late payments. Financial reserves were exhausted, and the U.S. Congress and State Department decided to withhold significant portions of the regular UN budget. The United States is legally obliged to pay one fourth of UN costs, but in October it decided to pay just $100 million of the $210 million it owed.

To cover the gap in the short term, UN Secretary-General Javier Pérez de Cuéllar realized $67 million in savings by curtailing travel, documentation, meetings, and hiring. Some countries speeded payments, and others (including China, the USSR, and France) contributed long-withheld arrears. This just enabled the UN to make its December payroll.

Most of the withholdings imposed by Washington stemmed from the feeling that, while the poorest Third World countries pay a total of less than 2% of the UN budget, they have used their voting majority to mandate wasteful spending. The United States and other contributors demanded more than economies. They sought changes in decision-making procedures that would enable the donors to exercise more control over how much is spent and what it is spent on. The Third World resisted the loss of the political power to set priorities, charging that the real objective of UN critics was to weaken the institution because of its perceived anti-Americanism.

Recommendations for resolving the long-term financial problems were put forward in August by a committee of 18 intergovernmental experts and became the major focus of the fall session of the General Assembly. The panel called for saving money by cutting the 14,000-person UN staff by 15%, curbing meetings, and phasing out outdated and duplicated activities.

On the crucial issue of reforming the budget process, the Assembly agreed at the end of December on a compromise that offered the donors more influence over fiscal decisions in return for promises that most of the withheld funds would be paid. U.S. officials endorsed the package, expressing hope that Congress would accept the reforms—and pay up in 1987.

In the midst of this controversy, the General Assembly and the Security Council acted by acclamation on October 10 to appoint Pérez de Cuéllar to a second five-year term as secretary-general, through 1991. The 66-year-old Peruvian appeared to be fully recovered from quadruple heart bypass surgery in July, and he was unopposed for the secretary-generalship. The office was tarnished, however, by charges that Pérez de Cuéllar's predecessor, Austria's President Kurt Waldheim, had served on the Balkan front with the Nazi army in World War II, was involved in brutal operations against Yugoslav partisans there, and then covered up his record. Part of the information was found in restricted files entrusted to the UN by an international war crimes commission. Waldheim denied the charges. (*See* BIOGRAPHY.)

The superpowers were allied on both the financial issue and the renaming of Pérez de Cuéllar, but East-West tensions were dramatized by a U.S. demand in March that the Soviets reduce the staff of their UN mission from 275 to 170, in three stages over a two-year period. Washington defended this unprecedented move on the ground that Soviet diplomats had habitually engaged in espionage in the United States. Moscow denounced the demand at the UN as illegal, and the secretary-general concurred, urging the two sides to negotiate.

The matter became part of a more serious dispute over the August 23 arrest in New York of Gennadi Zakharov, a Soviet employee of the UN Secretariat, on spy charges, and the subsequent detention in Moscow of U.S. journalist Nicholas Daniloff (*see* BIOGRAPHY). Later, after the failure of the Iceland summit between U.S. President Ronald Reagan and Soviet leader Mikhail Gorbachev, the United States in mid-October ordered 25 specified members of the Soviet UN mission to leave the country.

General Assembly. The 40th Assembly session reconvened in April to consider the financial crisis, and in May it approved the secretary-general's money-saving proposals.

From May 27 to June 1, the Assembly held a special session on the economic crisis in Africa. On the final day it adopted by consensus a declaration calling on developed nations to contribute $45.5 billion in new aid over five years and to forgive debts of approximately the same amount. The document called on African governments to make major fiscal reforms.

In another special session, on Namibia, a resolution was passed September 30, by a vote of 126–0 with 24 abstentions, calling for that territory's independence from South Africa.

The 41st regular session opened September 16 and elected Humayun Rashid Choudhury, the foreign minister of Bangladesh, as its president. The session adopted resolutions on some 145 agenda items, including 67 on disarmament and several each on the Middle East, apartheid in South Africa, and human-rights violations in Iran, Afghanistan, Chile, Guatemala, and El Salvador.

The United States was subjected to criticism on two new issues. One resolution condemned the U.S. attack on Libya in April; it was adopted November 20 by a vote of 79–28, with 33 abstentions. And a resolution calling for "full and immediate compliance" with a World Court decision ordering an end to U.S. support for rebels in Nicaragua won approval November 3 by a 94–3 vote, with 47 abstentions.

The Soviet Union and its ally, Vietnam, were criticized in resolutions that got record support. One calling for the withdrawal of Soviet troops from Afghanistan was adopted 122–20, with 11 abstentions, on November 4. A call for the pullout of Hanoi's troops from Cambodia won on October 21 by 115–21, with 13 abstentions.

In an odd historic footnote, the three Axis powers of World War II—Japan, Italy, and West Germany—were elected to the Security Council together for two-year terms.

Security Council. The 15-nation Security Council adopted several resolutions and released unanimous statements on South Africa, the Iran-Iraq war, and the Middle East. But for the most part, significant action by the UN organ entrusted with primary responsibility for maintaining world peace was blocked by contentious debates that ended in vetoes by the United States, occasionally joined by its allies.

The closest the Security Council came to a significant step toward dispute settlement was a resolution adopted unanimously on February 24 calling for an immediate cease-fire in the Persian Gulf, the withdrawal of all forces from foreign territories, and UN mediation. In an attempt to placate Iran, the resolution deplored the "initial acts" that launched the war as well as the use of poison gas against Iranian troops, but it did not blame Iraq by name. Iran remained critical of the Council, charging it with a pro-Iraq tilt and rejecting a truce.

The Council debated the South Africa situation on five occasions, but twice the United States and Great Britain vetoed resolutions calling for "selective" political and economic sanctions against Pretoria. The proposed sanctions were similar to those imposed by the U.S. Congress over the veto of President Reagan.

Nicaragua, complaining of Washington's decision to resume military aid to "contra" rebel forces, convened four debates. It asked the Council to call for U.S. compliance with the June 27 decision of the World Court barring actions to overthrow the Sandinista regime. On July 29, Nicaragua's President Daniel Ortega appeared before the Council to press the case, but the resolution was blocked by a U.S. veto.

The Council renewed the mandate of the UN Interim Force in Lebanon (UNIFIL), but French troops in the force were the targets of attacks by a pro-Iran group of Lebanese. Four were killed and 33 wounded in August and September, and 500 of the French left the force in southern Lebanon. UNIFIL lost $18 million in April, when the United States halved its contribution, but the Soviet Union, which had refused to pay any costs since the force

was created in 1978, voted its support on April 19 and announced that it would begin to contribute.

Secretariat. Pérez de Cuéllar's own efforts at dispute settlement slowed in 1986, as he was more preoccupied with the fiscal crisis. His representative, Diego Cordovez, pursued negotiations between Afghanistan and Pakistan on Soviet troop withdrawal. During a visit to the area in November, Cordovez succeeded in winning approval of a plan for UN observers to monitor the Soviet pullout and the Pakistani and U.S. guarantees that aid to the Afghan rebels would end. The final issue was the timetable for a Soviet pullout. Moscow asked for four years, while Pakistan insisted on four months. A new round of talks was set for February 1987.

The secretary-general himself arbitrated the dispute between France and New Zealand over the July 1985 bombing by French agents of the Greenpeace protest ship *Rainbow Warrior* in Auckland harbor. In a decision on July 6, accepted by both sides, Pérez de Cuéllar called on France to apologize and pay a $7 million indemnity, while New Zealand was to turn over the captured French agents.

The secretary-general on March 29 also proposed the terms of an agreement between the Turkish and Greek communities on Cyprus, but the Greek Cypriot side rejected the plan.

Pérez de Cuéllar in April launched a new mediation effort between Morocco and the Polisario Liberation Front on the future of the Western Sahara. A second round began in May, but no progress was made.

In his administrative role, Pérez de Cuéllar shifted or replaced a score of his undersecretaries at the end of the year, leaving at least ten jobs vacant and signaling his intention of streamlining the UN's departmental structure. Earlier, an in-house audit unearthed some 50 cases of fraud by UN staffers who bilked the organization of thousands of dollars in unwarranted education grants and other benefits.

Specialized Agencies. The various UN agencies involved in the massive campaign to feed the millions of famine victims in Africa wound down in 1986 on a successful note. The UN office that coordinated all global relief efforts closed on October 31, announcing that by August all food needs had been met and that prospects for 1987 harvests were good. It cautioned, however, that 15 nations still faced a plague of locusts and that ongoing civil wars in Sudan, Mozambique, and Angola threatened further famine. Outside Africa, according to the Food and Agriculture Organization (FAO), hunger was on the decline.

The UN Children's Fund (UNICEF) reported in December—on its 40th anniversary —that 1.5 million children had been saved over the previous 12 months by advances in inoculation coverage and the spread of oral dehydration therapy. It warned, however, that 14 million children still die needlessly each year and that 7 million of them could be saved just by creating the will and the funding to spread existing low-cost health technology.

The World Health Organization (WHO) appealed for $200 million per year in new funds to launch a top-priority global battle to stem the spread of Acquired Immune Deficiency Syndrome (AIDS). It warned that 100 million people could be infected with the AIDS virus within four years.

William Draper of the United States succeeded Bradford Morse on April 28 as the head of the UN Development Program, the United Nations' major funding agency for aid projects.

The International Atomic Energy Agency (IAEA) adopted two conventions on nuclear safety in the wake of the April radiation release at the Chernobyl reactor in the Soviet Union.

One pact requires early notification in the event of a radiation leak across borders, and the other mandates nations to provide help on request if disaster strikes. (*See* page 218.)

The United States in August canceled a $25 million donation to the UN Fund for Population Activities because the agency operates in China, which has a controversial abortion policy.

In May the UN Trusteeship Council approved a U.S. request for the termination on September 30 of the last UN trust territory—Micronesia. But the Americans delayed the action indefinitely when a court in Palau, one of the Pacific island groups in the territory, demanded another referendum in December.

Amadou M'Bow, the controversial head of the UN Educational, Scientific and Cultural Organization (UNESCO), announced in October that he would not seek a third term in 1987.

MICHAEL J. BERLIN, *"The Washington Post"*

ORGANIZATION OF THE UNITED NATIONS

THE SECRETARIAT

Secretary-General: Javier Pérez de Cuéllar (until Dec. 31, 1991)

THE GENERAL ASSEMBLY (159 member nations, 1986) *President:* Humayun Rasheed Choudhury, Bangladesh

COMMITTEES

General: Composed of 29 members as follows: The General Assembly president; the 21 General Assembly vice-presidents (heads of delegations or their deputies of Benin, Brazil, the Byelorussian Soviet Socialist Republic, China, Cyprus, the Dominican Republic, Fiji, France, the Libyan Arab Jamahiriya, Malaysia, Mozambique, Oman, Rwanda, Sierra Leone, Somalia, Suriname, Sweden, Turkey, the Union of Soviet Socialist Republics, the United Kingdom of Great Britain and Northern Ireland, the United States of America); and the chairmen of the following main committees, which are composed of all 159 member countries.

First (Political and Security): Siegfried Zachmann (German Democratic Republic)
Special Political: Kwam Kouassi (Togo)
Second (Economic and Financial): Abdalla Saleh Al-Ashtal (Democratic Yemen)
Third (Social, Humanitarian and Cultural): Alphons C. M. Hamer (Netherlands)
Fourth (Decolonization): James Victor Gbeho (Ghana)
Fifth (Administrative and Budgetary): Even Fontaine Ortiz (Cuba)
Sixth (Legal): Laurel B. Francis (Jamaica)

THE SECURITY COUNCIL

Membership ends on December 31 of the year noted; asterisks indicate permanent membership.

Argentina (1988)	Ghana (1987)	United Kingdom*
Bulgaria (1987)	Italy (1988)	United States*
China*	Japan (1988)	Venezuela (1987)
Congo (1987)	USSR*	Zambia (1988)
France*	United Arab	
Germany, Federal	Emirates (1987)	
Republic of (1988)		

THE ECONOMIC AND SOCIAL COUNCIL

President: Manuel Dos Santos (Mozambique)
Membership ends on December 31 of the year noted

Australia (1988)	Guinea (1987)	Sierra Leone
Bangladesh (1987)	Haiti (1987)	(1988)
Belgium (1988)	Iceland (1987)	Somalia (1989)
Belize (1989)	India (1987)	Spain (1987)
Bolivia (1989)	Iran (1989)	Sri Lanka (1989)
Brazil (1987)	Iraq (1988)	Sudan (1989)
Bulgaria (1989)	Italy (1988)	Syrian Arab
Byelorussian Soviet	Jamaica (1988)	Republic
Socialist Republic	Japan (1987)	(1988)
(1988)	Morocco (1987)	Turkey (1987)
Canada (1989)	Mozambique (1988)	USSR (1989)
China (1989)	Nigeria (1987)	United Kingdom
Colombia (1987)	Norway (1989)	(1989)
Denmark (1989)	Oman (1989)	United States
Djibouti (1988)	Pakistan (1988)	(1988)
Egypt (1988)	Panama (1988)	Uruguay (1989)
France (1987)	Peru (1988)	Venezuela (1987)
Gabon (1988)	Philippines (1988)	Zaire (1989)
German Democratic	Poland (1989)	Zimbabwe (1987)
Republic (1988)	Romania (1987)	
Germany, Federal	Rwanda (1989)	
Republic of (1987)	Senegal (1987)	

THE TRUSTEESHIP COUNCIL

President: Laurent Rapin (France)

China[2] France[2] USSR[2] United Kingdom[2] United States[1]

[1] Administers Trust Territory. [2] Permanent member of Security Council not administering Trust Territory.

THE INTERNATIONAL COURT OF JUSTICE

Membership ends on February 5 of the year noted

President: Nagendra Singh (India, 1991)
Vice-President: Guy Ladreit De Lacharrière (France, 1991)

Roberto Ago (Italy, 1988)	Kéba Mbaye (Senegal,
Mohammed Bedjaoui	1991)
(Algeria, 1988)	Ni Zhengyu (China, 1994)
Taslim O. Elias	Shigeru Oda (Japan, 1994)
(Nigeria, 1994)	José María Ruda (Argentina,
Jens Evensen (Norway, 1994)	1991)
Robert Y. Jennings	Stephen Schwebel (United
(United Kingdom, 1991)	States, 1988)
Manfred Lachs (Poland,	José Sette Camara (Brazil,
1994)	1988)
	Nikolai Konstantinovich
	Tarasou (USSR, 1988)

INTERGOVERNMENTAL AGENCIES

Food and Agricultural Organization (FAO); General Agreement on Tariffs and Trade (GATT); International Atomic Energy Agency (IAEA); International Bank for Reconstruction and Development (World Bank); International Civil Aviation Organization (ICAO); International Fund for Agricultural Development (IFAD); International Labor Organization (ILO); International Maritime Organization (IMO); International Monetary Fund (IMF); International Telecommunication Union (ITU); United Nations Educational, Scientific and Cultural Organization (UNESCO); United Nations Industrial Development Organization (UNIDO); Universal Postal Union (UPU); World Health Organization (WHO); World Intellectual Property Organization (WIPO); World Meteorological Organization (WMO).

A late-in-the-year scandal over the sale of U.S. arms to Iran led to the resignation of Vice Adm. John Poindexter (right) as the president's national security adviser and caused Chief of Staff Donald Regan (second from left) to come under fire.

UNITED STATES

"Tonight we thank God for the many blessings He has bestowed on our land," said President Ronald Reagan on July 3 as, with French President François Mitterrand at his side, he rekindled the torch of a refurbished Statue of Liberty in observance of the statue's centennial as a symbol of hope to the world. "We affirm our faithfulness to His rule and to our own ideals; and we pledge to keep alive the dream that brought our forefathers and mothers to this brave new land."

The ceremony in New York Harbor officially began an elaborate and enthusiastic celebration of Independence Day. And indeed Americans had good reason to rejoice in the blessings they enjoyed. But the explosion of the space shuttle *Challenger* on January 28 was a tragic reminder of the cost of continually fulfilling the historic dream mentioned by the president (*see* page 36). Moreover, as some critics pointed out, there was evidence that much remained to be done if the nation was to keep faith with the ideals that the statue symbolized. On November 13 the country's Roman Catholic bishops issued a pastoral letter, "Economic Justice for All," which condemned current poverty levels as "a social and moral scandal," and called for long-range, fundamental reforms to come to grips with the "unfinished business in the American experiment in freedom and justice for all."

The president's oratory and the bishop's manifesto delineated a major theme underlying public affairs in 1986. While Americans took pride in the principles and accomplishments of the past, they often disagreed sharply on how to best defend and advance these principles in the present and the future.

An Overview

Iran-Contra Scandal. For Americans increasingly threatened by terrorism and hostage seizures linked to deep-rooted Middle East antagonisms, news from Lebanon on Nov. 2, 1986, seemed to offer relief. On that day, David P. Jacobsen, a U.S. citizen held hostage for more than 17 months, was set free by his captors, members of a Muslim Shiite group with ties to Iran. In Washington, President Ronald Reagan issued a statement hailing Jacobsen's release, and there was speculation that more American hostages might soon be freed, perhaps in time to give the president and his Republican Party a boost in the November 4 midterm elections.

That prospect never materialized. Far from being the harbinger of political success, Jacobsen's release turned out to be the opening episode in a bizarre and tangled chronicle that in a few short weeks would shake the public's faith in the Reagan presidency and cast a cloud of uncertainty over the remaining two years of Reagan's tenure in the White House.

In rough outline, the story which emerged by year's end was that the Reagan administration, concerned for the fate of American hostages held by Muslim groups and hopeful of bolstering U.S. strategic relationships in the Middle East, had arranged for shipments of arms to Iran for use in its bloody war against Iraq. By doing so the administration had clearly contravened its own oft-reiterated policy against providing weaponry to the country still ruled by the despotic Ayatollah Khomeini and arguably breached various legislative restrictions on executive power.

Moreover, it was subsequently revealed that some profits gained from dealing with the Iranians had gone to support the "contra" guerrillas opposing the left-wing Sandinista regime in Nicaragua. And these transactions had taken place during a period when U.S. support for the rebels, or "freedom fighters," as President Reagan preferred to call them, had been specifically prohibited by Congress. After nearly two months filled with revelations and allegations, much still remained unknown about the actions and motives of the president and those around him involved in the Iran-contra affair. But whatever the truth turned out to be, it was already clear that the Reagan administration, facing the darkest political scandal since Watergate, by its disordered and often contradictory presentation of information had done critical and perhaps irreparable damage to its own credibility.

The pattern of confusion and dissembling was established from the start. In releasing the 55-year-old Jacobsen, the Islamic Jihad ("holy war") group issued a statement referring to "certain approaches" made by the United States which, if continued, could lead "to a solution to the hostage issue." The White House immediately denied that it had made any concessions to gain Jacobsen's freedom. But right after Jacobsen was given his freedom, a Beirut magazine called *Al Shiraa* reported that President Reagan's former top national security adviser, Robert McFarlane, had made a secret visit to the Iranian capital of Tehran the previous month. His purpose, the magazine reported, was to propose that Iran stop supporting terrorist groups and guarantee the security of Persian Gulf states in return for the United States providing Iran spare parts for military equipment.

Al Shiraa's world scoop was followed by published reports in the United States that McFarlane's visit was only one of a number of parleys between U.S. and Iranian officials that had been going on for more than a year, at a time when the U.S. government was publicly opposing the sale of arms to Iran and any concessions for the release of the hostages. Also involved in the negotiations, which were kept secret even from the congressional committees with jurisdiction in the intelligence field, were Vice Adm. John M. Poindexter, McFarlane's successor as White House national security adviser, and Marine Lt. Col. Oliver North, who was on the staff of the National Security Council (NSC).

Not until November 13, about ten days after *Al Shiraa* broke the story, did President Reagan publicly confirm that the United States had secretly sent arms to Iran. In a nationally televised address, Reagan claimed that total shipments amounted to less than a planeload, an estimate that was called into question by later disclosures. The president contended that the arms shipments were not part of a deal to gain the freedom of the hostages, although he listed as one of the objectives of the transactions, along with improving relations with Iran, "to effect the safe return of all hostages." The president also denied that he had failed to comply with the various laws requiring him to notify Congress about arms shipments to Iran, asserting that the appropriate congressional committees "are being and will be fully informed." But congressional leaders who were briefed by the president on the day before his speech told reporters they had not been informed before that. And in one of the first rumbles of the political thunder building against Reagan's actions, Senate Democratic leader Robert Byrd of West Virginia called the dealings with the Iranians "a foreign-policy blunder."

A week later, in a November 19 televised press conference, the president again defended his actions as based on diplomatic and strategic goals "that justify taking risks." To mollify his critics Reagan announced an end of all arms sales to Iran. He also continued to argue that the arms shipments—which he said totaled 1,000 TOW antitank missiles along with spare parts for Hawk antiaircraft missiles—had not been intended as a trade for hostages. Nevertheless the president claimed that the release of three American hostages in the past year was a sign that his dealings with the Iranians had achieved a measure of success.

Asked about reports that the United States had approved a shipment of arms to Iran by Israel as early as September 1985, Reagan claimed that U.S. arms had been shipped to Iran only after he himself had signed a secret order Jan. 17, 1986, authorizing specific exceptions in the Iranian arms embargo. And he denied that Israel or any other country had ever been involved in such shipments. Shortly after the press conference ended, however, the White House took the extraordinary step of issuing a statement correcting Reagan's response and conceding that "there was a third country involved in our secret project with Iran."

Administration hopes that the controversy might subside were wrecked by new disclosures. On November 25, Reagan told reporters that as a result of an inquiry conducted by his attorney general, Edwin Meese III, he had come to realize that he had not been "fully informed" about "one of the activities" connected with the Iranian arms transactions. This activity, as Meese then revealed, was the diversion of proceeds from the arms sales to aid the contras in Nicaragua. Acting on this information, the president accepted Admiral Poindexter's resignation as chief national security adviser and dismissed Lieutenant Colonel North. To help prevent such episodes in the future, Reagan announced he would establish a special review board to study the role and activities of the NSC staff.

In describing the contra venture, Meese said that between January and September 1986 the Central Intelligence Agency (CIA), under the direction of the NSC, sent $12 million in weapons stocks to Israelis who, acting as brokers, sold the arms to Iran at a profit of $10 million to $30 million. After the Israelis reimbursed the Defense Department through the CIA, the extra money was transferred to Swiss bank accounts, which according to Attorney General Meese were controlled by contra representatives.

The president knew nothing of all this, said Meese, who contended that the only government official familiar with the details of the diversion of funds to the contras was Lieutenant Colonel North. Though North had been little known to the public prior to the Iran arms uproar, press inquiries established him as a swashbuckling type of officer whose advice was highly valued by the president.

Whether or not North had actually engineered the contra funding on his own, as many doubted, the disclosure of the Nicaragua connection turned the Iranian arms affair into a full-blown scandal and stirred demands for a broader investigation. Reagan responded on December 2 by announcing that he would ask for the appointment of an independent Watergate-style prosecutor, or counsel, to probe charges of illegality in the Iran-contra affair. He also announced the appointment of Frank C. Carlucci, former undersecretary of defense, as his new national security adviser. Although the president seemed crisp and controlled during his brief televised remarks, he evidently was seething inwardly. "I have to say there is bitter bile in my throat these days," Reagan told a *Time* magazine interviewer Thanksgiving week. "I have never seen the sharks circling like they are now with blood in the water." Blaming most of his troubles on the "great irresponsibility" of the press, he predicted that "as the truth comes out, people will see what we were trying to do was right."

In the meantime though, the tide of public opinion was clearly running against him. Political analysts said that the public was indignant at the administration for helping to arm the regime in Tehran which had humiliated the U.S.

during the 1979–80 hostage crisis. Another negative reaction was disillusionment that Reagan, who had previously enjoyed a reputation for integrity, had been duplicitous enough to secretly sell weapons to the Iranians while publicly denouncing any such ideas. A New York Times-CBS News poll conducted November 30 showed that Reagan's approval rating had plummeted to 46%, a one-month 21% drop which was the sharpest ever recorded by presidential poll takers. Despite his denials, a majority of those surveyed believed that Reagan had known of the so-called contra connection beforehand. An overwhelming 75% opposed selling arms to Iran, and 58% were against helping the contras.

"I pledge to you I will set things right," the president told his countrymen in his weekly radio speech on December 6. But this would be no easy task. One complicating factor was the refusal of Poindexter and North to testify before congressional investigating committees, both pleading their 5th Amendment rights against self incrimination. Another problem was the turmoil in the upper echelons of the administration. Many of Reagan's advisers urged him to dismiss White House Chief of Staff Donald Regan, but this was a step he refused to take. Adding to the uncertainties Reagan faced, CIA Director William Casey underwent surgery for removal of a cancerous brain tumor December 18, and it was unclear when and if he would be able to resume his responsibilities.

To coordinate White House strategy on the multifaceted controversy, Reagan appointed retiring NATO Ambassador David M. Abshire as a special counselor with cabinet rank. Abshire's main responsibility would be to respond to requests for information from congressional and other investigators.

That would certainly keep him busy. Abshire would have to deal with the special commission which Reagan had appointed to look into NSC procedures under the chairmanship of former Texas Republican Sen. John Tower, and the independent counsel whose appointment Reagan had been prodded into seeking. That post was filled by former Federal Judge Lawrence E. Walsh, who was given broad authority to look into both the arms sales and the diversion of funds to the contras. Some of this ground would also be gone over by Watergate-style select committees created in both houses of Congress, headed by Sen. Daniel K. Inouye (D-HI) and Rep. Lee H. Hamilton (D-IN). These panels had many complex and sensitive areas to explore, ranging from accounting for the millions of dollars involved in the secret international transactions to establishing responsibility for the fateful decisions that precipitated the crisis. To resolve these issues countless witnesses would need to be called and voluminous evidence sifted.

Congress. Despite partisan tension between the Democratic controlled House of Representatives and Republican dominated Senate, which at times was exacerbated by the midterm election campaign (*see* page 550), the second session of the 99th Congress could look back on a year marked by significant accomplishments. Probably the most far reaching action was enactment of the much heralded proposal for tax reform, the most sweeping revision of the tax code in four decades (*see* TAXATION).

Another accomplishment that approached tax reform in importance, and was just about as controversial, was adoption of a broad immigration reform bill. For years Congress had been frustrated in efforts to find a practical way to cope with the problems created by the flood of illegal immigrants across U.S. borders. The economic and civil liberties controversies and the bitter conflicts between business, labor, and other interest groups had made prospects of action seem all but hopeless. But then in the fall of 1986 the road to passage was cleared by a series of behind the scenes compromises on Capitol Hill. Negotiators were spurred by Democratic Rep. Peter J. Rodino of New Jersey, chairman of the House Judiciary Committee, who cited estimates that 8 to 12 million illegal aliens already live in the United States and that six million more try to get in each year. "We're in a crisis," Rodino declared. The final version of the measure, approved by House-Senate conferees on October 14 represented the biggest change in immigration law in 20 years and would affect millions of employers around the country. On the one hand the bill would give legal status to several million illegal aliens, those who had entered the country before Jan. 1, 1982. Such aliens would have to apply for legal status in the 18-month period starting six months after the bill became law. On the other hand the new immigration law cracks down on employers who hire illegal aliens, imposing fines ranging from $250 to $10,000 for each illegal alien hired. Employers would have to ask all job applicants for documents, such as a passport or a driver's license, to confirm their status as either citizens or aliens authorized to work in the United States. The law prohibits employers from discriminating against legal aliens.

The environment was another area of major legislative activity. In October, Congress enacted a five-year extension of the so-called Superfund—money designated to clear up hazardous toxic wastes. The legislation sets the level of the fund for the five-year period 1987–91 at $8.5 billion and provides for financing chiefly from a tax on crude oil, a new tax on a broad base of businesses, and a previous duty on raw chemicals. The legislation requires the Environmental Protection Agency (EPA) to start work on 375 toxic waste sites in the next five years and also establishes standards aimed

UNITED STATES · Information Highlights

Official Name: United States of America.
Location: Central North America.
Area: 3,618,770 sq mi (9 372 614 km²).
Population (mid-1986 est.): 241,000,000.
Chief Cities (July 1, 1984 est.): Washington, DC, the capital, 622,873; New York, 7,164,742; Los Angeles, 3,096,721; Chicago, 2,992,472; Houston, 1,705,697; Philadelphia, 1,646,713; Detroit, 1,088,973.
Government: *Head of state and government,* Ronald Reagan, president (took office for second term, Jan. 20, 1985). *Legislature*—Congress: Senate and House of Representatives.
Monetary Unit: Dollar.

at eliminating dangerous wastes instead of merely burying them. Though President Reagan expressed reservations about the method of financing the fund and the scope of the program, he signed the bill into law on October 17.

Earlier in the year on June 19 the president also signed legislation greatly changing the Safe Drinking Water Act passed in 1974. The new law requires EPA to set maximum allowable limits for 83 toxic chemicals that can show up in household drinking water. On still another environmental front, President Reagan vetoed legislation strengthening the Clean Water Act, even though the bill had swept through both houses of Congress without dissent. The measure would have authorized almost $20 billion in appropriations in grant and loan money to help communities build sewage-treatment plants. Reagan objected because he said this sum was triple the amount he had requested.

Perhaps the most emotional issue to confront the lawmakers stemmed from alarming evidence of the spreading use of dangerous drugs. Public concern over the problem had intensified during the summer as a result of the widely publicized drug-related death of University of Maryland basketball star Len Bias, and widespread media coverage of a new form of cocaine, "crack." After a period in which legislators in both parties appeared to vie with each other in the search for tougher anti-drug measures the House and Senate on October 17 adopted a bill that increased most existing penalties for federal drug crimes and authorized nearly $1.7 billion in spending for such measures as law-enforcement grants to the states and educational grants to states, local governments, and colleges and universities.

Defense and national security was another area where Congress seemed to be reacting to the mood of the electorate which, as the lawmakers interpreted it, had become considerably more skeptical about Pentagon spending than it had been during the early days of the Reagan presidency when Congress went along with the president and voted big hikes in the defense budget. Accordingly, the lawmakers made a series of moves to curb increases in defense spending and streamline military operations. The new military budget called for about $290 billion in spending, an increase of only $3.5 billion, nearly $30 billion below the level sought by Reagan. House Democrats attempted to force the president's hand on arms control by attaching arms-control measures to the omnibus spending bill. This led to a bitter dispute with the president on the eve of his Iceland summit meeting in October with Soviet leader Mikhail Gorbachev. Finally, in the face of the president's insistence that their proposals would limit his ability to negotiate with the Russians, the Democrats abandoned their demands.

But the Congress did push through a continuation of the ban on the testing of antisatellite weapons and got the White House to agree to forward two nuclear testing treaties negotiated long ago to the Senate for ratification. In addition the Congress cut spending for next year on the president's proposed Strategic Defense Initiative (SDI), popularly known as Star Wars, from $5.3 billion to $3.5 billion.

Meanwhile, in a move intended to create a more efficient defense establishment by eliminating interservice rivalries, Congress legislated a drastic overhaul in the Pentagon's command structure. Under the new law the chairman of the Joint Chiefs of Staff would become the principal military adviser to the president, rather than merely serving as a spokesman for the views of the chiefs of the different services.

In other areas Congress approved legislation on May 6 that significantly relaxed federal gun laws by lifting the ban on interstate sales

U.S. District Judge Harry E. Claiborne became the first federal official in 50 years to be impeached and convicted.

of rifles and shotguns and allowing gun owners to transport their weapons interstate. On October 17, Congress approved legislation that prohibited most employers from setting a mandatory age for retirement.

The judiciary occupied an unusually prominent place on the congressional docket in 1986. In addition to holding hearings on and confirming President Reagan's two Supreme Court nominations, Justice William H. Rehnquist to be chief justice and Antonin Scalia to be an associate justice, the Senate became embroiled in controversies over two lower court nominees (*see* LAW). The nomination of Jefferson B. Sessions III, a 39-year-old U.S. attorney in Mobile, AL, to be a federal district judge was disapproved by the Senate Judiciary Committee on June 5. Sessions, the first Reagan judicial nominee to be rejected by the Senate, came under criticism for his 1985 prosecution of Alabama civil-rights activists on charges of vote fraud and because of racially insensitive remarks he had allegedly made.

The president had better luck with another controversial judicial selection, Daniel A. Manion, whom he chose for the Federal Appeals Court in Chicago. Democrats charged that Manion was lacking in courtroom experience, but the nominee's supporters contended that the real reason for the opposition had to do with Manion's oft expressed conservative views. The Judiciary Committee disapproved of his nomination but voted to send it to the floor. After delaying moves by his Democratic foes, Manion was confirmed by the Senate 50 to 49 on July 23, with Vice-President George Bush casting the deciding vote.

Another and rarer type of congressional involvement with the judicial branch involved the impeachment action against U.S. District Judge Harry E. Claiborne of Las Vegas, NV, who was serving a two-year federal sentence for tax evasion. The first sitting judge in U.S. history to be convicted of a felony, Claiborne refused to resign and give up his $78,000 annual salary. On July 22 the House approved four articles of impeachment by a vote of 406 to 0, the first unanimous impeachment vote ever recorded. On October 9 the Senate voted to convict him on three of the four counts, by a margin well over the required two thirds. Claiborne was the fifth federal official to be impeached and convicted by the Senate.

In a nonlegislative but nevertheless historic action, the Senate decided to follow the example of the House of Representatives and allow live television coverage of its proceedings. After a six-week trial period the Senate voted 78-21 to make coverage permanent. Proceedings of the House of Representatives have been televised since 1979.

In a personal sense the conclusion of the second session of the 99th Congress marked the end of an era, at least in the House of Representatives where Democratic Rep. Thomas P. O'Neill, Jr., of Massachusetts retired at 74 after serving ten consecutive years as speaker, a record, and 34 years in the House. His successor as speaker would be the Democratic majority leader in the 99th Congress, Jim Wright of Texas. In the Senate, among the notable figures retiring were Republican Sen. Barry Goldwater of Arizona and Sen. Russell Long of Louisiana, onetime Finance Committee chairman.

The election returns resulted in a transfer of control of the Senate to the Democrats and brought a host of other changes that would affect the 100th Congress. Democratic senators expected to take over the chairmanship of key committees include Lloyd Bentsen of Texas, finance; Lawton Chiles of Florida, budget; Joseph R. Biden, Jr., of Delaware, judiciary; Ernest F. Hollings of South Carolina, commerce; J. Bennett Johnston of Louisiana, energy; Edward M. Kennedy of Massachusetts, labor and human resources; Sam Nunn of Georgia, armed services; William Proxmire of Wisconsin, banking; Claiborne Pell of Rhode Island, foreign relations; and John C. Stennis of Mississippi, appropriations.

The Administration. Despite the adoption in 1985 of the Gramm-Rudman balanced budget law, the huge federal budget deficit continued to plague the Reagan administration and to constitute probably the nation's most serious domestic problem. And the mechanisms provided under Gramm-Rudman which were designed to automatically phase out the more than $200 billion 1986 deficit over five years did little to resolve the basic conflicts over spending priorities between the president and his opponents on Capitol Hill, including some in his own party. On February 5 the president released his fiscal 1987 budget, calling for $994 billion in outlays and revenues of $850.4 billion. This would leave a deficit of $143.6 billion, just under the $144 billion maximum allowed for the year under the Gramm-Rudman deficit reduction schedule.

But critics contended that the administration had asked for too much in defense spending—$320 billion—and had made up the difference by taking too much out of programs intended to aid low income and otherwise disadvantaged citizens. On March 3 the president's proposal was rejected by the Republican-controlled Senate budget committee by a 16-6 vote, and it gained only 12 supporting votes on the floor of the Democratic-controlled House. Those votes meant that for all practical purposes the budget process was turned over to Congress whose members had difficulty reaching agreements that the administration would accept. Consequently the 99th Congress failed to complete action on any of the 13 separate appropriations bills that normally fund federal programs. Instead all these proposals were combined into one omnibus spending bill, which at $576 billion amounted to the largest such bill in history and which in effect constituted the 1987 budget. Even at that the president had to sign four stop gap spending bills to keep the government from going broke and shutting down while details of the omnibus bill were ironed out.

Unable to reach the $144 billion Gramm-Rudman target, Congress took advantage of the $10 billion leeway allowed under the law to increase the deficit figure to $154 billion. Reaching that level was made possible by counting in extra first year proceeds from the new tax reform law, sales of federal assets, bookkeeping changes, and freezing many appropriations.

Meanwhile, the Supreme Court ruled July 7 in a 7-2 decision that the Gramm-Rudman automatic spending cut mechanism was unconstitutional because it operated by granting executive branch authority to an officer of the legislative branch, the comptroller general. The law's original sponsors introduced new legislation designed to cure that defect but the House refused to consider the measure. As the year ended it was unclear how much of a role Gramm-Rudman would play in future efforts to slash the deficit. But it was certain, as the president underlined publicly during the fall congressional campaign while barnstorming on behalf of Republican candidates, that he would continue to oppose any attempts to trim the deficit by raising taxes.

There was one major change in the Reagan cabinet in 1986. Agriculture Secretary John R. Block announced January 7 that he would resign effective in mid-February. A member of the original Reagan cabinet, Block had served during a period when because of severe drops in farm income, agriculture was one of the most controversial areas of domestic policy. On January 29, Reagan named Richard E. Lyng, Jr. (*see* BIOGRAPHY), to succeed Block.

Meanwhile the president had another sort of personal problem to worry about. He faced potential embarrassment as a result of charges of misconduct against officials who had formerly served in his administration. In addition to the investigation of alleged influence peddling by Michael Deaver, former White House deputy chief of staff (*see* BIOGRAPHY), another longtime Reagan associate and former political aide, Lyn Nofziger, came under federal investigation for allegedly violating conflict of interest laws by lobbying his former White House colleagues.

As 1986 drew to a close, President Reagan was faced with the task of regaining the confidence of the citizens he governs, and the first session of the 100th Congress was preparing to deal with such items as Gramm-Rudman and the continuing deficit problem.

ROBERT SHOGAN
Washington Bureau, "Los Angeles Times"

The Elections

From the start of the long and costly 1986 U.S. election campaign, leaders of both political parties agreed on at least one point: The richest prize at stake was control of the U.S. Senate.

Senate Races. Republicans had ended long years of Democratic control of that body in the landslide that swept Ronald Reagan into office in 1980 and had maintained their majority in the two subsequent elections in 1982 and 1984. But the scope of the Republican Senate gains in 1980 had created a big mathematical advantage for the Democrats in 1986. Of the 34 seats at stake, 22 were controlled by Republicans, a number of whom had been elected to the Senate for the first time in 1980. The Democrats needed only a net gain of four seats to overturn the 53 to 47 Republican majority.

Democratic leaders predicted early in the campaign that they would retake the Senate. Their confidence was bolstered by the big gains made by opposition parties in past "six-year-itch elections"—those that take place when one party has held the White House for six consecutive years. Nevertheless the Republicans insisted that they would hold on to the Senate, because of the relatively healthy state of the U.S. economy and the continued popularity of

Barbara Mikulski (D) smiles confidently as she leaves a Baltimore voting booth. The five-term congresswoman easily defeated Linda Chavez in Maryland's Senate race.
AP/Wide World

the president, who campaigned intensively for Republican candidates.

In the end, though, the Democrats prevailed in the November 4 balloting. By winning nine Republican seats and losing only one of their own, the Democrats gained a 55 to 45 majority in the new Senate. Their success immediately prompted claims by some of their leaders that the Reagan revolution was ended. For their part, Republicans took comfort in the fact that they suffered only minimal losses in the contest for the House of Representatives, where the Democrats maintained control as expected. And GOP leaders also were encouraged by significant gains made by their candidates in contests for governorships.

Dissatisfaction with economic conditions, specifically with depressed farm prices, helped Democrats win at least two seats—North Dakota where Kent Conrad defeated Republican Sen. Mark Andrews and South Dakota where Democratic Rep. Thomas Daschle ousted GOP incumbent James Abdnor. But in the main the Democratic victories were a result of local issues and the ability of the Democratic candidates to exploit them.

In regional terms the most impressive Democratic gains were in the South, where they won four seats from the Republicans. In Alabama, Democratic Rep. Richard Shelby defeated Republican Sen. Jeremiah Denton; in Florida, Democratic Gov. Bob Graham replaced Republican incumbent Paula Hawkins; in Georgia, Democratic Rep. Wyche Fowler, Jr., upset Republican Sen. Mack Mattingly; and in North Carolina former Democratic Gov. Terry Sanford defeated Republican James Broyhill, who had been appointed to complete the term of the late Sen. John P. East. The Democrats also gained the seats vacated by retiring Republican Sen. Paul Laxalt in Nevada and retiring Republican Sen. Charles Mathias, Jr., in Maryland. In Nevada, Democratic Rep. Harry Reid defeated Republican Jim Santini, a former congressman, and Rep. Barbara Mikulski won over Linda Chavez, a former aide to President Reagan, in Maryland's Senate contest. And in Washington, Brock Adams, a former transportation secretary in the Carter administration, ousted Republican Sen. Slade Gorton. Democrats also elected two new senators to seats formerly held by their party: In Louisiana, Rep. John Breaux succeeded retiring Sen. Russell Long, and in Colorado, Rep. Tim Wirth replaced outgoing Sen. Gary Hart.

Against their loss of nine seats, the Republicans took only one seat away from the Democrats. That was in Missouri where former Republican Gov. Christopher (Kit) Bond defeated Democrat Lt. Gov. Harriett Woods for the seat being vacated by Sen. Thomas Eagleton (D). Republicans elected another new senator in Arizona where Rep. John McCain replaced retiring GOP Sen. Barry Goldwater.

AP/Wide World

Sen. Phil Gramm (right) *joins in the celebrations for the GOP as William Clements* (left) *regains the Texas governorship.*

House and Gubernatorial Races. Results in the House elections ran close to expectations with the Democrats scoring a net gain of five seats. In advance of the vote Democrats had contended that their chances of scoring gains in the House as large as those made by opposition parties in past midterm elections were reduced by the fact that they entered the election with a substantial House majority of 253 to 180, with 2 vacancies. The new House will consist of 258 Democrats to 177 Republicans.

In the governorship races the Republicans enjoyed a numerical advantage comparable to that held by the Democrats in the Senate races. Of the 36 governorships at stake 27 were held by Democrats and 15 Democratic incumbents were retiring. The Republicans made a net gain of 8 governorships, winning 11 from the Democrats and losing 3 of their own. This brought the national totals of governorships to 26 for the Democrats and 24 for the Republicans. The two biggest states gained by Republicans were Florida where Tampa mayor and former Democrat Bob Martinez defeated Steve Pajcic for the seat held by Bob Graham, and Texas where former Republican Gov. William Clements unseated Democratic Gov. Mark White.

Probably the most surprising GOP success was in Alabama where Republican Guy Hunt defeated Democrat Bill Baxley for the seat held by Democrat George Wallace. Hunt, the first Republican governor elected in Alabama since post-Civil War Reconstruction was helped by a bitter dispute among Democrats over their nominating process. The Republicans took another Southern governorship away from the Democrats in South Carolina where they elected Rep. Carroll A. Campbell, Jr., to replace outgoing Democrat Richard Riley. Other Republicans elected to seats formerly held by

Democrats included Evan Mecham in Arizona, Mike Hayden in Kansas, John R. McKernan, Jr., in Maine, Kay Orr in Nebraska, Garrey E. Carruthers in New Mexico, Henry Bellmon in Oklahoma, and Tommy G. Thompson in Wisconsin.

The biggest state where Democrats took a governorship away from the Republicans was Pennsylvania, where Robert Casey defeated Lt. Gov. William W. Scranton III. Democrats also gained governorships from Republicans in Oregon where they elected Neil Goldschmidt, another transportation secretary under President Carter, to replace Republican Victor Atiyeh, and in Tennessee where Democrat Ned R. McWherter took the seat being vacated by Republican Lamar Alexander, who could not constitutionally seek another term.

The Republican gains in governorships bolstered party hopes of ultimately achieving their long cherished goal of party realignment, since control of state political machinery is the key to party building. But these gains at the state level were partly offset by the balloting for state legislatures where Democrats made a net gain of one state Senate and two House chambers, bringing their total to 32 state Senates and 35 state Houses.

Referenda. In results on ballot initiatives, Vermont voters defeated a proposal to add an equal rights amendment to the state constitution; voters in Massachusetts, Rhode Island, Oregon, and Arkansas defeated proposals to ban state-financed abortions; and five states approved—and one, North Dakota, rejected—state lotteries. In California voters approved measures to prevent toxic contamination and to declare English to be the state's official language.

Robert Shogan

551

The Economy

Measured by the broadest economic gauge, the year 1986 was a dull one for the U.S. economy. The nation's output of goods and services, the gross national product (GNP), rose less than 3% in spite of repeated White House promises of better times to come.

But the description simply did not fit when you lifted the veneer of official indicators and viewed the separate elements and events that make up the economy. Then the year was seen as one of the most unusual, even bizarre, ones in some time. It was a rare one too, since the economy late in the year was beginning its fifth straight year of growth, double the life span of most recent expansions. While not strong, that expansion showed few signs of terminal illness. The year-end consensus of forecasters was for at least another year of life, and maybe more. The White House said the expansion would last another six years.

In the view of the experts, nothing was more unexplainable than the behavior of consumers, the "cautious consumers" as they had come to be called over the past decade. In 1986 they lived beyond their means, saving very little, borrowing a lot, and raising the total of household debt to more than 80% of disposable income, compared with 35% three decades earlier.

The Tax Reform Act of 1986 passed Congress and was signed by President Ronald Reagan, who promised that over a five-year period it would transfer $130 billion of tax liability from individuals to business. What had happened to one of Reagan's fundamental goals, the strengthening of the nation's producing sec-

tor? He did not say, but some members of the business community felt abandoned by the tax act.

Stocks, Borrowing, Inflation. Nevertheless, Wall Street was able to shake off its disappointment. The stock market continued to strengthen, with the Dow Jones industrial average reaching a record high of 1955.57 points on December 2, more than 400 points higher than on January 1. The market seemed to absorb the impact of a scandal too, revealed when the Securities and Exchange Commission (SEC) accused prominent brokers of having made illegal profits through the use of inside information. The biggest of those named was Ivan Boesky, a 49-year-old Wall Street investor who was forced to repay $50 million and pay a $50 million fine for his misuse of confidential information on impending mergers. *See also* STOCKS AND BONDS.

In keeping with the surprising nature of events, the cost of borrowing money declined sharply. From a high of 9.5% in January, the prime interest rate to the soundest corporate customers stood at 7.5% as the year ended. Single-digit home mortgages returned too, after a descent from 15% in the summer of 1982. And wonder of wonders, inflation as measured by the Consumer Price Index fell to just 1.9% from 3.54% a year earlier. During some months, prices actually declined, and automobile dealers resorted to deep discounts, rebates, or low interest charges in order to keep car lots from becoming overcrowded.

Deficits, Diverse Economies, and Predictions. Why this good news should occur in spite of a budget deficit of $221 billion in fiscal 1986 and a record-high trade deficit of $148 billion, plus an estimated $100 billion of uncollectible Third World debts owed to American banks, was difficult to fathom. Eventually, critics said, the impact would be felt. But when and how remained for time to reveal.

Just as peculiar was the existence of national economic statistics that depicted continued growth while an enormous part of the country suffered deep wounds that might take years to heal. The United States in 1986 was not one vast economy but many. During early fall, the economic research firm of Sindlinger & Co. listed 31 states in recession, most of them bogged down by poor farming or mining conditions, or by the presence of old, heavy industries such as steel. But in the nation's four extreme geographical corners, especially those already into the information-computer age, stronger conditions overwhelmed statistics from other areas.

In one respect at least there might have been something inconsistent in the December 8 remark of Beryl Sprinkel, chairman of the Council of Economic Advisers. Speaking to reporters, Sprinkel stated: "You can eliminate recession as a major risk." He projected 1987

Americans turned increasingly to buying on credit in 1986. However the new tax act eliminates deductions for such purchasing and could influence consumer buying habits.

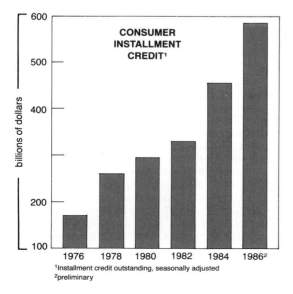

CONSUMER INSTALLMENT CREDIT[1]

billions of dollars

600

500

400

200

100

1976   1978   1980   1982   1984   1986[2]

[1]Installment credit outstanding, seasonally adjusted
[2]preliminary

growth of 3.2% in GNP, higher than anticipated by most private forecasters but, nevertheless, below earlier White House estimates of 3.5%. "We want a credible forecast," Sprinkel explained.

Credibility, however, remained a problem for the Reagan administration, a consequence of having repeatedly overestimated economic conditions. Critics contended, in fact, that optimism in the White House was intended to be an economic spur. But the repeated expectation of more from the economy than it could deliver could not be ignored. It showed up in a rate of consumer spending that exceeded income growth; in a stock market where price increases exceeded earnings growth; in factories, which operated at only 78% of total capacity.

Growth and Indicators. Still, while the pace of economic growth was slow, it produced the nation's first $4 trillion economy. Although the current-dollar measuring stick included some inflation, the final figure was close to $4.2 trillion, a gain of more than $200 trillion for the year.

After-tax corporate profits improved to about $140.5 billion from $131.4 billion a year earlier, an important gain even if its significance was reduced somewhat by the realization that it merely brought the total back to the 1984 level. Late in the year, the rate of improvement was picking up, and many business forecasts called for another increase in real corporate profits during 1987.

Automobile sales rose to 11.3 million units, but many of these units came from abroad. Domestic sales of 8.2 million were about the same as in 1985 and about 200,000 higher than in 1984. While auto analysts considered such figures strong, they wonder if they had been bolstered by sales "stolen" from 1987, especially since the new tax law made it more advantageous to buy in the earlier year, before sales taxes were eliminated as an income tax deduction. Indeed, many 1987 projections were for domestic car sales to fall by 1 million units. *See* AUTOMOBILES.

Housing markets remained strong, and that condition was expected to continue in 1987. More than 720,000 new, single-family houses were sold, up from 689,000 in the previous year, while transactions involving existing houses rose to 3.48 million from 3.2 million. Economists at the National Association of Realtors forecast only a small decline in sales for 1987, mainly because the new tax law would permit mortgage interest and real-estate taxes to remain deductible. *See* HOUSING.

In fact, since the new law ended the deductibility of credit-card and installment-loan interest, homeowners were in an enviable position. Many closed old credit accounts and, with encouragement from banks, borrowed on their home equity instead. It represented an amazing turnabout in the attitude of Americans toward the home. Just a few decades before, the clearest and most certain goal of millions of Americans was to pay off the mortgage. Now, they sought to take on as much debt as possible, thus risking the roof over their heads. Interest on home-mortgage debt climbed to 5% of disposable income. In 1952 the percentage was just a bit more than one.

A sense of job security, at least in relation to conditions five years earlier, helped to explain the willingness to incur debt. While the third quarter jobless rate of 6.9% represented an improvement of only two tenths of 1% over the rate for all of 1985, and 8 million Americans were without work, more than 2 million jobs were created. Some idleness was chronic, but many of those listed as jobless remained so for a few weeks only before others took their place.

Some of the idleness was produced by an amazing spate of mergers, leveraged buyouts and corporate raids, often financed with high-rise "junk" bonds that rewarded holders with high returns. In the first ten months of 1986, more than 2,800 deals of $1 million or more were completed, for a total value of more than $130 billion. But perhaps of even greater significance were deals that were avoided. Some of the biggest names in American industry—Bank America, Gillette, Goodyear, and U.S. Steel (now USX)—were forced to fight off unwelcome takeover attempts. In some instances the raiders were bought off with premium prices for their shares, leading to charges of "greenmail," and in some instances to shareholder suits against management.

Throughout the year the Federal Reserve System was compelled to deal not just with domestic interest rates but with the trade value of the dollar, the unpayable debts of Third World nations, and the terrible twins: the trade imbalance with other nations and the federal-budget deficit. The trade deficit reached a record $148 billion, but for the first time in years there was real hope. With the dollar having fallen 35% since January against European and Japanese currencies, U.S. goods would become less expensive abroad and thus more exportable. Simultaneously, U.S. imports would be discouraged by higher prices.

That, at least, was the hope and the forecast. But there existed a growing cynicism about such expectations. The economic expansion was growing old, and even during the best of it the reality fell short of the expectations. There was some sense of foreboding; time seemed to be running out, and big problems remained unsolved. Americans seemed ready to settle for another mediocre economy in 1987.

See also BUSINESS AND CORPORATE AFFAIRS; INDUSTRIAL REVIEW; TAXATION.

JOHN CUNNIFF, *The Associated Press*

The Trend Toward Privatization

In La Mirada, CA, Dial-A-Ride Transit provides transportation in comfortable vans. The Los Angeles County city is a prime example of a community that has turned to private companies to operate its public services.

© Barr/Gamma-Liaison

By the late 1970s, with the public sector accounting for more than a third of the output in virtually every modern nation, policies were introduced to shrink the role of government. One such policy was the effort to privatize—to change to private control or ownership—public services and public facilities.

Partly, privatization is an effort to reduce the role of government as a producer of services by selling state-owned businesses back to the private sector or by contracting with private firms. Partly, it is an effort to restrain government in its policy role by reducing regulations, by cutting back its obligation to pay for certain services and people, and by introducing fees and charges for public services.

In Great Britain the Conservative government of Margaret Thatcher began after 1979 to sell off the industries nationalized by previous Labour governments. Public housing units were sold to their occupants, for example, and half of British Telecom was sold to the public in 1984. In the United States there have been proposals to sell the National Railroad Passenger Corporation (Amtrak), weather satellites, or the public-power systems. But the United States has few nationalized industries, so privatization has been mainly at the state and local level. In the United States, privatization has taken the form of proposals for government to contract with private firms for services previously run by government agencies.

Governments traditionally have bought buildings, roads, vehicles, and other equipment from private suppliers, and have used private contractors for such services as refuse collection, building cleaning, and vehicle repair. What was startling with the privatization trend were the proposals for private firms to build, own, and run hospitals, waste treatment plants, schools, and especially prisons.

Pros and Cons. Two controversies have developed regarding privatization. The first involves the proposal simply to privatize the running of the service; the other arises when government would drop its policy and financial responsibility as well.

The first controversy is intensely practical. Both the private firms and the public employees want the government's business. Opponents of privatization point to a history of corruption in contracting and warn of a loss of public control. Proponents assert that costs will be lower under the private system, and argue that contractors will be more responsive than public bureaus.

The second controversy has to do with equity. Those who oppose privatization say it is wrong to cut back government services and benefits. Proponents respond that it is necessary, and argue that cuts in services for all are worse than charges to people who can pay. Opponents respond that people who are charged for services may then be unwilling to pay again, through taxes, to assist the poor.

Every service area—even security and education—is a mixture of what government buys and does for people and what people buy and do privately and for themselves and others. During the 1960s and 1970s, government expanded significantly its financing of public services (including some privately delivered). By the mid-1980s, the prospect of a continued fiscal squeeze by government seems certain to ensure a continuing effort to reduce spending. As the debate over privatization continues, however, the argument is growing that efficiency and effectiveness result less from the use of private organization than from changes that introduce competition among producers, public and private.

Ted Kolderie

Foreign Affairs

There is little question that 1986 was the most momentous year to date for Ronald Reagan's foreign policy—and quite possibly for his entire presidency. During the first five years of his presidency, Reagan remained slightly aloof from messy foreign-policy fights. In 1986 he finally got involved, but with as many failures as successes and damaged credibility the main result. A strong president suddenly looked weak. On almost every front, changing events were rapidly outdistancing the administration's policies. The policies, as a result, were under fire and in some cases had to be revised or even cast aside. Controversy was the only constant.

The low point came at the very end of the year, with a storm of public criticism over revelations about secret arms dealings with Iran and the disbursement of the profits from such sales to the "contra" rebels fighting the Sandinista government in Nicaragua. But it followed by only several weeks a hastily called and unsuccessful summit meeting in Iceland with Soviet leader Mikhail Gorbachev. Earlier in the year, Reagan faced continuing turmoil in South Africa, the Philippines, and Central America. And, as a U.S. military attack against Libya in April proved, terrorism remained unchecked.

The year brought to the surface concerns about people as well as policy. In fact in the face of the Iran-contra revelations, the president's national security adviser Vice Adm. John Poindexter—the fourth man to hold the job during Reagan's presidency—resigned, and a member of the National Security Council (NSC) staff, Lt. Col. Oliver North, was fired. Perhaps worse for Reagan, it appeared for a while that the Iran incident might lead to the resignation of Secretary of State George P. Shultz, who, at least among members of Congress, was the most respected and trusted of the entire spectrum of Reagan's cabinet secretaries and close advisers. The year ended, however, with Secretary Shultz remaining as head of the State Department and with the appointment of Frank C. Carlucci as the president's newest national security adviser.

The arms-to-Iran fiasco was not a classic foreign-policy crisis. In this instance the president's adversary was not a foreign power but American public opinion, his chief ally for the first six years of his presidency. The U.S. public appeared repulsed by the notion of sending arms to Iran in order to free the handful of American hostages held in Lebanon by forces linked to Iran. The incident undoubtedly reawakened dormant American outrage toward the regime that held 52 Americans hostage from late 1979 to early 1981. It also seemed a direct contradiction of Reagan's hard-line policy of never dealing with terrorists; this was a chief concern for Shultz. Finally, it contradicted stated U.S. neutrality in the Iran-Iraq war as well as U.S. urgings that other countries not sell arms to Iran. Lost in the uproar was the other element of Reagan's policy shift, praised by some foreign-policy experts, that it was in the long-term U.S. strategic interest to repair its relations with Iran.

Arms Control and USSR Relations. Arms control was President Reagan's other major failing in 1986. It was the primary topic at the October 11–12 summit between Reagan and Soviet leader Gorbachev at Reykjavik, Iceland. The summit was perceived as a failure for the American president, not only because no arms-control accord was reached, but because Reagan and his advisers appeared to be caught off guard by the Soviet Union's arms-control proposals, and then made far-reaching disarmament proposals themselves that caused confusion and required clarification later.

The Iceland summit was dramatic because it was unexpected. Until it was announced in late September, attention had been focused on a proposed Reagan-Gorbachev meeting in the United States in late 1986 or 1987. In addition to the surprise timing, the Iceland meeting was notable because it turned unpredictable: It ran nearly a full day longer than expected and then ended suddenly in stalemate, right at the brink of a major breakthrough in arms control, not to mention U.S.-Soviet relations. It ended because of continued U.S.-Soviet disagreement over the Reagan administration's so-called Strategic Defense Initiative (SDI or "Star Wars") program. Before they would agree to reductions in long-range and medium-range nuclear forces, the Soviets wanted the United States to agree to changes in the 1972 ABM treaty that would require significant restric-

Frank C. Carlucci, 56-year-old former government official, was named President Reagan's national security adviser.

tions on both testing and deployment of space-based defensive weapons. Reagan rejected the deal because of his desire to continue testing as well as research.

As a result, when Reagan and Gorbachev literally parted company at Reykjavik on the SDI issue, they left on the table almost-completed agreements on cutbacks in medium-range missiles, mostly in Europe, and long-range strategic nuclear missiles. There was hope, at least on the U.S. side, that those agreements would be the basis for further discussions in the formal arms-control talks in Geneva in 1987. But a November meeting in Vienna between Shultz and his Soviet counterpart, Foreign Minister Eduard Shevardnadze, failed to move the talks further. Despite the setbacks U.S. arms-control negotiators in Geneva termed the year "most productive" because both sides moved closer toward agreement on significant reductions in both long- and medium-range missiles. The talks were to resume in 1987.

The Reykjavik summit itself grew out of one of the year's many bizarre foreign-policy events: the arrest of U.S. News & World Report correspondent Nicholas Daniloff. Daniloff, an experienced Moscow correspondent, was arrested on August 30 by Soviet authorities and charged with espionage. His case quickly became linked to the U.S. arrest and detention of a suspected Soviet spy, Gennadi Zakharov, who ostensibly was an employee of the United Nations in New York. The Soviets, it appeared, arrested Daniloff to obtain Zakharov's freedom.

The issue was resolved only after several weeks of high-level diplomacy involving Secretary of State Shultz and Foreign Minister Shevardnadze. Daniloff was released first, then Zakharov was expelled from the United States and returned to Moscow. At the same time, the Soviets released dissident Yuri Orlov and his wife and allowed them to emigrate to the United States. As an adjunct to the deal, Reagan agreed to a Soviet idea for a summit to focus on arms control. The administration had insisted from the start it would not trade Daniloff, who it said was innocent, for a Soviet spy, and the agreement appeared to be constructed to allow the United States to claim that Daniloff was freed unconditionally, while Zakharov received his freedom in exchange for the Orlovs. But the administration was unable to avoid some damage from the incident. The Soviets achieved their apparent goal—the release of Zakharov—while the administration was left to explain why what looked like a trade was not one.

Terrorism. Recognized as the overriding international dilemma of the 1980s, terrorism remained a pressing issue for the administration in 1986. This was illustrated dramatically in April when President Reagan ordered air strikes against Libya after Libya's Muammar Qaddafi was linked to a bombing in West Berlin, in which two U.S. servicemen were killed. (One serviceman died at the time of the incident; a second died of his wounds in June.) Although the bombing of Libya initially brought criticism from U.S. allies in Europe, the criticism died down as it became apparent that the raid dampened Libya's terrorist activities.

Syria was the other Middle East state accused by the United States and its allies of terrorism. After Syrian government officials were linked to a foiled attempt to place a bomb aboard an El Al 747 jet in London, Great Britain and the United States took diplomatic measures to show their displeasure with Syrian policies. The United States, for example, withdrew its ambassador from Damascus and restricted trade with Syria.

No suspects were arrested in another terrorist incident during 1986, in which a bomb was placed aboard a TWA airliner in Cairo and exploded as the plane prepared to land in Athens. Four Americans were killed. In the year's other major terrorist incident involving Americans, a total of 21 persons died when a Pan Am jet was taken over and fired on by terrorists in Karachi, Pakistan. No government was linked to the incident.

Although there were no breakthroughs in fighting terrorism, the United States and its major allies seemed closer to agreeing on joint diplomatic sanctions whenever possible. Following the British action in the wake of the El Al incident, for example, all but one member of the European Community adopted some sanctions against Syria to protest the incident.

Terrorism also caused some unexpected fallout at home. In early October a controversy grew out of reports of a "disinformation" campaign on the part of the Reagan administration, the purported purpose of which was to make Qaddafi think the United States was preparing further military action against Libya. Besides Reagan, the controversy damaged the credibility of national security adviser Poindexter. And the incident, along with Poindexter's key role in the Iran arms transfer and the apparent involvement of his staff in helping supply the contra rebels in Nicaragua, aroused the ire of some members of Congress. They were concerned that too many risky foreign policy operations were being run out of the White House, whose staff is largely exempt from congressional oversight. In late November, President Reagan appointed a three-member board, headed by former Sen. John Tower (R-TX), to "conduct a comprehensive review of the role and procedures" of the NSC.

Middle East. Nor was there any "good" news from the Middle East to offset terrorism. Efforts by the United States, Israel, and Jordan to move forward on setting up direct negotia-

AP/Wide World

Secretary of State George Shultz (left) and Chester Crocker, assistant secretary of state for African affairs, testify on South Africa. In the fall, Congress overrode a presidential veto and enacted economic sanctions against Pretoria.

tions between Israel, Jordan, and representatives of the Palestinians proved unsuccessful, as they had in 1985. Political will on the part of the United States, Jordan, and Israel did not appear lacking; rather, no representatives of the Palestinians could be found that were acceptable to all parties.

U.S. policy toward the Middle East was tested on at least one other front during 1986, as Congress and the Reagan administration tangled over arms sales to U.S. allies in the region. Congress refused to approve arms sales to Jordan until that country engages in direct peace talks with Israel, a development that reflected the power of the Israeli lobby in Washington. And although Reagan was able to win approval of an arms sale to Saudi Arabia, it came only after most of the controversial items were removed from the package.

Nicaragua. Congress also was a major player in the continuing battle over U.S. policy toward Nicaragua. In 1986, after a two-year congressional ban, Reagan won approval of $70 million in military aid and $30 million in nonlethal supplies for the contras fighting the Sandinistas government in Nicaragua. The victory came on close votes in both the House and Senate and this assured reexamination of the issue in 1987. Congressional review also was certain in the wake of the Iran-contra scandal, and after a U.S.-based supply plane was shot down inside Nicaragua in the fall of 1986. It was carrying weapons and other supplies to the contras, and documents on board suggested that the Reagan administration may have been giving logistical support to the privately funded operation.

In Nicaragua itself, the prospects for the contras were uncertain by the end of 1986, despite the infusion of U.S. aid. The various factions of the rebel coalition suffered a number of disagreements during the year over civilian control of the military, and there were disputes over military strategy.

South Africa and the Philippines. The other major foreign policy dispute between Congress and the Reagan administration was on South Africa. On this issue, an angry, bipartisan congressional majority in the fall overrode a presidential veto and imposed economic sanctions on the white South African government. Because the South African government had not responded to Reagan's conciliatory approach with any ironclad commitment to dismantle the apartheid system, Congress chose to send a message of impatience and anger rather than give Pretoria more time.

The other major foreign policy issue facing Reagan in 1986, the Philippines, began on a positive note: the peaceful transition of political power from dictator Ferdinand Marcos to Corazon Aquino. The event showed the United States able to manage peaceful transitions from dictatorships to at least the seeds of democracy. And Reagan's role in backing the presidency of Aquino was surprising because Marcos had considered Reagan a close ally, and few foreign-policy observers predicted Reagan would desert him.

See also feature article on The Philippines (page 26); CENTRAL AMERICA; TERRORISM; and articles on individual countries.

CHRISTOPHER MADISON
Staff Correspondent, "National Journal"

The Peace Corps 1961–1986

In the wee hours of Oct. 14, 1960, presidential candidate John F. Kennedy asked 10,000 students at the University of Michigan: "How many of you are willing to spend years in Africa or Latin America or Asia working for the United States and working for freedom?" The students' enthusiastic response to that challenge marked the true beginnings of the Peace Corps. The idea of an overseas people-to-people program was first promoted by Sen. Hubert Humphrey and Rep. Henry Reuss in the 1950s, but it took the presidential leadership and vigor of John Kennedy to bring it to fruition.

On March 1, 1961, Kennedy, now president, signed an Executive Order providing for the establishment of a Peace Corps. R. Sargent Shriver was appointed as its first director. The following August 30, the first Peace Corps volunteers were sent out to eight different countries—Ghana, Nigeria, Tanganyika (now part of Tanzania), the Philippines, Chile, Colombia, India, and Pakistan—and to the British dependency of Saint Lucia to fulfill the "three goals" of the corps. According to the September 1961 legislation that approved the Peace Corps, the three goals are: to help the people of interested countries and areas in meeting their needs for trained manpower; to help promote a better understanding of Americans on the part of the people served; and to help promote a better understanding of other peoples on the part of Americans.

Since that time, the Peace Corps has sent more than 120,000 volunteers to 93 developing countries in Africa, Asia, and Latin America. The volunteers have introduced new agricultural methods and seeds and fertilizers; they have built schools, youth centers, and hospitals; they have demonstrated energy, soil, and water conservation techniques; they have helped to establish small businesses and family stores; they have taught math, science, and English; they have served as nurses, midwives, and nutritionists. Most of all, they have helped people in villages throughout the world to learn to help themselves.

The Peace Corps today shares the same basic goals and ideals as at its inception. However, under Director Loret Ruppe, the Peace Corps of the 1980s has striven to be more relevant in the fight against hunger, poverty, and lack of opportunity. Volunteers in the 1980s are older: the average age in 1985 was 29, while in 1962 it was 24. They have more technical and professional skills, and they spend more time in their tour of service (three years rather than two). Today's Peace Corps is just as committed to development as it is to promoting goodwill.

The celebration of the 25th anniversary of the Peace Corps was a yearlong affair. In a tribute to President Kennedy's now-famous speech, Vice-President George Bush, Director Loret Ruppe, and Sargent Shriver staged a kickoff celebration at the University of Michigan in October 1985. On March 1, the anniversary of the day President Kennedy signed the Executive Order that brought the Corps to life in 1961, a gala event was held at the Kennedy Library in Boston. Thousands of alumni, friends, and supporters of the Peace Corps attended similar events in 30 states. Finally, to mark the historic departures of those first volunteers, there was a massive reunion on Independence Mall in Washington, DC, Sept. 19–21, 1986.

CHRISTOPHER J. DODD
United States Senate

Editor's Note: Christopher J. Dodd, a U.S. senator from Connecticut, is a member of the Senate Foreign Relations Committee. The senator considers his time as a Peace Corps volunteer in the Dominican Republic (1966–68) as "enormously satisfying." The senator is "convinced, however, that the real value of a Peace Corps tour is more intangible: the communities that have accepted volunteers have been enriched by the vitality of bright, young people who were inspired by the challenge of creating a new and better world; and the volunteers have been afforded an opportunity to contribute significantly, to people much less fortunate than they."

URUGUAY

The democratically elected President Julio Maria Sanguinetti devoted his attention in 1986 to solidifying the elected constitutional civilian regime and to rebuilding the country's weakened economy.

Military Crimes. The most serious problem endangering the full transition from military dictatorship to a secure democratic regime was that of possible punishment of military men guilty of abuses during the 1973–85 dictatorship. In the early months of the year, extensive negotiations were held on the subject among the four groups represented in parliament: the president's Colorado Party, the Nationalist (Blanco) Party, the Broad Front coalition, and small Catholic Civic Union Party.

When these negotiations failed, the Colorados introduced a bill granting a general amnesty for all crimes committed between 1962 and March 1, 1985, "directly or indirectly related to the antisubversive fight." When this was defeated late in September, the Blancos introduced an alternative measure proposing amnesty for all except the 38 cases already pending in the courts. This, too, failed to pass when the Broad Front refused to support it.

However as the year drew to a close, parliament passed and the president signed a bill granting a general amnesty for soldiers accused of human-rights violations during 1973–85. The action prevented a possible showdown between the elected government and the military.

Economy. One major economic problem dealt with by President Sanguinetti was that of the country's foreign debt. Late in February agreements were reached on rescheduling $2 billion owed to 115 private banks that was to come due between 1985 and 1989. New terms provided for ten-year maturities, a two-year grace period, and lower interest rates. This settlement paved the way for new international financing. The World Bank granted a $45 million loan at the end of February for a hydroelectric project. In June the International Monetary Fund (IMF) extended Uruguay a $120 million standby loan, and further agreements were reached with private foreign creditors.

The Sanguinetti administration also sought to rationalize and make more efficient certain government-controlled segments of the economy. In March, ANCAP, the government oil monopoly, raised prices by between 5% and 8% to offset a devaluation of the peso. The state railways were forced to close 59 of their stations during the year in order to save money.

President Sanguinetti also sought to gain wider access in foreign markets for Uruguay's products. In June he visited the United States, announcing that the main purpose of the trip was to seek entry for Uruguayan goods. In July economic integration agreements were reached

---

URUGUAY • Information Highlights

Official Name: Oriental Republic of Uruguay.
Location: Southeastern coast of South America.
Area: 68,037 sq mi (176 215 km²).
Population (mid-1986 est.): 3,000,000.
Capital (1980): Montevideo, 1,260,573.
Government: *Head of state,* Julio María Sanguinetti, president (took office March 2, 1985). *Legislature* —National Congress: Senate and House of Deputies.
Monetary Unit: Peso (166.0 pesos equal U.S.$1, Oct. 19, 1986).
Gross Domestic Product (1984 U.S.$): $5,200,000,000.
Economic Index (Montevideo, 1985): *Consumer Prices* (1980 = 100), all items, 636.5; food, 595.1.
Foreign Trade (1985 U.S.$): *Imports,* $708,000,000; *exports,* $854,000,000.

---

with Argentina and Brazil, and in the following month Sanguinetti and Brazilian President José Sarney concluded agreements to increase bilateral trade from $300 million to $600 million. Five hundred Uruguayan industrial products were given free entry into Brazil, and the Brazilians agreed to increase significantly shipments of beef, rice, chicken, and other Uruguayan commodities. In addition, agreements for technical assistance were reached with Israel in July. In May, Mexico agreed to lift restrictions on importation of 8,000 Uruguayan products.

The government's economic policies provoked some vigorous opposition from organized labor, evidenced by a two-hour general strike on February 27 and an all-day strike on March 12. The unions were particularly critical of the administration's move to pass legislation restricting the right to strike for workers in "essential services."

There was evidence throughout the year that the Sanguinetti administration's economic policies were showing at least some success. In March it was announced that the inflation rate, which had been 83.1% in the period between December 1984 and December 1985, had fallen to only 15.4% during the first quarter of 1986. The government had a goal of 40% for the year.

GATT Conference. In September the Uruguayan resort of Punta del Este was host to a conference of nations belonging to the General Agreement on Tariffs and Trade (GATT). The conference scheduled a new round of GATT trade talks, to be known as the Uruguay Round.

ROBERT J. ALEXANDER, *Rutgers University*

UTAH

Midterm elections and state budget cuts were two dominant issues in Utah in 1986.

Elections. The 1986 off-year election was marked primarily by the return of a Democrat to the state's congressional delegation for the first time since 1980 and by an increase in Dem-

AP/Wide World

Sen. Jake Garn of Utah leaves a Washington hospital with daughter Susan a week after donating a kidney to her.

ocratic representation in the state legislature. Wayne Owens (D), a former congressman who had made unsuccessful bids for the U.S. Senate and the governorship, defeated former Salt Lake County Commissioner Tom Shimizu by a comfortable margin for the seat vacated by David S. Monson (R). In other congressional races, James V. Hansen (R) and Howard C. Nielson (R) retained their seats.

UTAH • Information Highlights

Education 84,899 sq mi (219 889 km²).
Population (1985 est.): 1,645,000.
Chief Cities (1980 census): Salt Lake City, the capital (July 1, 1984 est.), 164,844; Provo, 74,108; Ogden, 64,407.
Government (1986): *Chief Officers*—governor, Norman H. Bangerter (R); lt. gov., W. Val Oveson (R). *Legislature*—Senate, 29 members; House of Representatives, 75 members.
State Finances (fiscal year 1985): *Revenue,* $3,133,000,000; *expenditure,* $2,818,000,000.
Personal Income (1985): $17,259,000,000; per capita, $10,493.
Labor Force (June 1986): *Civilian labor force,* 750,800; *unemployed,* 40,800 (5.4% of total force).
Education: *Enrollment* (fall 1984)—public elementary schools, 289,340; public secondary, 100,801; colleges and universities, 103,994. *Public school expenditures* (1983–84), $754,000,000 ($2,119 per pupil).

Although the GOP had dominated both houses of the state legislature by more than a two-thirds margin, Democrats were able to reduce that margin, primarily by victories in Salt Lake County. Republican incumbents retained virtually all seats elsewhere in the state. Major Democratic victories in several local contests, plus numerous other close races, led Democratic State Chairman Randy Horiuchi to claim that "our party is back."

Although Utah, the most predominantly Republican state in the nation, seems to have returned to a two-party system, Democratic gains were overshadowed by the 3–1 sweeping victory of incumbent U.S. Sen. Jake Garn (R) over challenger Craig S. Oliver.

Three proposed changes to the state constitution were also on the ballot. The first, exempting nonprofit hospitals and nursing homes from the property tax, was defeated, permitting counties to continue to tax such institutions if they cannot prove they operate solely for charitable purposes. The constitution was amended to allow the legislature to exempt farm equipment and machinery from the property tax, effective Jan. 1, 1987. Also approved was a revision of the education article of the constitution to clarify the structure and governance of education in Utah and conform to current practices.

State Budget. An upwardly revised $48 million revenue shortfall projected for the 1986 fiscal year presented Gov. Norman Bangerter with a major financial crisis. Since state legislative leaders rejected the idea of a preelection special session to deal with appropriations, the governor was forced to balance the budget (a constitutional requirement) by reducing operating budgets for various state agencies. His plan included a hiring freeze and an across-the-board percentage cutback of funds for nearly all state agencies. Of particular concern was the impact on public education. Plans for implementing the imposed budget cuts ranged from reducing or eliminating kindergarten to terminating certain graduate programs at state institutions of higher learning. Staff and faculty positions were cut at all levels, resulting in the loss of highly qualified faculty to other institutions and a general adverse effect on morale throughout the educational system.

Other. A Utah concern, Morton Thiokol Inc., made headlines during investigations of the January explosion of the space shuttle *Challenger.* The company had manufactured the defective booster rocket that caused the tragedy.

The Kennecott Corporation reached an agreement with its unions that included a promise to reopen Bingham Canyon, the nation's largest copper mine, in about mid-1987. This would provide jobs for about 2,000 laid off workers.

LORENZO K. KIMBALL, *University of Utah*

VENEZUELA

On July 18, 1986, President Jaime Lusinchi announced a 21-point economic program designed to save foreign currency, pull the economy out of another year of zero growth, and provide benefits for low-income families.

Austerity Plan. The program came in response to official estimates of a $5.5 billion decrease in 1986 oil revenues and increased pressures on Venezuela's $12.2 billion foreign reserves. Principal points included a partial devaluation of the bolívar, liberalized foreign investment laws, additional controls on agricultural imports, efforts to increase nontraditional exports, and reduced government red tape and regulations.

Lusinchi announced that dollars for payment of private-sector debts owed to foreign banks would no longer be available at the previously subsidized rate of 4.3 bolívars to the dollar, due to the drop in price of Venezuelan oil. Bolívars would be exchanged only at a rate of 7.5 to the dollar.

Oil Income. Reflecting the drop in world oil prices and the government's reluctant acceptance of the need to shift away from dependence on oil revenues to finance the government, the 1987 budget, introduced in June, was based on 35% of government revenues coming from oil income, down from 60% in 1986 and as much as 80% in previous years. The $17.2 billion budget looks to an increase in taxes from 33% to 46% of revenues to make up a $3.2 billion deficit.

On September 5, Energy Minister Arturo Hernández Grisanti announced that Venezuela was increasing its prices 30–50 cents a barrel on various types of crude and between 40–60 cents on various petroleum derivatives. An average price of about $14.00 per barrel would be maintained on some 30 different types of products the rest of the year. Average production the first four months of 1986 was 1.43 million barrels per day (bpd). Prices recovered to an average price of $16.18 per barrel for crude in April after falling from $23.25 in January to $12.75 in March.

The Venezuelan Petroleum Corporation—a state-owned company—helped guarantee itself a market for 200,000 bpd through the purchase in February of 50% of the stock of CITGO Petroleum (formerly Cities Services) from the Southland Corporation. CITGO refines and markets petroleum products through 8,000 service stations in 30 U.S. states.

Improved Farm Supplies. Production of grains, meat, oil seeds, milk, sugar, and other farm products improved. Milk imports fell to an estimated 50,000 tons in 1986 from 100,000 tons in 1984. An increase, however, in powdered milk prices designed to stimulate the production domestically of fresh milk led to decreased consumption. The Caracas govern-

AP/Wide World

Venezuela's Energy Minister Arturo Hernández Grisanti takes a break during a June OPEC conference. With prices down, the nation sought to limit its reliance on oil.

ment announced the sale in August of pork and livestock to several Caribbean nations, which would be followed by the export of poultry and eggs.

Other Economic Matters. The Lusinchi government achieved some success in reducing unemployment from a high of 14.6% for the first half of 1985 to 11.8% by the end of June 1986. On the other hand, an estimated 40% of the six million work force is underemployed; recently the work force has been expanding by about 200,000 annually.

VENEZUELA • Information Highlights

Official Name: Republic of Venezuela.
Location: Northern coast of South America.
Area: 352,143 sq mi (912 050 km²).
Population (mid-1986 est.): 17,800,000.
Chief Cities (1981 est.): Caracas, the capital, 2,299,700; Maracaibo, 929,000; Valencia, 523,000.
Government: *Head of state and government,* Jaime Lusinchi, president (took office Feb. 2, 1984). *Legislature*—National Congress: Senate and Chamber of Deputies.
Monetary Unit: Bolívar (21.97 bolívars equal U.S.$1, Oct. 19, 1986).
Gross Domestic Product (1985 U.S.$): $47,000,-000,000.
Economic Index (Caracas, 1985): *Consumer Prices* (1980 = 100), all items, 170.0; food, 198.5.
Foreign Trade (1985 U.S.$): *Imports,* $7,559,000,000; *exports,* $12,272,000,000.

Inflation fell to an estimated rate of 8% annually in 1986 compared with 9.1% for 1985. In his July 18 speech, Lusinchi also said his government would freeze price controls on 30 basic food items and expand the preschool and school milk programs to improve nutrition for school children and pregnant women. The government also would invest more than $666 million in low-cost housing while developing six-month job-training programs for 50,000.

The 1988 Nominations. Lusinchi is not eligible for reelection in 1988. Minister of the Interior Octávio Lepage resigned his post on September 2 to improve his chances for nomination as a presidential candidate of the Democratic Action (AD) against former President Carlos Andrés Pérez, for whom he also was minister of the interior. Former President Rafael Caldera is the leading contender for COPEI, the other major party.

Foreign Policy. President Lusinchi visited Argentina, Uruguay, and Brazil in March. In August he joined Mexican President Miguel de la Madrid in renewing a program to supply 130,000 bpd of oil to Central American and Caribbean nations on favorable terms.

NEALE J. PEARSON, *Texas Tech University*

VERMONT

With statewide contests held only for the Republican nomination for U.S. senator and lieutenant governor in 1986, the Vermont primaries attracted only 15% of the electorate and produced no upsets. At a poorly attended state Republican platform convention, however, delegates voted to retract support for a proposed equal rights amendment (ERA) to the state constitution. Despite continued ERA support by all leading candidates of both parties, the proposed amendment was defeated by the voters by a 52 to 48% margin.

The general election gubernatorial contest pitted incumbent Gov. Madeleine Kunin (D)

VERMONT • Information Highlights

Area: 9,614 sq mi (24 900 km²).
Population (1985 est.): 535,000.
Chief Cities (1980 census): Montpelier, the capital, 8,241; Burlington, 37,712; Rutland, 18,436.
Government (1986): *Chief Officers*—governor, Madeleine M. Kunin (D); lt. gov., Peter Smith (R). *General Assembly*—Senate, 30 members; House of Representatives, 150 members.
State Finances (fiscal year 1985): *Revenue,* $1,109,000,000; *expenditure,* $1,034,000,000.
Personal Income (1985): $6,482,000,000; per capita, $12,117.
Labor Force (June 1986): *Civilian labor force,* 284,600; *unemployed,* 12,500 (4.4% of total force).
Education: *Enrollment* (fall 1984)—public elementary schools, 62,730; public secondary, 27,351; colleges and universities, 31,416. *Public school expenditures* (1983–84), $282,000,000 ($3,148 per pupil).

---

against Lt. Gov. Peter Smith (R). The race was complicated by the left-wing challenge of Burlington Mayor Bernard Sanders running as an Independent. Kunin, who ran on a record of moderation and fiscal conservatism, garnered 47% of the popular vote to Smith's 38% and Sanders' 15%. Since no candidate received a majority, the election would be decided by the state legislature in secret ballot and the outcome officially determined in January 1987. However, the Democrats strengthened their hold on the new legislature, picking up one seat in the Senate (19D-11R), and four in the House (76D-74R).

U.S. Sen. Patrick Leahy (D), was reelected with 63% of the vote over former four-term Gov. Richard Snelling (R). Also reelected was Congressman James Jeffords (R), who ran with both Republican and Democratic endorsement. In a mild upset Howard Dean (D) was elected lieutenant governor over Susan Auld.

Legislature and Budget. Notably contentious, the 1986 legislature passed 200 bills. At adjournment it concluded the longest biennial session in state history and left 700 bills not acted upon. Its major accomplishments were bills to enhance water quality; to establish a $5.5 million tax-relief program for homeowners, tenants, and farmers; to expand state aid to local schools by more than 12%; and to raise the drinking age gradually to 21.

For the first time in six years, the state recorded a budget surplus, closing the books on a record-high $35.8 million deficit incurred at the end of fiscal 1984. Though Vermont is the only state without a constitutional or statutory prohibition against running deficits, the legislature had responded to the 1984 shortfall with a deficit-reduction plan, to which the Kunin administration adhered. Thanks to a strong economy that brought in unanticipated revenues, the surplus was even larger than planned.

Other News. Vermont's reputation for probity was challenged by local scandals involving a town clerk accused of drug dealings; another town clerk alleged to have misappropriated half a million dollars in town funds; a school superintendent who reportedly covered up a $2 million shortage; a state college accreditation of phantom courses; and an assistant judge accused of misusing county funds. The last case, while involving relatively small sums, led to a Judicial Conduct Board investigation of three of Vermont's five Supreme Court justices who were linked to the matter. The assistant judge, a popularly elected lay person, was defeated in her bid for renomination and subsequently indicted for giving false testimony.

A long-simmering dispute over South African stock divestiture was resolved when the trustees of Middlebury College and the University of Vermont voted to divest.

SAMUEL B. HAND AND ROBERT V. DANIELS
University of Vermont

VIETNAM

The Vietnamese government began the year 1986 by trying to improve relations with the United States. As the year progressed the Vietnamese found themselves under growing pressure from their Soviet allies to resolve their conflict with China. Meanwhile, the Vietnamese Communist Party Sixth Congress met in December. The parley resulted in new leadership for the ruling party.

Politics. The death in July of Le Duan, the secretary general of the Vietnamese Communist Party, marked the end of an era. The 78-year-old Le Duan helped found the Vietnamese Communist Party in 1930 and became its secretary general in 1960. His successor in this post was 79-year-old Truong Chinh, a staunchly doctrinaire Communist who was responsible for an unsuccessful program to collectivize agriculture in the 1950s. Le Duan completed the program, despite the resistance of many peasants, while Truong Chinh went on to become the party's main theoretician.

The Sixth Congress of the Vietnamese Communist Party in December brought a new group of leaders into the government and the ruling Politburo. Nguyen Van Linh, chosen as secretary general of the party, replaced the ailing Truong Chinh, who retired along with Premier Pham Van Dong and key Politburo member, Le Duc Tho. The retirement of so many key leaders was unprecedented in Vietnamese history and unique in the Communist world. Linh, who had been expelled from the Politburo in 1982 and reinstated in 1985, was considered responsible for recent economic reforms in southern Vietnam. The new vice-premier, Vo Chi Cong, formerly agriculture minister, has supported agricultural reforms that allowed farmers to sell their surplus produce for a profit. The positions of chairman of the council of ministers (premier) and chairman of the state council (president), which were vacated by the resignations of Pham Van Dong and Truong Chinh, were not filled at the parley. The congress approved a draft law on marriage and the family, adopted development and budget plans for 1987, and supported the USSR's call for a nuclear-free world.

Economics. Vietnam's technocrats—government officials with economic expertise but often without a strong commitment to party ideology—are beginning to insist on a greater voice in shaping economic policies. There are plenty of problems for them to address.

Food production is increasing slowly but still lags behind population growth. A large portion of the population, especially in overcrowded Hanoi, lives in wretched housing and subsists on very meager food rations. The people seem to have little confidence in their government's ability to manage the economy. For the third time in less than two years, Vietnam

VIETNAM · Information Highlights

Official Name: Socialist Republic of Vietnam.
Location: Southeast Asia.
Area: 127,300 sq mi (329 707 km²).
Population (mid-1986 est.): 62,000,000.
Chief Cities (1985 est.): Hanoi, the capital, 2,000,000; Ho Chi Minh City (1986 est.), 4,000,000.
Government: Communist Party secretary, Nguyen Van Linh.
Monetary Unit: Dong (80 dongs equal U.S.$1, November 1986).
Gross National Product (1984 U.S.$): $18,100,000,000.
Foreign Trade (1984 U.S.$): *Imports,* $1,823,000,000; *exports,* $763,000,000.

devalued its currency, the dong, in mid-November. With inflation remaining rampant the dong was devalued from 15 to 80 to the U.S. dollar. Meanwhile, the black-market rate for the U.S. dollar rose from 270 dong in August to 430 dong in November.

There is an obvious need to provide more market incentives to encourage production of food and other commodities. While some steps toward economic liberalization have been taken, any sustained reform has been hampered by opposition within the bureaucracy and the party.

Foreign Affairs. Vietnam's occupation of neighboring Cambodia in 1979 led to its virtual isolation in the world community. Every year since, an overwhelming majority of nations have voted for United Nations' resolutions calling for the withdrawal of Vietnamese troops from Cambodia. Many nations also have withheld trade and aid. Although Vietnam is allied with the Soviet Union and receives hundreds of millions of dollars a year in aid from the Soviet bloc, the aid money has led to few completed projects.

The Soviet Union has serious economic problems of its own. In July 1986, Soviet leader Mikhail Gorbachev gave a speech in Vladivostok in which he advocated the development of much closer economic ties with the prosperous Asian-Pacific region. Gorbachev also indicated a desire to resolve the Cambodian problem, which is the main obstacle to improved relations with China and the Association of Southeast Asian Nations (ASEAN). He strongly urged Vietnam to enter into direct talks with China and its other neighbors.

Meanwhile, the Vietnamese have been trying to improve relations with the United States in exchange for resolving the issue of U.S. soldiers missing in action in Indochina since the end of the Vietnam War. The United States insists that the MIA issue is not negotiable, and that Vietnam's withdrawal from Cambodia must precede any improvement in relations.

See also CAMBODIA.

PETER A. POOLE
Author, "Eight Presidents and Indochina"

VIRGINIA

The state's largest tax increase in 20 years, U.S. congressional elections, and white-collar crime attracted interest in 1986.

Legislature. Gov. Gerald I. Baliles announced just two days after the January 11 inauguration that the state was in desperate need of money to build new roads and improve transportation. In an effort to break with the state's longtime "pay-as-you-go" highway financing system, he created a special commission to handle the roads question and called a special legislative session to pass on its recommendations. The governor asked the General Assembly for $571 million in tax increases to finance a ten-year, $10 billion construction program. The legislature reduced the request to $422 million. In 1987, Virginia residents, therefore, would pay an extra .5% in sales tax, at least 2½ cents more per gallon of gasoline, and more for titling new vehicles.

In regular session the legislature passed a new budget increasing state aid to local schools and established a Farmers Market Board to create local markets for Virginia-grown crops.

Elections. In November, Virginians voted only for their congressional delegation and in local races. The elections brought one new face to the state's ten-member delegation—that of former state legislator Owen B. Pickett, who would replace the retiring Republican Rep. G. William Whitehurst. The election of Pickett, a Democrat, brought the delegation to five Republicans and five Democrats.

Crime. In what was apparently the first ever proposed censure of a Virginia lawmaker, a state Senate panel ruled in 1986 that state Sen. Peter K. Babalas of Norfolk violated conflict-of-interest rules by voting on a bill that helped a corporate client of his law firm.

Clyde Pitchford, a flamboyant 31-year-old Richmond stockbroker, disappeared in mid-February. Amid mounting allegations of fraud and theft, the subject of his whereabouts became a cottage industry, spawning T-shirts, posters, and endless jokes. Pitchford, sporting dyed hair and saying nothing of where he had been, finally gave himself up on May 19 in Washington, DC. He later was sentenced to 25 years in prison and ordered to repay some of the $1.1 million he had stolen.

Other. In September, after the school board voted that Norfolk's elementary schools had been integrated, 15 years of busing ended.

James McGill Buchanan of George Mason University won the 1986 Nobel Prize for Economics for his work in applying economic principles to political decision-making. Another Virginia professor, the University of Virginia's Woodford McClellan, was reunited with his wife Irena. He married the Soviet English teacher on a 1974 visit to the USSR but had not been allowed to see her for 11 years.

J. Lindsay Almond, Jr., the state's governor from 1958 to 1962, died in April. While governor, Almond abandoned his opposition to school desegregation. July brought the deaths of former Gov. John N. Dalton and state Senate Finance Chairman Edward E. Willey. The 55-year-old Dalton had held the state's top post from 1978 to 1982 and was a key figure in the state Republican Party; many had hoped he would run again for governor. Willey had long been considered the most powerful man in the legislature.

ED NEWLAND
"The Richmond Times-Dispatch"

WASHINGTON

In Washington's 1986 U.S. Senate race, Brock Adams, former Democratic congressman and U.S. transportation secretary, defeated the incumbent, Slade Gorton. Eight incumbents—five Democrats and three Republicans—were reelected to the U.S. House of Representatives. State Democrats scraped through with a minimum number of votes to maintain control of the state Senate and kept a much larger majority in the House.

Economy. Tourists traveling to neighboring Vancouver's Expo 86 helped boost the state's economy somewhat, but personal bankruptcy filings in Seattle increased by 72% over 1985. The bankruptcy rate was higher in Washington than in any area of the country except Alaska.

The Boeing Company announced it would be a part of a team building a prototype of the new Advanced Tactical Fighter—more than 50 years after assembling its last fighter. At the same time Boeing completed work on its final cruise missile on deadline and more than $98 million under budget.

Legislature. Gov. Booth Gardner (D) backed away from an earlier plan to endorse a

---

VIRGINIA · Information Highlights

Area: 40,767 sq mi (105 586 km²).

Population (1985 est.): 5,706,000.

Chief Cities (July 1, 1984 est.): Richmond, the capital, 219,056; Virginia Beach, 308,664; Norfolk, 279,683; Newport News, 154,560; Chesapeake, 126,031.

Government (1986): *Chief Officers*—governor, Gerald L. Baliles (D); lt. gov., L. Douglas Wilder (D). *General Assembly*—Senate, 40 members; House of Delegates, 100 members.

State Finances (fiscal year 1985): *Revenue,* $9,030,000,000; *expenditure,* $7,833,000,000.

Personal Income (1985): $82,980,000,000; per capita, $14,542.

Labor Force (June 1986): *Civilian labor force,* 2,955,300; *unemployed,* 149,900 (5.1% of total force).

Education: *Enrollment* (fall 1984)—public elementary schools, 667,215; public secondary, 298,007; colleges and universities, 292,416. *Public school expenditures* (1983–84), $2,670,000,000 ($2,968 per pupil).

---

state income tax. Instead he planned to overhaul the present tax system to provide more money for the state's underfunded educational system. For the first time in 60 years, the state legislature ended its session one day early. More than 300 bills were passed, including a Puget Sound cleanup plan and a comparable worth scheme for state workers.

Fisheries. Technology developed at the University of Washington's School of Fisheries has resulted in a neutered Pacific oyster—allowing it to be edible the entire year. A boost in state oyster production should result.

WPPSS and Nuclear Issues. Several piping contractors to Washington's Public Power Supply System (WPPSS) as well as to a number of other nuclear projects in the country were being investigated for paying millions of dollars in kickbacks to ignore fraudulently inflated costs. A nationwide conspiracy was uncovered by a Seattle federal grand jury. Six corporations and seven individuals were indicted.

Two U.S. congressional subcommittees uncovered an earlier report by the Department of Energy technical staff in which the state's Hanford site was rated the least desirable of five potential U.S. nuclear dump sites.

Mishandling of radioactive plutonium by employees at two Hanford facilities operated by the Rockwell Corporation led to the halting of production in September. An audit for Rockwell cited several potential safety problems.

Hunthausen Case. Following a two-year investigation prompted by complaints from conservative Roman Catholics in the Seattle Archdiocese, the Vatican demoted Seattle's Liberal Archbishop Raymond Hunthausen, charging that he had deviated from Catholic norms and forcing him to share authority with Auxiliary Bishop Donald Wuerl.

Crime. Convicted of racketeering and murder, ten Neo-Nazi members of the Order (the Silent Brotherhood) were sentenced to prison terms of between 40 and 100 years.

WASHINGTON • Information Highlights

Area: 68,139 sq mi (176 479 km²).
Population (1985 est.): 4,409,000.
Chief Cities (July 1, 1984 est.): Olympia, the capital (1980 census), 27,447; Seattle, 488,474; Spokane, 173,349; Tacoma, 159,433.
Government (1986): *Chief Officers—*governor, Booth Gardner (D); lt. gov., John A. Cherberg (D). *Legislature—*Senate, 49 members; House of Representatives, 98 members.
State Finances (fiscal year 1985): *Revenue,* $9,781,000,000; *expenditure,* $9,012,000,000.
Personal Income (1985): $61,185,000,000; per capita, $13,876.
Labor Force (June 1986): *Civilian labor force,* 2,233,300; *unemployed,* 172,600 (7.7% of total force).
Education: *Enrollment* (fall 1984)—public elementary schools, 502,392; public secondary, 238,785; colleges and universities, 231,553. *Public school expenditures* (1983–84), $2,144,000,000 ($3,106 per pupil).

The list of unsolved murders in Green River (King County), one of the country's largest serial murder cases, grew to 36.

JEREMIAH J. SULLIVAN
Pacific Northwest Executive

WASHINGTON, DC

Washington's black mayor, Marion Barry, was reelected to an unprecedented third term in the November 1986 balloting. Council Chairperson David A. Clarke was reelected with the highest vote total of any candidate. Betty Ann Kane and Hilda Mason won their reelection bids to citywide seats on the council; Nadine P. Winter and Frank Smith, Jr., retained their ward-based seats. Harry L. Thomas and James E. Nathanson won positions from wards that had no incumbents in the race.

Walter E. Fauntroy won a ninth term as the nonvoting delegate in the U.S. House of Representatives.

Legislation. The legal age for drinking beer and wine was raised from 18 to 21, to match the minimum age for drinking liquor and to conform to laws in neighboring states. The change will be phased in gradually by exempting those who were 18 years old at the time it took effect.

Health and life-insurance companies were prohibited from denying coverage or raising insurance premiums to persons who test positive for exposure to the AIDS virus. Attempts to overturn the law by court action, referendum, and congressional veto failed.

The auto-insurance law that required District motorists to carry no-fault car insurance was amended to make no-fault coverage optional. A referendum drive to restore mandatory no-fault coverage failed to gain the necessary number of petition signatures.

The 1984 initiative guaranteeing overnight shelter for homeless people, that was struck down by a 1985 DC Superior Court judge's ruling, was upheld by the DC Court of Appeals.

Education. The Antioch School of Law, a private institution committed to social action, was acquired by the city to merge with the University of the District of Columbia. Gallaudet College, the 122-year-old school for the deaf, achieved university status.

New Attractions. The National Building Museum, to honor the nation's architectural arts and design, opened as the 70th museum located in the District. It is located in the century-old Pension Building. The Willard Hotel, rebuilt and restored to its turn-of-the-century grandeur, reopened. (*See* page 79.)

The Metro subway system, reaching far into the Virginia suburbs, opened a 9.1 mi (14 km) Orange line extension, with four new stations.

MORRIS J. LEVITT, *Howard University*

WEST VIRGINIA

Against a familiar backdrop of fiscal distress and high unemployment, West Virginians experienced a lackluster election with neither the governorship nor a U.S. Senate seat involved.

Election Results. All four incumbent Democratic representatives were returned to Washington with comfortable margins. Democrats retained control of both houses of the state legislature, with only scattered upsets marring an otherwise predictable picture. Speaker of the House of Delegates Joseph Albright was defeated after a tax reappraisal plan he had championed proved all but unworkable in some sectors and unpopular in most.

Voters, apparently expressing their discontent with the legislature's and governor's efforts to end the state's fiscal slide, defeated two proposed amendments that had wide bipartisan support: they soundly whipped a plan that would have authorized $500 million in new road money while raising the consumer's sales tax by 20% (from 5 to 6 cents), and another that would have permitted the sale of $200 million in bonds for public-school building improvements. Also rejected for a second time was one that would have allowed a sheriff to serve more than two consecutive terms.

The defeat of the two major amendments was viewed widely as evidence of the public's unwillingness to put the state any more deeply into debt or to approve any new taxes without evidence of a change in direction and emphasis in Charleston—a situation that reached near-ridiculous proportions in October when Gov. Arch A. Moore, Jr., a Republican, and state Auditor Glen B. Gainer, Jr., a Democrat, publicly disagreed as to whether there was enough money in the treasury to meet the state's payroll.

Three amendments were approved, however—a free-port agreement that will exempt from taxes materials stored in warehouses en route through the state; a second that prohibits the election to a county school board of more than two members from the same magisterial district; and a third that reiterates the "right to bear arms."

Economy. The continuing economic slump occupied most of the legislature's attention during a regular and two special sessions. Double-digit unemployment continued to be among the worst in the nation. Employment in the mining industry—26,200 in September—was down a full 7,000 from the record low figure of a year before and down from some 250,000 in the 1950s. Meanwhile, coal production maintained and slightly exceeded levels of the previous few years, reflecting additional reliance on automation and suggesting further layoffs among mine workers. The latter became fact in October as four more companies announced additional cuts.

Flood Damage. Reflecting the twin factors of economic hardship and public discontent was the painfully slow recovery from the disastrous flood of November 1985, when 29 of the state's 55 counties were hit with record high water, 48 deaths, and property loss of near $500 million. There was persistent criticism of a federal bureaucracy that has made flood relief programs both unpredictable and inadequate.

DONOVAN H. BOND
West Virginia University

WISCONSIN

An upset in the November gubernatorial election reflected some of the issues facing Wisconsin during 1986.

Elections. Gov. Anthony Earl, a liberal Democrat who had converted a $350 million state deficit into a surplus during his first term, ran for reelection on his record. His Republican challenger, Tommy G. Thompson, favored cutting taxes and state spending and encouraged the perception that Earl was more interested in social causes than in creating jobs. A conservative who had been the Assembly minority leader, Thompson argued that Wisconsin was becoming a magnet for those seeking welfare aid. He also differed with Earl on the site for a new prison; Earl proposed the Milwaukee area, while Thompson backed Waupun.

Although Thompson easily defeated Earl, capturing 53% of the vote, he will have to contend with a Democratic state legislature. Democrats gained one more seat in the Senate, for a 19–11 majority, with three vacancies. In the Assembly the Democrats gained two seats, for a 54–45 majority.

In another notable upset, Donald Hanaway, a Republican state senator, defeated Bronson La Follette, who was seeking his sixth term as

---

Gov. Anthony Earl signs legislation raising Wisconsin's drinking age from 19 to 21.

AP/Wide World

state attorney general. The grandson of former U.S. Sen. Robert M. ("Fighting Bob") La Follette had been fined $500 for an ethics violation less than a month before the election.

The race between Republican U.S. Sen. Robert W. Kasten, Jr., and his Democratic challenger, Ed Garvey, considered one of the most vicious in state history, was eventually won by Kasten. Garvey made an issue of Kasten's December 1985 arrest for drunk driving in Washington, DC. Kasten alleged that $750,000 had disappeared from the National Football League Players Association while Garvey led it, and Garvey filed a $2 million libel suit.

The state's nine U.S. congressmen—five Democrats and four Republicans—were re-elected.

The Legislature. In the most politically charged action of the session, legislators agreed to raise the state drinking age from 19 to 21, conforming with the four states bordering Wisconsin. The bill had been opposed by the Tavern League of Wisconsin, one of the state's most powerful lobbying groups. After Governor Earl reversed himself to favor raising the drinking age when faced with a loss of federal highway funds, the legislature agreed to raise the age effective September 1. Those who were 19 by that date were able to continue drinking legally.

The legislature also gave first approval to constitutional amendments that would allow a state lottery and pari-mutuel betting. Other actions included measures to renew a state-guaranteed crop-planting loan program and to order electric utilities and other industries to reduce sulfur-dioxide emissions in half by the year 1993.

Economy. Wisconsin's nonfarm economy picked up in 1986. Statewide employment was up 2.1% over 1985, although manufacturing employment rose only slightly. Personal income increased by 3.9%, and net farm income was expected to rise by 5.1%.

Other. A Madison courtroom was the focus of attention in July when three former University of Minnesota basketball players went on trial, charged with 12 counts of sexual assault. An 18-year-old art student had accused them of assaulting her in a hotel room after a game. Following a two-week trial, a jury acquitted the players, who had been dismissed by the university.

PAUL SALSINI
"The Milwaukee Journal"

WISCONSIN • Information Highlights

Area: 56,153 sq mi (145 436 km²).
Population (1985 est.): 4,775,000.
Chief Cities (July 1, 1984 est.): Madison, the capital, 170,745; Milwaukee, 620,811; Green Bay (1980 census), 87,899.
Government (1986): *Chief Officers—*governor, Anthony S. Earl (D); lt. gov., James T. Flynn (D). *Legislature—*Senate, 33 members; Assembly, 99 members.
State Finances (fiscal year 1985): *Revenue,* $9,740,000,000; *expenditure,* $8,718,000,000.
Personal Income (1985): $62,815,000,000; per capita, $13,154.
Labor Force (June 1986): *Civilian labor force,* 2,418,300; *unemployed,* 159,200 (6.5% of total force).
Education: *Enrollment* (fall 1984)—public elementary schools, 497,175; public secondary, 270,367; colleges and universities, 275,069. *Public school expenditures* (1983–84), $2,506,000,000 ($3,553 per pupil).

WOMEN

Women played a major role in the 1986 U.S. elections, with 80 women candidates seeking major offices around the country. In the workplace women formed the majority in the professions for the first time, and demands for equity in pay continued to make headway. But problems and challenges remained.

Politics. Women faced women as the major party candidates in two statewide contests— for a Senate seat in Maryland and the governorship in Nebraska. Elsewhere four other women were running for the U.S. Senate, 54 for the House of Representatives, 7 for governor, and 11 for lieutenant governor. The numbers were unprecedented.

The increase in the number of women candidates reflected recruiting drives by both major parties, who were alert to the fact that women make up 52% of the voters. It also reflected broader acceptance of women candidates by voters and, some analysts said, the example of Geraldine Ferraro's nomination for vice-president in 1984.

In most races the women candidates were able to keep pace with their male opponents in fund-raising, but polls showed that they still faced strong prejudices among voters. A poll conducted by *U.S. News & World Report,* for example, showed that a majority of voters rated women high in compassion for the poor and in concern for women's rights but considered them less qualified than men in dealing with crises, arms control, tax matters, and the Soviet Union.

What effect such attitudes may have had on the vote was unclear, but the women candidates generally did not fare well. The number of women in Congress remained the same: two in the Senate (including Democratic newcomer Barbara Mikulski from Maryland) and 23 in the House. Gov. Madeleine Kunin of Vermont (D) won reelection, and Kay Orr (R) won the Nebraska race, but the five other women gubernatorial candidates all lost their bids. Four women were elected lieutenant governors.

Business and Professions. U.S. Labor Department figures released in February showed that women held a narrow majority over men in the professions. Among the previously male-dominated fields in which women had gained the edge were psychology, statistics, and journalism; men continued to dominate such fields as medicine and law. The study also pointed to an earnings gap between the sexes: the median weekly earnings of the men in the study were $581, while those of women were $419. Other studies showed that, while women had made significant inroads in middle management, they were still underrepresented in upper management positions, holding 2% of top-level jobs.

Sears, Roebuck & Co. successfully defended itself in a suit charging discrimination against women in commission sales and management jobs, contending that women preferred less competitive jobs. The U.S. Equal Employment Opportunity Commission, which brought the suit, relied on statistics rather than personal accounts of discrimination; the court held that numbers alone did not prove the case.

In its first decision in a sexual harassment case, the Supreme Court ruled June 19 that harassment by an employee's supervisor which is "sufficiently severe or pervasive" to create a "hostile or abusive work environment" violates Title VII of the 1964 Civil Rights Act *(Meritor Savings Bank v. Vinson).*

Among public workers the concept of comparable worth—that women should receive equal pay for work of equal value to that done by men—gained ground. The American Federation of State, County, and Municipal Workers estimated in January that pay-equity decisions had already put some $200 million in workers' pockets. In a suit settled Dec. 31, 1985, the state of Washington agreed to wipe out salary differences between jobs of comparable worth held by women and men. The settlement was expected to cost the state $482 million over seven years. And in November 1986 voters in San Francisco approved a charter amendment requiring annual pay-equity reviews. It was the first time a U.S. city sent the issue to voters.

Other Concerns. Among other issues of concern to women in 1986 were divorce, retirement, and the future of women's movements in the United States and abroad.

Debate emerged on the effect of the "no-fault" divorce laws adopted by most states in the 1970s. Some reports showed that women had suffered under the laws, and women's groups urged courts to take a closer look at earning power and other factors in deciding divorce settlements. Meanwhile programs to help displaced homemakers learn new job skills suffered under federal budget cuts. Some state governments picked up the tab.

U.S. government figures showed that women were retiring in better health and with more benefits than ever. But the retirees' income still lagged significantly behind that of men, and women made up 71% of the elderly poor.

Under its new president, Eleanor Smeal, the National Organization for Women (NOW) took to the streets in several pro-abortion demonstrations in 1986. But debate on the future direction of the women's movement, which lost steam in the early 1980s, continued.

In a follow-up to the 1985 United Nations Decade for Women conference, 700 delegates from around the world met in Washington, DC, in October to discuss practical goals for women's advancement. Speakers at the meeting warned that traditional beliefs and customs continued to block progress in many countries.

ELAINE PASCOE, *Free-lance Writer*

WYOMING

A drop in crude oil prices in the spring of 1986 was good news for most energy consumers, but in the energy-producing state of Wyoming it meant substantial unemployment, marginal out-migration of population, very tight governmental budgets, and political debate over how to revive and diversify the stagnating economy.

The Economy. With the minerals sector at low ebb, statewide unemployment rose to about 10%, the highest rate in two decades. The oil rig count, an index of petroleum activity, was down by 50% from 1985 and the lowest since 1971. Coal production dropped by 4%, although the state remained second only to Kentucky in output. Banking, agriculture, and construction suffered as well. Only Cheyenne, buoyed by federal funds for the MX missile project, was relatively unscathed by the economic downturn.

The Budget Crunch. In February the Republican-controlled state legislature authorized a state budget of $773 million, $25 million less than the amount recommended by Democratic Gov. Ed Herschler, who vetoed other proposed cuts. The state's foundering workman's compensation fund was restructured in a brief special session in June. By then it was apparent that state revenues would fall far short of official projections made in December 1985. State and local agencies trimmed expenditures as tax receipts, federal mineral royalties, and the tax base followed the downward trend of oil prices.

Politics. The general elections in November sparked statewide discussion of the economic situation and how to deal with it. In the gubernatorial campaign, Republican candidate Pete Simpson stressed his experience as a college administrator and two-term legislator and his dedication to traditional Wyoming values. Democratic candidate Mike Sullivan, a political newcomer, emphasized his knowledge of the energy business and the need for innovative and aggressive executive action to spur eco-

nomic development. Although Simpson, the brother of U.S. Sen. Alan K. Simpson and son of former Gov. Milward L. Simpson, was favored in a state with about twice as many registered Republicans as Democrats, Sullivan eventually won with 54% of the vote.

Two of the remaining four state offices also went to Democrats—incumbent Lynn Simons won a third term as superintendent of public instruction and Kathy Karpan was elected secretary of state. Republican incumbent Stan Smith retained the post of state treasurer, and the race for state auditor was won by Republican Jack Sidi. Republican Richard Cheney, Wyoming's lone representative in the U.S. House, easily won a fifth term. The Democrats gained two seats in the lower house of the state legislature for a total of 20 seats to 44 for the Republicans. The party alignment in the state senate, with 19 Republicans and 11 Democrats, remained unchanged.

On May 21 the U.S. Senate confirmed the appointment of Lynne Cheney, the wife of Rep. Richard Cheney, as chairman of the National Endowment for the Humanities.

H. R. DIETERICH
University of Wyoming

WYOMING • Information Highlights

Area: 97,809 sq mi (253 326 km²).
Population (1985 est.): 509,000.
Chief Cities (1980 census): Cheyenne, the capital, 47,283; Casper, 51,016; Laramie, 24,410.
Government (1986): *Chief Officers*—governor, Ed Herschler (D); secretary of state, Thyra Thomson (R). *Legislature*—Senate, 30 members; House of Representatives, 64 members.
State Finances (fiscal year 1985): *Revenue,* $1,946,000,000; *expenditure,* $1,497,000,000.
Personal Income (1985): $6,734,000,000; per capita, $13,223.
Labor Force (June 1986): *Civilian labor force,* 262,000; *unemployed,* 24,300 (9.3% of total force).
Education: *Enrollment* (fall 1984)—public elementary schools, 73,049; public secondary, 28,212; colleges and universities, 24,204. *Public school expenditures* (1983–84), $420,000,000 ($4,488 per pupil).

AP/Wide World

Tragedy struck the town of Cokeville, WY, May 16 when former town marshall David Young and his wife seized control of the elementary school, right, demanding $300 million ransom. Their bomb accidentally detonated, and Young then shot his wife and himself. Some 78 persons, mostly children, suffered second-degree burns.

YUGOSLAVIA

In 1986, Yugoslavia faced its worst political-economic crisis since World War II. Its foreign debt totaled about $20 billion; its industrial production and exports were declining; and its rate of inflation had reached about 85% annually. More than 1.2 million people (13% of the labor force) were unemployed. With central authority waning, the country increasingly resembled a loose confederation of six republics and two autonomous provinces. Even the Yugoslav Communist Party (League of Communists of Yugoslavia—LCY) seemed to be losing its authority, cohesiveness, and popular appeal. Some 75,000 members, mostly blue-collar workers, left its ranks.

Domestic Affairs. The 13th Congress of the LCY took place in June in a glum, self-critical atmosphere. Current party leader Vidoje Zarković, addressing the 1,700 delegates, admitted the country's grave situation but offered no practical solutions. Yugoslavs were exhorted to place national interests over regional ones and to reduce consumption and spending on nonproductive social services. The party was urged to provide determined leadership. Responding, the congress elected a largely new central committee (replacing 127 of its 165 members), which in turn elected a new party presidium (replacing 17 of the 23 members). Within the state government, Sinan Hasani, an ethnic Albanian from the Kosovo province, took office for one year as president of the collective state presidency in May. Branko Mikulić, a Croat known as a strong disciplinarian and efficient organizer, became president of the Federal Executive Council (prime minister).

Domestic dissidence and ethnic tensions were on the rise. Attempts to "demythologize" the dead Yugoslav leader, Josip Broz Tito, provoked controversy. In late 1985 Dragoljub Petrović, a lecturer in history at the University of Novi Sad, was expelled from the Communist Party and given a 60-day prison sentence for an article charging that Yugoslav Communists had mistreated their opponents at the end of World War II. In October 1986 an unpublished 70-page manifesto prepared by the Serbian Academy of Sciences circulated, alleging that Tito (a Croat) and his deputy, Edvard Kardelj (a Slovene), had conspired to "destroy Serbia." Even the Serbs, comprising 8 of the 23 million Yugoslavs and considered the cement of the nation, and the Slovenes, the most quiescent and prosperous group within the country, betrayed growing separatist desires.

Ethnic tensions were highest in the Kosovo Autonomous Province, where Albanians number 78% of the population. There was a steady exodus of Serbs and Montenegrins, who faced assault, rape, and vandalism. They charged that ethnic Albanians, with the backing of Albania itself, were trying to drive them out and

YUGOSLAVIA • Information Highlights

Official Name: Socialist Federal Republic of Yugoslavia.
Location: Southeastern Europe.
Area: 98,766 sq mi (255 804 km²).
Population (mid-1986): 23,200,000.
Chief Cities (1981 census): Belgrade, the capital, 1,470,073; Osijek, 867,646; Zagreb, 768,700.
Government: *Head of state,* collective state presidency, Sinan Hasani, president (took office May 1986). *Head of government,* Branko Mikulić, president of the Federal Executive Council (took office May 1986). *Legislature*—Federal Assembly: Federal Chamber and Chamber of Republics and Provinces.
Monetary Unit: Dinar (402.78 dinars equal U.S.$1, Oct. 19, 1986).
Gross National Product (1984, est. at 1983 prices, U.S.$): $122,300,000,000.
Economic Indexes (1985): *Consumer Prices* (1980 = 100), all items, 694.0; food, 720.8. *Industrial Production* (1980 = 100), 114.
Foreign Trade (1985 U.S.$): *Imports,* $12,164,-000,000; *exports,* $10,641,000,000.

detach Kosovo from Yugoslavia. Polemics over the "endangered national rights" of ethnic Albanians and "Albanian interference in Yugoslav affairs" raged between the two countries. In May 1986 Yugoslavia sentenced 46 ethnic Albanians to prison terms ranging from 3 months to 13 years for trying to create an Albanian republic in Yugoslavia.

Foreign Relations. Two incidents caused friction with the United States: On a visit to Belgrade in December 1985, U.S. Secretary of State George Shultz expressed public anger at the suggestion of Yugoslav Foreign Minister Raif Dizdarević that the hijacking of the liner *Achille Lauro* in October 1985 by Palestinian terrorists might have been justified; secondly, in October 1986, Peter Ivezaj, an ethnic Albanian with dual U.S.-Yugoslav citizenship, was tried in Titograd for anti-Yugoslav activities in the United States. As a member of an Albanian-American student group, Ivezaj had taken part in demonstrations over the Kosovo issue in Chicago, Detroit, and Washington, DC. He was sentenced to seven years in prison. The U.S. State Department protested.

Despite mutual hostility Yugoslavia remained Albania's strongest trading partner, signing a new trade agreement for 1986–90 worth $680 million, an increase of 20% over the 1981–85 figure. In August 1986 it completed a new railroad link from Titograd in Montenegro to Shkodër in northwest Albania, providing Albania with its first connection with the European railway network.

Artukovic Case. In May, Andrija Artukovic, interior minister in the World War II pro-German government of Croatia, was convicted of war crimes and sentenced to death by a Zagreb court. Artukovic, 86, had been living in the United States for 37 years.

JOSEPH FREDERICK ZACEK
State University of New York at Albany

YUKON

In 1986 the major news in the Yukon Territory was of economic resurgence.

Economy. The reopening of the large lead and zinc mine at Faro by Curragh Resources Corporation highlighted the beginning of an economic upsurge that promised to break the back of the Yukon's two-year recession. Record high construction activity, a dropping unemployment rate, a vigorous tourism industry, and the lowest inflation rate in Canada all contributed to the economic renewal.

The value of building permits issued by the city of Whitehorse alone topped C$35 million as of September 1986, surpassing by more than $11 million the $24 million record set in 1978. An additional $19 million was being spent on construction in other Yukon communities.

Mineral production in the Yukon in 1985 was valued at $57 million, including $43 million in gold and $13 million in silver. With the reopening of the Faro mine, this total was expected to double in 1986.

Meanwhile, tourism dollars reached near record amounts in 1986 of $91.2 million, partly as a result of Expo 86 in Vancouver.

Government. Whitehorse lawyer Alan Nordling retained for the Progressive Conservative Party the seat vacated in the Yukon legislature following the highway death a year earlier of Conservative legislative member Andrew Philipsen. The by-election returned the legislative balance of power to eight New Democrats, six Conservatives, and two Liberals.

Indian Land Claims. While negotiators for the Yukon and federal governments and the Council for Yukon Indians initialed a federally sponsored Memorandum of Understanding, no formal talks began. Tentative proposals on some aspects of land selection and Indian self-government were discussed, but the federal cabinet balked on two items in the memorandum: the provision of a veto for Yukon Indians over any future transfer from Ottawa to the Yukon of additional political powers and apparent predetermined solutions to issues that may come up later in negotiations.

DON SAWATSKY, *Whitehorse*

ZAIRE

Zaire's improved economic situation was the most significant event of the year.

Economic Developments. Since 1983, Zaire's government has implemented sweeping economic reforms, including currency devaluation, spending cutbacks, and restrictions on wages. Although urban residents suffered from scarcities and high unemployment, these measures helped check inflation, improve the climate for foreign investment, and increase agricultural productivity. The International Monetary Fund (IMF) responded by awarding Zaire a loan of $165 million for 1986, and foreign creditors agreed to reschedule Zaire's $4 billion external debt. The World Bank planned to lend Zaire $550 million between 1986 and 1988, 20% of which would be used to aid in rehabilitating Gécamines, the state-owned cobalt and copper mining company.

Domestic Policy. President Mobutu Sese Seko's *Mouvement populaire de la revolution* (MPR), the only recognized political party, continued to control all levels of government. Attempts to create opposition parties were harshly repressed, and Amnesty International reported numerous human-rights violations in Shaba Province.

Foreign Policy. Tenuous relations with Belgium were further strained in April, when an Air Zaire plane was seized in connection with a lawsuit filed by a Belgian pilot. Mobutu revoked landing rights for Belgian aircraft, and moved Air Zaire's European personnel from Brussels to Paris. In July, Mobutu met with Angolan President José dos Santos in Angola. Mobutu promised to intercept any supplies in Zaire destined for UNITA rebel forces in Angola. Mobutu also conferred with President Reagan at the White House late in the year.

At the Organization of African Unity (OAU) meeting in Ethiopia in July, Mobutu campaigned covertly against harsh sanctions against South Africa, with which Zaire continued to trade. He agreed, however, to support comprehensive and mandatory OAU sanctions against the white minority regime.

HARRY A. GAILEY
San Jose State University

YUKON • Information Highlights

Area: 186,660 sq mi (483 450 km²).
Population (Jan. 1986 est.): 22,700.
Chief cities (1985 est.): Whitehorse, the capital, 17,265.
Government (1986): *Chief Officers*—commissioner, J. Kenneth McKinnon; government leader, Tony Penikett (New Democratic Party). *Legislature*—16-member Legislative Assembly.
Public Finance (1986–87 fiscal year budget est.): *Revenues,* C$251,384,000; *expenditures,* C$252,-000,000.
Personal Income (average weekly earnings, May 1986): C$447.76.
Education (1986–87) *Enrollment*—elementary and secondary schools, 4,470 pupils.

ZAIRE • Information Highlights

Official Name: Republic of Zaire.
Location: Central equatorial Africa.
Area: 905, 563 sq mi (2 345 409 km²).
Population (mid-1986 est.): 31,300,000.
Chief City (1981 est.): Kinshasa, the capital, 2,338,200.
Government: *Head of state,* Mobutu Sese Seko, president (took office 1965). *Legislature* (unicameral)—National Legislative Council.
Monetary Unit: Zaire (54.15 zaires equal U.S.$1, April 1986).
Foreign Trade (1984 U.S.$): *Imports,* $1,102,000,000; *exports,* $1,846,000,000.

ZIMBABWE

The future status of whites was a central issue in Zimbabwean domestic politics during 1986, while antagonisms with South Africa and growing differences with the United States highlighted the nation's foreign affairs.

Politics. At Zimbabwe's sixth anniversary of independence in April, Prime Minister Robert Mugabe declared that within the next year he intended to abolish the 20 seats reserved for whites in the 100-member House of Assembly. Under the constitution of 1979 these seats could be removed in mid-1987 if the government had the support of 70 members of the Assembly. In 1986 the ruling Zimbabwe African National Union—Patriotic Front (ZANU-PF) held 64 seats, opposition leader Joshua Nkomo's Zimbabwe African People's Union (ZAPU) had 15 seats, and the Conservative Alliance of former Prime Minister Ian Smith had 15 of the white-reserved seats.

In April, Smith was forced to apologize to the House of Assembly for remarks he had made on British television in which he maintained that majority rule in Zimbabwe was a "negation of democracy" because most Zimbabweans were "uneducated and uncivilized." At the anniversary celebration, Prime Minister Mugabe also reiterated his intention to change the constitution to allow for the creation of a one-party state. Meanwhile, Mugabe continued talks with Nkomo on a possible merger of ZANU and ZAPU.

South African Raid. In June, while the so-called Eminent Persons Group (EPG) was in South Africa to investigate political conditions on behalf of the British Commonwealth, South African forces raided African National Congress (ANC) targets in Zimbabwe, Botswana, and Zambia. Prime Minister Mugabe charged that South African forces had violated Zimbabwe's border and had attacked buildings in and near Harare. There were no casualties in either of the bombings. In protest of the attacks, however, the seven-member EPG cut short its visit.

Sanctions Against South Africa. In August, Prime Minister Mugabe announced that his government would impose economic sanctions against South Africa. Mugabe and the leaders of five other Commonwealth nations, including Zambia in Africa, had agreed to the sanctions at a summit meeting in London, August 2–5. Pretoria responded by implementing long delays in border inspections of all cargo coming from Zimbabwe and Zambia. With close to 90% of Zimbabwe's exports passing through South Africa, and with alternative transportation corridors through Mozambique under frequent attack by the South African-backed Mozambique National Resistance (MNR), the border disruptions were potentially crippling. Prime Minister Mugabe said that Zimbabwe was prepared to suffer whatever consequences might follow the imposition of sanctions, but by year's end he seemed more cautious regarding the extent and nature of the sanctions.

U.S. Relations. In 1986 relations between the United States and Zimbabwe reached their lowest point since Zimbabwe obtained independence in 1980. U.S. Ambassador David C. Miller, Jr., resigned in April after only two years in Harare, reportedly because of his inability to establish rapport with Prime Minister Mugabe and his government.

On July 4 former President Jimmy Carter, then on a visit to Zimbabwe, and Acting U.S. Ambassador Gibson Lanpher walked out of an official Independence Day reception because of an attack on U.S. policy toward South Africa in a speech written by Foreign Minister Witness Mangwende (and read on his behalf by the minister of youth, sport and culture). Prime Minister Mugabe subsequently apologized to Carter, but he refused to apologize to the Reagan administration because he considered the remarks "appropriate."

Later in July, Washington announced that it would delay disbursement of $13.5 million in U.S. aid until it received a satisfactory answer from Harare. Then in September the State Department announced that the United States would not be giving any new aid to Zimbabwe because of its "unwillingness to conduct relations . . . according to accepted norms of diplomatic civility and practice." In addition, the $13.5 million in aid promised for 1986 would be canceled.

Nonaligned Summit. Some 2,000 delegates, including 50 heads of state, met September 1–7 in Harare for the eighth summit conference of the Nonaligned Movement. In his keynote address, Prime Minister Mugabe, who took over as chairman of the movement for a three-year term, called on participants to provide economic aid to front-line states that cut off trade with South Africa.

PATRICK O'MEARA, *Indiana University*

ZIMBABWE · Information Highlights

Official Name: Republic of Zimbabwe.
Location: Southern Africa.
Area: 151,000 sq mi (391 090 km²).
Population (mid-1986 est.): 9,000,000.
Chief Cities (provisional census, Aug. 1982): Harare (formerly Salisbury), the capital, 656,000; Bulawayo, 413,800; Chitungwiza, 172,600.
Government: *Head of state,* Canaan Banana, president (took office April 1980). *Head of government,* Robert Mugabe, prime minister (took office March 1980). *Legislature*—Parliament: Senate and House of Assembly.
Monetary Unit: Zimbabwe dollar (1.745 Z dollars equal U.S.$1, May 1986).
Economic Indexes (1985): *Consumer Prices* (1980 = 100), all items, 200.9; food, 212.0. *Industrial Production* (1980 = 100), 108.
Foreign Trade (1984 U.S.$): *Imports,* $959,000,000; *exports,* $1,003,000,000.

The Burnet Park Zoo reopened in Syracuse, NY, following a four-year, $13 million renovation.

© Don Moore

ZOOS AND ZOOLOGY

Zoos and aquariums in North America opened a variety of new exhibits in 1986 that continued the trend toward displaying animals in their natural habitats and depicting diverse geographic regions and environments. Far from the menageries of former times, today's zoos and aquariums have become oases dedicated to protecting and breeding rare and endangered species, as well as arousing concern for the natural world.

Exhibits. After being closed for renovation for four years, the Burnet Park Zoo in Syracuse, NY, reopened in August. The $13-million face-lift focuses on animal life of the past and present. A four-sequence exhibit portrays the evolution of life on earth. Zoo visitors first find themselves in a cave depicting the past 600 million years—tidal pools inhabited by anemones, mollusks, and other invertebrates; a freshwater tank with bony fishes; neotropical woodlands for frogs and toads; and a river inhabited by present-day dinosaurs, the crocodilians. Then, a tropical walk-through aviary demonstrates the diversity in size, shape, color, and lifestyle of a number of different birds. Nocturnal exhibits inhabited by clouded leopards, sugar gliders, and fennec foxes show the various adaptations that animals have evolved to live in different environments. And troops of vervet monkeys, colonies of bees, and a white-handed gibbon family focus on social structures and interactions. A separate exhibit, called the Wild North, illustrates the types of animals found in the northern latitudes of North America—bison, elk, wolves, caribou, and prairie dogs.

Aquatic exhibits opened in a number of places during 1986. The Oklahoma City Zoo's new Aquaticus features an array of water habitats for creatures from Oklahoma and three U.S. coastal regions. In addition, visitors can see leopard sharks, kelp bass, and señorita fish swimming among the seaweeds of the California Kelp Bed, and explore a cave inhabited by sea anemones, sunflower stars, and a giant Pacific octopus. The New England Tidal Marsh display is filled with cordgrass, fiddler crabs, and periwinkles. Blue parrotfish, yellowtail snapper, and shrimps dwell in the Gulf of Mexico display.

In May, the Vancouver (B.C., Canada) Public Aquarium unveiled the Max Bell Marine Mammal Centre, in which visitors can view spectacular black-and-white killer whales from above and below the water. And the San Antonio (TX) Zoo has recreated a portion of Australia's Great Barrier reef in its Children's Zoo.

Primates received their fair share of attention. The St. Louis (MO) Zoo opened its Jungle of the Apes on June 14. A trail weaving among banyan trees, lianas, lush ferns, and bromeliads passes a group of chimpanzees grooming one another, then rises to treetop level, where orangutans spend most of their day, and drops down past a troop of resting lowland gorillas. Field notebooks provide information on primate social behavior, habits, and survival skills.

The Philadelphia (PA) Zoological Gardens also opened a primate exhibit in June. The World of Primates consists of a series of outdoor islands planted to resemble natural habitats for great apes and monkeys. Along with islands for gorillas and orangutans, there is a simulated jungle in which ring-tailed lemurs—primitive primates with foxlike faces—show off their climbing ability. Gibbons swing agilely among huge London plane trees; and drills, a type of baboon, live in large groups among grasses and thorny shrubs of a savanna.

Several new zoo projects were designed around geographical themes. The African

Veldt Exhibit at the Phoenix (AZ) Zoo provides a panorama of Kenya, with reticulated giraffes, ellipsis waterbuck, Thomson gazelles, ostriches, and vultures sharing 7 acres (2.8 ha). At the San Diego (CA) Zoo, rocky hillsides of the Kopje Exhibit are inhabited by a variety of East African mammals, including klipspringers and hyraxes. To demonstrate the diversity of life in mountain habitats, the Arizona-Sonora Desert Museum in Tucson has recreated montane zones from 4,500 to 7,000 ft (1 300 m to 2 100 m), as well as a section of rockwork resembling the Tucson Mountains. As visitors wind through the natural habitats, they see black bears, mountain lions, and Mexican gray wolves on high rocky outcrops. In September the Bronx (NY) Zoo unveiled to the public its Himalayan Highlands, which displays the critically endangered snow leopard as well as red pandas, tragopan pheasants, and white-naped cranes.

Breeding and Preservation. Among the significant births of 1986 was that of a false killer whale on May 1 at Sea Life Park in Honolulu, HI. It is the first of its species to be born and bred in captivity.

On September 26, Baby Shamu celebrated her first birthday at Sea World of Florida, in Orlando. She is the first killer whale to be born and thrive in captivity. At birth, Baby Shamu measured 6 ft (1.8 m) and weighed 350 lbs (159 kg). During her first year she grew to 9 ft (2.7 m) and 850 lbs (385 kg).

In early February, two captive-bred Guam rails were shipped to their native Pacific island from the Bronx Zoo in New York. At one time, the tiny island was filled with the sounds of birds, but habitat destruction, pesticide use, hunting, and disease wiped out many populations. But the worst culprit has been the brown tree snake, which is native to Australia, New Guinea, and the Solomon Islands. At the end

---

ZOOS AND ZOOLOGY / SPECIAL REPORT

Vivisection

The use of live animals in laboratory testing, research, and education—or vivisection—has become one of the most controversial practices of the 1980s—and one in which a small but vocal minority has begun to effect change through governmental legislation and public pressure.

The Issue. An estimated 17 to 22 million animals are used each year for testing, research, and education in government, industry, hospital, and university laboratories throughout the United States. Most are mice and rats, with smaller numbers of dogs, cats, hamsters, rabbits, guinea pigs, and nonhuman primates. Lab animals have been used for decades to test the effectiveness and safety of detergents, cosmetics, shampoos, toothpaste, shaving creams, and other products in daily use. Animal research on such medical problems as pain, heart disease, diabetes, cancers, AIDS, polio, diphtheria, whooping cough, and tetanus has, in many cases, led to medications which prevent, cure, or alleviate these serious or fatal afflictions.

While an Associated Press poll indicates that 80% of the U.S. public supports the use of animals for medical research, the use of live laboratory animals has been sharply challenged in recent years. Long the concern of only a few radical animal-rights activists, the issue has moved squarely into the mainstream of public concern. Groups ranging from long-established humane societies to radical animal-rights groups have risen in strong vocal opposition to laboratory use of animals. Their concern focuses on the extent of animal suffering, the manner in which research is conducted, and the purpose of the research—in short, whether the ends justify the means.

Out of these groups, two schools of thought have emerged. One weighs animal interests against human benefit. It allows that research on animals (or on humans) may sometimes be justified by potential gains in human (or animal) welfare, but insists that most experimentation causes too much suffering for too little gain. The other school holds that all animal research, however profitable, violates the moral rights of the experimental subjects.

Restrictions and Reforms. With aggressive campaigning and the recommendation of alternatives, the animal-rights movement has lobbied successfully for scores of bills in state and federal legislatures to restrict animal research. One of the most powerful measures is the Health Research Extension Act requiring the National Institutes of Health (NIH) to establish a special committee to review animal research projects at each institution that receives or requests NIH funding. Soon after the measure took effect on Jan. 1, 1986, several violations were uncovered. In February, NIH suspended a portion of funding to Columbia University after an unannounced site inspection revealed serious animal-care deficiencies. Funds also were suspended for the University of Pennsylvania and the City of

of World War II, the snake was accidentally introduced to Guam, where the species thrived by eating birds. Fortunately, the Guam Aquatic and Wildlife Resources Division took quick action to save the rail. In 1984, with the help of the Bronx Zoo and the National Zoo in Washington, DC, several pairs of wild-caught birds were sent to the United States for captive breeding. The two rails sent back to Guam will become part of a captive-breeding effort there until the birds can be released in the wild.

And in a Cuban forest, scientists discovered two ivory-billed woodpeckers, a North American species that many experts believed was extinct.

DEBORAH A. BEHLER, *Free-lance Writer*

The Max Bell Marine Mammal Centre, which opened at the Vancouver (B.C.) Public Aquarium in May 1986, is an outdoor "gallery" dedicated to Canada's marine mammals.

Finn Larsen

Hope Medical Center in Duarte, CA, until deficiencies were corrected.

In addition to new restrictive measures considered or enacted by state legislatures around the country, recent years have seen a number of private industries underwriting the refinement of existing procedures and the development of alternative research methods. Cosmetics firms, for example, have contributed some $5 million to the effort. Among the refinements being examined are the use of noninvasive imaging technology, greater use of anesthetics and tranquilizers, the early euthanasia of test animals, and the more efficient collection and distribution of test data. Among the alternatives being studied are *in vitro* cultures of animal components, electronic and mechanical simulators, and the use of cell cultures and microorganisms instead of larger live animals. For example, producing monoclonal antibodies from cancer cells grown in culture instead of mouse tumors may eliminate the need for millions of "mouse factories." Computer modeling of biological functions may also reduce the number of animals needed in the laboratory.

As a result of these developments, the number of animals used in research labs has fallen dramatically. In Great Britain animal use has dropped 35% in the past ten years. In Switzerland three large drug companies have reduced their use of animals by one half over the past decade. In the United States some companies report a 75% reduction in animal use.

Complexities. But the use of animals in the laboratory is far from over. Current technology is not adequate to eliminate animal research in the foreseeable future. And researchers argue that a total and immediate ban on vivisection would jeopardize the health and safety of life on our planet.

Today more than 50,000 chemicals are authorized for consumer and industrial use, with 500 to 1,000 being added each year. To protect human, plant, and animal life from possible toxicity, the properties and effects of these chemicals must be understood. The development and validation of many alternative testing techniques cannot be done without the use of animals (unless humans are used instead). A total ban, many contend, would cause delay in the marketing of drugs and pesticides, creating possible health hazards for the public.

Thus, the problem encompasses complex and serious legal, political, ethical, scientific, and economic issues. No simple answers exist. The concern of the federal government is to satisfy society's need for progress in research, toxicity testing for public health and safety, and medical education.

In February 1986, the congressional Office of Technology Assessment (OTA) issued a massive report on alternatives to animal testing, research, and education. The authors of the report contended that much animal experimentation is unnecessary and often poorly regulated, that alternatives to such procedures are becoming available, and that new alternatives should be developed. The document also included an outline of evolving technologies that could substantially reduce the number of animals needed for laboratory research.

By way of conclusion, the report recommended a balancing of competing concerns. A complete ban on animal testing "must be considered dangerous," it held, but alternatives to animal research should begin to be phased in.

DENNIS L. MAMMANA

Statistical and Tabular Data

NATIONS OF THE WORLD

A Profile and Synopsis of Major 1986 Developments

Nation, Region	Population in millions	Capital	Area Sq mi (km²)	Head of State/Government
Angola, S.W. Africa	8.2	Luanda	481,351 (1 246 700)	José Eduardo dos Santos, president

Rebels continued to fight the Soviet-backed Angolan government, which was aided by about 35,000 Cuban troops. In January rebel leader Jonas Savimbi visited Washington seeking support, and the Reagan administration later acknowledged it was providing covert aid, including antiaircraft missiles. It also urged American oil companies to leave Angola, a move that could have serious impact on the country's deteriorating economy. The Angolan government in June and September called for top-level talks with the United States as a first step in reestablishing diplomatic relations, which Angola had ended in 1985. In June in one of several actions taken in support of the rebels throughout the year, South Africa attacked Namibe harbor, sinking a Cuban ship and damaging two Soviet ships. Rebels opened a front in the north, near Angola's main oil fields, in the fall. Gross Domestic Product, GDP (1985 est.): $4 billion. Foreign Trade (1985): Imports, $1.7 billion; exports, $2.03 billion.

Antigua and Barbuda, Caribbean	0.1	St. John's	171 (443.6)	Sir Wilfred E. Jacobs, governor-general; Vere C. Bird, prime minister

Antigua and Barbuda joined the International Maritime Organization in January, and established diplomatic relations with Thailand in March. GDP (1984): $158 million. Foreign Trade (1984): Imports, $146.9 million; exports, $41 million.

Bahamas, Caribbean	0.2	Nassau	5,380 (13 934)	Sir Gerald C. Cash, governor-general Lynden O. Pindling, prime minister

The Bahamian vice-consul in Ottawa, Janet Rahming, was held hostage for 15 hours on April 1–2 by a single gunman. She was released unharmed, and the gunman, a former convict who had demanded aid for Ottawa's homeless, was apprehended. In May, Bank Leu International, the Bahamian branch of the Swiss Bank Leu Ltd., was implicated in a U.S. Securities and Exchange Commission suit involving charges of insider trading. Gross National Product, GNP (1984): $1.8 billion. Foreign Trade (1984): Imports, $4.01 billion; exports, $3.39 billion.

Bahrain, W. Asia	0.4	Manama	261 (676)	Isa bin Sulman Al Khalifa, emir Khalifa bin Salman Al Khalifa, prime minister

On April 26, helicopters from Qatar strafed a disputed coral reef in the Persian Gulf where Bahrain was constructing a coast-guard station and took 30 foreign construction workers prisoner. Saudi Arabia announced that it would mediate in the dispute, and 17 of the workers were released May 12. A billion-dollar causeway linking Bahrain to Saudi Arabia was completed, but its opening was delayed while the government studied the potential impact of the increase in visitors the causeway was expected to bring. GDP (1985 est.): $4.468 billion. Foreign Trade (1985): Imports, $2.6 billion; exports, $2.86 billion.

Barbados, Caribbean	0.3	Bridgetown	166 (430)	Sir Hugh Springer, governor-general Errol Barrow, prime minister

The Democratic Labour party won a sweeping victory in general elections May 27, taking 24 of 27 seats in the House of Assembly. The victory ended ten years of rule by the Labour Party, led by Bernard St. John. GDP (1984): $1.152 billion. Foreign Trade (1985): Imports, $607 million; exports, $352 million.

Benin, W. Africa	4.1	Porto Novo	43,483 (112 622)	Mathieu Kérékou, president

Benin began working with the International Monetary Fund to restructure its debt and institute economic controls. GNP (1984 est.): $974.2 million. Foreign Trade (1984): Imports, $225.4 million; exports, $172.5 million.

Bhutan, S. Asia	1.4	Thimphu	18,000 (46 620)	Jigme Singye Wangchuck, king

GDP (fiscal year 1984–85): $300 million. Foreign Trade (fiscal year 1984–85): Imports, $69.4 million; exports, $15.1 million.

Botswana, S. Africa	1.1	Gaborone	231,804 (600 372)	Quett Masire, president

South African commandos May 19 attacked a village near Gaborone where they claimed guerrillas of the African National Congress (ANC) were training. One person was reported killed. Botswana denied that ANC personnel were in the area and was joined by many nations in condemning the raid. U.S. civil-rights activist Jesse Jackson visited Botswana in August, speaking against apartheid in South Africa. GDP (1984): $905 million. Foreign Trade (1984): Imports, $690 million; exports, $670 million.

Brunei, S.E. Asia	0.2	Bandar Seri Begawan	2,235 (5 788)	Sir Hassanal Bolkiah, sultan and prime minister

Former Sultan Sir Omar Ali Saifuddin III, the current sultan's father, chief adviser, and defense minister, died September 8. In November the government took over the National Bank of Brunei and arrested its chairman and two others for allegedly using unsecured loans to companies related to the family of the bank's chairman. Late in the year, Brunei was reported to have contributed several million dollars to a secret Swiss bank account set up by U.S. government officials to aid Nicaraguan rebels. GDP (1984): $1.7 billion. Foreign Trade (1983): Imports, $728 million; exports, $3.4 billion.

Burkina Faso, W. Africa	7.1	Ouagadougou	92,741 (240 200)	Thomas Sankara, head of government

A brief border war with Mali that broke out late in 1985 was settled in January. Sankara dissolved the government in August, for the third year in a row, and named three military leaders "general coordinators" for a new government. GDP (1984): $66 million. Foreign Trade (1984): Imports, $207 million; exports, $79 million.

Burundi, E. Africa	4.9	Bujumbura	10,747 (27 834)	Jean-Baptiste Bagaza, president

At a two-day meeting in Bujumbura in May, member countries of the Preferential Trade Area (a group of 15 eastern and southern African nations) agreed to grant preferential tariffs to companies that were at least 51% locally owned. GDP (1984 est.): $963 million. Foreign Trade (1985): Imports, $186 million; exports, $110 million.

Nation, Region	Population in millions	Capital	Area Sq mi (km²)	Head of State/Government
Cameroon, Cen. Africa	10.0	Yaounde	183,567 (475 439)	Paul Biya, president

Poisonous gas from volcanic Lake Nios, near Wum, killed approximately 1,700 people on August 21. The exact cause of the disaster remained unclear. The United States and Western European nations were among those that sent aid. In another development, Cameroon and Israel resumed diplomatic ties that had been broken in 1973, and Israeli Prime Minister Shimon Peres visited Cameroon August 25–26, the first Israeli leader to do so in 20 years. GDP (1984–85): $7.934 billion. Foreign Trade (1984): Imports, $1.1 billion; exports, $882 million.

Cape Verde, W. Africa	0.3	Praia	1,560 (4 040)	Aristides Pereira, president Pedro Pires, prime minister

President Pereira, who had held his post since 1975, was unanimously reelected by the National Assembly January 13 for another five year term. Prime Minister Pires was also reelected.

Central African Republic, Cen. Africa	2.7	Bangui	240,534 (622 984)	André-Dieudonne Kolingba, president

Former self-proclaimed emperor Jean-Bedel Bokassa, who was sentenced to death in absentia after he fled the country in 1979, returned from exile in France October 23 and was promptly arrested. In another event, in March, the crash of a French military jet into a school near Bangui killed 22 people and set off violent anti-European protests. GDP (1984): $764 million. Foreign Trade (1984): Imports, $139.6 million; exports, $114.6 million.

Chad N.-Cen. Africa	5.2	Ndjamena	495,998 (1 284 634)	Hissein Habré, president

Northern Chad remained under the control of Libyan troops and rebel forces. In February these forces launched an offensive, and French jets backed Chadian troops by bombing a Libyan-built airfield near Wadi Doum. The rebel forces responded by bombing the Ndjamena airport, and France then sent in more troops and planes. The United States provided Chad with $10 million in military aid. In November former President Goukouni Oueddi was reported to have been replaced by Acheikh Ibn Oumar as rebel leader, after breaking with Libya and offering to negotiate with Ndja-mena. Most of his troops then joined Habré's forces in an attempt to drive out Libyan troops from Chad. Renewed fighting broke out late in the year, and the United States and France sent additional emergency equipment to Chad. Meanwhile, in March, President Habré shuffled his cabinet to include several former leaders of the southern rebels who had made peace with the government late in 1985. GDP (1984 est.): $360 million.

Comoros, E. Africa	0.5	Moroni	838 (2 171)	Ahmed Abdallah Abderemane, president

President Abdallah granted amnesty Dec. 31, 1985, to 58 of 67 prisoners convicted of a 1985 coup attempt. The country's budget for 1986 showed that the cost of servicing the foreign debt had risen 80%. GNP (1984): $92 million. Foreign Trade (1984): Imports, $27 million; exports, $16 million.

Congo, Cen. Africa	1.8	Brazzaville	132,046 (342 000)	Denis Sassou-Nguesso, president Ange Edouard Poungui, prime minister

A drop in oil prices reduced revenues, causing the government to cut spending nearly in half and accept International Monetary Fund supervision for the rescheduling of its debt. In July, President Sassou-Nguesso was elected to a one-year term as chairman of the Organization of African Unity. (OAU). GDP (1984 est.): $1.8 billion. Foreign Trade (1984): Imports, $618 million; exports, $1.18 billion.

Djibouti, E. Africa	0.3	Djibouti	8,494 (22 000)	Hassan Gouled Aptidon, president Barkat Gourad Hamadou, premier

Thousands of foreigners, many of them Soviets, were evacuated from South Yemen to Djibouti in January in a joint British-Soviet operation. The refugees fled factional fighting in South Yemen. GDP (1984 est.): $331.955 million. Foreign Trade (1984): Imports, $200 million; exports, $88 million.

Dominica, Caribbean	0.1	Roseau	291 (752.7)	Clarence A. Seignoret, president (Mary) Eugenia Charles, prime minister

Frederick Newton, former commander of the armed forces, was hanged August 8 for his role in a 1981 attempt to overthrow the government. GNP (1984): $85.4 million. Foreign Trade (1984): Imports, $55.8 million; exports, $25.6 million.

Dominican Republic, Caribbean	6.4	Santo Domingo	18,816 (48 734)	Joaquin Belaguer, president

Joaquin Belaguer, 78, defeated Senate president Jacobo Majluta Azar in a close presidential election May 16. Although judged fair by observers, the vote was marred by charges of fraud and was followed by clashes between rival political groups, including one in which soldiers opened fire and killed five persons. Belaguer, who had served as president in the 1960s and 1970s, took office August 16. GNP (1984): $11 billion. Foreign Trade (1985): Imports, $1.38 billion; exports, $741 million.

Equatorial Guinea, Cen. Africa	0.4	Malabo	10,830 (28 051)	Teodoro Obiang Nguema Mbasogo, president Cristino Seriche Bioko, premier

A coup attempt was foiled July 20 and its leader, Eugenio Abeso Mondu, was executed August 19. Several other civilian and military officials were sentenced to prison. GNP (1983): $75 million.

Fiji, Oceania	0.7	Suva	7,095 (18 376)	Sir Penaia Ganilau, governor-general Sir Kamisese Mara, premier

In June, Fiji agreed to discuss trade and technical exchanges with the Soviet Union. Member nations of the South Pacific Forum met in Fiji in August and expressed disapproval of continued French rule in New Caledonia. GDP (1984): $1.32 billion. Foreign Trade (1985): Imports, $442 million; exports, $236 million.

Gabon, Cen. Africa	1.2	Libreville	103,346 (267 667)	El Hadj Omar Bongo, president Léon Mébiame, premier

Gabon refused asylum to ousted Haitian dictator Jean-Claude Duvalier in February. In presidential elections November 9, President Bongo was the only candidate. GDP (1984): $3.331 billion. Foreign Trade (1984): Imports, $900 million; exports, $2 billion.

Gambia, W. Africa	0.8	Banjul	4,361 (11 295)	Sir Dawda Kairaba Jawara, president

Early in the year, several leading politicians broke with President Jawara's People's Progressive Party to form a new group, the Gambian People's Party, led by former Vice-President Assan Camara. In March the legislature passed a new treason law that permitted the death penalty for anyone convicted on the testimony of a single witness of plotting to overthrow the government. GDP (1984): $125 million. Foreign Trade (1984): Imports, $98 million; exports, $47 million.

Nation, Region	Population in millions	Capital	Area Sq mi (km²)	Head of State/Government
Ghana, W. Africa	13.6	Accra	92,100 (238 538)	Jerry Rawlings, chairman of the Provisional National Defense Council (PNDC)

Seven persons convicted of taking part in a 1985 attempted coup were executed June 22. The plot was one of at least a dozen since Rawlings seized power in 1981. GDP (1985 est.): $5.794 billion. Foreign Trade (1984): Imports, $591 million; exports, $571 million.

Grenada, Caribbean	0.1	St. George's	133 (344)	Sir Paul Scoon, governor-general Herbert A. Blaize, prime minister

Former Deputy Prime Minister Bernard Coard and 13 others were sentenced to death December 4 for their role in the 1983 killing of Prime Minister Maurice Bishop. In other news, U.S. President Reagan attended a summit of Caribbean leaders in Grenada February 20 and was welcomed enthusiastically in St. George's. Grenada's economy was reported to be growing with the help of U.S. aid, but unemployment remained at about 25%. GDP (1984 est.): $86.8 million. Foreign Trade (1983): Imports, $55.6 million; exports, $18.9 million.

Guinea, W. Africa	6.2	Conakry	94,964 (245 957)	Lansana Conté, president

President Conté shuffled his cabinet late in 1985, removing several political rivals. The International Monetary Fund (IMF) announced in February 1986 that it had granted Guinea a standby credit arrangement; $200 million of the country's foreign debt was rescheduled in April. U.S. black militant Stokely Carmichael was arrested in Guinea in August. The charges against Carmichael, who had lived in Guinea since 1969, were not immediately made known. GDP (1984): $1.546 billion. Foreign Trade (1984 est.): Imports, $403 million; exports, $537 million.

Guinea-Bissau, W. Africa	0.9	Bissau	14,000 (36 260)	João Bernardo Vieira, president

Fifty-six people were convicted July 12 of plotting a coup against President Vieira in November 1985. Six, including former Vice-President Paulo Coreia, were executed July 21 despite international appeals. GDP (1984 est.): $183.544 million. Foreign Trade (1983): Imports, $57 million; exports, $8.6 million.

Guyana, Northeast South America	0.8	Georgetown	83,000 (214 970)	Hugh Desmond Hoyte, president Hamilton Green, prime minister

A new cabinet was named January 28, and President Hoyte announced that it would concentrate on policy, delegating routine business to new supervisory councils. The formation of a new opposition group, the Patriotic Coalition for Democracy, was announced January 9. GNP (1984): $399 million. Foreign Trade (1984): Imports, $230 million; exports, $189 million.

Haiti, Caribbean	5.9	Port-au-Prince	10,714 (27 749)	Henri Namphy, head of governing council

GNP (fiscal year 1984): $1.8 billion. Foreign Trade (1984): Imports, $472 million; exports, $179 million. See page 166.

Ivory Coast, W. Africa	10.5	Yamoussoukro	124,503 (322 463)	Félix Houphouët-Boigny, president

In January, Liberia reopened its border with Ivory Coast, which had been closed since late 1985. Ivory Coast sent a peacekeeping force to supervise a January truce in a border dispute between Mali and Burkina Faso. GDP (1984): $6.1 billion. Foreign Trade (1985): Imports, $1.74 billion; exports, $2.9 billion.

Jamaica, Caribbean	2.3	Kingston	4,244 (10 991)	Florizel Glasspole, governor-general Edward Seaga, prime minister

Prime Minister Seaga's Jamaica Labour Party won just 43% of the vote in local elections July 29, compared with 57% for Michael Manley's People's National Party. An economy that was deteriorating, chiefly because of a 50% drop in bauxite income, and government austerity measures were seen as reasons for the defeat. In the fall, Seaga announced that he would not seek reelection in 1988, but he later retracted the statement, saying that his continued tenure in office was critical to economic recovery. GNP (1984): $2 billion. Foreign Trade (1985): Imports, $1.11 billion; exports, $564 million.

Kiribati, Oceania	0.06	Tarawa	278 (719)	Reginald Wallace, governor-general Ieremia Tabai, president

Kiribati allowed its $1 million fishing-rights agreement with the Soviet Union to lapse in October. Instead it joined with 16 other Pacific nations in an agreement with the United States that would direct $60 million to the region over five years in exchange for fishing rights. GDP (1984 est.): $25 million.

Kuwait, W. Asia	1.8	Kuwait	6,880 (17 818)	Jabir al-Ahmad Al Sabah, emir Sa'd al-Abdallah Al Sabah, prime minister

Under pressure from the legislature, the Kuwaiti cabinet resigned July 1. Two days later, citing danger from the Iran-Iraq war and an economic crisis, the emir dissolved the legislature, imposed press censorship, and suspended parts of the constitution. The cabinet was reinstated with minor changes July 12, but no date was set for the return of the legislature. In other news, a proposal to grant Kuwaiti women the vote was defeated in March, and Britain promised to aid Kuwait should the war between Iran and Iraq spread across its borders. In October the Organization of the Petroleum Exporting Countries (OPEC) granted Kuwait an increase of 78,000 barrels per day in its oil-production quota. GNP (1984): $21.8 billion. Foreign Trade (1984): Imports, $7.7 billion; exports, $10.75 billion.

Lesotho, S. Africa	1.6	Maseru	11,761 (30 460)	Moshoeshoe II, king Justin Lekhanya, chairman, council of ministers

Prime Minister Leabua Jonathan was ousted in a military coup January 20, ending 20 years of rule. The coup was preceded by a South African blockade of Lesotho, imposed to curb the presence of members of the anti-Pretoria African National Congress (ANC) there. Following the coup, the new leaders said they would fly ANC members out of Lesotho but not hand them over to South Africa, and the blockade was lifted. GDP (1983): $300 million.

Liberia, W. Africa	2.3	Monrovia	43,000 (111 370)	Samuel K. Doe, president

Doe was sworn in as president January 6, following a 1985 election widely reported as rigged, and released 18 political opponents and journalists from prison. However, several opposition leaders who formed a coalition and demanded new elections were arrested later in the year and released only after international pressure. One, Ellen Johnson-Sirleaf, fled the country after receiving what she said were threats against her life. Continued reports of human-rights abuses prompted both houses of the U.S. Congress to pass resolutions calling for an end to aid to Liberia. GDP (1984): $1.14 billion. Foreign Trade (1985): Imports, $284 million; exports, $436 million.

Liechtenstein, Cen. Europe	0.03	Vaduz	62 (160)	Franz Josef II, prince Hans Brunhart, prime minister

A conservative coalition was returned to power in elections February 2. The vote was the first in which women took part. Prime Minister Brunhart was reappointed by the legislature April 30. GNP (1984 est.): approximately $15,000 per capita. Foreign Trade (1984): exports, $440 million.

Nation, Region	Population in millions	Capital	Area Sq mi (km²)	Head of State/Government
Luxembourg, W. Europe	0.4	Luxembourg	998 (2 586)	Jean, grand duke Jaques Santer, prime minister

Following reports of Libyan involvement in terrorism and a U.S. retaliatory raid on Libya in April, the government ordered Libya to cut the levels of its diplomatic personnel in Luxembourg. The Luxembourg franc was revalued April 6 along with other currencies of the European Monetary System. GDP (1985 est.): $3.338 billion.

Madagascar, E. Africa	10.3	Antananarivo	228,919 (592 900)	Didier Ratsiraka, head of government Desire Rakotoarijaona, premier

Thirteen people, including Defense Minister Rear Adm. Guy Sibon and other government officials, were killed in a plane crash in Madagascar's central mountains May 3. In other developments, the government in January claimed a 200-mile offshore limit that encompassed the "scattered islands," which France also claimed, and signed a general trade and economic agreement with Egypt in February. GDP (1984): $2.4 billion.

Malawi, E. Africa	7.3	Lilongwe	45,747 (118 484)	Hastings Kamuzu Banda, president

In a meeting in Zimbabwe January 30–31, Malawi joined other members of the African Development Coordination Conference in calling for an economic boycott of South Africa. The country devalued its currency by 10% in August to increase the competitiveness of its exports. In November, several thousand refugees from fighting in Mozambique were reported to have crossed into Malawi. GDP (1985): $1.053 billion.

Maldives, S. Asia	0.2	Malé	115 (298)	Maumoon Abdul Gayoom, president

Mali, W. Africa	7.9	Bamako	478,764 (1 240 000)	Moussa Traoré, president

A brief border war with Burkina Faso was resolved in January. Rains eased a two-year drought but were followed by an invasion of locusts that threatened crops. In other news, Sabine Thierry, the French adventurer who established the grueling Paris-Dakar car rallly, was killed in a helicopter crash in Mali January 14, during the 1986 race. GDP (1984): $1.098 billion. Foreign Trade (1984): Imports, $345 million; exports, $165 million.

Malta, S. Europe	0.4	Valletta	121 (313)	Agatha Barbara, president Karmenu Mifsud Bonnici, prime minister

Four people were shot and wounded November 30 by the police during a conflict between followers of Prime Minister Mifsud Bonnici and the opposition Nationalist Party. One person was killed by shots fired from a passing car outside a Nationalist club in Gudia December 7. GDP (1984): $1 billion. Foreign Trade (1985): Imports, $758 million; exports, $400 million.

Mauritania, W. Africa	1.9	Nouakchott	397,954 (1 030 700)	Maaouiya Ould Sid Ahmed Taya, president and prime minister

The International Monetary Fund (IMF) reached a standby credit agreement with Mauritania in April. The government announced plans for local council elections, the first since a 1984 coup, but no date was set for the vote. GDP (1984 est.): $847.923 million. Foreign Trade (1985): Imports, $234 million; exports, $374 million.

Mauritius, E. Africa	1.0	Port Louis	720 (1 865)	Sir Veerasamy Ringadoo, governor-general Aneerood Jugnauth, prime minister

Governor-General Sir Seewoosagur Ramgoolam died in December 1985, and Sir Veerasamy Ringadoo, a former minister of finance, was appointed to the post in January 1986. Prime Minister Jugnauth shuffled his cabinet in January, after four ministers resigned to protest his handling of the arrest of four members of parliament in the Netherlands on drug-smuggling charges. His government survived a censure motion brought against it in parliament in May, and an inquiry into the drug charges began at midyear. GDP (1984–85): $1 billion.

Monaco, S. Europe	0.03	Monaco-Ville	0.7 (1.9)	Rainier III, prince M. Jean Ausseil, minister of state

M. Jean Ausseil was appointed minister of state to replace Jean Herly, who retired.

Mongolia, E. Asia	1.9	Ulan Bator	604,100 (1 564 619)	Jambyn Batmonh, chairman of the Presidium Dumaagiyn Sodnom, chairman, Council of Ministers

In January, Chinese vice foreign minister Qian Qichen listed the continuing presence of Soviet troops in Mongolia as a major roadblock to improved Sino-Soviet relations. Soviet leader Mikhail Gorbachev said in July that he envisioned substantial troop withdrawals, but he gave no date or specifics. China and Mongolia signed a consular agreement August 9. GDP (1985 est.): $2.123 billion. Foreign Trade (1981): Imports, $655 million; exports, $436 million.

Mozambique, E. Africa	14.0	Maputo	302,328 (783 030)	Joaquím A. Chissano, president

President Samora Moises Machel was killed in a plane crash in South Africa October 19, while returning from a meeting in Zambia. South Africa denied charges that it had caused the crash. On November 3, Foreign Minister Joaquím A. Chissano was elected president by the Central Committee of the Mozambique Liberation Front. Mozambique's leftist government continued to fight South African-supported rebels throughout the year. The rebels were reported to have captured the district capital of Ulongwe, near the Mali border, in November. GNP (1985 est.): $2 billion.

Nauru, Oceania	0.008	Nauru	8 (20.7)	Hammer DeRoburt, president

GNP (1984): $160 million. Foreign Trade (1984): Exports, $93 million.

Nepal, S. Asia	17.4	Katmandu	54,359 (140 791)	Birendra Bir Bikram, king Marish Man Singh Shrestha, prime minister

At least seven people were injured in unrest during general elections May 12. The vote was marked by threats of bombings by terrorists opposed to the monarchy. As a result of the elections, Marish Man Singh Shrestha was appointed prime minister June 13. A new council of ministers was named June 16. GDP (fiscal year 1984–85): $2.4 billion. Foreign Trade (fiscal year 1984–85): Imports, $450 million; exports, $157 million.

Niger, W. Africa	6.7	Niamey	489,189 (1 267 000)	Seyni Kountché, president Hamid Algabid, prime minister

Representatives of Niger and Mali met in May to establish a commission that would clarify their common border. GDP (1985 est.): $1.2 billion. Foreign Trade (1983): Imports, $324 million; exports, $298 million.

Oman, W. Asia	1.3	Muscat	ca. 82,000 (212 380)	Qaboos bin Said, sultan and prime minister

British and Omani naval, air, and ground forces held joint exercises in November. GNP (1984): $7.7 billion. Foreign Trade (1984): Imports, $2.75 billion; exports, $4.42 billion.

Nation, Region	Population in millions	Capital	Area Sq mi (km²)	Head of State/Government
Papua New Guinea, Oceania	3.4	Port Moresby	178,259 (461 691)	Sir Kingsford Dibela, governor-general Paias Wingti, prime minister

A friendship treaty signed with Indonesia drew fire from opposition leaders, who said it would help Indonesia suppress guerrillas in neighboring Irian Jaya. In August, Papua New Guinea's parliament voted to delay the introduction of television, for fear of diluting the culture with American and Australian ideas. GNP (1984): $2.2 billion.

Qatar, W. Asia	0.3	Doha	4,247 (11 000)	Khalifa bin Hamad Al Thani, emir and prime minister

Qatar staged a raid April 26 on the Fasht al-Dibal reef in the Persian Gulf, which both it and Bahrain claimed. The target of the raid was a coast guard station being built by a Dutch company for Bahrain. Thirty foreign workers were taken prisoner. Qatar freed 17 of them May 12, and Saudi Arabia announced that it would mediate in the dispute. GDP (1985): $3.050 billion. Foreign Trade (1984): Imports, $1 billion; exports, $4.5 billion.

Rwanda, E. Africa	6.5	Kigali	10,169 (26 338)	Juvénal Habyarimana, president

The Rwandan government announced in July that the country, as Africa's most densely populated, had no room for the return of approximately 2,000 of its citizens who were living in neighboring countries, mostly as refugees. GDP (1984): $1.6 billion. Foreign Trade (1985): Imports, $368 million; exports, $141 million.

Saint Christopher and Nevis, Caribbean	0.04	Basseterre	101 (261)	Clement A. Arrindell, governor-general Kennedy A. Simmonds, prime minister

Saint Christopher and Nevis established diplomatic relations with Thailand in March. GNP (1983): $61.9 million. Foreign Trade (1983): Imports, $47.3 million; exports, $30.6 million.

Saint Lucia, Caribbean	0.1	Castries	239 (619)	Sir Allen Lewis, governor-general John Compton, prime minister

St. Lucia established diplomatic relations with Thailand in March. GDP (1984): $148.1 million. Foreign Trade (1983): Imports, $106.8 million; exports, $49.7 million.

Saint Vincent and the Grenadines, Caribbean	0.1	Kingstown	150 (389)	Joseph Lambert Eustace, governor-general James F. Mitchell, prime minister

The English cricket team, arriving in St. Vincent January 31 to begin a test series against the West Indies, was met by antiapartheid demonstrators who objected to the fact that some British players had played in South Africa. (The West Indies took the series, 5–0.) GNP (1983): $88.9 million.

San Marino, S. Europe	0.023	San Marino	24 (62)	Co-regents appointed semi-annually

In July, the parliament approved a new government program that had been put forward by a coalition of the Communist and Christian Democratic parties. It was the first coalition between these parties, which were the largest in parliament.

São Tomé and Principe, W. Africa	0.1	São Tomé	372 (963)	Manuel Pinto da Costa, president

President Pinto da Costa shuffled his cabinet in February, giving up the posts of foreign affairs and planning and reducing the number of ministers. In April, a group of 76 São Tomean nationals in a 50-ft (15-m) fishing boat were rescued by South African naval forces off the coast of Namibia. The group said they were seeking military aid from South Africa to depose the government of President Pinto da Costa.

Senegal, W. Africa	6.9	Dakar	75,750 (196 192)	Abdou Diouf, president

President Diouf presented a plan for African economic recovery to the United Nations May 27. The plan, developed by the Organization for African Unity (OAU), called for changes in the agricultural system, greater reliance on private enterprise, and a "new set of relationships" between African countries and developed countries. GDP (1984): $2.3 billion. Foreign Trade (1984): Imports, $1.0 billion; exports, $534 million.

Seychelles, E. Africa	0.1	Victoria	108 (280)	France Albert René, president

President René named three new ministers to his cabinet in September, including the first woman cabinet minister, Rita Sinon, who was named interior minister. GDP (1984 est.): $148.748 million.

Sierra Leone, W. Africa	3.7	Freetown	27,699 (71 740)	Joseph Momoh, president

One-party parliamentary elections held May 30 led to a large turnover in the legislature. President Momoh named a new cabinet in June. GDP (1983–84 est.): $1 billion. Foreign Trade (1985): Imports, $156 million; exports, $112 million.

Solomon Islands, Oceania	0.3	Honiara	11,500 (29 785)	Sir Baddeley Devesi, governor-general Sir Peter Kenilorea, prime minister

The worst typhoon to hit the Solomon Islands in history struck May 19, flattening entire villages and killing at least 97 people. Officials estimated that it would take the islands five years to recover from the damage. GNP (1982): $131 million. Foreign Trade (1985): Imports, $69 million; exports, $70 million.

Somalia, E. Africa	7.8	Mogadishu	246,200 (637 657)	Mohamed Siad Barre, president

Refugees from Ethiopia continued to swell Somalia's population, prompting disputes between the United Nations and Somalia on aid levels and the handling of the refugees, most of whom were restricted to crowded camps near the border. President Siad Barre was severely injured in a traffic accident in Mogadishu that killed six people in May. GDP (1984 est.): $1.149 billion. Foreign Trade (1985): Imports, $561 million; exports, $107 million.

Suriname, S. America	0.4	Paramaribo	63,037 (163 265)	Desire Bouterse, head of National Military Council Willem Udenhout, prime minister

The Bouterse government faced a small rebel force and a deteriorating economy in 1986. While government troops fought guerrillas of the Surinamese Liberation Army (led by a former army commander, Ronny Brunswijk), 14 people were charged in the United States with planning to overthrow the Surinamese government. The leader of that group, Tommy Denley of Mississippi, was sentenced November 5 to two concurrent 30-month terms for violating the Neutrality Act. Meanwhile, a Surinamese military official was convicted in Miami September 17 on drug charges. On December 2, after 21 people were killed in four days of fighting in Suriname, the government declared a state of emergency in remote areas. GDP (1984): $1.1 billion. Foreign Trade (1984): Imports, $346 million; exports, $356 million.

Nation, Region	Population in millions	Capital	Area Sq mi (km²)	Head of State/Government
Swaziland, S. Africa	0.7	Mbabane	6,704 (17 363)	Mswati III, king

Prince Makhosetive Dlamini, 18, was installed April 25 as King Mswati III, ending three years of power struggles in the royal family. The new king was one of 70 sons of the previous king, Sobhuza II, who died in 1982. A month after the ceremony, Mswati abolished the ruling council that had controlled Swaziland since Sobhuza's death. Prince Bhekimpi Dlamini, the head of the council, was convicted of plotting against his political opponents and sentenced to five years in prison. GDP (1984): $478 million. Foreign Trade (1984): Imports, $498 million; exports, $360 million.

Nation, Region	Population in millions	Capital	Area Sq mi (km²)	Head of State/Government
Togo, W. Africa	3.0	Lomé	22,000 (56 980)	Gnassingbé Eyadéma, president

A small group of terrorists, infiltrating across the border from Ghana, failed in a coup attempt September 24. At the request of the Togolese government, troops and aircraft from France and Zaire were sent to secure the situation. In August, Togolese security forces thwarted an attempt by a group allegedly backed by Libya to blow up the U.S. embassy in Lomé. GNP (1984 est.): $668 million. Foreign Trade (1983): Imports, $284 million; exports, $162 million.

Nation, Region	Population in millions	Capital	Area Sq mi (km²)	Head of State/Government
Tonga, Oceania	0.1	Nuku'alofa	385 (997)	Taufa'ahau Tupou IV, king; Prince Fatafehi Tu'ipelehake, premier

In talks concluded in October in Tonga, 16 Pacific nations agreed to grant the American tuna industry fishing rights in exchange for a package of fees and government aid that would total $60 million over five years. GNP (1984): $65 million. Foreign Trade (1984): Imports, $41 million; exports, $9 million.

Nation, Region	Population in millions	Capital	Area Sq mi (km²)	Head of State/Government
Trinidad and Tobago, Caribbean	1.2	Port-of-Spain	1,980 (5 128)	Ellis E. Clarke, president; A. N. R. Robinson, prime minister

A four-party opposition coalition, the National Alliance, won a landslide victory over the ruling People's National Movement (PNM) in elections in mid-December. The National Alliance took 33 of the 36 seats contested in the House of Representatives. The PNM's handling of the nation's oil revenues was said to be responsible for its defeat. As a result of the voting, A. N. R. Robinson, the founder of the Alliance, became prime minister. Earlier, union leaders had called for a boycott of cricket matches between the West Indies and England February 8–April 1, objecting to the fact that some English players had played in South Africa. The effort was only partly successful, and 16 protesters were arrested March 4. GNP (1984): $8.6 billion. Foreign Trade (1985): Imports, $1.53 billion; exports, $2.16 billion.

Nation, Region	Population in millions	Capital	Area Sq mi (km²)	Head of State/Government
Tuvalu, Oceania	0.008	Funafuti	10 (26)	Sir Tupua Leupena, governor-general; Tomasi Puapua, prime minister

Tuvalu refused a goodwill visit from a French warship in February as a protest against continued French nuclear testing in the South Pacific. Sir Tupua Leupena was sworn in as governor-general March 1, replacing Sir Fiatau Penitala Teo. In May the government announced that the constitution would be amended to end the governor-general's power to reject the advice of the government. GNP (1984): $4 million. Foreign Trade (1981): Imports, $2.8 million; exports, $26,789.

Nation, Region	Population in millions	Capital	Area Sq mi (km²)	Head of State/Government
United Arab Emirates, W. Asia	1.4	Abu Dhabi	32,278 (83 600)	Zayid bin Sultan Al Nuhayyan, president; Rashid bin Sa'id Al Maktum, prime minister

U.S. military officials held talks with officials of the United Arab Emirates in March amid concern that war between Iran and Iraq might expand to include the Persian Gulf states. GDP (1984): $28.2 billion. Foreign Trade (1984): Imports, $6.9 billion; exports, $14.1 billion.

Nation, Region	Population in millions	Capital	Area Sq mi (km²)	Head of State/Government
Vanuatu, Oceania	0.1	Port-Vila	5,700 (14 763)	George Ati Sokomanu, president; Walter Lini, prime minister

Vanuatu established diplomatic relations with the Soviet Union June 30, ending its policy of denying recognition to both superpowers. Prime Minister Lini also began negotiating a fishing agreement with the Soviets. Vanuatu led a campaign among South Pacific Forum nations to protest France's continued rule of New Caledonia to the United Nations. At the conclusion of the 17th meeting of the forum in August, Prime Minister Lini said that the forum should be concerned with international issues and vote as bloc at the United Nations. He also called for recognition for the Palestine Liberation Organization and the South-West African People's Organization. GDP (1984): $77 million. Foreign Trade (1985): Imports, $71 million; exports, $30 million.

Nation, Region	Population in millions	Capital	Area Sq mi (km²)	Head of State/Government
Vatican City, S. Europe	0.001	Vatican City	0.17 (0.438)	John Paul II, pope

Nation, Region	Population in millions	Capital	Area Sq mi (km²)	Head of State/Government
Western Samoa, Oceania	0.2	Apia	1,133 (2 934)	Malietoa Tanumafili II, head of state; Va'ai Kolone, prime minister

Former Prime Minister Tofilau Eti resigned late in 1985 after his 1986 budget proposal was rejected by Parliament. Opposition leader Va'ai Kolone was sworn in in his place. GNP (1984): $50 million. Foreign Trade (1984): Imports, $57 million; exports, $19.5 million.

Nation, Region	Population in millions	Capital	Area Sq mi (km²)	Head of State/Government
Yemen, North, S. W. Asia	6.3	San'a	75,000 (194 250)	Ali Abdallah Salih, president; Abdel Aziz Abd al-Ghani, prime minister

In the aftermath of the U.S. bombing raid on Libya, a communications officer at the U.S. embassy in San'a was shot and wounded April 25. No one took credit for the attack. President Salih met with South Yemen President Haydar Abu Bakr al-Attas in Libya in June. It was the first meeting between heads of state of the two countries since civil war had broken out in South Yemen in January. GNP (1984): $3.36 billion.

Nation, Region	Population in millions	Capital	Area Sq mi (km²)	Head of State/Government
Yemen, South, S.W. Asia	2.3	Aden	124,698 (322 968)	Haydar Abu Bakr al-Attas, president

Factional fighting between extreme Marxists and supporters of more moderate President Ali Nasir Muhammad al-Hasani broke out January 13 and widened during the next 12 days, leaving several thousand people dead. Attas, the nation's prime minister since February 1985, who was abroad when the fighting broke out, became president with the support of the USSR. Ali Salim al-Bid became secretary-general of the ruling Yemen Socialist Party. GDP (1984): $1.1 billion. Foreign Trade (1984): Imports, $1.54 billion; exports, $674 million.

Nation, Region	Population in millions	Capital	Area Sq mi (km²)	Head of State/Government
Zambia, E. Africa	7.1	Lusaka	290,585 (752 614)	Kenneth David Kaunda, president; Kebby Musokotwane, prime minister

In December 1986 a 120% rise in the price of corn meal was halted after four days of rioting, sparked by the increase, left at least 15 persons dead. During the unrest, a curfew was imposed and the nation's land borders were closed. On May 19, South African air and ground forces had attacked a camp outside Lusaka that South Africa said was a center for guerrillas of the African National Congress (ANC) but that Zambia said was a refugee camp. Two persons were reported killed, and the raid was condemned widely. President Kaunda attended the early August summit of seven Commonwealth heads of state at which limited economic sanctions against South Africa were imposed. GDP (1984): $2.6 billion. Foreign Trade (1985): Imports, $698 million; exports, $539 million.

POPULATION

Vital Statistics of Selected Countries

	Estimated population mid-1986 (millions)	Birthrate per 1,000 population	Death rate per 1,000 population	Infant mortality [1]	Life expectancy at birth	Urban population (%)
World	4,942.0	27	11	82	62	43
Afghanistan	15.4	47	23	194	37	16
Albania	3.0	26	6	43	71	34
Algeria	22.8	43	11	88	60	52
Angola	8.2	47	22	143	42	25
Argentina	31.2	24	8	35.3	70	83
Australia	15.8	15	7	9.6	75	86
Austria	7.6	12	12	11.4	73	55
Bangladesh	104.1	44	17	128	48	13
Belgium	9.9	12	11	10.7	73	95
Bolivia	6.4	43	15	119	51	47
Brazil	143.3	31	8	71	63	69
Burma	37.7	33	14	70	58	24
Cambodia	6.4	41	18	160	43	16
Cameroon	10.0	44	17	103	51	42
Canada	25.6	15	7	8.1	75	76
Cen. Afr. Republic	2.7	47	19	142	43	41
Chile	12.3	22	6	19.6	70	83
China	1,050.0	18	8	50	64	32
Colombia	30.0	28	7	53	64	67
Cuba	10.2	17	6	15	73	70
Cyprus	0.7	21	8	12	74	53
Czechoslovakia	15.5	15	12	15.7	71	74
Denmark	5.1	10	11	7.8	75	84
Ecuador	9.6	36	8	70	64	45
Egypt	50.5	37	11	100	58	44
El Salvador	5.1	34	10	67	65	39
Ethiopia	43.9	44	23	168	41	15
Finland	4.9	13	9	6.6	74	60
France	55.4	14	10	8.2	75	73
Germany, East	16.7	14	13	10	72	77
Germany, West	60.7	10	11	9.6	74	85
Ghana	13.6	47	13	90	54	31
Greece	10.0	13	9	14.1	74	70
Guatemala	8.6	38	7	71.2	59	39
Haiti	5.9	36	13	108	53	26
Hungary	10.6	12	14	20.2	70	56
India	785.0	35	13	110	53	23
Indonesia	168.4	34	13	84	55	22
Iran	46.6	41	12	115	57	51
Iraq	16.0	46	13	77	62	68
Ireland	3.6	18	9	10.1	72	56
Israel	4.2	23	7	14.4	74	89
Italy	57.2	10	9	11.6	74	72
Japan	121.5	13	6	6.2	77	76
Jordan	3.7	44	7	63	67	60
Kenya	21.0	54	12	72	53	16
Korea, North	20.5	30	7	30	65	64
Korea, South	43.3	23	7	30	66	57
Laos	3.7	41	18	122	44	16
Lebanon	2.7	29	9	48	65	76
Liberia	2.3	48	17	132	49	39
Libya	3.9	44	11	97	58	76
Malaysia	15.8	31	7	30	67	32
Mexico	81.7	32	6	53	66	70
Morocco	23.7	37	11	97	58	42
Netherlands	14.5	12	8	8.3	76	88
New Zealand	3.3	16	8	12.5	74	84
Niger	6.7	51	23	140	43	16
Nigeria	105.4	48	18	127	49	28
Norway	4.2	12	10	8.3	76	71
Pakistan	101.9	43	15	120	50	28
Panama	2.2	26	5	26	71	49
Paraguay	4.1	35	7	45	65	43
Peru	20.2	35	10	99	59	66
Philippines	58.1	33	8	51	62	37
Poland	37.5	19	10	19.1	71	60
Portugal	10.1	14	9	19.3	73	30
Romania	22.8	14	10	23.9	71	49
Saudi Arabia	11.5	42	12	100	61	70
South Africa	33.2	33	10	86	54	53
Spain	38.8	13	8	9.6	76	91
Sweden	8.4	11	11	6.4	77	83
Syria	10.5	47	9	59	64	47
Taiwan	19.6	20	5	8.9	73	67
Tanzania	22.4	50	15	115	51	17
Thailand	52.8	28	8	48	63	17
Tunisia	7.2	33	6	85	61	53
Turkey	52.3	35	10	92	62	46
Uganda	15.2	50	17	112	49	14
USSR	280.0	20	11	31	69	65
United Kingdom	56.6	13	11	9.6	74	90
United States	241.0	16	9	10.5	75	74
Uruguay	3.0	18	9	29.9	70	85
Venezuela	17.8	33	6	39	69	76
Vietnam	62.0	34	9	59	59	19
Yugoslavia	23.2	16	9	28.9	70	47
Zaire	31.3	42	14	106	50	34
Zambia	7.1	48	15	88	53	43
Zimbabwe	9.0	47	12	80	56	24

[1] Deaths under age one per 1,000 live births   Source: 1986 World Population Data Sheet, Population Reference Bureau, Inc., Washington, DC

DEFENSE EXPENDITURE AND MILITARY MANPOWER 1981–86

Country	$ million[a] 1981	1984	$ per capita 1981	1984	% of government spending[b] 1981	1984	% of GDP/GNP[c] 1981	1984	Numbers in armed forces (000) 1986
WARSAW PACT[d]									
Bulgaria	1,245	1,491	140	166	5.6	5.6	3.0	3.9	148.5
Czechoslovakia	3,632	5,052	236	326	7.4	8.3	3.7	4.0	201.0
Germany, East	6,446	7,710	385	457	7.8	8.0	5.0	7.7	179.0
Hungary	2,095	2,136	195	199	8.1	7.3	4.1	3.9	105.0
Poland	5,532	5,911	156	160	5.2	7.5	2.8	3.7	402.0
Romania	1,264	1,345	57	58	3.9	4.3	1.6	1.4	189.7
Soviet Union							12–17		5,130.0
NATO[e]									
Belgium	3,385	2,452	342	248	8.8	7.8	3.5	3.2	91.4
Britain	25,691	23,294	459	416	10.8	11.9	5.0	5.5	323.8
Canada	5,246	7,196	215	288	9.3	9.3	1.8	2.1	83.0
Denmark	1,446	1,260	281	245	6.9	6.9	2.5	2.3	29.5
France	23,867	20,212	444	370	18.3	18.8	4.2	4.1	557.5
Germany, West[f]	23,094	20,125	375	328	22.4	22.3	3.4	3.3	485.8
Greece	2,578	2,412	269	237	19.5	19.4	7.0	7.2	209.0
Italy	8,681	9,353	152	161	5.6	5.6	2.5	2.7	385.1
Luxembourg	46	39	127	106	3.1	3.5	1.1	1.1	0.7
Netherlands	4,527	3,978	319	276	7.2	7.2	3.2	3.2	101.2
Norway	1,650	1,555	402	375	6.6	6.2	2.9	2.8	37.3
Portugal	844	629	79	62	8.6	9.4	3.5	3.2	68.3
Spain	3,655	4,534	97	117	12.3	10.2	1.9	2.8	325.5
Turkey	2,815	2,190	61	45	20.4	20.0	4.9	4.4	654.4
United States	169,888	237,052	754	1,001	25.0	27.8	5.8	6.4	2,144.0
OTHER EUROPEAN									
Albania	188	130	68	43	11.5	11.0	7.9	5.5	42.0
Austria	818	792	109	106	3.8	3.6	1.2	1.2	54.7
Cyprus	25	21	40	31	5.0	4.0	1.2	0.9	13.0
Finland	712	815	206	168	5.3	5.7	1.4	1.6	34.9
Ireland	319	283	93	80	3.0	2.9	1.7	1.6	14.1
Sweden	3,919	2,862	470	341	8.4	7.2	3.5	3.0	64.7
Switzerland	1,912	1,958	303	301	21.4	21.3	2.0	2.1	20.0
Yugoslavia[g]	2,914	1,599	129	69	14.9	19.1	4.6	3.8	210.0
MIDDLE EAST									
Algeria	811	930	41	44	5.2	4.4	1.8	2.0	169.0
Egypt	2,100	3,786	48	80	14.3	19.6	8.5	9.6	445.0
Iran	8,043	20,162	203	463	22.4	42.9	7.6	12.3	704.5
Iraq	7,958	13,831	582	928	46.8	n.a.	40.1	51.1	845.0
Israel	5,815	5,798	1,472	1,380	30.7	39.5	26.3	24.4	149.0
Jordan	554	533	183	158	30.8	28.0	14.4	13.4	70.2
Lebanon	245	312	92	115	23.4	19.2	n.a.	n.a.	15.3
Libya	n.a.	n.a.	n.a.	n.a.	n.a.	n.a.	n.a.	n.a.	71.5
Morocco	1,102	595	53	25	20.2	13.5	7.4	5.0	170.0
Saudi Arabia	24,400	22,674	2,534	2,096	29.0	36.9	15.9	20.9	67.5
Sudan	311	212	14	9	13.9	10.3	3.5	n.a.	56.8
Syria	2,459	3,372	259	324	28.8	29.9	14.5	15.1	392.5
Tunisia	229	437	35	61	9.2	9.6	2.7	5.4	37.0
Yemen, North	587	598	89	80	29.1	30.1	20.4	17.8	36.6
Yemen, South	162	194	80	88	46.3	21.0	17.5	16.3	27.5
AFRICA									
Angola	688	n.a.	100	n.a.	22.6	n.a.	16.9	n.a.	50.0
Chad	55	55	12	11	46.9	63.8	n.a.	n.a.	14.2
Ethiopia	440	548	13	16	27.6	28.4	10.0	11.4	227.0
Nigeria	893	1,215	11	14	3.7	9.3	1.2	1.9	94.0
South Africa	3,081	2,634	121	98	15.2	16.8	4.0	4.1	106.4
Zimbabwe	407	295	53	36	21.6	13.1	6.3	4.8	42.0
ASIA									
Afghanistan	326	209	20	12	29.0	37.5	12.0	6.9	50.0
Australia	4,032	4,954	270	319	10.1	9.7	2.6	2.8	70.5
China	6,000	6,455	6	6	15.4	11.9	1.7	1.6	2,950.0
India	5,022	6,907	7	9	18.5	19.3	2.7	3.9	1,260.0
Indonesia	2,846	2,420	19	15	13.0	12.4	3.4	3.0	281.0
Japan	10,728	12,018	91	100	5.2	5.8	1.0	1.0	243.0
Korea, North	3,201	4,086	168	208	14.8	14.7	9.0	10.2	840.0
Korea, South	4,285	4,494	111	111	28.6	27.2	6.2	5.4	601.0
Malaysia	2,037	1,997	143	131	17.4	16.8	8.1	5.9	110.0
New Zealand	380	400	121	124	3.9	4.4	1.6	1.8	12.6
Pakistan	1,649	1,957	19	21	32.6	39.8	6.1	7.1	480.6
Philippines	798	504	16	9	16.1	15.0	2.1	1.5	113.0
Singapore	707	1,046	290	415	19.7	15.2	5.2	5.8	55.5
Thailand	1,665	1,752	35	35	25.5	21.7	4.6	4.2	256.0
LATIN AMERICA									
Argentina	3,573	2,282	129	77	12.8	17.1	2.9	3.3	73.0
Brazil	1,559	1,055	12	8	2.2	5.8	0.6	0.5	283.4
Chile	2,103	1,622	188	135	20.9	25.2	6.4	8.5	101.0
Colombia	374	427	14	15	8.2	10.0	1.0	1.1	66.2
Cuba	1,272	1,357	128	134	9.6	10.3	7.7	7.9	162.0
El Salvador	116	205	27	39	16.7	23.1	3.4	4.5	42.6
Guatemala	91	180	13	22	6.3	15.0	1.1	1.9	32.0
Honduras	45	90	12	21	4.6	6.6	1.7	2.9	19.2
Mexico	1,403	562	20	7	1.2	1.3	0.6	0.3	139.5
Nicaragua	192	625	67	195	20.0	23.2	7.5	11.7	72.0
Peru	403	1,327	22	67	9.3	27.0	5.7	7.8	127.0
Venezuela	907	1,069	59	63	4.6	8.7	1.4	2.2	71.0

[a] Current U.S. dollars, subject to exchange rate fluctuations. Some military expenditures include internal security expenditures. [b] Calculations are based on local currency; this series is designed to show national trends only. [c] Based on local currency. [d] The difficulty of calculating suitable exchange rates makes conversion to dollars and international comparisons imprecise and unreliable.
[e] Defense expenditures are based on NATO definition. [f] Excluding aid to West Berlin. [g] Government spending is the total of federal government budget, plus state and regional government budgets. Gross material product is used instead of GDP.
Source: "The Military Balance 1986–1987," International Institute for Strategic Studies

WORLD MINERAL AND METAL PRODUCTION

ALUMINUM, primary smelter (thousand metric tons)

	1984	1985
United States	4,099	3,500
USSR	2,100	2,200
Canada	1,227	1,282
Australia	758	851
West Germany	777	745
Norway	761	724
Brazil	455	540 [e]
China [e]	400	410
Venezuela	386	396
Spain	381	370
France	342	293
United Kingdom	288	275
Yugoslavia	268	270
India	269	268
Other countries [a]	3,153	3,165
Total	15,664	15,289

ANTIMONY, mine [b] (metric tons)

	1984	1985
China [e]	15,000	15,000
USSR [e]	9,300	9,400
Bolivia	9,281	8,600 [e]
South Africa	7,440	7,400 [e]
Mexico	3,064	3,000 [e]
Thailand	1,970	2,040 [e]
Yugoslavia [e]	950	1,270
Canada	553	1,093
Australia	920	1,000
Czechoslovakia [e]	1,000	1,000
Morocco	972	1,000 [e]
Turkey	1,017	1,000 [e]
Other countries [a]	3,323	3,191
Total	54,790	54,994

ASBESTOS [c] (thousand metric tons)

	1984	1985
USSR [e]	2,300	2,400
Canada	837	742
South Africa	167	165 [e]
Zimbabwe	165	165 [e]
China [e]	135	140
Italy	147	140 [e]
Brazil	131	135
Other countries [a]	224	224
Total	4,106	4,111

BARITE [c] (thousand metric tons)

	1984	1985
China [e]	1,000	1,000
United States	703	670
India	420	610 [e]
USSR [e]	525	540
Mexico	426	490 [e]
Morocco	425	425 [e]
Ireland	220	220 [e]
Other countries [a]	2,043	2,097
Total	5,762	6,052

BAUXITE [d] (thousand metric tons)

	1984	1985
Australia	32,182	32,400
Guinea [e]	13,160	13,100
Brazil	6,433	6,650 [e]
Jamaica	8,734	6,239
USSR [e]	6,185	6,185
Yugoslavia	3,347	3,250
Surinam	3,454	3,000 [e]
Hungary	2,994	2,815
Greece	2,296	2,500 [e]
India	1,994	2,038
Guyana	1,333	1,675 [e]
China [e]	1,600	1,650
France	1,607	1,484
Other countries [a]	4,439	3,732
Total	89,758	86,718

CEMENT [c] (thousand metric tons)

	1984	1985
China	121,080	142,500 [e]
USSR	129,866	131,000
Japan	78,860	72,857
United States	71,395	71,540
Italy	37,782	40,000
India	29,030	33,050
West Germany	28,909	29,000 [e]
Brazil [e]	25,000	27,000
Spain	25,435	25,500 [e]
France	22,724	23,000 [e]
Mexico	18,436	20,580
South Korea	20,413	20,424
Turkey	15,738	16,000 [e]
Other countries [a]	322,777	319,349
Total	947,445	971,800

CHROMITE [c] (thousand metric tons)

	1984	1985
South Africa	3,006	3,340
USSR [e]	2,940	2,940
Albania	720	825
India	423	553
Zimbabwe	477	500 [e]
Finland	446	450 [e]
Turkey	487	450 [e]
Brazil	256	275 [e]
Philippines	259	258
Other countries [a]	341	344
Total	9,355	9,935

COAL, anthracite and bituminous [c] (million metric tons)

	1984	1985
China	772	850
United States	792	741
USSR	556	557 [e]
Poland	192	192
South Africa	160	169
India	146	149
Australia	125	136
United Kingdom	51	96
West Germany	79	82
Canada	48	51
North Korea [e]	36	36
Other countries [a]	166	177
Total	3,123	3,236

COAL, lignite [c] [f] (million metric tons)

	1984	1985
East Germany	296	312 [e]
USSR	156	169 [e]
West Germany	127	121
Czechoslovakia	105	100
Yugoslavia	64	69
United States	57	63
Poland	50	58
Turkey	27	36
Other countries [a]	217	216
Total	1,099	1,144

COPPER, mine [b] (thousand metric tons)

	1984	1985
Chile	1,291	1,356
United States	1,103	1,106
Canada	713	724
USSR [e]	590	600
Zaire	520	560 [e]
Zambia	541	483
Poland	431	431 [e]
Peru	375	397
Mexico	304	290
Australia	236	258 [e]
Philippines	233	226
South Africa	198	202
China [e]	180	185
Papua New Guinea	164	175
Other countries [a]	1,116	1,121
Total	7,995	8,114

COPPER, refined, primary and secondary (thousand metric tons)

	1984	1985
United States	1,490	1,436
USSR [e]	939	953
Japan	935	936
Chile	880	884
Canada	539	522
Zambia	522	480 [e]
West Germany	379	414
Belgium	428	400 [e]
China [e]	310	400
Poland	372	387
Peru	219	228
Zaire	225	227
Australia	207	199
South Africa	156	162
Spain	156	155 [e]
Other countries [a]	1,378	1,447
Total	9,135	9,230

DIAMOND, natural (thousand carats)

	1984	1985
Zaire	18,459	19,617
Botswana	12,914	12,900 [e]
USSR [e]	10,700	10,800
South Africa	10,143	10,202
Australia	5,690	7,059
China [e]	1,000	1,000
Namibia	930	941
Angola	1,000 [e]	625
Other countries [a]	2,681	3,227
Total	63,517	66,371

FLUORSPAR [g] (thousand metric tons)

	1984	1985
Mongolia	740	740
Mexico	699	729
China [e]	650	650
South Africa	319	560 [e]
USSR [e]	550	560
Spain	296	270 [e]
Thailand	287	240 [e]
France	232	220 [e]
Other countries [a]	1,008	810
Total	4,781	4,779

GAS, natural [h] (billion cubic feet)

	1984	1985
USSR	20,700	22,700
United States	18,230	17,218
Netherlands	2,728	2,851
Canada	2,506	2,831
Indonesia	1,386	1,450
United Kingdom	1,363	1,389
Algeria	1,260	1,320 [e]
Mexico	1,193	1,145
Romania	1,127	1,110 [e]
Other countries [a]	9,102	9,931
Total	59,595	61,945

GOLD, mine [b] (thousand troy ounces)

	1984	1985
South Africa	21,907	21,566
USSR [e]	8,650	8,700
Canada	2,638	2,747
United States	2,085	2,475
Brazil [e]	1,750	2,000
China [e]	1,900	1,950
Australia	1,257	1,833
Colombia	800	1,150
Papua New Guinea	835	1,050
Other countries [a]	4,586	4,746
Total	46,408	48,217

GYPSUM [c] (thousand metric tons)

	1984	1985
United States	12,900	13,359
Canada	7,756	8,437
Japan [e]	6,080	6,260
France	5,401	5,400 [e]
Spain	5,365	5,260 [e]
China [e]	4,800	5,000
Iran	5,000	5,000 [e]
USSR [e]	4,900	4,900
United Kingdom	3,138	3,074
Mexico	2,129	2,800 [e]
West Germany [e]	2,200	2,000
Romania [e]	1,800	1,550
Poland	1,297	1,350 [e]
Italy	1,264	1,270 [e]
Other countries [a]	14,684	15,279
Total	78,714	80,939

IRON ORE [c] (thousand metric tons)

	1984	1985
USSR	247,104	248,000 [e]
Brazil	112,057	120,000 [e]
Australia	88,969	100,000 [e]
China [e]	75,000	80,000
United States	52,092	49,533
India	41,026	44,546
Canada	41,065	39,889
South Africa	24,647	24,393
Sweden	18,123	20,454
Venezuela	13,054	15,480 [e]
Liberia	15,100	15,300 [e]
France	14,839	14,681
Other countries [a]	87,472	86,541
Total	830,548	858,817

IRON, steel ingots (thousand metric tons)

	1984	1985
USSR	154,238	155,000
Japan	105,586	105,281
United States	83,940	80,067
China	43,370	46,700 [e]
West Germany	39,389	40,500
Italy	24,026	23,744
Brazil	18,386	20,456
France	19,000	18,832
Poland	16,533	16,100
United Kingdom	15,121	15,722
Czechoslovakia	14,831	15,036
Canada	14,715	15,000 [e]
Spain	13,484	14,235
Romania	14,437	13,800
South Korea	13,033	13,500 [e]
India	10,344	10,860 [e]
Belgium	11,303	10,694
East Germany	7,573	7,900
South Africa	7,827	7,500 [e]
Mexico	7,509	7,271
Other countries [a]	74,782	76,772
Total	709,427	714,970

LEAD, mine [b] (thousand metric tons)

	1984	1985
Australia	441	491
USSR [e]	440	440
United States	334	424
Canada	264	278
Peru	205	210
Mexico	203	200 [e]
China [e]	160	160
Yugoslavia	114	110
Morocco	101	101
Other countries [a]	994	978
Total	3,256	3,392

LEAD, refined, primary and secondary [i] (thousand metric tons)

	1984	1985
United States	1,072	1,124
USSR [e]	755	760
Japan	363	367
West Germany	357	356
United Kingdom	338	299
Canada	252	240
France	207	231
Australia	220	212 [e]
China [e]	195	195
Mexico	187	190 [e]
Spain	160	155
Italy	141	125
Other countries [a]	1,219	1,262
Total	5,466	5,516

MAGNESIUM, primary (thousand metric tons)

	1984	1985
United States	144	136
USSR[e]	85	87
Norway	49	54[e]
France	13	13[e]
Italy	7	8
Canada[e]	8	7
China[e]	7	7
Other countries[a]	14	15
Total	327	327

MANGANESE ore[c] (thousand metric tons)

	1984	1985
USSR	10,089	9,900[e]
South Africa	3,049	3,600
Brazil	2,693	2,700[e]
Gabon	2,119	2,351
Australia	1,829	1,989
China	1,600	1,600
India	1,081	1,140
Other countries[a]	931	901
Total	23,391	24,181

MERCURY (76-pound flasks)

	1984	1985
USSR[e]	64,000	65,000
Spain	44,093	45,000[e]
Algeria	23,000	25,000
China[e]	20,000	20,000
United States	19,048	16,530
Other countries[a]	25,145	24,720
Total	195,286	196,250

MOLYBDENUM, mine[b] (metric tons)

	1984	1985
United States	47,021	49,174
Chile	16,861	18,390
USSR[e]	11,200	11,300
Canada	11,557	7,590
Peru	3,079	3,828
Mexico	4,054	3,700
Other countries[a]	3,528	3,621
Total	97,300	97,603

NATURAL GAS LIQUIDS (million barrels)

	1984	1985
United States	597	587
USSR[e]	160	175
Saudi Arabia	130	146
Canada	139	124
Algeria	119	120[e]
Mexico[e]	100	96
Other countries[a]	223	278
Total	1,468	1,526

NICKEL, mine[b] (thousand metric tons)

	1984	1985
USSR[e]	175	180
Canada	174	152
Australia	76	85
New Caledonia	57	73
Indonesia	48	49[e]
Cuba	32	32[e]
Dominican Republic	24	26[e]
South Africa[e]	25	25
Other countries[a]	144	155
Total	755	777

NITROGEN, content of ammonia (thousand metric tons)

	1984	1985
USSR[e]	15,000	15,500
China[e]	14,000	15,000
United States	12,127	12,009
India	3,975	4,100[e]
Canada	3,493	3,500[e]
Romania	2,700	2,700[e]
Netherlands	2,311	2,260
France[e]	2,000	2,100
Mexico	1,773	1,800
United Kingdom	1,836	1,800[e]
Other countries[a]	25,180	24,780
Total	84,395	85,549

PETROLEUM, crude (million barrels)

	1984	1985
USSR	4,500	4,370
United States	3,250	3,274
Saudi Arabia	1,645	1,231
Mexico	983	960
United Kingdom	882	890
China	836	874
Iran	798	809
Venezuela	658	614
Nigeria	502	537
Canada	526	530

PETROLEUM, crude (cont'd)

	1984	1985
Iraq	438	521
Indonesia	517	484
Libya	391	386
United Arab Emirates	405	386
Other countries[a]	3,426	3,499
Total	19,757	19,365

PHOSPHATE ROCK[c] (thousand metric tons)

	1984	1985
United States	49,197	50,835
USSR	31,900	32,200
Morocco	21,245	20,737
China[e]	14,210	12,000
Jordan	6,263	6,067
Tunisia	5,346	4,530
Brazil	3,855	4,214
Israel	3,312	4,076
Togo	2,696	2,452
South Africa	2,585	2,421
Other countries[a]	11,879	11,831
Total	152,488	151,363

POTASH, K_2O equivalent basis (thousand metric tons)

	1984	1985
USSR	9,776	10,000[e]
Canada	7,527	6,600
East Germany	3,465	3,475[e]
West Germany	2,644	2,580
France	1,739	1,750
United States	1,564	1,296
Other countries[a]	2,633	2,917
Total	29,348	28,618

SALT[c] (thousand metric tons)

	1984	1985
United States	35,615	34,820
USSR[e]	16,500	17,000
China	16,286	14,446
West Germany[e]	11,200	10,500
Canada	10,235	10,042
India	7,728	7,505[e]
United Kingdom	7,126	7,200
France	7,007	7,130
Mexico	6,157	6,000[e]
Poland	4,441	4,858
Brazil	4,527	4,650[e]
Australia	4,600	4,600[e]
Romania[e]	4,600	4,600
Netherlands	3,674	4,450[e]
Other countries[a]	31,489	31,440
Total	171,185	169,241

SILVER, mine (thousand troy ounces)

	1984	1985
Mexico	75,340	69,000
Peru	56,523	60,395
USSR	47,400	47,900
United States	44,440	39,357
Canada	42,655	38,889
Australia	31,183	35,000[e]
Poland	23,920	24,000[e]
Chile	15,766	16,633
Japan	10,403	10,899
South Africa	6,997	6,721
Sweden	5,793	6,102
Yugoslavia	4,051	5,015
Other countries[a]	50,616	52,362
Total	415,087	412,273

SULFUR, all forms[j] (thousand metric tons)

	1984	1985
United States	10,652	11,609
USSR[e]	9,700	9,725
Canada	6,606	6,748
Poland	5,210	5,096
China[e]	2,650	2,900
Japan	2,592	2,510[e]
Mexico	1,985	2,190[e]
France	1,862	1,694
West Germany	1,530	1,605[e]
Spain	1,231	1,259
Other countries[a]	8,589	9,520
Total	52,607	54,856

TIN, mine (thousand metric tons)

	1984	1985
Malaysia	41,307	36,884
USSR[e]	23,000	23,000
Indonesia	23,223	22,115
Brazil	19,957	22,000[e]
Thailand	21,920	20,000[e]
Bolivia	19,911	18,000[e]

TIN, mine (cont'd)

	1984	1985
China[e]	15,000	15,000
Other countries[a]	34,114	34,104
Total	198,432	191,103

TITANIUM MINERALS[c][k] (thousand metric tons)

ILMENITE

	1984	1985
Australia	1,159	1,269
Norway	661	735
USSR[e]	440	445
Malaysia	235	275[e]
India	140	170[e]
China[e]	140	140
Other countries[a]	311	281
Total	3,086	3,315

RUTILE

	1984	1985
Australia	181	204
Sierra Leone	91	81[e]
South Africa[e]	56	55
Other countries[a]	24	25
Total	352	365

TITANIFEROUS SLAG

	1984	1985
Canada	726	844
South Africa	417	435
Total	1,143	1,279

TUNGSTEN, mine (metric tons)

	1984	1985
China[e]	13,500	15,000
USSR[e]	9,100	9,200
Canada	3,328	3,174
South Korea	2,702	2,572
Mongolia	2,000	2,000
Australia	1,772	1,912
Portugal	1,493	1,751
Austria	1,632	1,565
Bolivia	1,893	1,551
Brazil	1,037	1,175[e]
North Korea[e]	1,000	1,000
United States	1,203	996
Other countries[a]	5,903	5,748
Total	46,563	47,644

URANIUM OXIDE (U_3O_8)[l] (metric tons)

	1984	1985
Canada	10,272	12,800
South Africa	6,762	5,744
United States	6,713	5,080
Namibia	4,400	4,000[e]
Australia	5,177	3,834
France	3,736	3,774
Niger	3,276	3,236
Other countries[a]	1,769	1,942
Total	42,105	40,410

ZINC, mine[b] (thousand metric tons)

	1984	1985
Canada	1,207	1,175
USSR[e]	810	810
Australia	659	734
Peru	558	589
Mexico	304	300[e]
Japan	253	252
United States	278	252
Spain	230	228
Sweden	206	207
Ireland	206	192[e]
China[e]	160	190
Poland	191	187
Other countries[a]	1,502	1,560
Total	6,564	6,676

ZINC, smelter, primary and secondary (thousand metric tons)

	1984	1985
USSR[e]	945	950
Japan	754	740
Canada	683	692
West Germany	356	368
United States	331	312
Australia	306	293
Belgium	271	277
France	259	247
Italy	170	216
Spain	207	205
Netherlands	210	203
China	185	190
Poland	176	180
Mexico	167	170
Other countries[a]	1,443	1,524
Total	6,463	6,567

[a] Estimated in part. [b] Content of concentrates. [c] Gross weight. [d] Includes calculated bauxite equivalent of estimated output of aluminum ores other than bauxite (nepheline concentrate and alunite ore). [e] Estimate. [f] Includes coal classified in some countries as brown coal. [g] Gross weight of marketable product. [h] Marketed production (includes gas sold or used by producers; excludes gas reinjected to reservoirs for pressure maintenance and that flared or vented to the atmosphere which is not used as fuel or industrial raw material, and which thus has no economic value). [i] Excludes bullion produced for refining elsewhere. [j] Includes (1) Frasch process sulfur, (2) elemental sulfur mined by conventional means, (3) by-product recovered elemental sulfur, and (4) elemental sulfur equivalent obtained from pyrite and other materials. [k] Excludes output in the United States, which cannot be disclosed because it is company proprietary information. [l] Excludes output (if any) by Albania, Bulgaria, China, Czechoslovakia, East Germany, Hungary, North Korea, Mongolia, Poland, Romania, and Vietnam.

Compiled by Charles L. Kimbell primarily from data collected by the U.S. Bureau of Mines, but with some modifications from other sources.

THE UNITED STATES GOVERNMENT

(selected listing, as of Jan. 1, 1987)

President: Ronald Reagan

Vice-President: George Bush

Executive Office of the President
The White House

Chief of Staff and Assistant to the President: Donald T. Regan

Assistant to the President and Press Secretary: James S. Brady

Assistant to the President and Director of Communications: Patrick J. Buchanan

Assistant to the President for Political and Intergovernmental Affairs: Mitchell E. Daniels, Jr.

Counsel to the President: Peter J. Wallison

Assistant to the President: William Henkel

Cabinet Secretary and Assistant to the President: Alfred H. Kingon

Assistant to the President for Legislative Affairs: William L. Ball III

Assistant to the President for National Security Affairs: Frank C. Carlucci

Assistant to the President and Principal Deputy Press Secretary: Larry M. Speakes[1]

Assistant to the President: W. Dennis Thomas

Office of Management and Budget, Director: James C. Miller III

Council of Economic Advisers, Chairman: Beryl W. Sprinkel

Office of United States Trade Representative, U.S. Trade Representative: Clayton Yeutter

Council of Environmental Quality, Chairman: A. Alan Hill

Office of Science and Technology Policy, Director: William R. Graham

Office of Administration, Director: Johnathan S. Miller

The Cabinet

Secretary of Agriculture: Richard Lyng

Secretary of Commerce: Malcolm Baldrige

Secretary of Defense: Caspar W. Weinberger

Joint Chiefs of Staff, Chairman: Adm. William J. Crowe, Jr.

Secretary of the Air Force: Edward C. Aldridge, Jr.

Secretary of the Army: John O. Marsh, Jr.

Secretary of the Navy: John Lehman

Secretary of Education: William J. Bennett

Secretary of Energy: John S. Herrington

Secretary of Health and Human Services: Otis R. Bowen

National Institutes of Health, Director: James B. Wyngaarden

Surgeon General: C. Everett Koop

Commissioner of Food and Drugs: Frank E. Young

Social Security Administration, Commissioner: Dorcas R. Hardy

Secretary of Housing and Urban Development: Samuel R. Pierce, Jr.

Secretary of the Interior: Donald Paul Hodel

Department of Justice, Attorney General: Edwin Meese III

Federal Bureau of Investigation, Director: William H. Webster

Secretary of Labor: William E. Brock III

Women's Bureau, Director: Shirley M. Dennis

Commissioner of Labor Statistics: Janet L. Norwood

Secretary of State: George P. Shultz

Secretary of Transportation: Elizabeth H. Dole

Secretary of the Treasury: James A. Baker III

Internal Revenue Service, Commissioner: Lawrence B. Gibbs

Independent Agencies

ACTION, Director: Donna M. Alvarado

Central Intelligence Agency, Director: William J. Casey

Commission on Civil Rights, Chairman: Clarence M. Pendleton, Jr.

Commission of Fine Arts, Chairman: J. Carter Brown

Consumer Product Safety Commission, Chairman: Terrence M. Scanlon

Environmental Protection Agency, Administrator: Lee M. Thomas

Equal Employment Opportunity Commission, Chairman: Clarence Thomas

Export-Import Bank, President and Chairman: John A. Bohn, Jr.

Farm Credit Administration, Chairman: Frank W. Naylor

Federal Communications Commission, Chairman: Mark S. Fowler

Federal Deposit Insurance Corporation, Chairman: L. William Seidman

Federal Election Commission, Chairman: Scott E. Thomas

Federal Emergency Management Agency, Director: Julius W. Becton, Jr.

Federal Home Loan Bank Board, Chairman: Edwin J. Gray

Federal Labor Relations Authority, Chairman: Jerry L. Calhoun

Federal Maritime Commission, Chairman: Edward V. Hickey, Jr.

Federal Reserve System, Chairman: Paul A. Volcker

Federal Trade Commission, Chairman: Daniel Oliver

General Services Administrator: Terence C. Golden

Interstate Commerce Commission, Chairman: Heather J. Gradison

National Aeronautics and Space Administration, Administrator: James C. Fletcher

National Foundation on the Arts and Humanities

National Endowment for the Arts, Chairman: Francis S. M. Hodsoll; National Endowment for the Humanities, Chairman: Lynne V. Cheney

National Labor Relations Board, Chairman: Donald L. Dotson

National Science Foundation, Chairman: Erich Bloch

National Transportation Safety Board, Chairman: James E. Burnett

Nuclear Regulatory Commission, Chairman: Lando W. Zech, Jr.

Peace Corps, Director: Loret M. Ruppe

Postal Rate Commission, Chairman: Janet D. Steiger

Securities and Exchange Commission, Chairman: John S. R. Shad

Selective Service System, Director: Wilfred E. Ebel (acting)

Small Business Administrator: Charles L. Heatherly (acting)

Tennessee Valley Authority, Chairman: C. H. Dean, Jr.

U.S. Arms Control and Disarmament Agency, Director: Kenneth L. Adelman

U.S. Information Agency, Director: Charles Z. Wick

U.S. International Trade Commission, Chairman: Susan W. Liebeler

U.S. Postmaster General: Preston R. Tisch

Veterans Administrator: Thomas K. Turnage

The Supreme Court

Chief Justice, William H. Rehnquist

William J. Brennan, Jr.

Lewis F. Powell, Jr.

Byron R. White

John Paul Stevens

Thurgood Marshall

Sandra Day O'Connor

Harry A. Blackmun

Antonin Scalia

[1] Resignation announced.

SENATE MEMBERSHIP

(As of January 1987: 55 Democrats, 45 Republicans) Letters after senators' names refer to party affiliation—D for Democrat, R for Republican. Single asterisk (*) denotes term expiring in January 1989; double asterisk (**), term expiring in January 1991; triple asterisk (***), term expiring in January 1993.

Alabama
** H. Heflin, D
*** R. C. Shelby, D

Alaska
** T. Stevens, R
*** F. H. Murkowski, R

Arizona
* D. DeConcini, D
*** J. McCain, R

Arkansas
*** D. Bumpers, D
** D. Pryor, D

California
*** A. Cranston, D
* P. Wilson, R

Colorado
** W. L. Armstrong, R
*** T. E. Wirth, D

Connecticut
* L. P. Weicker, Jr., R
*** C. J. Dodd, D

Delaware
* W. V. Roth, Jr., R
* J. R. Biden, Jr., D

Florida
* L. Chiles, Jr., D
*** B. Graham, D

Georgia
** S. Nunn, D
*** W. Fowler, Jr., D

Hawaii
*** D. K. Inouye, D
* S. M. Matsunaga, D

Idaho
** J. A. McClure, R
*** S. Symms, R

Illinois
*** A. J. Dixon, D
** P. Simon, D

Indiana
* R. G. Lugar, R
*** D. Quayle, R

Iowa
*** C. E. Grassley, R
** T. Harkin, D

Kansas
*** R. J. Dole, R
** N. Kassebaum, R

Kentucky
*** W. H. Ford, D
** M. McConnell, R

Louisiana
** J. B. Johnston, D
*** J. B. Breaux, D

Maine
** W. Cohen, R
* G. Mitchell, D

Maryland
* P. S. Sarbanes, D
*** B. A. Mikulski, D

Massachusetts
* E. M. Kennedy, D
* J. F. Kerry, D

Michigan
* D. W. Riegle, Jr., D
** C. Levin, D

Minnesota
* D. F. Durenberger, R
** R. Boschwitz, R

Mississippi
* J. C. Stennis, D
** T. Cochran, R

Missouri
* J. C. Danforth, R
*** C. S. Bond, R

Montana
* J. Melcher, D
** M. Baucus, D

Nebraska
* E. Zorinsky, D
** J. J. Exon, Jr., D

Nevada
* C. Hecht, R
*** H. Reid, D

New Hampshire
** G. Humphrey, R
*** W. Rudman, R

New Jersey
** B. Bradley, D
* F. R. Lautenberg, D

New Mexico
** P. V. Domenici, R
* J. Bingaman, D

New York
* D. P. Moynihan, D
*** A. D'Amato, R

North Carolina
** J. Helms, R
*** T. Sanford, D

North Dakota
* Q. N. Burdick, D
*** K. Conrad, D

Ohio
*** J. H. Glenn, Jr., D
* H. M. Metzenbaum, D

Oklahoma
* D. L. Boren, D
*** D. Nickles, R

Oregon
** M. O. Hatfield, R
*** B. Packwood, R

Pennsylvania
* J. Heinz, R
*** A. Specter, R

Rhode Island
** C. Pell, D
* J. H. Chafee, R

South Carolina
** S. Thurmond, R
*** E. F. Hollings, D

South Dakota
** L. Pressler, R
*** T. A. Daschle, D

Tennessee
* J. R. Sasser, D
** A. Gore, Jr., D

Texas
* L. M. Bentsen, D
** P. Gramm, R

Utah
*** E. J. Garn, R
* O. G. Hatch, R

Vermont
* R. T. Stafford, R
*** P. J. Leahy, D

Virginia
** J. Warner, R
* P. S. Trible, Jr., R

Washington
* D. J. Evans, R
*** B. Adams, D

West Virginia
* R. C. Byrd, D
* J. D. Rockefeller IV, D

Wisconsin
* W. Proxmire, D
*** R. W. Kasten, Jr., R

Wyoming
* M. Wallop, R
** A. K. Simpson, R

HOUSE MEMBERSHIP

(As of January 1987, 258 Democrats, 177 Republicans) "At-L," in place of Congressional district number means "representative at large." * Indicates elected Nov. 4, 1986; all others were reelected in 1986.

Alabama
1. H. L. Callahan, R
2. W. L. Dickinson, R
3. W. Nichols, D
4. T. Bevill, D
5. R. Flippo, D
6. B. Erdreich, D
7. *C. Harris, D

Alaska
At-L. D. Young, R

Arizona
1. J. J. Rhodes, III, R
2. M. K. Udall, D
3. B. Stump, R
4. *J. Kyl, R
5. J. Kolbe, R

Arkansas
1. W. V. Alexander, Jr., D
2. T. Robinson, D
3. J. P. Hammerschmidt, R
4. B. Anthony, Jr., D

California
1. D. H. Bosco, D
2. *W. Herger, R
3. R. Matsui, D
4. V. Fazio, D
5. S. Burton, D
6. B. Boxer, D
7. G. Miller, D
8. R. V. Dellums, D
9. F. H. Stark, Jr., D
10. D. Edwards, D
11. T. Lantos, D

12. *E. L. Konnyu, R
13. N. Y. Mineta, D
14. N. Shumway, R
15. T. Coelho, D
16. L. E. Panetta, D
17. C. Pashayan, Jr., R
18. R. Lehman, D
19. R. J. Lagomarsino, R
20. W. M. Thomas, R
21. *E. Gallegly, R
22. C. J. Moorhead, R
23. A. C. Beilenson, D
24. H. A. Waxman, D
25. E. R. Roybal, D
26. H. L. Berman, D
27. M. Levine, D
28. J. Dixon, D
29. A. F. Hawkins, D
30. M. G. Martinez, Jr., D
31. M. Dymally, D
32. G. M. Anderson, D
33. D. Dreier, R
34. E. Torres, D
35. J. Lewis, R
36. G. E. Brown, Jr., D
37. A. McCandless, R
38. R. K. Dornan, R
39. W. Dannemeyer, R
40. R. E. Badham, R
41. W. D. Lowery, R
42. D. Lungren, R
43. R. Packard, R
44. J. Bates, D
45. D. L. Hunter, R

Colorado
1. P. Schroeder, D
2. *D. Skaggs, D

3. *B. N. Campbell, D
4. H. Brown, R
5. *J. Hefley, R
6. D. Schaefer, R

Connecticut
1. B. Kennelly, D
2. S. Gejdenson, D
3. B. Morrison, D
4. S. B. McKinney, R
5. J. G. Rowland, R
6. N. L. Johnson, R

Delaware
At-L. T. R. Carper, D

Florida
1. E. Hutto, D
2. *B. Grant, D
3. C. E. Bennett, D
4. W. V. Chappell, Jr., D
5. B. McCollum, Jr., R
6. K. H. MacKay, D
7. S. M. Gibbons, D
8. C. W. Young, R
9. M. Bilirakis, R
10. A. Ireland, R
11. B. Nelson, D
12. T. Lewis, R
13. C. Mack, 3d, R
14. D. A. Mica, D
15. E. C. Shaw, Jr., R
16. L. Smith, D
17. W. Lehman, D
18. C. Pepper, D
19. D. B. Fascell, D

Georgia
1. R. L. Thomas, D
2. C. Hatcher, D
3. R. Ray, D
4. P. L. Swindall, R
5. *J. Lewis, D
6. N. Gingrich, R
7. G. Darden, D
8. J. R. Rowland, Jr., D
9. E. L. Jenkins, D
10. D. Barnard, Jr., D

Hawaii
1. *P. Saiki, R
2. D. K. Akaka, D

Idaho
1. L. Craig, R
2. R. Stallings, D

Illinois
1. C. A. Hayes, D
2. G. Savage, D
3. M. Russo, D
4. *J. Davis, R
5. W. O. Lipinski, D
6. H. J. Hyde, R
7. C. Collins, D
8. D. Rostenkowski, D
9. S. R. Yates, D
10. J. Porter, R
11. F. Annunzio, D
12. P. M. Crane, R
13. H. W. Fawell, R
14. *J. D. Hastert, R
15. E. R. Madigan, R
16. L. Martin, R
17. L. Evans, D

18. R. H. Michel, R
19. T. L. Bruce, D
20. R. Durbin, D
21. C. M. Price, D
22. K. J. Gray, D

Indiana
1. P. J. Visclosky, D
2. P. R. Sharp, D
3. J. Hiler, R
4. D. Coats, R
5. *J. Jontz, D
6. D. Burton, R
7. J. T. Myers, R
8. F. McCloskey, D
9. L. H. Hamilton, D
10. A. Jacobs, Jr., D

Iowa
1. J. Leach, R
2. T. Tauke, R
3. *D. R. Nagle, D
4. N. Smith, D
5. J. R. Lightfoot, R
6. *F. Grandy, R

Kansas
1. C. P. Roberts, R
2. J. C. Slattery, D
3. J. Meyers, R
4. D. Glickman, D
5. B. Whittaker, R

Kentucky
1. C. Hubbard, Jr., D
2. W. H. Natcher, D
3. R. L. Mazzoli, D
4. *J. Bunning, R
5. H. Rogers, R
6. L. Hopkins, R
7. C. C. Perkins, D

Louisiana
1. R. L. Livingston, Jr., R
2. C. C. Boggs, D
3. W. J. Tauzin, D
4. C. E. Roemer III, D
5. T. J. Huckaby, D
6. *R. Baker, R
7. *J. Hayes, D
8. *C. Holloway, R

Maine
1. *J. Brennan, D
2. O. Snowe, R

Maryland
1. R. Dyson, D
2. H. D. Bentley, R
3. *B. L. Cardin, D
4. *T. McMillen, D
5. S. Hoyer, D
6. B. Byron, D
7. *K. Mfume, D
8. *C. A. Morella, R

Massachusetts
1. S. O. Conte, R
2. E. P. Boland, D
3. J. D. Early, D
4. B. Frank, D
5. C. G. Atkins, D
6. N. Mavroules, D
7. E. J. Markey, D
8. *J. P. Kennedy II, D
9. J. J. Moakley, D
10. G. E. Studds, D
11. B. Donnelly, D

Michigan
1. J. Conyers, Jr., D
2. C. D. Pursell, R
3. H. Wolpe, D
4. *F. Upton, R
5. P. B. Henry, R
6. B. Carr, D
7. D. E. Kildee, D
8. B. Traxler, D
9. G. Vander Jagt, R
10. B. Schuette, R
11. R. Davis, R
12. D. E. Bonior, D
13. G. Crockett, Jr., D
14. D. Hertel, D
15. W. D. Ford, D
16. J. D. Dingell, D
17. S. Levin, D
18. W. S. Broomfield, R

Minnesota
1. T. J. Penny, D
2. V. Weber, R
3. B. Frenzel, R

4. B. F. Vento, D
5. M. Sabo, D
6. G. Sikorski, D
7. A. Stangeland, R
8. J. L. Oberstar, D

Mississippi
1. J. L. Whitten, D
2. *M. Espy, D
3. G. V. Montgomery, D
4. W. Dowdy, D
5. T. Lott, R

Missouri
1. W. L. Clay, D
2. *J. Buechner, R
3. R. A. Gephardt, D
4. I. Skelton, D
5. A. Wheat, D
6. E. T. Coleman, R
7. G. Taylor, R
8. W. Emerson, R
9. H. L. Volkmer, D

Montana
1. P. Williams, D
2. R. Marlenee, R

Nebraska
1. D. Bereuter, R
2. H. Daub, R
3. V. Smith, R

Nevada
1. *J. Bilbray, D
2. B. Vucanovich, R

New Hampshire
1. R. C. Smith, R
2. J. Gregg, R

New Jersey
1. J. J. Florio, D
2. W. J. Hughes, D
3. J. J. Howard, D
4. C. Smith, R
5. M. Roukema, R
6. B. J. Dwyer, D
7. M. J. Rinaldo, R
8. R. A. Roe, D
9. R. G. Torricelli, D
10. P. W. Rodino, Jr., D
11. D. A. Gallo, R
12. J. Courter, R
13. H. J. Saxton, R
14. F. Guarini, D

New Mexico
1. M. Lujan, Jr., R
2. J. Skeen, R
3. W. B. Richardson, D

New York
1. *G. J. Hochbrueckner, D
2. T. J. Downey, D
3. R. J. Mrazek, D
4. N. F. Lent, R
5. R. McGrath, R
6. *F. H. Flake, D
7. G. L. Ackerman, D
8. J. H. Scheuer, D
9. T. J. Manton, D
10. C. E. Schumer, D
11. E. Towns, D
12. M. R. Owens, D
13. S. J. Solarz, D
14. G. V. Molinari, R
15. B. Green, R
16. C. B. Rangel, D
17. T. Weiss, D
18. R. Garcia, D
19. M. Biaggi, D
20. J. J. DioGuardi, R
21. H. Fish, Jr., R
22. B. A. Gilman, R
23. S. S. Stratton, D
24. G. B. H. Solomon, R
25. S. L. Boehlert, R
26. D. Martin, R
27. G. C. Wortley, R
28. M. F. McHugh, D
29. F. Horton, R
30. *L. M. Slaughter, D
31. J. Kemp, R
32. J. J. LaFalce, D
33. H. J. Nowak, D
34. *A. Houghton, Jr., R

North Carolina
1. W. B. Jones, D
2. T. Valentine, D

3. *M. Lancaster, D
4. *D. E. Price, D
5. S. L. Neal, D
6. H. Coble, R
7. C. Rose, D
8. W. G. Hefner, D
9. J. A. McMillan III, R
10. *C. Ballenger, R
11. *J. McC. Clarke, D

North Dakota
At-L. B. Dorgan, D

Ohio
1. T. A. Luken, D
2. W. D. Gradison, Jr., R
3. T. Hall, D
4. M. Oxley, R
5. D. L. Latta, R
6. B. McEwen, R
7. M. DeWine, R
8. *D. Lukens, R
9. M. Kaptur, D
10. C. E. Miller, R
11. D. E. Eckart, D
12. J. R. Kasich, R
13. D. J. Pease, D
14. *T. C. Sawyer, D
15. C. P. Wylie, R
16. R. Regula, R
17. J. A. Traficant, Jr., D
18. D. Applegate, D
19. E. F. Feighan, D
20. M. R. Oakar, D
21. L. Stokes, D

Oklahoma
1. *J. M. Inhofe, R
2. M. Synar, D
3. W. W. Watkins, D
4. D. McCurdy, D
5. M. Edwards, R
6. G. English, D

Oregon
1. L. AuCoin, D
2. R. F. Smith, R
3. R. Wyden, D
4. *P. A. DeFazio, D
5. D. Smith, R

Pennsylvania
1. T. Foglietta, D
2. W. H. Gray, III, D
3. R. A. Borski, Jr., D
4. J. P. Kolter, D
5. R. T. Schulze, R
6. G. Yatron, D
7. *C. Weldon, R
8. P. H. Kostmayer, D
9. B. Shuster, R
10. J. M. McDade, R
11. P. E. Kanjorski, D
12. J. P. Murtha, D
13. L. Coughlin, R
14. W. Coyne, D
15. D. Ritter, R
16. R. S. Walker, R
17. G. W. Gekas, R
18. D. Walgren, D
19. W. F. Goodling, R
20. J. M. Gaydos, D
21. T. J. Ridge, R
22. A. J. Murphy, D
23. W. Clinger, Jr., R

Rhode Island
1. F. J. St Germain, D
2. C. Schneider, R

South Carolina
1. *A. Ravenel, Jr., R
2. F. D. Spence, R
3. B. C. Derrick, Jr., D
4. *L. J. Patterson, D
5. J. Spratt, Jr., D
6. R. M. Tallon, Jr., D

South Dakota
At-L. *T. Johnson, D

Tennessee
1. J. H. Quillen, R
2. J. J. Duncan, R
3. M. Lloyd, D
4. J. Cooper, D
5. W. H. Boner, D
6. B. Gordon, D
7. D. Sundquist, R
8. E. Jones, D
9. H. E. Ford, D

Texas
1. *J. Chapman, D
2. C. Wilson, D
3. S. Bartlett, R
4. R. Hall, D
5. J. Bryant, D
6. J. Barton, R
7. B. Archer, R
8. J. Fields, R
9. J. Brooks, D
10. J. J. Pickle, D
11. J. M. Leath, D
12. J. C. Wright, Jr., D
13. E. B. Boulter, R
14. D. M. Sweeney, R
15. E. de la Garza, D
16. R. Coleman, D
17. C. Stenholm, D
18. M. Leland, D
19. L. Combest, R
20. H. B. Gonzalez, D
21. *L. Smith, R
22. T. DeLay, R
23. A. G. Bustamante, D
24. M. Frost, D
25. M. Andrews, D
26. R. Armey, R
27. S. P. Ortiz, D

Utah
1. J. Hansen, R
2. *W. Owens, D
3. H. C. Nielson, R

Vermont
At-L. J. M. Jeffords, R

Virginia
1. H. H. Bateman, R
2. *O. B. Pickett, D
3. T. J. Bliley, Jr., R
4. N. Sisisky, D
5. D. Daniel, D
6. J. R. Olin, D
7. D. F. Slaughter, Jr., R
8. S. Parris, R
9. F. C. Boucher, D
10. F. Wolf, R

Washington
1. J. Miller, R
2. A. Swift, D
3. D. L. Bonker, D
4. S. Morrison, R
5. T. S. Foley, D
6. N. D. Dicks, D
7. M. Lowry, D
8. R. Chandler, R

West Virginia
1. A. B. Mollohan, D
2. H. O. Staggers, Jr., D
3. R. E. Wise, Jr., D
4. N. J. Rahall, II, D

Wisconsin
1. L. Aspin, D
2. R. W. Kastenmeier, D
3. S. Gunderson, R
4. G. D. Kleczka, D
5. J. Moody, D
6. T. E. Petri, R
7. D. R. Obey, D
8. T. Roth, R
9. F. J. Sensenbrenner, Jr., R

Wyoming
At-L. D. Cheney, R

AMERICAN SAMOA
Delegate, Fofó Sunia, D

DISTRICT OF COLUMBIA
Delegate, W. E. Fauntroy, D

GUAM
Delegate, Ben Garrido Blaz, R

PUERTO RICO
Resident Commissioner
J. B. Fuster, D

VIRGIN ISLANDS
Delegate, Ron de Lugo, D

588

THE U.S. BUDGET

On Feb. 5, 1986, President Ronald Reagan submitted to Congress his budget for fiscal year 1987. The proposed budget called for total outlays of $994.0 billion and revenues of $850.4 billion. The projected deficit of $143.6 billion was just below the deficit target of $144 billion called for under the recently enacted Gramm-Rudman anti-deficit act. In October, Congress passed and the president signed a $576 billion omnibus spending bill to fund the federal government's activities through fiscal 1987. It was known as a continuing resolution because it would keep the government operating until the end of the fiscal year, Sept. 30, 1987. Between the beginning of fiscal 1987 (Oct. 1, 1986) and enactment of the continuing resolution, Congress passed four separate stopgap measures to keep the government from going out of business. The comprehensive spending legislation was necessary because none of the 13 appropriation bills that were used to fund the federal departments and agencies had been enacted. Not part of the final legislation—the largest and most detailed financial measure ever passed by Congress—were outlays (exceeding $400 billion) for activities that are funded on a permanent basis, including Social Security, interest payments on the federal debt, and the bulk of Medicare spending. Details of the continuing appropriations measure (PL 99-500) follow.

	BUDGET REQUEST	PASSED BY HOUSE	PASSED BY SENATE	FINAL AMOUNT
AGRICULTURE				
Agriculture Programs	$2,248,832,000 [1]	$19,242,918,000	$2,546,703,000	$19,286,452,000
Rural Development Assistance	$6,911,784,000	$6,209,193,000	$7,426,776,000	$6,077,067,000
Domestic Food Programs	$14,510,231,000	$14,910,403,000	$15,688,563,000	$14,900,300,000
International Programs	$1,239,333,000	$1,269,840,000	$1,072,164,000	$1,171,715,000
Agencies	$459,643,000	$466,207,000	$468,727,000	$468,070,000
Total [2]	$28,604,019,000	$45,401,271,000	$30,486,017,000	$45,206,688,000
COMMERCE, JUSTICE, STATE, AND JUDICIARY				
Commerce Department	$1,741,327,000			$2,099,160,000
Related Agencies	$3,197,505,000			$879,442,000
Justice Department	$4,204,705,000			$4,673,090,000
Related Agencies	$507,821,000			$498,620,000
State Department	$3,920,195,000			$2,585,697,000
Related Agencies	$1,159,879,000			$980,184,000
The Judiciary	$1,227,183,000			$1,192,592,000
Total	$15,958,615,000			$12,908,785,000
DISTRICT OF COLUMBIA				
Federal Funds	$560,380,000	$530,027,000	$580,380,000	$580,380,000 [3]
District of Columbia Funds	$2,989,598,000	$2,989,598,000	$3,009,098,000	$3,060,407,000
DEFENSE				
Military Personnel	$74,202,900,000	$72,404,112,000	$72,678,798,000	$72,737,378,000
Operations and Maintenance	$85,773,000,000	$78,109,862,000	$77,923,000,000	$78,050,372,000
Procurement	$95,656,700,000	$79,502,330,000 [4]	$84,897,136,000 [4]	$84,875,632,000
Research and Development	$41,929,900,000	$33,956,074,000 [4]	$36,391,125,000	$35,804,214,000
Other Programs	$1,469,638,000	$1,179,238,000	$2,221,338,000	$2,531,410,000
Total	$299,032,138,000	$267,769,416,000 [4]	$274,695,897,000 [4]	$273,999,006,000
ENERGY AND WATER DEVELOPMENT				
Energy Department	$11,483,101,000	$10,847,046,000	$10,087,517,000	$10,404,917,000
Corps of Engineers	$3,069,500,000	$3,226,052,000	$2,992,287,000	$3,126,080,000
Bureau of Reclamation	$851,200,000	$863,930,000	$850,068,000	$867,647,000
Independent Agencies	$466,342,000	$610,972,000	$599,383,000	$608,633,000
Total	$15,870,143,000	$15,548,000,000	$14,529,255,000	$15,007,277,000
FOREIGN OPERATIONS				
Multilateral Aid	$1,578,002,125	$1,260,444,000	$1,043,657,676	$1,186,591,927
Bilateral Aid	$6,860,252,000	$5,875,204,000	$6,628,783,000	$6,345,212,500
Military Aid	$6,726,280,000	$4,987,523,284	$4,987,523,284	$4,996,441,284
Total [5]	$15,474,534,125	$13,023,171,284	$13,559,963,960	$13,428,245,711
HOUSING AND URBAN DEVELOPMENT AGENCIES				
Housing and Urban Development Dept.	$6,385,220,000	$13,271,483,300	$12,872,553,800	$13,061,040,300
Independent Agencies	$40,102,827,000	$40,734,685,400	$40,805,486,000	$42,950,762,400
Total	$46,488,047,000	$54,006,168,700	$53,678,039,800	$56,011,802,700
INTERIOR				
Interior Department	$3,632,714,000	$4,010,119,000	$4,004,040,000	$4,125,802,000
Related Agencies	$2,984,261,000	$4,180,027,000	$4,037,441,000	$4,182,603,000
Total	$6,616,975,000	$8,190,146,000	$8,041,481,000	$8,308,405,000
LABOR, HEALTH AND HUMAN SERVICES, (HHS), AND EDUCATION				
Labor Department	$4,872,614,000	$5,524,294,000	$5,758,198,000	$5,668,002,000
Health and Human Services Dept.	$70,273,063,000	$71,403,502,000	$75,315,314,000	$76,085,576,000
Education Department	$16,265,881,000	$13,380,231,000	$19,018,427,000	$19,442,818,000
Related Agencies	$620,436,000	$600,924,000	$761,904,000	$761,954,000
Total	$92,031,994,000	$90,908,951,000	$100,853,843,000	$101,958,350,000
LEGISLATIVE BRANCH				
Congressional Operations		774,838,100	$1,112,801,214	$1,104,789,214
Related Agencies		$530,426,000	$535,401,000	$530,401,000
Total		$1,305,264,100	$1,648,202,214	$1,635,190,214
MILITARY CONSTRUCTION				
Army	$1,695,200,000	$1,200,070,000	$1,262,570,000	$1,260,110,000
Navy	$1,814,100,000	$1,224,290,000	$1,282,985,000	$1,376,715,000
Air Force	$1,773,200,000	$1,220,130,000	$1,250,620,000	$1,242,530,000
Defense Agencies	$762,100,000	$541,563,000	$505,110,000	$543,170,000
NATO Infrastructure	$247,000,000	$247,000,000	$232,000,000	$232,000,000
Reserve and National Guard	$451,200,000	$435,541,000	$472,296,000	$479,904,000
Family Housing	$3,417,568,000	$3,110,375,000	$3,234,568,000	$3,140,413,000
Total [6]	$10,520,200,000	$8,390,801,000	$8,651,981,000	$8,686,674,000
TRANSPORTATION				
Transportation Department	$6,453,896,000	$9,724,652,000	$9,638,548,000	$9,822,404,500
Related Agencies	$560,618,569	$560,248,569	$559,198,569	$560,968,569
Total	$7,014,514,569	$10,284,900,569	$10,197,746,569	$10,383,373,069
TREASURY, POSTAL SERVICE, AND GENERAL GOVERNMENT				
Treasury Department	$5,950,261,000	$6,236,721,000	$5,875,165,000	$6,359,591,000
Postal Service	$40,049,000	$690,049,000	$650,000,000	$650,000,000
Executive Office of the President	$100,899,000	$95,491,000	$95,726,000	$101,301,000
Independent Agencies	$6,765,021,000	$6,772,118,000 [7]	$6,663,971,800	$6,678,593,000
Total	$12,856,230,000	$13,651,757,000	$13,284,862,800	$13,789,485,000

[1] The administration had sought a permanent indefinite appropriation for the Commodity Credit Corporation Reimbursement. The Senate Appropriations Committee incorporated the proposal into its bill; the House rejected the plan. [2] Obligational authority. [3] Includes $20,000,000 in advance 1988 funds. [4] Includes funds transferred from prior appropriations. [5] Includes debits and credits for the Housing Guaranty program, Overseas Private Investment Corporation, Export-Import Bank total limitation, Export-Import Bank direct loans, and Fair Export Financing Program. [6] Excludes portion applied to debt reduction. [7] Excludes a general reduction under a House-passed amendment making a 9.75% reduction in certain accounts.

Source: "Congressional Quarterly Weekly Report"

UNITED STATES: Major Legislation Enacted During the Second Session of the 99th Congress

SUBJECT	PURPOSE
Tobacco Advertising	Prohibits radio and television advertising of chewing tobacco and snuff. Signed February 27. Public Law 99-252.
Gun Control	Lifts the ban on interstate sales of rifles and shotguns and limits the number of people who are required to obtain licenses to sell firearms. Allows gun owners to transport their firearms interstate. Bans the future sales and possession of machine guns by private citizens. Signed May 19. Public Law 99-308.
Presidential Libraries	Helps to defray the federal cost of future presidential libraries. Private foundations that raise funds for the construction of presidential libraries must establish an endowment equal to 20% of building costs to help cover operational costs of such libraries, which now are paid by the federal government. Signed May 27. Public Law 99-323.
Federal Pensions	Creates a new federal retirement system for workers hired after December 31, 1983. Signed June 6. Public Law 99-335.
Drinking Water	Requires the Environmental Protection Agency to set maximum allowable limits for 83 toxic chemicals that can appear in public drinking water. Signed June 19. Public Law 99-339.
Daylight Saving Time	Authorizes that daylight saving time begins on the first Sunday of April instead of the last Sunday of April. Signed July 8. Public Law 99-359.
Attorneys' Fees	Allows courts to award attorneys' fees to parents who win legal disputes involving the education rights of handicapped children. Signed August 5. Public Law 99-372.
Embassy Security	Authorizes $2.4 billion for a five-year program to strengthen and rebuild security measures at U.S. embassies and other diplomatic missions. Signed August 27. Public Law 99-399.
Military Reorganization	Shifts bureaucratic power within the Defense Department from the separate armed services to the senior officials intended to coordinate the services, i.e. the chairman of the Joint Chiefs of Staff and the commanders in chief of the combat forces in the field. Signed October 1. Public Law 99-433.
South Africa	Imposes economic sanctions against South Africa. The House and Senate overrode a presidential veto on September 29 and October 2, respectively. Public Law 99-440.
National Flower	Establishes the rose as the national floral emblem. Signed October 7. Public Law 99-449.
Handicapped Education	Renews handicapped-education programs, putting increased emphasis on helping disabled children in their preschool years. Signed October 8. Public Law 99-457.
Export-Import Bank	Approves a six-year reauthorization of the Export-Import Bank. Establishes a $300 million trade "war chest" to combine grants and direct loans to make U.S. exports more attractive. Signed October 15. Public Law 99-472.
Reading	Designates 1987 as the "Year of the Reader." Signed October 16. Public Law 99-494.
Hydroelectric Power	Establishes guidelines to be used by the Federal Energy Regulatory Commission in renewing the licenses for hydroelectric power plants. Signed October 16. Public Law 99-495.
College Aid	Reauthorizes for five years various federal aid programs for higher education. Signed October 17. Public Law 99-498.
"Superfund" Toxic Waste	Funds the toxic-dump cleanup program at $8.5 billion for fiscal years 1987–91. Sets new schedules for the Environmental Protection Agency to follow in cleaning up toxic-waste dump sites. Signed October 17. Public Law 99-499.
Federal Spending	Appropriates $575.9 billion in budget authority for fiscal 1987. Includes $70 million in military aid and $30 million in non-military aid for the "contras" in Nicaragua. Signed October 18. Public Law 99-500.
Vocational Training	Reauthorizes for five years vocational training programs that were established in 1973. Signed October 21. Public Law 99-506.
Electronic Privacy	Extends privacy guarantees to communications transmitted by new technology. Signed October 21. Public Law 99-508.
Tax Reform	Reduces income tax rates for corporations and individuals. Curtails or eliminates dozens of tax breaks. *See* page 508. Signed October 22. Public Law 99-514.
School Asbestos	Orders the nation's schools to clean up hazardous asbestos and requires the federal government to establish standards for school inspections for asbestos. Signed October 22. Public Law 99-519.
Anti-drugs	Authorizes $1.7 billion in new funds for drug interdiction, eradication, enforcement, education, treatment, and rehabilitation. *See* page 208. Signed October 27. Public Law 99-570.
Age Discrimination	Makes it illegal for most employers to have mandatory retirement policies. Signed October 31. Public Law 99-592.
Immigration	Transforms the nation's immigration laws. *See* page 442. Signed November 6. Public Law 99-603.
Water Resources Development	Authorizes more than 300 public works, including harbor and waterway, projects nationwide at a cost of $16 billion, for which the federal government would pay $9 billion and state and local users and beneficiaries would pay about $7 billion. Also imposes a new user fee on cargo using American harbors and channels, increases the inland waterway fuel tax, establishes new cost-sharing formulas, and authorizes 12 new Corps of Engineers or Interior Department water-resource programs. Signed November 17. Public Law 99-662.

Contributors

ADRIAN, CHARLES R., Professor of Political Science, University of California at Riverside; Coauthor, *Governing Urban America:* CALIFORNIA; LOS ANGELES

ALEXANDER, ROBERT J., Professor of Economics and Political Science, Rutgers University: BOLIVIA; ECUADOR; URUGUAY

ALTER, STEWART, Senior Reporter, *Advertising Age:* ADVERTISING

AMBRE, AGO, Economist, Bureau of Economic Analysis, U.S. Department of Commerce: INDUSTRIAL REVIEW

ATTNER, PAUL, National Correspondent, *The Sporting News:* SPORTS—*Basketball*

BARMASH, ISADORE, Business-Financial Writer, *The New York Times;* Author, *Always Live Better Than Your Clients, More Than They Bargained For,* and *The Chief Executives:* THE BUSINESS OF ADVICE; RETAILING

BATRA, PREM P., Professor of Biochemistry, Wright State University: BIOCHEMISTRY

BECK, KAY, School of Urban Life, Georgia State University: GEORGIA

BEHLER, DEBORAH A., Free-lance Writer: ZOOS AND ZOOLOGY

BERLIN, MICHAEL J., United Nations Correspondent, *The Washington Post:* BIOGRAPHY—*Kurt Waldheim;* LAW—*International;* UNITED NATIONS

BEST, JOHN, Chief, *Canada World News:* NEW BRUNSWICK; PRINCE EDWARD ISLAND; QUEBEC

BITTON-JACKSON, LIVIA E., Professor of Judaic and Hebraic Studies, Herbert H. Lehman College of City University of New York; Author, *Elli: Coming of Age in the Holocaust, Madonna or Courtesan: The Jewish Woman in Christian Literature:* RELIGION—*Judaism*

BOLUS, JIM, Free-lance Sports Writer; Author, *Run for the Roses:* SPORTS—*Horse Racing*

BOND, DONOVAN H., Professor Emeritus of Journalism, West Virginia University: WEST VIRGINIA

BOULAY, HARVEY, Systems Manager, Rogerson House; Author, *The Twilight Cities:* MASSACHUSETTS

BOWER, BRUCE, Behavioral Sciences Editor, *Science News:* ANTHROPOLOGY; ARCHAEOLOGY

BRAMMER, DANA B., Associate Director, Public Policy Center, University of Mississippi: MISSISSIPPI

BRANDHORST, L. CARL, and JOANN, Western Oregon State College: OREGON

BURANELLI, VINCENT, Free-lance Writer and Editor; Author, *The Trial of Peter Zenger, Louis XIV;* Coauthor, *Spy/Counterspy: An Encyclopedia of Espionage:* ESPIONAGE

BURKS, ARDATH W., Professor Emeritus Asian Studies, Rutgers University; Author, *Japan: A Postindustrial Power:* JAPAN

BUSH, GRAHAM W. A., Associate Professor of Political Studies, University of Auckland; Author, *Local Government & Politics in New Zealand;* Editor, *New Zealand—A Nation Divided?:* NEW ZEALAND

BUTWELL, RICHARD, President and Professor of Political Science, California State University; Author, *Southeast Asia: A Political Introduction, Southeast Asia Today and Tomorrow, U Nu of Burma, Foreign Policy and the Developing State:* ASIA; BURMA; LAOS

CASPER, GRETCHEN, Department of Political Science, Grinnell College: THE PHILIPPINES: A NATION IN CHANGE

CASPER, LEONARD, Professor of English, Boston College: THE PHILIPPINES: A NATION IN CHANGE

CHALMERS, JOHN W. Concordia College, Edmonton, Alberta; Editor, *Alberta Diamond Jubilee Anthology:* ALBERTA

CHRISTENSEN, WILLIAM E., Professor of History, Midland Lutheran College; Author, *In Such Harmony: A History of the Federated Church of Columbus, Nebraska, New Song to the Lord:* NEBRASKA

CHRISTGAU, GEORGIA, Free-lance Writer: MUSIC—*Popular;* RECORDINGS

CLARKE, JAMES W., Professor of Political Science, University of Arizona: ARIZONA

COLE, JOHN N., Cofounder, *Maine Times;* Author, *In Maine, Striper, Salmon, House Building:* MAINE

COLLINS, BUD, Sports Writer, *The Boston Globe:* SPORTS—*Tennis*

COMMANDAY, ROBERT P., Music Critic, *San Francisco Chronicle:* MUSIC—*Classical*

CONRADT, DAVID P., Professor of Political Science, University of Florida; Author, *The German Polity, Comparative Politics, The German Voter 1949–1987:* GERMANY

COOPER, MARY H., Staff Writer, *Editorial Research Reports:* THE LIABILITY INSURANCE CRISIS

CORLEW, DR. ROBERT E., Dean, School of Liberal Arts, Middle Tennessee State University: TENNESSEE

CORNWELL, ELMER E., JR., Professor of Political Science, Brown University: RHODE ISLAND

COSSER, ANNE, Free-lance Journalist: ICELAND

CRAIG, PAUL P., Professor of Applied Science, University of California, Davis; Coauthor, *Nuclear Arms Race: Technology and Society:* ENERGY—*The Chernobyl Accident*

CUNNIFF, JOHN, Business News Analyst, The Associated Press; Author, *How to Stretch Your Dollar:* UNITED STATES—*The Economy*

CUNNINGHAM, PEGGY, *Insight Magazine:* MARYLAND

CURRIER, CHET, Financial Writer, The Associated Press; Author, *The Investor's Encyclopedia, The 15-Minute Investor:* STOCKS AND BONDS

CURTIS, L. PERRY, JR., Professor of History, Brown University: IRELAND

DANIELS, ROBERT V., Professor of History, University of Vermont: VERMONT

DARBY, JOSEPH W., III, Reporter, *The Times-Picayune/State Item:* LOUISIANA

DAVIS, GRANT M., Distinguished Professor of Business Administration and Chairholder, Oren Harris Chair of Transportation, University of Arkansas; Author, *Carrier Management, Physical Logistics Management, Motor Carrier Economics, Regulation, Operation:* TRANSPORTATION

DEEB, MARIUS, Professor, Center for Contemporary Arab Studies, Georgetown University; Author, *The Lebanese Civil War, Party Politics in Egypt: The Wafd and Its Rivals 1919–1939:* JORDAN; LEBANON; SYRIA

DeGREGORIO, GEORGE, Sports Department, *The New York Times;* Author, *Joe DiMaggio, An Informal Biography:* SPORTS—*Boxing, Ice Skating, Skiing, Swimming, Track and Field*

DELZELL, CHARLES F., Professor of History, Vanderbilt University; Author, *Italy in the Twentieth Century, Mediterranean Fascism, Mussolini's Enemies:* ITALY

DENNIS, LARRY, Free-lance Golf Writer: SPORTS—*Golf*

DIETERICH, H. R., Professor of History, University of Wyoming: WYOMING

DODD, CHRISTOPHER, U.S. Senator: UNITED STATES—*The Peace Corps 1961–1986*

DRIGGS, DON W., Chairman, Department of Political Science, University of Nevada; Coauthor, *The Nevada Constitution: Origin and Growth:* NEVADA

DUFF, ERNEST A., Professor of Politics, Randolph-Macon Woman's College; Author, *Agrarian Reform in Colombia, Violence and Repression in Latin America, Leader and Party in Latin America:* COLOMBIA

DUNN, CHRISTOPHER, Professor of Political Science, University of Saskatchewan: SASKATCHEWAN

DuPONT, ROBERT L., M.D., Clinical Professor of Psychiatry, Georgetown University Medical School; Author, *Getting Tough on Gateway Drugs: A Guide for the Family;* Editor, *Phobia: A Comprehensive Summary of Modern Treatments:* PHOBIAS

ELKINS, ANN M., Fashion Director, *Good Housekeeping Magazine:* FASHION; FASHION—*The New Male Seeks the Perfect Look*

ELVING, PHYLLIS, Free-lance Travel Writer: TRAVEL

ENSTAD, ROBERT H., Writer, *Chicago Tribune:* CHICAGO; ILLINOIS

EVANS, DAVID A., Professor, Department of Food Science and Nutrition, University of Massachusetts: FOOD

EWEGEN, BOB, Editorial Writer, *The Denver Post:* COLORADO

FAGEN, MORTON D., AT&T Bell Laboratories (retired); Editor, *A History of Engineering and Science in the Bell System,* Vols. I and II: COMMUNICATION TECHNOLOGY

FISKE, EDWARD B., Education Editor, *The New York Times;* Author, *Selective Guide to Colleges, Best Buys in College Education:* EDUCATION—*Early Schooling*

FRANCIS, DAVID R., Economic Columnist, *The Christian Science Monitor:* BIOGRAPHY—*Barber B. Conable, Jr.;* INTERNATIONAL TRADE & FINANCE

FREDERICK, WILLIAM H., Professor of History, Ohio University: INDONESIA

FRIEDMAN, ROBERT, Reporter, *The San Juan Star:* PUERTO RICO

FRIIS, ERIK J., Editor and Publisher, *The Scandinavian-American Bulletin:* DENMARK; FINLAND; SWEDEN

GAILEY, HARRY A., Professor of History and Coordinator of African Studies, San Jose State University: NIGERIA; SUDAN; ZAIRE

GARFIELD, ROBERT, Associate Professor of History, DePaul University: KENYA; TANZANIA; UGANDA

GEIS, GILBERT, Professor, Program in Social Ecology, University of California, Irvine; Author, *On White Collar Crime:* CRIME; CRIME—*Product Tampering;* LAW—*Pornography*

GIBSON, ROBERT C., Regional Editor, *The Billings Gazette:* MONTANA

GJESTER, THØR, Former Editor, *Økonomisk Revy,* Oslo: NORWAY

GLANVILLE, BRIAN, Soccer Correspondent, *The Sunday Times,* London; Author, *The Olympian, A Cry of Crickets, Diamond, The Comic, A Second Home:* SPORTS—*Soccer*

GOODMAN, DONALD, Associate Professor of Sociology, John Jay College of Criminal Justice, City University of New York: PRISONS

GORDON, MAYNARD M., Editor, *Motor News Analysis;* Author, *The Iacocca Management Technique:* AUTOMOBILES

GRAYSON, GEORGE W., John Marshall Professor of Government and Citizenship, College of William and Mary; Author, *The Politics of Mexican Oil, The United States and Mexico: Patterns of Influence:* BRAZIL; PORTUGAL; SPAIN

GREEN, MAUREEN, Author-Journalist, London: GREAT BRITAIN—*The Arts;* LITERATURE—*English;* LONDON

GREGORY, BARBARA, Production Editor, *The Numismatist:* COINS AND COIN COLLECTING

GROTH, ALEXANDER J., Professor of Political Science, University of California, Davis; Author, *People's Poland;* Coauthor, *Contemporary Politics: Europe, Comparative Resource Allocation, Public Policy Across Nations:* POLAND

GUTH, JAMES, Professor of Political Science, Furman University: BIOGRAPHY—*Lyndon LaRouche*

GUTMAN, RICHARD J. S., Coauthor, *American Diner:* THE DINER IS BACK

HADWIGER, DON F., Professor of Political Science, Iowa State University; Author, *Politics of Agricultural Research;* Coauthor, *Policy Process in American Agriculture;* Coeditor, *World Food Interdependence:* AGRICULTURE; BIOGRAPHY—*Richard Lyng*

HAND, SAMUEL B., Professor of History, University of Vermont: VERMONT

HARVEY, ROSS M., Assistant Deputy Minister of Culture and Communications, Government of the Northwest Territories: NORTHWEST TERRITORIES

HELMREICH, ERNST C., Professor Emeritus of History, Bowdoin College; Author, *The German Churches under Hitler: Background, Struggle, and Epilogue:* AUSTRIA

HELMREICH, J. E., Professor of History, Allegheny College; Author, *Belgium and Europe: A Study in Small Power Diplomacy, Gathering Rare Ores: The Diplomacy of Uranium Acquisition, 1943–54:* BELGIUM

HELMREICH, PAUL C., Professor of History, Wheaton College; Author, *From Paris to Sèvres: The Partition of the Ottoman Empire at the Peace Conference of 1919–1920:* SWITZERLAND

HENBERG, MARVIN, Department of Philosophy, University of Idaho: IDAHO

HINTON, HAROLD C., Professor of Political Science and International Affairs, The George Washington University; Author, *An Introduction to Chinese Politics, Korea Under New Leadership: The Fifth Republic:* KOREA

HOOVER, HERBERT T., Professor of History, University of South Dakota; Author, *To Be an Indian, The Chitimacha People, The Sioux, The Practice of Oral History:* SOUTH DAKOTA

HOPKO, THE REV. THOMAS, Assistant Professor, St. Vladimir's Orthodox Theological Seminary: RELIGION—*Orthodox Eastern*

HOYT, CHARLES K., Senior Editor, *Architectural Record;* Author, *More Places for People:* ARCHITECTURE

HULBERT, DAN, *The Dallas Times Herald:* TELEVISION AND RADIO; THEATER

HUTH, JOHN F., JR., Reporter (retired), *The Plain Dealer,* Cleveland: OHIO

JEWELL, MALCOLM E., Professor of Political Science, University of Kentucky; Coauthor, *American State Political Parties and Elections, Kentucky Politics:* KENTUCKY

JOHNSTON, ROBERT L., Editor/Associate Publisher, *The Chicago Catholic:* RELIGION—*Roman Catholicism*

JONES, H. G., Curator, North Carolina Collection, University of North Carolina at Chapel Hill: NORTH CAROLINA

KARNES, THOMAS L., Professor of History Emeritus, Arizona State University; Author, *Latin American Policy of the United States, Failure of Union: Central America 1824–1960:* CENTRAL AMERICA

KASH, DON E., George Lynn Cross Research Professor of Political Science, University of Oklahoma; Coauthor, *Our Energy Future, Energy Under the Oceans;* Author, *U.S. Energy Policy: Crisis and Complacency:* ENERGY

KIMBALL, LORENZO D., Professor of Political Science, University of Utah: RELIGION—*The Mormons and the Mormon Church;* UTAH

KIMBELL, CHARLES L., Senior Foreign Mineral Specialist, U.S. Bureau of Mines: STATISTICAL AND TABULAR DATA—*World Mineral and Metal Production*

KING, PETER J., Associate Professor of History, Carleton University, Ottawa: ONTARIO; OTTAWA

KINNEAR, MICHAEL, Professor of History, University of Manitoba; Author, *The Fall of Lloyd George, The British Voter:* MANITOBA

KISSELGOFF, ANNA, Chief Dance Critic, *The New York Times:* DANCE

KOLDERIE, TED, Senior Fellow, Hubert H. Humphrey Institute of Public Affairs, University of Minnesota: UNITED STATES—*The Trend Toward Privatization*

KRAUSE, AXEL, Economic Correspondent, *International Herald Tribune,* Paris: BIOGRAPHY—*Jacques Chirac;* FRANCE

KRONISH, SYD, Stamp Editor, The Associated Press: STAMPS AND STAMP COLLECTING

LAI, CHUEN-YAN DAVID, Associate Professor of Geography, University of Victoria, British Columbia: HONG KONG

LAWRENCE, ROBERT M., Professor of Political Science, Colorado State University; Author, *The Strategic Defense Initiative Bibliography and Reference Guide:* ARMS CONTROL; MILITARY AFFAIRS; MILITARY AFFAIRS—*The Weapons Market;* OBITUARIES—*Hyman Rickover*

LEE, STEWART M., Chairman, Department of Economics and Business Administration, Geneva College; Coauthor, *Economics for Consumers:* BUSINESS AND CORPORATE AFFAIRS; CONSUMER AFFAIRS

LEEPSON, MARC, Contributing Editor and Columnist, *American Politics Magazine:* DRUGS AND ALCOHOL; SOCIAL WELFARE

LEVINE, LOUIS, Professor, Department of Biology, City College of New York; Author, *Biology of the Gene, Biology for a Modern Society:* GENETICS; MICROBIOLOGY

LEVITT, MORRIS J., Professor, Department of Political Science, Howard University; Coauthor, *Of, By, and For the People: State & Local Government and Politics:* WASHINGTON, DC

LEWIS, JEROME R., Director for Public Administration, College of Urban Affairs and Public Policy, University of Delaware: DELAWARE; HOUSING

LOBRON, BARBARA L., Writer, Editor, Photographer: PHOTOGRAPHY

LOESCHER, GIL, Associate Professor, University of Notre Dame; Author, *Calculated Kindness: Refugees and America's Half-Open Door, The Global Refugee Problem: U.S. and World Response:* REFUGEES AND IMMIGRATION

MABRY, DONALD J., Professor of History, Mississippi State University; Author, *Mexico's Acción Nacional, The Mexican University and the State;* Coauthor, *Neighbors—Mexico and the United States:* MEXICO

MADISON, CHRISTOPHER, Staff Correspondent, *National Journal:* U.S.—*Foreign Affairs*

MAMMANA, DENNIS L., Free-lance Science Writer/Photographer: SPACE EXPLORATION—*Uranus;* ZOOLOGY—*Vivisection*

MARCOPOULOS, GEORGE J., Associate Professor of History, Tufts University: CYPRUS; GREECE

MASOTTI, LOUIS H., Professor of Political Science, Urban Affairs and Public Policy Research, Northwestern University; Author, *The New Urban Politics, The City in Comparative Perspective:* CITIES AND URBAN AFFAIRS

MATHESON, JIM, Sports Writer, *Edmonton Journal:* SPORTS—*Ice Hockey*

MATTHEWS, WILLIAM H., III, Professor of Geology, Lamar University: GEOLOGY

MAYER, BARBARA, Home Furnishings Writer, The Associated Press: INTERIOR DESIGN

McCORQUODALE, SUSAN, Political Science Department, Memorial University of Newfoundland: NEWFOUNDLAND

McFADDEN, ROBERT D., Reporter, *The New York Times;* Coauthor, *No Hiding Place:* NEW YORK CITY

McGILL, DAVID A., Professor of Marine Science, U.S. Coast Guard Academy: OCEANOGRAPHY

MELIKOV, GREG, State News Desk, *Miami Herald:* FLORIDA

MICHAELIS, PATRICIA A., Curator of Manuscripts, Kansas State Historical Society: KANSAS

MITCHELL, GARY, Professor of Physics, North Carolina State University: PHYSICS

MORTIMER, ROBERT A., Professor, Haverford College; Author, *The Third World Coalition in International Politics:* ALGERIA

MORTON, DESMOND, Professor of History and Principal, Erindale College, University of Toronto; Author, *A Short History of Canada, Bloody Victory: Canadians and the D-Day Campaign, Working People: An Illustrated History of the Canadian Labour Movement, A Military History of Canada:* CANADA

MULLINER, K., Assistant to Director of Libraries, Ohio University; Coeditor, *Malaysia Studies: Archaeology, Historiography, Geography, and Bibliography, Southeast Asia: An Emerging Center of World Influence?:* MALAYSIA; SINGAPORE

MURPHY, ROBERT F., *The Hartford Courant:* CONNECTICUT

NADLER, PAUL S., Professor of Finance, Rutgers University; Author, *Commercial Banking in the Economy, The Banking Jungle:* BANKING AND FINANCE

NAFTALIN, ARTHUR, Professor Emeritus of Public Affairs, University of Minnesota: MINNESOTA

NELSON, BILL, U.S. Representative from Florida; Chairman, House Subcommittee on Space Science and Applications: THE LOSS OF "CHALLENGER" AND AMERICA'S FUTURE IN SPACE

NEUMANN, JIM, *The Forum,* Fargo, ND: NORTH DAKOTA

NEWLAND, ED, Assistant State Editor, *Richmond Times-Dispatch:* VIRGINIA

NOLAN, WILLIAM C., Professor of Political Science, Southern Arkansas University: ARKANSAS

NYREN, KARL, Senior Editor, *Library Journal:* LIBRARIES

OCHSENWALD, WILLIAM, Professor of History, Virginia Polytechnic Institute; Author, *The Hijaz Railroad, Religion, Society, and the State in Arabia:* SAUDI ARABIA

O'CONNOR, ROBERT E., Associate Professor of Political Science, The Pennsylvania State University; Author, *Politics and Structure: Essentials of American National Government:* PENNSYLVANIA

OLSEN, MICHAEL L., Professor, New Mexico Highlands University: NEW MEXICO

O'MEARA, PATRICK, Director, African Studies Program, Indiana University; Coeditor, *Africa, International Politics in Southern Africa, Southern Africa, The Continuing Crisis:* AFRICA; SOUTH AFRICA; ZIMBABWE

OSTLING, RICHARD N., Religion Editor, *Time* magazine: RELIGION—*The Television Factor*

PALMER, NORMAN D., Professor Emeritus of Political Science and South Asian Studies, University of Pennsylvania; Author, *The United States and India: The Dimensions of Influence, Elections and Political Development: The South Asian Experience:* INDIA; SRI LANKA

PARKER, FRANKLIN, Distinguished Visiting Professor, Center for Excellence in Education; Author, *Education in the People's Republic of China, Past and Present, British Schools and Ours, What Can We Learn from the Schools of China?, Battle of the Books Kanawha County:* EDUCATION

PASCOE, ELAINE, Free-lance Writer and Editor; Author, *Racial Prejudice:* BIOGRAPHY—*Whoopi Goldberg, Joan Rivers;* FAMILY; OBITUARIES—*Henry Moore, Georgia O'Keeffe:* WOMEN

PAWEL, MIRIAM, Albany Bureau Chief, *Newsday:* NEW YORK

PEARSON, NEALE J., Professor of Political Science, Texas Tech University: CHILE; PERU; VENEZUELA

PERETZ, DON, Professor of Political Science, State University of New York at Binghamton; Author, *The West Bank—History, Politics, Society & Economy, Government and Politics of Israel, The Middle East Today:* EGYPT; IRAN; IRAQ

PERKINS, KENNETH J., Assistant Professor of History, University of South Carolina: LIBYA; RELIGION—*Islam*

PIOTROWSKI, WILLIAM L., National Aeronautics and Space Administration: SPACE EXPLORATION (article written independent of NASA)

PIPPIN, LARRY L., Professor of Political Science, University of the Pacific; Author, *The Remón Era:* ARGENTINA; PARAGUAY

PLATT, HERMANN K., Professor of History, Saint Peter's College: NEW JERSEY

POOLE, PETER A., Author, *The Vietnamese in Thailand, Eight Presidents and Indochina:* CAMBODIA; THAILAND; VIETNAM

POULLADA, LEON B., Professor of Political Science, Center for Afghanistan Studies, University of Nebraska; Author, *Reform and Rebellion in Afghanistan:* AFGHANISTAN

PREBLE, CECILIA, Transport Editor, *Aviation Week & Space Technology:* TRAVEL—*Airline Security and Safety*

RAGUSA, ISA, Research Art Historian, Department of Art and Archaeology, Princeton University: ART

RALOFF, JANET, Policy/Technology Editor, *Science News:* ENVIRONMENT

REUNING, WINIFRED, Writer, Polar Program, National Science Foundation: POLAR RESEARCH

RICHTER, WILLIAM L., Professor and Head, Department of Political Science, Kansas State University: BANGLADESH; PAKISTAN

RIGGAN, WILLIAM, Associate Editor, *World Literature Today,* University of Oklahoma; Author, *Picaros, Madmen, Naifs, and Clowns, Comparative Literature and Literary Theory:* LITERATURE—*World*

ROBINSON, LEIF J., Editor, *Sky and Telescope:* ASTRONOMY; ASTRONOMY—*Halley's Comet*

ROBOCK, ALAN, Professor, Department of Meteorology, University of Maryland: METEOROLOGY

ROSS, RUSSELL M., Professor of Political Science, University of Iowa; Author, *State and Local Government and Administration, Iowa Government and Administration:* IOWA

ROWEN, HERBERT H., Professor, Rutgers University, New Brunswick; Author, *John de Witt: Statesman of the "True Freedom," The King's State: Proprietary Dynasticism in Early Modern France, John de Witt: Grand Pensionary of Holland, 1625–1672:* NETHERLANDS

RUBIN, JIM, Supreme Court Correspondent, The Associated Press: BIOGRAPHY—*William H. Rehnquist, Antonin Scalia;* LAW; LAW—*The Burger Court*

RUFF, NORMAN J., Assistant Professor, University of Victoria; Coauthor, *Reins of Power: Governing British Columbia:* BRITISH COLUMBIA

SALSINI, PAUL, *The Milwaukee Journal:* WISCONSIN

SARRATT, WILLIAM A., Executive Editor, *The Fish Boat:* FISHERIES

SAVAGE, DAVID, Professor of English (retired), Simon Fraser University: CANADA—*The Arts, Expo 86;* LITERATURE—*Canadian*

SAWATSKY, DON, Free-lance Writer/Broadcaster, Author, *Ghost Town Trails of the Yukon:* YUKON TERRITORY

SCHLOSSBERG, DAN, Author, *Baseball Stars 1986:* SPORTS—*Baseball*

SCHROEDER, RICHARD, Washington Bureau Chief, *Vision;* Syndicated Writer, U.S. Newspapers: CARIBBEAN; CARIBBEAN—*Haiti;* INTERNATIONAL TRADE & FINANCE—*The Effects of Cheap Oil;* LATIN AMERICA

SCHWAB, PETER, Professor of Political Science, State University of New York at Purchase; Author, *Ethiopia: Politics, Economics and Society:* ETHIOPIA

SENSER, ROBERT A., Free-lance Labor Writer, Washington, DC: LABOR

SETH, R. P., Professor of Economics, Mount Saint Vincent University, Halifax: CANADA—*The Economy;* NOVA SCOTIA

SEYBOLD, PAUL G., Professor, Department of Chemistry, Wright State University: CHEMISTRY

SHEPRO, CARL E., Professor, North Slope Higher Education Center, University of Alaska at Barrow: ALASKA

SHOGAN, ROBERT, National Political Correspondent, Washington Bureau, *Los Angeles Times;* Author, *A Question of Judgment, Promises to Keep:* BIOGRAPHY—*Michael Deaver;* UNITED STATES—*Overview; The Elections*

SIEGEL, STANLEY E., Professor of History, University of Houston; Author, *A Political History of the Texas Republic, 1836–1845, Houston: Portrait of the Supercity on Buffalo Bayou:* TEXAS

SIMON, JEFFREY, The Rand Corporation, Santa Monica, CA: TERRORISM

SMALLOWITZ, HOWARD, Associate News Editor, *Civil Engineering Magazine:* ENGINEERING, CIVIL

SNODSMITH, RALPH L., Ornamental Horticulturist; Author, *Ralph Snodsmith's Tips from the Garden Hotline:* GARDENING AND HORTICULTURE; GARDENING AND HORTICULTURE—*The Cut-Flowers Boom*

SOLER, MARK I., Executive Director, Youth Law Center: LAW—*Juvenile Justice*

SPERA, DOMINIC, Professor of Music, Indiana University; Author, *The Prestige Series—16 Original Compositions for Jazz Band:* MUSIC—*Jazz;* OBITUARIES—*Benny Goodman*

STARR, JOHN BRYAN, Lecturer, Department of Political Science, Yale University; Executive Director, Yale-China Association; Author, *Continuing the Revolution: The Political Thought of Mao;* Editor, *The Future of U.S.-China Relations:* CHINA; TAIWAN

STERN, JEROME H., Associate Professor of English, Florida State University; Editor, *Studies in Popular Culture:* LITERATURE—*American*

STEWART, WILLIAM H., Associate Professor of Political Science, The University of Alabama; Coauthor, *Alabama Government and Politics:* ALABAMA; ALABAMA—*The Wallace Era Ends*

STOUDEMIRE, ROBERT H., Distinguished Professor Emeritus, University of South Carolina: SOUTH CAROLINA

SULLIVAN, CHERYL, *The Christian Science Monitor:* ETHNIC GROUPS

SULLIVAN, JEREMIAH H., Associate Professor of Business Communications, University of Washington; Author, *Pacific Basin Enterprise and the Changing Law of the Sea, Foreign Investment in the U.S. Fishing Industry:* WASHINGTON

SUNY, RONALD GRIGOR, Alex Manoogian Professor of Modern Armenian History, University of Michigan; Author, *The Baku Commune, 1917–18: Class and Nationality in the Russian Revolution, Armenia in the Twentieth Century:* USSR

SUTTON, STAN, Sportswriter, *The Courier Journal,* Louisville, KY: SPORTS—*Auto Racing*

SYLVESTER, LORNA LUTES, Associate Editor, *Indiana Magazine of History,* Indiana University: INDIANA

TABORSKY, EDWARD, Professor of Government, University of Texas at Austin; Author, *Communism in Czechoslovakia, 1948–1960, Communist Penetration of the Third World:* CZECHOSLOVAKIA

TAYLOR, WILLIAM L., Professor of History, Plymouth State College: NEW HAMPSHIRE

TESAR, JENNY, Medicine and Science Writer: BIOGRAPHY—*Robert Peter Gale;* COMPUTERS; COMPUTERS—*Artificial Intelligence;* INDUSTRIAL REVIEW—*The Plastics Revolution;* MEDICINE AND HEALTH; MEDICINE AND HEALTH—*Dentistry*

TESSLER, MARK, Professor of Political Science, University of Wisconsin-Milwaukee; Coauthor, *Political Elites in Arab North Africa:* MOROCCO; TUNISIA

THEISEN, CHARLES W., Assistant News Editor, *The Detroit News:* MICHIGAN

TOWNE, RUTH W., Professor of History, Northeast Missouri State University: MISSOURI

TRIEGEL, LINDA, Free-lance Writer and Editor: BIOGRAPHY—*Louis L'Amour;* OBITUARIES—*Cary Grant, Kate Smith*

TURNER, ARTHUR CAMPBELL, Professor of Political Science, University of California, Riverside; Coauthor, *Power and Ideology in the Middle East:* MIDDLE EAST

TURNER, CHARLES H., Free-lance Writer: HAWAII

TURNER, DARRELL J., Associate Editor, Religious News Service: RELIGION—*Protestantism*

VAN RIPER, PAUL P., Professor Emeritus and Head, Department of Political Science, Texas A&M University: POSTAL SERVICE

VOLSKY, GEORGE, Center for Advanced International Studies, University of Miami: CUBA

WATTERS, ELSIE M., Vice President—Research, Tax Foundation, Inc.: TAXATION; TAXATION—*The Tax Reform Act of 1986*

WEIKER, WALTER F., Professor of Political Science, Rutgers University: ISRAEL; TURKEY

WEISBERGER, BERNARD A., Author, *The Statue of Liberty: The First Hundred Years, The American Heritage History of the American People:* LADY LIBERTY AT 100

WENTZ, RICHARD E., Professor of Religious Studies, Arizona State University; Author, *The Contemplation of Otherness: The Critical Vision of Religion, More Than You Know, Saga of the American Soul:* RELIGION—*Far Eastern*

WESTIN, ALAN, Professor of Public Law and Government, Columbia University: DRUGS AND ALCOHOL—*Drug Testing*

WILLIS, F. ROY, Professor of History, University of California, Davis; Author, *France, Germany and the New Europe, 1945–1968, Italy Chooses Europe, The French Paradox:* EUROPE

WILMS, DENISE MURCKO, Assistant Editor, Children's Books, The Booklist, American Library Association: LITERATURE—*Children*

WINDER, DAVID, British Isles Correspondent, *The Christian Science Monitor:* GREAT BRITAIN

WOLF, WILLIAM, Film Critic, Gannett News Service; Author, *The Marx Brothers, The Landmark Films, The Cinema and Our Century:* BIOGRAPHY—*Geraldine Page;* MOTION PICTURES; OBITUARIES—*James Cagney*

WOOD, JOHN, Professor of Political Science, University of Oklahoma: OKLAHOMA

YAMASHITA, ELIZABETH S., Professor, School of Journalism and Mass Communication, University of Oklahoma: PUBLISHING

YOUNGER, R. M., Author, *Australia and the Australians, Australia's Great River, Australia! Australia! March to Nationhood:* AUSTRALIA

ZACEK, JOSEPH FREDERICK, Professor of History, State University of New York, Albany; Author, *Palacky: The Historian as Scholar and Nationalist:* ALBANIA; BULGARIA; HUNGARY; ROMANIA; YUGOSLAVIA

Index

Main article headings appear in this index as bold-faced capitals; subjects within articles appear as lower-case entries. Both the general references and the subentries should be consulted for maximum usefulness of this index. Illustrations are indexed herein. Cross references are to the entries in this index.